PATAGONIA

WAYNE BERNHARDSON

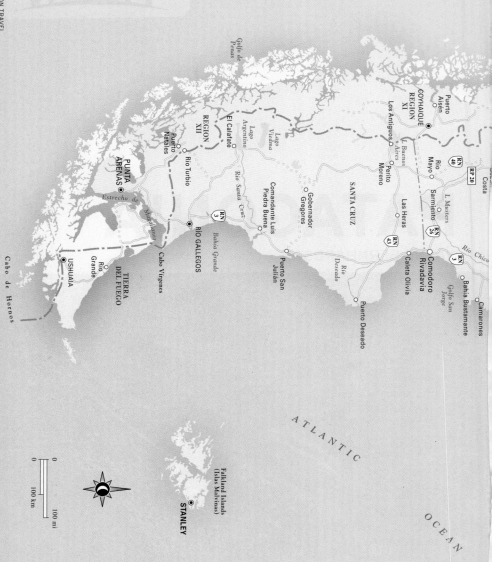

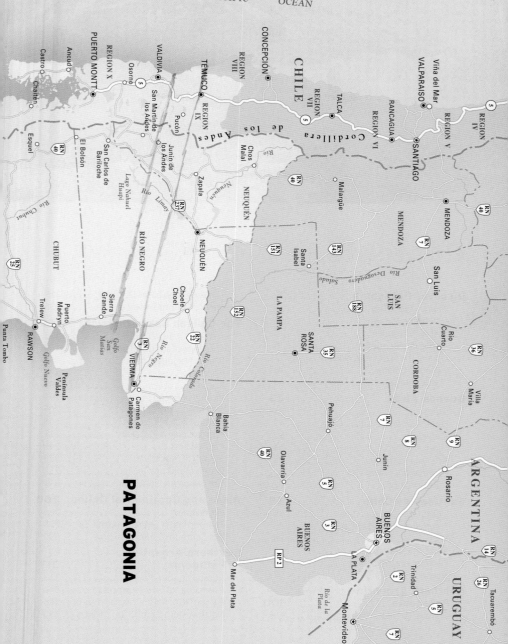

PACIFIC   OCEAN

CHILE

Cordillera de los Andes

PATAGONIA

ARGENTINA

URUGUAY

Contents

DISCOVER
Patagonia

Patagonia has excited the imagination since Magellan's account of hidden cities of gold first reached the Old World. Even today, when air travel has made much of the exotic familiar, Patagonia's staggering landscapes evoke mystery and inspire exploration.

The diversity of this region is unparalleled, with fjords, big-sky steppes, and truly wild coastlines. Glaciar Perito Moreno is a grinding river of ice that's a feast for the eyes and the ears. Hiking trails trace the pinnacles of Torres del Paine and elephant seals crowd the coastline of Península Valdés. The aboriginal rock art of Cueva de las Manos gives glimpses of the pre-Columbian past. The Falkland Islands offer the greatest assemblage of Antarctic wildlife—including penguins—this side of the frozen continent. Patagonia is also rich with culture. Chile's lakes district is home to the resilient Mapuche people, who defended their territory against the Spaniards for centuries, and in Tierra del Fuego, sheep farmers have created a distinctive cultural landscape.

Five centuries after its discovery by Europeans, Patagonia remains an enduring symbol of the unknown, still luring the adventurous to the end of the earth.

Clockwise from top left: wild horse in Parque Nacional Chiloe; the harbor at Ushuaia; Laguna de Los Tres with Cerro Fitz Roy in the background; black-browed albatrosses at The Rookery on Saunders Island, Falkland Islands; interior of the Capilla de Mármol; Cerro Castillo.

Clockwise from top left: Plaza de Mayo in Buenos Aires; Parque Nacional Torres del Paine; guanaco crossing the river; a solitary araucaria in front of Volcán Lonquimay; rockhopper penguins at Cape Bougainville, East Falkland.

© AVALON TRAVEL

Planning Your Trip

Where to Go

Patagonia is notoriously hard to define. For the purposes of this guide, it's a pragmatic matter that corresponds closely to political geography.

BUENOS AIRES

Patagonia's primary gateway is also South America's **highest-profile capital.** Many visitors spend weeks or even months enjoying its **first-rate hotels,** innovative cuisine, all-night entertainment, nonstop shopping, and **matchless cultural resources.** Despite its international sophistication,

it's also a city of intimate neighborhoods where no one is truly anonymous.

SANTIAGO DE CHILE

Patagonia's other gateway remains one of the continent's most underrated cities. While it lacks the international profile of its Argentine neighbor, Santiago's setting at the **base of the Andes** is more impressive, and its hotels, food, and entertainment scenes are catching up rapidly—not least because Chile is the continent's most **politically stable** and **prosperous** country.

If You Have . . .

- **ONE WEEK:** Visit Buenos Aires, El Calafate and the Glaciar Perito Moreno, and Torres del Paine.

- **TWO WEEKS:** Add El Chaltén, Tierra del Fuego (possibly including the Cruceros Australis voyage from Punta Arenas to Ushuaia), and Santiago. Alternatively, add Laguna San Rafael, including parts of the Carretera Austral and Termas de Puyuhuapi, or the ferry from Puerto Natales to Puerto Montt.

- **THREE WEEKS:** Add Península Valdés and Bariloche, or Parque Pumalín and Pucón.

- **FOUR WEEKS:** Add the Falkland Islands or Chiloé and vicinity.

- **SIX WEEKS:** Add a road trip along RN 3 and RN 40 (Argentina) or the entire Carretera Austral (Chile).

NORTHERN ARGENTINE PATAGONIA

In this guide, northern Argentine Patagonia comprises **Neuquén** and **Río Negro,** plus northwesterly parts of **Chubut.** While most of Argentine Patagonia is arid steppe, the densely forested sector near the Chilean border boasts numerous national parks. **San Carlos de Bariloche** is the country's playground for hiking, skiing, rafting, kayaking, and fly-fishing.

THE CHILEAN LAKES DISTRICT

The **Sur Chico,** popularly called the Chilean lakes district, is a wonderland of rivers, lakes, forests, and volcanoes. It comprises **La Araucanía** and **Los Lagos;** the latter includes the **Chiloé archipelago.** It is common to cross the Andes into Argentine Patagonia here. It's also the official starting point for the **Carretera Austral,** the southern highway that links parts of southern Chile to the mainland.

AISÉN AND CONTINENTAL CHILOÉ

Chile's Aisén is mostly **wild islands-and-highlands country.** In this guide, it also includes the southernmost part of Los Lagos, often known as "continental Chiloé." Running most of the region's length, the **Carretera Austral** is one of Patagonia's greatest road trips. Off-highway sights like **Laguna San Rafael** and **Parque Pumalín,** one of South America's most audacious private conservation initiatives, are also highlights.

SOUTHERN ARGENTINE PATAGONIA

In this guide, southern Argentine Patagonia consists of Chubut province and Santa Cruz province. Its coastline is a scenic cornucopia of **whales, seals, penguins,** and other wildlife. It's also famous for **Glaciar Perito Moreno,** a crackling outlier of the Campo de Hielo Sur, the southern Patagonian ice sheet. Two legendary highways, the coastal **RN 3** and the interior **RN 40,** connect the region with northerly provinces.

MAGALLANES

South of Aisén are jagged mountains and islands set among inland seas. Copious rain and snow feed rivers and the glaciers of the **Campo de Hielo Sur.** Pristine woodlands still cover the mountainsides in much of the region, whose biggest draw is the igneous spires of **Parque Nacional Torres del Paine.** The only significant city is **Punta Arenas,** though growing **Puerto Natales** is a gateway to Torres del Paine. **Puerto Williams** is the last major settlement north of Antarctica. Local cruise ships now visit **Cape Horn,** South America's southernmost point.

ARGENTINE TIERRA DEL FUEGO

Across the Strait of Magellan from the continent, Chile and Argentina share the **broad steppes** and **mountainous** sub-Antarctic grandeur of the Isla Grande de Tierra del Fuego, where **Ushuaia**

Defining Patagonia

Patagonia does not lend itself to any easy, precise definition. Like the people, plants, and animals that migrate with the season, the years, the decades, the centuries, and even millennia, it shifts with time and perspective. In Argentina, there's broad agreement that it is the vast territory south of the Río Colorado, from Neuquén and Río Negro provinces to Tierra del Fuego. Chilean Patagonia has no formal boundaries, though nearly everybody would agree that Region XI (Aisén) and Region XII (Magallanes) are at least part of it.

Ecologically speaking, Patagonia comprises four main vegetation zones: Patagonian steppe, *coigüe*-dominated southern beech forest, Magellanic moorland, and ice fields and glaciers. No definition should omit its indigenous peoples, many of whom were mobile hunter-gatherers, like the land-based Tehuelche and the coastal Kawéskar, Selk'nam, and Yámana, or the trans-Andean Mapuche, who disregarded political borders. It was the combative Mapuche people, in fact, whose presence marked the frontier on both sides of the border—deterring colonial Spain and making early Argentine and Chilean colonization precarious.

is the world's southernmost city and **Parque Nacional Tierra del Fuego** was Argentina's first coastal national park.

THE FALKLAND ISLANDS
More than 500 kilometers east of the mainland, the Falkland Islands acquired international notoriety in 1982, when an Argentine dictatorship invaded to enforce a long-standing territorial claim to the **British-held islands.** The British regained them 10 weeks later. Since then, the Falklands have prospered under a commercial-fishing-license regime. They've also become a magnet for cruise ships and a handful of **independent adventurers** who come to see abundant **sub-Antarctic wildlife** and enjoy local hospitality.

When to Go
The southern hemisphere's spring, summer, and fall months correspond to the north's coldest seasons, adding to Patagonia's appeal. Still, seasonal wildlife migrations and Andean ski resorts make it a destination even during the austral winter.

The Andean **lakes district** is a traditional **summer destination,** with locales like Bariloche and Pucón as busy as the ocean beaches. It's also a magnet for fly-fishing enthusiasts **October to April.** Bariloche is the focus of Argentina's ski industry June-August.

Farther south, **El Calafate,** gateway to Glaciar Perito Moreno, offers many services **October to April,** and even for the July holidays. **Península Valdés** is a special case that depends on South Atlantic wildlife—July's midwinter arrival of right whales brings the first tourists, who keep coming with the influx of elephant seals, orcas, and penguins until the **end of March.**

Tierra del Fuego is primarily a **summer** destination, though it also has a ski season. The city of Ushuaia is the gateway to Antarctica, where the spring breakup of pack ice determines the season.

Falklands tourism depends on the wildlife calendar. Migratory Magellanic and rockhopper penguins and elephant seals begin arriving in **October** and stay until **March,** or even a little later. That said, there's some wildlife at all seasons, even though access becomes more difficult in winter.

Before You Go
Patagonia covers an **enormous territory,** far larger than most of the world's countries, and **logistics can be complicated.** Capital cities like Buenos Aires and Santiago are compact and easy to travel around. Visiting other high-profile

destinations like Argentina's Perito Moreno Glacier and Chile's Torres del Paine require 2- to 3-hour **flights** or 15- to 30-hour **bus trips.** Driving is an option, but for most visitors this will mean a rental car from a provincial airport or city.

PASSPORTS AND VISAS

U.S. and Canadian citizens traveling to **Argentina** and **Chile** need **passports** but not advance visas. Passports are also necessary for checking into hotels, cashing traveler's checks, or even credit card transactions. Both countries routinely grant foreign visitors **90-day entry permits** in the form of a tourist card. Both also collect a substantial **reciprocity fee** from certain nationalities, including Canadians and Australians, at all border crossings.

Visitors to the **Falkland Islands,** including Britons, must have passports, return or onward tickets, and sufficient funds to cover their stay. They may need to arrange accommodations in advance. A Visa or MasterCard is proof of sufficient funds. Visitors must also have adequate medical coverage, including emergency evacuation insurance.

VACCINATIONS AND
HEALTH INSURANCE

Argentina and Chile demand **no proof of vaccinations,** but if you are coming from a tropical country where yellow fever is endemic, authorities could ask for a vaccination certificate. Traveling to Patagonia or elsewhere without adequate **medical insurance** is risky. Before leaving home, purchase a policy that includes evacuation in case of serious emergency.

TRANSPORTATION

Most visitors arrive by air, via the international airports of **Buenos Aires** (EZE) or **Santiago** (SCL). Some arrive overland and others by ship. Chile's LATAM has the only commercial flights to the Falkland Islands.

Argentina has an extensive network of **domestic airports,** serving many destinations from Buenos Aires south to Ushuaia, Tierra del Fuego. Chile's domestic airports are located in Temuco, Pucón, Osorno, Puerto Montt, Chaitén, Balmaceda, and Punta Arenas.

Argentina and Chile share numerous **border crossings.** In both countries' lakes districts, **trans-Andean bus service** is fairly common, but many southerly crossings lack public transportation. In both countries, **buses** along the principal highways are frequent, spacious, and comfortable. Fares are reasonable by international standards.

For those choosing an aquatic route, the main international crossings are the popular **bus-boat-bus shuttle** between Argentina's San Carlos de Bariloche and Chile's Puerto Montt, and the cruise between Punta Arenas and Ushuaia.

WHAT TO PACK

Budget travelers should pack a spacious but **lightweight backpack** and a small daypack for excursions. Even for non-backpackers, **light luggage** is advisable. Use sturdy **locks** on all luggage.

Good **rain gear** and **warm footwear** are essential for hikers. **Warm clothing, sleeping bags,** and a **sturdy tent** are imperative at high elevations and high latitudes. In **southernmost Patagonia** and **Tierra del Fuego,** state-of-the-art wet-weather gear is advisable. In some national parks, wood fires are prohibited. An adaptable multi-fuel **camp stove** is the best choice. **Binoculars** are a good idea for watching wildlife. Rental gear is available in the gateways to prime hiking areas.

In much of the region, drinking water is potable straight from the stream, but a **purification system** is a good idea. Public restrooms sometimes lack **toilet paper,** so travelers should always carry some.

southern sea lion in the Falkland Islands

Best of Patagonia

This 10-day itinerary focuses on highlights for first-timers, including Argentina's Glaciar Perito Moreno, Chile's Torres del Paine, and one of South America's largest penguin colonies. A possible extension goes to the "uttermost part of the earth" at Ushuaia, the world's southernmost city, in Argentine Tierra del Fuego.

Day 1

Plan a morning arrival in **Buenos Aires,** leaving the afternoon free for sightseeing and the evening for a tango floor show.

Days 2-3

After breakfast, fly to **El Calafate** (3 hours) and take an afternoon excursion to a nearby *estancia* for a traditional *asado* (barbecue). The following morning, take a full-day excursion to the groaning, deep blue **Glaciar Perito Moreno.**

Days 4-5

Take a scenic morning bus trip or drive to **El Chaltén** (3 hours), the trekking mecca of **Parque Nacional Los Glaciares.** With an early arrival and good weather, it'll be a swift hike to view the glaciated needle of **Cerro Torre.** Spend the next morning on a full-day hike to **Laguna de los Tres,** with stupendous views of **Cerro Fitz Roy,** followed by an evening return to El Calafate.

Days 6-8

Bus to bustling **Puerto Natales** (5 hours), gateway to **Parque Nacional Torres del Paine.** Stay overnight in Natales. The next day, plan on a scenic day hike in the vicinity or in the park (2 hours north), with afternoon options for short hikes or a horseback ride. The next morning, hike the short but strenuous trail to the tarns beneath the Torres themselves. In the evening, return to Puerto Natales.

Day 9

Travel across the Magellanic steppe to **Punta Arenas** (3 hours), with a short detour to the

Magellanic penguin colony at **Pingüinera Seno Otway,** or, if the timing is right, ride the afternoon ferry to the larger colony on **Isla Magdalena,** in the Strait of Magellan. There are also quicker Zodiac trips to Isla Magdalena.

Day 10

From Punta Arenas, a morning flight to Chile's underrated capital, **Santiago** (3 hours), leaves the afternoon free for sightseeing and a seafood lunch at the **Mercado Central,** followed by a nighttime departure. A later departure from Punta Arenas could mean time to visit that city's exceptional **Museo Regional Salesiano** and then transfer directly to the international flight home.

Extension: Ushuaia and Tierra del Fuego

DAY 10

From Punta Arenas, take a day tour to the Chilean side of **Tierra del Fuego,** to see the king penguin

colony at **Parque Pingüino Rey.** It's a long trip via ferry and road so, returning to Punta Arenas, have a relaxing dinner at one of the city's outstanding restaurants.

DAYS 11-12

From Punta Arenas, take the 50-minute flight to **Ushuaia,** the capital of Tierra del Fuego. This is the starting point for wildlife-viewing on the legendary **Beagle Channel.** Spend half a day on the water. The next day, plan an excursion to **Parque Nacional Tierra del Fuego,** which has multiple short hiking trails. Save time for Ushuaia's **Museo Marítimo,** which is actually a prison museum.

DAY 13

Fly over Argentina's endless Atlantic coastline back to **Buenos Aires.** The afternoon and evening are free for sightseeing and a tango show before the flight home.

Glaciar Perito Moreno

Santiago's Mercado Central

Nearly the entire Patagonian coastline abounds in wildlife, with elephant seals, penguins, sea lions, and birds. These are the destinations for prime wildlife viewing.

PENÍNSULA VALDÉS

(page 326)
On Argentina's Atlantic coast, this World Heritage Site is famous for southern right whales, which breed and birth here during the winter months. Yet at different seasons, there are also orcas, elephant seals, Magellanic penguins, and sea lions, while grazing guanacos and sprinting rheas roam the interior grasslands.

ÁREA NATURAL PROTEGIDA PUNTA TOMBO

(page 338)
The South American continent's largest single Magellanic penguin colony is a top destination for penguin watchers: 250,000 pairs come ashore each spring to nest. In addition, giant petrels, kelp and dolphin gulls, king and rock cormorants, oystercatchers, and steamer ducks all breed here.

PARQUE INTERJURISDICCIONAL MARINO COSTERO PATAGONIA AUSTRAL

(page 340)
In Chubut province, this new park consists of a wildlife-rich coastal strip, including islands, that extends from Camarones to Cabo dos Bahías, with an easy access point and accommodations at Bahía Bustamante. Expect to see Magellanic penguins, cormorants, and sea lions.

PARQUE MARINO FRANCISCO COLOANE

(page 408)
One of Chile's first maritime reserves, this park was created to investigate the southern humpback whale's feeding grounds. Orcas, Magellanic pen-

southern right whale off Península Valdés

guins, sea lions, cormorants, and many other southern seabirds populate the 67,000-hectare park.

FALKLAND ISLANDS

(page 472)
The Falkland Islands are rich with elephant seals, fur seals, sea lions, and massive nesting colonies of penguins (five or sometimes more species), black-browed albatrosses, cormorants, and many unusual smaller birds. Prime destinations include Volunteer Point and wildlife lodges at Carcass Island, Pebble Island, Sea Lion Island, and Saunders Island. Whales can be found offshore near Saunders February to May.

A king cormorant scavenges for nesting material on Saunders Island, in the Falklands.

Explore the Natural World

Patagonia offers an astonishing diversity of natural environments. The coastline abounds in wildlife, including elephant seals, penguins, and sea lions, but the great distances require time and money to see it. Public transportation is fine along the main highway but poor off it. The same is true of the Patagonian steppes, home to the llama-like guanaco and the ostrich-like rhea, and the southern Andean forests beyond the main tourist clusters.

Northern Argentine Patagonia boasts major paleontological sites in and around the city of Neuquén, and in and around the city of Trelew, near Puerto Madryn, as well as the wildlife mecca of Península Valdés. Along much of the Andes, particularly on the Chilean side, volcanism is an active presence.

Day 1

After an early-morning arrival in **Santiago,** start sightseeing. Plan on a seafood lunch at the picturesque **Mercado Central** and a visit to the information offices of Conaf, the country's main national parks and conservation agency. Alternatively, in lieu of a hotel, ride a comfortable sleeper bus to **Temuco,** gateway to the upper Biobío's araucaria forests.

Day 2

From Temuco, reached by sleeper bus (roughly nine hours) or a two-hour flight from Santiago, rent a car to explore the streams, gallery forests, and araucaria woodlands of **Parque Nacional Tolhuaca** and the upper Biobío, with accommodations at **Curacautín** or **Malalcahuello.** Bring binoculars for **bird-watching.**

Day 3

Plan a full-day hiking excursion to **araucaria forests** above Malalcahuello, on the slopes of **Volcán Lonquimay,** with a post-hike soak at the nearby **hot springs.**

Measuring some 16,800 square kilometers, the Campo de Hielo Sur (Southern Continental Ice Field) feeds some of the most southerly glaciers this side of Antarctica. On ferries and cruise ships, visitors can watch the ice meet the sea. On land, they can drive to some of the largest glaciers, with catamaran alternatives on some larger lakes. More adventurous travelers can climb atop the ice and explore glacial caverns.

LAGUNA SAN RAFAEL

(page 276)
Catamarans, small cruise ships, and even some modest launches sail to remote Laguna San Rafael, where the Campo de Hielo Norte meets the sea. A natural laboratory for global warming studies, it's receding rapidly.

GLACIAR O'HIGGINS

(page 310)
From Villa O'Higgins, the terminus of the Carretera Austral, the vessel that carries cyclists to the alternative Cruce de Lagos, the rugged overland border crossing to El Chaltén, continues to this scenic outlier of the Campo de Hielo Sur.

PARQUE NACIONAL LOS GLACIARES

(page 368)
Parque Nacional Los Glaciares is home to famous Glaciar Perito Moreno, 250 square kilometers in area and 30 kilometers in length, which is easily reached overland. It intermittently explodes from the weight of the water behind it as the advancing ice dams a nearby lake.

In the same park, the even larger Upsala and Viedma glaciers are accessible by catamaran. It's also possible to go ice-climbing on each with experienced guides. Don't overlook El Calafate's ice museum, the Glaciarium.

THE FJORDS OF FUEGIA

(page 412)
Luxury cruises on relatively small vessels visit Chilean Tierra del Fuego's Avenida de los Glaciares on weekly circuits between Punta Are-

Glaciar Upsala

nas and Ushuaia. Most visitors take the trip in one direction or the other. If the weather cooperates, the luckiest get to go ashore at Cape Horn.

THE CHANNELS OF THE KAWÉSKAR

(page 426)
On multiple-day cruises of the Channels of the Kawéskar, from Puerto Natales to Puerto Edén and back, passengers can catch a glimpse of South America's longest glacier, Glaciar Pío XI, a staggering 62 kilometers in length and 6 kilometers wide. Many others, such as Glaciar Amalia, also get views up close and personal.

Days 4-5

Take a leisurely drive in the upper Biobío through **Lonquimay** and forested, thinly populated land of the Pehuenche people, entering **Parque Nacional Conguillío** via the southern Melipeuco approach. It's about 150 kilometers, but plan on a full day with sightseeing and photographic stops. After an orientation visit to the visitors center, camp or find cabaña accommodations nearby.

On the following day, try any of several hikes among Conguillío's **lava fields** and **araucaria forests.**

Days 6-7

Make a morning departure for **Lago Villarrica** (100 kilometers), with accommodations in **Villarrica** or **Pucón** (20 kilometers farther). The drive is only a couple of hours, leaving most of the day free. Plan an excursion to the **Termas Geométricas** hot springs or an afternoon **rafting** on the **Río Trancura.**

The next morning, tackle a strenuous full-day **climb** to the crater of **Volcán Villarrica,** one of the continent's most active volcanoes. Alternatively, spend a full day hiking to the Andean lakes of nearby **Parque Nacional Huerquehue** where, with luck, Andean condors glide overhead.

Day 8

Return to Temuco and bus to **Puerto Varas** (5 hours), spending a leisurely afternoon on the shores of **Lago Llanquihue,** in the shadow of **Volcán Osorno**'s perfect snowcapped cone— Chile's counterpart to Mount Fuji. Alternatively, take a shuttle to the **ski area,** where, even in summer, the lifts carry hikers close to the snow line for panoramic views.

Days 9-10

Hope for fine weather on the classic, full-day bus-boat shuttle to **Bariloche,** Argentina, via **Lago Todos los Santos.** Stay in or near Bariloche.

The next morning, tour Bariloche and its **Museo de la Patagonia Francisco P. Moreno,** which emphasizes natural history and conservation. In the afternoon, plan an excursion on **Parque Nacional Nahuel Huapi**'s Circuito Chico, a loop that includes

Volcán Llaima from Parque Nacional Conguillío

Bariloche

a stiff trail hike to **Cerro López** for panoramic views of the Andes and **Lago Nahuel Huapi.** Alternatively, boat to the lake's **Isla Victoria,** formerly home to the park system's ranger school.

Day 11

From Bariloche, a smooth paved highway rounds Nahuel Huapi's eastern shore and then turns northwest to **Villa La Angostura** (1 hour's drive). A long but not taxing day hike leads to the myrtle forest of **Parque Nacional Los Arrayanes** and back. Those with less stamina can take a boat one-way or round-trip. Return to Bariloche for a comfortable overnight sleeper bus to **Puerto Madryn** (14 hours).

Days 12-13

Start the day with a visit to the **Ecocentro Puerto Madryn,** an environmental museum. In the afternoon, take time for in-town beach activities such as diving or windsurfing.

The following morning, depart early by tour bus or rental car for **Península Valdés** (about 1 hour away). Depending on the season, there'll be elephant seals, penguins, orcas, or right whales. Many other species—rheas, guanacos, and sea lions, for instance—are present year-round.

Day 14

Catch a morning flight to **Buenos Aires,** with the afternoon free for and lunch and sightseeing. Plan an evening departure flight for home.

Classic Patagonia Road Trips

Because of Patagonia's vast expanses, overland travel tends to be for those with plenty of time. Most routes are well served by reasonably priced public transportation, but renting a vehicle can be more efficient. A 4WD vehicle is rarely necessary, but a high-clearance vehicle can be worth the extra bucks.

Parallel to RN 3, the mother of all Argentine roads is RN 40, from the Bolivian border in Jujuy province to the Chilean border in Patagonia's Santa Cruz province. It's in Patagonia, though, that **RN 40** has acquired an international reputation as the **adventurous route** between the northern lakes and southern glaciers. Only in the last few years has there been any semiregular public transportation on the route from Bariloche to El Calafate. The southern segment from the town of Perito Moreno to El Calafate is in the process of being fully paved, but parts of any trip south of Río Mayo still seem like an expedition. Travelers should be prepared for several days' rugged travel, or weeks, if they want to explore off the main route.

Coastal RN 3 is entirely paved (though discontinuous), and parts of the connector roads through Chilean Tierra del Fuego remain unsurfaced. Still, RN 3 glows with the charisma of **the world's southernmost highway,** the Patagonian road that leads from Buenos Aires to Tierra del Fuego's tip. To grasp the vastness that so impressed early European visitors, and to view prodigious wildlife concentrations, "Ruta Tres" is still a matchless itinerary.

The following section suggests week-long itineraries that can be combined to explore this intriguing region for a longer period, up to 15 days or ideally more. Unfortunately, drop-off charges for rental vehicles are expensive except at the point of rental.

DAY 1

Whichever route you choose, begin by arriving at Aeropuerto Internacional Ministro Pistarini (Ezeiza) and transfer to a **Buenos Aires** hotel, leaving the afternoon free for sightseeing. Get a good night's sleep before beginning the road trip of a lifetime.

The Northern Coast

Best for those with limited time and flexibility, this segment is logistically simpler and close to major airports with plenty of other services, including rental cars.

DAY 2

Take a morning flight to **Trelew** and transfer north on RN 3 to the coastal city of **Puerto Madryn** (1 hour's drive). Make an afternoon visit to the **Ecocentro Puerto Madryn,** an environmental museum. This leaves time for the beach, more active pursuits such as diving or windsurfing, or even an excursion to **Área Natural Protegida Punta Loma,** which has a big sea lion colony and many seabirds.

DAY 3

It's barely an hour's drive to **Península Valdés.** Spend the full day viewing wildlife, including elephant seals, penguins, orcas, or right whales (depending on the season), as well as guanacos, rheas, and sea lions (present year-round). Consider a night at one of the peninsula's accommodations, such as **Estancia Rincón Chico.**

DAY 4

Depart in the morning, heading south on RN 3 back to **Trelew** (1 hour's drive) to visit **Museo Paleontológico Egidio Feruglio,** a state-of-the-art paleontology museum, followed by a badlands hike through the in situ paleontological park at **Bryn Gwyn,** near Gaiman. Enjoy a late afternoon Welsh tea and overnight at **Gaiman.**

DAYS 5-6

From Gaiman, make an eastbound lateral from RN 3 to **Punta Tombo** (about 150 kilometers, roughly 2 hours). Its massive Magellanic penguin colony is the continent's largest. After exploring Punta Tombo, drive along the desolate but scenic coastline past Cabo Raso to isolated **Camarones** (about 150 kilometers, 3 hours) for lunch. Continue onward to **Bahía Bustamante** (140 kilometers, 2.5 hours) for accommodations and excursions to offshore islands or a nearby petrified forest. From here, it's possible to return to Trelew (roughly 250 kilometers, about 4 hours) and fly back to Buenos Aires.

Cerro Fitz Roy

Travelers with more time can continue south on RN 3 to Comodoro Rivadavia (roughly 200 kilometers, 3 hours) to tour the Southern Coast.

The Southern Coast

DAY 2

Fly from Buenos Aires to **Comodoro Rivadavia.** Make a brief stop at its first-rate **Museo Nacional del Petróleo** before continuing along smoothly paved highway to picturesque **Puerto Deseado** (300 kilometers, 3.5 hours) and its unique estuary, the **Reserva Natural Provincial Ría Deseado.** Take a short excursion on the Ría Deseado, home to penguins, cormorants, many other seabirds, and especially dolphins. Spend the night at Deseado.

DAY 3

Sea conditions permitting, sail to offshore **Isla Pingüino,** site of the world's northernmost rockhopper colony, along with Magellanics and many sea lions. Spend the night at Deseado or, if there's enough daylight, continue south via RN 281 and RN 3 to **Puerto San Julián** (about 380 kilometers, 5 hours). Its harbor and offshore islands are also home to large populations of dolphins and Magellanic penguins. Spend the night in San Julián.

DAY 4

Continue south on RN 3 to the stunning headlands of **Parque Nacional Monte León** (150 kilometers, roughly 2.5 hours), a short detour off the main road. Before leaving the highway, check tide tables at the park visitors center in order to be able to walk the beach, enter the sea caves, and approach the cormorant-covered **Isla Monte León.** Camp at the park or find accommodations in the nearby town of **Comandante Luis Piedra Buena.**

DAYS 5-6

Departing in the morning or afternoon, head south on RN 3 to **Río Gallegos** (200 kilometers, 3 hours). Find accommodations in town or at **Estancia Monte Dinero,** near the large Magellanic penguin colony at **Reserva Provincial Cabo Vírgenes,** the easternmost point of the Strait of Magellan. From Gallegos, it's possible to fly back to Buenos Aires.

Travelers with more time can continue onward to tour the Andes. Start on RN 3, then turn onto RP 5, which becomes contiguous with RP 40 at Esperanza until the junction with RP 11 east to El Calafate.

The Andes

DAYS 2-3

From Buenos Aires, fly to **El Calafate,** gateway to Parque Nacional Los Glaciares. Time permitting, visit a working *estancia.* Otherwise, dine at one of El Calafate's fine restaurants. The following morning, begin a full-day overland excursion to the **Glaciar Perito Moreno** in Parque Nacional Los Glaciares. Overnight in El Calafate.

DAYS 4-6

East of El Calafate, take the excellent paved northbound RN 40 and then westbound RP 23, to **El Chaltén** (about 250 kilometers, 3-4 hours) in Sector Fitz Roy of **Parque Nacional Los Glaciares.** With an early arrival and good weather, there's time for a swift hike to view **Cerro Torre**'s namesake glaciated needle. Find accommodations in or near town.

The following day, plan on a demanding full-day hike to **Laguna de los Tres,** for views of **Cerro Fitz Roy.** On the next day, do another hike to **Loma del Pliegue Tumbado** for its panoramas of Fitz Roy. Return to El Calafate for the flight back to Buenos Aires.

Buenos Aires

Look for ★ to find recommended
sights, activities, dining, and lodging.

Highlights

★ **Plaza de Mayo:** Buenos Aires's historic center is ground zero for public life in Argentina (page 33).

★ **Café Tortoni:** Avenida de Mayo's traditional gathering place has been an island of stability in a tumultuous ocean of political, social, and economic upheaval (page 33).

★ **Teatro Colón:** Having celebrated Argentina's bicentennial with a major restoration, the continent's most important performing arts venue retains its style and dignity (page 36).

★ **Plaza Dorrego:** Antiques vendors and spirited performers clog San Telmo's principal plaza and surrounding streets every Sunday (page 39).

★ **Cementerio de la Recoleta:** For both the living and the dead, the barrio of Recoleta is the capital's prestige address (page 44).

★ **Museo de Arte Latinoamericano de Buenos Aires (MALBA):** Argentina has had a thriving modern art scene for decades, but Palermo's Latin American art museum has given it a new focal point (page 46).

★ **Museo Eva Perón:** Promoted by Evita's partisans, Argentina's first museum dedicated to a woman is as notable for its omissions as its inclusions (page 46).

★ **Museo Argentino de Ciencias Naturales:** In the decidedly untouristed barrio of Caballito, this museum sheds light on Argentina's impressive dinosaur discoveries (page 48).

South America's highest-profile capital has evolved dramatically since its shaky colonial origins. Massive postindependence immigration and prosperity turned a cozy "Gran Aldea" (Great Village) into a "Paris of the South" with

broad avenues, colossal monuments, and mansard-capped mansions. In the 20th century, Buenos Aires experienced spectacular spurts of growth and even more spectacular economic and political disasters. Yet somehow, like its melancholy signature music and dance, the tango, it has retained its identity and mystique.

Despite Argentina's problems, the Río de la Plata's megalopolis still has much to offer urban explorers in a city that truly never sleeps. It's one of the most underrated destinations on an underrated continent—*Travel + Leisure* has called it Latin America's top tourist city.

Foreign visitors often conflate the city with Argentina—though provincial Argentines adamantly assert that "Buenos Aires is *not* Argentina." Despite a cosmopolitan outlook, many Porteños ("residents of the port") identify more strongly with their own barrios or neighborhoods. Like New Yorkers, they often seem brashly assertive, their accent setting them apart from provincial residents.

Buenos Aires has a humid coastal climate resembling that of Washington DC for most of the year, with hot and muggy summers. Unlike Washington, though, it has mild winters, and it has snowed only once in the last century. The daily maximum temperature averages 30.4°C in January; it's slow to cool off until the early morning hours. In July, the coolest month, the daily maximum averages 13.9°C.

PLANNING YOUR TIME

Buenos Aires deserves as much time as possible, but Patagonia-bound visitors may have to pick and choose. Anyone planning an extended stay should consult *Moon Buenos Aires*.

Presuming no more than two days in town, visitors should focus on central highlights like the Plaza de Mayo and vicinity, the Teatro Colón, the southern barrios of San Telmo and La Boca, the famous Recoleta cemetery, and the art museums of Palermo.

Previous: street performers at Feria Plaza Francia; the Casa Rosada presidential palace. **Above:** The Congreso Nacional.

Buenos Aires

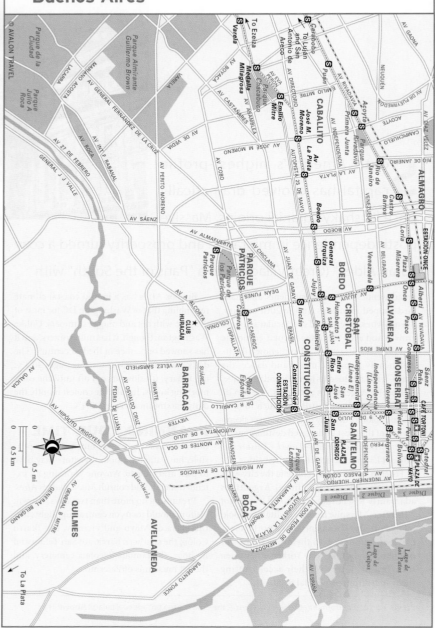

© AVALON TRAVEL

Parque Almirante Guillermo Brown

Parque de la Ciudad

Parque Julio A Roca

LACARRA

MARIANO ACOSTA

AV GENERAL FERNÁNDEZ DE LA CRUZ

AV INT F RABANAL

AV ROCA

AV 27 DE FEBRERO

GENERAL J J VALLE

VARELA

AV DE VEDIA

AV CASTAÑARES

AV PERITO MORENO

AV JOSE M MORENO

AV COBO

AV SÁENZ

AV ALMAFUERTE

GENERAL BELGRANO

AV GAICIA

AV HIPÓLITO YRIGOYEN

PEDRO DE LUJAN

AV OSVALDO CRUZ

SUAREZ

IRIARTE

VIEYTES

DR R CARRILLO

AV MONTES DE OCA

BRANDSEN

SUÁREZ

AV REGIMIENTO DE PATRICIOS

AV ALMIRANTE BROWN

AV DON PEDRO DE MENDOZA

AUTOPISTA LA PLATA

SARGENTO PONCE

To La Plata

QUILMES

AVELLANEDA

LA BOCA

BARRACAS

AV VÉLEZ SARSFIELD

CLUB HURACÁN

Parque Patricios

Parque de los Patricios

PARQUE PATRICIOS

AV A ALCORTA

COLONIA

USPALLATA

CASEROS

DEAN FUNES

AV CASEROS

AV JUAN DE GARAY

AV CHICLANA

BOEDO

General Urquiza

Julyy

Inclan

Pichincha

Entre Ríos

San José

BRASIL

SAN CRISTOBAL

Humberto 1°

AV SAN JUAN

AV JUJUY

CONSTITUCIÓN

Constitución

ESTACIÓN CONSTITUCIÓN

Plaza España

San Juan

AV JUAN DE GARAY

Parque Lezama

AV INGENIERO HUERGO

AV PASEO COLÓN

AV INDEPENDENCIA

AV 9 DE JULIO

SAN TELMO

PLAZA DORREGO

PERÚ

BELGRANO

Bolivar

Piedras

Lima

AV 9 DE JULIO

Moreno

Independencia (Línea C)

Independencia (Línea E)

San José

Entre Ríos

MONSERRAT

BALVANERA

AV ENTRE RÍOS

Saenz Peña

Congreso

Pasco

Alberti

ESTACIÓN ONCE

Plaza Once

Plaza Misere

RÍO DE JANEIRO

AV PUEYRREDÓN

AV RIVADAVIA

AV BELGRANO

Loria

Castro Barros

Rio de Janeiro

Venezuela

AV BOEDO

Boedo

AV LA PLATA

AUTOPISTA 25 DE MAYO

VENEZUELA

ALMAGRO

AV DÍAZ VÉLEZ

AV DR PUEYRREDÓN

CAMPICHUELO

ACOYTE

NEUQUEN

AV GAONA

Acoyte

Parque Rivadavia

Primera Junta

AV INDEPENDENCIA

Av La Plata

José M. Moreno

Emilio Mitre

CABALLITO

Parque Chacabuco

AV DIRECTORIO

AV RIVADAVIA

EMILIO MITRE

AV EVA PERÓN

Medalla Milagrosa

Chacabuco

AV BOYACA

AV ASAMBLEA

AV CASTAÑARES

Varela

Carabobo

To Luján and San Antonio de Areco

To Ezeiza

Puán

0   0.5 mi

0   0.5 km

To La Plata

Ruchuelo

Dique 1

Dique 2

Dique 3

Lago de los Patos

Lago de los Coipos

AV ESPAÑA

CAFÉ TORTONI

Catedral

PLAZA DE MAYO

CÁCERES

CÁCERES

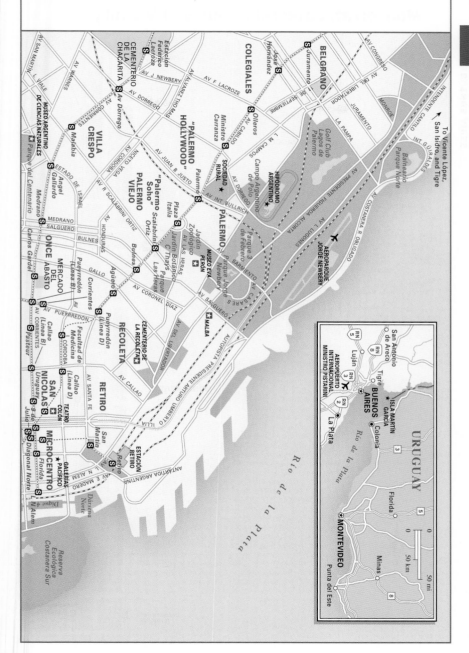

BUENOS AIRES

Monserrat/Catedral al Sur and Vicinity

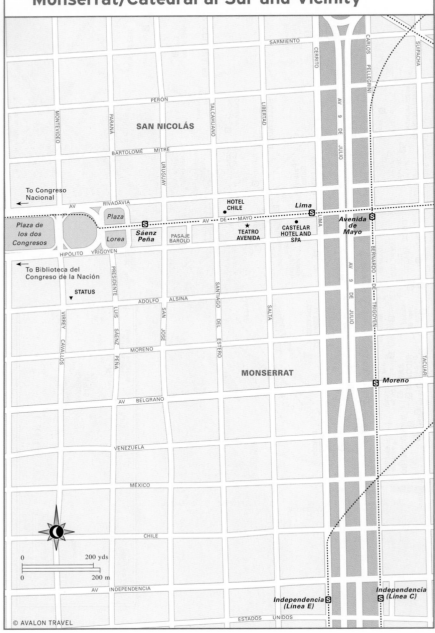

SARMIENTO

CERRITO

CARLOS PELLEGRINI

SUIPACHA

PERÓN

MONTEVIDEO

PARANÁ

TALCAHUANO

LIBERTAD

SAN NICOLÁS

AV 9 DE JULIO

BARTOLOMÉ MITRE

URUGUAY

To Congreso Nacional ←

AV RIVADAVIA

Plaza

HOTEL CHILE ●

Lima S

S

Plaza de los dos Congresos

Lorea

Sáenz Peña S

PASAJE BAROLO

AV DE MAYO

★ TEATRO AVENIDA

● CASTELAR HOTEL AND SPA

LIMA

Avenida de Mayo S

HIPÓLITO YRIGOYEN

← To Biblioteca del Congreso de la Nación

PRESIDENTE

▼ STATUS

ADOLFO ALSINA

SANTIAGO DEL ESTERO

SALTA

AV 9 DE JULIO

BERNARDO DE IRIGOYEN

LUIS SÁENZ

SAN JOSÉ

VIRREY CAVALLOS

PEÑA

MORENO

MONSERRAT

S *Moreno*

TACUARI

AV BELGRANO

VENEZUELA

MÉXICO

CHILE

| 0 | 200 yds |
| 0 | 200 m |

AV INDEPENDENCIA

Independencia S (Línea E)

Independencia S (Línea C)

ESTADOS UNIDOS

© AVALON TRAVEL

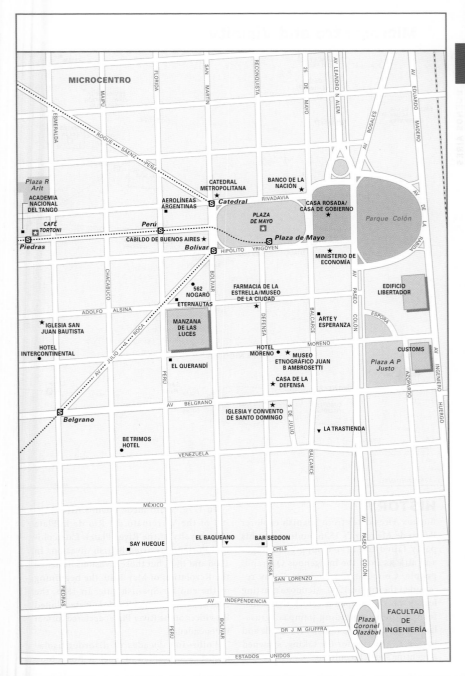

MICROCENTRO

FLORIDA
MAIPÚ
ESMERALDA
SAN MARTÍN
RECONQUISTA
25 DE MAYO
AV LEANDRO N ALEM
AV EDUARDO MADERO
AV ROSALES
AV DE LA RABIDA

ROQUE SAENZ PEÑA

Plaza R Arlt

ACADEMIA NACIONAL DEL TANGO

CATEDRAL METROPOLITANA ★
AEROLÍNEAS ARGENTINAS ■
🄢 Catedral
Perú
RIVADAVIA

BANCO DE LA NACIÓN ★

CASA ROSADA/ CASA DE GOBIERNO ★

Parque Colón

PLAZA DE MAYO ✪

CAFÉ TORTONI 🄻
🄢 Piedras
🄢
CABILDO DE BUENOS AIRES ★
Bolívar 🄢
HIPÓLITO YRIGOYEN
Plaza de Mayo

MINISTERIO DE ECONOMÍA ★

CHACABUCO
BOLÍVAR
ADOLFO ALSINA
DEFENSA
BALCARCE
AV PASEO COLÓN
ESPORA
AV INGENIERO HUERGO
AZOPARDO

562 NOGARÓ ●
ETERNAUTAS ■

FARMACIA DE LA ESTRELLA/MUSEO DE LA CIUDAD

EDIFICIO LIBERTADOR

ARTE Y ESPERANZA ■

IGLESIA SAN JUAN BAUTISTA ★

MANZANA DE LAS LUCES

HOTEL INTERCONTINENTAL ●

AV JULIO A ROCA
PERÚ

EL QUERANDÍ ■

HOTEL MORENO ●
MORENO
MUSEO ETNOGRÁFICO JUAN B AMBROSETTI ★

CUSTOMS

Plaza A P Justo

CASA DE LA DEFENSA ★

AV BELGRANO

🄢 Belgrano

IGLESIA Y CONVENTO DE SANTO DOMINGO ★

5 DE JULIO

LA TRASTIENDA ▾

BE TRIMOS HOTEL ●

VENEZUELA

BALCARCE

MÉXICO

EL BAQUEANO ▾
SAY HUEQUE ■
BAR SEDDON ■
CHILE

DEFENSA
AV PASEO COLÓN

SAN LORENZO

PIEDRAS
AV INDEPENDENCIA
PERÚ
BOLÍVAR

DR J M GIUFFRA

Plaza Coronel Olazábal
FACULTAD DE INGENIERÍA

ESTADOS UNIDOS

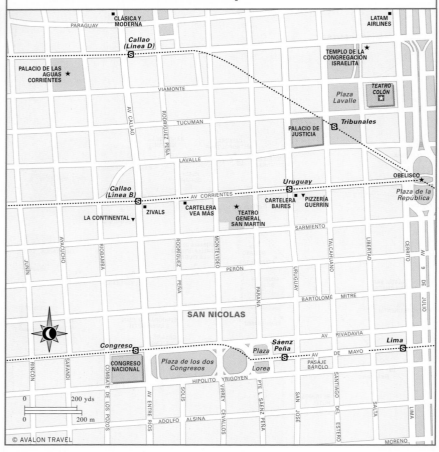

Microcentro and Vicinity

PARAGUAY
CLÁSICA Y MODERNA
LATAM AIRLINES ★

Callao (Linea D) Ⓢ

PALACIO DE LAS AGUAS CORRIENTES ★

TEMPLO DE LA CONGREGACIÓN ISRAELITA ★

VIAMONTE

AV CALLAO
RODRIGUEZ PEÑA
TUCUMAN

Plaza Lavalle

TEATRO COLÓN ✚

PALACIO DE JUSTICIA Ⓢ Tribunales

LAVALLE

Uruguay Ⓢ

OBELISCO ★

Callao (Linea B) Ⓢ
AV CORRIENTES

Plaza de la República

CARTELERA BAIRES
PIZZERÍA GUERRÍN

LA CONTINENTAL ▾
ZIVALS
CARTELERA VEA MÁS ★
TEATRO GENERAL SAN MARTÍN

SARMIENTO

AVACUCHO
RIOBAMBA
JUNIN
RODRIGUEZ
PEÑA
MONTEVIDEO
PERÓN
URUGUAY
PARANA
TALCAHUANO
LIBERTAD
CERRITO
AV 9 DE JULIO

BARTOLOME MITRE

SAN NICOLAS

AV RIVADAVIA

Congreso Ⓢ
Plaza Sáenz Peña Ⓢ
Lima Ⓢ

CONGRESO NACIONAL
Plaza de los dos Congresos
Lorea
DE MAYO
PASAJE BAROLO

RINCON
SARANDI
COMBATE DE LOS POZOS
AV ENTRE RIOS
SOLIS
HIPOLITO YRIGOYEN
VIRREY
CEVALLOS
PTE L. SÁENZ PEÑA
SAN JOSE
SANTIAGO DEL ESTERO
SALTA
LIMA

| 0 | 200 yds |
| 0 | 200 m |

ADOLFO ALSINA

MORENO

© AVALON TRAVEL

HISTORY

Buenos Aires dates from Spanish explorer Pedro de Mendoza's 1536 landing, but his party failed to survive supply shortages and attacks from the indigenous Querandí people. Conquistador Juan de Garay refounded the city in 1580. Mendoza's lasting legacy was the escaped livestock that transformed the surrounding pampas (grasslands) into a fenceless ranch. Feral cattle and horses, nearly free for the taking, spawned Argentina's gaucho culture.

In 1776, Spain made Buenos Aires capital of the Virreinato del Río de la Plata (Viceroyalty of the River Plate). Late colonial Porteños resisted British invasions in 1806 and 1807, but those invasions hastened the Revolution of May 1810, the beginning of the end for Spanish rule. In 1816, the Provincias Unidas del Río de la Plata (United Provinces of the River Plate) declared formal independence.

Following decades of disorder, isolationist caudillo Juan Manuel de Rosas took

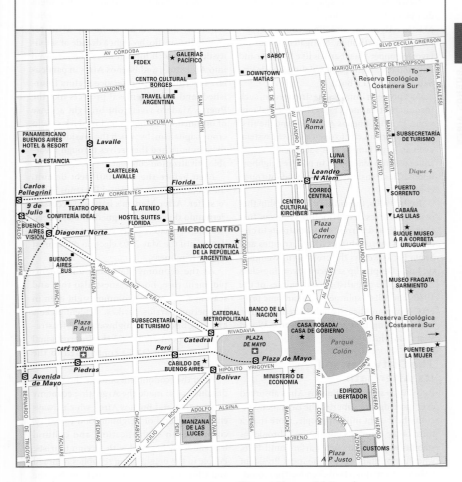

command of Buenos Aires province, ruling it from 1829 until 1852. When Rosas took power, the provincial capital's population was nearly 60,000; shortly after his departure, it reached 99,000.

Rosas's overthrow and exile brought explosive growth—the city's population more than doubled, to 230,000, by 1875. In 1880, it became the federal capital and, by the early 20th century, the region's first city with more than a million inhabitants.

From Gran Aldea to Cosmopolitan Capital

Federalized Buenos Aires's first mayor, Torcuato de Alvear, soon imposed his vision on the newly designated capital. Instead of the intimate Gran Aldea (Great Village), Buenos Aires would become a cosmopolitan showpiece. Where single-story houses once lined narrow colonial streets, broad boulevards like the Avenida de Mayo soon linked majestic public buildings.

Newly landscaped spaces like the Plaza de Mayo, Plaza del Congreso, and Plaza San Martín reflected an ambitious country's aspirations. Some, though, castigated Alvear for favoring upper-class barrios like Recoleta and Palermo over immigrant neighborhoods like San Telmo and La Boca.

As European immigrants streamed in, such inequitable treatment exacerbated social tensions. In 1913, Buenos Aires became the first South American city to open a subway system, even as large families on subsistence wages squeezed into tenements in poorer neighborhoods. Class tension often exploded into open conflict.

In the 1930s, the military dictatorship that overthrew President Hipólito Yrigoyen further obliterated narrow colonial streets to create broad thoroughfares like Corrientes and Santa Fe, as well as the crosstown Avenida 9 de Julio. Despite lip service to working-class interests, the populist Perón regimes of the 1940s and 1950s splurged on pharaonic projects, heavy and heavily subsidized industry, and spending that squandered post-World War II surpluses.

The Dirty War and Its Aftermath

By 1970, as sprawling Buenos Aires absorbed ever more distant suburbs, the capital and vicinity held eight million people, more than a third of the country's population. Chronic instability approached open warfare until 1976, when the military ousted the inept President Isabelita Perón (Juan Perón's widow) in a bloodless coup that became a bloody reign of terror.

One pretext for taking power was civilian corruption, but the military and their civilian collaborators similarly attracted international loans to demolish vibrant but neglected neighborhoods for colossal public works. Much of the money found its way into offshore bank accounts.

Following 1983's return to constitutional government, Argentina underwent several years' hyperinflation in which President Raúl Alfonsín's administration squandered enormous amounts of good will. President Carlos Menem's succeeding Peronist government, directed by Economy Minister Domingo Cavallo, brought a decade of stability during which foreign investment flowed into Argentina, and Buenos Aires in particular. The financial and service sectors flourished, and urban renewal projects like the Puerto Madero riverfront brought a sense of optimism. The boom had its dark side in crony capitalism, by which the president's associates enriched themselves through favorable privatization contracts.

Even before the late-2001 debt default, the economy contracted and Porteños began to suffer. After Menem's hapless successor, Fernando de la Rúa, resigned in December, the country had a series of caretaker presidents until the May 2003 election of Peronist Néstor Kirchner.

As the economy stagnated and unemployment rose, homelessness also rose and scavengers became a common sight even in prosperous barrios. Strikes, strident pickets blocking bridges and highways, and frustration with politicians and the International Monetary Fund (IMF) contributed to the aggravation.

After the economy hit bottom, though, the devalued peso made the Argentine economy competitive, and Buenos Aires, which always enjoyed a blend of neighborhood integrity, cosmopolitan sophistication, and cultural life, suddenly boomed with foreign tourists. People in the neighboring republics of Brazil and Chile were the first to catch on, but the rest of the world soon caught up.

Kirchner (who died in 2010) and Cristina Fernández, his wife and successor, governed controversially for a dozen years before city mayor Mauricio Macri defeated her hapless protégé Daniel Scioli for the presidency in 2015. Macri, like others before him, drew accusations of favoritism toward wealthier barrios, but his government did move municipal offices into the southerly working-class barrio of Parque Patricios and made significant improvements in transportation infrastructure.

ORIENTATION

Also known as the Capital Federal, Buenos Aires lies within the boundaries formed by the Río de la Plata, its Riachuelo tributary, and the ring roads of Avenida General Paz and Avenida 27 de Febrero. Most visitors see only a handful of its 47 barrios.

The historic center is **Monserrat** (also known as Catedral al Sur, "South of the Cathedral"), whose Plaza de Mayo has been the flashpoint for spectacle and debacle in Argentina's tumultuous politics. Immediately north, **San Nicolás** includes the compact, densely built **Microcentro** (also known as Catedral al Norte, "North of the Cathedral"), with the shopping and theater districts, and the local Wall Street in "La City." Eastward, stretching north-south along the river, redeveloped **Puerto Madero** is the city's newest barrio.

Southern Monserrat gives way to **San Telmo**'s cobbled colonial streets, peopled with artists and musicians, tango bars, and the Plaza Dorrego flea market, plus a scattering

of old-money families and more than a scattering of *conventillos* (tenements) abandoned by old money. To the southeast, **La Boca** has never been prosperous, but it has a colorful history, an extravagantly colorful vernacular architecture and artists' colony, and an enviable community solidarity.

Across Avenida Córdoba, elegant **Retiro** marks a transition to the upper-middle-class residential barrios to the north and northwest. Immediately northwest, **Recoleta** retains that elegance in one of the world's most exclusive graveyards, where many affluent Argentines have elected to spend eternity. **Barrio Norte,** a mostly residential area overlapping Retiro and Recoleta, is more a real estate contrivance than a barrio per se.

Beyond Recoleta, broad avenues lead to the open spaces of **Palermo,** a middle- to upper-middle-class barrio with the city's finest dining and wildest nightlife. Woodsy **Belgrano** is a mostly residential barrio with an assortment of museums and other cultural resources.

Sights

Buenos Aires's sights are mostly easily grouped by the more central barrios, though some outlying barrios have scattered points of interest.

MONSERRAT/CATEDRAL AL SUR AND VICINITY

The barrio's axis is the **Avenida de Mayo,** which links the **Casa Rosada** presidential palace (1873-1898) with the **Congreso Nacional** (National Congress, 1908). The perpendicular **Avenida 9 de Julio** splits Monserrat in half.

★ Plaza de Mayo

The **Plaza de Mayo** derives its name from the date of the Revolution of 1810, but it owes its fame to the massive demonstrations that have taken place here in support and protest of

the Peróns, the Falklands/Malvinas war, and other political causes.

At its northwest corner, the imposing **Catedral Metropolitana** (1827) holds the remains of national icon José de San Martín. At the southwest corner, only part of the colonial **Cabildo de Buenos Aires** (1725-1765) survived construction of the Avenida de Mayo. If the economy were as solid as the northeast corner's neoclassical **Banco de la Nación** (1939), Argentina would be a global powerhouse.

★ Café Tortoni

First among the Avenida de Mayo's surviving landmarks, the legendary **Café Tortoni** (Av. de Mayo 825, tel. 011/4342-4328, www.cafetortoni.com.ar) dates from 1858. One of Buenos Aires's most quietly traditional places, the Tortoni has made no concessions to the 21st century and only a few to the 20th: upholstered chairs and marble tables stand among sturdy columns beneath a ceiling punctuated by stained-glass panels; within dark-stained wooden trim, the wallpaper looks original; and the walls are decorated with pictures, portraits, and *filete,* the traditional calligraphy of Porteño sign-painters.

Among the patrons acknowledged on the walls are tango singer Carlos Gardel, La Boca painter Benito Quinquela Martín, dramatists Luigi Pirandello and Federico García Lorca, and pianist Arthur Rubinstein. More recently, the Tortoni has hosted King Juan Carlos I of Spain and Hillary Rodham Clinton.

Other Sights

At the west end of Avenida de Mayo, the **Plaza del Congreso** (officially, Plaza de los dos Congresos, 1904), another frequent site for political demonstrations, faces the Congreso Nacional (1908), Argentina's notoriously dysfunctional legislature.

South of Plaza de Mayo, Monserrat's major colonial landmark is the **Manzana de las Luces,** comprising several ecclesiastical and educational institutions filling an entire block bounded by Alsina, Bolívar, Moreno, and Perú.

At Alsina and Defensa, the **Farmacia de la Estrella** (1900) is a classic apothecary distinguished by magnificent woodwork and health-oriented ceiling murals. Its exterior windows exhibit materials from the upstairs **Museo de la Ciudad** (Defensa 219, tel. 011/4331-9855, www.farmaciadelaestrella. com, 11am-6pm daily, US$0.35, free Mon. and Wed.), specializing in elements of everyday Porteño life.

A block south, the **Museo Etnográfico Juan B. Ambrosetti** (Moreno 350, tel. 011/4345-8196, www.museoetnografico.filo. uba.ar, 1pm-7pm Tues.-Fri., 3pm-7pm Sat.-Sun., US$2) has superb archaeological, ethnographic, and ethnohistoric displays on the Tierra del Fuego archipelago. There are guided tours at 4pm Saturday-Sunday.

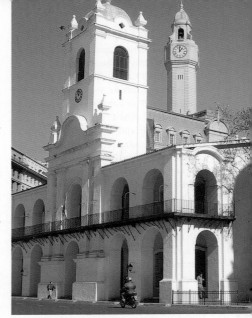

The Cabildo is one of few remaining colonial buildings in downtown Buenos Aires.

From the roof of the **Casa de la Defensa** (Defensa 372), Porteños poured boiling oil on British invaders in 1806-1807. Half a block south, at Avenida Belgrano, the 18th-century **Iglesia y Convento de Santo Domingo** shares grounds with the Instituto Nacional Belgraniano, a patriotic institute that contains the tomb of Argentine flag designer General Manuel Belgrano.

MICROCENTRO AND VICINITY

Formally known as San Nicolás, the area bounded by Avenida Córdoba, Avenida Madero, Avenida Rivadavia, and Avenida Callao encompasses the city's traditional financial, commercial, and entertainment centers. The area between Avenida 9 de Julio and the riverfront, immediately north of the Plaza de Mayo, is commonly called the **Microcentro** and, occasionally, "Catedral al Norte." North of Rivadavia, Calle San Martín is the axis of the financial district, known as "La City."

Organized Tours

Some of the city's best guided tours are available through the municipal tourist office throughout the week, often but not always with English-speaking guides. The complete schedule appears on the city government's website (www.bue.gov.ar). In case of rain, tours are canceled, and they usually do not take place in the summer months of January and February.

For conventional tours of the capital and vicinity, including the Microcentro, Recoleta and Palermo, and San Telmo and La Boca, a frequent choice is **Buenos Aires Visión** (Esmeralda 356, 8th Fl., tel. 011/4394-2986, www.buenosaires-vision.com.ar).

Highly recommended **Eternautas** (Av. Presidente Julio A. Roca 584, 7th Fl., tel. 011/5031-9916 or 011/15-4173-1078, www.eternautas.com) is an organization of professional historians who offer inexpensive walking tours and longer half-day excursions, such as El Otro Sur, a fascinating three-hour bus tour (US$35 pp) through working-class southern barrios like Barracas, Nueva Pompeya, Parque Patricios, and Boedo. They also go farther afield to such places as La Plata and San Antonio de Areco.

By its very name, **Tangol** (Florida 971, Local 31, tel. 011/4363-6000, www.tangol.com) combines those two Porteño passions, tango and soccer (¡go-o-ol!), in its offerings. It also does excursions farther afield in Buenos Aires province and elsewhere. For a commercial website, it's also surprisingly informative.

Travel Line Argentina (Viamonte 640, 9th Fl., tel. 011/4393-9000, www.travelline.com.ar) conducts specialty excursions such as its Evita Tour (4 hours, US$90), which takes in the CGT labor headquarters, Luna Park Stadium, the Perón and Duarte residences, and other locales associated with Evita's meteoric career.

One unique option is **Cicerones de Buenos Aires** (J. J. Biedma 883, Caballito, tel. 011/4431-9892, www.cicerones.org.ar), a nonprofit that matches visitors with enthusiastic nonprofessional guides who can provide a resident's perspective on the city.

For self-guided visitors, another option is **Buenos Aires Bus** (Av. Roque Sáenz Peña 846, 10th Fl., tel. 011/5239-5160, www.buenosairesbus.com), an on-and-off transportation system that links various attractions and destinations, with a dozen stops throughout the city from La Boca to Palermo (9am-8pm daily). A 24-hour ticket costs US$25 pp, but a two-day ticket is only US$8 more.

Named for Argentina's independence day, the broad **Avenida 9 de Julio** separates the Microcentro from the rest of the barrio. **Calle Florida,** a pedestrian mall that became the city's smartest shopping area in the early 20th century, is less fashionable than it once was, except for the restored **Galerías Pacífico,** an architectural landmark occupying nearly an entire block. Don't miss its dome murals, inspired by the famous Mexican muralist David Alfaro Siqueiros.

East-west **Avenida Corrientes,** the traditional axis of Porteño nightlife, now takes a back seat to trendier areas like Puerto Madero and Palermo. Widened sidewalks, though, have encouraged pedestrian traffic to return in an area still important for its theaters, cinemas, and other cultural activities.

At the foot of Corrientes, the former **Correo Central** (central post office, 1928) is a Beaux-Arts landmark whose original architect, Norberto Maillart, based his design on New York City's General Post Office. It is now the **Centro Cultural Kirchner,** named for the late president Néstor Kirchner.

Argentina's central bank, the Italianate **Banco Central de la República Argentina,** has identical facades on the 200 blocks of San Martín and Reconquista. Its **Museo Numismático Dr. José E. Uriburu** (Reconquista 266, tel. 011/4348-3882, 10am-4pm Mon.-Fri., free) helps explain the country's volatile economic history.

At Avenida 9 de Julio and Corrientes, the 67.5-meter **Obelisco** (Obelisk, 1936) is a city symbol erected for the 400th anniversary of Pedro de Mendoza's landing. From the Obelisco, the Diagonal Roque Sáenz Peña ends at **Plaza Lavalle,** where the **Palacio de Justicia** ("Tribunales" or Law Courts, 1904) has lent its colloquial name to the neighborhood.

Across Plaza Lavalle is the stately, newly renovated **Teatro Colón** (1908) opera house. To its north, fronting on Libertad and protected by bulky concrete planter boxes, the **Templo de la Congregación Israelita** (1932) is the capital's largest synagogue. Do not photograph this or any other Jewish community site without express permission.

★ Teatro Colón

Possibly the continent's most important performing arts venue, the ornate **Teatro Colón** (Tucumán 1171, tel. 011/4378-7127, www.teatrocolon.org.ar, tours 9am-5pm daily, US$14, free under age 7) reopened in 2010 after a bicentennial makeover. Moved from an earlier Plaza de Mayo site, the current theater dates from 1908; Francesco Tamburini's Italian Renaissance structure replaced the city's first railroad station here.

Occupying a floor space of nearly 38,000 square meters on seven levels, the Colón opened with a performance of Verdi's *Aida*.

Seating 2,478 patrons, with standing room for another 700, it's one of the country's most ornate buildings, its **Gran Hall** outfitted with Verona and Carrara marble, the **Salón de los Bustos** studded with busts of famous figures from European classical music, and the **Salón Dorado** (Golden Salon) modeled on palaces like Paris's Versailles and Vienna's Schönbrunn. Guided tours last 50 minutes and go behind the scenes as well.

The theater presents some 200 events annually between May and November (contact the box office at tel. 011/4378-7109, www.teatrocolon.org.ar). The main theater itself follows lines of French and Italian classics, with world-class acoustics; a rotating disk aids rapid scene changes. Seating ranges from comfortably upholstered rows to luxury boxes, including a presidential box with its own phone line and a separate exit. Presidential command performances take place on the winter patriotic holidays of May 25 and July 9.

Since its opening, the current theater's who's who of performers has included Igor Stravinsky, Maria Callas, Mikhail Baryshnikov, George Balanchine, and Yo-Yo Ma, not to mention world-renowned orchestras and dance companies. At times, though,

The Puente de la Mujer has become a Puerto Madero landmark.

it's let its hair down to accommodate performers like folksinger Mercedes Sosa, the rhythm-and-blues unit Memphis La Blusera, and rockers Luis Alberto Spinetta and Charly García.

PUERTO MADERO

Born amidst 19th-century corruption, modern **Puerto Madero** has reclaimed a riverfront that languished off-limits during the 1976-1983 dictatorship. Comparable, in some ways, to Baltimore's Inner Harbor and London's Docklands, its focus is four rectangular basins bordered by brick warehouses recycled into stylish lofts, offices, restaurants, bars, and cinemas.

Sequentially numbered from south to north, the four basins include a 450-berth yacht harbor at Dique No. 3; docked on the west side, the **Museo Fragata Sarmiento** (tel. 011/4334-9386, 10am-7pm daily, US$0.70, free under age 5) is an early-20th-century naval training vessel.

Spanish architect Santiago Calatrava's **Puente de la Mujer** is a modernistic pedestrian suspension bridge whose rotating center section allows vessels to pass between Dique No. 3 and Dique No. 2. At the northernmost Dique No. 4, the **Buque Museo**

A.R.A. Corbeta Uruguay (tel. 011/4314-1090, 10am-7pm daily, US$0.35) rescued Norwegian explorers Carl Skottsberg and Otto Nordenskjöld from Antarctica in 1903. Dating from 1874, it's the oldest Argentine vessel still afloat.

Toward the barrio's north end, the **Hotel de Inmigrantes** was Argentina's Ellis Island for European immigrants. It's now the **Museo Nacional de la Inmigración** (Av. Antártida Argentina 1355, tel. 011/4893-0322, www.untref.edu.ar, noon-8pm Tues.-Sun., free), which documents the immigrant experience.

SAN TELMO

San Telmo, with its narrow colonial streets, antiques shops, and street fairs, appeals to Argentines and foreigners alike. Six blocks south of Plaza de Mayo, it's a fine walkers' neighborhood—especially on Sunday, when authorities close most of Calle Defensa to motor vehicles.

After elite families fled an 1870s yellow fever epidemic and moved to northern barrios like Palermo and Belgrano, San Telmo became an area where impoverished immigrant families could find a foothold in *conventillos*, abandoned mansions where large families filled small spaces—often a single

Teatro Colón

San Telmo

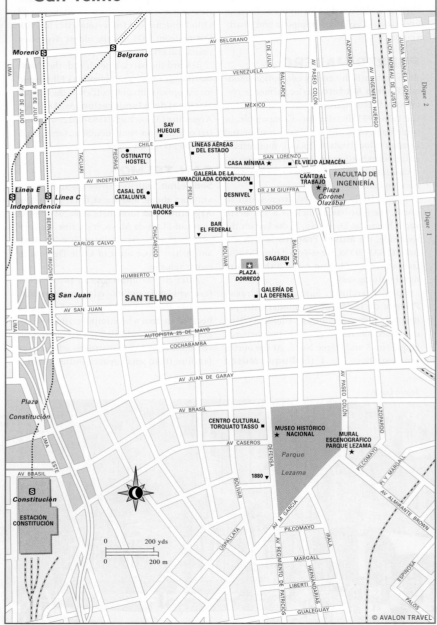

room. Today it's a mixed neighborhood where *conventillos* still exist, but young professionals have also recycled crumbling apartment buildings and even industrial sites into lofts. It's also closely linked to tango, or at least the high-priced spectacle with professional dancers.

While colonial Spanish law dictated rectangular city blocks of equal size, San Telmo breaks the rules. North-south **Calle Balcarce,** for instance, doglegs between Chile and Estados Unidos, crossing the cobblestone alleyways of **Pasaje San Lorenzo** and **Pasaje Giuffra.** The **Casa Mínima** (Pasaje San Lorenzo 380) takes the vernacular *casa chorizo* (sausage house) style to an extreme: This two-story adobe is barely wider than an average adult male's arm spread.

To the east, on Paseo Colón's **Plaza Coronel Olazábal,** Rogelio Yrurtia's *Canto al Trabajo* (Ode to Labor), a sculptural tribute to hardworking pioneers, is a welcome antidote to the pompous equestrian statues elsewhere.

San Telmo's heart, though, is **Plaza Dorrego** (Defensa and Humberto Primo), site of the hectic weekend flea market. At Defensa and Avenida Brasil, a statue of Pedro de Mendoza guards the entrance to **Parque Lezama,** where Mendoza ostensibly founded the city in 1536.

★ Plaza Dorrego

Six days a week, **Plaza Dorrego** is a shady square where Porteños sip *cortados* and nibble lunches from nearby cafés. On Sunday, however, it swarms with visitors who stroll among antiques stalls at the **Feria de San Pedro Telmo** (9am or 10am-late afternoon Sun.), the capital's most famous street fair. Items range from soda siphons to brightly painted calligraphy plaques with *piropos* (aphorisms), oversize antique radios, and many other items. The plaza and side streets also fill with *tangueros* (tango dancers), puppet theaters, hurdy-gurdy men, and "living statues" (costumed mimes). The sidewalk and balcony cafés overlooking the plaza are ideal for enjoying the show.

Parque Lezama

Like many Argentine museums, **Parque Lezama**'s **Museo Histórico Nacional** (Defensa 1600, tel. 011/4307-1182, http://museohistoriconacional.cultura.gob.ar, 11am-6pm Wed.-Sun., US$1.50, free Wed.) underwent an overhaul for the 2010 bicentennial, but it has since retreated from controversial contemporary topics to focus on the distant past, including improved coverage of pre-Columbian Argentina's indigenous peoples. There are guided tours in English (noon Wed.-Fri.).

More conventionally, there are portrait galleries of figures such as San Martín and independence intellectual Mariano Moreno, and massive oils that romanticize General Julio Argentino Roca's brutal Patagonian campaigns. The building itself deserves a look.

LA BOCA

On the twisting Riachuelo's west bank, **La Boca** owes its origins to French Basque and Genovese immigrants who manned packing plants and warehouses during the mid-19th-century beef export boom. Perhaps more than any other city neighborhood, it remains a community, symbolized by fervent identification—some would say fanatical obsession—with the Boca Juniors soccer team.

La Boca is literally the city's most colorful neighborhood, thanks to the brightly painted houses with corrugated zinc siding that line the curving **Caminito,** once a rail terminus. One of the country's most polluted waterways, the **Riachuelo** has undergone a visible cleanup of the corroded hulks that oozed contamination along the meander known as the **Vuelta de Rocha,** but there's a long way to go—the riverside is more presentable, but it's still not for sensitive noses.

Socially and politically, La Boca has a reputation for disorder and anarchy, but the late Benito Quinquela Martín, whose oils sympathetically portrayed its hardworking inhabitants, helped make it an artists' colony. Many

Porteños consider the barrio dangerous, and some visitors prefer guided tours starting at the Caminito.

La Boca's real gateway, though, is Avenida Almirante Brown, at Parque Lezama's southeast corner. Here, the Catalinas del Sur theater group has erected the **Mural Escenográfico Parque Lezama,** a sprawling mural depicting community life through colorful three-dimensional caricatures. From the foot of the avenue, where it intersects Avenida Pedro de Mendoza, the remaining massive girders of the former **Puente Nicolás Avellaneda** (1940), towering above the Riachuelo, are a civil engineering landmark.

Caminito

The starting point for most visitors remains the cobbled, curving **Caminito.** Once the terminus of a railroad line, it's now a pedestrian mall where painters display their watercolors (with more artists on weekends than weekdays). Taking its name from a popular tango, the passageway veers northwest, between brightly colored houses with corrugated zinc siding, from Avenida Pedro de Mendoza.

Initially, these bright colors came from marine paints salvaged from ships in the harbor. The colors are inviting, but the poorly insulated buildings can be stifling in summer and frigid in winter.

Museo de Bellas Artes de La Boca

East of the Caminito, Quinquela Martín's former studio is now the **Museo de Bellas Artes de La Boca** (Pedro de Mendoza 1835, tel. 011/4301-1080, www.buenosaires.gob.ar, 11:15am-6pm Tues.-Sun. and holidays Jan.-Feb., 10am-6pm Tues.-Fri., 11:15am-6pm Sat.-Sun. and holidays Mar.-Dec., US$2).

Estadio Alberto J. Armando

For residents, the neighborhood's key landmark is the **Estadio Alberto J. Armando** (Brandsen and Del Valle Iberlucea), the soccer stadium better known as **La Bombonera.** Murals of barrio life cover the walls along the Brandsen side. It's now home to the **Museo de la Pasión Boquense** (Brandsen 805, tel. 011/4362-1100, www.museoboquense.com, 10am-6pm daily, US$8, US$10.50 with a guided stadium tour), a thunderous homage to the passion for soccer and its role in the community.

La Boca's vibrant Caminito

RETIRO

Popularly describing the area surrounding **Plaza San Martín, Retiro** takes in much of the terrain north of Avenida Córdoba and overlaps the Barrio Norte sector. Once literally a retreat, it began as an isolated colonial monastery on the *barranca* (terrace) above the river, but by 1862, General San Martín's equestrian statue marked its definitive urbanization. On the centennial of the liberator's birth in 1878, the original property was declared Plaza San Martín.

From the late 19th century, the streets surrounding Plaza San Martín became Buenos Aires's most elite residential area. The most extravagant residence, dating from 1909, was the **Palacio Paz** (Av. Santa Fe 750), a 12,000-square-meter Francophile mansion built for newspaper magnate José C. Paz. On the north side, the art nouveau **Palacio San Martín** (1905) was originally a three-house complex built for the Anchorena family. At the plaza's southeastern edge, dating from 1935, the 33-story **Edificio Kavanagh** (Florida 1035) was the city's first skyscraper.

The marble **Monumento a los Caidos de Malvinas** (northeast corner of Plaza San Martín) commemorates those who died in the 1982 Falkland/Malvinas war with Britain. Across Avenida del Libertador, the former Plaza Britania is now the **Plaza Fuerza Aérea Argentina** (the air force was the only branch of the Argentine military to perform competently in the war). Its enduring centerpiece, though, remains the **Torre Monumental** (formerly the Torre de los Ingleses, 1916), a Big Ben clone donated by the Anglo-Argentine community.

Immediately across Avenida Ramos Mejía, **Estación Retiro** (1915) is a restored relic of the railroad era, when British-operated trains served Argentina's northern and northwestern provinces. Today it receives mostly suburban commuter trains.

Retiro is a barrio where people purchase rather than make art, and the contemporary galleries around Plaza San Martín are almost all worth a look. Its major museum is the **Museo Municipal de Arte Hispanoamericano Isaac Fernández Blanco** (Suipacha 1422, tel. 011/4327-0228, www.buenosaires.gob.ar, 1pm-7pm Tues.-Fri., 11am-7pm Sat.-Sun., US$0.75, free Wed.), which stresses colonial and early independence-era art. The museum sometimes closes in January or February.

Retiro's Palacio Paz

Retiro

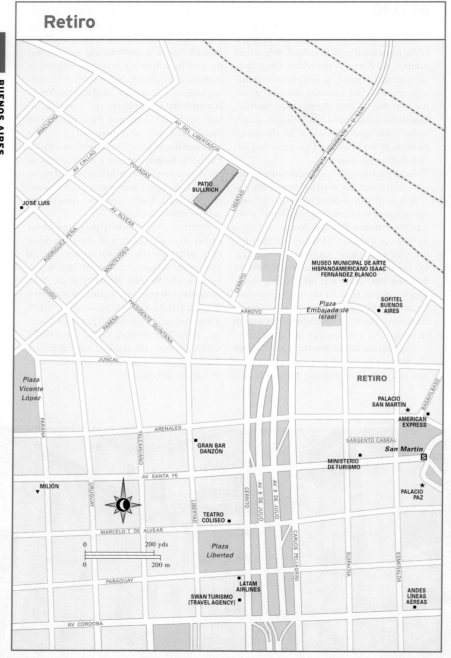

JOSÉ LUIS

PATIO
BULLRICH

MUSEO MUNICIPAL DE ARTE
HISPANOAMERICANO ISAAC
FERNÁNDEZ BLANCO ★

Plaza
Embajada de
Israel

SOFITEL
BUENOS
● AIRES

Plaza
Vicente
López

RETIRO

PALACIO
SAN MARTÍN ★

AMERICAN
EXPRESS

SARGENTO CABRAL

San Martín

GRAN BAR
DANZÓN ■

MINISTERIO
DE TURISMO ■

PALACIO
PAZ ★

MILIÓN ▼

TEATRO
COLISEO ■

Plaza
Libertad

0   200 yds

0   200 m

LATAM ■
AIRLINES

SWAN TURISMO
(TRAVEL AGENCY) ■

ANDES
LÍNEAS
AÉREAS ■

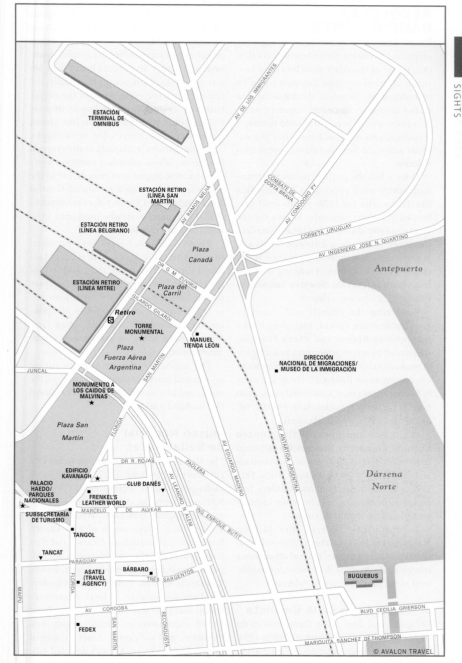

ESTACIÓN
TERMINAL DE
OMNIBUS

AV DE LOS INMIGRANTES

COMBATE DE
COSTA BRAVA

AV COMODORO PY

ESTACIÓN RETIRO
(LÍNEA SAN
MARTÍN)

AV RAMOS MEJÍA

CORBETA URUGUAY

ESTACIÓN RETIRO
(LÍNEA BELGRANO)

Plaza
Canadá

AV INGENIERO JOSÉ N QUARTINO

Antepuerto

DR G M ZUVIRÍA

ESTACIÓN RETIRO
(LÍNEA MITRE)

Plaza del
Carril

GILARDO GILARDI

Retiro
S

TORRE
MONUMENTAL
★

MANUEL
TIENDA LEÓN

Plaza
Fuerza Aérea
Argentina

SAN MARTÍN

DIRECCIÓN
NACIONAL DE MIGRACIONES/
MUSEO DE LA INMIGRACIÓN

JUNCAL

MONUMENTO A
LOS CAÍDOS DE
MALVINAS
★

AV ANTÁRTIDA ARGENTINA

Dársena
Norte

Plaza San
Martín

FLORIDA

DR R ROJAS

PAOLERA

AV EDUARDO MADERO

EDIFICIO
KAVANAGH ★

AV LEANDRO N ALEM

CLUB DANÉS
▼

PALACIO
HAEDO/
PARQUES
NACIONALES

FRENKEL'S
LEATHER WORLD

MARCELO   T DE ALVEAR

ING ENRIQUE BUTIT

SUBSECRETARÍA
DE TURISMO

TANGOL

TANCAT
▼

PARAGUAY

ASATEJ
(TRAVEL
AGENCY)

BÁRBARO
■

TRES SARGENTOS

BUQUEBUS

MAIPÚ

FLORIDA

AV CÓRDOBA

RECONQUISTA

BLVD CECILIA GRIERSON

FEDEX

SAN MARTÍN

MARIQUITA SÁNCHEZ DE THOMPSON

© AVALON TRAVEL

RECOLETA/ BARRIO NORTE

Recoleta, where the line between vigorous excess and serene but opulent eternity is a thin one, is one of the city's most touristed barrios, and one of its prime shopping zones. In everyday usage, "Recoleta" describes the area in and around its namesake cemetery, but it also encompasses much of **Barrio Norte,** a residential area of vague boundaries that extends westward from Retiro and north into Palermo.

Once a bucolic outlier, Recoleta urbanized rapidly when upper-class Porteños fled San Telmo after the 1870s yellow fever outbreaks. It is internationally known for the **Cementerio de la Recoleta** (Recoleta Cemetery, 1822), whose elaborate crypts and mausoleums cost more than many—if not most—Porteño houses. Flanking it is the Jesuit-built **Iglesia de Nuestra Señora de Pilar** (1732), a baroque church.

Bordering the church and cemetery are sizable green spaces, including **Plaza Intendente Alvear** and **Plaza Francia,** frequented by street performers and a legion of professional dog walkers. On the southeastern corner, along Robert M. Ortiz, are some of Buenos Aires's most traditional cafés, most notably **La Biela** (Av. Quintana 596/600, tel. 011/4804-0449, www.labiela.com).

Alongside the church, the **Centro Cultural Ciudad de Buenos Aires** (Junín 1930, tel. 011/4803-1040, www.centrocultural recoleta.org, 1:30pm-8:30pm Tues.-Fri., 11:30am-8:30pm Sat.-Sun. and holidays, free except for some areas) is one of the capital's most important cultural centers.

Facing Plaza Francia, the **Museo Nacional de Bellas Artes** (1933) is the national fine-arts museum. Several other plazas stretch along Avenida del Libertador, northwest of the museum toward Palermo.

★ Cementerio de la Recoleta

For quick and dead alike, **Cementerio de la Recoleta** (Junín 1790, tel. 011/4803-1594, www.cementeriorecoleta.com.ar, 7am-5:45pm daily, free) is Buenos Aires's most prestigious address; its roster of postmortem residents represents wealth and power as surely as the inhabitants of surrounding Francophile mansions and luxury apartments hoard their assets in overseas bank accounts. Socially, the cemetery is more exclusive than the neighborhood—enough cash can buy an impressive residence, but not a surname like Alvear, Anchorena, Mitre, Pueyrredón, or Sarmiento.

Its top attraction, though, is the crypt of Eva Perón, whose relentless ambition overcame humble origins and brought her to the pinnacle of power with her husband, General and President Juan Perón, before her death in 1952. Even Juan Perón, who lived until 1974, failed to qualify for Recoleta.

There were other ways into Recoleta, though. One unlikely occupant is boxer Luis Angel Firpo (1894-1960), the "wild bull of the Pampas," who nearly beat Jack Dempsey for the world heavyweight championship in 1923. Firpo, though, had pull—his sponsor was landowner Félix Bunge, whose family owns some of the cemetery's most ornate constructions.

The cemetery is the site of many guided on-demand tours through travel agencies; the municipal tourist office provides occasional free weekend tours.

Museo Nacional de Bellas Artes

The **Museo Nacional de Bellas Artes** (Av. del Libertador 1473, tel. 011/5288-9900, www. mnba.gob.ar/en, 12:30pm-8:30pm Tues.-Fri., 9:30am-8:30pm Sat.-Sun., free, free guided tours in English 1pm Tues., Wed., and Fri., 4:15pm Sat.) mixes works of well-known European artists such as Picasso and Van Gogh with Argentine counterparts, including Antonio Berni, Cándido López, Benito Quinquela Martín, Prilidiano Pueyrredón, and Lino Spilimbergo. In total, Argentina's traditional fine-arts museum houses about 12,000 oils, watercolors, sketches, engravings, tapestries, and sculptures. Among the most interesting works are López's detailed oils, which recreate the history of the Paraguayan war (1864-1870) despite his having lost his right arm to a grenade.

PALERMO

Buenos Aires's largest barrio, **Palermo** boasts wide-open spaces thanks to 19th-century dictator Juan Manuel de Rosas, whose estate stretched almost from Recoleta all the way to Belgrano. After his exile, the property passed into the public domain and, ironically enough, the sprawling **Parque 3 de Febrero** takes its name from the date of his defeat in 1852.

Once part of the capital's unsavory margins, its street corners populated by stylish but capricious bullies immortalized in Jorge Luis Borges's stories, Palermo hasn't entirely superseded that reputation—in some areas, poorly lighted streets still make visitors uneasy. Yet it also has exclusive neighborhoods such as **Barrio Parque,** also known as **Palermo Chico,** with embassies, single-family mansions, some of Buenos Aires's highest property values, and several key museums.

Across Avenida del Libertador, the **Botánico** is an upper-middle-class enclave taking its name from the **Jardín Botánico Carlos Thays** (Av. Santa Fe 3951, tel. 011/4831-4527, www.jardinbotanico.buenosaires.gob.ar, 8:30am-6:45pm Mon.-Fri., 9:30am-6:45pm Sat.-Sun. and holidays, free), a lovely botanical garden regrettably infested with feral cats. Once a neighborhood of imposing mansions, the Botánico is still affluent but less exclusive than when, in 1948, Eva Perón enraged the neighbors by making one of those mansions into a home for single mothers; it's now a museum in her memory.

The real action is slightly northwest at **Palermo Viejo,** where **Plaza Serrano** (also known as **Plaza Cortázar**) has become a major axis of local nightlife. Palermo Viejo further subdivides into **Palermo Soho** and the more northerly **Palermo Hollywood,** where many TV and radio producers have located their facilities. Shaded by sycamores, many streets still contain low-rise *casas chorizos* (sausage houses) on deep, narrow lots. At the northern end of the barrio, **Las Cañitas** is a gastronomic and nightlife area challenging Palermo Viejo among partygoers.

Museo de Arte Popular José Hernández

Named for the author of the *gauchesco* epic *Martín Fierro,* **Museo de Arte Popular José Hernández** (Av. del Libertador 2373, tel. 011/4803-2384, www.buenosaires.gob.ar, 2pm-7pm Tues.-Fri., 10am-8pm Sat.-Sun. Mar.-Jan., US$0.75, free Wed.) specializes in rural Argentiniana. It's tempting to call it the "museum of irony": Argentina's most gaucho-oriented institution stands in one of the country's most urbane, affluent, and cosmopolitan neighborhoods. Even more ironically, oligarch Félix Bunge built the French-Italianate residence with marble staircases and other lavish features, and exhibits depict gentry like the Martínez de Hoz family—one of whom was the 1976-1983 dictatorship's economy minister—as symbols of a romanticized open-range lifestyle. That said, the museum's worthwhile collections range from magnificent silverwork and vicuña textiles by contemporary Argentine artisans to pre-Columbian pottery, indigenous crafts, and even a typical *pulpería* (rural store).

Museo Nacional de Arte Decorativo

Chilean diplomat Matías Errázuriz Ortúzar and his widow, Josefina de Alvear de Errázuriz, lived less than 20 years in the ornate beaux arts building (1918) that now houses the national decorative art museum. The inventory of the **Museo Nacional de Arte Decorativo** (Av. del Libertador 1902, tel. 011/4802-6606, www.mnad.org.ar, 2pm-7pm Tues.-Sun. mid-Jan.-mid-Dec., US$1.50, free Tues.) comprises 4,000 items from the family's collections, ranging from Roman sculptures to contemporary silverwork, but mostly Asian and European pieces from the 17th to 19th centuries. Many items are anonymous; the best-known are by Europeans like

Manet and Rodin. Guided English-language tours (2:30pm Tues.-Fri., US$3) are available.

★ Museo de Arte Latinoamericano de Buenos Aires (MALBA)

Dedicated to Latin American art, the **Museo de Arte Latinoamericano de Buenos Aires** (Av. Figueroa Alcorta 3415, tel. 011/4808-6500, www.malba.org.ar, noon-9pm Wed., noon-8pm Thurs.-Mon. and holidays, US$6.50, US$3 Wed.) is a striking steel-and-glass structure that devotes one entire floor to Argentine businessman and founder Eduardo F. Constantini's private collections, featuring prominent artists like Mexico's Frida Kahlo and Diego Rivera. There are also works by Antonio Berni, Chile's Roberto Matta, Uruguay's Pedro Figari, and others. The second floor offers special exhibitions. The museum also has a cinema and hosts many events.

★ Museo Eva Perón

Eva Perón, the charismatic spouse of populist president Juan Domingo Perón, made a point of antagonizing her political opponents, or, in her words, "the oligarchy." At her most combative, to the anger and dismay of neighbors, she chose the upscale Botánico neighborhood for the Hogar de Tránsito No. 2, a shelter for single mothers from the provinces. Even more galling, her Fundación de Ayuda Social María Eva Duarte de Perón took over an imposing three-story mansion to house city-bound transients.

Since Evita's 1952 death, middle-class multistory apartment blocks have mostly supplanted the elegant single-family houses and distinctive apartments that then housed the Porteño elite; many have moved to exclusive northern suburbs. Fifty years later, on the July 26 anniversary of her death—supporting novelist Tomás Eloy Martínez's contention that Argentines are "cadaver cultists"—Evita's great-niece María Carolina Rodríguez officially opened the **Museo Eva Perón** (Lafinur 2988, tel. 011/4807-0306, www.museoevita.

org, 11am-6:30pm Tues.-Sun., US$5) "to spread the life, work, and ideology of María Eva Duarte de Perón." What's missing is a critical perspective. Rather than a balanced account of her life, the museum is a professionally presented chronological homage that sidesteps the demagoguery and personality cults that typified both Evita and her charismatic husband.

There's a museum store with a selection of Evita souvenirs on site and a fine café-restaurant as well. Guided English-language tours (US$7) are bookable in advance.

BELGRANO

North of Palermo, linked to downtown by Subte, bus, and train, **Belgrano** remains a barrio apart. In fact, it was once a separate city and then, briefly in the 1880s, the country's capital; the Congress met at what is now the **Museo Histórico Sarmiento** (Cuba 2079, tel. 011/4781-2354, http://museosarmiento. cultura.gob.ar, 1pm-6pm Mon.-Fri., 2pm-7pm Sat.-Sun., US$1.50, free Thurs. and Sat.), honoring President Domingo F. Sarmiento. Sarmiento never lived here, but the exhibits contain many personal possessions and a model of his provincial San Juan birthplace. The museum also chronicles the near-civil war of the 1880s that resulted in Buenos Aires's federalization. Guided tours take place at 4pm Sunday.

Only a block off Cabildo, **Plaza General Manuel Belgrano** hosts the **Feria Plaza Belgrano** (11am-8pm Sat.-Sun.), a popular crafts market. Immediately east, the 1865 landmark **Iglesia de la Inmaculada Concepción** (Vuelta de Obligado 2042), known as **La Redonda** for its circular floor plan, figures in Ernesto Sabato's psychological novel *On Heroes and Tombs*.

The **Museo Casa de Yrurtia** (O'Higgins 2390, tel. 011/4781-0385, http://museoyrurtia.cultura.gob.ar, 11:30am-6pm Wed.-Fri., 10:30am-6pm Sat.-Sun., US$1.50) was home to sculptor Rogelio Yrurtia (1879-1950), creator of San Telmo's *Canto al Trabajo* and other works that challenged the pomposity of

Evita on Tour

Eva Perón became famous for her visit to Europe in 1947. As representative of an Argentina that emerged from World War II as an economic powerhouse, she helped legitimize a shaky Franco regime in Spain. Despite some missteps, she impressed other war-ravaged European countries with Argentina's potential. But even her death, five years later, didn't stop her from touring.

In 1952, millions of Argentines said their *adiós* in a funeral cortege that took hours to travel up Avenida de Mayo from the Casa Rosada to the Congreso Nacional, where her corpse lay in state. She then found a temporary resting place at the headquarters of the Confederación General del Trabajo (CGT, the Peronist trade union), where the shadowy Spanish physician Pedro Ara gave the corpse a mummification worthy of Lenin in hopes of a monument to honor her legacy.

Evita remained at the CGT until 1955, when anti-Peronist General Pedro Aramburu took power and ordered her removal. Eventually, after a series of whistle stops that included the office of a mummy-smitten military man, Aramburu shipped her to an anonymous grave near Milan, Italy—even as a cadaver, Evita symbolized Peronism's durability.

Despite banning the party, Aramburu had reason to worry. For many years, while Perón lived in luxury near Madrid, Argentines dared not even speak his name. In 1970, though, as Argentine politics came undone, left-wing Montoneros guerrillas kidnapped Aramburu and demanded to know Evita's whereabouts.

When Aramburu refused to answer, they executed him and announced that they would hold the body hostage until Evita was returned to "the people." A common slogan of the time was "*Si Evita viviera, sería Montonera*" (If Evita were alive, she would be a Montonera); the cynical Perón encouraged leftist militants to help return him to power, even as he privately despised them.

The police found Aramburu's body before any postmortem prisoner swap could take place, but a notary to whom Aramburu had confided came forward with information on Evita's whereabouts. In September 1971, Perón was stunned when a truck bearing Evita's casket and corpse arrived at his Madrid residence; remarried to dancer María Estela (Isabelita) Martínez, he never expected any such thing. Still, his bizarre spiritualist adviser, José López Rega, used the opportunity to try to transfer Evita's essence into Isabelita's body, as the mummy remained in the attic.

In 1973, Perón finally returned—leaving Evita in Madrid—and was soon elected president with Isabelita as his vice president. Meanwhile, the Montoneros once again kidnapped Aramburu—from his Recoleta crypt—until Evita's return.

Angry but ill and senile, Perón died the next year, but his widow—now president—flew Evita's corpse on a charter from Madrid to Buenos Aires. Evita remained at the presidential residence at Olivos, just north of the capital, until March 1976, when General Jorge Rafael Videla's junta overthrew Isabelita.

At Recoleta, a resentful Evita finally achieved the respectability that she envied in others during her rise to power. Though she was an illegitimate child who went by her mother's surname, Ibarguren, she landed in the family crypt of her father, Juan Duarte, a provincial landowner—only a short walk from Aramburu's tomb.

Even now, Evita's wanderings may not be over. There have been rumors of yet another move—to San Telmo's Franciscan convent at Defensa and Alsina (ironically enough, it was set afire by Peronist mobs in 1955, but it's also the burial place of her confessor, Pedro Errecart). Another possibility is the new mausoleum at Juan Perón's *quinta* (country house) in the southern suburb of San Vicente, which holds his remains.

Isabelita, for her part, was even willing to see Evita lie alongside her late husband. The main objection, it seems, is that Isabelita, former caretaker president Eduardo Duhalde, and other Peronist politicians like the idea better than the Duarte heirs do.

Argentine public art. Guided tours (3pm Fri., 4:30pm Sat.-Sun., US$1) are available.

OUTER BARRIOS

Beyond its most touristed barrios, Buenos Aires has a variety of worthwhile sights ranging from the mundane to the morbid. Some are less accessible by Subte, but have regular *colectivo* (city bus) service.

★ Museo Argentino de Ciencias Naturales

The westerly barrio of Caballito gets few tourists, but its largest open space, **Parque Centenario,** is a good area to see an unadorned but improving neighborhood popular with urban homesteaders. Its impressive natural history museum, **Museo Argentino de Ciencias Naturales Bernardino Rivadavia** (Angel Gallardo 490, tel./fax 011/4982-6595, www.macn.secyt.gov.ar, 2pm-7pm daily, US$2, free under age 7), veers between the stuff-in-glass-cases approach and more sophisticated exhibits offering ecological, historical, and cultural context. Dating from 1937, its quarters are far smaller than the original grandiose project but include decorative details such as bas-relief spiderwebs around the main entrance and sculpted owls

flanking the upper windows. A major expansion with an annex is under consideration.

The main floor contains geological and paleontological exhibits, including the massive Patagonian specimens *Giganotosaurus carolini* (the world's largest carnivorous dinosaur) and *Argentinosaurus huinculensis* (an herbivore whose neck alone measures 12 meters). The second floor stresses South American mammals (including marine mammals), comparative anatomy, amphibians and reptiles, birds, arthropods, and botany.

The museum is about equidistant from the Malabia and Angel Gallardo stations on Subte Línea B.

Cementerio de la Chacarita and Vicinity

For most cadavers, Buenos Aires's second cemetery is more affordable than Recoleta, but eternity at the **Cementerio de la Chacarita** (Guzmán 680, tel. 011/4553-9338, www.cementeriochacarita.com.ar, 7am-5pm daily) can still mean notoriety. Many high-profile Argentines, in fields ranging from entertainment to religion and politics, reside here, and the lines between these categories can be blurry.

The most universally beloved is tango singer Carlos Gardel, victim of a 1935 plane

exterior friezes at Museo Argentino de Ciencias Naturales

crash. Hundreds of admirers from around the globe have left dedicatory plaques, many thanking him for miracles, and every June 26 *Gardelianos* jam the cemetery's streets—platted like a small city—to pay homage.

In terms of devotion from the public, only faith healer to the aristocracy Madre María Salomé can approach Gardel; on the second of each month—she died October 2, 1928—white carnations cover her crypt. Other famous figures include aviator Jorge Newbery, tango musicians Aníbal "Pichuco" Troilo and Osvaldo Pugliese, poet Alfonsina Storni, painter Benito Quinquela Martín, and theater and film comedian Luis Sandrini.

The most notorious resident, though, was Juan Domingo Perón, who moved to a new mausoleum at his San Vicente country house a few years ago. In June 1987, stealthy vandals entered his crypt here, amputating and stealing the caudillo's hands; anti-Peronists speculated, despite lack of evidence, that the thieves sought Perón's fingerprints for access to supposed Swiss bank accounts.

The Cementerio de la Chacarita covers 95 blocks with 12,000 burial vaults, 100,000 gravesites, and 350,000 niches. It's a short walk from Estación Federico Lacroze (Subte Línea B). Free guided tours take place at 11am on the second and fourth Saturday of each month.

Besides Chacarita, there are two contiguous but formally separate cemeteries: the **Cementerio Alemán** (German Cemetery, Av. Elcano 4530, tel. 011/4553-3206, 7am-5pm daily) and the **Cementerio Británico** (British Cemetery, Av. Elcano 4568, tel. 011/4554-0092, 7am-5pm daily).

The Británico is more diverse, with tombs belonging to Armenian, Greek, Irish, Jewish, and other immigrant nationalities. Lucas Bridges, the son of pioneer Anglican missionaries in Tierra del Fuego and author of the classic Fuegian memoir *The Uttermost Part of the Earth*, lies here after dying at sea en route from Ushuaia to Buenos Aires.

Entertainment

Buenos Aires is a 24-hour city with as much to offer as New York or London. Argentines in general and Porteños in particular are night people—discos and dance clubs, for instance, may not even *open* until 1am or so and stay open until dawn. Not everything takes place at those hours, though; there are some municipal restrictions on live music venues and hours.

Every Buenos Aires daily has thorough event listings, especially in end-of-the-week supplements. For tickets to events at many major venues, contact **Ticketek** (tel. 011/5237-7200, www.ticketek.com. ar), which adds a US$1 service charge per ticket. It has brick-and-mortar outlets in the Microcentro at the Teatro Ópera (Av. Corrientes 860) and in Palermo at Groove (Av. Santa Fe 4389).

For discount tickets to tango shows, cinemas, and live theater, try these ticket agencies *(carteleras):* **Cartelera Lavalle** (Lavalle 742, Local 2, tel. 011/4322-1559, www.cartel-eralavalle.com.ar), **Cartelera Baires** (Av. Corrientes 1382, Local 24, tel. 011/4372-5058, www.cartelerabaires.com), and **Cartelera Vea Más** (Av. Corrientes 1660, Local 2, tel. 011/6320-5319).

CAFÉS

No single place embodies tradition better than Monserrat's **Café Tortoni** (Av. de Mayo 825, tel. 011/4342-4328, www.cafe-tortoni.com.ar). Most come for coffee and croissants, but there's live tango, and the bar serves good mixed drinks, accompanied by a selection of cold cuts and cheeses that easily feeds two people.

Despite a partial rehab, the **Confitería Ideal** (Suipacha 384, tel. 011/5265-8069, www.confiteriaideal.com) remains one of the city's most traditional settings. With its worn upholstery and cracked floors, the Ideal served as a set for Madonna's cinematic debacle *Evita*. It hosts downstairs tango shows (for spectators) and upstairs informal dance clubs (for aspiring dancers) around 3pm daily Wednesday-Monday.

Opposite the historic cemetery, Recoleta's **La Biela** (Av. Quintana 596/600, tel. 011/4804-0449, www.labiela.com) is a classic breakfast and coffee spot. In good weather, try the patio, beneath the palm and *palo borracho* trees and the giant *gomero* or *ombú*, which needs wooden beams to prop up its sprawling branches. It's slightly more expensive to eat outside, where the service can be inconsistent.

BARS AND CLUBS

The distinction between cafés and bars is more a continuum than a dichotomy. Some bars call themselves pubs, pronounced as in English, and many of those call themselves Irish.

Relocated to Monserrat, **Bar Seddon** (Defensa 695, tel. 011/4342-3700) has made a successful transition to the capital's oldest neighborhood. Behind its street-side restaurant, **La Trastienda** (Balcarce 460, tel. 011/4342-7650, www.latrastienda.com) has recycled a Monserrat warehouse into an attractive theater hosting both live music and drama. **Downtown Matías** (Reconquista 701, tel. 011/4311-0327, www.downtownmatias.com) is the Microcentro branch of Buenos Aires's oldest Irish-style pub.

Retiro's **Bárbaro** (Tres Sargentos 415, tel. 011/4311-6856, www.barbarobar.com.ar) takes its punning name from a *lunfardo* (street slang) term roughly translatable as "cool." Bordering Barrio Norte, **Milión** (Paraná 1048, tel. 011/4815-9925, www.milion.com.ar) is a tapas bar set in a magnificent 1913 mansion, with a garden, a patio, and interior seating. **Gran Bar Danzón** (Libertad 1161, tel. 011/4811-1108, www.granbardanzon.com.ar) is a sophisticated wine bar with a sushi special at happy hour (7pm-9pm daily), and doubles as a restaurant with separate dining area.

Recoleta's **Buller Brewing Company** (Presidente Ramón Ortiz 1827, tel. 011/4808-9061, www.bullerpub.com) is a brewpub offering seven different styles of beer served with tapas, seafood, and pizza. Palermo Hollywood's cavernous **Niceto Club** (Niceto Vega 5510, tel. 011/4779-9396, www.nicetoclub.com, Thurs.-Sat. nights) has become one of the area's top live music venues. The nearby **Roxy Live Bar** (Niceto Vega 5542, tel. 011/4777-0997, www.theroxybsas.com.ar) draws performers of the stature of Charly García.

Buenos Aires has a vigorous gay scene, centered mostly around Recoleta, Barrio Norte, and Palermo Viejo, with a handful of venues elsewhere. Lots of gay men hang out on Avenida Santa Fe between Callao and Pueyrredón, a good area to meet people. The **Buenos Aires Gay Travel Guide** (www.thegayguide.com.ar) is a comprehensive site for gay visitors.

TANGO

Many but not all tango venues are in the southerly barrios of Monserrat and San Telmo. Professional shows range from straightforward, low-priced programs to extravagant productions at high (often excessive) cost. *Milongas* are participatory bargains for those who want to learn.

Monserrat's legendary **Café Tortoni** (Av. de Mayo 825, tel. 011/4342-4328, www.cafetortoni.com.ar, US$20 pp) offers song-and-dance shows at its Sala Alfonsina Storni, separated from the main part of the café.

Dating from 1920, the elegant **El Querandí** (Perú 302, tel. 011/5199-1770, www.querandi.com.ar, US$140 pp) is another classic, with a nightly dinner (8:30pm) and show (10:30pm). The show alone costs US$60.

One of San Telmo's classic venues, occupying a late-18th-century building, is **El Viejo Almacén** (Balcarce and Av. Independencia, tel. 011/4307-6689, www.viejoalmacen.com.ar, US$140 pp). The price includes dinner at its restaurant, directly across the street.

In the shadow of the Mercado del Abasto, the **Esquina Carlos Gardel** (Carlos Gardel 3200, tel./fax 011/4867-6363, www.esquina-carlosgardel.com.ar) has nightly shows from US$99 pp (show only) to US$140 pp (with dinner). There are also more expensive VIP seats. It's part of a project to sustain the legacy of Gardel, perhaps the most prominent musician in the history of tango, who was called the "Morocho del Abasto."

For those who want to play instead of watch, the best options are neighborhood *milongas* (informal dance clubs). Organized events charge US$5-10 with live music, less with recorded music. For classes, a good clearinghouse is Monserrat's **Academia Nacional del Tango** (Av. de Mayo 833, tel. 011/4345-6968, www.anacdeltango.org.ar), alongside the Café Tortoni. For the truly committed, it even offers a three-year tango degree.

San Telmo's **Centro Cultural Torquato Tasso** (Defensa 1575, tel. 011/4307-6506, www.torquatotasso.com.ar) offers outstanding live tango music shows (but no dancing) on Friday and Saturday, usually at 10pm; a cheap Sunday-night *milonga* at 10pm; and tango lessons every day.

Constitución's **Niño Bien** (Humberto Primo 1462, tel. 015/4147-8687) has an elegant *milonga* from 10:30pm Thursday night that gets crowded early, as it has one of the best dance floors. Palermo's **Salón Canning** (Scalabrini Ortiz 1331, tel. 011/4832-6753) hosts the **Parakultural** (www.parakultural.com.ar, from 11pm Mon.-Tues. and Thurs.), a more avant-garde *milonga* that incorporates electronica.

JAZZ

Clásica y Moderna (Av. Callao 892, tel. 011/4812-8707, www.clasicaymoderna.com, 8am-2am Sun.-Thurs., 8am-4am Fri.-Sat.) is a hybrid bookstore-café-live jazz venue that has occupied the same Barrio Norte location since 1938. Performers here have included Susana Rinaldi, Mercedes Sosa, and Liza Minnelli. Regulars get better service than newcomers.

CLASSICAL MUSIC AND OPERA

The classical music and opera season runs March to November but peaks in winter, June to August. For nearly a century the premier venue has been the **Teatro Colón** (Cerrito 628, tel. 011/4378-7100, www.teatrocolon.org.ar).

Other options include Monserrat's **Teatro Avenida** (Av. de Mayo 1212, tel. 011/4812-6369, www.balirica.org.ar), and Retiro's **Teatro Coliseo** (Marcelo T. de Alvear 1125, tel. 011/4814-3056, www.teatrocoliseo.org.ar).

CULTURAL CENTERS

Adjacent to the Galerías Pacífico, the **Centro Cultural Borges** (Viamonte and San Martín, tel. 011/5555-5359, www.ccborges.org.ar, 10am-9pm Mon.-Sat., 11:30am-9pm Sun., US$4.50 pp) features permanent exhibits on Argentina's most famous literary figure, Jorge Luis Borges, plus rotating fine-arts programs and performing-arts events.

Recoleta's **Centro Cultural Ciudad de Buenos Aires** (Junín 1930, tel. 011/4803-1040, www.centroculturalrecoleta.org, 1:30pm-8:30pm Tues.-Fri., 11:30am-8:30pm Sat.-Sun. and holidays) is one of the city's outstanding cultural venues, with many free or inexpensive events.

EVENTS

Buenos Aires observes all the usual Roman Catholic holidays and many special events as well. The summer months of January and February are quiet; things pick up after school starts in early March.

Dates for the pre-Lenten **Carnaval,** in February or March, vary from year to year. Unlike Brazil's massive festivities, Carnaval here means neighborhood *murgas* (street musicians and dancers). Celebrations take place on weekends rather than during the entire week.

Mid-April's **Feria del Libro** (www.el-libro.com.ar) is Latin America's largest book fair, a fixture on the literary scene since 1974. Late April's **Festival Internacional de Cine Independiente** (International Independent

Buenos Aires Street Fairs

For sightseers and spontaneous shoppers alike, Buenos Aires's diverse *ferias* (street fairs) are one of its greatest pleasures. The most prominent is Sunday's **Feria de San Pedro Telmo** (www.feriadesantelmo.com, around 10am-5pm Sun.), which fills Plaza Dorrego and surrounding streets—closing Calle Defensa to vehicular traffic—with booths full of antiques, *filete* paintings, and other crafts. There are professional tango musicians and dancers, and dozens more street performers range from embarrassingly mundane to truly innovative. Sidewalk cafés and upscale antiques shops are also on offer.

In La Boca, the **Feria Artesanal Plazoleta Vuelta de Rocha** (Av. Pedro de Mendoza and Puerto de Palos, 10am-6pm Sat.-Sun. and holidays) takes place weekends and holidays. Along the length of the nearby Caminito, painters, illustrators, and sculptors sell their works in the **Feria del Caminito** (10am-6pm daily).

After San Telmo, the most frequented *feria* is probably Recoleta's crafts-oriented **Feria Plaza Francia** (www.feriaplazafrancia.com, 11am-8pm Sat.-Sun. and holidays), which is also strong on street performers. Immediately northeast of the Centro Cultural Recoleta, it stretches south along Junín.

On weekends and holidays, crafts stalls cover most of Belgrano's main square at the easygoing **Feria Artesanal Plaza General Manuel Belgrano** (Juramento and Cuba, 11am-8pm Sat.-Sun.).

Film Festival, www.bafici.gov.ar) has grown over the past decade-plus.

For more than a century, late July's **Exposición Internacional de Ganadería, Agricultura y Industria Internacional** (www.exposicionrural.com.ar), the annual livestock show at Palermo's Predio Ferial, has been one of the capital's biggest events.

The **Festival Buenos Aires Tango** (http://festivales.buenosaires.gob.ar) starts around mid-August, immediately before the Mundial de Tango (World Tango Championships), which run to the end of the month. It's a decentralized series of performances at smaller, often intimate venues, offering opportunities to see and hear not just established artists but also developing performers.

Shopping

The main shopping areas are the Microcentro, along the Florida pedestrian mall toward Retiro; Retiro, around Plaza San Martín and along Avenida Santa Fe; Recoleta, near the cemetery; and the tree-lined streets of Palermo Viejo, with stylish shops among the newest restaurants and bars. Street markets take place in San Telmo, Recoleta, and Belgrano.

SHOPPING CENTERS

Over the past decade-plus, developers have recycled many older buildings into upmarket malls for one-stop shopping. The most notable is the Microcentro's magnificent **Galerías Pacífico** (Florida and Córdoba, tel. 011/5555-5100, www.galeriaspacifico.com.ar).

ANTIQUES

Sunday's **Feria de San Pedro Telmo** (www.feriadesantelmo.com, around 10am-5pm Sun.), one of the city's biggest tourist attractions, fills Plaza Dorrego with antiques and bric-a-brac. There are also many dealers in galleries with small street-side frontage, including **Galería de la Inmaculada Concepción** (Defensa 845, tel. 011/4307-0259) and **Galería de la Defensa** (Defensa 1179, no phone).

ART GALLERIES

Buenos Aires has a thriving modern-art scene, with the most innovative galleries in Retiro and Recoleta. **Galería Rubbers** (Av. Alvear 1595, Recoleta, tel. 011/4816-1864, www.rubbers.com.ar) is an excellent contemporary gallery.

In new quarters at Villa Crespo, **Galería Ruth Benzácar** (Juan Ramírez de Velasco 1287, tel. 011/4857-3322, www.ruthbenzacar.com) showcases some of the capital's and the country's most avant-garde artists.

BOOKS AND MUSIC

Buenos Aires's signature bookstore is the Microcentro's **El Ateneo** (Florida 340, tel. 011/4325-6801, www.yenny-elateneo.com), which has a huge selection of Argentine history, literature, and coffee-table books, plus domestic travel titles.

The most elegant outlet, though, is Barrio Norte's affiliated **El Ateneo Grand Splendid** (Av. Santa Fe 1880, tel. 011/4813-6052), a recycled cinema that made *The Guardian*'s list of the world's 10 best bookstores; the former stage is now a café. **Zivals** (Av. Callao 395, Congreso, tel. 011/4371-6978, www.zivals.com) is an excellent independent store. In addition to books, El Ateneo, El Ateneo Grand Splendid, and Zivals all carry quality CDs.

Librerías Turísticas (Paraguay 2457, tel. 011/4963-2866, www.libreriaturistica.com.ar) has a wide choice of maps and guidebooks, including its own guides to the capital's cafés.

San Telmo's **Walrus Books** (Estados Unidos 617, tel. 011/4300-7135, www.walrus-books.com.ar, noon-8pm Tues.-Sun.) carries an ample selection of English-language books well beyond the usual Stephen King potboilers.

CRAFTS

Monserrat's **Arte y Esperanza** (Balcarce 234, tel. 011/4343-1455, www.arteyesperanza.com.ar) stocks a representative sample of indigenous crafts from around the country. Palermo's **Arte Étnico Argentino** (El Salvador 4656, tel. 011/4832-0516, www.arteetnicoargentino.com) specializes in textiles, specifically clothing from the Andean northwest and woolen rugs from the Mapuche people of Patagonia, along with rustically styled furniture.

LEATHER GOODS AND FOOTWEAR

Retiro has several leather specialists, starting with **Frenkel's Leather World** (Florida 1075, tel. 011/4311-2300, www.frenkel.com.ar), which sells crafts as well. Italian immigrant Luciano Bagnasco created one of the capital's most enduring shoemakers in **Guido Mocasines** (Rodríguez Peña 1290, Barrio Norte, tel. 011/4813-4095, www.guidomocasines.com.ar).

WINE

English sommelier Nigel Tollerman operates **0800-VINO** (tel. 011/4966-2500, www.0800-vino.com), which offers a wide selection of Argentine wines and delivers throughout the city.

Near the U.S. Embassy, Palermo's **Terroir** (Buschiazzo 3040, tel. 011/4778-3408, www.terroir.com.ar) is an elite wine shop, with access to limited vintages in addition to the usual fine wines, but it's not utterly unaffordable.

Food

While prices are rising, dining out remains affordable by global standards, at quality ranging from good to world-class.

MONSERRAT

Almost but not quite in San Telmo, ★ **El Baqueano** (Chile 494, tel. 011/4342-0802, www.restoelbaqueano.com, 8pm-midnight Tues.-Sat., eight-course tasting menu US$67 pp, US$100 pp with paired wines) is a one-of-a-kind restaurant specializing in Patagonian products and wild game dishes from throughout the country. To sample the kitchen's diversity, the best choices are the nightly six-course tasting menus, which samples items such as *ñandú* (rhea) carpaccio and *yacaré* (caiman) empanadas, in addition to more conventional dishes such as Patagonian lamb and duck pâté (there's also a vegetarian option). It's a quiet place, with soothing decor and assiduous service.

MICROCENTRO AND VICINITY

★ **Pizzería Guerrín** (Av. Corrientes 1372, tel. 011/4371-8141, from 8am daily) is a one-of-a-kind that sells pizza by the slice at the stand-up counter—the oniony *fugazza* (and *fugazzetta*) are exquisitely simple and simply exquisite. **La Continental** (Callao 361, tel. 011/4374-1444, www.lacontinental.com, 7am-1am Sun.-Thurs., 7am-2am Fri.-Sat.), which has more than a dozen branches around town, is a good backup.

Several tourist-oriented *parrillas* make a fetish of staking their steaks over hot coals in circular barbecue pits, tended by bogus gauchos in full regalia, behind picture windows. While they play for the cliché and serve too many people for individual attention, the quality is good and prices are moderate at **La Estancia** (Lavalle 941, tel. 011/4326-0330, www.asadorlaestancia.com.ar, noon-1am daily).

Perhaps downtown's best restaurant, the banker's favorite ★ **Sabot** (25 de Mayo 756, tel. 011/4313-6587, noon-4pm Mon.-Fri., US$15-20) serves Italian-Argentine dishes of the highest quality in a masculine environment—women are few but not unwelcome—with good-humored professional service. Entrées include *matambre de cerdo* (pork flank steak) and *chivito* (roast goat), plus some fish dishes. A pleasant surprise is the *mate de coca,* a tea made from fresh coca leaves (for digestive purposes only, of course).

PUERTO MADERO

Even though Puerto Madero's food is mostly unimpressive, the barrio draws foreigners from nearby luxury hotels because its restaurants don't flinch at dinnertimes as early as 7pm.

Opposite Dique No. 4, the best *parrilla* is ★ **Cabaña Las Lilas** (Alicia Moreau de Justo 516, tel. 011/4313-1336, www.laslilas.com, noon-4pm and from 8pm daily). Often packed for lunch despite soaring prices, it offers complimentary champagne and snacks while you wait. Its admittedly fine *bife de chorizo* (resembling a porterhouse) has skyrocketed upward of US$40.

Puerto Sorrento (Alicia Moreau de Justo 410, tel. 011/4319-8731, www.sorrentorestaurant.com.ar, noon-1:30am daily, midday special US$30) is the best seafood choice. It has an excellent three-course *almuerzo ejecutivo* (midday special, literally "businessman's lunch") including a soft drink, beer, or wine.

SAN TELMO AND VICINITY

Despite San Telmo's tourist allure, most restaurants here are better lunchtime bargains than dinnertime indulgences, but the scene is improving.

Dating from 1864, ★ **Bar El Federal** (Carlos Calvo 399, tel. 011/4300-4313, from

8am daily, US$8) looks its age—in a positive way, with its worn tiled floors and intricate carved wooden bar. The house specialty is turkey ravioli with a choice of sauces. There is refreshingly cold hard cider on tap.

Despite the large multiple dining rooms at **DesNivel** (Defensa 855, tel. 011/4300-9081, lunch Tues.-Sun., dinner daily), Sunday visitors to Plaza Dorrego form long queues outside for *parrillada* and pasta at bargain prices. Opposite Parque Lezama, **1880** (Defensa 1665, tel. 011/4307-2746, www.parrilla1880.com.ar, lunch and dinner Tues.-Sat.) is a traditional *parrilla* full of barrio atmosphere, including *filete* ornaments by Martiniano Arce.

Reopened in its classic dining room—dark mahogany woodwork and Moorish tiles—the **Casal de Catalunya** (Chacabuco 863, tel. 011/4361-0191, www.casal.org.ar, lunch Tues.-Sun., dinner daily) specializes in Catalonian seafood, tapas, and the occasional standard Argentine item. Suckling pig is the house specialty.

Really two restaurants in one, **Sagardi** (Humberto Primo 319, tel. 011/4361-2538, www.sagardi.com.ar, noon-4pm and from 8pm daily) serves elaborate Basque and Spanish seafood in its semi-private dining room, but the street side is a tapas bar with varied *pintxos* (bar snacks) ideal for a light but diverse and relatively inexpensive lunch. Pay by the toothpick for prosciutto, salmon, artichoke with chopped tomato, sardines, and the like. There's also a good selection of wines by the glass.

LA BOCA

La Boca's offerings are limited, but the food is good enough for lunch—most people visit during the daytime, anyway—and the occasional dinnertime foray.

Banchero (Suárez 396, tel. 011/4301-1406, noon-4pm and from 8pm daily) is the original site of the pizzeria that claims to have invented the onion-and-mozzarella *fugazzeta*. Whether or not that's true, theirs is one of the best.

In an area where taxis are obligatory at night and maybe advisable even in the daytime (though some cabbies have trouble finding it), ★ **El Obrero** (Agustín Cafferena 64, tel. 011/4362-9912, noon-4:30pm and from 8:30pm Mon.-Sat., US$6-10) is where celebrities go slumming for steaks. Its walls plastered with images of soccer icon Diego Maradona and little else, it draws an international clientele on the order of Bono and Robert Duvall. There's no printed menu—check the chalkboards.

San Telmo's Sagardi

At the other extreme, celebrity chef Francis Mallman's **Patagonia Sur** (Rocha 801, tel. 011/4303-5917, www.restaurante-patagoniasur.com, lunch Thurs.-Sun., dinner Thurs.-Sat., 3-course dinner without wine US$200 pp), one of his several gourmet restaurants in Argentina and Uruguay, seems out of place here. It's expensive, but Mallman's Argentine beef, seafood, and other regional dishes are always worth consideration.

RETIRO

Danish *smørrebrød* might seem an improbable alternative here, but the **Club Danés** (Av. Leandro N. Alem 1074, 12th Fl., tel. 011/4312-9266, lunch Mon.-Fri., US$11) is cheap *and* appetizing. It also has exceptional views of Puerto Madero.

★ **Tancat** (Paraguay 645, tel. 011/4312-5442, www.tancatrestaurante.com, noon-12:30am Mon.-Sat., lunch US$10-15) is a first-rate *tasca,* an informal Spanish bar-restaurant with good-natured service. Don't miss the prosciutto-ish *jamón serrano* appetizer. There are few tables, but lunch-goers jam into the long wooden bar, backed by shelves of wine covered with business cards, posters, and photos.

RECOLETA/ BARRIO NORTE

José Luis (Av. Quintana 456, tel. 011/4807-0606, lunch and dinner Mon.-Sat., dinner around US$30) is an Asturian seafood restaurant that stresses fresher and lighter dishes than most of its counterparts.

Internationally recognized **Oviedo** (Beruti 2602, tel. 011/4822-5415, www.oviedoresto.com.ar, noon-2am Mon.-Sat., lunch US$30) has moved to a more contemporary menu but still stresses seafood, such as grilled fish with a variety of sauces. It also serves Patagonian lamb and standards like beef.

PALERMO

Palermo is, without question, the center of innovation in Argentine dining, mostly in Palermo Soho but also in Palermo Hollywood, the Botánico, and Las Cañitas.

Among the Botánico's best, ★ **Bella Italia Café Bar** (Repúblic Arabe Siria 3330, tel. 011/4807-5120, www.bellaitalia-gourmet.com.ar, 7am-1am daily, US$11) serves items such as spinach-ricotta gnocchi with a subtle cream sauce, fine shrimp risotto (US$12), and salads.

Guido (Blv. Cerviño 3943, tel. 011/4802-1262, www.guidorestaurant.com.ar, from 7pm Tues.-Sun., entrées US$12, 3-course dinner US$20) is a trattoria that has expanded an already outstanding menu notable for a nightly risotto and a separate three-course dinner, plus inexpensive pizzas. The decor is classically cinematic, the service is attentive, there's an extensive list of wines by the glass, and a 7pm-9pm happy hour nightly.

Mark's Deli & Coffee House (El Salvador 4701, tel. 011/4832-6244, www.markspalermo.com.ar, 8:30am-9:30pm Mon.-Sat., 10:30am-9pm Sun. and holidays, sandwiches US$7-8) is a U.S.-style deli, bright and cheerful with indoor and patio seating and outstanding sandwiches. There's a small selection of wines by the glass and large and tasty glasses of lemonade.

In the Botánico, cozy ★ **Nemo** (Cabello 3672, tel. 011/4802-5308, www.nemoresto.com.ar, lunch and dinner daily, entrées US$12-20) serves light entrées, including seafood-based pastas and a diverse fish menu with at least one freshwater catch every night. It has limited sidewalk seating. The late *Buenos Aires Herald* food writer Dereck Foster called it the capital's "consistently best seafood restaurant."

Just when it seems that Peruvian fusion here can't get any better, along comes **Bardot** (Honduras 5237, tel. 011/4831-1112, 8pm-midnight Tues.-Fri., 1pm-5pm and 8pm-midnight Sat.-Sun.), with dishes such as *mero a lo macho* (grouper with a shrimp sauce, US$15), Buenos Aires's best *pisco* sours (two-for-one on Wed.), and nearly flawless service.

The *parrilla* of the moment remains **La Cabrera** (Cabrera 5099, tel. 011/4832-5754, www.parrillalacabrera.com.ar,

12:30pm-4:30pm and from 8:30pm nightly, lunch US$20), where the *bife de chorizo* can feed two hungry diners and comes with a sampler of side dishes. There's also a nightly happy hour (7pm-8pm), with 40 percent menu discounts.

For an excellent and cheaper alternative, try the distinctly unfashionable **El Trapiche** (Paraguay 5099, tel. 011/4772-7343, lunch and dinner daily), where a single portion of beef can suffice for two or even three diners.

It's fallen out of favor in some circles, but Palermo Hollywood's **Olsen** (Gorriti 5870, tel. 011/4776-7677, olsen@fibertel.com.ar, from noon Tues.-Sat., from 10am Sun., entrées from US$12) serves what might be called Scandinavian criollo cuisine, with dishes like ravioli with goat cheese and pork roast with raspberry sauce. The bar serves the standard aperitifs but also a literally dizzying variety of vodka-based cocktails. Also serving Sunday brunch, Olsen has devoted part of its deep lot to a sculpture garden replicating a Scandinavian boreal forest of birches, cypresses, and pines.

BELGRANO

On a quiet Belgrano block, the stylishly cozy ★ **Pura Tierra** (3 de Febrero 1167, tel. 011/4899-2007, www.puratierra.com.ar, 8pm-12:30am Mon.-Sat., entrées US$20, 8-course tasting menu US$60 without wine) is one of the city's top restaurants for a creative menu that incorporates fresh, natural, local ingredients including tantalizing starters, entrées such as *bondiola* (pork shoulder), and remarkable desserts; there's also an eight-course tasting menu. On top of that, its sommelier provides some of the savviest wine recommendations, at reasonable prices, to accompany them. One of the best options for a romantic dinner or a small group of friends, Pura Tierra offers a 10 percent discount for cash payments.

Palermo's Olsen

Accommodations

Buenos Aires has abundant accommodations in all categories. Some opportunistic hoteliers have established higher rates for foreigners; if they insist on this, there's little you can do except go elsewhere or try to argue the point. Advertised rates at top-end hotels often exclude the 21 percent IVA, but prices listed here do include taxes. There is now an IVA exemption for foreigners paying with credit or debit cards.

Note that many accommodations, especially hostels that have both dorms and private rooms, have rates that overlap the categories below.

US$25-50

In recent years, hostels have sprung up like tango halls in Gardel's time, and most of them are good to excellent at modest prices. Some are Hostelling International affiliates, but most are independent. Some basic inexpensive hotels also remain.

Near the Facultad de Medicina, **Hotel del Prado** (Paraguay 2385, tel. 011/4961-1192, www.hoteldelprado-ba.com.ar, US$33 s or d) is a plain but tastefully remodeled older building with a quiet interior, good beds, and friendly owner-operators. Rooms have private bath, cable TV, telephone, and ceiling fans but no air-conditioning; there are discounts for extended stays.

Congreso's ★ **Hotel Chile** (Av. de Mayo 1297, tel./fax 011/4383-7877, www.hotelchile.com.ar, US$33 s, US$38 d) is an art nouveau monument offering modernized rooms with private baths, cable TV, and telephones. Corner balcony rooms on the upper floors enjoy panoramic views of the Congreso and, by craning your neck eastward, the Plaza de Mayo and Casa Rosada; the decibel level rises from the street, though.

It's not quite the design hostel it purports to be, but San Telmo's ★ **Ostinatto Hostel** (Chile 680, tel. 011/4362-9639, www.ostinatto.com.ar, US$17-19 pp dorm, US$39-54 s or d

with private bath) has done some daring innovations while keeping prices modest, even low, in an ideal location. It features a bar-restaurant, a rooftop terrace that hosts barbecues, and even a mini-cinema, and offers at least one free-of-charge activity per day.

US$50-100

In a primo location, the Microcentro's **Hostel Suites Florida** (Florida 328, tel. 011/4325-0969, www.hostelsuites.com, US$19 pp dorm, US$43 s, 56 d) is a converted hotel with institutional architecture, but they've spiced it up with decorative touches and theme floors for Carlos Gardel, Che Guevara, and other figures from Argentine history. While it's lively and occasionally rowdy, the sleeping quarters are far from the common areas; an activities board shows what's going on around town.

On a block-long street where original cobbles still show through slabs of pavement, Palermo Soho's **Che Lulu Guest House** (Emilio Zolá 5185, tel. 011/4772-0289, www.chelulu.com, US$50-100 d with breakfast) is an artist-inspired B&B where nine small but colorful rooms with rustically styled furniture go for bargain prices; the cheaper rooms have a shared bath; there are also a couple of even cheaper dorm rooms. The main drawback here is limited closet space, which can mean living out of a suitcase or backpack.

Originally built and run with the gay market in mind, but now under new ownership, Monserrat's **Be Trimos Hotel** (Venezuela 647, tel. 011/4136-9393, www.betrimoshotel.com.ar, US$60-73 s or d) is on the edge of San Telmo. Architecturally, its creative use of transparent glass in the reception area, staircases, and even the rooftop health club pool—its shimmering waters visible from the ground level—still suggest, metaphorically at least, that those who stay here have nothing to hide. The decor of its 48 midsize guest rooms and common areas is modern and boutiquey.

In Palermo's Villa Freud neighborhood, the French-run ★ **Hotel Costa Rica** (Costa Rica 4137, tel. 011/4864-7390, www.hotelcostarica.com.ar, US$49 d with shared bath, US$63-84 d with private bath) falls at the affordable end of the boutique hotel scale. Restored to their original configurations, with high ceilings in what was once a crowded family hotel, its 25 rooms are well-furnished but plain and frills-free (no TV, for instance). While less convenient than some barrio hotels, it's still in easy walking distance to the restaurants and bars of Palermo Soho.

In a painstakingly remodeled *casa chorizo* (sausage house), ★ **Malabia House** (Malabia 1555, tel./fax 011/4832-3345, www.malabia-house.com.ar, US$77-103 s, US$86-115 d) is a bed-and-breakfast with magnificent natural light, glistening wood floors, handsome furnishings, and small but verdant patios. Standard ground-floor rooms have external private baths; the more expensive upstairs rooms have air-conditioning and interior baths.

Built from scratch, rather than recycled, Palermo Soho's deceptively named **Five Cool Rooms Buenos Aires** (Honduras 4742, tel. 011/4774-8783, www.fivehotelbuenosaires.com, US$81-152 s or d) is a design hotel with 17 rooms in three categories: small, medium, and large (the "five" derives from the number of brothers and sisters who own the place). The management deserves truth-in-labeling credit for the 11 "smalls," but in truth they're bigger than the name implies; king beds, however, fill most of the floor space. The capacious common areas, including a reading room, two large patios, and an even larger rooftop terrace with a whirlpool tub, compensate for any small interior spaces. The entire hotel enjoys a quiet seclusion uncommon among the abundant restaurants, bars, and shops.

One of the capital's most historic lodgings, dating from 1929, Monserrat's **Castelar Hotel & Spa** (Av. de Mayo 1152, tel. 011/4383-5000, www.castelarhotel.com.ar, from US$95 s or d) has hosted the likes of Spanish dramatist Federico García Lorca (whose restored room is now a museum), Chile's Nobel Prize-winning poet Pablo Neruda, and Nobel Prize-winning scientist Linus Pauling. Embellished with Carrara marble, it offers comfortable, well-equipped rooms with breakfast and access to its own spa.

US$100-150

In a recycled six-story print shop, Monserrat's **Hotel Moreno** (Moreno 376, tel. 011/6091-2001, www.morenobuenosaires.com,

Monserrat's Hotel Moreno

US$100-127 d) calls itself a "no-frills deluxe" hotel with 39 large rooms and lofts with limited decor and amenities—little or no artwork, for instance, and relatively small flat-screen TVs. It retains classic features, such as grillwork elevators and staircase stained-glass panels; a rooftop bar and terrace offer fine views. In low season (Apr.-July, except Easter), some rooms can go for even less.

Monserrat's four-star ★ **562 Nogaró** (Diagonal Presidente Julio A. Roca 562, tel. 011/4331-0091, www.562nogarohotel.com, from US$100 s or d) dates from 1930 but benefits from contemporary renovations. This French-style 150-room hotel offers occasional discount rates.

Barrio Norte's bright **Design Suites** (Marcelo T. de Alvear 1683, tel./fax 011/4814-8700, www.designsuites.com, US$137-197 s or d) has a heated pool, gym, restaurant room service, and daily newspaper delivery (of the guest's choice). Each of its 40 suites has cable TV, a telephone, Internet connections, a kitchenette, a minibar, air-conditioning, a strongbox, and a hot tub.

Monserrat's high-rise **Hotel Intercontinental** (Moreno 809, tel. 011/4340-7100, www.intercontinental.com, US$138-273 s or d) consistently makes best-hotels lists in magazines like *Travel + Leisure*. Corporate and other discount rates are possible for its 305 rooms.

US$150-200

Every taxi driver in town knows about ★ **Hotel Home Buenos Aires** (Honduras 5860, tel. 011/4779-1008, www.homebuenosaires.com, US$160 s or d). Even U2 stayed here (and welcomed other hotel guests to *their* party) when they played Buenos Aires, but you needn't be a big name to enjoy its imaginative design, spacious rooms and suites, and ample common spaces, including a large garden with pool that is uncommon in this part of town.

Near the Obelisco, the **Panamericano Buenos Aires Hotel and Resort** (Carlos Pellegrini 551, tel. 011/4348-5000, www.panamericano.us, US$165-265 s or d, with more expensive suites) consists of an older (slightly cheaper) south tower and a newer north tower. Both are comfortable, but the north-tower rooms are technologically superior. All 400 rooms have access to amenities, including the gym and rooftop pool. Its restaurant, **Tomo I**, is widely considered one of the capital's best.

OVER US$200

Of all the city's hotels, Retiro's **Sofitel Buenos Aires** (Arroyo 841, tel. 011/4131-0000, www.sofitel.com, from US$296) comes closest to matching the Alvear Palace's classic Parisian elegance. Its lobby is an architectural masterpiece. This modernization of the neoclassical Torre Mihanovich (1929) manages to blend the Francophile tradition with current design trends and modern functions. The slightly more expensive "luxury" rooms have larger baths and slightly better views on one of the city's quietest blocks, known for its upscale art galleries.

Each of the 11 rooms at Palermo Soho's **Legado Mítico Buenos Aires** (Gurruchaga 1848, tel. 011/4833-1300, www.legadomitico.com, US$300-425) takes its theme from a historic figure in Argentina's past (this is perhaps the first time that such bitter enemies as Eva Perón and writer Victoria Ocampo have appeared under the same roof). Its decor is a blend of classic and contemporary, with French-style furnishings often side by side with modern designs. Ironically, one of the largest and most luxurious rooms is "The Idealist," dedicated to Ernesto "Che" Guevara, but Guevara's family background placed him among the Argentine elite.

Since 1928, the ★ **Alvear Palace Hotel** (Av. Alvear 1891, tel. 011/4805-2100, www.alvearpalace.com, from US$650 s or d) has symbolized elegance and luxury—not to mention wealth and privilege. This is one place that, despite devaluation, maintains both its standards and its prices for accommodations, with Egyptian-cotton sheets and Hermès toiletries. Francophobes, though, may find the *ancien régime* decor cloying.

There's no faux modesty in the name of French architect Philippe Starck's latest project, which transformed a landmark Puerto Madero granary into the five-star-plus **Faena Hotel & Universe** (Marta Salotti 445, tel. 011/4010-9000, www.faenahotelanduniverse. com, from US$395 s or d). From outside, it's not evident that this redbrick structure is even a hotel, but its interior is a revelation of continental style. The rooms and their furnishings look so Parisian as to be incongruous with the building, but there's no denying their quality and sophistication. The Faena also sells "experiences," such as polo with pros and workshops with famous photographer Aldo Sessa. If you've ever thought of paying upward of US$12,000 for a hotel room, the Faena's for you.

Information and Services

INFORMATION

The **Ministerio de Turismo** (Av. Santa Fe 883, Retiro, tel. 011/4312-2232 or 0800/555-0016, www.turismo.gov.ar, 9am-5pm Mon.-Fri.) has a branch at Aeropuerto Internacional Ezeiza (tel. 011/4480-0292, 8am-8pm daily) and another at Aeroparque Jorge Newbery (tel. 011/4771-0104, 8am-8pm daily).

The municipal **Subsecretaría de Turismo** (www.bue.gov.ar) maintains several information kiosks: in the Microcentro (Florida 100, 11am-6pm Mon.-Fri., 9am-6pm Sat.-Sun.); in Recoleta (Quintana 596, tel. 011/4806-0904, 11am-6pm Mon.-Fri., 9am-6pm Sat.-Sun.); at Puerto Madero's Dique 4 (Av. Alicia Moreau de Justo 200, tel. 011/4315-4265, 11am-6pm Mon.-Fri., 9am-6pm Sat.-Sun.); in Retiro (Florida and Marcelo T. de Alvear, 10am-6pm Mon.-Fri.); and at the Retiro bus terminal (tel. 011/4313-0187, 7:30am-2:30pm Mon.-Fri., 7:30am-9:30am Sat.-Sun.). All distribute maps and brochures, and usually have English-speaking staff.

SERVICES

Money

The ubiquitous ATMs are most convenient for changing money, but their fees make cash more convenient at exchange houses, *cuevas* (informal exchange houses), or even more informal street changers (use caution, however). Traveler's checks are normally charged a commission or exchanged at a lower rate than cash, but **American Express** (Arenales 707, Retiro, tel. 011/4310-3000, www.americanexpress.com.ar) cashes its own checks for no commission.

Postal Services

There are many offices throughout the city, but international parcels exceeding one kilogram must go from the **Correo Internacional** (Antártida Argentina near Retiro train station, tel. 011/4316-7777, 11am-5pm Mon.-Fri.).

Federal Express (Maipú 753, tel. 011/4630-0300) offers private courier service.

Communication

Locutorios for faxes and long-distance calls are not so common as they used to be, but some still exist and have Internet connections. Wi-Fi is almost ubiquitous.

Travel Agencies

North of Plaza San Martín, Retiro's **American Express** (Arenales 707, tel. 011/4310-3000, www.americanexpress.com. ar) offers the usual services of a travel agency.

Swan Turismo (Cerrito 822, 9th Fl., Retiro, tel. 011/4129-7926, www.swanturismo. com.ar) is a full-service agency with a reputation for navigating some of the Argentine travel system's eccentricities.

In the Galería Buenos Aires, the nonprofit **Asatej** (Florida 835, Oficina 205, Retiro, tel. 011/4114-7528, www.almundo.com.ar) is good at searching out the best airfares for anyone, not just students; it is also a Hostelling International affiliate. Another good choice is **Say Hueque** (www.sayhueque.com), which has branches in San Telmo (Chile 557, tel. 011/4307-3451) and Palermo (Thames 2062, tel. 011/5258-8740), especially for independent travelers.

Libraries

The **Biblioteca Nacional Mariano Moreno** (National Library, Agüero 2502, Recoleta, tel. 011/4808-6000, www.bn.gov.ar, 9am-9pm Mon.-Fri., noon-7pm Sat.-Sun.) holds frequent special exhibitions, lectures and literary events, and free concerts.

Immigration

For visa extensions, head to the **Dirección Nacional de Migraciones** (Av. Antártida Argentina 1355, tel. 011/4317-0237, www.migraciones.gov.ar, 7:30am-2pm Mon.-Fri.).

the Correo Central

Medical Services

Public hospitals include Recoleta's **Hospital Rivadavia** (Av. Las Heras 2670, tel. 011/4809-2000) and Palermo's **Hospital Municipal Juan Fernández** (Cerviño 3356, tel. 011/4808-2600), which provide emergency services at little or no cost. Wait times can be long.

The **Hospital Británico** (Perdriel 74, Barracas, tel. 011/4309-6400, www.hospital-britanico.org.ar) is a highly regarded private hospital. Cardiology is the specialty at the **Fundación Favaloro** (Av. Belgrano 1746, tel. 011/4378-1200, www.fundacionfavaloro.org).

Argentine presidents have had arthroscopies and soccer star Diego Maradona did his detox at Belgrano's **Clínica Fleni** (Montañeses 2325, tel. 011/5777-3200, www.fleni.org.ar), but it does not handle every specialty.

Transportation

AIR

Buenos Aires has two airports, both operated by the private concessionaire **Aeropuertos Argentinos 2000** (tel. 011/5480-6111, www.aa2000.com.ar). Most international flights arrive and depart from the suburban airport **Aeropuerto Internacional Ministro Pistarini** (EZE), 35 kilometers southwest of downtown, popularly called **Ezeiza** after its namesake suburb. Palermo's **Aeroparque Jorge Newbery** (AEP, Av. Costanera Rafael Obligado s/n) is primarily domestic but handles some international flights from neighboring countries.

Renationalized **Aerolíneas Argentinas** (Perú 2, Monserrat, tel. 0810/222-86527, www.aerolineas.com.ar) flies erratically to destinations as far south as Ushuaia in Tierra del Fuego. Though it serves fewer destinations, **LATAM Argentina** (Cerrito 866, tel. 0810/999-9526) is more reliable.

Aeroparque-based **Andes Líneas Aéreas** (Av. Córdoba 673, 4th Fl., tel. 0810/7772-6337, www.andesonline.com) flies to Puerto Madryn.

Líneas Aéreas del Estado (LADE, Perú 714, San Telmo, tel. 0810/810-5233, www.lade.com.ar) is the Argentine air force's commercial aviation branch. Miraculously surviving budget crises and privatizations, it flies to southern Buenos Aires province and Patagonia on a wing and a subsidy.

International passengers leaving from Ezeiza pay a US$41.50 **departure tax,** payable in local currency or U.S. dollars; some of this may be collected on departure. On flights shorter than 300 kilometers to neighboring countries, such as Uruguay, the tax is only US$10; on domestic flights from Aeroparque, it's about US$3. These latter fees are normally included in the ticket price.

Transportation to the Airport

There are various options for getting to and from the airports, ranging from *colectivos* (city buses) to shuttles, metered taxis, and *remises* (meterless taxis). The ride-sharing app Uber now operates in Buenos Aires, but faces vigorous opposition from taxi drivers.

Colectivos are the cheapest option, but they are more practical for close-in Aeroparque than distant Ezeiza, as they take circuitous routes on surface streets. To Aeroparque (about US$0.50), the options are No. 33 from Plaza de Mayo, the Microcentro, and Retiro; No. 37-C (Ciudad Universitaria) from Plaza del Congreso, Avenida Callao, Avenida Las Heras, and Plaza Italia; No. 45 northbound from Plaza Constitución, Plaza San Martín, or Retiro; and No. 160-C or 160-D from Avenida Las Heras or Plaza Italia. Return buses leave from the Avenida Costanera Rafael Obligado, just outside the terminal.

Manuel Tienda León (Av. Madero and San Martín, Retiro, tel. 011/4315-5115 or 0810/888-5366, www.tiendaleon.com.ar) runs frequent buses to and from Ezeiza (US$13) and to Aeroparque (US$5); buses from Ezeiza make connections to Aeroparque for domestic flights and also include door-to-door taxi service from Tienda León's Retiro terminal.

Offering door-to-door services, **taxis** and *remises* are no more expensive than shuttles for three or more people. Manuel Tienda León and many other companies, such as **Transfer Express** (tel. 0800/444-4872) and **Naon Remises** (tel. 011/4545-6500), have *remises* to Aeroparque (US$18) and Ezeiza (US$40). Fares usually include tolls to Ezeiza.

SUBWAY

Operated by the private concessionaire **Metrovías** (www.metrovias.com.ar), the state-owned Subterráneos de Buenos Aires, popularly known as the **Subte** (5am-11pm Mon.-Sat., 8am-10:30pm Sun. and holidays, about US$0.50 per ride), comprises six alphabetically designated lines *(líneas),* four of which (A, B, D, and E) begin in Monserrat or the Microcentro and serve outlying northern and western barrios with numerous stations in between. Service is less frequent on Sunday and holidays. The rechargeable SUBE ticket is now obligatory. Two or more people may legally use the same ticket by passing it back and forth across the turnstile; you do not need a ticket to exit the system.

Before going through the turnstiles, be sure of the direction that you're headed; at some stations, trains in both directions use the same platform, but at others the platforms are on opposite sides. Some stations have one-way traffic only; in those cases, the next station down the line usually serves one-way traffic in the other direction.

For complaints or problems, contact Metrovías's **Centro de Atención al Pasajero** (tel. 011/4555-1616 toll-free).

Routes

Línea A begins at Plaza de Mayo in Monserrat and runs beneath Avenida Rivadavia to San Pedrito, in the barrio of Flores.

Look for ★ to find recommended
sights, activities, dining, and lodging.

Highlights

★ **Museo Chileno de Arte Precolombino:** In an elegant colonial building, this museum houses an irreplaceable assortment of indigenous artifacts from throughout the Americas (page 73).

★ **Mercado Central:** North of the Plaza de Armas, this former colonial rubbish dump is today a produce market and a tourist draw for its fine seafood eateries (page 73).

★ **Palacio de la Moneda:** The public is once again welcome to stroll the passages of Santiago's colonial presidential palace. On the side facing the Alameda, it also offers a spectacular subterranean cultural center (page 78).

★ **Cerro Santa Lucía:** In the late 19th century, visionary mayor Benjamín Vicuña Mackenna started the transformation of a barren quarry,

where Pedro de Valdivia founded Santiago, into what it is today: a true garden spot (page 78).

★ **La Chascona:** On a cul-de-sac in bohemian Barrio Bellavista, Nobel-winning poet Pablo Neruda's whimsical Santiago residence is a literary pilgrimage site (page 84).

★ **Viña Cousiño Macul:** Though surrounded by the sprawling capital, the surviving vineyards and subterranean bodegas of this classic Chilean winery are close enough—just a short hike from the Metro—for tours and tasting (page 85).

★ **Viña Concha y Toro:** In the southeastern suburb of Pirque, a bit more distant than Cousiño Macul, one of Chile's best-known vineyards and wineries is still a prime visitor destination (page 85).

M

Most visitors get their first impressions of Chile in sprawling Santiago, with its Mediterranean hillsides and snow-covered Andean crest. Santiago may lack the high profile of Buenos Aires, but its finest attractions can match

or, in some cases, surpass those of Argentina's capital.

Since the 1990 return to constitutional government and subsequent economic expansion, the city has improved greatly. Both individuals and businesses, for instance, have restored or rehabbed houses and buildings in once run-down Barrio Brasil. Entrepreneurs have replaced unsalvageable structures with tasteful contemporary apartments. Barrio Bellavista has enjoyed a gastronomic and nightlife boom, and international commerce flourishes in Providencia and Las Condes. Despite the publicity, the powerful 8.8 earthquake of February 2010 barely slowed the city down.

The mega-city of Santiago is really many cities, made up of 32 different *comunas* (boroughs) with separate governments. Most sights and services are in the colonial nucleus and adjacent boroughs like Recoleta, Independencia, and Quinta Normal, and

eastern suburbs like Providencia, Las Condes, and Ñuñoa.

Six million people, more than a third of all Chileans, live in Gran Santiago (Greater Santiago). The locus of political and economic power, the capital has grown at the expense of the regions, but unevenly so. Some boroughs have become prosperous, while others remain desperately poor.

Class-based residential segregation is striking, though less extreme than in cities like Lima and Mexico City. There are also environmental costs: More than a million automobiles sometimes clog narrow colonial streets. Though sooty diesel buses are mostly a thing of the past, smokestack industry adds its share, aggravating one of the world's worst smog problems, especially in the almost windless autumn months of March and April.

The Mediterranean climate has a pronounced dry season, November to April, and wet winters, although droughts are not

Previous: the Palacio de la Moneda; the highrises of Las Condes. **Above:** the Catedral Metropolitana.

Gran Santiago

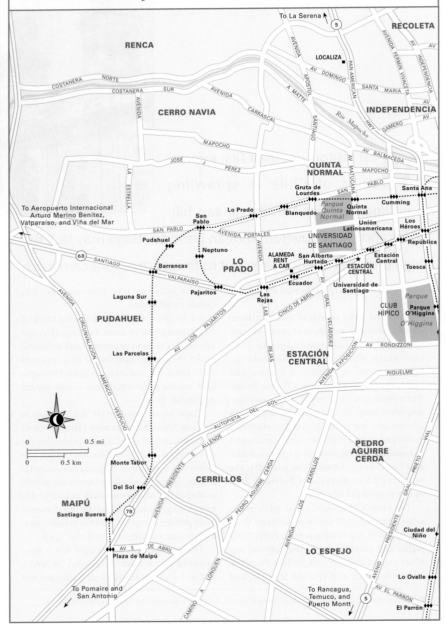

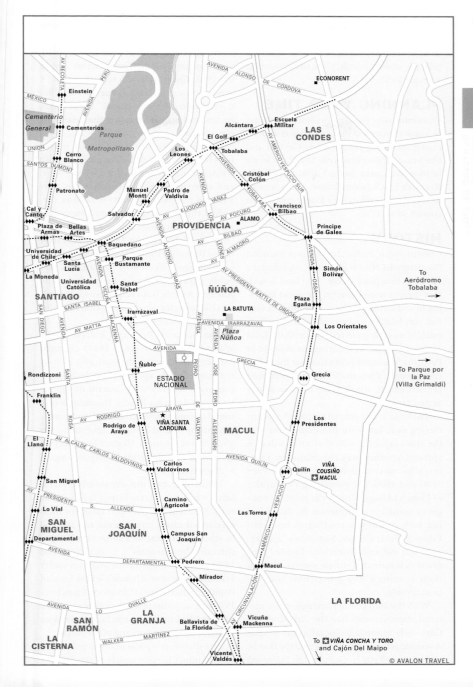

© AVALON TRAVEL

unusual. The daily maximum temperature averages 28°C in January, but it almost always cools off at night thanks to the elevation. In July, the coolest month, the daily maximum averages 10°C.

PLANNING YOUR TIME

Presuming only two days, visitors should get to know the central Plaza de Armas and vicinity, including the Mercado Central and the Museo Precolombino, the Palacio de la Moneda, Cerro Santa Lucía, poet Pablo Neruda's La Chascona house, and a winery or two. Anyone planning a longer stay should consult *Moon Chile*.

HISTORY

Conquistador Pedro de Valdivia founded "Santiago del Nuevo Extremo" on February 12, 1541, in a place where "The land is such that there is none better in the world for living in and settling down . . . because it is very flat, very healthy, and very pleasant." Valdivia established early good relations with the local Mapuche people but, during his absence in Peru, the Spaniards began to abuse the indigenous people. Their rebellion nearly destroyed the settlement, which became a precarious armed camp.

Valdivia's chosen site proved an enduring one, but with problems. One was the Río Mapocho, which often flooded in spring. Another was the Mapuche raiders, who made its defense costly. Between 1600 and 1606, the governing viceroyalty of Lima had to quadruple the military budget to maintain its presence. By the end of the 16th century, according to historian Eduardo Solar Correa, Santiago's "appearance was sad and miserable." Landed proprietors dominated urban society, though their economic and power base was the countryside.

With the 18th century, though, came material improvements like the cathedral, the Casa de la Moneda (colonial mint) to spur economic activity, dikes to contain the floods, and improved roads. Cultural life improved with the establishment of what later became the Universidad de Chile.

When independence came in 1810, Santiago was a modest, nondescript city. In the 1830s Charles Darwin remarked that "it is not so fine or so large as Buenos Aires, but it is built after the same model." Earthquakes encouraged utilitarian rather than elaborate construction.

Postindependence Santiago was poised for a boom. The 1850s California Gold Rush created a market for Chilean wheat, wine, and other produce. The beneficiaries were a landed elite who built city mansions, furnished them extravagantly, and supported exclusive institutions like the Club Hípico (Racing Club). By the 1870s, progressive mayor Benjamín Vicuña Mackenna was transforming areas like Cerro Santa Lucía into public parks. Venezuelan-born scholar and educator Andrés Bello helped enrich the cultural life of a city whose population exceeded 100,000 by midcentury.

Conflict with Peru and Bolivia in the War of the Pacific (1879-1884) changed both city and country dramatically, in ways not immediately apparent. Chilean interests grew wealthy with control of the nitrate-rich Atacama Desert, financing a new round of conspicuous consumption by mining magnates and bringing revenue to the government treasury. Neglect lost much of sprawling, vaguely defined Patagonia region to Argentina.

Industrialization initially absorbed excess labor when the nitrate mines failed in the early 20th century, but rural labor conflicts accelerated urban immigration and resulted in squatter settlements known as *callampas* (literally, "mushrooms"). In the 1960s and 1970s, these exploded with activism under President Salvador Allende's leftist Unidad Popular. After General Augusto Pinochet's 1973 coup, activists bided their time as eastern suburbs like Las Condes reached for the skies in high-rise apartments and office blocks.

The dictatorship's economic policies—largely intact despite nearly three decades of constitutional government—also encouraged suburban sprawl and private automobile ownership that have contributed to traffic congestion and air pollution. That over a third of Chile's 17 million inhabitants live in Gran Santiago suggests that these problems will not disappear soon, but some central city neighborhoods are becoming increasingly livable.

ORIENTATION

Between the high Andes and the lower coast range, Gran Santiago sprawls from north of the Río Mapocho to south of the Río Maipo. The meandering Mapocho unites with the Maipo near Talagante, to the southwest. Andean outliers like 635-meter Cerro Santa Lucía and 869-meter Cerro San Cristóbal rise above the city's sedimentary plain, 550 meters above sea level.

Santiago's colonial core lies south of the Río Mapocho, north of the east-west Avenida del Libertador General Bernardo O'Higgins (the "Alameda"), and east of the Vía Norte Sur, downtown's segment of the Carretera Panamericana. Its center is the rectangular **Plaza de Armas.** Some narrow downtown streets have become pedestrian malls.

Santiago Centro comprises several informal but distinctive barrios or neighborhoods. In the **Barrio Cívico,** southwest of the Plaza de Armas, major government offices surround the Plaza de la Constitución. Farther west, once-dilapidated **Barrio Brasil** is undergoing a residential renaissance. South of the Alameda, **Barrio París Londres**'s winding streets break the grid pattern, as do those of **Barrio Lastarria,** east of Cerro Santa Lucía.

Beyond Santiago Centro, several other boroughs have sights and services, most notably the easterly suburbs of **Providencia** and **Las Condes.** Some of these boast their own distinctive neighborhoods: North of the Mapocho, the restaurant and nightlife mecca of **Barrio Bellavista** lies half in Recoleta, half in Providencia. **Providencia**'s traditional point of identification is Plaza Baquedano, universally known as **Plaza Italia,** where the eastbound Alameda becomes Avenida Providencia.

Las Condes and Vitacura are affluent eastward extensions of Providencia. Independencia, Quinta Normal, and Estación Central have fewer sights, except for major museums and parks, and a few key services such as long-distance bus terminals.

Sights

Central Santiago has the highest density of sights in or around the Plaza de Armas, Plaza de la Constitución, Cerro Santa Lucía, and Barrio Bellavista, with a handful elsewhere. The municipal tourist authority, with separate offices near the Plaza de Armas and on Cerro Santa Lucía, offers free walking tours that include admission to some of the best museums; check for the most current itineraries.

For the city's best panoramas, take the elevator to the observation deck at Providencia's **Costanera Center** (Av. Andrés Bello 2425, tel. 02/2916-9226, www.skycostanera.cl, 10am-10pm daily, Mon.-Thurs. US$7.50 adults, US$4.50 ages 4-12, US$6 students

and seniors, Fri.-Sun. and holidays US$12 adults, US$7.50 ages 4-12, US$8 students and seniors), which rises 300 meters above its surroundings.

La Bicicleta Verde (Loreto 6, tel. 02/2570-9338, www.labicicletaverde.com) offers a variety of bicycle tours around the city, including winery visits.

PLAZA DE ARMAS AND VICINITY

On its west side, the plaza's oldest surviving landmark is the **Catedral Metropolitana,** begun in 1748 but, because of earthquakes and fires, not completed until 1830. Italian architect Joaquín Toesca designed its neoclassical facade, modified with late-19th-century Tuscan touches.

On the north side, the next oldest structure is the **Municipalidad de Santiago** (1785). Immediately west, the **Palacio de la Real Audiencia** (1804) houses the **Museo Histórico Nacional**. At the corner of Paseo Puente, the Francophile **Correo Central** (Post Office, 1882) replaced the original government house. Half a block east of the plaza, dating from 1769, the **Casa Colorada** (Merced 860) houses the municipal tourist office and city museum.

One block from the southwest corner of the plaza, the **Palacio de la Real Aduana** (Royal Customs House, Bandera 361) now holds the exceptional **Museo Chileno de Arte Precolombino** (Chilean Museum of Pre-Columbian Art).

One block north of the plaza, built of massive blocks, the **Templo de Santo Domingo** (21 de Mayo and Monjitas) was constructed in 1747-1808. Two blocks north is the **Mercado Central,** the landmark central market that's a tourist draw for its seafood restaurants.

From 1913 until 1987, trains to Valparaíso, northern Chile, and Mendoza (Argentina) used Eiffel-influenced architect Emilio Jecquier's monumental **Estación Mapocho.** Closed in 1987 and reopened as a cultural center, it hosts events like Santiago's annual book fair. In the nearby Cal y Canto Metro station, foundations of the colonial **Puente Cal y Canto** bridge over the Río Mapocho are now open to view.

Museo Histórico Nacional

During the 17th century, the Palacio de la Real Audiencia housed Chile's colonial supreme court, but earthquakes destroyed its quarters in both 1647 and 1730. Architect Juan José de Goycolea y Zañartu designed the current neoclassical building (1808), whose clock tower dates from Mayor Benjamín Vicuña Mackenna's late-19th-century term.

During the independence struggle, the first Congreso Nacional met here. Royalists restored the Real Audiencia from 1814 to 1817. That same year, the Cabildo de Santiago met here to make Argentine general José de San Martín head of state, but San Martín declined in favor of Bernardo O'Higgins. After President Manuel Bulnes moved government offices to the Casa de la Moneda, the building became municipal offices and then a museum.

Today, the building houses the **Museo Histórico Nacional** (Plaza de Armas 951, tel. 02/2411-7010, www.museohistoriconacional. cl, 10am-6pm Tues.-Sun., free). Thematically, its collections encompass Mapuche silverwork, colonial and republican furniture and art, material folklore, textiles, weapons, and photography. Chronologically, it traces Chile's development from indigenous times through Spanish colonial rule, the subsequent establishment of church and state, collapse of the Spanish empire, the early republic and its 19th-century expansion, the oligarchy that ruled parliament, and the failed reforms that ended with the 1973 coup—when the story abruptly ends.

Museo de Santiago

Perhaps Santiago's best-preserved colonial house, the Casa Colorada was home to Mateo de Toro y Zambrano, who became Chile's interim governor at age 83, after the colonial governor resigned. Named for its reddish paint, it hosted both José de San Martín and Bernardo O'Higgins after the battle of Chacabuco (1817), and the famous mercenary Lord Cochrane later lived here. Abandoned for many years, it underwent restoration after 1977. Only the two-story facade facing Merced, with its forged iron balconies, is truly original.

Inside the Casa Colorada, the **Museo de Santiago** (Merced 860, tel. 02/2386-7400, www.santiagocultura.cl, 10am-6pm Tues.-Fri., 10am-5pm Sat., 11am-2pm Sun. and holidays, US$1 pp) chronicles the city's development from pre-Columbian times through its founding by Valdivia, the evolution of colonial society, the independence era, and its transformation under 19th-century mayor

Benjamín Vicuña Mackenna. The history is vivid in the models of historical buildings and dioramas of events, such as the 1863 fire that destroyed the Iglesia de la Compañía. As of late 2016, the museum was closed for a major restoration.

★ Museo Chileno de Arte Precolombino

The late architect Sergio Larraín García-Moreno donated a lifetime's acquisitions to stock the **Museo Chileno de Arte Precolombino** (Bandera 361, tel. 02/2352-7510, www.precolombino.cl, 10am-6pm Tues.-Sun., US$6.50, US$3 students, free under age 13), housed in the former colonial Real Casa de Aduana (Royal Customs House, 1805). Following independence, the neoclassical building became the Biblioteca Nacional (National Library) and then the Tribunales de Justicia (Law Courts) until a 1968 fire destroyed most of its interior and archives. Flanked by twin patios, a broad staircase leads to the upstairs exhibits. The permanent collections from Mesoamerica and the central and southern Andes are impressive. There are smaller displays on the Caribbean, the Amazon, and Andean textiles. Particularly notable are the carved wooden *chemamull*, larger-than-life-size Mapuche funerary statues. The museum also possesses Aguateca's Stele 6, from a Late Classic Maya site in Guatemala's Petén lowlands that has suffered severe depredations from looters.

★ Mercado Central

In 1817, Bernardo O'Higgins himself shifted the disorderly market on the Plaza de Armas to an area once known as "the Dominican rubbish dump" on the Río Mapocho's south bank, a few blocks north. When fire destroyed the informal installations on the new Plaza de Abasto in 1864, municipal authorities hired Manuel Aldunate to create more permanent facilities. But the current **Mercado Central** (San Pablo 967, tel. 02/2696-8327, www.mercadocentral.cl, 7am-5pm Sun.-Thurs.,

7am-8pm Fri., 7am-6pm Sat.) structure, from 1872, is mainly the work of Fermín Vivaceta.

Street-side storefronts have concealed the original facade except on the Ismael Valdés Vergara side, where it faces the river and opens onto a new plaza. There are entrances, however, on all four sides. From the interior, the wrought-iron superstructure, embellished with the Chilean flag's recurring lone star, provides an airy setting for merchants to display their fresh fruit, vegetables, and seafood—according to journalist Robb Walsh, "a display of fishes and shellfish so vast and unfamiliar that I felt I was observing the marine life of another planet."

Lunching and people-watching at tables set among the produce is a popular pastime for locals and tourists alike. The smallish restaurants on the periphery are cheaper and nearly as good as the two or three that monopolize the prime central sites.

BARRIO CÍVICO AND VICINITY

Straddling the Alameda, several blocks southwest of the Plaza de Armas, the **Barrio Cívico** is the country's political and administrative center. Facing the **Plaza de la Constitución,** the late-colonial **Palacio de la Moneda** is the locus of presidential authority. At 10am on even-numbered days, there's a presidential changing-of-the-guard ceremony here.

In a development that rankles Pinochet diehards, a statue of former President Salvador Allende overlooks the plaza's southeast corner, with an inscription from his last radio address: "I have faith in Chile and her destiny," September 11, 1973.

Across the street, the **Intendencia de Santiago** (Moneda and Morandé), built in 1914-1916, features an attractive corner entrance and a spectacular interior cupola. French architect Emilio Jecquier designed the flatiron-style **Bolsa de Comercio** (Stock Exchange, La Bolsa 84), begun in 1914 but delayed when World War I disrupted the arrival of materials from New York. Immediately south, reached by a cobbled passageway but

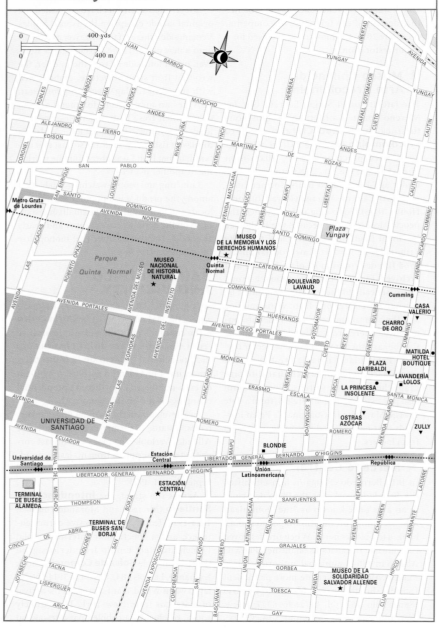

Santiago West

0 — 400 yds
0 — 400 m

JUAN DE BARROS

YUNGAY

LIBERTAD

AVENIDA

YUNGAY

ROBLES

GENERAL BARBOZA

VILLASANA

LOURDES

HERRERA

RAFAEL SOTOMAYOR

CUETO

CAUTIN

ALEJANDRO

MAPOCHO

ANDES

EDISON

FIERRO

RIVAS VICUÑA

PATRICIO LYNCH

MARTINEZ

DE

ANDES

CORONEL

F. LOBOS

ROZAS

CAUTIN

SAN ENRIQUE

SAN PABLO

LOURDES

Metro Gruta de Lourdes

SANTO

AVENIDA

DOMINGO

NORTE

AVENIDA MATUCANA

CHACABUCO

MAIPU

HERRERA

ROSAS

SANTO DOMINGO

LIBERTAD

Plaza Yungay

AVENIDA RICARDO CUMMING

ACACIAS

MUSEO DE LA MEMORIA Y LOS DERECHOS HUMANOS

LAS

ROBERTO OPAZO

Parque
Quinta Normal

AVENIDA DEL MUSEO

MUSEO NACIONAL DE HISTORIA NATURAL ★

Quinta Normal

CATEDRAL

COMPANIA

BOULEVARD LAVAUD ▼

BULNES

Cumming

CASA VALERIO ▼

AVENIDA

AVENIDA PORTALES

AVENIDA DEL INSTITUTO

HUERFANOS

MAIPU

SOTOMAYOR

CHARRO DE ORO ▼

CUMMING

AVENIDA DIEGO PORTALES

CUETO

REYES

GENERAL

MATILDA HOTEL BOUTIQUE ●

SOPHORAS

AVENIDA DEL

MONEDA

LAS

ERASMO

CHACABUCO

LIBERTAD

RAFAEL

ESCALA

GARCIA

PLAZA GARIBALDI ▼

LA PRINCESA INSOLENTE ●

LAVANDERIA LOLOS ■

SANTA MONICA

AVENIDA

SUR

AVENIDA

ROMERO

AVENIDA RICARDO

OSTRAS AZOCAR ▼

ZULLY ▼

UNIVERSIDAD DE SANTIAGO

AVENIDA

ECUADOR

MAIPU

ROMERO

Universidad de Santiago

BERNAL DEL MERCADO

Estación Central

LIBERTADOR GENERAL BERNARDO O'HIGGINS

BLONDIE ■

Unión Latinoamericana

República

LIBERTADOR GENERAL BERNARDO O'HIGGINS

ESTACIÓN CENTRAL ★

REPUBLICA

LATORRE

TERMINAL DE BUSES ALAMEDA

THOMPSON

BORJA

SANFUENTES

ESPAÑA

AVENIDA

ECHAURREN

ALMIRANTE

TERMINAL DE BUSES SAN BORJA

ABRIL

SAN

SAZIE

LATINOAMERICANA

MOLINA

CINCO

DE

DOLORES

AVENIDA EXPOSICION

ALFONSO

GUERRERO

UNION

ABATE

GRAJALES

JOTABECHE

TACNA

CONFERENCIA

SAN

GORBEA

MUSEO DE LA SOLIDARIDAD SALVADOR ALLENDE ★

HIPICO

LISPERGUER

TOESCA

CLUB

ARICA

BASCUÑAN

GAY

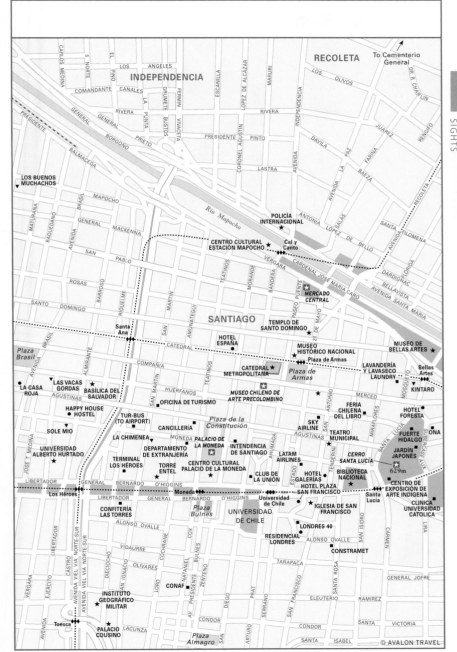

© AVALON TRAVEL

Santiago East

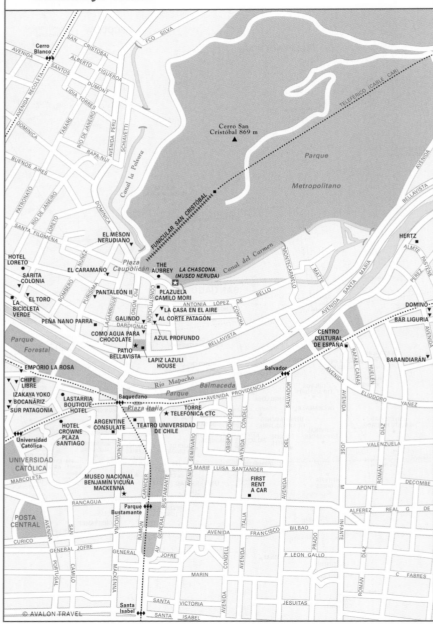

Cerro Blanco

Cerro San Cristóbal 869 m

Parque

Metropolitano

TELEFERICO (CABLE CAR)

Canal la Palmera

FUNICULAR SAN CRISTÓBAL

Canal del Carmen

Parque Forestal

EL MESON NERUDIANO

HOTEL LORETO

SARITA COLONIA

EL TORO

LA BICICLETA VERDE

PEÑA NANO PARRA

EL CARAMAÑO

Plaza Caupolicán

PANTALEÓN II

GALINDO

COMO AGUA PARA CHOCOLATE

PATIO BELLAVISTA

EMPORIO LA ROSA

THE AUBREY

LA CHASCONA (MUSEO NERUDA)

PLAZUELA CAMILO MORI

ANTONIA LÓPEZ DE BELLO

LA CASA EN EL AIRE

AL CORTE PATAGÓN

AZUL PROFUNDO

LAPIZ LAZULI HOUSE

DOMINÓ

BAR LIGURIA

CENTRO CULTURAL DE ESPAÑA

BARANDIARÁN

HERTZ

ALMTE

Salvador

CHIPE LIBRE

IZAKAYA YOKO

BOCANÁRIZ

SUR PATAGONIA

LASTARRIA BOUTIQUE HOTEL

ARGENTINE CONSULATE

HOTEL CROWNE PLAZA SANTIAGO

Baquedano

Plaza Italia

Rio Mapocho

Parque

Balmaceda

AVENIDA PROVIDENCIA

TORRE TELEFÓNICA CTC

TEATRO UNIVERSIDAD DE CHILE

Universidad Católica

UNIVERSIDAD CATÓLICA

MUSEO NACIONAL BENJAMÍN VICUÑA MACKENNA

MARIE LUISA SANTANDER

FIRST RENT A CAR

VALENZUELA

DECOMBE

MARCOLETA

RANCAGUA

Parque Bustamante

POSTA CENTRAL

CURICO

GENERAL JOFRE

ALFEREZ REAL G DE

AVENIDA

FRANCISCO

BILBAO

P LEON GALLO

MARIN

JESUITAS

C FABRES

Santa Isabel

SANTA VICTORIA ISABEL

© AVALON TRAVEL

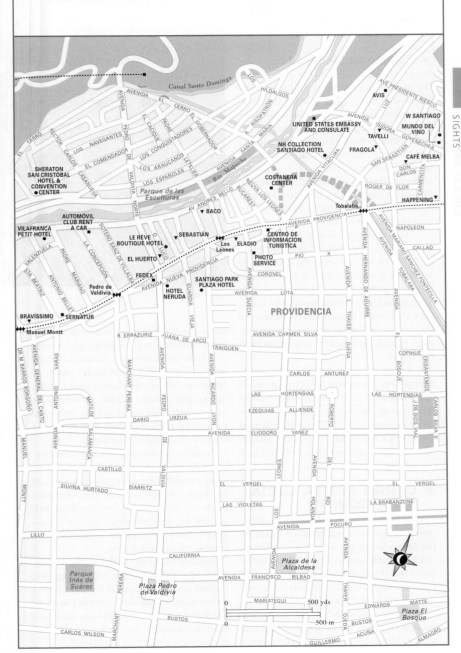

fronting on the Alameda, the **Club de la Unión** (1925) gave stockbrokers a place to schmooze on their lunch hours.

★ Palacio de la Moneda

Never intended as the seat of government, the neoclassical **Palacio de la Moneda** (Morandé 130, tel. 02/2269-4000, http://visitasguiadas.presidencia.cl, 10am-6pm Mon.-Fri.) became the presidential palace in 1846, when Manuel Bulnes moved his residence and offices to the former colonial mint. It made global headlines in 1973, when the air force strafed and bombed it in General Pinochet's coup against President Salvador Allende, who shot himself to death before he could be taken prisoner.

Pinochet's regime restored the building to architect Joaquín Toesca's original design by 1981, but it's no longer the presidential residence. Ricardo Lagos, the first socialist elected president since Allende, opened the main passageway for one-way public traffic from the Plaza de la Constitución entrance to the Plaza de la Libertad exit. For a more thorough guided tour, make a request through the website.

Between the palace and the Alameda, beneath the lawns and reflecting pools of the Plaza de la Ciudadanía, broad pedestrian ramps descend to a luminous subterranean facility, the **Centro Cultural Palacio La Moneda.** Its gigantic atrium flanked by special exhibit galleries and other facilities.

★ CERRO SANTA LUCÍA AND VICINITY

East of Paseo Ahumada and north of the Alameda, the promontory called Welén by the Mapuche people was where Pedro de Valdivia held out against the indigenous forces that threatened to expel the Spaniards from the Mapocho valley. Nearly three centuries later, in 1822, the Scotswoman María Graham marveled at the view of "the city, its gardens, churches, and its magnificent bridge all lit up by the rays of the setting sun . . . what

Cerro Santa Lucía

pen or pencil can impart a thousandth part of the sublime beauty of sunset on the Andes?"

It took visionary mayor Benjamín Vicuña Mackenna to realize Santa Lucía's potential. His efforts, along with convict labor and donations from wealthy citizens, transformed a barren quarry into an urban Eden with more than 60 hectares of gardens, fountains, and statuary, including his own tomb.

From the summit, approached by meandering footpaths and reached by a steep climb to a tiny parapet, there are stupendous views of the Andes—at least on a clear day—and panoramas of the city and Cerro San Cristóbal. A lower but broader terrace offers less panoramic but still impressive views toward Providencia and the Andes.

Royalists built **Fuerte Hidalgo** (1816) toward the park's north end to defend against Chilean revolutionaries. On its lower northeastern slope, the **Jardín Japonés** (Japanese Garden) is a more recent addition. Along the Alameda, look for the tile mural of Nobel Prize-winning poet Gabriela Mistral.

Fenced except around its lowest periphery and steepest slope, **Cerro Santa Lucía** (9am-8pm daily) has two main entrances: from the Alameda just east of Plaza Vicuña Mackenna, where twin staircases nearly encircle the fountains of **Plaza Neptuno,** and by a cobbled road from the east end of Agustinas. There's also a modern glass elevator, at the east end of Huérfanos, that is often out of service. In an exaggerated effort to improve security, authorities require all visitors to sign in (as if muggers would do so), but the park's not really dangerous.

The best introduction is a **guided tour** (11am Sat.-Sun., 10am Mon.) in English and Spanish, starting from its municipal tourist-office branch. Tours include Vicuña Mackenna's tomb and the still-functioning gun emplacement (several years ago, authorities halted the startling midday cannon shot because of neighbors' complaints; broader public pressure restored the tradition at a lower decibel level).

Between Cerro Santa Lucía and Paseo Ahumada, the most imposing landmark is the classicist **Biblioteca Nacional** (National Library, facing the Alameda between MacIver and Miraflores), built in 1914-1927. Two blocks north, the neoclassical **Teatro Municipal** (Municipal Theater, 1857) has seen performances by Sarah Bernhardt, Igor Stravinsky, Plácido Domingo, Anna Pavlova, and the Chilean classical pianist Claudio Arrau.

BARRIO PARÍS LONDRES AND VICINITY

South of the Alameda, the major landmark is the **Iglesia y Convento de San Francisco** (Alameda 834), Chile's oldest colonial building (1618) and a survivor of repeated fires and earthquakes.

Until the early 1920s, the Franciscans controlled much of this area, but a financial crisis forced them to sell 30,000 square meters to developer Walter Lihn. Lihn demolished several buildings and patios, and their gardens, but architects Roberto Araya and Ernesto

Holzmann replaced them with an intimately livable neighborhood of meandering cobbled streets.

Betraying the neighborhood's legacy, the house at **Londres 40** was a torture center during Pinochet's dictatorship. Two blocks west of Iglesia San Francisco, the **Casa Central de la Universidad de Chile** (1863-1872), the state university's main campus, stretches along the Alameda.

Iglesia y Convento de San Francisco

Pedro de Valdivia himself established the Ermita del Socorro to house an image of the Virgen del Socorro that he had brought to Chile. Valdivia credited the Virgen del Socorro with Santiago's survival from Mapuche attacks. In 1554, in exchange for 12 city lots, the Franciscans built a church to house the image, but a 1583 earthquake destroyed the original structure. After finishing the present church in 1618, they built a pair of cloisters and gradually added patios, gardens, a refectory, and other structures. Earthquakes toppled the towers in 1643 and 1751, but Fermín Vivaceta's 19th-century clock tower has withstood every tremor since. The interior is notable for its Mudéjar details and carved cypress doors.

Over four and a half centuries, the Franciscans have kept faith with Valdivia by continuing to host the Virgen del Socorro. In addition, the church houses an ecclesiastical art collection, the **Museo de Arte Colonial** (Londres 4, tel. 02/2639-8737, www.museo-sanfrancisco.com, 9:30am-1:30pm and 3pm-6pm Mon.-Fri., 10am-2pm Sat.-Sun. Mar.-Dec., 9:30am-1:30pm and 3pm-7pm Mon.-Fri., 10am-2pm Sat.-Sun. Jan.-Feb., closed on religious holidays, US$2 pp, US$1 students and seniors).

BARRIO LASTARRIA AND VICINITY

East of Cerro Santa Lucía, between Parque Forestal and the Alameda, **Barrio Lastarria** is a neighborhood of narrow streets and cul-de-sacs that's become a dining and nightlife focus, but also has multiple cultural attractions.

The barrio's main axis is its namesake street, José Victorino Lastarria, whose **Plaza del Mulato Gil de Castro** is an adaptive reuse uniting several early-20th-century buildings into a commercial and cultural cluster with two notable museums: the **Museo Arqueológico de Santiago** and the eye-catching **Museo de Artes Visuales.** Between Rosal and Merced, Lastarria has become an attractive pedestrian mall.

To the north, the Río Mapocho's banks and floodplain were home to slums and rubbish dumps until the early 20th century, when mayor Enrique Cousiño redeveloped the area as the **Parque Forestal,** stretching from Estación Mapocho on the west to the Pío Nono bridge on the east. Shaded with mature trees and dotted with statues and fountains, it's a verdant refuge from summer's midday heat.

Toward the west, directly north of Cerro Santa Lucía, stands the **Museo Nacional de Bellas Artes,** the city's traditional fine arts museum. South across the Alameda, toward downtown, is the central campus of the **Universidad Católica** (Catholic University, 1913).

Museo de Artes Visuales

Privately owned and financed, the **Museo de Artes Visuales** (MAVI, Lastarria 307, tel. 02/2638-3502, www.mavi.cl, 11am-6:30pm Tues.-Sun., US$1.50 adults, US$0.75 students) boasts a permanent collection of 1,400 pieces by 300 contemporary Chilean artists, among them Roberto Matta and Alfredo Jaar. About 140 of these pieces, ranging from engravings to paintings, photographs, and sculptures, are on display at any one time. The MAVI is located in the Plaza del Mulato Gil complex.

Architect Cristián Undurraga's design incorporates 1,400 square meters of display space. Flawless lighting accentuates individual pieces in half a dozen spacious galleries, which feature high ceilings and polished

wooden floors. The English translations are better than at some Chilean museums.

The MAVI now subsumes the **Museo Arqueológico de Santiago** (Lastarria 321, tel. 02/2638-3502), with excellent exhibits on Chile's indigenous peoples from pre-Columbian times to the present. The price of admission to MAVI provides access to both museums.

Museo de Bellas Artes

Built for Chile's independence centennial and fashioned after Paris's Petit Palais, Santiago's neoclassical fine arts museum **Museo de Bellas Artes** (José Miguel de La Barra s/n, tel. 02/2499-1660, www.mnba.cl, 10am-6:45pm Tues.-Sun., closed Jan. 1, May 1, Sept. 18-19, and Dec. 25, free), is the pride of Parque Forestal. Collections range from colonial and religious art to nearly contemporary figurative and abstract works by artists like the late Roberto Matta. It also has a sample of French, Italian, and Dutch paintings and prestigious special exhibits. While Bellas Artes is a traditional museum, its ambitious website is making the works of 2,000 Chilean artists accessible to the world in a "museum without walls."

BARRIO BRASIL AND VICINITY

West of the Vía Norte Sur, **Barrio Brasil** was a prestigious early-20th-century residential area that fell upon hard times but has since experienced a resurgence. The best way to approach the barrio is the Huérfanos pedestrian suspension bridge that crosses the Vía Norte Sur to an area where private universities have rehabbed buildings, salvaged libraries, built collections, and introduced a youthful vigor. It's also a good area for moderately priced food and accommodations.

The barrio's focus is its lovingly landscaped namesake, **Plaza Brasil.** Dating from 1892, its most impressive landmark has been the neo-Gothic **Basílica del Salvador** (Huérfanos 1781), but severe damage from the 1985 and 2010 earthquakes could require its

The Puente Huérfanos connects downtown Santiago with Barrio Brasil.

fields, tennis courts, skating rinks, pools, and a cluster of museums. Parque Quinta Normal's main entrance is on Matucana at the west end of Compañía, with other gateways on Avenida Portales, Santo Domingo, and Apostól Santiago; it now has its own Metro station.

Having suffered some damage in the 2010 earthquake, the restored **Museo Nacional de Historia Natural** (Natural History Museum, tel. 02/2680-4603, www.mnhn.cl, 10am-5:30pm Tues.-Sat., 11am-5:30pm Sun., closed Jan. 1, Easter Sun., May 1, Sept. 18-19, Nov. 1, and Dec. 25, free) is a research facility that also has public exhibits on archaeology, ethnography, physical anthropology, mineralogy, paleontology, botany, and zoology. The museum collection began in 1830, when the government contracted French naturalist Claude Gay to inventory Chile's natural resources.

demolition. Dating from 1926, the most idiosyncratic building is the German Gothic **Universidad Albert Hurtado** (Cienfuegos 41), whose grinning gargoyles and smiling skulls jutting from its facade always attract attention.

Beyond Barrio Brasil proper, wooded **Parque Quinta Normal** offers relief from a densely built area and is home to several museums. The other main attraction is the **Museo de la Solidaridad Salvador Allende** (Av. República 475, tel. 02/2689-9761, www.mssa.cl, 11am-7pm. Tues.-Sun. Dec.-Jan., 10am-6pm Tues.-Sun. Apr.-Nov., US$1.50, free Sun.), a modern-art collection and cultural center.

Parque Quinta Normal

At the western edge of Santiago Centro, **Parque Quinta Normal** (8am-8:30pm Tues.-Sun.) is a traditional open space whose 40 hectares were the city's first de facto botanical garden. It is also home to playgrounds, soccer

Palacio Cousiño

South of the Alameda, 19th-century Calle Dieciocho was an aristocratic area of Parisian-style mansions long before the oligarchy moved to the eastern suburbs. One of its keystone families was the Cousiños, Portuguese immigrants who made fortunes in wine and mining. Funds for the 1878 **Palacio Cousiño** (Dieciocho 438, tel. 02/2698-5063) came from the estate of Luis Cousiño, an art collector who inherited his father's mining fortune. Luis Cousiño died young, but his widow Isidora Goyenechea continued construction. The three-story house has marble staircases, a music hall, a winter garden, and even a one-person elevator, the country's first. The Palacio remained in family hands until 1941, when the city purchased it for a museum and as a guesthouse for high-profile visitors like Charles DeGaulle, Marshal Tito, and Golda Meir. Following severe earthquake damage in 2010, the Palacio Cousiño has been undergoing a painstaking restoration. The date of its reopening is yet to be determined.

Torture Tours

It's harder to tell in happier times but, from 1973 to 1990, Chile experienced one of the most vicious and durable military dictatorships ever on a continent that was notorious for them. Yet there are numerous reminders of those sad years, even if most of them are relatively inconspicuous (such as the headquarters of Constramet metal workers union, Avenida Santa Rosa 101, which simply displays a plaque with the names of some 60 members who disappeared under General Augusto Pinochet's rule). A couple of them, though, are more outspokenly eloquent.

PARQUE POR LA PAZ

Perhaps the most subtly eloquent memorial to the dictatorship's victims, Peñalolén's **Parque por la Paz** (Av. Arrieta 8401, tel. 02/2292-5229, www.villagrimaldi.cl, 10am-6pm daily, guided tours 10:30am, noon, and 3pm Tues.-Fri., free) occupies the grounds of the former Villa Grimaldi, the principal torture center for the Directorio de Inteligencia Nacional (DINA), General Manuel Contreras's ruthless intelligence service. Before it closed, more than 200 political prisoners died at the isolated mansion, and many more were interrogated and tortured.

In the regime's final days, the military bulldozed nearly every building to destroy evidence, but the nonprofit Fundación Parque por la Paz has transformed the property into a pilgrimage site that commemorates the victims without any overt political posturing. It has permanently locked the original street-side gates, by which prisoners entered the grounds, with a declaration that they are "never to be opened again."

From Metro Plaza Egaña (Línea 4), Transantiago buses 513 and D09 make stops nearby.

MUSEO DE LA MEMORIA Y DE LOS DERECHOS HUMANOS

More central and more comprehensive than Villa Grimaldi, the **Museo de la Memoria** (Matucana 501, tel. 02/2597-9600, www.museodelamemoria.cl, 10am-6pm Tues.-Sun. Mar.-Dec., 10am-8pm Tues.-Sun. Jan.-Feb., donation) is a three-story monument whose glass exterior and reflecting pool establish transparency as an architectural and cultural value. Its interior exhibits vividly document the abuses of the Pinochet years and the gradual return to democracy.

On the ground level, the museum starts innocuously enough in displaying the written accounts of human rights violations, such as the Rettig Report, that began to appear in the aftermath of the

PROVIDENCIA AND VICINITY

At the east end of the Alameda, lively **Plaza Italia** (formally Plaza Baquedano) marks the boundary of the borough of **Providencia,** the westernmost of the affluent suburbs that also include Las Condes, Vitacura, and Ñuñoa. While this mostly staid middle-to upper-middle-class area has shopping malls that seem straight out of the suburban United States, it also has Bohemian enclaves like Barrio Bellavista (Santiago's main restaurant and nightlife area) and bar-hopping zones like Avenida Suecia. Except in compact Bellavista, points of interest are more spread out than in Santiago Centro, but public transportation is good.

From Plaza Italia, the northbound Pío Nono bridge crosses the Mapocho to Barrio Bellavista. The area's most conspicuous landmark is the 31-story **Torre Telefónica CTC** (Av. Providencia 111), the company headquarters in the form of a (now antique) 140-meter-tall cell phone.

South of Plaza Italia, Avenida Vicuña Mackenna separates the boroughs of Santiago Centro on one side and Providencia and Ñuñoa on the other. On the Providencia side, the **Museo Nacional Benjamín Vicuña Mackenna** (Av. Vicuña Mackenna 94, tel. 02/2222-9642, www.museovicunamackenna.cl, 9:30am-5:30pm Mon.-Fri., free) honors the mayor, historian, journalist, and diplomat responsible for the capital's 1870s modernization.

Museo de la Memoria

regime. The powerful visual material begins with huge wall photos of the violent coup against President Salvador Allende, along with live footage of the events on multiple screens (though the English subtitles are sometimes misleading) and a sample of the front pages of Santiago dailies (whose coverage was truly disgraceful).

In addition, the material here includes a site-by-site catalog of detention camps and torture centers with video links. The second floor covers demands for accountability for the missing, with a computer database of individual cases. A separate exhibit deals with popular culture, stressing the contributions of folk musicians and quilters as indicators of resistance. The third floor is open for special exhibitions.

The Museo de la Memoria has its own access to the Metro Quinta Normal station (Línea 5).

On the Mapocho's north bank, between the Padre Letelier and Pedro de Valdivia bridges, the open-air **Parque de las Esculturas** (Av. Santa María 2201, tel. 02/2340-7303, 10am-7:30pm daily, free) showcases abstract and figurative works by contemporary Chilean sculptors. It also has an enclosed gallery with rotating exhibitions.

BARRIO BELLAVISTA AND VICINITY

At the foot of massive Cerro San Cristóbal, compact **Bellavista** is a walker's delight. In daytime, Santiaguinos cross the Pío Nono bridge to stroll its leafy streets, parks, and plazas and enjoy modest lunch specials at innovative restaurants. At night, they crowd the same places for elaborate dinners before a night at nearby bars, discos, salsa clubs, theaters, and other diversions. Daytime visitors, by the way, may not even realize that this is a nightlife center—most dance clubs, for instance, don't even *open* until 1am or so, and few have prominent signs.

While most visitors see Bellavista as a single neighborhood, the recently rehabbed **Avenida Pío Nono** is a dividing line between the two *comunas* (boroughs) that compose the barrio—rough-edged Recoleta to the west and modish Providencia to the east. There's more style than substance to this, as security-obsessed Providencia makes more conspicuous efforts to prevent auto burglaries and other petty crime in what is, for the most part, a safe area.

On weekends, Pío Nono itself is a frenetic blend of crafts market, cheap sidewalk restaurants, and beer joints. While not as bad as that might sound, it's less appealing than the perpendicular and parallel side streets.

For a notion of Bellavista's best, relax on a bench at **Plazuela Camilo Mori** (Antonia López de Bello and Constitución), a small triangular plaza. Walking north on Constitución, turn into the cul-de-sac of Márquez de la Plata, where poet Pablo Neruda lived at the house he called **La Chascona**, now a museum. A short walk northwest, **Plaza Caupolicán** is the main entry point to the 722-hectare **Parque Metropolitano**, a hillside and hilltop public park. A funicular railroad carries visitors past the city zoo to the summit, whose terrace offers exceptional views on clear days. From here, a *teleférico* (cable gondola) connects the park to eastern Providencia.

On the Recoleta side, at the north end of Avenida La Paz, famous figures from Chile's past are among the two million reposing in the **Cementerio General** (General Cemetery, 1897).

★ La Chascona

Inconspicuous from the street side of its cul-de-sac, Pablo Neruda's hillside home **La Chascona** today houses the **Museo Neruda** (Márquez de La Plata 0192, tel. 02/2737-8712, www.fundacionneruda.org, 10am-6pm Tues.-Sun. Mar.-Dec., 10am-7pm Tues.-Sun Jan.-Feb., US$9 adults, US$3 students). It may be the most conventional of his three houses (the others, also open for visits, are in Valparaíso and the beach community of Isla Negra). Opposite the house, a small amphitheater tucked into the slope is an ideal complement to the residence, which has been restored since its military sacking in 1973 (Neruda, a committed Salvador Allende supporter, died about a month after the coup). Audio-guided tours are available in English, French, German, and Portuguese on a first-come, first-served basis. The museum also operates a café, a bookstore, and a souvenir shop.

Cementerio General

All but two of Chile's presidents are interred among the Gothic, Greek, Moorish, and Egyptian-style sepulchres of the **Cementerio General** (Av. La Paz s/n, tel. 02/2637-7800, www.cementeriogeneral.cl, 8:30am-6pm Mon.-Fri., 8am-6pm Sat.-Sun. and holidays). Bernardo O'Higgins's remains are at rest in the Alameda's Altar de la Patria, Gabriel González Videla lies in his native La Serena, and General Augusto Pinochet—if he qualifies—was cremated. Other notable figures include diplomat Orlando Letelier (killed by a car bomb in Washington DC under orders from a Pinochet subordinate); Venezuelan-born educator Andrés Bello; and cultural icon, folksinger, and songwriter Violeta Parra. Nobel Prize-winning poets Gabriela Mistral and Pablo Neruda originally rested here as well, but Mistral's body was moved to her Elqui valley birthplace and Neruda's to his Isla Negra beach residence. Salvador Allende's remains moved in the other direction—after 17 years in Viña del Mar, he regained his freedom to travel after the Pinochet dictatorship's demise and has a monumental memorial here. Another indicator of change is sculptor Francisco Gazitúa's *Rostros* (Faces), memorializing the regime's victims. The cemetery offers a number of guided tours, including occasional nighttime visits, by reservation only.

OUTLYING SIGHTS
Los Dominicos

One of few survivors from colonial Las Condes, the **Iglesia y Convento San Vicente Ferrer de los Dominicos** sits on lands that Pedro de Valdivia seized from Mapuche cacique Apoquindo for Valdivia's mistress, Inés de Suárez. Eventually willed to the Dominican order, the property deteriorated during a century-plus of litigation, but the Dominicans managed to add its twin Byzantine domes in 1847.

Alongside the church, where Avenida Apoquindo dead-ends at Padre Hurtado, **Los Graneros del Alba** (Av. Apoquindo 9085, tel. 02/2896-9841, www.paseolosdominicos.

cl, 10am-7pm Tues.-Sun. fall-spring, 10am-8pm Tues.-Sun. summer), popularly known as "Los Dominicos," is Santiago's biggest crafts market, also popular for its country cuisine and impromptu entertainment. Since the extension of the Metro's Línea 1, it's much easier to reach.

Estadio Nacional

South of Providencia, middle-class Ñuñoa has few landmarks but enjoys a vigorous cultural life on and around **Plaza Ñuñoa**, thanks partly to the nearby campuses of Universidad Católica and Universidad de Chile.

With the Andean front range in the distance, Ñuñoa's major landmark is the **Estadio Nacional** (National Stadium, Av. Grecia 2001). First famous for the 1962 World Cup, it became infamous as an impromptu prison camp after the 1973 coup, incarcerating some 7,000 Allende sympathizers and suspected sympathizers. Many were tortured and more than a few executed, including folksinger Victor Jara and U.S. citizens Charles Horman and Frank Teruggi. Today, the stadium is once again the site of the country's most important soccer matches, and it's within reasonable walking distance of Línea 5's Ñuble station.

★ Viña Cousiño Macul

In the southeastern borough of Peñalolén,

Viña Cousiño Macul (Av. Quilín 7100, tel. 02/2351-4135, www.cousinomacul.cl, tours 11am, noon, 3pm, and 4pm Mon.-Fri., 11am and noon Sat.-Sun., US$15-30 depending on the wines) is one of Chile's oldest wineries. It has been in the same family since Matías Cousiño purchased the vineyards in 1856. Its cellars and wine museum are open for Spanish- and English-language tours. The basic tasting, held in an attractive bar-cum-sales room, includes one varietal and two reserve vintages in a souvenir glass. The house produces cabernet, merlot, chardonnay, sauvignon blanc, and riesling. Viña Cousiño Macul is a 20-minute walk from Quilín station on the Metro's Línea 4.

★ Viña Concha y Toro

In suburban Pirque, **Viña Concha y Toro** (Victoria Subercaseaux 210, tel. 02/2476-5269, www.conchaytoro.com, tastings 9am-6pm daily, US$19-38) offers guided English-language tours of its vineyards, grounds, cellars, and museum, along with tastings. Reservations are advisable. It's sometimes possible to join an existing group that might include—who knows?—Mick Jagger, Bono, Helmut Kohl, Nicaraguan poet Ernesto Cardenal, and others who have toured the facilities. A separate wine bar, with a diverse food menu, is open 9:30am-6:30pm daily.

Entertainment and Shopping

ENTERTAINMENT AND EVENTS

Just as it's the center of Santiago's restaurant scene, Barrio Bellavista is the city's nightlife focus. In a neighborhood where most clubs don't *open* until after midnight and hardly anybody goes before 2am, it's hard to believe that, during Pinochet's dictatorship, Santiaguinos endured an 11pm curfew.

There are also nightspots in and around Santiago Centro, around Providencia's Avenida Suecia, and near Plaza Ñuñoa in the largely middle-class borough of the same name. Many bars and dance clubs, especially gay venues, have no obvious public signs except during opening hours.

Bars

Bellavista's **La Casa en el Aire** (Antonia López de Bello 0125, tel. 02/2735-6680, www.lacasaenelaire.cl) is a direct descendant of 1960s and 1970s *peñas*, with folkloric music, storytelling, films, and the like in an alternative milieu. **Peña Nano Parra** (Ernesto

Pinto Lagarrigue 80, tel. 02/2735-6093) is more strictly traditional. The consistently best rock-music locale is Plaza Ñuñoa's **La Batuta** (Jorge Washington 52, tel. 02/2274-7096, www.batuta.cl).

Discos and Dance Clubs

Blondie (Alameda 2879, Metro Unión Latinoamericana, tel. 02/2681-7793, www.blondie.cl, from US$6) is a four-floor dance club, featuring occasional live acts, that accommodates up to 2,000 people at a time, two-thirds of those on the main floor.

Nightclubs

Several venerable venues hold stage and floor shows, often featuring cultural staples such as the *cueca,* along with typical cuisine such as *pastel de choclo* (Chilean corn casserole). In the landmark Palacio Iñíguez, **Confitería Las Torres** (Alameda 1570, tel. 02/2688-0751, www.confiteriatorres.cl), hosts live tango on weekends. If you can't visit Buenos Aires's Café Tortoni, this magnificent 19th-century building is a worthy alternative.

South of the Alameda, the garish **Los Adobes de Argomedo** (Argomedo 411, tel. 02/2222-2104, www.losadobesdeargomedo.cl) is popular for foreign tour groups' farewell dinners (around US$29-33), but it attracts plenty of Chileans as well. The floor show is participatory—get ready to *cueca.*

In the same location since 1939, Barrio Brasil's cavernous **Los Buenos Muchachos** (Av. Ricardo Cumming 1031, tel. 02/2698-0112, www.losbuenosmuchachos.cl) seats up to 1,000 people for lunch or dinner and floor shows (around US$28-35) with its own orchestra. The above-average food is not that far above average—prices are farther above average, but the service is excellent.

Cultural Centers

The subterranean **Centro Cultural Palacio La Moneda** (Plaza de la Ciudadanía 26, tel. 02/2355-6500, www.ccplm.cl, 9am-9pm daily, US$7.50 foreign adults, US$3.75 students, free until noon) is in a class of its own. In

addition to its gigantic atrium and special exhibit galleries, facilities include the **Cineteca Nacional** (national film archive, with regular repertory programs) and a sprawling crafts shop displaying museum-quality pieces from artisans around the country (not all of these are for sale). Free guided tours (11:30am and 1pm Sat.-Sun.) are given.

The **Instituto Chileno-Norteamericano de Cultura** (Moneda 1467, tel. 02/2677-7070, www.norteamericano.cl) sponsors art exhibits and other events and has an English-language library. The most elaborate and active foreign cultural center, though, is Providencia's **Centro Cultural de España** (Av. Providencia 927, tel. 02/2795-9700, www.ccespana.cl), which sponsors events nearly every night.

Performing Arts

Santiago has many live theater and music venues, with offerings ranging from serious classical and contemporary drama to vulgar burlesque, and from traditional folk to rock and classical. The best source of information is the entertainment section of the daily *El Mercurio.*

The landmark **Teatro Municipal** (Agustinas 794, tel. 02/2463-1000, www.municipal.cl) is Santiago's most prestigious performing-arts venue, hosting classical music, opera, and occasional popular musicals. Only opening performances are truly formal, and Santiaguinos sometimes appear in surprisingly casual clothes. During operas, a translation of the libretto is projected above the stage so that it's easier to follow the plot (presuming you read Spanish).

Musicians rave about the acoustics at the **Teatro Universidad de Chile** (Av. Providencia 043, tel. 02/2978-2480, www.teatro.uchile.cl), best known for ballet and classical music, though it hosts the occasional rock event.

Festivals

September's patriotic holidays are an excuse for parties and parades, but the month can also be contentious. September 11, the date of Pinochet's coup, still sees disturbances around

Providencia's Avenida 11 de Septiembre, recently renamed Avenida Nueva Providencia. September 18, **Día de la Independencia** (Independence Day), means cheerful barbecues in the parks, but September 19's **Día del Ejército** (Armed Forces Day) has been more divisive.

From late October, at the Estación Mapocho, the two-week **Feria de Libro** (Book Festival, www.filsa.cl) draws both Chilean writers and internationally recognized authors.

SHOPPING

Santiago may not be a shopping mecca, but quality handicrafts and antiques from around the country are widely available. Many visitors, of course, take home Chilean wines.

Books

The **Feria Chilena del Libro** (Huérfanos 670, Local 1, tel. 02/2345-8316, www.feriachilenadellibro.cl) is a chain with several branches elsewhere.

Handicrafts

Cerro Santa Lucía's **Centro de Exposición de Arte Indígena** (Alameda 499, tel. 02/2632-3668, 10am-6pm Mon.-Sat. fall-spring, 10am-7pm Mon.-Sat. summer), in the

semi-subterranean Grutas del Cerro Welén, has Mapuche, Aymara, and Rapanui crafts.

In the Bellas Artes neighborhood, **Ona** (Victoria Subercaseaux 295, tel. 02/2632-1859, www.onachile.com) carries a wide selection of Andean handicrafts from throughout Chile and even parts of Bolivia and Peru, commissioned from notable artisans. The best include delicately carved and painted wooden birds, *krin* (woven horsehair items including dolls and butterflies), Mapuche silver, textiles, and pre-Columbian reproductions.

Bellavista is best for lapis lazuli jewelry, at locales like **Lapiz Lazuli House** (Bellavista 08, tel. 02/2732-1419, www.lapislazulihouse.cl).

Wine

If visiting wineries isn't on your agenda but buying wine is, Providencia's **Baco** (Santa Magdalena 116, tel. 02/2231-4444) is the retail outlet of its nearby restaurant. In the same building as the W Hotel, Las Condes's **El Mundo del Vino** (Isidora Goyenechea 3000, tel. 02/2584-1173, www.elmundodelvino.cl) is a wine supermarket.

Antiques

On the pedestrian segment of Calle Lastarria, there's an active weekend antiques fair.

Calle Lastarria is home to an active weekend antiques fair.

Food

On a global level, Santiago's diverse and innovative gastronomy is an underappreciated secret. The distribution of restaurants mirrors that of hotels, with cheaper eateries downtown and most upscale restaurants in Providencia and Las Condes. Barrio Bellavista, across the Río Mapocho, offers some of the most original dining and creative ambience.

SANTIAGO CENTRO

Santiago cafés have finally broken through the "coffee with legs" barrier to become places such as **Emporio La Rosa** (Merced 291, tel. 02/2638-9257, www.emporiolarosa.cl, 8am-9pm Mon.-Fri., 9am-10pm Sat., 9am-9pm Sun., breakfast and lunch less than US$10), which serves excellent breakfasts and lunches, with outstanding juices and Argentine-style *medialunas* (croissants) and empanadas. The ice cream is above average, and there are several other branches around town.

For whimsical decor, traditional Chilean food, and equally reasonable prices, there's **La Chimenea** (Príncipe de Gales 90, tel. 02/2697-0131, www.lachimenea.cl, 9:30am-2am Mon.-Thurs., 9:30am-4am Fri., noon-4am Sat., under US$10). In the same location since 1952, it keeps long hours and often has live music, including tango, and even films.

In Barrio Lastarria, near Cerro Santa Lucía, **Sur Patagónico** (Lastarria 96, tel. 02/2638-6651, 8am-1am Mon.-Fri., 9am-1am Sat.-Sun., US$9-21) is a full-fledged restaurant and wine bar that enjoys one of the neighborhood's widest sidewalks for outdoor dining. Entrées include pastas and lamb with polenta, but it's probably still best for sandwiches. The *parrillada patagónica* of grilled beef, lamb, venison, wild boar, and vegetables (US$44 for two, with a glass of wine each) is a special here.

Down the block, though, **Bocanáriz** (Lastarria 276, tel. 02/2638-9893, www.bocanariz.cl, noon-midnight Mon.-Wed., noon-12:30am Thurs.-Sat., 7pm-11pm Sun., US$12-15) carries a selection of 400 Chilean vintages, including a large selection of flights and wines by the glass, and a food menu that complements those wines beautifully. The ceviche's outstanding, but there are many other delightful small plates, plus Francophile touches such as onion soup.

Under the same ownership, next-door **Chipe Libre** (Lastarria 282, tel. 02/2664-0584) is a *pisco* bar with similar menu offerings, but occasional touches like sweet potato chips to accompany the ceviche.

Kintaro (Monjitas 460, tel. 02/2638-2448, www.kintaro.cl, 12:30pm-3pm and 7:30pm-11pm Mon.-Thurs., 12:30pm-3pm and 7:30pm-11:30pm Fri., 1pm-3:30pm and 8pm-11:30pm Sat., US$11-16) is one of Santiago's cheapest sushi options, with large fresh fish and shrimp plates. The portions are more than most diners can consume in a sitting. Sashimi and rice-based plates like *donburi* are also on the menu. Not quite so good or diverse, but notably cheaper, is **Izakaya Yoko** (Monjitas 296-A, tel. 02/2632-1954, www.izakayayoko.cl, noon-3:30pm and 7:30pm-11:30pm Mon.-Thurs., noon-3:30pm and 7:30pm-12:30am Fri., 12:30pm-4pm and 7:30pm-12:30pm Sat., 12:30pm-4pm Sun.).

BARRIO BRASIL

Barrio Brasil's dining options are getting steadily better and, since Chile tightened its tobacco laws, the air quality has improved.

Long after its opening, **Las Vacas Gordas** (Cienfuegos 280, tel. 02/2697-1066, noon-midnight Mon.-Thurs., noon-12:30am Fri.-Sat., noon-5:30pm Sun., US$15) still manages to combine high standards with high volume and low prices. It's almost always crowded and noisy. The fare is primarily *parrillada* (mixed grill), but pasta and fish are also on the menu. For US$2, it may not have the city's best *pisco* sour, but it may be the best value.

Prepared to a soundtrack of *narcocorridos* (Mexican border ballads about drug traffickers), the bargain-priced Mexican tacos, *antojitos* (short orders such as enchiladas), and more elaborate dinner plates at **Charro de Oro** (Av. Ricardo Cumming 342-A, tel. 02/2698-0400, 12:30pm-12:30am Mon.-Fri., 6:30pm-12:45am Sat., 12:30pm-4pm Sun., tacos US$3) are too spicy for some Chilean palates, but it won't bother those who have eaten Mexican food elsewhere. It sometimes keeps erratic hours.

The best Mexican option, **Plaza Garibaldi** (Moneda 2319, tel. 02/2699-4278, www.plazagaribaldi.cl, noon-4pm and 7pm-midnight Mon.-Thurs., noon-4pm and 7pm-1am Fri.-Sat., US$8-12) continues to draw diners who at one time wouldn't be caught dead in this area. Brightly decorated, it's operated by the improbably named Jane Holmes, a Chilean who lived many years in exile in Mexico City. The diverse regional Mexican menu merits a visit even for those who live in areas where such food is common (the *enchiladas de mole* are a personal favorite). The Mexican beers and strong margaritas are more than authentic.

Under the same ownerships as Las Vacas Gordas, **Sole Mio** (Moneda 1816, tel. 02/2672-6342, 12:30pm-12:30am Mon.-Sat., 12:30pm-4:30pm Sun., US$10-15) is a stylish but moderately priced Italian choice. It occupies a spectacularly recycled building with a stunning mezzanine (though its acoustics are a little too good). Unlike many Chilean restaurants, it offers ample distance between tables. Truly unusually for a Chilean restaurant, the ground-floor kitchen is open to public view.

After recovering from a disastrous fire, the classic **Ostras Azócar** (Bulnes 37, tel. 02/2681-6109, www.ostrasazocar.cl, 12:30pm-11:30pm Mon.-Sat., 12:30pm-4:30pm Sun., US$30) has retained its traditional approach to serve a more affluent clientele. Before being seated, everyone enters the oyster bar for freshly shucked samples accompanied by a shot-plus of chardonnay. A wide selection of

sauces accompanies very fresh fish dishes, and the Peruvian-style *pisco* sours are outstanding.

It's a reflection of the changing neighborhood (and city) that the Peruvian restaurant and *pisco* bar **Casa Valerio Pan** (Compañía 2280, tel. 02/2696-8009, www.casavalariorest.cl, noon-midnight daily, US$15) has taken over what was a sprawling family-style Chinese restaurant until not so long ago. Ceviche, fish, and seafood are the menu staples in this handsomely renovated locale, but there are also embellished versions of Peruvian beef, lamb, and pork dishes (try the *lechón adobado*, marinated suckling pig).

The barrio's star is ★ **Zully** (Concha y Toro 34, tel. 02/2696-1378, www.zully.cl, noon-11pm Mon.-Sat., US$25-30), an audacious restoration and modernization of a once-crumbling mansion in Barrio Concha y Toro, an intriguing maze of streets just off the Alameda. Expat Michigander Joe Westrate has created an intimate destination-in-itself bar-restaurant with multiple dining rooms plus a spectacular basement wine bar with an adjacent sunken patio and an equally impressive rooftop terrace. The furniture and place settings, though, are ultramodern. That's not to mention a creative, visually spectacular menu that changes frequently but includes entrées such as "ostrich" (actually rhea). It's expensive, but the three-course weekday lunch is a more economical option (with a glass of wine and coffee). There's a big wine list, including a good by-the-glass selection, mostly from Chilean bodegas.

In a similar vein, **Boulevard Lavaud** (Compañía 2789, tel. 02/2682-5243, www.boulevardlavaud.cl, 10am-midnight Mon.-Sat., 10am-6pm Sun., lunch US$15, dinner US$25) has recycled an 1868 building into a combination bar-restaurant that also serves, in daytime hours, its historic function as a barbershop (for men and women). Even that doesn't say everything, as it has also integrated an antiques shop into the restaurant—much of the decor along its redbrick walls is for sale. With all that, the food might seem an afterthought, but dishes such as coq au vin and duck à l'orange are relatively expensive specialties. It also serves breakfast, plus a midday menu; drinks are fairly expensive.

BARRIO BELLAVISTA

North of the Mapocho via the Pío Nono bridge, Bellavista is Santiago's gourmet ghetto, with dozens of fine restaurants virtually side-by-side—but not on Pío Nono itself, where most options are still greasy spoons. The bulk of the choices are east of Pío Nono, on the Providencia side of the barrio, but there are still fine options on the Recoleta side, to the west.

Flourishing amid rampant gentrification by serving outstanding sandwiches and Chilean comfort food such as *pastel de choclo* (corn casserole) to a Bohemian clientele, **Galindo** (Dardignac 098, tel. 02/2777-0116, www.galindo.cl, noon-1am Sun.-Tues., noon-2am Wed.-Thurs., noon-3am Fri.-Sat., US$13) is one of the Providencia side's oldest eateries. With its bright new facade, **El Caramaño** (Purísima 257, tel. 02/2737-7043, 1pm-11pm Mon.-Sat., 1pm-5pm Sun., from US$10) is less casual than it once was. In the past, it lacked even a street sign and you used to need to bang on the door to get in, lending it a slumming sort of "members only"

atmosphere. In the back rooms, diners can still scribble on the walls, and the Chilean specialties are reliable.

Dining at **Azul Profundo** (Constitución 111, tel. 02/2738-0288, www.restauranteazul-profundo.cl, 1pm-5pm and 7pm-midnight Mon.-Fri., 1pm-5pm and 7pm-12:30am Sat.-Sun., US$15-18) might be the closest possible experience to eating at Pablo Neruda's. Its whimsical decor, including its signature navy-blue exterior, a doorway bowsprit, and maritime memorabilia within, could have come straight from the poet's beloved Isla Negra residence. They've put as much effort into its kitchen as its character. Seafood is the specialty, with a diversity of ceviches, shellfish, and fish dishes.

On the Recoleta side of the barrio, the food at **Pantaleón II** (Antonia López de Bello 98, tel. 02/2735-8785, www.restaurant-pantaleon.cl, 12:45pm-midnight Mon.-Sat., 12:45pm-11pm Sun. and holidays, US$15) belies its modest appearance: This is an excellent Peruvian restaurant, with a superb *ceviche mixto* starter suitable for two or three diners. Main courses include a fine *chupe de mariscos* that comes with shrimp, squid, octopus, and scallops. They also serve superb Peruvian *pisco* sours.

traditional restaurant Galindo

Occupying a classic Bellavista mansion, with a small shaded terrace offering views of densely wooded Cerro San Cristóbal, **El Mesón Nerudiano** (Dominica 35, tel. 02/2737-1542, www.elmesonnerudiano. cl, 12:30pm-4pm and 7pm-1am Mon.-Sat., US$25) prepares exceptional fish (especially corvina) and seafood dishes, as well as pastas with seafood sauces. Downstairs, it has live music, ranging from folk to jazz, several nights per week.

Looking like a movie set based on its Mexican namesake novel, ★ **Como Agua Para Chocolate** (Like Water for Chocolate, Constitución 88, tel. 02/2777-8740, www. comoaguaparachocolate.cl, 12:30pm-4pm and 7:30pm-2am daily, US$18-22) is one of Bellavista's smartest restaurants. The menu has shifted from Mexican-Caribbean entrées more toward creative Chilean cuisine, but the seafood fajitas (US$35 for 2) suggest it hasn't abandoned its origins.

Al Corte Patagón (Mallinkrodt 184, tel. 02/2800-3890) imports its beef and lamb from the northern Patagonian region of Aisén, but also works them into dishes such as ravioli and adds touches like a *merquén*-spiced puree. The *pisco* sours are good, and the service is excellent.

It's stretching things to call it Bellavista—it's really in Recoleta's Patronato garment district—but the casual Argentine-run ★ **El Toro** (Loreto 33, tel. 02/2936-6715, www.eltoro.cl, 1pm-1:30am Mon.-Sat., US$15) has earned a loyal following for its crepes, moderately priced lunches, and nonconformist sidewalk atmosphere. Across the street, ★ **Sarita Colonia** (Loreto 40, tel. 02/2881-3937, www.saritacoloniarestoran.cl, 8am-midnight Mon.-Wed., 8am-1am Thurs.-Sat.) is a self-proclaimed "Peruvian transvestite restaurant" named for a folk saint followed by immigrants, prisoners, and LGBT minorities. The decor is quality kitsch, while the food is a colorful fusion of Peruvian and Chilean dishes with global touches.

On the Providencia side, the latest development in neighborhood gastronomy is the expanding **Patio Bellavista** (Constitución 70, tel. 02/2249-8700, www.patiobellavista.cl, 10am-2am Sun.-Tues., 10am-3am Wed., 10am-4am Thurs.-Sat.), a refashioned interior patio between Avenida Pío Nono and Constitución that's home to new branches of several successful restaurants and numerous newer establishments. The Peruvian institution **Barandiarán** (Constitución 38, Local 52, tel. 02/2737-0725, www.barandiaran.cl, 12:30pm-midnight Sun.-Thurs., noon-midnight Fri.-Sat., US$20) and the well-established Colombian **La Casa en el Aire** (Constitución 40, Local D, tel. 02/2762-1161, 10am-3am Wed., 10am-4am Thurs.-Sat., US$22) have locales here, while **Backstage Experience** (tel. 02/2247-3885) is a bar and blues club.

PROVIDENCIA

Liguria (Av. Providencia 1353, tel. 02/2235-7914, www.liguria.cl, 10am-1:30am Mon.-Sat., US$10) is a traditional hangout with plain but reliable Chilean meals at moderate prices. Nearby **Dominó** (Av. Providencia 1355, www.domino.cl, 8:30am-10pm Mon.-Fri., 11am-4:30pm Sat., US$7) has excellent sandwiches, fresh juices, and quick service, with several other branches around town.

Eladio (Av. Nueva Providencia 2250, 5th Fl., tel. 02/2231-4224, www.eladio.cl, 1pm-midnight Mon.-Sat., 1pm-4pm Sun., US$10-20) specializes in beef, but its varied menu will satisfy most anyone, with inexpensive entrées and good cheap *pisco* sours.

★ **El Huerto** (Orrego Luco 054, tel. 02/2233-2690, www.elhuerto.cl, 12:15pm-11pm Mon.-Wed., 12:15pm-11:30pm Thurs.-Sat., 12:30pm-4:30pm Sun., US$10-12) is a landmark vegetarian restaurant, with dishes so appetizing that even the most eager carnivores hardly notice the absence of meat. There is now abundant sidewalk seating.

In an aging but spacious Providencia house, painted in exuberant primary colors, **Barandiarán** (Manuel Montt 315, tel. 02/2236-6854, www.barandiaran.cl,

1pm-11:45pm Mon.-Thurs., 1pm-12:45am Fri.-Sat., 1pm-3:45pm Sun., US$12-15) prepares tangy appetizers and ceviches, spicy Peruvian entrées, and a diverse dessert menu. Other Peruvian options have caught up.

Set back from a shady but busy street, ★ Baco Vino y Bistró (Nueva de Lyon 113, tel. 02/2231-4444, 12:30pm-1am Mon.-Sat., 12:30pm-midnight Sun., US$8-14) is a wine bar with a mostly Francophile menu such as beef bourguignon and crepes, but also the occasional oddity such as gnocchi. The main dining room features a semicircular bar and natural woods. There's a big wine-by-the-glass selection displayed on the chalkboard, with quality vintages from niche wineries alongside the traditional giants (each glass bears a circular label around the stem so you don't forget what you're drinking).

Providencia has some of the city's better ice creameries, including Bravíssimo (Av. Providencia 1406, tel. 02/2421-7596, www. bravissimo.cl) and Sebastián (Andrés de Fuenzalida 26, tel. 02/2231-9968, www.heladeriasebastian.cl). Both also offer sandwiches and light lunches.

LAS CONDES AND VITACURA

For lunches and Sunday brunch, the hands-down choice is Kiwi-run ★ Café Melba (Don Carlos 2898, tel. 02/2232-4546, www. cafemelba.cl, 8am-6pm Mon.-Sat., 8:30am-6pm Sun., US$6-10). There's sidewalk seating, and the sandwiches, omelets, fresh juices, and breakfast fare are unmatchable in their category.

Except for a few boned cuts, nearby Happening (Av. Apoquindo 3090, tel. 02/2233-2301, www.happening.cl, 12:30pm-12:30am Mon.-Sat., from US$18) imports its beef directly from Argentina (sanitary regulations prohibit shipping boned meats across the border). The results are well above average, as are the prices. There are a couple of fish dishes, the odd pasta, fine desserts, and a giant wine list. The building is an older house, its interior walls demolished to form a single spacious, luminous dining room.

Las Condes now has two fine ice creameries within sight of each other: Fragola (Av. El Bosque Norte 0166, tel. 02/2333-2029, www. fragola.cl) and Tavelli (Isidora Goyenechea 2891, tel. 02/2586-2523, www.tavelli.cl). Like their Providencia counterparts, both serve sandwiches and light lunches as well.

Accommodations

Nearly all the budget to mid-range accommodations are in and around Santiago Centro, with luxury hotels in Providencia and Las Condes. Most mid-range and top-end hotels discount the IVA (value-added tax) for foreign visitors. Many upper-range hotels belong to international chains.

Unless otherwise indicated, accommodations listed here are in Santiago Centro; some of them are more closely defined by barrio. Many hotels in other boroughs are oriented toward business travelers but still welcome ordinary travelers.

US$25-50

In the winding cobbled streets south of the Alameda and such a good value that reservations are imperative, ★ Residencial Londres (Londres 54, tel. 02/2633-9192, www.londres.cl, US$29 s, US$40 d with shared bath, US$43-60 s, US$60-70 d with private bath) has real charm, but it may not be able to keep pace with some of the newer backpacker favorites.

In a handsomely transformed art deco building that was once an old folks home, La Princesa Insolente (Moneda 2350, tel. 02/2671-6551, www.princesainsolente.cl,

US$11-14 dorm, US$46 d) is ideal for back-packers and even has a few private rooms (some with external bath). It's part of a small hostel chain that also has accommodations in Pucón.

US$50-100

Barrio Brasil's **Happy House Hostel** (Moneda 1829, tel. 02/2688-4849, www. happyhousehostel.com, US$18-20 dorm, US$43-57 s, US$50-64 d) has truly turned a century-old mansion into a "boutique design hostel." It has huge private rooms with state-of-the-art overhead showers, high ceilings, a modern kitchen for dorm backpackers, and a swimming pool with a bar and two large wooden decks. Two of the ground-level bedrooms get noise from the busy street.

A dull burgundy facade masks the interior of nearby ★ **La Casa Roja** (Agustinas 2113, tel. 02/2696-4241, www.lacasaroja.cl, US$15 dorm, US$52-70 d), a sprawling 19th-century mansion that bids to become a backpacker boutique hostel—though with 85 or so beds, it's perhaps a bit too large for that. Australian owner Simon Shalders restored period details while modernizing the baths and creating a contemporary kitchen, not to mention a garden pool with a swim-up bar and a batting cage (for cricket, but adaptable for baseball). Even the eight-bed dorms don't feel cramped, and with large common areas scattered through the building, the place never seems crowded. There are also private rooms with or without private baths.

Nicely modernized, the central **Hotel España** (Morandé 510, tel. 02/2770-4500, www.hotelespania.com, US$55 s, US$60 d) has spacious cheerful rooms with contemporary baths and exceptional natural light on the fourth floor in particular. Well located at the north end of Cerro Santa Lucía, the under-rated ★ **Hotel Foresta** (Subercaseaux 353, tel. 02/2639-6261, www.forestahotel.cl, US$53 s, US$63 d with a so-so breakfast) offers excellent value for money.

Few traditional townhouses survive among Providencia's high-rises, but a Catalan couple has converted two of them into the ★ **Vilafranca Petit Hotel** (Pérez Valenzuela 1650, tel. 02/2235-1413, www.vilafranca.cl, US$75 s, US$90 d with breakfast), whose only drawback is the rush-hour drone from nearby Avenida Andrés Bello. Engagingly furnished, the eight rooms vary from cozy attic doubles to spacious suites, all with private baths, plus amenities such as cable TV and Wi-Fi. The

La Casa Roja is the only Santiago hostel with a swim-up bar.

common areas include a comfortable living room with plenty of reading material and a shady patio.

US$100-150

Under the same ownership as La Casa Roja, next-door **Matildas Hotel Boutique** (Agustinas 2149, tel. 02/2661-9700, www. matildashotel.com, US$100-230 s or d) is a renovated Francophile mansion with high ceilings and burnished period details in its 17 rooms and common areas. It also enjoys a secluded garden, and high walkability scores for its access to nearby restaurants and downtown attractions as well as public transportation, including the Metro.

Decorated with museum-piece artifacts from the Chilean countryside, downtown's ★ **Hotel Galerías** (San Antonio 65, tel. 02/2470-7400, www.hotelgalerias.cl, US$99 s, US$120-215 d) is a theme hotel with 162 rooms that, despite its romantic ruralism, has contemporary conveniences, including Wi-Fi and a terraced pool. Its deceptively inconspicuous street-side entrance leads to spacious facilities that are an enclave of calm in a busy neighborhood.

A converted apartment building, **Hotel Neruda** (Av. Pedro de Valdivia 164, tel. 02/2679-0700, www.hotelneruda.cl, US$110-146 s, US$135-177 d) is a business-oriented facility with contemporary conveniences that include free Wi-Fi, plus a gym, a sauna, and a rooftop pool in an adjacent building.

US$150-200

Business-oriented **Hotel Plaza San Francisco** (Alameda 816, tel. 02/2639-3832, www.plazasanfrancisco.cl, US$140-178 s or d) often gets celebrity clientele such as Mia Farrow, Plácido Domingo, and even the Dalai Lama. Some of its 148 rooms have Asian design touches. In the summer off-season, there may be discounts for "standard" rooms.

Las Condes's **NH Collection Plaza Santiago Hotel** (Av. Vitacura 2610, tel. 02/2433-9000, www.nh-collection.com, US$143-203 s or d) caters primarily to

business travelers. Each room comes with its own cell phone, for instance, and it occupies part of Santiago's World Trade Center. There are also, of course, amenities such as a rooftop pool, a gymnasium, whirlpool tubs, and Andean panoramas.

Providencia's **Le Rêve Boutique Hotel** (Orrego Luco 023, tel. 02/2757-6000, www.le-revehotelcl, US$147-161 s, US$155-199 d) appeals to Francophiles in its architecture and furnishings (except for the lobby, which is surprisingly modernist). According to the front desk personnel, at least, Parisians have said they feel at home here.

The Patronato garment district's not known for its accommodations but, on the edge of Bellavista's nightlife and gourmet ghetto, **Hotel Loreto** (Loreto 170, tel. 02/2777-1060, www.loretohotel.cl, US$150 s, US$160 d) is a nicely renovated building with simple but comfortable rooms (some with balconies), plus garden spaces and a sunny terrace. It doesn't claim to be a "boutique" facility, but similar accommodations elsewhere do.

At Providencia's **Hotel Santiago Park Plaza** (Ricardo Lyon 207, tel. 02/2372-4000, www.parkplaza.cl, US$160-200 s or d), the antique-studded foyer belies the modernity of its wired rooms and recreational facilities, including a glassed-in rooftop plunge pool. The 104 rooms in this European-style hotel vary considerably in size.

Alongside the Parque Arauco shopping center, Las Condes's copper-plated ★ **Marriott Santiago Hotel** (Av. Kennedy 5741, tel. 02/2426-2000, www.marriott.cl, from US$199 s or d) is one of Santiago's tallest buildings. It projects a contemporary gentility, especially in its luminous atrium. Still, nonconformist celebrities are often among its clientele—check to see if Ozzy Osbourne's in the adjacent suite.

OVER US$200

At the base of Cerro San Cristóbal, ★ **The Aubrey** (Constitución 299, tel. 02/2940-2800, www.theaubrey.com, US$195-575 s or d) has

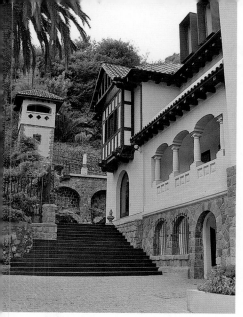

The Aubrey is a former mansion recycled as a boutique hotel..

www.crowneplaza.cl, from US$115-256 s or d) features recreational facilities, including a gymnasium, swimming pool, dozens of shops, and even its own post office. All 293 rooms in this 22-story hotel have luxury furniture and marble baths, and Internet access is included in the rates.

Overlooking the Mapocho from the base of Cerro San Cristóbal, with garden space that other luxury hotels lack, Providencia's **Sheraton San Cristóbal Hotel & Convention Center** (Av. Santa María 1742, tel. 02/2233-5000, www.sheraton.com/santiago, US$145-273 s or d, suites up to US$1,039) is where Bob Dylan holes up when he plays Santiago. The rooms are stylishly decorated and feature beautiful views. For those who want to explore the city, though, this hotel is a little isolated and definitely not pedestrian-friendly.

In Las Condes, the 310-room high-rise ★ **Grand Hyatt Santiago** (Av. Kennedy 4601, tel. 02/2950-1234, www.hyatt.cl, from US$213 s or d) has made *Condé Nast Traveler*'s top 10 list of Latin American hotels several times. Its lofty atrium, topped by a glass dome, lets natural light stream inside. Rates for mid-size to capacious rooms, some with stupendous Andean panoramas, also include access to a gymnasium, a swimming pool, and tennis courts.

The first of its kind in South America, Las Condes's **W Santiago** (Isidora Goyenechea 3000, tel. 02/2777-0000, www.whotels.com, from US$272 s or d) is a 196-room unit that occupies the upper 17 floors of a 21-story convention center complex, crowned by its panoramic swimming pool and rooftop bar. Including several restaurants, two bars, and a clothing boutique, it aims to provide casual luxury. It's pet-friendly, so if you want to bring along your howler monkey, they won't object.

seamlessly transformed a derelict 1930s residence into a 15-room boutique hotel (four rooms, newly constructed, occupy a separate wing). While the street can get busy and the zoo is next door, the double-paned windows keep this handsomely restored and recycled building quiet.

In downtown's most fashionable neighborhood, the **Lastarria Boutique Hotel** (Bueras 188, tel. 02/2840-3700, www.lastarriahotel. com, US$169-189 s, US$249-399 d) is a beautifully renovated mansion within easy walking distance of many attractions and some of the city's best dining. All the furnishings are contemporary, and it has a secluded garden swimming pool.

Virtually self-contained, downtown's business-oriented **Hotel Crowne Plaza Santiago** (Alameda 136, tel. 02/2638-1042,

Information and Services

INFORMATION

Santiago is home to Chile's central tourism agency but also to municipal authorities and some private information sources.

Tourist Offices

Redesigned for user-friendliness, the national tourism service **Sernatur** (Av. Providencia 1550, tel. 02/2731-8336, www. sernatur.cl, 9am-6pm Mon.-Fri., 9am-2pm Sat.) has numerous touch-screen computers, mural maps of the city, and English-speaking personnel who provide maps and information on city attractions and brochures on the rest of the country. It also has a branch at Alameda 221 (tel. 02/2731-8627, noon-6pm Mon., 10am-7pm Tues. and Thurs., 10am-6pm Wed. and Fri., 10am-2pm Sat.) and an international airport office (tel. 02/2601-9320, 9am-6pm daily).

In new quarters on the north side of Plaza de Armas, the municipal **Oficina de Turismo** (Plaza de Armas s/n, tel. 02/2713-6745, turismo@munistgo.cl, 9am-6pm Mon.-Fri., 10am-6pm Sat.-Sun.) also has a satellite office on Cerro Santa Lucía (tel. 02/2386-7185, 9am-6pm Mon.-Thurs., 9am-5pm Fri.).

The borough of Providencia has its own **Centro de Información Turística** (Av. Providencia 2359, tel. 02/2374-2743, www. citi.providencia.cl, 9am-2pm and 3pm-7pm Mon.-Fri., 10am-4pm Sat.-Sun. and holidays).

National Parks

South of the Alameda, the **Corporación Nacional Forestal** (Conaf, Av. Bulnes 265, tel. 02/2663-0125, www.conaf.cl, 9am-5:30pm Mon.-Thurs., 9am-4:30pm Fri.) provides information on national parks and other protected areas. It also has inexpensive maps, and a selection of pamphlets on parks throughout the country.

Libraries

The **Biblioteca Nacional** (national library, Alameda 651, tel. 02/2360-5400, www.bibliotecanacional.cl) hosts special exhibitions on history, archaeology, and art.

Newspapers

The notoriously conservative—many would say reactionary—daily *El Mercurio* still publishes paeans to Pinochet, but now does it through guest columnists rather than its own editorial staff. It partially compensates for that with broad international, business, cultural, and entertainment coverage.

SERVICES

Like accommodations and restaurants, most services are in Santiago Centro, Providencia, and Las Condes, with a few addresses elsewhere.

Money

ATMs are so abundant that exchange houses have become virtual dinosaurs except for changing traveler's checks or leftover cash. The many branches of BancoEstado have the lowest surcharge for foreign ATM cards, but they work with MasterCard only. Most exchange houses are downtown on Agustinas, between Bandera and Ahumada. There are others in Providencia and at the airport, where rates are notably lower.

Postal Services

The **Correo Central** (Plaza de Armas 983, 8am-7pm Mon.-Fri., 9am-2pm Sat.) offers general delivery services, as well as a good postal museum, a philatelic office, and branch offices around town. For courier service, try **FedEx** (Av. Providencia 1951, tel. 02/2231-5250).

Communications

Long-distance *centros de llamados* (calling centers), at Metro stations and on the streets, are so ubiquitous that none needs individual mention. Many of these provide Internet access as well, but there are also Internet specialists charging US$1 per hour or less.

Immigration

For visa extensions, visit the **Departamento de Extranjería** (San Antonio 580, Santiago Centro, tel. 02/2486-3200, 8:30am-2pm daily). Replacing a lost tourist card requires a trip to the **Policía Internacional** (Eleuterio Ramírez 852, Santiago Centro, tel. 02/2708-1043, 8am-2pm Mon.-Fri.).

Laundry

Laundries include Santiago Centro's **Lavandería y Lavaseco Laundry** (Monjitas 507, tel. 02/2664-2948) and Barrio Brasil's **Lavandería Lolos** (Moneda 2296, tel. 02/2699-5376).

Travel Agencies

Upscape (Tegualda 1352, Providencia, tel. 02/2244-2750, www.upscapetravel.com) has extensive experience in arranging excursions, along with the usual travel services.

Photography

For the most complex digital service, visit **Photo Service** (Av. Suecia 84, Oficina 61, Providencia, tel. 02/2335-4460, www.photo-service.cl).

Medical Services

The **Posta Central** (Av. Portugal 125, Santiago Centro, tel. 02/2568-1100, www.huap.cl) is a public clinic; the private **Clínica Universidad Católica** (Lira 40, tel. 02/2384-6000, www.clinicauc.cl) is nearby. The private **Clínica Alemana** (Av. Vitacura 5951, Vitacura, tel. 02/2210-1111, www.alemana.cl) is highly regarded.

Transportation

AIR

Santiago has international air links to most South American capitals, Europe, North America, and the Caribbean, and across the Pacific. Domestic destinations include Puerto Montt, the gateway to Chilean Patagonia, and the Patagonian cities of Coyhaique and Punta Arenas.

Serving all international and virtually all domestic flights, the state-of-the-art **Aeropuerto Internacional Arturo Merino Benítez** (SCL, tel. 02/2690-1752 or 02/2690-1798, www.nuevopudahuel.cl) is 26 kilometers west of Santiago Centro, in the borough of Pudahuel.

Domestically, **LATAM/LAN** (Estado 82, tel. 02/2687-2941) flies south to Punta Arenas and points between. Its main competitor, **Sky Airline** (Huérfanos 815, tel. 02/2632-9449,

www.skyairline.cl) has fewer destinations and flights but is growing steadily.

Airport Transportation

For airport transport to Pudahuel, the cheapest option is **Centropuerto** (tel. 02/2601-9883, US$3 pp), which has some 40 buses daily from Plazoleta Los Héroes, just off the eastbound lanes of the Alameda outside Los Héroes Metro station. The slightly more expensive **Tur-Bus** (Moneda 1523, tel. 02/2822-7741) has similar services.

For shuttle services, it's best to ring a day in advance. **Transvip** (tel. 02/2677-3000) provides door-to-door service for the entire city, starting around US$10 to Santiago Centro; Providencia, Las Condes, and other eastern boroughs are slightly more expensive. This is the best option for travelers with heavy luggage or those who arrive late at night.

Hotels can help arrange taxi or radio-taxi service, which can be cost-effective if shared by several people.

METRO

Carrying upward of 200 million passengers per year, Santiago's quiet, clean, and efficient **Metro** (www.metrosantiago.cl, 6:30am-10:30pm Mon.-Sat., 8am-10:30pm Sun. and holidays) would be the pride of many European cities. Five interconnected lines cover most points of interest; others lines and extensions of existing lines are under construction. For most visitors, Línea 1, running beneath the Alameda and Avenida Providencia to Los Dominicos, is the most useful (at present, there is no Línea 3, though it and a Línea 6 are under construction, but there is a Línea 4A).

Fares depend on the hour of the day. A *punta* (peak hour) ticket, good 7:15am-9am and 6pm-7:30pm Monday-Friday, costs US$1.10. During the day and on Saturday-Sunday, the *valle* (mid-hour) fare is about US$0.95, while the early morning and late night *bajo* fare is US$0.90. The turnstile swallows the ticket, which is not needed to exit the system.

A *tarjeta bip!* (multi-trip ticket) is more convenient, but the electronic ticket itself requires a US$3 investment that's almost pointless for short-term users. More than one person, though, may use a *bip!* ticket by passing it back across the turnstile; this is not illegal.

BUS

Santiago's four bus terminals are all on or near the Alameda; some companies have offices at more than one.

Tur-Bus and **Pullman Bus** are based at the **Terminal de Buses Alameda** (Alameda 3750, Metro: Universidad de Santiago, tel. 02/2270-7500) and travel to a wide variety of destinations. Most southbound carriers use nearby **Terminal Santiago** (also known as Terminal de Buses Sur, Alameda 3848, tel. 02/2376-1750, www.terminaldebusessanti-ago.cl). Some Terminal Santiago buses pick up additional passengers at **Terrapuerto Los Héroes** (Tucapel Jiménez 21, tel. 02/2420-0099, www.terrapuertolosheroes.co.cl).

Fares can fluctuate both seasonally and among companies, so comparison shopping is advisable. Distance and fare don't necessarily correlate—longer trips can be cheaper when competition is greater. Sample domestic destinations, journey times, and fares include Temuco (9 hours, US$13-45), Villarrica

Santiago's Metro carries more than 200 million passengers per year.

(11 hours, US$22-53), and Puerto Montt (15 hours, US$17-66).

Nar-Bus (tel. 02/2778-1235, www.narbus.cl) goes to Argentina's Patagonian cities of Junín de los Andes, San Martín de los Andes, and Neuquén, with a change of buses in Temuco. **Cruz del Sur** (tel. 02/2776-9973, http://busescruzdelsur.cl) goes to Bariloche, but this requires changing buses in Osorno.

For getting around Santiago, city buses, called **micros,** are numerous and cheap. They run all day and all night to virtually every part of town—often faster than they should. **Transantiago** (www.transantiago. cl) plans to replace nearly all buses with smart new cleaner-burning articulated buses. Along the Alameda are dedicated bus lanes and fixed stops, intended to speed up traffic, and the hope is that the new system will reduce traffic congestion. After the Metro closes, it is the main means of getting around town. Destinations are marked on window signs and at fixed stops. Buses have automatic fare machines that accept coins but also work with the *tarjeta bip!*; hold onto your tickets, as inspectors often ask for them.

Taxis Colectivos

Carrying four or sometimes five passengers on fixed routes, *taxis colectivos* cover much of the same ground as Transantiago buses but are slightly more expensive (though often quicker).

Taxis

Black with yellow roofs, regular taxis charge about US$0.50 to start the meter and US$0.20 more for every subsequent 200 meters. There is also a system of radio taxis with fixed fares within certain zones; among the choices are **Radio Taxi Arauco** (tel. 02/2206-2151) and **Radio Taxi Alameda** (tel. 02/2776-4730).

CAR RENTALS

Santiago's numerous car rental agencies, both international franchises and generally cheaper local companies, are scattered throughout the city. Most airport rentals are franchises. Note that demand is high for economy cars, so reserve well in advance for the best rates.

- **Alameda** (Av. Libertador Bernardo O'Higgins 4709, Estación Central, tel. 02/2779-0609, www.alamedarentacar.cl)

- **Alamo** (Av. Francisco Bilbao 2846, Providencia, tel. 02/2655-5255, www.alamochile.com)

- **Automóvil Club de Chile** (Av. Andrés Bello 1863, Providencia, tel. 02/2431-1313, www.automovilclub.cl)

- **Avis** (Luz 2934, Las Condes, tel. 02/2795-3928, www.avis.cl)

- **Econorent** (Av. Manquehue Sur 600, Las Condes, tel. 02/2202-9002, www.econorent.cl)

- **First** (Rancagua 0514, Providencia, tel. 02/2225-6328, www.firstrentacar.cl)

- **Hertz** (Av. Costanera Andrés Bello 1469, Providencia, tel. 02/2360-8618, www.hertz.cl)

- **Localiza** (Av. Eduardo Frei Montalva 1762, Renca, tel. 02/2478-9000, www.eurorentacar.cl)

Northern Argentine Patagonia

On a bridge over the Río Colorado, midway between Bahía Blanca and the Río Negro, a roadside sign reads "Patagonia Starts Here." No other part of the continent so stimulates the imagination.

Ever since Magellan's chronicler Antonio Pigafetta concocted encounters with a giant "so tall that the tallest among us reached only to his waist," the remote southern latitudes have projected a mystique that blends anticipation and apprehension. Geographically, Patagonia is more diverse than simple statistics would suggest, with a long Atlantic coastline, boundless steppes, and Andean lakes, forests, and peaks. Its wildlife sites and national parks draw visitors from around the globe, and its gateway towns and cities are also worth exploring. Increasing numbers of *estancias* (ranches) have become enticing getaways.

In Argentina, Patagonia encompasses the area south of the Río Colorado, primarily the provinces of Neuquén, Río Negro, Chubut, and Santa Cruz. While the four provinces' approximately 2 million residents are nearly 5 percent of the country's 40.1 million population, according to the 2010 census, they cover more than 27 percent of Argentine territory,

an area roughly equivalent to Texas (whose population exceeds 27 million).

Between them, Neuquén and Río Negro provinces contain most of the Argentine lakes district, a popular vacation area on the eastern Andean slope. Along the Chilean border, its alpine peaks and glaciers, indigo finger lakes, and dense forests have long been a prime destination. If Patagonia were a country, its logical capital might be the Río Negro resort of San Carlos de Bariloche.

Together, the two provinces extend from the Andes to the Atlantic. The coastal zone features the colonial city of Carmen de Patagones (actually part of Buenos Aires province) and the Río Negro provincial capital of Viedma, plus a scattering of wildlife reserves and beach resorts. An energy storehouse for its petroleum reserves and hydroelectric resources, the intervening steppe is the site of some of the world's most momentous dinosaur discoveries.

Previous: Lago Nahuel Huapi; Llao Llao Hotel & Resort. **Above:** The Río Arrayanes runs through Parque Nacional Los Alerces

Look for ★ to find recommended
sights, activities, dining, and lodging.

Highlights

★ **Volcán Lanín:** In the northernmost sector of Argentina's fabled lakes district, the snow-capped centerpiece of Parque Nacional Lanín is perhaps the region's most recognizable summit (page 126).

★ **Parque Nacional Los Arrayanes:** *Arrayán* forests are the highlight of this park on the shore of Lago Nahuel Huapi. The town of Villa La Angostura provides easy access (page 130).

★ **Centro Cívico:** The buildings surrounding the central square of San Carlos de Bariloche represent the best of Argentine Patagonia's architecture with their steep roofs and arched arcades (page 135).

★ **Lago Nahuel Huapi:** From the alluring shoreline of this glacial finger lake, the terrain of Parque Nacional Nahuel Huapi rises to the forests, pinnacles, and ice fields of the Andes (page 145).

★ **Feria Artesanal:** This three-times-a-week market surrounding El Bolsón's Plaza Pagano is the perfect place to find local crafts and sample regional food and drink (page 149).

★ **Cerro Piltriquitrón:** This 2,284-meter granite summit rises east of El Bolsón, where a clear day reveals snow-covered peaks along the Chilean border (page 155).

★ **Circuito Lacustre:** The most popular excursion in Parque Nacional Los Alerces is this lake circuit, by boat and by foot, starting at Puerto Limonao, on Lago Futalaufquen's south end, and ending at Puerto Sagrario (page 165).

In addition to Río Negro and Neuquén in northern Argentine Patagonia, this chapter includes parts of Chubut province, most notably the city of Esquel and vicinity, including Parque Nacional Los Alerces, which are most frequently visited from southern Río Negro. The Southern Argentine Patagonia chapter includes coastal segments of Chubut and all of Santa Cruz province.

PLANNING YOUR TIME

Patagonia's highlights could consume a lifetime, so even repeat visitors have to be selective about what they see and do. Distances are great, so it's often necessary to fly, especially if visiting widely separated areas like the northerly lakes of Neuquén and Río Negro, and southern Patagonia's coastal wildlife areas and massive Andean glaciers.

Unlike the coast, where sights and settlements are often far apart, the Andean lakes district of Neuquén, Río Negro, and northwestern Chubut is a more compact area with dense infrastructure and easy accessibility. A week here can be rewarding for special-interest visitors like fly-fishing aficionados. Most travelers would easily enjoy two weeks or more. Dedicated adventure travelers like climbers could spend a month or an entire summer.

San Carlos de Bariloche makes an ideal hub for excursions in and around the lakes, but towns like San Martín de los Andes, Villa La Angostura, El Bolsón, and Esquel are also good choices. Rural lodges and ranches are another option.

January and February are the main vacation months, but they are also the most expensive. The shoulder months of November-December and March-April have small crowds and lower prices, with almost equally good and sometimes better weather. By April, days are getting shorter, but the region becomes a winter destination, thanks to skiing in Bariloche, San Martín de los Andes, and a few other areas.

Throughout Patagonia, overland transportation schedules change from season to season and year to year, and may be disrupted by weather.

Coastal Río Negro Province

CARMEN DE PATAGONES

Carmen de Patagones, founded in 1779 on the Río Negro's north bank, was once Spain's farthest outpost in what is now Argentina. It's the only Patagonian city with any genuine colonial feel. "Patagones" is also Buenos Aires province's most southerly city. The south bank city of Viedma has more services, including hotels and restaurants.

Befitting its dual heritage, the city's name is a hybrid of the indigenous (Patagones, after the aboriginal inhabitants) and the European (after its patron, the Virgen del Carmen). The original colonists came from Maragatería, in the province of León. In 1827, in a conflict over the buffer state of Uruguay, their descendants fended off Brazilian invaders. Locals still go by the nickname *maragatos.*

Carmen de Patagones (pop. 20,533) is 279 kilometers south of Bahía Blanca and 961 kilometers south of Buenos Aires via Ruta Nacional (RN) 3, which continues west and then south to Chubut, Santa Cruz, and Tierra del Fuego. Two bridges connect it to Viedma, but locals also shuttle across the river on motor launches.

Sights

Patagones's most conspicuous landmark, the twin towers of the Salesian-built **Iglesia Parroquial Nuestra Señora del Carmen** (1885) rise above the **Plaza 7 de Marzo,** which commemorates the victory over Brazil in 1827. Immediately west, the **Torre del Fuerte** (1780) is the sole remnant of Patagones's frontier fortifications.

Northern Argentine Patagonia

PACIFIC OCEAN

Golfo Corcovado

Chaitén

Puerto Aisén

Coyhaique

Los Antiguos

Perito Moreno

Lago Buenos Aires

SANTA CRUZ

Las Heras

Pico Truncado

RP 43

RP 12

RN 3

RN 281

Puerto Deseado

FERIA ARTESANAL

El Bolsón

CERRO PILTRIQUITRÓN

RN 40

El Maitén

PN Los Alerces

PN Lago Puelo

Cholila

Leleque

CIRCUITO LACUSTRE

Esquel

Trevelin

Tecka

RP 62

Gobernador Costa

Alto Río Senguer

RP 20

RN 26

RN 40

Río Mayo

RP 22

Lago Musters

Sarmiento

Lago Colhué Huapi

RN 26

RN 25

Río Chubut

CHUBUT

Rada Tilly

Comodoro Rivadavia

Golfo San Jorge

Bahía Bustamante

RP 28

RP 30

RN 3

RP 1

Camarones

Reserva Provincial Punta Tombo

Gaiman

Trelew

Rawson

Puerto Madryn

RP 2

Reserva Natural Península Valdés

ATLANTIC OCEAN

0 50 km

0 50 mi

© AVALON TRAVEL

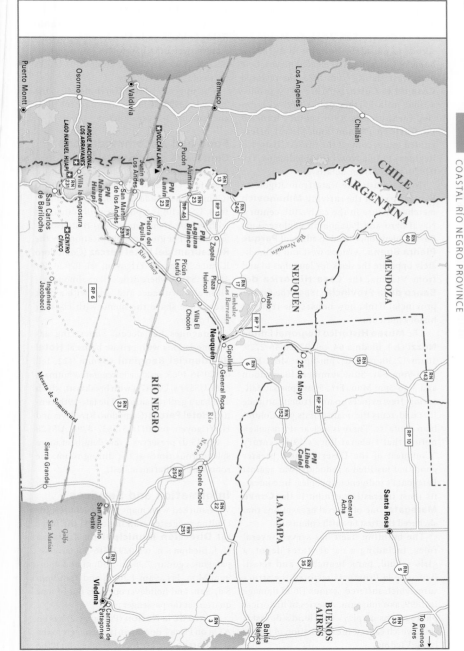

Puerto Montt

Osorno

Valdivia

Temuco

Los Ángeles

Chillán

CHILE

ARGENTINA

Los Andes

PARQUE NACIONAL
LOS ARRAYANES

VOLCÁN LANÍN

Pucón

Alumine

RN 13

RN 23

RN 242

RN 40

LAGO NAHUEL HUAPI

RN 231

PN Nahuel Huapi

Villa la Angostura

CENTRO CÍVICO

San Carlos de Bariloche

Junín de los Andes

San Martín de los Andes

PN Lanín

PN Lanín

RP 46

RP 13

Zapala

RN 237

Piedra del Águila

Río Limay

Laguna Blanca

PN Laguna Blanca

Plaza Huincul

RN 242

Río Neuquén

NEUQUÉN

MENDOZA

RN 40

Ingeniero Jacobacci

RP 6

Picún Leufú

Villa El Chocón

RN 17

Los Barreales

Embalse

Añelo

RP 7

Cipolletti

RN 6

General Roca

Neuquén

25 de Mayo

RN 151

RP 20

RN 143

Meseta de Somuncurá

RÍO NEGRO

RN 23

Río Negro

RN 152

RP 10

Sierra Grande

Choele Choel

RN 250

PN Lihué Calel

General Acha

Santa Rosa

LA PAMPA

San Antonio Oeste

RN 22

RN 251

RN 35

RN 5

Golfo San Matías

Viedma

RN 3

Carmen de Patagones

RN 3

Bahía Blanca

BUENOS AIRES

RN 33

To Buenos Aires

Immediately south of the tower, between a set of antique cannons, the broad staircase of **Pasaje San José de Mayo** descends to the adobe **Rancho Rial** (1820s), home of Carmen's first elected mayor. One block east, dating from 1823, the restored **Casa de la Cultura** (Mitre 27) was once a flour mill. Farther east, fitted with period furniture, the 19th-century **Rancho La Carlota** (Bynon and Mitre) offers guided tours; contact the Museo Histórico Regional Emma Nozzi (J.J. Biedma 64, tel. 02920/46-2729) for details.

To the south, the waterfront Rigoletto Bar was part of the thriving **Mihanovich** merchant house in the early 20th century. Naval hero and Patagonian explorer Luis Piedra Buena once lived in adjacent **Parque Piedra Buena.** A block west and immediately opposite the dock for launches to and from Viedma, the **Casa Histórica del Banco de la Provincia** (1884), the former provincial bank, now houses the regional history museum.

The **Museo Histórico Regional Emma Nozzi** (J. J. Biedma 64, tel. 02920/46-2729, 10am-12:30pm and 7pm-9pm Mon.-Fri., 7pm-9pm Sat.-Sun. summer, 10am-noon and 3pm-5pm Mon.-Fri., 5pm-7pm Sat. fall-spring, free) evinces an unfortunate attitude that undercuts the quality of its pre-Columbian artifacts. There is a clear if unspoken notion that General Roca's 19th-century "Conquest of the Desert" was a greater good that justified a genocidal war against Patagonia's indigenous peoples. In context, its most interesting exhibit is the **Cueva Maragata,** one of several excavations that sheltered the first Spanish colonists.

The building itself has served several roles, including a naval-stores depot, a girls school, bank branches, and retail. Banco de la Provincia restored the structure, which suffered serious flood damage in 1899, as a museum. A series of historical photographs displays the flood's devastation, which caused the evacuation of lower-lying Viedma.

Entertainment and Events

The week-long **Fiesta de la Soberanía Patagónica** in early March commemorates victory over Brazilian forces. Most festivities take place on railroad grounds, 11 blocks north of Plaza 7 de Marzo.

The upgraded **Cine Garibaldi** (España 205, tel. 02920/41-0019) shows recent films and even has 3-D capability.

Food and Accommodations

Confitería Sabbatella (Comodoro Rivadavia 218, tel. 02920/46-3662) is fine for breakfast, coffee, or sandwiches. **Neptuno** (Comodoro Rivadavia 310, tel. 02920/46-1493, US$7-10) is a popular grill restaurant with *bife de lomo* (tenderloin) that also offers pizza. For greater sophistication, try the **Restaurant del Hotel Percaz** (Comodoro Rivadavia and H. Yrigoyen, tel. 02920/46-4104, US$12), where dishes like salmon ravioli in a prawn sauce and lamb with a dark beer sauce share the menu with cheaper short orders.

Patagones has decent shoestring accommodations with private baths at **Hotel Residencial Reggiani** (Bynon 422, tel. 02920/46-1065, residencialreggiani@hotmail.com, US$31 s, US$47 d with breakfast), which also has a grill restaurant. The late-19th-century **Hotel Percaz** (Comodoro Rivadavia and H. Yrigoyen, tel. 011/15-5837-8794, US$28 s, US$45 d) preserves a few details of more splendorous times at the dining room; the rooms are utilitarian at best.

Information and Services

Well-stocked with maps and brochures, including suggested walking tours, the helpful **Dirección Municipal de Turismo** (J. J. Biedma s/n, tel. 02920/46-5406, www.patagones.gov.ar, 7:30am-1:30pm and 4pm-9pm Mon.-Fri., 9am-1:30pm and 4pm-9pm Sat.-Sun. and holidays) operates out of new quarters at the passenger pier.

Banco de la Nación (Paraguay 2) has an ATM on Plaza 7 de Marzo. Immediately to the east, **Correo Argentino** (Paraguay 38) is the post office; the postal code is 8504. Phone and Internet access are available at **Cyber Speed** (Suipacha 291).

Transportation

Services to and from Patagones's **Terminal de Ómnibus** (Barbieri 300, tel. 02920/46-3585), four blocks north and three blocks east of Plaza 7 de Marzo, are less frequent than Viedma's; several long-distance buses stop at both, however. Nearby Viedma has an airport.

On-demand *lanchas* (passenger launches, 6:30am-10:45pm Mon.-Fri., US$0.50) frequently cross the river to Viedma.

VIEDMA

While Viedma lacks Patagones's colonial character, it long ago surpassed its neighbor in services and significance. Viedma is the provincial capital of Río Negro, which stretches from the Atlantic to the Andes. Locals swim and kayak along the willow-shaded riverfront, with its restaurants and sailing school.

In 1779, founded simultaneously with Patagones, Viedma became Patagonia's de facto capital a century later. Following the "Conquest of the Desert," it became capital of Río Negro territory and then, in 1955, capital of the new Río Negro province. In the 1980s, President Raúl Alfonsín tried to move the federal capital here from Buenos Aires—a boondoggle that never came to be.

Viedma (pop. 52,789) is 280 kilometers south of Bahía Blanca and 440 kilometers northeast of Puerto Madryn via coastal RN 3. It's 982 kilometers east of Bariloche, Río Negro's largest city, via the Río Negro Valley and Neuquén.

Sights

On the southwest side of **Plaza Alsina,** the block bounded by Yrigoyen, Colón, Rivadavia, and Álvaro Barros is a national historical monument dating from the 1880s, when the Salesian order installed itself here. Among its works were the **Vicariato Apostólico de la Patagonia Septentrional** (Vicarage of Northern Patagonia, 1884-1897), with its neo-Renaissance brick facade and tower.

Today, it houses the **Centro Histórico Cultural Salesiano,** comprising two separate museums: the **Museo Salesiano Cardenal Cagliero** (Rivadavia 34, tel. 02920/15-61-3355, 10:30am-1pm and 2:30pm-5pm Mon.-Fri., free), presenting the Salesian viewpoint on Patagonian evangelization, and the irrigation-focused **Museo Tecnológico del Agua y el Suelo** (Colón 498, 1st Fl., tel. 02920/42-6096, 10am-1pm and 6pm-8pm Mon.-Fri. summer, 8:30am-6pm Mon.-Fri. fall-spring, free).

Part of the same complex but facing Plaza Alsina, the **Catedral de la Merced** (1912) replaced an earlier church that came down after the 1899 flood. Alongside it, the neoclassical **Obispado de Viedma** (Bishopric of Viedma, 1945) replaced the **Hospital San José.**

Key public buildings cluster around Plaza San Martín, including the **Casa de Gobierno** (Government House), the **Municipalidad,** and the dignified **Residencia del Gobernador** (Governor's Residence).

The catamaran **Currú Leuvú II** (tel. 02920/15-40-8599) offers 1.5-hour river excursions (6pm Thurs.-Sun. summer, US$13 adults, US$6.50 under age 13) from the **Muelle de Lanchas,** at the foot of 25 de Mayo.

Events

Viedma's biggest event is January's **Regata del Río Negro** (www.regatadelrionegro.com.ar), a more-than-300-kilometer kayak race from Neuquén. It's one of the 10 races included in the Classic Canoe Marathon World Series.

Shopping

While a provincial **Mercado Artesanal** (Belgrano 305; also Av. Villarino and Belgrano) sells varied handicrafts made by Mapuche artisans, informal craftspeople usually populate Plaza Alsina. For wines and other local produce, try **Vinoteca Vinopolitan** (Rivadavia 890, tel. 02920/42-6225).

Food

For its varied menu of generous portions, the most popular choice in town is the family-friendly **Sahara Pizza & Pasta** (Saavedra 336, tel. 02920/42-1092, lunch and dinner daily, US$8-18), where half-pizzas are also available at half the price. Pasta, beef, lamb, chicken, fish, and seafood dishes complete the list together with creative salads. A popular pizzeria is **Los Tíos** (Belgrano 387, tel. 02920/42-2790, lunch and dinner daily, from US$7).

The waterside **Sal y Fuego** (Av. Villarino 55, tel. 02920/43-1259, lunch and dinner daily, US$12-20) specializes in fish and seafood with a few pricey dishes, but the location trumps the food. Right alongside it, under the same ownership, **Café del Sauce** (Av. Villarino 27, tel. 02920/43-1259) offers cheaper short orders and a terrace ideal for lunch beneath the riverside willow trees.

Facing the river, **Fiore Helados** (Belgrano 19, tel. 02920/42-0700) is a fine ice creamery.

Accommodations

In a quiet residential area nine blocks east of downtown, **Residencial Río Mar** (Rivadavia 897, tel. 02920/42-4188, www.hotelriomar-viedma.com, US$27 s, US$39 d) is a decent utilitarian option with Wi-Fi.

Close to Plaza San Martín, **Residencial Roca** (Roca 347, tel. 02920/43-1241, US$29 s, US$39 d, with breakfast) is another decent choice with parking and baths with tubs.

Overlooking Plaza Alsina, the no-frills **Hotel Peumayén** (Buenos Aires 334, tel. 02920/42-5222, www.hotelpeumayen.com. ar, US$39 s, US$56 with breakfast) remains a good mid-range choice. It has a helpful staff, Wi-Fi, air-conditioning, parking, and TV.

Friendly **Hotel Nijar** (Mitre 490, tel. 02920/42-2833, www.hotelnijar.com, US$53 s, US$66 d) is a modern hotel with good service, comfortable rooms, parking, restaurant, and amenities that include air-conditioning and Wi-Fi. Though well-run, it's showing signs of wear.

Overlooking the river, there's **Hotel Austral** (Av. Villarino 292, tel. 02920/42-2615,

www.hotelesaustral.com, US$51-57 s, US$64-76 d), which has similar amenities but a better location than the Nijar. It's worth considering the larger rooms with river views; the cheaper standard rooms at the back are smallish.

Information

The helpful **Oficina de Informes Turísticos** (Av. Francisco de Viedma 51, tel. 02920/42-7171, www.viedma.gov.ar, 9am-9pm daily summer, 8am-7pm Mon.-Fri., 11am-7pm Sat.-Sun. fall-spring) is on the riverfront.

The **Ministerio de Turismo** (Av. Caseros 1425, tel. 02920/42-2150, www.rionegrotur. gov.ar) provides information and printed matter for the province.

Services

Mona Tour (San Martín 225, tel. 02920/42-2933, www.monatour.com.ar) organizes city and coastal tours, as well as excursions with *La Trochita* train from Ingeniero Jacobacci if available. For motorists, **ACA** (RN 3, Km 962, tel. 02920/42-2441) provides limited roadside assistance.

Banco Patagonia (Buenos Aires 184) has one of many ATMs. **Tritón Turismo** (Namuncurá 78, tel. 02920/43-1131, tritontur@speedy.com.ar) changes money, rents cars, and arranges excursions.

The postal code for **Correo Argentino** (Rivadavia 151) is 8500. **Locutorio Balda** (Colón 639) offers telephone services. **Laverap** (Mitre 343, tel. 02920/15-66-4086) does the laundry. **Hospital Artémides Zatti** (Rivadavia 391, tel. 02920/42-0307, ext. 109) is the public hospital.

Transportation

Aeropuerto Gobernador Castello (VDM, tel. 02920/42-3276) is five kilometers south of town on Ruta Provincial (RP) 51. **Aerolíneas Argentinas** (Colón 246, tel. 02920/42-2018) has services to and from Aeroparque (Buenos Aires) and Bariloche. Taxis to the airport cost about US$5.

Viedma's **Terminal de Ómnibus** (Guido 1660, tel. 02920/42-6850) is 13 blocks south of downtown. Tickets for **Vía Bariloche** group are also sold downtown (San Martín 57, tel. 02920/42-1300). Sample destinations, times, and fares include Las Grutas (2.5 hours, US$15), Puerto Madryn (7 hours, US$30-45), Trelew (8 hours, US$36-41), Neuquén (8 hours, US$43), Comodoro Rivadavia (13 hours, US$63-73), Buenos Aires (12-14 hours, US$70-91), and Río Gallegos (24 hours, US$116-170).

From Estación Viedma, at the southeast edge of town, the **Tren Patagónico** (Cagliero s/n, tel. 02920/42-2130, www.trenpatagonico-sa.com.ar) ostensibly travels Friday evenings to Bariloche in summer, but it's recently been suspended.

On-demand *lanchas* (passenger launches, 6:30am-10:45pm Mon.-Fri., US$0.50) frequently cross the river to Carmen de Patagones from the Muelle de Lanchas at the foot of 25 de Mayo.

Tritón Turismo (Namuncurá 78, tel. 02920/43-1131) has rental cars. **Avis** (tel. 02920/42-9800, viedma@avis.com.ar) is at Hotel Nijar (Mitre 490) and at the airport.

GOLFO SAN MATÍAS AND VICINITY

From Viedma, RN 3 turns west and slightly inland toward the port of San Antonio Oeste, paralleling the Golfo San Matías shoreline. Visitors with their own vehicles should consider a detour along coastal RP 1. Here, about 30 kilometers southeast of Viedma at the mouth of the Río Negro, **Balneario El Cóndor** draws beachgoers from the provincial capital. From Viedma's terminal, **Empresa Ceferino** (tel. 02920/42-6691, US$1.50) has five buses daily, adding services in summer.

The scenic coastline is a prime **birdwatching** area. Along 12 kilometers starting immediately west of El Cóndor, the headlands host about 35,000 active nests of burrowing parrots in the world's largest known colony of Psittaciformes. The area is best visited in the breeding season from November to early January.

RP 1 and La Comarca buses continue another 30 kilometers to **La Lobería,** where the **Reserva Faunística Provincial Punta Bermeja** is one of the continent's largest southern sea lion colonies.

West of La Lobería, the pavement ends but the scenery improves to include massive dunes at **Bahía Creek** and another sea lion colony at **Reserva Provincial Caleta de los Loros,** where more nesting parrots burrow into the headlands. At Punta Mejillón, the highway swerves inland; it's possible to return to RN 3 via unpaved RP 52, or else continue west toward Puerto San Antonio Este, before which a paved road also turns north to RN 3.

Some 187 kilometers west of Viedma but east of RN 3, summer and weekend visitors swarm the beaches of **Las Grutas** (permanent pop. 2,708), named for the wave-cut grottoes that have penetrated the sedimentary headlands. Because of a wide tidal range, the beachfront can recede to just tens of meters, suitable for only the most gregarious beachgoers. There are nearly a hundred hotels and campgrounds; for suggestions, visit the **Secretaría Municipal de Turismo** (Peatonal Viedma, Segunda Bajada, tel. 02934/49-7463, www.lasgrutas-turismo.gob.ar). Las Grutas has frequent buses to San Antonio Oeste, 16 kilometers northeast.

About 125 kilometers south of San Antonio Oeste and 140 kilometers north of Puerto Madryn, RN 3 passes through **Sierra Grande** (pop. 6,768), an iron-mining town that's the northernmost point to purchase gasoline at Patagonian prices, cheaper than in Las Grutas or San Antonio Oeste.

NEUQUÉN AND VICINITY

Capital of its namesake province, Neuquén is a gateway to the northern Patagonian lakes but also a base for visiting a triangle of nearby dinosaur sites and cluster of wineries. At the confluence of two major rivers, it's a clean modern city that benefits from abundant energy resources, its productive financial sector, and the upper Río Negro valley's agricultural plenty. It also has an active cultural life, best exemplified by its fine arts museum.

Where the Río Neuquén and the Río Limay meet, Neuquén (pop. 232,000) is 537 kilometers west of Bahía Blanca via RN 22, about 559 kilometers southwest of Santa Rosa via several paved highways, and 412 kilometers northeast of San Carlos de Bariloche via RN 40 and RN 237. Through the upper Río Negro Valley and west toward Zapala, RN 22 is a narrow highway with heavy truck traffic and dangerously impatient drivers.

Sights

Nearly all the sights are in the **Parque Central,** the recycled railyard bounded by Avenida San Martín-Avenida Independencia and the streets of Manuel Láinez, Tierra del Fuego, and Sarmiento-Mitre.

In luminous contemporary quarters in the Parque Central, **Museo Nacional de Bellas Artes** (Mitre and Santa Cruz, tel. 0299/443-6268, www.mnbaneuquen.gov.ar, 10am-9pm Tues.-Fri., 10am-2pm and 6pm-10pm Sat., 6pm-10pm Sun. and holidays, free) is the first provincial branch of the national fine arts museum, with permanent collections of European and Argentine art, supplemented by rotating exhibits. Walls on wheels separate its 2,000-square-meter interior into manageable spaces as needed.

The **Sala de Arte Emilio Saraco** (Av. Olascoaga s/n, tel. 0299/449-1200, ext. 4390, 8am-8pm Mon.-Fri., 4pm-8pm Sat.-Sun. and holidays, free) occupies the railroad station's former cargo terminal with exhibits of contemporary art.

Two blocks east, in a former railroad workers residence, the **Museo de la Ciudad Paraje Confluencia** (Av. Independencia and Pasaje Héroes de Malvinas, tel. 0299/15-576-4658, 8am-8pm Mon.-Fri., 6pm-10pm Sat.-Sun. and holidays summer, 8am-8pm Mon.-Fri., 4pm-8pm Sat.-Sun. and holidays fall-spring, free) traces Neuquén's urban evolution.

Entertainment and Events

O'Connell's (Roca 234, tel. 0299/448-2272) is a bar with occasional live music. For current films, there's the **Cine Teatro Español** (Av. Argentina 235, www.cineteatroespanol. com tel. 0299/448-2486), which also has live music and theater.

January's **Regata del Río Negro** (www. regatadelrionegro.com.ar) is a kayak marathon of over 300 kilometers that starts here and ends a week later in Viedma. It is included in the Classic Canoe Marathon World Series.

Neuquén's Museo Nacional de Bellas Artes is a branch of Argentina's national fine arts museum.

Shopping

The province of Neuquén sponsors **Artesanías Neuquinas** (Carlos H. Rodríguez 174, tel. 0299/442-3806, www. artesaniasneuquinas.com), with a diverse crafts selection at reasonable prices. **Cardón** (Ministro González 54, tel. 0299/447-7331) sells leather goods, silverwork, and *mate* gourds and accessories.

Food

Neuquén is strong on pizza and pasta at places like the traditional **La Nonna Francesca** (9 de Julio 56, tel. 0299/430-0930, www.lanonnafrancescanqn.com, 11am-3pm and 8pm-midnight Mon.-Sat., US$10-15) and **La Tartaruga** (Roca 193, tel. 0299/443-6888, lunch and dinner daily, US$10-15). **Franz y Peppone** (9 de Julio and Belgrano, tel. 0299/448-2299, www. franzypeppone.com.ar, lunch and dinner daily, US$8) blends the Teutonic and the Mediterranean, including *salchichas con chucrut* (sausage and sauerkraut) and pizzas, in its varied menu.

★ **Benjamina** (Irigoyen 490, tel. 0299/442-7258, 9am-12:30am daily, US$10-20) concocts fresh healthy dishes including sandwiches, wraps, and salads that are more flavorful than you might expect. The chicken salad with cherry tomatoes and sliced fruit is satisfying in quantity and quality. The fresh juices are exceptional.

Piré (Diagonal Alvear 29, tel. 0299/443-0575) has fine ice cream, but the El Bolsón import **Jauja** (Santa Fé 195, tel. 02944/43-4589, www.heladosjauja.com) is among the country's best when it comes to ice cream.

Accommodations

Most accommodations lie in the scruffy but not unsafe retail area between RN 22 and the Parque Central.

Rooms at friendly, centrally located **Hostería Belgrano** (Rivadavia 283, tel. 0299/442-4311, US$28 s, US$41 d) are small—some very small—but also immaculate.

The local classic **Hotel Iberia** (Av. Olascoaga 294, tel. 0299/442-2372, www. iberia-hotel.com.ar, US$37 s, US$72 d) offers tidy, ample rooms with standard conveniences, including Wi-Fi. It's worth paying extra for the more comfortable suite for two people. Parking costs extra.

Though showing some wear, **Hotel El Prado** (Perito Moreno 484, tel. 0299/448-6000, www.hotel-elprado.com.ar, US$43-64 s, US$64-79 d) remains one of the city's better values, with large, well-furnished rooms with Wi-Fi. In addition, there's an abundant buffet breakfast and superb service.

Hotel Huemul (Tierra del Fuego 335, tel. 0299/442-2344, www.huemulhotel.com.ar, US$73 s, US$84 d) is another decent choice, with responsive service. It's quiet, with firm beds and Wi-Fi.

The best downtown value, ★ **Hotel Suizo** (Carlos H. Rodríguez 167, tel. 0299/442-2602, www.hotelsuizo.com.ar, US$76-90 s, US$83-96 d) has comfortable rooms, attentive service, Wi-Fi, parking, and a buffet breakfast.

Downtown's four-star **Hotel del Comahue** (Av. Argentina 377, tel. 0299/443-2040, www.hoteldelcomahue.com, US$123-264 s, US$145-364 d) is the overpriced pick of the litter. The highest price corresponds to the presidential suite.

Information and Services

The **Subsecretaría de Turismo** (Félix San Martín 182, tel. 0299/442-4089, www. neuquentur.gov.ar, 8am-9pm daily) is directly on RN 22 through downtown. In content, accuracy, and usefulness, their maps and brochures are among the country's best. **ACA** (Diagonal 25 de Mayo 165, tel. 0299/442-4860) is a resource for motorists.

Banco de la Provincia de Neuquén (Av. Argentina 13) has one of many ATMs. **Cambio Olano** (J. B. Justo 107, tel. 0299/442-6192) and **Cambio Pullman** (Alcorta 144, tel. 0299/442-2438) are exchange houses.

The postal code for **Correo Argentino** (Avenida Santa Fe 101) is 8300. **Ciber One** (Av. Olascoaga 331, tel. 0299/443-7333) has both telephone and Internet access.

Neuquén has a **Chilean consulate** (La Rioja 241, tel. 0299/442-2727) and a **Migraciones** (Santiago del Estero 466, tel. 0299/442-2061) office. **Lava Ya** (Av. Independencia 326, tel. 0299/443-4318) does the washing. The **Hospital Provincial Castro Rendón** (Buenos Aires 450, tel. 0299/449-0800) can handle emergencies and routine care.

Transportation

Aeropuerto Internacional J. D. Perón (NQN, Av. San Martín 5901, tel. 0299/444-0486) is seven kilometers west of town via RN 22; despite its name, there are no international flights. **Aerolíneas Argentinas** (Santa Fe 52, tel. 0299/442-2409) averages three or four flights daily from Buenos Aires, with additional services to Comodoro Rivadavia, Córdoba, and Mendoza. **LATAM Argentina** (Hipólito Yrigoyen 347, tel. 0299/444-1210) also has daily flights to Buenos Aires's Aeroparque. **LADE** (tel. 0299/443-1153) offers Patagonian services south to Bariloche and Comodoro, and thence to Mar del Plata and Buenos Aires.

An airport taxi costs US$10; to the bus terminal, it's about US$5. The main car rental agencies are all at the airport: **Avis** (tel. 0299/444-1297), **Hertz** (tel. 0299/444-0146), and **Localiza** (tel. 0299/444-0440).

About five kilometers west of downtown, Neuquén's shiny **Terminal de Ómnibus** (Planas and Solalique, tel. 0299/445-2300, www.terminalneuquen.com.ar) is a hub for provincial, national, and some international bus services (for example, to the Chilean city of Temuco; reservations are advised).

Sample provincial and long-distance destinations, times, and fares include Zapala (3 hours, US$13-20), Bariloche (5.5 hours, US$26-37), San Martín de los Andes (7 hours, US$32-62), Villa La Angostura (7 hours, US$48-67), Puerto Madryn (9-11 hours, US$50-57), El Bolsón (7-8 hours, US$34-40), Mendoza (11-13 hours, US$49-81), Esquel (9.5-10.5 hours, US$42-49), Buenos Aires (14-17 hours, US$64-95), Comodoro Rivadavia

(14-20 hours, US$80-92), and Río Gallegos (27-29 hours, US$132-150).

Bus companies for Temuco (Chile) via Zapala and the Pino Hachado pass (9.5-11 hours, US$28) include **Albus** (tel. 0299/445-2522), **Igi Llaima/Narbus** (tel. 0299/445-2295), and **Vía Bariloche** (tel. 0299/445-2265).

The Dinosaur Triangle

Where there's oil, there are dinosaurs, and Neuquén's sedimentary steppe is one of Argentina's late-Cretaceous hot spots. By rental car, a triangle of sites northwest, west, and southwest of the provincial capital makes an ideal (if long) full-day excursion. One of these, Lago Los Barreales, is currently difficult to visit. The other two, Plaza Huincul and Villa El Chocón, are accessible by public transportation.

CENTRO PALEONTOLÓGICO LAGO LOS BARREALES

At the **Centro Paleontológico Lago Los Barreales,** on a reservoir northwest of Neuquén, paleontologists demonstrate the separation and rescue of fossil deposits as well as the cleaning and extraction of the fossils themselves. Beasts in the sediments here include the sauropod *Futalognkosaurus* (a long-tailed quadruped with a long neck and small head), theropods (bipedal carnivores with huge claws, such as *Megaraptor*), and ornithopods (small bipedal herbivores), along with bivalves, crocodiles, turtles, and pterosaurs.

Unfortunately, the site remains closed to the public due to a political controversy. Determined visitors should contact the provincial Subsecretaría de Turismo (Félix San Martín 182, Neuquén, tel. 0299/442-4089, www.neuquentur.gov.ar, 8am-9pm daily) in the city of Neuquén for more information.

MUSEO MUNICIPAL CARMEN FUNES

At the oil town of **Plaza Huincul,** midway between Neuquén and Zapala, is the **Museo Municipal Carmen Funes** (Av. Córdoba 55,

Giganotosaurus skeleton at Villa El Chocón

The dinosaur takes its name from amateur paleontologist Rubén Carolini, who discovered the fossil. Measuring 14 meters in length and 4.65 meters high at the hip, it weighed up to eight tons.

Above an enormous hydroelectric reservoir southwest of Neuquén, the **Museo Paleontológico Municipal Ernesto Bachmann** (Centro Cívico s/n, tel. 0299/490-1230, museoernestobachmann@gmail.com, 8am-8pm daily, US$1.50) features models of *Carnotaurus* and the smaller *Pianitzkysaurus,* as well as exhibits on the area's archaeology and a whitewashed account of the dam and former ranch owner Manuel Bustigorry. There are also dinosaur tracks in the vicinity. Unfortunately, because the massive hydroelectric dam drowned the Río Limay's sedimentary canyon here, many probable paleontological sites have disappeared beneath the water.

Villa El Chocón, 80 kilometers southwest of Neuquén via RN 22 and RN 237, originated as a company town during the dam's construction. **Dirección Municipal de Turismo** (RN 22 junction, tel. 0299/490-1223, turismochocon@gmail.com, 8am-7pm daily) is the town's tourist office.

On the shoreline, **La Posada del Dinosaurio** (tel. 0299/490-1200, www.posadadeldinosaurio.com.ar, US$65 s, US$80 d) offers excellent accommodations, with a good, reasonably priced restaurant and outstanding service. There's also camping nearby.

ZAPALA

Argentine backpackers once used forlorn Zapala, the erstwhile end of the line for the Ferrocarril Roca's northern spur, as a takeoff point to the lakes district's least-visited sectors. Since the railroad shut down, the town and the bleak surrounding steppe is mainly a convenient stopover en route to San Martín de los Andes, and a gateway to bird-rich Parque Nacional Laguna Blanca.

Zapala (pop. about 40,000) is 184 kilometers west of Neuquén via RN 22 and 244 kilometers northeast of San Martín de los Andes via RN 40 and RN 234. From Zapala, RN 40 continues

tel. 0299/496-5486, museo_cfunesph@yahoo.com.ar, 9am-7pm Mon.-Fri., 10:30am-8:30pm Sat.-Sun., free). The prize exhibit is a replica skeleton of *Argentinosaurus huinculensis,* which measures 35 meters long and 18 meters high. This herbivore is so large that an adult male human barely reaches its knee, and one of its dorsal vertebrae measures 1.6 meters.

In 1987, former oil worker Guillermo Heredia found the fossil three kilometers away, along the highway. In addition to the imposing skeleton, there are models of the carnivorous *Mapusaurus* and several smaller dinosaurs, a clutch of dinosaur eggs some 80 million years old, and remains of crocodiles found in Picún Leufú, about 75 kilometers south. There are also exhibits on the town's history. Buses from Neuquén are frequent.

MUSEO PALEONTOLÓGICO MUNICIPAL ERNESTO BACHMANN

Plaza Huincul boasts the world's largest herbivore, but **Villa El Chocón** claims its carnivorous counterpart in *Giganotosaurus carolinii.*

northwest toward Las Lajas, from where RN 242 reaches the Chilean border at Pino Hachado. The main drag is Avenida San Martín, which leads south from a traffic circle on RN 22.

Museo Olsacher

The modernized **Museo Olsacher** (Etcheluz and Ejército Argentino, tel. 02943/42-2928, 8:30am-7:30pm Mon.-Fri., free) fills a recycled warehouse with minerals from around the world and paleontological exhibits from Neuquén. Its prize exhibit is the remains of the herbivorous dinosaur *Zapalasaurus bonapartei*. There are also displays on marine reptiles, paleobotany, systematic mineralogy, Argentine economic minerals, and invertebrate and vertebrate paleontology, along with a specialized library.

Shopping

Zapala's **Escuela de Cerámica** (Luis Monti 240, tel. 02942/15-58-7901) has a long tradition in artisanal pottery.

Food and Accommodations

Directly on RN 22 near the traffic circle, **El Fogón** (Houssay and Bolivia, tel. 02942/42-4665, US$12) is a good *parrilla* (grill restaurant). **Heladería Don Héctor** (Etcheluz 527, tel. 02942/43-0000) sells ice cream and also sandwiches.

While accommodations and dining are limited, the quality of lodging and food is good. The cheapest options are **Hotel Coliqueo** (Etcheluz 159, tel. 02942/42-1308, US$31 s, US$45 d) and the immaculate **Pehuén Hotel** (Etcheluz and Elena de la Vega, tel. 02942/42-3135, US$32 s, US$45 d with breakfast). **Hotel Hue Melén** (Almirante Brown 929, tel. 02942/42-2407, www.hotelhuemelen.com.ar, US$90 s, US$103 d) also has a restaurant and a casino.

At the west edge of town, the new **Hotel Mac Royal Suites** (RN 40 and RN 22, tel. 02942/42-2128, www.macroyalsuites.com, US$157 s, US$236 d, US$424 suite) is an outpost of the Howard Johnson empire. It includes a casino and a restaurant.

Information and Services

Providing information on the province's northernmost lakes district, the **Centro de Informes Turísticos Portal del Pehuén** (RN 22, Km 1398, tel. 02942/42-4296, portaldelpehuen@zapala.gob.ar, 7am-9pm daily) occupies quarters near the ACA gas station, on the eastern approach to town.

The **Administración de Parques Nacionales** (APN, 12 de Julio 686, tel. 02942/43-1982, lagunablanca@apn.gov.ar) provides information on Parque Nacional Laguna Blanca.

Banco de la Provincia del Neuquén (Cháneton 410) has an ATM. The postal code for **Correo Argentino** (Av. San Martín 324) is 8340. **Telecenter** (Etcheluz 527) has long-distance telephones and improved Internet. For medical needs, try the **Hospital Regional** (Luis Monti 155, tel. 02924/43-1555).

Transportation

Downtown's **Terminal de Ómnibus** (Etcheluz and Uriburu, tel. 02924/43-1090) has provincial and long-distance services; some Chile-bound carriers will pick up passengers here. Sample destinations, times, and fares include Neuquén (3 hours, US$16-20), San Martín de los Andes (4 hours, US$20-31), and Buenos Aires (16-20 hours, US$103-128). Often, for Buenos Aires, it's easier to transfer in Neuquén.

PARQUE NACIONAL LAGUNA BLANCA

In the stark volcanic steppe southwest of Zapala, alkaline **Laguna Blanca** is a shallow, plankton-rich interior drainage lake with breeding populations of the black-necked swan. Designated a major international wetland under the Ramsar Convention, it's also an ideal **birdwatching** site to spot coots, ducks, grebes, gulls, upland geese, and the occasional flamingo. Even the flightless *choique* (rhea) scurries along the barren shoreline for a drink.

The park comprises 11,250 hectares of undulating terrain at 1,276 meters above sea level. Covering 1,700 hectares, the lake reaches a depth of 10 meters.

Directly on RP 46, the **Centro de Visitantes** (9am-7pm daily mid-Dec.-Mar., 9am-7pm Sat.-Sun. Apr.-mid-Dec.) has helpful rangers, informative exhibits, and clean restrooms.

From the center, a short nature trail leads across the steppe to the shoreline for glimpses of the swans, which are always here. Though birdlife is most abundant November-March, the unfortunate introduction of nonnative fish species such as *perca* decades ago has affected the birds' diet and, hence, diminished its population. A fishing season in the colder months has been set up to try to reverse the situation.

Transportation and Services

From a junction 10 kilometers south of Zapala via RN 40, paved RP 46 leads 20 kilometers southwest to the park. On the north side of RP 46, about two kilometers east of the visitors center, a free **APN campground** offers little shelter from the westerlies that gust across the steppe. Laguna Blanca really makes a better day trip than an overnight. There's no food or water available—bring everything necessary.

Public transportation is limited, and the only two companies that pass Parque Nacional Laguna Blanca en route to Aluminé do so in the afternoon, after which there are no services back on the same day. Hiring a *remise* (fixed-rate taxi) for a quick visit and return costs about US$30.

The Argentine Lakes District

ALUMINÉ AND VICINITY

West of Laguna Blanca, paved RP 46 passes 2,839-meter Cerro Chachil, with more distant views of Volcán Lanín on the Chilean border, and of fuming Volcán Villarrica, across the line. From the Cuesta de Rahue, where the first araucaria (monkey-puzzle) trees make their appearance, the zigzag road descends into the Río Aluminé valley. Río Aluminé is a prime trout and white-water river whose singularly appropriate name derives from a Mapuche compound meaning "glittering jewel."

Aluminé proper is nothing special, but for visitors with their own vehicles, it offers the best services in an area with exceptional recreational opportunities in northernmost Parque Nacional Lanín. The southbound route through the Aluminé valley, to Junín de los Andes and San Martín de los Andes, is more scenic than RN 40.

Aluminé (pop. 4,861, elev. 900 meters) is 138 kilometers southwest of Zapala via RN 40, RP 46 (which is mostly paved), and a paved stretch of RP 23. It is also 102 kilometers north of Junín de los Andes via RP 23, a good but still mostly gravel road.

White-Water Rafting

November and December's heavy runoff makes the Class II-IV Río Aluminé a challenging white-water opportunity, but low water the rest of the year makes much of the rock-strewn riverbed hazardous. Class III-IV trips (from US$67 pp) are over by December, but Class II-III (from US$17 pp) rafting continues through the summer. For details, contact **Aluminé Rafting** (RP 23 Sur, Km 2, tel. 02942/15-69-5331, aluminerafting@yahoo. com.ar, www.interpatagonia.com).

Events

Mid-March's **Fiesta del Pehuén** pays homage to the distinctive araucaria tree that provided sustenance to the region's aboriginal inhabitants. Mapuche people still harvest the fallen nuts.

Food and Accommodations

Across from Plaza San Martín, looking better without than within, **Hostería Aluminé** (Cristián Joubert 312, tel. 02942/49-6174, www.hosteriaalumine.com.ar, US$44 s, US$63 d) has spacious if Spartan rooms. Breakfast costs US$3 extra.

Aluminé's best lodging, **Hotel de la Aldea** (RP 23, Km 82, tel. 02942/49-6340, www.hoteldelaldea.com.ar, US$46 s, US$68-77 d), is a multistory Euro-style chalet with comfortable rooms, some with river views. Lodging and meal packages are also available.

Transportation and Services

Aluminé's **Terminal de Ómnibus** (4 de Caballería 139, tel. 02942/49-6048) occupies a triangular block immediately south of Plaza San Martín. **Albus** leaves a few times daily to Zapala (3 hours, US$16) and Neuquén (5.5-6 hours, US$32). In summer it goes daily also to Junín de los Andes (2.5 hours, US$12) and to San Martín de los Andes (3 hours, US$14), with fewer weekly services the rest of the year.

For information, consult the diligent **Secretaría de Turismo** (Cristián Joubert and Julio Ayoso, tel. 02942/49-6001, www.alumine.gob.ar), directly on the central Plaza San Martín. In summer, it also operates a **Centro de Informes** (junction of RP 46 and RP 23) in the hamlet of Rahue.

Banco de la Provincia del Neuquén (Villegas 392) has an ATM. The postal code for **Correo Argentino** (Villegas 560) is 8345. There's a *locutorio* (call center) at Juan Benigar 334. **Nex Sur** (Av. Regimiento de Infantería de la Montaña 26, No. 848) has Internet access.

JUNÍN DE LOS ANDES

Where the steppe meets the sierra, the Río Chimehuín gushes from the base of 3,776-meter Volcán Lanín to become one of Argentina's top trout streams near Junín de los Andes. Calling itself Neuquén's "trout capital," Junín also offers access to the central sector of Parque Nacional Lanín, which takes its name from the symmetrical cone along the Chilean border.

In addition to its natural attractions, Junín promotes itself as a pilgrimage site for links to the beatified Chilean Laura Vicuña and its ostensible blend of Roman Catholic and Mapuche traditions. Founded in 1883, during General Roca's so-called "Conquista del Desierto," Junín is Neuquén's oldest city.

Near the confluence of the Río Chimehuín and its Curruhué tributary, Junín (pop. about 18,000) is 387 kilometers southwest of Neuquén via RN 22 and RN 40, and 41 kilometers northeast of San Martín de los Andes via RN 40. It's 218 kilometers north of San Carlos de Bariloche via RN 40.

The main thoroughfare is north-south RN 40. The city center, a compact grid around Plaza San Martín, lies east between the highway and the river.

Sights

Junín draws religious tourists to its modernized **Santuario Nuestra Señora de las Nieves y Beata Laura Vicuña** (Ginés Ponte and Don Bosco, tel. 02972/49-1199, 8am-8pm daily, US$3), which focuses on Laura Vicuña, a young girl who (legend says) willed her own death to protest her widowed mother's affair with an Argentine landowner. The airy, luminous structure incorporates Mapuche elements; it also holds an urn with one of Laura Vicuña's vertebrae.

The **Museo Mapuche** (Padre Milanesio 750, tel. 02972/49-1178, 8am-2pm and 4pm-7pm Mon.-Fri., 9am-1pm Sat., free) focuses on indigenous artifacts and historical exhibits. It also displays fossils.

In the western foothills, the **Vía Christi** is a Stations of the Cross footpath climbing 2.5 kilometers to the summit of **Cerro de la Cruz.**

Entertainment and Events

January's **Encuentro de Artesanos Mapuches** and mid-July's **Semana de Artesanía Aborigen** let the Mapuche showcase their crafts.

Late January's **Feria y Exposición Ganadera** is the landowners' extravaganza of blue-ribbon cattle, horses, and sheep, plus

Horse gear waits for its riders at Estancia Huechahue.

daily). For nonresidents of the country, licenses cost US$24 per day, US$72 per week, or US$96 for the season (Nov.-Apr.), with an additional charge for a trolling permit; passports are required.

The **APN office** (Padre Milanesio 570, tel. 02972/49-2748) provides information on hiking and climbing Volcán Lanín and other excursions within the park.

Estancia Huechahue

On the Río Aluminé, about 30 kilometers east of Junín via RN 234, the 6,600-hectare Anglo-Argentine **Estancia Huechahue** (no phone, www.huechahue.com) is a woodsy ranch that doubles as a recreational getaway for serious gaucho-style riders, those who want to become serious riders, and increasing numbers of fishing enthusiasts. October to April, Jane Williams's well-trained horses carry a maximum of 12 guests at a time over mountainous terrain into Parque Nacional Lanín, or undertake a circuit of other nearby *estancias* (cattle or sheep ranches).

For accompanying nonriders, or for a change of pace, there's hiking, birding, swimming, and even tennis. Huechahue also features volcanic caves, Tehuelche rock-art sites, and wildlife, including Andean condor nesting sites, not to mention deer and feral boars.

Most visitors arrange packages from overseas. Drop-ins are not possible, but with at least a few days' notice it may be possible to arrange a stay (3-day minimum). The basic rate of US$400 pp, in 11 twin-bed rooms, includes all meals, drinks (beer, wine, and spirits), a hot tub and sauna, and activities (fishing guides and massages are extra). The food is traditional Patagonian fare rather than European-style cuisine, though Huechahue can accommodate vegetarians. The basic package also includes transfers between Huechahue and San Martín de los Andes' Aeropuerto Chapelco; transport to or from Bariloche is possible for an additional charge. For details, contact Jane Williams at Estancia Huechahue (www.huechahue.com).

rabbits and poultry. Gauchos show off their skills as well, but they take center stage at mid-February's **Festival del Puestero.**

The pre-Lenten **Carnaval del Pehuén** fills the streets with parades, costumed celebrants, water balloons, and confetti.

Shopping

Junín's **Paseo Artesanal** (Padre Milanesio 590) and **Paseo del Centenario** (Don Bosco and Coronel Suárez) house a cluster of artisans working in ceramics, leather, wood, and wool.

Sports and Recreation

Both Argentines and foreigners flock here for **fishing** on the Río Chimehuín, the Río Aluminé, their tributaries, and Parque Nacional Lanín's glacial lakes. Catch-and-release is the norm for riverine fishing. For licenses and suggested guides, visit the tourist office on Plaza San Martín: **Secretaría de Turismo** (Padre Milanesio 590, tel. 02972/49-1160, www.junindelosandes.gov.ar, 8am-9pm

Food

In an attractive building styled after Bariloche's landmark civic center, the awkwardly named **Centro de Turismo** (Padre Milanesio 586, tel. 02972/49-2555, lunch and dinner daily, US$14) has a mostly standard Argentine menu. The standout item is the butter-grilled trout.

Primarily a grill restaurant, ★ **Ruca Hueney** (Padre Milanesio and Coronel Suárez, tel. 02972/49-1113, www.ruca-hueney.com.ar, lunch and dinner daily, US$15) has a more diverse menu, including trout and venison (try the *pollo al ajillo*, garlic chicken, or a similar trout) in enormous portions. It's generous with wine by the glass, and offers good service even with large numbers of diners.

Accommodations

The well-kept riverside **Camping y Albergue Mallín Laura Vicuña** (Ginés Ponte 867, tel. 02972/49-1149, mallinlaura@gmail.com, US$10 pp) also offers shoestring accommodations in dorms and in small apartments for four to eight people.

The roadside **Residencial Marisa** (Blv. Juan Manuel de Rosas 360, tel. 02972/49-1175, residencialmarisa@jdeandes.com.ar, US$28 s, US$44 d) has basic but comfortable rooms with private baths and Wi-Fi.

Aging but agreeable, the riverside **Hostería Chimehuín** (Coronel Suárez and 25 de Mayo, tel. 02972/49-1132, hosteriachimehuin@fronteradigital.net.ar, US$47 s, US$60 d) has 23 comfortable rooms with private baths as well as apartments. Breakfast includes homemade scones and other specialties.

The self-consciously rustic **The Río Dorado Lodge & Fly Shop** (Pedro Illera 448, tel. 02972/49-2451, www.riodoradolodge.com, US$70 s, US$90 d, with buffet breakfast) has become the default option for foreign tour groups, especially but not exclusively for fly-fishing enthusiasts. Packages with meals are also available.

Information and Services

Facing Plaza San Martín, the helpful **Secretaría de Turismo** (Padre Milanesio 596, tel. 02972/49-1160, www.junindelosandes.gov.ar, 8am-9pm daily) answers questions, provides brochures, and sells fishing permits.

Immediately north, the **APN office** (Padre Milanesio 570, tel. 02972/49-2748, erratic hours) provides information on Parque Nacional Lanín.

Picurú Viajes y Turismo (Coronel Suárez 373, tel. 02972/49-2829) organizes rafting and hiking excursions. It also rents bicycles from its offices on the plaza.

Banco de la Provincia del Neuquén (Av. San Martín 511) has an ATM. The postal code for **Correo Argentino** (Don Bosco 602) is 8371. For long-distance, use the *locutorio* (Padre Milanesio 530) half a block north of the tourist office. **Arroba Computación** (Lamadrid 342) has Internet access.

Laverap Pehuén (Ginés Ponte 330) does the washing. For medical services, contact the **Hospital de Área** (Av. Antártida Argentina 50, tel. 02972/49-2143).

Transportation

Aeropuerto Aviador Carlos Campos-Chapelco (CPC, RN 234, Km 24, tel. 02972/42-8388) lies midway between Junín and San Martín de los Andes. Air and bus schedules change frequently, especially in ski season. **Aerolíneas Argentinas** (Belgrano 949, San Martín de los Andes, tel. 02972/41-0588) flies regularly from Buenos Aires.

Services at Junín's **Terminal de Ómnibus** (Olavarría and Félix San Martín, tel. 02972/49-2038) resemble those at San Martín de los Andes, including trans-Andean buses to Chile. **Castelli** (tel. 02972/49-1557) buses go hourly to San Martín de los Andes (50 minutes, US$2), except on Sunday, when they go less often.

SAN MARTÍN DE LOS ANDES

Barely a century since its founding as a frontier fortress, San Martín de los Andes has become one of the lakes district's most fashionable resorts. Nestled in the hills near Lago Lácar, it owes its appeal to its surrounding scenery, the trout that thrash in Parque Nacional Lanín's lakes and streams, and the ski resorts at nearby Chapelco.

San Martín itself is picturesque, thanks to the legacy of architect Alejandro Bustillo, whose rustically styled Centro Cívico built on his designs at Bariloche. San Martín has shunned the high-rise horrors that have degraded Bustillo's legacy there, but the height limit has its own downside in promoting San Martín's perceived exclusivity. However, its biggest blight is the increasingly aggressive marketing of timeshares.

At Lago Lácar's east end, 642 meters above sea level, San Martín (pop. 28,599) is 189 kilometers north of Bariloche via recently rerouted RN 40; it's 109 kilometers north of Villa La Angostura by the same route. Via Junín and La Rinconada, it's 259 kilometers.

Sights

The masterpiece of lavishly landscaped **Plaza San Martín** is Bustillo's former **Intendencia del Parque Nacional Lanín,** which matches the style of its Bariloche counterpart and has influenced architects and designers throughout the region. The exterior consists of roughly hewn blocks, rustically carved beams, dormers that jut out from the main structure, and wooden roof shingles. The **Museo del Parque Nacional Lanín** (Emilio Frey 749, tel. 02972/42-0664, 8am-9pm daily summer, 8am-7pm Mon.-Fri. fall-spring, free) combines a small museum on the park's origins and natural history with a traditional information center.

Across the plaza, the **Museo Primeros Pobladores** (Rosas 758, tel. 02972/41-2306, 9am-2pm and 4:30pm-8:30pm Mon.-Fri., 5:30pm-7:30pm Sat.-Sun. summer, 2pm-6pm Tues.-Sat. fall-spring, free; hours may vary from year to year) is a modest effort at acknowledging all the area's cultural influences, from pre-Columbian hunter-gatherers to settled Mapuche farmers and their struggles with the Spanish and Argentine invaders, and the Euro-Argentine colonists who helped create the contemporary city. Exhibits include items such as arrowheads, spear points, and ceramics. There's also an account of Parque Nacional Lanín's creation.

For four nights in 1952, Ernesto "Che" Guevara Lynch and his buddy Alberto Granados crashed on hay bales in the national park's barn in San Martín. That, apparently, was reason enough to turn the barn

Museo del Parque Nacional Lanín, in San Martín de los Andes

San Martín de los Andes

Lago Lácar

To Playa Catritre, Villa La
Angostura, Bariloche,
Chapelco, and Siete Lagos

RUKALHUÉ HOSTEL

LA COSTA DEL PUEBLO
HOSTERÍA LA POSTA DEL CAZADOR
HOSTERÍA ANTIGUOS PATAGONIA
NAVIERA LÁCAR Y NONTHUÉ
LA CASA DE EUGENIA
HOSTERÍA DEL CHAPELCO
HOSTERÍA MONTE VERDE

GRAL ROCA
AV COSTANERA
GRAEFF
JUEZ DEL VALLE
CORONEL ROHDE
BROWN
M MORENO

EL CLARO VIAJES & TURISMO
HOTEL ANTIGUOS
HOSTERÍA ANTARES PATAGONIA
TERMINAL DE ÓMNIBUS
SIETE LAGOS TURISMO
HOSTAL DEL ESQUIADOR
LANÍN TURISMO
HOSPITAL ZONAL RAMÓN CARRILLO
BUMPS
CHARLOT
HERTZ

G OBEID
M MORENO
TTE CNEL PÉREZ
GRAL VILLEGAS

HOTEL PATAGONIA PLAZA
LA COLINA
AV SAN MARTÍN
ROSAS
CAP DRURY

FREY
Plaza San Martín

HOSTERÍA LAS LUCARNAS
P MORENO
R ROCA
CALDERÓN

CORONEL DÍAZ
A FOSBERY
R ROCA
CALDERÓN
RIVADAVIA
MARIANO MORENO
CNEL PÉREZ
CAP DRURY
BELGRANO
3 DE CABALLERÍA
C WEBER

PUMA HOSTEL

HOTEL CRISMALÚ

SEE DETAIL

LAVERAP
VONHAUS
DOÑA QUELA
Plaza Sarmiento
ASOCIACIÓN DE ARTESANOS
HG RODADOS
LA OVEJA NEGRA
COTESMA
LA PASTERA MUSEO DEL CHE
HOTEL TURISMO

HOTEL DEL VIEJO ESQUIADOR
CENTRO CULTURAL
COTESMA

JORGE CARDILLO FLY SHOP
EL REGIONAL

LOS CIPRESES
RAMAYÓN
E ELORDI
SARMIENTO
MASCARDI

AV DE KOESSLER

To Junín de los Andes, Airport,
Parque Nacional Lanín,
and VOLCÁN LANÍN

CAMPING DEL ACA

© AVALON TRAVEL

0   200 yds
0   200 m

Detail

HOTEL & SPA LA CHEMINEE
CHAPELCO AVENTURA
DOWNTOWN MATÍAS
MAMUSIA
DUBLIN PUB
AEROLÍNEAS ARGENTINAS
COLORADO
GRAL VILLEGAS

AV SAN MARTÍN
BANCO DE LA NACIÓN
CAFÉ DE LA PLAZA
AVIS
PIZZERÍA LA NONNA
HOTEL INTERMONTI

MUSEO DEL PARQUE NACIONAL LANÍN
SECRETARÍA MUNICIPAL DE TURISMO
ARTESANÍAS NEUQUINAS
FREY
Plaza San Martín
ROSAS
ABUELA GOYE
CHAPELCO TURISMO
HOTEL ROSA DE LOS VIAJES
KOSEM
ANDINA / CHAPELCO TURISMO
LAVERAP

POST OFFICE
MUSEO PRIMEROS POBLADORES
TEATRO SAN JOSÉ
ABOLENGO
HERTZ
PATALIBRO
KOSEM
HOTEL CHAPELCO SKI

GENERAL ROCA
CAPITÁN DRURY
BELGRANO

into the interactive **La Pastera Museo del Che** (Sarmiento and Rudecindo Roca, tel. 02972/41-1994, www.lapasteramuseoche. org.ar, 9am-1:30pm and 2:30pm-9pm Wed.-Mon., US$3), complete with video of Che's career and a shop to market Che souvenirs, including his books and those of his admirers. In truth, it's more a shrine than a museum.

Entertainment and Events

At February 4's **Día de la Fundación,** the anniversary of San Martín's 1898 founding, the military still marches down the avenues, followed by firefighters and an equestrian array of gauchos and polo players.

The main performing-arts outlet is the **Centro Cultural Cotesma** (General Roca 1154, tel. 02972/42-8399, www.centrocultural. cotesma.com.ar), which offers recent movies at its **Cine Amankay.** The **Teatro San José** (Capitán Drury 743, tel. 02972/42-8676) hosts live theater.

This is also a bar-goer's town with places like **Dublin Pub** (Av. San Martín 599, tel. 02972/41-0141) and **Downtown Matías** (Av. San Martín 598, tel. 02972/41-3386, www. downtownmatias.com), which offer beer, reasonably priced mixed drinks, pub grub, sidewalk seating, and Wi-Fi.

Shopping

San Martín's souvenir outlets start with Mapuche weavings, silverwork, and carvings at **Artesanías Neuquinas** (Rosas 790, tel. 02972/42-8396), a provincially sponsored crafts cooperative. There's also a good selection at Plaza Sarmiento's **Asociación de Artesanos** (Av. San Martín 1050, tel. 02972/42-9097).

For textiles, try **La Oveja Negra** (Av. San Martín 1025, tel. 02972/42-8039) or **Kosem** (Capitán Drury 836, tel. 02972/42-7562). **Mamusia** (Av. San Martín 601, tel. 02972/42-7560) is a traditional chocolate shop. **Patalibro** (Av. San Martín 884, tel. 02972/41-1485, www.patalibro.com.ar) carries books on Patagonia, including some in English.

Sports and Recreation

Thanks to Lanín's proximity, San Martín is a mecca for hiking, climbing, mountain biking, white-water rafting, trout fishing, and skiing.

Overlooking San Martín de los Andes, at a maximum elevation of 1,980 meters, **Cerro Chapelco ski resort** draws enthusiastic winter crowds to 28 different runs, whose longest combination is about 5.3 kilometers. The diversity of conditions means it's suitable for both experienced skiers and novices. Several winter sports events take place annually, including the snowboard world cup, snow polo tournaments, and many ski championships. Lift-ticket prices depend on timing; the season runs mid-June to mid-October but is subdivided into low, mid-, and peak season (when daily lift rates are roughly US$70). **Chapelco Aventura** (Mariano Moreno 859, tel. 02972/42-7845, www.chapelco.com) is the resort office in San Martín. Rental equipment is available on-site but also in town at **Bumps** (Villegas 465, tel. 02972/42-8491, www.skibumps.com.ar) and **La Colina** (Av. San Martín 350, tel. 02972/42-7414, www.lacolinarentalski.com.ar).

HG Rodados (Av. San Martín 1061, tel. 02972/42-7345) rents mountain bikes, which are ideal for secondary roads around Lago Lácar and the park, as well as motorcycles.

Argentine rivers generally have lower flows and fewer rapids than their Chilean counterparts, but the Class II-IV **Río Aluminé** flows through spectacular scenery a couple of hours north of San Martín. Rafting is best with the spring runoff in November and December. Contact **Siete Lagos Turismo** (Villegas 313, tel. 02972/42-7877, www.sietelagosturismo. com.ar) or **Lanín Turismo** (Av. San Martín 437, local 3, tel. 02972/42-5808, www.laninturismo.com).

Closer to San Martín, the Class II **Río Hua Hum** provides a gentler experience; contact **El Claro Viajes & Turismo** (Coronel Díaz 751, tel. 02972/42-8876, www.elclaroturismo. com.ar).

For hiking and climbing, contact **Rumbo Patagonia** (tel. 0294/15-463-4070, www.

rumbopatagonia.com.ar). For fishing gear and advice, visit the **Jorge Cardillo Fly Shop** (Villegas 1061, tel. 02972/42-8372, www.jorge-cardillo.com).

Food

Try **Café de la Plaza** (Av. San Martín and Teniente Coronel Pérez, tel. 02972/42-8488) for coffee, croissants, sandwiches, desserts, and good short orders. Cozy, comfortable **Abolengo** (Av. San Martín 806, tel. 02972/42-7732) is ideal for rich hot chocolate on a cool night. More excellent chocolate and cakes are at **Abuela Goye** (Av. San Martín 807, tel. 02972/42-9409), also with outstanding ice cream. **La Casa de Eugenia** (Coronel Díaz 1186, tel. 02972/42-7206, www.lceugenia. com) doubles as accommodations and a tearoom open to nonguests.

Pizzería La Nonna (Capitán Drury 857, tel. 02972/42-2223, from US$10) serves about 30 varieties of pizzas, including wild boar, trout, and venison, plus calzones and empanadas. It gets crowded and noisy, though—take earplugs, go early or late, or consider takeout.

★ **Colorado** (Villegas 659, tel. 02972/42-7585, lunch and dinner daily, US$10-15) is an eclectic restaurant with pastas, stir-fry dishes, and regional specialties like trout in an almond sauce or venison. The wine list takes some chances, and most of them succeed. The service is casually attentive.

For lunch or dinner with lake views, there are few tables with the setting to match **La Costa del Pueblo** (Av. Costanera, by the pier, tel. 02972/42-9289, US$8-20), where the menu includes Argentine standards and regional specialties.

A former hotel, dating from 1910, houses **Doña Quela** (Av. San Martín 1017, tel. 02972/42-0670, www.interpatagonia.com/donaquela, from US$12), with a varied menu including pasta and trout. The olive oil dip with jalapeños adds some welcome spice to local dishes.

For ice cream, try **Charlot** (Av. San Martín 467, tel. 02972/42-8561), with dozens of imaginative flavors. **Vönhaus** (Av. San Martín 941,

tel. 02972/41-3565) carries ice cream from El Bolsón's Jauja, with a relatively small selection of their flavors.

★ **El Regional** (Av. San Martín and Mascardi, tel. 02972/41-4600, www.elregionalpatagonia.com.ar, lunch and dinner daily, US$19-25) offers pastas such as trout ravioli in a saffron sauce and varied meat dishes. There's also the distinctive *picada patagónica,* a mixed platter of smoked venison, smoked salmon, wild boar rolls, smoked cheese, and deer pâté.

Accommodations

Accommodations are abundant, but the best values go fast. Reservations are advisable and single occupants usually have to pay double rates in summer, at Semana Santa, and throughout ski season. The municipal tourist office, though, will make every effort to help find the best accommodations in your price range. The credit-card surcharge is often high.

UNDER US$25

On the Junín highway, the wooded **Camping del ACA** (Av. Koessler 2176, tel. 02972/42-9430, US$12 pp summer) is spacious and shady. The best sites go early. There are other campgrounds north and south of town, in Parque Nacional Lanín.

US$25-50

Rukalhue Hostel (Juez del Valle 682, tel. 02972/42-7431, www.rukalhue.com.ar, US$20 pp dorm, US$57 d) offers respectable hostel accommodations, private rooms, and small apartments. Amenities include Wi-Fi and breakfast.

Peak-season reservations are imperative at HI-affiliated ★ **Puma Hostel** (Fosbery 535, tel. 02972/42-2443, www.pumahostel.com.ar, US$25 pp dorm, US$80 s or d), an attractive and well-run facility north of the arroyo.

US$50-100

The handsome classic **Hotel Crismalú** (Rudecindo Roca 975, tel. 02972/42-7283, www.interpatagonia.com, US$43 s, US$67 d) is showing its age but is still a reasonable option. It has Wi-Fi.

With responsive management, **Hostería Las Lucarnas** (Teniente Coronel Pérez 632, tel. 02972/42-7085, www.hosterialaslucarnas.com, US$60 s, US$77 d) is a homey choice, with only 10 smallish rooms, a breakfast buffet, and amenities that include cable TV, Wi-Fi, strongboxes, and parking. Expect lower rates off-season.

Hotel Rosa de los Viajes (Av. San Martín 817, tel. 02972/42-7484, www.interpatagonia.com, US$77 s or d) is small and homey, but both foot and auto traffic are heavy in this part of town. Sedate **Hotel Intermonti** (Villegas 717, tel./fax 02972/42-7454, www.hotelintermonti.com.ar, US$80 d) has 24 well-furnished midsize rooms, plus attractive common areas and Wi-Fi.

After Chilean poet Pablo Neruda fled over the Andes on horseback to avoid political persecution in 1949, he may have shared drinks with Juan Perón in the gallery bar of **Hostería Parque Los Andes** (RN 40, Km 2215, tel. 02972/42-8211, www.interpatagonia.com, US$44 s, US$80 d). At the east end of town, before the road turns north toward Junín, it retains its classic style, with bright and improved rooms, but it's only open from New Year's until Easter, and then again in ski season.

For its exterior and the dining room's style, well-located **Hotel Turismo** (Mascardi 517, tel. 02972/42-7592, www.patagoniahotelturismo.com, US$52 s, US$84 d) belongs to another era. One of the best values in town, it has Wi-Fi, self-service breakfast, and comfortable rooms—brighter alongside the street and newer upstairs. Thin walls are its main drawback.

Central **Hotel Chapelco Ski** (Belgrano 869, tel. 02972/42-7480, www.chapelcoskihotel.com.ar, US$67 s, US$84 d) is a little worn and has limited parking but is otherwise acceptable.

Near the lake, **Hostería del Chapelco** (Brown 297, tel. 02972/42-7610, www.delchapelco.com.ar, US$80 s, US$94 d) has the best location of any hotel in its range. Its dining room has lake views, but the rooms themselves are on the smallish side.

US$100-150

Some upstairs rooms have lake views at **Hostería La Posta del Cazador** (Av. San Martín 175, tel. 02972/42-7501, www.lapostadelcazador.com.ar, US$106 s or d), a family-run Middle European-style place on a quiet block near the lake. It has large, superior rooms, Wi-Fi, and parking.

Hotel Antiguos (Coronel Díaz 753, tel. 02972/41-1876, www.hotelantiguos.com.ar, US$120 s, US$133 d) is a luminous 12-room hotel with natural wood details and some luxuries, including whirlpool tubs in every bath. While rooms are on the small side, they are stylish.

Try also **Hostal del Esquiador** (Coronel Rohde 975, tel. 02972/42-7674, www.hostaldelesquiador.com.ar, US$110 s, US$135 d), a block from the bus terminal, which has clean pleasant rooms with appealing designer touches.

Immaculately maintained, the modest ★ **Hotel del Viejo Esquiador** (Av. San Martín 1242, tel. 02972/42-7690, www.delviejoesquiador.com, US$90 s, US$140 d) is a congenial place that even has some legitimate single rooms. The breakfast is fine, but the tiny parking area will test any driver's skills.

US$150-200

In a quiet location, **Hostería Monte Verde** (Rivadavia 1165, tel. 02972/41-0129, www.hosteriamonteverde.com.ar, from US$147 s or d) is functional and comfortable, with a swimming pool and sauna. More expensive rooms have their own whirlpool tub and fireplace.

Sited on a leafy cul-de-sac, the boutique-ish ★ **La Casa de Eugenia** (Coronel Díaz 1186, tel. 02972/42-7206, www.lceugenia.com, US$170 d) stands out as a 1927 wooden residence in impeccable condition. The best choice in town, this family-run B&B perfectly combines historic ambience with modern functionality. Of the nine rooms, five are suites that face a manicured garden with a small heated pool. Breakfast's sweet delicacies are also served at the tearoom, which is open to nonguests as well.

OVER US$200

Four-star ★ **Hotel Patagonia Plaza** (Av. San Martín and Rivadavia, tel./fax 02972/42-2280, www.hotelpatagoniaplaza.com.ar, US$200 s, US$234 d) has become one of the city's premier accommodations, with 90 rooms ranging from relatively simple doubles to sprawling suites.

Hotel & Spa La Cheminée (General Roca and Mariano Moreno, tel. 02972/42-7617, www.lachemineehotel.com, US$230-297 s or d) has upgraded into one of the town's most stylish hotels, featuring an indoor pool, a sauna, a wine bar, an art gallery, and other distinctive amenities.

San Martín's latest luxury option, **Hostería Antares Patagonia** (Av. San Martín 251, tel. 02972/42-7670, www.antarespatagonia.com.ar, from US$295-340 s or d), is a recycled and expanded family mansion on a large lot. There are 10 spacious suites (superior ones have their own whirlpool tub and fireplace), a heated pool, a sauna, a business center, and other spacious common areas.

Information

At Plaza San Martín's east end, the **Secretaría Municipal de Turismo** (Av. San Martín and Rosas, tel. 02972/42-7347, www.sanmartindelosandes.gov.ar, 8am-9pm daily) provides advice, maps, and brochures, plus an up-to-the-minute database of accommodations and rates. In peak season, high demand can test its resources.

The APN's **Centro de Visitantes del Parque Nacional Lanín** (Emilio Frey 749, tel. 02972/42-0664, lanin@apn.gov.ar, 8am-8pm daily) provides park information with a selection of maps and brochures.

Services

Banco de la Nación (Av. San Martín 687) and several others have ATMs. **Andina**

Internacional (Capitán Drury 876) is the only exchange house. **Correo Argentino** (General Roca 690) is the post office. **Cotesma** (General Roca and Sarmiento) has telephone and Internet.

Chapelco Turismo (Capitán Drury 876, Local 1, tel. 02972/42-7550) offers conventional excursions to Parque Nacional Lanín, Villa La Angostura, and other destinations.

For laundry, **Laverap** (Capitán Drury 880, tel. 02972/42-8820; Villegas 972, tel. 02972/42-7500) has two locations. **Hospital Zonal Ramón Carrillo** (Av. San Martín and Coronel Rohde, tel. 02972/42-7211) is centrally located.

Transportation

Air and bus schedules change frequently, especially in ski season. **Aeropuerto Aviador Carlos Campos-Chapelco** (CPC, RN 234, Km 24, tel. 02972/42-8388) is midway between San Martín and Junín de los Andes. A taxi into town costs around US$18. **Aerolíneas Argentinas** (Mariano Moreno 859, tel. 02972/41-0588) flies regularly from Buenos Aires.

San Martín's **Terminal de Ómnibus** (Villegas 231, tel. 02972/42-7044) has regional, long-distance, and Chilean bus connections. **Castelli** (tel. 02972/42-2800) goes hourly to Junín de los Andes (50 min., US$2), except on Sunday, when it goes less often. Most services to Bariloche (4 hours, US$14-16) use the longer but smoother Rinconada route with **Vía Bariloche** (tel. 02972/42-3808). In the same office, **Ko Ko** goes to Villa La Angostura (2.5 hours, US$11) in summer via the scenic Siete Lagos route, continuing to Bariloche. It also goes to the Chilean border at Paso Hua Hum and to nearby lakes.

Albus (tel. 02972/42-8100) also goes to Villa La Angostura three or four times daily by the Siete Lagos route. **Igi-Llaima** (tel. 02972/42-8878) and **Transporte San Martín** (tel. 02972/42-7294) alternate service to Pucón (5 hours, US$50) and Temuco, Chile (7 hours, US$55) Monday-Saturday. Transporte San Martín continues to Valdivia.

Other typical destinations include Neuquén (7 hours, US$32-49) and Buenos Aires (19-22 hours, US$123-141).

Naviera Lácar y Nonthué (Av. Costanera s/n, at Obeid, tel. 02972/42-7380, www.lagolacarynonthue.com.ar) sails three to eight times daily to the beach community of Quila Quina (US$20 round-trip, national park admission fee not included), on Lago Lácar's south shore, and daily in summer to Hua Hum (US$60 round-trip, park admission not included).

For rental cars, try **Avis** (Teniente Coronel Pérez and Av. San Martín, tel. 02972/41-1141) or **Hertz** (Rivadavia 880, tel. 02972/42-0280).

PARQUE NACIONAL LANÍN

In westernmost Neuquén, **Parque Nacional Lanín** comprises 412,000 hectares of arid steppe, mid-elevation forests, alpine highlands, and volcanic summits. When eastward-flowing Pleistocene glaciers receded, they left a series of deep finger lakes draining into the Río Limay's upper and lower tributaries. These lakes and the Valdivian forests surrounding them have suffered less commercial development than those of Parque Nacional Nahuel Huapi to the south. They are recovering from the timber exploitation and livestock grazing that persist in some areas.

The park stretches from Lago Ñorquinco in the north to a diagonal that runs between Lago Nonthué on the Chilean border and Confluencia on RN 40. From Aluminé in the north to San Martín de los Andes in the south, several longitudinal highways intersect graveled westbound access roads. Most visitors use either Junín or San Martín as their base.

Flora and Fauna

Up to 3,000 millimeters of precipitation per annum supports dense, humid Valdivian woodlands. Lanín's signature species is the coniferous *pehuén* or araucaria tree *(Araucaria araucana)*, a subsistence resource for the Mapuche and Pehuenche people (a sub-group whose own name stresses their dependence

on the tree's edible nuts). Along with the broadleaf deciduous southern beech, *raulí, the pehuén* forms part of a transitional forest overlapping southern beech species that dominate more southerly Patagonian forests, such as the *coihue, lenga,* and *ñire.* In places, the solid bamboo *colihue* forms almost impenetrable thickets.

At higher elevations, above 1,600 meters, cold and wind reduce the vegetative cover to shrubs and grasses. At lower elevations, the drier climate supports shrubs and steppe grasses.

Except for trout, Lanín is less celebrated for its wildlife than for its landscapes. Fortunate visitors may see the secretive spaniel-size deer known as the *pudú* or the larger Andean *huemul.* The major predator is the puma, present on the steppes and in the forest, while torrent ducks frequent the faster streams, and the Andean condor glides on the heights. The lakes and rivers attract many other birds.

Sector Aluminé

Immediately west of Aluminé, RP 18 follows the south bank of the Río Rucachoroi for 23 kilometers to Lago Rucachoroi, site of a Mapuche reserve. From Rahue, 16 kilometers south of Aluminé, RP 46 leads west to **Lago Quillén,** an area of dense forests that's also home to Mapuche families.

Nineteen kilometers north of Aluminé via RP 23, scenic RP 11 climbs westward through the araucaria forests along the Río Pulmarí and **Lago Ñorquinco,** the park's northernmost access point. On what would be an excellent mountain-bike route, the road loops north-northeast toward the Chilean border at Icalma and the small Argentine resort of Villa Pehuenia.

Sector Lago Tromen

From a junction 16 kilometers north of Junín, northwesterly RP 60 leads to the Chilean border at Paso Mamuil Malal, where **Lago Tromen** marks the most convenient approach to **Volcán Lanín**'s summit. Because of the northeasterly exposure, hiking and climbing routes open earlier here than on the southern side, which lies partly in Chile.

★ VOLCÁN LANÍN

Looming above the landscape, straddling the Chilean border at 3,776 meters elevation, lopsided **Lanín** is the literal and metaphorical center of its namesake park. Covered by permanent snow and rising 1,500 meters above any other nearby peak, its irregular cone is a beacon for hundreds of kilometers to the east and, where the rugged terrain permits, to the north and south.

Unless you hire a registered national park guide, the APN requires written permission from its on-site **Centro de Informes,** which may inspect your gear. Gear should contain crampons, an ice ax, plastic tools, a VHF radio, a helmet, a portable stove, a first-aid kit, and appropriate clothing and peripherals (gloves, hats, insulated jackets, sunglasses, and sunscreen). As the maximum number of hikers authorized to climb at the same time is 60 and reservations are not possible, you might have to wait at the Centro de Informes.

From the Centro de Informes, it's one hour to start the ascent along **Espina de Pescado,** and another hour for the steeper **Camino de Mulas,** which leads after three hours to the **Refugio Militar Nuevo** (elev. 2,315 meters). Less than an hour above is the **Refugio Club Andino Junín de los Andes** (CAJA, elev. 2,600 meters). Beyond here, snow gear is essential for the following six to seven long hours up to the summit.

Sector Lago Huechulafquen

About four kilometers north of Junín, RP 61 leads northwest along the Río Chimehuín and Lago Huechulafquen's north shore for 52 kilometers to Puerto Canoa and **Lago Paimún** (at road's end). En route, a few trailheads lead north; the most interesting is the **Cara Sur** (Southern Face) approach to Volcán Lanín along the wooded Arroyo Rucu Leufú.

From the Piedra Mala campground at Lago Paimún, a 30-minute hike goes to **Cascada**

Volcán Lanín

El Saltillo, a 20-meter waterfall. In summer, when the Río Paimún and Arroyo Frutillar are usually fordable, it's possible to walk around Lago Paimún. Otherwise, summer hikers can do the boat crossing (US$3) at La Unión narrows, which separates Huechulafquen and Paimún, to basic **Camping Ecufén** (US$8 pp) on Paimún's south shore, one of several Mapuche family-run campsites in the park.

From La Unión, the trail continues through *coihue* and *pehuén* forest for about three hours to **Aila** campground and another eight hours to **Termas de Epulafquen,** where a new resort has exclusive use of the hot springs there. From Epulafquen, RP 62 returns to Junín de los Andes.

For nonhikers, the *Catamarán José Julián* (Av. San Martín 881, Local 6, San Martín de los Andes, tel. 02972/42-8029, www.catamaranjosejulian.com.ar, US$30 pp) offers a 90-minute lake excursion from Puerto Canoa over Huechulafquen and Epulafquen three to five times daily in summer, less frequently the rest of the year.

One Trail for the Lakes

In 2011, Argentina opened the first 22 sections of the **Huella Andina** (www.huellaandina.desarrolloturistico.gov.ar), a public footpath now covering about 30 percent of the total 560 kilometers across the lakes district's woodlands. Most of the area is protected under Argentina's national park administration and also as part of UNESCO's Andina Norpatagónica World Biosphere Reserve.

The first of its kind in Argentina, the north-south trail will eventually connect Neuquén's Lago Aluminé with northwestern Chubut's Lago Baguilt. Like the longer Sendero de Chile, it uses existing but rehabbed paths for pedestrians, allowing cyclists and horseback riders in some sections as well, and requiring a few lake crossings. Signs with distinctive blue and white striped markers identify the route.

As the trail improves, more information will be available at the local APN and tourist offices.

Lago Lolog and Lago Lácar

San Martín's own **Lago Lácar** is wilder toward the Chilean border, where there is camping, hiking, and white-water rafting at the outlet of the Río Hua Hum. About 15 kilometers north of San Martín, **Lago Lolog** has several campgrounds and regular summer transportation. It's particularly popular with windsurfers.

Naviera Lácar y Nonthué (Av. Costanera s/n at Obeid, tel. 02972/42-7380, www.lagolacarynonthue.com.ar) sails three to eight times daily to the beach community of Quila Quina (US$20 round-trip; national park admission fee not included), on Lago Lácar's south shore, and daily in summer to Hua Hum (US$60 round-trip; park admission fee not included).

Food and Accommodations

Except in nearby towns, accommodations and food options are few. Organized campgrounds with hot showers and other services charge slightly more than so-called *agreste* (wild) sites, which cost around US$6 pp.

SECTOR LAGO TROMEN

Reservations are essential for the four singles and six twin rooms at **Hostería San Huberto** (RP 60, Km 12.5, tel. 02972/42-1875, www.sanhubertolodge.com.ar, US$680 pp all-inclusive), which appeals chiefly to fly-fishing fanatics. Fishing licenses cost extra.

SECTOR LAGO HUECHULAFQUEN

Several Mapuche community-run organized campgrounds offer good services along the shores of Lago Huechulafquen and Lago Paimún, including **Camping Bahía Cañicul** (RP 61, Km 48, US$7 pp), which has a small store, but supplies are cheaper and more diverse in Junín. **Camping Raquithué** (RP 61, Km 54, US$4 pp) is another option.

A few kilometers before Lago Paimún, **Hostería Huechulafquen** (RP 61, Km 51, tel. 02972/42-7598, www.hosteriahuechulafquen.com, US$115 pp with 2 meals) is pleasant enough, with kayaks, mountain bikes, and other recreational possibilities. **Hostería Paimún** (RP 61, Km 57, tel. 02972/49-1758, www.hosteriapaimun.com.ar, US$100 pp with 2 meals, US$140 pp with all meals) is primarily a fishing lodge. Drinks are extra.

LAGO LOLOG

Basic **Camping Puerto Arturo** (tel. 02972/42-6353) charges US$9 per adult, slightly less for children. It has hot showers and picnic tables.

HUA HUM

Westbound from San Martín, gravel RP 48 follows Lago Lácar's and Nonthué's north shores to the Chilean border at Hua Hum. En route, open mid-December through Easter, **Café Quechuquina** (RP 48, Km 34, noon-7:30pm daily) is a rustic teahouse with exceptional cakes and cookies. It serves lunch and tea. Though lacking accommodations, the café enjoys lake access and makes an ideal day trip.

Transportation and Services

In addition to the **APN visitors center** at San Martín, there are **ranger stations** at all major lakes and some other points. While the rangers are helpful, they do not, in general, have maps or other printed matter. The US$10 pp (for foreigners) admission fee must be paid at the various park entrances.

San Martín de los Andes and Junín de los Andes are the main gateways, but public transportation is limited. From Junín, **Castelli** (tel. 02972/42-2800) buses go twice daily to and from Huechulafquen and Paimún (US$6) and twice more to Tromen (US$6.50). On international buses to Chile, via the Tromen (or Mamuil Malal) pass, through-passengers have priority.

VILLA LA ANGOSTURA AND VICINITY

On Lago Nahuel Huapi's north shore, Villa La Angostura lies within Bariloche's economic orbit. Its proximity to less developed parts of the lake, to Parque Nacional Los Arrayanes, and to the Cerro Bayo winter-sports center, however, has helped established its own identity—with an air of exclusivity—for both Argentines and foreigners. It has excellent accommodations and restaurants, with prices on the high side because it gets hordes of Chilean visitors thanks to the paved international highway.

Villa La Angostura (pop. 11,100) is 80 kilometers northwest of Bariloche via RN 40 and RN 231 (the highway to Osorno, Chile) and 109 kilometers south of San Martín de los Andes via RN 234 via the scenic Siete Lagos (Seven Lakes) route that's now completely paved. It's at 870 meters elevation, but the mountains rise sharply from the lakeshore.

"El Cruce" is that part of town where the highway crosses the street to the lakeside district, referred to as **"La Villa."** Many services line both sides of RN 231 (Av. Arrayanes and its westward extension, Av. Siete Lagos) as it passes directly through El Cruce. Three kilometers south, residential La Villa (also referred to as El Puerto) has another cluster

Windsurfers flock to Lago Lolog.

of hotels and restaurants. Parque Nacional Los Arrayanes occupies all of Península Quetrihué, the southward-jutting peninsula linked to La Villa by the isthmus that gives Villa La Angostura its name (The Narrows).

Sights

Foot, bicycle, and kayak are the best ways to see Villa La Angostura and nearby sights. For hiking in the mountains, where the trails are too steep and narrow for bicycles, take a taxi or *remise* to the trailhead.

At La Villa, the **Museo Histórico Regional** (Blv. Nahuel Huapi 2177, no phone, 10am-5pm Tues.-Sat., free) is an attenuated version of the local museum, relocated to a tiny space that only allows it to focus on the lake's navigation and settlement history.

From June to September, nine kilometers east of El Cruce, the **Centro de Ski Cerro Bayo** (Los Maquis 98, in town, tel. 0294/449-4189, www.cerrobayoweb.com) operates 12 kilometers of runs ranging 1,050 to 1,782 meters in elevation, with eight chairlifts and four

Villa La Angostura

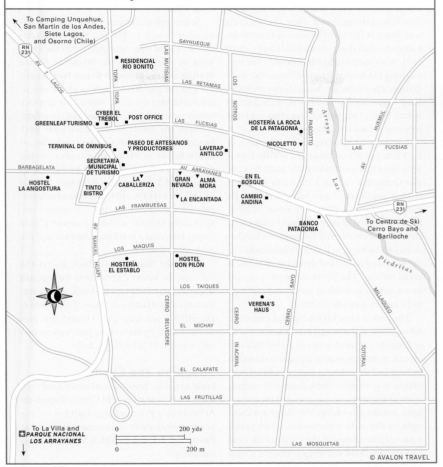

To Camping Unquehue,
San Martín de los Andes,
Siete Lagos,
and Osorno (Chile)

RN 231

AV 7 LAGOS

SAYHUEQUE

RESIDENCIAL
RÍO BONITO

LAS MUTISIAS

TOPA

TOPA

LAS RETAMAS

LOS NOTROS

CYBER EL
TREBOL   POST OFFICE
GREENLEAF TURISMO

LAS FUCSIAS

HOSTERÍA LA ROCA
DE LA PATAGONIA

BV PASCOTTO

Arroyo

HUEMUL

TERMINAL DE ÓMNIBUS

PASEO DE ARTESANOS
Y PRODUCTORES

LAVERAP
ANTILCO

NICOLETTO

LAS   FUCSIAS

BARBAGELATA

SECRETARÍA
MUNICIPAL
DE TURISMO

AV ARRAYANES

AV Las

HOSTEL
LA ANGOSTURA

TINTO
BISTRO

LA
CABALLERIZA

GRAN
NEVADA

ALMA
MORA

EN EL
BOSQUE

LA ENCANTADA

CAMBIO
ANDINA

RN 231

LAS FRAMBUESAS

To Centro de Ski
Cerro Bayo and
Bariloche

BV NAHUEL HUAPI

LOS MAQUIS

BANCO
PATAGONIA

Piedritas

HOSTERÍA
EL ESTABLO

HOSTEL
DON PILÓN

LOS TAIQUES

CERRO BAYO

MILLAQUEO

CERRO BELVEDERE

VERENA'S
HAUS

CERRO

EL MICHAY

IN ACAYAL

TOTORAL

EL CALAFATE

LAS FRUTILLAS

To La Villa and
PARQUE NACIONAL
LOS ARRAYANES

0   200 yds

0   200 m

LAS MOSQUETAS

tow bars. Cerro Bayo also has restaurants and rental equipment on-site; for lift ticket prices, consult the website.

From Avenida Siete Lagos, 800 meters west of El Cruce, the Cacique Antriao road leads to a wide parking area, from which a two-kilometer trail reaches **Mirador Belvedere.** From Mirador Belvedere, there are views along Lago Correntoso to the north; the implausibly short Río Correntoso that connects

it to Lago Nahuel Huapi; and the hoary western peaks that mark the Chilean border.

About midway up the forest trail, an eastbound trail leads to **Cascada Inacayal,** a 50-meter waterfall. For experienced trekkers only, another trail to 1,992-meter **Cerro Belvedere** climbs through *coihue* forest before dipping into a saddle and then ascending steeply over Cerro Falso Belvedere before continuing to the summit.

★ Parque Nacional Los Arrayanes

Local folklore says Walt Disney modeled *Bambi*'s cartoon forest after the *arrayán* woodland at the tip of Península Quetrihué, a former ranch that became a national park in 1971. With their bright white flowers, the eye-catching red-barked forests of *Luma apiculata* do bear a resemblance, but a Disney archivist has pointed out that *Bambi* was in production before Walt's 1941 trip to Argentina, and that he never visited the area.

Los Arrayanes is larger than the town of La Villa, but it's so close to La Villa that it feels more like a sprawling city park. It occupies Quetrihué's entire 1,753 hectares, which stretch south into Lago Nahuel Huapi. Its namesake forest covers only about 20 hectares, but the rest of the peninsula bristles with trees like the *maitén* and the southern beeches *coihue* and *ñire*, as well as colorful shrubs like the *notro* and *chilco*, and dense bamboo thickets of *colihue*. The floral standout is the *arrayán*, whose individual specimens reach up to 25 meters and 650 years old.

The park is ideal for hiking and mountain biking: The undulating 12-kilometer trail to or from the peninsula's tip is a perfect half-day excursion (on a bicycle or doing one direction by boat and the other on foot) or a full day by hiking in both directions. Argentine rangers often exaggerate the time needed on certain trails, but the three hours they suggest is about right for this walk in the woods, which passes a pair of lakes. Only at the park portal, near La Villa, are there any steep segments; a slide has forced partial relocation of the route here.

Before starting any hike in the park and within the previous 48 hours to the date of the hike, a free form must be filled in to keep a record at the national park's *Registro de Trekking* and to show upon park rangers' request. The form is provided at **APN's offices** (Blv. Nahuel Huapi 2193, tel. 0294/449-4152, 9am-3pm Mon.-Fri.), online on the park's website (www.parquesnacionales.gob.ar), and at Bariloche's **Club Andino** (20 de Febrero 30, tel. 0294/452-7966, www.clubandino.org).

Access for hikers is permitted only up to 1pm, and up to 2pm for bikers. Bikes can be rented at La Villa.

At the portal, rangers collect a US$10 admission charge (US$6 for Argentina residents). Those who only plan to do the short walk to the panoramic **Mirador Bahía Mansa** and the **Mirador Brazo Norte** need not pay the fee. Near the dock at the peninsula's southern tip, a café with a cozy fireplace serves sandwiches, coffee, and hot chocolate.

From the Bahía Mansa dock near park headquarters, nonhikers can reach the *arrayán* forest in about 45 minutes on the **Catamarán Futaleufú**, run by El Cruce's **Greenleaf Turismo** (Av. Arryanes 360, 1st Fl., tel. 0294/449-4404, www.bosquelosarrayanes.com.ar), which runs one to three services daily; the cost is US$25 one-way, US$33 round-trip, plus a small boarding tax and the park admission fee.

From the Bahía Brava dock across the isthmus, the newer **Catamarán Patagonia Argentina** (tel. 0294/449-4463, www.catamaranpatagonia.com.ar) runs a similar service (US$23 one-way, US$33 round-trip, plus a small boarding tax and the park's admission fee), also one to three times daily.

Shopping and Events

Local artisans, brewers, and other food producers sell their stuff at El Cruce's **Paseo de Artesanos y Productores** (just behind the bus terminal, daily in summer) and also at **Paseo del Puerto** (at Bahía Mansa, daily in summer).

For four days, early February's provincial **Fiesta de los Jardines** (Garden Festival) occupies center stage.

Sports and Recreation

Hikers must register at La Villa's **APN office** (Blv. Nahuel Huapi 2193, tel. 0294/449-4152, 9am-3pm Mon.-Fri.) or online (www.nahuelhuapi.gov.ar) within 48 hours prior to starting any hike in the parks.

English-speaking Anthony Hawes operates **Alma Sur Eco Trips** (tel. 0294/15-456-4724, www.almasur.com), with activities ranging from hiking and riding to mountain biking, fly-fishing, and white-water rafting and kayaking.

Food

In addition to hotel restaurants, Villa La Angostura offers a diversity of dining options at moderate to upmarket prices.

Alma Mora (Av. Arrayanes 156, tel. 0294/448-8145, lunch and dinner daily) is a fine modern café and bistro with Wi-Fi, a few tables, and comfortable couches.

★ **Nicoletto** (Blv. Pascotto 165, tel. 0294/449-5619, noon-3pm and 8:30pm-11:30pm daily, US$13) is a go-to place for pasta and dishes like trout-stuffed *sorrentinos* with a leek sauce. There is a small but memorable selection of wines by the glass. Nicoletto has luminous surroundings with mountain views.

Highly regarded as a budget choice, **Gran Nevada** (Av. Arrayanes 106, tel. 0294/449-4512, lunch and dinner daily, US$5-8) offers generous portions of Argentine standards at low prices. In new quarters behind the tourism office, **Hub** (Av. Arrayanes 21, tel. 0294/449-5700, lunch and dinner daily) is a pub-restaurant with a more elaborate and expensive menu.

Not necessarily the area's best, but perhaps its best value, ★ **La Encantada** (Cerro Belvedere 69, tel. 0294/449-5515, 1pm-3:30pm and 9pm-11:30pm daily, US$15-18) has a mud oven for roasting trout and lamb. It serves exceptional *ahumados* (smoked appetizers), exquisite trout empanadas, and fine pizzas and pastas, with attentive service, including savvy wine recommendations.

About one kilometer west of El Cruce, **Villa Franca** (Av. Siete Lagos 908, tel. 0294/448-5969, 12:30pm-11pm daily) is a cozy, moderately-priced family-run pasta and risotto restaurant, with a handful of game dishes and a noteworthy assortment of wines by the glass. A small but excellent dessert selection includes lemon pie.

Set on wooded grounds, Puerto Manzano's ★ **Cocina Waldhaus** (Av. Arrayanes 6431, tel. 0294/447-5323, www.leomorsella.com.ar, from US$20) serves continental-style dishes like fondue, goulash, and raclette with a Patagonian touch. Chef Leo Morsella's restaurant is open for lunch and for dinner (when reservations are obligatory). The menu is accompanied by a fine wine list.

Under the same ownership as Waldhaus, **La Caballeriza** (Av. Arrayanes 44, tel. 0294/449-4248, www.lacaballeriza.com, lunch and dinner daily) is a *parrilla* (grill restaurant) that has several branches in and around Buenos Aires (and in Brazil and Chile), but this is the first in Patagonia. *Cordero a las brasas* (grilled lamb) is served for two people (US$30). It has kept the pastas and desserts of chef Morsella's previous restaurant, La Macarena. Try *negra tentación,* a highly rich chocolate blend.

Unless you're content to sit at the small bar, reservations are critical at the star of the cuisine scene, ★ **Tinto Bistro** (Blv. Nahuel Huapi 34, tel. 0294/449-4924, www.tintobistro.com, from 8:30pm daily, US$16-21). Owned by brother-to-royalty Martín Zorreguieta (his sister Máxima is Queen of the Netherlands), it offers Asian-Mediterranean-Americas fusion food with Patagonian ingredients on a seasonal variation. Open for dinner only, it offers the area's finest wine list (including expensive vintages). After 1am on Thursday in high season, it opens as a bar.

For the best ice cream, try **En El Bosque** (Av. Arrayanes 218, tel. 0294/449-5738), which also carries a selection of chocolates. Lines are long.

Accommodations

In the past, Villa La Angostura was almost exclusively upscale, but several fine budget options are now available.

Some 500 meters west of the tourist office, **Camping Unquehué** (Av. Siete Lagos 727, tel. 0294/449-4103, www.campingunquehue.com.ar, US$9 pp plus US$3 per tent) offers wooded sites, with hot showers in the communal baths. They also have small modern apartments (US$70-133 for 2-4 people, depending on the season).

The well-organized and lively Hostelling International (HI) affiliate **Hostel La Angostura** (Barbagelata 157, tel. 0294/449-4834, www.hostellaangostura.com.ar, US$23 pp, US$63 d with breakfast) is an imposing alpine-style building on spacious grounds with Wi-Fi; all rooms have private baths.

Two blocks north of the bus terminal, homey **Residencial Río Bonito** (Topa Topa 260, tel. 0294/449-4110, www.riobonitopatagonia.com.ar, US$60 s or d) enjoys a quiet garden setting and has been attractively refurbished thanks to young new owners. It has Wi-Fi and ample parking.

On attractive wooded grounds, ★ **Bajo Cero Hostel** (Av. Siete Lagos 1200, tel. 0294/449-5454, www.bajocerohostel.com, US$20 pp, US$63 d) is well-run and has the usual amenities. All rooms have private baths, and double rooms have large TVs and DVD players.

El Cruce's ★ **Don Pilón** (Belvedere and Los Maquis, tel. 0294/449-4269, www.hosteldonpilon.com, US$23 pp, US$53 s, US$68 d) is a well-kept place run by Luis and Agustina, heirs of a local pioneer. Delicious homemade breakfasts, a fireplace, Wi-Fi, and parking attract families and couples alike. Discounts for longer stays apply. All rooms have private baths.

About one kilometer west of El Cruce, the eight-room **Hostería Las Cumbres** (Av. Siete Lagos s/n, tel. 0294/449-4945, www.hosterialascumbres.com, US$67 s, US$87 d) is a cozy, owner-operated hotel that offers good value, despite a forgettable breakfast.

In Puerto Manzano, about six kilometers southeast of El Cruce, the eight-room **Hostería Naranjo en Flor** (Chucao 62, tel. 0294/482-6484, www.naranjoenflor.com.ar, US$74-88 s or d) occupies a forested lot with views of Lago Nahuel Huapi and the Andes. Premium rooms have their own fireplace and whirlpool tub. It also has a pool and a restaurant that pulls in nonguests as well.

El Cruce's **Hostería Verena's Haus** (Los Taiques 268, tel. 0294/449-4467, www.verenas-haus.com.ar, US$94 s or d) is a bed-and-breakfast with comfortable beds and small but functional baths. It also has off-street parking in a large garden, and Wi-Fi through most of the building.

On a large lot in a quiet area, with friendly management and traditional Euro-Andean style, **Hostería La Roca de la Patagonia** (Blv. Pascotto 155, tel. 0294/449-4497, www.larocadelapatagonia.com.ar, US$117 s or d) offers six large rooms and an upper-floor lounge with great views. The dining room is at street level.

Dating from 1938, originally built for the APN, La Villa's lakeside classic ★ **Hotel Angostura** (Nahuel Huapi 1911, tel. 0294/449-4224, www.hotelangostura.com, US$100-120 s or d) has 20 TV-free rooms, some with lake views, and three separate bungalows sleeping up to six people. While its aged floors are creaky and the hot water seeps slowly through the pipes for the morning shower, this once-romantic hotel still has style, personality, good beds, Wi-Fi, a restaurant, and friendly service.

Set among large lush gardens, **Hostería El Establo** (Los Maquis 56, tel. 0294/449-4142, www.hosteriaelestablo.com.ar, US$115 s, US$150 d) is an Andean lodge that offers 14 comfortable rooms with tastefully individualized decor, plus engaging common areas and an excellent buffet breakfast. It's still one of Villa La Angostura's best values, though the floors are getting a little creaky with age.

A short distance west of town, the **Sol Arrayán Hotel & Spa** (RN 231, Km 64.5, tel. 0294/448-8000, www.solarrayan.com, US$156-1,930 s or d) benefits from a sloping lot that isolates it from highway noise. It benefits even more from assiduous service and 42 luminous lake-view rooms with balconies, plus common areas that include a restaurant, a wine bar, and a spa with an indoor-outdoor pool.

The area's traditional standout is the Relais & Chateaux affiliate ★ **Las Balsas Gourmet Hotel & Spa** (tel. 0294/449-4308, www.lasbalsas.com, from US$625 d), a

15-room, three-suite classic south of El Cruce. All rooms have lake views. Rates include unlimited spa access and breakfast, and there's a highly regarded hybrid restaurant with French and traditional Argentine dishes.

Across the Río Correntoso, three kilometers northwest of El Cruce, the historic ★ **Correntoso Lake & River Hotel** (Ruta de los 7 Lagos y Río Correntoso, tel. 0294/15-461-9728, tel. 011/4803-0030 in Buenos Aires, www.correntoso.com, US$450-650 s or d) started as a fishing lodge in 1917 and became a major attraction before burning down. Once nearly abandoned, it has undergone a rehab that restored it to its former glory, plus there's a spa, a lakeside fishing bar, a wine bar, and an outstanding restaurant as well.

Information and Services

The **Secretaría Municipal de Turismo** (Av. Arrayanes 9, El Cruce, tel. 0294/449-4124, www.villalaangostura.gov.ar, 8:30am-9pm daily spring-fall, 8:30am-8pm daily winter) provides information to travelers.

The APN's **Seccional Villa La Angostura** (Blv. Nahuel Huapi 2193, tel. 0294/449-4152, 9am-3pm Mon.-Fri.) is in La Villa, where hikers must register for Parque Nacional Los Arrayanes (if they haven't done so already online at www.nahuelhuapi.gov.ar). There's another office at the Quetrihué entrance to the park.

Virtually all services are in El Cruce, where **Banco Patagonia** (Millaqueo 10) has an ATM. **Cambio Andina** (Av. Arrayanes 256) is an exchange house. The postal code for **Correo Argentino** (Las Fucsias 121) is 8407. **Cyber El Trébol** (Las Fucsias and Topa Topa) has long-distance phones and Internet connections. **Laverap Antilco** (Los Notros 57) handles the laundry.

Transportation

El Cruce's convenient **Terminal de Ómnibus** (Av. Siete Lagos and Av. Arrayanes) has frequent connections to Bariloche, several buses daily to San Martín de los Andes via the scenic Siete Lagos route, and long-distance

services to Neuquén. Chile-bound buses from Bariloche stop here, but reservations are advised because they often run full.

Sample destinations include Bariloche (1.5 hours, US$5), San Martín de los Andes (2.5 hours, US$11), and Neuquén (6-7 hours, US$48-67).

SAN CARLOS DE BARILOCHE AND VICINITY

If Patagonia ever became independent, its logical capital might be San Carlos de Bariloche, the highest-profile destination in an area explorer Francisco P. Moreno called "this beautiful piece of Argentine Switzerland." Bariloche, with its incomparable Nahuel Huapi setting, is the lakes district's largest city, transportation hub, and gateway to Argentina's first national park. Moreover, in the 1930s, the carved granite blocks and rough-hewn polished timbers of its landmark Centro Cívico set a promising precedent for harmonizing urban expansion with wilder surroundings.

Dating from 1902, Bariloche was slow to grow. When former U.S. president Theodore Roosevelt visited in 1913, he observed:

> Bariloche is a real frontier village....
> It was like one of our frontier towns in
> the old-time West as regards the diversity in ethnic type and nationality
> among the citizens. The little houses
> stood well away from one another on the
> broad, rough, faintly marked streets.

When Roosevelt crossed the Andes from Chile, Bariloche was more than 400 kilometers from the nearest railroad, but it boomed after completion of the Ferrocarril Roca's southern branch in 1934. Its rustically sophisticated style has spread throughout the region—even to phone booths. Unrelenting growth, promoted by unscrupulous politicians and developers, has detracted from its Euro-Andean charm. For much of the day, for instance, the Bariloche Center, a multistory monstrosity authorized by the brief and irregular repeal of height-limit legislation, overshadows the Centro Cívico.

San Carlos de Bariloche

© AVALON TRAVEL

CAMPICHUELO

To Hotel Llao Llao
and Cruce de Lagos

GRISÚ

ROKET

CEREBRO

AV JUAN M DE ROSAS

LAGO NAHUEL HUAPI

Lago Nahuel Huapi

200 yds

200 m

BARILOCHE
HOSTEL

PATAGONIA
RAFTING

To Cerro
Otto

AVENIDA DE LOS PIONEROS

24 DE SEPTIEMBRE

DON
MOLINA

FREIXA VINOS

PATAGONIA
VINOS

HOTEL
PANAMERICANO

TANGO INN
CLUB HOTEL

WILKENNY
IRISH PUB &
RESTAURANT

CHILEAN
CONSULATE

MIGRACIONES

SECRETARÍA
MUNICIPAL
DE TURISMO

MUSEO DE LA
PATAGONIA

PUERTO
SAN CARLOS

CENTRO CÍVICO

TUCUMAN

MAROPOLO INN

AV SAN MARTIN

ESPAÑA

LIBERTAD

BACCIO

PAGANO

TORRE RELOJ

CERRO OTTO

20 DE JUNIO

HOSTERIA
GÜEMES

RUCA CHELI
SKI HOTEL

AV GENERAL BELGRANO

HOTEL INN
BARILOCHE
EDELWEISS

LAVADERO
HUEMUL

BUS STOP

AVIS

INTENDENCIA DEL
PN NAHUEL HUAPI

CLUB ANDINO
BARILOCHE

GÜEMES

20 DE FEBRERO

CÉSARE

HOSTERIA
LAS
MARIANAS

J F PASO

JURAMENTO

HOSTERIA LA
PASTORELLA

Plaza
Belgrano

20 DE FEBRERO

KANDAHAR

VEGETARIANO

ALTO EL
FUEGO

SOUTH
BAR

SAAVEDRA

HOTEL TRES
REYES

SEE
DETAIL

EXTREMO
SUR

PERIKO'S
HOSTEL

AGUAS BLANCAS

ANTARES

HERTZ

EL BOLICHE
DE ALBERTO

BYPASS

H ANASAGASTI

E B MORALES

L DE QUAGLIA

A GALLARDO

LA MONTAÑA
SPANISH SCHOOL

A ROLANDO

MARTÍN
PESCADOR

VÍA
BARILOCHE

ABUELA
GOYE

AHUMADERO
FAMILIA WEISS

Plaza Italia

S ALBARRACIN

CIVILLEGAS

ATISCORNIA

ANTIGUO
SOLAR

PALACIOS

THE ROXY
BARILOCHE

NEBBIOLO

LA BARCA

IGLESIA
CATEDRAL

URQUIZA

COCODRILO'S

BARUZZI FLY
SHOP &
OUTDOORS

ABUELA
GOYE

CAMBIO
ANDINA

F BESCHTEDT

LATAM
AIRLINES

LOCAL BUS
STATION

BARILOCHE BIKES

LA VIZCACHA

To Cervecería Bachmann and
Kospi Boutique Guesthouse

TEATRO
LA BAITA

HELADOS
JAUJA

LA ALPINA

P MORENO

L DE QUAGLIA

CAU
CAU

B MITRE

BANCO DE LA
NACIÓN

AEROLÍNEAS
ARGENTINAS

LOCUTORIO
QUAGLIA

E FREY

AM ELFLEIN

HOSPITAL ZONAL

P MORENO

LA CAVA

BUDGET

EL MUNDO
PIZZA Y
PASTA

RAID

B MITRE

CHEVALLIER

POST OFFICE

PASEO DE LOS
ARTESANOS

TURISUR

SITURISMO

CIVILLEGAS

J O'CONNOR

O GOEDECKE

LADE

ACA

AV 12 DE OCTUBRE

E O'CONNOR

To Terminal de Ómnibus,
Train Station, Airport, Villa
La Angostura, and Neuquén

As the population has grown from near 50,000 in 1980 to over 110,000 in 2010, its *microcentro* has become a clutter of chocolate shops, hotels, and timeshares and is notorious for high-school graduation bashes that leave hotel rooms in ruins. Student tourism is declining, in relative terms at least, but Bariloche still lags behind aspirations that were once higher than Cerro Catedral's ski areas. Like other Patagonian destinations, it booms in the summer months of December, January, and February.

Bariloche holds a unique place in Argentine cinema as the location for Emilio Vieyra's *Sangre de Vírgenes* (Blood of the Virgins), a Hammer-style vampire flick that was ahead of its time when shot in 1967 (it's available on DVD). Perhaps Vieyra envisaged the unsavory things to come, but Bariloche's bloodsuckers are only part of the story. The city and its surroundings still have much to offer, and at reasonable cost. Many of the best accommodations, restaurants, and other services lie along or near Avenida Bustillo between Bariloche proper and Llao Llao, about 25 kilometers west.

Orientation

On Lago Nahuel Huapi's southeastern shore, at 764 meters elevation, Bariloche (pop. 112,887) is 1,596 kilometers from Buenos Aires and 429 kilometers southwest of Neuquén via RN 237 and RN 40. It is 835 kilometers west of Viedma, Río Negro province's coastal capital, via RN 3, RP 23, and RN 40. It is 123 kilometers north of El Bolsón via RN 40.

As RN 40 enters Bariloche from the east, it becomes Avenida 12 de Octubre, Avenida Juan Manuel de Rosas, and then Avenida Bustillo, continuing west to Llao Llao. En route, it skirts the landmark Centro Cívico. One block south, the parallel Bartolomé Mitre is the main commercial street. North-south streets—some of them staircases—climb steeply from the lakeshore.

★ Centro Cívico

Even with the kitsch merchants who pervade the plaza with Siberian huskies and St. Bernards for photographic poses, and the graffiti defacing General Roca's equestrian statue, the array of buildings that border it would be the pride of many cities around the globe. The view to Lago Nahuel Huapi is a bonus, even when the boxy Bariloche Center blocks the sun.

The **Centro Cívico** was a team effort, envisioned by architect Ernesto de Estrada in 1936 and executed under APN director Exequiel Bustillo until its inauguration in 1940. When the municipal **Torre Reloj** (Clock Tower) sounds at noon, figures from Patagonian history appear to mark the hour. The former **Correo** (post office, but now the tourism office) is one of several buildings of interest, with steep-pitched roofs and arched arcades that offer shelter from inclement weather.

At the Centro Cívico's northeast corner, **Museo de la Patagonia Francisco P. Moreno** (Centro Cívico s/n, tel. 0294/442-2309, www.museodelapatagonia.nahuel-huapi.gov.ar, 10am-12:30pm and 2pm-7pm Tues.-Fri., 10am-5pm Sat., from US$1.25) attempts to place the region (and more) in ecological, cultural, and historical context. Its multiple halls touch on natural history through taxidermy (better than most of its kind); insects (inexplicably including subtropical Iguazú); Patagonia's population from antiquity to the present; the aboriginal Mapuche, Tehuelche, and Fuegian peoples; caudillo Juan Manuel de Rosas; the "Conquista del Desierto" that displaced the indigenous people; and Bariloche's own urban development. There is even material on Stanford geologist Bailey Willis, a visionary consultant who did the region's first systematic surveys in the early 20th century.

Exequiel Bustillo's brother, architect Alejandro Bustillo, designed the **Intendencia del Parque Nacional Nahuel Huapi** (Nahuel Huapi National Park Headquarters, San Martín 24), one block north, to harmonize with the Centro Cívico. As a collective national monument, they represent Argentine Patagonia's best.

Entertainment

Teatro La Baita (Moreno 39, tel. 0294/443-4439, www.teatrolabaita.com) hosts a diversity of musical and theater events. **Cine Sunstar** (at Shopping Patagonia, Onelli 447, tel. 0294/443-3128, www.cinesunstar.com) shows current movies.

A cluster of downtown bars offers palatable pub grub. Choices include the **Wilkenny Irish Pub & Restaurant** (Av. San Martín 435, tel. 0294/442-4444, 11am-4am daily) and **South Bar** (Juramento 30, tel. 0294/412-3456). Popular **Antares** (Elflein 47, tel. 0294/443-1454, www.cervezaantares.com, 1pm-3am or 4am daily) is a brewpub with a decent food menu of German specialties and sandwiches to complement the suds.

At the east end of downtown, **Cervecería Bachmann** (Vice Almirante O'Connor 1348, tel. 0294/443-6337, www.cerveceriabachmann.com.ar) is a cozy friendly bar with half a dozen craft brews on tap and a good sandwich menu, supplemented with pizza and a few other items. A more secluded brewpub is **La Cruz** (Nilpi 789, uphill from Av. Bustillo, Km 6.1, tel. 0294/444-2634, www.cervecerialacruz.com.ar, from 6pm Tues.-Sun.); it serves snacks and a few meals with its excellent ales.

For live music, **The Roxy** (Palacios 287, tel. 0294/445-9950, 8pm-4am Mon.-Sat.) is a bar-restaurant that's a branch of its Buenos Aires namesake.

Bariloche nightspots open late—around 1am—and close around daybreak. The most central is the youthful **By Pass** (Rolando 157, tel. 0294/443-5681, www.bypass.com.ar). Several others lie a few blocks west of the Centro Cívico: **Cerebro** (Av. Juan Manuel de Rosas 406, tel. 0294/442-4948, www.cerebro.com.ar), **Roket** (Av. Juan Manuel de Rosas 424, tel. 0294/443-1940, www.roket.com), and **Grisú** (Av. Juan Manuel de Rosas 584, tel. 0294/442-2269, www.grisu.com).

Events

More than just a pretty landscape, Nahuel Huapi has an active cultural life. Llao Llao's **Camping Musical Bariloche** (Vivaldi s/n, tel. 0294/441-2345 www.campingmusicalbche.org.ar) sponsors chamber music and brass concerts throughout the year.

Around Semana Santa, the week before Easter, the **Fiesta Provincial del Chocolate** promotes the obvious. June's **Fiesta Nacional de la Nieve** (National Snow Festival) marks the start of ski season.

For one week every October, Llao Llao Hotel & Resort hosts the **Semana Musical Llao Llao** (tel. 011/4800-1914 in Buenos Aires, www.semanamusical.com), an exclusive musical event.

Mid-December brings the **Navidad Coral** (Christmas Chorus) at the cathedral.

Shopping

Local artisans live off souvenir hunters who frequent the **Paseo de los Artesanos** (Villegas and Perito Moreno, 10am-9pm daily).

Patagonia Vinos (Av. San Martín 598, tel. 0294/443-3813, www.clubpatagoniavinos.com.ar) probably carries the widest selection of premium wines. Across the street, **Freixa Vinos** (Av. San Martín 597, tel. 0294/443-6300) also carries a good selection of reds and whites, and **La Cava** (Mitre 812, tel. 0294/445-9893) also deserves a look. Chocoholics flock to **Abuela Goye** (Mitre 252, tel. 0294/442-9856, www.abuelagoye.com) and similar locales.

La Barca (Mitre 534, Local 3, tel. 0294/443-6744) has a fine selection of books and maps.

Sports and Recreation

Because of Parque Nacional Nahuel Huapi, Bariloche is the base for outdoor activities that include fishing, hiking, climbing, mountain biking, horseback riding, white-water rafting, kayaking, and skiing.

November to April, the region is a **fishing** enthusiast's paradise for its lakes, where trolling is the rule, and streams, for fly-fishing. The **Asociación de Pesca y Caza Nahuel Huapi** (Av. 12 de Octubre and Onelli, tel. 0294/442-1515) is a good information source. For rental gear, try **Baruzzi Fly Shop & Outdoors** (Urquiza 250, tel. 0294/442-4922, www.barilochefishing.com) or **Martín Pescador** (Rolando 257, tel. 0294/442-2275, martinpescadorbariloche@speedy.com.ar).

Non-Argentines can purchase **fishing licenses** (US$24 per day, US$72 per week, US$96 per season, passport required) at the APN's Intendencia del Parque Nacional Nahuel Huapi on the Centro Cívico; there are additional charges for trolling permits.

The **APN** (San Martín 24, tel. 0294/442-3111, www.nahuelhuapi.gov.ar) provides **hiking** and **climbing** information, but the best source is the **Club Andino Bariloche** (20 de Febrero 30, tel. 0294/442-2266, www.clubandino.org), which also organizes excursions and sells trail maps. Before starting any hike in the park and within the 48 hours before the date of the hike, hikers must obtain a permit for the national park's *Registro de Trekking,* to show upon park rangers' request, from APN offices; also available on the park's website (www.nahuelhuapi.gov.ar) and at the Club Andino.

Bariloche's roads, both paved and gravel, and many wide trails make **cycling** an attractive option. Mountain bike rental, with gloves and helmet, costs from US$20 per day. **Dirty Bikes** (Lonquimay 3908, tel. 0294/442-2743, www.dirtybikes.com.ar) rents bikes and also offers half-day to multiple-day excursions that include other activities as well. **Bariloche Bikes** (Moreno 520, tel. 0294/442-4657) also rents bikes. **Bike Cordillera** (Av. Bustillo, Km 18.6, tel. 0294/452-4828, www.cordillerabike.com) starts its tours beyond the busiest, narrowest sector of the Circuito Chico. **Bike Way** (Av. Bustillo 12521, tel. 0294/15-461-7723, www.bikeway.com.ar) has similar offerings and longer trips.

Local **horseback riding** trips can last from two hours (about US$55) to a full day (US$75, with lunch), with multiple-day excursions also possible. The main operators are **Cabalgatas Carol Jones** (Modesta Victoria 5600, tel. 0294/442-6508, www.caroljones.com.ar) and **Cabalgatas Tom Wesley** (Av. Bustillo 15500, tel. 0294/444-8193, www.cabalgatastomwesley.com).

For **rafting** and **kayaking,** mostly from September to April, the Río Manso between Lago Steffen and Río Villegas is a Class II-III float (from US$90) midway between Bariloche and El Bolsón to the south, ideal for beginners and families. Downstream and near the international border, the Río Manso becomes more challenging with some taxing Class IV rapids (about US$105, discounts for cash). On some multiple-day trips, which may include a border crossing, trekking, horseback riding, or cycling is added.

River operators include **Aguas Blancas** (Morales 564, tel. 0294/443-2799, www.aguasblancas.com.ar) and **Extremo Sur** (Morales 765, tel. 0294/442-7301, www.extremosur.com).

Pura Vida Patagonia (tel. 0294/15-441-4053, www.puravidapatagonia.com) runs half-day (US$37) to four-day-plus kayak touring trips across nearby lakes and on the Río Limay.

After decades of decline and eclipse by resorts like Las Leñas (Mendoza), Bariloche is reestablishing itself as a ski destination with new investment and technological improvements at **Catedral Alta Patagonia** (Base Cerro Catedral, tel. 0294/440-9000, www.catedralaltapatagonia.com), only a short hop west of town. It's still more popular with Argentines and Brazilians than intercontinental travelers, but new snowmaking and grooming gear has complemented the blend of 50 beginner to advanced runs, and lift capacities have also improved. From a base of 1,030 meters elevation, the skiable slopes rise another 1,100 meters. As elsewhere, ticket prices depend on timing; the season runs mid-June to mid-October but is subdivided into low, mid-, and peak season. Basic rental equipment is cheap, but quality gear is more expensive. In addition to on-site facilities, try downtown's **Raid** (Mitre 860, tel. 0294/452-2178, ramos1157@hotmail.com) for ski rentals. There are also cross-country opportunities at close-in Cerro Otto.

Food

For breakfast, coffee, sandwiches, and sweets, try a café like **La Alpina** (Perito Moreno 98, tel. 0294/442-5693, www.laalpinabariloche.com.ar, 10am-3am daily), which also has brews on tap.

Bariloche abounds in pizzerias, starting with the unpretentious **Cocodrilo's** (Mitre 5, tel. 0294/442-6640, lunch and dinner daily, pizza from US$12). **El Mundo Pizza y Pasta** (Mitre 759, tel. 0294/442-3461, www.elmundopizzas.wix.com, noon-3pm and 8pm-midnight daily) has greater variety and slightly lower prices. In addition to pizza, similarly priced **Césare** (20 de Febrero 788, tel. 0294/443-2060, 11am-11pm Mon.-Sat., 7pm-11pm Sun.) prepares around 20 varieties of empanadas.

El Vegetariano (20 de Febrero 730, tel. 0294/442-1820, noon-3pm and 8pm-11pm Mon.-Sat., US$10) occupies an attractive residence screened by two large *pehuén* trees. The three or five courses offered as the meal of the day may include fish.

Uphill from the Club Andino, ★ **Alto El Fuego** (20 de Febrero 451, tel. 0294/443-7015, www.altoelfuego.com.ar, noon-3pm and 8pm-midnight Mon.-Sat., US$15) is a grill restaurant in a comfortably informal house. It keeps it simple with well-prepared cuts like *entraña* (skirt steak) and alternatives like trout, with exceptional service. The by-the-glass house wine can be an unusual blend, such as malbec-bonarda.

On the Llao Llao road, the **Cervecería Berlina Brew House & Restaurante** (Av. Bustillo, Km 11.750, tel. 0294/452-3336, www.cervezaberlina.com, noon-1am or later daily, US$13) offers beer samplers and excellent sandwiches, plus pizzas, pastas, and a few standard Argentine dishes such as *bife de chorizo* (sirloin). It has an outdoor beer garden with a 6pm-8pm daily happy hour. Almost

Cervecería Berlina is one of several brewpubs on Bariloche's western outskirts.

next door, for snacks, pizzas, and draft beer, there's **Cervecería Blest** (Av. Bustillo, Km 11.6, tel. 0294/446-1026, www.cervezablest.com.ar, noon-midnight daily).

For smoked venison, wild boar, and trout, visit tourist-oriented **Restaurant Familia Weiss** (Palacios and V. A. O'Connor, tel. 0294/443-5789, www.ahumaderoweiss.com, noon-midnight daily, US$10-15), where specialties include *ciervo a la cazadora* (a venison stew with a side of spaetzle). On the downside, they overcook the accompanying vegetables.

La Vizcacha (Eduardo O'Connor 630, tel. 0294/442-2109, lunch and dinner Wed.-Mon.) is a venerable downtown grill restaurant. **Asador Criollo Don Molina** (San Martín 605, tel. 0294/443-6616, US$18) is a more elaborate grill restaurant whose half-portion of Patagonian lamb looks larger than full portions elsewhere. Its three-course lunches are an excellent value.

The full-size *bife de chorizo* (sirloin) at ★ **El Boliche de Alberto** (Villegas 347, tel. 0294/443-4564; Villegas and Elflein, tel. 0294/440-1040; Av. Bustillo, Km 8.8, tel. 0294/446-2285, www.elbolichedealberto.com, noon-3pm and 8pm-midnight daily, US$20) will challenge all but the most ravenous adolescents. Even the half portion may be too large for a single diner and some couples.

Despite the name, ★ **Kandahar** (20 de Febrero 698, tel. 0294/442-4702, www. kandahar.com.ar, 8pm-11pm Mon.-Sat., US$18) does not serve Afghan food, rather Patagonian game dishes such as a venison casserole garnished with applesauce and red cabbage. In intimate surroundings with a Sinatra soundtrack, the service is excellent, the kitchen involved, but the dessert menu is weak.

Nebbiolo (Palacios 156, tel. 0294/489-0023, 11:30am-4pm and 8pm-1am daily, www. nebbiolo.com.ar, US$12) has a sophisticated Italian-Patagonian menu, with more thoughtful preparation than most downtown restaurants. The stuffed pasta with goat cheese and a shrimp sauce typify something that goes beyond the generic dishes available elsewhere in the area. The service is exemplary, and there's an extensive wine list that includes good by-the-glass choices.

Despite its intimidating size, cavernous ★ **El Patacón** (Av. Bustillo, Km 7, tel. 0294/444-2898, www.elpatacon.com, noon-11:30pm daily, from US$14) has personalized service and meticulously prepared food served in generous portions. Former U.S. president Bill Clinton dined on dishes such as the black hake.

Bariloche has exceptional ice creameries, starting with **Abuela Goye** (Quaglia 219; Mitre 252, tel. 0294/443-3861, www. abuelagoye.com) and **Baccio** (España 7, tel. 0294/442-2305), whose outstanding fruit flavors include raspberry mousse and blueberry. The real standout, though, is **Helados Jauja** (Moreno 48, tel. 0294/443-7888, noon-midnight daily), whose dizzying diversity includes unconventional wild fruit flavors and half a dozen or more chocolates.

Accommodations

Bariloche has plentiful accommodations options in all categories, from camping to hostels, B&Bs, hotels, and luxury lodges. Hostels, in particular, have proliferated. Most of the finest hotels are west of the city proper, on and along the Llao Llao road. Though it's usual to find the highest rates in ski season, it's not necessarily the rule.

The municipal tourist office keeps a thorough accommodations database, and when summer demand is high, they're an excellent resource. Since many low-priced to mid-range hotels cater to high school graduation trips, it's better to avoid them toward the end of December.

UNDER US$25

The lakefront **Camping Petunia** (Av. Bustillo, Km 13.5, tel. 0294/446-1969, www. campingpetunia.com, US$10 pp adults, US$5 pp children) is one of numerous campgrounds west of town.

US$25-50

Most places in this price range are hostels that, in addition to dorms, also have private rooms that are mostly better value than an average hotel. They also include breakfast and offer amenities such as Wi-Fi. One hostel even includes dinner in its rates.

On wooded grounds in a quiet barrio west of town, the **Alaska Hostel** (Lilinquén 326, tel. 0294/446-1564, www.alaska-hostel.com, US$14 pp, US$43-57 d) is walking distance from Avenida Bustillo, Km 7.5. Several buses, including Nos. 10, 20, and 21, will drop passengers here.

Downtown, ★ **Periko's Hostel** (Morales 555, tel. 0294/452-2326, www.perikos.com, US$21 pp, US$50-57 s or d) has mostly dorm rooms but also some stylish and spacious doubles on the upper floors. The secluded garden is uncommon in this part of town.

Only 500 meters west of the bus terminal, the **Tango Inn Soho** (Av. 12 de Octubre 1915, tel. 0294/443-0707, www.tangoinn.com, US$21 pp dorms, US$57-70 s or d) has all dorms and private rooms with their own baths along with a restaurant, a cafeteria, and a bar.

On a narrow street with lake views, friendly **Bariloche Hostel** (Salta 528, tel. 0294/442-5460, www.barilochehostel.com.ar, US$23 pp, US$57 d) is a converted residence where both dorms and doubles have private baths. The lake panoramas are even better from the deck on the slope behind the house, where there's a magnificently productive pear tree and other fruit trees.

Nearby, the Hostelling International affiliate **Marcopolo Inn** (Salta 422, tel. 0294/440-0105, www.marcopoloinnbariloche.com, US$22 pp, US$75 d) is a converted hotel whose rooms are more spacious than most hostels. All rooms come with private baths and most with bathtubs. Rates include breakfast and dinner.

US$50-100

In a former family residence dating from the 1950s, the ★ **Antiguo Solar** (Ángel Gallardo 360, tel. 0294/440-0337, www.antiguosolar.com, US$50 s, US$83 d) is a lovely B&B. Its young operators offer warm, attentive service and comfort.

Slightly uphill on the Llao Llao road, cozy **Hostería Pájaro Azul** (Av. Bustillo, Km 10.8, tel. 0294/446-1025, www.hosteriapajaroazul.com.ar, US$60 d) has eight pine-paneled rooms with mountain views through relatively small windows. They also have Wi-Fi.

Some of the 13 rooms at **Hostería La Pastorella** (Belgrano 127, tel. 0294/442-4656, www.lapastorella.com.ar, US$40 s, US$70 d) are a little too cozy for comfort, but it does offer a diverse buffet breakfast. Amenities include a sauna.

The Tango Inn Soho recently opened the more elaborate **Tango Inn Club Hotel** (Av. San Martín 547, tel. 0294/442-4628, www.tangoinn.com, US$67-93 s or d), a converted hotel that includes a spa.

At the east end of downtown, the ★ **Kospi Boutique Guesthouse** (Mitre 1361, tel. 0294/442-3407, www.kospihouse.com.ar, US$62 s, US$84 d) is both less and more than

it sounds. Rather than a stylish contemporary lodge, it's a lovingly retro restoration of a traditional *residencial,* a family house with a few short-term rooms to rent. The rooms and baths are both small, but the common areas are spacious, with decor from decades past. Breakfast (US$6) is above average, with homemade bread and pastries, and fresh fruit.

Well-located **Hostería Güemes** (Güemes 715, tel. 0294/442-4785, www.hosteriaguemes.com.ar, US$50 s, US$92 d), in Barrio Belgrano, is one of the city's oldest and most hospitable B&Bs. In the same neighborhood, upgraded **Ruca Cheli Village Ski Hotel** (24 de Setiembre 275, tel. 0294/442-4528, www.rucacheli.com.ar, US$91 s or d, with buffet breakfast) has reasonably large rooms and obliging management.

The lakefront ★ **Hotel Tres Reyes** (Av. 12 de Octubre 135, tel. 0294/442-6121, www.hotel3reyes.com, US$88-145 s or d), a stylishly rehabbed classic dating from 1951, is a reliable downtown hotel whose higher rates correspond to lake views. Some rooms are smallish, but even these almost double their rates in ski season.

Almost across the street, built in an Austrian style, Barrio Belgrano's **Hostería Las Marianas** (24 de Septiembre 218, tel. 0294/443-9876, www.hosterialasmarianas.com.ar, from US$98 s or d) is a friendly, family-run inn with only 16 rooms—each named for a nearby Andean peak.

US$100-150

Highly regarded **Los Juncos Patagonian Lake House** (Av. Bustillo 20063, tel. 0294/495-7871, www.posadalosjuncos.com, US$126-170 s or d) is an exclusive five-suite facility with a restaurant on Bahía Campanario.

US$150-200

Part of a small exclusive chain, ★ **Design Suites Bariloche** (Av. Bustillo, Km 2.5, tel. 0294/445-7000, www.designsuites.com, US$150-270 s or d) differs from all its kin in setting and architecture. In this case, the common areas consist of a luminous clubhouse

On Bariloche's outskirts, the Casco Art Hotel contains a sculpture garden.

the area's top choice were it not for the nearby Llao Llao Hotel & Resort.

Built into the slopes of Península San Pedro, the **Aldebarán Hotel & Spa** (Av. Bustillo, Km 20.4, Península San Pedro, tel. 0294/444-8678, www.aldebaranpatagonia. com, US$207-340 s or d) is a strikingly modern view hotel with panoramas to Cerro Campanario, Cerro López, and beyond. The 10 rustically stylish rooms are enormous, 35 to 55 square meters, plus they have huge baths and balconies overlooking the lake. It also boasts a good restaurant and enjoys contemporary spa facilities.

Now part of a Spanish chain, **Hotel NH Bariloche Edelweiss** (Av. San Martín 202, tel. 0294/444-5500, www.edelweiss.com.ar, from US$224 s or d) has 100 spacious standard to superior rooms, plus more elaborate suites. A minimum stay of four nights is obligatory in ski season.

Halfway to Llao Llao, each of the 33 rooms at the **Casco Art Hotel** (Av. Bustillo, Km 11.5, tel. 0294/446-3131, www.hotelelcasco. com, US$350-1,800 s or d, plus taxes) is its own mini-gallery, featuring original works by individual Argentine artists. Created by a Buenos Aires gallery owner, it's a one-of-a-kind lakeside spa hotel whose grounds also constitute a sculpture garden.

Not just a hotel but a landmark in its own right, ★ **Llao Llao Hotel & Resort** (Av. Bustillo, Km 25, tel. 0810/222-5526, www.llaollao.com, US$415-785 s or d) is an Alejandro Bustillo classic dating from 1940. Rates depend on the room size (22 to 160 square meters), views, and amenities, as well as the season.

Information

The **Secretaría Municipal de Turismo** (Centro Cívico s/n, tel. 0294/442-9850, www. barilochepatagonia.info, 8am-9pm daily June-Apr., closed Jan.1, Nov.8, and Dec. 25) gets overrun with visitors seeking accommodations and other information in the peak season. There are satellite offices at the bus terminal (Av. 12 de Octubre s/n) and at the airport.

with cathedral ceilings and views over Nahuel Huapi, as well as an indoor-outdoor pool, a gym, and sauna facilities. The accommodations occupy three separate buildings with greater setbacks from the busy avenue. All rooms enjoy lake views and whirlpool tubs, some of them with views as well.

Downtown's most prestigious option is **Hotel Panamericano** (Av. San Martín 536/570, tel. 0294/440-9200, www.panamericanobariloche.com, US$175-325 s or d), a sprawling complex on both sides of the avenue linked by glassed-in elevated bridges. It also holds a casino, a spa, and several restaurants. However, it's not up to the standards—not to mention the style or location—of places like the Llao Llao. Rates vary according to view (some rooms lack views, others have lake views).

OVER US$200

Llao Llao's ★ **Hotel Tunquelén** (Av. Bustillo, Km 24.5, tel. 0294/444-8600, www. tunquelen.com, US$195-580 s or d) might be

The APN's **Intendencia del Parque Nacional Nahuel Huapi** (San Martín 24, tel. 0294/442-3111, www.nahuelhuapi. gov.ar) is one block south of the tourist office. It is where hikers must register within 48 hours prior to the start of any hike in the park. Another block south, the **Club Andino Bariloche** (20 de Febrero 30, tel. 0294/442-2266, www.clubandino.org, 9am-9pm Mon.-Sat. summer, afternoons only Mon.-Sat. fall-spring) provides hiking information.

Services

ACA (Av. 12 de Octubre 785, tel. 0294/442-3000) is a resource for motorists. **Cambio Andina** (Mitre 102) changes foreign cash and traveler's checks. **Banco de la Nación** (Mitre 180) is one of many downtown banks with ATMs. The postal code foe **Correo Argentino** (Moreno 175) is 8400. **Locutorio Quaglia** (Quaglia 220) has phone, fax, and Internet service.

Siturismo (Villegas 222, tel. 0294/443-6215, www.siturismo.com) is a full-service agency that will arrange a variety of excursions around the area. **La Montaña Spanish School** (Elflein 251, tel. 0294/452-4212, www. lamontana.com) has programs starting at US$140 per week for 20 hours of instruction.

There is a **Chilean consulate** (España 275, tel. 0294/442-3050) in town. For visa matters, visit the **Dirección Nacional de Migraciones** (Libertad 191, tel. 0294/442-3043).

Lavadero Huemul (Juramento 36, tel. 0294/452-2067) is one of many laundries. For medical services, there's the **Hospital Zonal Bariloche Dr. Ramón Carrillo** (Perito Moreno 601, tel. 0294/442-6100, www.hospitalbariloche.com.ar).

Transportation

AIR

Bariloche is this region's transportation hub. **Aerolíneas Argentinas** (Mitre 185, tel. 0810/2228-6527) flies to Buenos Aires and El Calafate. Twice a week, there is a flight to Mendoza, Salta, and Iguazú. **LATAM/LAN**

(Mitre 534, Local 1, tel. 0810/442-7755) flies daily to Buenos Aires. **LADE** (John O'Connor 214, tel. 0294/442-3562) has cheap flights to Buenos Aires and other Patagonian destinations, but most are only weekly, and schedules often change. **Aeropuerto Teniente Candelaria** (BRC, Ruta Provincial 80 s/n, tel. 0294/440-5016) is 15 kilometers east of Bariloche via RN 40 and RP 80. Micro Ómnibus 3 de Mayo's No. 72 bus goes directly there (US$1.50). Cabs and *remises* to the airport cost about US$18. City buses now use rechargeable magnetic cards, though it's possible to pay cash from the airport and to Cerro Catedral.

BUS

On the eastern outskirts of town, across the Río Ñireco, Bariloche's **Terminal de Ómnibus** (Av. 12 de Octubre 2400, tel. 0294/443-2860) is immediately east of the train station. There are services to Chile, long-distance buses throughout the country, and provincial and regional routes. Some bus companies keep downtown ticket offices, including **Chevallier** (Moreno 107, tel. 0294/442-3090) and the **Vía Bariloche** group (Mitre 321, tel. 0294/442-9012).

Four bus companies cross the Andes to the Chilean cities of Osorno (4-6 hours, US$24-33), Puerto Varas (5.5-6.5 hours), and Puerto Montt (6-7.5 hours): **Andesmar** (tel. 0294/442-2288); **Bus Norte/Cruz del Sur** (tel. 0294/442-2818); and **Vía Bariloche** (tel. 0294/443-2444). Sample domestic destinations include Villa La Angostura (1.5 hours, US$5), El Bolsón (2-2.5 hours, US$6-8), San Martín de los Andes (4 hours, US$14-15), Esquel (4.5 hours, US$16-23), Neuquén (5.5 hours, US$25-40), Comodoro Rivadavia (13-15 hours, US$60), Río Gallegos (24 hours, US$115), El Calafate (30 hours, US$125), El Chaltén (30 hours, US$130), and Buenos Aires (20-25 hours, US$112-145).

From Moreno between Palacios and Beschtedt, where **Micro Ómnibus 3 de Mayo** (Moreno 480, tel. 0294/442-5648) has its office, Línea Catedral goes to Cerro

Catedral (US$1.50) hourly 7am-8pm daily, via Avenida de los Pioneros or via Avenida Bustillo, alternately. For most of the day, 3 de Mayo's bus No. 20 goes every 20 minutes to Llao Llao and Puerto Pañuelo (US$1.50), while bus No. 10 goes to Colonia Suiza seven times daily (four of which reach Bahía López), on the Circuito Chico route through Parque Nacional Nahuel Huapi.

BUS-BOAT SHUTTLE

Cruce Andino (www.cruceandino.com) operates the **bus-boat shuttle** over the Andes to Puerto Montt, Chile (US$280 pp without lunch; national park admission fee and boarding tax not included), via Puerto Pañuelo, Puerto Blest, Puerto Frías, Peulla (Chile), Petrohué, and Puerto Varas. With an overnight at Peulla, the trip costs US$400-450 pp, depending on the hotel. For bookings, contact **Turisur** (Mitre 219, tel. 0294/442-6109, www.turisur.com.ar). It's also possible to do this trip in segments or as a round-trip, say from Puerto Pañuelo to Puerto Blest and back.

CAR RENTAL

Bariloche has several car rental agencies, including **Avis** (San Martín 162, 1st Fl., tel. 0294/443-1648), **Budget** (Mitre 717, tel. 0294/442-2482), and **Hertz** (Elflein 190, tel. 0294/442-3457).

TRAIN

Immediately west of the bus terminal, the **Tren Patagónico** (Av. 12 de Octubre s/n, tel. 0294/442-3172, www.trenpatagonico-sa.com. ar) provides weekly rail transport to Viedma, but service is often subject to interruptions.

PARQUE NACIONAL NAHUEL HUAPI

In 1903, Patagonian explorer Francisco Pascasio Moreno donated three square leagues of "the most beautiful scenery my eyes had ever seen," at Lago Nahuel Huapi's west end, near the Chilean border, to "be conserved as a natural public park." Citing the United States' example, Moreno's burst of idealism returned

part of a personal land grant to the Argentine state. First known as Parque Nacional del Sur, the property became today's Parque Nacional Nahuel Huapi.

Since then, countless Argentine and foreign visitors have enjoyed Moreno's generosity in a reserve that now encompasses a far larger area of glacial lakes and limpid rivers, forested moraines and mountains, and snow-topped Andean peaks that mark the border. So many have done so, in fact, that it's debatable whether authorities have complied with Moreno's wish that "the current features of their perimeter not be altered, and that there be no additional constructions other than those that facilitate the comforts of the cultured visitor."

Prior to the "Conquest of the Desert," Mapuche peoples freely crossed the Andes via the Paso de los Vuriloches south of 3,554-meter Cerro Tronador. The pass lent its name to Bariloche, which, over a century since its 1903 founding, has morphed from lakeside hamlet to a sprawling city whose wastes imperil the air, water, and surrounding woodlands.

For all that, Nahuel Huapi remains a beautiful place connecting two countries via a series of scenic roads and waterways. In 1979, Argentine and Chilean military dictatorships fortified the borders and mined the approaches because of a territorial dispute elsewhere, but a papal intervention cleared the air and perhaps reflected Moreno's aspirations:

> This land of beauty in the Andes is home to a colossal peak shared by two nations: Monte Tronador unites both of them.... Together, they could rest and share ideas there; they could find solutions to problems unsolved by diplomacy. Visitors from around the world would mingle and share with one another at this international crossroads.

Orientation

Now stretching from the northerly Lago Queñi, west of San Martín de los Andes, to

Parque Nacional Nahuel Huapi

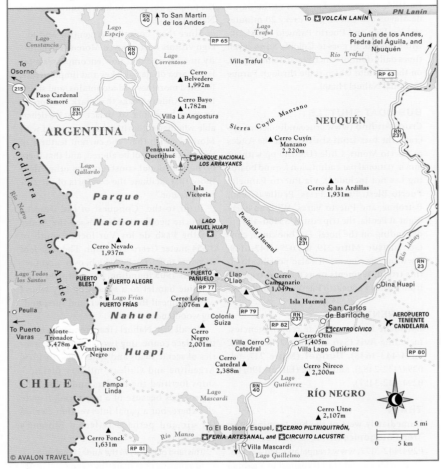

To San Martín
de los Andes

RN 40

Lago
Espejo

Lago
Constancia

RN 40

Lago
Correntoso

To
Osorno

215

Paso Cardenal
Samoré

RN 231

ARGENTINA

Lago
Gallardo

Cerro
▲ Belvedere
1,992m

Cerro Bayo
▲ 1,782m

Villa La Angostura

Península
Quetrihué

◆PARQUE NACIONAL
LOS ARRAYANES

Isla
Victoria

To
San Martín

Lago
Traful

RP 65

Villa Traful

To **VOLCÁN LANÍN**

PN Lanín

To Junín de los Andes,
Piedra del Águila, and
Neuquén

Río Traful

RP 63

Sierra Cuyín Manzano

NEUQUÉN

▲ Cerro Cuyín
Manzano
2,220m

RN 237

Cordillera de los Andes

Río Negro

Parque

Nacional

▲ Cerro Nevado
1,937m

Lago Todos
los Santos

PUERTO
BLEST

PUERTO ALEGRE

Lago Frías
PUERTO FRÍAS

Peulla

To Puerto
Varas

Monte
Tronador
3,478m

Ventisquero
Negro

CHILE

Pampa
Linda

Cerro Fonck
1,631m

RP 81

LAGO
NAHUEL HUAPI
★

Península Huemul

▲ Cerro de las Ardillas
1,931m

RN 231

Río Limay

RN 23

PUERTO
PANUELO

RP 77

Llao
Llao

Cerro
Campanario
1,049m

Dina Huapi

Cerro López
2,076m ▲

Nahuel

Colonia
Suiza

RP 79

Cerro
Negro
2,001m

Cerro
Catedral ▲
2,388m

Huapi

Villa Cerro
Catedral

Isla Huemul

RN 237

RP 82

San Carlos
de Bariloche

CENTRO CÍVICO

Cerro Otto
1,405m

Villa Lago Gutiérrez

Cerro Ñireco
▲ 2,200m

Lago
Gutiérrez

RÍO NEGRO

AEROPUERTO
TENIENTE
CANDELARIA

RP 80

Lago
Mascardi

RN 40

Cerro Utne
▲ 2,107m

To El Bolsón, Esquel, ★**CERRO PILTRIQUITRÓN,**
★**FERIA ARTESANAL, and** ★**CIRCUITO LACUSTRE**

Villa Mascardi

Río Manso

Lago Guillelmo

0   5 mi

0   5 km

© AVALON TRAVEL

the southerly Río Manso, midway between Bariloche and El Bolsón, the park covers 717,000 hectares in southwestern Neuquén and western Río Negro. Together with Parque Nacional Lanín to the north, it forms an uninterrupted stretch well over one million hectares, but part of that is a *reserva nacional* that permits some commercial development. At the park's western edge, Tronador is the highest of a phalanx of snow-covered border peaks.

Flora and Fauna

The flora and fauna resemble those of Lanín to the north and Los Alerces to the south, with minor differences. There are three principal ecosystems: the easterly Patagonian steppe, the Andean-Patagonian forest, and the high Andes above 1,600 meters elevation, which consists of low shrubs and sparse grasses adapted to cold, wind, and snow.

Guanacos graze the semiarid steppe grasslands, stalked by foxes and even pumas, while raptors like the cinereous harrier and American kestrel patrol the skies. Toward the west, open woodlands of coniferous cypress, *ñire* (southern false beech), and *maitén* stand among rocky soils.

Farther west, at slightly higher elevations, dense southern beech forests of *coihue, lenga,* and *ñire* cover the slopes. The shoreline and stream banks burst with a flowering understory of *notro* and climbing vines like *mutisia,* with clusters of the cinnamon-barked *arrayán.*

Near Puerto Blest, rainfall up to 4,000 millimeters per year supports a humid Valdivian forest of Guaiteca cypress, *Podocarpus,* and tree ferns. Nahuel Huapi, though, lacks Lanín's araucaria forests, and the more southerly *alerce* tree is less abundant than in Chubut.

Sightings of the *huemul* (Andean deer) and the miniature *pudú* deer are rare. Other mammals include the carnivorous *huillín* (otter) and the *tuco-tuco,* an endemic gopher-like rodent.

Normally ocean-going, the king cormorant has a colony along Lago Nahuel Huapi, where the kelp gull often trails the boats that sail the lake. Nahuel Huapi, its tributary streams, and other lakes teem with trout and other fish.

★ Lago Nahuel Huapi

Nahuel Huapi's focal point is its namesake lake, whose finger-like channels converge near the Llao Llao peninsula to form the main part of its 560-square-kilometer surface. With a maximum depth of 454 meters, it drains eastward into the Río Limay, a Río Negro tributary.

In the middle of Nahuel Huapi's northern arm, **Isla Victoria** once housed the APN's park ranger school (now at Córdoba), which trained rangers from throughout the Americas. From Puerto Pañuelo, Turisur's *Modesta Victoria* (Mitre 219, tel. 0294/442-6109, www.turisur.com.ar, US$53 plus US$10 national park admission fee) sails once a day to the island, while the *Cau Cau* (Mitre 139, tel. 0294/443-1372, www.islavictoriayarrayanes.com, US$53 plus US$10 national park admission fee) goes twice. Both continue to Parque Nacional Los Arrayanes (which is more accessible from Villa La Angostura, on the north shore).

Circuito Chico

The Circuito Chico is the most popular way to explore the national park from Bariloche. Following the route takes about a day. There are several possible hikes along the way, as

Lago Nahuel Huapi

The Legacy of Perito Moreno

The career of Francisco Pascasio Moreno (1852-1919) began improbably at his father's Buenos Aires insurance agency but, by age 20, the inquisitive young man had founded the Sociedad Científica Argentina (Argentine Scientific Society). From 1875, when much of Patagonia was still hostile territory, he explored the Río Negro and Limay valleys up to Lago Nahuel Huapi (twice), and the Río Santa Cruz to its source at Lago San Martín. On his 1879-1880 Nahuel Huapi expedition, he fell prisoner to previously friendly Manzanero people—for whom he evinced a sympathy that was unfashionable during General Roca's Conquest of the Desert—and escaped down the Río Limay on a precarious log raft.

In 1884, dedicated to the public good, Moreno donated his natural history collections to the Museo Antropológico y Etnológico de Buenos Aires, which became the Museo de Historia Natural de La Plata (which U.S. surveyor Bailey Willis compared with the Smithsonian Institution). In 1897, recognizing Moreno's knowledge of the region, the government named the *perito* (expert) its delegate to a commission settling border differences with Chile. Five years later, he oversaw the placement of permanent boundary markers.

The following year, honoring his services, the government granted Moreno a Nahuel Huapi property near the Chilean border, which the altruistic public servant returned on the stipulation that it become the cornerstone of a national park system. In 1908, he founded the Argentine Boy Scouts; in 1913 he hosted former U.S. president Theodore Roosevelt at Bariloche.

Only a few years later, dismayed by changes in a country that ignored his ideas, feeling betrayed and bitter like San Martín a century earlier, Moreno died in near poverty in Buenos Aires. In Patagonia, his public legacy is a few frequently confused place-names: a street in Bariloche, his namesake lake to the west, the dusty provincial town of Perito Moreno, Parque Nacional Perito Moreno, and the famous Glaciar Perito Moreno.

Yet according to Willis (whose own name graces a peak near Bariloche), Moreno was the first to grasp Patagonia's potential as a "national asset" that needed impartial research to be properly unlocked: "Among men of Moreno's nationality, personal ambition is more often than not the ruling motive. But he was selfless where knowledge of the truth was his objective."

well as spots where you might want to linger, depending upon your interest and the amount of time you have. The roughly 45-kilometer excursion leads west, out along Avenida Bustillo to Península Llao Llao, and returns via the hamlet of Colonia Suiza, at the foot of Cerro López, which makes a good stop for lunch. It's easily accessible by car, bicycle, or public transportation. Public buses will pick up and drop off passengers almost anywhere along the route. Many Bariloche agencies offer the Circuito Chico as a half-day tour (about US$20 pp), but it's cheaper to use public transportation.

For exceptional panoramas of Nahuel Huapi and surroundings, take the chairlift **Aerosilla Campanario** (Av. Bustillo, Km 17.5, tel. 0294/442-7274, 9am-6:30pm daily, US$12 pp) to the 1,050-meter summit of

Cerro Campanario. There's a *confitería* at the summit.

The bus-boat Cruce Andino trip to Chile starts at **Puerto Pañuelo,** but excursions to Isla Victoria and Parque Nacional Los Arrayanes (across the lake) also leave from here. The outstanding cultural landmark is the **Llao Llao Hotel & Resort** (Av. Bustillo, Km 25, tel. 0294/444-8530, www.llaollao.com), a Bustillo creation opened to nonguests for guided tours (US$3 pp, advance reservation required).

Almost immediately west of Puerto Pañuelo, a level footpath from the parking area leads southwest to an *arrayán* forest in **Parque Municipal Llao Llao;** the trail rejoins with the paved road near **Lago Escondido.** The road itself passes a trailhead for **Cerro Llao Llao,** a short but stiff climb offering fine panoramas of Nahuel Huapi and the Andean crest. On the descent, the trail joins a gravel road that rejoins the paved road from Puerto Pañuelo, which leads south before looping northeast toward Bariloche. A gravel alternative heads east to **Colonia Suiza,** known for its Sunday crafts fair, which also occurs on Wednesday in summer. There's a spectacular assortment of foods available, including sweets, desserts, and *curanto* (a mixture of beef, lamb, pork, chicken, sausage, potatoes, sweet potatoes, and other vegetables, baked on heated earth-covered stones). The *curanto* requires reservations, which can be made at Abuela Goye shops or by phone (tel. 0294/444-8605).

On any day, try the regional menu at **Fundo Colonia Suiza** (tel. 0294/444-8619, noon-8pm daily summer, noon-7pm daily fall-spring, US$15). The individual *tabla* of smoked venison, pork, trout, salami, and cheese is an unusual but welcome practice; most such restaurants have a two-person minimum.

From Colonia Suiza, a zigzag dirt road suitable for 4WD vehicles and mountain bikes climbs toward **Refugio López** (tel. 0294/15-458-0321, www.cerrolopez.com, mid-Dec.-late Mar., US$15 pp, with kitchen use), at 1,620 meters elevation. Farther west and near the junction of the paved and gravel roads, a steep footpath climbs 2.5 hours to Refugio López.

From Refugio López (a good place for a break and a beer), the route continues to **Pico Turista,** a strenuous scramble over rugged volcanic terrain. With an early start, experienced hikers may reach the 2,076-meter summit of **Cerro López.**

Cerro Otto

From Bariloche's Barrio Belgrano, Avenida de los Pioneros intersects a gravel road that climbs gently and then steeply west to Cerro Otto's 1,405-meter summit. While it's a feasible eight-kilometer hike or mountain-bike ride, it's easier via the gondolas of **Teleférico Cerro Otto** (Av. de los Pioneros, Km 5, tel. 0294/444-1035, www.telefericobariloche.com.

ar, 10am-6:30pm daily, US$20 adults, US$15 seniors and ages 6-12). A free transfer from the ticket office, downtown at Avenida San Martín and Independencia, is included.

On the summit road, at 1,240 meters elevation, the Club Andino's **Refugio Berghof** (tel. 0294/15-427-1527) serves meals and drinks. Its **Museo de Montaña Otto Meiling** honors a pioneering Andeanist who built his residence here.

Cerro Catedral

Cerro Catedral's 2,388-meter summit overlooks **Villa Catedral,** the ski village that serves **Catedral Alta Patagonia,** the area's major winter-sports resort. From Villa Catedral, the chairlifts **Telesilla Princesa I, II, and III** (9:30am-4:45pm daily, US$24 adults, US$19 children) carry visitors to **Confitería Punta Princesa.** Hikers can continue along the ridgetop to the Club Andino's 40-bed **Refugio Emilio Frey** (tel. 0294/15-435-2222, www.refugiofrey.com, US$12 pp, US$3 for kitchen privileges), at 1,700 meters elevation and open year-round, with meals available. The spire-like summits nearby are a magnet for rock climbers.

Monte Tronador

Its inner fire died long ago, but Tronador's ice-clad volcanic summit still merits its name ("Thunderer") when frozen blocks plunge off its face into the valley below. The peak that surveyor Bailey Willis called "majestic in savage ruggedness" has impressed everyone from Jesuit explorer Miguel de Olivares to Perito Moreno, Theodore Roosevelt, and the hordes that view it every summer. Its ascent, though, is for skilled snow-and-ice climbers only.

Source of the Río Manso, Tronador's icy eastern face gives birth to the **Ventisquero Negro** (Black Glacier), a jumble of ice, sand, and rocky detritus, and countless waterfalls. At Pampa Linda, at the end of the Lago Mascardi road, whistle-blowing rangers prevent hikers from getting too close to the **Garganta del Diablo,** the area's largest accessible waterfall.

From Pampa Linda, hikers on a two-day trek (requiring access to Chile) can visit Club Andino's basic **Refugio Viejo Tronador** (a kiln-shaped structure that sleeps a maximum of 10 climbers in bivouac conditions) via a trail on the road's south side. Information is available at Bariloche's **Club Andino** (20 de Febrero 30, tel. 0294/452-7966, www.cluban-dino.org). On the north side, another trail leads to the 60-bed **Refugio Otto Meiling** (tel. 0294/15-421-3921, www.refugiomeiling. com, US$20 pp, meals extra, camping possible), at 2,000 meters elevation. Between early January and March, well-equipped backpackers can continue north to Laguna Frías via the 1,335-meter Paso de las Nubes and return to Bariloche on the previously booked bus-boat shuttle via Puerto Blest and Puerto Pañuelo.

Reaching the Tronador area requires a roundabout drive via southbound RN 40 to Lago Mascardi's south end, where westbound RP 81 follows the lake's southern shore. At Km 9, a northbound lateral road crosses Río Manso and becomes a single-lane dirt road to Pampa Linda and Tronador's base. Because it is narrow, morning traffic (10:30am-2pm daily) is one-way inbound, afternoon traffic (4pm-6pm daily) is one-way outbound, and at other times (7:30pm-9am daily) the road is open to cautious two-way traffic. From December to Easter holidays, **Active Patagonia** (tel. 0294/452-9875, www.active-patagonia.com.ar) provides transportation from Club Andino's Bariloche headquarters to Pampa Linda at 8:30am daily, returning at 5pm (reservations required, 2 hours, US$14 each way).

Food and Accommodations

Campgrounds are numerous, especially in areas accessible by road. Club Andino *refugios* (shelters) also provide moderately priced meals. Though *refugios* don't take reservations for bunks, which are limited, it is always advisable to check first at **Club Andino** (20 de Febrero 30, tel. 0294/452-7966, www.cluban-dino.org) in Bariloche in case a large group is

already accommodated. Day hikers can buy simple meals and cold drinks.

Hotels and other accommodations are scattered around various park sectors. At Lago Mascardi's northwest end, on the Pampa Linda road, **Hotel Tronador** (tel. 0294/449-0550, www.hoteltronador.com, US$86-135 s, US$103-185 d with all meals) is a lakes-district classic in the Bustillo tradition. Rates vary according to the room and the season; it's open mid-November to mid-April.

Near road's end, **Hostería Pampa Linda** (tel. 0294/449-0517, www.hosteriapampal-inda.com.ar, US$85 s, US$135 d with breakfast, US$105 s, US$180 d with 2 meals, US$130 s, US$215 d with all meals) is a rustically contemporary inn that also organizes hikes and horseback rides (at additional cost).

Information and Services

For detailed park information and hiking registration, contact the **APN** (San Martín 24, tel. 0294/442-3111, www.nahuelhuapi.gov.ar) or **Club Andino Bariloche** (20 de Febrero 30, tel. 0294/452-7966, www.clubandino.org). The shelters are also good sources of information within the park.

With 48 hours of starting any hike in the park, it is obligatory to inform the national park's *Registro de Trekking* by filling out a free form provided at APN offices, also available on the park's website (www.nahuelhuapi.gov. ar) or at the Club Andino, to be shown to park rangers upon request.

The Club Andino's improved **trail map,** *Refugios, Sendas y Picadas,* at a scale of 1:100,000 with more detailed versions covering smaller areas at a scale of 1:50,000, is a worthwhile acquisition. Pixmap (www.pix-map.com) publishes more sophisticated versions of some areas.

EL BOLSÓN

El Bolsón, Argentine Patagonia's counterculture capital, may be the place to replace your faded tie-dyes. It's also a beautiful spot in a fertile valley between stunning longitudinal mountain ranges ideal for hiking. So far, despite completion of the paved highway from Bariloche, this self-styled "ecological municipality" has managed to stymie five-star hotels and ski areas in favor of simpler, earthier services and activities.

El Bolsón's alternative lifestyle, dating from the 1960s, grew as an island of tolerance and tranquility even during the Dirty War dictatorship. More affordable than Bariloche, it embraces visitors, turns its agricultural bounty of apples, cherries, pears, raspberries, and strawberries into delectable edibles, and makes local hops into distinctive brews.

El Bolsón (pop. 19,000, elev. 300 meters) is 123 kilometers south of Bariloche via RN 40 and 167 kilometers north of Esquel via RN 259 and RN 40. West of the south-flowing Río Quemquemtreu, the Cordón Nevado's snowy ridge marks the Chilean border, while Cerro Piltriquitrón's knife-edge crest rises to the east. Surrounding an artificial lake, the elliptical Plaza Pagano is the town's civic center and the site of its popular street fair.

★ Feria Artesanal

Buskers, bakers, candle-makers, flower arrangers, and other craft workers have transformed El Bolsón's street fair from a once-a-week gathering to a Tuesday, Thursday, and Saturday event that nearly encircles Plaza Pagano. In summer, there's also a smaller version on Sunday. Forgo a restaurant lunch and snack to the max on the Belgian waffles, empanadas, sandwiches, sausages, and sweets, and wash them all down with freshly brewed draft beer. It starts about 10am and winds down around 4pm.

Shopping

The Mapuche-oriented **Centro Artesanal Cumei Antu** (Av. San Martín 1920, tel. 0294/445-5322) sells indigenous textiles. **Cabaña Micó** (Islas Malvinas 2753, tel. 0294/449-2691, www.mico.com.ar) sells fresh fruit from its own vines in season, and homemade preserves the rest of the year.

Entertainment and Events

Founded in 1926, the city celebrates its **Aniversario** on January 28. Local brewers take center stage in mid-February's four-day **Festival Nacional del Lúpulo** (National Hops Festival, www.festivaldelacosechadelupulo.com). In high season, a few evenings a week at the Auditorio El Pitío in Villa Turismo, **Languedoc** (Tres Cipreses s/n,

Waffles with fresh raspberries are a staple of Bolsón's Feria Artesanal.

El Bolsón

To Bariloche

HOSTERÍA CARPE DIEM

25 DE MAYO

BALCARCE

STO CABRAL

MERINO

HOTEL COMARCA

AMANCAY HOTEL

Plaza España

LAVERAP EL BOLSÓN

HERNÁNDEZ

ISLAS MALVINAS

ONELLI

AV. SACRAMENTO

RIVADAVIA

LARREA

AZCUÉNAGA

To Río Azul and Cabeza del Indio

HOSTERÍA LA ESCAMPADA

ALTE BROWN

CYBERIA

POST OFFICE

JAUJA

DORREGO

INFORMES DE MONTAÑA

BANCO PATAGONIA

PULMARI

CARLITOS

OTTO TIPP

SECRETARÍA DE TURISMO

GRAL ROCA

CLUB ANDINO PILTRIQUITRÓN

VÍA BARILOCHE

CABAÑA MICÓ

ULIEDIN

AV. SAN MARTÍN

Plaza Pagano

HOSPITAL DE ÁREA

FELICIANO

SAAVEDRA

MIGUEL ANDEN

LINIERS

AMEGHINO

FERIA ARTESANAL

PELLEGRINI

BANCO DE LA NACIÓN

MITSKI COCOA

LA NONA

MAPUTUR/ MAR Y VALLE

RANCHONET

PABLO   HUBE

GRADO 42/TRANSPORTES ESQUEL / TAQSA/ MARGA

PERITO

AVENIDA BELGRANO

ACA

FRENCH

LA SALTEÑITA

ANDESMAR

PASIONES ARGENTINAS

BERUTTI

CASTELLI

0   200 yds

0   200 m

MORENO

GÜEMES

To Parque Nacional Lago Puelo

To El Hoyo, Parque Nacional Los Alerces, Villa Turismo, and Esquel

© AVALON TRAVEL

www.languedoc.com.ar, tel. 0294/449-2723) performs theatrical medieval and renaissance music concerts.

Sports and Recreation

Several travel agencies arrange excursions such as boating on Lago Puelo, hiking and climbing, horseback riding, mountain biking, rafting on the Río Azul and the more distant Río Manso, and parasailing. Where logistics are complex, as in reaching some trailheads, these excursions can be a good option.

Local operators include **Grado 42** (Av. Belgrano 406, tel. 0294/449-3124, www. grado42.com), **Maputur** (Av. San Martín 2501, tel. 0294/449-1440, www.maputur. com.ar), and **Pulmari** (Perito Moreno 2871, tel. 0294/449-3093, www.pulmariturismo. com.ar).

Food

Given the fresh fruit and vegetables, El Bolsón's food exceeds expectations, though it lacks sophistication. Give up one lunch in favor of snacking at Plaza Pagano's **Feria Artesanal**. Most places in El Bolsón stay open all day, serving breakfast, lunch, and dinner, and many of them have Wi-Fi.

La Salteñita (Av. Belgrano 515, tel. 0294/449-3749) serves spicy northern empanadas for takeout. **Mitski Cocoa** (Av. San Martín 2526, tel. 0294/449-1878) is an ideal breakfast spot for succulent croissants and hot chocolate. Nonspicy and still tasty empanadas are served at the popular bakery **La Nona** (Av. San Martín 2525, tel. 0294/449-2413), which also has a few tables outside.

Otto Tipp (Islas Malvinas and Roca, tel. 0294/448-3780) is stylishly Teutonic, with free beer samples in addition to pastas, pizzas, and a *picada* for two that includes smoked venison and wild boar (US$20).

In new quarters east of the main drag, **Carlitos** (Roca and Isla Malvinas, tel. 0294/445-5654, US$13) is a grill restaurant, serving lamb and *bife de chorizo*

(sirloin). **Pasiones Argentinas** (Av. Belgrano and Beruti, tel. 0294/448-3616, noon-4pm and 8pm-midnight Tues.-Sun., US$9-12) serves more elaborate versions of standards such as *bife de chorizo*, pastas, and grilled lamb.

★ **Jauja** (Av. San Martín 2867, tel. 0294/449-2448, noon-4pm and 8pm-11:30pm daily, US$12) is probably the best downtown restaurant. Vivid flower arrangements set the stage for succulent pastas such as gnocchi with a morel mushroom sauce, vegetarian dishes such as quinoa and millet burger with a side of vegetable aioli, trout with a white wine sauce, outstanding homemade bread, and local brews.

Ignore Jauja's in-house desserts and step just outside to ★ **Helados Jauja** (www. heladosjauja.com), one of the country's top ice creameries, with an almost paralyzing choice of nearly 60 inventive flavors. Longstanding favorites include *calafate con leche de oveja* (calafate berry with sheep's milk) and *mate cocido con tres de azúcar* (boiled and slightly sweetened *mate*, though some Argentines blanch at consuming their favorite bitter infusion in frozen form). *Chocolate profundo*, a bittersweet chocolate mousse, is also interesting.

Set among lavender gardens 10 minutes' drive south on the road to Esquel, **Pirque** (RN 40, Km 1903, El Hoyo, tel. 0294/447-1867, US$13-18) offers a sophisticated menu, including native *perca* fish and cypress mushrooms.

Accommodations

El Bolsón has quality accommodations for every budget, except the luxury category (though character often compensates for lack of luxury). Some of the best values are not in town but scattered around the outskirts.

At the north end, directly on the Bariloche highway, **Camping El Bolsón** (RN 40, Km 123.9, tel. 0294/449-2595, www.campingelbolsonruta40@gmail.com, US$7 pp plus US$3 per vehicle) operates its own brewery and beer garden (for another US$1, the rate includes a daily beer).

About three kilometers north of town, **El Pueblito Hostel** (Barrio Luján s/n, tel. 0294/449-8730, www.elpueblitohostel.com.ar, US$15 pp dorms, US$40-46 d), with 40 beds, is a comfortable, sociable place on a large property. There are also separate cabañas, some with shared baths and others with private baths, and Wi-Fi. From downtown El Bolsón, there are hourly buses between 7:45am and 8:45pm, except at 7:45pm; the first transfer is deducted from the bill.

Six kilometers north of town, by a signed dirt road that diverges from the Bariloche highway, the riverside **La Casona de Odile** (Barrio Luján s/n, tel. 0294/449-2753, www.odile.com.ar, US$16 dorms, US$41 d) has reinvented itself as a hostel on lovingly maintained grounds. It's open from late spring to early fall.

On secluded grounds in Barrio Turismo, just off the road to Cerro Piltriquitrón, Hostelling International affiliate ★ **El Mirador Hostel** (Tres Cipreses 1237, tel. 0294/449-8844, www.elmiradorhostel.com.ar, US$18 pp, US$48 d, US$68 house, with breakfast) has four- and six-bed dorms, plus a couple of doubles and a detached house for four, all with private baths. Its pristine facilities and amenities (which include two hectares of woodlands, an orchard, a library, satellite TV, and Wi-Fi) make it El Bolsón's best hostel.

West of the highway on El Bolsón's northern outskirts, **Hostería del Campo** (RN 40 s/n, tel. 0294/449-2297, www.cabaniasdelcampo.com.ar, from US$60 s or d) has quiet motel-style rooms with Wi-Fi and covered parking, set among spacious gardens. Breakfast is extra (US$4).

The **Amancay Hotel** (Av. San Martín 3207, tel. 0294/449-2222, hotelamancay@elbolson.com, US$50 s, US$69 d) is aging, but still serviceable, showing wear but not tear. The four-room **La Posada de Hamelin** (Granollers 2179, tel. 0294/449-2030, www.posadadehamelin.com.ar, US$70 s, US$90 d) is one of El Bolsón's best B&Bs.

Toward the north end of downtown, tranquil ★ **Hostería Carpe Diem** (Perito Moreno 3443, tel. 0294/445-5280, www.carpediemelbolson.com.ar, US$98 s or d) has spacious garden suites with flat-screen TVs, Wi-Fi, a mini-bar, and even whirlpool tubs in every bath. In high season, there's a three-night minimum.

At the edge of Villa Turismo's wooded slopes, the ★ **Buena Vida Social Club** (tel. 0294/449-1729, www.buenavidasocialclubpatagonia.com, Dec.-May, US$80 s, US$100 d) is a delightful five-room B&B run by an artistic Argentine-American couple who designed the place in an aesthetic fusion of styles. Simple comfort and no TV make a relaxing stay. In January and February, single rates rise to US$100; there is a two-night minimum, with no children, smoking, or pets allowed.

In a quiet east-side location, **Hostería La Escampada** (Azcuénaga and 25 de Mayo, tel. 0294/448-3905, www.laescampada.com, US$60 s, US$95-110 d) is a cozy B&B with Wi-Fi, friendly management, and regional style. For a slightly higher rate, superior doubles have their own whirlpool tubs.

Historically, El Bolsón lacks full-service hotels, but the recently renamed **Cumbres Hotel** (Av. San Martín 3220, tel. 0294/449-2235, www.cumbreshotel.com.ar, US$106-125 s or d) is an attempt to fill the vacuum with a modern 36-room construction. The best rooms have balconies that face toward Piltriquitrón.

Information and Services

At Plaza Pagano's north end, the **Secretaría de Turismo** (Av. San Martín and Roca, tel. 0294/449-2604, www.turismoelbolson.gob.ar, 8am-9pm Mon.-Fri., 9am-9pm Sat.-Sun. summer, 8am-8pm Mon.-Fri., 9am-8pm Sat.-Sun. fall-spring) provides decent maps of accommodations and other services. It even employs an accommodations specialist who makes suggestions and books hotels.

For hiking and climbing suggestions, visit the **Club Andino Piltriquitrón** (Sarmiento between Roca and Ulieldin, tel.

0294/449-2600, www.capiltriquitron.com.ar, 6pm-8pm Mon.-Fri.). For information on mountain huts and camping in the vicinity, contact **Informes de Montaña** (Onelli and Roca, tel. 0294/445-5810, cerros_elbolson@hotmail.com).

For motorists, **ACA** (Av. Belgrano and Av. San Martín, tel. 0294/449-2260) is a resource. **Banco de la Nación** (Av. San Martín 2598) and **Banco Patagonia** (Av. San Martín 2831) have ATMs.

The postal code for **Correo Argentino** (Av. San Martín 2806) is 8430. **Ranchonet** (Av. San Martín and Pablo Hube) has the best Internet connections. Phones and Internet access are also available at **Cyberia** (Av. San Martín and Dorrego).

Laverap El Bolsón (José Hernández 223, tel. 0294/449-3243) not only does the washing, but they will also pick up and deliver. The **Hospital de Área** (Perito Moreno s/n, tel. 0294/449-2240) is immediately east of Plaza Pagano.

Transportation

El Bolsón lacks a central bus terminal, but most companies are within a few blocks of each other, and several travel agencies are not only sales offices but bus stops too.

Andesmar (Belgrano and Perito Moreno, tel. 0294/449-2178) buses go to Bariloche, Buenos Aires (with a change in Bariloche), and south to Esquel. **Vía Bariloche** (Roca and Onelli, tel. 0294/445-5554) buses go to Esquel, Bariloche, Comodoro Rivadavia, Puerto Madryn, Buenos Aires, and northbound destinations as far as San Salvador de Jujuy. **Mar y Valle** (San Martín 2501, tel. 0294/449-1440) goes to Esquel and Puerto Madryn.

Grado 42 (Belgrano 406, tel. 0294/449-3124, www.grado42.com) represents Taqsa/Marga, which goes to El Calafate and El Chaltén, and Transportes Esquel, which goes to Esquel via Parque Nacional Los Alerces, running transfer services to its northernmost stop at Lago Puelo. Grado 42 also operates its own regular service to El Maitén (8:30pm Mon.-Fri., 1:30pm Sat. US$8).

The usual destinations are Bariloche (2-2.5 hours, US$6-8) and Esquel (2-3 hours, US$15-17). For most coastal destinations, like Puerto Madryn, it's better to backtrack to Bariloche. There are regular services to Comodoro Rivadavia (US$51-59). Fares to other northbound destinations are slightly more expensive than those from Bariloche; fares to southbound destinations are slightly cheaper.

For a small town, El Bolsón has fine public transportation for excursions like Cerro Piltriquitrón and Lago Puelo. There are also abundant radio taxis.

VICINITY OF EL BOLSÓN

One of El Bolsón's virtues is its convenience to trailheads for hiking and secondary roads for mountain biking. Most are just far enough away, though, to require an early start for those without their own vehicle. Consider hiring a *remise* (radio taxi) to the trailheads. Hikers should look for *Guía Educativa: Informes de Montaña,* an inexpensive local hiking guide for sale in El Bolsón's tourist office, whose separate **Informes de Montaña** (Onelli and Roca, tel. 0294/445-5810) will have the latest unprinted info. Although it's in Spanish, it summarizes trail descriptions in English, and its basic orientation maps are adequate for initial planning. Try also the **Club Andino Piltriquitrón** (Sarmiento between Roca and Ulieldin, tel. 0294/449-2600, www.capiltriquitron.com.ar, 6pm-8pm Mon.-Fri.).

Both east and west of town, there's a growing number of backcountry *refugios* (shelters) where hikers can either camp or hire a bunk or floor space, and cook or purchase meals. These are fairly basic, but inexpensive and comfortable enough, and the *refugieros* who run them have built a series of connector trails to supplement the access points and create a hikers' circuit.

Two blocks north of Plaza Pagano, westbound Azcuénaga crosses the Quemquemtreu and continues six kilometers to a footpath overlooking its southerly confluence with the Río Azul and, in the distance, Lago Puelo. The short but precipitous northbound trail leads to the natural metamorphic silhouette colloquially known as the **Cabeza del Indio** (Indian's Head). There's now a small admission charge.

About six kilometers north of town via the Bariloche road, a northwesterly gravel road leads to a signed southwesterly turnoff to the municipal **Reserva Forestal Loma del Medio-Río Azul** (US$2). Its main attraction is an 800-meter loop trail to the **Cascada Escondida,** where the river follows a fault before tumbling down the titled face in a classic bridal veil. It's best during spring runoff, when the volume of water turns the single falls into two or three larger ones.

About 10 kilometers north of town by the same main road, but via a northeasterly lateral road, the **Cascada Mallín Ahogado** (US$2) is a 20-meter waterfall on the Quemquemtreu tributary of the Arroyo del Medio. Diverted for agriculture, it's also best in early spring. The caretaker has carved scale models of traditional oxcarts, wheelbarrows, and the like.

A parallel main road continues 15 kilometers northwest to Club Andino's 70-bunk **Refugio Perito Moreno** (tel. 0294/448-3433, US$13 pp). A small ski area, at a base elevation of 1,000 meters, has a chairlift and a T-bar lift to 1,450 meters. From the *refugio,* the 2,206-meter summit of **Cerro Perito Moreno** is about a three-hour hike. The *refugio* is busiest in summer; meals are also available here.

Cajón del Azul

Immediately west of Mallín Ahogado, 15 kilometers northwest of El Bolsón, a signed gravel road drops steeply into the Río Azul canyon. Río Azul waters flow eastward before turning sharply south at the confluence with the Río Blanco. Where the rivers meet, only accessible by 4WD vehicle, **La Confluencia Lodge & Farm** (tel. 02944/49-8329, www.laconfluencia.com, US$95-165 s, US$115-185

d, with breakfast) is a new sustainable development project with six double rooms and one suite, plus an organic restaurant using produce from its own gardens (lunch costs US$20, dinner US$30). Transfers in and out are free; there is also "The Roost," a separate bunkhouse that provides backpacker-friendly accommodations.

Beyond the Arco Iris campground, where the road ends, two precarious pedestrian bridges cross the rivers before the trail becomes an up-and-down hike leading to a sheer-sided gorge. Here, beneath a sturdy log bridge, the spring runoff explodes like a cannon shot.

Just across the bridge, about 3.5 hours from the confluence, **Refugio Cajón del Azul** (US$6 pp camping, US$22 pp dorms) is open year-round. Run by an English-speaking semi-hermit named Atilio, the *refugio* (shelter) also offers camping and mattresses for overnighters in a communal dorm. Atilio provides free coffee, tea, or *mate* to every arrival. Though dark, the rustically comfortable *refugio* even has a water-driven turbine for electricity. Most supplies arrive on horseback, though in summer and fall Atilio's irrigated grounds provide fresh apples, cherries, peaches, plums, raspberries, and the like. The westbound trail continues another hour or more to **Refugio El Retamal** (refugioelretamal@hotmail.com, US$16 pp bunks, US$6 pp camping).

An alternative northwesterly trail from the Arco Iris trailhead dead-ends at **Refugio Dedo Gordo** (US$13 pp bunks, US$5 pp camping), providing access for experienced hikers to its namesake 2,065-meter summit. Before the final climb to Refugio Cajón del Azul, a new but poorly signed trail climbs steeply southward and then drops into the Arroyo Teno drainage and **Refugio Hielo Azul** (tel. 0294/445-5532, www.refugiohieloazul.com.ar, US$19 pp bunks, US$6 pp camping). This route allows overnighters to loop back to El Bolsón.

★ Cerro Piltriquitrón

East of El Bolsón, the piedmont rises steadily and then sharply to 2,284-meter **Cerro Piltriquitrón**'s granite summit. Clear days reveal the snow-covered phalanx of peaks along the Chilean border, from Tronador and beyond in the north to Lago Puelo and beyond the Cordón Esperanza in the south. When the clouds clear, Volcán Osorno's Fuji-perfect cone, in Chile, appears almost immediately west of Tronador.

From El Bolsón, a winding dirt road climbs 13 kilometers to a parking area at the 1,200-meter level, where a steep footpath leads to the **Bosque Tallado** (US$5 pp). Here, chainsaw carvers have transformed trunks from a scorched *lenga* forest into 50 memorable sculptures.

Beyond the Bosque Tallado, the trail climbs to the Club Andino's **Refugio Piltriquitrón** (US$10 pp bunks, camping free) at 1,400 meters elevation. You need your own sleeping bag for the bunks; meals are also available. This was once a ski area, and the path climbs even more steeply along the rusty T-bar cable before leveling off and rounding Piltriquitrón; marked by paint blazes, it then climbs steeply over loose talus to the summit. From the *refugio,* it takes two or three hours to reach the summit. Carry water and high-energy snacks.

In summer, by reservation only, **Grado 42** (Av. Belgrano 406, tel. 0294/449-3124, www.grado42.com) goes to the parking area at 9am daily, returning at 12:30pm. The fare is US$19 round-trip, while a radio taxi costs about US$30.

Cerro Piltriquitrón rises behind El Bolsón's Plaza Pagano.

Interior Chubut Province

PARQUE NACIONAL LAGO PUELO

Fed by four rivers and numerous arroyos, nearly surrounded by forested peaks, Lago Puelo is the turquoise showpiece of its namesake national park. In addition to its scenery, it's popular for camping, swimming, boating, and hiking, and it offers a little-used option for crossing into Chile that may become a ferry-vehicle shuttle. Unlike most Argentine lakes, Puelo drains toward the Pacific.

Just 15 kilometers south of El Bolsón, Lago Puelo lies across the Chubut provincial line. It encompasses 27,674 hectares of mountainous forested land. The Río Azul's lakeshore deltas lie to the north and the Río Turbio is across the lake to the south. The lake is only 200 meters above sea level, but the summits rise above 1,500 meters.

Flora and Fauna

The park's flora and fauna resemble those of Nahuel Huapi to the north and Los Alerces to the south. Its relatively low elevations and exposure to Pacific storms, though, create a mild lakeshore microclimate that permits the growth of tree species like the *ulmo,* with its showy white flowers, and the *lingue.* The *huemul* (Andean deer) and *pudú* (miniature deer) are present but rarely seen.

Sports and Recreation

Several trailheads start near the Oficina de Informes. The most popular is the **Sendero al Mirador del Lago** to the east, which climbs 130 meters to an overlook.

To the west, the **Senda Los Hitos** fords the Río Azul and leads five kilometers to Arroyo Las Lágrimas, where Chile-bound hikers can complete Argentine border formalities. Thirteen kilometers farther west, well into Chilean territory, Carabineros finish the paperwork; from there, continue to the Chilean

town of Puelo, with onward connections to Puerto Montt.

For most visitors, sailing the lake is the main attraction. The **Juana de Arco** (tel. 0294/449-8946, tel. 0294/15-463-3838, www.interpatagonia.com, from 11am daily) and other smaller boats carry passengers on half-hour excursions (US$13 pp) and also on longer rides, including to the Chilean border (US$20 pp).

Camping

Near the passenger pier, **Camping Delta del Río Azul** (tel. 0294/15-420-1664, US$11 pp), has limited services. In addition, there are free campsites at **Arroyo Las Lágrimas,** about five kilometers west on the footpath to the border, and other sites at **Río Turbio** (free), at the lake's south end.

Transportation and Services

Near the park entrance, where rangers collect US$6 pp for Argentina residents, US$10 per person for foreigners, the helpful **Oficina de Informes** (tel. 02944/49-9232, lagopuelo@apn.gov.ar, 9am-8pm daily summer, more limited hours fall-spring) provides practical information on attractions and activities.

From El Bolsón, Transporte La Golondrina **buses** (9am-10:30pm daily summer) shuttle down Avenida San Martín to the pier and back 14 times daily. There are two early morning runs that only reach the park entrance, which is also the terminal point for all off-season services.

EL MAITÉN

In 1979, Paul Theroux's dyspeptic opus *The Old Patagonian Express* made the dying narrow-gauge railroad a local legend. Its antique steam locomotives no longer traverse the entire 402-kilometer route, but the dusty township of El Maitén, with its rusting rails, weathered workshops, and twirling turntables, is the best place to savor this picturesque economic folly. Like Esquel, it retains enough rolling stock that committed train-spotters can board this living anachronism and fill their photo albums in the process.

El Maitén (pop. 6,300) is 70 kilometers southeast of El Bolsón via RN 40 and RP 70. It's 130 kilometers north of Esquel via RN 40 and its spur RN 1s40.

La Trochita

Gringos may cite the Gospel of Theroux, but Argentines know the train as **La Trochita** (a diminutive for "gauge") or El Trencito (Little Train). The yards are still open, although only a couple of locomotives (an American Baldwin and a 1922 German Henschel) are in running order. The mostly Belgian cars date from 1922 to about 1960.

February's **Fiesta Nacional del Tren a Vapor** (National Steam Train Festival) fills the handful of hotels and campgrounds. Celebrating the railroad, it also features live music on a custom-built stage, horseback races, bronco-busting, and regional delicacies.

Excursions to Desvío Thomae (2.5 hours, US$32 pp for foreigners), the first station south of El Maitén, and back usually run from January to the Easter holidays once or twice weekly, more frequently in January and during the steam train festival. Excursions include a visit to a small but interesting museum at the old station and to the nearby workshops. For reservations, contact **Grado 42** (Av. Belgrano 406, El Bolsón, tel. 0294/449-3124; Av. San Martín 1135, El Maitén, tel. 02945/49-5585, www.grado42.com).

For current schedules, contact El Maitén's **Dirección de Turismo** (Av. San Martín 992, tel. 02945/49-5016, www.turismoelmaiten.com.ar, 8am-8pm daily), near the railroad tracks, or **Estación El Maitén** (Pellegrini 841, tel. 02945/49-5190, ferroelmaiten@gmail.com).

Accommodations

The **Camping Municipal** (US$3 pp plus US$3 per vehicle) is on the nearby Río Chubut. **Hostería Refugio Andino** (Av.

San Martín 1179, tel. 02945/49-5309, refugioandino12@hotmail.com, US$11 pp) has accommodations, a restaurant, and long-distance phones.

Transportation

Grado 42 (tel. 02945/49-5585) has minibus service to El Bolsón (US$8) Monday to Saturday, while Transporte La Golondrina (tel. 02944/15-66-4730) goes four times daily. **Jacobsen** (tel. 02945/49-5007) goes to Esquel (2 hours, 4pm Tues. and Thurs.-Fri., US$7).

ESQUEL

Across the Chubut border, the gateway to Parque Nacional Los Alerces and end of the line for the "Old Patagonian Express," Esquel is a deceptively tranquil town of wide avenues divided by densely planted medians. It's also a city divided by a plebiscite that rejected a nearby gold mine that would have used toxic cyanide to leach the mineral wealth. Mapuche militancy is also palpable here: the graffiti says "Neither Argentine nor Chilean, but Mapuche."

A compact grid on the north bank of its namesake arroyo, Esquel (pop. 32,343) is 167 kilometers south of El Bolsón via smoothly-paved RN 40 and RN 259. Alternatively, many visitors take RP 71, south of the town of Epuyén, directly to Parque Nacional Los Alerces. Esquel is also 608 kilometers west of Trelew via several paved highways across the Patagonian steppe, and 581 kilometers northwest of Comodoro Rivadavia via equally good roads. Southbound RN 259 leads to a junction to Parque Nacional Los Alerces, the Welsh-settled town of Trevelin, and the Chilean border at La Balsa.

Sights

From its railroad station, next to the old one converted into a museum, **La Trochita** still makes entertaining excursions to the Mapuche hamlet of Nahuel Pan. Its wooden passenger wagons, with salamander stoves and hard-backed benches, are classics of their era. The entire line is a national historical monument.

Esquel

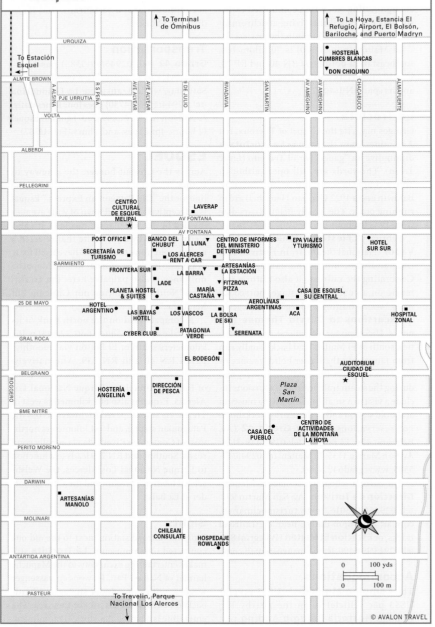

To Terminal de Ómnibus

To La Hoya, Estancia El Refugio, Airport, El Bolsón, Bariloche, and Puerto Madryn

URQUIZA

To Estación Esquel

HOSTERÍA CUMBRES BLANCAS

DON CHIQUINO

ALMTE BROWN

A ALSINA
PJE URRUTIA
R S PEÑA
AVE ALVEAR
AVE ALVEAR
9 DE JULIO
RIVADAVIA
SAN MARTÍN
AV AMEGHINO
AV AMEGHINO
CHACABUCO
ALMAFUERTE

VOLTA

ALBERDI

PELLEGRINI

CENTRO CULTURAL DE ESQUEL MELIPAL ★

LAVERAP

AV FONTANA

AV FONTANA

POST OFFICE

SECRETARÍA DE TURISMO

BANCO DEL CHUBUT

LA LUNA

LOS ALERCES RENT A CAR

CENTRO DE INFORMES DEL MINISTERIO DE TURISMO

EPA VIAJES Y TURISMO

HOTEL SUR SUR

SARMIENTO

FRONTERA SUR

LA BARRA

ARTESANÍAS LA ESTACIÓN

PLANETA HOSTEL & SUITES

LADE

MARÍA CASTAÑA

FITZROYA PIZZA

CASA DE ESQUEL, SU CENTRAL

25 DE MAYO

HOTEL ARGENTINO

LAS BAYAS HOTEL

LOS VASCOS

LA BOLSA DE SKI

AEROLÍNAS ARGENTINAS

ACA

HOSPITAL ZONAL

CYBER CLUB

PATAGONIA VERDE

SERENATA

GRAL ROCA

EL BODEGÓN

AUDITORIUM CIUDAD DE ESQUEL ★

BELGRANO

ROGGERO

HOSTERÍA ANGELINA

DIRECCIÓN DE PESCA

Plaza San Martín

BME MITRE

CENTRO DE ACTIVIDADES DE LA MONTAÑA LA HOYA

CASA DEL PUEBLO

PERITO MORENO

DARWIN

ARTESANÍAS MANOLO

MOLINARI

CHILEAN CONSULATE

HOSPEDAJE ROWLANDS

ANTÁRTIDA ARGENTINA

0   100 yds

0   100 m

PASTEUR

To Trevelin, Parque Nacional Los Alerces

As the train departs, residents leave their houses and cars to wave as it chugs past their backyards and crosses the highway. Each passenger coach has a guide, but the rolling stock is so noisy that understanding the narration is difficult.

The train takes about an hour to reach Nahuel Pan, where there are good oven-baked empanadas, drinks, Mapuche crafts, and short horseback rides, as well as spare time to visit the **Museo de Culturas Originarias Patagónicas** (open for train arrivals). La Trochita remains for about an hour before returning to Esquel.

Excursions (US$40 pp foreigners, cash only) usually run from October to the Easter holidays, plus winter holidays, operating up to thrice daily in summer and reducing in frequencies the rest of the season to Saturday-only service. It's advisable to buy tickets in advance. For details, contact **Estación Esquel** (Roggero and Urquiza, tel. 02945/45-1403).

In the utterly transformed old bus terminal, the **Centro Cultural de Esquel Melipal** (Av. Fontana and Av. Alvear, tel. 02945/45-7154, 7am-9pm Mon.-Fri., 5pm-10pm Sat.-Sun.) encompasses a variety of art and performing arts spaces. The **Auditorium**

Ciudad de Esquel (Belgrano 330, tel. 02945/45-1929) shows first-run movies.

Shopping

Artesanías La Estación (Sarmiento 630, tel. 02945/45-6388) sells crafts, textiles, and other regional products. For wood carvings, try **Artesanías Manolo** (Alsina 483). **Casa de Esquel** (25 de Mayo 415, tel. 02945/45-2544) is a crafts outlet and a bookstore focused on Patagonia. Though adapted to contemporary times, **Los Vascos** (9 de Julio 1000, tel. 02945/45-2352, www.losvascosesquel.com.ar) still displays the diversity of a classic general store.

Sports and Recreation

Hiking, climbing, fishing, horseback riding, and rafting and kayaking are all on the docket. Argentina's Río Corcovado is a Class II-III starter river, but the Class V Futaleufú, across the Chilean border, has world-class white water.

Patagonia Verde (9 de Julio 926, tel. 02945/45-4396, www.patagonia-verde.com.ar) arranges activities like hiking, climbing, and riding. **Frontera Sur** (Sarmiento 784, tel. 02945/45-0505, www.fronterasur.net) organizes water sports like rafting (US$75 for a

La Trochita, the famous narrow gauge steam train, steams out of Esquel.

full day) and kayaking on the Corcovado, as well as hiking, riding, and mountain biking. **Epa Viajes y Turismo** (Av. Fontana 482, tel. 02945/45-7015, www.grupoepa.com) also does rafting and other activities.

For fishing licenses, contact the **Secretaría de Pesca** (Belgrano 722, tel. 02945/45-1063); licenses can also be purchased at some shops and gas stations. The fishing season runs November to April. **Andrés Müller** (Sarmiento 120, tel. 02945/45-4572, framumi@ar.inter.net) is a reliable independent fishing guide.

Food

María Castaña (25 de Mayo 605, tel. 02945/45-1752, 8am-midnight daily) serves breakfast, coffee, good sandwiches, and short orders. **Serenata** (Rivadavia 939, tel. 02945/45-5999, noon-11pm daily) is a good choice for coffee and pastries, and has Esquel's finest ice cream.

La Luna (Av. Fontana 656, tel. 02945/45-3800, lunch and dinner daily, US$12) serves versions of Argentine standards, including grilled trout and a massive *milanesa La Luna,* with bacon, fried eggs, and potatoes. La Luna also offers patio seating. **La Barra** (Sarmiento 638, tel. 02945/45-4321, lunch and dinner daily, US$9) is an unpretentious but excellent grill restaurant that has unexpected treats, such as giant ravioli stuffed with lamb. When it gets busy, the service can suffer.

★ **Fitzroya Pizza** (Rivadavia 1050, tel. 02945/45-0512, lunch and dinner daily, from US$8) is a first-rate pizzeria, with an enormous variety of toppings. Solo diners can order half portions. Flamboyantly decorated, created by a magician, ★ **Don Chiquino** (Av. Ameghino 1641, tel. 02945/45-0035, lunch from noon daily, dinner from 8pm daily, US$8-15) has outstanding pastas and individual pizzas. The atmosphere is casual, and there's a decent wine list and locally brewed craft beer.

Hotel Argentino (25 de Mayo 862, tel. 02945/45-5237) has a great bar with a classic kitchen-sink collection of memorabilia and junk as well as friendly staff. **El Bodegón** (Rivadavia 860, tel. 02945/15-42-8117) is a pizzeria and live blues bar.

Accommodations

Esquel has increased its accommodations, but availability can be limited in summer and in ski season.

Basic **Hospedaje Rowlands** (Rivadavia 330, tel. 02945/45-2578, US$13 pp) serves no breakfast but offers kitchen privileges and Wi-Fi. The Hostelling International affiliate **Casa del Pueblo** (San Martín 661, tel. 02945/45-0581, www.esquelcasadelpueblo.com.ar, US$19 pp, US$61 d) is a well-run hostel with a bar and a tidy garden. Also HI-affiliated, **Planeta Hostel & Suites** (Av. Alvear 1021, tel. 02945/45-6846, www.planetahostel.com, US$19-20 pp dorms, US$68 d) occupies a rehabbed building whose compact suites have upgraded baths and flat-screen TVs.

Hotel Sur Sur (Av. Fontana and Chacabuco, tel. 02945/45-3858, www.hotelsursur.com, US$51 s, US$61 d) has excellent-value accommodations with functional, light, and simply decorated rooms. Amenities include an ample breakfast and Wi-Fi. A commonplace facade conceals the spacious, well-furnished rooms at ★ **Hostería Angelina** (Av. Alvear 758, tel. 02945/45-2763, info@hosteriaangelina.com.ar, US$60-70 s, US$65-85 d). Rates include Wi-Fi, cable TV, parking, and central heating. Baths in the larger superior rooms have tubs. The buffet breakfast has 35 different items, including croissants, rice pudding, cakes, ham, cheese, bread, cereal, fruit and fruit salad, coffee, and tea.

In the Villa Ayelén neighborhood, opposite the racetrack just south of the town center, ★ **Hostería Canela** (Los Notros and Los Radales, tel. 02945/45-3890, www.canelaesquel.com, US$135 s or d) is a former teahouse turned bed-and-breakfast with five spacious rooms on immaculate grounds. Hosts Jorge Miglioli and Verónica Ayling speak fluent English, provide an ample breakfast, and offer dining and excursion suggestions.

The 20 midsize-plus rooms at the somewhat overpriced **Hostería Cumbres Blancas** (Av. Ameghino 1683, tel. 02945/45-5100, www.cumbresblancas.com.ar, US$104-164 s, US$145-234 d) look as good as the day the small hotel opened in 1997. It also has Wi-Fi, a sauna, a restaurant, and grounds that include a mini-golf course and a duck pond. If business is slow, try asking for the lower Argentine rates.

With every contemporary comfort but no extravagances, the **Las Bayas Hotel** (Av. Alvear 985, tel. 02945/45-5800, www.lasbayas-hotel.com, US$169-385 s or d) has 10 spacious suites, including a split-level apartment for four. There is a long list of amenities, attentive room service, and a restaurant also open to nonguests.

Information

The **Secretaría de Turismo** (Av. Alvear 1120, tel. 02945/45-1927, www.esquel.gov.ar, 8am-10pm daily summer, 8am-9pm daily fall-spring) maintains a thorough database on accommodations and other services here and in Parque Nacional Los Alerces. In summer only, a satellite office (6am-8am and 6pm-10pm Fri.-Sun. summer) at the bus terminal keeps limited hours.

For information on all of Chubut province, there is a **Centro de Informes del Ministerio de Turismo** (Sarmiento 635, tel. 02945/45-0458, infoturismoprovincia@gmail.com, 8am-1pm Mon.-Fri.).

Services

For motorists, **ACA** (25 de Mayo and Av. Ameghino, tel. 02965/45-2382) is an important resource. **Banco del Chubut** (Av. Alvear 1131) has one of several downtown ATMs. For money exchange, try **Artesanías La Estación** (Sarmiento 630). The postal code for **Correo Argentino** (Av. Alvear 1192) is 9200. **Su Central** (25 de Mayo 415) has both phone and Internet access, as does **Cyber Club** (Av. Alvear 961).

There is an honorary **Chilean consulate** (Molinari 754, tel. 02945/45-1189, 8:30am-1:30pm Mon.-Fri.) here. For laundry, try **Laverap** (Av. Fontana 649, tel. 02945/45-1838). For medical services, contact the **Hospital Zonal** (25 de Mayo 150, tel. 02945/45-0009).

Transportation

Esquel has limited air services, better bus connections, and rail fantasies.

Aerolíneas Argentinas (25 de Mayo 451, tel. 02945/45-3614) flies three times a week to Buenos Aires. **LADE** (Av. Alvear 1085, tel. 02945/45-2124) usually flies weekly to Bariloche, Mar del Plata, and Buenos Aires, but schedules change frequently. **Aeropuerto Brigadier General Parodi** (EQS, tel. 02945/45-1676) is 20 kilometers east of town on RN 40; transfer services arranged by travel agencies, and taxis are the only options to get to the airport.

The **Terminal de Ómnibus** (Av. Alvear 1871, tel. 02945/45-1584) is a contemporary facility eight blocks northeast of downtown. It has good local and regional services, but long-distance links are better in Bariloche; a small boarding tax is charged.

Transporte Jacobsen (tel. 02945/45-4676) connects Esquel with El Maitén (2 hours, 1:30pm Tues. and Thurs.-Fri., US$7). Jacobsen also serves nearby Trevelin (frequently), La Balsa (2 or 3 times weekly), Corcovado (4 times weekly), and other minor destinations in west and northwestern Chubut. Twice daily in summer, it goes to Lago Puelo via Parque Nacional Los Alerces (7:30am and 1:30pm daily summer). Most notable, though, are its services to the Chilean border at Futaleufú (1 hour, 8am and 6pm Mon., Wed., and Fri., US$8).

In summer, **Transportes Esquel** (tel. 02945/45-3529, www.transportesesquel.com.ar) goes to Parque Nacional Los Alerces and Lago Puelo (8am daily summer), connecting with lake excursions. Fares are US$4 to La Villa, US$5 to Bahía Rosales, US$6.50 to Lago Verde and to Lago Rivadavia, US$7 to Cholila, and US$11 to Lago Puelo (6 hours), where there are easy connections to El Bolsón.

An open ticket (US$14), valid throughout the season either north- or southbound, allows passengers to stop anywhere en route and continue on any succeeding bus in the same direction. Bikes not allowed. Winter services are limited to three per week.

Typical destinations include Trevelin (30 minutes, US$1), La Balsa (1.5 hours, US$6), El Maitén (2 hours, US$6), El Bolsón (2-3 hours, US$9-13), Bariloche (4.5 hours, US$16-23), Trelew (8-8.5 hours, US$41-68), Puerto Madryn (9 hours, US$60-72), Comodoro Rivadavia (8 hours, US$50-57), and Buenos Aires (24 hours, US$150).

Los Alerces Rent a Car (Sarmiento 763, tel. 02945/45-6008, www.losalercesrentacar.com.ar) has rental cars.

VICINITY OF ESQUEL

In addition to Parque Nacional Los Alerces, Esquel has many other points of interest within an hour or two.

La Hoya

Only 12 kilometers north of Esquel, **La Hoya** is a modest **ski area** that, thanks to its location on the Andes's drier eastern side, gets a fine powder that compensates for its relatively small size. It's substantially cheaper than Bariloche, and the infrastructure is improving. Limited capacity can mean long lift lines.

Ranging from 1,350 to 2,075 meters elevation, La Hoya has 25 runs totaling about 22 kilometers on 60 hectares. Its modern lifts include the 1,100-meter Telesilla del Bosque, which also carries hikers to high-country trailheads in summer (US$6), and the 1,018-meter Telesilla del Cañadón. In season, it also has a ski school and celebrates the **Fiesta Nacional del Esquí** (National Ski Festival).

Equipment can be rented on-site or in Esquel at several shops, including **Bolsa de Ski** (Rivadavia and 25 de Mayo, tel. 02945/45-2379, www.bolsadeski.com.ar). For other details, contact **Centro de Actividades de Montaña La Hoya** (Av. Ameghino 670, tel. 02945/45-3018, www.skilahoya.com).

Museo Leleque

Midway between Esquel and El Bolsón, on what was one of Argentina's largest ranches, the **Museo Leleque** (RN 40, Km 1440, tel. 011/4326-5156, www.benetton.com, 11am-5pm Thurs.-Tues. Mar.-Apr., July-Aug., and Oct.-Dec., 11am-7pm Thurs.-Tues. Jan.-Feb., US$2) covers Patagonia from prehistory to the present. It is funded by fashion icon Carlo Benetton, who purchased the Argentine Southern Land Company and several other Patagonian properties.

The museum houses the collections of Ukrainian immigrant Pablo S. Korschenewski, who left Buenos Aires half a century ago to explore the Patagonian countryside on foot and by horseback. In the process, Korschenewski amassed over 14,000 artifacts, including arrowheads, bone drills, ceremonial axes, grinding stones, and pottery shards. Striking a chord with Benetton, he persuaded the Italian to turn Leleque's historic buildings, once a general store, hotel, and school, into a contemporary museum that now gets nearly 10,000 visitors every year. Not just archaeological, the exhibits stress contact and post-contact history of the region's first peoples, regional and oral histories, photographs, and documents. One prize is a receipt signed by Butch Cassidy, who lived in nearby Cholila from 1901 to 1905, under the alias Santiago Ryan.

Administered by the Fundación Ameghino, the Museo Leleque is 90 kilometers north of Esquel. The museum has a souvenir shop and a *boliche* for snacks and coffee.

Cholila

Though it's barely a wide spot in the road, the village of Cholila has become an offbeat pilgrimage site ever since U.S. author Anne Meadows pinpointed it as the location of the cabins where outlaws Robert Leroy Parker and Harry Longabaugh—mythologized as **Butch Cassidy and the Sundance Kid**—made their last stand in her historical travelogue *Digging Up Butch and Sundance* (Lincoln, NE: University of Nebraska Press, 2003). Bruce

Chatwin also told of the Cholila cabin, perhaps taking literary license, in his classic *In Patagonia* (New York: Summit Books, 1977).

Butch and Sundance presumably attempted to reform at this cabin hideout, but fled to Chile in 1905 when accused of a robbery in Río Gallegos after the Pinkertons got on their scent. After the 1999 death of the house's elderly occupant, Aladín Sepúlveda, souvenir hunters looted the unoccupied and crumbling cabin, but the municipality has restored the buildings. In fact, they look livable enough that you almost expect to see cardboard cutouts of Paul Newman and Robert Redford, but there are no exhibits within. In theory, a caretaker collects a small admission charge.

Near Parque Nacional Los Alerces's northeastern entrance, a few kilometers north of Cholila at Km 21 on RP 71 near the signed junction to the Casa de Piedra teahouse, the cabin is visible on the west side of the highway; in fact, buses between Puelo and Esquel via Los Alerces pass within sight of it.

TREVELIN AND VICINITY

Few settlements in Chubut's Andean interior retain the Welsh imprint, but tranquil Trevelin, with historic houses and teahouses, is the exception. Only half an hour from Esquel, it owes its name to a Welsh compound meaning "mill town," after its first flour mill, now a history museum.

Trevelin (pop. 12,000), 24 kilometers south of Esquel via RN 259, is also unique for its disorienting octagonal Plaza Coronel Fontana, from which the highway continues south as Avenida San Martín. It's the main commercial street and thoroughfare toward the Chilean border post of Futaleufú. Other streets fan out from the plaza.

Chile-bound motorists should fill the tank here. Though Futaleufú has a new gas station, Chilean prices are substantially higher.

Sights

In 1922, Welsh immigrants founded the Molino Harinero de la Compañía Andes, the flour mill that's now the **Museo Histórico**

Regional Molino Viejo (Molino Viejo 488, tel. 02945/48-0189, 11am-8pm Mon.-Fri., 2pm-6:30pm Sat.-Sun. Jan.-Feb., 11am-6pm Sat.-Sun. Mar.-Dec., US$7.50 adults, US$2 under age 12). Its exhibits include period clothing, furniture, carriages, and agricultural machinery as well as photographs, maps, documents, and even tea ware. It also devotes space to the Mapuche and Tehuelche.

Two blocks northeast of the plaza, the offbeat **Museo Cartref Taid** (Malacara s/n, tel. 02945/48-0108, www.caballomalacara.com.ar, 5pm-7pm daily, US$5) holds the **Tumba de Malacara,** the final resting place of a horse that helped its rider, Trevelin founder John D. Evans, flee a Mapuche raid during the Argentine army's 1880s war against the indigenous people. Admission includes a guided tour and a visit to a pioneer's rebuilt cottage.

At the south end of town, the brick **Capilla Bethel** (Ap Iwan and Laprida) is a Welsh chapel dating from 1910. It has also served as a school.

About 17 kilometers south of Trevelin via RN 259 and a short southbound lateral road, **Reserva Provincial Nant-y-Fall** (8am-8pm daily, US$2.50 Argentines, US$7.50 foreigners) is a provincial park with a 400-meter footpath to a string of waterfalls, the highest of which is 64 meters. Nant-y-Fall's source is **Lago Rosario,** a subalpine lake on a Mapuche reservation, 26 kilometers southeast of Trevelin via RN 259, RP 17, and a short eastbound lateral road.

Six kilometers west of the access to Nant-y-Fall, the provincial **Estación de Salmonicultura** (salmon hatchery, no phone, free tours 8am-8pm daily in summer, shorter hours fall-spring) offers guided tours. There are several campgrounds and cabañas along RN 259, which leads to the Chilean border. One of these is the oddly named **Motor Home Eco-Parking** (RN 259, Km 52.5, tel. 02945/15-51-5021, cocineros@yahoo.com.ar) which, more notably, is also the site of **Viñas del Nant y Fall**—the continent's southernmost winery, though it may shortly be displaced. The first vintages of Pinot Noir have just appeared on the market; it also sells a variety of local products from other farms, and even offers accommodations.

In the Valle 16 de Octubre, about five kilometers east of Trevelin via gravel road, the historic **Escuela No. 18** stands near the site of a 1902 plebiscite that determined that Trevelin would stay on the Argentine side of the border (the original adobe building no longer exists). Commemorating those events, the onetime school now holds the **Museo del Plebiscito de 1902** (no phone, 12:30pm-6:30pm daily summer, free), an outlier of Trevelin's regional museum.

In summer, Plaza Coronel Fontana hosts a weekend **crafts market** that also takes place on holidays. The rest of the year, it takes place on alternate Sundays.

Food

The Welsh teahouses are outstanding. The traditional favorite, in modern quarters, is ★ **Nain Maggie** (Perito Moreno 179, tel. 02945/48-0232, www.nainmaggie.com, 8am-8pm daily, US$15 pp), but there's nothing wrong with **La Mutisia** (Av. San Martín 170, tel. 02945/48-0165, www.casadetemutisia.com.ar, US$15 pp). Both serve filling late-afternoon teas.

Oregon (Av. San Martín and John Murray Thomas, tel. 02945/48-0408, lunch and dinner Wed.-Mon., US$15) is a popular grill restaurant with an all-you-can-eat option. **Sabores** (Av. San Martín 924, tel. 02945/15-40-7621) is a mostly take-out venue whose *empanadas árabes* (chopped lamb with a touch of lemon) are uncommon in this part of the country.

Serenata (Plaza Fontana s/n, tel. 02945/48-0126) is a branch of Esquel's fine ice creamery.

Accommodations

Except for cabañas, which are best for family groups, accommodations are few. **Hospedaje Familiar Pezzi** (Sarmiento 351, tel. 02945/48-0146 or 02945/15-68-1196, hpezzi@intramed.net, summer only, US$48 d) provides an ample breakfast, a neat backyard, and discounts for

longer stays. **Hostería Estefanía** (Perito Moreno and Sarmiento, tel. 02945/48-0148, hosteriaestefania@gmail.com, US$50 d) has Wi-Fi. **Hostería Casa de Piedra** (Brown 244, tel. 02945/48-0357, www.casadepiedratrevelin.com, US$78 s, US$86 d) is a 10-room, two-story bed-and-breakfast of stone and polished natural wood. There are king beds, continental or buffet breakfast, and Wi-Fi. There are more lodging choices in nearby Esquel.

About midway between Trevelin and the Futaleufú border crossing, the misleadingly named **Motor Home Eco-Parking** (RN 259, Km 52.5, tel. 02945/51-5021, cocineros@yahoo.com.ar, US$10 pp tent camping, US$14 pp RVs, US$20 pp dorm, US$57 pp s or d) is also the campground and accommodations of the pioneer Nant y Fall winery. There are ample sites for RVs and camper vehicles, with electricity, Wi-Fi, and baths equipped with hot showers, but tents are also welcome. In addition, there's a two-room guesthouse sleeping up to seven. One room is a double with an additional single bed and private bath, while the other is a four-bed dorm that has a single external bath with a shower. Meals are also available on an ad hoc basis.

Information and Services

The **Dirección de Turismo** (Plaza Coronel Fontana s/n, tel. 02945/48-0120, www.trevelin.gob.ar, 8am-9pm daily Jan.-Feb., 8am-7pm daily Mar.-Dec.) is on the plaza.

Banco del Chubut (Av. San Martín and Brown) has an ATM. **Correo Argentino** (Av. San Martín 99) is across from the bank. The postal code is 9203.

Gales al Sur (Av. Patagonia 186, tel. 02945/48-0427, www.galesalsur.com.ar) organizes excursions and activities in and around town. **Hospital Trevelin** (Av. San Martín 995, tel. 02945/48-0132) is nine blocks south of Plaza Coronel Fontana.

Transportation

In daylight hours, **Transporte Jacobsen** shuttles between Esquel and Trevelin (US$1) frequently. Futaleufú-bound travelers can catch the bus that continues to the Chilean border crossing at La Balsa (8:30am and 6:30pm Mon. and Fri., US$5), but everyone else has to return to Esquel.

PARQUE NACIONAL LOS ALERCES

Parque Nacional Los Alerces owes its existence and name to *Fitzroya cupressoides,* the coniferous monarch of the humid Valdivian forests, also known as *lahuán,* false larch or Patagonian cypress. Western Chubut's most popular attraction, the park draws campers and fishing aficionados to its forests and finger lakes. Despite a magnificent setting, with snowy Andean summits to the west, hikers find it frustrating because a scant trail network often forces them to walk the shoulders of dusty roads with heavy auto traffic. Colloquially known as **La Villa,** Villa Futalaufquen is the park headquarters and also offers a cluster of services at Lago Futalaufquen's south end, where **Puerto Limonao** serves as a point of arrival and departure.

About 45 kilometers west of Esquel via RN 259 and RP 71, Los Alerces is a 263,000-hectare unit on the eastern Andean slope. Its highest point is 2,253-meter Cerro Torrecillas, but Pacific storms that penetrate the lower cordillera here make it wetter than most of Argentine Patagonia. Past glaciations have left navigable finger lakes that provide access to some of the park's finest sights. Summers are mild, with temperatures reaching 24°C with cool nights. Winters average barely 2°C, with ample snowfall.

Flora and Fauna

Besides the *alerce,* the park's other conifers include the Chilean incense cedar and the Guaiteca cypress, both with limited geographical distribution. Most of the rest of the forest consists of the broadleaf southern beeches *coihue, lenga,* and *ñire.* The *arrayán* nears the southern limit of its range here.

For hikers, one of the worst plagues is the *colihue,* a solid bamboo that forms impassable thickets. The aggressive and exotic *rosa mosqueta,* a European introduction, is displacing native plants.

In this dense forest, Los Alerces's fauna is less conspicuous. The Andean deer or *huemul* is present, along with its distant miniature relative the *pudú.* Birds include the *chucao* (a common songbird), the austral parakeet, and the Patagonian woodpecker.

Sights and Recreation

The long-distance **Huella Andina** footpath, which begins in Neuquén province, now passes through the park en route to Lago Baggilt.

On the Río Desaguadero, the **Sendero de las Pinturas Rupestres** (west of RP 71 at the south end of Lago Futalaufquen) is an easy 500-meter nature trail that passes a natural overhang with fading pre-Columbian rock art, some of it clearly geometrical. It then climbs through forest to an overlook with expansive panoramas to the north.

Register with rangers for the steep hike to the 1,916-meter summit of **Cerro El Dedal,** reached by a trailhead from La Villa; figure about six or seven hours round-trip. From the road to Puerto Limonao (3.5 kilometers north of La Villa), **Cinco Saltos** is a shorter and easier hike to a series of waterfalls.

From Puerto Limonao, four kilometers north of La Villa, the 25-kilometer **Sendero Lago Krüger** follows Lago Futalaufquen's south shore to the smaller Lago Krüger, which has a campground and a lodge. Register with rangers before beginning the hike (a portable stove is obligatory). The hike has only one campsite, at Playa Blanca, between the trailhead and the lodge, for an overnight stay (for inbound hikers only). Daily boat service to Lago Krüger costs about US$30 pp round-trip.

★ Circuito Lacustre

Los Alerces's traditional excursion is the "lake circuit" from Puerto Limonao, at Lago Futalaufquen's south end, to the Río Arrayanes outlet of Lago Verde. At **Puerto Mermoud,** a catwalk crosses to Lago

Menéndez's **Puerto Chucao,** where another boat continues to **Puerto Sagrario.**

From Puerto Sagrario, passing blue-green **Lago Cisne,** a looping nature trail goes to the **El Alerzal** grove and the landmark **El Abuelo,** the oldest and most impressive single *alerce.* While there are guides on the hike to and from El Abuelo, it's possible to separate from the group. It's not possible, though, to hike elsewhere in an area that's mostly an off-limits *zona intangible.*

It's possible to start the excursion at either Puerto Limonao (US$55 pp) or Puerto Chucao (US$45 pp). Low water often eliminates the Limonao-Chucao segment. Scheduled departures vary, and in summer an extra afternoon service from Limonao is added to the usual morning excursion. Any Esquel travel agency can make reservations, but it's possible (though not recommended) to purchase tickets here on a space-available basis.

Food and Accommodations

Los Alerces has numerous campgrounds and other accommodations, mostly near Lago Futalaufquen. In addition to organized campgrounds, formerly free *agreste* (wild) sites now charge for limited services. These sites are much cleaner than in the past.

Accessible by road, organized campgrounds all have picnic tables, fire pits, restrooms, hot showers, and access to groceries and restaurants; some have electrical outlets. Among them are **Camping Los Maitenes** (tel. 02945/47-1006, US$11 pp), 800 meters from the Intendencia at Futalaufquen's south end; **Camping Bahía Rosales** (tel. 02945/15-68-5901, www.bahiarosales.com, US$11 pp), 15 kilometers from La Villa on the eastern lakeshore; and **Camping Lago Rivadavia** (tel. 02945/45-4381, US$12 pp), 46 kilometers north of La Villa at its namesake lake's south end.

At Lago Verde, 35 kilometers from La Villa, **El Aura Patagonia Lodge** (tel. 011/4813-4340, www.elaurapatagonia.com, US$95-115 s or d in dome tents, US$304-333 s or d) features comfortable bungalows and an upscale restaurant. Meals and packages with fly-fishing or more conventional activities like hiking, riding, and kayaking are considerably more expensive.

Reached only by a 25-kilometer footpath or launch from Puerto Limonao, the former **Hostería Lago Krüger** is now open as a free backcountry *refugio* for hikers, but it has no services, though there's a ranger nearby.

Lago Menéndez is part of Los Alerces' Circuito Lacustre.

The nearby camping area is closed because of treefall hazards.

For groups of any size, the cheapest non-camping options are places like **Cabañas Tejas Negras** (RP 71, tel. 02945/47-1046, www.tejasnegras.com, US$140 d), about 12 kilometers north of La Villa.

About five kilometers north of La Villa, **Hostería Quimé-Quipán** (RP 71 s/n, tel. 02945/47-1021, www.quimequipan.com.ar, US$66-120 s or d) has simple but comfortable rooms, some with lake views. The restaurant is adequate.

Four kilometers north of La Villa, the park's prestige lodging is the Bustillo-built ★ **Hostería Futalaufquen** (tel. 02945/47-1008, www.hosteriafutalaufquen. com, US$160-200 s or d, with breakfast in high season). With only nine rooms—prices depend on whether you get a forest or lake view—it enjoys a privileged end-of-the-road site on Lago Futalaufquen's western shore. Distinctive features include beamed Tudor-style ceilings, a walk-in granite fireplace, copper chandeliers, and a polished wooden bar. The restaurant is open to nonguests (reservations only for dinner); a fixed-price meal costs US$22 with drinks. The hotel also has separate cabaña accommodations.

Information and Services

At the park headquarters in La Villa, the APN's **Museo y Centro de Informes** (tel. 02945/47-1015, losalerces@apn.gov.ar, 8am-9pm daily mid-Dec.-Mar., 9am-8pm daily Apr.-mid-Dec.) is both a museum, with history and natural history exhibits, and a helpful ranger information center.

At both the northern Lago Rivadavia (Portada Norte) and eastern La Portada (Portada Centro) entrances, rangers collect a US$10 pp admission charge for foreigners. After 9pm, when the tollbooths close, there's no one to collect the charge, but they check on the way out.

La Villa also has a grocery, public telephones, and a first-aid station.

Transportation

Transportes Esquel and **Transporte Jacobsen** buses between Esquel and Lago Puelo pick up and drop off passengers along RP 71 within the park. Off-season Transportes Esquel buses go only thrice a week to Lago Puelo, and on Monday only to La Villa.

GOBERNADOR COSTA

Some 180 kilometers south of Esquel, Gobernador Costa is a cow town with the best services on the long haul between Esquel and Río Mayo on RN 40. Its early-February **Fiesta Provincial del Caballo** is the town's major event.

Food and Accommodations

Across from the tourist office, **El Petiso** restaurant (Av. Roca s/n, no phone, lunch and dinner daily) is best for beef. North of the highway, the **Camping Municipal** (2 de Abril and Los Suecos) has hot water and electricity, and there are several modest accommodations.

Transportation and Services

The **Oficina de Informes Turísticos** (Av. Roca s/n, tel. 02945/15-60-5737, turismogobernadorcosta@hotmail.com, 8am-8pm Mon.-Fri., hours vary Sat.-Sun.) is helpful. **Banco del Chubut** (Sarmiento and San Martín) has an ATM.

The bus terminal has services northbound to Esquel, eastbound to Trelew, and southbound to Sarmiento and Comodoro Rivadavia. Summer buses between Bariloche and El Calafate pass through here.

RÍO MAYO

Because public transportation is limited on RN 40 between Gobernador Costa and Perito Moreno, only self-propelled southbound travelers normally see the crossroads town of Río Mayo. In fact, few vehicles of any kind use the dull segment that intersects RP 43, the paved route between Comodoro Rivadavia and the Chilean border, 124 kilometers to the south. Despite having little to see, it's a stopover for

Look for ★ to find recommended
sights, activities, dining, and lodging.

Highlights

★ **Sector Conguillío:** Over a century ago, conservationist John Muir went far out of his way to see the famed monkey-puzzle tree. Today, this park protects much of South America's endemic araucaria forests (page 187).

★ **Parque Nacional Villarrica:** Climb the snow-covered slopes of Chile's most active volcano in its namesake national park (page 201).

★ **Parque Nacional Huerquehue:** This is the place for shaded woodland hikes alongside rushing streams (page 203).

★ **Anticura:** See Parque Nacional Puyehue's most impressive sight: the barren high country wrought by the lava flows and ash from its namesake volcano (page 210).

★ **Puerto Varas Historic District:** On Lago Llanquihue's western shore, charming Puerto Varas is studded with shingled houses that recall the Middle European origins of its earliest settlers, as well as the Lakes District's finest restaurants and services (page 218).

★ **Parque Nacional Vicente Pérez Rosales:** On the eastern shore of Lago Llanquihue, Volcán Osorno is a summer favorite for hikers and a winter destination for skiers (page 225).

★ **Cochamó:** The Cochamó backcountry boasts granite monoliths surrounded by lush rainforests. Hiking the muddy trails can be a slog, so some visitors prefer horseback excursions (page 230).

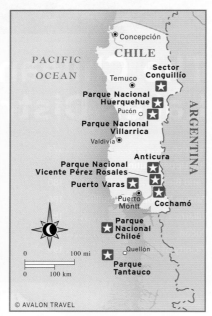
© AVALON TRAVEL

★ **Parque Nacional Chiloé:** On Chiloé's wild west coast, hikers can still wander through dense dwarf native woodlands (page 254).

★ **Parque Tantauco:** In a roadless wilderness, former Chilean president Sebastián Piñera has created a forest reserve that is becoming a top ecotourism destination (page 258).

S outh of the Río Biobío, the Sur Chico ("Lesser South") has long enticed Chileans and Argentines with ice-capped volcanic cones soaring above dense native forests. The region is popularly known as the lakes district for the scenic

finger lakes left by receding Pleistocene glaciers.

More adventurous travelers venture beyond conventional lakeside resorts into the Andean backcountry for hiking, horseback riding, and white-water rafting. National parks and reserves cover large swaths of the cordillera.

Politically, the Sur Chico comprises La Araucanía (Region IX), Los Ríos (Region XIV, not covered in this book), and Los Lagos (Region X), which includes the Chiloé archipelago and, on the mainland across an inland sea, what is colloquially known as continental Chiloé. Economically diverse cities such as Temuco, Osorno, and Puerto Montt, which rely on forestry, agricultural services, and manufacturing, are the gateways, but smaller lakeside towns such as Villarrica, Pucón, and Puerto Varas make better bases for excursions and sightseeing. There are several trans-Andean routes to Argentina, which has its own lakes region centered on the city of Bariloche.

Puerto Montt, the de facto terminus of the continental Panamericana, is the hub for air, land, and sea access to Chilean Patagonia and also a gateway to the Argentine side.

Southeast of Temuco, Lago Villarrica is a beehive of activity for access to national parks such as Villarrica and Huerquehue. The district's heart is farther south, where Lago Todos los Santos may be Chile's single most beautiful body of water. Near the picturesque town of Puerto Varas, Volcán Osorno, an almost perfectly symmetrical cone rising above Lago Llanquihue, offers some of the most breathtaking views. Still, there are dozens of other volcanic summits, scenic lakes and rivers, and shores and estuaries to fill weeks or months of sightseeing and activities.

Like La Araucanía, Los Lagos has a vigorous tourism sector. There's tension between defenders of the natural landscape and resource-based industries such as forestry and fisheries—water pollution from large-scale

Previous: Lago Todos los Santos, in the Parque Nacional Vicente Pérez Rosales; Volcán Villarrica as seen from Pucón. **Above:** rusting farm equipment in front of Volcán Osorno.

The Chilean Lakes District

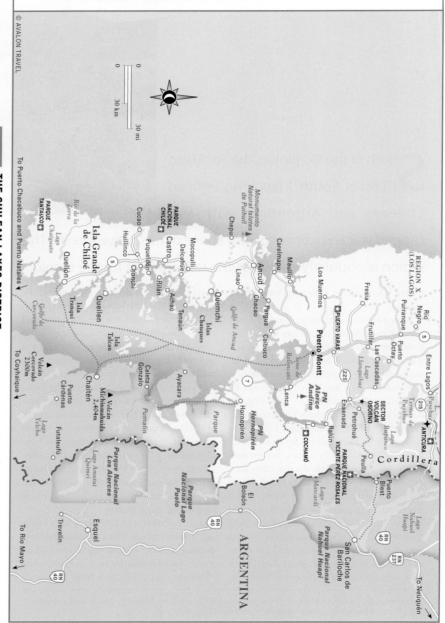

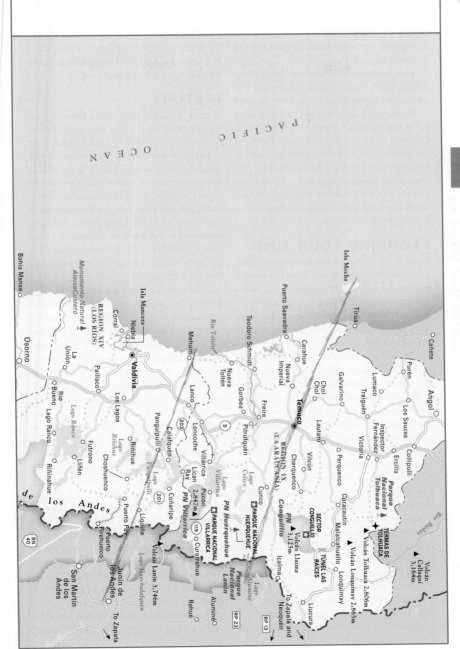

PACIFIC OCEAN

Isla Mocha

Bahía Mansa

Monumento Natural
Alerce Costero

Isla Mancera

REGION XIV
(LOS RÍOS)

Corral

Niebla

Osorno

La
Unión

Paillaco

Río
Bueno

Puerto Saavedra

Carahue

Teodoro Schmidt

Nueva
Toltén

Río Toltén

Mehuín

Valdivia

Lanco

Nueva
Imperial

Chol
Chol

Gorbea

Freire

Pitrufquén

Temuco

Galvarino

Lumaco

Traiguén

Cañete

Purén

Los Sauces

Angol

Inspector
Fernández

Collipulli

Ercilla

Parque
Nacional
Tolhuaca

Volcán Tolhuaca 2,806m ▲
TERMAS DE
TOLHUACA ★

Lago
Ranco

Los Lagos

Lago
Riñihue

Riñihue

Panguipulli

Loncoche

Villarrica

Lago
Villarrica

Lago
Calafquén

Cunco

Curarehue

Cherquenco

Vilcún

Lautaro

Perquenco

Victoria

Curacautín

Malalcahuello

Lonquimay

Volcán Lonquimay 2,865m ▲

Río Biobío

Volcán
Callaqui
3,164m ▲

Furrono

Llifén

Río Bueno

REGION IX
(LA ARAUCANÍA)

SECTOR
CONGUILLIO

PN
Conguillío

Volcán Llaima
3,125m ▲

TÚNEL LAS
RAÍCES

Icalma

Liucura

Riñinahue

Choshuenco

Lago
Riñihue

Lago
Panguipulli

Lican
Ray

Pucón

Lican
2,847m ▲

PN Villarrica

PARQUE NACIONAL
VILLARRICA

PN Huerquehue

PARQUE NACIONAL
HUERQUEHUE

Lago
Huilipilún

Puerto Fuy

Liquiñe

Coñaripe

Volcán
Villarrica

Lago
Calafquén

Coñaripe

Puerto
Pirehueico

Junín de
los Andes

Volcán Lanín 3,746m ▲

Parque
Nacional
Lanín

Lago Huechulafquen

Rahué

Aluminé

RP 23

RP 13

To Zapala and
Neuquén

San Martín
de los
Andes

To Zapala

RN
40

de   los   Andes

5

203

201

119

PACIFIC
OCEAN

salmon farming in both freshwater lakes and saltwater estuaries continues to cause concern. Overexploitation of native finfish as well as shellfish such as abalone and giant mussels is a problem.

This chapter also includes the Chiloé archipelago, easily reached by shuttle ferries, and parts of continental Chiloé, south to the town of Hornopirén, also known as Río Negro. From Hornopirén, a summer-only ferry usually sails to the tiny cove of Caleta Gonzalo, the de facto start of the Carretera Austral. Because of continental Chiloé's physical isolation from the rest of Region X, only air taxis, catamarans, slow-moving ferries, and roundabout buses through Argentina connect it to Puerto Montt and Castro.

PLANNING YOUR TIME

Because the lakes district is relatively compact, with fine highways and secondary roads, plus abundant public transportation, travel is straightforward. Still, in the summer tourism peak, hotel and rental-car reservations are advised, although some accommodations are usually available.

The best bases are the Lago Villarrica resorts of Villarrica and Pucón to the north, and the Lago Llanquihue town of Puerto Varas or the mainland city of Puerto Montt to the south. For visitors with vehicles, staying at any of these locales keeps driving to a minimum, but good public transportation reduces the need for a car. For those staying outside of town, it's helpful to have a car.

Seeing the main sights in either of these two clusters requires around a week. This would permit a day trip to Parque Nacional Conguillío and perhaps an overnight near the thermal-baths complex at Malalcahuello, or looping around the park from Temuco via the upper Biobío. In Villarrica or Pucón, there would be ample time for hiking in Parque Nacional Huerquehue, climbing Volcán Villarrica, rafting the Río Trancura, or simply relaxing on the black-sand beaches.

From either Puerto Varas or Puerto Montt, attractions such as Parque Nacional Vicente Pérez Rosales, the wild Cochamó backcountry, the seafood port of Angelmó, and the Chiloé archipelago are almost equally accessible. Many visitors prefer Puerto Varas, which is quieter and more picturesque, with better services in a more compact area.

HISTORY

Human presence here dates from at least 13,000 years ago, when hunter-gatherers roamed the area around Monte Verde, west of Puerto Montt. One of the continent's oldest archaeological sites, Monte Verde offered ideal preservation conditions: Despite the humid climate, more than a meter of volcanic ash and peat covered the remains of mastodons, shellfish, seeds, fruits, and roots consumed by a dozen or so families who lived here. Researchers have determined that these groups hunted and foraged within a radius of about 100 kilometers.

Unlike the Andean highlands of Peru and Bolivia, this region never developed cities or monuments in pre-Columbian times. Its people developed agricultural skills, but they were shifting cultivators in dispersed settlements, lacking centralized political authority. In practice, this benefited their resistance to the Inca Empire and, later, Spanish invaders; the Mapuche used guerrilla tactics to harass their opponents. More egalitarian than hierarchical, their leadership was interchangeable rather than irreplaceable.

Thus, by the early 1600s, Mapuche resistance had reduced most Spanish settlements beyond the Biobío to ashes and ruin. Except for the river port of Valdivia, which was reestablished in the mid-17th century, the area remained precarious for settlers until a series of treaties between the Chilean government and the indigenous people in the 1880s. Several northerly cities and towns—Victoria, Curacautín, Lonquimay, Temuco, Cunco, Villarrica, and Pucón—were originally fortresses along the Mapuche frontier.

Chile counts more than a million Mapuche people among its 17 million citizens. Many have left for the cities, but large numbers still remain in the countryside, where, in the post-Pinochet political climate, they have become more assertive of their rights to ancestral lands.

Part of the controversy dates from the officially encouraged immigration that took place after the mid-19th century, when Santiago recruited German émigrés to settle on and around Lago Llanquihue. In the ensuing years, Llanquihue and other lakes to the north became the region's highways, linking towns like Puerto Varas and Puerto Octay via sail and steamer until the railroad's early-20th-century arrival.

German immigrants have left a palpable imprint on the economy, through commerce and manufacturing; the landscape, through dairy farming and other agricultural pursuits; architecture, with some of the finest European-style houses; and food—Germanic goodies known collectively as kuchen are almost universal. Many other nationalities, mostly Spaniards and Italians, also flowed into the region.

Temuco

Fast-growing Temuco is the gateway to the lakes, numerous national parks, and many other attractions, though its own tourist appeal is limited. While it is a Mapuche market town, the architecture is utilitarian, and economically it relies on agricultural and forest products. Unfortunately, it suffers air-pollution problems, especially in winter, as widespread use of wood-burning stoves has contributed to respiratory infections.

HISTORY

Temuco dates from February 24, 1881, when President Aníbal Pinto sent Interior Minister Manuel Recabarren, General Gregorio Urrutia, engineer Teodoro Schmidt, and the Chilean army to found Fuerte de Temuco (originally Fuerte Recabarren). Later that year, the Chileans averted an attack by reaching a treaty agreement with the Mapuche people. Within 15 years the railroad had arrived. Before the new century, colonists had flooded into the region, their farmers displacing the aboriginal Mapuche people, and the population exceeded 7,000. The early push from the railroad sustained that growth well into the 20th century, providing easy access to metropolitan markets and technology.

ORIENTATION

On the north margin of the braided Río Cautín, Temuco (pop. about 270,000) is 677 kilometers south of Santiago and 339 kilometers north of Puerto Montt via the Panamericana, which bypasses the city center. The diagonal Avenida Caupolicán—formerly the Panamericana—divides the city into a compact original grid to the east and an irregular residential area to the west.

SIGHTS

Temuco's focal point is the lushly landscaped **Plaza de Armas Aníbal Pinto,** whose showpiece is the massive **Homenaje a la Región de la Araucanía,** a sculpture representing a Mapuche female healer, a soldier of the pacification, an early colonist, the conquistador and epic poet Alonso de Ercilla, and the Mapuche leader Kallfulifan (Caupolicán). The bandshell gallery hosts rotating cultural exhibits.

Most other landmarks are scattered, such as the gingerbread-style **Iglesia Anglicana Santa Trinidad** (Vicuña Mackenna and Lautaro), the century-old Anglican church, as well as several museums and markets. Sadly, the former **Mercado Municipal**—home to many restaurants and crafts outlets—burned to the ground in early 2016.

Chile's national flower, the *copihue (Lapageria rosea),* flaunts its autumn

Temuco

N

0   200 yds
0   200 m

HOTEL
DREAMS
ARAUCANÍA

PIZZERÍA
MADONNA

POSADA
SELVA NEGRA

HOCHSTETTER

AVENIDA ESPAÑA

MANUEL RODRÍGUEZ

AVENIDA

FRANCIA

SENADOR ESTÉBANEZ

ALEMANIA

HOLANDESA

AVENIDA

SAN MARTÍN

AVENIDA

GALLO

LEÓN

URUGUAY

O'HIGGINS

SAN FEDERICO

TRIZANO

PEDRO DE VALDIVIA

Estero Temuco

Estero Collaco

LA SUERTE

CARRILO

DR

DINAMARCA

PHILLIPPI

THIERS

MUSEO REGIONAL
DE LA ARAUCANÍA

AUTOMÓVIL
CLUB DE CHILE

SANTA MARGARITA

To Aeropuerto
Araucanía, Valdivia,
and Puerto Montt

LAS QUILAS

SUR

PRIETO

IMPERIAL

GALLO

LEÓN

Plaza

AVENIDA CAUPOLICÁN

BELLO

FREIRE

EL BOSQUE

ARRAYÁN

ARAUCANA

STA LAURA

CARMINE

CABO RIQUELME

AVENIDA PRIETO

NORTE

BLANCO

BALMACEDA

MIRAFLORES

LAUTARO

LYNCH

V MACKENNA

Cementerio

Monumento
Natural

Cerro Ñielol

AULA MAGNA
UNIVERSIDAD
CATÓLICA

Plaza Teniente
Dagoberto Godoy

HOSPITAL
DR. HERNÁN
HENRÍQUEZ
ARAVENA

IGLESIA
ANGLICANA

CARRERA

CARRERA

VARAS

CLARO

SOLAR

MANUEL

LAS HERAS

CARRERA

MANUEL RODRÍGUEZ

O'HIGGINS

IMPERIAL

Plaza Manuel
Recabarren

EL CORRALERO

HOTEL DON
EDUARDO

AVIS

HERTZ

TUR-BUS

GOHAN

MONTT

LAGOS

MACKENNA

VICUÑA

HOTEL
FRONTERA

Plaza de
Armas
Aníbal Pinto

SERNATUR

HOTEL
RP

Plaza
Teodoro
Schmidt

POST
OFFICE

HOTEL NICOLÁS

MULTITOUR

TERMINAL
BÍO BÍO

BULNES

PRAT

To Rodoviario
Araucario, Chillán
and Santiago

CONAF

HOSTAL
ALDUNATE

LAVANDERÍA MI ZU

LATAM AIRLINES

HOTEL
FRONTERA

HOTEL
AITUE

BANCOESTADO

CASA DE
CAMBIO GLOBAL

MERCADO
MUNICIPAL

ALDUNATE

DIEGO PORTALES

MACKENNA

GENERAL

GENERAL CRUZ

BARROS ARANA

AVENIDA

SAN MARTÍN

GENERAL MACKENNA

MATTA

ZENTENO

BALMACEDA

BUSES JAC

BUSES
INTERCOMUNAL
SUR

TERMINAL DE
BUSES RURALES

FERIA LIBRE
ANÍBAL PINTO

BUSES IGI
LLAIMA/NAR-BUS

ESTACIÓN
FERROCARRILES
DEL ESTADO

BILBAO

PAITZKE

JANEQUEO

AVENIDA A PINTO

To Museo
Nacional
Ferroviario

Río Cautín

blooms in the deciduous lowland forest of **Monumento Natural Cerro Ñielol** (8:30am-11pm daily, US$3 adults, US$1.50 children), a hilly 90-hectare reserve reached by strolling north on Prat from the Plaza de Armas for about one kilometer. Several short trails thread among the mixed woodlands, but it's also a historical site. Under the shade of **La Patagua del Armisticio,** in 1881, Mapuche leaders finally acceded to the city's founding. For most of its numerous yearly visitors, though, it's a place for weekend picnics and similar recreation. Note the numerous **Chemamüll,** the imposing carved Mapuche statues.

Museo Regional de la Araucanía

Housed in the former Carlos Thiers residence (1924), a German immigrant-style national monument, the **Museo Regional de la Araucanía** (Av. Alemania 084, tel. 045/274-7948, www.museoregionalaraucania. cl, 9:30am-5:30pm Tues.-Fri., 11am-5pm Sat., 11am-2pm Sun. and holidays, free) recently underwent a major rehab and reorganization, with greater attention to little-known topics such as Mapuche cooking and culinary artifacts. In the past, though, the museum has seen frequent clashes of philosophy in a region where the indigenous presence is so strong. The museum is about 10 blocks west of the Plaza de Armas.

Museo Nacional Ferroviario Pablo Neruda

Soon after the railroad's arrival from Angol in 1893, Temuco became a rail hub, where long-distance trains changed locomotives. Its original roundhouse opened in 1920, housed locomotives used on several branch lines, and also held repair facilities. By the 1930s these installations were inadequate; the current roundhouse was completed between 1937 and 1941. Temuco was the last Chilean base for steam locomotives. The Empresa de los Ferrocarriles del Estado (EFE) maintained it as a repair and reserve center until 1983, but

it closed soon after. There were no permanent diesel facilities here until the 1980s.

In the aftermath, EFE wanted to tear down the roundhouse and sell off its 14 antique steam engines and other rolling stock for scrap. The Asociación Chilena de Conservación del Patrimonio Ferroviario (ACCPF, Chilean Association for Conservation of Railroad Heritage) managed to get all of them declared national monuments. Finally, in February 2004, President Ricardo Lagos dedicated a museum to Pablo Neruda during the poet's centennial year; Neruda's father was a railroad laborer, and Neruda himself wrote many poems about rail travel.

In a 19-hectare facility, the **Museo Nacional Ferroviario Pablo Neruda** (Av. Barros Arana 0565, tel. 045/293-7940, www. museoferroviariodetemuco.cl, 9am-6pm Tues.-Fri., 10am-6pm Sat.-Sun., closed holidays, US$1.50 adults, US$0.50 children) includes the roundhouse and extensive lawns, with additional stock elevated on rails. Highlights include a luxury presidential railcar that was in service until 2003, an antique sleeper also in service until 2003, and President Carlos Ibáñez del Campo's 1928 Packard limousine, custom-designed so that it could use the rails as well as Chile's then-rudimentary roads. The museum also features an art gallery. Closed after the 2010 earthquake, the historic roundhouse can now be visited only with a guide.

The museum is about one kilometer north of the station. Northbound buses and *taxis colectivos* on Barros Arana go within two short blocks of the site, saving an unappealing walk through a grubby neighborhood. An occasional summer steam train does a five-hour excursion to and from Victoria (US$10 adults, US$6 children).

Feria Libre Aníbal Pinto

Comprising more than 700 different stalls, **Feria Libre Aníbal Pinto** (8am-5pm daily) is a lively, mainly Mapuche, sometimes disagreeably fragrant produce market. It fills several blocks south along Avenida Aníbal Pinto and Avenida Barros Arana from the Terminal de Buses Rurales south to the EFE railroad station. The Aníbal Pinto sector is a roofed pedestrian area that is more handsome and tidier than in past years—though it's not immaculate. In addition to fruits and vegetables, there are cheap eateries and assorted Mapuche crafts.

ENTERTAINMENT AND EVENTS

Temuco isn't exactly a 24-hour city, but there's usually something going on at local cultural facilities or at its two universities. The biggest single celebration is February's **Aniversario de la Ciudad,** commemorating the city's founding on February 24, 1881. At the time of its founding, it was really a fortress. During the festivities, a high-quality crafts fair nearly fills the Plaza de Armas.

The **Aula Magna Universidad Católica** (Manuel Montt 56, tel. 045/220-5421, www.extension.uct.cl) has an annual events schedule that includes live theater, music, and films.

FOOD

Downtown's only notable restaurant, **El Corralero** (Vicuña Mackenna 811, tel. 045/240-1355, lunch and dinner daily, US$10-15) specializes in beef but also offers a sample of fish and seafood dishes. It provides excellent and congenial service as well. **Gohan** (España 390, tel. 045/274-1110, www.gohan.cl) is the go-to choice for sushi.

In residential Temuco, only a couple blocks west of Hochstetter and just south of Avenida Alemania, the popular **Restaurant Oregon** (Recreo 530, tel. 045/238-5776, lunch daily, dinner Mon.-Sat., US$10-13) is a step-plus above most of its *parrilla* (grill restaurant) competitors, with fish and pastas to supplement the beef. The service is attentive and good-natured, and they're flexible about wine-by-the-glass selections.

The popular **Pizzería Madonna** (Av. Alemania 0660, tel. 045/232-9393, www.madonnapizza.com, noon-4pm and 6pm-midnight Mon.-Fri., noon-midnight Sat., noon-11pm Sun., US$15) has fine pastas and a greater diversity of pizzas, ranging from individual to family-size, than most Chilean pizzerias.

ACCOMMODATIONS

Temuco's budget accommodations are only so-so, but travelers spending just a little more can get better value. Upper-range choices are generally good.

US$25-50

Hostal Aldunate (Aldunate 864, tel. 045/264-2438, hostalaldunate864@hotmail.com, US$15 pp shared bath, US$22 s, US$37 d private bath, breakfast included) occupies a quiet but still central neighborhood. **Hotel Nicolás** (General Mackenna 420, tel. 045/221-0020, www.hotelnicolas.cl, US$43 s, US$49 d, with private bath and TV) is undistinguished but central.

US$50-100

On the residential west side, ★ **Posada Selva Negra** (Tirzano 110, tel. 045/223-6913, www.hospedajeselvanegra.cl, US$43 s, US$56 d) is a German-run B&B with quiet garden rooms and unexpected touches like soft bathrobes (unusual in this price range). Some singles are small but contain a writing desk, and there's Wi-Fi. The breakfast nook has a world-class collection of Teutonic kitsch.

Downtown's **RP Hotel** (Portales 779, tel. 045/297-7777, www.hotelrp.cl, from US$80 s or d) is a modern 23-room boutique hotel that includes one suite.

★ **Hotel Frontera** (Bulnes 733, tel. 045/220-0400, www.hotelfrontera.cl, from US$89 s or d) is a complex of two facing buildings that include one business-oriented hotel and a convention center. The one across the street has greater amenities (a swimming pool, a gym, and the like), but its only advantage is easier access, as guests at either building are entitled to use all facilities. Ask for IVA (sales tax) discounts.

Hotel Aitué (Antonio Varas 1048, tel.

045/221-2512, www.hotelaitue.cl, US$75 s, US$90 d) is a business-oriented facility with responsive service. Insist on IVA discounts.

US$100-150

At **Hotel Don Eduardo** (Andrés Bello 755, tel. 045/221-4133, www.hoteldoneduardo.cl, from US$106 s or d), the small dark lobby is a misleading approach to a modern downtown business hotel. It has smallish but spotless standard rooms, Wi-Fi, a decent buffet breakfast, and secure parking. Double-paned windows keep the street noise to a minimum.

US$150-200

The five-story **Hotel Dreams Araucanía** (Av. Alemania 0945, tel. 045/237-9000, www.mundodreams.com, from US$189-213 s or d) is a glass palace that's an integral part of the city's casino. In this mostly residential area, it has better access to the restaurant-and-nightlife strip than do its downtown counterparts.

INFORMATION

On the north side of the Plaza de Armas, **Sernatur** (Bulnes 590, tel. 045/240-6205, infoaraucania@sernatur.cl, 9am-6pm Mon.-Fri.) distributes free city maps and regional leaflets. For motorists, the **Automóvil Club de Chile** (San Martín 0278, tel. 045/299-5755) is west of the former Panamericana. **Conaf** (Av. Bilbao 931, 2nd Fl., tel. 045/229-8114) provides national parks information.

SERVICES

There are worthwhile excursions in all directions, but most visitors focus on the Andes to the east. Temuco's **Multitour** (tel. 09/9818-1358, www.chile-travel.com/multitour) has English-speaking guides and a good track record for excursions in and around Temuco, primarily toward the Andean national parks and reserves, but also to westerly Mapuche villages.

Though it's primarily an administrative and commercial center, Temuco has a full complement of traveler's services. **BancoEstado** (Claro Solar 931) has the best

ATMs; the nearby **Casa de Cambio Global** (Bulnes 655, Local 1) is an exchange house. **Correos de Chile** (Diego Portales 801) is the post office. For laundry, try **Lavandería Ni-Zu** (Aldunate 842, tel. 045/223-6893). The **Hospital Dr. Hernán Henríquez Aravena** (Manuel Montt 115, tel. 045/255-9000) is west of the former Panamericana.

TRANSPORTATION

Temuco is La Araucanía's major transportation hub, with air connections north and south as well as abundant bus connections north and south along the Panamericana and east into and over the Andes.

Air

LATAM (Bulnes 687, tel. 045/221-1339) flies several times daily to Santiago and once or twice daily to Puerto Montt. **Sky Airline** (www.skyairline.cl) still flies to Santiago and to Puerto Montt, but sells tickets online or at the airport.

Temuco's new **Aeropuerto Araucanía** (ZCO, Ruta 5, Km 692, Freire, tel. 045/220-1901, www.aeropuertoaraucania.cl) is 30 kilometers south of town. **Transfer Temuco** (tel. 045/233-4033, www.transfertemuco.cl) picks up downtown passengers (US$7.50) outside the Hotel Frontera (Bulnes 733).

Bus

The chaos of long-distance carriers that once congested downtown streets has been relieved by construction of the **Rodoviario Araucario** (Reyes Católicos 1420, tel. 045/222-5005), at the eastern foot of Cerro Ñielol. This has not completely concentrated services. The **Terminal de Buses Rurales** (Av. Aníbal Pinto 032, tel. 045/221-0494) hosts regional carriers, and several long-distance companies have ticket offices and even terminals around the axis formed with the perpendicular Avenida Balmaceda.

Among the regional carriers at Buses Rurales are **Flota Erbuc** (tel. 045/227-2204), which goes several times daily to Curacautín via Lautaro or Victoria, continuing to

Malalcahuello and Lonquimay; **Nar-Bus** (tel. 045/240-7777) and **Intercomunal Sur** (Av. Balmaceda 1395, tel. 045/221-4864), which travel to Cherquenco (for the Llaima sector of Parque Nacional Conguillío), Icalma, Cunco, and Melipeuco; and **Buses Jac,** servicing Villarrica and Pucón, though departures are more frequent from its other office. From its own terminal, **Buses Biobío** (Lautaro 853, tel. 045/265-7876) links Temuco to Angol.

From the Rodoviario, many carriers connect Temuco with Panamericana destinations from Santiago to Puerto Montt and Chiloé. Some have downtown ticket offices, including **Tur-Bus** (Claro Solar 625, tel. 045/268-6602) and **Igi Llaima,** which shares facilities with **Nar-Bus** (Balmaceda 995, tel. 045/240-7700). **Buses Jac** (Av. Balmaceda 1005, tel. 045/299-3117) shuttles frequently to Villarrica and Pucón, and has a daily service to Curarrehue.

Sample domestic destinations, with approximate times and fares, include Villarrica (1 hour, US$3-6), Pucón (1.5 hours, US$4-7), Curacautín (1.5 hours, US$5), Osorno (4 hours, US$6-15), Puerto Montt (5.5 hours, US$8-14), and Santiago (9 hours, US$13-30).

Most Argentina-bound buses use the Paso Mamuil Malal crossing southeast of Pucón (to Junín de los Andes and San Martín de los Andes). But some take the Paso Pino Hachado route, directly east of Temuco via Curacautín and the upper Biobío town of Lonquimay (to Zapala and Neuquén). In addition, there are connections to Bariloche via the Panamericana to Osorno and Ruta 215 east over Paso Cardenal Samoré.

Since the distances are long, the terrain mountainous, and the roads partly gravel, some trans-Andean buses leave early—sometimes as early as 3am. Carriers serving Junín de los Andes and San Martín de los Andes (6 hours, US$20) include **Buses San Martín/ Andesmar Chile** (tel. 045/225-8626). **Igi Llaima** and **Nar-Bus** (both at Balmaceda 995, tel. 045/240-7700) alternate 5am daily services to Zapala and Neuquén (10 hours, US$56) and also go to San Martín. **Vía Bariloche** (tel. 045/225-7904) also goes to Neuquén.

Getting Around

From downtown to the Rodoviario, catch northbound Micro 7 Troncal or Micro 9 from Portales and Bulnes, or *taxi colectivo* 11P from the corner of Prat and Claro Solar.

For excursions into the backcountry in and around Temuco, especially the circuit through Parque Nacional Conguillío or the upper Biobío, scarce public transportation makes renting a car a more convenient option. Rental agencies include the **Automóvil Club de Chile** (Acchi, San Martín 0278, tel. 045/224-8903), **Avis** (San Martín 755, tel. 02/2795-3967, airport tel. 02/2795-3978), **Europcar** (Ruta 5 Sur 4750, Padre Las Casas, tel. 045/291-8940, airport tel. 045/291-8927), and **Hertz** (Longitudinal Sur 2715, Padre Las Casas, tel. 045/231-8585, airport tel. 045/254-4548).

The Upper Cautín and Biobío

From Victoria, 58 kilometers north of Temuco on the Panamericana, a smooth and scenic two-lane highway goes to Curacautín, Lonquimay, and the upper Biobío, an underrated area north of Parque Nacional Conguillío. Blessed with its own native forests, rushing rivers, and volcanic grandeur, the upper Biobío is, along with Conguillío, part of a UNESCO World Biosphere Reserve declared to protect its remaining araucaria stands.

In addition to the main road, this area is also accessible via a shorter paved alternative that heads northeast from Lautaro (30 kilometers north of Temuco). From the upper Biobío, it's also possible to loop back around on good gravel roads to Melipeuco (Conguillío's southern gateway) or back to Temuco.

CURACAUTÍN

Dating from 1882, when the military established Fuerte Ultra Cautín in Pehuenche territory, Curacautín (pop. 16,508) is now the northern access point to Parque Nacional Conguillío and gateway to the upper Río Cautín and upper Biobío. It is 87 kilometers northeast of Temuco via Lautaro or 119 kilometers via the Panamericana and Victoria.

In Curacautín, it's also possible to organize adventure travel activities such as mountain biking and rafting on the Río Cautín, a gentle Class II stream that, in spring runoff, has some Class III segments.

Food and Accommodations

There are few places to eat, the best of which is probably Hotel Plaza's **La Cabaña** (Yungay 157, tel. 045/288-1256, breakfast, lunch, and dinner daily), opposite the plaza. **Café Vizzio's** (Serrano 248, tel. 045/288-1653, lunch and dinner daily) has sandwiches, desserts, and coffee. **Terra** (Prat 539, tel. 045/288-1237) is a café with pizza, pasta, sandwiches, and snacks, plus beer and cocktails and an appealing patio. The service is amateurish, though.

Facing the Plaza from the south side of the highway, **Hostal Epu Pewen** (Manuel Rodríguez 705, tel. 045/288-1793, www.epupewen.cl, US$18 dorm with shared bath, US$49 s or d with private bath, breakfast included) is a rustically stylish hybrid offering hostel dorms with shared baths and a couple of suites with private baths; it's also a center for arranging outdoor activities. Despite the roadside frontage, the rooms themselves are at the back and nighttime is quiet, although the walls are a little thin.

Facing the highway a couple of blocks west, **Hospedaje Aliwen** (Manuel Rodríguez 540, tel. 09/7899-0910, www.alojamientocuracautin.cl, US$26 pp with shared bath, US$52 s or d with private bath) also includes breakfast in its rates.

About 15 kilometers east of Curacautín, the rushing Río Cautín and dense forest shield the immaculate ★ **Hotel Andenrose** (Ruta 181, Km 68.5, tel. 09/9869-1700, www.andenrose.com, US$50-60 s, US$73-82 d) from any noise or visual pollution on the nearby highway. The B&B accommodations, in luminous pinewood rooms with firm beds, include a diverse buffet breakfast; there are also somewhat more expensive *cabañas* and apartments and a new swimming pool. Its gregarious Bavarian owner, English-speaking Hans Schöndorfer, provides transfers from the Curacautín bus terminal and is also a talented chef.

Transportation and Services

The **Oficina de Informaciones Turísticas** (Manuel Rodríguez s/n, tel. 045/246-4858, 8am-9pm Mon.-Fri., 9am-5pm Sat., 9am-2pm Sun.) is on the north side of the Plaza de Armas.

BancoEstado (O'Higgins 562) has an ATM. **Correos de Chile** (Yungay 265) is the post office. There are several call centers and Internet options on O'Higgins and around the plaza.

Three blocks west of the Plaza de Armas, Curacautín's **Terminal Rodoviario** (Ruta 181 and Arica) is directly on the Lonquimay highway. At a separate office, **Tur-Bus** (Serrano 101, tel. 045/268-6629) has direct service to Santiago (8.5 hours, US$20-28). **Flota Erbuc** has five buses daily to and from Temuco (US$5) via Victoria and four via Lautaro; there are five to Lonquimay. Recently, **Araucanía Express** has begun to offer better services with newer buses. Getting to Parque Nacional Conguillío is possible only by taxi. **Igi Llaima** and **Nar-Bus** pass through town daily en route to Zapala and Neuquén, Argentina (9 hours, US$26); make reservations in Temuco to guarantee a seat.

PARQUE NACIONAL TOLHUACA

Native woodlands of araucarias and other species adorn the foothill slopes of **Parque Nacional Tolhuaca** (US$8 adults, US$4.50 children), where the Río Malleco drains south-southwest into marshy Laguna Malleco

The Chilean Path to Conservation

One of Latin America's most far-sighted conservation projects is the former Lagos administration's **Sendero de Chile,** a foot, bicycle, and horse path linking the altiplano, near the Peruvian border, with southern Patagonia's sub-Antarctic tundra. Intended for both environmental and recreational purposes, its initial segments opened in 2001. The ambitious goal was to finish the project by 2010, the bicentennial of Chilean independence. The bicentennial has passed, but progress continues.

Comparable to the United States' Pacific Crest Trail in the terrain it covers, but more like the older Appalachian Trail in that authorities hope to encourage community maintenance, the trail passes through a representative sample of foothill and upper Andean ecosystems. There is even the possibility of cooperation with Argentina, where the route passes through the vicinity of the Campo de Hielo Sur, the southern Patagonian ice sheet that once engendered a bitter border dispute between the two countries.

Conama, the state environmental agency entrusted with the project, prohibits motorized transport on the two-meter-wide dirt and gravel trail. Mostly following the Andean foothills, the route suggests detours to important natural, cultural, or even commercial features, such as archaeological sites, wineries, and crafts markets.

Conama hopes the trail will attract both Chileans and international outdoors enthusiasts to hike some or all of its length. Along the route there will be rustic cabins and campsites, in locally appropriate styles, as well as mileage markers and informational panels on flora and fauna. Because one project goal is to encourage local development, there will be special emphasis on local place-names and cultural monuments.

Since 2001, when Ricardo Lagos himself inaugurated the first segment at Parque Nacional Conguillío, thousands of kilometers have opened to the public. This progress may not be so great as it implies, though—parts of it link preexisting trails in national parks, reserves, and monuments. Some segments will pass through private land, and private companies and individuals will become involved.

Conama and its tourism counterpart, Sernatur, are promoting this as the world's longest hiking trail, in excess of 8,500 kilometers by its presumed completion—whenever that is. To follow its progress, visit the Sendero de Chile website (www.senderodechile.cl), which details access, services, and routes.

before plunging toward the coast. Improved access roads have increased visitation, especially in summer and on weekends, but most people stay near Laguna Malleco. The rest of the park remains ideal for camping, hiking, and fishing.

Geography and Climate

In the Andean foothills, ranging from 1,000 meters elevation at Laguna Malleco to 1,821 meters on its northern summits and ridgelines, Tolhuaca is a compact 6,374-hectare unit on the north bank of the Río Malleco. It has a cool, humid climate, with an average annual temperature of 9°C and 2,500 to 3,000 millimeters of rainfall. Summers are mild and relatively dry. The park's namesake

peak, 2,806-meter Volcán Tolhuaca, lies beyond its southeastern boundaries.

Flora and Fauna

At higher elevations, Tolhuaca has nearly pure araucaria stands in well-drained soils. The dense gallery forests along the Río Malleco consist of *coigüe, olivillo,* and other evergreen species, along with deciduous *raulí* and *roble. Quila* forms almost impenetrable bamboo thickets in some areas. *Junquillos* (reeds) grow in the lakeside sediments, while rhubarb-like *nalcas,* ferns, firecracker fuchsias, mosses, and other water-loving plants grow on the riverbanks.

Except for waterfowl and coypu in Laguna Malleco, Tolhuaca's fauna is inconspicuous.

Pumas, *pudú* (miniature deer), foxes, and skunks all exist here.

Sights and Recreation

As ash and other sediments from the surrounding ridges and peaks sluice into the river and downstream, water-loving reeds are colonizing the shoreline of 76-hectare **Laguna Malleco,** a glacial remnant where Conaf keeps a loaner rowboat for anglers and birders. It's an easy walk from the campground, and swimming is possible in several nearby pools.

From Laguna Malleco's north shore, the 1,800-meter **Sendero El Salto** winds through thick native forest to **Salto Malleco,** a 50-meter cascade that plummets over basalt into the lower drainage. Also from Laguna Malleco, the **Sendero Prados de Mesacura** switchbacks up the north shore to intersect the **Sendero Lagunillas,** which follows the contour east through nearly waterless araucaria woodlands (porous volcanic soil absorbs almost all precipitation). From a spot about five kilometers east of Laguna Malleco, toward hot springs resort Termas de Tolhuaca, the eight-kilometer **Sendero Laguna Verde** skirts 1,606-meter Cerro Laguna Verde's southwestern slope to arrive at its namesake lake.

Food and Accommodations

At Laguna Malleco, Conaf's shady **Camping Inalaufquén** (tel. 045/229-8210 in Temuco, US$18) has 25 sites with barbecue pits, picnic tables, running water, and clean restrooms with flush toilets and cold showers. Single travelers can seek a discount if it's not crowded. Nine kilometers south of the park, accommodations at the 100-bed **Hotel Termas Malleco** (tel. 045/229-9500, www. tolhuaca.viaje.cl, US$111 pp with breakfast, US$60 under age 10) include unlimited access to pools and baths. It has its own restaurant, and packages with meals are available.

Transportation and Services

Tolhuaca lacks a formal visitors center, but rangers at Laguna Malleco offer daily chats at the outdoor amphitheater.

From Curacautín, 87 kilometers northeast of Temuco via Lautaro or 119 kilometers via Victoria, an improved gravel road reaches hot springs resort Termas de Tolhuaca, 33 kilometers to the north. From there, a once-hazardous 4WD road to Laguna Malleco is now passable for ordinary vehicles, at least in summer. *Taxis colectivos* from Curacautín go as far as Termas de Tolhuaca, but it's another nine kilometers to Malleco.

MALALCAHUELLO

Ten kilometers east of Manzanar, the hamlet of Malalcahuello occupies a high valley in the shadow of 2,865-meter Volcán Lonquimay, known also as Volcán Mocho. At 980 meters, Malalcahuello is cooler than areas to the west, and nights can get chilly even in summer. Its highest-profile assets are the hot-springs resort Centro Termal Malalcahuello and the new Corralco ski area.

Malalcahuello makes an ideal destination for hikers and riders thanks to its accessibility to its namesake national reserve. Trailheads start near the highway.

Reserva Nacional Malalcahuello

Combined with the contiguous Reserva Las Nalcas to the north, the **Reserva Nacional Malalcahuello** comprises 25,000 hectares of wild country. At higher elevation than Parque Nacional Tolhuaca, it contains overlapping forest flora of araucaria with deciduous Andean forest of evergreen *coigüe* and *lenga,* and araucaria with *coigüe* mixed with *ñire.* The fauna resembles Tolhuaca's, though the Andean condor and the *carpintero negro* (black woodpecker) are more common here.

Symmetrical **Volcán Lonquimay (Mocho)** is the reserve's focal point, its summit crater filled by a glacier that spills onto the adjoining flanks. Slightly northeast of town, it dates from the late Pleistocene but erupted as recently as 1933, almost simultaneously with nearby Volcán Llaima, and lava spilled down its northeastern flanks in 1990. Trails to nearby Cerro Cautín (2.5 hours) and Lonquimay's summit start at the ski area. Sendero de Chile rounds Lonquimay before descending into town and then continuing toward the Sierra Nevada and Conguillío. Trekking maps, for sale at Suizandina Lodge, make hiking here easier.

On the site of an older ski area that was nearly in ruins, Malalcahuello also has a sparkling new option, the **Corralco Mountain & Ski Resort** (Callao 3602-A, Las Condes, Santiago, tel. 02/2206-0741, www.corralco.com, US$120 s, US$183 d, with breakfast, meal packages available). After a slow start, the resort has provided a lift for businesses in nearby communities as well as itself. Lift tickets cost about US$56 per day during the mid-June to October season, but it's also open for summer excursions such as climbing Volcán Lonquimay.

Food and Accommodations

★ **Suizandina Lodge** (Camino Internacional, Km 83, tel. 045/197-3725 or tel. 09/9884-9541, www.suizandina.com, US$23-27 pp dorms, US$48-59 s, US$71-82 d, ask for IVA discounts) is a hybrid hostel, *cabaña,* and guesthouse west of town on the north side of the highway. Founder Tom Buschor is no longer here, but the new Swiss-Chilean owners have matched his exacting standards, still serving specialties such as fondue and *rösti* for reasonably priced lunches or dinners, accompanied by fresh desserts and Chilean wines. While they no longer promote Suizandina as a campground, individuals and small parties can still camp here economically (US$9-12 pp, breakfast US$8). The newest offerings are horseback riding in summer and ski-touring in winter.

The **Malalcahuello Thermal Resort & Spa** (Ruta 181, Km 86, tel. 09/6617-4605, www.malalcahuello.cl, from US$287 s or d) is a hot springs megaproject that fits surprisingly well into its setting, about two kilometers south of the highway via a paved spur. With indoor pools, spa treatments, and physical therapists, it also has a handful of *cabañas* and bungalows (from US$300 for up to 6 people, including access to baths but not breakfast), and a so-so restaurant. There are IVA discounts for foreigners. Nonguests can access the pools (US$30 adults, US$13 ages 3-12, US$4.50 under age 3). Additional services include massages, mud baths, whirlpool tubs, saunas, and the like.

the Malalcahuello Thermal Resort & Spa

the traditional starting point for descending what was Chile's wildest white-water river until a series of downstream dams submerged the rapids.

Instead of a standard grid, Lonquimay (pop. about 3,500) has a peculiar ovoid town plan, though still centered on the handsomely refurbished Plaza de Armas. For information, it has an obliging **Oficina Municipal de Turismo** (O'Higgins and Colón, tel. 045/265-6096, www.mlonquimay.cl, 8:30am-2pm and 3pm-5:30pm Mon.-Fri., 10am-2pm and 3pm-7pm Sat.-Sun.). From Malalcahuello, a steep eastbound dirt road over Cuesta las Raíces is a shorter alternate route to Lonquimay, which is 900 meters above sea level. This road is open in summer and autumn only.

Lonco Patagonia (Ruta 89, Km 106.5, tel. 09/9283-0846, www.loncopatagonia.ga-leon.com) offers horseback excursions in the vicinity.

Hostal Nativo (Caupolicán 915, tel. 045/289-1111, www.hostalnativo.cl, US$30-45 s, US$37-52 d) is a pleasant guesthouse with smallish but comfortable rooms, the cheaper of which have shared baths. Its restaurant has one of the more diverse menus in town. **Hostería Donde Juancho** (O'Higgins 1130, tel. 045/289-1140, www.dondejuancho.cl, US$40 s, US$48 d) also offers accommodations and has a 50-seat restaurant with beef and traditional Chilean dishes.

At least five daily **Biobío** and **Flota Erbuc** buses connect Lonquimay's Terminal de Buses (O'Higgins and Portales) with Temuco.

ALTO BIOBÍO

South of Lonquimay, a gravel road tracks south over the Cuesta La Fusta past Lago Galletué, the Biobío's official source and part of Conaf's **Reserva Nacional Galletué.** The road continues southeast past the border post of Icalma (for the Argentine town of Aluminé), but there is no public transportation across this route. There are numerous simple campgrounds along this main road, which then turns west toward Melipeuco and Parque Nacional Conguillío. From

This former railway tunnel is now used by auto traffic.

Transportation and Services

Conaf's Malalcahuello ranger station is a good source of advice. Speakers of English, German, French, and Italian can try La Suizandina. **Biobío** and **Flota Erbuc** buses between Temuco and Lonquimay pass directly by La Suizandina's gates and the ranger station.

LONQUIMAY

From Malalcahuello, the highway heads southeast to enter the 1930s' **Túnel Las Raíces** (toll US$0.60). Now open to vehicular traffic, the single-lane, 4.5-kilometer tunnel has been upgraded with new pavement and a reinforced roof. A second parallel tunnel to permit two-way traffic, rather than alternating traffic as at present, remains in the planning stages. This improvement would simplify access to the Pino Hachado border crossing.

Beyond the tunnel, where cyclists must hitch a lift with a passing pickup, the highway veers northeast to the village of **Lonquimay,** in the placid upper Biobío drainage. This was

Lonquimay, newly paved Ruta 181 crosses Conaf's **Reserva Nacional Alto Biobío** via the 1,884-meter Paso Pino Hachado, the route used by buses to the Argentine cities of Zapala and Neuquén.

MELIPEUCO

In the Río Allipén valley, sited on an ancient mudflow 92 kilometers east of Temuco and 45 kilometers west of Icalma, the Mapuche town of Melipeuco is Parque Nacional Conguillío's southern access point and an alternative route into the upper Biobío loop around Lonquimay. In the 1970s, this was a conflict area in the agrarian reform movement, and the issue remains alive today.

Melipeuco (pop. 2,500) operates a summer-only tourist office on Pedro Aguirre Cerda, across from the YPF gas station. There's a crafts market here as well, and balky but free public Wi-Fi in the vicinity of the municipal offices.

For the cheapest accommodations, try friendly **Hospedaje Icalma** (Pedro Aguirre Cerda 729, tel. 09/9280-8210, www.melipeucohospedaje.cl, US$21 pp with private bath, breakfast, and Wi-Fi). The rooms are unheated but have lots of blankets. Under new management, in a remodeled house of some architectural distinction, **Hospedaje Hue Telén** (Pedro Aguirre Cerda 1, tel. 045/258-1005, pabloparrak1@hotmail.com, US$45 d, not including breakfast) is in a sprawling motel-style place with its own restaurant. The best place to eat may be **Las Terrazas de Melipeuco** (Pedro Aguirre Cerda 87, tel. 09/8769-0163, 9am-6pm Mon.-Thurs., 9am-midnight Fri.-Sat., 9am-11pm Sun.), which serves fixed-price lunches plus excellent sandwiches on their homemade *pan amasado*.

Nar-Bus runs frequent buses to and from Temuco's Terminal de Buses Rurales (1.5 hours, US$5). There is no scheduled public transportation to Conguillío, but taxis or pickup trucks will take passengers to the visitors center for about US$25 one-way.

Parque Nacional Conguillío

Directly east of Temuco, 3,125-meter Volcán Llaima's smoldering crater is Conguillío's most eye-catching feature. Since colonial times, Chile's second most active volcano has recorded dozens of violent eruptions. On New Year's Day 2008, in fact, a sudden eruption and lava flow closed the northern access road from Curacautín and forced evacuation of 150 travelers.

Within its 60,833 hectares, this UNESCO biosphere reserve abounds with dozens of other lava flows, secondary cones, alpine lakes, river canyons, and the araucaria forest that it was created to protect. The name Conguillío derives from the Mapudungun *kongüjim*, "to enter the *pewen* forest." In late 1911, drawn by the *pewen*'s fame, the aging pioneer U.S. conservationist John Muir traveled in the area simply to see, sketch, and photograph the tree in its native habitat—"A glorious and novel sight, beyond all I had hoped for." As he so often did in California's Sierra Nevada, Muir slept in the open air, beneath the trees he came to visit.

For foreigners and Chileans alike, Conguillío is one of Temuco's most popular excursions. It justifies a day trip but merits at least an overnight.

GEOGRAPHY AND CLIMATE

From Temuco, Conguillío's western limit is only about 80 kilometers away via Cherquenco; by either Curacautín or Melipeuco, it's about 120 kilometers. Elevation ranges from around 900 meters in the Truful Truful valley to 3,125 meters on Llaima's summit. In its northeastern corner, the ruggedly glaciated Sierra Nevada averages above 2,500 meters.

Since most of Conguillío's 2,500 millimeters of precipitation falls as snow between May and September, the mild summers, averaging around 15°C, make its lakes and streams popular recreational destinations. Even in summer, occasional heavy rains—if not lava flows—can make the Curacautín road impassable even with a 4WD vehicle.

FLORA AND FAUNA

Conguillío was originally two separate parks. The other park was named Los Paraguas after the umbrella shape of the mature araucaria that, above 1,400 meters, mixes with the southern beeches *coigüe, ñire,* and *lenga. Coigüe* is also common at lower elevations, but mixed with *roble.* Above 1,200 meters, *raulí* succeeds *roble.*

Traditionally, Pehuenche people collected the coniferous araucaria's nuts, much as indigenous people gathered *piñon* nuts in western North America. The name Pehuenche means "people of the *pewen,*" the local species of an endemic southern hemisphere genus that once enjoyed a greater distribution throughout the Americas.

Because much of the terrain consists of barren volcanic slopes, lava fields, and open woodlands, prime wildlife habitat is scarce, and so is wildlife. Birds are most common and resemble those at Tolhuaca or Malalcahuello. The small reptile *lagartija* flourishes in drier environments.

VOLCÁN LLAIMA

Towering west of the park's geographic center, glacier-covered **Volcán Llaima** is a Holocene structure of accumulated lava flows within an eight-kilometer-wide caldera that exploded about 7,200 years ago. It has two active craters, one on the summit and another on its southeastern shoulder. In good weather, the northern access road is passable for normal-sized vehicles.

★ SECTOR CONGUILLÍO

In **Sector Conguillío,** east of Llaima, the sprawling lava flows of **El Escorial** dammed

the Río Truful Truful to form **Laguna Arco Iris** and **Laguna Verde.** To the north, beneath the Sierra Nevada, **Laguna Conguillío** has a similar origin.

Near Conaf's Centro de Información Ambiental at the southwest corner of Laguna Conguillío, the **Sendero Araucarias** is a short woodland trail suitable for any hiker. For a longer and more challenging excursion, try walking from **Playa Linda,** at the east end of Laguna Conguillío, to the base of the **Sierra Nevada,** which offers hikers overwhelming views through nearly solid araucaria stands. This extension across the mountains to Termas Río Blanco is a hazardous one on which hikers have died.

At **Laguna Captrén,** at the northern entrance, the **Sendero de Chile** was the initial section of the nonmotorized trail intended to unite the country from the Peruvian border to Tierra del Fuego. At Laguna Arco Iris, to the south, an early settler built the wooden **Casa del Colono** as a homestead cabin. From Laguna Verde, also known as Laguna Quililo, a short wooded footpath reaches the beach at **La Ensenada.**

Conaf's **Sendero Cañadon Truful-Truful,** a 900-meter nature trail, follows the river's course where erosion has uncovered the rainbow chronology of Llaima's eruptions and ash falls. Along the 800-meter **Sendero Los Vertientes,** subterranean springs emerge from the volcanic terrain.

SECTOR LOS PARAGUAS

From **Sector Los Paraguas,** on the park's west side, well-equipped climbers can scale Llaima. Camping is possible in summer, and there's also a *refugio* (shelter). There is an alternative route from Captrén, which has better public transportation, on the north side. Before climbing, get permission from Conaf in Temuco.

Skiing takes place at Los Paraguas's **Centro de Ski Las Araucarias** (tel. 045/256-2313, www.skiaraucarias.cl, lift tickets US$32-38). It also has Temuco offices (Bulnes 351, Oficina 47, tel. 045/227-4141).

ACCOMMODATIONS

Along Laguna Conguillío's south shore, Conaf has five **campgrounds** (tel. 045/229-8114, US$24-48 for up to 6 people in summer and during Semana Santa) under private concession: The campground administration is at **Los Ñirres** (42 sites), while there are smaller clusters at **Los Carpinteros** (12 sites), **La Caseta** (12 sites, private baths), **El Estero** (16 sites), and **El Hoyón** (10 sites, private baths). Conaf also sets aside a handful of El Estero sites for bicyclists and backpackers (US$10 pp).

At the **Conguillío Lodge** (US$191 for up to 3 people, US$225 for up to 7, off-season rates about 20 percent lower), *cabañas* are one kilometer west of park headquarters. There are also dorm accommodations at the winter-only **Refugio Kalfukura** (US$30 pp). For details and reservations at all park facilities, contact **Sendas Conguillío** (tel. 02/2840-6809, www.sendasconguillio.cl).

At Laguna Verde, 18 kilometers northeast of Melipeuco, the private **La Baita Conguillío** (Casilla 492, Villarrica, tel. 045/258-1073, www.labaitaconguillio.cl, from US$83 s, US$106 d) has *cabañas* sleeping four to eight people and a modular "eco-lodge" that's more suitable for individuals or couples.

The modern **Centro de Ski las Araucarias** (tel. 045/256-2313, www.ski-araucarias.cl) has a variety of accommodations. Its **Refugio Paraguas** (US$18 pp dorms with your own sleeping bag, US$45 d) has dorm beds and a triple room with shared baths. The **Refugio Pehuén** also has dorms (US$18 pp) and doubles (US$45) with shared baths. Facilities at the **Edificio Araucarias** can sleep up to eight.

INFORMATION

At Laguna Conguillío, Conaf's **Centro de Información Ambiental** (tel. 02/2840-6818, parque.conguillio@conaf.cl, 8:30am-7:30pm daily Jan.-Feb., 8:30am-1pm and 2:30pm-6:30pm daily Mar.-Dec.) has good natural-history exhibits and a cozy fireplace. It organizes children's programs and hiking excursions, and provides evening naturalist talks.

Conaf also has ranger stations at the Laguna Captrén and Truful Truful park entrances (park admission US$7 pp). At the Paraguas ski area, admission is US$2.50.

TRANSPORTATION

Because public transportation is inconvenient to almost every sector of the park, it's worth considering renting a car, but it's not absolutely essential. Even with a car, the steep, narrow, and often muddy road between Laguna Captrén and the park administration can be difficult in either direction.

Reaching Curacautín and Melipeuco, the northern and southern gateways to the main park loop, is easy enough by public bus. From Curacautín, **Curacautín Express** (tel. 045/225-8125) provides twice-daily bus service (6am and 6pm daily) to the northern park entrance at Laguna Captrén. From Melipeuco, it's possible to hire a taxi or pickup truck to get to the park.

Sector Los Paraguas is most difficult to reach by public transportation as there is no bus service beyond Vilcún, 35 kilometers east; from there, it's another 42 kilometers to the Los Paraguas ski lodge. A rugged alternative route goes from Captrén to Los Paraguas, but with no public transportation.

Villarrica

Volcán Villarrica's fiery eruptions may have deterred some settlers, but Mapuche resistance to the Spaniards and Chileans was more effective. In 1552, the 50 colonists under Gerónimo de Alderete established Santa María Magdalena de Villarrica, but the Mapuche people forced its abandonment several times despite speculation about precious metals nearby (the overly optimistic founding name Villarrica means "Rich Town"). After expelling the Spaniards in 1602, the Mapuche enjoyed nearly three centuries of uninterrupted possession until, in 1883, Chilean colonel Gregorio Urrutia reached an agreement with Mapuche chief Epuléf to regularize the Chilean presence.

Villarrica's 1897 declaration of city status brought an influx of immigrants, many of them German, who transformed the area into a dairy zone and, eventually, a durable resort area with an international reputation.

ORIENTATION

Some 87 kilometers southeast of Temuco via the Panamericana and Ruta 199, an international highway to Argentina, Villarrica (pop. about 40,000) lies at Lago Villarrica's southwestern edge, at its Río Toltén outlet. While the town has a regular grid pattern, the focus of activity is not the Plaza de Armas but rather the lakeshore, along with the commercial thoroughfare Avenida Pedro de Valdivia and its perpendicular Camilo Henríquez-Gerónimo de Alderete.

SIGHTS AND RECREATION

Stone tools, early Mapuche ceramics, and contemporary indigenous jewelry, silver, and leatherwork constitute the collections of the **Museo Histórico y Arqueológico de Villarrica** (Pedro de Valdivia 1050, tel. 045/241-5706, 9am-2pm and 3pm-7pm Mon.-Fri., 6pm-10pm Sun., US$0.50).

The rejuvenated lakefront **Embarcadero,** with a cluster of small jetties toward the foot of General Körner, is the starting point for water-based excursions. Another of its attractions is the new **Centro Cultural Liquen** (Arturo Prat and General Körner, tel. 045/275-8088, www.culturaliquen.cl), which hosts a variety of performing arts events and films.

ENTERTAINMENT AND SHOPPING

In recent years, **The Travellers** (Valentín Letelier 753, tel. 045/241-3617) has morphed from a diverse fusion restaurant into a bar that serves primarily pub grub. It remains popular, and smokers congregate on the patio. **Dinner's** (Pedro Montt 390, tel. 045/241-0361) is a pub-restaurant that draws a younger crowd.

Immediately west of the tourist office, the **Feria Artesanal** (midday-late afternoon daily) showcases Mapuche crafts and food in summer, but fall-spring it's moribund. **Tejidos Ray-Ray** (Anfión Muñoz 386, tel. 045/241-2006) is a clothing store strong on woolens.

FOOD

At the Mercado Fritz crafts market, inexpensive **La Cocina de María** (Aviador Acevedo 612, tel. 09/9675-1418) is a good lunch option for typical Chilean dishes such as chicken with rice, fried chicken, and empanadas. **El Sabio** (Julio Zegers 393, tel. 045/241-9918, www.elsabio.cl, 12:30pm-4pm and 6pm-10:30pm Thurs.-Sun.) prepares moderately priced Argentine-style pizza, including the delicious cheese-and-onion *fugazzeta.*

The unpretentious **Tejuelas** (Gerónimo de Alderete 632, tel. 045/241-0619, lunch and dinner daily) delivers great value for the price, especially with some of the country's finest homemade bread for sandwiches. The pizza is

Lago Villarrica and Vicinity

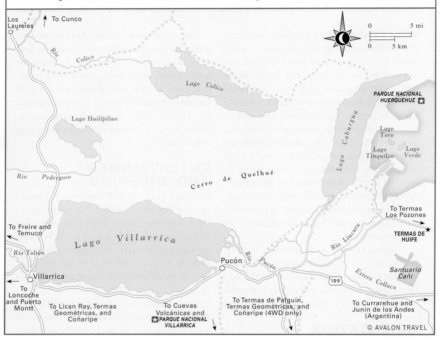

Los Laureles · To Cunco · Río Colico · Lago Colico · Lago Huilipilun · Río Pedregoso · Río · Cerro de Quelhué · Lago Caburgua · PARQUE NACIONAL HUERQUEHUE · Lago Toro · Lago Tinquilco · Lago Verde · To Termas Los Pozones · TERMAS DE HUIFE · To Freire and Temuco · Río Tolten · Lago Villarrica · Pucón · Río Pucón · Río Liucura · Estero Collaco · Santuario Cañi · Villarrica · To Loncoche and Puerto Montt · To Lican Ray, Termas Geométricas, and Coñaripe · To Cuevas Volcánicas and PARQUE NACIONAL VILLARRICA · To Termas de Palguín, Termas Geométricas, and Coñaripe (4WD only) · 199 · To Currarehue and Junín de los Andes (Argentina) · © AVALON TRAVEL · 0 5 mi · 0 5 km

less appealing, its crust a little heavy despite a diversity of appetizing toppings.

The expanded **Sweet & Gourmet** (Camilo Henríquez 331, tel. 045/241-4087) serves sandwiches and light meals, but its strength is Chile's finest kuchen: The raspberry kuchen topped with flakes of white chocolate is beyond exquisite. Next-door **Huerto Azul** (Camilo Henríquez 341, www.huertoazul.cl) serves rich ice cream and other desserts.

Near the lake, **Fuego Patagón** (Pedro Montt 40, tel. 045/241-2207, 12:30pm-3:30pm and 7:30pm-11:30pm Mon.-Sat., 12:30pm-4pm Sun., US$19) serves the usual beef cuts but also Patagonian lamb (with a distinctive asparagus side dish) and game dishes such as *jabalí* (wild boar) and venison. The service is assiduous. The wine list offers only the biggest wineries, though they're flexible on by-the-glass selections. A newer grill restaurant,

Brazas (Körner 153, tel. 045/241-1631) occupies the former Hotel Yachting Kiel.

In a lakeside setting, the local classic **El Rey del Marisco** (Valentín Letelier 1030, tel. 045/241-2093, www.elreydelmarisco.cl, lunch and dinner daily, US$10-15) remains popular for fish and shellfish dishes. More often than not, the ambitious **Mesa del Mar** (Gerónimo de Alderete 835, tel. 045/241-9515, www.mesadelmar.cl, noon-4pm and 7pm-midnight daily) is good, but it can be hit or miss.

ACCOMMODATIONS

As in other lakes district resorts, room rates peak in January and February. Semana Santa (the week before Easter), September's Fiestas Patrias, and the ski season can all see higher prices as well.

The mostly dorms **Mapu Hostel** (General Urrutia 302, tel./fax 045/241-2098, www.

Villarrica

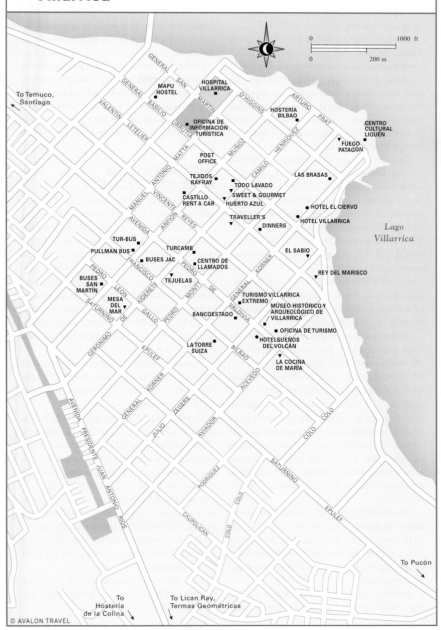

To Temuco, Santiago

GENERAL SAN MARTIN

GENERAL BASILIO

VALENTIN LETELIER

URRUTIA

MATTA

ANTONIO

MANUEL

VINCENTE

AVENIDA

ANFION REYES

O'HIGGINS

MARTIN

FRANCISCO

PEDRO LEON

AIDERETE

SATURNINO DE

GALLO

PEDRO

MONT DE

PEDRO

KORNER

GERONIMO

EPULEF

KORNER

GENERAL

JULIO

ZEGERS

AVIADOR

RODRIGUEZ

COLO

COLO

CAUPOLICAN

AVENIDA PRESIDENTE JUAN ANTONIO RIOS

ARTURO PRAT

CAMILO HENRIQUEZ

MUÑOZ

VALDIVIA

BILBAO

ACEVEDO

SATURNINO

COLO

COLO

EPULEF

MAPU HOSTEL

HOSPITAL VILLARRICA

OFICINA DE INFORMACIÓN TURÍSTICA

POST OFFICE

TEJIDOS RAY-RAY

CASTILLO RENT A CAR

TUR-BUS

PULLMAN BUS

BUSES JAC

TURCAMB

BUSES SAN MARTIN

MESA DEL MAR

TEJUELAS

CENTRO DE LLAMADOS

LA TORRE SUIZA

BANCOESTADO

HOSTERÍA BILBAO

TODO LAVADO

SWEET & GOURMET

HUERTO AZUL

TRAVELLER'S

DINNERS

LAS BRASAS

EL SABIO

TURISMO VILLARRICA EXTREMO

CENTRO CULTURAL LIQUEN

FUEGO PATAGON

HOTEL EL CIERVO

HOTEL VILLARRICA

REY DEL MARISCO

MUSEO HISTÓRICO Y ARQUEOLÓGICO DE VILLARRICA

OFICINA DE TURISMO

HOTELSUEÑOS DEL VOLCÁN

LA COCINA DE MARÍA

Lago Villarrica

0   1000 ft

0   200 m

To Hostería de la Colina

To Lican Ray, Termas Geométricas

To Pucón

© AVALON TRAVEL

mapuhostel.com, US$15-18 pp, US$45 d) has done a lot with a little, including recycling wood pallets as casually stylish furniture with Mapuche touches.

Cyclists in particular flock to ★ La Torre Suiza (Bilbao 969, tel./fax 045/241-1213, www.torresuiza.com, US$18 pp dorms, US$30 s, US$42 d with shared bath, US$53 s or d), with firm, comfortable beds, easily regulated hot showers, but squeaky floors. The higher rates are for larger rooms with private baths in a new wing. Everyone shares a substantial European-style breakfast.

Comfy, rustically styled **Hostería Bilbao** (Camilo Henríquez 43, tel. 045/241-1186, hosteriabilbao@gmail.com, US$53 s, uS$83 d) enjoys a lakeshore site. On Villarrica's busiest commercial avenue, the **Hotel Sueños del Volcán** (Pedro de Valdivia 1011, tel. 045/241-1050, www.suenosdelvolcan.cl, US$57-113 s, US$73-128 d) has simple but nicely decorated rooms and a restaurant.

Hotel Villarrica (Körner 255, tel./fax 045/241-1641, www.cajalosandes.cl, US$91 s or d) offers good value for its tranquil lakeside location in a residential area.

Under new ownership, overlooking the lake from secluded high ground, the eight-room ★ **Hostería de la Colina** (Las Colinas 115, tel. 045/241-1503, www.hosteriadelacolina. com, ma.elortegui@gmail.com, US$91-117 s or d) provides a full American-style breakfast, attractive gardens with a hot tub, and a large English-language book exchange on the honor system. The best volcano views are from a garden overlook. The highest rates correspond to spacious garden *cabañas*. The homemade ice cream alone makes the restaurant worth a visit.

Set among lush gardens, near the lakeshore, **Hotel El Ciervo** (Körner 241, tel. 045/241-1215, www.hotelelciervo.cl, US$127-181 s or d) is a traditional favorite. Some rooms have fireplaces. Rates include an ample European-style breakfast.

Midway between Villarrica and Pucón, the area's only legitimate five-star hotel is the lakeside ★ **Villarrica Park Lake Hotel** (Camino Villarrica Pucón, Km 13, tel. 045/245-0000, www.hotelvillarricaparklake. com, from US$285 s or d), a tasteful contemporary place with 70 expansive rooms (nearly all with balconies), all of which face the lake. Its relatively small private beach is rockier than it is sandy, but it compensates partly with indoor and outdoor pools as well as a spa, two bars, and a restaurant. Serious high rollers opt for the presidential suite (US$1,375, usually reserved well ahead of time).

INFORMATION AND SERVICES

Well-stocked with maps, brochures, and a roster of accommodations but no prices, Villarrica's municipal **Oficina de Información Turística** (Pedro de Valdivia 1070, tel. 045/220-6619, www.visitvillarrica. cl, 8am-11pm daily Jan.-Feb., 8:30am-1pm and 2pm-6pm Mon.-Fri., 9am-pm and 2pm-5:30pm Sat.-Sun. Mar.-Dec.) keeps long hours in January and February. There is an additional **Oficina de Información Turística** (Urrutia s/n, tel. 045/241-9819) directly on the Plaza de Armas.

Turcamb (Camilo Henríquez 576, Local 6) is the main exchange house. **BancoEstado** (Pedro de Valdivia 957) collects minimal ATM commissions.

Correos de Chile (Anfión Muñoz 315) is the post office. The **Centro de Llamados** (Camilo Henríquez 587) provides both long-distance telephone and Internet service. For laundry service, try **Todo Lavado** (General Urrutia 699, Local 7, tel. 045/241-4452).

It used to be necessary to organize excursions such as climbing Volcán Villarrica in Pucón, but **Turismo Villarrica Extremo** (Pedro de Valdivia 910, tel. 045/241-0900, www.villarricaextremo.com) works with Pucón agencies.

For medical assistance, there's the **Hospital Villarrica** (San Martín 460, tel. 045/255-5250).

TRANSPORTATION

Villarrica has a central **Terminal de Buses** (Av. Pedro de Valdivia 621), but some carriers have individual offices nearby. At the main terminal, **Vipu Ray** (tel. 09/6835-5798) has frequent buses to Pucón (40 minutes, US$1.25), where there are connections to other regional destinations such as Curarrehue and Puesco. **Buses Jac** (Bilbao 610, tel. 045/246-7777) shuttles at least every 15-30 minutes between Temuco (1 hour, US$2.50) and Pucón (30 minutes, US$1).

Northbound services to Santiago and intermediates on the Panamericana are frequent, but some southbound services require backtracking to Temuco. Alternatively, you can transfer at Freire from any Temuco-bound bus. Many companies go to Santiago, including **Pullman Bus** (Bilbao 598, tel. 045/241-4217), Buses Jac, and **Tur-Bus** (Anfión Muñoz 657, tel. 045/220-4102), which also has direct services to Osorno, Puerto Varas, and Puerto Montt. Santiago fares start around US$23, with sleepers around US$45 but ranging up to US$75. More southerly destinations, like Osorno (3 hours, US$11) and Puerto Montt (4 hours, US$15) sometimes require backtracking to Temuco.

Local carriers also serve the Argentine cities of Junín de los Andes, with connections to San Martín de los Andes (5 hours, US$20); these buses daily leave from Temuco and board additional passengers in Villarrica and Pucón. **Buses San Martín** (Pedro León Gallo 559, tel. 045/241-1584) and **Igi Llaima** (tel. 045/241-2733), at the main terminal, alternate daily service. For services to Bariloche, it's necessary to return to Temuco or make connections in Osorno (or from San Martín).

Castillo Rent A Car (Valentín Letelier 585, tel. 045/241-1618, www.castillorentacar.cl) is the only car-rental option.

Pucón

At the base of smoldering Volcán Villarrica, Pucón has gained a name as *the* destination for hikers, climbers, mountain bikers, windsurfers, and white-water rafters and kayakers. Still popular with Chilean holidaymakers, it enjoys a longer season than most lakes district resorts because hordes of youthful international travelers frequent the area from November to April. It has no sights of its own because almost everything worth seeing or doing is outside town. But at day's end, everyone swarms to local hotels, restaurants, and bars to party.

That doesn't mean Pucón lacks a serious side. Over the past several years, the landmark cooperative Hostería ¡Ecole!, along with the affiliated Fundación Lahuen, has actively promoted regional forest conservation.

ORIENTATION

Where the Río Pucón enters the lake, 25 kilometers east of Villarrica via Ruta 119, Pucón (pop. about 23,000) occupies a compact grid bounded by the lakeshore to the north and west, Avenida Colo Colo to the east, and Volcán Villarrica's lower slopes to the south. Its commercial axis is Avenida Bernardo O'Higgins, which continues as Ruta 119 toward Curarrehue and the Argentine border at Paso Mamuil Malal.

ENTERTAINMENT AND EVENTS

There are few formal entertainment venues, but somehow Pucón has plenty to do.

The **Enjoy Pucón** (Ansorena 121, tel. 600/700-6000, www.enjoy.cl) casino attracts performers of the stature of Spain's Joan Manuel Serrat.

There's a lot of turnover in bars, but several have managed to last more than a few seasons, most notably **Krater** (O'Higgins 447, tel. 09/6628-9724) and **Mamas & Tapas** (O'Higgins 587, tel. 045/244-9002).

Both places serve food as well, but that's not their forte.

Early February's **Ironman Internacional de Pucón** (Pucón International Triathlon) grows in popularity every year. February 27's **Aniversario de Pucón** celebrates the city's founding.

SHOPPING

The **Mercado Artesanal Municipal** (Ansorena 445, tel. 045/244-3171, daily) and the **Centro Artesanal Pucón** (Alderete 370, tel. 09/8207-3163, 10am-9pm daily) both have ample crafts selections. There are also abundant street vendors.

FOOD

Pucón's food ranges from simple regional cuisine and fast food—no greasy chain outlets, fortunately—to sophisticated international fare. **La Suiza** (O'Higgins 116, tel. 045/244-1241, breakfast, lunch, and dinner daily) is the classic breakfast spot for tasty pastries. **Kuchenladen** (Fresia 248, tel. 045/244-1782, 9am-8:30pm daily) is a branch of Frutillar's outstanding sandwich and pastry place. The latest entry in the race for espresso, desserts, and the like is the contemporary **Café Berlín** (Ansorena 160,

tel. 045/263-9849), which really is reminiscent of something plucked out of Germany's modern capital.

★ **Latitude 39** (Gerónimo de Alderete 324, tel. 09/7430-0016, www.latitude39.cl, 11am-9pm Mon.-Sat.) is a U.S.-run café with a diverse menu that includes moderately priced sandwiches, Mexican food, and Thai dishes. Breakfast is available all day. Latitude 39 has also introduced a local novelty, shaved ice, for hot summer days.

Even if there's no room at the inn, consider the vegetarian menu at ★ **Hostería ¡Ecole!** (Urrutia 592, tel. 045/244-1675, 8am-11pm daily, US$8-10), which focuses on seasonal, locally produced organic products, including Mapuche-derived dishes and spices. With low prices, this remains some of the country's best-value food.

The menu at ★ **Trawen** (O'Higgins 311, tel. 045/244-2024, www.trawen.cl, 8am-midnight daily) does a lot with standards such as ravioli (stuffed with prosciutto, for instance), creative vegetarian dishes, and the freshest local ingredients. There's also a respectable selection of wines by the glass.

Puerto Pucón (Fresia 246, tel. 09/9863-1348, lunch and dinner daily, US$15) is the standard seafood option, but prices have risen

Volcán Villarrica looms above the beach at Pucón.

Pucón

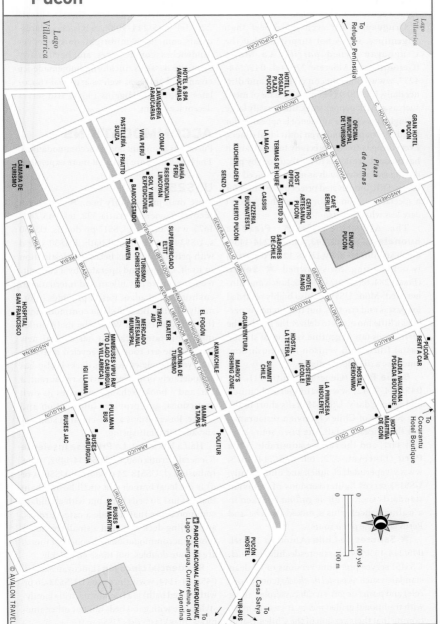

Lago Villarrica

Lago Villarrica

To Refugio Peninsula

CAUPOLICAN

C. HOLZAPFEL

GRAN HOTEL PUCÓN

Plaza de Armas

ANSORENA

HOTEL & SPA ARAUCARIAS

HOTEL LA POSADA PLAZA PUCÓN

LINCOYAN

OFICINA MUNICIPAL DE TURISMO

PEDRO DE VALDIVIA

FRESIA

LAVANDERIA ARAUCARIAS

PASTELERIA SUIZA

FRIATTO

CONAF

VIVA PERÚ

BANCO ESTADO

LA MAGA

TERMAS DE HUIFE

POST OFFICE

CENTRO ARTESANAL PUCÓN

CAFÉ BERLIN

KUCHENLADEN

BAHIA PERÚ

RESIDENCIAL LINCOYAN

SOL Y NIEVE EXPEDICIONES

SENZO

PIZZERIA BUONATESTA

PUERTO PUCÓN

CASSIS

LATITUD 39

SABORES DE CHILE

ENJOY PUCÓN

CAMARA DE TURISMO

PJE CHILE

FRESIA

SUPERMERCADO ELIT

AVENIDA LIBERTADOR

TRAWEN

TURISMO CHRISTOPHER

GENERAL BASILIO URRUTIA

HOTEL RANGI

GERONIMO DE ALDERETE

PALGUIN

HOSPITAL SAN FRANCISCO

ANSORENA

EL FOGON

TRAVEL AID

KRATER

AVENIDA LIBERTADOR BERNARDO O'HIGGINS

BERNARDO O'HIGGINS

OFICINA DE TURISMO

AGUAVENTURA

KAYAKCHILE

MARIO'S FISHING ZONE

SUMMIT CHILE

HOSTAL LA TETERA

HOSTERIA ¡ECOLE!

LA PRINCESA INSOLENTE

PUCÓN RENT A CAR

ARAUCO

ALDEA NAUKANA POSADA BOUTIQUE

HOSTAL GERONIMO

HOTEL MARTINA DE GONI

To Cocurantu Hotel Boutique

MERCADO ARTESANAL MUNICIPAL

IGI LLAIMA

PALGUIN

MINIBUSES VIPU RAY (TO LAGO CABURGUA & VILLARICA)

PULLMAN BUS

BUSES CABURGUA

BUSES JAC

ARAUCO

MAMA'S & TAPAS

POLITUR

COLO COLO

BRASIL

URUGUAY

BUSES SAN MARTIN

PARQUE NACIONAL HUERQUEHUE, Lago Caburgua, Currarehue, and Argentina

PUCÓN HOSTEL

TUR-BUS

To Casa Satya

0   100 yds
0   100 m

© AVALON TRAVEL

significantly. **El Fogón** (O'Higgins 480, tel. 045/244-4904, lunch and dinner daily, US$10-15) is a conventional *parrilla*.

Uruguayans eat even more beef than Argentines, so it's not surprising that the Uruguayan-owned *parrilla* **La Maga** (Gerónimo de Alderete 276, tel. 045/244-4277, www.lamagapucon.cl, lunch and dinner daily, US$28) serves massive slabs of meat, such as a thick pepper steak that's easily large enough for two. The ambience is appealing for families, couples, and even individual diners. Everything is cooked precisely to order, and it has made concessions to local custom by producing side dishes such as *merkén*-spiced potatoes. Still, the elevated prices make it best for a special occasion or for those who couldn't care less what it costs.

The Argentine-style ★ **Pizzería Buonatesta** (Fresia 243, tel. 045/244-1434, lunch and dinner daily, US$8-12 for pizzettas) is outstanding. Swiss-owned ★ **Senzo** (Fresia 284, tel. 045/244-9005, lunch and dinner Wed.-Mon., US$14) is also highly regarded for pastas and risottos, but the kitchen is perhaps a little too quick to deliver the goods. The *sorrentinos* (an Argentine version of stuffed pasta) filled with venison in a mushroom sauce are a distinctive dish.

Bahía Perú (General Urrutia 211, tel. 045/244-4942, www.bahiaperu.cl, lunch and dinner daily, US$8-15) falls short of the top echelon of Chile's Peruvian restaurants, but the prices are fair, the *pisco* sours suitably tart, and the service admirable. **Viva Perú** (Lincoyán 372, tel. 045/244-4025, www.vivaperudeli.cl, lunch and dinner daily, US$13) serves lighter versions of Peruvian standards such as *ají de gallina* (chicken in a walnut sauce), plus a mixed ceviche and Peruvian-style *pisco* sours.

★ **Sabores de Chile** (Ansorena 212, tel. 045/244-1330, www.saboresdechilepucon.cl, US$15) serves premium versions of Chilean standards such as *pastel de choclo* (corn casserole) and *pastel de jaiva* (crab casserole), along with traditional grilled meats. It's worth mentioning that their version of the Chilean salad

(tomato and onion) may surprise some diners with its spiciness.

In remodeled quarters, **Cassis** (Fresia 223, tel. 045/244-9088, www.chocolates-cassis.com, 9am-midnight daily) serves sandwiches, coffee, juices, and particularly exquisite desserts, including homemade ice cream and crepes as well as artisanal chocolates. **Friatto** (O'Higgins 136-B) also serves decent ice cream.

ACCOMMODATIONS

Pucón has abundant budget accommodations. The best values are just a bit more expensive.

US$25-50

More than just a comfy bed, ★ **Hostería ¡Ecole!** (General Urrutia 592, tel. 045/244-1675, www.ecole.cl, US$17 pp dorms, US$30 s, US$34 d with shared bath, US$50 s or d with private bath) has become a destination in itself. Owned and operated by a committed cooperative of Chilean and international environmental advocates, it provides informally stylish B&B-style accommodations (breakfast is extra). While the main building's a bit ramshackle, it has several new state-of-the-art rooms in recycled quarters, with volcano views from its deck. It also has a moderately priced vegetarian restaurant, a bar, and a book exchange, operates its own excursions, and provides information and advice. Reservations are essential in summer and advisable fall-spring.

Half a block east, **La Princesa Insolente** (General Urrutia 660, tel. 045/244-1492, www.tpihostels.cl, US$18-24 pp dorms, US$60 s or d) is the local branch of a small hostel chain that has just 30 beds here, but with abundant common areas that include a café, gardens, a sprawling deck and even a small treehouse (not for accommodations). A couple of rooms are private doubles, but those go quickly.

Residencial Lincoyán (Lincoyán 323, tel. 045/244-1144, www.lincoyan.cl, US$23-26 pp with shared bath) is a friendly no-frills family-style place with good beds but few other amenities. Breakfast costs US$5 more.

US$50-100

Just beyond the town's central grid, **Pucón Hostel** (Av. O'Higgins 771, tel. 045/244-1381, www.puconhostelchile.com, US$19-27 pp, US$52-82 s or d) is a purpose-built facility that has mostly private rooms with just a few dorm bunks. While it may lack the liveliness of its competitors, it compensates with a friendly family approach.

In a quiet site only about 100 meters north of the Tur-Bus terminal, Swiss-run **Casa Satya** (Blanco Encalada 190, tel. 045/244-4093, www.casasatya.com, US$56-68 s or d, with breakfast) has upgraded doubles and triples with either shared or private bath, plus Wi-Fi, access to a full modern kitchen, and even spa facilities. The higher rates correspond to doubles with private baths. There are also massage options ranging from reiki to Thai, along with yoga classes and a sauna.

Alongside ¡Ecole!, the more subdued ★ **Hostal La Tetera** (General Urrutia 580, tel./fax 045/244-1462, www.tetera.cl, US$57 s, US$57 d with shared bath, US$57 s, US$69 d with private bath) offers equally stylish, comfortable rooms with good beds and individual reading lights. The walls are a little thin. Still, it attracts a quiet clientele and has some of Pucón's best breakfasts. There's also a good book exchange. Ask for one of the front rooms, whose balconies offer views of Volcán Villarrica. If possible, avoid room 4 (Meli), shaded by a dense fir tree.

It's a little ragged in some aspects—the rooms have irregular shapes, for instance, and the bathroom linoleum undulates across the floor—but the Hostelling International (HI) affiliate **Refugio Península** (Holzapfel 11, tel. 045/244-3398, www.refugiopeninsula.cl, US$30 pp dorms, US$52 s, US$75 d) compensates with coziness and a quiet lakeshore location. HI members get a small discount.

With its spa and other upgrades, **Hotel & Spa Araucarias** (Caupolicán 243, tel. 045/244-1286, www.araucarias.cl, US$70 s, US$105 d) is a fine value with IVA discounts. It also has a small but impressive museum of Mapuche artifacts.

US$100-150

Hostal Gerónimo (Gerónimo de Alderete 665, tel. 045/244-3762, www.geronimo.cl, US$102 s or d) offers immaculate small to midsize rooms, some with terrace views of the volcano. The personnel are gracious and helpful, and there's also a pasta-oriented restaurant.

The main drawback at **Hotel Malalhue** (Camino Internacional 1615, tel. 045/244-3130, www.malalhue.cl, US$97 s, US$106-130 d) is that it fronts on the eastbound road out of town and, consequently, has traffic day or night. Still, it's an impressive structure with luminous rooms and contemporary Euro-Andean style.

New in late 2015, adjacent to the Gerónimo and under the same ownership, the **Hotel Martina de Goñi** (Colo Colo 224, tel. 045/267-8192, www.hotelmartina.cl, US$118 s, US$132 d) is a purpose-built four-story hotel with decorative inconsistencies—Mapuche weavings in some rooms and Francophile sofas in the bar—but it's unquestionably a bargain for the price (suites with volcano views are dearer). It shares the Gerónimo's restaurant, and the rooftop deck also offers great volcano views and a hot tub.

Set on ample grounds, with a large pool, **Hotel La Posada Plaza Pucón** (Pedro de Valdivia 191, tel. 045/244-1088, www.hotelplazapucon.cl, US$90-138 s, US$115-174 d) has midsized rooms in an upgraded older building. The service is accommodating and attentive.

US$150-200

Its Asian-inflected restaurant may have folded, but the **Aldea Naukana Posada Boutique** (Gerónimo de Alderete 656, tel. 045/244-3508, www.aldeanaukana.com, US$157-174 s or d) survives toward the top end of the creative design continuum here. The exterior and all the rooms feature soothing natural woods, though some of them are on the smallish side.

On the quiet edge of town, a block north of the Martina the **Cocurantu Hotel Boutique**

(Colo Colo 103, tel. 045/244-1746, www.cocurantu.cl, US$179 s or d) is an intimate structure of natural wood and stone that's currently expanding from nine to 15 rooms. All the rooms have either balconies or garden access, though its wooded grounds provide seclusion rather than views.

The **Hotel Rangi Pucón** (Palguín 212, tel. 045/268-5400, www.hotelrangipucon.cl, US$150-184 s or d) is a handsome design hotel with luminous midsize rooms and impressive views of the volcano from its fourth-story deck.

Over US$200

On Pucón's eastern outskirts, under new ownership, the **Hotel Pucón Green Park** (Camino Internacional 4150, tel. 045/246-7960, www.pucongreenpark.cl, US$209-294 s or d) is a spa hotel on expansive grounds with an ample setback from the international highway. For those who prefer being close to town but away from frenetic summer crowds, this is a good option.

Two kilometers west of town on the Villarrica road, poised among wooded hillside gardens with immaculate flower beds, pools, and cascades, the Bauhaus-style ★ **Hotel Antumalal** (tel. 045/244-1011, www.antumalal.com, from US$339 s or d) was arguably one of the world's earliest design hotels. It prides itself on personal service. When you arrive, staff members may even wash your car, and your room door features your name rather than a number. Each of its 22 rooms boasts lake views and a modernized fireplace. The common areas have panoramic views through giant plate-glass windows, and there is now Wi-Fi throughout. In addition to a heated pool and a private beach, it has also added the Spa Antumaco with a hot tub, a sauna, and massage services. Half-board rates are also available. The restaurant has been gaining clientele from nonguests as well.

Enjoying its own black-sand beach, the mammoth lakefront **Gran Hotel Pucón** (Holzapfel 190, tel. 045/244-1001, www.hotelpucon.cl, US$177-200 s or d) dates from the 1930s, when the state railroad agency Ferrocarriles del Estado chose Pucón as Chile's next great tourist destination. Despite its acquisition by the Enjoy group, which also operates the new casino and has money to burn, its character remains that of an aging grand hotel.

On Pucón's eastern outskirts, the **Vira Vira Hacienda Hotel** (Parcela 22-A Quetroleufú, tel. 045/237-4000, www.hotelviravira.com, US$480-670 pp) is a sprawling all-inclusive facility, with audacious contemporary architecture and even its own dairy, producing premium cheeses. It's one of only four Relais & Chateaux affiliates in Chile.

INFORMATION

In summer, Pucón's **Oficina Municipal de Turismo** (O'Higgins 483, tel. 045/229-3002, www.destinopucon.com, 8:30am-10pm daily summer, 8:30am-7pm daily fall-spring) keeps longer hours. There's a secondary office (Pedro de Valdivia and Fresia (no phone, 11:30am-7pm daily) on the Plaza de Armas. The private **Cámara de Turismo** (Brasil 115, tel. 045/244-1671, www.puconturismo.cl, 9am-midnight daily Jan.-Feb., 10am-1:30pm and 4pm-7pm daily Mar.-Dec.) is another resource for visitors. For national parks info, **Conaf** (Lincoyán 336, 1st Fl., tel. 045/244-3781) has centrally convenient offices.

SERVICES

Turismo Christopher (O'Higgins 261) and **Supermercado Eltit** (O'Higgins 336) change U.S. and Argentine cash. **BancoEstado** (O'Higgins 240) is the most convenient of several ATM options. **Correos de Chile** (Fresia 183) handles the mail.

Speaking Spanish, English, and German, Swiss-run **Travel Aid** (Ansorena 425, Local 4, tel. 045/244-4040, www.travelaid.cl) is a well-informed travel agency, tour broker, and apartment rental agency that also sells books and maps of the area, region, and country. It's also the local agent for the Navimag ferries and Andino shuttle.

Going to the Dogs

In wintertime, skiing and snowboarding are no longer the only outdoor activities in and around Pucón. While it may not be Alaska or the Yukon, German expat Konrad Jakob has 50 working huskies that, on the western slopes of Volcán Villarrica, he uses for guided tours on individual sleds for experienced or aspiring amateur mushers. In summer, though, the same animals are available to pull carts on the area's back roads. Full-moon rides are another option.

In August 2013, Jakob organized the first Volcán Villarrica Challenge, which brought mushers from around southernmost South America for a 160-kilometer race on the snow. It is becoming an annual event.

About midway between Villarrica and Lican Ray, **Aurora Austral Husky Adventure** (tel. 09/8901-2574, www.auroraaustral.com) offers day trips for visitors to Pucón and Villarrica. It also sells packages that include accommodations in *cabañas* on Jakob's own secluded property.

Lavandería Araucarias (General Urrutia 108, Local 4, tel. 045/244-1963) is one of several efficient laundry services.

For medical assistance, contact **Hospital San Francisco** (Uruguay 325, tel. 045/229-0400).

TRANSPORTATION

Most flights arrive at the airport at Freire, 30 kilometers south of Temuco. In the past there have been occasional summer flights into Pucón, but its airfield is not really suitable for commercial flights.

Long-distance bus service is an extension of that from Villarrica. The three main carriers have their own terminals: **Tur-Bus** (O'Higgins 910, tel. 045/268-6101), **Buses Jac** (Uruguay 505, tel. 045/299-0880), and **Pullman Bus** (Palguín 555, tel. 045/244-3331). **Intersur** shares the Tur-Bus terminal, while other companies have separate terminals around the east end of town.

Buses Jac, Tur-Bus, Intersur, and **Igi Llaima** (Palguín 598, tel. 045/244-4762) go frequently to Santiago. Tur-Bus also goes to Puerto Montt. Igi Llaima and **Buses San Martín** (Colo Colo 612, tel. 045/244-3595) both cross the cordillera to Junín de los Andes and San Martín de los Andes, Argentina.

Minibuses Vipu Ray (Palguín 550, tel. 09/6835-5798) and Buses Jac both go frequently to Villarrica (30-40 minutes, US$1.25); Vipu Ray has nine buses daily to Caburgua (US$1), while Jac has three or four daily to Curarrehue (US$1.50). In summer, **Buses Caburgua** (Uruguay 540, tel. 09/9838-9047) has four rides daily to Parque Nacional Huerquehue (US$4 one-way, US$7 round-trip); fall through spring, there are at least two per day.

Several adventure travel companies along Avenida O'Higgins also rent mountain bikes. For rental cars, try **Pucón Rent A Car** (Pedro de Valdivia 636, tel. 09/8998-0294, www.puconrentacar.cl).

Vicinity of Pucón

The locus of adventure travel in the Andean lakes district, Pucón offers activities ranging from climbing Volcán Villarrica to rafting the Río Trancura, hiking at Huerquehue, horseback riding, fly-fishing, skiing, and visits to nearby thermal baths. Competition, often cutthroat, can keep prices low and temperatures high among local operators. Occasionally,

though, they cooperate in putting groups together, especially outside the summer peak.

Commercial operators include French-run **Aguaventura** (Palguín 336, tel. 045/244-4246, www.aguaventura.com), **Kayakchile** (O'Higgins 524, tel. 045/244-1584, www.kayakchile.net), **Politur** (O'Higgins 635, tel./fax 045/244-1373, www.politur.com), and **Sol y**

Nieve Expediciones (Lincoyán 361, tel./ fax 045/244-4761, www.solynievepucon.cl), and **Summit Chile** (General Urrutia 585, tel. 045/244-3259, www.summitchile.org).

Best known for its accommodations, noncommercial **Hostería ¡Ecole!** (General Urrutia 592, Pucón, tel. 045/244-1675, www.ecole.cl) organizes groups to visit the Fundación Lahuén's nearby Santuario Cañi forest reserve and other excursions. The staff also offers suggestions for independent excursions.

Mario's Fishing Zone (O'Higgins 590, tel. 09/9760-7280, www.flyfishingpucon. com) is a fly-fishing operator who also sells and rents gear.

PARQUE CUEVAS VOLCÁNICAS

On Volcán Villarrica's southern slopes, but outside the national park, the misleadingly named "volcanic caves" are really lava tubes that descend 340 meters into the mountainside (unless you're a bat, the darkness at the bottom is absolute). Reached by a fork off the road to Parque Nacional Villarrica, the **Cuevas Volcánicas** (tel. 045/244-2002, US$28 adults, US$23 children, free under age 6) are 14.5 kilometers south of the main Villarrica-Pucón highway. Some guides can manage English if necessary. Although the service has declined, it's an interesting sight in its own right.

RÍO TRANCURA

Barely half an hour east of Pucón, the **Trancura** is not one of Chile's premier whitewater rivers—there are long calm floats between rapids—but the Class IV waterfalls make parts of the upper river a wild ride indeed. Heavy competition has kept prices down to about US$45 pp for the Alto Trancura, US$23 for the calmer Bajo Trancura. Both are half-day excursions, either morning or afternoon, but the Alto Trancura means a little longer on the water.

Summit Chile's climbing wall at its Pucón offices

HOT SPRINGS

The entire volcanic cordon of the Sur Chico is dotted with *termas* (hot springs), and there's a particularly dense concentration around Pucón. Several have been turned into retreats or resorts that vary from basic day-use facilities to upmarket but not-quite-lavish hotels.

On the Río Liucura northeast of Pucón, **Hotel y Termas Huife** (Gerónimo de Alderete 324, Pucón, tel./fax 045/244-1222, www.termashuife.cl, US$163-193 s, US$208-267 d) is the most upscale option, a modern chalet-style resort with spa facilities in 40°C waters and massage therapy. Day-trippers can use the outdoor pools (US$24 summer, US$19 fall-spring). The resort provides its own transportation from Pucón (US$33 round-trip, including outdoor pool access). Infrequent buses also pass near the entrance. Restaurant and cafeteria meals are available. Termas Huife is 30 kilometers northeast of Pucón via Paillaco, on the road to Parque Nacional Huerquehue. The higher rates are in effect mid-December-mid-March only.

Just two kilometers beyond Huife, the minimalist **Termas Los Pozones** (tel. 045/197-2350, www.termaslospozones.cl, US$12 pp daytime, US$15 pp at night) is a backpacker's alternative. It features a series of riverside pools ranging 30-40°C open during the day and at night (when some Pucón travel agencies run tours). Bring food and other supplies, as there's little on-site. There are usually one or two buses daily (US$3 one-way).

On the highway to Argentina, the **Parque Termal Menetúe** (Camino Internacional, Km 30, tel. 045/232-4800, www.menetue.com, pool use US$27 adults, US$14 children summer, US$21 adults, US$11 children fall-spring) has the best indoor installations in the area. There are pools, mud baths, and massages. Menetúe also has *cabaña* accommodations (with breakfast US$127 pp summer, US$112 pp fall-spring, with all meals US$142 pp summer, US$127 pp fall-spring). Menetúe runs its own daily transfers from Pucón, which includes access to the baths (US$35 summer, US$29 fall-spring); the transfer is free for those housed at Menetúe.

Southeast of Villarrica, beyond the town of Coñaripe, Ruta 201 leads to a turnoff to the **Termas Geométricas** (Ruta 201, Km 16, tel. 09/9442-5420, www.termasgeometricas.cl, 10am-10pm daily summer, 11am-8pm daily fall-spring, US$30-36 adults, US$15-18 under age 15), a Zen-like hot-springs retreat that has drawn raves for its 17 thermal pools, linked by boardwalks in a lush sylvan setting. There's also a café, but no accommodations. Alcohol is forbidden.

RANCHO DE CABALLOS

At Palguín Alto, near Termas de Palguín, the German-run **Rancho de Caballos** (Casilla 142, Pucón, tel. 09/8346-1764, www.ranchodecaballos.com) offers a series of three-hour to 10-day riding tours of the backcountry in and around Parque Nacional Villarrica. In addition to tours, Rancho de Caballos provides simple *cabaña* accommodations (US$17-23 pp), with meals available at extra cost.

CORRAL DEL AGUA

At Curarrehue, about 40 kilometers east of Pucón, a narrow gravel road leads northeast toward Reigolil. At about the 14-kilometer point, an even narrower road dead-ends 11 kilometers later at **Corral del Agua** (tel. 09/8398-9774, www.corraldelagua.cl), a small private nature reserve and lodge that organizes hiking and horseback excursions into the much larger backcountry of Reserva Nacional Villarrica, along the Argentine border.

One of Corral del Agua's most impressive sights is the **Salto Malal-co,** a waterfall that spills vertically over a columnar basalt wall that resembles California's Devil's Postpile. There's abundant birdlife, including nesting condors and many lacustrine and riverine species.

SANTUARIO CAÑI

In a high, roadless area about 21 kilometers east of Pucón, the Fundación Lahuen administers 400 hectares of mixed araucaria forest in the **Santuario Cañi** (US$7), Chile's initial private nature reserve. A project to create a "Sendero Pehuén" to connect the reserve with Parque Nacional Huerquehue, as part of the ambitious Sendero de Chile project, is advancing slowly. In the meantime, it is possible to camp here (US$4.50 pp in addition to the admission fee).

For the moment, access is limited to guided hikes (US$23-34 pp depending on group size) under the auspices of the Fundación Lahuen through Manuel Venera at the **Grupo de Guías del Cañi** (Camino Pucón Huife, Km 21, tel. 09/9837-3928, www.ecole.cl) and other local operators. For information in the United States, contact Ancient Forests International (P.O. Box 1850, Redway, CA 95560, U.S. tel. 707/923-4475, www.ancientforests.org).

★ PARQUE NACIONAL VILLARRICA

Dominating the skyline south of Pucón, 2,847-meter Volcán Villarrica's glowing crater is a constant reminder that what Spanish conquistador poet Alonso de Ercilla called its "great neighbor volcano" could, at any moment, bury the town beneath a cloud of ash or a lahar of lava and melting snow, or set it aflame in a cataclysm of volcanic bombs. Closely monitored and occasionally closed to climbers, its summit remains one of Pucón's most popular excursions.

More than just the volcano, the park comprises 63,000 hectares of mostly wooded Andean cordillera stretching from Pucón to the 3,746-meter summit of Volcán Lanín, most of which lies within Argentina's Parque Nacional Lanín (would-be climbers must cross to the Argentine side).

Geography and Climate

Immediately south of Pucón, the park ranges from 600 meters elevation on the lower slopes to 3,746 meters at Volcán Lanín. Barren lava flows and volcanic ash cover much of its surface, but unaffected areas are lushly forested. The other major summit is 2,360-meter Volcán Quetrupillán, halfway to the Argentine border. From Quetrupillán to the east, several alpine lakes are accessible on foot.

Summertime temperatures range from a minimum of about 9°C to a maximum of around 23°C, while wintertime lows average 4°C. Most precipitation falls between March and August, when Pacific storms can drop up to two meters of snow. Rain can fall at any time. The park receives 2,500 to 3,500 millimeters of rainfall per year.

Flora and Fauna

At lower elevations, up to about 1,500 meters, mixed araucaria and *Nothofagus* woodlands cover the slopes. The araucaria reaches its southernmost point at Volcán Quetrupillán. The *mañío* (*Podocarpus*), an ornamental in the northern hemisphere, also makes an appearance. Native bunch grasses have colonized some volcanic areas.

Among the mammals are pumas, *pudú*, foxes, and skunks, as well as the aquatic coypu. Waterfowl such as coots and ducks inhabit the lakes and other watercourses. Large raptors such as the black-shouldered kites and peregrine falcons are occasionally sighted in the skies.

Volcán Villarrica

Chile's most active volcano, Villarrica is a cauldron of bubbling lava and venting steam that has erupted dozens of times, including a 1971 event that expelled 30 million cubic meters of lava in a flow that spread over 14 kilometers. Nothing since has approached that level of hazard.

A strenuous but nontechnical climb, Villarrica requires crampons, an ice ax, rain- and wind gear, high-energy snacks, and a guide, except for those who manage to wrangle one of Conaf's few individual private permits. For those who contract a tour with one of Pucón's adventure travel agencies, the tour involves a mountaineering crash course. In good weather, the summit is about six hours from the ski area, but bad weather sometimes forces groups to turn back. When the sulfurous crater is especially active, Conaf closes the route.

While the ascent can be a slog through wet snow, the descent involves body-sledding down the volcano's flanks with only an ice ax for braking. Rates for the trip (around US$120 pp) can vary considerably among agencies.

When winter snows cover the lower slopes, the **Centro de Ski Volcán Villarrica** (lift tickets US$54 peak season, US$39 shoulder season) operates four lifts with nine runs ranging 500-1,500 meters in length. In addition to one-day lift tickets, there are three-day, one-week, and season passes. For more information, contact **Pucón Ski** (Holzapfel 190, tel. 045/244-1901, www.skipucon.cl) in the Gran Hotel Pucón.

Sector Quetrupillán

About midway between Volcán Villarrica and **Volcán Quetrupillán,** a rough, summer-only road crosses the park from Termas de Palguín to the hot-springs town of Coñaripe. Best suited to 4WD or at least high-clearance vehicles, it passes through a scenic araucaria forest that includes the park's only campground.

From Volcán Villarrica's southern slopes, hiking trails cross the park to Termas de Palguín and continue to Puesco, where Buses Jac has a daily bus back to Pucón. For more detail on this hike, which has some hard-to-follow segments, see Tim Burford's *Chile and Argentina: The Bradt Trekking Guide* (Chalfont St. Peter, UK: Bradt Travel Guides, 2001) or Carolyn McCarthy's *Trekking in the Patagonian Andes* (Melbourne: Lonely Planet, 2009). Conaf now levies a US$12 fee for hikers on this trail.

Food and Accommodations
In Sector Quetrupillán on the park's southern boundary, on the steep, narrow road between Termas de Palguín and Coñaripe, Conaf's **Camping Chinay** (US$10 per site) lies in the midst of an araucaria forest. It sometimes suffers water shortages.

Skiers sleep in Pucón, but they can eat at the ski area: **Refugio Villarrica** serves cafeteria meals.

Information
On the road to the ski area, eight kilometers from Pucón, Conaf's Guardería Rucapillán is the best source for information. Rangers collect park admission here (US$7.50 adults, US$4.50 children). There are ranger stations at Sector Quetrupillán and Sector Puesco.

Transportation
Transportation is limited except for organized tours. To Sector Rucapillán, only a few kilometers south of Pucón, taxis are the only non-tour option.

★ PARQUE NACIONAL HUERQUEHUE
In the scenic Andean foothills, dotted with alpine lakes, rushing rivers, and waterfalls within dense native forest, 12,500-hectare **Huerquehue** has become one of the area's most popular parks. Its proximity to Pucón and a small but accessible network of hiking trails make it ideal for day trips. Overnights are also possible.

Geography and Climate
Huerquehue is 35 kilometers northeast of Pucón via the hamlet of Paillaco. Elevations range from about 720 meters near Lago Tinquilco to the 2,000-meter summit of Cerro Araucano, but glaciers and rivers have eroded deep canyons. It receives just over 2,000 millimeters of rainfall per year, mostly between May and September, with snow at higher elevations. While temperatures are mild, rain can fall at any time.

Flora and Fauna
On the lower slopes, the dominant forest species is the *coigüe*, while *lenga* gives way gradually to araucarias at higher elevations. Birds, ranging from woodpeckers to thrushes, flit within the forest, while Andean condors sometimes soar among the ridgetops and summits.

Sendero Ñirrico
Huerquehue is a hiker's park, beginning with **Sendero Ñirrico,** the signed nature trail that parallels the shore of Lago Tinquilco. It starts at the parking lot just beyond the park gate. Thanks to this trail, it's no longer necessary to walk along the gravel road leading to the Lago Verde trailhead, where the park's most popular walk starts (the gravel road is closed to vehicles other than those belonging to Conaf or park inholders).

Sendero Lago Verde
From the north end of Lago Tinquilco, reached by the Sendero Ñirrico, the well-watered **Sendero Lago Verde** (Lago Verde Trail) zigzags from an elevation of 700 meters at the trailhead to 1,300 meters at its namesake lake. Gaps in the *coigüe* woodlands yield glimpses of Volcán Villarrica to the south, while the surrounding ridges sport araucaria forests.

From Tinquilco, it's about two-plus hours of steady hiking to **Lago Chico,** where the terrain levels off. At a trail junction beyond Lago Chico, the left fork goes to **Lago Verde,** while the right fork goes to **Lago El Toro** and continues to Conaf's simple **Camping Renahue,** the only authorized backcountry campground. From here an eastbound trail continues to **Termas de Río Blanco,** thermal springs linked by gravel road to Cunco, Lago Colico, and Lago Caburgua's north end.

Sendero Quinchol and Sendero San Sebastián

From the parking lot beyond the park gate, the gravel road north soon intercepts the **Sendero Quinchol,** which climbs even more steeply than the Sendero Lago Verde through shady southern beech forests to an araucaria-studded Pampa Quinchol, with a short loop through even denser araucaria forests. At roughly the three-kilometer mark, the first stunted araucaria tree appears. It's another kilometer or so to the junction with **Sendero San Sebastián,** which leads north toward the Pampa Quinchol, with expansive views of nearly all the area's volcanoes. On a clear day, Villarrica, Lanín, and Choshuenco, plus Lago Caburgua, are all within view.

The five-kilometer trail to Pampa Quinchol takes about two hours. The descent is not much shorter because of its steepness, and there is little or no water. On the return, for variety, take the Sendero Quinchol loop back to the trail junction before returning to the park headquarters.

Food and Accommodations

On Lago Tinquilco's eastern shore, near the park gate, Conaf's 22-site **Camping Tinquilco** (US$27 per site) can accommodate up to five people at each of its wooded sites.

Just beyond the park entrance, near the Lago Verde trailhead, the rustically chic Canadian-Chilean ★ **Refugio Tinquilco** (tel. 09/9539-2728, Santiago tel. 02/2278-9831, www.tinquilco.cl, US$20 pp dorm, US$43 d with shared bath, US$54 d with private bath) has hostel-type bunks as well as rooms with king beds. Set on densely wooded grounds, it has its own beach and offers fixed-price breakfasts, lunches, and dinners to guests or nonguests. More elaborate multicourse dinners include aperitifs and wine.

Information

At the Lago Tinquilco entrance is Conaf's **Centro de Educación e Interpretación Ambiental** (10am-8pm daily summer). Rangers at the park gate collect an admission fee (US$7.50 adults, US$4.50 children). **Refugio Tinquilco** (tel. 09/9539-2728, tel. 02/2278-9831 in Santiago, www.tinquilco.cl) is also a good source of information for hiking alternatives beyond the main Lago Verde route.

Transportation

From Pucón, **Buses Caburgua** (Uruguay 580, tel. 09/9838-9047) now offers summer service to Huerquehue (US$4) four times daily starting at 8:30am; fall-spring, however, it's just twice daily. Most Pucón travel agencies also offer Huerquehue excursions.

Osorno

More a crossroads than a destination, Osorno thrives on dairying, forestry, and manufacturing. It's also the gateway to destinations such as Lago Puyehue, Parque Nacional Puyehue, and Argentina's own Andean lakes region. The city dates from 1558, but the Mapuche uprising of 1599 destroyed it and six other cities within five years, and resulted in the death of Spanish governor Martín García Oñez de Loyola.

Spanish authorities needed nearly two centuries to refound the city in 1793 with the construction of Fuerte Reina Luisa, a riverside fortification that helped keep out the Mapuche people. It failed to flourish until the mid-19th century, as overland communications were too arduous, even hazardous, to permit rapid growth of internal markets. This began to change with the mid-19th-century arrival of German immigrants. It accelerated after the so-called "pacification" south of the Biobío in the 1880s, followed by the railroad's arrival in 1895 and its extension to Puerto Montt by 1911. Through most of the 20th century, it achieved stable prosperity.

ORIENTATION

Osorno (pop. about 150,000) is 913 kilometers south of Santiago and 109 kilometers north of Puerto Montt via the Panamericana. An east-west crossroads, it's 126 kilometers from the Argentine border at Paso Cardenal Samoré via paved Ruta 215.

Central Osorno, about two kilometers west of the Panamericana, has a slightly irregular grid bordered by the Río Damas to the north, Calles Angulo and Eduvijes to the east, Manuel Rodríguez to the south, and the Río Rahue to the west.

SIGHTS

Despite its colonial origins, Osorno has few venerable sights. The so-called **Distrito Histórico** west of the Plaza de Armas includes early-20th-century landmarks such as the restored Francophile **Estación de Ferrocarril** (1912). It now houses the **Museo Interactivo Osorno** (Mackenna 555, tel. 064/221-2996, 9am-1pm and 2:30pm-5:30pm Mon.-Thurs., 9am-1pm and 2:30pm-5pm Fri., 2:30pm-6pm Sat., shorter hours in winter, free), a hands-on science museum.

Other area sights include the restored **Sociedad Molinera de Osorno,** a flour mill now occupied by a pasta factory, and many weathered private residences. The ramparts and towers of **Fuerte Reina Luisa** (Condell s/n), all that remains of the late colonial fortress at the foot of Eleuterio Ramírez, stand out more now that they have a **Sala de Exposiciones** (Condell s/n, tel. 064/222-6184, 9am-6pm Mon.-Fri., 2pm-7pm Sat.-Sun., free) with rotating historical exhibits and interpretive material.

The de facto historical district is on Juan Mackenna between Avenida Matta and Freire, where half a dozen pioneer houses are national monuments: the **Casa Mohr Pérez** (Mackenna 939), **Casa Enrique Schüller** (Mackenna 1011), **Casa Sürber** (Mackenna 1027), **Casa Germán Stückrath** (Mackenna 1047), **Casa Federico Stückrath** (Mackenna 1069), and **Casa Conrado Stückrath** (Mackenna 1095).

The **Museo Histórico Municipal** (Av. Matta 809, tel. 064/223-3717, 9:30am-5:30pm Mon.-Thurs., 9:30am-5pm Fri., 2pm-6pm Sat., free) exhibits diverse materials ranging from Paleo-Indian archaeology and Mapuche culture to Osorno's colonial founding, its destruction by the Mapuche and subsequent refounding, the 19th-century city and immigration, and naval hero Eleuterio Ramírez. A natural-history room and a child-oriented interactive basement display round out the features. It occupies the former Schilling Buschmann residence (1929), a handsome neocolonial building with a neglected exterior.

East of town, the **Auto Museum Moncopulli** (Ruta 215, Km 25, tel. 064/221-0744, www.moncopulli.cl, 10am-8pm daily Jan.-Feb., 10am-6pm daily Mar.-Dec., US$4.50 adults, US$3 students and seniors, US$1.50 children) contains more than 80 historic vehicles, many restored and others awaiting restoration, along with supplementary advertising and marketing materials and other artifacts of the early to mid-20th century. German collector Bernardo Eggers, its creator, specializes in the now-obscure Studebaker, from its 1850s beginnings as a horse-cart manufacturer in South Bend, Indiana, to its first electric automobile (1902) and the plant's closure (1966). With its futuristic design, the late 1940s and early 1950s Studebaker vehicle was one of the most distinctive automobiles ever manufactured, but it never really caught on with the public.

Professionally arranged, the museum has one shortcoming: a failure to provide any narrative beyond its creator's enthusiasm (there is more info on the Spanish-only website). That said, for anyone traveling the highway to Parque Nacional Puyehue and the Argentine border, it's worth at least a brief stop. Classic car lovers might want to go out of their way to see it.

Casa Enrique Schüller, in Osorno's historic district

ENTERTAINMENT

Cine Lido (Ramírez 650, tel. 064/204-9540) shows current movies. The municipal **Centro Cultural Osorno** (Av. Matta 556, tel. 064/223-2522, 8:30am-1:45pm and 4pm-5:15pm daily) hosts theater and music events, along with rotating art exhibits.

SHOPPING

Detalles Hecho a Mano (Mackenna 1100, tel. 064/223-8462) sells regional crafts, but the biggest selection is at **Alta Artesanía** (Mackenna 1069, tel. 064/223-2446), which sells wood carvings, woolens, ceramics, copper, and jewelry. At the **Pueblito Artesanal** (Mackenna 1113), artisans sell directly to the public along a block of the city's most heavily traveled street.

FOOD

For real budget meals, nothing's better than the seafood at the simple eateries in the **Mercado Municipal** (Prat and Errázuriz, roughly 8am-6pm daily)—but avoid the often greasy fried fish in favor of the far superior grilled fish.

Upstairs from its namesake bakery, **Pastelería Rhenania** (Ramírez 977, tel. 064/221-7610, www.rhenania.cl, 9am-8:30pm Mon.-Fri., 10am-8pm Sat.) serves sandwiches and pastries. **Dino's** (Ramírez 898, tel. 064/223-3880, 8:30am-midnight Mon.-Sat.) also specializes in sandwiches and light meals, as does its franchise rival **Bavaria** (O'Higgins 747, tel. 064/223-1303, www.bavaria.cl, 9:30am-10:30pm Mon.-Fri., 11am-10pm Sat., 11:30am-9pm Sun.). **Bocatto** (Ramírez 938, tel. 064/223-8000, breakfast, lunch, and dinner daily) has similar offerings but also pizza and Osorno's best ice cream.

The **Club Alemán,** also known as the **Deutscher Verein** (O'Higgins 563, tel. 064/223-2784, www.clubalemanosorno.cl, lunch and dinner Mon.-Sat., lunch Sun.), reflects the German community's significance more in name than in menu, which is standard Chilean. The **Club de Artesanos** (Juan Mackenna 634, tel. 064/223-0307, noon-11pm Mon.-Sat., noon-3:30pm Sun.) is a labor-union restaurant with a good Chilean menu.

In the historic Casa Conrado Stückrath, **La Parrilla de Pepe** (Mackenna 1095, tel. 064/223-9653, lunch and dinner Mon.-Sat., lunch Sun.) lacks ambience but serves meats cooked to order, with diligent service.

In conservative Osorno, the Asian-Peruvian fusion dishes at **Mumbai-Lima** (Manuel Rodríguez 1701, tel. 064/242-1337, www.mumbailima.cl, 1pm-3pm and 8pm-midnight Mon.-Sat., US$15) may be a tough sell, but, so long as it survives—it changed hands recently—this is likely to be the city's most creative option. Peruvian dishes like *picante de camarón* (a shrimp chowder with jasmine rice) are exquisite, and the cocktail menu is wide-ranging.

ACCOMMODATIONS

Except in the upper categories, Osorno's accommodations are only so-so.

East of the bus terminal, **Hospedaje Sánchez** (Los Carrera 1595, tel./fax 064/223-2560, US$15 pp) is a modest but passable shoestring choice. About 15 blocks east of the Plaza, in an improving area, **Hostel Vermont** (Toribio Medina 2020, tel. 064/224-7030, www.hostelvermont.cl, US$22 dorm, US$30 s, US$52 d) is the first of its kind here.

Hotel San Pedro (Bulnes 630, tel. 064/231-4126, www.hotelsanpedro.cl, US$44 s, US$56 d) is a contemporary business-oriented hotel.

Under the same ownership, **Hostal Bilbao Express** (Bilbao 1019, tel. 064/226-2200, www.hotelbilbao.cl, US$42-45 s, US$59 d) and the art deco-style **Hotel Bilbao** (Juan Mackenna 1205, tel. 064/226-4444, www.hotelbilbao.cl, US$52 s, US$68 d) are among the best in their range; both have Wi-Fi throughout.

Four blocks south of the terminal, **Hotel Villa Eduviges** (Eduviges 856, tel. 064/223-5023, www.hoteleduviges.cl, US$41 s, US$63 d, with breakfast) occupies a rambling older building that's undergone a haphazard modernization. The shower stalls, in particular, are tiny, but it inhabits a less congested and quieter neighborhood than some other places.

Half a block off the plaza, **Hotel Lagos del Sur** (O'Higgins 564, tel. 064/224-5222, www.hotelagosdelsur.cl, US$72 s, US$87 d) is a nearly new hotel with handsomely decorated rooms.

The classic **Hotel Waeger** (Cochrane 816, tel. 064/223-3721, www.hotelwaeger.cl, US$90 s, US$99 d) is an art deco-style lodging where German speakers get special attention. The more contemporary **Hotel García Hurtado de Mendoza** (Mackenna 1040, tel. 064/223-7111, www.hotelgarciahurtado.cl, US$89 s, US$106 d) is holding its own in a city with mostly unexceptional accommodations.

INFORMATION

On the west side of the Plaza de Armas, **Sernatur** (O'Higgins 667, tel. 064/223-4104, infosorno@sernatur.cl, 8:30am-5:30pm Mon.-Thurs., to 4:30pm Fri.) occupies a ground-floor office at the Edificio Gobernación Provincial.

The municipal **Departamento de Turismo** (tel. 064/221-8740, www.osorno-chile.cl, 9am-7pm Mon.-Fri., 11am-6pm Sat. mid-Dec.-mid-Mar., 11am-1pm or 3pm Mon.-Fri. mid-Mar.-mid-Dec.) is located on the Plaza de Armas. For national parks information, contact **Conaf** (Martínez de Rozas 430, tel. 064/222-1304).

SERVICES

Turismo Frontera (Ramírez 959, Local 12) changes cash and traveler's checks, while **BancoEstado** (Eleuterio Ramírez 741) has one of many ATMs.

On the west side of the Plaza de Armas, **Correos de Chile** (O'Higgins 645) is the postal service. There is free municipal Wi-Fi in and around the Plaza de Armas, and in some other parts of town.

Lavandería Limpec (Arturo Prat 678, tel. 064/223-8966) offers prompt laundry service. For medical help, contact the **Hospital Base** (Av. Bühler 1765, tel. 064/233-6200, www. hospitalbaseosorno.cl); Avenida Bühler is the southward extension of Arturo Prat.

TRANSPORTATION

Osorno has limited air connections, but it's a hub for bus services along the Panamericana, throughout the region, and across the Andes to Argentina. **LAN** (Ramírez 802, tel. 600/526-2000) flies at least daily to Santiago, usually via Temuco or Concepción. **Aeropuerto Carlos Hott Siebert** (ZOS, tel. 02/2222-8400), also known as Cañal Bajo, is seven kilometers east of Osorno via Avenida Buschmann. It's off the city bus routes, but a taxi costs only about US$5.

The **Terminal de Buses** (Av. Errázuriz 1400, tel. 064/223-4149) is the long-distance facility. Some but not all regional buses use the Mercado Municipal's **Terminal de Buses Rurales** (Errázuriz 1300, tel. 064/220-1237), where **Expreso Lago Puyehue** (tel. 064/224-3919) offers 8 to 10 daily services to Puyehue and Aguas Calientes (US$3.50).

At the main terminal, **Buses Arriagada** (tel. 064/223-4371) goes to the eastern Lago Llanquihue destination of Las Cascadas (1 hour-plus, US$3) up to seven times daily. **Buses Vía Octay** (tel. 064/223-7043) and **Octay Bus** (tel. 064/221-3065) go frequently to the northern Lago Llanquihue town of Puerto Octay (US$2).

Many carriers connect Osorno with Panamericana destinations between Santiago in the north and Puerto Montt to the south. Sample destinations, times, and fares include Puerto Montt (1.5 hours, US$3-10), Temuco (3 hours, US$8-14), and Santiago (12 hours, US$22-59).

Services to Punta Arenas (28 hours, US$80) and to Coyhaique (19 hours, US$56) start in Puerto Montt and pick up passengers here. Note that buses to Chilean Patagonian destinations use Paso Cardenal Samoré, east of Osorno, but carry through-passengers only— Chilean domestic bus lines may not drop passengers within Argentina.

Most buses across the Andes to Bariloche (5 hours, US$27) and other Argentine destinations also begin in Puerto Montt and use Paso Cardenal Samoré.

Servimaq (Eleodoro Vásquez 130, tel. 064/221-6086, rentacar@servimaq.cl) provides rental cars.

Parque Nacional Puyehue

Barely an hour from Osorno, Puyehue still has plenty of wild terrain among its 106,772 hectares of Valdivian rainforest, at least where lava flows and ash from its volcanic vents and summits have not left it as barren as the Atacama. In 2011 the Cordón Caulle experienced a major volcanic eruption that nearly buried the Argentine resort of Villa La Angostura beneath countless tons of ash.

Statistically, Puyehue is one of Chile's most visited parks, but statistics can deceive. The developed hot-springs resort at Aguas Calientes and its Antillanca ski area draw mostly Chilean crowds. Except for trails near its hotels and campgrounds, the backcountry gets few hikers, and the park is under threat from a proposed hydroelectric project.

GEOGRAPHY AND CLIMATE

Ranging from the lower Río Golgol valley, at about 250 meters elevation, to the 2,240-meter summit of **Volcán Puyehue,** the park is about 80 kilometers east of Osorno and extends to the Argentine border. **Volcán Casablanca** (1,980 meters) is another major landmark. The park has abundant creeks,

Ash from the 2011 Cordón Caulle eruption can still be seen on the shoulders of the highway.

and the 2011 Cordón Caulle event have left the landscape so barren that grasses and shrubs have only recently begun to colonize the area, despite substantial rainfall.

Pudú may inhabit the dense forest, but it's difficult to see them or other woodland and riverine species such as foxes, otters, and coypus. Some 100 or so bird species flit from tree to tree, along with waterfowl such as the *pato cortacorriente* (torrent duck), which fishes in the river rapids. Condors soar on the thermals overhead.

SIGHTS AND RECREATION

Puyehue consists of three distinct sectors: Aguas Calientes at its southwestern border, Antillanca at its southeastern border, and Anticura, mostly north of Ruta 215.

Aguas Calientes

From the Termas de Puyehue junction, a paved road leads four kilometers south to **Termas Aguas Calientes** (tel. 064/233-1710, www.termasaguascalientes.cl), whose highlight is its namesake thermal baths, open to hotel guests, campers, and day-trippers alike. Under the same management as Termas de Puyehue, its rates are more affordable.

Several short nature trails and one longer hike start here. The six-kilometer **Sendero El Pionero** switchbacks through dense forest to a ridgetop with panoramic northern vistas of Lago Puyehue, the wooded Golgol Valley, and Volcán Puyehue's barren cone, before continuing to Lago Espejo and then returning along the Antillanca road. Along its namesake river, the **Sendero Rápidos del Chanleufú** traverses 1,200 meters of gallery forest. The 11-kilometer **Sendero Lago Bertín** climbs steadily to its namesake lake, where backcountry camping is possible.

Antillanca

Beyond Aguas Calientes, the road becomes a gravel surface leading another 18 kilometers to the base of Volcán Casablanca, where **Antillanca** houses skiers from early June to

rivers, and lakes that are ideal for fishing and kayaking.

The annual rainfall, about 5,000 millimeters, with snow at higher elevations, supports verdant Valdivian forest. Temperatures are relatively mild at lower elevations, averaging about 14°C in summer and 5°C in winter, with highs near 25°C and lows around freezing.

FLORA AND FAUNA

Puyehue's lower Valdivian forest is a lush mixed woodland of species such as *ulmo,* which can reach 40 meters or more in height, along with *olivillo, tineo, mañío,* and *coigüe.*

Beneath the canopy grow smaller trees such as the myrtle relative *arrayán,* while the bamboo-like *quila* forms impassable thickets. The endemic *chilco,* along with intensely green ferns and mosses, provides spots of color. The striking *nalca* sports umbrella-size leaves at the end of edible stalks, up to two meters in height.

At some higher elevations, lava flows and ash from the 1960 Volcán Puyehue eruption

THE CHILEAN LAKES DISTRICT PARQUE NACIONAL PUYEHUE

late October. In summer it's open for hikers, mountain bikers, anglers, and general recreationists, even though there's no campground nearby.

Where the public road ends, the Club Andino Osorno maintains a toll road (8am-9pm daily, US$15 per vehicle) to the 1,262-meter **Cráter Raihuén**, an extinct volcanic crater, and **Cerro Mirador**, the starting point for several high-country trails. Pay at the hotel office, which opens the gate and provides a helpful topographic map.

Ranging from 1,050 meters at its base to 1,514 meters elevation on Cerro Haique, the ski area itself has beginner, intermediate, and expert slopes. For more details, contact **Hotel Antillanca** (tel. 064/261-2070, www.antillanca.cl).

★ Anticura

From Termas de Puyehue, Ruta 215 leads northeast up the Golgol Valley for 17 kilometers to **Anticura** before continuing to Chilean customs and immigration at Pajaritos and on to the Argentine border. At Anticura, there is camping and access to several short trails and some longer ones.

The 950-meter **Sendero Educativo Salto del Indio** is a signed nature trail leading to a waterfall on the Golgol. Its name comes from a local legend that a fugitive Mapuche hid to avoid forced labor in a colonial mine. An overnight excursion up the Río Anticura Valley leads to **Pampa Frutilla,** now part of the Sendero de Chile. Areas east of Pajaritos, the Chilean border post, require Conaf permission to hike or otherwise explore because it's a legal no-man's-land and, unfortunately, this means limited access to large sectors of the park.

From El Caulle, two kilometers west of Anticura, a 16-kilometer trail climbs the abrupt flanks of **Volcán Puyehue,** where there's a simple *refugio* (shelter) and camping is also possible; alternatively, continue through a barren landscape of hardened lava flows where it's also possible to camp. At the trailhead, former senator Marcos Cariola's

Turismo El Caulle (Ruta 215, Km 90, tel. 09/5008-6367, www.elcaulle.com) demands a US$19 toll for the right to pass through his property; this includes use of the *refugio,* but Cariola's cattle have eroded parts of the trail. It's possible to hike through to Riñinahue, at Lago Ranco's south end (where there's a US$4 toll), rather than return to El Caulle.

Volcán Puyehue itself is a flat-topped Holocene caldera, measuring 2.4 kilometers in diameter. It sits within a larger caldera measuring five kilometers across. The most recent eruptions have come not from the summit caldera but from the Cordón Caulle's vents on its western flanks.

FOOD AND ACCOMMODATIONS

Some visitors stay at Termas de Puyehue, but park accommodations also include campgrounds and *cabañas.*

Aguas Calientes

Termas Aguas Calientes (tel. 064/233-1710, www.termasaguascalientes.cl) operates the 36-site **Camping Chanleufú** (year-round, US$37 for up to 4 people). Fees at Chanleufú include firewood and electricity. Access to pools is an additional cost. There are also the **Domos Termas Aguas Calientes** (US$96-125 d, including access to pools).

Accommodations at **Cabañas Aguas Calientes** (tel. 064/233-1710, US$185 for up to 4 people) include access to the baths. It also has a cafeteria with a sandwich menu, the more elaborate restaurant **El Arrayán,** and an outdoor grill restaurant in summer only.

Antillanca

At the ski area, the 73-room **Hotel Antillanca** (Ruta 215, Km 98, tel. 064/261-2070, www.antillanca.cl, US$54 s, US$60 d with breakfast; packages with 2 meals available) has a contemporary sector and an older but passable *refugio* (shelter) that's closed in summer. In the peak season, July to mid-August, hotel rates reach US$1,600 per week for a

Anticura

West of Anticura, **El Caulle** (Ruta 215, Km 90, tel. 09/9641-2000, www.elcaulle.com) operates a grill restaurant just off the highway.

Patagonia Expeditions (tel. 09/9104-8061, www.anticura.com) runs the eight-site **Camping Catrué** (US$7-10 pp), whose facilities include running water, picnic tables, fire pits, showers, and flush toilets. There's also a 14-bed hostel (US$19 pp, with shared bath and kitchen facilities) and *cabañas* (around US$70 d).

Termas de Puyehue

Alone on a winter's night, walking the corridors and circuitous staircases at Hotel Termas de Puyehue, you might expect a deranged Jack Nicholson to turn the corner swinging an ax. Unlike *The Shining*'s isolated alpine hotel, though, the Sur Chico's hot-springs resort borders a major international highway, stays open year-round, and is never isolated by weather, so you're not likely to be snowed in with a madman.

Only a small wing of the original building remains, but the all-inclusive **Termas de Puyehue Wellness & Spa Resort** (Ruta 215, tel. 064/233-1400, www.puyehue. cl, US$195-275 s, US$300-430 d) retains the stately elegance of a grand country hotel while adding contemporary conveniences to ensure its premier position among Chilean hot-springs resorts. From modest beginnings in 1908, on sprawling wooded grounds near the border of Parque Nacional Puyehue, it now houses up to 300 guests in 138 spacious rooms, some with balconies. Guests pay a lower rate for open access to nearly all services (including full board with both alcoholic and nonalcoholic drinks), or more for a package that includes activities such as horseback riding, mountain biking, tennis, and enjoying its thermal pools. Only premium wines and spa treatments are additional.

Its thermal spa boasts a huge covered pool and an Olympic-size outdoor pool, and offers whirlpool tubs, massages, mud baths, and algal treatments. For food, there are three restaurants, including the Italian **Olivia Nova,** and a bar. Other amenities include a small museum, a library, game rooms, and even an events hall that hosts classical music concerts. Since 1939, electricity has come from the resort's own small hydroelectric installation.

The resort sits at the junction where the main highway continues toward Anticura and the Argentine border. A paved lateral road heads to Aguas Calientes, a more modest hot springs, and the Antillanca sector of Parque Nacional Puyehue.

Around major holidays, there may be a minimum stay of three or four days. Outside the peak summer season (Jan.-mid-Mar.), rates drop 20-25 percent or more. Fall to spring, day passes for nonguests (US$103 Mon.-Fri., US$114 Sat.-Sun. and holidays summer) also drop in price by 20-25 percent.

INFORMATION

At Aguas Calientes, Conaf's **Centro de Información Ambiental** (tel. 064/197-4572, www.parquepuyehue.cl, 9am-1pm and 2pm-6pm daily) offers daily slide talks in late afternoon during the summer. Permanent exhibits focus on natural history (flora and fauna) and topics such as volcanism. Conaf also maintains an information center at Antillanca, generally open in ski season only.

TRANSPORTATION

Paved all the way to the border, Ruta 215 passes directly through the park. From Osorno's Mercado Municipal (Errázuriz 1300), **Expreso Lago Puyehue** (tel. 064/224-3919) serves Termas de Puyehue and Aguas Calientes (US$3.50) with buses and *taxis colectivos*, with additional service to Anticura and the Chilean border post at Pajaritos.

In winter, the **Club Andino Osorno** (O'Higgins 1073, tel. 064/223-2297) shuttles between Osorno and the Antillanca ski area.

double room with all meals and lift tickets. In the shoulder ski season, prices drop by about 25 percent.

Puerto Octay and Vicinity

From prosaic 19th-century beginnings as a port at Lago Llanquihue's north end, idyllic Puerto Octay has become one of the region's most picturesque locales, with magnificent views across the lake to Volcán Osorno. Local pleasure boats have supplanted the steaming freighters that once connected Octay with Puerto Varas, and it has become a low-key destination for summer holidaymakers who arrive by paved road from Osorno, 50 kilometers northwest. The German immigrant presence is palpable in the architecture, food, checkerboard landscape of dairy farms and woodlands, and in its apparent middle-class contentment.

Puerto Octay (pop. about 3,500) also includes Península Centinela, a wooded lakeside spit that's home to campgrounds and a classic that's closed because of apparently municipal ineptitude. From town, it's possible to travel Llanquihue's western shore to the resort village of Frutillar, or its eastern shore to Ensenada and Parque Nacional Vicente Pérez Rosales, via a now paved road that's ideal for cycling.

SIGHTS

Puerto Octay dates from 1852, but its architectural legacy of European-style neoclassical and chalet houses dates from the early 20th century. While no structure within Puerto Octay is a recognized national monument, at least a dozen private residences and other buildings contribute to a captivating ambience.

One of those buildings is the **Casa de la Cultura Emilio Winkler** (Independencia 591, tel. 064/239-1523, 10am-1pm and 3pm-7pm daily, US$1.50), housing part of the **Museo El Colono,** a well-organized collection of maps, photographs, and other materials on early German colonization. The building is too small to accommodate an assortment of antique farm equipment that spills out of a

barn and onto the grounds of a separate facility (at the point where the gravel road to Península Centinela splits off the paved road to Frutillar). Admission is valid for both sites.

FOOD

Puerto Octay has little out of the ordinary. The food is mostly Chilean standbys such as at **Baviera** (Germán Wulf 582, tel. 064/239-1460, lunch and dinner daily). The ice cream and desserts at **Benhaus** (Amunátegui 604, tel. 09/7846-2334), opposite the Plaza de Armas, are a welcome new addition.

About one kilometer north of town on the Osorno highway, ★ **El Fogón de Anita** (tel. 064/239-1276, lunch daily, dinner Mon.-Sat., US$12) is a fine grill restaurant. Try the *asado de tira* (short ribs). It also prepares exceptional *pisco* sours and has attentive service in attractive surroundings.

Another option is the **Rancho Espantapájaros** (Camino a Frutillar, Km 6, tel. 065/233-0049, www.espantapajaros.cl, noon-10pm daily, buffet US$25), whose specialty is barbecued boar as the centerpiece of a buffet that includes wine or beer. There's also a sandwich menu for those who don't care to gorge themselves.

ACCOMMODATIONS

Downtown has camping and basic *hospedajes* (family-run lodging). One intriguing option is the **Hotel Haase** (Pedro Montt 344, tel. 064/239-1302, www.hotelhaase.cl, US$22-27 s, US$52 d), an architectural monument whose common areas are approaching their onetime grandeur. The rooms do lag a little behind, and the floors are squeaky, but the style is classic. The management is friendly and the restaurant has become more consistent.

About two kilometers north of town on the Osorno road, the Swiss-Chilean ★ **Puerto Octay Hostal Zapato Amarillo** (tel. 064/221-0787, www.zapatoamarillo.cl, US$19 pp dorms, with breakfast and shared bath, US$50-59 d) has become a destination in its own right as much as a place to stay. It arranges taxi transfers to La Picada for a five-hour hike to Petrohué (US$45 for up to four people, US$75 for the return from Petrohué). Comfortably stylish dorm accommodations on ample grounds, with kitchen facilities, are slightly cheaper outside of the peak October-April months. Zapato Amarillo also offers several doubles with shared or private baths, some of them in truly distinctive freestanding, sod-roofed houses. There are fine views of Volcán Osorno across the lawns. In addition, Zapato Amarillo offers initial transfers from Puerto Octay, information, Wi-Fi, laundry, rental bikes, a small sailboat, and rental scooters for day trips. Proprietors Armin Dübendorfer and Nadia Muñoz can handle Spanish, German, English, and French.

INFORMATION AND SERVICES

Opposite the Plaza, the **Caseta de Informaciones Turísticas** (Esperanza 555, tel. 064/239-1764, www.turismopuertooctay.cl) provides useful info. Opposite Hotel Haase, **BancoEstado** (Pedro Montt 345) has an ATM.

TRANSPORTATION

Buses and minibuses leave from the **Terminal de Buses** (La Esperanza and Balmaceda), half a block south of the Plaza de Armas. **Via Octay** (tel. 064/223-7043) and **Buses Norambuena** (tel. 064/223-0240) travel to Osorno's main bus terminal (US$2) several times daily, while **Thaebus** goes half a dozen times daily to Puerto Montt (US$3) via Frutillar and Puerto Varas. **Buses Arriagada** goes south to Las Cascadas (5pm daily, US$2.50), roughly halfway to Ensenada.

FRUTILLAR

The region's most self-consciously immaculate example of German colonization, the western Llanquihue village of Frutillar can seem a caricature of Teutonic orderliness. The lakefront is so tidy that, when a thoughtless smoker flips a cigarette butt, some burgher might well materialize to catch it before it hits the ground.

Still, with its almost perfectly preserved European-style houses, Frutillar exudes both style and charm. For a town its size, it has impressive cultural resources in a fine museum, a state-of-the-art theater, and one of Chile's most important music festivals. Mirrored in

Hotel Haase, Puerto Octay

Llanquihue's waters, Volcán Osorno soars symmetrically to the east.

Orientation

Frutillar (pop. about 18,000) is 63 kilometers south of Osorno and 50 kilometers north of Puerto Montt via the Panamericana. It comprises two separate sectors: Frutillar Alto's busy commercial zone adjoins the Panamericana; Avenida Carlos Richter leads to tranquil Frutillar Bajo, pinched between the sandy lakeshore and a steeply rising hill, about two kilometers east. Avenida Philippi runs north-south along the lakeshore, linked to the parallel Vicente Pérez Rosales by a series of block-long streets. Most services and other points of interest face the lake from the west side of Philippi.

Sights

Middle European-style architecture is Frutillar Bajo's trademark, in structures such as the 1911 **Iglesia Luterana** (Lutheran Church, Philippi 1000), but Germanic houses and other handsome buildings face the entire lakefront.

The highlight is the **Museo Colonial Alemán de Frutillar** (Vicente Pérez Rosales s/n, tel. 065/242-1142, www.museosaustral.

cl, 9am-7:30pm daily, US$4 adults, US$1 children), an indoor-outdoor facility set among immaculate gardens at the base of the hill. Antique farm machinery in mint condition adorns the grounds. Buildings such as the **Molino** (a water-powered mill), the **Casa del Herrero** (a working smithy), the **Campanario** (a storage structure with a conical roof supported by a central pillar), and the **Casa del Colono** (a residence filled with period furniture and household implements) are precise historical reconstructions. Built partly with German aid, the museum is at the west end of Arturo Prat, one short block from the lakeshore. The museum shop sells souvenirs such as horseshoes forged in the smithy and carvings of museum buildings.

Events

Frutillar's major annual event is the **Semanas Musicales de Frutillar** (www.semanasmusicales.cl), a 10-day extravaganza that has showcased classical, jazz, and ethnic music since 1968. From January 27 to February 5, events take place both during the daytime and at night, when performances are both more formal and more expensive. Some recitals take place at the magnificent **Teatro del Lago** (Av. Philippi 1000, tel. 065/242-2900, www.

Teatro del Lago, Frutillar

teatrodellago.cl, guided tours noon daily, US$7), a state-of-the-art theater built on pilings over the lake. Seating about 1,000 spectators within, its exterior glistens with strips of veneer from native woods. The series also includes concerts in regional cities such as Osorno and Puerto Montt.

In the second week of November, the next-largest event is **Semana Frutillarina**, celebrating Frutillar's founding as a lake port in 1856.

Food

In summer, look along the lakeshore for stands with fresh raspberries, raspberry jam, and raspberry kuchen, all local specialties. Compared with its accommodations, Frutillar's restaurant are only average, but it has several breakfast and *onces* (afternoon tea) places, starting with the **Salón de Té Trayén** (Philippi 963, tel. 065/242-1346, breakfast and lunch daily).

O'Clock (Vicente Pérez Rosales 690, tel. 065/242-1660) serves fixed-price lunches, sandwiches, and a diversity of craft beers as well as coffee. **Kuchenladen** (Philippi 1155, tel. 065/242-2917, 9am-8:30pm daily) specializes in kuchen, but also has some well-crafted ice cream. **Crambussa** (Pérez Rosales 814, tel. 09/9799-5840, www.crambussa.cl) is a specialist chocolate shop, with fruit-flavored truffles and other dark chocolate goodies.

In the old fire station, **Don René** (Av. Philippi 1065, tel. 065/242-1884, US$10-12) serves a variety of fish and shellfish dishes; its midday special offers a variety of choices in that regard. The service is friendly and attentive.

Guten Apetit (Balmaceda 98, tel. 065/242-1145, lunch and dinner daily) is a *parrilla* (grill restaurant) with lunchtime specials and assiduous service. The traditional **Club Alemán** (San Martín 22, tel. 065/242-1249, lunch and dinner daily, US$15) is more formal and more expensive. It serves dishes such as *pastel de jaiva* (crab soufflé) among otherwise more Germanic specialties, slightly sugary *pisco* sours, and generous servings of limited wine-by-the-glass selections.

On the southern outskirts of town, **Lavanda** (Camino Quebrada Honda, Km 1.5, tel. 09/9458-0804, www.lavandacasadete.cl, 1pm-8pm Tues.-Sun.) is now an established teahouse, with nearly 50 different teas and creative sandwiches that include wild boar and rhea fillings. Their chocolate cake falls short—stick with the kuchen. The sandwiches (on bagels) are moderately priced. The teas and sweets are fairly expensive at US$5-6 each. They now offer horseback rides as well.

Accommodations

Frutillar's accommodations scene is strong at the mid- to upscale range, but budget alternatives are limited. During the music festival, prices can spike even higher than regular summer rates. All listings provided here are in Frutillar Bajo, but Frutillar Alto has a handful of cheaper options.

Only a block from the beach, **Hospedaje Tía Clarita** (Vicente Pérez Rosales 743, tel. 065/242-1806, US$45 pp, with breakfast) is a friendly, family-run place lacking the elaborate German colonial style of Frutillar's pricier options. Rates include both private bath and cable TV.

Also notable for its teahouse, **Hostería Trayén** (Philippi 963, tel. 065/242-1346, tttrayen33@hotmail.com, US$53 s, US$68 d, with breakfast) has rooms with private baths and cable TV. Some rooms have balconies with lake views. **Hotel Residenz am See** (Philippi 539, tel. 065/242-1539, US$111 s, US$118 d) offers rooms with Wi-Fi, private baths, a European-style breakfast, and parking. Some rooms enjoy lake views.

On the northern outskirts of town, via a newly paved road, the **Salzburg Hotel & Spa** (Camino Playa Maqui s/n, tel. 065/242-1579, www.salzburg.cl, US$98-128 s or d) is a venerable spa hotel, most of whose TV-free rooms are in a modern new wing overlooking lush gardens with views to Lago Llanquihue and Volcán Osorno (there are several small TV lounges). In addition to having a restaurant, it may be Chile's only accommodations with its own brewery on the grounds (open for tours and tastings).

On a hillock with colorful flower gardens, **Hotel Frau Holle am See** (Antonio Varas 54, tel. 065/242-1345, www.frauholle-frutillar.com, US$143 s, US$162-280 d) embodies traditional Frutillar. It's a lovingly maintained, family-run hotel with no frills but is utterly reliable.

★ **Hotel Ayacara** (Philippi 1215, tel./fax 065/242-1550, www.hotelayacara.cl, US$143-189 s or d) occupies a gabled century-old lakefront mansion. Each of its eight rooms is distinctive. The more expensive rooms enjoy lake views. Rates include a full German-style breakfast with homemade kuchen.

At the southern edge of town, the 14 rooms at **Hotel Elun** (Camino Punta Larga, Km 2, tel. 065/242-0055, www.hotelelun.cl, US$135 s, US$165-190 d) feature natural wood interiors, with lake and volcano views, surrounded by lush gardens. Set back from the street, it's quiet and attractive, with friendly ownership and staff. The Wi-Fi may only reach the rooms nearest the lobby. The restaurant normally opens only in summer, but will serve meals on request fall to spring.

Information and Services

Frutillar's **Centro de Información Turística** (Philippi and O'Higgins, tel. 065/246-7450, infoturismo@munifrutillar.cl, 9am-8pm daily summer, 9am-1pm and 2pm-6pm Mon.-Fri. fall-spring) sometimes opens outside its regular days and hours.

Frutillar has no exchange houses, but **BancoEstado** (Philippi 403) has an ATM. **Lavandería Thieck's** (Philippi 1227, Local 2, tel. 09/9829-3601) handles the washing. For medical services, contact the **Hospital de Frutillar** (Las Piedras s/n, tel. 065/232-6903).

Transportation

Buses arrive at and leave from Frutillar Alto; *taxis colectivos* shuttle back and forth to Frutillar Bajo. The major long-distance carriers are **Tur-Bus** (Alianza Cristiana y Misionera 150, tel. 065/249-3419) and **Cruz del Sur** (Alessandri 32, tel. 065/242-1552). Both run north to Santiago and intermediate destinations and south to Puerto Montt along the Panamericana. From a small new terminal alongside the Bigger supermarket, **Thaebus** (Alessandri 381, tel. 065/242-1047) runs half a dozen buses daily to Puerto Octay (US$1.80) and to Puerto Montt (US$2.50).

Puerto Varas

North of Puerto Montt, picturesque Puerto Varas appeals to conventional tourists who loll on Lago Llanquihue's beaches, admire its century-old mansions, sup in some of Chile's best restaurants, and indulge themselves on the scenery of the bus-boat crossing to the Argentine resort of Bariloche. Increasing numbers of more adventurous visitors also appreciate the nearby Río Petrohué's white-water rafting, Volcán Osorno's snow-clad slopes, Cochamó's wild backcountry, and other outdoor attractions. To the southeast, beyond Cochamó, a bridge over the Río Puelo also provides an alternative route to Hornopirén and the Carretera Austral.

Varas's architectural heritage, stemming from its German colonization as a 19th-century lake port, lends it its character. A recent building boom has resulted in nondescript housing developments on the outskirts, but it has also brought more stylish infill downtown. Many visitors prefer Varas to nearby Puerto Montt, and not just as a base for excursions.

ORIENTATION

On Llanquihue's southwestern shore, Puerto Varas (pop. 41,000) is 996 kilometers south of Santiago, 20 kilometers north of Puerto Montt, and a short distance east of Ruta 5,

Puerto Varas

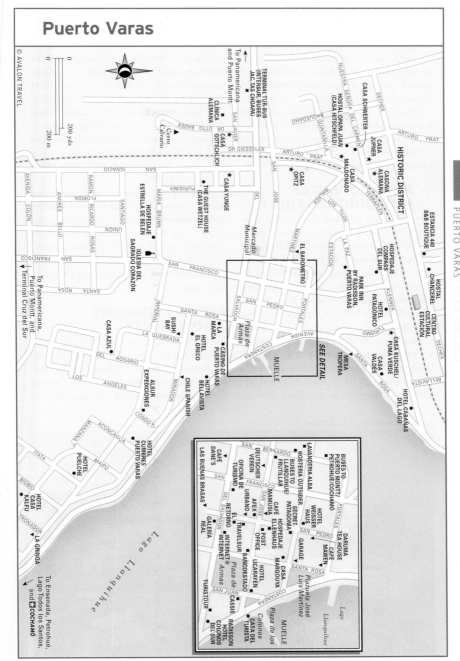

© AVALON TRAVEL

0 — 200 yds
0 — 200 m

To Panamericana
and Puerto Montt

Cerro Calvario

HISTORIC DISTRICT

TERMINAL TUR-BUS
(INTERSUR, BUSES
JAC, TAS CHOAPA)

CLINICA ALEMANA

CASA GOTSCHLICH

HOSTAL OPARA JUAN
(CASA HITSCHFELD)

CASA SCHWERTER

CASA JUPNER

CASA ALEMANA

CASONA ALEMANA

CASA MALDONADO

CASA OPITZ

CASA YUNGE

THE GUEST HOUSE
(CASA WETZEL)

HOSPEDAJE
ESTRELLA DE BELEN

IGLESIA DEL
SAGRADO CORAZON

Mercado Municipal

EL BAROMETRO

HOSPEDAJE
COMPASS
DEL SUR

PARK INN
BY RADISSON
PUERTO VARAS

HOTEL
PATAGONICO

CASA KUSCHEL/
PUMA VERDE

MESA
TROPERA

CASA
VALDES

HOTEL CABAÑAS
DEL LAGO

ESTANCIA 440
B&B BOUTIQUE

HOSTAL
CHANCEREL

CENTRO
CULTURAL
ESTACION

CASA AZUL

ALSUR
EXPEDICIONES

LA
MARCA

CASINO DE
PUERTO VARAS

SUSHI
BAY

HOTEL
EL GRECO

HOTEL
BELLAVISTA

CHILE SPANISH

Plaza de
Armas

MUELLE

SEE DETAIL

HOTELES
CUMBRES
PUERTO VARAS

HOTEL
PUELCHE

HOTEL
CASA
KALFU

LA GRINGA

Lago Llanquihue

To Panamericana,
Puerto Montt, and
Terminal Cruz del Sur

To Ensenada, Petrohué,
Lago Todos los Santos,
and ⚓ COCHAMÓ

Streets: NUESTRA SEÑORA DEL CARMEN, DECHER, ARTURO PRAT, BAQUEDANO, QUINTANILLA, SAN JAVIER, DR OTTO BADER, DR GIESSELER, ARTURO PRAT, WALKER, TERRABEN, LOS SOTI, DEL SOL, SAN JOSE, DEL SALVADOR, SAN PEDRO, PORTALES, AVENIDA COSTANERA, ESTACION, LA PAZ, KLEENER, SANTA ROSA, SANTA ROSA, BELLAVISTA, SAN IGNACIO, RAMON RICARDO, ANDRES BELLO, COLON, FLORIDA, SANTIAGO, MARIA BRUNN, PURISMA, SAN FRANCISCO, AVENIDA, ROSAS, SAN FRANCISCO, SANTA ROSA, IMPERIAL, LA QUEBRADA, MIRADOR, CONDOR, DEL ROSARIO, LOS ANGELES, ACONCAGUA, MANZANO, ITATA, MAIPO, BIOBIO, TRONADOR

SEE DETAIL (inset):

CAFÉ DANE'S

LAS BUENAS BRASAS

GALERIA REAL

LAVANDERIA ALBA

HOSTERIA OUTSIDER

DEUTSCHER VEREIN

OFICINA DE TURISMO

EL RETORNO
INTERNET®

BUSES TO
PUERTO MONTT/
PETROHUE/COCHAMO

BUSES TO
LLANQUIHUE/
FRUTILLAR

BUSES TO
OUTSIDER

SECRET
PATAGONIA

CAFÉ
MAMUSIA

HOSPEDAJE
ELLENHAUS

POST
OFFICE

AFEX

URBANO

INTERNET®

Plaza de
Armas

BANCOESTADO

HOTEL
LICARAYEN

CASA
MARGOUYA

HOTEL
WEISSER
HAUS

GARAGE

DARUMA
TEA HOUSE

CAFÉ
MAVEN

Plazuela José
Luis Martínez

TURISTOUR

CASSIS

RADISSON
HOTEL
COLONOS
DEL SUR

CASA DEL
TURISTA

Plaza de los
Colonos

MUELLE

Lago
Llanquihue

the Panamericana. The boundaries of its compact central grid are the lakeshore to the east, Diego Portales to the north, San Bernardo to the west, and Del Salvador to the south. On all sides except the shoreline, hills rise steeply toward quiet residential neighborhoods that include many places to stay.

From the corner of Del Salvador, the Costanera becomes paved Ruta 225 to the village of Ensenada, the lake port of Petrohué in Parque Nacional Vicente Pérez Rosales, and toward the Cochamó backcountry.

★ PUERTO VARAS HISTORIC DISTRICT

Other than the lake and its inspiring views toward Volcán Osorno, Varas's main attraction is its Germanic colonial architecture. The most imposing single structure is the **Iglesia del Sagrado Corazón** (1915), a national monument whose steeple soars above the town from the corner of San Francisco and María Brunn. When lit at night, it's best seen from the corner of Imperial and Santa Rosa.

Numerous private residences are national monuments, mostly in residential neighborhoods northwest and west of downtown. The city emphasizes its architectural heritage with explanatory signs with brief histories alongside many of these residences. Examples include 1910's **Casa Kuschel** (Klenner 299), 1914's **Casona Alemana** (Nuestra Señora del Carmen 788), 1915's deteriorating **Casa Maldonado** (Quintanilla 852), 1910's **Casa Jupner** (Miraflores 96), 1913's **Casa Opitz** (Terraplén 861), 1932's **Casa Gotschlich** (Dr. Otto Bader 701-05), and 1932's **Casa Yunge** (San Ignacio 711). A couple of impressive non-monuments serve as accommodations: the 1941-1942 **Casa Schwerter** (Nuestra Señora del Carmen 873) and 1930's **Casa Hitschfeld** (Arturo Prat 107).

For some years after the Santiago-Puerto Montt railroad closed, the former **Estación del Ferrocarril** (Klenner s/n) sat empty, but today it has been revamped as the Centro Cultural Estación, a gallery and events center. After a brief revival, rail service has been suspended, but work is underway on the tracks and sleepers.

ENTERTAINMENT AND EVENTS

Puerto Varas has less nightlife than might be expected in a town with its tourist traffic. Roulette wheels and slots cram the unsightly and pharaonically oversize **Casino de Puerto Varas** (Del Salvador 21, tel.

Puerto Varas on Lago Llanquihue

065/249-2000), alongside the Hotel de los Volcanes.

Far better, though, is **Garage** (Walker Martínez 220, tel. 09/8755-7640), a low-key bar that was once an auto repair shop alongside the Copec gas station, but now has live music, including jazz. **Urbano** (San Pedro 418, tel. 09/8710-1452) is also popular for drinks and dancing.

More a wine bar than a restaurant, though it does serve food and stronger alcohol, the Costanera's **Bravo Cabrera** (Vicente Pérez Rosales 1071, tel. 065/223-3441, www.bravocabrera.cl) has a diverse selection of wines by the glass, not all of them from the biggest producers.

Commemorating the city's 1854 founding, the **Aniversario de Puerto Varas** lasts two weeks in late January and early February. Soon thereafter, painters from around the country display their work at the **Concurso de Pintura El Color del Sur.**

SHOPPING

At the headquarters for Parque Pumalín, **Puma Verde** (Klenner 299, tel. 065/225-0079) is the crafts outlet for residents of its surrounding communities. Items for sale range from locally produced honey to

souvenirs and quality woolens. In addition, there's a good selection of books on Chilean conservation topics, mostly in Spanish.

On the Costanera, behind the Ibis restaurant, **La Vinoteca** (Av. Pérez Rosales 1069, tel. 065/248-0066, www.lavinoteca.cl) has the biggest and best selection of wines in town.

FOOD

In Puerto Varas, even run-of-the-mill restaurants can be pretty good. **Café Dane's** (Del Salvador 441, tel. 065/223-2371, breakfast, lunch, and dinner daily) wins no style points, but its breakfasts, *onces* (afternoon tea), and Chilean specialties, such as *pastel de choclo* (corn casserole), stand out among similar fare elsewhere.

The location may change from year to year but, somewhere along the lakefront, there's a diversity of ★ **food trucks** where the choices include ceviche, sandwiches, shawarma, sushi, tacos, and even a creative assortment of sheep's milk ice cream flavors at **8 Reinas** (www.8reinas.cl). There are sit-down tables but, depending on the specific location, little shade or shelter from wet weather.

In the Mercado Municipal, **Donde El Gordito** (San Bernardo 560, Local 7, tel. 065/223-3425, 11:30am-11pm daily) is a

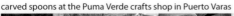

carved spoons at the Puma Verde crafts shop in Puerto Varas

modest seafood venue that is good value for the price. For nontraditional seafood, **Sushi Bay** (Mirador 123, tel. 065/223-7593, www. sushibay.cl, US$15) serves a diversity of sushi and sashimi, plus donburi, tempura, and pot stickers. The surroundings are spacious and attractive, there's also outdoor seating, and the service is attentive without being overbearing.

At **La Gringa Bakery Café** (Imperial 605, tel. 065/223-1980, www.lagringa.cl, 8am-8pm Mon.-Fri., 10am-8pm Sat.), coffee and kuchen are morning fare, but there are also tasty lunches and an adjacent wine bar and shop, in a historic building. The salads merit special mention.

In new and more expansive quarters, **Casa Mawen** (Santa Rosa 218, tel. 065/223-6971, 8am-8pm daily) serves fine salads and sandwiches as well as desserts that include kuchen. It is probably most notable for a variety of espresso drinks. **Cassis** (San Juan 431, Local 3, tel. 065/244-1529, 8:30am-midnight daily) is a branch of Pucón's outstanding sandwich, sweets, and coffee shop. When it gets busy, though, the quality of the food is inversely proportional to its appalling service.

New in late 2016, **Daruma Tea House** (San Pedro 251, 8am-10pm Mon.-Fri., 9am-10pm Sat.-Sun. and holidays) is Varas's first dedicated teahouse, but that's a bit misleading in that it also serves a wide variety of juices, coffees, desserts, and sandwiches. The chicken pesto on ciabatta, with caramelized peppers (US$9), really breaks the mold for Chilean sandwiches, and the space itself is luminously appealing.

Puerto Madero (Santa Rosa and Imperial, tel. 065/223-7525) is an Argentine-run coffee shop with trans-Andean specialties such as *medialunas* (croissants) and the *submarino* (a bar of bittersweet chocolate dissolved in hot milk).

Café Mamusia (San José 316, tel. 065/223-3343, lunch and dinner daily, US$9-12) serves fine Chilean specialties, especially *pastel de choclo* (corn casserole), with a cheaper

fixed-price *menú de casa* at midday. The *pisco* sours are strong, and the kuchen sweet with fresh fruit. Service is erratic.

Specializing in seafood, the traditional **Club Alemán** (German Club, San José 415, tel. 065/223-2246, www.clubalemanpvaras. cl, lunch and dinner daily) offers fixed-price midday meals for about US$10.

The best seafood choice, ★ **Casa Valdés** (Santa Rosa 040, tel. 09/9079-3938, 12:30pm-4pm and 7pm-11pm daily, US$13) specializes in fish, such as corvina (croaker) in squid ink and outstanding shellfish appetizers such as *machas a la parmesana* (razor clams) and live oysters. Though the Peruvian *pisco* sour lacks tanginess, the lake views are memorable, and service is above average.

From its name ("The Good Coals"), ★ **Las Buenas Brasas** (San Pedro 543, tel. 065/223-4154, www.lbb.cl, lunch and dinner daily, US$12) sounds like a *parrilla* (grill restaurant), but it's proudest of its fish dishes, especially conger eel and seafood sauces. The attractive **La Marca** (Santa Rosa 539, tel. 065/223-2026, www.restaurantlamarca.cl, noon-11:30pm daily, from US$12), though, does draw praise for grilled meats—some say it's the best restaurant in town. In this location, however, space is limited and reservations strongly advised.

In the same building as Hostería Outsider, **Trattoria Di Carusso** (San Bernardo 318, tel. 065/223-3478, 12:30pm-1am daily) makes tremendous pizza (the crust is especially notable) and seafood. A direct descendant of the Mediterráneo restaurant that formerly occupied its space, **Almendra** (Santa Rosa 68, tel. 065/223-7268) prepares a variety of ceviches, fish and even game dishes, and especially pastas at surprisingly moderate prices in upscale surroundings. It also offers an ample selection of wines by the glass.

Astonishingly, the website of **Hotel El Greco** (Mirador 134, tel. 065/223-3880, www.hotelelgreco.cl) doesn't even mention its fine restaurant, which is a slightly offbeat Peruvian-Chilote fusion (though it does contain a couple of photos). Seafood is the specialty, though there are also meats and Chinese-Peruvian platters. The Peruvian *pisco* sour may be the best in town.

Other pizza options include moderately-priced ★ **El Retorno** (San Pedro 465, tel. 065/234-6441, lunch and dinner daily) and **Da Alessandro** (Av. Costanera 1290, tel. 065/231-0583, www.daalessandro.com, lunch and dinner daily), which earns good marks from knowledgeable locals for its pizzas, pastas, and seafood.

The best new choice, under the same ownership as Coyhaique's Mamma Gaucha, is **Mesa Tropera** (Santa Rosa 161, tel. 065/223-7973, www.mesatropera.cl, 10am-2am Mon.-Sat.), which has transformed the once stuffy yacht club into a casual but energetic restaurant with numerous artisanal beers on tap at separate bars at each end of the building; in between, the staff assembles fresh stuffed pasta in the open kitchen. The lakeside dining area has great views toward the volcanos but, on sunny days, it can be blindingly bright.

Ibis (Vicente Pérez Rosales 1117, tel. 065/223-5533, www.ibisrest.cl, dinner daily, from US$15) has been one of southern Chile's finest dining experiences, with prices to match, but there are signs it's slipping. With drinks and side orders, it's easy to spend upward of US$40 pp. There may be better places to splurge.

For fish and seafood, ★ **La Olla** (Ruta 225, Km 0.9, tel. 065/223-3540, www.laolla. cl, noon-4pm daily and 7pm-10:30pm Mon.-Sat., US$12) falls into the upmarket end of the "hearty Chilean cooking" category, serving traditional dishes plus a few, such as corvina with a razor clam sauce, that transcend the stereotype. In new quarters at the eastern outskirts of town, it still gets crowded, especially on weekends, and parking can be a problem.

ACCOMMODATIONS

Puerto Varas has abundant and often distinctive accommodations, but not much that's truly cheap.

US$25-50

With Spanish, English, and French spoken, **Casa Margouya** (Santa Rosa 318, tel. 065/251-1648, www.margouya.com, US$17 pp, US$27 s, US$39 d) can lodge up to 17 guests in a variety of singles, doubles, and dorms, which share just two baths. Rates include tea and coffee and Internet access. Half-price breakfasts are available at a nearby café. One of Varas's livelier accommodations, this is not for the early-to-bed crowd.

Downtown's labyrinthine **Hospedaje Ellenhaus** (San Pedro 325, tel. 065/223-3577, www.ellenhaus.cl, US$20 pp dorm, US$22 s, US$39 d with shared bath, US$65 s or d with private bath) is a step above most other budget places.

In a quiet hilltop neighborhood about a 10-minute walk from the Plaza de Armas, German-run ★ **Casa Azul** (Manzanal 66, tel. 065/223-2904, www.casaazul.net, US$15 pp dorms, US$30 s, US$43 d with shared bath, US$55 d with private bath) has become a favorite for its rustically stylish and comfortable rooms, which enjoy central heating. Rates include kitchen access, but the huge breakfast of muesli and homemade bread costs US$5 extra. The garden includes a bonsai-bounded koi pond and an imposing but friendly Brazilian Fila dog named Butch.

Still nearly pristine after more than a decade, ★ **Hostería Outsider** (San Bernardo 318, tel./fax 065/223-2910, www.turout.com, US$37 s, US$48 d) has consistently provided some of Varas's best value for the price, and has done it with style.

US$50-100

Located alongside the Iglesia Sagrado Corazón, **Hospedaje Estrella de Belén** (Verbo Divino 422, tel. 065/271-6551, www. hospedaje-estrelladebelen.cl, US$30-40 s, US$52-58 d) has drawn enthusiastic praise for many years. Services include cable TV and Wi-Fi. Rates vary according to shared or private bath.

Easy walking distance from downtown, but in a quiet barrio opposite the old railroad station, ★ **Hostal Compass del Sur** (Klenner 467, tel. 065/223-2044, www.compassdelsur.cl, US$20 pp dorms, US$42 s, US$55 d with shared bath, US$50 s, US$66 d with private bath) occupies a German colonial-style house with large rooms and kitchen privileges. Rates include a standard breakfast, but extras such as muesli, eggs, and real coffee (not Nescafé) cost more. Laundry service and camping (US$14 pp, including breakfast and access to the house's common areas) are also available.

Named a national monument for its architecture, the shingled Casa Hitschfeld also houses **Hostal Opapa Juan** (Arturo Prat 107, tel. 065/223-2234, www.opapajuan.cl, US$52 s, US$72 d, with private bath and breakfast), a respectable B&B.

In quiet surroundings, some rooms at the **Park Inn by Radisson, Puerto Varas** (La Paz 471, tel. 065/223-5555, www.radisson.com, US$68-88 s, U$72-94 d, with breakfast) have truly grand views, and, compared with some other places, it has kept its prices stable. However, it now serves more as overflow for when its rebuilt lakeside sister hotel (the Radisson Hotel Colonos del Sur) is full.

Its exterior restored to pioneer style, ★ **The Guest House** (O'Higgins 608, tel. 065/223-7577, www.theguesthouse.cl, US$50 s, US$75 d) occupies the German-colonial Casa Kortmann, a national monument. With smartly furnished rooms and ample well-lighted common spaces, it provides some of Varas's most intimate accommodations, though it has recently changed hands.

It may look remote on the map, but **Hostal Chancerel** (Decher 400, tel./fax 065/223-4221, www.turismochancerel.com, US$65 s, US$75 d) is still just a 15-minute walk from the Plaza de Armas. Rates include spacious rooms with private baths, breakfast, cable TV, Wi-Fi, and central heating. Other meals and German-style *onces* (afternoon tea) are available.

If its rooms had views, the 25-room **Puerto Chico Hotel** (Av. Colonos 60, tel. 065/223-1000, www.puertochicohotel.cl,

US$88 s, US$101 d) would command higher prices than it does, as the decor and amenities match or exceed those of many better-known accommodations. At the same time, it's easy walking distance from lakeshore restaurants along the eastern Costanera.

Downtown's **Hotel Weisser Haus** (San Pedro 252, tel. 065/234-6479, www.weisserhaus.cl, US$80 s, US$99 d) is a 10-room B&B that consists of a handsome and architecturally suitable addition to a traditional German colonial-style residence. A couple of rooms are small but still well designed, and slightly cheaper.

US$100-150

One of Varas's most distinctive accommodations, featuring natural wood walls enhanced with work by regional artists, **Hotel El Greco** (Mirador 134, tel. 065/223-3880, www.hotelelgreco.cl, US$101 s, US$109 d) might be the world's greenest hotel in terms of building materials. When the nearby German school moved to new quarters, El Greco's owners salvaged everything from the building to convert a single-story hotel into a four-story building with legitimately traditional style. The current floors, for instance, were once part of the school's gymnasium, and the room doors once opened into classrooms.

The 98-room lakefront **Radisson Hotel Colonos del Sur** (Del Salvador 024, tel. 065/223-1100, www.radisson.com, US$93-210 s, US$102-220 d) is the expanded reconstruction of an earlier fire-ravaged hotel, now under the Radisson umbrella. Standard rooms are smaller than premiums and suites. Rooms on the lakeside seventh floor are preferable to those facing the casino across the street. In addition to a restaurant, it has a small pool and spa, and a great top-floor view lounge.

On a quiet site above the Costanera, **Hotel Casa Kalfu** (Tronador 1134, tel. 065/275-1261, www.casakalfu.cl, US$115 s or d) has adapted and expanded a traditional Varas-style house into a striking hotel surrounded by lush gardens, with 17 rooms that vary in size; the smallest room still benefits from a balcony with views toward Volcán Osorno.

Near the Chancerel, ★ **Estancia 440 Bed & Breakfast Boutique** (Decher 440, tel. 065/223-3921, www.estancia440.cl, US$100 s, US$120 d) is a seven-room facility that occupies an exquisitely restored 1930s house with finely burnished woodwork, hand-crafted furniture, and breakfast delicacies from the owner's own Café Dane's.

Hotel Puelche (Imperial 695, tel. 065/223-3600, www.hotelpuelche.com, US$112-127 s or d) is a handsome, 21-room boutique hotel on a hill just above the lakeshore, with rustically sophisticated stone-and-wood style. It includes a gym and spa, and is within easy walking distance to Varas's best restaurants. In clear weather, some balconied rooms enjoy volcano views.

US$150-200

On the lakeshore just south of the casino, the modernizing **Hotel Bellavista** (Vicente Pérez Rosales 60, tel. 065/223-2011, www.hotelbellavista.cl, US$142-214 s or d) has outstanding lake views and improved amenities. Popular with foreign tour groups, it's notably cheaper off-season.

Stretching impressively above the lakeshore, the hillside **Hotel Cabañas del Lago** (Klenner 195, tel. 065/223-2291, www.cabanasdellago.cl, US$159-270 s or d, with breakfast) has equally impressive views and a heated pool. The more expensive corner suites offer views of Osorno as well as the lake and Calbuco.

Over US$200

Under the same ownership as the adjacent casino, the **Hotel de los Volcanes** (Del Salvador 021, tel. 065/249-2000, www.mundodreams.com, US$200 s or d) deserves consideration even by non-gamblers. Its 50 tastefully decorated rooms, including several more expensive suites, enjoy spectacular lake and volcano views. Amenities include a pool, a spa, and an elaborate buffet breakfast.

Nearby **Hotel Cumbres Puerto Varas** (Imperial 0561, tel. 065/222-2000, www.cumbrespuertovaras.com, US$179-189 s, US$279-289 d) is a spa hotel whose luminous common areas stress locally quarried volcanic stone and native woods. On a hillock behind the Costanera, it has some of Varas's finest unobstructed views. The 90 rooms include 23 luxury rooms with their own balconies, and four suites, including the priciest presidential suite.

Across from the old train station, the Spanish Meliá chain rehabbed the once run-down casino, but then divested itself of the glistening **Hotel Patagónico** (Klenner 349, tel. 065/220-1000, www.hotelpatagonico.cl, US$210-400 s or d), with 91 contemporary rooms with elaborate common areas and gardens as well as a spa. Some of the rooms suffer minor limitations associated with the remodeling of an existing building, but this still stands among Varas's top hotels.

"Inconspicuous consumption" might be the motto of the **Quincho Casa Hotel** (Ruta 225, Km 7.5, tel. 065/233-0737, www.quinchocasahotel.cl, US$440-682 s, US$660-870 d), which lacks even a road sign to identify its sprawling four-suite lodge on the eastern outskirts of town. It also offers multiple-night all-inclusive packages with airport pickups, all meals, and guided day trips.

INFORMATION

The municipal **Oficina de Turismo** (Del Salvador 320, tel. 065/236-1194, 8:30am-8:30pm daily Dec.-Mar., 8:30am-5:30pm Mon.-Fri. Apr.-Nov.) is a helpful resource. At the foot of the pier on the Avenida Costanera, the private **Casa del Turista** (Piedraplén s/n, tel. 065/223-7956, www.puertovaras.org, 8:30am-9pm Mon.-Fri., 10am-7pm Sat.-Sun. mid-Dec.-mid-Mar., 9am-7pm Mon.-Fri., 10am-7pm Sat.-Sun. mid-Mar.-mid-Dec.) usually has an English speaker available.

Informatur (San José and Santa Rosa, tel. 065/223-7773, www.informatur.com), sponsored by an alliance of various service operators, keeps a selective database of accommodations and other services.

SERVICES

Afex (San Pedro 414, tel. 065/223-2377) is the local exchange house; TravelSur (San Pedro 451, tel. 065/223-6000, www.travelsur.cl) is a general travel agency that also changes money. The ATM at BancoEstado (Santa Rosa 414) adds only a minimal service charge on transactions.

Correos de Chile (San José 242) is the post office. The most durable phone and cyber outlet is Internet@Internet (Del Salvador 264, Local 102). Chile Spanish (Mirador 20, tel. 09/8361-2500, www.chile-spanish.cl) offers Spanish-language classes.

Lavandería Alba (Walker Martínez 511, tel. 065/223-2908) washes clothes. Atop Cerro Calvario in southwestern Puerto Varas, the Clínica Alemana (Dr. Otto Bader 810, tel. 065/258-2100, www.clinicapv.cl) provides medical assistance.

TRANSPORTATION

Puerto Varas is close to the area's principal airport at Puerto Montt, has good regional and long-distance bus connections, and is also on the scenic bus-boat route to Argentina.

Air

LATAM (Av. Gramado 560, tel. 065/243-7572) flies out of Puerto Montt, as does Sky Airline (Benavente 405, Puerto Montt, tel. 065/243-4755). Turistour (tel. 065/234-7127) will drop off or pick up Varas passengers (US$18 pp); otherwise it's necessary to make the connection indirectly via ETM bus from Puerto Montt.

Bus

There is no central terminal, but some regional and long-distance bus companies share central offices near the Plaza de Armas as well as less central terminals. Some long-distance carriers from Puerto Montt, including those bound for Argentina, pick up passengers here; some area carriers have no fixed offices but pick up and drop off passengers en route through the city.

Numerous carriers serve Santiago (12-13 hours, US$15-48) and intermediates,

including Cruz del Sur (San Francisco 1317, tel. 065/223-6969), Buses Jac (tel. 065/223-7255), Cóndor Bus (tel. 065/238-3800), and Pullman Bus (terminal at San Francisco 1004, tel. 065/223-4612) as well as Intersur, Tas Choapa, and Tur-Bus (all at Del Salvador 1093, tel. 065/223-3787). Santiago fares can be higher, depending on the season and service level. The most expensive are nighttime buses with fully reclining seats.

Bus Norte Internacional (Andrés Bello 204, Oficina 20, tel. 065/223-4298) goes daily to San Carlos de Bariloche, Argentina (6 hours, US$27). Thaebus (tel. 09/9475-5666) shuttles frequently to Puerto Montt (US$1.40), stopping at the corner of San Bernardo and Walker Martínez, as does Expreso Puerto Varas (tel. 065/223-2253), commonly known as "Mitsubishi" for its minibus fleet. Between them, Buses Ensenada (tel. 09/9987-3249) and Thaebus shuttle at least half-hourly to Ensenada (US$3) and Petrohué (US$3.50), in Parque Nacional Vicente Pérez Rosales. Intercity J. M. (tel. 09/9647-1716) also goes to Ensenada and Petrohué, but less often.

From Puerto Montt, Buses Río Puelo (tel. 09/7408-9199, www.busesriopuelo.cl) goes to Cochamó (7:45am, noon, 2pm, and 4:30pm daily, US$4), with the 7:45am bus continuing to Puelo (US$6) and Tagua Tagua (US$8); Varas departures are about half an hour later. Transhar (tel. 065/225-4187) also serves this route.

Boat Shuttle

Puerto Varas is one of the intermediate points on the Cruce Andino bus-boat shuttle (US$280 pp) from Puerto Montt to Bariloche (Argentina) via Lago Todos los Santos, so it's possible to purchase tickets and board the bus to Petrohué here. Most of the year, buses leave Puerto Montt at 7:45am daily for Petrohué; April-mid-September, though, they leave Puerto Montt at 9am Wednesday-Sunday only. For details, contact Turistour (Del Salvador 72, tel. 065/243-7127, www.turistour.cl, www.cruceandino.cl).

Vicinity of Puerto Varas

Puerto Varas is the gateway for sights such as Volcán Osorno and Lago Todos los Santos, in Parque Nacional Vicente Pérez Rosales, and the Cochamó backcountry. It's also the staging point for adventure activities such as white-water rafting, hiking, climbing, mountain biking, horseback riding, and fishing. Paved Ruta 225 follows the lakeshore east to Ensenada; at a fork two kilometers farther east, the main road goes northwest to Petrohué, while another paved route heads southeast to Ralún, Cochamó, and Puelo.

Conventional travel agencies include **Turistour** (Del Salvador 72, Puerto Varas, tel. 065/243-7127, www.turistour.cl) and **TravelSur** (San Pedro 451, tel./fax 065/223-6000, www.travelsur.cl). For activities-oriented operators, try **Alsur Expediciones** (Aconcagua 8, Puerto Varas, tel. 065/223-2300, www.alsurexpeditions.com), and **Secret Patagonia** (San Pedro 311, Puerto Varas, tel. 065/223-2921, www.secretpatagonia.com), a consortium of several operators in the Ensenada-Cochamó area.

Most adventure-travel agencies rent mountain bikes and other outdoor-sports equipment. Just north of the pier, rental canoes and kayaks are available for lake use. **KoKayak** (San Pedro 311, Puerto Varas, tel. 065/223-3004; Ruta 225, Km 40, Ensenada, tel. 09/9310-5272, www.kokayak.cl) organizes more ambitious kayak trips on the Río Petrohué. Birding-oriented **Birds Chile** (San Pedro 311, Puerto Varas, tel. 09/9269-2606, www.birdschile.com) shares the office.

ENSENADA

At Lago Llanquihue's east end, 45 kilometers from Puerto Varas, the shoreline village of Ensenada lies midway between Volcán Osorno's symmetrical cone to the northeast and Volcán Calbuco's serrated caldera to the southwest. Most services are at or near the junction with the northbound road to Las Cascadas and Puerto Octay.

On the south side of the highway, a three-kilometer gravel lateral road leads to the French-run **Quila Hostal** (Camino a Ensenada, Km 37, Sector El Tepú, tel. 09/6760-7039, www.quilahostal.com, US$53-76 s, US$61-83 d, two-night minimum), a five-room B&B with panoramic views of Lago Llanquihue, Volcán Osorno, and Puntiagudo, or Calbuco. Most rooms have private baths, but two of them share a bath. Meals may be available on request. Quila does require a car, or at least a bicycle, for easy access.

Several daily buses use Ruta 225 between Puerto Varas, Ensenada, and Petrohué; others continue to Ralún, Cochamó, and Puelo.

From Ensenada, the newly paved road follows the eastern lakeshore for 22 kilometers to Las Cascadas, where it continues to Puerto Octay. There is no public transportation on this segment, but four daily buses link Las Cascadas to Puerto Octay.

★ PARQUE NACIONAL VICENTE PÉREZ ROSALES

Established in 1926, Chile's first national park is a geographical extravaganza whose dominant features are Volcán Osorno, a symmetrical snowcapped cone that's the "Mount Fuji of South America," and Lago Todos los Santos, an elongated lacustrine highway leading toward the Argentine border. The 251,000-hectare park also contains rushing rivers, steep forested canyons, and a scattering of alpine lakes.

It takes its name from Vicente Pérez Rosales, an adventurer whose mid-19th-century travels literally cleared the way for European pioneers—he hired the indigenous Huilliche people to set fire to the forests near Lago Llanquihue. Pérez Rosales later made

Vicinity of Puerto Varas

To Osorno, Temuco, and Santiago

To Osorno

Purranque

Puerto Octay

Puerto Klocker

Volcán Puntiagudo 2,493m

Las Cascadas

Sector Volcán Osorno

Lago Llanquihue

Frutillar

Volcán Osorno 2,652m

CENTRO DE SKI & MONTAÑA VOLCÁN OSORNO

Lago Todos los Santos

Petrohué

To Peulla and Bariloche (Argentina)

Llanquihue

225

Ensenada

PARQUE NACIONAL VICENTE PÉREZ ROSALES

Río Petrohué

⭐ PUERTO VARAS

Volcán Calbuco 2,015m

Monumento Natural Lahuén Nadi

5

Ralún

✈ AEROPUERTO EL TEPUAL

Puerto Montt

Río Chamiza

Correntoso

Lago Chapo

⭐ COCHAMÓ

Pelluco

Chinquihue

Angelmó

Isla Tenglo

Laguna Sargazo

Panitao

Isla Maillén

Parque

To Ancud, ⭐ PARQUE NACIONAL CHILOÉ, ⭐ PARQUE TANTAUCO, and Castro (Chiloé)

Lenca

Nacional

S e n o   d e

Alerce Andino

de Reloncaví

Isle Guar

Caleta La Arena

Estuario

Puelo

Caleta Puelche

Calbuco

R e l o n c a v í

Volcán Yates 2,187m

Isla Puluqui

0   5 mi

0   5 km

Volcán Hornopirén

Parque Nacional Hornopirén

To Chaitén, Puerto Chacabuco, and Puerto Natales

7

To Hornopirén and ferry to Caleta Gonzalo

© AVALON TRAVEL

himself a name during the California gold rush, once even operating a restaurant in San Francisco.

Boat traffic began to cross Todos los Santos around 1890, with the first tourists arriving in 1903. In 1913, Theodore Roosevelt was one of them. Long before Europeans saw the area, though, indigenous peoples had used the southerly Paso de Vuriloche to traverse the Andes, and Jesuit missionaries used a slightly different route south of Volcán Tronador, the area's highest peak.

Geography and Climate

Some 50 kilometers northeast of Puerto Varas via Ruta 225, the park ranges from 50 meters elevation near Ensenada to about 3,460 meters on the summit of Cerro Tronador, a dormant glaciated volcano on the Argentine border. Volcán Osorno's 2,652-meter summit is its most conspicuous feature. Other high peaks include 2,493-meter Volcán Puntiagudo on the park's northern border and 1,710-meter Cerro La Picada, northeast of Volcán Osorno.

Several rivers, most notably the Río Negro, drain into Lago Todos los Santos. At 191 meters above sea level, Todos los Santos is the source of the Río Petrohué, diverted southward into the Golfo de Reloncaví by lava flows that reached Lago Llanquihue's shores just north of Ensenada.

The park receives about 2,500 millimeters of rainfall per year at lower elevations and up to 4,000 millimeters, much of it as snow, near the border. The lake moderates the ambient temperature, which averages about 16°C in summer and 6.5°C in winter, though higher elevations get colder. Summertime highs reach about 25°C.

Flora and Fauna

Ecologically, up to 1,000 meters above sea level, the dense Valdivian rainforest consists of the southern beech *coigüe* mixed with glossy-leaved *ulmos* and the dense bamboo *quila,* as well as ferns and climbing vines. Up higher, *coigüe* mixes with the related

lenga. The coniferous *alerce* grows in a few steep areas.

Within the park, 33 mammal species include pumas, *pudús,* foxes, and skunks. Among 117 bird species are torrent ducks, kingfishers, coots, woodpeckers, and hummingbirds. Rainbow and brown trout have been introduced into lakes and streams, though there are also native trout.

Sector Volcán Osorno

While not erupting since the mid-19th century, **Volcán Osorno**'s youthful but potentially dangerous Holocene crater has active fumaroles. From the deck of the *Beagle,* Charles Darwin observed the eruption of January 19-20, 1835:

> At midnight the sentry observed something like a large star, which gradually increased in size until about three o'clock, when it presented a very magnificent spectacle. By the aid of a glass, dark objects, in constant succession, were seen, in the midst of a great glare of red light, to be thrown up and to fall down. The light was sufficient to cast on the water a long bright reflection.

Adventure operators in Puerto Octay and Puerto Varas offer one-day guided climbs of Osorno, for about US$400 for one person, US$300 pp if there are two. Starting around 4am, it's a challenging ascent, requiring either technical skills on snow and ice or guides with those technical skills, especially to cross crevasses. Conaf, which issues permits, requires one guide for every two climbers on commercial trips. Independent climbers must provide proof of experience and present their gear.

Recent improvements have made Osorno's ski area a viable recreational option in both summer and winter, though it's not likely to draw big crowds away from more elaborate ski areas resorts as Portillo and Valle Nevado. Most skiers stay in either Puerto Varas or other lakeside communities, as the only accommodations are two basic nearby *refugios* (shelters), though plans for a small hotel near the lifts are on hold.

Facilities include a pair of lifts that carry skiers nearly 500 meters above the base elevation of 1,200 meters. At the base, reached by a paved road just north of Ensenada, there's a small cafeteria and a larger restaurant, seating up to 150 patrons for lunch. Lift tickets are moderately priced, and rental gear is available. Outside ski season, visitors can still take the lifts (US$24 adults, US$12 children) for access to the views and high country walks.

For more information on the ski area in both winter and summer, contact the **Centro de Ski & Montaña Volcán Osorno** (tel. 09/9158-7337, www.volcanosorno.com). They also provide round-trip van shuttles (US$22 pp) for day trips from Puerto Varas.

Sector Petrohué

At the west end of Todos los Santos, the source of its namesake river, **Sector Petrohué** is most popular as the port for the Peulla passenger ferry, which leaves mid-morning and returns early afternoon. Since most of the sector lacks an integrated trail network, visiting remote areas requires either hiring a private launch or contracting an activities-oriented tour, but there are a few accessible options. From **Playa Larga,** the black-sand beach north of Petrohué Lodge, the five-kilometer **Sendero Rincón del Osorno** follows the lake's western shore. In the La Picada sector, the **Sendero Paso Desolación** is a five-hour (one-way) hike that traverses the volcano's northeastern slopes to a gravel road that continues to Las Cascadas.

A short walk from the jetty, the **Museo Pioneros de la Patagonia** (no phone, 9am-7p daily summer, on request off-season, US$2.25) is a privately built facility depicting local history from pre-Columbian times to the present. It focuses on the trans-Andean connection pioneered by the Roth-Schirmer family since the mid-19th century, emphasizing commercial links to Argentina and creation of the Cruce Andino shuttle that now carries tourists there.

Six kilometers southwest of Petrohué, on the south side of the highway, Conaf manages the **Sendero Saltos del Petrohué** (US$3), a short riverbank trail that follows a series of basalt bedrock rapids and falls that are too rough for rafting or kayaking. Below the falls, Puerto Varas operators start their Class III-IV descents of the **Río Petrohué** (US$52), which is suitable for novices but still interesting for

Volcán Osorno

those with more experience. Rock climbing sites are nearby.

Sector Peulla

Where the Río Negro and the Río Peulla empty into Todos los Santos, 20 nautical miles (37 kilometers) east of Petrohué, the hamlet of **Peulla** traditionally earns its livelihood from tourist traffic patronizing Hotel Peulla and its restaurant, whether overnight, on day excursions from Petrohué, or en route to Bariloche. A newer luxury hotel has mostly supplanted the Peulla, which primarily serves as overflow. Chilean customs and immigration is a short distance east.

Day-trippers and through-travelers have enough time to walk to **Cascada de Los Novios,** a waterfall just a few minutes from Hotel Peulla. Only overnighters will have time for the eight-kilometer climb of the **Sendero Laguna Margarita.**

Food and Accommodations

Park food and accommodations are limited; hotel reservations are advised.

Just below Volcán Osorno's permanent snow line, at 1,200 meters elevation, the 40-bunk **Refugio Teski Ski Club** (tel. 09/9159-5147, www.teskiclub.cl, US$25 pp dorm, US$63 d with shared bath, US$81 d with private toilet but external shower) also serves meals. Near the ski lift itself, the **Restaurant y Cafetería Mirador** serves very good sandwiches and kuchen, and some more complex dishes. From a turnoff three kilometers north of the Ensenada junction, both are a 13-kilometer climb on a smoothly paved road.

On the Río Petrohué's south bank, reached by rowboat shuttle from the road, the no-frills **Hospedaje Kuschel** (tel. 09/5665-9872, US$22 pp dorm, US$52 d, with breakfast) also has camping and serves meals for US$12. North of the museum, Conaf's 24-site **Camping Playa Petrohué** (tel. 09/9499-3226, parque.perezrosales@conaf.cl, US$20 for up to 5 people) includes firewood in the camping cost. As of early 2017, however, it was closed for lack of potable water.

The Middle European-style ★ **Petrohué Lodge** (tel./fax 065/221-2025, www.petrohue. com, US$194 s, US$264-293 d, with breakfast) has always been a fine hotel. Rate options include two meals (US$218 s, US$312-341 d) and all meals with activities (US$296 s, US$466-498 d). The fourth floor has the best views, but there are no elevators. There is Wi-Fi but no TV, and its restaurant and bar are open to the public. Otherwise, the only shop offers limited supplies at high prices, and Cruce Andino has a modest snack bar at the dock.

At the east end of the lake, the venerable Hotel Peulla's ownership has built the new, separately managed **Hotel Natura** (tel. 065/297-2289, www.hotelnatura.cl, US$211 s, US$220 d, with buffet breakfast) in the manner of an Andean design hotel, with spacious four-star rooms and magnificent natural light throughout. It remains open year-round. Lunch or dinner (US$36 pp) costs extra.

In 1913, when **Hotel Peulla** (tel. 065/221-2053, www.hotelpeulla.cl, US$138 s, US$146 d, with buffet breakfast) opened at the east end of the lake, Theodore Roosevelt was among the first-year visitors. Now serving as an overflow from the Natura, it usually closes in winter. Many rooms have been renovated, though it retains a Euro-Andean style and squeaky floors. If space is available, the hotel offers a backpackers' special with two meals included. Many Cruce Andino passengers take the buffet lunch at its restaurant, **Tejuela,** en route to Bariloche. Both hotels have slow Internet connections.

Tent camping is possible near the Conaf cabin on the road leading from the dock to the hotels.

Transportation and Services

At Saltos del Petrohué, the private **Centro de Visitantes** offers information, a café, souvenirs, and activities throughout the park.

Buses Ensenada and **Thaebus** connect Petrohué with Puerto Varas (US$3.50) and Puerto Montt every half hour or so, and there are occasional additional services with **Intercity J. M.** Mid-September to mid-April,

Puerto Montt's **Turistour** operates buses (7:45am Mon.-Sat.) to Ensenada and Petrohué via Puerto Varas, connecting with its own bus-boat crossing to Bariloche (US$280 pp). Mid-April to mid-September, the Bariloche crossing takes two days, with an obligatory overnight at Hotel Peulla; buses leave Puerto Montt at 8:30am Monday-Friday.

At Petrohué, a dockside kiosk sells tickets for the three-hour voyage to Peulla, where it connects with the bus to the Argentine border at Puerto Frías and a relay of bus-boat links to Bariloche. Hikers and cyclists can also take this route. Round-trip tickets to Peulla cost US$40 adults, slightly less for children; lunch at Hotel Peulla costs an additional US$20 pp. From Puerto Varas, the fare is US$57; for more details, contact **Turistour** (Del Salvador 72, tel. 065/243-7127, www.turistour.cl).

★ COCHAMÓ

Two kilometers east of Ensenada, where international Ruta 225 continues to Petrohué, another paved road follows the Río Petrohué southeast for 30 kilometers, where it forks as the river enters the Estuario de Reloncaví. The graveled left fork crosses the bridge over the Petrohué and continues to **Ralún,** where another gravel road forks north to **Cayutué,** on the south arm of Lago Todos los Santos.

The main road, however, continues another 15 kilometers to Cochamó, where the 2,111-meter Volcán Yates provides a backdrop for the shingled **Iglesia Parroquial María Inmaculada** and its soaring steeple. The area's big attraction is the grandeur of the upper **Río Cochamó,** where ribbon-like waterfalls tumble over exfoliated granite domes that rise above luxuriant rainforest. Still, relatively small numbers of hikers, technical climbers, and horseback riders challenge the muddy trail, part of which follows a log road that once crossed the Andes to Argentina, to the scenic valley of **La Junta** and beyond.

From the Río Cochamó's outlet, the gravel road continues south over a new bridge across the Río Puelo and then joins Ruta 7,

the Carretera Austral, to **Caleta Puelche.** Here it's possible to double back north toward Puerto Montt via the ferry shuttle to Caleta La Arena, or continue south to Hornopirén, the summer ferry port for southbound travelers.

Campo Aventura Cochamó

Cochamó is the base for **Campo Aventura Cochamó,** (tel. 09/9289-2318, www.campo-aventura.com) an eco-lodge and horse-trekking company offering 1- to 10-day riding trips to its backcountry camp at La Junta, 17 kilometers east and 300 meters above sea level. Under U.S. owners, it has expanded its hiking programs, with a full-time guide for those who prefer foot travel. They've also trained new horses to replace those that were getting long in the tooth.

The present trail follows the river's north bank as far as La Junta. New catwalks help avoid the muddiest sections and bridges now cross most of the streams. At La Junta, it's no longer necessary to ford the river to Cochamó Aventura's south-bank camp, as they installed their own cable car to simplify access to comfortable lodging, camping (US$7 pp, with shower access), and its own network of hiking trails. Its classic four-day, three-night horseback-riding package costs US$700 pp; for more details, especially on longer excursions, go to Cochamó Aventura's website. In addition, the company offers sea kayaking, fly-fishing, and trekking.

Both horseback-tour clients and non-riders stay overnight in three tasteful *cabañas* and the separate Casa Gris (sleeping six) at the ★ **Riverside Lodge** (US$100 pp with all meals), five kilometers south of Cochamó proper and 500 meters east of the Puelo road, on the south side of the bridge over the Río Cochamó. Walk-ins are accommodated if space is available. It's also possible to camp (US$8 pp, with flush toilets and showers). Fixed-menu lunches and dinners are also available at its restaurant, **La Mesa de los Sabores,** which can accommodate most dietary restrictions (except for veganism) on request.

Open mid-September-mid-May, Cochamó Aventura has equally stylish if simpler dormitory accommodations at La Junta's **Cochamó Aventura Mountain Lodge** (US$85 pp with all meals), with wood-fired hot showers and a campground as well. There is also the dorm-style **Mountain Cabin** (bunks with a mattress US$25 pp, bring your own sleeping bag). Meals, wine, and fresh bread are available, but it's best to make advance arrangements for meals at the riverside lodge. Camping is possible at both sites but, for quality control, on a limited basis only.

Transportation

In summer, from Puerto Montt, **Buses Río Puelo** (tel. 09/7408-9199) goes to Cochamó (US$4) four times daily via Puerto Varas. Cochamó Aventura can also arrange transfers in a private vehicle.

LAGO TAGUA TAGUA AND VICINITY

East of the town of Puelo, surrounded by wooded mountains, **Lago Tagua Tagua** is the starting point for an adventurous border crossing that begins with a vehicle and passenger ferry at the hamlet of El Canelo.

From Puerto Maldonado, at the east end of the lake, daily bus service continues another 32 kilometers to Llanada Grande, where it's another 70 kilometers on foot or horseback to the Argentine border at Lago Puelo, about half an hour south of the town of El Bolsón.

At the lake's east end, the **Hotel Mítico** (Walker Martínez 807, Puerto Varas, tel. 065/223-4892, Tagua Tagua tel. 02/2196-1001, www.miticopuelo.com, US$174-229 s, US$268-353 d) has reinvented itself as a diverse, activities-oriented lodging instead of the fly-fishing destination it once was (though fly-fishing is still part of the mix). Open year-round, the 2,400-square-meter structure has expansive ground-floor common areas in natural wood and midsize rooms with ample private baths. Rooms on the second floor have large balconies with lake views (partially blocked by dense forest). There are also packages that include activities.

Buses Río Puelo (tel. 09/7408-9199) goes at 7:45am daily from Puerto Montt via Puerto Varas to El Canelo (5 hours, US$8), connecting at 1pm with the ferry *Caupolicán* to Puerto Maldonado (US$1.50 passengers, US$10 vehicles), where another bus continues to Llanada Grande.

the riverside camp at Cochamó Aventura Mountain Lodge

Puerto Montt and Vicinity

No Chilean city enjoys a more impressive setting than Puerto Montt, where a cordon of forested mountains and snowcapped volcanoes stretches south along Chile's island-studded "Inside Passage." Unfortunately, this midsize port can't match the prosperity and cultural diversity of cities in comparable surroundings, such as Seattle and Vancouver, Canada. Unfortunately, attempts at improvements haven't managed to raise the standard. Part of the waterfront, with its dramatic views, has become a park, but the lawns have died for lack of maintenance, graffiti vandals have defaced new constructions, and traffic clogs downtown streets.

Puerto Montt owes its growth to shipbuilding, extractive industries such as forestry, and the fish-farming sector. As a city whose potential, to this point, exceeds its achievements, the capital of Region X (Los Lagos) is mainly a gateway to the Andean lakes district, the Chiloé archipelago, Chilean Patagonia, and parts of Argentina. As a transport hub where mainland Chile ends and archipelagic Chile begins, it enjoys air, land, and sea connections in all directions but west. Cruise ships call at its port of Angelmó, though there's barely room for them to maneuver in and out of the congested harbor; the largest vessels have to anchor offshore and shuttle passengers to the pier.

HISTORY

Puerto Montt dates from 1853, when German colonists landed at the north end of the Seno de Reloncaví in what was then called Melipulli, a Huilliche word whose definition—"Four Hills"—aptly described the site. It grew slowly until 1912, when the railroad cut travel time to Santiago to 26 hours and it became the jumping-off point for southbound colonists headed for continental Chiloé, Aisén, and Magallanes.

In 1960, a massive earthquake destroyed the port and most of what Jan Morris called "structures in the Alpine manner, all high-pitched roofs and quaint balconies." Rebuilt in a mostly utilitarian style, Puerto Montt is only now beginning to sport newer buildings of distinction. The earlier style survives in nearby Puerto Varas.

ORIENTATION

Puerto Montt (pop. about 240,000) is 1,016 kilometers south of Santiago via the Panamericana, which now bypasses the city center en route to Chiloé. Like Valparaíso, it occupies a narrow shelf at the foot of a series of hills. Westbound Avenida Diego Portales becomes Avenida Angelmó, the main approach to the ferry, fishing, and forest-products port of Angelmó, which draws visitors to its crafts fair and seafood restaurants. Eastbound Avenida Diego Portales becomes Avenida Soler Manfredini, starting point for the discontinuous Carretera Austral, a series of both paved and gravel highways linked, where necessary, by ferries. This highway ends at Villa O'Higgins, 1,240 kilometers to the south in Region XI (Aisén). Most travelers cover at least part of the route via air or ferry from Puerto Montt or Chiloé.

SIGHTS

Puerto Montt's strength is its magnificent setting, but a handful of architectural monuments have survived, along with other sights. On the south side of **Plaza Manuel Irarrázaval,** built of *alerce,* the copper-domed, Parthenon-style **Catedral de Puerto Montt** (1856) is the city's oldest building. Surrounded by woods, the hillside **Torre Campanario del Colegio San Francisco Javier** (1894) rises behind the **Iglesia de los Jesuitas** (1872), at the corner of Guillermo Gallardo and Rengifo.

Puerto Montt

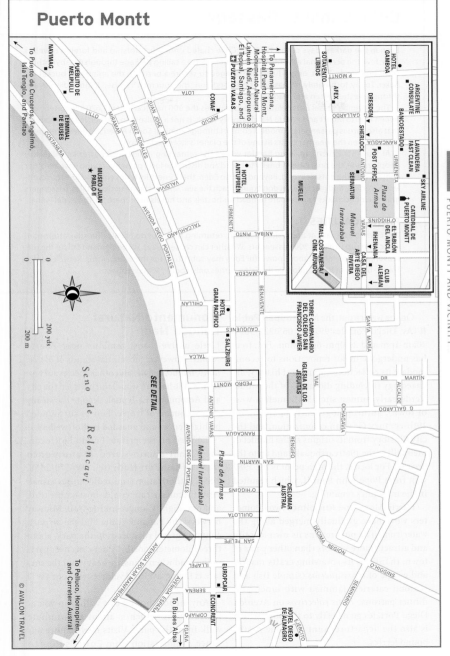

To Panamericana,
Hospital Puerto Montt,
Monumento Natural
Lahuén Nadi, Aeropuerto
El Tepual, Santiago, and
PUERTO VARAS

To Puerto de Cruceros, Angelmó,
Isla Tenglo, and Panitao

NAVIMAG

PUEBLITO DE
MELIPULLI

TERMINAL
DE BUSES

MUSEO JUAN
PABLO II

CONAF

LOTA

LILLO

MIRAMAR

PÉREZ ROSALES

JUAN JOSÉ MIRA

ANCUD

COSTANERA

VALDIVIA

AVENIDA DIEGO PORTALES

TALCAHUANO

RODRIGUEZ

FREIRE

URMENETA

BAQUEDANO

ANIBAL PINTO

BENAVENTE

BALMACEDA

CHILLAN

CAUQUENES

TALCA

AVENIDA DIEGO PORTALES

PEDRO MONTT

ANTONIO VARAS

RANCAGUA

SAN MARTIN

O'HIGGINS

QUILLOTA

SAN FELIPE

ILLAPEL

SERENA

COPIAPO

EGAÑA

Seno de Reloncaví

Plaza de Armas

Manuel Irarrázabal

HOTEL
ANTUPIREN

HOTEL
GRAN PACÍFICO

SALZBURG

TORRE CAMPANARIO
DEL COLEGIO SAN
FRANCISCO JAVIER

IGLESIA DE LOS
JESUITAS

CIELOMAR
AUSTRAL

EUROPCAR

ECONORENT

HOTEL DIEGO
DE ALMAGRO

SANTA MARÍA

DR MARTIN

ALCALDE

G GALLARDO

OCHAGAVIA

RENGIFO

DÉCIMA REGIÓN

O'HIGGINS

SEMINARIO

EJERCITO

To Pelluco, Hornopirén,
and Carretera Austral

AVENIDA SOLAR MANFREDINI

AVENIDA ESPAÑA

To Buses Absa

SEE DETAIL

Detail

SOTAVENTO
LIBROS

HOTEL
GAMBOA

ARGENTINE
CONSULATE

BANCOESTADO

DRESDEN

SHERLOCK

AFEX

P MONTT

GALLARDO

RANCAGUA

ANTONIO

SERNATUR

MUELLE

MALL COSTANERA
CINE MUNDO

LAVANDERIA
FAST CLEAN

POST OFFICE

URMENETA

VARAS

RHENANIA

EL TABLON
DEL ANCLA

Plaza de
Armas

Manuel
Irarrázabal

SKY AIRLINE

CATEDRAL DE
PUERTO MONTT

O'HIGGINS

CASA DEL
ARTE DIEGO
RIVERA

CLUB
ALEMAN

0   200 yds
0   200 m

© AVALON TRAVEL

Chile's Inside Passage

Even in the darkest days of the 1970s, as Chile chafed under dictatorship and foreign travelers were few, the occasional adventurer still went seeking a sailing passage through its labyrinthine southern canals. Then, only a handful managed to secure a berth on the aging rust bucket *Río Baker*. Today, fortunately, it's easier to find a berth on "the poor man's cruise," a three-day voyage through western Aisén and Magallanes.

The Navimag vessel *Evangelistas*, which shuttles the 900 nautical miles (1,670 kilometers) between Puerto Montt and Puerto Natales every week, is not a cruise ship. Rather, it's a cargo ferry that also carries passengers in modest comfort through some of South America's finest scenery—at least when the weather clears in one of the planet's stormiest regions.

At **Puerto Edén,** a fishing hamlet where the remaining indigenous Kawéskar (Alacaluf) people reside, the boat pauses briefly to board and discharge local passengers who have no other contact with the outside world. Beyond Puerto Edén, the scenery includes emerald forests, countless waterfalls, and glaciers that don't quite reach the sea. Approaching Puerto Natales, passengers grab their backpacks and prepare to head for hostels and hotels to prepare for Torres del Paine.

PRACTICALITIES

The *Evangelistas* sails at 8pm Friday evening, returning from Puerto Natales Tuesday afternoon, and carries up to about 300 passengers. Weather can cause delays. When demand falls in the off-season, the smaller but more powerful *Edén* may substitute for the *Evangelistas*. Recycled from France by way of Baja California, the Edén carries only about 150 passengers.

On the waterfront, the **Museo Juan Pablo II** (Av. Diego Portales 997, tel. 065/222-3029, 10am-1pm and 2:30pm-6pm Mon.-Fri., free) has undergone major renovations to accommodate its collections on natural history, archaeology (including dioramas of the Monte Verde early human site 35 kilometers west of town), anthropology, early Spanish and 19th-century German colonization, and the city's history from its origins as the hamlet of Melipulli to the 1960 earthquake and up to the present. For locals, the high point is the 1987 visit from Pope John Paul II, which resulted in the museum's renaming.

Puerto Montt and **Angelmó,** two kilometers west, have gradually merged along the waterfront. The port retains its own identity and attracts more visitors than other parts of town, thanks to its sprawling crafts market and gaggle of *marisquerías* (simple fish and seafood eateries) jammed with lunch and dinner patrons. *Taxis colectivos* on Avenida Diego Portales go directly to the port, which is also the departure point for some southbound ferries.

Monumento Natural Lahuén Ñadi

Little native forest remains near Puerto Montt. However, substantial stands of *alerce, ulmo, mañío, coigüe,* and other species survive in this 200-hectare woodland between the city and Aeropuerto El Tepual, despite the steady encroachment of trophy houses surrounded by high fences and guarded by Rottweilers.

Located on the private Fundo El Rincón, the Conaf-administered **Monumento Natural Lahuén Ñadi** (tel. 09/8570-2388, US$6, authorization required) features a small visitors center, a cafeteria, a short nature trail, and one slightly longer hiking trail. Midway between the Panamericana and the airport, a bumpy gravel road leads to the park, about three kilometers north. Water can cover parts of the road when rains are heavy, but the surface is firm gravel and vehicles without 4WD pass easily.

Any airport-bound bus will drop you at the junction, which is about a 30-minute walk from the park. Visits now require advance authorization from **Conaf's Puerto**

The *Evangelistas* has a self-service cafeteria and dining room, and spacious upper decks and terraces. Its AAA cabins have two bunks, each with individual reading lights, private bath, writing desk, chair, and an exterior window. AA cabins have four bunks, while A cabins have exterior shared baths. BB cabins lack exterior windows. The CC cabins have four bunks, one of them above another, no exterior windows, and shared baths.

The food is cafeteria food, palatable and reasonably abundant. If the boat is full, lunch and dinner require two shifts. Both bridge and cabin staff are friendly, and bar prices are moderate. Some people bring their own wine, though the vessel is now officially dry. Smoking is allowed outdoors only.

Navimag carries about twice as many foreigners as Chileans on this route, which can still be delayed by bad weather. At the outset, there are orientation and safety talks in Spanish and English in the cafeteria *and* auditorium. There's ready access to the bridge, the crew are personable and informative, and it's possible to follow the route on their charts. Some passengers, though, bring their own GPS devices.

With the Evangelistas back in service on this route, there is more space for passengers. Still, reservations are imperative in the summer peak season; contact **Navimag** (Av. Diego Portales 2000, Puerto Montt, tel. 065/243-2360, www.navimag.com). Fares depend on the season and the level of accommodations but range US$550-2,100 pp with all meals. Bicycles now go for free, but motorcycles cost an additional US$125, passenger cars US$405, and light trucks US$430; other vehicles pay a linear meter rate.

Montt office (Urmeneta 977, 5th Fl., tel. 065/248-6115).

ENTERTAINMENT

Built with Mexican aid after the 1960 quake and named for the famous muralist, the **Casa del Arte Diego Rivera** (Quillota 116, tel. 065/226-1836, www.teatrodiegorivera.cl, 10am-7pm Mon.-Sat., 3pm-7pm Sun. and holidays, free) is Montt's main venue for theater, dance, and the occasional film. It also includes several display halls: the **Sala Mexicana**, with rotating exhibits; the **Sala Hardy Wistuba**, named for a mid-20th-century Chilean painter; and the **Pinacoteca Municipal**, the municipal art museum.

Puerto Montt has a smattering of pubs and bars, including the **Salzburg** (Cauquenes 128, tel. 065/229-3000), which specializes in Frutillar's namesake microbrew, and the **Sherlock** (Antonio Varas 452, tel. 065/228-8888).

In the former train station, miraculously transformed into the Mall Costanera, the **Cinemundo** (Illapel 10, Local 303, tel. 065/234-8877, www.cinemundo.cl) shows current movies.

SHOPPING

Directly opposite the bus terminal, the **Pueblito de Melipulli** (Av. Diego Portales s/n, tel. 065/226-3524) is a permanent artisans market. Crafts stalls also line both sides and cover the sidewalks of Avenida Angelmó west of Independencia. Typical items include woolens, copperware, and standard souvenirs.

Sotavento Libros (Av. Diego Portales 580, tel. 065/225-6650) specializes in local and regional history and literature.

FOOD

The gastronomic scene is pretty basic, with minor exceptions. For sandwiches, *onces* (afternoon tea), coffee, and desserts such as German-style kuchen, try **Café Rhenania** (Antonio Varas 328, tel. 065/228-2606, www.rhenania.cl, 9am-9pm Mon.-Fri., 10am-9pm Sat., noon-8:30pm holidays) or **Dresden** (Antonio Varas 500, tel. 065/225-0000). **El Tablón del Ancla** (Antonio Varas 350, tel.

065/236-7554, from 10am Mon.-Sat., from 11am Sun., US$8-15) is a cheerful bar/restaurant that's worth a look for sandwiches and short orders.

The rejuvenated **Club Alemán** (German Club, Antonio Varas 264, tel. 065/229-7000, www.elclubaleman.cl, lunch and dinner daily, US$12-20) is a step up in both price and quality, with seafood starters, meats, and even game dishes such as venison and wild boar. At Angelmó, there are numerous basic fish-and-seafood restaurants such as **Don Raúl** (Av. Angelmo 2176, tel. 065/236-9627).

Hard to find, but well worth the effort (take a cab rather than hiking the steep hills up from the terminal), ★ **Chile Picante** (Vicente Pérez Rosales 567, tel. 09/8454-8923, www.chilepicanterestoran.cl, 12:30pm-3pm and 7pm-10pm Mon.-Sat., US$15) changes its menu daily, depending on what's fresh and local in fish, seafood, meat, and complementary items. The fixed-price menu includes three options for a starter, main course, and dessert, but even then the choice is difficult.

Heladería La Reina (Urmeneta 508, tel. 065/225-3979) continues to produce the city's finest ice cream.

ACCOMMODATIONS

Puerto Montt's accommodations are adequate, but the lower-end options are unremarkable if not quite dire; even most at the top lack distinction. Many visitors taking the ferry prefer to stay in Puerto Varas, 20 minutes north, and visit Puerto Montt for the afternoon.

Northwest of the bus terminal, ★ **Casa Perla** (Trigal 312, tel. 065/226-2104, www.casaperla.com, US$19-25 pp, with breakfast) offers rooms with shared or private baths, kitchen privileges, and laundry facilities. While it's not Puerto Montt's most appealing neighborhood, the sociable owners speak English, and the cozy common areas include a small library.

Nearer the port, **Hospedaje Rocco** (Pudeto 233, tel./fax 065/227-2897, www.

hospedajerocco.cl, US$18 pp in dorms, US$30 s, US$37 d, with breakfast) also gets high marks for hospitality, but all the rooms have shared baths.

Hotel Gamboa (Pedro Montt 157, tel. 065/225-2741, US$23-30 pp) is a vintage hotel with character but also deferred maintenance. The sizable rooms retain most of their original style, though the modern furniture can be tacky. Rates vary according to shared or private baths.

Business-oriented **Hotel Antupirén** (Freire 186, tel. 065/236-7800, www.antupirenhotel.cl, US$38 s, US$64 d) is a utilitarian hotel with attentive, efficient service and a good buffet breakfast. The exterior shows signs of wear.

Up the hill from downtown, with expansive views of the sound and surrounding volcanoes, the chain affiliate **Hotel Diego de Almagro** (Ejército 516, tel. 065/232-0200, www.dahoteles.com, US$130 s, US$140 d) is probably the best value, but its location is not pedestrian-friendly.

The business-oriented **Hotel Gran Pacífico** (Urmeneta 719, tel. 065/248-2100, www.hotelgranpacifico.cl, US$98-112 s or d, suites US$144-192 s or d) has spacious, comfortable, and immaculate rooms with outstanding views, especially facing southeast, from the higher floors (eighth and ninth are best). Amenities include a gym, a sauna, and what may be the city's best view restaurant, on the tenth floor.

INFORMATION

Sernatur (Antonio Varas 415, tel. 065/222-3016, 8:30am-9pm Mon.-Fri., hours vary Sat.-Sun. mid-Dec.-mid.-Mar., 8:30am-1pm and 3pm-5:30pm Mon.-Fri. mid-Mar.-mid-Dec.) provides tourist information. Conaf's **Patrimonio Silvestre** unit (Urmeneta 977, 5th Fl., tel. 065/248-6401) can provide national parks information.

Downtown is an **Argentine consulate** (Pedro Montt 160, 6th Fl., tel. 065/225-3996, 8am-1pm Mon.-Fri.).

SERVICES

Exchange houses include **Afex** (Av. Diego Portales 516, tel. 065/225-6604) and the bus terminal's **La Moneda de Oro** (Av. Diego Portales s/n, tel. 065/225-5108). **BancoEstado** (Urmeneta 444) has one of many downtown ATMs.

Correos de Chile (Rancagua 126) is the post office. **Lavandería Fast Clean** (San Martin 167, Local 6, tel. 065/225-8643) lives up to its name in laundry service.

The state-of-the-art **Hospital Puerto Montt Dr. Eduardo Schütz Schroeder** (Los Aromos s/n, tel. 065/236-2000) is at the northern approach to town.

TRANSPORTATION

Other than Santiago, Puerto Montt is the main gateway for air, land, and sea connections to Chilean Patagonia and across the Andes to Argentina. For southbound travelers on the Carretera Austral, maritime services may vary seasonally.

Air

LATAM/LAN (O'Higgins 167, Local 1-B, tel. 065/225-3315) flies several times daily to Santiago, usually nonstop but sometimes via Valdivia, Temuco, or Concepción, or a combination of those. It also flies at least twice daily to Balmaceda-Coyhaique and three or four times daily to Punta Arenas, occasionally stopping in Balmaceda-Coyhaique. Occasionally it flies from Santiago to Puerto Montt and on to San Carlos de Bariloche, Argentina.

Sky Airline (Benavente 405, Local 4, tel. 065/243-7555) flies frequently to Santiago, less frequently to Balmaceda-Coyhaique, and to Punta Arenas and occasionally Puerto Natales.

No carrier has lasted long on the air-taxi route to Chaitén, a major starting point for overland trips on the Carretera Austral. **Aerocord** (tel. 065/226-2300, www.aerocord. cl) and **Cielomaraustral** (Quillota 245, Local 1, tel. 065/226-4010, www.cielomaraustral.cl) fly to nearby Santa Bárbara (US$75 one-way, US$135 round-trip). Flights depart from Aeródromo La Paloma, on the hill immediately north of downtown.

Bus

Having undergone a major renovation that includes a modern hotel, Puerto Montt's **Terminal de Buses** (Av. Diego Portales 1001, tel. 065/228-3000, www.terminalpm.cl) is about one kilometer southwest of the Plaza de Armas. Services are frequent to rural, regional, and most long-distance destinations, as well as to Bariloche, Argentina. Buses to the Chilean Patagonia destinations of Coyhaique and Punta Arenas, which pass through Argentina, are less frequent but reliable.

From the bus terminal, **Buses Andrestour** (tel. 065/254-2161, US$4) connects to inbound and outbound flights at **Aeropuerto El Tepual** (PMC, tel. 065/225-2019), which is 16 kilometers west via the Panamericana and a paved lateral road.

Cruz del Sur (Av. Salvador Allende and Av. Presidente Ibáñez, tel. 065/248-3127) and its affiliated companies have opened a new terminal on higher ground near the Panamericana but continue to use the downtown terminal as well.

From a dedicated platform, several companies go to Puerto Varas (US$1.40, 30 minutes), including **Expreso Puerto Varas** and **Thaebus** (tel. 065/242-0120). Thaebus also passes through Varas en route to Frutillar and Puerto Octay.

Buses Fierro (tel. 065/225-2909) goes to Lenca (US$2.50), the southerly access point to Parque Nacional Alerce Andino, at noon and 4:30pm daily. **Buses JB** (tel. 065/229-0850) goes to Correntoso (US$2), the northern access point to Alerce Andino, five times daily between 7:40am and 8:30pm, except Sunday, when it goes at 9:10am and 8:30pm.

Kémelbus (tel. 065/225-6450) goes to Hornopirén, also known as Río Negro (4 hours, 7am, 8am, 1pm, and 3:30pm daily, US$6). The first bus daily continues to Chaitén (12 hours, US$15) via the Ruta Bimodal, which involves ferry crossing from Hornopirén to

Leptepu and Fiordo Largo to Caleta Gonzalo. This is now the main overland option for Futaleufú, but involves catching another bus in Chaitén. **Trans Hornopirén** (tel. 09/5414-9726) also offers services to Hornopirén.

At 6:20am Monday and Thursday, **Buses Absa** (Bilbao 13, tel. 065/238-0982, www.busesabsa.cl) provides service to Futaleufú (11 hours, US$38) via Osorno and Argentina, where passengers may not disembark at interim points. Absa does not use Puerto Montt's bus terminal; rather, passengers board downtown at the Plaza de Armas.

Numerous carriers serve the capital city of Santiago (12-13 hours, US$27-47) and intermediates including Temuco (5.5 hours, US$10). Chiloé destinations include Ancud (2 hours, US$6-10) and Castro (3 hours, US$9-12).

Buses Trans Austral (tel. 065/227-0984) goes to Bariloche (US$24), El Bolsón (US$33), Esquel (US$50), Comodoro Rivadavia (US$65), Caleta Olivia, Trelew (US$90), and Puerto Madryn (US$90).

Several companies operate between Puerto Montt and Punta Arenas (28 hours, US$75) via Argentina, including **Pullman Bus** (tel. 065/225-4399), **Queilen Bus** (tel. 065/225-3468), and **Turibús** (tel. 065/225-2872), all of which normally begin in Castro (Chiloé) and pick up passengers here and in Osorno. These are through-buses, not permitted to drop passengers in Argentina. Queilen also goes to Coyhaique (24 hours, US$60) at noon Wednesday, but schedules and frequencies are subject to change.

Five companies cross the Andes to San Carlos de Bariloche, Argentina (6 hours, US$23-27), via Osorno and the Cardenal Samoré pass: **Andesmar** (tel. 065/231-2123), **Buses Norte Internacional** (tel. 065/223-3319), **Cruz del Sur** (tel. 065/225-2872), **Tas Choapa** (tel. 065/225-4828), and **Vía Bariloche** (tel. 065/223-3633).

Sea

From Puerto Montt there are passenger and passenger-vehicle ferries or bus-ferry combinations to Chiloé and Chaitén in Region X,

Puerto Chacabuco (the port of Coyhaique) in Region XI (Aisén), and Puerto Natales in Region XII (Magallanes). Since these routes mostly follow the sheltered inland sea, seasickness is usually a minor problem except on the open-ocean crossing of the Golfo de Penas (literally, Gulf of Sorrows), en route to Puerto Natales. In the new passenger terminal, the two main companies are **Naviera Austral** (Av. Angelmó 1673, tel. 065/227-0430, www.navieraustral.cl) and **Navimag** (Av. Diego Portales 2000, tel. 02/2869-9900, www.navimag.com). Naviera vehicles still board at the **Terminal de Transbordadores** (Av. Angelmó 2187), about 500 meters west, though Navimag ferries sail from the **Extrapuerto** (Chinquihue Alto, Km 9), reached via a narrow paved road west of Angelmó.

Naviera Austral runs routes between Puerto Montt and Chaitén (8-12 hours) on the *Barcaza Jacaf* (US$30 pp) at least three times weekly. Vehicle rates are US$135 for passenger vehicles and small trucks; bicycles cost US$15 and motorcycles US$30.

The return of the *Evangelistas* on Navimag's Puerto Montt-Puerto Natales route has eased the pressure, but reservations are still imperative in the summer peak. If in Santiago, visit the Navimag office there. Still, it's worth trying for a last-minute berth or cabin. Fares depend on the season and the level of accommodations but start around US$550 per person with all meals included. Bicycles go for free, but motorcycles pay an additional US$125, passenger cars US$405, and light trucks US$430; other vehicles pay a linear meter rate. Northbound rates are significantly cheaper.

On Navimag's Puerto Chacabuco route, the *Edén* sails Thursday and Sunday mornings. Rates for accommodations ranging from quadruple bunks with shared baths to compact cabins with private baths vary from US$56 to US$225 pp. As on the Puerto Natales route, bicycles go for free, while motorcycles pay an additional US$115, passenger cars US$255, and light trucks US$320; other vehicles pay a linear meter rate. Passengers with their own vehicles board the previous evening and sleep on board.

From September to May, **Cruceros Marítimos Skorpios** (Av. Angelmó 1660, tel. 065/227-5646, www.skorpios.cl) operates **luxury cruises** to Laguna San Rafael that begin in Puerto Montt; rates on the 130-passenger *Skorpios II* range US$1,400 to US$3,300 pp.

Car Rentals

For car rentals, try **Econorent** (Antonio Varas 144, tel. 065/248-1261) or **Europcar** (Antonio Varas 162, tel. 065/228-6277). Note that taking a vehicle into Argentina requires notarial permission.

PARQUE NACIONAL ALERCE ANDINO

Occupying most of the peninsula only a short distance east of Puerto Montt and south of Lago Chapo, adjoining the Carretera Austral, **Alerce Andino** takes its name from the Andean false larch, which survives in and around the 39,255-hectare unit. Hiking its woodland trails is the main attraction and, because of its proximity to Puerto Montt, the park is best for day trips. Camping is possible, but the lack of through trails makes trekking impossible.

Geography and Climate

Park elevations range from sea level just east of La Arena, on the Estuario de Reloncaví, to 1,558 meters on Cerro Cuadrado, in the easternmost sector. While elevations are not extreme, the precipitous terrain and dense forest make off-trail travel difficult. At upper elevations, there are more than 50 lakes and tarns of glacial origin.

The park consists of three distinct sectors. From the village of Colhuin, nine kilometers east of Puerto Montt via the Carretera Austral, a smooth paved road leads 19 kilometers east to the northerly Sector Correntoso and, another nine kilometers farther south, a good gravel road goes to Sector Sargazo. The

Carretera Austral passes near the westerly entrance to Sector Chaicas, about 32 kilometers southeast of Puerto Montt.

With its maritime west coast climate, Alerce Andino gets up to 4,500 millimeters of rainfall per year at lower elevations and substantial snowfall above 700 meters. Temperatures are mild, averaging about 7°C in winter and 15°C in summer.

Flora and Fauna

Officially designated a national monument, the long-lived *alerce* spurred the park's creation in 1982. Ranging about 400 to 700 meters elevation, it mixes with other species such as *coigüe, tineo, mañío,* and *canelo.* Evergreen rainforest of *coigüe, tepa,* and *ulmo* reaches from sea level up to 900 meters or more, while nearly prostrate *lenga* covers the highest areas.

In such dense forest, wildlife is rarely seen, but there are pumas, *pudús,* gray foxes, and skunks. *Pudús* have even been sighted in Sector Correntoso's Pangal campground. Birdlife includes the Andean condor, the kingfisher, and waterfowl such as the *pato real* (Chiloé wigeon).

The most conspicuous wildlife, abundant in early summer, is the large but slow-moving, biting fly known as the *tábano.* Insect repellent, long trousers, light-colored clothing, and long sleeves are all good precautions, but they're no guarantee of invulnerability.

Sights and Recreation

Because of deadfalls and landslides, the footpath that once connected the Sargazo and Chaicas sectors is no longer viable, but shorter hikes through dense forests are still feasible at both. Rangers close the trails at 4pm, and hikers must return by 6pm.

From Sector Sargazo, **Sendero Laguna Frías** climbs 9.5 kilometers up the Río Sargazo Valley to **Laguna Frías,** where camping is no longer allowed, but it's a feasible day hike with an early start. There are several shorter spur trails, including a 45-minute climb to placid **Laguna Sargazo** itself, where there's a picnic

The Redwoods of the South

Like California's redwoods, the coniferous *alerce* is long-lived (up to 4,000 years), tall (up to 70 meters), and an attractive, easily worked, and water- and insect-resistant timber. Colonial Spanish shipwrights built vessels from it, and some of Chile's historical monuments, most notably Chiloé's churches, consist of *alerce* timber. Much of the Sur Chico's vernacular architecture, from Puerto Varas's Germanic houses to Chiloé's *palafitos,* also use its lumber.

In Chile, the *alerce's* natural habitat ranges from coastal Valdivia south to archipelagic and continental Chiloé. It has a narrower distribution across the border in Argentina. Although it grows mostly between 400 and 700 meters above sea level, it also occurs in poorly drained *ñadi* marshlands. The branches of younger specimens touch the ground, but the reddish-barked trunks of mature trees are barren.

Known to the Mapuche people as the *lawen,* the species is a national monument thanks to the efforts of the conservation organization Codeff, which somehow persuaded the Pinochet dictatorship to protect the remaining *alerce* forests in 1976, a time when any activism was risky. Charles Darwin gave the tree its botanical name, *Fitzroya cupressoides,* after the famous commanding officer of his equally famous vessel. Still, *The Voyage of the Beagle* offers only a general description.

site with rustic tables (no camping allowed). Most of the Laguna Sargazo trail now consists of boardwalks and staircases through the humid forest, plus one hanging bridge over the Río Lenca.

At Sector Chaicas, the **Sendero Laguna Chaiquenes** up the Río Chaicas Valley leads to **Laguna Chaiquenes** (5.5 kilometers), where the **Sendero Laguna Triángulo** continues another four kilometers to its namesake lake.

For the most up-to-date information on park trails, contact Conaf's **Patrimonio Silvestre** office (Urmeneta 977, 5th Fl., Puerto Montt, tel. 065/248-6401) in Puerto Montt or rangers at the park entrances.

Food and Accommodations

At Sector Correntoso, now under a private concessionaire, **Camping Pangal** (tel. 09/8610-8892, US$5 pp) has six wooded sites with reasonable privacy but only two toilets and cold showers for all of them. At the Sector Sargazo entrance, Conaf's tidy **Refugio Luis Levicán** (US$8 pp, with kitchen access and hot showers) makes a good base for day hikers. It can bunk up to 18 people, mostly four to a room, but there's only one bathroom.

At the head of the Río Chaicas valley,

Conaf's walk-in **Camping Chaicas** (US$3 pp) is the only option in the southern sector.

By the southern approach, on the highway to Hornopirén, Austrian-run **Hostal Mozart** (Carretera Austral, Km 25, tel. 09/8378-7566, hostalmozart@gmail.com, US$20 pp, US$70 s or d) is a comfortable guesthouse with spacious rooms that range from a five-bed dorm with a shared bath to a sea-view double with its own small deck. The Austrian owners will shuttle guests to Sector Chaicas (US$20 pp round-trip).

Just outside the park boundaries, the secluded **Alerce Mountain Lodge** (Carretera Austral, Km 36, tel. 065/228-6969, www.mountainlodge.cl, 3-day, 2-night package from US$1,100 s, US$1,976 d) is a luxury lodge that specializes in multiple-day packages, including activities such as hiking and horseback riding. Off-season (May-Oct.) rates are 15-20 percent lower.

Other Practicalities

Conaf has ranger posts at Sector Correntoso, Sector Sargazo, and Sector Chaicas. Park admission is US$6, except at Correntoso, where there's no charge.

From Puerto Montt, **Buses JB** (tel. 065/229-0850) goes to the village of **Correntoso** (1 hour, US$2), the park's northern access point, every two hours or so. There's no public transportation to Sector Sargazo, which means a nine-kilometer walk for those without their own vehicles.

HORNOPIRÉN (RÍO NEGRO)

At La Arena, 45 kilometers southeast of Puerto Montt, the mouth of the Estuario de Reloncaví interrupts the graveled Carretera Austral. Frequent ferries cross the water to Puelche, where the road continues to **Hornopirén** (also known as Río Negro), 48 kilometers farther south. Hornopirén (pop. 1,500) is the access point for its little-visited Parque Nacional Hornopirén, only a few kilometers east. It is also the northern port for the vehicle/passenger ferry shuttle to Leptepu and Parque Natural Pumalín.

Food and Accommodations

At the ferry ramp, several simple eateries prepare fresh fish for those awaiting Transporte Austral ferries.

Rates at the aging but charming **Hotel Hornopirén** (Ignacio Carrera Pinto 388, tel. 065/221-7256, h.hornopiren@gmail.com, US$22 pp with shared bath, US$44-64 d with private bath) include breakfast; lunch and dinner are optional. In addition, there's a cluster of inexpensive *hospedajes* (family-run lodgings) opposite the ferry ramp, as well as the more developed **Hostería Catalina** (Ingenieros Militares s/n, tel. 065/221-7359, www.hosteriacatalina.cl, US$43 s, US$55 d, with private bath).

Transportation

From Puerto Montt, **Kémelbus** (tel. 065/225-6450, www.kemelbus.cl) goes to Hornopirén (3.5 hours, US$6) three or four times Monday to Saturday; on Sunday they go only twice. One Kémelbus service continues to Chaitén via the ferry shuttle to Leptepú and Caleta Gonzalo.

Both buses and private vehicles must cross from La Arena to Puelche over the Estuario de Reloncaví, where **Naviera Puelche** (tel. 065/227-0000, www.navieraparedes.cl, US$1 pp, US$14 cars and light trucks, US$10 motorcycles, US$4 bicycles) shuttles the ferries *Trauco* and *Gobernador Figueroa* (6:15am-4:30am daily) for the half-hour voyage.

From Hornopirén, Transportes Austral's ferry *Comau* sails to **Leptepú** three times daily. At 3:30pm at Fiordo Largo, at the south end of the Leptepú road, the ferry *Tehuelche* continues to **Caleta Gonzalo,** the gateway to Parque Pumalín. Passengers pay US$8 pp, cyclists an extra US$8, and motorcyclists US$12. Automobiles and light trucks pay US$48, while larger vehicles pay per linear meter; only the driver goes for free.

From Puerto Montt, **Kémelbus** (tel. 065/225-6450) covers this route as far as Chaitén (12 hours, US$16), including the ferry portions.

The Chiloé Archipelago

The heartland of Chilean folklore, greener than Washington and Oregon, rain-soaked Chiloé is an archipelago whose wild western woodlands are darker than the Black Forest and traversed by trails leading to secluded ocean beaches with rolling dunes. Its cultural landscape is a mosaic of field and forest—it's a center of genetic diversity for potatoes—and its seas yield some of Chile's most diverse seafood.

Chiloé also includes the associated mainland area that is inaccessible overland. The main island is the Isla Grande de Chiloé—some 180 kilometers long and 50 kilometers wide, one of about 40 islands in the group, it is South America's second largest; only Tierra del Fuego is larger. The sheltered inlets on its more densely populated east coast are ideal for sea kayaking, linking subsistence villages

Crossing the Lakes

In Walter Salles's 2004 film *The Motorcycle Diaries*, a youthful Ernesto "Che" Guevara and his friend Alberto Granados push their dying motorcycle through a freak summer snowstorm around Lago Frías en route to Chile. The two Argentines were following the Cruce de Lagos, a route that's become one of South America's classics since it opened in the early 20th century.

Connecting the Chilean and Argentine lake districts, the Cruce de Lagos is a boat-bus-boat shuttle between Puerto Montt, Chile, and Bariloche, Argentina. While many people do it in a day, there are accommodations at each end of Lago Todos los Santos that offer opportunities for exploratory hikes.

The more active can go white-water rafting on the Río Petrohué, hike up steep ravines, or even scale snowcapped Volcán Osorno, a 2,652-meter peak that's a technical challenge. There are fewer places to stay on the Argentine side, except between Bariloche and Puerto Pañuelo. A good network of footpaths makes it possible to hike part of the route. Quite a few cyclists pedal the roads between the water segments of the trip.

Cruce de Lagos is now known as the **Cruce Andino** (www.cruceandino.com). It is open year-round but best from October to April. While through-trips cost around US$280 pp, budget-conscious travelers can do it for less by paying for each leg separately, on the spot if space is available. For day-trippers and overnighters, **Turistour** (tel. 09/5217-2489, www.turistour.cl) has excursions to Peulla at 10:30am (full-day, US$40) and at 3pm (half-day, US$26 pp). Bicycle rentals are also available.

with a unique vernacular architecture of elaborately shingled houses—a handful of them on stilts—and churches.

Though it can rain in any season, summer is the best time to visit, as days are long enough at least to hope for a break in the drizzle. On the Pacific side, penguins breed in summer. The ranges of the Humboldt and Magellanic penguin species overlap here.

HISTORY

Pre-Columbian Chiloé was the province of the Huilliche people, the southernmost branch of the Mapuche, who netted and trapped fish, gathered shellfish such as sea urchins, and cultivated maize and especially potatoes in its cool, damp climate. Their insularity bred a self-reliance that persists to the present, as residents have adapted native materials into technologically simple but useful artifacts.

Spain founded the city of Castro in 1567, but Jesuit missionaries soon established a circuit around this "last outpost of Christianity." Before their 1767 expulsion from the Americas, the Jesuits encouraged the construction of wooden churches and chapels that were predecessors of the 50-plus scattered around the archipelago, which led to its designation as a UNESCO World Heritage Site.

Mainland refugees from the early 17th century Mapuche insurrection found a haven here, creating the first permanent European presence. Their geographical isolation took political form in a conservatism that made them the Spanish empire's last holdouts in Chile, which failed to conquer the fortress of Ancud until 1826.

Economically, isolation meant poverty, though not starvation. A few years after Spain's expulsion, Charles Darwin remarked that "there is no demand for labor, and consequently the lower orders cannot scrape together money sufficient to purchase even the smallest luxuries," and that barter was pervasive. Emigration for employment became a way of life. Buses still leave the Isla Grande for southern Patagonia every day, but developments of the past two decades have improved the economy and reduced isolation. Ferries constantly shuttle across the Canal Chacao to the mainland, and salmon farming, despite serious environmental drawbacks, has brought a measure of prosperity. In summer and sometimes beyond, the tourist trade makes an increasing contribution.

Strong earthquakes are not uncommon here. A magnitude 7.7 earthquake in 2016 was the biggest since 1960's estimated 9.4 event at Valdivia. Despite damage to roads and other infrastructure, there were no fatalities.

ANCUD

On a sheltered harbor with good ocean access, the late colonial outpost of **San Carlos de Ancud** defended Spain's Pacific coastline from foreign powers and privateers so well that it held out for nearly a decade after Chile's 1818 declaration of independence. Only the Peruvian port of Callao stayed in Spanish hands longer.

The former fortress was once a major port of entry, but the 1912 arrival of the railroad to Puerto Montt undercut its economic base, and it now relies on fishing for its livelihood. Its headlands provide exceptional coastal views.

Orientation

On the Isla Grande's northern coast, facing the Canal Chacao, which divides the archipelago from the mainland, San Carlos de Ancud (pop. 40,000) is 90 kilometers southwest of Puerto Montt, and 27 kilometers west of the Pargua-Chacao ferry crossing. Some 87 kilometers north of Castro via the Panamericana, which skirts the city's eastern approach, it occupies a hilly peninsular site whose irregular terrain has generated an equally irregular but compact city plan around the trapezoidal Plaza de Armas.

Sights

At the southwest corner of the Plaza de Armas, the **Museo Azul de las Islas de Chiloé** (Libertad 370, tel. 065/262-2413, www.museoancud.cl, 10am-5pm Tues.-Fri., 10:30am-3:30pm Sat.-Sun. Jan.-Feb., 10am-5:30pm Tues.-Fri., 10am-1:30pm Sat.-Sun. and holidays Mar.-Dec., free), alternatively known as the **Museo Aurelio Bórquez Canobra,** is the regional museum. Colloquially known as

the Museo Chilote, it offers improved exhibits on the archipelago's natural environment and wildlife (with a major nod to Charles Darwin), regional archaeology, European settlement (including Dutch exploration), ecclesiastical art and architecture, stunning photographs of the 1960 earthquake and tsunami (which literally shook the island into the present), the Castro-Ancud railroad (destroyed by the quake), and a vivid relief map of the archipelago. The patios feature items such as petrified logs and a full blue whale skeleton.

The **Fundación Amigos Iglesias de Chiloé** (Errázuriz 227, tel. 065/262-1046, www.iglesiasdechiloe.cl, 9:30am-6pm Mon.-Fri., 10:30am-5:30pm Sat.-Sun., free) has converted a former convent into a museum that provides an outstanding overview of Chiloé's UNESCO heritage of wooden churches. It has not only meticulously crafted models of many of them, with descriptions in good English, but also a sample of doors, windows, and other architectural items salvaged from the original structures.

Guarding the harbor from a promontory just west of the intersection of Cochrane and San Antonio, the colonial **Fuerte San Antonio** (9am-8pm daily, free), dating from 1770, was Spain's last Chilean stronghold during the independence struggles. Revolutionary forces finally lowered the Spanish flag and raised their own in 1826. Its cannon emplacements are still intact.

Entertainment and Events

Performing-arts events take place at the **Teatro Municipal de Ancud** (Blanco Encalada 660), on the east side of the Plaza de Armas, and the **Casa de la Cultura** (Libertad 663, tel. 065/262-8164), alongside the museum.

Late January's **Semana Ancuditana** (Ancud Week) celebrates the city's founding, the island's folkloric music and dance, and traditional food. Throughout December and January there are similar events in nearby communities.

Ancud

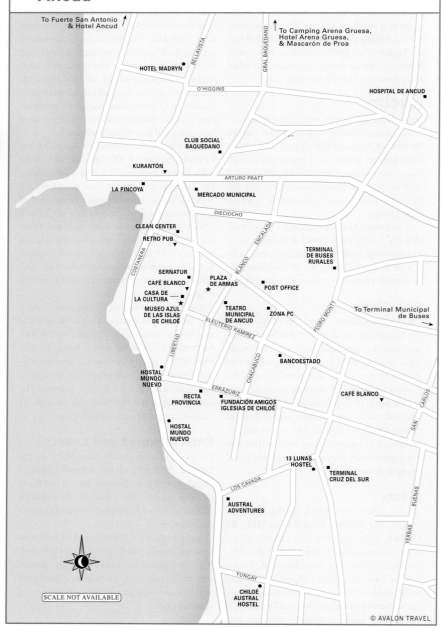

To Fuerte San Antonio
& Hotel Ancud

To Camping Arena Gruesa,
Hotel Arena Gruesa,
& Mascarón de Proa

HOTEL MADRYN

BELLAVISTA

GRAL BAQUEDANO

O'HIGGINS

HOSPITAL DE ANCUD

CLUB SOCIAL
BAQUEDANO

KURANTÓN

ARTURO PRATT

LA PINCOYA

MERCADO MUNICIPAL

DIECIOCHO

CLEAN CENTER

RETRO PUB

ENCALADA

BLANCO

TERMINAL
DE BUSES
RURALES

COSTANERA

SERNATUR

CAFÉ BLANCO

CASA DE
LA CULTURA

MUSEO AZUL
DE LAS ISLAS
DE CHILOÉ

PLAZA
DE ARMAS

POST OFFICE

TEATRO
MUNICIPAL
DE ANCUD

ZONA PC

ELEUTERIO RAMÍREZ

PEDRO MONTT

To Terminal Municipal
de Buses

LIBERTAD

CHACABUCO

BANCOESTADO

HOSTAL
MUNDO
NUEVO

ERRÁZURIZ

RECTA
PROVINCIA

FUNDACIÓN AMIGOS
IGLESIAS DE CHILOÉ

CAFÉ BLANCO

SAN CARLOS

HOSTAL
MUNDO
NUEVO

13 LUNAS
HOSTEL

TERMINAL
CRUZ DEL SUR

LOS CAVADA

BUENAS

AUSTRAL
ADVENTURES

YERBAS

YUNGAY

CHILOÉ
AUSTRAL
HOSTEL

SCALE NOT AVAILABLE

© AVALON TRAVEL

Shopping

Chiloé's crafts offerings include ceramics, wood carvings, and woolens. Outlets include the **Museo Chilote** (Libertad 370) and the **Mercado Municipal** (Dieciocho between Libertad and Blanco Encalada).

Food

Many restaurant menus are similar in content—fish and shellfish—and in price, mostly in the US$9-12 range for menu items. Salads are easily large enough for two.

For coffee and desserts, there are two branches of **Café Blanco** (Libertad 669, facing the plaza, tel. 065/262-2567; Ramírez 359, a few blocks east, tel. 065/262-0197). The latter is more spacious and comfortable.

In new quarters, the **Retro Pub** (Pudeto 44, tel. 065/262-6410, lunch and dinner daily) breaks the local mold by daring to serve pizza and even some Mexican dishes. **Recta Provincia** (Errázuriz 215, tel. 09/7752-0972) puts creative touches on Chilean sandwich standards, such as pork burgers, plus a wide selection of beers and mixed drinks.

At **Kurantón** (Prat 94, tel. 065/262-2216, lunch and dinner daily, US$12) the specialty is, obviously, their signature seafood stew, *curanto,* but the menu also stresses fish, mostly

hake and salmon, with seafood sauces. It has an eclectic decor of folkloric figures from Chiloé (with a soundtrack to match), plus bullfight posters, maritime memorabilia, and photos. The kitchen can be slow.

More elaborate seafood venues include the nearby **La Pincoya** (Prat 61, tel. 065/262-2613, lunch and dinner daily), **Polo Sur** (Av. Salvador Allende 630, tel. 065/262-2200, lunch and dinner daily), and especially **Mascarón de Proa** (Baquedano 560, tel. 065/262-1979, lunch and dinner daily), which offers the best views.

The new favorite, though, is the **Club Social Baquedano** (Baquedano 469, tel. 065/262-3633), a magnificent conversion of an existing building that was a police property. It specializes in fish and seafood, most notably local oysters and ceviche, but also pizzas and pastas, plus meats such as the relatively uncommon *entraña* (skirt steak). Native local potatoes are a significant asset, along with a respectable selection of wines by the glass, and there's also live music some nights.

Accommodations

Ancud has plenty of accommodations, ranging from camping and hostels to mostly mid-range choices, with a handful of not-quite-upmarket alternatives.

Ancud's Museo Azul de las Islas de Chiloé includes a full blue whale skeleton.

For the truly budget-conscious, at the **Chiloé Austral Hostel** (Yungay 282, tel. 065/262-5818, chiloeaustralhostel@gmail. com, US$18 pp dorms, US$42 s or d), most of the accommodations are dorms, but a couple of nicely furnished private doubles have spectacular views. All rooms have shared bath access, however.

Opposite the Cruz del Sur bus terminal, the **13 Lunas Hostel** (Los Carrera 855, tel. 065/262-2106, www.13lunas.cl, US$20-22 pp dorms, US$33 s, US$48-52 d) occupies a magnificently recycled house with vast common spaces and attractive furnishings, plus a deck and garden for barbecues. Most of the private rooms lack natural light because they occupy part of the basement on this sloping lot.

All rooms at **Hotel Madryn** (Bellavista 491, tel. 065/262-2128, www.hotelmadryn.cl, US$37 s, US$56 d) come with private baths, cable TV, and breakfast, and some have sea views. Some rooms are a little irregular in shape but still functional.

Arguably Ancud's best value, the nearly pristine Swiss-run ★ **Hostal Mundo Nuevo** (Av. Costanera Salvador Allende 748, tel. 065/262-8383, www.newworld.cl, US$21 pp dorms, US$43-58 s, US$61-77 d) provides spacious rooms, firm beds, panoramic sunsets through the glassed-in porch, a fine breakfast, an ample kitchen for the budget-conscious, and secure parking. Given its popularity, reservations are advised, although it has recently added several new rooms with private baths.

Surveying the shoreline from its location above Playa Gruesa, about 600 meters north of downtown, **Camping Arena Gruesa** (Costanera Norte 290, tel. 065/262-3428, www.hotelarenagruesa.cl, US$10 pp) has 60 lighted sites with improved privacy, hot showers, firewood, and other conveniences. At the same site, it's also added the cheerful new **Hotel Arena Gruesa** (US$44 s, US$62 d, with private bath). In this residential neighborhood, the major drawbacks are barking dogs and crowing roosters.

Hotel Galeón Azul (Libertad 751, tel. 065/262-2567, www.hotelgaleonazul.cl, US$49 s, US$67 d) is cheerful and central but wins no points for truth in labeling—the "Blue Galleon" sports a bright banana-yellow paint job.

For the best views, at least from the common areas, there's **Hotel Ancud** (San Antonio 30, tel. 065/262-2340, Santiago tel. 02/2234-9610, www.panamericanahoteles. cl, US$109 s or d). Since its acquisition by the Panamericana group, the facilities and service have improved. Still, the common areas outshine the rooms, which are on the small side.

About six kilometers west of town, the shoreline **Chil-hué** (Camino Lechagua, Km 6.4, tel. 09/9644-2578, www.chil-hue. com, US$120-200 s or d) offers a diversity of accommodations for up to six people, including a sea-view tower. Excellent meals, including Peruvian dishes, are also available. English is spoken.

Information and Services

Sernatur (Libertad 665, tel. 065/262-2800, infochiloe@sernatur.cl, 8:30am-5pm Mon.-Thurs., 8:30am-4:30 Fri.) has maps, brochures, and up-to-date accommodations data. The **Oficina Municipal de Turismo** (tel. 065/262-8183, www.ancud.cl) now depends on Sernatur, but its website provides a complete listing of services (in Spanish only).

Ancud has no exchange houses, but **BancoEstado** (Ramírez 229) has an ATM. For postal services, go to **Correos de Chile** (Pudeto 201). **Zona PC** (Pudeto 243, Local 4) has Internet access and phones.

Clean Center (Pudeto 45, tel. 065/262-3838) does the washing. The **Hospital de Ancud** (Almirante Latorre 301, tel. 065/232-6478, www.hsopitalancud.gov.cl) handles medical matters.

Transportation

Ancud's long-distance **Terminal Municipal de Buses** (Aníbal Pinto 1200), about 1.2 kilometers east of downtown, is relatively new but less central than the private terminal operated by **Cruz del Sur** (Los Carrera 850, tel. 065/262-2249, www.busescruzdelsur.cl).

There are many northbound buses to Puerto Montt and on to Santiago and intermediates, southbound buses to Castro and Quellón, and services to Punta Arenas via Argentina with **Queilen Bus** (tel. 065/262-1140) and **Turibús** (tel. 065/262-7247), the latter an affiliate of Cruz del Sur.

Typical destinations, times, and fares include Castro (1 hour, US$3), Chonchi (1.5 hours, US$4), Puerto Montt (2 hours, US$6), Temuco (7 hours, US$15), Santiago (15 hours, US$39-50), and Punta Arenas (33 hours, US$56).

The **Terminal de Buses Rurales** (Pedro Montt and Colo Colo) is for buses to destinations other than those on or along the Panamericana.

Transmarchilay (www.tmc.cl) and **Cruz del Sur** ferries sail between Pargua and Chacao (US$18 automobiles and light trucks, US$12 motorcycles, US$3 bicycles, free for foot passengers).

VICINITY OF ANCUD

Ancud's U.S.-Peruvian **Austral Adventures** (Av. Costanera 904, tel./fax 065/262-5977, www.austral-adventures.com) conducts multiple-day hikes along the island's wild northwest coast as well as custom sea kayak trips.

In a kiosk at the Mercado Municipal, **Aki Turismo** (Dieciocho s/n, tel. 065/262-0868, www.akiturismochiloe.cl) arranges local excursions, such as trips to the Puñihuil penguin colony and to the island's churches and chapels.

Monumento Natural Islotes de Puñihuil

About 27 kilometers southwest of Ancud via a newly paved road, the islets of **Puñihuil** are home to summer breeding colonies of both Magellanic and Humboldt penguins, whose ranges overlap here. Chilote fishermen use fiberglass launches to shuttle penguin-watchers (US$10 pp) from the sandy beach into the surrounding waters. Two hours advance notice is advisable; those with reservations have priority. For details, contact **Pingüineras Puñihuil** (tel. 09/8317-4302, www.pinguineraschiloe.cl).

Bahía Puñihuil (US$10), one of several restaurants along the beach, serves simple but artful fish and seafood dishes at modest prices. **Costa Pacífico** (tel. 09/9455-0434) is another good option.

Chepu

About 40 kilometers southwest of Ancud via Ruta 5 and a gravel road, set among Chiloé's rugged western mountains, the village of **Chepu** has a nascent kayak scene on wetlands created by the massive 1960 tsunami that struck the area. Today its "sunken forest" is a prime **birding** destination. Now under new management, this small guesthouse complex features wind turbines, solar-powered hot water, and simple but stylish four-bed dormitories (US$15 pp for kayaker clients, US$10 more for breakfast), and newer ones with private baths (US$75-97 s or d, including breakfast). There are no kitchen facilities, but packages with meals are also available.

In addition to kayaking, there are excursions to a nearby penguin colony, reached by boat and a hike. Children under 14 are not permitted because of safety concerns about the river, and those ages 14 to 17 must be accompanied by an adult. For more information, contact Juan Puentes at **Chepu Adventures** (tel. 065/284-0583, www.chepuadventures.com).

Only a couple of kilometers west, the more rustic **Los Senderos de Chepu** (tel. 09/9260-2423, www.actiweb.es/senderos-chepu, US$30 pp with all meals) gets high marks from local operators and guests alike for charm and graciousness, as well as excursions including guided horseback rides (4 hours, US$20). There's also the unique *maderocarril* (a short-line railcar that runs on wooden rails and ends at a forest grove where there's a good hour's hike).

Every Monday, Wednesday, and Friday, there are two buses daily from Ancud to Chepu that pass directly by the entrance to Chepu Adventures but turn around before reaching Los Senderos de Chepu. From the **Terminal de Buses Rurales** (Pedro

Montt and Colo Colo), the first leaves at 6am, the second at 4pm. On request, the proprietors will also pick up those who have booked *cabañas* or kayak trips at Km 25 on the Panamericana. A taxi from Ancud costs about US$30 but can be shared by several people. From the new airport at Mocopulli, the price is about US$75.

CASTRO

The Isla Grande's first urban settlement, **Castro** dates from 1567, when Martín Ruiz de Gamboa made it the base for evangelizing the southern Huilliche and Chonos peoples. Despite the activities of Franciscan, Mercedarian, and Jesuit missionaries, it remained a poor and isolated backwater, subject to earthquakes, tsunamis, fires, and sacking by privateers.

In 1834, barely two decades after Chilean independence was declared, Charles Darwin found Castro to be "a most forlorn and deserted place." Even in the early 20th century, it had barely 1,000 inhabitants, and its isolation had fostered a distinctive townscape still characterized by its surviving *palafitos,* the stilted waterfront houses with their elaborately carved shingles. By 1912, a narrow-gauge railroad linked it with Ancud and the rest of the country as farm products increased port activity.

The 1960 earthquake devastated the city—as sea level rose from the tsunami, it saturated the soils and undercut many buildings—but salmon farming sparked a recovery that has continued to this day and, in recent years, it has gained a new airport, a hotel-casino, and a sore-thumb shopping mall that dominates the downtown. On the brighter side, the northern *palafitos* along Avenida Pedro Montt have begun to sprout new businesses and rehabbed houses, a process that began on the south side some years ago.

Orientation

Castro (pop. 43,000), 88 kilometers south of Ancud via the Panamericana, is a central location for Isla Grande excursions. Its compact central grid occupies a broad plain above the Estero de Castro, a sheltered ocean inlet, while Avenida Pedro Montt, route of the former rail line, curves around the shoreline just above sea level.

Sights

Castro's sights give it greater tourist appeal than any other city on the island, but it's also a fine base for excursions.

The interior of Castro's Iglesia San Francisco glistens with polished alerce timber.

Castro

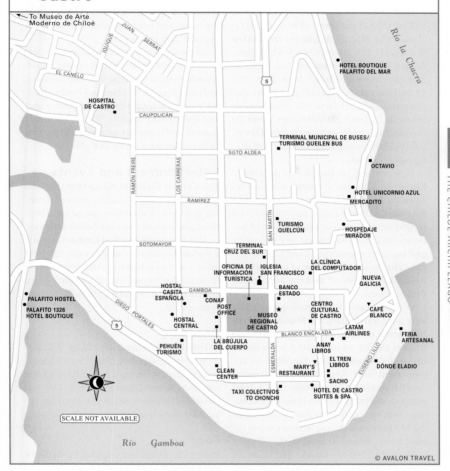

← To Museo de Arte
Moderno de Chiloé

JUAN
SERRAT
IQUIQUE

EL CANELO

HOSPITAL
DE CASTRO

CAUPOLICÁN

5

HOTEL BOUTIQUE
PALAFITO DEL MAR

Río la Chaura

TERMINAL MUNICIPAL DE BUSES/
TURISMO QUEILEN BUS

SGTO ALDEA

OCTAVIO

RAMÓN FREIRE
LOS CARRERAS

RAMÍREZ

HOTEL UNICORNIO AZUL
MERCADITO

SAN MARTÍN

TURISMO
QUELCÚN

HOSPEDAJE
MIRADOR

SOTOMAYOR

TERMINAL
CRUZ DEL SUR

OFICINA DE   IGLESIA
INFORMACIÓN SAN FRANCISCO
TURÍSTICA

LA CLÍNICA
DEL COMPUTADOR

NUEVA
GALICIA

HOSTAL
CASITA   GAMBOA
ESPAÑOLA

PALAFITO HOSTEL

DIEGO   PORTALES

CONAF

BANCO
ESTADO

PALAFITO 1326
HOTEL BOUTIQUE

5

POST
OFFICE

HOSTAL
CENTRAL

MUSEO
REGIONAL
DE CASTRO

CENTRO
CULTURAL
DE CASTRO

CAFÉ
BLANCO

PEHUÉN
TURISMO

LA BRÚJULA
DEL CUERPO

BLANCO ENCALADA

LATAM
AIRLINES

FERIA
ARTESANAL

ESMERALDA

ANAY
LIBROS

EUSEBIO LILLO

CLEAN
CENTER

MARY'S
RESTAURANT

EL TREN
LIBROS

DÓNDE ELADIO

SACHO

SCALE NOT AVAILABLE

TAXI COLECTIVOS
TO CHONCHI

HOTEL DE CASTRO
SUITES & SPA

Río   Gamboa

© AVALON TRAVEL

On the north side of the refurbished Plaza de Armas, the landmark **Iglesia San Francisco** represents both change and continuity in Chiloé's architectural tradition. After fire destroyed its Franciscan-built predecessor in 1902, ecclesiastical authorities broke with tradition in hiring an Italian architect, Eduardo Provasoli, who incorporated both neo-Gothic and classical elements into the twin-tower structure. At the same time, employing local master builders and artisans ensured that Chilote elements would survive in the ironclad wooden building, which was begun in 1906 but not completed until 1912.

Now a national monument, the church has changed its colors without surrendering its flamboyance. Instead of salmon and violet, its galvanized-iron exterior is now a fading banana-yellow with violet towers and dashes of reddish trim. The burnished-wood interior is more somber, embellished with traditional

Catholic statuary, with grisly renderings of the crucifixion.

Half a block south of the Plaza de Armas, still bursting at the seams of its cramped facilities, the **Museo Regional de Castro** (Esmeralda 255, tel. 065/263-5967, 9:30am-6:30pm Mon.-Fri., 9:30am-1pm Sat., 10:30am-1pm Sun. summer; 10am-6:30pm Mon.-Fri., 10am-1pm Sat. fall-spring, donation) displays Huilliche artifacts and ethnographic materials, "appropriate technology" from the surrounding countryside, accounts of the island's urban development, and excellent photographic exhibits.

Now sitting in the newly developed **Plazuela El Tren**, a waterfront park on Avenida Pedro Montt, the **Locomotora Ancud-Castro** hauled passengers and freight on the narrow-gauge railroad between 1912 and 1960, when an earthquake and tsunami ended the island's train service. The route either followed or paralleled Avenida Pedro Montt and the present-day Panamericana.

Occupying airy, well-lighted quarters that were once warehouses, the **Museo de Arte Moderno de Chiloé** (MAM, Galvarino Riveros s/n, tel. 065/263-5454, www.mam-chiloe.cl, 10am-6pm daily Jan.-Mar., by appointment only Apr.-Dec., free) stresses up-and-coming Chilean (mostly Chilote) painters, sculptors, and multimedia specialists. On the grounds of the Parque Municipal, the MAM is open during summer, when invited artists show their latest work.

Until the 1960 earthquake and tsunami, shingled *palafitos* (houses on stilts) lined nearly all the Isla Grande's eastern shore estuaries. Only a handful survive today, most notably in Castro and vicinity. Traditionally, Chilote fishermen would tie their vessels to the pilings out their back doors, but the houses themselves front on city streets.

Castro has the largest remaining assortment of this unique vernacular architecture, in the **Barrio Pedro Montt** at the northern approach to town and in **Barrio Gamboa** on both sides of the Río Gamboa bridge,

southwest of the city center. Both areas are home to new accommodations, cafés, and art-oriented businesses. Residents are also receiving grants and subsidies to preserve and even upgrade their properties.

At the south end of the Costanera, the waterfront **Feria Artesanal** integrates tourist appeal—typical woolens, souvenir basketry, and *palafito* seafood restaurants—with practical items such as food (including edible algae) and fuel (blocks of peat). While Dalcahue's Sunday crafts market gets more hype, this daily market rates nearly as highly.

Entertainment and Events

The **Centro Cultural de Castro** (Serrano 320, tel. 065/263-5531) is the main performing-arts venue. It also offers special art exhibitions, plus myriad classes and other activities.

Mid-February's **Festival Costumbrista** is a weekend event with island crafts, folkloric music and dance, traditional foods such as *curanto* (seafood stew) and *yoco* (a pork dish), and liquors such as *chicha* (cider, usually made from apples).

Shopping

El Tren Libros (Thompson 229, tel. 065/263-3936) is an outstanding bookstore with local works. After suffering a fire at its longtime location, **Anay Libros** (Blanco 140, tel. 065/263-0158, www.anaylibros.com) has relocated to new quarters.

Food

Facing the plaza, the popular **La Brújula del Cuerpo** (O'Higgins 308, tel. 065/263-3229) offers a café menu of breakfasts, sandwiches, coffee, and desserts. There are several new smaller but similar offerings, such as highly recommended **Café Blanco** (Blanco Encalada 268, tel. 065/253-4636).

Most of the best dining options are seafood venues, such as **Sacho** (Thompson 213, tel. 065/263-2079, noon-3:30pm and 8pm-11pm Tues.-Sat., noon-3:30pm Sun.) and **Dónde Eladio** (Lillo 97, tel. 065/263-5285, lunch and dinner daily). **Octavio** (Av. Pedro Montt

261, tel. 065/263-2855, lunch and dinner daily, US$10) offers waterfront dining with style and fine service at moderate prices with a diverse menu. Entrées range from chicken to king crab, with many fish dishes in between. **Mary's Restaurant** (Thompson 244, tel. 065/263-1429, noon-3:30pm and 8pm-midnight Mon.-Sat.) has a particularly choice *chupe de centolla* (king crab casserole) and other appealing fish and seafood dishes. Beef, pork, and poultry are also on the menu.

One of Castro's best, ★ **Nueva Galicia** (Pedro Montt 38, tel. 065/253-2828, 1:30pm-4:30pm and 7:30pm-10:30pm daily, US$13) has a fairly simple menu but superb execution in dishes like *chupe de jaiva* (crab casserole) and king crab lasagna—not to mention ten varieties of *pisco* sours. The glistening open kitchen is uncommon even in Santiago, and downright rare in this region. There is limited sidewalk seating, but traffic can block views of the sea.

The best new choice, probably the best overall, is the deceptively casual ★ **Mercadito** (Pedro Montt 210, tel. 065/253-3866, www.elmercaditodechiloe.cl, 12:30pm-4:30pm and 7pm-11pm Mon.-Sat., 12:30pm-4:30pm Sun.), whose colorful decor masks unanticipated professionalism in its menu, preparation, and service. The seared tuna with grilled vegetables (US$15) is exquisite, the frozen *pisco* sour surprisingly satisfying, and the wine-by-the-glass selection admirable—premium selections at moderate prices, rather than mediocre mini bottles. It also has an outdoor deck for fine weather.

Accommodations

Of several budget accommodations, the best value may be **Hospedaje Mirador** (Barros Arana 127, tel. 065/263-3795, www.hostalelmiradorcastro.cl, US$22 pp, US$45 d, with breakfast), an immaculate place on a pedestrian staircase overlooking the port. The more expensive rooms have private baths. One block from the Plaza de Armas, **Hostal Central** (Los Carrera 316, tel. 065/263-7026, ogalindo@entelchile.net, US$24 pp with shared bath, US$38 s, US$45 d with private bath and breakfast) is a three-floor warren of smallish rooms—many legitimate singles—with exceptionally helpful staff.

Near the Gamboa bridge, the ★ **Palafito Hostel** (Ernesto Riquelme 1210, tel. 065/253-1008, www.palafitohostel.com, US$24 pp, US$50-71 s, US$71-93 d) is a remodeled *palafito* (house on stilts) turned into a luminous eight-room designer hostel-B&B. All rooms, even the dorms, have private baths, and the building incorporates elements of the island's maritime heritage, such as curved walls. Even travelers wary of hostels should consider staying here.

At the northern edge of town, the **Hotel Boutique Palafito del Mar** (Pedro Montt 567, tel. 065/263-1622, www.palafitodelmar.cl, US$74-148 d) is a luminous, seven-room guesthouse with natural wood and just enough irregularities to make it seem more traditional than it really is (such as lack of a railing on a slightly inclined staircase). It also has several comparably priced apartments that can hold more guests.

Despite its offbeat chalet design (on an island that rarely gets snow), the **Hotel de Castro Suites & Spa** (Chacabuco 202, tel. 065/263-2301, www.hosteriadecastro.cl, US$65-79 s, US$81-154 d) traditionally vies for the honor of being Castro's top hotel in its price range. Amenities include sea views, a restaurant and bar, an indoor pool, and Wi-Fi. It has remodeled two rooms into more elaborate (and expensive) suites. Embellished with native wood and carpeted floors, **Hostal Casita Española** (Los Carrera 359, tel. 065/263-5186, www.hosteriadecastro.cl, US$44 s, US$58 d) operates under the same management.

Dating from 1910, a hotel only since 1986, the quirky ★ **Hotel Unicornio Azul** (Pedro Montt 228, tel. 065/263-2359, www.hotelunicornioazul.cl, US$108 s or d) was once a budget hotel, but steady improvements have driven prices upward. Rooms vary considerably in size, shape, and view, so don't take anything without seeing it first.

Seemingly taking its cues from the nearby Palafito Hostel, the **Palafito 1326 Hotel Boutique** (Ernesto Riquelme 1326, tel. 065/253-0053, www.palafito1326.cl, US$110-144 s or d) has done an even more spectacular transformation and expansion of a stilted house, with a dozen smartly furnished rooms decorated with native woods. Rates vary according to whether the room has street-side or sea views. Everyone can make use of the decks and spectacular rooftop terrace, which face the water.

In a class of its own, in an isolated location 20 kilometers out of town, **Tierra Chiloé** (Playa San José, tel. 02/2207-8861, www.tierrachiloe.com, 2-night minimum US$1,620 s, US$2,700 d) is an architecturally bold, all-inclusive resort with a gourmet restaurant, geared primarily toward multiple-day packages with excursions. They will accept one-nighters or short-termers on a space-available basis. Getting here with your own vehicle requires elaborate directions, but they do provide transfers.

Information and Services

The municipal **Oficina de Información Turística** (tel. 065/254-7706, www.visitchiloe.cl, 10am-9pm daily summer, 10am-6pm daily fall-spring) is directly on the Plaza de Armas, opposite the church. **Conaf** (Gamboa 424, tel. 065/253-2501, 8:30am-5pm Mon.-Fri.) can provide information on Parque Nacional Chiloé.

BancoEstado (San Martín 397) has an ATM. **Correos de Chile** (O'Higgins 338) handles the mail. **La Clínica del Computador** (Serrano 428, tel. 065/253-6733) has public Internet access.

The **Clean Center** (Balmaceda 220, tel. 065/263-3132) does laundry for about US$2 per kilogram. For medical assistance, contact the **Hospital de Castro** (Freire 852, tel. 065/249-0548, www.hospitalcastro.gov.cl).

Transportation

LATAM (Blanco 180, tel. 065/249-4425) is the only airline flying out of **Aeródromo Mocopulli** (MHC, tel. 02/2222-8400, www.aeropuertochiloe.com), 20 kilometers north of Castro via Ruta 5, although Sky Airline may begin flights. There is one LATAM flight (Tues.-Wed. and Fri.-Sun.). **Transfer Chiloé** (tel. 09/8899-4441, www.transferchiloe.cl) provides transfer to and from the airport for US$6.

Most local and long-distance bus companies use the **Terminal Municipal de Buses**

Tierra Chiloé is a bold design hotel that diverges from the island's humble image.

(San Martín 667, tel. 065/263-5666), which desperately needs an upgrade or replacement. **Cruz del Sur** (San Martín 486, tel. 065/263-5152) has its own terminal, also used by **Turibús** and **Transchiloé**. Some companies have ticket windows at both sites. Cruz del Sur goes south to Chonchi and north to Ancud and Puerto Montt, offering continuing service to Santiago and intermediates. Transchiloé has similar routes. Several carriers go to Punta Arenas, including **Queilen Bus** (tel. 065/263-2173) and Turibús.

At the Terminal de Buses Rurales, **Buses Ojeda** (tel. 09/9887-4129) and **Unión Express** (tel. 09/6668-3531) have frequent services to Cucao and Parque Nacional Chiloé (US$3) between 7:45am and 6pm. Various minibuses leave frequently for Dalcahue (US$1.50). **Buses Lemuy** and **Buses Gallardo** (tel. 065/263-0529) serve Chonchi (US$1.50). *Taxis colectivos* to Chonchi leave from the corner of Chacabuco and Esmeralda.

Sample destinations, times, and fares include Ancud (1 hour, US$3), Puerto Montt (3 hours, US$9), Temuco (8 hours, US$16), Santiago (17 hours, US$27-37), and Punta Arenas (34 hours, US$75).

VICINITY OF CASTRO

Several companies conduct day trips and longer tours, including destinations such as Dalcahue, Chonchi, Parque Nacional Chiloé, and offshore islands. Among them are **Turismo Quelcún** (San Martín 581, tel. 065/263-2396, www.hostalyturismoquelcun. cl), **Turismo Queilen Bus** (San Martín 667, tel. 065/263-2594, www.queilenbus.cl), at the Terminal de Buses Rurales, and **Pehuén Turismo** (Chacabuco 498, tel. 065/263-5254, www.turismopehuen.cl).

Dalcahue

Artisans from around Chiloé customarily present their best at **Dalcahue**'s Sunday market, which is still its biggest attraction. This modest fishing village (pop. 5,000), about 20 kilometers northeast of Castro, is gaining importance as a base for sea kayaking among the islands off the archipelago's sheltered eastern shore.

Nothing remains of Dalcahue's original *palafitos* (houses on stilts), obliterated by the 1960 tsunami, but a handsome new construction, housing a gaggle of seafood eateries, puts a modern twist on the typical Chilote style. Alongside it, the vendors and their clients at the sharp new **Mercado Artesanal** no longer need dodge the rain squalls that pass through here, and additional waterfront improvements are underway. Also on the waterfront, a block or so to the east, the **Museo Histórico Etnográfico de Dalcahue** (Pedro Montt s/n, 8am-7pm Mon.-Fri., 10am-7pm Sat.-Sun.) displays a representative sample of local material culture, including the *dalcas* (canoes) that gave the town its name.

The restored 19th-century **Iglesia Parroquial** is one of the architectural monuments that helped the island's wooden churches gain UNESCO World Heritage Site status.

Mid-February's **Semana Dalcahuina** is the town's major festival. **Willi Mapu** (Manuel Rodríguez 200, tel. 09/6762-1440) does kayaking and birding excursions.

Dalcahue makes a good day trip, but improved accommodations make an overnight stay more appealing. For those on a budget, **Hostal Encanto Patagón** (Ramón Freire 026, tel. 065/264-1651, www.hostalencantopatagon.blogspot.com, US$18-23 pp) is a rambling house whose higher rates correspond to rooms with private baths. There's also a camping option, with kitchen privileges.

Until recently, the best option exception was the locally styled **Hotel La Isla** (Av. Mocopulli 113, tel. 065/264-1241, hotellaisla@hotmail.com, US$53 s, US$68 d), which has some modern comforts, especially in its newer annex, and its own grill restaurant, **Sal y Leña.**

As accommodations, though, it can't beat the congenial ★ **Refugio de Navegantes Chiloé** (San Martín 165, tel. 065/264-1128, www.refugiodenavegantes.cl, US$153-230 s or d), a boutique unit offering five spacious rooms with glistening natural woods and private terraces on the upper floors (the highest price corresponds to a top-floor suite). A short walk from the church, facing the plaza, it has an equally attractive café open to the public, with espresso drinks and kuchen.

Mostly interchangeable, the *palafito* restaurants have fried and grilled fish and empanadas, and the Chilote potato pancake known as *milcao*.

Well-meaning youngsters staff the **Oficina de Información Turística** (Pedro Montt s/n, www.dalcahue.cl, 9am-7pm daily summer), a sidewalk kiosk at the waterside market plaza. **BancoEstado** (Freire 645) has an ATM.

Frequent buses to and from Castro stop at the waterfront Feria Artesanal. There are also *taxis colectivos* to and from Castro.

Chonchi

Nicknamed the Ciudad de los Tres Pisos (City of Three Levels) for its sheer hillsides and steep streets, **San Carlos de Chonchi** (pop. about 5,300) was one of Chiloé's first Jesuit missions, thanks to its strategically central location. Not founded officially until 1767, it managed to keep its own spontaneous street plan—the hilly topography defeating the imposition of the regulation Spanish colonial grid. With one of the island's best concentrations of traditional architecture, Chonchi is 22 kilometers south of Castro.

The historic **Iglesia San Carlos de Chonchi** (1900) and many equally historic residences line **Calle Centenario,** an area designated a *zona típica* national monument. The church's exterior has undergone palpable restoration. The **Museo de las Tradiciones Chonchinas** (Centenario 116, tel. 065/267-2802, 9:30am-1:30pm and 2:30pm-6pm Mon.-Fri., 9:30am-1:30pm Sat., US$1) replicates a typical Chilote kitchen and displays impressive photographs of the 1960 tsunami.

The **Mercado Municipal** (Irarrázaval s/n) has helped renovate Chonchi's waterfront, where regular cleanups are keeping the beach presentable. Like its counterpart in Dalcahue, the market blends the traditional and the contemporary and contains a clutch of modest seafood restaurants with ocean views. Taggers have defaced parts of it.

Late January's **Semana Verano Chonchi** is the city's summer festival, featuring folkloric music, dance, and art along with rural skills such as rodeo. Chonchi is renowned for its *licor de oro,* a milk-based liqueur resembling Drambuie.

Having undergone substantial restoration, the classic **Hotel Huildín** (Centenario 102, tel. 065/267-1388, www.hotelhuildin.com, US$30 pp with breakfast and private bath) once again deserves consideration.

Don't miss the *pastel de jaiva* (crab soufflé) at the waterfront **El Trébol** (Irarrázaval 187, tel. 065/267-1203, lunch and dinner daily, US$10). The lack of frills keeps prices down, and the service is excellent. The *mostaza de ajo* (garlic mustard) enhances the homemade bread. One block inland, **La Quila** (Andrade 183, tel. 065/267-1389, lunch and dinner daily) is comparable. **Los Tres Pisos** (O'Higgins 359, tel. 065/267-1433, lunch and dinner daily) serves sandwiches, empanadas, and kuchen.

The municipal **Oficina de Información Turística** (Sargento Candelaria and Centenario, tel. 065/267-1522, www.municipalidadchonchi.cl, 9:30am-8:30pm daily summer only) has a branch at the Mercado Municipal. **BancoEstado** (Centenario 28) has an ATM. **Correos de Chile** (Sargento Candelaria 134) is the post office.

In shared offices, **Cruz del Sur** and **Transchiloé** (Pedro Montt 233, tel. 065/267-1218) have frequent services between Castro and Chonchi; *taxis colectivos* to Castro (US$2) are also frequent. Buses from Castro bound for Cucao (Parque Nacional Chiloé) stop at Chonchi's **Terminal Municipal** (Alonso de Ercilla s/n).

★ PARQUE NACIONAL CHILOÉ

South of Ancud and west of the Panamericana, Chiloé's Pacific coast is an almost roadless area of abrupt headlands, broad sandy beaches, and sprawling dunes at the foot of forested mountains dissected by transverse rivers. Much of this landscape, in fact, differs little from Charles Darwin's description in *The Voyage of the Beagle* as he rode west toward Cucao, now the gateway to Parque Nacional Chiloé:

> At Chonchi we struck across the island, following intricate winding paths, sometimes passing through magnificent forests, and sometimes through pretty cleared spots, abounding with corn and potato crops. This undulating woody country, partially cultivated, reminded me of the wilder parts of England, and therefore had to my eye a most fascinating aspect. At Vilinco [Huillinco], which is situated on the borders of the lake of Cucao, only a few fields were cleared.

Since its creation in 1982, **Parque Nacional Chiloé** has guarded a representative sample of the Isla Grande's natural habitat and wildlife, while providing recreational access to growing numbers of outdoors enthusiasts, both Chileans and foreigners. For many years, the Conaf administration failed to integrate the area's indigenous Huilliche people into its activities. Matters had changed little from the 19th century when Darwin observed "they are very much secluded from the rest of Chiloé, and have scarcely any sort of commerce." Substantial areas of former parkland are now under Huilliche administration.

Geography and Climate

On the thinly settled, densely forested Pacific coast, Parque Nacional Chiloé comprises 42,567 hectares in five discrete sectors: **Sector Anay,** west of Chonchi near the village of Cucao; **Sector Chepu,** southwest of Ancud; **Sector Cole Cole,** north of Chanquín; the 50-hectare **Sector Islote Metalqui,** a rugged offshore island; and the Conaf administration area west of Cucao.

Elevations range from sea level to 850 meters in the Cordillera de Piuchén. Annual rainfall varies from about 2,000 millimeters on the coast to 3,000 millimeters at the highest elevations. Temperatures are mild, averaging about 10°C over the course of the year, with few extremes of either heat or cold.

Flora and Fauna

At some lower elevations, mixed evergreen forest of the endemic *coigüe* or *roble de Chiloé* covers the valleys and slopes, along with the coniferous *mañío* and climbing vines. In others, enormous ferns cover the soil beneath the *ulmo, arrayán,* and the twisted *tepu.* Near its northern limit, the world's most southerly conifer, the *ciprés de los Guaitecas,* grows in swampy soils alongside the *tepu.* The *alerce* reaches the southern limit of its geographical range at elevations above 600 meters.

In such dense forest, it's rare to see mammals, though the *pudú* and the Chiloé fox (*Dusicyon fulvipes,* first identified by Darwin) survive here. Both sea otters and sea lions inhabit coastal areas, while the 110 bird species include Magellanic and Humboldt penguins, oystercatchers, and cormorants on the coast. The dense forest is home to the elusive *chucao* (a species of bird).

Sights and Recreation

Chanquín is the base for visiting Sector Anay, the park's most accessible area, which has hiking trails of varying length. The damp climate makes wool socks and water-resistant boots advisable for hikers.

Near Conaf's Centro de Información Ambiental at Chanquín, just across the river from the village of Cucao, the 750-meter **Sendero Interpretivo El Tepual** makes as many twists and turns as the *tepu* trunks over which it passes in boggy, slippery terrain. A short distance west, the **Sendero Playa de Cucao** winds through vestigial forest and traverses a broad dune field to arrive at a long white sandy beach, 1.4 kilometers west. At about the midway point, a short lateral path climbs to a scenic overlook. Violent surf, treacherous currents, and frigid Pacific waters make it unsuitable for swimming, so the scenery is the main attraction.

North of Cucao, the road continues eight kilometers past **Lago Huelde** to the Río

Chanquil. From there, it's necessary to walk to the **Río Cole Cole,** which has a 10-site campground administered by the community of Huentemó. Eight kilometers beyond Cole Cole, Conaf has a *refugio* (shelter) on the north bank of the **Río Anay,** but until a pedestrian suspension bridge is completed, it will not be open.

For nonhikers, inexpensive rental horses are available at Chanquín, but they're not suitable for forest trails such as El Tepual, and because they're untrained for amateur riders, there have been accidents.

Food and Accommodations

In and around Chanquín, there are several Huilliche-run campgrounds (US$3-4 pp). Conaf's **Camping Chanquín** (US$7.50 pp), nearby *cabañas* (US$53 d, US$90 for up to 5 people) have reopened under concessionaire Bernabé Leal (tel. 09/9507-2559, tel. 09/8221-2078, www.parquechiloe.cl). There are Conaf shelters (US$5 pp, camping free) along the trails.

Across the Chanquín bridge, the exterior is a bit weathered at **Hostal El Fogón de Cucao** (tel. 09/9946-5685, US$23 pp, US$52 d), but the interior is immaculate and attractive. It has one tiny single and two more comfortable doubles with shared bath downstairs, plus four more elaborate rooms with private baths upstairs. The reception is at its namesake grill restaurant, just across the road, where it also operates a campground.

Just across the Chanquín bridge, handsomely built of native woods, the **Palafito Cucao Lodge** (tel. 065/297-1154, www.hostelpalafitocucao.cl, US$25 pp dorms, US$65 s, US$82 d) is distancing itself a bit from its hostel side, but it still gets plenty of backpackers in what's clearly the best local option.

Cucao and **Chanquín** both have mini markets, and it's possible to buy fresh fish, potatoes, and the like from local fisherfolk and farmers. Supplies are more diverse and cheaper in **Castro** and **Chonchi.**

Information

About 500 meters beyond the concrete bridge over the Río Cucao, rangers collect a US$6 pp admission at Chanquín. Here, Conaf's glistening **Centro de Información Ambiental** (9am-6pm Mon.-Fri., 9am-5pm Sat.-Sun. and holidays) provides an informative map (in Spanish only). The information center contains exhibits on the park's flora and fauna, the aboriginal Huilliche people, mining history, and regional legends and traditions. The surrounding grounds contain samples of Chilote technology, including a cider press and wooden sleighs used to drag heavy loads over boggy ground.

Getting There and Around

Cucao, the park's easiest access point, is 52 kilometers southwest of **Castro** and 32 kilometers west of **Chonchi** via the Panamericana and a paved road with a few potholes; public transportation now continues to **Chanquín.** From Castro and Chonchi and back, **Buses Ojeda** (at the Terrazas de Cucao restaurant, tel. 09/9887-4129) and **Unión Express** (kiosk across from the Los Arrayanes restaurant, tel. 09/6668-3531) provide numerous buses daily (1 hour, US$3).

QUELLÓN

Nondescript **Quellón** is a 20th-century port that really only came into its own after an alcohol and acetone distillery, using native woods from dense nearby forests, installed itself here in 1905. After the 1960 tsunami, most inhabitants moved to higher ground away from the port, which is home to a small fishing fleet and regular ferries to continental Chiloé and Aisén. It is technically the Chilean terminus of the Panamericana, though an alternative route goes farther south in Argentine Patagonia.

Quellón hopes for a tourist influx because of the presence of a large **blue whale feeding colony** in the waters to the southwest. Commercial operators have only recently begun to make inroads here. At the kelp-gathering hamlet of **Chaiguao,** 11 kilometers east of town, it's sometimes possible to observe blue whales and humpbacks from shore. To the southwest, former Chilean president Sebastián Piñera has created Parque Tantauco, a conservation project similar to Parque Pumalín. For the moment, though, it's still the ferries that bring the tourists.

Orientation

On the southeastern coast of the Isla Grande, Quellón (pop. about 12,000) is 92 kilometers south of Castro via the Panamericana, which becomes Calle Ladrilleros as it enters town. The town site rises steeply above the harbor. Most points of interest and services are on or near the Costanera Pedro Montt, which runs along the shoreline.

Food and Accommodations

Seafood restaurants dot the waterfront, with a handful of venues elsewhere. **Hostería Romeo Alfa** (Capitán Luis Alcázar 554, tel. 065/268-0177, lunch and dinner daily, US$10) has an exceptional *chupe de jaiva* (crab casserole). It's good enough to overlook the slow, if well-intentioned, service. They also do pretty good grilled fish (salmon, hake, conger eel, corvina), which comes with a side dish, such as *merkén*-spiced mashed potatoes.

El Madero (Ramón Freire 430, tel. 065/268-1330, 12:30pm-11pm Mon.-Sat., US$12) has better atmosphere than the Patagonia Insular, and a similarly interesting menu. The kitchen can be slow and the service erratic. On a good day, it gets raves from diners, but it overcooks the barbecued lamb; the most reliable items are the sandwiches (around US$6) and the homemade ice cream, especially Swiss chocolate and pistachio.

Residencial Esteban (Aguirre Cerda 353, tel. 065/268-1438, esteban.amt@gmail.com, US$18 pp with shared bath, US$23 pp with private bath) is on a quiet block. Rates include breakfast and cable TV. The newer rooms at the back, with private baths, are more spacious and comfortable. **Hostal Chiloé Verde** (Ladrilleros 186, tel. 065/268-0683, cafeislasandwich@gmail.com, US$27 pp with shared bath, US$45 s or d with private bath) has everything going for it but its location along Quellón's busiest street, though all three rooms (two of which share a bath) face in the other direction. The downstairs **Café Isla Sandwich** serves the obvious as well as kuchen and coffee.

On the waterfront, **Hotel Tierra del Fuego** (Pedro Montt 445, tel. 065/268-2079, tdfhotel@gmail.com, US$30 s, US$45 d, with private bath) also has a restaurant with a unique boat-shaped bar. Down the block, **Hotel El Chico Leo** (Pedro Montt 325, tel. 065/268-1567, irma1.0@hotmail.com, US$27 s, US$48 d) has a choice of rooms with shared or private baths, and a restaurant with good seafood and service.

Atop a wooded slope at the west end of town, Quellón's top accommodations is cordial **Hotel Patagonia Insular** (Ladrilleros 1737, tel. 065/268-1610, www.hotelpatagoniainsular.cl, US$93 s, US$102 d), whose clientele often consists of Japanese fishing entrepreneurs. It has 30 spacious rooms with built-in work areas and cable TV. Some rooms have French balconies with views to snow-covered Andean peaks across the water, and the suites have whirlpool tubs and walk-in closets. In a town not known for its accommodations, the Patagonia Insular is a pleasant surprise. Its mostly seafood restaurant (US$15) is no more expensive than several lesser choices, but it lacks atmosphere. Try the seafood risotto.

Information and Services

Between the Municipalidad and the post office, just east of Juan Ladrilleros, Quellón's **Oficina de Información Turística** (22 de Mayo s/n, www.muniquellon.cl, 10am-6:30pm daily Oct.-Apr.) has improved dramatically.

Services are fewer than in Ancud or Castro. **BancoEstado** (22 de Mayo 399) has an ATM. **Correos de Chile** (22 de Mayo 397) handles the mail. There are numerous call centers and Internet locales along Ladrilleros. For medical help, try the **Hospital de Quellón** (Dr.

Whale-Watching from Chiloé

For decades now, Argentina's Península Valdés, where southern right whales spend the winter mating and giving birth, has been South America's prime whale-watching site. Chile's Isla Carlos Tercero, in the western Strait of Magellan, is a feeding ground for southern humpbacks. More recently, biologists have identified the Golfo de Corcovado south and east of Chiloé as a major feeding ground for both blue whales (largest of the whales) and humpbacks.

While whale-watching from shore is possible (if uncertain) at the hamlet of Chaiguao, near Quellón. The surest place to see the whales is at Melinka, in the Archipiélago de las Guaitecas, about two hours south of Quellón via high-speed launch. At Quellón, English-speaking veterinarian Jorge Oyarce has founded the company **Darwin Adventure** (tel. 09/9530-4355, www.darwinadventure.cl) to offer day trips to Melinka and longer charter photo-safaris around the Golfo de Corcovado. Oyarce is also interested in birds and dolphins, and sometimes works in tandem with **Excursiones Quellón** (Av. Jorge Vivar 382-B, tel. 065/268-0234, www.excursionesquellon.cl), which also offers other excursions in the vicinity.

At Melinka, there are accommodations as well as boats that will take passengers more cheaply than from Quellón, as it's closer to the feeding grounds.

Ahués 305, tel. 065/232-6600, www.hospitaldequellon.cl).

Transportation

Cruz del Sur and **Transchiloé** (both at Aguirre Cerda 52, tel. 065/268-1284) have frequent service to Chonchi, Castro, Ancud, and Puerto Montt. There are also *taxis colectivos* to Castro.

Naviera Austral (Pedro Montt 355, tel. 065/268-2207, www.navieraustral.cl) sails to Puerto Chacabuco (28 hours) on the *Barcaza Queulat* (11pm Wed. and Sat., US$25 pp in reclining *butaca,* US$11 bicycles, US$36 motorcycles, US$197 cars or light trucks).

Naviera's *Barcaza Jacaf* sails to Puerto Cisnes, Aisén (7pm Tues., US$25 pp, US$115 for cars or light trucks) via Melinka (US$10 pp). The same vessel sails to Chaitén (10am Tues., 5 hours, US$18 pp in *butaca,* US$15 bicycles, US$23 motorcycles, US$98 cars or light trucks).

★ PARQUE TANTAUCO

Doug Tompkins may have started something. After the late U.S. environmental philanthropist succeeded in having Parque Pumalín declared a formal nature sanctuary under Chilean law, Sebastián Piñera, Chile's president from 2010 to 2014, created his own private nature reserve in the virtually roadless southwestern sector of the Isla Grande de Chiloé.

Since acquiring the property in 2006, Piñera—who consulted with Tompkins about the project—has built an attractive guesthouse, an elegant campground with modern baths and a spacious *quincho* for cooking, several hiking trails, and a series of *refugios* (shelters) along those trails for hikers who brave the nearly incessant rain and soggy forests. At the same time, he's created a plant nursery to reforest areas damaged by fire and logging, most notably near the park's overland entrance at Chaiguata, near the city of Quellón.

Parque Tantauco's centerpiece is its headquarters at **Caleta Inío,** a settlement created some 30 years ago to exploit the area's extensive kelp beds. Accessible only by foot or motor launch from Quellón (2.5-6 hours, depending on the vessel), Inío has a permanent population of about 50. Many are now park employees; others benefit from the park's presence by offering lodging, meals, and handicrafts for sale. Given Inío's isolation, they also benefit because Tantauco's daily launch takes them to and from Quellón for free, on a space-available basis (paying passengers have priority).

Though Tantauco is still in early days, one trek appears likely to become an instant classic: the five-day, 52-kilometer **Sendero Transversal** from Chaiguata (reachable by bus from Quellón) to Caleta Inío, where hikers catch the launch back to Quellón. En route, they stay at four simple shelters with bunks, which eliminate the need to carry a tent. They also have cooking facilities and latrines (not flush toilets).

At first glance, the daily distances suggested, ranging 7.5-15 kilometers per day, sound pretty modest for experienced hikers at low elevations (the highest point is only about 250 meters above sea level). That's misleading, though, because much of the route crosses soggy (sometimes muddy) terrain and involves climbing up, over, and down fallen tree trunks. Many but not nearly all those trunks have steps cut into them. Even then, they are often slippery and require caution to avoid falls and sprains. In some areas, boardwalks and staircases make things easier.

For visitors who arrive at Inío, there are shorter hikes, such as the **Sendero Punta Rocosa,** which climbs to a solar-powered lighthouse and then loops through a rocky peninsula with several small, secluded beaches. Tantauco, in fact, may have some of South America's most secluded beaches, even if the South Pacific here is too chilly for swimming except on the warmest summer days.

Another worthwhile excursion is the **Sendero Quilantar,** a two-day, 22-kilometer loop from Inío that includes a night at Refugio Quilantar. All trails are clearly marked with bright metallic triangles every 100 meters. At regular intervals, they also have numbers that indicate progress along the route. Still, given the area's copious rainfall and winter storms that often knock down trees, maintenance is a major issue.

Combined with **whale-watching** in the Golfo de Corcovado, Parque Tantauco could make the area a huge ecotourism destination. At the same time, it lacks some of the attention to detail that Tompkins brought to Pumalín and his other projects. Tantauco's guesthouse, for instance, lacks double-paned windows, there are no books (though there are bookshelves), and there are no towels (bring your own). Electricity comes from a diesel generator (there are no suitable sites for a hydropower turbine, but wind power is a real possibility).

It's hard to imagine that Piñera can't afford a wind turbine for Tantauco. His fortune, made largely through LATAM Airlines and the pioneering implementation of credit card payment systems, must be immeasurably larger than Tompkins's. On the other hand, for the former Chilean president, Tantauco is just one of many projects; Tompkins's entire life was conservation.

For more information, contact the Castro **offices of Parque Tantauco** (Ruta 5 Sur, Km 1826, tel. 065/263-3805, www.parquetantauco.cl). Before visiting the park, it's imperative to make arrangements for transportation and accommodations, including the park *refugios* (shelters), which hold a maximum of eight people. There is a central office in Santiago at the **Fundación Futuro** (Apoquindo 3000, 19th Fl., Las Condes, tel. 02/2422-7322, www.fundacionfuturo.cl).

Tantauco has three authorized tour operators: **Chiloetnico** (Ernest Riquelme 1228, Castro, tel. 09/9135-3448, www.chiloetnico.cl), **Chiloé Natural** (Pedro Montt 210, Castro, tel. 09/9969-9344, www.chiloenatural.com), and **Excursiones Quellón** (Av. Jorge Vivar 382-B, Quellón, tel. 065/268-0324, www.excursionesquellon.cl).

Aisén and Continental Chiloé

With the smallest population of any Chilean region, Aisén is a natural wonderland of islands, mountains, fjords, lakes, rivers, and forests that's been drawing ever more visitors since the Carretera Austral's completion from Caleta Gonzalo in the north to Villa O'Higgins in the south.

Its only sizable city, the regional capital of Coyhaique, has a modern airport and makes a good base for exploring the area. Some visitors, though, begin at the ferry port of Chaitén and move south by road. Others arrive at Coyhaique's nearby Puerto Chacabuco via ferry from Puerto Montt or Chiloé.

Aisén's biggest single sight, accessible only by sea or by air taxi, is Parque Nacional Laguna San Rafael, where the ice meets the ocean. The climate resembles that of coastal British Columbia, with the seasons reversed (December, January, and February are summer). Consequently, weather can be wet, windy, and cool at any time, especially at higher elevations. Hikers should carry good trekking and rain gear and hope for the best. Summer highs can climb above 25°C around Coyhaique, but cooler temperatures are the rule. Midsummer days are long, with sunsets around 10pm.

Thanks to tourism, Aisén is increasingly prosperous, but agriculture, forestry, and mining are also important. The salmon-farming industry has brought both prosperity and controversy, as its environmental cost is greater than some residents believe it's worth.

PLANNING YOUR TIME

Because distances are great, public transportation is limited, and roads are few and slow, Aisén justifies a rental car, preferably with high clearance. Vehicles are also few, so rental reservations are imperative for visitors flying into Balmaceda-Coyhaique, the Carretera Austral's approximate midpoint.

Coyhaique is the best base for excursions north, south, and to Laguna San Rafael by catamaran or air taxi. Northbound on the Carretera Austral, it takes at least a week or 10 days to see roadside or near-roadside

Previous: the Río Futaleufú; visitors approach Glaciar Laguna San Rafael on a rigid inflatable. **Above:** the Carretera Austral.

Look for ★ to find recommended
sights, activities, dining, and lodging.

Highlights

★ **Parque Nacional Laguna San Rafael:**
The ice still reaches the sea at Laguna San
Rafael—though it's receding fast (page 276).

★ **Parque Nacional Queulat:** The hanging glacier at this park once reached the present-
day Carretera Austral. While it has receded over
the past two centuries, it still suggests what
Yosemite Valley might have looked like before its
own glaciers melted (page 280).

★ **Puyuhuapi Lodge & Spa:** It's not really
on an island, but this hot springs resort might as
well be, due to its splendid isolation (page 283).

★ **Futaleufú:** Almost every rafter and kayaker
places the Río Futaleufú among the world's top
10 white-water rivers (page 285).

★ **Parque Pumalín:** This private conservation area preserves huge extents of mid-latitude
rainforest, making it accessible to the public
(page 292).

★ **Reserva Nacional Cerro Castillo:** The
trek beneath the spires of this readily accessible
reserve makes it second only to Torres del Paine
in its popularity (page 295).

★ **Capilla de Mármol:** Accessible by water
only, the sinuous walls of these blue-white grottos line the western shores of Lago General
Carrera (page 298).

★ **Parque Patagonia:** This conservation
project's sprawling steppes and woodlands
are rich with wildlife, including guanacos, the
region's signature species (page 304).

★ **Caleta Tortel:** The only way to get around
this quaint seaside village is on foot, via the
boardwalks and staircases that connect its waterfront and scattered houses (page 308).

© AVALON TRAVEL

★ **Villa O'Higgins:** In scenic mountain
surroundings, this outpost of bureaucracy is
almost the end of the road—the Carretera
Austral stops just south of here—but it's also
the start of the rugged Cruce de Lagos trek to
El Chaltén (page 310).

highlights like Parque Nacional Queulat, the Puyuhuapi hot springs, Parque Pumalín, and the Río Futaleufú's world-class white water.

Southbound on the highway, it requires at least a week to enjoy Cerro Castillo, Lago General Carrera, the singular seaside village of Caleta Tortel, and the road's end wilderness at Villa O'Higgins.

For visitors heading south from Puerto Montt with rental cars, ferry reservations are advisable, especially for the service between Hornopirén-Leptepú and Fiordo Largo-Caleta Gonzalo.

HISTORY

Europeans first viewed Aisén's channels in 1553, when Pedro de Valdivia ordered Francisco de Ulloa to explore the Strait of Magellan from the Pacific side. When Ulloa landed on Península Taitao, though, the forerunners of today's Kawéskar (Alacaluf) people had been navigating those waterways for millennia. On the nearby continent, the Tehuelche (Aónikenk) people and their predecessors had long stalked the steppes for guanaco and the forests for *huemul*.

Aisén's thinly populated, rugged recesses held little for the Spaniards. At first, tales of "Trapananda" drew a few fortune hunters in search of the fabled but fictitious "City of the Caesars" (tales of hidden riches persist to the present, and a small reserve near Coyhaique still bears the name Trapananda). As gold fever subsided, the Spaniards settled temperate areas where they could exact tribute and labor from the indigenous population, a more dependable source of wealth until introduced diseases reduced their numbers.

In the 1670s, both Bartolomé Díaz Gallardo and Antonio de Vea came upon Laguna San Rafael and the Campo de Hielo Norte, the northern continental ice sheet. The most dedicated explorers, though, were Jesuit missionaries, working their way south from insular Chiloé by land and sea until their expulsion from the Americas in 1767. The list of non-Spaniards reads like a who's who: John Byron, grandfather of poet George Gordon (Lord Byron), suffered a shipwreck in the late 18th century, and Robert FitzRoy and Charles Darwin saw Laguna San Rafael on board the *Beagle* a few decades later. Under Admiral Thomas Baker, commanding the British navy's South American Squadron, the latter pair charted the area's waters, their work supplemented by Chilean naval officer Enrique Simpson in the 1870s.

In 1798, Spain made the region's first land grant, an enormous tract between the northern Río Yelcho and the southern Río Bravo. Argentine overland travelers were the first nonindigenous people to see much of the area. Despite concern about the Argentine presence, which led to territorial disagreements that are now resolved, Chile had trouble enough controlling areas south of the Biobío, let alone remote Aisén. Consequently, settlement lagged until the early 20th century, when it granted the Valparaíso-based Sociedad Industrial Aisén a concession for sheep ranching and forestry near present-day Coyhaique.

News of the concession set off a land rush, from the heartland and Argentina's Chubut province, by settlers who challenged the company's state-sanctioned dominance. While these smallholders held their own against the company, both of them, along with the Chilean state, bear responsibility for massive deforestation under a misguided law that encouraged cutting and burning to establish land titles. Today, when hillsides of deciduous *ñire* turn red in autumn, it's a pale reminder of what the region must have looked like decades ago, before both deliberate and unintentional wildfires denuded countless slopes, leaving pale trunks scattered among pasture grasses from Mañihuales in the north to Puerto Ibáñez in the south. Triggered by deforestation and grazing, silt carried by the Río Simpson clogged Puerto Aisén's harbor, forcing a shift to Puerto Chacabuco.

Since the 1970s, the major development has been construction of the Carretera Austral, now gradually being paved, to Villa O'Higgins. Improved relations with Argentina have brought better cross-border contacts,

Aisén and Continental Chiloé

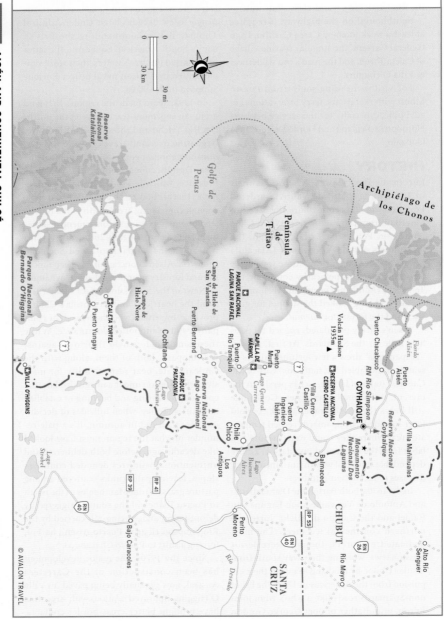

0
0

30 mi
30 km

Reserva
Nacional
Katalalixar

*Golfo de
Penas*

*Península
de
Taitao*

*Archipiélago de
los Chonos*

Parque Nacional
Bernardo O'Higgins

Campo de Hielo de
San Valentín

Campo de
Hielo Norte

PARQUE NACIONAL
LAGUNA SAN RAFAEL

Puerto Yungay

CALETA TORTEL

Puerto Bertrand

Cochrane

Puerto
Río Tranquilo

CAPILLA DE
MÁRMOL

Volcán Hudson
1905m ▲

Puerto Chacabuco

*Fiordo
Aisén*

Puerto
Aisén

RN Río Simpson

RESERVA NACIONAL
CERRO CASTILLO

COYHAIQUE

Reserva
Nacional
Coyhaique

Villa Manihuales

7

VILLA O'HIGGINS

Lago
Cochrane

PARQUE
PATAGONIA

Reserva Nacional
Lago Jeinimeni

Puerto
Murta

Lago
General
Carrera

7

Puerto
Ingeniero
Ibáñez

Villa Cerro
Castillo

★
Monumento
Nacional Dos
Lagunas

Balmaceda

Lago
Strobel

Chile
Chico

Los
Antiguos

Lago
Buenos
Aires

RP 39

RP 41

RN
40

Bajo Caracoles

Perito
Moreno

Río Desecado

RP 55

CHUBUT

RN
40

RN
26

Río Mayo

Alto Río
Senguer

**SANTA
CRUZ**

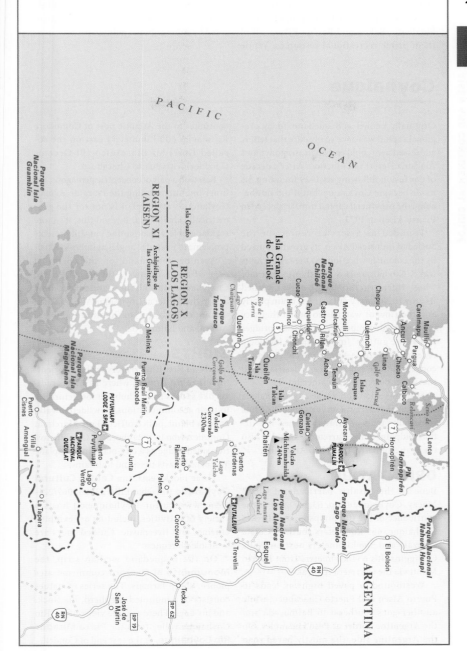

PACIFIC

OCEAN

Parque Nacional Isla Guamblin

Isla Guafo

REGION XI (AISÉN)

Archipiélago de las Guaitecas

Isla Grande de Chiloé

Parque Nacional Chiloé

REGION X (LOS LAGOS)

Parque Tantauco

Melinka

Parque Nacional Isla Magdalena

Puerto Raúl Marín Balmaceda

PUYUHUAPI LODGE & SPA

Puerto Cisnes

La Junta

Puerto Puyuhuapi

PARQUE NACIONAL QUEULAT

Lago Verde

Villa Amengual

La Tapera

José de San Martín

Lago Chaiguata

Río de la Zorra

Cucao

Huillinco

Puqueldón

Chonchi

Castro

Dalcahue

Mocopulli

Quemchi

Rilán

Achao

Tenaún

Quellón

Queilén

Isla Tranqui

Islas Chauques

Isla Talcán

Caleta Gonzalo

Golfo de Ancud

Linao

Chacao

Ancud

Carelmapu

Maullín

Quellón

Golfo de Corcovado

Volcán Corcovado 2300m

Puerto Ramírez

Palena

Corcovado

FUTALEUFÚ

Puerto Cárdenas

Lago Yelcho

Chaitén

Volcán Michinmahuida 2404m

PARQUE PUMALÍN

Ayacara

Parque Nacional Pumalín

Hornopirén

PN Hornopirén

Lenca

Seno de

Reloncaví

Calbuco

Pargua

Chepu

PARQUE NACIONAL LOS ALERCES

Lago Amutui Quimei

Lago Quimei

Parque Nacional Lago Puelo

El Bolsón

Parque Nacional Nahuel Huapi

Trevelín

Esquel

RN 40

Tecka

RP 62

RP 19

RN 40

ARGENTINA

5

7

7

7

and pressure has increased to open up the area to controversial hydroelectric projects on the Futaleufú, Baker, and Pascua Rivers, all of them prime recreational resources. While Aisén seems likely to grow, it seems unlikely to attract the large-scale immigration advocated by some regional politicians.

Coyhaique

Originally known as Baquedano, today's regional capital was once so obscure that letters addressed here could end up in an eponymous Atacama Desert rail junction. After a decade of confusion following its 1929 founding, its name became Coyhaique, but it did not become the provincial capital until it succeeded Puerto Aisén in 1973.

Founded as a service center for the Sociedad Industrial Aisén, its growth spurred by the colonists who flooded the region in its wake, Coyhaique is a mostly modern city whose infrastructure hasn't quite matched its growth. In heavy rain, streets drain poorly and the flow of water is so broad that city workers place temporary pedestrian bridges across the gutters. Improvements include a redesigned Plaza de Armas and conversion of congested Calle Horn into a pedestrian mall that's become a popular gathering place.

Still the region's only true city, Coyhaique has a complete array of services, including fine restaurants, pubs, and travel agencies. The virtual midpoint of the Carretera Austral, it also offers an alternative route into Argentina.

ORIENTATION

Beneath the basaltic barricade of Cerro Macay, Coyhaique (pop. 63,567) sits at the confluence of the Río Simpson and the Río Coyhaique, 455 kilometers south of Caleta Gonzalo and 566 kilometers north of Villa O'Higgins. It's 634 kilometers from Puerto Montt via the Carretera Austral.

Westbound, a paved highway leads to Puerto Aisén and Puerto Chacabuco, while another goes southeast to Balmaceda and the Argentine border at Paso Huemules. On the Argentine side, the mostly paved road

continues to the Atlantic port of Comodoro Rivadavia, 600 kilometers east on the so-called Corredor Bioceánico (Bi-Oceanic Corridor) with Puerto Chacabuco.

Based on a pair of concentric pentagons, the inner one surrounding the Plaza de Armas, Coyhaique's street plan is not for the geometrically challenged. Beyond this, it's more regular and less disorienting but still presents problems of irregular angles at intersections.

Avenida Baquedano, on the northeast edge of town, connects the paved Puerto Chacabuco road with the gravel road leading east to the border at Coyhaique Alto. Avenida Ogana leads to the southbound Carretera Austral and Balmaceda.

SIGHTS

Nearly all first-time visitors to the disorienting **Plaza de Armas,** where 10 streets radiate like spokes from a hub, get lost returning to their accommodations. Bewildered walkers can blame police officer Luis Marchant González, who in 1929 chose the Carabineros' five-sided badge as a city-planning template. The plaza boasts trees and fountains.

Three blocks east, the **Centro Cultural Coyhaique** (Eusebio Lillo 23, tel. 067/221-1596, www.culturalcoyhaique.cl) hosts a variety of activities, including art exhibits, cinema, and live music. Guided tours are available on request.

On the Baquedano median strip, the **Monumento al Ovejero** commemorates pioneer sheep farmers. The series of statues consists of a mounted shepherd, his flock, and his dogs. There are fine views of the Río Coyhaique valley from the **Plaza Mirador Río Coyhaique,** at the east end of Condell.

Coyhaique

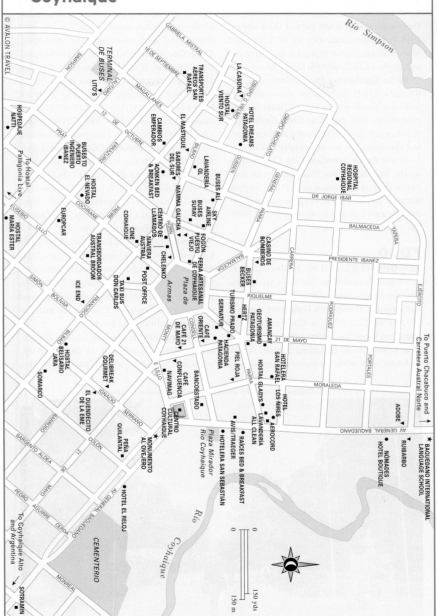

© AVALON TRAVEL

Río Simpson

Río Coyhaique

CEMENTERIO

0   150 yds
0   150 m

To Puerto Chacabuco and
Carretera Austral Norte

★ BAQUEDANO INTERNATIONAL
   LANGUAGE SCHOOL

● NÓMADES
  HOTEL BOUTIQUE

● RUIBARBO

ADOBE ●

AV GENERAL BAQUEDANO

● HOTELERA SAN SEBASTIAN

Plaza Mirador
Río Coyhaique

● RAÍCES BED & BREAKFAST

AVISTRAEGER ■

LAVANDERIA ■
ALL CLEAN

AEROCORD ■

HOTEL ■
LOS ÑIRES

HOTELERA ■
SAN RAFAEL

HOSTAL GLADYS ●

MORALEDA

PORTALES

EJÉRCITO

MONUMENTO
AL OVEJERO ■

CENTRO
CULTURAL
COYHAIQUE

● HOTEL EL RELOJ

PEÑA
QUILANTAL ■

EL DUENDECITO
DE LA EME ■

DELIBREAK
GOURMET ▼

HOSTAL
BELISARIO
JARA ■

SOMARCO ■

BARROSO

SARGENTO ALDEA

PEDRO
AGUIRRE
CERDA

To Coyhaique Alto
and Argentina

SOTRAMIN ■

MONREAL

MAYO

COLÓN

SERRANO

IGNACIO

E LILLO

AV GENERAL BAQUEDANO

SIMÓN
BOLÍVAR

FRANCISCO

MONTT

CONDELL

BILBAO

BAQUEDANO

ICE END ■

TRANSBORDADORA ■
AUSTRAL BROOM

EUROPCAR ■

HOSTAL
MARÍA ESTER ■

EUSEBIO
LILLO

HOSPEDAJE
NATTI ■

LATINASUR
LITO'S ▼

To Hostal
Patagonia Live

COCHRANE

HOSTAL
EL NEVADO ■

CINE
COIHAIQUE ■

TAXI BUS
DON CARLOS ■

POST OFFICE ■

NAVIERA
AUSTRAL ■

CHELENCO ■

CENTRO DE
LLAMADOS ■

AONIKEN BED
& BREAKFAST ■

SABORES
DEL SUR ▼

MAMMA GAUCHA ▼

HORN

FREIRE

PRAT

12 DE OCTUBRE

PAT BRUN ERSTZ

BUSES TO
PUERTO
INGENIERO
IBÁÑEZ ■

CAMBIOS
EMPERADOR ■

EL MÁSTIQUE ■

LAVANDERIA,
OL. ■

BUSES ALÍ ■

SKY
AIRLINE ■

BUSES
SURAY ■

FOGÓN
PUESTO
VIEJO ■

FERIA ARTESANAL
DE COYHAIQUE ■

Plaza de
Armas

Plaza de

BUSES
BECKER ■

CASINO DE
BOMBEROS ■

SERNATUR ■

TURISMO PRADO ▼

HERTZ ■

CAFÉ
ORIENTE ▼

CAFÉ 21
DE MAYO ▼

HACIENDA
PATAGONIA ▼

PIEL ROJA ■

GEOTURISMO
PATAGONIA ▼

AMANCAY ■

CAFÉ
CONFLUENCIA ■

NAVIMAG ▼

BANCOESTADO ■

RIQUELME

BALMACEDA

21 DE MAYO

PRESIDENTE IBÁÑEZ

DR JORGE IBAR

BALMACEDA

CARRERA

PARRA

RODRIGUEZ

CONDELL

GENERAL PARRA

OBISPO MICHELATO

OBISPO VIELMO

DISSEN

TERMINAL
DE BUSES ■

SIMPSON

GABRIELA MISTRAL

18 DE SEPTIEMBRE

MAGALLANES

LA CASONA ■

TRANSPORTES
AÉREOS SAN
RAFAEL ■

HOSTAL
VIENTO SUR ■

HOTEL DREAMS
PATAGONIA ●

HOSPITAL
REGIONAL
COYHAIQUE ■

TAPERA

ENTERTAINMENT AND SHOPPING

Coyhaique has a growing number of bars, but their aspirations often exceed their appeal. **Piel Roja** (Moraleda 495, tel. 067/223-6635, www.pielroja.cl), for instance, has pizza and pub grub, and a 7pm-9pm happy hour.

Peña Quilantal (Baquedano 791, tel. 067/223-4394) sometimes showcases live folkloric music but is just as likely to offer run-of-the-mill pop. The **Cine Coihaique** (Cochrane 321) shows occasional recent films, but also hosts live music, usually folkloric.

At the **Feria Artesanal de Coyhaique,** on the west side of the Plaza de Armas, local horse gear is the main attraction, supplemented by wood carvings and woolens. **Amancay** (21 de Mayo 340, tel. 067/221-6099) has custom chocolates.

FOOD

Café Oriente (Condell 201, tel. 067/223-1622, lunch and dinner Mon.-Sat.) is a traditional spot for sandwiches, *onces* (afternoon tea), and desserts. **Delibreak Gourmet** (Serrano 143, tel. 067/221-1522, 8:30am-1:30pm and 2pm-7pm Mon.-Sat.) offers a diversity of takeaway baked goods, including cinnamon rolls and Argentine-style *medialunas* (croissants).

For inexpensive light meals, try **Café de Mayo** (21 de Mayo 543, tel. 09/6217-4897, 10am-9pm Mon.-Sat.), whose offerings include sandwiches, quiches, kuchen, espresso drinks, and garden seating. Across the street, **Café Confluencia** (21 de Mayo 548, tel. 067/224-5080, 10am-11:30pm Mon.-Sat.) has similar offerings and a bit more indoor space.

Despite an almost foreboding exterior, **Lito's** (Lautaro 147, tel. 067/225-4528, lunch and dinner Mon.-Sat., US$9-12) has a spacious dining area with an attractive bar and above-average versions of Chilean beef, fish, and seafood. In more appealing surroundings, ★ **Sabores del Sur** (12 de Octubre 308, tel. 067/221-0801, US$12-15) is also notable for seafood—its mixed shellfish appetizer (US$13), in a slightly spicy *pil pil* sauce, makes an excellent light lunch.

Another fine option, best for seafood, is ★ **La Casona** (Obispo Vielmo 77, tel. 067/223-8894, noon-3pm and 7:30pm-midnight Mon.-Sat., noon-3pm Sun. and holidays, US$10-15), for lamb, *pastel de jaiva* (crab soufflé), and other regional entrées. The service matches the high quality of the food.

The sign outside may say "Adobe Bistro," but **Adobe** (Baquedano 9, tel. 067/224-0486, www.adobecoyhaique.cl, US$10) is more a

Coyhaique's Plaza de Armas features stands of mature conifers and smaller deciduous trees.

brews and pub grub type of place. The menu does include ceviches and tapas, however.

With a Chilean menu enhanced by top-quality ingredients, the **Casino de Bomberos** (General Parra 365, tel. 067/223-1437, lunch and dinner daily) is an institution and one of the country's more expensive fire-station restaurants. **El Duendecito de la Eme** (Serrano 150, tel. 09/9499-9291, 12:30pm-3:30pm and 6pm-11pm Mon.-Fri., 1pm-4pm and 6pm-11pm Sat., 12:30pm-4pm Sun.) does all-you-can-eat pizza, but also has individual pie options for the less ravenous.

★ **Mamma Gaucha** (Paseo Horn 47, tel. 067/221-0721, 10am-12:30am Mon.-Sat., US$10) has been an overwhelming success for remarkable thin-crusted pizzas, light on cheese, with a far greater variety of toppings than available even in Santiago's best pizzerias—think shredded chicken with sautéed red onions and cilantro. The kitchen may be a little slow, but the service is cheerful.

For light cooking to international standards, Hotel El Reloj's ★ **El Ovejero** (Baquedano 828, tel. 067/223-1108, lunch and dinner daily, US$15) comes highly recommended for entrées such as *congrio al ajillo* (conger eel with garlic) and Patagonian desserts, including rhubarb mousse. Grab a window table for views over the river.

Chelenko (Paseo Horn 47, tel. 09/5419-3246, 9am-11pm Mon.-Sat.) is the direct successor of the historic Café Ricer, reinvented as a "Patagonian steakhouse" in smaller quarters—they occupy only the ground level of a local institution whose upstairs dining room fed generations here. Chelenko also operates an ice cream stand that's sometimes out on the sidewalk.

New in late 2016, **Fogón Puesto Viejo** (Prat 230, tel. 067/7529-2532, www.fogonpuestoviejo.cl, 12:30pm-3:30pm and 8pm-11:30pm Mon. and Wed.-Sat., 12:30pm-4pm Sun., US$13) is an upscale steakhouse that suggests locals are demanding more of their traditional grill restaurants. Certain cuts, though, still come in "local" and slightly more expensive "premium" versions.

Far more imposing, ★ **Hacienda Patagonia** (21 de Mayo 461, tel. 067/223-3933, www.haciendapatagonia.cl, US$15-20) is the similarly upscale restaurant of an events center that serves grilled meats with a varied menu that includes lamb, fish and seafood, pastas, and even sandwiches. It's a good option for an end-of-trip splurge.

In a similar category, ★ **Ruibarbo** (Baquedano 208, tel. 067/221-1826, www.ruibarborestaurant.cl, US$15-20) is a more intimate and sophisticated dining experience, with specialties like lamb tongue risotto on the menu. The menu changes seasonally.

Probably Coyhaique's most stylish dining option, ★ **Ice End** (Bilbao 563, tel. 067/222-3006, lunch Tues.-Sun., dinner Tues.-Sat., US$20) uses local touches to accentuate Chilean standards—such as adding the exquisite wild mushroom *morilla* to its fish sauces. There are also meat dishes, and an extensive pasta menu.

ACCOMMODATIONS

Coyhaique's accommodations scene is unusual, with plenty of budget and mid-range choices and few upmarket options. With some exceptions, budget accommodations are only so-so.

US$25-50

One of the cheapest options is **Hospedaje Natti** (Almirante Simpson 417, tel. 067/223-1047, natividad.eulalia@gmail.com, US$18 pp with shared bath); camping (US$10 pp) is also possible. Breakfast costs extra.

Under new ownership, the backpackers' best is ★ **Hostal Salamandras** (Sector los Pinos s/n, tel. 067/221-1865, www.salamandras.cl, US$23 pp with shared bath, US$38 s, US$61 d with private bath and kitchen access), on piney grounds about two kilometers southwest of downtown on the old airport road. Most rooms in this attractive building, with large communal spaces, are dorms, but there are a few doubles. Camping (US$10 pp) is also possible.

US$50-100

For the price, it's hard to find anything better than pristine, friendly **Hostal María Ester** (Lautaro 544, tel. 067/223-3023, hospedajemariaester@hotmail.com, US$20-37 s, US$36-53 d). Rates vary according to shared or private bath; breakfast (US$4) costs extra.

Quiet, well-located, spotless, and tobacco-free, ★ **Hostal Gladys** (General Parra 65, tel. 067/224-5288, www.hostalgladys.cl, US$30-53 s, US$53-68 d with cable TV and Wi-Fi) has transformed a simple but pleasant family-run B&B into stylish accommodations with spacious new rooms and high ceilings. Only the street-side rooms have windows (though all have skylights), and a couple older rooms are cramped with too many beds. Breakfast, which costs extra, varies in quality.

Another of Coyhaique's best values, in a central but residential area, **Hostal El Nevado** (Cochrane 495-A, tel. 09/9624-2533, www.hostalelnevado.cl, US$30 s US$60 d with shared bath, US$67 s or d with private bath, breakfast included) offers comfortable mid-size rooms and accommodating ownership. All rooms have flat-screen TVs.

Central and tranquil, the unadorned **Aonken Bed & Breakfast** (12 de Octubre 338, tel. 067/223-4792, www.contactaonken. wixsite.com, US$37 pp with private bath) is a rambling family home transformed into a comfy B&B with ample common areas (the family still lives in a newer house out back). The rooms vary in size, the decor is utilitarian—except when it's kitschy—and there's an ample if unimaginative breakfast, and secure parking as well.

In a residential neighborhood, **Hostal Español** (Sargento Aldea 343, tel. 067/224-2580, www.hostalcoyhaique.cl, US$52 s, US$70 d with continental breakfast) is a polished product with upstairs view rooms.

★ **Hostal Patagonia Live** (Eusebio Lillo 826, tel. 067/223-0892, www.hostalpatagonialive.cl, US$53 s, US$65-79 d) is a friendly four-room B&B that features stylish furniture, central heating, double-paned windows, flat-screen TVs, and Wi-Fi in all rooms. The above-average breakfast is a bonus.

On a quiet block, **Hostal Viento Sur** (Obispo Vielmo 71, tel. 067/223-2707, www. hostalvientosur.cl, US$53 s, US$68 d) is luminous and spacious. However, the open floor plan lets noise carry into the upstairs sleeping quarters.

In some rooms at **Hotel Los Ñires** (Av. Baquedano 315, tel. 067/223-2261, www.hotellosnires.cl, US$68 s, US$81 d), large beds occupy most of the floor space, but the baths are spacious and it has a quality restaurant.

Hotelera San Rafael (Moraleda 343, tel. 067/223-3733, www.hotelerasanrafael.cl, US$74 s, US$83 d) has tasteful, spacious, and sunny hotel rooms along with *cabaña*-style accommodations.

US$100-150

Overseas tour operators often choose **Hostal Belisario Jara** (Bilbao 662, tel./fax 067/223-4150, www.belisariojara.cl, US$100 s, US$127 d), which has more architectural distinction and personality than most hotels here. It has just eight rooms.

On a site overlooking the Río Coyhaique, genial ★ **Hotel El Reloj** (Baquedano 828, tel./fax 067/223-1108, www.elrelojhotel.cl, US$99 s, US$129 d with breakfast) has fine accommodations and an exceptional restaurant as well.

Also overlooking the river, **Raíces Bed & Breakfast** (Baquedano 444, tel. 067/221-0490, www.raicesbedandbreakfast.com, US$90 s, US$130 d) enjoys modern conveniences but a rustic style, with blond pine details.

US$150-200

Part of the widespread casino franchise, **Hotel Dreams Patagonia** (Magallanes 131, tel. 067/226-4717, US$175 s or d) is a handsomely overbuilt structure, with 20 suites and 17 standard rooms, in a region that can hardly support it—except, perhaps, in summer.

The **Nómades Hotel Boutique** (Baquedano 84, tel. 067/223-7777, www.

nomadeshotel.com, US$120 s, US$155-240 d) is a seven-room facility with a stylishly imposing exterior, vast common areas and large rooms with wood accents, and views over the Río Coyhaique from all of them. It's ostensibly adding a pool.

INFORMATION

Sernatur (Bulnes 35, tel. 067/224-0290, infoaisen@sernatur.cl, 9am-8pm Mon.-Fri., 10am-8pm Sat., 10:30am-4:30pm Sun. summer, 9am-6:30pm Mon.-Fri., 9am-6pm Sat. fall-spring) has capable English-speaking staff.

Directly on the Plaza de Armas, Coyhaique's private **Cámara de Turismo** (tel. 067/222-1403, www.aysenpatagonia.cl, 9am-7pm Mon.-Sat., 9am-1pm and 3pm-7pm Sun.) operates a summer-only office.

South of downtown, Conaf's **Patrimonio Silvestre** (Los Coihues s/n, tel. 067/221-2125, aysen@conaf.cl) provides information on national parks and reserves.

SERVICES

Coyhaique has the region's most complete services. Changing money, in particular, is easier than elsewhere on the Carretera Austral.

Turismo Prado (21 de Mayo 417, tel. 067/223-4843) and **Cambios Emperador** (Freire 171, tel. 067/223-3727) both exchange cash and traveler's checks. **BancoEstado** (Moraleda 502) and several other banks have ATMs.

For postal services, **Correos de Chile** (Cochrane 226) is near the Plaza de Armas. The **Centro de Llamados** (Paseo Horn 40) has phones and fax service.

Intensive **Spanish classes** with homestay room and full board are offered at **Baquedano International Language School** (Baquedano 20, tel. 067/223-2520, www.balasch.cl, from US$600 per week). Rates include four hours of instruction Monday-Saturday, plus accommodations, meals, and laundry.

For laundry, try **Lavandería QL** (Bilbao 160, tel. 067/223-2266) or **Lavandería All**

Clean (General Parra 55, Local 2, tel. 067/221-9635), alongside Residencial Gladys.

For medical attention, contact the **Hospital Regional Coyhaique** (Dr. Jorge Ibar 068, tel. 067/226-2002, www.hospitalregionalcoyhaique.cl).

TRANSPORTATION

Coyhaique is the region's transportation hub, with flights north and south as well as bus service along the Carretera Austral to Region X (Los Lagos) and Region XII (Magallanes), and to Argentina. Chilean buses to destinations in other regions cannot drop passengers in Argentina.

Air

Commercial jets land at modern **Aeropuerto Balmaceda,** (BBA, tel. 02/2222-8400, www.aeropuertobalmaceda.com) 50 kilometers southeast of Coyhaique. Small planes still use convenient **Aeródromo Teniente Vidal,** only five kilometers southwest of town. **Taxis** to Aeropuerto Teniente Vidal are cheap enough (about US$8), but air-taxi companies usually provide their own transfers. To Aeropuerto Balmaceda, about 45 minutes away, door-to-door minivan services (US$10 pp) include **Transfer Velásquez** (tel. 09/8505-0886, transfer.velasquez@gmail.com) and **Transfer Valencia** (tel. 067/223-3030, www.transfervalencia.cl).

LATAM (tel. 0600/526-2000, www.latam.com) has closed its Coyhaique office in favor of Internet and telephone sales, but still flies several times daily from Balmaceda to Puerto Montt and Santiago, occasionally to Punta Arenas, and in summer to Puerto Natales. **Sky Airline** (Prat 203, tel. 067/224-0825) flies daily to Puerto Montt and the Chilean capital, and south to Punta Arenas.

Transportes Aéreos San Rafael (18 de Septiembre 469, tel. 067/257-3083, www.transportesaereossanrafael.cl) flies to the island settlement of Melinka (US$38) and on to Quellón (US$30 more) Tuesday and Thursday. **Aerocord** (General Parra 21, tel. 067/224-6300, www.aerocord.cl) flies to Villa

The Dictator's Highway?

The road where Santiaguinos come to test their SUVs, the Carretera Austral is so crucial to Aisén that Coyhaique's former museum devoted its largest exhibit to the road. Some residents still give General Pinochet credit—one conspicuous photo showed a grandfatherly Pinochet, in civilian dress, beaming at a local schoolboy. A frequent comment is that the military regime was "the last one to pay attention to the region," and one Pinochet partisan proclaimed that "the politicians would never have built this highway. There are no votes here."

But Pinochet may get more credit than he deserves. The original highway studies date from 1968, during President Eduardo Frei Montalva's Christian Democrat government, and the project advanced during Salvador Allende's Socialist administration until Pinochet's 1973 coup. Work accelerated during the dictatorship, but civilian contractors did more than the military.

The Carretera's final irony is that the man who finished it, President Ricardo Lagos (in office 2000-2006), is the man who stared down Pinochet in 1988 through a TV camera: "You promise the country another eight years of torture, disappearances, and human rights violations." Lagos's bravery probably turned the tide in a plebiscite that ended Pinochet's reign. Maps once labeled "Carretera Longitudinal Austral Presidente Pinochet" now say "Carretera Longitudinal Austral."

Despite its sympathy for the far-right UDI (Unión Demócratica Independiente), the entire town

O'Higgins (US$43) Monday and Thursday, a route on which local residents have priority.

Bus

More carriers now use the **Terminal de Buses** (Lautaro 109, tel. 067/223-2067), but several still prefer their own offices elsewhere. Services north and south along the Carretera Austral are most frequent in summer and may be considerably fewer in winter.

To Puerto Aisén (1 hour, US$3), there are frequent departures with **Buses Suray** (Prat 265, tel. 067/223-8387, www.suray.cl) and **Buses Alí** (Dussen 283, tel. 067/223-2788, www.busesali.cl), but continuing to Puerto Chacabuco requires changing buses in Aisén.

At the main terminal, **Buses São Paulo** (tel. 067/225-5726) goes north to Mañihuales (1 hour, US$5) and Puerto Cisnes (4pm Mon.-Sat., 6 hours, US$9) via the paved Viviana junction. **Terra Austral** (tel. 067/225-4335) goes to Cisnes (6am Mon.-Sat., 10am Sun.), and to Chaitén (8am Tues., Thurs., and Sun. summer only, US$30).

Águilas Patagónicas (tel. 067/221-1288, www.aguilaspatagonicas.cl) goes to Puerto Puyuhuapi (3pm daily, US$12) and La Junta (US$15), and south to Puerto Río Tranquilo

and Cochrane (US$22). **Buses Bronco** (tel. 09/6610-5214) does the Puyuhuapi-La Junta route (8am Tues.), as does **Buses Don Pedro** (tel. 067/221-2916, at 5pm daily). **Transporte Laguna** (tel. 09/9372-8591, 8am Sat.), which picks up passengers at their home address or hotel, also travels this route. **Transportes ECA** (Alejandro Gutiérrez 79, tel. 09/7378-4094) goes to Puerto Guadal (1pm Tues. and Fri., US$16).

Buses Becker (General Parra 329, tel. 067/223-2167, www.busesbecker.com) normally goes to Chaitén (10.5 hours, US$36) three times weekly via Puerto Puyuhuapi (US$13), La Junta (7 hours, US$18), and intermediates. In summer there is Friday service to Futaleufú (US$36).

To Puerto Ingeniero Ibáñez (2 hours, US$8), on Lago General Carrera's north shore, **Buses Carolina** (tel. 067/221-9009) connects with the Chile Chico ferry. Ibáñez-bound minibus drivers, such as **Miguel Acuña** (Manuel Rodríguez 143, tel. 067/225-1579) usually pick up passengers at their homes or hotels, but some also stop at the corner of Moraleda and General Carrera.

Other southbound minibuses go as far as Villa Cerro Castillo (1.5 hours, US$6-7),

of Villa O'Higgins showed up in April 2000, when Pinochet's nemesis Lagos, as president, formally dedicated the Río Bravo–Villa O'Higgins segment, the final piece in the puzzle.

The notoriously timid *huemul*, the emblematic, endangered Andean deer that graces Chile's coat of arms (along with the Andean condor and the motto "by reason or force") is surprisingly common and even docile along this last segment. In a sense, it's a tangible symbol of change and the openness that the highway represents—not force alone, but reason as well. The highway that began as a military exercise now belongs to everyone.

Some pioneer settlements along the Carretera Austral are acquiring an air of permanence, but this is still wild country, with just enough creature comforts for those on bigger budgets. Prices are highest and public transport most frequent in January and February, when most Chileans take their vacations. The spring months of October and November and the autumn months of March and April can be good times to travel, though public transportation is less frequent.

While this may be one of the continent's loveliest roads—there's no bad scenery—it's still one of the most hazardous. Paved segments are steadily increasing, but blind curves in dense forests and sheer mountains, narrow segments with steeply sloping shoulders, and frequent loose gravel still require drivers to pay the closest attention to avoid head-on collisions, rollovers, and other accidents.

where the pavement ends on the Carretera Austral: **Minibuses Javier Alí** (tel. 09/9313-1402) leaves from Prat and Lautaro, opposite the Unimarc supermarket, but with a day's notice they'll come to your hotel. **Minibus Víctor Vidal** (tel. 09/9932-9896) goes to Puerto Río Tranquilo (9am Wed. and Sat., 5 hours, US$12).

From the main terminal, **Acuario 13** (tel. 067/225-5726) goes beyond Cerro Castillo to Cochrane (9am Wed., Fri., and Sun., 9 hours, US$22) and intermediates, as does **Buses São Paulo** (Tues., Thurs., Sat.), at the same office, and **Don Carlos** (Subteniente Cruz 63, tel. 067/223-2981, 9am Sun.-Tues. and Thurs.-Fri.). **Transportes Seguel** (Errázuriz 1358, tel. 09/8473-8731) goes to Puerto Guadal (1pm Wed.).

Other southbound fares include Puerto Río Tranquilo (5.5 hours, US$15), Puerto Guadal (7 hours, US$16), and Puerto Bertrand (8 hours, US$19).

In summer, from the main terminal, **Queilen Bus** (tel. 067/224-0760) goes to Puerto Montt (2pm Mon., Wed., and Fri., 24 hours, US$60) via Argentina. Fall to spring, the service runs only on Friday.

In the same main terminal office,

TransAustral (tel. 067/223-2067) serves Comodoro Rivadavia (9am Mon. and Fri., 9 hours, US$42), Argentina, via Río Mayo and Sarmiento, with northbound connections to Esquel and Bariloche.

Sea

Coyhaique is not a seaport, but the local office of **Navimag Ferries** (Eusebio Lillo 91, tel. 067/222-3306) sells ferry berths from Puerto Chacabuco to Puerto Montt (3pm Tues. and 5pm Fri.).

Naviera Austral (Paseo Horn 40, Oficina 101, tel. 067/221-0727, www.navieraustral.cl) operates ferries from Puerto Chacabuco to Quellón (Chiloé) (8pm Mon. and noon Fri.).

Transbordador Austral Broom (Lillo 377, 2nd Fl., tel. 067/221-4771, www.tabsa.cl) sells space on the new car-passenger ferry that connects Puerto Yungay (Caleta Tortel) with Puerto Natales.

Car Rental

Even shoestring travelers indulge themselves on car rentals in Aisén, since public transportation is less frequent than elsewhere and some sights are off the main north-south route. Because the fleet is small and demand can be high, summer reservations are essential.

Among Coyhaique's rental agencies are **Traeger** (Av. Baquedano 457, tel. 067/223-1648, www.traeger.cl), **Europcar** (Errázuriz 454, tel. 067/267-8652), and **Hertz** (General Parra 280, tel. 067/229-4104).

VICINITY OF COYHAIQUE

Coyhaique is an ideal base for activities like hiking, fly-fishing, rafting, and even winter skiing. **Fishing** probably tops the list, as the season runs November to May in the numerous lakes and rivers. For day trips, Luis Miranda's **Patagone Travelling** (tel. 09/4207-1314, www.patagonetravelling.com) offers horseback rides and a float trip that, in its latter stages, becomes Class III white water.

U.S.-run, Puerto Bertrand-based **Patagonia Adventure Expeditions** (Casilla 8, Cochrane, tel. 09/8182-0608, www.adventurepatagonia.com) offers extended fishing and backcountry trips; U.S.-Chilean **Salvaje Corazón** (Casilla 311, tel. 067/221-1488, www.salvajecorazon.com; U.S. tel. 0415/990-7748) is a reliable operator that can handle English, Hebrew, Portuguese, and some French.

Geoturismo Patagonia (21 de Mayo 398, tel. 067/258-3173, www.carretera-austral.net) helps organize driving tours of the Carretera Austral with its own vehicles and 24-hour logistical support in case of problems on this still-challenging route.

Reserva Nacional Coyhaique

Few cities anywhere have so much wild country so nearby as the mountainous 2,676-hectare **Reserva Nacional Coyhaique,** with its top-of-the-world views of Coyhaique, Cerro Macay, and Cerro Castillo to the south; the Río Simpson Valley to the west; and the Patagonian plains sprawling eastward. Local residents enjoy weekend picnics and barbecues here, only five kilometers north of town. There's always space away from the crowds, and on weekdays it's almost empty.

Elevation ranges from 400 meters to 1,361 meters on Cerro Cinchao's summit. More than 1,000 millimeters of rain and snow fall throughout the year. Summers are mild and fairly dry, with an average temperature of 12°C.

While the reserve is wild and almost undeveloped, it's not exactly pristine. Forests of *coigüe (Nothofagus betuloides)* and *lenga (Nothofagus pumilio)* blanket the hillsides, but plantations of exotic pines and larches—some of them now being removed—replaced some of the native forest devastated in the 1940s. So close to the city, birds are the most conspicuous wildlife.

The main sights are literally that—the seemingly infinite panoramas in every direction. Several trails offer different perspectives on those panoramas: the 800-meter **Sendero Laguna Verde,** the four-kilometer **Sendero Laguna Venus,** and the **Sendero Las Piedras,** which leads to Cerro Cinchao's summit.

Most visitors stay in town, but **Conaf** (tel. 067/221-2125 in Coyhaique, camping US$7 for up to six people) has a rustic 6-site campground at **Laguna Verde** and a 10-siter at **Casa Bruja.** Two of the Laguna Verde sites have roofed shelters. All sites have picnic tables, potable water, and fire pits. Casa Bruja has toilets and hot showers. Bring as much food as necessary. At the entrance, Conaf collects an admission charge (US$4.50 adults, US$2 children).

Three kilometers north of town via the paved highway to Puerto Chacabuco, a dirt lateral road climbs steeply east to the reserve. The road is passable for most vehicles in summer but can be difficult with rain. It's close enough to the city that anyone in decent physical condition should be able to hike from the highway to the park entrance in about half an hour.

Reserva Nacional Río Simpson

Northwest of Coyhaique, midway to Puerto Chacabuco, paved Ruta 240 passes through the Río Simpson Valley, flanked by the steep walls and canyons that form the accessible 41,634-hectare **Reserva Nacional Río Simpson.**

Elevations are about 100 meters along the river but rise to 1,878 meters in the cordillera. Because it's mostly lower than Reserva Nacional Coyhaique, the weather is milder (15-17°C in summer). It's also wetter, as westerly storms drop up to 2,500 millimeters of precipitation en route inland.

As at Coyhaique, Río Simpson's forests are mostly native southern beeches (*Nothofagus* species). The rainfall fosters verdant undergrowth of ferns, fuchsias, and the like. *Huemul* are found in the more remote areas, as are puma and *pudú.* Bird species, which include the Andean condor, diminish in autumn and winter, returning in spring.

At Km 37, look for the **Cascada La Virgen,** a waterfall that plunges vertically through intense greenery on the highway's north side. Two kilometers east of park headquarters, Conaf's eight-site **Camping San Sebastián** (Ruta 240, Km 30, US$11 per tent) has baths with hot showers.

Conaf's **Centro de Información Ambiental** (Ruta 240, Km 32) boasts a small **natural-history museum** (8:30am-5:30pm daily, US$4.50 adults, US$2 children) and botanical garden. From Coyhaique, Suray buses will drop passengers at the campground, museum, or anywhere along the route.

Puerto Chacabuco and Vicinity

The forests that thrived here before the 1940s wildfires were more than just landscape embellishments. Their foliage softened the impact of heavy storms and impeded soil erosion. One effect of the fire-fed devastation was to clog Puerto Aisén's harbor with Río Simpson's sediments, forcing authorities to build new port facilities at Puerto Chacabuco, 14 kilometers west.

Now the region's main maritime gateway, Chacabuco is also the departure point for excursions to Parque Nacional Laguna San Rafael and a stopover on some voyages between Puerto Montt and Laguna San Rafael.

Food and Accommodations

With 60 rooms in three separate modules, ★ **Hotel Loberías del Sur** (J. M. Carrera 50, tel. 067/235-1112, www.loberiasdelsur. cl, US$166 s or d, with buffet breakfast) may be the region's best pure hotel (as opposed to lodges and resorts, though it also does

Reserva Nacional Río Simpson

promote its own packages). Everything runs like clockwork, including a fine restaurant and catamaran excursions to Laguna San Rafael. It even has its own 250-hectare forest reserve nearby. The rooms are spacious, with bay windows and king beds. Amenities include a gym, a sauna, and Wi-Fi.

Transportation

Buses shuttle frequently between Puerto Chacabuco and Coyhaique, 82 kilometers east via Ruta 240.

Both long-distance ferries and excursions to Parque Nacional Laguna San Rafael leave from the **Terminal de Transbordadores,** part of the port complex. **Naviera Austral** (Coyhaique tel. 067/221-0727) operates the passenger and vehicle ferry *Barcaza Queulat* (11pm Mon. and noon Fri., US$25 pp, vehicles US$198, motorcycles US$36, bicycles US$11) to Quellón (Chiloé).

★ PARQUE NACIONAL LAGUNA SAN RAFAEL

Flowing ice meets frigid sea at Laguna San Rafael. Frozen pinnacles tumble from the crackling face of Ventisquero San Rafael, a 60-meter-high glacier that descends from the Campo de Hielo Norte, to become bobbing icebergs. Misleadingly named, **Laguna San Rafael** is really an ocean inlet, though its salinity is low as the icebergs slowly thaw and the receding glacier—a palpable victim of global warming that may no longer reach the sea within a few years—discharges freshwater into it.

One of Chile's largest national parks with 1.74 million hectares of rugged terrain, Laguna San Rafael is a UNESCO World Biosphere Reserve for its extraordinary scenery and environments. While remote from any settlement, it's a popular summer excursion for Chileans and foreigners and is accessible year-round.

History

For a place so thinly populated and rarely visited, Laguna San Rafael has an intriguing history. Its first European visitor was Spaniard Bartolomé Díaz Gallardo, who crossed the low-lying Istmo de Ofqui (Isthmus of Ofqui) from the Golfo de Penas. Jesuit missionaries visited in 1766 and 1767, bestowing its present name, but the Spanish king soon expelled them from the continent.

British naval officer John Byron, grandfather of poet Lord Byron, once spent a winter marooned here. During the voyage of the *Beagle,* Charles Darwin made extensive observations, while Chilean naval officer Enrique Simpson delivered the first official report in 1871. In 1940, the government began a canal across the isthmus to simplify communications with the far south but soon gave up the project. In 1959 it declared the area a national park, but as late as the 1980s it entertained proposals to build a road for cargo transshipments.

Geography and Climate

Laguna San Rafael is 225 kilometers southwest of Puerto Chacabuco via a series of narrow channels, but only 190 kilometers from Coyhaique as the air taxi flies. To the east rises the rugged Patagonian mainland; to the west lie the myriad islands of the Archipiélago de Chonos and the Península de Taitao.

Elevations range from sea level to 4,058-meter Monte San Valentín, the southern Andes's highest peak. Sea-level temperatures are fairly mild, about 8°C, with upward of 2,500 millimeters of rainfall per year. At higher elevations, precipitation doubles, temperatures are colder, and the snowfall feeds 19 major glaciers that form the 300,000-hectare Campo de Hielo Norte. Pacific storms can darken the skies for weeks on end, but views are stunning when the overcast lifts.

Flora and Fauna

In areas not covered by ice, up to about 700 meters elevation, mixed Valdivian forest grows so dense that, wrote Darwin, "our faces, hands and shin-bones all bore witness to the maltreatment we received, in attempting to penetrate their forbidding recesses."

The main trees are two species of the southern beech *coigüe*, the coniferous *mañío macho (Podocarpus nubigena), tepu,* and other species, with an understory of shrubs, ferns, mosses, and vines. Above 700 meters, there is almost equally dense forest of the southern beeches *lenga* and *ñire*, with occasional specimens of the coniferous Guaitecas cypress.

Most of the easily visible wildlife congregates around the shoreline, beginning with eye-catching seabirds, such as the flightless steamer duck and Magellanic penguin, black-browed and sooty albatrosses, and various gulls. Marine mammals include the southern elephant seal, southern sea lion, and southern sea otter.

Forest-dwelling animals are harder to see, but *pudú* and *huemul* graze the uplands, while foxes and pumas prowl for prey.

Sights and Recreation

Calving off the face of **Ventisquero San Rafael,** indigo icebergs bob and drift in the waters of **Laguna San Rafael,** an oval body of water measuring six to nine kilometers in width and connected to the southern canals by the narrow Río Témpanos. The world's lowest-latitude tidewater glacier, Ventisquero San Rafael may not be so much longer. In continuous retreat since 1960, it could become a casualty of global warming.

Few visitors actually set foot in the park, as most arrive by ferry or catamaran, transferring to inflatables to meander among the bergs and approach the glacier's face. Those who manage to land can hike through seven kilometers of evergreen forest on the **Sendero al Ventisquero** to a glacial overlook.

Accommodations

At park headquarters, Conaf's three-site **Camping Laguna Caiquenes** (US$8 pp for up to 6 campers) allows no campfires. Contact Conaf's Coyhaique Patrimonio Silvestre office (Los Coihues s/n, tel. 067/221-2125) reservations. Dome tents are also available via package excursions with **Turismo**

Río Exploradores (tel. 09/8259-4017, www. exploradores-sanrafael.cl).

No supplies except potable water are available. Bring everything from Coyhaique or Puerto Chacabuco. Ferries and catamarans feed their passengers; the catamarans usually have an open bar and chill the whiskey with ice chipped off passing bergs.

Information

Conaf's administration and ranger station is on Laguna San Rafael's northeastern shore. Anyone who sets foot in the park pays a US$11 admission fee, but boat people do not, as offshore waters fall under naval jurisdiction. According to Conaf statistics, which exclude maritime passengers, the park received only 4,728 visitors in 2015.

Transportation

There's no cheap and easy way of reaching the park. Air travel usually means only an overflight, while sea travel can be relatively fast (in a catamaran) or slow (on a cruise ship) but still expensive. Catamarans spend only a couple of hours at the glacier, while cruise ships spend longer but are even more expensive. From the town of Puerto Río Tranquilo, on the north arm of Lago General Carrera, a new gravel road has reached Bahía Exploradores, only about 65 kilometers north of the glacier. The road's completion has not eliminated the need for boat travel, only shortened it.

Air taxis rarely land at the 775-meter gravel airstrip, but Coyhaique-based charters can carry up to seven passengers on overflights for a price that may be negotiable. The current option is **Transportes Aéreos San Rafael** (18 de Septiembre 469, tel./fax 067/257-3083, www.transportesaereossanrafael.cl).

September to May, **Cruceros Marítimos Skorpios** (Augusto Leguía 118, Las Condes, Santiago, tel. 02/2231-1030, www.skorpios.cl) offers six-day, five-night cruises from Puerto Montt on the 130-passenger *Skorpios II* (from US$1,400 pp low season to US$3,300 pp mid-Dec.-Feb.). Rates depend on the season and on the cabin. Some voyages include a side trip to hot springs in the Quitralco fjord.

From Puerto Chacabuco, the catamaran *Chaitén* offers day trips (US$200-285 pp) that include full meals and an open bar. For details, contact **Loberías del Sur** (Pedro de Valdivia 0210, Providencia, tel. 02/2231-1902 in Santiago; José Miguel Carrera 50, tel. 067/235-1112 in Puerto Chacabuco, www.loberiasdelsur.cl).

It's possible for hikers to reach the park by sea for day trips and for one- to three-night packages with dome-tent camping. It's not cheap—about US$220 for the day trip and US$350 for overnighting, not counting transportation from Puerto Río Tranquilo to the end of the Río Exploradores valley road—but the price compares favorably to the catamaran and cruise-ship excursions. For details, contact English-speaking Ian Farmer at **Turismo Río Exploradores** (tel. 09/8259-4017, www.exploradores-sanrafael.cl).

The Northern Carretera Austral

From Coyhaique, the paved Carretera Austral is briefly contiguous with Ruta 240 to Puerto Aisén and Puerto Chacabuco, but after nine kilometers it becomes a gravel road veering northeast to Villa Ortega. Ruta 240 continues west and, passing through the **Túnel Farellón** above the Río Simpson, it reaches the Viviana junction after 39 kilometers. Here, a smooth paved highway turns northeast up the Río Mañihuales Valley and intersects the Carretera Austral about 13 kilometers southeast of Villa Mañihuales.

Heavy rains can and do close the highway north to Chaitén, sometimes for several days. The rapid pace of paving may soon reduce or eliminate the problem.

VILLA MAÑIHUALES

Villa Mañihuales is a pioneer village 76 kilometers north of Coyhaique via the Viviana junction. It is the headquarters for **Reserva Nacional Mañihuales,** a 3,596-hectare forest reserve that takes its name from the native *mañío (Podocarpus)* forest. Most services in town are along the Carretera Austral, known here as Eusebio Ibar.

Practicalities

Residencial Mañihuales (Ibar 280, tel. 067/243-1403, US$15 pp, without breakfast) has ample common spaces, Wi-Fi, and rooms with shared baths only (though the baths are numerous). There are a few simple eateries, most notably the roadside **La Posada del Mate** (Ibar 2563, tel. 09/5705-5344), toward the north end of town, for coffee, pastries, and short orders.

All buses from Coyhaique pass through town en route to and from northerly Carretera Austral destinations.

VILLA AMENGUAL

About 58 kilometers north of Villa Mañihuales, overlooking the Río Cisnes Canyon beneath 2,095-meter Cerro Alto Nevado, **Villa Amengual** dates from 1983. It owes its existence to the Carretera Austral. A few kilometers south, an eastbound gravel road climbs the valley to the settlement of La Tapera and a rarely used border crossing to Argentina.

Distinguished by its shingled chapel, built in the Chilote immigrant style, Amengual is an important stop for cyclists, as one of few places with food and accommodations between Mañihuales and Puerto Puyuhuapi, another 60 kilometers north over rugged terrain.

Practicalities

There are several modest *hospedajes* (family-run lodgings) in the US$10-12 pp range, including **Residencial El Encanto** (Pasaje Plaza 3, tel. 067/221-5412, US$12 pp) and **Residencial El Paso** (Arias 12, tel. 067/221-5413, US$18 pp), both of which also serve meals. Permanently parked near the highway, at the entrance to town, **Bus Melinda** serves sandwiches but keeps erratic hours.

Amengual's spiffy **Oficina de Información Turística** (Arias and Castro, tel. 067/221-5400, 2pm-8pm Mon.-Sat. summer only) doubles as a crafts shop.

All northbound buses from Coyhaique pass through Amengual. Some go no farther than Puerto Cisnes from a junction 33 kilometers northwest of town.

PUERTO CISNES

At the mouth of its namesake river, **Puerto Cisnes** (pop. 2,000) owes its origins to a 1920s lumber mill but still serves as a key port for scattered fishing hamlets in and around Canal Puyuhuapi. Visitors can hire a launch to the 157,616-hectare **Parque Nacional Isla Magdalena,** occupying most of its namesake island and several others, through Jorge Coronado at **Tour Bella Vista** (Séptimo de Línea 112, tel. 067/234-6408, www.tourbellavista.cl). **Viva La Lluvia** (Av. Arturo Prat s/n, tel. 09/8742-6545, www.vivalalluvia.cl) does a variety of excursions, including fly-fishing, and rents kayaks and bicycles.

Food and Accommodations

Puerto Cisnes has several passable accommodations, starting with the reasonably priced **Hospedaje Bella Vista** (Séptimo de Línea 112, tel. 067/234-6408, US$18 pp with shared bath). Well-kept ★ **El Guairao** (Av. Arturo Prat 373, tel. 067/234-6473, www.guairao.cl, US$38 s, US$45 d) has motel-style rooms with satellite TV, along with a good restaurant. Additional dining options are along the waterfront, most notably **Pimienta Canelo** (Av. Arturo Prat s/n, tel. 09/7802-7317), which prepares creative versions of standards like *chupe de jaiva* (crab casserole) and even credible quesadillas.

Information

Occupying municipal offices, **Sernatur** (Sotomayor and José María Caro, tel. 09/7663-7208, pepabecker@gmail.com, 10am-1:30pm and 3pm-7pm daily) has a seasonal representative. This as well as their hours are subject to change.

Transportation

Several companies go to Coyhaique (6 hours, US$9), including **Transportes Terra Austral** (Piloto Pardo 369, tel. 067/234-6757) and **Buses São Paulo** (Carlos Condell 150, tel.

the Carretera Austral

067/234-6559, 6am Mon.-Fri.). Note that schedules change often.

Buses Entre Verdes (Gabriela Mistral s/n, tel. 09/9510-3196) goes to La Junta (4pm Mon. Wed., and Fri., 3.5 hours, US$7). Otherwise, for northbound connections, wait at the highway junction or backtrack toward Coyhaique.

At noon every Wednesday, **Naviera Austral** (Av. Arturo Prat 07, tel. 067/234-6558, www.navieraustral.cl) sails the *Barcaza Jacaf* to Quellón (US$25 pp, US$115 cars or light trucks) via Melinka, on the Isla Grande de Chiloé.

★ PARQUE NACIONAL QUEULAT

From the Cisnes junction, the Carretera Austral zigzags over the 500-meter Portezuelo Queulat as it enters 154,093-hectare **Parque Nacional Queulat,** which rises from the fjords of Canal Puyuhuapi through nearly impenetrable evergreen forests that, except on a few well-kept trails, deter all but the most intrepid hikers. Beneath snowcapped summits, meltwater cascades off hanging indigo glaciers into frigidly limpid rivers that have cut deep canyons en route to the sea.

Queulat's accessibility has made it a popular destination for those exploring the Carretera Austral, but most see only a sample of its attractions. Many visitors come to enjoy fishing in particular.

Queulat could be a poster child for climate change. As late as 1837, its hanging glacier came within 100 meters of the sea, but that distance is now 7.8 kilometers. Much of this change dates from a 1960 flood.

Geography and Climate

Roughly midway between Chaitén and Coyhaique, elevations in Queulat range from sea level on Canal Puyuhuapi to the 2,225-meter summit of Cerro Alto Nevado. Up to 4,000 millimeters of precipitation, evenly distributed throughout the year, feeds its upper snowfields and glaciers, rushing rivers, and peaceful finger lakes; the more westerly areas

are wettest. The mean annual temperature is around 8°C.

Flora and Fauna

At lower elevations, Queulat's humid climate fosters dense evergreen forests of the southern beech *coigüe* and *tepa,* reaching heights of 30 meters or more, with a dense understory of bamboo-like *quila,* fuchsia, and ferns. On some slopes, the coniferous Guaiteca cypress shades massive specimens of the broadleaf *nalca* (resembling rhubarb, it's also edible) while at higher elevations the *coigüe* mixes with the related *lenga.*

Even along the highway, look for the timid *pudú,* no bigger than a border collie, as it emerges from the forest. Foxes, pumas, and Patagonian skunks are also present. The seldom-seen *chucao* is a solitary songbird that, legend says, brings good luck if it sings on your right, but bad luck if it sings on your left. The elegant black-necked swan paddles the fjords and even some lakes.

Sights and Recreation

Many points of interest are on or near the highway. The best operations base is **Sector Ventisquero,** where Conaf's Centro de Información (22 kilometers south of Puerto Puyuhuapi via the highway and a short east-bound lateral road) marks the start of several dead-end trails. Even the most sedentary can walk the 200-meter **Sendero El Mirador** to a vista point that looks up the valley to the **Ventisquero Colgante,** a hanging glacier that suggests what California's Yosemite Valley must have looked like before the ice melted. Even when the sun shines brightly, the trail winds through rainforest so dark that you nearly need a flashlight at midday.

Crossing its eponymous river on a suspension bridge, the 600-meter **Sendero Río Guillermo** trail arrives at **Laguna Témpanos** (Iceberg Lake). Despite the name, it's iceberg-free. On the turbulent river's north bank, the 3.5-kilometer **Sendero Ventisquero Colgante** climbs unrelentingly to even better views of the hanging glacier. As the afternoon sun warms the atmosphere, ice chunks tumble onto the rocks below.

West of the bridge crossing, on the south bank, the 350-meter **Sendero Interpretativo El Aluvión** loops through part of the valley where the 1960 flood carried huge boulders and flattened tall trees. It's signed in Spanish and pretty good English.

Just beyond Guardería Pudú, the park's southern entrance, the 1.7-kilometer **Sendero Río de las Cascadas** trail winds through dripping rainforest before arriving at a granite amphitheater where ribbons of glacial meltwater mark the river's source. Farther on, where the highway begins to switchback into the Río Queulat Valley, a short staircase trail approaches the **Salto Río Padre García,** a waterfall named for the Chiloé-based Jesuit who, in 1766-1767, may have been the first European to see the area.

Queulat's numerous rivers and lakes, particularly the northern **Lago Risopatrón** and **Lago Rosselot,** are prime fly-fishing destinations.

Food and Accommodations

Accommodations are decentralized, to say the least, but there are options from La Junta in the north to the Río Ventisquero and vicinity in the south. Other nearby accommodations can be found in Puerto Puyuhuapi and La Junta.

Near the main trailheads, Conaf's **Camping Ventisquero** (US$9 per site) has 10 relatively barren sites with sheltered cooking areas, immaculate restrooms, and hot showers. Cheap firewood is also available.

On Lago Risopatrón's western shore, 12 kilometers north of Puerto Puyuhuapi, Conaf's five-site **Camping Angostura** (US$9 per site) has similar facilities in a humid temperate rainforest with soggy soils.

Thirty kilometers south of Puerto Puyuhuapi, fly-fishing is the focus at **Posada Estuario Queulat** (tel. 09/9919-3520 in Coyhaique, www.posadaqueulat.cl, US$180 s, US$205 d with 2 meals). It has branched out to include other activities such as hiking and sea-kayaking, leaving directly from its own property. Formerly just a cluster of *cabañas,* it added a handsome new clubhouse with a fireplace and comfortable common areas, with 24-hour electricity from a water-driven turbine and solar panels. It also offers a variety of excursions, including hiking and kayaking.

About half an hour north of Puerto Puyuhuapi on Lago Risopatrón, ★ **Cabañas El Pangue** (Km 240, tel. 067/252-6906, www.elpangue.cl, US$150 s, US$175 d) offers spacious cabins with natural wood, large double beds, and sunken tubs in a woodsy setting. Off-season rates are about 40 percent lower. Larger units, sleeping up to seven, cost less on a per-person basis. Breakfasts and other meals, including lamb barbecues, are also available, along with a hot tub and a sauna. The management also rents canoes, rowboats, motorboats, and horses. El Pangue offers multiple-day all-inclusive packages as well.

Other Practicalities

At Conaf's informative **Centro de Información Ambiental** at Sector Ventisquero, rangers provide guidance on hiking and other activities. Visitors can also consult with rangers at Guardería Pudú (the park's southern entrance) and Guardería El Pangue (northern entrance). Conaf collects the admission fee (US$7.50 adults, US$4 children) at Sector Ventisquero only.

Buses from Coyhaique to Puerto Puyuhuapi and Chaitén pass directly through the park, but they drop passengers at least 30 minutes' walk west of Sector Ventisquero.

PUERTO PUYUHUAPI

A pioneer port established by Sudeten German immigrants in the 1930s, **Puerto Puyuhuapi** has a greater air of permanence than any other Carretera Austral settlement between Coyhaique, 225 kilometers south, and Chaitén, 195 kilometers north. Many of its streets, residents, and businesses still bear names like Hopperdietzel, Grosse, Ludwig, Rossbach, and Übel.

At the north end of Seno Ventisquero, a sheltered extension of the larger Canal Puyuhuapi, Puerto Puyuhuapi (pop. 600) is also a gateway to Parque Nacional Queulat and the hot springs of Puyuhuapi Lodge.

Alfombras de Puyuhuapi

Since its 1940 founding by textile engineer Walter Hopperdietzel, **Alfombras de Puyuhuapi** (Aysén s/n, tel. 09/9359-9515, www.puyuhuapi.com, sales office 10am-1:30pm and 3pm-6:30pm Mon.-Sat., 9:30am-noon Sun., guided tours 10am-1:30pm and 3pm-6:30pm Mon.-Sat., US$4) has produced handmade woolen carpets, tinted with Swiss dyes, for both local and export markets. Some sell for nearly US$5,000, but there are smaller, more affordable pieces as well. Most of the 20 or so employees are female weavers from Chiloé. The benchmark price is about US$375 per square meter. There are guided tours of the factory and a sales office.

Termas Ventisquero de Puyuhuapi

Six kilometers south of town, nestled between the road and the shoreline, **Termas Ventisquero de Puyuhuapi** (tel. 09/7966-6862, www.termasventisqueropuyuhuapi.cl, 9am-8pm daily, US$27 pp for use of the baths) is an upstart hot-springs center with outdoor pools suitable for a hot soak and, for the more daring, a plunge into the sea. Given its accessibility, Ventisquero gets visitors who otherwise might spend the day at upscale Puyuhuapi Lodge & Spa (accessible only by boat).

Upstairs from the baths, Ventisquero de Puyuhuapi has a handsome café that prepares espresso, quality teas, sandwiches, and kuchen.

Food and Accommodations

Aonikenk (Hamburgo 16, tel. 067/232-5208, lunch and dinner daily) is a cafeteria with a limited menu but pleasing decor. **El Muelle** (Av. Übel s/n, 7654-3598, lunch and dinner daily) prepares Chilean standards in a sea-view setting, with notable raspberry kuchen. **Los Mañíos del Queulat** (Av. Circunvalación s/n, tel. 09/7664-9866, www.losmaniosdelqueulat.cl, 9:30am-11pm daily) has comparable offerings, plus an extensive pastry menu, in cozier surroundings. The most sophisticated option is the Euro-Patagonian **Mi Sur** (Av. Übel 36, tel. 09/7550-7656), which is cozier yet—make reservations for dinner, as seating is limited.

Puyuhuapi has numerous basic accommodations along the highway, which runs through the middle of town.

Open November to April, but due to close at the end of the 2018 summer season, ★ **Casa Ludwig** (Av. Übel 202, tel./fax 067/232-5220, www.casaludwig.cl, US$30-67 s, US$67-82 d) is a 10-room B&B in a cavernous four-story house that's now a national historical monument. Glistening *mañío* woodwork and abundant windows fill it with natural light. Attic rooms with shared baths are cheaper than the downstairs rooms (some of which have sea views) but are still comfy and cozy, and the breakfast is excellent. Owner Luisa Ludwig speaks fluent English and German, the sitting room has a German-language library with a few English titles, and there is Wi-Fi as well. It's possible new ownership may take over.

Hostal Comuy Huapi (Llautureo 143, tel. 09/7766-1984, www.comuy-huapi.cl, US$30 pp) is a family-run B&B whose spacious and luminous rooms all have private baths. The restaurant menu consists of simple Chilean dishes, but they do a lot with them—the grilled chicken with sautéed potatoes in their skins, for instance, is a tasty variation on an everyday item that would usually include fries or mashed spuds.

Set among lush gardens, the seven-room **Hostería Alemana** (Av. Übel 450, tel. 067/232-5118, www.hosteriaalemana.cl, US$46 s, US$61 d) also includes an attractive conservatory setting for breakfast. The downstairs rooms are more spacious, as those upstairs have to cope with an angled roof.

Information and Services

Staffed with enthusiasm and talent, the local

Oficina de Información Turística (Otto Übel s/n, tel. 067/232-5244, www.puertopuyuhuapi.cl, 10:30am-1:30pm and 4:30pm-8pm Wed.-Mon. Oct.-Mar.) provides flyers for self-guided tours to the town and its surroundings, written in good English.

Transportation

Bus services change rapidly, but as of early 2017 **Buses Becker** (Übel s/n, tel. 067/223-2167) connects to Coyhaique (4:30pm Wed. and Sun., US$16) en route to Chaitén (4:30pm Tues.) and intermediates, with connections to Futaleufú. **Terraustral** (O'Higgins s/n, tel. 067/232-5119) also connects northbound to La Junta and Chaitén (Mon. and Fri.), and southbound to Coyhaique (US$14).

Starting from Puerto Cisnes, **Buses Entre Verdes** (tel. 09/9510-3196) passes through Puyuhuapi (3pm Mon., Wed., and Fri.) en route to La Junta, and returning to Cisnes from La Junta (8am Mon., Wed., and Fri.).

★ PUYUHUAPI LODGE & SPA

South of Puerto Puyuhuapi, the secluded **Puyuhuapi Lodge & Spa** (Bahía Dorita s/n, tel. 067/245-0305) isn't literally an island but, since there's no road and the only access is by

launch across the Seno Ventisquero (Glacier Sound), it might as well be. Both hotel guests and day visitors (except in Jan.-Feb.) can enjoy naturally heated outdoor pools and hiking trails that veer through the forest understory of dense *quila* (solid bamboo) thickets, *chilco* (firecracker fuchsia), rhubarb-like *nalcas* with leaves the size of umbrellas, and colossal tree ferns.

Hotel guests only, though, have access to spa facilities, including a gym, a heated indoor pool, and a massage room (perched in a tower, it enjoys 360-degree views of its scenic surroundings). When the clouds lift, the panorama is Queulat's Andean front range, where snow lingers even at summer's end.

Spacious waterfront rooms, stocked with terrycloth robes and individual umbrellas, look onto the dock. Rising behind the shore, newer buildings are equally comfortable but have balconies. Activities like hiking, fly-fishing, and excursions along the Carretera Austral cost extra.

While the hotel works mainly with packages, overnight accommodations (from US$320 s or d, with buffet breakfast) are possible on a space-available basis. Peak season is mid-November to mid-March; rates are about 20 percent lower mid-March to

the Puyuhuapi Lodge & Spa

mid-November. There are fixed-price lunches and dinners (US$34), with a choice of courses. Spa access is available for B&B guests (US$14 adults, US$9 children).

Except in the peak season, Puyuhuapi also lets the riffraff in for day use of the outdoor pools, baths, and spa (US$80 pp, including transfer and lunch, not including drinks). Located between the outdoor pools, **Café Verde** (noon-7pm daily) has a cheaper salad-and-sandwich menu than the restaurant.

Launches (round-trip US$15 adults, US$9 children) from its mainland information center on the Carretera Austral, 14 kilometers south of Puerto Puyuhuapi, are free for package guests. Scheduled departures from the hotel are at 9:30am, 12:30pm, 3pm, and 6:30pm daily, returning half an hour later. There are occasional unscheduled crossings as well.

Termas de Puyuhuapi's central office is **Patagonia Connection** (Fidel Oteíza 1951, Oficina 1006, Providencia, Santiago, tel. 02/2225-6489, www.puyuhuapilodge.com).

LA JUNTA AND VICINITY

At the crossroads town of **La Junta,** roads proceed west along the Río Palena toward the port of Raúl Marín Balmaceda and east up the Río Figueroa valley toward the Argentine border. Local businesses are placing themselves as a "place of encounter" for exploring the Cuenca de Palena, the Río Palena drainage.

At the confluence of the two rivers, just south of the regional border between Aisén and Los Lagos, La Junta (pop. 1,200) is the main access point to **Reserva Nacional Lago Rosselot,** a 12,725-hectare forest reserve whose longitudinal finger lake is known for its fishing.

La Junta gained a measure of notoriety when, in 2001, local authorities erected an unauthorized monument to General Pinochet, who is still popular with some residents for building the north-south highway. Others, though, find it embarrassing.

Sights

Only 200 meters south of Hotel Espacio y Tiempo, Conaf's **Sendero Mirador Los Ciruelillos** leads to two scenic overlooks within Reserva Nacional Lago Rosselot. Climbing steeply from the highway for about 25 minutes, the first viewpoint looks west toward the dormant snow-covered cone of 2,400-meter Cerro Melimoyu. At the second, about 15 minutes on, there are even better views of the Rosselot-Palena confluence and the Córdon Barros Arana to the northeast.

From the north end of town, **Buses Willy** (tel. 09/8474-0784) has minibus service (Mon., Wed., and Fri.) on a scenic road that leads 65 kilometers northeast, including a short free ferry connection, to the modest island port of **Raúl Marín Balmaceda** (US$3). At Km 17, **Termas El Sauce** (tel. 09/8737-5645) is a rustic hot springs and campground.

Food and Accommodations

For breakfasts, lunches, and desserts, **Mi Casita de Té** (Carretera Austral and Patricio Lynch, tel. 067/231-4206) makes an ideal break. It also offers Wi-Fi and has outdoor seating—a mixed blessing when trucks pass by on the dusty highway.

At Balmaceda proper, the modest **Hospedaje Melimoyu** (Ministro Palma s/n, tel. 09/6222-4944, US$18 pp, with breakfast) is a good budget alternative that serves additional meals. **Fundo Los Leones Lodge** (tel. 09/7898-2956, www.fundolosleones. cl, US$123 s, US$165 d, cash only) is a seaside eco-lodge whose excursions include sea kayaking, visits to a nearby sea lion colony (contracted separately), and horseback-riding. Formerly the property of environmental philanthropists Doug Tompkins and Kris McDivitt, its four *cabañas* still bear the founders' rustically elegant style, and the food is remarkable—light but flavorful quiches and pies, diverse salads, and even homemade truffles.

La Junta has many simple accommodations, the best of which is probably **Hostería Valdera** (Antonio Varas s/n, tel.

067/231-4105, hosteriavaldera@gmail.com, US$18-23 pp), where rates include breakfast. The higher price corresponds to rooms with private baths. Along the highway, **Alto Melimoyu B&B** (Carretera Austral 375, tel. 067/231-4320, www.altomelimoyu.cl, US$94-123 s, US$131-145 d) is a shiny new construction with luminous common areas. Two smaller rooms share a bath, while 10 larger ones have private baths and TVs.

The elite choice, though, is the nine-room, Chilean-Colombian ★ **Hotel Espacio y Tiempo** (Carretera Austral 399, tel. 067/231-4141, www.espacioytiempo.cl, US$109 s, US$138 d, with breakfast, private bath, and Wi-Fi), where a cordon of conifers encloses the lawns and gardens of a small but appealing roadside inn. The rooms themselves are spacious and even sophisticated. The restaurant, which is open to the public, serves a diverse menu of meats and fish, and there's even a Mapuche-run brewery on-site.

Information

La Junta's **Oficina de Información Turística** (1 de Noviembre and Diego Portales, 10:30am-1pm and 3pm-8:30pm Mon.-Fri., 10am-1pm and 3pm-5pm Sat.) faces the Plaza de Armas.

Transportation

Like other Carretera Austral villages, La Junta is a regular stop for buses en route between Coyhaique and continental Chiloé. **Entre Verdes** (Antonio Varas s/n, tel. 09/9510-3196) goes to Puerto Cisnes (7am Mon., Wed., and Fri., 3.5 hours, US$7). **Terra Austral** (Manuel Montt s/n, tel. 067/231-4400, tel. 09/8241-5526) also goes to Coyhaique.

LAGO YELCHO

About 30 kilometers north of La Junta, where the highway bridges the Río Palena, lies the boundary between Region XI (Aisén) and Region X (Los Lagos). Los Lagos's first major attraction is elongated **Lago Yelcho,** stretching from Puerto Cárdenas in the north to Puerto Ramírez in the southeast, which formed the lacustrine part of the highway

between Chaitén and Futaleufú until the overland route eliminated the need for ferries. Kayakers can still paddle from Puerto Ramírez to Puerto Cárdenas and even to the Pacific.

At **Villa Santa Lucía,** 70 kilometers north of La Junta and 78 kilometers south of Chaitén, the main highway continues north but the eastbound lateral Ruta 235 drops steeply to the lakeshore and **Puerto Ramírez,** continuing southeast toward Palena and a minor border crossing. The alternative Ruta 231 proceeds northeast toward the white-water capital of Futaleufú and a more efficient crossing.

Midway between Villa Santa Lucía and Puerto Cárdenas, on the west side of the highway, the north side of the **Puente Ventisquero** (Glacier Bridge) is the trailhead for a two-hour hike through soggy evergreen forest to the **Ventisquero Cavi,** a hanging glacier.

Across the highway here, the lakeside **Hotel Yelcho en la Patagonia** (tel. 065/257-6005, www.yelcho.cl, US$175 s, US$190 d) is a fashionable fishing lodge that has expanded its base to families. The comfortable upstairs rooms offer lake views through groves of *arrayanes.* The ground-level bar-restaurant has high-beamed ceilings and decent-enough food for a place that traditionally specializes in fly-fishing holidays. On the same grounds, it also has 15 campsites (US$46 for up to 7 people) with electricity, roofed shelters, and hot showers; smaller groups can get a discount.

★ FUTALEUFÚ

Given its reputation for white water—some say it is the world's best—**Futaleufú** draws outdoor recreationists like a magnet. The spectacular natural beauty, cleanliness, and isolation work for this tidy village, its forested mountains, and its namesake river.

Until recently, the 2,700 or so people who live here have been fending off Endesa, the powerful Spanish electric utility company that wanted to build three massive dams where at least three international rafting and kayaking enterprises have elaborate summer

Futaleufú

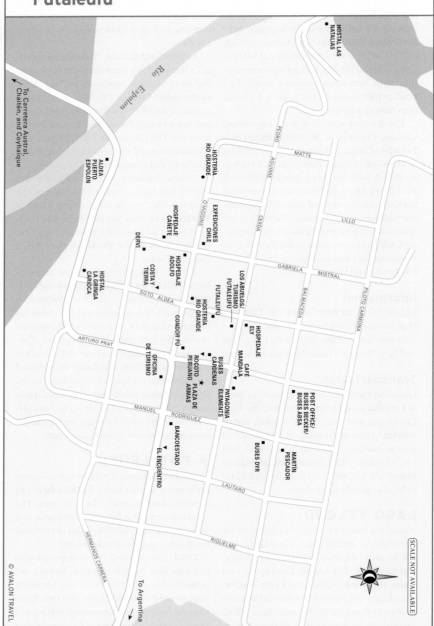

HOSTAL LAS
NATALIAS

Río Espolón

To Carretera Austral,
Chaitén, and Coyhaique

ALDEA
PUERTO
ESPOLON

HOSTERIA
RIO GRANDE

PEDRO

AGUIRRE

MATTE

CERDA

O'HIGGINS

EXPEDICIONES
CHILE

LILLO

HOSPEDAJE
CANETE

DERVI

HOSPEDAJE
ADOLFO

COSTA Y
TIERRA

HOSTAL
LA GRINGA
CARIOCA

SGTO. ALDEA

GABRIELA   MISTRAL

BALMACEDA

LOS ABUELOS/
TURISMO
FUTALEUFÚ

HOSTERIA
RIO GRANDE

CONDOR FÚ

HOSPEDAJE
ELY

CAFÉ
MANDALA

PILOTO CARMONA

ARTURO PRAT

OFICINA
DE TURISMO

ROCOTO
PERIANO

BUSES
CARDENAS

PLAZA DE
ARMAS

PATAGONIA
ELEMENTS

POST OFFICE/
BUSES BECKER/
BUSES ABSA

MANUEL

RODRIGUEZ

BANCOESTADO

EL ENCUENTRO

BUSES DYR

MARTIN
PESCADOR

LAUTARO

HERMANOS CARRERA

RIQUELME

To Argentina

© AVALON TRAVEL

SCALE NOT AVAILABLE

The *Huaso* and the Rodeo

Less celebrated than the Argentine gaucho, the Chilean *huaso* resembles his trans-Andean counterpart in many ways but differs in others. Both, of course, are horsemen, but the gaucho arose from a background of fierce independence on the Pampas, while the subservient *huaso* originated on the landed estates that dominated economic and social life in colonial and republican Chile. The *huaso* was a hired hand or even a peon attached to the property.

On Sundays, *huasos* could blow off steam by racing horses, betting, and drinking. As the spontaneous rodeo grew too raucous, it drew the disapproval of landowners, who responded by organizing competitions that, over time, became versions more genteel than their *huaso* origins. Though Chilean rodeo remains popular, it is now, according to historian Richard Slatta, a nostalgic exercise that's "a middle- and upper-class pastime, not a profession," as it has become in North America. Riders wear colorful ponchos, flat-brimmed *chupallas,* oversize spurs, and elaborately carved wooden stirrups.

The signature event is the *atajada,* in which a pair of *jinetes* (riders) guide and pin a calf or steer to the padded wall of the *medialuna,* the semicircular rodeo ring. Since it's harder to control the steer by the body than the head—the chest is best—the horsemen get more points for this. They lose points if the steer strikes any unpadded part of the wall or escapes between the horses.

There are no cash prizes. The event ends by acknowledging the champions and other riders with wine and empanadas. Compared to Canada, the United States, and even Mexico, Chilean rodeo is truly *machista* (male chauvinist). Women prepare and serve food, dress in costume, and dance the traditional *cueca* with the men, but they do not ride.

An hour south of Santiago, Rancagua is the capital of Chilean rodeo, drawing thousands of spectators to March's national festival. In small settlements along the Carretera Austral, though, rodeo probably comes closest to its historic roots.

---

camps and several Chilean operators spend at least part of the season. Endesa finally backed off, but some worry that others may step into the vacuum.

The unfortunate introduction of invasive *Didymosphenia germinata* (the so-called "toilet paper algae") has also threatened the clear waters in some tributaries but, despite these challenges, the "Fu" remains one of the world's cleanest and most challenging rivers. Both foreign and Chilean operators hope to kindle local and national enthusiasm for preserving the river and its surroundings. Fly-fishing also has a presence here.

Orientation

Only eight kilometers west of the Argentine border, at the confluence of the Río Espolón and the Río Futaleufú, the village is 155 kilometers southeast of Chaitén via the Carretera Austral, Ruta 235 from Villa Santa Lucia, and Ruta 231 from Puerto Ramírez.

Futaleufú's plan is a rectangular grid whose focus, if not its precise center, is the manicured Plaza de Armas. On the plaza's south side, Bernardo O'Higgins leads east toward the Argentine border, while Arturo Prat, on the west side, leads south toward westbound Ruta 231.

Recreation

White water is the main attraction here. But this is a multiple-sport destination, where hiking, climbing, horseback riding, and mountain biking are also grabbing attention. Several U.S. **rafting and kayaking** operators maintain summer camps in the vicinity October to April.

The Class III Espolón is a good starter river. Parts of the "Fu" (Futaleufú) are suitable for those with limited experience, though rapids like the Class V Terminator can challenge even top professionals. It's less common for inexperienced rafters to become "swimmers" than it once was, but it's certainly not unheard of.

For a half-day Class IV descent on the Fu, figure about US$75-100 pp, though groups might be able to negotiate a discount with some Chilean companies. This involves descent of the river "between the bridges," a nonstop succession of Class III-IV rapids. Novices get out before tackling the Class V Casa de Piedra rapid. Rates normally include lunch and transfer from town and back.

For river rafting and other activities, drop-in visitors can try local operators and offices. **Cara del Indio** (Ruta 231, Km 35, tel. 09/8971-0514, www.caradelindio.cl) has a camp and *cabañas* on the Fu, 35 kilometers west of town. **Cóndor Fu** (O'Higgins 463, tel. 09/6488-7484, www.condorfu.cl) draws praise from overseas operators. Other possibilities include **Patagonia Elements** (Pedro Aguirre Cerda 549, tel. 09/7499-0296, www.patagoniaelements.com), and the U.S. operator **Expediciones Chile** (Gabriela Mistral 296, tel. 065/272-1386, www.exchile.com).

For horseback riding, there's now **Turismo Antuhuya** (Sector Espolón, tel. 065/272-1901, www.turismoantuhuya.com).

Food

The food here is better than in most other towns of Futaleufú's size. Chilean standards like beef, chicken, and sandwiches are the rule. In addition to Hostería Río Grande's grill restaurant, choices include **El Encuentro** (O'Higgins 653, tel. 065/272-1247, lunch and dinner daily) and the rather bland **Futaleufú** (Sargento Aldea 265, tel. 09/6288-6722, lunch and dinner daily).

The **Café Mandala** (Pedro Aguirre Cerda 545, tel. 09/6168-4925) is great for coffee, pastries, salads, and pizza. Argentine-run **Costa y Tierra** (Sargento Aldea 348, tel. 09/9210-5841) has a daily changing menu of entrées, but specializes in a diversity of thin-crusted pizzas. Another welcome arrival is **Rocoto Peruano** (Prat 262 Interior, tel. 09/7499-0296), a tiny locale with a surprisingly diverse menu of Peruvian specialties.

Though overbuilt for a burg of Futaleufú's size, **Martín Pescador** (Balmaceda 603, tel.

White-water rafters take on the mighty Río Futaleufú.

065/272-1279, lunch and dinner daily) offers a cozy living-room-style atmosphere. Enjoy an aperitif, a crunchy seared salmon, and a small English-language library (although not a book exchange). Prices have risen dramatically—figure upward of US$30 for lunch or dinner. In fact, they're comparable to prices at the luxury view restaurant at the **Uman Lodge** (Fundo La Confluencia s/n, tel. 065/272-1700, www.umanlodge.cl), which has a more diverse menu and a bigger wine selection.

Accommodations

Futaleufú has more and better accommodations than any other place its size on or along the Carretera Austral. Most lodgings are utilitarian, but several have both character and style.

Just south of town on Ruta 231, prior to crossing the bridge over the river, **Aldea Puerto Espolón** (www.aldeapuertoespolon.blogspot.com, tel. 09/5324-0305, campsites US$9 pp, domes US$24 d) has grassy campsites with shade, clean restrooms, and hot showers. It also offers domes on elevated platforms.

At Wi-Fi-equipped **Hospedaje Adolfo** (O'Higgins 302, tel. 065/272-1256, hospedajoeadolfo@gmail.com, US$19 pp with shared bath, US$37 s or d with private bath) some rooms have low ceilings and the floors are creaky, but the ownership is exceptionally accommodating. **Hospedaje Cañete** (Gabriela Mistral 347, tel. 065/272-1214, elocovi@hotmail.com, US$16-18 pp) gets high marks from local operators for their overseas clients who want to stay within a limited budget, though the rooms vary in size and comfort. **Posada Ely** (Balmaceda 409, tel. 065/272-1205, posada.ely.futaleufu@gmail.com, US$22 pp with breakfast) has rooms with private baths.

About a 10-minute walk from the western edge of town, **Hostal Las Natalias** (Pedro Aguirre Cerda s/n, tel. 09/6283-5371 or 09/9631-1330, www.hostallasnatalias.info, US$18 pp in dorms, US$40-46 d) is a luminous building on an imposing site that offers the best possible views. Operated by Argentine-American Nathaniel Mack, it has a couple of private rooms and also offers rental bikes and kitchen access.

Hostal La Gringa Carioca (Sargento Aldea 498, tel. 065/272-1260, www. hostallagringacarioca.cl, US$95 s or d) offers more spacious B&B accommodations in a remodeled older house on expansive grounds.

Hostería Río Grande (O'Higgins 397, tel. 065/272-1320, www.pachile.com, US$80 s, US$115 d) has pleasant common areas, a bar-restaurant, and a dozen simple, tastefully decorated rooms with twin beds in the main building. A new annex has half a dozen larger doubles, and it has also added a grill restaurant.

Rooms at rustically styled, family-run ★ **Hotel El Barranco** (O'Higgins 172, tel. 065/272-1314, www.elbarrancochile.cl, US$198 d with breakfast, meal package options available) look into lush woods at the west end of town. Its restaurant deserves consideration, especially its locally sourced fruit-flavored ice cream.

About 20 kilometers west of Futaleufú, **Tineo Patagonia** (Ruta 231, tel. 09/6868-1597, www.tineopatagonia.com, US$180-225 s, US$300-450 d, with 2 meals) is a backwoods lodge that also arranges a variety of excursions—some on its own property—including hiking, mountain biking, horseback riding, fly-fishing, kayaking, and rafting. The roadside approach, including a ramshackle barn, is a deceptive introduction to

The Uman Lodge, outside Futaleufú, is built into the mountainside.

facilities that include decentralized accommodations linked by boardwalks as well as a hot tub, a sauna, and a restaurant (which is open to nonguests).

On nearly 500 verdant hectares, the **Uman Lodge** (Fundo La Confluencia s/n, tel. 065/272-1700, www.umanlodge.cl, US$465 s or d with breakfast, US$585 s or d with 2 meals, US$645 s or d with all meals) is a new luxury spa lodge on a hill overlooking the river, about 10 kilometers southwest of town. With contemporary style, its own restaurant, and 10 luxurious suites, Uman Lodge is light-years ahead of anything else in the vicinity. It also offers extensive activity packages, including fly-fishing. The outstanding view restaurant is open to nonguests.

Information and Services

Futaleufú's municipal **Oficina de Turismo** (O'Higgins 536, tel. 065/272-1629, www.futaleufu.cl, 8:30am-10pm daily Dec.-Mar., 10:30am-6:30pm daily Apr.-Nov.) is on the south side of the Plaza de Armas. For visitors arriving from or bound for Argentina, the **border** is open 8am-9pm daily.

BancoEstado (O'Higgins 603) has had the only ATM, which only takes MasterCard. **Correos de Chile** (Balmaceda 501) is the post office. **Los Abuelos** (Pedro Aguirre Cerda 436) has long-distance phone and Internet service. **Dervi** (Gabriela Mistral 393, tel. 065/272-1469) handles the washing.

Transportation

Bus services to and from Futaleufú via Argentina are subject to abrupt changes. There is no bus terminal, and companies will either pick you up or tell you where to wait, especially as services often begin in La Junta.

Turismo Futaleufú (Pedro Aguirre Cerda 436, tel. 065/272-1458) go to the Argentine border (9am and 7pm Mon., Wed., and Fri.); there are no taxis. After border formalities, passengers board **Transporte Jacobsen** (tel. 02945/45-4676 in Argentina) to continue to Trevelin and Esquel.

Buses Cárdenas (Prat 268, tel. 065/272-1214) goes to Chaitén (1pm daily, US$4), and makes connections for La Junta (Mon., Wed., and Fri.) in Villa Santa Lucía. **Buses DyR** (Manuel Rodríguez 115, tel. 09/4262-0432) goes to Chaitén (6am daily).

Buses Becker (Balmaceda 501, tel. 065/272-1360) goes to Coyhaique (11:30am Sun., US$36).

To Osorno and Puerto Montt (7:20am Tues. and Fri., 11 hours, US$38), **Buses Absa** (Balmaceda 501, tel. 065/272-1360, www.busesabsa.cl) operates the only long-distance services via Argentina (where passengers cannot disembark at interim points).

CHAITÉN

Between the snowy volcanic cones of Michinmahuida and Corcovado, the modest port of **Chaitén** was long the main gateway to continental Chiloé. Receiving regular ferries and occasional catamarans from Puerto Montt and insular Chiloé, it's the starting point for many trips down the Carretera Austral and the year-round access point for Parque Natural Pumalín, the late U.S. entrepreneur Douglas Tompkins's controversial conservation initiative.

The town of Chaitén is still continuing its slow recovery from the eruption of its namesake volcano in 2008. The current population is no more than 1,500 (before the eruption, it exceeded 4,000). Ferries are again arriving, and accommodations, food, and fuel are all available, though some parts of town still show signs of devastation.

About 20 kilometers southeast of Chaitén, on the south side of the highway, stands one of the region's most offbeat landmarks. In 1974, well before the road's completion, the Chilean Air Force crashed a DC-3 nearby; unable to fly it out, they salvaged the engines and left the fuselage. Using two oxcarts, farmer Carlos Anabalón hauled it to his roadside property, divided it into three rooms, and lived in the **Casa Avión** (Airplane House) until 2000, when he traded it to a Chaitén police officer for a 4WD Jeep. Now a rusting roadside curiosity, it is up for sale.

Orientation

Chaitén is 46 kilometers north of Puerto Cárdenas by a totally paved segment of Carretera Austral, and 56 kilometers south of Caleta Gonzalo, a summer-only ferry port that's the northern gateway to Parque Pumalín.

Food

Chaitén has relatively few eateries. The most distinctive is **Natour** (O'Higgins 166, tel. 09/4234-2803, www.natour.cl), a tour operator that also runs a green food bus across the street from its offices. For espresso, sandwiches, pastries, ice cream, and even Chinese dishes, prices are moderate and quality is high. **Pizzería Reconquista** (Diego Portales 269, tel. 09/7153-1738) serves above-average pizza and sandwiches, but **El Rincón del Mate** (Libertad 274, tel. 09/7764-5891)—in domed tent facilities—has surpassed it in variety and quality. They'll also do half-and-half pizzas, which is unusual in Chile, and have good but inexpensive house wine by the glass.

El Quijote (O'Higgins 42, tel. 065/273-1204, lunch and dinner daily) serves huge sandwiches, such as the steak-and-cheese Barros Luco, and good fresh fish. **El Refugio** (Todesco 2, lunch and dinner daily) is a longtime favorite. With a small but well-executed menu, fine sandwiches, and a limited wine-by-the-glass selection, **Flamengo** (Corcovado 218, tel. 09/6678-9718, lunch and dinner daily) deserves a look. There's no really sophisticated food in town, but **El Volcán** (Arturo Prat 65, tel. 065/273-1136) comes pretty close for seafood—try the spiny but savory *sierra* (sawfish)—though it can get crowded.

Accommodations

Budget favorite **Hospedaje Rita** (Arturo Prat 229, tel. 09/9778-2351, ritagutierrezgarcia@hotmail.es, US$15 pp with shared bath) also has *cabaña* accommodations (US$90 for up to 4 people). At the waterfront, **Hostería**

Llanos (Corcovado 378, tel. 09/9084-1978, US$20 s with shared bath, US$54 s or d with private bath and breakfast), some rooms have awkward configurations.

The best new place is **Hostal Trekanpangui** (Piloto Pardo 136, tel. 09/8268-7067, trekanpangui@gmail.com, US$22 pp), a cozy B&B with youthful vibes and comfy common spaces, plus an adjacent campground (US$7.50 pp) with ample kitchen facilities. **Hospedaje Don Carlos** (Almirante Riveros 53, tel. 065/273-1287, doncarlos.palena@mail.com, US$22-30 s, US$53-57 d) offers greater space and comfort.

Popular **Cabañas Pudú** (Corcovado 668, tel. 09/8227-9602, puduchaiten@hotmail.com, US$75 d) is close to everything. Attractive **Hotel Schilling** (Corcovado 230, tel. 09/6826-0680, hotelschilling@hotmail.com, US$90 s or d with private bath) is another step up.

Rooms at renovated **Hotel Mi Casa** (Av. Norte 206, tel. 065/273-1285, www.hotelmicasa.cl, US$76 s, US$94 d) have the drawback of relatively small size, but the furnishings and decoration have seen a significant upgrade. Its hillside location offers some fine views, but not from every direction. On the waterfront, **Cabañas Brisas del Mar** (Corcovado 278, tel. 09/9515-8808, cababrisas@telsur.cl, US$106 for up to 4 people) is immaculate and spacious.

Information and Services

The municipal **Oficina de Información Turística** (Corcovado and O'Higgins, www.patagoniaverde.org, 8am-9pm daily Jan.-Apr.) is a kiosk on the Costanera.

At the bus terminal, Nicholas La Penna's **Chaitur** (O'Higgins 67, tel. 09/7468-5608, www.chaitur.com) is a good year-round information source, with Spanish-, English-, and French-speaking staff. In addition to leading trips to Pumalín, including hikes to the volcano's cinder cone, Nicholas also rents bicycles, sells maps, has a small book exchange, and provides the latest bus schedules. The German-Chilean **Natour** (O'Higgins 166, tel. 09/4234-2803, www.natour.cl) has comparable excursions.

BancoEstado (Libertad 298) has the only ATM between Futaleufú and Puerto Montt. **Blu Bazar** (Pedro Aguirre Cerda 41) offers long-distance telephone and Internet access.

Transportation

Chaitén has air links with Puerto Montt, sea links with Puerto Montt and Chiloé, and roads south to Futaleufú and Coyhaique and north to Caleta Gonzalo. All services are subject to change and, in the case of buses, to demand.

The sparkling new **Aeródromo Nuevo Chaitén** (WCH) is at Santa Bárbara, about 10 kilometers north of town. Two air taxi companies fly to Puerto Montt: **Aerocord** (Diego Portales 287, tel. 09/7669-4515, jpineda@ aerocord.cl) and **Pewen Servicios Aéreos** (Todesco 153, tel. 09/8687-3612, www.pewen-chile.cl).

Chaitén's ferry dock is a short distance northwest of town via the Costanera. In new quarters, **Naviera Austral** (Almirante Riveros 181, tel. 065/273-1011, www.navieraustral.cl) sails Tuesday to Quellón (5 hours, US$18, US$2 infants, US$15 bicycles, US$24 motorcycles, US$99 cars and light trucks, US$25 per linear meter for other vehicles) with the *Barcaza Jacaf.*

With the same vessel, there is direct service to Puerto Montt (Mon., Thurs., Fri., 9 hours, US$25, US$15 bicycles, and US$31 motorcycles, US$138 cars and light trucks, US$36 per linear meter for other vehicles).

Nearly all buses stop at the main **Terminal de Buses** (O'Higgins 67, tel. 065/273-1429), but services are also in flux here. The main destinations are Futaleufú, Coyhaique, and intermediates. Schedules change frequently; for monthly updates, check the Chaitur website (www.chaitur.com).

Kémelbus (tel. 065/225-6450 in Puerto Montt) goes to Puerto Montt (11am daily, 12 hours, US$15) on the subsidized Ruta Bimodal, which includes two ferry shuttles along the Carretera Austral. **Buses**

Becker services to La Junta (US$18), Puerto Puyuhuapi (US$23), and Coyhaique (11:30am Wed. and Sun., 12 hours, US$43). **Buses Terraustral** goes as far as La Junta (5pm Mon. and Fri.). **Buses Cárdenas** goes to Futaleufú (6pm daily, 3.5 hours, US$4, a subsidized fare that could rise), while **Buses DyR** has similar services at noon daily.

★ PARQUE PUMALÍN

In 1991, U.S. businessman Douglas Tompkins and his wife, Kris McDivitt Tompkins, cashed out their equity from the Esprit and Patagonia clothing empires to purchase blocks of temperate rainforest that became **Parque Pumalín,** a 317,000-hectare private nature reserve straddling the highway north of Chaitén. Since then, says the *New York Times,* only General Pinochet's name has appeared more in the Chilean press than Tompkins's. Before his death in a kayaking accident in 2015, he even received death threats from ultranationalists who accused him of trying to split the country in half, though most criticisms were not so extreme.

Tompkins allayed much of that criticism by building trails, cabins, campgrounds, and a restaurant and visitors center that have lured visitors from Chaitén to the summer ferry port of Caleta Gonzalo, on the Reñihué fjord, and other points along the highway and the park's extensive shoreline. In late 2004, at a ceremony in Santiago, Pumalín finally received formal legal recognition from President Ricardo Lagos's government. In 2017, the government of President Michelle Bachelet agreed to accept the donation of Pumalín as part of a new Ruta de los Parques (Route of the Parks) in northern Chilean Patagonia.

Geography and Climate

Pumalín stretches from 42 degrees south latitude, where it is contiguous with Parque Nacional Hornopirén, to nearly 43 degrees south, east of Chaitén at its southern end. Most visitors see the areas along both sides of the Carretera Austral between Chaitén and Caleta Gonzalo.

Elevations range from sea level to snow-capped 2,404-meter Volcán Michinmahuida, in the southernmost sector, but even these statistics can be misleading. The topography rises so steeply that some trails require ladders rather than switchbacks. The forests owe their verdant color to rainfall that probably exceeds 4,000 millimeters per annum. At higher elevations, of course, it accumulates as snow.

Flora and Fauna

Pumalín takes its name from the puma or mountain lion, but it owes its creation to the temperate southern rainforest, whose single most significant species is the *alerce* (false larch). There are also several species of southern beech, not to mention other rainforest species common to southern Chile.

In addition to the puma, the *pudú* inhabits the sopping woodlands, while foxes prowl along the shoreline and other open areas. Southern sea lions inhabit headlands and rookeries, stealing salmon from the fish farms that float just beyond the park boundaries—and placing themselves at risk from the powerful companies that bring in much of the region's income.

Hikers here and in other parts of the southern rainforests should watch for tiny *sanguijuelas* (leeches), which can work their way into boots and trousers (some leeches are used for medical purposes in Chile).

Sights and Recreation

From a trailhead near Café Caleta Gonzalo, the **Sendero Cascadas** climbs and winds through thick rainforest to a high falls; figure about 1.5 hours each way. At the Centro de Información, it's possible to arrange a tour of the apiaries at **Fundo Pillán,** across the Fiordo de Reñihué, and to obtain fishing licenses.

From a trailhead about 12 kilometers south of Caleta Gonzalo, west of the highway, the **Sendero Laguna Tronador** crosses a *pasarela* (hanging bridge) before ascending a string of slippery stepladders to the **Mirador Michinmahuida** where, on

clear days, a platform provides astounding views of the volcano's wintry summit. The trail continues through nearly pristine forest, dropping gradually to the amphitheater lake where park staff have built a stylish two-site campground with picnic tables, a deck, and an outhouse. It's about 1.5 hours to or from the trailhead.

A short distance farther south, on the highway's east side, the mostly board-walk **Sendero los Alerces** crosses the Río Blanco to a large *alerce* grove. Just a little farther south on the west side, the **Sendero Cascadas Escondidas** is longer and more strenuous than the signposted three hours might suggest. It's mostly boardwalk, through the swampy, soggy forest, and catwalk along precipitous rock walls, with steep stepladders as well. The toughest part, though, is boulder-hopping the river on slippery granite or, better and perhaps safer, wading across. On the other side, the trail climbs steeply another 15 to 20 minutes, then drops into a narrow canyon where, on a dangerous-looking stepladder anchored by a rope, the bravest hikers can circle the rock to get the best view of the "hidden" falls.

Seventeen kilometers south of Caleta Gonzalo, at its namesake campground, **Sendero Lago Negro** leads 800 meters through dense forest to reed-lined Lago Negro. Just north of the park entrance on the Chaitén-Caleta Gonzalo road, the **Sendero Interpretativo** is a 1.8-kilometer walk in the woods starting from the Volcán ranger station, which provides an explanatory map.

Five kilometers farther south, the **Sendero Volcán Chaitén is** a new knee-breaking trail leading to the lip of the crater that nearly obliterated its namesake town. The sign that suggests a three-hour round-trip is probably a stretch even for the physically fit—ideally, allow twice the time—but the views are an ample reward.

From Chaitén, it's possible to reach the southern **Sendero Ventisquero Amarillo,** via a northbound road at the highway's junction of the turnoff to Termas El Amarillo.

The Legacy of Douglas Tompkins

One of Chile's largest landholders, the late Douglas Tompkins was a polarizing figure, but not in the usual sense. In the years after he purchased 17,000 hectares of temperate rainforest on continental Chiloé's Fiordo Reñihué, he became the gringo Chileans knew best—or at least the one they thought they knew best.

Tompkins, founder of the Esprit clothing empire, turned conventional politics on its head. Taking advantage of openness toward foreign investment, he used the proceeds from selling Esprit to consolidate undeveloped properties not for profit, but for preservation. As other entrepreneurs were clear-cutting native forest and replanting with fast-growing exotics for a quick profit, Tompkins formed a Chilean trust to turn his lands into a private nature sanctuary.

Tompkins expected that his Pumalín project, in a thinly populated area south of Hornopirén and north of Chaitén, would make him a hero. In fact it did—within a growing Chilean environmental movement. On the other hand, Tompkins's actions aroused the distrust and hostility of conservative sectors. He ran afoul of business, military, and religious interests, all with different but overlapping objections for opposing the project. The project's supporters included the Lagos

Organized Tours

Al Sur Expediciones (Aconcagua 8, Puerto Varas, tel./fax 065/223-2300, www.alsurex-peditions.com) arranges activity-oriented excursions—hiking, sea kayaking, and sailing—throughout the park.

Food and Accommodations

Dignified by a stone fireplace with a copper vent, the airy ★ **Café Caleta Gonzalo** (near the ferry ramp, 7:30am-10pm daily, breakfast US$12, lunch and dinner US$25) serves quality organic fruit, vegetables, dairy products, meat, and seafood. The breakfast really shines with homemade bread, local honey, butter, and cheese. There's also a sandwich menu, omelets, and juices. Four-course lunches and dinners are served with fresh bread.

At Caleta Gonzalo, the walk-in **Camping Río Gonzalo** (US$5 pp camping, US$12 roofed shelter) has forested sites with fire pits (firewood is for sale), clean restrooms, and cold showers. There's a separate large shelter for cooking. Those without tents can rent one of three *fogones*, roofed shelters with fire pits normally reserved for picnickers during the daytime. *Fogón* No. 3 has wide benches that can sleep three comfortably, presuming they have their own sleeping pads.

Fourteen kilometers south of Caleta

Gonzalo, **Auto-Camping Cascadas Escondidas** (US$11 pp) has three drive-in sites with clean restrooms, cold showers, and roofed decks for pitching tents and eating without having to sit on soggy ground.

Seventeen kilometers south of Caleta Gonzalo, **Camping Lago Negro** (US$11 pp) resembles Cascadas Escondidas, with three roofed sites and an open tent-camping area. Accessible by an 800-meter footpath, the nearby **Camping Punta del Lago** has two lakeside sites. Three kilometers farther south, **Camping Lago Blanco** (US$11 pp) resembles Camping Lago Negro, with half a dozen roofed sites. Slightly beyond, near the park entrance, **Camping El Volcán** (US$11 pp) has a dozen sites, plus a small store at the ranger station.

Tompkins's seven cozy but stylish ★ **Cabañas Caleta Gonzalo** (Puerto Varas tel. 065/225-0079, reservas@parquepumalin. cl, US$111 s, US$137 d) accommodate three to six people each. All have private baths and hot water, but no kitchen facilities. So bring your own food and cook at the campground, or eat at the nearby café.

Information

At Caleta Gonzalo, Pumalín's **Centro de Visitantes** distributes brochures, provides

administration, which approved the conversion of Pumalín into a natural sanctuary in 2005. As the project has developed, public access has improved through hiking trails, campgrounds, *cabañas*, a restaurant, and a visitors center, not to mention sustainable agriculture experiments and other features to benefit the small local population.

Today, Tompkins's widow Kris McDivitt Tompkins manages **Conservación Patagónica** (www.conservacionpatagonica.org). **Parque Pumalín** (Klenner 299, Puerto Varas, tel. 065/225-0079 or 065/225-1911, www.parquepumalin.cl) has been so successful that Chile's former president Sebastián Piñera used is as a model in creating **Parque Tantauco** (www.parquetantauco.cl) at the southern tip of the Isla Grande de Chiloé. And Tompkins' legacy continues with **Parque Patagonia,** based on a former sheep ranch in the Aisén region. The proposed Parque Nacional Patagonia would create a protected area almost from Lago General Carrera to Lago Cochrane. Tompkins' ultimate vision also incorporates Reserva Nacional Jeinimeni and Reserva Nacional Tamango, with its key *huemul* habitat. All are part of the Ruta de los Parques (Route of the Parks) established by President Michelle Bachelet in 2017.

information, and displays informational panels with large black-and-white photographs of the park. It also sells books, maps, film, park products like organic honey and jam, and local crafts. If it's not open, café personnel can unlock it on request. At El Amarillo, the park's southern approach, there's an informational kiosk.

Pumalín (www.parquepumalin.cl, in Spanish and English) maintains additional **information offices** in Puerto Varas (Klenner 299, tel. 065/225-0079, info@parquepumalin.cl) and in California (The Conservation Land Trust, Bldg. 1062, Fort Cronkhite, Sausalito, CA 94965, U.S. tel. 0415/229-9339, www.theconservationlandtrust.org).

Transportation

There is now daily transportation to and from Puerto Montt via the Ruta Bimodal, which uses ferry crossings from Hornopirén to Leptepu and Fiordo Largo to Caleta Gonzalo. Buses run from Puerto Montt or Chaitén. Vehicle space is limited and requires reservations through Naviera Austral.

The Southern Carretera Austral

Even more thinly settled than north of Coyhaique, southern Aisén is wild country, with few and scattered services; barely 10,000 people live in nearly 46,000 square kilometers. The only towns with more than 1,000 inhabitants are Chile Chico, near the Argentine border on Lago General Carrera, and Cochrane, directly on the Carretera Austral.

The highway is paved to Villa Cerro Castillo, 98 kilometers south of Coyhaique, where work is once again proceeding, but beyond there, it's still narrow and rugged. In late 1999, it finally reached its terminus at Villa O'Higgins, though the last 100-kilometer stretch still requires a ferry shuttle from Puerto Yungay to Río Bravo.

★ RESERVA NACIONAL CERRO CASTILLO

Straddling the Carretera Austral beyond the Balmaceda turnoff, marking the divide between the Río Simpson and Río Ibáñez drainages, **Cerro Castillo** is a 179,550-hectare unit whose map boundaries look like jigsaw puzzle pieces. Its signature landmark is Cerro Castillo itself, whose soaring basaltic battlements above the tree line do resemble a medieval castle.

Elevations range from about 500 meters to Cerro Castillo's 2,320-meter summit, embellished by three south-facing glaciers. Like most of the region, it gets substantial rainfall and snow at higher elevations, but some east-facing areas enjoy a rain-shadow effect.

Nearly pure stands of the southern beech *lenga* dominate the forest up to about 1,200 meters elevation, along with the related *coigüe, ñire,* and many shrubs. Steppe-like grasslands typify the rain-shadow areas.

Mammals include the puma, *huemul,* two fox species, and skunks. Birds are common, including the Andean condor, various owls, the *tordo* (austral blackbird), and the *cachaña* (austral parakeet).

Sights and Recreation

About eight kilometers south of Laguna Chiguay, an inconspicuous sign marks the faint westbound road that's the starting point for **Sendero Las Horquetas,** a four-day backpacking trail that climbs the Estero la Lima Valley to pass beneath the spires of Cerro Castillo before descending to Villa Cerro Castillo. This is easier from the north than from the south, where the approach is steeper.

Practicalities

At the reserve's northeastern edge, Conaf's woodsy five-site **Camping Laguna Chiguay** (Km 67, US$7.50 per site) is just west of the highway. At the southern approach, there are simple accommodations at Villa Cerro Castillo, just outside the reserve boundary. Conaf maintains a **ranger station** on the highway opposite the Laguna Chiguay campground.

All public transportation between Coyhaique, to the north, and Puerto Ibáñez and Villa Cerro Castillo, to the south, passes through the reserve's northern sector.

PUERTO INGENIERO IBÁÑEZ

Prior to the Carretera Austral's completion, **Puerto Ibáñez** was a major lake port, connecting Coyhaique with Chile Chico and other settlements on Lago General Carrera's south shore. Its current livelihood derives from agriculture, both livestock and tree fruit like apples and pears.

Reserva Nacional Cerro Castillo

Since completion of the highway bypass, it has lost economic clout. However, the ferry from here to Chile Chico remains an easy border crossing to Argentina, quicker and cheaper than the roundabout (albeit scenic) roads. It's about 110 kilometers south of Coyhaique via the Carretera Austral and a paved lateral that bears south about 10 kilometers east of Villa Cerro Castillo. There's also a rugged road but scenic border crossing along the lake's north shore (in Argentina, it's called Lago Buenos Aires).

Accommodations

Lodging is available at **Cabañas Emmanuel** (Ronchi 210, tel. 09/8358-6514, nancy-calderon@hotmail.com, US$53 s or d).

Getting There and Around

Several companies operate minibuses to and from Coyhaique (2 hours, US$7.50), combining with the ferry in either direction: **Buses Carolina** (tel. 067/221-9009), **Minibus Eben Ezer** (tel. 067/242-3203), **Minibus Lukas** (tel. 067/252-1045), **Transporte Alonso** (tel. 09/4247-1135), and **Mini Bus Fredy Morales** (tel. 09/8944-8847). In Coyhaique, these services pick up passengers at homes or hotels.

Somarco (Terminal de Transbordadores, tel. 09/6586-6431; Bilbao 736, Coyhaique, tel. 067/224-7400, www.barcazas.cl, US$3 adults, US$2.50 bicycles, US$6 motorcycles, US$28 cars and light trucks, US$10 per linear meter for larger vehicles) operates the ferry *La Tehuelche* to Chile Chico (daily, 2-plus hours). Schedules are subject to change, and reservations are strongly advised for both passengers and vehicles.

VILLA CERRO CASTILLO

Founded in 1966 and 98 kilometers from Coyhaique, the frontier outpost of **Villa Cerro Castillo** is finally acquiring an air of permanency, though its exposed site makes it one of the Carretera Austral's bleaker settlements. Just south of here, work on the highway is now advancing rapidly. Hikers who begin the trek through Reserva Nacional Cerro Castillo at Las Horquetas will exit the reserve here. Horseback riding has become increasingly popular, with several operators along the highway.

Alero de las Manos

Five kilometers south of town, via a lateral road off the highway, the positive and negative hands of the pre-Columbian rock art at **Alero de las Manos** (9am-noon and 2pm-6pm daily, US$1.50 pp includes guided tour) resemble those of the famous Argentine site at Cueva de las Manos. Beneath a volcanic overhang, these paintings differ in that they are fewer, younger (only about 3,000 years old), and include no animals. In some cases, rocks have split from the overhang and fallen to the ground, probably concealing even more images. There's a small visitors center with tidy restrooms.

Practicalities

Though improving, accommodations, other than inexpensive campgrounds, are limited and fill up fast.

Hospedaje Villarrica (O'Higgins 592, tel. 09/6628-3585, hospedaje.villarrica@gmail.com, US$18 pp with shared bath, US$42 d) has five upgraded rooms, and runs a cheerful restaurant. **La Querencia** (O'Higgins 520, tel. 09/9503-0746) no longer offers accommodations but still has good food. The sandwiches at **La Cocina de Sole** (Ruta 7 s/n), a complex of two buses on the west side of the highway as it passes through town, may be the region's roadside food highlight.

Open long hours November-March only, the **Oficina de Información Turística** (O'Higgins s/n, www.rioibanez.cl) provides a town map and list of services.

Several **minibus** services have early morning departures for Coyhaique (1.5 hours, US$8). All regularly scheduled services between Coyhaique, to the north, and Puerto Río Tranquilo and Cochrane, to the south, pass by the entrance to town.

PUERTO RÍO TRANQUILO AND VICINITY

Until the Carretera Austral's completion, **Puerto Río Tranquilo** (pop. 500) was a port with a weekly supply boat from Puerto Ibáñez. Today it's a small settlement at Lago General Carrera's west end, 130 kilometers southwest of Puerto Murta, burgeoning with excursion operators. At the north end of town, a new road toward Bahía Exploradores, an inlet of the larger Estero Capquelán, permits summer boat-and-hike connections to Laguna San Rafael.

★ Capilla de Mármol

The area's most popular excursion is a launch trip to **Capilla de Mármol,** a string of swirling marble grottos on the shoreline. The 1.5-hour trip costs around US$15 pp for a minimum five passengers, but it's difficult if winds are high. It's best in late summer or fall, when water levels permit launches to approach more closely and explore more thoroughly. In season, there are several roadside stands that assemble groups to visit the site, so the wait is rarely long.

Valle Exploradores

Westbound from Río Tranquilo, a smooth but narrow penetration road has finally reached the Pacific, so that it's now possible to reach Laguna San Rafael this way. At the 60-kilometer point, past Lago Bayo and the Glaciar Exploradores, an impressive but receding continental glacier has scoured the mountainside, leaving lateral and terminal moraines. Small icebergs still calve off its face and float down its namesake river.

At Km 52, **El Puesto** (tel. 09/6207-3794 in Río Tranquilo) charges US$6 for climbing the trail to its Mirador Exploradores, a 20-minute woodland walk that yields spectacular views from a hilltop deck. More ambitious hikers can organize a full-day ice hike (US$105 pp) from Tranquilo or even here, if guides are on-site.

In Tranquilo itself, **Destino Patagonia** (Gilberta Flores 208, tel. 09/9158-6044, www.destinopatagonia.cl) offers overland and boat day trips (US$220 pp) and two- to three-day packages to Laguna San Rafael. Demand is high, particularly for day trips, so reserve as far ahead as possible. **Excursiones Exploradores** (Los Arrayanes 205, tel. 067/261-4681, www.explorandopatagonia.cl) has similar offerings, and it may be a bit easier to get a spot.

A launch emerges from within the Capilla de Mármol.

Food and Accommodations

Right along the highway in town, immediately south of Hostería Costanera, the **Cervecería Río Tranquilo** (Carretera Austral s/n, tel. 09/7646-2825, US$15) is the town's brew pub, with an appropriate menu to accompany it. Immediately south of it, **Pía** (Carretera Austral 257, tel. 09/4231-9698) has made an admirable attempt to introduce Peruvian dishes here, but the *lomo saltado* (stir-fried beef and vegetables, US$13) is more noteworthy for quantity than quality.

Two blocks southwest of the highway, budget favorite **Residencial Darka** (Los Arrayanes 330, tel. 09/9126-5292, darkaresidencial@gmail.com, US$18 pp) has smallish rooms with twin beds and shared baths. A block north, **Residencial La Cabañita** (Los Arrayanes 253, tel. 09/8278-2217, US$19 pp with a good optional breakfast) has accommodating ownership and simple but immaculate rooms—shared bath only—with firm new beds. It also offers lunch, but not dinner.

With ten rooms divided by a corridor, family-run **Hostería Los Pinos** (Godoy 51, tel. 067/241-1572, lospinos_hosteriasuite@outlook.com, US$30 s, US$45 d) offers worn but tidy accommodations with breakfast and private baths. Its restaurant is also above average, serving fixed-price lunches or dinners (US$13).

Right on the highway, rebuilt after a major fire, **Hostería Costanera** (Pedro Lagos 9, tel. 09/5743-2175, ipinuerhostal@gmail.com, US$50 s, US$90 d) is a major upgrade over its predecessor, with an additional floor, larger rooms, private baths, and a newly expanded restaurant. **Hostal El Puesto** (Pedro Lagos 258, tel. 09/6207-3794, www.elpuesto.cl, US$107 s, US$139 d) is closer in style to high-end fishing lodges than to roadside accommodations (actually, it's a few blocks from the highway).

In the Valle Exploradores, German-owned **Campo Alacaluf** (Km 44, www.campoalacaluf.com, US$42-66 s, US$48-72 d, English and Spanish spoken) has four rooms with either shared or private baths in a rustically handsome house with 24-hour electricity from its own water-driven turbine. Rates include breakfast; other simple home-cooked meals (US$15) are also available. Camping's also possible, but even more rustic—no electricity, for instance, though there are wood-fired showers.

Information

From mid-November to mid-April, there's a log-cabin **Oficina de Información Turística** (Pedro Lagos and Los Arrayanes, no phone, 10am-9pm Wed.-Mon.) on the Plaza de Armas, two blocks southwest of the highway.

On the west side of the highway, across from Hostería Costanera, the **Casa del Turista** (Carretera Austral 257, tel. 09/9133-6363, 9am-noon and 2pm-8pm daily) helps arrange excursions up the Valle Exploradores, plus kayak trips to the Capilla de Mármol.

Transportation

Scheduled buses between Coyhaique and Cochrane drop off and pick up passengers here. Many backpackers try hitching, with heavy competition for a handful of rides.

Transporte Bellavista (tel. 09/8152-8505) goes to Coyhaique (9pm Tues. and 2pm Sun.). At **Víctor Vidal** (tel. 09/9932-9898) has minibus service to Coyhaique (10:30am Thurs. and Sun., 5 hours, US$12).

Transporte Carrera (tel. 09/8739-2544) goes to Chile Chico (1:30pm Wed. and Sun. US$24). In summer, **Martín Pescador** (tel. 067/241-1033) goes from Cabañas Silvana (Dagoberto Godoy 197, 5pm daily, US$30). Also in summer, **Buses Aldea** (tel. 09/8180-1962) offers service to Caleta Tortel (6:30am Mon.-Tues. and Fri.-Sat., 5 hours, US$20).

HACIENDA TRES LAGOS

Cruce El Maitén, about 50 kilometers south of Puerto Río Tranquilo at Lago General Carrera's westward outlet, is only a crossroads with the eastbound highway to Puerto Guadal and Chile Chico. Almost at the junction, **Hacienda Tres Lagos** (Ruta 7, Km 273, tel. 067/241-1323, www.haciendatreslagos.com, from US$240 s or d) is one of the highway's best accommodations.

Oriented toward packages of three days or more, its spacious, well-lighted *cabañas* are appealing enough, but its newer suites, separated from the main building, are even more so—especially the floating suites on the lake. Amenities include a good restaurant, a sauna, a game room and a bar, Wi-Fi, and even a cinema and an art gallery, while activities include horseback riding, fishing, and excursions to sights along and off the highway. In Santiago, contact Hacienda Tres Lagos (Monseñor Eyzaguirre 485, Ñuñoa, tel. 02/2333-4122).

PUERTO GUADAL

Another former lake port, at Lago General Carrera's west end, **Puerto Guadal** is 13 kilometers east of El Maitén. From here, a rugged and narrow road leads northeast to Chile Chico and the Argentine border at Los Antiguos.

There are simple accommodations and *cabañas* in town, such as those at **La Perla del Lago** (Los Lirios s/n, tel. 067/243-1229, US$22 s, US$52 d, with breakfast), half a block south of the plaza. On Guadal's eastern outskirts, the wooded grounds at elegantly simple **Terra Luna Patagonia** (Camino a Chile Chico, Km 1.5, tel. 067/243-1263, www.terraluna.cl, from US$100-180 s or d, with breakfast) enjoy lake panoramas, and it also offers affordable "mini studio" accommodations (US$70 s or d). Other meals are extra (lunch or dinner US$25, both for US$45), and the kitchen can do a lot with a little, even on short notice. While the French-run resort (English is also spoken) specializes in weeklong activities-oriented packages, including jet-boat excursions and helicopter tours, it has had some safety issues.

A short distance beyond the Terra Luna, the Dutch-Chilean **El Mirador de Guadal** (tel. 09/9234-9130, www.elmiradordeguadal.com, US$105 s, US$125 d) is a lakeside lodge that consists of nine freestanding rooms—not *cabañas*, because they lack full kitchens—on a wooded site that allows maximum privacy. Three of these are family suites that accommodate up to four, and the hilltop reception area also includes a restaurant-bar for guests only.

Other than the Terra Luna, **Café de la Frontera** (Los Lirios 399, tel. 067/243-1234, lunch and dinner daily) is the best option for standard Chilean food.

The **Delegación Municipal de Turismo** (Los Lirios and Los Notros, 8am-1pm and 2pm-5:15pm Mon.-Thurs., 8am-1pm and 2pm-4pm Fri.) is at the southwest corner of the Plaza de Armas.

To Chile Chico (3 hours, US$12), try **Turismo Seguel** (tel. 067/241-2214, 7am Mon. and Thurs.) or **Transportes ECA** (Las Magnolias 306, tel. 067/243-1224, 5pm Tues.-Wed. and Fri.). ECA also goes to Coyhaique (7:30am Sun. and Wed. 6 hours, US$18) and intermediates.

CHILE CHICO AND VICINITY

Settled from Argentina in the early 20th century, on Lago General Carrera's south shore, **Chile Chico** developed in isolation from the rest of Chile, and connections are still better with Argentina. One of the region's easiest border crossings, it also enjoys access to protected areas like Reserva Nacional Lago Jeinimeni—starting point for a new long-distance trekking option—and is also the starting (or finishing) point for the wild rugged highway to or from Puerto Guadal.

Despite brief mining booms, the enduring economic base has been the production of temperate fruits, thanks to its mild lakeshore microclimate, but this has not exactly brought prosperity. Even after the 1952 completion of the first motor road from Coyhaique to Puerto Ibáñez, Chile Chico remained remote from any sizable market. Argentines do cross the border for shopping trips because of greater product availability and lower prices.

Improvements are under way, with many more paved streets, a refurbished Plaza Ciudadana, a waterfront promenade, and a paved road to the border town of Los Antiguos. From Los Antiguos, travelers can make connections to the town of Perito Moreno and the Atlantic-coast city of Caleta Olivia, the northern Argentine Patagonian cities of Esquel and Bariloche, and southern Argentine Patagonian destinations such as El Chaltén and El Calafate.

Motorists can fill the tank more cheaply in Los Antiguos.

Orientation

Only five kilometers west of the border, Chile Chico (pop. about 3,500) is 122 kilometers northeast of Cruce El Maitén via the winding gravel road along Lago General Carrera's south shore. Avenida O'Higgins, one block south of the lakeshore, is the main thoroughfare. The central grid extends about 10 blocks from east to west, and four blocks from north to south. The Plaza Ciudadana is in the northwest corner of town.

Sights

For panoramic views of the town, Lago General Carrera and Lago Buenos Aires (as it's called in Argentina) climb the steps at the west end of O'Higgins to the aptly named **Plaza del Viento** (Plaza of Wind).

The reconstruction of Chile Chico's museum continues to lag behind schedule, but the restored vessel **Los Andes,** which once ferried passengers and cargo around the lake, remains at the corner of O'Higgins and Lautaro.

East of town, an improved gravel road parallels the border to **Reserva Nacional Lago Jeinimeni** (US$4.50 adults, US$2 children), a protected area of 161,000 hectares that now has a hiking trail to Parque Patagonia, at Valle Chacabuco. There is little infrastructure except a **campground** (US$15, discounts possible for individuals or small groups).

Food

There's not much of a food scene here. Centrally located **Café Antu Mapu** (O'Higgins 266, tel. 09/6647-9558) serves good Chilean sandwiches on homemade bread, but stay away from the pizza. The **Taberna Restobar** (O'Higgins 416-B, tel. 09/8757-1098) also has decent sandwiches, pizzas, and mixed drinks.

On the east side of the plaza, **Café Yamila y Beatriz** (González 25, tel. 09/9301-6374) serves reliable breakfasts, lunches, and even Middle Eastern dishes. **Valle de la Luna** (O'Higgins 257, tel. 09/8192-2455) serves

Young kayakers get their start on Lago General Carrera.

well-prepared but no-frills Chilean dishes such a grilled chicken and an avocado-tomato salad at bargain prices.

For a more varied menu, **J&D** (O'Higgins 501, tel. 067/241-1815) has comparable Chilean comfort food but also a variety of pastas including trout ravioli, and is also moderately priced. With lakefront views, **Facundo** (Manuel Rodríguez 253, tel. 09/8895-5020) is the most ambitious restaurant here, but the quality of the food falls short of the prices, the presentation, and the ambiance. The grilled salmon with a shrimp sauce (US$18) is probably the best option.

Accommodations

The quantity of accommodations is increasing, and their quality is improving. Half a block south of the plaza, all the rooms at tidy **Hospedaje Don Luis** (Balmaceda 175, tel. 09/8441-4970, www.hospedajedonluis.com, US$15 pp with shared bath, US$22 pp with private bath, US$66 for *cabañas* sleeping up to 5) take their names from native trees and other flora. Even the rooms without baths are spacious; an above-average breakfast (US$7.50) is extra.

In a distinctive art deco-style brick structure, run by an obliging family, **Hotel Plaza** (Balmaceda 102, tel. 09/8444-0867, hotelplaza. chilechico@gmail.com, US$15 pp) has cheerful rooms but no frills (shared baths only and so-so Wi-Fi, no breakfast). Some interior walls are a bit thin, but the major downside is that one exterior wall adjoins a thunderous Friday-Saturday disco (the proprietors are candid about potential noise). On other nights, it's fine.

Hotel Ventura (Carrera 290, tel. 067/241-1311, hotelventurachch@hotmail.com, US$22 s with shared bath, US$45 s or d with private bath) is conveniently central but starting to show its age. **Hotel Austral** (O'Higgins 501, tel. 067/241-1815, jjdiazbar@yahoo.es, US$37 s, US$52 d with private bath and breakfast) is a spacious modern construction. Near the lakeshore, **Hospedaje Brisas del Lago** (Manuel Rodríguez 443, tel. 067/241-1204,

brisasdellago@gmail.com, US$22 pp, US$52-60 s or d) also has *cabaña* accommodations.

On the eastern outskirts, the Belgian-Chilean ★ **Hostería de la Patagonia** (Camino Internacional s/n, tel. 067/241-1337, www.hosteriadelapatagonia.cl, US$53-63 s, US$72-94 d with private bath) is an ivy-covered inn with large, rustically decorated cozy rooms with private baths and breakfast (with excellent homemade bread). There's one tiny single with a shared bath and some slightly larger ones, and separate rooms built into a land-based vessel that used to work the lake. Camping and additional meals are available.

Within walking distance of the border complex, under new ownership, the **Posada del Río Jeinimeni** (Camino Internacional, Km 5, tel. 09/9452-0759, www.chile-chico.cl, US$100 s or d) is a purpose-built lodge that has expanded to 14 spacious rooms and two apartments, plus inviting common areas.

Information and Services

Sernatur (O'Higgins 333, tel. 067/241-1303, www.chilechico.cl, gneira@sernatur. cl, 8:30am-1pm and 2:30pm-8pm Mon.-Fri., 10am-6pm Sat.-Sun. summer, shorter winter hours) provides thorough information. For national parks information, contact **Conaf** (Blest Gana 121, tel. 067/241-1325).

Turismo Garnik Bike (Baquedano 51, tel. 09/9949-6899, ciclismogarnikbike@gmail. com) rents bicycles but also offers excursions to Jeinimeni (full-day US$60 pp) and other attractions as far afield as the Capillas de Mármol at Río Tranquilo. **Turismo La Huella** (Baquedano 5, tel. 09/5667-9576, www.turismolahuella.com) has similar offerings.

Banco del Estado (González 112, 10am-1pm Mon.-Fri.) changes both U.S. cash and traveler's checks and has an ATM that only takes MasterCard. **Martín Pescador** (O'Higgins 479) will change U.S. and Argentine cash.

Correos de Chile (O'Higgins 223) is the post office. The **Centro de Llamados**

(O'Higgins 426) provides long-distance services and Internet access. **Lavados Pelusa** (Santiago Ericksen 151, tel. 09/9614-5331) can handle the washing.

Hospital Chile Chico (Lautaro 275, tel. 067/241-1334) provides medical services.

Transportation

Transportation out of town can be difficult. Bus and boat capacity is limited, so reserve as early as possible. Backpackers crossing from Argentina have been stranded here for several days until space has become available.

A new bus terminal is under construction at O'Higgins and González, at the southeast corner of the Plaza de Armas, but until it becomes operational, services will continue to leave from individual offices.

Note that, because of an ill-advised Argentine tax, there is no longer minibus service to nearby Los Antiguos, though there's hope it will resume at some point. Meanwhile, local taxis will take up to three passengers to the Chilean border post (about US$10), but then it's necessary to walk six kilometers to Argentine immigration and customs.

Transportes Seguel (Los Notros 560, tel. 09/9847-8731) goes to Puerto Guadal (4pm Mon. and Thurs., 3 hours, US$12) from the Supermercado Sur (O'Higgins 394). **Transportes ECA** (Las Magnolias 306, tel. 067/243-1224) goes to Guadal (1pm Tues.-Wed. and Fri., US$16). **Transporte Carrera** (Manuel Rodríguez 253, tel. 09/8739-2544) goes to Puerto Río Tranquilo (11am Tues. and Fri., US$24), as does **Martín Pescador** (O'Higgins 479, tel. 067/241-1033, 10:30am daily, US$30). **Transporte Marfer** (Pedro Antonio González 182, tel. 09/7756-8234) goes to Cochrane (8am Mon., Wed., and Fri., US$20).

From dockside offices, **Somarco** (tel. 067/241-1093, www.barcazas.cl, US$3 adults, US$2.50 bicycles, US$6 motorcycles, US$28 cars and light trucks, US$10 per linear meter for larger vehicles) sails the ferry *La Tehuelche* to Puerto Ibáñez (daily, 2-plus hours). Schedules are subject to change. It's possible

to purchase through tickets to Coyhaique (US$7.50) with minibus services that leave from the port at Ibáñez.

PUERTO BERTRAND AND VICINITY

Separated from Lago General Carrera by a short and narrow channel, Lago Bertrand is the source of the Río Baker, Chile's largest river in terms of discharge. Beautifully sited on the lake's southeastern shore, 11 kilometers south of Cruce El Maitén, the village of **Puerto Bertrand** makes a convenient base for exploring the area, though it's a bit moribund recently.

Sights and Recreation

For water sports—rafting, kayaking, and fly-fishing—the **Río Baker** itself is the big draw. Because it has few rocks and play spots, the Class II and III rapids draw fewer rafters and kayakers than the rugged Futaleufú. Its fast current, huge flow, large waves, and occasional deep holes make it lively enough for beginners. Fly-fishing lodges line the highway south of town.

September to April, Bertrand-based U.S.-run **Patagonia Adventure Expeditions** (tel. 09/8182-0608, www.adventurepatagonia.com) arranges adventure excursions nearby; there is also a specialist fly-fishing guide. It no longer does half-day trips down the Baker but has added more ambitious expeditions, such as the 212-kilometer, eight-day descent to the ocean. Its specialty is the Aysén Glacier Trail, a 10-day trek with porter-guides that goes through nearly uncharted territory on the eastern edge of Parque Nacional Laguna San Rafael and ends with a float down the Río Baker to Caleta Tortel.

Meanwhile, **Baker Patagonia Aventura** (Costanera s/n, tel. 09/8817-7525, www.bakerpatagonia.com) has taken over the half-day rafting trips on the Río Baker (US$50 pp), but also does a five-day river descent to Caleta Tortel.

Practicalities

There are primarily budget accommodations in Bertrand. A string of accommodations along the southbound highway toward Cochran includes some package-oriented fishing lodges. If space is available, lodges will take drop-in guests.

On a steep S-curve street up from the lakefront, **Hospedaje Buena Vista** (Ventisquero Nef s/n, tel. 09/7881-4999, cabanasbertrand@gmail.com, US$18 pp with breakfast, *cabañas* US$90) is probably the best budget choice.

On the highway just south of town, the rustically appealing **Green Baker Lodge** (Lote C, Lago Bertrand, tel. 09/9159-7757, www.greenbakerlodge.com, from US$124 s or d with IVA discount) has both *cabañas* and hotel rooms along the lake, offers Wi-Fi, and has a decent restaurant with three-course lunches or dinners (US$23).

Eight kilometers south of town, inspired by Caleta Tortel, the architecturally distinctive **Lodge BordeBaker** (tel. 09/9234-5315, www.bordebaker.cl, US$260 s or d) features one main building and seven stylish free-standing rooms linked by boardwalks. It also has a restaurant open to the public, river access for fishing, and will add a spa.

Buses between Coyhaique and Cochrane, and between Chile Chico and Cochrane, pass at the highway junction.

★ PARQUE PATAGONIA AND VICINITY

At the confluence of the Río Baker and Río Nef, 15 kilometers south of Puerto Bertrand, the Cascada Nef Baker is a thunderous waterfall. Since the highway was rerouted, it's no longer visible from the road, but there's free trail access to the river from a clearly signed parking area on the west side of the highway—only about a 10-minute walk from the falls. Visitors must carry out their trash, must not start fires, and may not camp.

The highway continues south to Cochrane and Villa O'Higgins, while an eastbound lateral ascends the Río Chacabuco Valley to 647-meter Paso Roballos, the region's most southerly border crossing for motor vehicles (others farther south are for non-motorized transport only). Across the border, at the bleak crossroads of Bajo Caracoles (where gasoline sometimes runs out), Argentina's once dusty RN 40 is steadily being paved south to El Calafate and Chile's Parque Nacional Torres del Paine.

On the grounds of the former sheep ranch known as Estancia Valle Chacabuco, the

The architecture at Lodge BordeBaker mimics the settlement of Caleta Tortel.

the West Winds Campground at Valle Chacabuco

headquarters of **Parque Patagonia** (Ruta X-83 Km 11, www.patagoniapark.org) sits among sprawling steppes at the base of forested Andean slopes and craggy volcanic uplands. Only a few kilometers from the highway over rolling terrain, this private conservation initiative is recovering a wildness that ranching had diminished but could not destroy. The removal of sheep (and the wire fences that kept them from becoming roadkill) has allowed grazing guanacos—the region's signature species—to thrive.

The park is the vision of conservationist Kris McDivitt Tompkins, who heads the nonprofit Conservación Patagonia. McDivitt and her late husband, Doug Tompkins, also founded Parque Pumalín. On a continent where skeptics have traditionally viewed large landholdings, especially those controlled by foreigners, with suspicion, both parks have become an inspiration. Chile's Socialist President Michelle Bachelet has lauded Tompkins as a "world-class philanthropist." While Parque Patagonia began as a private initiative, McDivitt's idea has always been a national park that would expand to include two adjacent state-protected areas, Reserva Nacional Jeinimeni to the south and Reserva Nacional Coyhaique (also known as Tamango) to the north. In early 2017, McDivitt and Bachelet signed an agreement that will grant those areas and others park status.

Sights and Recreation

There's plenty to see here—most notably the guanaco herds that hang out within easy view, but also birds. The park's own guides lead excursions along the rivers and wetlands that host flocks of flamingos, geese, swans and coots, and raptors such as common and crested caracaras. There's also fly-fishing and, on the nearby Río Baker, Puerto Bertrand operators offer rafting and kayaking.

The only long-distance trekking trail is the 50-km Sendero Avilés, south to Jeinimeni, which is still 70 km from the town of Chile Chico by a dirt road. It's mainly suitable for experienced and well-equipped hikers. A footpath connects Parque Patagonia and Jeinimeni, offering an extended trekking option, but Tamango is a cross-country option.

Food and Accommodations

The park's central compound invites comparisons to California's Yosemite Village, though the new visitors center has not yet opened. Near park headquarters, there are luxury accommodations in the solar-powered **Lodge at Valle Chacabuco** (US$350 s, US$500 d), with half a dozen stylish suites and another four double rooms in a nearby annex. Breakfast takes place in the lounge, but lunch and dinner (both extras) are available at the park's restaurant **El Rincón Gaucho**—also open to non-guests—where there's a gift shop as well.

Two kilometers from the restaurant, the poplar-sheltered **West Winds Campground** (US$11 pp) offers covered cooking shelters, flush toilets, and solar-powered showers (though their capacity may be insufficient at times). Closer to the Argentine border, at the confluence of the Río Avilés and the Río Chacabuco, the **Stone House Campground** (Ruta X-83 Km 36, US$11 pp) has similar facilities.

Transportation

There is no public transportation to park headquarters or along the road to the Argentine border, but southbound buses from Puerto Bertrand and northbound buses from Cochrane will drop intending visitors at the junction. From there it may be possible to hitch to headquarters or hike the 11 kilometers in a few hours. Alternatively, it may be possible to hire a car and driver in Cochrane.

COCHRANE

Once literally the end of the road, the tidy town of **Cochrane** may still have more horses than automobiles, but, says one immigrant, "If you park your horse in front of the bar now, you'll get a ticket for shitting on the sidewalk." It's tidy enough for a frontier settlement, thanks to a neatly landscaped Plaza de Armas and broad paved streets. Its main appeal lies in the surrounding countryside of **Reserva Nacional Lago Cochrane,** north and northeast of town. When Parque Patagonia achieves protected status, Cochrane could see a major outdoor recreation boom.

Cochrane is still an obligatory stop for southbound wanderers, partly because it offers the last accommodations and food for nearly 300 kilometers and partly because it's home to **Casa Melero,** Chilean Patagonia's greatest general store. It's *the* place to buy camping gear, canoes, chainsaws, chocolate, fine wines, firearms, fishing gear, and almost anything else you can't find between here and Antarctica.

Orientation

Cochrane (pop. about 3,500) is 345 kilometers south of Coyhaique and 225 kilometers north of Villa O'Higgins. Its core is a rectangular grid that is only about three blocks from north to south but about nine blocks from west to east, where the Río Cochrane marks its limit.

Reserva Nacional Lago Cochrane

Informally known as Reserva Nacional Tamango, **Reserva Nacional Lago Cochrane** (admission fee at Guardería Húngaro entrance, US$7.50 adults, US$4 children) is most notable as home to the endangered *huemul,* the south Andean deer that appears on Chile's coat of arms. On the north shore of its namesake lake, the 6,925-hectare reserve is six kilometers northwest of Cochrane.

For **Huemul-watching excursions** (US$50 for up to 5 people) by launch to the east end of the lake, contact Francisco Melinao (tel. 09/6215-8374). While there's no regular public transportation to the reserve, it's near enough that hitching is possible, and even a taxi is not that expensive.

On the Río Cochrane's north bank, run by a private concessionaire, Conaf's **Camping Las Correntadas** (US$7.50) has four sites with picnic tables, wash basins, and fire pits. Accessible only by a 45-minute boat ride (US$30) or an eight-kilometer hike, Conaf's lakeside **Camping Playa Paleta** (also US$7.50) has another four campsites.

Food

El Fogón (San Valentín 651, tel. 09/8261-2017, lunch and dinner daily, US$8-12) is no longer the best, but it's still good. The name implies a *parrilla* (grill restaurant), but the menu is more diverse than beef alone, with fish (including conger eel, hake, and salmon) and fowl also available.

Thanks to outstanding homemade meals, family-run ★ **Ñirrantal** (O'Higgins 650-C, tel. 09/7878-2621, 10am-11pm daily, US$8) prepares diverse entrées ranging from sandwiches and salmon to beef and everything in between. Ñirrantal is so well intentioned and the food is so good that the erratic service is only a minor drawback.

Café Tamango (Esmeralda 464, tel. 09/9158-4521, 9am-9pm daily), on the east side of the plaza, is great for sandwiches, lunches, pastries, juices, and quality coffee. New in mid-2016, the **Taberna Tehuelche** (Teniente Merino 372, tel. 09/7879-4509) is Cochrane's lively brew pub, with massive sandwiches.

Next door **Ada's** (Teniente Merino 374, tel. 09/8399-5889, 11am-midnight daily, US$10) is a cheerful place whose offerings range from sandwiches to individual pizzas (a little heavy on the cheese), seafood, and roast lamb (US$15) in attractive surroundings. Upstairs from its namesake supermarket, the next-door **Comedor Rojitas** (Teniente Merino 501, tel. 09/8466-1928) has a more utilitarian ambiance, but it's a nice backup choice if Ada's is closed. Service is surprisingly good.

Accommodations

The simple **Residencial Cochrane** (Dr. Steffens 451, tel. 067/252-2377, pquintana13@gmail.com, US$13 pp without breakfast, US$18 pp with breakfast) also offers camping space (US$5 pp).

A rickety staircase leads to six simple rooms with shared baths at **Residencial El Arriero** (San Valentín 750, tel. 067/252-2137, rj.contrerasojeda@hotmail.com, US$15 pp). Rates include an above-average breakfast. The beds are comfortable, the shared baths are tidy and the showers excellent, and some rooms even have balconies, but the doors and floors are creaky. Ask at the downstairs supermarket to see the rooms.

The family-run **Hostal Latitud 47° Sur** (Lago Brown 564, tel. 067/252-2280, latitud-47sur_patagonia@hotmail.com, US$18 s, US$30 d with shared bath, US$30 s, US$45 d with private bath) is a budget favorite, but it sometimes fills up with local contract workers. The remodeled rooms vary at **Residencial Sur Austral** (Arturo Prat 334, tel. 067/252-2150, US$21-28 s, US$39-48 d) and, even if the walls are a little thin, the management is obliging.

Probably the best in town, Spanish-run ★ **Hotel Ultimo Paraíso** (Lago, tel./fax 067/252-2361, www.hotelultimoparaiso.cl, US$102 s, US$108 d) offers six well-heated spacious and attractive rooms with private baths. The guests-only restaurant serves lunch and dinner.

Information and Services

December-March only, the municipal **Oficina de Información Turística** (www.municochrane.cl, 9am-1:30pm and 2:30pm-6pm Mon.-Fri., 9am-1:30pm Sat.) works from a kiosk at the southeast corner of the Plaza de Armas. The staff are helpful but hours can be inconsistent. For information on nearby parks and reserves, visit **Conaf** (Río Nef 417, tel. 067/252-2164).

On the east side of the Plaza de Armas, **Banco del Estado** (Esmeralda 460) now has an ATM that only takes MasterCard. At the southwest corner of the plaza, **Correos de Chile** (Dr. Steffens and Golondrinas) handles postal needs. **Scarleth** (Dr. Steffen 576) provides public Internet access, including Wi-Fi, and also has espresso, fresh kuchen, and other sweets. **La Lavandería** (Los Helechos 336) washes and irons for about US$8.

Hospital Cochrane (O'Higgins 755, tel. 067/252-2131) provides medical assistance.

Transportation

Schedules into and out of Cochrane change frequently, so use these as a general guide. A new bus terminal is under construction on Tamango, across the arroyo at the north end of Las Golondrinas, behind the municipal gymnasium that fronts on San Valentín.

Several companies connect Cochrane with Coyhaique (9 hours, US$21) and intermediates, including **Buses Don Carlos** (Prat 334, tel. 067/252-2150, 9am Mon.-Sat.), **Buses São Paulo** (Río Baker 349, tel. 067/252-2143, 8am Mon., Wed., and Fri.), **Buses Acuario 13** (Río Baker 349, tel. 067/252-2143, 8am Mon., Thurs., and Sat.), and **Águilas Patagónicas** (San Valentín 466, tel. 067/252-3730, http://www.aguilaspatagonicas.cl, 7am daily).

Águilas also goes to Villa O'Higgins (7:30am Wed. and Sat.).

Buses Marfer (tel. 09/7756-8234) goes to Puerto Guadal and Chile Chico (4pm Mon., Wed., and Fri., 6 hours, US$20). **Buses Aldea** (Las Golondrinas 399, tel. 09/8180-9162) goes to Caleta Tortel (9:30am Tues., Thurs.-Fri., and Sun., 3 hours, US$13). **Buses Pachamama** (Teniente Merino 499, tel. 09/9411-1811) also goes to Caleta Tortel (6pm Sun.-Mon., 10am Wed., also 9am Sat. when there's a ferry). **Buses Tortel** (Dr. Steffen and Las Golondrinas, tel. 09/6614-0236) goes to Tortel (9:30am Mon., Wed., and Fri.), while **Buses Cordillera** (tel. 09/8134-4990) goes to Tortel (6pm. Mon. and Thurs.).

★ CALETA TORTEL

Where the Río Baker greets the sea, **Caleta Tortel** is a distinctive timber town with no streets in the traditional sense—rather, boardwalks and staircases link its homes and businesses. For nearly half a century the only access to this isolated hamlet, founded in 1955, was slow or expensive or both, by air, river, or sea. Since a lateral road opened from the Carretera Austral, it's now accessible overland.

Over the last few years, Tortel has seen a minor building boom of handsome-roofed riverside plazas as well as a larger Municipalidad, which have enhanced its traditional charm. In addition to the town itself, there is hiking to destinations such as **Cerro La Bandera** or, more ambitiously, to **Cascada Pisagua,** which requires hiring a launch to the trailhead.

Caleta Tortel (pop. 500) is 130 kilometers southeast of Cochrane via the Carretera Austral and a westbound lateral along the Río Baker's south bank. Motor vehicles arrive at a parking lot at the Rincón Alto sector, from which it's necessary to wheel or haul your baggage down the steep staircases (and back up when you leave).

Food and Accommodations

For the freshest fish, head to **El Mirador** (Sector Base s/n, tel. 09/8431-2106, lunch and dinner daily, 3-course meal US$12-15), whose picture windows provide broad panoramas of the harbor and mountains. This is river salmon, not farmed, and while the preparation may be unsophisticated, the quality is high. There are often catch-of-the-day specials, such as *merluza* (hake). **Sabores Locales** (Sector Base s/n, lunch and dinner daily, from US$8) is less elaborate but makes

Caleta Tortel's boardwalks are signed, making it easy to find your way around.

savory fresh seafood soups and larger plates as well. Nearer the parking area, **Ayllu Patagón** (Sector Rincón Alto, lunch and dinner daily) serves sandwiches and pizza.

Hostal Don Adán (Rincón Alto, tel. 09/8135-6931, hdonadan@gmail.com, US$23 pp) is a good budget choice, and also has more spacious *cabaña* accommodations (US$60).

Traditionally the town's best, **Hostal Costanera** (tel. 09/6677-0236, US$23 pp with shared bath) has one exceptional room with high ceilings and sea views. All the other rooms are more than acceptable. It has competition from several other places, including across-the-boardwalk **Hostal Estilo Tortel** (tel. 09/8255-8487, zuri_1@hotmail.com, US$30 pp), which also serves meals.

Under new ownership, the renovated **Casa Baker** (Rincón Alto, tel. 067/258-3173 in Coyhaique, www.caleta-tortel.cl, US$110 s or d) is a five-room B&B that's upgraded both exterior and interior without sacrificing traditional style. It's also close to the parking lot, which means not hauling luggage very far.

In a class of its own is the six-room ★ **Entre Hielos Lodge** (Sector Base, tel. 09/9579-3779, US$118 s, US$150 d), an engaging place remodeled by a Santiago architect who now lives here with her local husband. He, in fact, designed and built the furniture and decoration, which has a contemporary sensibility but with regard for local tradition. The rooms are midsize, all with private baths. A chef prepares meals for lodge guests only, and the wine list would be a good one even in a large city.

Information and Services

At the parking area, the town maintains a small but helpful **tourist office** (tel. 09/6230-4879, emerainiguez@gmail.com, 9am-11pm Mon.-Thurs., 10am-10pm Sat.-Sun. mid-Oct.-mid-Apr.) that has maps and offers suggestions for accommodations, hikes, and excursions. They can also help arrange six-hour boat trips to nearby glaciers (around US$525 for up to 8 people) with local operators such as **Expediciones Patagonia**

Tortel (tel. 09/7704-2651, Claudio.Landeras@ live.cl).

Transportation

From the parking area above town, **Buses Aldea** goes to Cochrane (3pm Mon. and Thurs., 6pm Fri., 4pm Sun., 3 hours, US$12). **Buses Tortel** has similar service to Cochrane (4pm Mon., Wed., and Fri.), as does **Bus Pachamama** (9am Mon.-Tues., 3pm Wed., 8:45pm Thurs., 4pm Fri.). **Buses Cordillera** (tel. 09/8134-4990) goes to Villa O'Higgins (4:30pm Mon., Thurs., and Sat., 4 hours, US$6).

PUERTO YUNGAY

Puerto Yungay, on Fiordo Mitchell, is the port for a free car and passenger ferry to a ramp at Río Bravo and the gateway to Villa O'Higgins, the highway's most southerly outpost. The CMT may someday carve a road along the sheer rock wall of the fjord's north side, but it will never be as fast as the half-hour ferry to Río Bravo, where the road resumes. Space on the ferry *Padre Antonio Ronchi* is available free on a first-come, first-served basis. From December to March, departures are at 10am, noon, 3pm and 6pm daily; return times from Río Bravo are at 11am, 1pm, 4pm, and 7pm daily. April to November, services may be reduced; for details, contact **Somarco** (Bilbao 736, Coyhaique, tel. 067/224-7400, www.somarco.cl).

As of mid-2016, there is weekly ferry service to Puerto Natales (US$180 adults, bicycles US$15, vehicles US$36 per linear meter) with the ferry *Crux Australis,* which formerly shuttled between the mainland port city of Punta Arenas and the town of Porvenir on Tierra del Fuego. Avoiding the rougher waters of the Golfo de Penas, through which Navimag ferries from Puerto Montt must pass, the vessel leaves Yungay at 8pm Saturday, but those without their own vehicle can catch it at Caleta Tortel. For reservations, contact **Transbordador Austral Broom** (Lillo 377, 2nd floor, tel. 067/221-4771, Coyhaique, www. tabsa.cl).

There are no other services at Puerto Yungay except for a waiting room and the small café **El Peregrino** that, in season, prepares hot tea or coffee and has a small selection of groceries and snacks. At Río Bravo, there's a modern passenger shelter with clean restrooms; late-arriving cyclists have slept inside the shelter.

★ VILLA O'HIGGINS

Tiny **Villa O'Higgins** has become something of a backpackers' mecca as the start or finish of the still rugged overland crossing to and from the Argentine trekking capital of El Chaltén. While waiting for the boat that begins the track south or the bus north to Caleta Tortel or Cochrane, there's not much choice but to stay here. Still, O'Higgins has plenty to do in its own right, including hiking and fishing amid extraordinary scenery, and its services are fast improving.

From its founding in 1954 until completion of the Carretera Austral in 1999, O'Higgins (pop. 600) was accessible only by air taxi from Coyhaique or by water from Argentina. It depended on Argentine supplies, and highway construction materials entered via Argentine roads and ferries on Lago O'Higgins (Lago San Martín to Argentines). Now, the Puerto Yungay ferry drops passengers and vehicles at Río Bravo, a boat ramp 100 kilometers to the northwest, for the Carretera Austral's last leg.

When the new road finally opened, said ex-police officer Arturo Gómez, curious tourists overran the town. "We were at full capacity, and most of the people here have scarce resources and couldn't arrange things so soon." People camped, slept in spare rooms, and rented a handful of *cabañas.* "We didn't evolve step-by-step," said then-mayor Alfredo Runín. "We went from horseback to jet."

Today, Villa O'Higgins is booming with summer visitors, and services are improving. Thanks to work on the Sendero de Chile trail, and the motor launch that helps link the town with remote parts of the lake and El Chaltén, the backcountry is increasingly hiker-friendly.

A new road has also been built to Río Mayer, on the Argentine border to the northeast, for a border crossing whose opening remains theoretical.

One measure of O'Higgins's growth is that its Copec gas station is the first south of Cochrane on the Carretera Austral (with the country's priciest fuel, around US$1.40 per liter). Still, services here remain at least 15 years behind El Chaltén's, though there are credible rumors of a project that would bring a three-star hotel and a small cruise ship for the lake.

Sights and Recreation

On the north side of the Plaza de Armas, the **Museo Antonio Ronchi** (no phone, 10am-1pm and 3pm-7pm daily, free) was the town's first church. It still preserves the Spartan bedroom of the apparently ascetic Italian priest whose name it bears. It also contains artifacts of early colonists.

At the east end of Río Pascua street, a footpath leads to a scenic overlook that's part of **Parque Cerro Santiago,** Chile's first municipal nature reserve. Hoping to attract adventurous hikers and climbers, local authorities have patched together a trail by signing existing forest paths to a backwoods shelter near the **Ventisquero Mosco** (Mosco Glacier), a 12-hour round-trip, but it's possible to view the glacier in half that time.

Villa O'Higgins lies in the broad valley of the **Río Mayer,** a prime trout stream. Just outside town, a southbound secondary road crosses the river on the **Puente Colgante August Grosse,** a 123-meter suspension bridge. From the bridge's south side, an exposed zigzag trail leads west above **Lago Ciervo,** a scenic route that eventually drops onto the shore of **Lago Negro,** where camping is possible. With an early start, this can also be a long day hike, but the trail is tiring because it conserves elevation poorly and is difficult to follow in some spots.

To the west, the steeply rising peaks of the **Campo de Hielo Sur,** the southern Patagonian icecap, may be the next big thing

The New Cruce de Lagos

The traditional lake-land-lake crossing from Chile to Argentina goes from Puerto Montt to Bariloche. If Aisén and Santa Cruz authorities have their way, the next big thing will be the route from Villa O'Higgins to El Chaltén.

Increasing numbers of hardy travelers are making the journey from Villa O'Higgins to the nearby lake port of **Bahía Bahamóndez** for the twice-weekly, 50-kilometer, 3.5-hour journey (US$65) on the 60-passenger motor launch *Quetru* to the Chilean border post of **Candelario Mancilla.** From Candelario Mancilla, the *Quetru* makes an optional excursion to Glaciar O'Higgins and **Glaciar Chico** (US$49 more) before returning to Mancilla (to pick up arrivals from Argentina) and return to Bahamóndez.

At Candelario Mancilla, where there are simple accommodations (US$39 pp with dinner and breakfast) and camping (US$6 per tent). Chilean Carabineros handle immigration and customs procedures. On foot or by bicycle, horseback, or vehicle, it's another 15 kilometers to the international border and 7.5 kilometers more to the Argentine Gendarmería, who handle customs and immigration there. In some cases, hikers may need to ford the appropriately named Río Obstáculo (Obstacle River); beyond the border, the existing road becomes a footpath unsuitable for cyclists, who may have to push or even carry their bikes. At Candelario Mancilla, it may be possible to get a lift to the border with a pickup truck (US$22 pp, US$15 per backpack, suspended as of early 2017) or with horses to Laguna del Desierto (US$60 pp plus US$60 for each pack animal); these leave the day after the boat's arrival. Make arrangements as far in advance as possible, as both horses and personnel are few, and the guide can take no more than three or four people.

From the Gendarmería post, at the north end of **Laguna del Desierto,** there are passenger launches (11am and 5pm daily, 30-45 minutes, US$32) to the south end of the lake. Alternatively, hikers can walk the 15 kilometers in about five hours. At the south end, where the launches leave for the border at 10am and 4pm daily, there is also **Camping Estancia Lago del Desierto** (US$13 pp), offering wooded sites with fire pits and restrooms with hot showers.

From Laguna del Desierto, there are buses to **El Chaltén** (2:30pm and 8:30pm daily, 1 hour, US$27). Buses from El Chaltén to Laguna del Desierto leave at 8:30am and 3pm daily; schedules are subject to change.

There are environmental issues here—deforestation and erosion, for example—and romantics may deplore the loss of frontier feeling as buses replace bicycles. Whatever the ultimate result, crossing the borders here is a huge improvement over the days when Chilean and Argentine forces exchanged gunfire, including an incident that killed a Carabinero in 1965, over what was one of the last outstanding border disputes between the two countries.

For the latest details about the crossing, contact **Robinson Crusoe Deep Patagonia** (tel. 067/243-1811, www.robinsoncrusoe.com) at the info tent immediately north of their lodge.

---

for hikers for whom Torres del Paine is too tame. Beyond the bridge, the road continues south to **Bahía Bahamóndez,** where the comfortable catamaran *MN Quetru* carries tourists up Lago O'Higgins to the **Glaciar O'Higgins** in a full-day excursion.

It is possible, however, to cross the Argentine border by taking the *Quetru* to the south end of **Lago O'Higgins** and making a long, sometimes difficult hike through rugged country to **Laguna del Desierto.** From this point, there's a road to the Argentine

village of **El Chaltén,** in Parque Nacional Los Glaciares.

Food and Accommodations

O'Higgins now has two decent restaurants. In an attractive building at the north end of town, **Entre Patagones** (Carretera Austral 1, tel. 067/243-1810, www.entrepatagones.cl, lunch and dinner daily, US$20) makes great soups and a genuine effort to make its dishes visually appealing. The main menu consists of one or two dishes, usually beef-based, per night. It also offers *cabaña* accommodations (US$90 for up to 5 people).

Though less aesthetically appealing, **San Gabriel** (Lago O'Higgins s/n, tel. 067/243-1878, lunch and dinner Mon.-Sat.) has a more diverse menu (including lamb in the evening) and excellent service. Immediately south of Entre Patagones, ex-Mayor Runín's expanded **Quiyango** (tel. 09/8459-4546) specializes in grilled Patagonian lamb.

Hospedaje La Norteña (Lago Christie s/n, tel. 09/7547-1721, silvia_cuevas@live.cl, US$19 pp with breakfast) is an obliging family-run place whose shared-bath rooms vary in size. When it's busy, avoid rooms near the upstairs TV lounge.

Under obliging ownership, **Hostería Fitzroy** (Teniente Merino and Río Mayo, tel. 067/243-1839, hospedajefitzroy@gmail.com, US$18-37 pp depending on shared or private bath, breakfast included) is a pleasant surprise with some contradictions. In a recently built house, the spacious rooms have comfortable beds and double-paned windows, but they haven't bothered to paint or otherwise decorate the compressed plywood walls (which do not suppress noise very well). The shared baths have state-of-the-art showers, and one suite even has a jetted tub.

Hostería El Mosco (Carretera Austral, Km 1240, tel. 067/243-1819, www.elmosco.cl, US$13-18 pp dorms, US$27 s, US$45-67 d) is a hybrid B&B (six upstairs doubles, three of them with private baths), hostel (four six-bed dorms at street level), and a barren campground (US$9 pp). Both levels have ample common areas, including kitchens. Campers may also use the downstairs areas. Arguably, it's a travelers' social center, and also provides a sauna and a hot tub (for an extra charge).

Directly across from El Mosco, far more ambitious than anything else in town, the **Robinson Crusoe Deep Patagonia Lodge** (Carretera Austral s/n, tel. 067/243-1811, www.robinsoncrusoe.com, US$185 s, US$220 d) is a 12-room lodge with a big central clubhouse area and bar with high ceilings, plus two separate wings of comfortable doubles or triples with double-paned windows.

Information and Services

On the Plaza de Armas, there's a small but helpful **information kiosk** (10am-1pm and 2:40pm-7pm daily summer, www.municipalidadohiggins.cl). Some but not all accommodations have Wi-Fi.

Immediately north of its namesake lodge, **Robinson Crusoe Deep Patagonia** (tel. 067/243-1811, www.robinsoncrucoe.com) takes reservations for *MN Quetru,* which visits the O'Higgins glacier and drops Argentina-bound passengers at Candelario Mancilla.

Transportation

At the airstrip directly opposite the main drag, there's a handsome new terminal building. Coyhaique's **Aerocord** (tel. 067/224-6300, www.aerocord.cl) flies here (US$43) Monday and Thursday, a route on which local residents have priority.

There's a new bus terminal along the main road, but still only a handful of services. **Buses Cordillera** (tel. 09/8134-4990) goes to Caleta Tortel (8am Mon., Thurs., and Sat., 4 hours, US$6). **Buses Águilas Patagónicas** (tel. 067/221-1288) covers the highway to Cochrane (9am Thurs. and Sun., 6.5 hours, US$15).

Southern Argentine Patagonia

Look for ★ to find recommended
sights, activities, dining, and lodging.

Highlights

★ **Área Natural Protegida Península Valdés:** This wildlife reserve has everything: guanacos, rheas, penguins, elephant seals, sea lions, orcas, and great right whales—but not at the same time, so each season is different (page 326).

★ **Área Natural Protegida Punta Tombo:** Every austral spring, 200,000 pairs of Magellanic penguins waddle ashore to mate in this remote spot (page 338).

★ **Bahía Bustamante:** A unique kelp-gathering community hosts visitors in comfortable accommodations, close to the sights of the Parque Interjurisdiccional Marino Costero Patagonia Austral (page 340).

★ **Puerto Deseado:** This picturesque town is the base for exploring penguin, cormorant, and sea lion colonies (page 344).

★ **Parque Nacional Monte León:** The tides have molded varied shapes in this coastal park, where wildlife includes penguins, sea lions, and guanacos (page 350).

★ **Estancia Monte Dinero:** This model working ranch provides homey accommodations and access to the giant penguin colony at Cabo Vírgenes (page 355).

★ **Glaciar Perito Moreno:** The constantly-calving, 60-meter face of this groaning glacier is one of the continent's most awesome sights—and sounds (page 368).

★ **Sector Fitz Roy:** Experience some of the Andes's most exhilarating scenery, hiking, and climbing (page 371).

★ **Parque Nacional Perito Moreno:** What may be Patagonia's wildest park offers

endless vistas and varied terrain, ranging from sub-Antarctic forest to high Andean pastures (page 383).

★ **Cueva de las Manos:** This UNESCO World Heritage Site's rock art is nearly 10,000 years old (page 385).

S outhern Argentine Patagonia's most dramatic sight (and sound) is the Perito Moreno Glacier at Parque Nacional Los Glaciares. Many spend entire days gazing at and listening to the relentless river of ice. More adventurous visitors take the bus to El Chaltén, where trailheads offer access to wild backcountry and, for climbers, some of the continent's most challenging technical peaks. Even day hikers will appreciate its Andean scenery.

The barren coastline draws many visitors to Península Valdés and other sites where packs of penguins waddle ashore in the southern spring, elephant seals give birth in summer, and the great right whales breed and birth in sheltered shallows in winter and spring. The coast and steppe also feature picturesque towns, such as the Welsh settlement of Gaiman and the historic ports of Puerto Deseado and Puerto San Julián. On the Santa Cruz steppe, there are several petrified forests and the landmark rock art of Cueva de las Manos, a UNESCO World Heritage Site.

Argentina's second- and third-largest provinces, stretching from the Atlantic to the Andes, Santa Cruz and Chubut might be considered Argentina's "deep south." Their vast open spaces and scattered population lend themselves to Patagonia's wild-and-remote stereotype. That said, there are substantial cities and towns, many good roads, and decent public transportation.

Note that southern Argentine Patagonia, for the purposes of this guide, includes sections of Ruta Nacional (RN) 40 from Río Turbio, along the Chilean border, and north to the town of Perito Moreno; northern Argentine Patagonia includes northern RN 40, from the Río Negro provincial border to the southern Chubut town of Río Mayo.

PLANNING YOUR TIME

Southern Argentine Patagonia's highlights are bountiful, but distances are great, and flying is almost imperative for short-term visitors. Overland travel is too time-consuming to visit widely separated sights like Península Valdés's wildlife and the Perito Moreno Glacier.

Previous: valley of Los Altares; Glaciar Perito Moreno. **Above:** Sector Fitz Roy.

Southern Argentine Patagonia

PACIFIC OCEAN

CHILE

ARGENTINA

SANTA CRUZ

ATLANTIC OCEAN

Bahía Grande

SEE "PARQUE NACIONAL LOS GLACIARES" MAP

SECTOR FITZ ROY

SECTOR PERITO MORENO

GLACIER PERITO MORENO

Villa O'Higgins

Cochrane

★ PARQUE NATIONAL PERITO MORENO

ESTANCIA HELSINGFORS

El Chaltén

Lago Viedma

Lago Argentino

Lago Argentino

Eólo Lodge

El Calafate

■ LA LEONA

Tres Lagos

Río Turbio

Puerto Natales

To Punta Arenas

Río Gallegos

Río Santa Cruz

Comandante Luis Piedra Buena

PARQUE NACIONAL MONTE LEÓN

Puerto Santa Cruz

Reserva Provincial Marino Makenke

Parque Interjurisdiccional Marino Península de San Julián

Puerto San Julián

Estancia La María

Gobernador Gregores

Río Chico

Gran Bajo de San Julián

Parque Nacional Bosque Petrificado de Jaramillo

Bajo Caracoles

★ CUEVA DE LAS MANOS

★ PUERTO DESEADO

Parque Interjurisdiccional Marino Isla Pingüino

Reserva Natural Provincial Ría Deseado

Río Gallegos

ESTANCIA MONTE DINERO

Reserva Provincial Cabo Vírgenes

RN 7
RN 40
RN 40
RN 40
RN 288
RN 40
RN 40
RN 3
RN 3
RN 281

RP 23
RP 11
RP 7
RP 5
RP 9
RP 27
RP 29
RP 37
RP 39
RP 41
RP 97
RP 25
RP 1

0   50 km
0   50 mi

© AVALON TRAVEL

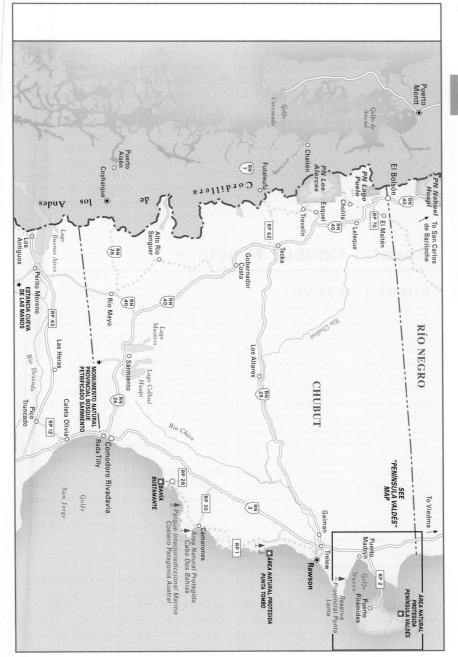

Perito Moreno Glacier visitors should make additional time, perhaps at least a week, to hike Parque Nacional Los Glaciares's Sector Fitz Roy and even Chile's Parque Nacional Torres del Paine (climbers may wait the entire summer for the weather to clear at these latitudes). Many choose an extension to Tierra del Fuego as well.

For those with time, money, and a vehicle, the ideal way to see the region is to drive south on RN 3 all the way to the Perito Moreno Glacier or even Tierra del Fuego and return via RN 40 to Bariloche or beyond. Besides a sturdy vehicle, this requires at least a month, preferably two, and ideally three.

Coastal Patagonia's best base is Puerto Madryn, which has the best services, and access to secondary attractions like the Welsh settlement of Gaiman. For the national parks along the Andes, El Calafate and El Chaltén, along with full-service cattle or sheep ranches, are the top options.

January and February are the most popular months, but also the most expensive. The shoulder months of November-December and March-April have less crowding, lower prices, and sometimes better weather. By April, days start getting short, but winter whale-watching has become big business at Puerto Pirámides.

Overland transportation schedules change seasonally and annually, and they can be disrupted by weather.

Coastal Chubut Province

PUERTO MADRYN

For foreigners and many Argentines, Puerto Madryn is the gateway to coastal Patagonia's wealth of wildlife. The Golfo Nuevo's sheltered waters and sandy shoreline have also made it a beach resort. In January and February, sunbathers, cyclists, in-line skaters, joggers, and windsurfers irrupt onto the *balnearios* (beach complexes) along Boulevard Brown, while divers seek out reefs and wrecks as the shallow waters warm with the season.

Madryn's tourist season weakens after Semana Santa (the week before Easter) until July, when Península Valdés's great right whales help fill hotels and restaurants. Conscious of this birthright, Madryn promotes itself as an ecofriendly destination. Its Ecocentro complex, focused on maritime conservation, is a positive development. At the same time, souvenir stores and chocolate shops have turned parts of the waterfront into tourist traps, and bright green suburban lawns have worsened the water deficit.

Stimulated by the Muelle Storni (commercial pier), the Aluar aluminum plant, and the fishing fleet, three-plus decades of growth have almost obliterated Madryn's Welsh heritage (though it still has a sister city in Nefyn, Gwynedd). On the positive side, cultural life has blossomed with a university campus, a theater, and a cinema.

Orientation

Puerto Madryn (pop. about 100,000) is 1,308 kilometers southwest of Buenos Aires and 1,219 kilometers northeast of Río Gallegos via RN 3. It is 670 kilometers east of Esquel via several paved highways; 680 kilometers southeast of Neuquén; and 960 kilometers from Bariloche via Esquel. It is 65 kilometers north of Trelew.

Most services are within a few blocks of the waterfront Avenida Roca and Boulevard Brown, with their sandy beaches and *balnearios,* which are the main points of interest in the city itself.

Sights

North of downtown, the **Museo del Hombre y del Mar** (Domecq García and Menéndez, tel. 0280/445-1139, museopujolmadryn@ yahoo.com.ar, 10am-4pm Mon.-Fri., 3pm-7pm Sat. and holidays, also morning Sat.-Sun. when cruise ships are in port, free) stresses

Puerto Madryn

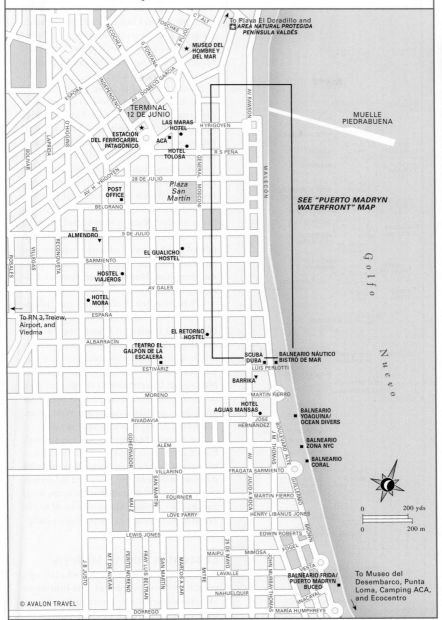

To Playa El Doradillo and
★ ÁREA NATURAL PROTEGIDA
  PENÍNSULA VALDÉS

★ MUSEO DEL
  HOMBRE Y
  DEL MAR

CT ALT

TOSCHKE

JOPPLN

NEOCHEA

G. FONTANA

INDEPENDENCIA

ESPORA

O'HIGGINS

LAPRIDA

BOLIVAR

RECONQUISTA

VILLEGAS

ROSALES

AV. DOMECQ GARCÍA

TERMINAL
12 DE JUNIO

★ LAS MARAS
  HOTEL

★ ESTACIÓN
  DEL FERROCARRIL
  PATAGÓNICO

ACA ●

● HOTEL
  TOLOSA

AV. H. YRIGOYEN

28 DE JULIO

■ POST
  OFFICE

Plaza
San
Martín

BELGRANO

EL
ALMENDRO ▼

9 DE JULIO

SARMIENTO

EL GUALICHO
HOSTEL ■

● HOSTEL
  VIAJEROS

AV. GALES

● HOTEL
  MORA

ESPAÑA

← To RN 3, Trelew,
  Airport, and
  Viedma

ALBARRACÍN

TEATRO EL
GALPÓN DE LA
ESCALERA ■

● EL RETORNO
  HOSTEL

ESTIVÁRIZ

BARRIKA ▼

MORENO

HOTEL
AGUAS MANSAS ■

RIVADAVIA

GOBERNADOR

MAI Z

ALEM

VILLARINO

SAN MARTÍN

FOURNIER

LOVE PARRY

LEWIS JONES

MT. DE ALVEAR

PERITO MORENO

FRAY LUIS BELTRÁN

J.B. JUSTO

SAN MARTÍN

MARCOS A. ZAR

MITRE

25 DE MAYO

MAIPÚ

LAVALLE

NAHUELQUIR

DORREGO

HYRIGOYEN

AV. RAWSON

R S PEÑA

GENERAL

MOSCONI

MALECÓN

MUELLE
PIEDRABUENA

SEE "PUERTO MADRYN
WATERFRONT" MAP

G o l f o

N u e v o

SCUBA
DUBA ■

● BALNEARIO NÁUTICO
■ BISTRÓ DE MAR

LUIS PERLOTTI

MARTIN FIERRO

JOSÉ
HERNÁNDEZ

■ BALNEARIO
  YOAQUINA/
  OCEAN DIVERS

BOULEVARD ALTE

J.M. THOMAS

■ BALNEARIO
  ZONA NYC

AV

■ BALNEARIO
  CORAL

FRAGATA SARMIENTO

JULIO A ROCA

MARTIN FIERRO

GUILLERMO

HENRY LIBANUS JONES

BROWN

EDWIN ROBERTS

FOGEL

MIMOSA

JOHN MURRAY THOMAS

VESTA

● BALNEARIO FRIDA/
  PUERTO MADRYN
  BUCEO

INACAYAL

MARÍA HUMPHREYS

To Museo del
Desembarco, Punta
Loma, Camping ACA,
and Ecocentro

0   200 yds
0   200 m

© AVALON TRAVEL

Puerto Madryn Waterfront

PAULINA

TEATRO DEL ■
MUELLE

ESCARDO

MUELLE
PIEDRABUENA

LOS
GARDELITOS ■ HIPÓLITO YRIGOYEN

HOTEL
YENE HUE
■ HOTEL
VASKONIA

● HOTEL BAHÍA NUEVA

CASA DE   MARGARITA
LA CULTURA   BAR ▼   ▼ AMBIGÚ
R S PEÑA
CAFÉ MAR ▼   ▼ BARRIKA
Y TIEMPO   25 DE MAYO   LADE
■ BANCO DEL
CHUBUT   ● HOTEL PENÍNSULA VALDÉS
HOTEL LOS   ● CUYUN-CO/FIORASI
GUINDOS   PLAYA HOTEL ●
● ■   ● BONAFIDE CAFÉ
28 DE JULIO   ▼ HAVANNA CAFÉ   *Golfo*
CINE TEATRO   TURISMO   ★
AUDITORIUM   PUMA ■   ● SECRETARÍA   *Nuevo*
PORTAL DE   DE TURISMO   M
MADRYN   A
ANDES   RENT A CAR   L
LÍNEAS AÉREAS ■   PATAGONIA   E
BELGRANO   ● ACA   C
■ HUINCA   ★ MONUMENTO A LA
TRAVEL   FLAMENCO   GESTA GALESA
TOUR

TRANSFER
PMY   LOCUTORIO
ROCA
9 DE JULIO
EL ■   AV. JULIO A. ROCA
DESCORCHE   AEROLÍNEAS
ARGENTINAS
MUSEO
NIEVEMAR/AVIS ■   ★ MUNICIPAL
CAMBIO THALER ■   DE ARTE
SARMIENTO
▼ PLÁCIDO
▼ BOMKE
■ MANOS DEL SUR
■ AQUATOURS
▼ LIZARD CAFÉ
AV GALES
▼   ● PRESTO-LAV
MAR Y
MESETA   ■ ANDES   BLV D AITE
LÍNEAS
AÉREAS
ESPAÑA   ALFONSINA STORNI
CHEPATAGONIA   GUILLERMO
0   100 yds   HOSTEL
0   100 m   BROWN
CANTINA EL NÁUTICO ▼
ALBARRACIN   LEOPOLD LUGONES
HOTEL GRAN
MADRYN
LOBO LARSEN ■
© AVALON TRAVEL

the interaction of the Tehuelche people and the pioneers with the regional environment through use of its natural resources, with excellent natural history and ethnographic material. It occupies the neoclassical **Chalet Pujol** (1917), built by businessman and Madryn mayor Agustín Pujol and topped by a domed hexagonal tower.

Immediately in front of the bus terminal, one of Madryn's oldest structures, dating from 1889, the former **Estación del Ferrocarril Patagónico** (train station) previously served as a bus terminal and now houses the **Centro de Estudios Históricos** (Av. Hipólito Yrigoyen and Independencia, tel. 0280/447-1777, 8:30am-11:30am Mon.-Fri., free), which has occasional exhibits about the town's history. On the waterfront is the modest **Museo Municipal de Arte** (Municipal Art Museum, Av. Roca 444, tel. 0280/445-3204, museodearte@madryn.gov.ar, 8am-8pm Mon.-Fri., 5pm-8pm Sat. summer, 9am-8pm Mon.-Fri., 5pm-8pm Sat. fall-spring, donation).

Where the first Welshmen came ashore in 1865, about three kilometers southeast of town via Boulevard Brown, the **Parque Histórico Punta Cuevas** preserves remnants of the shelters whose foundations they dug into the bluff above the high-tide mark. Its **Museo del Desembarco** (Blv. Brown 3600, tel. 0280/494-5054, 9am-1pm and 3pm-8pm Wed.-Sun. summer, 3pm-7pm Wed.-Mon. fall-spring, US$1) provides more details.

For Puerto Madryn's 1965 centennial, Porteño artist Luis Perlotti created two monumental sculptures: downtown's **Monumento a la Gesta Galesa** (Av. Roca and Belgrano), to honor the Welsh contribution to the area, and Punta Cuevas's **Monumento al Indio Tehuelche,** a tribute to the province's indigenous inhabitants.

Ecocentro Puerto Madryn

In season, southern right whales approach the promontory of this luminous Magellanic structure, crowned by a tower that yields views of distant Península

Valdés across the Golfo Nuevo. **Ecocentro Puerto Madryn** (Julio Verne 3784, tel. 0280/445-7470, www.ecocentro.org.ar, 5pm-9pm Wed.-Mon. Dec.21.-Feb., also 10am-1pm when cruise ships are in port, 3pm-7pm Wed.-Mon. Mar.-May 6 and July 6-Sept., 3pm-7pm Sat.-Sun. May 7-29, 3pm-7pm Wed.-Mon. Oct.-Dec. 20, foreigners US$12 adults, US$9 ages 6-12) is the work of a nonprofit institution striving to bring environmental education, research, and the arts under the same roof.

As a maritime-life educational center, the Ecocentro has superb displays of South Atlantic fauna, including birds, seals, and especially whales. One display is a living tidal pool. Even the surrounding gardens serve a didactic purpose—in lieu of residential Madryn's water-hungry lawns, they preserve the native coastal desert flora.

Reached by a spiral staircase, the three-level tower holds a library, an exhibition room for local artists and authors, and a reading room. Painting, photography, and sculpture are all on display. The ground-floor atrium accommodates the largest works. Other features include a 150-seat theater for concerts and lectures, a crafts and souvenir shop, and a café with a great view.

The Ecocentro is reached by Boulevard Almirante Brown, about five minutes from downtown by taxi, 15 minutes by bicycle, and 40 minutes on foot.

Entertainment and Events

Madryn has an active cultural calendar, starting with the **Teatro del Muelle** (Rawson 60, tel. 0280/445-0307), which offers theater programs, usually on weekends. The **Casa de la Cultura** (Roque Sáenz Peña 86, tel. 0280/447-2060, www.cultural.madryn.gov.ar) hosts a variety of events.

The **Cine Teatro Auditorium** (28 de Julio 129, tel. 0280/445-5653, www.cinemadryn. com) shows current movies and also offers live theater. The **Teatro El Galpón de la Escalera** (Estivariz and San Martín, tel. 0280/15-457-8922) is a cozy venue that does cutting-edge material.

For occasional live music, try the **Margarita Bar** (Roque Sáenz Peña 15, tel. 0280/447-2659), which has pub grub (outstanding midday specials from US$9) and costlier drinks. **Los Gardelitos** (Av. Hipólito Yrigoyen 144, tel. 0280/445-1052) is another popular bar, with live music on weekends and occasional tango during the week.

spiral staircase at the Chalet Pujol, Madryn's maritime museum

July 28's **Fundación de la Ciudad** celebrates the initial Welsh landing at Punta Cuevas. Festivities continue for several days.

Shopping

The waterfront avenues are full of souvenir shops, but the best option remains **Manos del Sur** (Av. Roca 516, tel. 0280/447-2539, www.manosdelsurap.com).

Barrika (Avenida Roca 109, tel. 0280/426-9677; Perlotti 74) has the biggest wine selection, but **El Descorche** (9 de Julio 132, tel. 0280/445-7725, www.eldescorche.com.ar, 9:30am-1pm and 5pm-9:30pm Mon.-Sat.) makes some more daring choices from lesser-known bodegas.

Sports and Recreation

Water sports are the attraction on the crescent of sandy beaches stretching from Muelle Storni in the north almost to Punta Cuevas in the south. In these sheltered waters, hazards like rip currents are nonexistent. At low tide, the water retreats hundreds of meters on the gently sloping beach.

At the beaches along Boulevard Almirante Brown, several *balnearios* (beach complexes) rent water-sports equipment and have snack bars and restaurants, including (from north to south and centrally located) **Naútico Bistró del Mar** (Blv. Brown 860, tel. 0280/445-7616), **Balneario Yoaquina** (Blv. Brown 1050, tel. 0280/441-4913), **Balneario Zona NYC** (Blv. Brown 1070, tel. 0280/447-5696), **Balneario Coral** (Blv. Brown 1300, tel. 0280/447-0070), and **Balneario Frida** (Blv. Brown 1980, tel. 0280/447-1668).

Balnearios also rent items like in-line skates and mountain bikes. Some operators who arrange diving excursions and other activities have space here; others are scattered around town.

Divers favor Madryn because of its clear waters, natural and artificial reefs, and shipwrecks. Most operators do initial dives for novices, PADI certification courses, and underwater photography. Operators working out of the *balnearios* include **Ocean Divers**

(Balneario Yoaquina, tel. 0280/15-466-0865, www.oceandivers.com.ar), **Patagonia Buceo** (Bajada 6, Blv. Brown and Castelli, tel. 0280/445-2278, www.patagoniabuceo. com), and **Puerto Madryn Buceo** (Bajada 5, Blv. Brown 1900, tel. 0280/15-456-4422, www.madrynbuceo.com). Operators elsewhere include **Aquatours** (Av. Roca 550, tel. 0280/445-1954, www.aquatours.com.ar), **Lobo Larsen** (Av. Roca 885, tel. 0280/447-0277, www.lobolarsen.com), and **Scuba Duba** (Blv. Brown 893, Local 2, tel. 0280/445-2699, www.scubaduba.com.ar).

Food

Among Puerto Madryn's dining scene there are a few standout restaurants. Note that beach-complex restaurants change hands frequently due to municipal concessions that may not be renewed, and are usually best for a quick lunch rather than a more elaborate dinner.

Good choices for breakfast, snacks, light lunches, and coffee include **Café Mar y Tiempo** (Roque Sáenz Peña and 25 de Mayo, tel. 0280/445-2046) and the **Lizard Café** (Av. Roca and Gales, tel. 0280/445-8333), which is also a decent pizzería. The **Bonafide Café** (Av. Roca and 28 de Julio, tel. 0280/447-0863) and the **Havanna Café** (28 de Julio and Roca, tel. 0280/447-3373) are probably the best *confiterías* (cafés with a menu of short orders).

Occupying a historic building, but with an eclectic sports-bar ambience that includes nine TVs in silent mode plus music, ★ **Ambigú** (Av. Roca 97, tel. 0280/447-2541, lunch and dinner daily, US$12) is an excellent value for its pastas and tasty sauces and top quality pizzas. It is also a popular choice that fills up fast in the evening.

Cantina El Náutico (Av. Roca 790, tel. 0280/447-1404, www.cantinaelnautico.com. ar, lunch and dinner daily) is a traditional seafood favorite.

Named for the almond tree that shades its entrance, ★ **El Almendro** (Marcelo T. de Alvear 409, tel. 0280/447-0525, dinner Tues.-Sun., US$12) is one of few Madryn restaurants that provides quiet dining in sophisticated surroundings at reasonable prices. They serve items such as stuffed pasta with Patagonian lamb and an herb sauce, plus simple well-executed dishes such as haddock with calamari and scallops. With good desserts, a decent wine list, and attentive service, this is probably the city's top choice.

The kitchen can be creative at **Plácido** (Av. Roca 506, tel. 0280/445-5991, www.placido.com.ar, lunch and dinner daily, US$12-17), but the appetizers, desserts, and drinks are unconscionably expensive by Argentine standards. A modest malbec by the glass, for instance, costs almost as much as a bottle of pretty good wine in some other places. However, entrées are reasonably priced.

Bomke (Av. Roca 540, tel. 0280/447-4094, www.bomke.com.ar) has new ownership and a slightly revised name, but it continues to serve the same fine ice cream.

Accommodations

In addition to current hotel prices, the Secretaría de Turismo keeps a register of rental apartments on a daily, weekly, or monthly basis. In peak season, most hotels charge double rates even for a single guest. Hotel occupancy is high, but the summer trend is toward apartments, as most Argentines come here to spend two weeks on the beach.

In addition to these options, Madryn has reasonably priced hostels, with Wi-Fi, for shoestring travelers.

UNDER US$25

On the Punta Cuevas road, the wooded Automóvil Club Argentino (ACA) 800-campsite **Complejo Turístico Punta Cuevas** (tel. 0280/445-2952, www.acamadryn.com.ar, US$14 for 2 people) offers discounts to members and foreign affiliates.

US$25-50

Under new ownership, **Hotel Los Guindos** (28 de Julio 149, tel. 0280/447-3742, losguindoshotel@gmail.com, US$24 s, US$32 d with

private bath, TV, and Wi-Fi) has spotless rooms and attractive shady patios, but serves no breakfast.

Though it's less central than others, all rooms at **Hotel Mora** (Juan B. Justo 654, tel. 0280/447-1424, www.morahotel.com.ar, US$28 s, US$42 d, with breakfast) have private baths, and it's a good choice. Wi-Fi only works in the lobby, however.

Freshly modernized, set among pleasing gardens, the motel-style **Hostel Viajeros** (Gobernador Maíz 545, tel. 0280/445-6457, www.hostelviajeros.com, US$13 pp dorm, US$28 s, US$42 d, US$51-63 d *hostería* rooms) is an amiable place with dorms, legitimate single rooms, and doubles with private baths. Newer private rooms at its small hotel in the same location offer comfort equivalent to a good modern hotel.

US$50-100

Only half a block from the beach, spotless and pleasant **Chepatagonia Hostel** (Alfonsina Storni 16, tel. 0280/445-5783, www.chepatagoniahostel.com.ar, US$18 pp dorm, US$53 d with shared bath) is an independent hostel with mostly dorm accommodations. It also offers free Wi-Fi and rental bikes.

Though it's a bit farther from the beach, homey **El Retorno Hostel** (Mitre 798, tel. 0280/445-6044, www.elretornohostel.com.ar, from US$22 pp dorm, US$60-78 d) is a beautifully appointed place, whose cheaper private rooms have shared baths.

Madryn's Hostelling International (HI) affiliate is the exceptional ★ **El Gualicho Hostel** (Marcos A. Zar 480, tel. 0280/445-4163, www.elgualichohostel.com.ar, US$22-31 pp dorm, US$65 d with shared bath, US$80 d with private bath). Comfortably furnished and attractively decorated, it also has a shady patio that encourages socializing. HI members get discounts.

Close to the beach, on a residential block, **Hotel Aguas Mansas** (José Hernández 51, tel. 0280/447-3103, www.hotelaguasmansas.com.ar, US$60 s, US$80 d) is a pleasant, contemporary place with a swimming pool, but there's a surcharge for credit card payments. The **Playa Hotel** (Av. Roca 187, tel. 0280/445-1446, www.playahotel.com.ar, US$75 s, US$95 d) draws its character from its patina of age, though the rooms themselves are utilitarian.

US$100-150

Recreating the style of Madryn's early Welsh houses, but with contemporary comforts, ★ **Hotel Bahía Nueva** (Av. Roca 67, tel. 0280/445-1677, www.bahianueva.com.ar, US$85 s, US$105 d) has spacious gardens and ample parking in a central beachfront location. Rooms are comfy, but not large, and there may be an extra charge for any of the four rooms with sea views.

Though lacking views, **Las Maras Hotel** (Marcos A. Zar 64, tel. 0280/445-3215, www.lasmarashotel.com.ar, US$106-139 s, US$126-162 d) is an attractive choice, in a convenient location with easy access to the beach and the bus terminal, choice superior rooms, and attentive staff.

Well-established, central **Hotel Tolosa** (Roque Sáenz Peña 253, tel. 0280/447-1850, www.hoteltolosa.com.ar, US$120-145 s or d) is keeping up with some of the newer places; the more expensive sea view suites are worth consideration.

US$150-200

Hotel Península Valdés (Av. Roca 155, tel. 0280/447-1292, www.hotelpeninsula.com.ar, US$160-402 s or d) has fine standard rooms, but spectacular ocean views make the larger eighth-floor rooms worth consideration.

Facing the beach, **Hotel Yenehue** (Av. Roca 33, tel. 0280/447-1496, www.hotelesaustralis.com.ar, US$130-175 s or d) is a spa hotel with high-rise ocean views from the rooms that front on the avenue. In addition to saunas, massages, and other treatments (which are open to nonguests), amenities include a restaurant, a swimming pool, and good accessibility for travelers with disabilities. The most expensive option is a sea-view suite.

OVER US$200

At the south end of town, emulating a massive shearing shed in its exterior style, **Hotel Territorio** (Blv. Brown 3251, tel. 0280/447-0050, www.hotelterritorio.com.ar, US$186-279 s or d) is a top-end, 36-room hotel offering high comfort, functionality, spectacular ocean views from all rooms, a spa, and a restaurant open only to guests. It's owned by the Ecocentro's founder. A protected dune field separates it from the coastal road.

Information

The exemplary **Secretaría de Turismo** (Av. Roca 223, tel. 0280/445-3504 or 0280/445-6067, www.madryn.travel, 7am-10pm Mon.-Fri., 8am-11pm Sat.-Sun. mid-Dec.-mid-Mar., 7am-9pm daily mid-Mar.-mid-Dec.) provides information in Spanish and English and helps find accommodations when beds are scarce. There is also an information point at the bus terminal (Dr. Ávila 350, tel. 0280/447-5971) with the same hours.

For motorists, **ACA** (Belgrano 13, tel. 0280/445-6684) can provide maps and info.

Services

Banco del Chubut (25 de Mayo 154) has one of many ATMs. The postal code for **Correo Argentino** (Gobernador Maíz 293) is 9120. **Locutorio Roca** (Av. Roca 395) has phone, fax, and Internet services. **Presto-Lav** (Av. Brown 605, tel. 0280/445-1526) can do the washing. The **Hospital Subzonal Dr. Andrés Ísola** (Roberto Gómez 383, tel. 0280/445-1999) provides medical services.

Transportation

Commercial flights traditionally land at **Trelew,** 65 kilometers south, but Madryn's own **Aeropuerto El Tehuelche** (PMY, RN 250, tel. 0280/445-6774) gets some commercial flights.

Andes Líneas Aéreas (Av. Belgrano 41, tel. 0280/447-5877, www.andesonline.com) flies to and from Buenos Aires. **LADE** (Av. Roca 119, tel. 0280/445-1256) flies to Bariloche, Mar del Plata and Buenos Aires, but schedules are always subject change. From Trelew, **Aerolíneas Argentinas** (Av. Roca 427, tel. 0280/445-1998) flies twice to thrice daily to Buenos Aires's Aeroparque and daily to El Calafate and Ushuaia (Aug.-Jan.).

Transporte Aitué (tel. 0280/15-427-2444, www.transporteaitue.com.ar, US$6 pp) provides shuttle service to or from Tehuelche airport. A taxi or *remise* (meterless radio taxi) is a bit more expensive. For flights to and from Trelew, **Transfer PMY** (25 de Mayo 364, 1st Fl., tel. 0280/15-487-3000, www.transferpmy.com) charges US$17 pp for door-to-door shuttle service, but a taxi or *remise* costs around US$50.

Madryn's bus terminal, **Terminal 12 de Junio** (Dr. Ávila s/n, tel. 0280/445-1789, www.terminalmadryn.com), stands directly behind the former railroad station. It has frequent service to Trelew with **Línea 28 de Julio** (tel. 0280/447-2056) and **Mar y Valle** (tel. 0280/445-0600), plus extensive regional and long-distance connections. **Mar y Valle** also goes five times daily to Puerto Pirámides in summer; fall-spring it goes only twice daily.

Sample destinations, times, and fares include Trelew (1 hour, US$4), Puerto Pirámides (1.5 hours, US$8), Comodoro Rivadavia (6 hours, US$35-45), Esquel (9 hours, US$58-70), Neuquén (9-11 hours, US$55-66), Río Gallegos (16-18 hours, US$94-107), and Buenos Aires (18-21 hours, US$99-113).

Because the area's attractions are spread out and the roads are decent, renting a car is a good option. Agencies include **Avis** (Av. Roca 493, tel. 0280/447-5422), **Fiorasi/Alamo** (Av. Roca 165, tel. 0280/445-6300), and **Rent A Car Patagonia** (Av. Roca 293, Local 8, tel. 0280/445-0295).

VICINITY OF PUERTO MADRYN

Madryn's tour agencies go farther afield to Trelew, Gaiman, Punta Tombo, and, of course, Península Valdés. Operators include **Cuyun-Co** (Av. Roca 165, tel. 0280/445-1845, www.cuyunco.com), **Flamenco Tour** (Belgrano 25, Local 1, tel. 0280/445-5505,

www.flamencotour.com), **Huinca Travel** (Belgrano 198, Oficinas 1 and 2, tel. 0280/445-4411, www.huincatravel.com), **Nievemar** (Av. Roca 493, tel. 0280/445-5544, www.nievemartours.com.ar), and **Turismo Puma** (28 de Julio 46, tel. 0280/445-1063, www.turismopuma.com). Full-day excursions to Península Valdés cost US$55, not including meals or park admission fees. While springtime excursions usually include a stop at Punta Delgada, later in summer they visit Punta Norte instead. Whale-watching starts at US$65 pp.

Wildlife Routes

For Patagonia travelers, arrow-straight **RN 3** is the quickest way south. Visitors with their own wheels (two or four) should consider coastal Chubut's dusty back roads. It's common enough to rent a car for **Península Valdés,** where a bicycle is difficult because camping is prohibited, but the loop from Rawson south to **Punta Tombo** and **Camarones,** returning via RN 3, is an intriguing alternative for automobiles, motorbikes, and bicycles.

Along southbound **Ruta Provincial (RP) 1,** the big attraction is Punta Tombo's penguins, which most visitors see on a tour. Rather than returning to Puerto Madryn or Trelew, the self-propelled can get a ranch owner's view of the thinly settled area by following the dusty, narrow, but smooth gravel road south past desolate **Cabo Raso,** with its steep gravel beach, and on to picturesque **Camarones.**

From Camarones, the provincial wildlife reserve at **Cabo Dos Bahías** makes an ideal excursion before returning to RN 3 via a paved lateral road and heading back north, perhaps for tea in **Gaiman,** or continuing south toward **Bahía Bustamante** and **Comodoro Rivadavia.** Bahía Bustamante is the kelp-gathering community that's part of the new **Parque Interjurisdiccional Marino Costero Patagonia Austral** along the Atlantic shoreline. With an early start, the Punta Tombo-Camarones-Gaiman circuit could be a day trip, but an overnight in Camarones is better.

Área Natural Protegida Punta Loma

Close enough to Madryn for a mountain-bike excursion, **Punta Loma** (8am-8pm daily, US$10) lacks Península Valdés's sheer numbers and diversity of wildlife, but its ample sea lion colonies, along with cormorants, giant petrels, gulls, terns, and snowy sheathbills, are reason enough to visit. Only 15 kilometers southeast of Madryn via an undulating gravel road, it gets few visitors. Near the sea lion colony, there's a visitors center and an overlook that permits good views of the animals. There's no scheduled transportation, but Madryn operators will arrange excursions, or a small group can go for about US$30 by meterless taxi.

Área Protegida Municipal El Doradillo

From **Playa El Doradillo**'s headlands, 15 kilometers northeast of Madryn via RP 42, deep water lets whales approach the shore—the next best choice to an in-the-water view at Península Valdés. Like Punta Loma, this is close enough for a bike ride or a shared taxi.

★ ÁREA NATURAL PROTEGIDA PENÍNSULA VALDÉS

Coastal Patagonia's top destination, World Heritage Site **Península Valdés** is the place where the great southern right whale arrives to breed and birth in winter. Protected since 1937, the *ballena franca* occupies a nearly unique position as a "natural monument"—a designation normally reserved for territorial ecosystems—within Argentina's national park system.

Península Valdés itself, a provincial reserve rather than a national park, has more to offer than just whales. Some marine mammal species, ranging from sea lions to southern elephant seals and orcas, cover the beaches or gather in the Golfo San José, Golfo Nuevo, or

the open South Atlantic year-round. There are also colonies of burrowing Magellanic penguins and flocks of other seabirds, plus herds of grazing guanacos and groups of sprinting rheas in the interior grasslands.

The main activity center is the hamlet of **Puerto Pirámides** (pop. about 600), which, like Puerto Madryn, enjoys a longer tourist season because of the whale- and orca-watching periods. Once the export point for salt from the Salina Grande depression, it has grown haphazardly, and water continues to be a problem in this desert environment. Since 2010, street names have changed: 25 de Septiembre (National Whale Day) replaces Primera Bajada, and 14 de Julio (the town's anniversary) replaces Segunda Bajada. Other street names include those of Antonio Soto and Facón Grande, leaders of the Santa Cruz anarchist rebellion of 1921, and of writer Osvaldo Bayer, whose book *Los Vengadores de la Patagonia Trágica* helped to reveal the facts.

Sometimes called Puerto Pirámide, the village has reasserted its plurality. According to local accounts, when the Argentine navy used the area as a firing range, they destroyed two of the three pyramidal promontories that gave the settlement its original moniker.

Geography and Climate

Connected to the mainland by the narrow Istmo Carlos Ameghino, Península Valdés is 45 kilometers northeast of Puerto Madryn via RP 2. Visiting the major wildlife sites involves a circuit of roughly 400 kilometers to Puerto Pirámides and Punta Delgada via RP 2, Caleta Valdés and Punta Norte via RP 47, RP 3 back to Puerto Pirámides, and RP 2 back to Puerto Madryn. Beyond Puerto Pirámides, inexperienced drivers may find the loose gravel and dirt trying, especially with low-clearance vehicles.

Broad sandy beaches line much of the coast. Unconsolidated sediments make the steep headlands that rise above them dangerous to descend. Sheep *estancias* (ranches) occupy most of the interior, whose Salina Grande depression (42 meters below sea level)

Península Valdés

RN 3

To Bahía Blanca
and Buenos Aires

RP 1

To Trelew and
Comodoro
Rivadavia

RN 3

Puerto
Madryn

ECOCENTRO

To Rawso

Punta
Cuevas

RP 42

Playa El Doradillo

Área Protegida
Municipal El
Doradillo

EL DESEMPEÑO

RP 2

Área Natural Protegida Punta Loma

Punta Loma

RP 5

Golfo

Nuevo

Punta Ninfas

CENTRO DE
INTERPRETACIÓN

Istmo
Carlos
Ameghino

Isla de
los Pájaros

Punta
Quiroga

Golfo San Matías

Golfo San José

Punta
Buenos Aires

Puerto Pirámides

Punta
Pirámide

Punta
Pardelas

RP 3

Salina
Grande

RP 2

ESTANCIA
RINCÓN CHICO

Salina
Chica

ÁREA NATURAL PROTEGIDA
PENÍNSULA VALDÉS

El Salitral

Bajo   de   Valdés

Punta Delgada
FARO PUNTA
DELGADA HOTEL DE
CAMPO

Península

Valdés

ESTANCIA
SAN LORENZO

RP 3

RP 52

Caleta
Valdés

RP 47

Punta
Norte

ATLANTIC OCEAN

0   10 km
0   10 mi

© AVALON TRAVEL

is one of the world's lowest points. The climate is dry, with high evaporation due to long hours of sunlight and perpetual winds.

Flora and Fauna

Most of Península Valdés consists of rolling *monte* (scrubland) with patches of pasture that expand in wet years. The stocking rate for sheep is low, permitting guanacos and rheas to thrive alongside them.

Marine mammals—whales, orcas, southern elephant seals, and sea lions—are the big draw, along with Magellanic penguin colonies. In addition to penguins, there are breeding populations of Dominican gulls, white herons, black-crowned night herons, olivaceous and black cormorants, steamer ducks, Patagonian crested ducks, and Magellanic and black oystercatchers. Several species of gulls, terns, and plovers are visitors, along with the Chilean flamingo and the snowy sheathbill.

From June to December, the breeding, breaching, blowing, and birthing of **whales** brings whale-watchers to the warm shallow waters of the Golfo Nuevo and Golfo San José. Since the first census in 1971, the population has grown from 580 to upward of 2,000.

Inhabiting the South Atlantic at latitudes from about 20 to 55 degrees south, the southern right whale reaches 17 meters in length and weighs up to 100 tons; females are larger than males. These are baleen whales, filtering krill and plankton as seawater passes through sieves in their jaws.

The species *Eubalaena australis* acquired its English name from whalers who sought them out because dead specimens, instead of sinking, floated to the surface; hence, they were the "right whales" for hunting. Identifiable by keratin calluses on their heads, about 1,300 of Valdés's population have names. This has allowed researchers to follow their movements and even trace their kinship.

After the cows give birth, their calves get closest to the catamarans that do commercial whale-watching from Puerto Pirámides. Over the season, it's possible to see all stages of the mating and breeding cycle.

For much of the year, **orcas** *(Orcinus orca)* swim the South Atlantic in search of squid, fish, penguins, and dolphins. In October-November and February-April, pods of these "killer whales" prowl the Punta Norte and Caleta Valdés shorelines for sea lions and southern elephant seal pups. A nine-meter orca can consume up to eight pups per day. The largest of the dolphin family, the 950-kilogram animal is conspicuous for its sleek

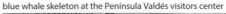
blue whale skeleton at the Península Valdés visitors center

black body, white underbelly, and menacing dorsal fin, which can rise two meters above the water.

Valdés's sandy beaches are the only continental breeding site for **southern elephant seals** *(Mirounga leonina)*, though there are also breeding colonies on sub-Antarctic islands in Chile, the Falkland (Malvinas) Islands, and at South Georgia. Largest of the pinnipeds, the southern elephant seal is a true seal with no external ear. Its distinguishing characteristic is the male's inflatable proboscis, which resembles an elephant's trunk.

Ungainly on land, 2,500- to 4,000-kilogram "beachmaster" males come ashore in spring to dominate harems that number up to 100 females (who weigh only about 500 kilograms each). Up to seven meters long, beachmasters defend their harems in fights with younger bachelors that leave all parties bloody, scarred, and even disfigured.

Females spend most of their pregnancy at sea, giving birth upon returning to land in spring. Pups spend only a few weeks nursing, gaining weight quickly, before the mothers abandon them (some die crushed beneath battling males). At sea, the elephant can plunge up to 600 vertical meters in search of squid before surfacing for air half an hour later.

Present year-round on the beaches and reefs beneath the peninsula's headlands, **sea lions** *(Otaria flavescens)* are common from southern Brazil and Uruguay all the way around the tip of South America and north to Peru. With its thick mane, the 300-kilogram 2.3-meter male resembles an African lion, but Spanish speakers call it *lobo marino* (sea wolf). The female, about 1.8 meters long, weighs only about 100 kilograms.

Unlike the larger southern elephant seal, the sea lion has external ears. Also unlike the southern elephant seal, it propels itself on land with both front and rear flippers, and the male is quick enough to drag away elephant pups. More often, though, it feeds on krill and the odd penguin.

For Spanish speakers, this is the *lobo marino de un pelo,* as opposed to the *lobo marino de dos pelos,* or southern fur seal *(Arctocephalos australis),* whose pelt was more valuable to commercial sealers and is found farther south.

Spheniscus magellanicus, also known as the "jackass penguin" for its braying, is normally the only **penguin** species here. From September to March or April, it breeds and raises its young at Caleta Valdés and Punta Norte. Summer swimmers have had close encounters at Puerto Pirámides.

Sights and Recreation

Many visitors book excursions in Madryn, but day trips are too brief for more than a glimpse of the best, especially if the operators spend too much time at lunch. Staying at Puerto Pirámides and contracting tours there is ideal for whale-watching, as you have the flexibility to pick the best time to go out.

Six Pirámides operators, some with offices in Madryn as well, offer whale-watching in semirigid rafts (which get closer to the animals) or larger catamarans: **Tito Bottazzi** (25 de Septiembre s/n, tel. 0280/449-5050, www.titobottazzi.com), **Hydrosport** (25 de Septiembre s/n, tel. 0280/449-5065, www.hydrosport.com.ar), **Whales Argentina** (25 de Septiembre s/n, tel. 0280/449-5015, www.whalesargentina.com.ar), **Punta Ballenas** (14 de Julio s/n, tel. 0280/449-5112, www.puntaballena.com.ar), **Peke Sosa** (14 de Julio s/n, tel. 0280/449-5010, www.pekesosa.com.ar), and **Southern Spirit** (25 de Septiembre s/n, tel. 0280/449-5094, www.southernspirit.com.ar), which offers the semi-submergible "Yellow Submarine." Prices start around US$60-75, but can cost more, depending on the vessel and the tour's duration.

In Golfo San José, 800 meters north of the isthmus, penguins, gulls, cormorants, and herons all nest on **Isla de los Pájaros,** an offshore bird sanctuary. It's off-limits to humans, but a stationary shoreline telescope magnifies the breeding birds. Near the telescope is a replica chapel of Fuerte San José, the area's first Spanish settlement (from 1779, but destroyed by Tehuelche people in 1810).

Puerto Pirámides has the most services, including the most affordable accommodations and food. June to December, whales are the main attraction, but beachgoers take over in January and February. Carless visitors can hike or bike to the sea lion colony at Punta Pirámide, four kilometers west, for vast panoramas and sunsets over the Golfo Nuevo.

Beneath the headlands at the peninsula's southeastern tip, **Punta Delgada** is home to southern elephant seal and sea lion colonies, reached by trail from the lighthouse at the former naval station (now a hotel-restaurant). Hotel concessionaires provide English-speaking guides to lead tour groups and individuals, but they charge US$10 pp for those who do not eat at the restaurant. They have also turned the lighthouse into a museum and offer horseback rides.

On the peninsula's eastern shore, about midway between Punta Delgada and Punta Norte, **Caleta Valdés** is a sheltered bay that's fast becoming a lagoon as its ocean outlet fills with sediment. Meanwhile, Magellanic penguins swim north to a breeding colony and southern elephant seals haul up onto shore in the mating season. Even kelp-seeking guanacos stroll along the beach.

Where RP 47 and RP 3 meet at the peninsula's northern tip, **Punta Norte** features a mixed colony of southern elephant seals and sea lions. October to April, this is also the best place to see orcas, which lunge onto the beach to grab unwary pups. The museum here places marine mammals in both a natural and cultural context, thanks to exhibits on the indigenous Tehuelche and a historical account of the sealing industry.

Near Punta Norte, reached by a northwesterly spur off RP 3, **Estancia San Lorenzo** (www.pinguinospuntanorte.com.ar) conducts tours of its own Magellanic penguin colony but does not offer accommodations.

Food and Accommodations

Puerto Pirámides continues sprouting more places to stay, eat, and recreate, but demand is high. Most accommodations, including the *estancias,* have added Wi-Fi service. In summer and during whale-watch season, reservations are advised. Rates rise notably in the second half of the year, and some hotels keep those well into the summer, while others apply lower rates once whale-watching is over. There are *estancia* accommodations scattered at and near Punta Delgada, but no camping is permitted beyond Puerto Pirámides.

Puerto Pirámides offers whale-watching services.

In a casual ambience blending traditional artifacts and artwork with pop music, **La Estación** (Av. de la Ballenas s/n, tel. 0280/449-5047, US$8-13) serves excellent fresh fish and salads, but the kitchen is slow and the service amateurish. **La Covacha** (Av. 25 de Septiembre s/n, tel. 0280/15-424-0838, US$12-15) serves a variety of fresh fish specials in a casual and friendly but still attentive atmosphere. There are good mixed drinks, including Cuban mojitos, with a happy hour 8pm-10pm nightly.

Immediately behind the dunes, the shoreline **Camping Municipal** (tel. 0280/449-5084, US$10 pp plus US$1 per vehicle) no longer charges separately for the timed showers. The baths are clean, and a store carries basic supplies. Few sites have any shade.

At the entrance to town, simple hostel accommodations are found at **Bahía Ballenas** (tel. 0280/15-456-7104, www.bahiaballenas.com.ar, US$11 pp), which hosts up to 24 people in two large gender-segregated dorms. For the same price, **Aloha Hostel** (Av. de las Ballenas s/n, tel. 0280/449-5040, alohahostel@hotmail.com.ar, US$11 pp) offers a bit more privacy.

At **Hostería La Estancia del Sol** (Av. de las Ballenas s/n, tel. 0280/449-5007, www.interpatagonia.com/estanciadelsolpiramides, US$78 d, with breakfast), plain but reasonably spacious and immaculately clean rooms are the rule. Its restaurant serves seafood and the usual Argentine standards.

Recently spruced up, the **Motel ACA** (tel. 0280/449-5004, www.motelacapiramides.com, members US$78 s, US$99 d, nonmembers US$111 s, US$142 d) was once Pirámides's top choice. Members of foreign affiliates are eligible for the member price. Its restaurant has also improved.

Set back from the main drag, the **Hostería Ecológica del Nómade** (Av. de las Ballenas s/n, tel. 0280/449-5044, www.ecohosteria.com.ar, mid-Aug.-mid-Apr., US$86-165 s or d) is an eight-room lodging designed to minimize its carbon footprint and water consumption in this desert area; it manages to do so without sacrificing style.

Its brick superstructure mimicking Chubut's Welsh heritage, the inviting ★ **Hostería The Paradise** (Av. de las Ballenas s/n, tel. 0280/449-5030, www.hosteriatheparadise.com.ar, US$160 s, US$185 d) is a substantial improvement on the usual utilitarian choices. Its restaurant (US$20) offers fixed-price lunches or dinners, with a menu that includes items such as scallops in a white wine sauce.

Top-end **Las Restingas Hotel de Mar** (tel. 0280/449-5101, www.lasrestingas.com, from US$168-210 s or d, plus 21 percent tax) is a seafront hotel with only 12 functional rooms, a few of which have balconies at the upper floor, others with decks and individual access to the beach, and some without ocean views at lower rates. It has a restaurant, a gym, and a spa. Rates are lower after whale-watching season.

On the bluffs overlooking Punta Delgada, alongside the lighthouse at RP 2's east end, ★ **Faro Punta Delgada Hotel de Campo** (tel. 0280/445-8444 or 0280/15-440-6304, www.puntadelgada.com, July-Apr., US$177 s, US$206 d with breakfast Sept.-Feb., 20-30 percent lower Mar.-Apr. and July-Aug.) is an upgraded property, with 27 comfortable rooms, on lease from the navy. It offers a scenic location and good access to wildlife, including penguins and southern elephant seals. Tour buses often stop at its restaurant, which is open to nonguests, and packages with all meals are available.

Near Punta Delgada, run by a Madryn couple, the best tourist-oriented ranch is ★ **Estancia Rincón Chico** (Blv. Brown 1783, tel. 0280/15-430-4581, Puerto Madryn tel. 0280/447-1733, www.rinconchico.com.ar, mid-Sept.-Mar., US$583 s, US$826 d, plus tax, 2-night minimum). Four kilometers southwest of RP 2, its purpose-built hotel has eight well-furnished doubles. From September to November they host elephant-seal researchers, as the seals frequent their long coastal frontage. Rates include all meals and activities but not drinks, transfers, or tips.

Information

At El Desempeño, at the west end of the Istmo de Ameghino, a provincial toll booth collects an **admission fee** (foreigners US$23 adults, US$10 ages 6-12, Argentines US$12, free under age 6). About 22 kilometers east, the **Centro de Interpretación** (7:30am-9pm daily) displays a complete right whale skeleton and also historical materials ranging from Tehuelche times to Spanish colonization and Argentine settlement for salt mining and sheep ranching. The informational panels are accompanied with good English translations. An observation tower offers panoramas across the northerly Golfo San José to the southerly Golfo Nuevo, and east across the peninsula's interior.

The **Dirección de Turismo** (25 de Septiembre s/n, tel. 0280/449-5048, www. puertopiramides.gov.ar, 8am-9pm daily summer, 8am-6pm daily fall-spring) is the municipal tourist office.

Transportation

In summer, from Puerto Madryn, **Mar y Valle** (tel. 0280/445-0600) has five buses daily to Puerto Pirámides (1.5 hours, US$8); from fall to spring this drops to as few as two buses daily. On a space-available basis, tour buses may allow passengers to disembark at Pirámides and return another day, but make advance arrangements.

Distances from Pirámides to other peninsula destinations are too great for nonmotorized transportation, so it's worth considering a **rental car** in Puerto Madryn. Many consider day trips from Madryn too rushed.

TRELEW

Less obviously tourist-oriented than Puerto Madryn, the Río Chubut city of **Trelew** retains more visible remnants of its Welsh birthright than its seaside sibling. It also offers access to the lower Chubut Welsh communities of Gaiman and Dolavon, the dolphin-watching beach resort of Playa Unión, and the massive penguin colonies at Punta Tombo. Its own main attraction, though, is

a state-of-the-art paleontological museum presenting Argentina's dramatic dinosaur discoveries.

Dating from 1886, when the railroad united Puerto Madryn with the lower Chubut's farm towns, Trelew takes its name from Welsh colonist and railroad promoter Lewis Jones (in Welsh, *tre* means town, while *lew* was an abbreviation of Lewis). It has since absorbed several waves of immigration—Italians and Spaniards, as well as Argentines from elsewhere in the country—and boom-and-bust cycles thanks to the wool industry, customs preferences, and industrial promotion.

Despite the changes, Trelew has retained its Welsh identity in events like the Eisteddfod del Chubut (a poetry and music festival) and other cultural activities.

On the Río Chubut's north bank, Trelew (pop. 105,000) is 65 kilometers south of Puerto Madryn and 375 kilometers northeast of Comodoro Rivadavia via RN 3. It is 608 kilometers west of Esquel via several paved highways.

Sights

On the pleasingly landscaped **Plaza Independencia,** the Victorian-style **Kiosco del Centenario** (1910) marked the centennial of Argentine independence. To the southwest, once isolated by walls and gates, the former **Distrito Militar** (army headquarters), dating from 1900, now houses the **Museo Municipal de Artes Visuales** (Mitre 351, tel. 0280/443-3774, 8am-7pm Mon.-Fri., 2pm-7pm Sat.-Sun., US$2), exhibiting historical photos as well as modern photography, painting, and sculpture. The tourist office occupies its adjacent **Anexo** (Annex, Mitre 387).

In 1920, Trelew's Spaniards built the **Teatro Español** (25 de Mayo 237), on the plaza's northwest side. Half a block east of the plaza, dating from 1914, the **Teatro Verdi** (San Martín 128) served the Italian community. The 1913 **Salón San David** (San Martín and Belgrano), originally a Welsh community center, used to host the Eisteddfod festival. Half a block northwest, the 1889 Welsh

Capilla Tabernacl (no phone, 9:30am-12:30pm Mon., Wed., and Fri., free) is Trelew's oldest surviving building.

Two blocks northeast of the plaza, early Patagonian tourists stayed at the **Hotel Touring Club** (formerly the Hotel Martino, dating from 1906), which underwent a major 1920s upgrade but now seems frozen in time (the moribund Touring Club Argentino once rivaled the Automóvil Club Argentino). It is still a popular local meeting place, however.

On the site of the old airport, a few kilometers north of the plaza, the **Centro Cultural por la Memoria** (RP 8 and RN 25, tel. 0280/442-6266, 8am-7pm Mon.-Fri., free) commemorates the Argentine navy's 1972 massacre of 16 escaped political prisoners who had laid down their weapons after failing to hijack a plane here.

Museo Regional Pueblo de Luis

An antique steam locomotive still stands outside Trelew's former train station, where, from 1889 to 1961, the Ferrocarril Central Chubut delivered passengers and freight from Puerto Madryn. The station now houses the **Museo Regional Pueblo de Luis** (Av. Fontana and Lewis Jones, tel. 0280/442-4062, 7am-7pm Mon.-Fri., 2pm-8pm Sat., US$2), which is packed with Welsh memorabilia, including historical photographs, furnishings, and clothing.

Museo Paleontológico Egidio Feruglio (MEF)

West of Trelew, the central Patagonian steppe is a prime dinosaur dig. The city's **Museo Paleontológico Egidio Feruglio** (MEF, Av. Fontana 140, tel. 0280/443-2100, www.mef.org.ar, 9am-6pm Mon.-Fri., 10am-7pm Sat.-Sun. Mar.-mid-Sept. except winter school holidays; 9am-7pm daily mid-Sept.-Mar. and winter school holidays, US$8 adults, US$6 children ages 6-12) features the magnificently mounted models of Argentine dinosaurs like the carnivorous *Piatnitzkysaurus floresi* and *Carnotaurus sastrei*. There are also dinosaur eggs, a genuine touchable dinosaur femur, and a working lab visible to the public.

At the same time, the museum acknowledges the achievements of pioneering Patagonian researchers like Florentino Ameghino, George Gaylord Simpson, and Alejandro Pianitzky in its hall of fame. It owes its name to an Italian paleontologist who came to Argentina in 1925 as a petroleum geologist for the state oil company YPF.

Piatnitzkysaurus at Trelew's Museo Paleontológico Egidio Feruglio

The museum has a small café (with Wi-Fi) and a souvenir shop. It also arranges excursions to the in situ fossil site at the Geoparque Paleontológico Bryn Gwyn, near Gaiman.

Entertainment and Events

The **Cine Coliseo** (Belgrano 375, tel. 0280/442-5300) shows recent films, while the **Teatro Verdi** (San Martín 128, tel. 0280/443-1398) provides live theater and music.

In odd-numbered years only, mid-September's **Certamen Internacional de Coros** draws on the Welsh choral tradition. October 20's **Aniversario de la Ciudad** marks Trelew's 1886 founding. Late October's **Eisteddfod del Chubut** (www.eisteddfod-patagonia.com) festival held at the Racing Club focuses on the lower Chubut valley's Welsh traditions, particularly folk music and poetry.

Shopping

For souvenirs and clothing, including horse gear, leather, and woolens, visit **El Jagüel** (La Rioja 382, tel. 0280/442-2949).

Roger Shop (Moreno 463, tel. 0280/443-0690) is the place to purchase traditional black cake and *teisenbach* (a Welsh cake), which are good as snacks.

Food

Even those who don't stay at the hotel should take breakfast or coffee at the **Confitería Touring Club** (Av. Fontana 240, tel. 0280/443-3998) to partake of its timeless ambience. **Café Balcarce** (9 de Julio 201, tel. 0280/442-4021, 8am-12:30am Mon.-Thurs., 8am-2am Fri., 8:30am-2am Sat., from US$8) is not only good for its sweets and desserts, but also for short orders, serving set menus and a daily special, including fish.

Sugar (25 de Mayo 247, tel. 0280/443-5978, 7:30am-12:30am daily, US$13) is a midday sandwich and short-order option, but also a more sophisticated dinner choice, with elaborate dishes such as squash-filled ravioli, seafood risotto, and lamb in herb sauce.

La Bodeguita (Belgrano 374, tel. 0280/443-7777, lunch and dinner daily, US$10-15) serves good pasta (particularly cannelloni) and pizza, with decent service.

For ice cream, try **Elke** (25 de Mayo 195, tel. 0280/443-3322, www.elkehelados.com) or **Vía Roca** (Belgrano 484, tel. 0280/443-1368).

Accommodations

For backpackers, Trelew has **Hostel El Ágora** (Edwin Roberts 33, tel. 0280/442-6899, www.hostelagora.com, US$17 pp, US$35 d), which has three- to eight-bed dorms, all with shared baths. It's four blocks from the bus terminal.

The serviceable staff of **Residencial Rivadavia** (Rivadavia 55, tel. 0280/443-4472, residencialrivadavia@gmail.com, US$25 s, US$38 d, breakfast US$3) helps overcome, at least in part, the basic comfort of the smallish rooms. Rooms include Wi-Fi and TV; in a so-so local hotel scene, this is one of the better values.

Hotel Centenario (San Martín 150, tel. 0280/442-6111, www.hotelcentenario.com.ar, US$57 s, US$63 d) is a large hotel with covered parking. It has undergone a relatively recent renovation.

For a touch of old Patagonia, perhaps because it's well past its prime, try the landmark **Hotel Touring Club** (Av. Fontana 240, tel. 0280/443-3998, www.touringpatagonia.com.ar, US$45 s, US$70 d). Though its rooms have been modernized, the building still retains a mystique from more glamorous times.

Hotel Galicia (9 de Julio 214, tel. 0280/443-3802, www.hotelgalicia.com.ar, US$61 s, US$72 d) has impressive common areas, including a startlingly beautiful spiral staircase, if slightly less impressive rooms.

The central 110-room **Hotel Rayentray** (Belgrano and San Martín, tel. 0280/443-4702, www.cadenarayentray.com.ar, US$50-60 s, US$60-80 d) has amenities including a restaurant, a gym, a sauna, and a swimming pool. The cheaper rooms are notably smaller.

Four-star in designation, the 80-room **Hotel Libertador** (Rivadavia 31, tel. 0280/442-0220, www.hotellibertador.com.ar, from US$67 s, US$83 d) has overcome a dull style thanks to steady renovation, offering now mostly comfortable standard rooms and suites in contemporary style.

Information

At Plaza Independencia's southwest corner, the municipal **Secretaría de Producción y Turismo** (Mitre 387, tel. 0280/442-0139, www.trelewpatagonia.gov.ar, 8am-8pm Mon.-Fri., 9am-9pm Sat.-Sun.) usually has an English speaker on hand. There are also offices at the bus terminal (keeping identical hours) and the airport (arriving flights only). **ACA** (Av. Fontana and San Martín, tel. 0280/443-5197) is a resource for motorists.

Services

Many visitors stay in Puerto Madryn, but Trelew agencies also do excursions to destinations like Rawson and Playa Unión, the lower Chubut valley's Welsh villages, Punta Tombo, and even Península Valdés.

Several banks have ATMs, including **Banco de la Nación** (25 de Mayo 2), which also exchanges money and travelers' checks. The postal code for **Correo Argentino** (Mitre 315) is 9100. Locutorio del Centro (25 de Mayo 219, tel. 0280/443-0176), at Plaza Independencia's northwest side, has telephone and Internet services. The area around Plaza Independencia is also a Wi-Fi zone.

Nievemar (Italia 20, tel. 0280/443-4114, www.nievemartours.com.ar) arranges excursions to the Welsh settlements and Punta Tombo (US$65). **Explore Patagonia** (Julio A. Roca 94, tel. 0280/443-7860, www.explorepatagonia.com.ar) also offers tours.

For medical needs, contact the **Hospital Zonal Adolfo Margara** (28 de Julio 160, tel. 0280/442-7543).

Transportation

Aeropuerto Internacional Marcos A. Zar (REL, RN 3 s/n, tel. 0280/443-3443, www.aeropuertotrelew.com) is five kilometers north of town on the east side of the Puerto Madryn highway. Cabs or meterless radio taxis cost about US$5.

Aerolíneas Argentinas (Rivadavia 548, tel. 0810/2228-6527) flies two or three times daily to Buenos Aires and daily to El Calafate and Ushuaia (Aug.-Jan.). **LADE** (Italia 170, tel. 0280/443-5740) flies sporadically to Buenos Aires as well as to some Patagonian destinations.

The **Terminal de Ómnibus** (Urquiza 150, tel. 0280/442-0121) is six blocks northeast of Plaza Independencia. A small boarding tax is charged on all long-distance tickets.

Mar y Valle (tel. 0280/443-2429) has regular service to Puerto Pirámides, leaving Trelew at 8:30am daily, with additional summer service. **El Ñandú** (tel. 0280/442-7499, elnandu_srl@hotmail.com) goes to the coastal town of Camarones (8am Mon., Wed., and Fri.). Typical destinations, times, and fares include Camarones (4 hours, US$15), Puerto Pirámides (3 hours, US$11), Comodoro Rivadavia (5 hours, US$30-40), Esquel (8-8.5 hours, US$40-66), Neuquén (10-12 hours, US$60-72), Río Gallegos (15-18 hours, US$89-101), and Buenos Aires (19-21 hours, US$104-120).

Mar y Valle (tel. 0280/443-2429) alternates with **Línea 28 de Julio** (tel. 0280/443-2429), running frequent buses to Puerto Madryn (1 hour, US$4). Línea 28 de Julio also goes every half hour to Gaiman (US$2) and less frequently to Dolavon (US$3), though weekend services are fewer. Both Línea 28 de Julio and **Empresa Rawson** (tel. 0280/448-1915) go frequently to Rawson (US$1.50), while **Transportes Bahía** (tel. 0280/448-2317) goes hourly to Puerto Rawson and Playa Unión (US$2), via Rawson.

Fiorasi (Urquiza 310, tel. 0280/443-5344) is the local car-rental option.

GAIMAN AND VICINITY

More than any other lower Chubut settlement, **Gaiman** has sustained and capitalized on its Welsh heritage. It's known for tourist teahouses, sturdy stone buildings, and community events like the youth Eisteddfod festival. Several agreeable B&Bs have made it more a destination than just an excursion.

Gaiman (pop. about 12,000), 17 kilometers east of Trelew via RN 25, dates from 1874, when Welsh farmers first harnessed the river to irrigate their fields and orchards. The Tehuelche people gave it the name Gaiman (Stony Point).

Sights

The best starting point is the **Amgueddfa Hanesyddol** (Sarmiento and 28 de Julio, tel. 0280/449-1007, 3pm-7pm daily, US$0.65), the regional historical museum in the former train station. Staffed by Welsh- and English-speaking volunteers, it holds documents, photographs, and possessions of early immigrants.

Two blocks northwest, Dolavon-bound trains no longer chug through the **Twnnel yr Hen Reilfford,** a 300-meter brick tunnel that's now open to pedestrians only. A block west of the tunnel exit, dating from 1906, the **Coleg Camwy** (Michael D. Jones and Bouchard) may have been Patagonia's first secondary school. Other original Welsh colony buildings can be seen nearby, such as the old post office, **Yr Hen Bost** (Michael D. Jones 222), and, dating from 1874, the town's first house, which opens as a small museum (J. C. Evans between Av. Eugenio Tello and 28 de Julio). Historic headstones, many of them in Welsh, dot the **Mynwent** (cemetery; east end of 28 de Julio).

Geoparque Paleontológico Bryn Gwyn

Exposed by meanderings of the Río Chubut after an earlier subtropical sea evaporated, the sedimentary badlands at **Geoparque Paleontológico Bryn Gwyn** (8 kilometers south of Gaiman via RP 7, 10am-6pm Tues.-Sun. summer and winter holidays, 11am-6pm Tues.-Sun. in other seasons, US$2 adults, US$1 children) are an open book of Tertiary fossils. The oldest beds are too recent for dinosaur bones, but there is evidence of marine mammals, such as seals, dolphins, and whales, along with penguins, giant anteaters, and ungulates from times when this was savanna.

The park is affiliated with Trelew's Museo Paleontológico Egidio Feruglio. Visitors can hike the well-organized trail, which climbs gradually and then steeply up the cliffs from the south-side café. There are at least a dozen excavations, with some fossils in the open and others preserved in glass cases. Groups larger than 20 can arrange guided visits.

There's no scheduled transportation, but meterless taxis from Gaiman are not unreasonable.

Shopping

For crafts, visit the **Paseo Artesanal Crefft Werin** (Av. Eugenio Tello and Michael D. Jones, tel. 0280/449-1134), opposite Plaza Roca.

Food

Gaiman may be picturesque, but it's pointless to come here without indulging yourself on cakes, jams, scones, pies, and a bottomless teapot. Since tea starts around 2:30pm-3pm, either skip lunch or go later and then skip dinner; for about US$15-20 pp, it's a de facto all-you-can-eat. When tour buses are parked outside, slow service is likely.

Gaiman's oldest teahouse is **Plas y Coed** (Michael D. Jones 123, tel. 0280/15-469-7069, www.plasycoed.com.ar), which wins points for exceptional sweets and personalized service. Ivy-covered **Ty Nain** (Av. Yrigoyen 283, tel. 0280/449-1126) is the most stylish, but **Ty Gwyn** (9 de Julio 111, tel. 0280/449-1009, www.tygwyn.com.ar) is also appealing. **Ty Cymraeg** (A. Mathews 74, tel. 0280/449-1010, www.casagalesa.com.ar) blends a traditional style but lacks the historical patina of, say, Plas y Coed; still, its scones, grape jam, and lemon pie are outstanding.

Quite a long way across the river, reached by a roundabout route over the bridge at the south end of J. C. Evans, **Ty Te Caerdydd** (Finca 202, tel. 0280/449-1510) is an enormous teahouse set among its own irrigated fields, which produce fresh fruits and berries for its own products, and elaborate flower gardens. Diana, Princess of Wales, was once a celebrity guest.

Enjoy Welsh tea in Gaiman.

Overnighters can't gorge themselves on Welsh teas every day. One alternative is **Cornel Wini** (Av. Eugenio Tello 199, tel. 0280/449-1397, 11:30am-2:30pm Wed., 11:30am-2:30pm and 8:30pm-midnight Thurs.-Mon.), a grill restaurant.

Accommodations
The quality of accommodations is fine, as top teahouses now offer B&Bs. Options are still limited, though, so reservations are advised.

In a handsome century-old house, friendly **Hostería Yr Hen Ffordd** (Michael D. Jones 342, tel. 0280/449-1394, www.yrhenffordd.com.ar, US$45 s, US$50 d, with breakfast) has simple and functional rooms. The classic brick facade at **Hostería Ty 'r Haul** (Sarmiento 121, tel. 0280/449-1880 or 0280/15-469-8350, www.hosteriatyrhaul.com.ar, US$52 s, US$58 d) is architecturally appealing, but the rooms themselves are strictly utilitarian. Despite the name, the owners are not Welsh nor even Welsh-Argentines.

★ **Hostería Plas y Coed** (Michael D. Jones 123, tel. 0280/449-1133, plasycoed@gmail.com, US$69-73 s or d) is a B&B annex of Gaiman's landmark teahouse, with just three comfortable rooms (and Wi-Fi).

★ **Hostería Ty Gwyn** (9 de Julio 111, tel. 0280/449-1009, www.tygwyn.com.ar, US$53 s, US$86 d) is a quality teahouse that also features several stylishly furnished rooms. The beds are handsome, and antique sewing machines serve as desks. Rooms have balconies facing the river that might be welcoming for summer mosquitoes. Breakfast is a delicious reprise of the previous afternoon's tea.

Transportation and Services
Next to the east end of the railroad tunnel is the municipal **Oficina de Informes** (Belgrano 574, tel. 0280/449-1571, 9am-8pm Mon.-Sat., 11am-8pm Sun. summer, 9am-6pm Mon.-Sat., 11am-6pm Sun. fall-spring).

Correo Argentino (J. C. Evans 114) is just north of the bridge over the river; the postal code is 9105. There's a *locutorio* (Av. Tello between 25 de Mayo and 9 de Julio), which is the telephone call center.

Línea 28 de Julio buses (Trelew tel. 0280/443-2429) traveling eastbound to Trelew and westbound to Dolavon stop on Plaza Roca. Note that a few bus services a day run the more attractive Trelew-Gaiman-Dolavon valley route in both directions across farmland and past some old Welsh chapels.

DOLAVON
Unlike Gaiman, sleepy **Dolavon** (pop. about 3,000) has never become a tourist town. The brick buildings along its silent streets display a greater architectural harmony than its larger neighbor, even though it's much newer (founded in 1919). Its major landmark, the **Molino Harinero** (1930), is a former grain mill with a restaurant annex; **La Molienda** (Maipú 61, tel. 0280/449-2290, www.molino-harinerodedolavon.com, 11am-4pm Tues.-Sun., US$10-20) serves pastas and lamb with local wines. *Norias* (waterwheels) decoratively set along the downtown canal represent what

was a common practice for the irrigation of the nearby fields and orchards.

From the Trelew terminal, **Línea 28 de Julio** (Trelew tel. 0280/443-2429) runs buses almost every hour daily to Dolavon via Gaiman. Try to take those along the valley route for a more picturesque journey.

LOS ALTARES

From Trelew, passing Gaiman and Dolavon, paved westbound RN 25 stays atop the steppe for about 150 kilometers before dropping into the Río Chubut valley at Valle de los Mártires. Here, the landscape resembles Utah's Bryce Canyon, with striking sandstone hoodoos resisting the ravages of erosion. The road continues through the Valle de las Ruinas, slightly less impressively, and from the floodplain hamlet of **Los Altares** through the Valle Paso de los Indios, where it rejoins the steppe.

At Los Altares, a wide spot on the road with only about 120 inhabitants, there's a municipal campground with decent facilities. The other lodging is the **ACA Motel** (RN 25, Km 321, tel. 0280/449-9003, US$23-32 s, US$35-50 d), a tidy but worn facility, where everything works and there's hot water. It's on such a shoestring budget that, when a light bulb fails, they have to go out and buy one. The rooms are Spartan and dark. The lower prices are for ACA members and members of foreign affiliates.

While the accommodations here are no prize, **Parrilla El Vasco** (tel. 0280/15-467-6880) across the highway offers better-than-expected food at reasonable prices.

★ ÁREA NATURAL PROTEGIDA PUNTA TOMBO

On barren South Atlantic shores, 126 kilometers south of Trelew, some 200,000 pairs of Magellanic penguins waddle ashore every austral spring to nest on only 210 hectares at Punta Tombo. Despite its isolation, more than 100,000 visitors a year, and up to 2,500 in a single day, find their way to **Área Natural Protegida Punta Tombo** (Sept.-Apr.,

foreigners US$17, Argentines US$7, plus a small fee per vehicle), following RN 3 and a shortcut to a dusty southeasterly lateral road and the continent's largest single penguin colony. Besides penguins, there are giant petrels, kelp and dolphin gulls, king and rock cormorants, and shorebirds that include oystercatchers and flightless steamer ducks—not to mention offshore whales.

Tours from Trelew (around US$65 pp) arrive around 11am daily, but the birds are so dispersed that it rarely seems crowded. Authorities have marked off the nesting grounds, and human visitors must stay on marked trails and boardwalks. Still, since penguins do not respect fences, it's possible to get up-close-and-personal photos. Just respect the birds' space (their beaks can inflict a nasty gash). Tombo's infrastructure remains limited, though the new **Centro de Interpretación de Pingüinos** has recently opened. No camping is permitted. The season runs from September to April; the park is closed for visits outside that period.

Despite their numbers, penguin populations here and at Península Valdés may be in trouble. An article in *Science* concluded that continued overfishing of the Patagonian anchovy, which constitutes half the penguins' diet (and also sustains elephant seals, dolphins, and other South Atlantic species) could cause a population collapse.

While it's also possible for a group to hire a taxi for a day trip to the reserve, renting a car in Trelew or Puerto Madryn would make it possible to follow the scenic desert coastline south past the ghost town of Cabo Raso to the picturesque fishing port of Camarones and Cabo Dos Bahías, a reserve with both penguins and sea lions. From Camarones, it's possible to return to Trelew or Puerto Madryn via paved RN 3.

CAMARONES AND VICINITY

Toward the south end of its namesake bay, **Camarones** is a sleepy fishing port with just two paved streets but so many wide gravel roads that it seems to be waiting for something to happen. Though its residents may wait a while, Camarones is just picturesque enough, close enough to the wildlife reserve at Cabo Dos Bahías, and an interesting enough jaunt from Punta Tombo via the Cabo Raso route that it's an ideal off-the-beaten-road loop for anyone with a vehicle. Its museum also deserves a look.

Alternatively, there's public transportation via RN 3 either southbound from Trelew or northbound from Comodoro Rivadavia, and then eastbound on RP 30, a distance of about 260 kilometers from either city. The town holds a **Fiesta Nacional del Salmón** (National Salmon Festival) in early February.

Museo de la Familia Perón

The **Museo de la Familia Perón** (Estrada 467, tel. 0297/496-3014, museoperon.cama-rones@gmail.com, 9am-6pm Mon.-Fri., 1pm-6pm Sat. and holidays, free) occupies a shiny new replica of Juan Domingo Perón's boyhood home. The caudillo's father, Tomás Perón, was justice of the peace and ran a sheep ranch on the town's western outskirts in the early 20th century (Juan Domingo was born in 1895). It differs from other Perón museums not in that it's professionally organized—so is Buenos Aires's Museo Eva Perón—but in that it acknowledges that Perón was a controversial and contradictory figure whose loyalists even engaged each other in firefights in the 1970s (right- and left-wing factions were each convinced the general was on their side).

While the museum leans toward the interpretations of Argentina's current left-of-center Peronists, it avoids the polemics so common in Argentine politics. Not only that, but the English translations that accompany the exhibits are above average.

Área Natural Protegida Cabo Dos Bahías

Only 30 kilometers southeast of Camarones, the 12,000-strong Magellanic penguin colony at **Dos Bahías** (free) is smaller than Punta Tombo's, but Dos Bahías's open terrain makes it easier to appreciate the colony's extent. In addition to penguins, it boasts a southern sea lion colony on offshore **Isla Moreno,** though they're hard to see without binoculars. Besides many of the same seabirds that frequent Punta Tombo, terrestrial wildlife includes armadillos, foxes, guanacos, and rheas.

Unlike at Punta Tombo, it's possible to camp at beaches en route to Dos Bahías, though there are no other services. There is no scheduled transportation either, though it's possible to contract a meterless taxi in Camarones.

Food and Accommodations

Open year-round, the waterfront **Camping Camarones** (Espora s/n, tel. 0297/15-436-9174, US$6 pp plus US$6 per vehicle and US$3 per tent, first day only) has sheltered sites with electricity, and there are clean baths with hot showers.

The **Indalo Inn** (Sarmiento and Roca, tel. 0297/496-3004, www.indaloinn.com.ar, US$52 s, US$59 d) has comfortable rooms and good *cabañas*. It also has a reliable restaurant (US$20) for fish and seafood.

Information and Services

Camarones' **Centro de Informes** (Belgrano and Estrada, tel. 0297/15-501-4285, 9am-8pm daily) is on the highway at the approach to town. There's a second office near the shoreline at the foot of Calle Roca, near the municipal campground.

Correo Argentino (Roca and Estrada) is the post office. **Banco Chubut** (San Martín 570) has an ATM.

Transportation

From the terminal at 9 de Julio and Rivadavia, **El Ñandú** (tel. 0280/442-7499 in Trelew) has buses to Trelew (4pm Mon., Wed., and Fri., 4 hours, US$15), while **ETAP** (tel. 0297/448-2750 in Comodoro Rivadavia) has buses to Comodoro Rivadavia (2pm Sat., 3.5 hours, US$22), but schedules and frequencies can change.

★ BAHÍA BUSTAMANTE

South of Camarones and Cabo Dos Bahías, **Parque Interjurisdiccional Marino Costero Patagonia Austral** comprises just a strip of the South Atlantic coastline, exactly one nautical mile (1.8 kilometers) out to sea and 1.5 kilometers inland. The easiest access point is **Bahía Bustamante,** 30 kilometers east of the main highway turnoff by a good gravel road.

From Bahía Bustamante, it's possible to take multiple excursions, including one to offshore islands that are part of the park and home to thousands of Magellanic penguins, cormorants, dolphin gulls, and steamer ducks as well as large colonies of southern sea lions and South American fur seals. This is possible only at high tide, though, as the five-meter tidal range makes it impossible for the flat-bottom launch to navigate at low tide. At low tide, there are other options: Beyond the park's limits, Bustamante possesses a remarkable badlands with a sprawling petrified forest equivalent to Santa Cruz province's Parque Nacional Bosques Petrificados de Jaramillo and Chubut's own Monumento Natural Bosque Petrificado de Sarmiento.

Bahía Bustamante is a company town based not on mineral extraction but rather on seaweed harvesting. Dating from about 1953, it once had 400 residents—most of them employees—but now has only about 40 or so. Many of them gather seaweed along the shoreline. It is then dried in the sun and trucked to Gaiman, where a factory processes it into food additives. All Bustamante's streets are named for species of seaweed.

Food and Accommodations

Accommodations at Bahía Bustamante (access at RN 3, Km 1674, tel. 0297/480-1000, Buenos Aires tel. 011/4156-7788, www.bahiabustamante.com, Aug.-Apr.) are at the former administrators' houses, which have been transformed into stylishly retrofitted guesthouses by the sea. **Casas del Mar**

rheas on the steppe behind Bahía Bustamante

(US$400-520 s, US$500-640 d, including all meals, lower rates for 3 or 4 people) are available at premium prices on an all-inclusive basis. The simpler **Casas de la Estepa** (US$145 for the house for up to 3 people, not including meals or activities) offers cheaper accommodations with kitchens. Meals and excursions on a space-available basis are extra. Rates vary according to seasonal peaks. **La Proveeduría** restaurant serves intriguing meals that often use seaweed as a condiment.

COMODORO RIVADAVIA

Comodoro Rivadavia's motto is "a city with energy," and Chubut's southernmost city is really Houston on the South Atlantic. For nearly a century, ever since water-seeking drillers hit a crude gusher instead, it has been the locus of Argentina's petroleum industry. Thanks to the former state oil company Yacimientos Petrolíferos Fiscales (YPF), it has an outstanding petroleum museum.

On surrounding hills, the landscape

remains a jumble of drilling rigs, pipelines, storage tanks, and seismic survey markers. Ironically, though, Cerro Chenque's high-tech windmills herald alternative energy.

A frequent stopover for southbound motorists, hilly Comodoro (pop. 202,800) is 375 kilometers southwest of Trelew and 780 kilometers north of Río Gallegos via RN 3; it's 581 kilometers southeast of Esquel via several paved highways. Most services are on or near east-west San Martín, within a few blocks of the sea.

Sights

For a panorama of Golfo San Jorge's curving coastline, take the road up to 212-meter **Cerro Chenque,** immediately north of downtown. Nearly barren and prone to landslides that have covered RN 3, it's now one of the sites of **Parque Eólico Antonio Morán,** South America's largest windmill farm. It's also possible to hike to the top, but the loose sediments demand caution.

About three kilometers north of the town center, the Universidad Nacional de la Patagonia's **Museo Nacional del Petróleo** (San Lorenzo 203, Barrio General Mosconi, tel. 0297/455-9558, museodelpetroleo@gmail.com, 9am-5pm Tues.-Fri., 3pm-6pm Sat., US$4) is a YPF legacy. On the grounds of Comodoro's initial gusher, it presents a professional account of Argentina's oil industry, from the natural and cultural environment to petroleum technology and its social and historical consequences. From San Martín between 25 de Mayo and Carlos Pellegrini, take the No. 4 Saavedra or No. 5 Universidad bus, and also other northbound buses.

Entertainment

A classic of its era, the **Cine Teatro Español** (San Martín 668, tel. 0297/447-7700, www.cinecr.com.ar) offers recent movies and theater productions. There's also the **Cine Coliseo** (San Martín 570, tel. 0297/444-5500), inside a mall.

Food

Barile Express (San Martín 514, tel. 0297/446-6953), a popular local bakery, has its own pleasant café, with good breakfasts.

Pizzería Giulietta (Belgrano 851, tel. 0297/446-1201, lunch and dinner daily, US$10-15) serves pizzas and fine pasta as well; in the same vein, there's **Cayo Coco** (Rivadavia 102, tel. 0297/447-3033, lunch and dinner daily).

Waterfront **Puerto Cangrejo** (Av. Costanera 1051, tel. 0297/444-4590, noon-3pm and 8pm-midnight daily, US$15-20) serves ample portions of fish and seafood.

The Hotel Austral Plaza's ★ **Tunet** (Moreno 725, tel. 0297/447-2200, 8pm-midnight daily, US$20) is Comodoro's top restaurant, with an elaborate fish and seafood menu that also includes tapas (US$10).

Chocolate's (San Martín 231, tel. 0297/446-4488) serves Comodoro's best ice cream.

Accommodations

Because Comodoro is the largest city in almost 1,000 kilometers of highway, hotels fill up fast, so reservations are advised.

Rehabbed **Hotel del Mar** (Ameghino 750, tel. 0297/447-2025, www.hotel-delmar.com.ar, US$42-53 s, US$60 d) is one of several utilitarian accommodations, but all rooms now have private baths, digital TV, and Wi-Fi. With improved services in a modern location, **Nuevo Hotel Español** (9 de Julio 940, tel. 0297/446-0116, www.hotelespanol.com.ar, US$60 s, US$75 d) also has a small restaurant.

Similarly upgraded, **Hotel Azul** (Sarmiento 724, tel. 0297/447-4628, www.hotelazul.com.ar, US$70 s, US$80 d) always had pretty good rooms. It now has Wi-Fi and more presentable common areas.

Really two hotels in one, the **Austral Express** (Moreno 725, tel. 0297/447-2200, www.australhotel.com.ar, US$70-94 s, US$104-118 d) and the newer ★ **Austral Plaza** (US$145-230 s, US$188-298 d) share a reception area, telephones, bar, café, and an excellent restaurant. The Express rooms are comfy enough, if a little small, but they're less extravagant than the Plaza's. Guests at both enjoy the same buffet breakfast.

Lucania Palazzo Hotel (Moreno 676, tel. 0297/449-9300, www.lucania-palazzo.com, from US$122 s, US$158 d) is a four-star highrise with amenities comparable to those of the Austral Plaza.

Information

The municipal **Centro de Informes** (Av. Hipólito Yrigoyen and Moreno, tel. 0297/444-0664, www.comodoroturismo.gob.ar, 8am-8pm Mon.-Fri., 1pm-8pm Sat., 3pm-8pm Sun.) provides information.

ACA (Dorrego and Alvear, tel. 0297/446-4036) is a resource for motorists.

Services

Banco de la Nación (San Martín 108) has one of several ATMs along the street. For currency exchange, try **Agencia Ceferino** (9 de Julio 880, Oficina 4, tel. 0297/447-3805).

The postal code for **Correo Argentino** (Av. San Martín 180) is 9000. There are several *locutorios* (call centers) with phone and Internet services, mainly on Avenida Rivadavia or on San Martín, and one at Moreno 830.

The **Chilean consulate** (Almirante Brown 456, Oficina 3, tel. 0297/446-2414) is a short distance from the bus terminal.

For medical assistance, try the **Hospital Regional** (Hipólito Yrigoyen 950, tel. 0297/444-2222).

Transportation

Aeropuerto General Mosconi (CRD, RN 3, tel. 0297/454-8190) is nine kilometers north of town. **Aerolíneas Argentinas** (Rivadavia 156, tel. 0297/444-0050) flies three to five times daily to Buenos Aires, and twice weekly to Neuquén. **LATAM Argentina** (tel. 0297/454-8171 at the airport) also flies to Buenos Aires.

Comodoro is a hub for **LADE** (Rivadavia 360, tel. 0297/447-0585), which flies northbound to Bariloche, Aeroparque in Buenos Aires, and intermediate towns; westbound to Perito Moreno; and southbound to El Calafate, Río Gallegos, and Ushuaia.

Comodoro's **Terminal de Ómnibus Teniente General Ángel Solari** (Pellegrini 730, tel. 0297/446-7305) has regional, long-distance, and limited international bus service to Coyhaique, Chile. **TransAustral** (tel. 0297/447-4841) departs for Coyhaique (8am Wed. and Sat., 10 hours, US$42); these buses usually run full and schedules can vary, so reservations are essential. The Palazzo Standard bus goes to and from the airport.

Other sample destinations, times, and fares include Caleta Olivia (1.5 hours, US$6-8.50), Puerto San Julián (6 hours, US$33-38), Trelew (5 hours, US$30-39), Puerto Deseado (4.5 hours, US$25), Puerto Madryn (6 hours, US$35-45), Los Antiguos (6.5 hours, US$35-39), Camarones (3.5 hours, US$22), Esquel (8 hours, US$48-56), Río Gallegos (10-11 hours, US$60-67), Bariloche (13-15 hours, US$58-67), and Buenos Aires (24-27 hours, US$110-126).

Car rental agencies include **Avis** (Moreno 725, at Austral Plaza Hotel, tel. 0297/446-4828, comodoro@avis.com.ar) and **Dubrovnik** (Moreno 941, tel. 0297/444-1844, www.rentacardubrovnik.com).

SARMIENTO

In what was once Tehuelche territory, the settlement of **Sarmiento** (pop. 11,000) is an oil town and farming service center. It sits between two large lakes, Lago Musters and Lago Colhué Huapi, part of whose waters flow eastward via a pipeline to relieve the thirst of arid Comodoro Rivadavia.

Monumento Natural Provincial Bosque Petrificado Sarmiento

Sarmiento is the gateway to the petrified forests of the **Monumento Natural Provincial Bosque Petrificado Sarmiento** (9am-7pm daily Oct.-Mar., 10am-6pm daily Apr.-Sept., donation), where fossil stumps, trunks, and chips of wood and bark litter the shale-and-sandstone landscape. Here, 75 million years ago, a two-tier tropical to subtropical forest covered what is now a Technicolor desert. Probably uprooted by hurricanes, then buried by ash blown westward as volcanism and tectonic uplift built the Andes, the fallen trees petrified as ensuing climatic change turned the densely vegetated fluvial landscape into a desert. The petrified trees, often exceeding a meter in diameter, may have reached 100 meters in height.

From the park **visitors center** (tel. 0297/489-8282), there's a scenic 1.5-kilometer nature trail that passes through the modern moonscape that was once the forest. It's best when the slanting afternoon sun brings out the hues of Cerro Colorado, to the southeast, but worthwhile at any time. Souvenir taking is absolutely prohibited.

The park entrance is reached by a southbound gravel road from Sarmiento. It's a common day tour from Comodoro, but it's also possible to hire a meterless taxi from Sarmiento for about US$50.

Food and Accommodations

There's no elaborate food, but low-priced **Heidy's** (Perito Moreno 600, tel. 0297/489-8308) serves large portions of pretty good ravioli and an excellent flan for dessert.

In a town with limited options, the best lodging is the motel-style **Hotel Ismar** (Patagonia 248, tel. 0297/489-3293, US$32 s, US$41 d, breakfast US$3 extra).

Transportation and Services

Sarmiento is 149 kilometers west of Comodoro Rivadavia via paved RP 20. **ETAP** (12 de Octubre and San Martín, tel. 0297/489-3058) has several buses to and from Comodoro, and others to Río Mayo and Esquel as well.

Sarmiento's hard-working **Dirección Municipal de Turismo** (Pietrobelli 388, tel. 0297/489-8220) keeps long hours daily.

fossil logs at Bosque Petrificado Sarmiento

Coastal Santa Cruz Province

CALETA OLIVIA

South of Comodoro Rivadavia, there's heavy truck traffic and plenty of reckless drivers on winding RN 3 (only the first 15 kilometers of a four-lane freeway are complete) before arriving at the gritty oil port of **Caleta Olivia** (pop. 63,700). Caleta Olivia, 79 kilometers from Comodoro, is a crossroads for westbound traffic to Lago Buenos Aires and the Chilean border at Chile Chico. It's 346 kilometers north of Puerto San Julián but only 216 kilometers northwest of Puerto Deseado, an underrated wildlife destination.

Caleta's only conspicuous sight, dominating a traffic circle that marks the town center, is the *Monumento al Obrero Petrolero* (1969), popularly known as "El Gorosito." Facing north, Pablo Daniel Sánchez's 10-meter sculpture of a muscular shirtless worker turning an oil valve symbolizes thinly peopled Patagonia's contribution to (or exploitation by) the populous heartland. It's also a dog-whistle reference to authoritarian president Juan Domingo Perón's most devoted followers, who were working-class *descamisados* ("shirtless ones").

Food and Accommodations

El Puerto (Av. Independencia 1060, tel. 0297/485-1313, lunch and dinner daily, US$13-20) is best for fish and seafood, serving salmon, shrimp, and a daily special. **Heladería Centro** (Av. Independencia 1175, tel. 0297/485-3721) has fine ice cream.

With helpful staff, **Hostería Don David** (Hipólito Yrigoyen 2385, tel. 0297/485-7661, www.posadadondavid.com.ar, US$40 s, US$46 d) is a fairly basic place that has a small restaurant and self-service breakfast. Expanded **Hotel Robert** (Av. San Martín 2151, tel. 0297/485-1452, www.hotelrobert. com.ar, US$60 s, US$67 d, small discount for cash, breakfast US$5) has comfortable rooms.

Its restaurant, **La Rosa** (US$8-16) comes recommended for fish.

Information and Services

The municipal **Oficina Central de Informes Turísticos** (Av. San Martín and Güemes, tel. 0297/485-0988, caletaolivia@ santacruz.gov.ar, 8am-8pm daily) is a helpful source of information.

Banco de la Nación (Av. Eva Perón 135) has one of several ATMs. **Correo Argentino** (Hipólito Yrigoyen 2194) is the post office. **Locutorio Monte de Horeb** (Gobernador Gregores 1300) has long-distance services. **Cyber Centro** (Av. San Martín 2281, tel. 0297/483-6933) has Internet services.

Transportation

From the **Terminal de Ómnibus** (Av. Tierra del Fuego 850), 16 blocks west of the Gorosito sculpture, there are northbound and southbound services along RN 3, plus westbound connections to Los Antiguos and Chile Chico.

Typical destinations, times, and fares include Comodoro Rivadavia (1.5 hours, US$6-9), Puerto Deseado (3 hours, US$18), Río Gallegos (10 hours, US$53-60), Los Antiguos (5 hours, US$30), and Buenos Aires (25-28 hours, US$151).

★ PUERTO DESEADO AND VICINITY

Bypassed by RN 3—but not by nature or history—**Puerto Deseado** is one of Patagonia's underrated pleasures. Visited by Magellan, settled by Spanish whalers, explored by Charles Darwin in 1833, and resettled half a century later, it clings to its pioneer ambience in what Francisco P. Moreno called "the most picturesque place on the eastern Patagonian coast." The star is the Ría Deseado, where strong tides rush up the estuary to create a wildlife-rich environment that supports a

Death Rode the Rails

At the corner of San Martín and Almirante Brown, Puerto Deseado's handsome wooden railcar is more than an object of train-spotter nostalgia. During the 1921 Santa Cruz anarchist rebellion (dramatized in Osvaldo Bayer's novel-based film *La Patagonia Rebelde*), it was the mobile command center for Colonel Héctor Benigno Varela, who led government forces against striking farm workers throughout the territory. At Jaramillo station, near the present-day junction of RN 281 and RN 3, Varela personally executed gaucho insurgent José Font (known as "Facón Grande" or "Big Knife") under false pretenses (Varela himself died from a bomb and bullets by German anarchist Kurt Gustav Wilckens in Buenos Aires in 1923).

In total, some 1,500 people died at the hands of Varela's forces. As a symbol of military brutality, the car is an enduring monument. In December 1980, in a defiant demonstration against Argentina's fiercest dictatorship ever, Deseado residents encircled the historic railcar with 40 private automobiles to prevent its removal by truck. Not only did the demonstrators challenge armed authority—in a town with a tank regiment—but they bravely signed their names and ID card numbers in a petition to Santa Cruz's military governor. Astonishingly, the dictatorship backed down.

growing ecotourism sector. Its wildlife-rich offshore islands and the shores are now part of Parque Marino Isla Pingüino. At the same time, Deseado has become a homeport for the South Atlantic shrimp fishery, and some businesses keep signs in Spanish, English, and Russian.

On the Ría Deseado's north shore, Puerto Deseado (pop. 15,000) is 216 kilometers southeast of Caleta Olivia and 295 kilometers from Comodoro Rivadavia via RN 3 and paved RN 281 (but 126 kilometers from the RN 3 junction).

Sights

For a small town, Deseado has plenty to see. The big draw is the Reserva Natural Ría Deseado, but various historical monuments all have good stories behind them.

By the late 19th century, Deseado seemed destined to become a rail port, as authorities planned a northwesterly freight-and-passenger line to Bariloche. It never advanced beyond Las Heras, 283 kilometers northwest, and closed in 1977, leaving the stately **Estación del Ferrocarril Patagónico** (Eufrasia Arias s/n, tel. 0297/487-0601, 4pm-7pm Mon.-Fri., donation) as a surprisingly good museum staffed by former railroad workers.

Several monuments date from this era, most notably the railroad's 1898 **Vagón Histórico** (San Martín and Almirante Brown), a historical railcar in a small plaza. Immediately across the street, **Banco de la Nación** has preserved its classic lava-block style. The former **Compañía Argentina del Sud** (1919) now hosts a supermarket that has sadly concealed its vintage details with painted signs on all sides. One block west stands the **Sociedad Española** (1915).

Along the waterfront, the **Museo Regional Mario Brozoski** (Colón and Belgrano, tel. 0297/487-1358, museo@deseado.gob.ar, 9am-7pm daily summer, 10am-5pm daily fall-spring, free) holds artifacts from the English corvette *Swift*, sunk nearby in 1770 and rediscovered in 1982. Four kilometers northeast, **Balneario Las Piletas** is a volcanic beach area where retreating tides leave pools warm enough for swimming, at least in summer.

Reserva Natural Provincial Ría Deseado

One of coastal Patagonia's prime wildlife sites, the **Ría Deseado** submerges a long narrow valley that once carried more fresh water. As the fresh water flow diminished, seawater penetrated farther and farther inland, creating new islands and other fauna-rich habitats.

Several operators organize wildlife-watching excursions in and around the *ría* (estuary) to locations such as the Magellanic penguin colonies at **Isla Chaffers** and **Isla de los Pájaros,** and cliff-side colonies of rock cormorants and gray or red-legged cormorants at **Barranca de los Cormoranes,** where deep water permits close approach to the nests. On any excursion, swiftly swimming *toninas overas* (Commerson's dolphins) breach and dive around and under the outboard launches. In mating season, they leap out of the water. Some operators also follow Charles Darwin's route up the *ría* where, the great naturalist wrote, "I do not think I ever saw a spot which appeared more secluded from the rest of the world, than this rocky crevice in the wild plain."

In handsome quarters that include a seaview café, **Darwin Expediciones** (España 2551, tel. 0297/15-624-7554, www.darwin-expeditions.com) has extensive experience here and also does sea kayaking. Half-day trips (US$50 pp with a 6-passenger minimum) run along the Ría Deseado; longer full-day trips along Darwin's estuary route are also possible.

Puerto Penacho (tel. 0297/15-405-8472, www.puertopenacho.com.ar) does similar maritime itineraries, and **Turismo Aventura Los Vikingos** (Prefectura Naval s/n, tel. 0297/487-0020, www.losvikingos.com.ar) adds other overland excursions to the usual nautical journeys.

Parque Interjurisdiccional Marino Isla Pingüino

Created in 2011, this park protects the wildlife-rich seashores south from Ría Deseado to Bahía Laura and several small offshore islands, including **Isla Pingüino.** Exploited until the 19th century for its populous sea lion colonies, this 1.25-square kilometer island, about 20 kilometers southeast of Deseado, has breeding sea lions, vagrant elephant seals, two species of skuas and their hybrids, and the world's northernmost colony of the tireless rockhopper penguin, which braves crashing waves up steep stone faces to reach its nesting sites.

For full-day boat excursions to Isla Pingüino (about US$100 pp with a 6-passenger minimum), contact Deseado operators **Darwin Expediciones** (España 2551, tel. 0297/15-624-7554, www.darwin-expeditions.com), **Puerto Penacho** (tel. 0297/15-405-8472, www.puertopenacho.com.ar),

a molting rockhopper chick at Isla Pingüino, off Puerto Deseado

and **Turismo Aventura Los Vikingos** (Prefectura Naval s/n, tel. 0297/487-0020, www.losvikingos.com.ar).

Food and Accommodations

In summer, reservations are advised for the limited accommodations.

El Refugio de la Ría (12 de Octubre and 15 de Julio, tel. 0297/487-2317, lunch and dinner daily) serves seafood and is a grill restaurant as well. **Puerto Cristal** (España 1698, tel. 0297/487-0387, lunch and dinner Thurs.-Tues., dinner Wed., US$10-15) has decent seafood, excellent pastas, and good service.

At the western approach to town, the sheltered **Camping Cañadón Giménez** (tel. 0297/15-466-3815, US$3 s or d) also charges US$5 per tent.

Some of the singles are tiny at labyrinthine **Residencial Los Olmos** (Gregores 849, tel. 0297/487-0077, www.losolmoshotel.com.ar, US$31 s, US$44 d, discounts for cash), but the management is friendly. Amenities include (balky) Wi-Fi and private parking. **Hotel Isla Chaffers** (San Martín and Moreno, tel. 0297/487-2246, administracion@hotelislachaffers.com.ar, US$46 s, US$56 d) has decent rooms at a central location.

At **Hotel Los Acantilados** (España 1611, tel. 0297/487-2167, reservas.losacantilados@gmail.com, US$47-59 s, US$59-95 d), downstairs rooms come with small but serviceable baths. Upstairs rooms have sea views and better furniture, but the baths are equally small. Its bar is one of the best places to watch the sunset.

Information and Services

The **Dirección Municipal de Turismo** (Av. San Martín 1525, tel. 0297/487-0220, 7am-8pm daily) provides tourist information.

Banco de la Nación (San Martín 1001) has an ATM. **Correo Argentino** (San Martín 1075) is the post office; the postal code is 9050. **Nuevo Centro** (Almirante Brown 571) has telephones and Internet connections.

For medical services, try the **Hospital Distrital** (España 991, tel. 0297/487-0200).

Transportation

From the **Terminal de Ómnibus** (Sargento Cabral 1302), about 10 blocks northeast of downtown, there are services to Caleta Olivia (3 hours, US$17) with **Andesmar,** and two buses daily to Comodoro Rivadavia (4.5 hours, US$25) with **Sportman** (tel. 0297/487-0013).

PARQUE NACIONAL BOSQUES PETRIFICADOS DE JARAMILLO

One of RN 3's most desolate stretches is the 350 kilometers between Caleta Olivia and Puerto San Julián, but just north of the halfway point, the 60,000-hectare badlands called **Parque Nacional Bosques Petrificados de Jaramillo** (9am-7pm daily Oct.-Mar., 10am-5pm daily Apr.-Sept., free) is an incomparable detour. In Jurassic times, before the Andes rose in the west, this was a humid region of coniferous *Proaraucaria* woodlands; after volcanic eruptions flattened the forests and buried them in ash 130 million years ago, water and wind gradually uncovered the now-petrified trunks.

Measuring up to 3 meters in diameter and 35 meters in length, *Proaraucaria* was a forerunner of the Andean araucaria. Until 1954, when the area became a natural monument (meriting Argentina's highest possible level of protection), the best and biggest specimens were regularly looted.

Solitary Bosques Petrificados, 50 kilometers west of RN 3 via graveled RP 49, gets only a few thousand visitors per year, mostly in summer. In addition to its petrified forests, it has desert steppe vegetation and wildlife, including guanacos and rheas. It has no water, and there is no public transportation, but Puerto Deseado operators will organize excursions to the site.

For camping, try **Estancia La Paloma** (tel. 0297/15-430-5255, nikourri@yahoo.com.ar, US$6 pp), roughly midway between the highway and the forest. About 40 kilometers south of the park's access point, on RN 3, a basic hotel and restaurant (tel. 02962/45-4294, estaciontrescerros@hotmail.com) is an annex of the Tres Cerros gas station.

For more information, contact Caleta Olivia's **Administración de Parques Nacionales (APN) office** (Ameghino s/n, Jaramillo, tel. 0297/483-1201, bosquespetrificados@apn.gov.ar).

PUERTO SAN JULIÁN AND VICINITY

Windswept **San Julián** was where Magellan's crew wintered in 1520 during the first circumnavigation of the globe. Both Magellan and Sir Francis Drake (half a century later) faced mutinies that they repressed ruthlessly, while Antonio de Viedma founded a short-lived Spanish colony at nearby Floridablanca— southern Patagonia's first European settlement—in 1780. Darwin, who found the countryside "more sterile" than Deseado, uncovered a llama-like fossil with an elephantine trunk here.

In the 1890s, British settlers from the Falkland Islands and Scotland finally established a permanent presence through the powerful San Julián Sheep Farming Company. Even in the late 1930s, according to John Locke Blake, "English was spoken freely round town," and the company's extensive holdings—175,000 hectares of pasture—dominated life into the 1960s. Today, it's a secondary ecotourism destination for dolphins and penguins, and a common stopover between Caleta Olivia and Río Gallegos. A long stretch of the coast and its ocean waters south from Cabo Curioso (25 kilometers to the north) are now part of the **Parque Interjurisdiccional Marino Makenke.**

San Julián (pop. 8,672) is 351 kilometers south of Caleta Olivia and 360 kilometers north of Río Gallegos via RN 3. It's a well-kept town whose main thoroughfare, Avenida San Martín, is an extension of the eastward lateral road that connects it with the highway.

Sights

In the bay just north of town, **Isla Cormorán** has a Magellanic penguin colony. There's a king cormorant colony nearby at the sardonically named **Isla Justicia,** where Magellan stopped a mutiny by decapitating one rebel, quartering another, and leaving two others to starve. Headquartered in an adapted shed, **Pinocho Excursiones** (Av. Costanera and Mitre, tel. 02962/45-4600, www.pinochoexcursiones.com.ar) takes visitors on harbor tours (US$43 pp), with English-speaking guides, that include dolphin- and penguin-watching; when winds are too strong, their rigid inflatables may not be able to sail.

At the foot of Avenida San Martín, San Julián's most conspicuous waterfront attraction is a Disneyish scale model of Magellan's ship that holds the **Museo Temático Nao Victoria** (no phone, daily 8am-9:30pm or dusk, whichever is earlier, foreigners US$2.50 adults, US$1 children, Argentines US$2 adults). It's tempting to dismiss this as "Pirates of the South Atlantic," but it does make an effort to cover local history.

The **Museo de los Pioneros Rosa Novak de Hoffman** (Vieytes and Rivadavia, no phone, 8am-10pm Mon.-Fri., 10am-8pm Sat.-Sun., free) is a small archaeological and historical museum. Immediately across from it, the memorial **Plazoleta Albino Argüelles** commemorates one of the army's victims in the 1921 anarchist rebellion. From here, the coastal Avenida Hernando de Magallanes leads north past the marked grave of *Beagle* crewman Robert Sholl, who died on the voyage prior to Charles Darwin's. The road continues to the **Frigorífico Swift,** a mutton freezer that operated from 1912 to 1967; its crumbling shell and pier appeal to postindustrial photographers.

About 50 kilometers south from Puerto San Julián on RN 3, there's a viewpoint onto the vast natural depression of the **Gran Bajo de San Julián,** whose lowest point at Laguna del Carbón is 105 meters below sea level, marking the continent's deepest site.

Food

Popular ★ **La Rural** (Ameghino 811, tel. 02962/45-4066, lunch and dinner daily, US$11) has a menu of Argentine standards, such as its *bife de chorizo,* plus very good fish and seafood, all at reasonable prices. Its fine pastas include stuffed *sorrentinos.*

Right on the waterfront, **Naos** (9 de Julio and Mitre, tel. 02962/45-2714, lunch and dinner daily, US$10-15) is another quality restaurant that may get crowded in the evening. It serves lamb, fish, and seafood. **M&M** (Av. San Martín 387, tel. 02962/45-4419) has superb ice cream.

Accommodations

The waterfront **Autocamping Municipal** (Av. Hernando de Magallanes 650, tel. 02962/45-4506, US$2 pp adults, US$1 children, plus US$4 per tent and US$4 per car, US$8 per motorhome) has well-sheltered sites with picnic tables and fire pits, clean baths, hot showers, laundry facilities, and even a playground.

In a recycled sea-view house, ★ **Hostería La Casona** (Av. Costanera s/n, tel. 02962/45-2434, www.hosteri-alacasona.com, US$37 s, US$50 d) is a B&B that's San Julián's most distinctively Patagonian lodging, and probably its best value. It has comfortable beds, spacious and attractive common areas with Wi-Fi, and a kitchen for a basic self-serve breakfast. Under the same ownership, the nearby **Hostería Miramar** (Av. San Martín 210, tel. 02962/45-4626, www.hosteria-miramar. com, US$50 s, US$63 d) looks better on the surface than La Casona, but the rooms are just okay.

Hotel Sada (Av. San Martín 1112, tel. 02962/45-2013, ketty_sanjulian@hot-mail.com, US$47 s, US$66 d) has 18 rooms with private baths. The comparably priced **Posada de Drake** (Mitre and Rivadavia, tel. 02962/45-2523, posadadedrake@speedy.com. ar, US$49 s, US$70 d) deserves attention for immaculate quarters and for its teahouse; it also has Wi-Fi.

Government-owned but privately run, **Hotel Municipal Costanera** (25 de Mayo and Urquiza, tel. 02962/45-2300, www.costanerahotel.com, US$70 s, US$85 d) has 23 comfortable, spotless (and occasionally stylish) rooms, a restaurant, and Wi-Fi.

Information and Services

At the bus terminal, the municipal **Centro de Informes "La Terminal"** (Av. San Martín 1570, tel. 02962/45-2301, www.sanjulian.gov. ar, 8am-9pm daily) works efficiently. There's a separate **Centro de Informes** (Av. San Martín s/n, no phone, 8am-8pm daily) near the Não Victoria museum on the waterfront.

Banco de la Nación (Mitre 101) has an ATM. The postal code for **Correo Argentino** (Av. San Martín 155) is 9310. For phone and Internet services, there is **Tree-com** (Av. San Martín and Saavedra), a block from the bus terminal.

For medical services, try the **Hospital Distrital Miguel Lombardich** (9 de Julio s/n, tel. 02962/45-2020).

Transportation

The **bus terminal** (Av. San Martín 1570, tel. 02962/45-2301) is 15 blocks northwest of several services on the shore.

On a highway the length of RN 3, somebody has to draw the short straw, and most San Julián buses arrive and leave between midnight and 4am. There are several services to Buenos Aires and intermediate towns, and also south to Río Gallegos. **Transportes Cerro San Lorenzo** (no phone) goes daily to Gobernador Gregores (4 hours, US$30).

COMANDANTE LUIS PIEDRA BUENA

When Charles Darwin and the *Beagle* crew ascended the Río Santa Cruz in 1834, swift currents beyond Isla Pavón obliged them to walk the shore and drag their boats on lines, limiting their progress to about 16 kilometers per day. Twenty-five years later, naval explorer Luis Piedra Buena first raised the Argentine flag where his namesake town now stands. Naval officer Valentín Feilberg first ascended the river in 1873 to its source at Lago Argentino, followed four years later by Perito Moreno, who sailed the lake and went beyond, reaching Lago Viedma and Lago San Martín.

Piedra Buena (pop. 6,400) has little to see in its own right, but its services can justify a lunch break or even an overnight stay before seeing Parque Nacional Monte León. On the Río Santa Cruz's north bank, it's 127 kilometers south of Puerto San Julián and 237 kilometers north of Río Gallegos via RN 3. About 45 kilometers south, westbound RP 9 provides a bumpy motorist's or cyclist's shortcut along the Río Santa Cruz valley to El Calafate.

While the town is nondescript, **Isla Pavón**, reached by a turnoff from the bridge over the Río Santa Cruz about three kilometers south of the highway junction, is a beautiful wooded spot that is popular for fishing. A small museum honors Piedra Buena's efforts; admission is free.

Food and Accommodations
On the access road, **Doña Ana** (Av. Belgrano and Benigno Fernández, tel. 02966/15-45-8719, lunch and dinner daily, US$10-15) serves local trout as well as traditional Patagonian lamb.

On the island, the campsite at **Complejo Turístico Isla Pavón** (tel. 02962/15-42-3361, complejoislapavon@hotmail.com, US$25 for up to 6 people) has electricity, clean restrooms, and hot showers.

Despite its uninviting name, the spacious rooms at ★ **Hotel Sur Atlantic Oil** (RN 3, Km 2404, tel. 02962/49-7054, suratlantic@infovia.com.ar, US$41 s, US$55 d, breakfast extra), part of the YPF gas station complex, fill up early, and it's sloppy with reservations. Popular with southbound travelers, it also has a surprisingly good restaurant (US$10-13) with particularly choice pastas (take lunch in the restaurant, rather than the adjacent café).

Across the highway, the newer **Hotel Río**

Santa Cruz (tel. 02962/49-7245, h_riosantacruz@yahoo.com.ar, US$45 s, US$55 d) is a good backup lodging choice.

Transportation
Northbound and southbound services along RN 3 use the **Terminal de Ómnibus** (Av. Ibáñez 157), but it's also possible to flag down buses on the highway. At the same terminal, check at the **Centro de Información Turística** (tel. 02966/15-57-3065, 9am-6pm Mon.-Fri., 3pm-8pm Sat.-Sun.) to see if there are regular transfer services for Parque Nacional Monte León; recently, there have only been taxis or *remises*.

★ PARQUE NACIONAL MONTE LEÓN
Monte León's 30-kilometer shoreline and headlands are an ecological wonderland of copious wildlife and uncommon landscapes. Little-known and less visited, this former cattle ranch is Argentina's second coastal national park, after Parque Nacional Tierra del Fuego. The 62,000 hectares of land were donated to the APN by the Fundación Vida Silvestre and the Patagonia Land Trust via environmental philanthropists Doug Tompkins and Kris McDivitt Tompkins.

Flora and Fauna
Monte León's coastline is home to some 150,000 Magellanic penguins, as well as gray and king cormorants, snowy sheathbills, Patagonian crested and steamer ducks, Dominican gulls, and sea lions. Its shelters armadillos and *liebres* (Patagonian hares) and is home to grazing guanacos and rheas. The vegetation is primarily grasses and prostrate shrubs of the Patagonian steppe. There are also pumas as well as red and gray foxes.

Sights and Recreation
While wildlife-watching is the principal activity, the landscape here is noteworthy. Where the tides meet the headlands, the sea has eroded deep caverns. The most famous of these, **La Olla** (The Kettle) took its name

from its almost perfectly circular opening. Heavy rains and seas caused it to collapse in 2006, but it remains one of park's top sights. The collapsed segment is visible along the beach at low tide; it's dangerous to approach at other times.

Unlike much of the South Atlantic, the coastline here abounds with offshore rocks and stacks. Guano collectors worked one of these, **Isla Monte León**, by stringing a still-existing cable tram from the headland. At low tide, exploring La Olla's remnants and Isla Monte León's base is possible. Be sure to know the tides to avoid being stranded in a dangerous situation—the rocks are slippery, and the water comes in fast. Try to descend about an hour before low tide. Park rangers there will advise on times.

Food and Accommodations

Unfortunately, after a death in the family, ★ **Hostería Monte León** (RN 3, Km 2399), the former *estancia*'s *casco* (manor house) managed by the former owners' family, is closed until further notice. The *casco* itself is a spacious, high-ceilinged beauty with four guest rooms and a small museum.

On barren sites at the park proper, camping is possible through the concessionaire at the **Proveeduría Monte León** (US$19 per site for up to 6 people). Basic supplies are also available here.

Transportation and Services

Six kilometers northeast of the park's entrance at the former *estancia*'s *casco* is the **Oficina de Informes del Centro Operativo Monte León**, where free registration is necessary prior to the visit and information is available, especially for the tides and the wash-out-prone road. Park access from RN 3, Km 2405, 31 kilometers south of Piedra Buena, is via graveled RP 63, which reaches the coast after about 20 kilometers. The park closes from April to November; after summer rains, the access road may occasionally close. The **APN's office** (San Martín 112, tel. 02962/49-8184, www.pnmonteleon.com.ar) is in Puerto Santa Cruz.

RÍO GALLEGOS

Travelers often dismiss windy **Río Gallegos** as merely a port and service center for Anglo-Argentine wool *estancias* and the petroleum industry. Dating from 1885, near continental Argentina's southern tip, it has a handful of museums, historical landmarks, and other distinctive Magellanic buildings, and a

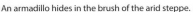

An armadillo hides in the brush of the arid steppe.

handsomely redeveloped waterfront. It's also the gateway to one of the continent's largest penguin colonies and several historic *estancias* open to visitors. It's no longer the main gateway to El Calafate since construction of the new international airport there, but travelers bound for Punta Arenas (Chile) and Tierra del Fuego may have to spend the night here.

Río Gallegos (pop. 109,200) is 780 kilometers south of Comodoro Rivadavia and 360 kilometers south of Puerto San Julián via RN 3, and 67 kilometers north of the Chilean border post of Monte Aymond. From Monte Aymond it's another 196 kilometers to Punta Arenas or, alternatively, 571 kilometers to Ushuaia, Tierra del Fuego (including a ferry crossing at Primera Angostura). It's 305 kilometers southeast of El Calafate via RN 3, RP 5, RN 40, and RP 11, all paved. The city's main thoroughfare, Avenida Roca, was renamed as Avenida Presidente Doctor Néstor C. Kirchner, only a few days after the Gallegos-born former president's death in 2010, in a political decision that has not pleased everyone.

Sights

Opposite Plaza San Martín, the **Catedral Nuestra Señora de Luján** (1899) was the work of Salesian priest Juan Bernabé, who was also responsible for the cathedrals of Punta Arenas and Ushuaia. Like other pioneer buildings, it reflects the wood-framed, metal-clad Magellanic style.

On the plaza's southwest side, the **Museo de Arte Eduardo Minnicelli** (Maipú 13, tel. 02966/43-6323, www.museominnicelli.santacruz.gov.ar, 8am-3pm Mon., 8am-7pm Tues.-Fri., 3pm-7pm Sat.-Sun. and holidays Feb. 11-Dec. 19, free) showcases provincial artists such as its namesake sculptor.

Three blocks southwest, the comprehensive **Museo Regional Provincial Padre Jesús Molina** (Ramón y Cajal 51, tel. 02966/42-3290, 9am-7pm Mon.-Fri., 11am-7pm Sat.-Sun. and holidays, free) holds material on geology, paleontology, natural history, ethnology, and local history, including a good photographic collection.

In a pioneer house that belonged to Arthur and Victor Fenton, the city's first physicians, the **Museo de los Pioneros** (Elcano and Alberdi, tel. 02966/43-7763, pioneros@riogallegos.gov.ar, 10am-5pm daily, free) documents southern Patagonia's early settlers. A guide may explain the details in English.

The late president Kirchner's family tomb is becoming something of a pilgrimage site at the **Cementerio Municipal** (Av. Beccar and Tucumán), southwest of downtown, though it appears to be deteriorating after shoddy construction.

Shopping

Rincón Gaucho (Av. Kirchner 617, tel. 02966/42-0669) specializes in horse gear and the like. **Artesanías Keokén** (Av. San Martín 336, tel. 02966/42-0335) specializes in woolens but also sells leather goods and food items such as preserves and candies.

Food

Highly regarded as a pizzeria and grill restaurant, **Don Bartolo** (Sarmiento 124, tel. 02966/42-7297, lunch and dinner daily, US$10-15) serves pizzas, lamb, and a full *parrillada* (mixed grill) for two (US$40).

Anyone who's ever been, or aspired to be, an Anglo-Argentine wool baron will want to dine at the atmospheric **British Club Restaurant** (Av. Kirchner 935, tel. 02966/43-2668, www.britishclub.com.ar, lunch and dinner daily, from US$10), which offers live jazz some nights. The menu is short but creative, including seafood, beef, fish, and lamb, even using a wok, and managing to combine the Andean quinoa grain with Yorkshire pudding in a single dish. Three-course lunches (US$15) are available Monday to Saturday.

Known for its chocolates and ice cream, **Delicias de la Abuela** (Errázuriz 26, tel. 02966/42-9996, US$12) is now stressing its role as a tea and waffle house, though it has a diversity of other lunchtime dishes. The local ice cream favorite is **Heladería Tito** (Zapiola 595, tel. 02966/42-2008, www.heladostito.com.ar).

Accommodations

Traditionally expensive, scarce, and mediocre, accommodations have substantially improved in comfort and amenities such as Wi-Fi, which is now present in all listed hotels. Demand is high, so reservations are advised.

With gracious and conscientious ownership, **Hotel Colonial** (Urquiza and Rivadavia, tel. 02966/42-0020, ines_frey@hotmail.com, US$25 s, US$38 d) is the best shoestring choice in a partly renovated 1930s building with spotless rooms. Though no breakfast is served, there is kitchen access.

Well-kept **Hotel Oviedo** (Alfonsín 746, tel. 02966/42-0118, www.hoteloviedo.com.ar, US$30 s, US$40 d, breakfast US$5 extra) is a very good value. The original mid-20th-century style has been preserved in its spacious rooms; all baths have bathtubs.

A reliable classic, **Hotel Covadonga** (Av. Kirchner 1244, tel. 02966/42-0190, hotelcovadongargl@hotmail.com, US$31-35 s, US$38-41 d) has preserved much of its original 1930s style, especially in its common areas. Rooms are simple with both shared and private baths (with minimal price difference), and there is parking.

Friendly **Hotel Punta Arenas** (Federico Sphur 55, tel. 02966/43-1924, www.hotelpuntaarenas.com, US$40-45 s, US$43-52 d) has newer comfortable rooms but also preserves older and cheaper ones. All rooms now have private baths. Breakfast takes place in its adjacent Something Café, which has a small but tasty snack menu.

Ill-planned remodeling has cost **Hotel París** (Av. Kirchner 1040, tel. 02966/42-0111, www.hotelparisrg.com.ar, US$37 s, US$42) most of its original charm, but renovation under new ownership brought respectable results. At the back, there are modern motel-style rooms with high ceilings and firm single beds.

Reservations are almost essential for friendly, well-kept **Hotel Sehuen** (Rawson 160, tel. 02966/42-5683, www.hotelsehuen.com, US$60 s, US$65-75 d), where singles are perhaps too small. Some doubles have baths with bathtubs.

Rehabbed **Hotel Comercio** (Av. Kirchner 1302, tel. 02966/42-0209, gerenciahotelcomercio@gmail.com, US$60 s, US$75 d) is a good-value, centrally located choice with comfortable rooms and a self-serve breakfast. There's a 10 percent discount for cash.

Nondescript **Hotel Santa Cruz** (Av. Kirchner 701, tel. 02966/42-0601, www.hotelsantacruzrgl.com.ar, US$65-80 s, US$90-102 d) has newer, superior rooms, though it is slightly overpriced.

The 85-room **Hotel Patagonia** (Fagnano 54, tel. 02966/44-4969, www.hotel-patagonia.com, US$135-220 s or d), under the same ownership as El Calafate's Hotel Los Alamos, has positioned itself as the city's best, with a gym, a spa, a business center, and a restaurant with a short and reasonably priced menu. The higher rates correspond to four larger suites.

Information

The well-organized **Secretaría de Estado de Turismo de la Provincia** (Av. Kirchner 863, tel. 02966/43-7412, www.santacruzpatagonia.gob.ar, 9am-4pm Mon.-Fri. Feb.-Dec., 10am-4pm Mon.-Fri. Jan.) has maps and details on accommodations, excursions, and transportation.

The **Dirección Municipal de Turismo** (Av. Beccar 126, tel. 02966/43-6920, www.turismo.riogallegos.gov.ar, 8am-7pm Mon.-Fri., 8am-noon and 4pm-8pm Sat.-Sun. and holidays) also maintains two other **Centros de Informes.** One occupies an old railcar known as **El Carretón** (Av. San Martín and Av. Kirchner, 1pm-8pm Mon.-Fri., 8am-10pm Sat.-Sun.), while the other is at the **bus terminal** (RN 3 and Charlotte Fairchild, tel. 02966/44-2159, 7am-8pm Mon.-Fri., 7am-noon and 4pm-8pm Sat.-Sun. and holidays).

For motorists, **ACA** (Gobernador Lista and San Martín, tel. 02966/42-0477) is at the north end of Avenida San Martín.

Services

Cambio Luis Lopetegui (Zapiola 469, tel. 02966/42-1202) exchanges U.S. dollars, Chilean pesos, and traveler's checks. **Banco**

de la Nación (Av. Kirchner 799) has one of many ATMs. Correo Argentino (Av. Kirchner 893) occupies a historic building; the postal code is 9400.

For visa issues, visit Migraciones (Monseñor Fagnano 95, tel. 02966/42-0205, 8am-4pm Mon.-Fri.). The Chilean consulate (Mariano Moreno 148, tel. 02966/42-2364, 8am-1pm Mon.-Fri.) is just a few blocks south of Avenida Kirchner, between Rivadavia and Fagnano.

Lavadero El Tumbaito (Alberdi 397, tel. 02966/42-2452) handles the laundry. For medical attention, try the Hospital Regional (José Ingenieros 98, tel. 02966/42-0025).

Transportation

Aeropuerto Internacional Piloto Civil Norberto Fernández (RGL, RN 3, Km 8, tel. 02966/44-2340) is on the north side of the highway, about five kilometers west of town. Taxis and meterless radio taxis (about US$8) are the only transportation to and from the airport.

Air services are fewer since El Calafate's airport opened. Aerolíneas Argentinas (Av. San Martín 545, tel. 0810/2228-6527) flies daily to Buenos Aires's Aeroparque Jorge Newbery and twice weekly to Ushuaia. LADE (Fagnano 53, tel. 02966/42-2316) flies northbound to Comodoro Rivadavia; westbound to the town of Perito Moreno; and southbound to Ushuaia.

LATAM Argentina (tel. 02966/45-7189) flies to Buenos Aires's Aeroparque four times a week, and once a month to the Falklands (Malvinas) Islands; for details, contact travel agencies.

About two kilometers southwest of downtown, Río Gallegos's Terminal de Ómnibus Manuel Álvarez (RN 3 and Charlotte Fairchild, tel. 02966/44-2159) fronts on RN 3 near Avenida Eva Perón. There are provincial, long-distance, and international bus connections to El Calafate and Parque Nacional Los Glaciares as well as the coal town of Río Turbio, and to Chile's Puerto Natales and Parque Nacional Torres del Paine;

southbound links are to Punta Arenas, Chile, and to Argentine Tierra del Fuego.

Daily in high season, Tecni-Austral (tel. 02966/44-2447) and Marga (tel. 02966/44-2671) offer direct service to Río Grande (8 hours, US$40) and Ushuaia (11 hours, US$52), in Argentine Tierra del Fuego.

Taqsa (tel. 02966/44-2194) goes weekdays to Gobernador Gregores (7 hours, US$38), the quasi-gateway to Parque Nacional Perito Moreno (not to the famous Perito Moreno Glacier), and to El Chaltén (6 hours, US$55) with a change of buses in El Calafate.

Other typical destinations, times, and fares include San Julián (4-6 hours, US$28-30), Río Turbio (5 hours, US$29-34), El Calafate (4.5 hours, US$29-34), Comodoro Rivadavia (10-11 hours, US$60-68), Trelew (15-18 hours, US$90-105), Puerto Madryn (16-18 hours, US$95-110), and Buenos Aires (36-38 hours, US$195-220).

Several carriers go to Punta Arenas, Chile (4 hours, US$23), including El Pingüino (tel. 02966/44-2169), Buses Ghisoni (tel. 02966/45-7047), and Pacheco/Magallanes Tour (tel. 02966/44-2765). For Puerto Natales, the gateway to Torres del Paine, it's possible to bus to Río Turbio, where there are frequent shuttles to Natales.

From downtown Avenida Kirchner, inexpensive city buses A and B go directly to the Terminal de Ómnibus, on the southwestern outskirts of town, while cabs charge about US$6.

Car-rental agencies include Localiza (Sarmiento 245, tel. 02966/43-6717) and Riestra (Av. San Martín 1508, tel. 02966/42-1321, www.riestrarentacar.com), near the traffic circle junction with RN 3.

VICINITY OF RÍO GALLEGOS

Given its proximity to historic *estancias* and wildlife sites, most notably the Cabo Vírgenes penguin colony, Río Gallegos is earning a newfound respect even though it's not a major destination itself. Gallegos travel agencies such as Macatobiano (Av. San Martín

1093, tel. 02966/42-2466, www.macatobiano. com) arrange excursions to outlying attractions such as Cabo Vírgenes (around US$200, but divisible by at least three passengers, plus US$3 reserve admission fee for foreigners, which is not always collected).

Returning from Cabo Vírgenes, Chile-bound travelers with their own vehicles can take the RP 51 shortcut to the Monte Aymond border post but should ask directions before doing so, as the route is not always obvious or clearly signed.

★ Estancia Monte Dinero

From a junction about 15 kilometers south of Río Gallegos, RP 1 swerves southeast through rolling pasturelands where gas-and-oil derricks remind you that Santa Cruz is an energy storehouse. The gravel road is smooth to the picture-postcard settlement of Estancia Cóndor.

Beyond Cóndor, the road deteriorates toward **Estancia Monte Dinero** (tel. 02966/42-8922, www.montedinero.com.ar, US$220-235 s, US$320-350 d with 2 meals, US$265-280 s, US$410-440 d with all meals, excluding drinks), a pioneer sheep farm open to overnighters. Some 120 kilometers from Río Gallegos, 26,000-hectare Monte Dinero has subdivided its fragile pastures into smaller paddocks to manage some 14,000 sheep more intensively. Also unlike other *estancias,* it trains its contract shearers to use manual rather than electric shears, pays them a premium to do so, and shears ewes early in the season to ensure a higher lambing rate. The sparkling café, **Al Fin y al Cabo,** has become the place to stop for lunch and sweets. Try the rhubarb cake. The quality is excellent and the building has magnificent shoreline views southeast to Punta Dungeness.

Founded by the Fentons, another pioneer Patagonian family, **Hostería Monte Dinero** has four downstairs bedrooms with private baths and two upstairs (with a shared bath), plus Wi-Fi and satellite TV. The manor's former sun porch has been expanded into an attractive and spacious, but not extravagant, bar and dining room. A small museum holds family keepsakes, and there's also a billiard table (not a pool table).

Reserva Provincial Cabo Vírgenes

Beyond Monte Dinero, the road improves as it approaches **Cabo Vírgenes** (foreigners US$3), a Magellanic **penguin colony** second only to Punta Tombo. With more than 130,000 breeding pairs, the colony continues to grow.

The abundance of brush here means the birds are less visible than at Dos Bahías, and there's no direct beach access. A 1,500-meter nature trail permits close approach to the birds, and there's an interpretive brochure in good English.

At the reserve's northeast corner, the rehabbed hilltop **Faro Cabo Vírgenes,** the historic Argentine lighthouse, includes a small museum. Outside, facing the ocean, there remain foxholes dug to repel British commandos who might have landed here during the 1982 Falklands war (Britain conducted operations in Argentine Patagonia and Tierra del Fuego, escaping into Chile with collusion from the Pinochet dictatorship, which feared an Argentine attack if the Brits lost).

At the so-called **Cementerio Histórico,** the only truly legitimate tomb may be that of Conrado Assinbom, a hermit who lived in the shack beneath the lighthouse. One older cross is almost illegible, and it's not certain anyone is buried here.

At the reserve's southern edge, visitors can cross the border—technically illegally— to see **Faro Punta Dungeness** (1897), the lighthouse at the east end of Chile's narrow latitudinal strip along the Strait of Magellan. When duties permit, Chilean navy personnel show visitors around the facility.

Estancia Monte Dinero has the nearest accommodations, and its café is a good place to stop for lunch.

Parque Nacional Los Glaciares

On the eastern Andean slopes, Parque Nacional Los Glaciares comprises over 750,000 hectares, where slowly flowing ice gives birth to clear frigid rivers and vast lakes, interspersed with Magellanic forests, along the Chilean border west and north of El Calafate. A UNESCO World Heritage Site, it's famous for the Glaciar Perito Moreno, which draws thousands of visitors as well as scientists absorbed in glaciology and climate studies. The northern sector draws those seeking to spend several days in vigorous exercise, for either trekking or the riskier technical climbing.

Exploring the Park

Hugging the Chilean border, the elongated park stretches well over 100 kilometers from north to south. There are four significant access points, but just two of those get the great majority of visitors.

Since nearly all visitors come to see Glaciar Perito Moreno, most stay at **El Calafate,** 80 kilometers east by paved highway; the only accommodations closer to the glacier are expensive ranches and lodges just outside park boundaries with small capacities. At the Río Mitre entrance, this main Glaciar Perito Moreno approach, the APN collects a US$22 admission fee (payable in pesos only) from nonresidents of Argentina. Lake excursions into the park leave from **Punta Bandera,** a short detour north from the Moreno Glacier road. Passengers on lake excursions from Punta Bandera must also pay the fee.

The other main access point is the village **El Chaltén,** 220 kilometers to the northwest by a paved but roundabout route, with abundant accommodations in all categories and easy trail access even for those without their own vehicles. This northernmost sector—a three-hour bus trip from El Calafate by paved highway—attracts hikers and serious mountaineers. Backpackers should note that no campfires are permitted within the park. Carrying a camp stove is obligatory for cooking. This southern approach includes the **APN visitors center** (tel. 02962/49-3004, 9am-5pm daily, occasionally until 8pm), which has natural history exhibits, provides a decent trail map (scale 1:75,000), and also issues climbing permits (free).

There is additional park access at Lago Roca, southwest of El Calafate, and at little-visited Helsingfors, to the northwest. Accessible by gravel road, the **Lago Roca sector** has campgrounds and some ranch accommodations, but few trails. To the northwest, on the south shore of Lago Viedma, reached from El Calafate by a roundabout combination of paved and gravel routes, the **Helsingfors sector** has limited but scenic hiking and private accommodations at its namesake lodge. There is no public transportation.

At present, the Lago Roca, Helsingfors, and El Chaltén sectors remain fee-free.

Resources

For an informed guide who leads backcountry trips in the El Chaltén sector, contact retired ranger **Adrián Falcone** (tel. 02962/49-3064, aefalcone@gmail.com), who speaks English and even a smattering of Japanese.

Hikers may want to consult Tim Burford's *Chile and Argentina: The Bradt Trekking Guide* (Chalfont St. Peter, UK: Bradt Travel Guides, 2001) or Carolyn McCarthy's *Trekking in the Patagonian Andes* (Melbourne: Lonely Planet, 2009). Both could use updates; the latter has better maps. There is also the 2nd edition of Miguel A. Alonso's locally-available, bilingual *Trekking en Chaltén y Lago del Desierto* (Buenos Aires: Los Glaciares, 2014), which covers numerous hikes in the vicinity. Alonso has also written the *Lago Argentino & Glaciar Perito Moreno Handbook* (Buenos

Parque Nacional Los Glaciares

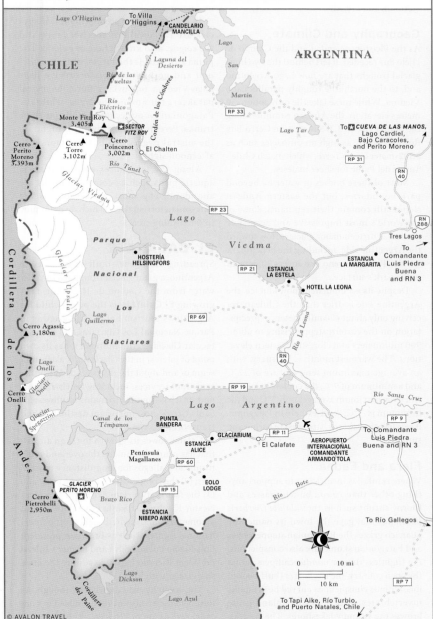

Lago O'Higgins

To Villa O'Higgins

CANDELARIO MANCILLA

Lago

ARGENTINA

CHILE

Laguna del Desierto

Río de las Vueltas

San

Martín

Río Eléctrico

Cordón de los Cóndores

RP 33

Monte Fitz Roy 3,405m

SECTOR FITZ ROY

Lago Tar

To CUEVA DE LAS MANOS, Lago Cardiel, Bajo Caracoles, and Perito Moreno

Cerro Perito Moreno 3,393m

Cerro Torre 3,102m

Cerro Poincenot 3,002m

El Chalten

RP 31

Glaciar Viedma

Río Túnel

RN 40

Lago

RP 23

RN 288

Parque

Viedma

Tres Lagos

Glaciar Upsala

HOSTERÍA HELSINGFORS

Nacional

RP 21

ESTANCIA LA ESTELA

ESTANCIA LA MARGARITA

To Comandante Luis Piedra Buena and RN 3

HOTEL LA LEONA

Cordillera

Cerro Agassiz 3,180m

Los

Lago Guillermo

RP 69

Río La Leona

Glaciares

de

Lago Onelli

RN 40

Glaciar Onelli

los

Cerro Onelli

Glaciar Spegazzini

RP 19

Río Santa Cruz

Lago   Argentino

RP 9

Andes

Canal de los Témpanos

PUNTA BANDERA

GLACIARIUM

RP 11

To Comandante Luis Piedra Buena and RN 3

ESTANCIA ALICE

El Calafate

AEROPUERTO INTERNACIONAL COMANDANTE ARMANDO TOLA

Península Magallanes

RP 60

EOLO LODGE

Río Bote

GLACIER PERITO MORENO

RP 15

Cerro Pietrobelli 2,950m

Brazo Rico

ESTANCIA NIBEPO AIKE

To Río Gallegos

0   10 mi

0   10 km

Lago Dickson

Cordillera del Paine

Lago Azul

RP 7

To Tapi Aike, Río Turbio, and Puerto Natales, Chile

© AVALON TRAVEL

Aires: Zagier & Urruty, 2004), a more general guide that's available in English, Italian, German, and French.

Geography and Climate

As the Pleistocene ended and the Campo de Hielo Sur receded, it left behind the two huge glacial troughs that are now Lago Argentino and, to the north, the roughly parallel Lago Viedma. While these lakes lie only about 250 meters elevation, the Andean summits along the border rise to 3,375 meters on Cerro Fitz Roy and nearly as high on pinnacles such as 3,102-meter Cerro Torre, which match Chile's Torres del Paine for sheer majesty.

Most of these bodies of water lie beyond park boundaries, but the eastern Andean slopes still contain their remnants, some of the world's most impressive and accessible glaciers. Thirteen major glaciers flow toward the Argentine side, including the benchmark Glaciar Perito Moreno. Ice covers 30 percent of the park's surface.

Despite its accumulated snow and ice, the Argentine side is drier than the Chilean, receiving only about 400 millimeters of precipitation on the eastern steppe, rising to about 900 millimeters at its forested western elevations. The warmest month is February, with an average maximum temperature of 22°C and a minimum of 9°C; the coolest is August, when the maximum averages only 5°C and the minimum is -1°C. As elsewhere in Patagonia, it gets ferocious winds, strongest in spring and summer.

Flora and Fauna

Where rainfall is insufficient to support anything other than *coirón* bunch grasses and thorny shrubs such as the *calafate (Berberis buxifolia)* that gave the town its name, the guanaco grazes the Patagonian steppe. Foxes and Patagonian skunks are also conspicuous, the flightless rhea or *ñandú* scampers across the open country, the *bandurria* (buff-necked ibis, with its conspicuous curved beak) stalks invertebrates, and flocks of upland geese browse the swampy lakeshores. The Andean condor soars above the plains and even the highest peaks, occasionally landing to feast on carrion.

In the forests, the predominant tree species are the southern beeches *lenga* and the *coigüe*, also known here as *guindo*. The puma still prowls the forest, while the *huemul* and perhaps the *pudú* survive near Lago Viedma. Squawking flocks of austral parakeets flit among the trees, while the Patagonian woodpecker pounds on their trunks. Perching calmly, awaiting nightfall, the austral pygmy owl is a common late-afternoon sight.

Along the lakeshores and riverbanks, aquatic birds such as coots and ducks are abundant. The most picturesque is the Patagonian torrent duck, which dives for prey in the rushing creeks.

EL CALAFATE

Spreading along the south shore of Lago Argentino, a giant glacial trough fed by meltwater from the Campo de Hielo Sur, fast-growing **El Calafate** is the poster child for Argentina's tourism boom. The gateway to Parque Nacional Los Glaciares and its spectacular Glaciar Perito Moreno, it has its own point of interest in the Glaciarium, a new museum of and about the rivers of ice. While the growth of services, including hotels and restaurants, has slowed, it remains southwestern Santa Cruz's most important destination and transport hub.

Calafate owes its growth to (1) an airport that has nearly eliminated the overland route from Río Gallegos for long-distance passengers; (2) the competitive Argentine peso; and (3) the fact that the late Argentine president Néstor Kirchner, a Santa Cruz native, built a home here and invited high-profile international figures, such as Brazilian president Luis Inácio Lula da Silva and former Chilean president Ricardo Lagos, to admire the massive glacier with him.

The boom has had drawbacks, though. As the population has more than doubled in a decade, real-estate prices have skyrocketed. A

El Calafate

AVENIDA PADRE AGOSTINI

AVE 17 DE OCTUBRE

CALLE 18

CALLE 1 DE MAYO

BOLIVAR

FEILBERG

AV DEL LIBERTADOR

GUERRERO

GOBERNADOR GREGORES

GOBERNADOR MOYANO

GOBERNADOR

7 DE DICIEMBRE

EZEQUIEL BUSTILLO

LOS GAUCHOS

25 DE MAYO

9 DE JULIO

COMANDANTE ESPORA

PERITO MORENO

JOSE PANTIN

CORONEL ROSALES

CORONEL

SAN JULIAN

PUERTO DESEADO

AV DEL LIBERTADOR

SERVICAR
LOCALIZA

MARAMBIO

Arroyo Calafate

To Reserva Municipal
Laguna Nimez

To Centro de
Interpretación Histórica

To Glaciarium and
Parque Nacional
Los Glaciares

DON DIEGO DE LA NOCHE

PATAGONIA QUEEN

CALAFATE
PARQUE
HOTEL

HOSPITAL MUNICIPAL
DR. JOSÉ FORMENTI

AEROLINEAS
ARGENTINAS

ADMINISTRACION DE
PARQUES NACIONAL
(APN)

PIZZERIA
LA LECHUZA

BANCO DE LA
PROVINCIA DE
SANTA CRUZ

LA
COCINA

LAGUNA
NEGRA

KAU
KALESHEN

HOTEL POSADA
LOS ALAMOS

HOTEL
KOSTEN AIKE

HOTEL
EL QUIJOTE

CASA
KIRCHNER

HOTEL
PUNTA
NORTE

HOSTERIA
DEL HOSTEL

CALAFATE
HOSTEL

DON LUIS

HOSTERIA
MADRE TIERRA
PATAGONIA

HOSPEDAJE CAMPING
LOS DOS PINOS

SEE DETAIL

To I Keu Ken
Hostel, Kelta Hotel

CAFÉ LA ESQUINA

BORGES Y ALVAREZ

NUNATAK

HOTEL
KAPENKE

LA ZAINA

CASIMIRO
BIGUA

CASIMIRO

OPEN
CALAFATE

HLS

HIELO Y
AVENTURA

Plazoleta Perito
Moreno

VIVA
AVENTURA

ANDINA

LA PEFA

CARDON

SOLO
PATAGONIA

HOSTEL
DEL GLACIAR
LIBERTADOR

LA TABLITA

MUSEO REGIONAL
EL CALAFATE

LA CASA DEL
GAUCHO ARGENTINO

LINEAS
AEREAS DEL
ESTADO

HOSTERIA
POSTA SUR

AMERICA
DEL SUR
HOSTEL

To Posada
Patagonia
Rebelde

HOTEL PICOS
DEL SUR

HOSTERIA
HAINEN

Camping
El
Overjero

Camping
El
Overjero

To Airport,
El Chaltén,
Rio Turbio, and
Rio Gallegos

RIO GALLEGOS

LOS PIONEROS

HOSTEL
DEL GLACIAR
PIONEROS

ROCA

TERMINAL DE
BUSES

S J BOSCO

JULIO A ROCA

CALLE 6

AV DEL DESIERTO

E DE VILLANUSTE

CAMPAÑA DEL DESIERTO

0   100 yds
0   100 m

SEE DETAIL

25 DE MAYO

AV DEL LIBERTADOR DE

JULIO

AVIS

CASABLANCA
PIZZA CAFÉ

CASABLANCA

EL LAVADERO/
CORDILLERA
DEL SOL

BANCO TIERRA
DEL FUEGO

LA VACA
ATADA

CHALTEN
TRAVEL

MUNDO
AUSTRAL

ACUARELA/
OVEJITAS DE
LA PATAGONIA

POST
OFFICE

MI VIEJO

ARTE
INDIO

9405
FOOD BAR

HELADOS
TITO

RUMBO
SUR

MARPATAG

CAL
TUR

BOUTIQUE
DEL LIBRO

CASINO CLUB
EL CALAFATE

EUROTUR

prime downtown location that once housed the old power plant, admittedly a noisy eyesore, has become the site of a quieter eyesore in the new casino.

Orientation

El Calafate (pop. 21,500) is 320 kilometers northwest of Río Gallegos and 32 kilometers west of northbound RP 40, which leads to the wilder El Chaltén sector of Parque Nacional Los Glaciares and an adventurous overland route to Chile. While only about 50 or 60 kilometers from Torres del Paine as the crow flies, the town is 215 kilometers from the Cerro Castillo border crossing and about 305 kilometers from Puerto Natales via Argentine highways RN 40, RP 5, and RP 11, plus a short distance on the Chilean side.

A former stage stop, El Calafate has an elongated city plan that has spread barelý a few blocks north and south of its main east-west thoroughfare, the pompously named Avenida del Libertador General José de San Martín (for Argentina's independence hero). Most services and points of interest are close to "Avenida Libertador" or "San Martín," as the street is variously called, but explosive hotel growth has taken place to the east, on and near the former airfield.

Sights

West of town on the road to the Glaciar Perito Moreno, the **Glaciarium** (RP 11, Km 6, tel. 02902/49-7912, www.glaciarium.com, 9am-9pm daily, US$20 adults, US$8 ages 6-12) places the Patagonian ice sheets in natural and historical perspective, in state-of-the-art hilltop facilities. Within its walls (shaped to mimic the angular ice blocks on a glacier's tongue), sophisticated exhibits focus on the formation of the southern Patagonian fields, their original coverage and present extent, and details on individual glaciers. There are also detailed accounts of discovery and research, with special emphasis on explorer and conservationist Francisco P. Moreno. In fact, there's even a robot of an elderly Moreno at his desk, writing his memoirs with a spoken narration of his thoughts. Built with private funds, the museum promotes public consciousness of climate change and environmental deterioration. The consulting glaciologist is Pedro Skvarca, an early mountaineer in the region who found his life's calling in the preservation of the massive rivers of ice and the summits that surround them. In addition to the regular exhibits, there is an art space and a 120-seat theater that offers a 3-D tour of the glaciers themselves, worthwhile for those who

the Glaciarium museum

lack time to visit all of them. There's also a café for snacks and sandwiches, as well as the **Glaciobar Branca**, a subterranean ice bar (US$12 more; US$6 under age 16). It's a good distance from town, so it offers its own free shuttles hourly.

In town, the **Centro de Interpretación Histórica** (Almirante Brown and Bonarelli, tel. 02902/49-2799, www.museocalafate.com. ar, 10am-8pm daily Sept.-Apr., 11am-5pm daily May-Aug., US$10 adults, US$6 over age 65, US$5 ages 6-12) offers a sophisticated timeline that puts southern Patagonia's natural, cultural, and historical events in context. It has many photographs, good English translations, and a quality library. Admission includes *remise* (meterless taxi) transportation from downtown.

The **Museo Regional El Calafate** (Av. Libertador 575, tel. 02902/49-1924, 8am-2pm Mon.-Fri., free) has sparse exhibits on paleontology, natural history, geology, and ethnology. The pioneer families' photographic histories show promise, but it still lacks an explanation of the 1920s labor unrest that led to several shooting deaths on the *estancias*.

At the north edge of town, **Reserva Municipal Laguna Nimez** is a freshwater body frequented by more than 100 bird species. Guides from the Universidad de la Patagonia now take visitors for interpretive walks (10am-8pm daily, US$6 pp) through the wetlands and along the lakeshore. Information is available at the municipal **tourist office** (Coronel Rosales s/n, tel. 02902/49-1090, www.elcalafate.tur.ar, 8am-8pm daily).

One sight that locals know but few foreigners recognize is the **Casa Kirchner** (Los Gauchos and Namuncurá), home of the late president Néstor Kirchner and his wife, former president Cristina Fernández de Kirchner.

Entertainment

El Calafate is surprisingly light on nightlife, which consists mostly of dining out and drinking venues such as **Don Diego de la Noche** (Av. Libertador 1603, tel. 02902/49-3270). **Borges y Álvarez** (Av. Libertador 1015, tel. 02902/49-1464, 10am-3am daily) is an upstairs literary bar with sidewalk seating in good weather. The food is nothing special, but it's acceptable for lunch. At night, it often hosts live folkloric music.

It's an architectural atrocity, but the **Casino Club El Calafate** (Av. Libertador 1061, tel. 02902/49-5911, www.casino-club. com.ar) does have live entertainment, mostly cabaret acts, and sometimes more rewarding programs that include folkloric performers.

Shopping

Downtown Avenida del Libertador is lined with souvenir shops such as **Open Calafate** (Av. Libertador 996, tel. 02902/49-1254), which also sells books and maps. **Boutique del Libro** (Av. Libertador 1033, tel. 02902/49-1363) carries a broad selection of books (many in English) on Antarctica, Argentina, and Patagonia, including Moon handbooks, as well as novels.

For premium homemade chocolates, try **Ovejitas de la Patagonia** (Av. Libertador 1197, tel. 02902/49-1315), **Laguna Negra** (Av. Libertador 1250, tel. 02902/49-2423), or any of several similar locales.

Cardón (Emilio Amado 835, tel. 02902/49-2074) is a casual clothing counterpart to Esprit or Patagonia. **Arte Indio** (Av. Libertador 1108, tel. 02902/49-2131, www.puebloindio.com.ar) carries high-end crafts from around the country, including ceramics, silverwork, and tapestries. **La Casa del Gaucho Argentino** (Av. del Libertador 351, tel. 02902/49-1281) stocks gaucho apparel and riding gear.

Food

El Calafate has the province's best restaurants, and in southernmost Argentine Patagonia, only Ushuaia can match it for quality. Prices have risen, although the quality remains high.

The best breakfast spot is **Cafetería Don Luis** (9 de Julio 265, tel. 02902/49-1550, 7am-10pm daily), with the best coffee, the most succulent croissants, and many other treats to try throughout the day. It has several other locations around town. Several decent *confiterías* (cafés) offer short orders, sandwiches, coffee, and the like. Among them are **Café La Esquina** (Av. Libertador 1002, tel. 02902/49-2334) and the **Casablanca Pizza Café** (Av. Libertador 1202, tel. 02902/49-1402).

★ **Pizzería La Lechuza** (Av. Libertador 1301, tel. 02902/49-1610, lunch and dinner daily, US$8-10) deserves special mention for its *super cebolla y jamón crudo* (onion and prosciutto) and its empanadas. The pasta-oriented **La Cocina** (Av. Libertador 1245, tel. 02902/49-1758, noon-midnight daily, from US$15) has expanded its menu to include high-end meats.

★ **Viva la Pepa** (Emilio Amado 833, Local 1, tel. 02902/49-1880, lunch and dinner daily, US$10-12.50) offers sweet and savory crepes that make an ideal antidote for anyone who's overdosed on beef, lamb, or other Patagonian staples. The small wine list stresses Patagonian vintages. **Kau Kaleshen** (Gobernador Gregores 1256, tel. 02902/49-1118, US$12) is a reinvented teahouse and vegetarian restaurant with entrées such as pumpkin-stuffed pasta and pizzas in a cozy environment. It also has beef and fish dishes.

Despite its name, **La Vaca Atada** (Av. Libertador 1176, tel. 02902/49-1227, lunch and dinner daily, US$12) is the best choice for fish, such as trout in a shrimp sauce, though it also serves beef, pastas, and soups. On the down side, the bread is basic, it gets a little noisy with families, and the small wine list relies on major bodegas, though there are some by-the-glass selections. The service can be absent-minded.

New in late 2015, the **9405 Food Bar** (Av. Libertador 1091, tel. 02902/49-4491, lunch and dinner daily, US$18) serves a creative tapas menu in distinctive surroundings—one table is a long tree trunk, its surface smoothed by chainsaws and then refinished. The best new choice in town, though, may be ★ **La Zaina** (Gobernador Gregores 1057, tel. 02902/49-6789, leonardosaracho@hotmail.com, 5pm-midnight daily, US$25), which combines a

Patagonian menu with what may be the town's most sophisticated wine bar. The ambience is deceptively but agreeably rustic, and reservations are advisable, though single diners may be able to squeeze in at the bar.

Despite utilitarian decor, ★ **Mi Viejo** (Av. Libertador 1111, tel. 02902/49-1691, noon-2:30pm and 7pm-11:30pm daily, US$20) serves fine lamb with roasted potatoes and exceptional pepper steak along with especially tasty creamed potatoes. The service is efficient, but the only style points come from the staked lamb in the window fire pit. **La Tablita** (Coronel Rosales 28, tel. 02902/49-1065, lunch and dinner daily) is also a well-regarded *parrilla* (grill restaurant), though it has shifted toward more innovative cuisine.

★ **Casimiro** (Av. Libertador 963, tel. 02902/49-2590, www.casimirobigua.com, lunch and dinner daily, US$25) would be a good choice almost anywhere in the world. The plate of smoked Patagonian appetizers is exquisite. There's a US$20 lunch that includes a main dish, dessert, and a glass of wine. Entrées such as almond-crusted lamb and black hake make this a special outing at dinnertime. It's also a by-the-glass wine bar, with an imposing list reaching several hundred dollars per bottle (but with other more affordable, and plenty of palatable, choices).

A few doors west, under the same ownership, **Casimiro Biguá** (Av. del Libertador 993, tel. 02902/49-3993, www.casimirobigua.com, 11:30am-late daily, from US$15) has an overlapping menu, but stick with its specialties of grilled beef and lamb. Like its sibling, rapidly rising prices make it a lesser value than it once was.

At the other end of town, ★ **Pura Vida** (Av. Libertador 1876, tel. 02902/49-3356, lunch and dinner Thurs.-Tues., US$13) gets few foreigners for quality versions of traditional Argentine and Patagonian dishes such as gnocchi with a saffron sauce, *carbonada* (a motley stew large enough for two hungry diners), and *cazuela de cordero* (a lamb casserole). Self-consciously casual—no two chairs or menu cards are alike—it has mezzanine seating with views over Laguna Nimes and, in the distance, Lago Argentino. The main floor, though, is cozier. The menu rarely changes, and the wine list is modest (with nothing by the glass).

El Calafate went nearly a decade without a quality ice creamery, but now it has two fine ones. **Acuarela** (Av. Libertador 1197, tel. 02902/49-1315) can aspire toward Buenos Aires's best, but nearby **Tito** (Av. Libertador 1100, tel. 02902/49-5413) is also outstanding.

Accommodations

El Calafate has diverse high-standard accommodations ranging from camping to five-star extravagance. Its custom-built hostels, with stylish architecture, engaging common areas with stunning views, and even restaurants and bars, far surpass the no-frills reputation that the word sometimes implies. In addition to dorms, several hostels have private rooms that shame some hotels.

Occupancy rates are high, and places that once stayed open only in summer now stay open year-round. Despite the increased capacity, high demand and Argentina's notorious inflation issues are driving prices upward. Unless otherwise indicated, prices listed are for high season, usually October to April, but dates vary, and if business is slow, rates can be negotiable. Every place in categories over US$50 includes breakfast; less expensive places may or may not provide it. Wi-Fi has become almost universal, but local service is miserably slow, with frequent outages. Argentine hotels, like those in Chile, now discount IVA (value-added tax) for foreign visitors who pay in U.S. cash or by credit card.

CAMPING

Flanking the Arroyo Calafate, the municipal **Camping El Ovejero** (José Pantín s/n, tel. 02902/49-3422, www.campingelovejero. com.ar, US$8 pp adults, US$5 ages 4-12) has reopened under a private concessionaire. Fenced and forested, it has good common restrooms and hot showers, and each site has its own fire pit. Areas east of the creek are for walk-in campers only. It's also added hostel quarters (US$10-15 pp) and a few private rooms (US$53 d).

Camping Los Dos Pinos (9 de Julio 218, tel. 02902/49-1271, www.losdospinos.com, US$10 pp) is a small tents-only area.

UNDER US$25

Custom-built **Hotel Punta Norte** (25 de Mayo 311, tel. 02902/49-6671, www.puntan-ortehotel.com, US$18-20 pp dorm, US$72-81 s or d) is a hostel with large and luminous common areas. Some dorms are cramped with up to a dozen beds, but other private rooms have balconies, which add a touch of style to its amenities.

Expanded **Hospedaje los dos Pinos** (9 de Julio 358, tel./fax 02902/49-1271, www.losdospinos.com, US$19 pp dorm, US$66 d) provides plain but spacious and immaculate rooms ranging from hostel dorms to private doubles and *cabañas* (its tours, though, have drawn some criticism). Breakfast costs extra.

US$25-50

Several hostels in this category also have private rooms that are excellent values in this range, which otherwise has few options.

East of the arroyo, open October to mid-April, the Hostelling International affiliate ★ **Hostel del Glaciar Pioneros** (Los Pioneros 251, tel./fax 02902/49-1243, www.glaciar.com, US$18 pp dorm, US$48-57 s, US$54-63 d) has extensive common spaces, including a large lounge with Wi-Fi, kitchen space, and laundry facilities. The higher rates are for larger and comfortable but no-frills hotel-style rooms with breakfast. It also offers its own Glaciar Perito Moreno excursions.

The I **Keu Ken Hostel** (Pontoriero 171, tel. 02902/49-5175, www.patagoniaikeuken.com. ar, US$22 pp, US$63 d, with breakfast) is a purpose-built hostel in the Magellanic style, with truly inviting common areas. All rooms are quadruple dorms with lockers and shared baths; rates include breakfast. The private rooms are free-standing *cabañas,* but with access to the common areas. It's a windy location uphill from downtown, but there are free transfers from the bus terminal.

"Think big" is the apparent motto at **Calafate Hostel** (Gobernador Moyano 1296, tel. 02902/49-2450, www.calafatehostels.com, US$25 pp dorm, US$56 s, US$75 d. with breakfast), which has dorms with shared baths and balconies in a stylish building with vast common areas. It also has single and double rooms with private baths.

Under the same management as the Pioneros, the newer and more stylish ★ **Hostel del Glaciar Libertador** (Av. Libertador 587, tel./fax 02902/49-2492, www.glaciar.com, US$23 pp dorm, US$70 s, US$80 d) has 22 rooms with private baths; some are four-bed dorms, while others are twins or doubles. Both hostels offer roughly 15 percent discounts for Hostelling International members, and 30 percent low-season discounts in October and April (except for Semana Santa, the week before Easter).

On the hilltop immediately east of the municipal campground, custom-built ★ **América del Sur Hostel** (Puerto Deseado 153, tel. 02902/49-3525, www.americahostel.com.ar, US$30 pp dorm, US$120 s or d) has friendly management, spectacular common spaces with panoramic views, and well-designed rooms in which the toilet and shower are separate and the vanity is outside of both. Rates include breakfast and free transfers from the bus terminal; off-season rates are about 20 percent less.

US$50-100

Near the old airfield, **Hotel Picos del Sur** (Puerto San Julián 271, tel. 02902/49-3650, www.hotelpicosdelsur.com.ar, US$86 s or d) has overcome some service shortcomings to become a good choice. The service is truly congenial now. Rates include airport pickup and drop-off.

Alongside the Calafate Hostel, under the same management but with a separate reception area, the **Hostería del Hostel** (25 de Mayo and Gobernador Moyano, www.

calafatehostels.com, US$75 s, US$90 d) is a smart, modern building with immaculate midsize rooms, all of which have Internet-connected computers. When business is slow, rates may fall by a third or so.

Directly across from the América del Sur hostel, **Hostería Hainén** (Puerto Deseado 118, tel. 02902/49-3874, www.hosteriahainen.com, US$90 s or d) is a handsome wooden structure with wainscoted midsize rooms in soothing colors. Owner-operated, it lacks elaborate amenities but compensates with peace and quiet (except for the nearly incessant winds at this exposed location).

US$100-150

The renovated **Hotel Kapenke** (9 de Julio 112, tel. 02902/49-1093, www.kapenke.com.ar, US$107 s or d) recently added a handsome new wing to an already attractive hotel, without dramatically raising rates.

The ★ **Kelta Hotel** (Portoriero 109, tel. 02902/49-5966, www.kelta.com.ar, US$113 s or d) is a handsome hillside lodge with views across the lake; the larger lake-view rooms are no more expensive than the smaller interior rooms and, on request, the staff will shift guests to better rooms as they open up.

At first glimpse, the interior of ★ **Posada Patagonia Rebelde** (José R. Haro 442, tel. 02902/49-4495, www.patagoniarebelde.com, US$110 s, US$130 d) seems more like a well-stocked antiques shop than a boutique hotel in distinctive Patagonian style. Ironically, much of the recycled material that built the building came from the Buenos Aires barrio of La Boca, and its own rustic sophistication contrasts dramatically with the sophisticated design hotels elsewhere in town. Though it's not for everyone, everyone who's read *In Patagonia* is likely to love it.

Near the Picos del Sur, the rooms at owner-operated **Hostería Posta Sur** (Puerto San Julián 490, tel./fax 02902/49-2406, www.hosteriapostasur.com.ar, US$142 s or d) are small for the price and some lack even closets, but it is well regarded. Off-season rates may fall by 30 percent.

When El Calafate was smaller, ★ **Hotel Kau Yatún** (tel. 02902/49-1259, www.kauya-tun.com, from US$137 s or d, with breakfast) was part of Estancia 25 de Mayo; the older part was the manor, whose suites have whirlpool tubs, fireplaces, and other amenities. But it has not kept pace with trends here. Note that its business address, Avenida Libertador 1190, is not the same as the property itself: The hotel is east of the arroyo and up the hill from the Hostel del Glaciar Pioneros.

US$150-200

The pastel rooms at well-located **Hotel El Quijote** (Gregores 1191, tel. 02902/49-1017, www.quijotehotel.com.ar, US$145 s, US$172 d) make it one of El Calafate's most stylish hotels. Its exterior was handsomely rehabbed in wood and glass. A recent remodel enlarged the rooms and made them more comfortable, but it has also meant thinner walls that conduct noise more easily.

Hotel Mirador del Lago (Av. Libertador 2047, tel. 02902/49-3176, www.miradordel-lago.com.ar, from US$192 s or d) is more than two decades old, but a rehab and expansion have left it looking like new. From its knoll on the south side of the road, it has fine lake views. Rooms in the newer wing are larger and significantly better than the older ones. It has a well-regarded restaurant, and the staff often anticipates (rather than reacts to) its guests' needs.

On a blustery bluff north of the old airfield, the architecturally audacious ★ **Design Suites Calafate** (Calle 598 No. 190, tel. 02902/49-4525, www.designsuites.com, from US$168 s or d) enjoys spectacular panoramas, at least from the higher-priced suites that face the lake. Slightly smaller standard rooms face an unappealing part of the steppe. Given its relative isolation, it's surprising that its hourly downtown shuttle doesn't begin until 6pm.

Located close to everything but just beyond the crowded center, **Patagonia Queen** (Av. Padre Agostini 49, tel. 02902/49-6701, www.patagoniaqueen.com.ar, US$160 s, US$190-210 d) is a 20-room boutique hotel done in

stunning natural wood with earnest Korean-Argentine ownership. The rooms are only midsize, but all the baths have whirlpool tubs.

A couple blocks north of Libertador, **Hostería Madre Tierra Patagonia** (9 de Julio 239, tel. 02902/49-8880, www.madre-tierrapatagonia.com, US$165-230 s or d) is an eight-room, boutique-style facility whose rooms are relatively small, but all the baths have whirlpool tubs. Amenities include flat-screen cable TV, Wi-Fi, and a buffet breakfast.

On the western outskirts of town, the **Imago Hotel & Spa** (Calle 669 No. 40, tel. 02902/49-6502, www.imagohotelspa.com, from US$150 s or d) is an outpost of the Kirchner empire, and a symbol of their presence in Santa Cruz province. It embodies a modern Patagonian style, with a quarried stone facade and glistening wood details, with midsize to large rooms and suites equipped with the latest technology. Some rooms have balconies with lake views. Its spa is one of the most complete in town, in a class with Hotel Posada Los Álamos and Design Suites Calafate. Rates include a free downtown shuttle.

Though well-regarded by its guests, rates for the midsize-plus rooms at **Calafate Parque Hotel** (7 de Diciembre and Gobernador Gregores, tel. 02902/49-2970, www.calafateparquehotel.com.ar, from US$179 s or d) seem a little high. Facilities include a third-floor gym and spa as well as a fairly elaborate restaurant. With discounted rates through its website, it can be an excellent value.

OVER US$200

Atop a hill near the eastern approach to town, the upper-midsize rooms at **Hotel Alto Calafate** (RP 11 s/n, tel. 02902/49-4110, www.hotelaltocalafate.com.ar, US$299 s or d) command views of the Lago Argentino basin and the Andes to the southwest, or of the "Balcón de Calafate" that rises immediately behind it. The service is exemplary, and its bar-restaurant precludes the need to dine or drink in town (though a free shuttle is available every

15 minutes). There are no neighbors to make any noise around this Kirchner-owned property, which has faced investigation for shady business practices, but the wind can wail at the exposed location.

The 60-room **Hotel Kosten Aike** (Gobernador Moyano 1243, tel. 02902/49-2424, www.kostenaike.com.ar, US$230-510 s or d) is an impressive four-star facility with every modern convenience, including a well-regarded restaurant, a gym and a spa, and facilities for guests with disabilities. Though it's not a view hotel, the large and comfy quarters, with Tehuelche-derived decor, have drawn uniformly positive comments, as has its personnel. Off-season rates can fall by half or more.

On the western outskirts of town, **Xelena Deluxe Suites** (René Favaloro 3548, tel. 02902/49-6201, www.xelena.com.ar, US$180, US$240 d) is a seven-story, 70-room hotel that looks smaller than that because three ample floors, including guest rooms and a spa (with an indoor-outdoor pool), lie below the street-level reception area. Even standard rooms have exceptional lake views, while the suites enjoy a more panoramic aspect. All the baths have whirlpool tubs.

Hotel Posada Los Álamos (Gobernador Moyano 1355, tel. 02902/49-1144, www.posadalosalamos.com, US$248 s, US$270 d) may be Calafate's most complete hotel, with a pool, a spa, and a convention center. Breakfast takes place in the restaurant across the street, where it also operates the compact nine-hole (three holes with three different tees each) Campo de Golf Pinar. The rooms are a little undersized for its category.

Information

At the eastern approach to town, at the roundabout just beyond the police checkpoint, the **Secretaría de Turismo de la Municipalidad de El Calafate** (Bajada de Palma 44, tel. 02902/49-1090, www.elcalafate.tur.ar, 8am-8pm daily) maintains a database of hotels and other services, as well as maps and brochures. A separate office at the current

Terminal de Ómnibus (Av. Roca 1004, tel. 02902/49-1476, 8am-8pm daily) is due to move when a new terminal opens at the old airport complex, but progress continues to be slow. Both offices have competent English speakers.

The **Administración de Parques Nacionales** (APN, Av. Libertador 1302, tel. 02902/49-1755 or 02902/49-1545, losglaciares@apn.gov.ar, 8am-4pm daily) is in town.

Services

El Calafate no longer has any custom exchange houses, but businesses along Av. San Martín will happily accept payment in U.S. dollars. **Banco de Santa Cruz** (Av. Libertador 1285) and **Banco Tierra del Fuego** (25 de Mayo 40) operate two of several ATMs.

Correo Argentino (Av. Libertador 1133) is the post office. **Open Calafate** (Av. Libertador 996, tel. 02902/49-1254) offers both telephone and Internet service, but its connections here are slow and sometimes nonexistent.

El Lavadero (25 de Mayo 43, tel. 02902/49-2182) charges around US$5 per laundry load. The **Hospital Municipal Dr. José Formenti** (Av. Roca 1487, tel. 02902/49-1001 or 02902/49-1173) handles medical issues.

Transportation

El Calafate is the transport hub for western Santa Cruz thanks to its new airport, road connections to Río Gallegos and El Chaltén, and improving links north and south along RN 40.

AIR

Aerolíneas Argentinas (Av. del Libertador 1361, tel. 0810/2228-6527) normally flies north to Trelew and Buenos Aires, and south to Ushuaia, but it sometimes has service to or from Bariloche as well. **LATAM Argentina** (airport tel. 02902/49-5548, www.latam.com) has an increasing number of flights; travel agencies such as **Rumbo Sur** (9 de Julio 81, tel. 02902/49-2155) can help make arrangements. **LADE** (Jean Mermoz 160, tel. 02902/49-1262, elcalafate_ld@lade.com.ar) occasionally flies northbound to Comodoro Rivadavia and Puerto Madryn, and southbound to Río Gallegos, with connections to Río Grande and Ushuaia.

Aeropuerto Internacional El Calafate (FTE, tel. 02902/49-1220, www.aeropuertoelcalafate.com) is 23 kilometers east of town and just north of RP 11. **Ves Patagonia** (tel. 02902/49-4355, www.vespatagonia.com.ar, US$7-11 pp) provides door-to-door shuttles to and from the airport. A *remise* (meterless taxi) costs about US$30 for up to four passengers.

BUS

El Calafate's **Terminal de Ómnibus** (Av. Roca 1004) overlooks the town. For pedestrians, the easiest approach is a staircase from the corner of Avenida Libertador and 9 de Julio. Progress on plans to move it to the former airfield terminal just west of the bridge over the arroyo has been slow but, whenever it happens, buses will no longer enter town and, for most accommodations, taxi rides will be longer. For long-distance connections to most of the rest of the country, it's necessary to backtrack to Río Gallegos, but there are northbound services along RN 40, and southbound to Puerto Natales and Torres del Paine, Chile.

Taqsa (tel. 02902/49-1843, www.taqsa.com.ar) and **Sportman** (tel. 02902/49-2680) shuttle between El Calafate and the Santa Cruz provincial capital of Río Gallegos (4 hours, US$29-34), where there are northbound connections to Buenos Aires and intermediate towns, and southbound connections to Punta Arenas (Chile). These buses will also drop passengers at the Río Gallegos airport.

Three carriers connect El Calafate with El Chaltén (3.5 hours, US$40) in the Fitz Roy sector of Parque Nacional Los Glaciares: **Cal Tur** (tel. 02902/49-1842), **Chaltén Travel** (tel. 02902/49-1833), and Taqsa. Most services leave 7:30am-8am daily, though there are sometimes afternoon buses 5pm-6pm daily. Winter services are fewer but normally go at least daily among the three companies.

From September to April, Taqsa now has a service to Perito Moreno (the town, not the glacier) and Los Antiguos (4am daily, 15 hours, US$70), along desolate RN 40, for connections to Chile Chico. This is more direct, quicker, and cheaper than the roundabout routes via coastal RN 3, especially if you factor in accommodations. Taqsa also goes daily to Bariloche (30 hours, US$125), but uses the longer coastal route before turning inland toward Esquel.

December to April or so, Chaltén Travel also provides daily bus service from El Calafate to Perito Moreno and Los Antiguos (12 hours, US$95); Bariloche-bound passengers have to spend the night in Perito Moreno. Passengers from El Chaltén can board the northbound bus from El Calafate at the junction of RN 40 and RP 23 without having to return to El Calafate. Buses depart Calafate on odd-numbered days and return from Los Antiguos on even-numbered days. **Cal Tur** operates the same route, as far as Perito Moreno and Los Antiguos.

In summer, **Turismo Zaahj/Bus Sur** (tel. 02902/49-1631, www.turismozaahj.co.cl) and **Cootra** (tel. 02902/49-1444) alternate daily services to Puerto Natales, Chile (4.5 hours, US$32); **Buses Pacheco** handles the route at 11am Monday, Wednesday, and Friday. In winter, these services may operate only weekly. Occasionally there are direct services to Parque Nacional Torres del Paine.

CAR AND BIKE RENTALS

Car-rental agencies include **Avis** (Av. Libertador 1078, tel. 02902/49-2877, elcalafate@avis.com.ar), **Hertz** (Av. Libertador 1822, tel. 02902/49-2525, elcalafate@hertz.com.ar), **Localiza** (Av. Libertador 687, tel. 02902/49-1398, localizacalafate@hotmail.com), **Nunatak** (Gobernador Gregores 1075, tel. 02902/49-1987, www.nunatakrentacar.com.ar), and **Servicar** (Av. del Libertador 695, tel. 02902/49-2301, www.servicar4x4.com.ar).

HLS (Perito Moreno 95, tel. 02902/49-3806, www.travesiasur.com.ar) rents bicycles and also does bike tours.

★ GLACIAR PERITO MORENO

Where a low Andean pass lets Pacific weather systems cross the cordillera, countless storms have deposited immeasurable meters of snow that, over millennia, have compressed into **Glaciar Perito Moreno,** a rasping river of ice that's one of the continent's greatest sights and sounds. Fifteen times during the 20th century, the advancing glacier blocked Lago Argentino's **Brazo Rico** (Rico Arm) to form a rising body of water that eventually, when the weight became too great for the natural dam, triggered an eruption of ice and water toward the lake's main glacial trough.

The last event took place on March 10, 2016, but the avalanche of ice and water could easily have been a metaphor for the flood of tourists that invaded El Calafate in anticipation. On any given day, massive icebergs still calve off the glacier's 60-meter face and crash into the **Canal de los Témpanos** (Iceberg Channel) with astonishing frequency.

Perched on newly modernized catwalks and overlooks, many visitors spend entire days either gazing at or simply listening to this rumbling river of ice. Descending to lake level is prohibited because of the danger of backwash and flying ice chunks.

Sights and Tours

Hielo y Aventura (Av. Libertador 935, El Calafate, tel. 02902/49-2205, www.hieloy-aventura.com) offers full-day "mini trekking" excursions onto the ice (US$140 pp includes transportation from El Calafate). Other options include the more strenuous Big Ice trip (US$152 pp with transportation) and a passive Safari Náutico navigation (1 hour, US$23 pp, transportation not included) that approaches the glacier's face.

Organized tours to the glacier, 80 kilometers southwest of El Calafate via RP 11, leave every day, as does scheduled transportation. Transportation usually costs extra for everything except bus tours.

In addition to regularly scheduled transportation, guided bus tours are frequent, but both are less frequent in winter. Competent operators include **Aventura Andina** (Av. del Libertador 761, Local 4, tel. 02902/49-1726, www.aventura-andina.com.ar), **Cal Tur** (Av. Libertador 1080, tel. 02902/49-1368, www.caltur.com.ar), **Cordillera del Sol** (25 de Mayo 43, tel. 02902/49-2822, www.cordil-leradelsol.com), **Eurotur** (Av. del Libertador 1025, tel. 02902/49-2190, www.eurotur.com. ar), **Mundo Austral** (Av. Libertador 1114, tel. 02902/49-2365, www.mundoaustral.com.ar),

Glaciar Perito Moreno

and **Rumbo Sur** (9 de Julio 81, Local 2, tel. 02902/49-2155, www.rumbosur.com.ar).

El Calafate's **Hostel del Glaciar** runs its own guided minivan excursions (US$40 pp), leaving about 8am daily and returning around 5pm. These include more hiking and navigation for a waterside view of the lake.

Food and Accommodations

There are no accommodations at the glacier, but there are options just outside the park entrance.

Formerly the *casco* of Estancia Alice, west of El Calafate en route to the Glaciar Perito Moreno, **El Galpón del Glaciar** (RP 11, Km 22) is open for day tours that may include activities such as birding and horseback riding, as well as exhibitions of sheep herding and shearing, afternoon tea, and a barbecued-lamb dinner. Rates are around US$60 pp plus transportation to and from the farm (US$6 pp); drinks and horseback rides are extra.

El Galpón also offers accommodations (US$135 s or d); there are also multiple-day programs, with limited activities included. For details, contact **Agroturismo El Galpón** (Av. Libertador 761, El Calafate, tel. 02902/49-1793, www.elgalpondelglaciar.com.ar).

On the 4,000-hectare Estancia Alice, ★ **Eolo Lodge** (RP 11, Km 23, tel. 02902/49-2042, www.eolo.com.ar, early Oct.-Apr., US$810-1,345 s, US$995-1,550 d with all meals, holiday rates higher) is an exclusive mountainside lodge with 17 spacious suites and equally spacious common areas. All the rooms at this Relais & Chateaux affiliate offer "big sky" views that include either Lago Argentino to the east, the Valle de Anita immediately south, the Brazo Rico to the west, or a combination of them. On a clear day, there are even glimpses across the border to Torres del Paine.

Eolo owes its style to the *cascos* of the great Patagonian wool *estancias,* with corrugated metal siding, antique furnishings, and English tea settings. Contemporary innovations such as double-paned windows allows far greater natural light and better views than the poorly insulated buildings of the late 19th and early 20th centuries. The baths are also modern.

Like those houses, the suites at Eolo lack television (though there's a satellite TV and DVD lounge) but do have Wi-Fi. There's a sheltered interior patio studded with Technicolor lupines in summer, a small indoor pool, and a restaurant (also open to non-guests, by reservation only).

Eolo also has a Gran Buenos Aires contact (Laprida 3278, Oficina 39, San Isidro, tel. 011/4700-0705). Eolo helps arrange excursions to the Perito Moreno Glacier and other nearby sights but does not organize them itself.

At the glacier, the only services belong to **Nativos de la Patagonia,** which operated a snack bar that burned to the ground in 2015, but it should reopen by the time this book appears in print. There is a separate restaurant with set meals (around US$20); there's also an à la carte menu. Expansion is supposed to include a sheltered picnic area for those who bring their own food.

Transportation

The Glaciar Perito Moreno is about 80 kilometers west of El Calafate via RP 11, which is now completely paved. The trip takes slightly over an hour. Both **Cal Tur** (tel. 02902/49-1842, www.caltur.com.ar) and **Taqsa** (tel. 02902/49-1843, www.taqsa.com.ar) at El Calafate's bus terminal have scheduled services (9am daily, US$30 round-trip), returning in the afternoon.

GLACIAR UPSALA

Even larger than the Glaciar Perito Moreno, 50 kilometers long and 10 kilometers wide at its foot, **Glaciar Upsala** is impressive for its sheer extent, the sizable bergs that have calved off it, and their shapes and colors. It's accessible only by crowded catamaran trips from Punta Bandera via Lago Argentino's Brazo Norte (North Arm).

Tours

At midday the boat anchors at Bahía Onelli. Bring a bag lunch (skip the restaurant) to

Hostería Helsingfors

In a dramatic setting at the base of glacier-covered mountains, on Lago Viedma's secluded south shore, Helsingfors was one of southwestern Santa Cruz's earliest *estancias*, and also one of the first to open its gates to tourists. Though its services, elevated prices, and isolation imply exclusivity, it's surprisingly unpretentious. The comfortable *casco* has an inviting reception area, a cozy sitting room with beamed ceilings, a large brick fireplace, a bar, and a dining room with an Italian-born chef.

One of Helsingfors's recreational highlights is a 2.5-hour hike through meadows and *lenga* forest to Laguna Azul, a cirque lake beneath a hanging glacier. Despite the name, it's more turquoise than blue. There is also a rigid inflatable Zodiac for excursions to Glaciar Viedma, wind and weather permitting.

Legally, Helsingfors may not even be an *estancia*, as the founders apparently never registered their title and the land probably belongs to Parque Nacional Los Glaciares. Laguna Azul and other surrounding areas certainly are part of the park. Helsingfors's owners are concerned that Calafate operators could bring an influx of day hikers that could impact a nearly pristine part of the park and, of course, reduce its appeal to affluent overnighters.

Most visitors spend two or three nights at Helsingfors, which is 179 kilometers from El Calafate via eastbound RP 11, northbound RN 40, and westbound RP 21. It has nine double rooms, some of them detached from the *casco*. Open mid-October to the end of March, **Hostería Helsingfors** (tel. 011/5277-0195 direct, tel. 02966/15-67-5753 in Río Gallegos, www.helsingfors.com.ar, US$450 s, US$790 d) includes transportation to and from El Calafate, excursions, and all meals, but not alcoholic beverages. Children under age eight pay half, while children three or younger cost nothing extra.

Tuesday, Thursday, and Saturday, Helsingfors provides its own transfers to and from El Calafate hotels or the airport for overnight guests.

---

hike to ice-clogged **Lago Onelli.** The land portion of this excursion is regimented, and the guide-suggested pace—30 minutes from dock to lakeshore—is appropriate for those on crutches. Smoking is prohibited on the forest trail.

Visitors should realize that this is a mass-tourism excursion that may frustrate hikers accustomed to having the freedom of the hills. If you take it, choose the biggest available ship, which offers the most deck space to see the Spegazzini and Upsala Glaciers. On board, the freshest air is within the cabin of the *ALM*, whose seats are cramped but where smoking is prohibited; on deck, desperate smokers congregate even in freezing rain. Reasonably priced cakes, sandwiches, coffee, tea, and hot chocolate are available on board.

Puerto Bandera is 45 kilometers west of Calafate via RP 11 and RP 8. For information and reservations, contact concessionaire **Solo Patagonia** (Av. Libertador 867,

El Calafate, tel. 02902/49-1155 or 02902/49-1428, www.solopatagonia.com). The full-day trip costs about US$110 pp, US$65 ages 8-16, with a four-course lunch and open bar; it does not include transfer to Puerto Bandera or the US$22 park fee.

On its small cruiser *Leal*, **Cruceros Marpatag** (9 de Julio 57, Local 10, El Calafate, tel. 02902/49-2118, www.crucerosmarpatag.com) offers a full-day excursion, with a six-course gourmet lunch (wine included), to the Spegazzini and Upsala glacier fields (US$270-340 pp, including transfers and park admission). The triple-deck 22-cabin catamaran *Santa Cruz* now offers three-day, two-night cruises to Upsala and Spegazzini (US$1,785-3,900 s, US$3,360-5,680 d), with a final day's lunch facing the Perito Moreno Glacier.

LAGO ROCA

Also known as La Jerónima, the park's little-visited southwesterly sector along **Lago**

Roca's Brazo Sur (South Arm) offers camping and cross-country hiking. There are no formal trails, only routes such as the one from the campground to the summit of **Cerro Cristal,** 55 kilometers from El Calafate. The most striking feature is the high shoreline, dry from the days when the lake backs up behind the advancing Glaciar Perito Moreno. Unlike other sectors, Lago Roca charges no admission fee.

Food and Accommodations

La Jerónima's **Camping Lago Roca** (RP 15, Km 50, tel. 02902/49-9500, lagoroca@yahoo.com.ar, US$13 pp adults, US$9 ages 4-11) also has four-bed dorm-style *cabañas* (US$56 d, US$85 quadruple) with exterior baths; linens cost extra. Hot showers are available, and its café serves decent meals.

At the terminus of RP 15, which is 56 kilometers southwest of El Calafate, the big house at Croatian-founded **Estancia Nibepo Aike** (El Calafate tel./fax 02966/49-2797, www.nibepoaike.com.ar, Oct.-Apr., US$170 pp with 2 meals, US$215 pp with all meals and activities) preserves its original rustic style but is now a 10-room guesthouse with contemporary conveniences. It also offers a separate **Quincho Don Juan** where day-trippers can lunch or dine; overnight guests can choose to dine there or in the main house's dining room. "Day in the country" excursions (US$95 pp, US$48 ages 4-10, for those with their own transportation US$70 pp, US$35 ages 4-10) include grilled lamb and dessert for either lunch or dinner. Three-hour horseback rides (US$85 pp extra) are available.

★ SECTOR FITZ ROY

In the park's most northerly sector, the **Fitz Roy** range has sheer spires to match Torres del Paine. Even if you're not a top technical climber, trails from the village of El Chaltén to the base of summits such as **Cerro Fitz Roy** and **Cerro Torre** make for exhilarating hikes. It's even possible to traverse the southern Patagonian ice fields. Visitors seeking a sedate outdoor experience will find a handful

of former sheep ranches, onetime Patagonian wool producers that have reinvented themselves as tourist accommodations.

Hiking and Trekking

From a signposted trailhead at El Chaltén's north end, the **Sendero Laguna Torre** is an 11-kilometer track gaining about 200 meters in elevation as it winds through southern beech forests to the climbers' base camp for Cerro Torre; figure 3 to 3.5 hours. At the lake, in clear weather, there are extraordinary views of Cerro Torre's 3,102-meter summit, crowned by the so-called ice-and-snow "mushroom" that technical climbers must surmount. While Italian Cesare Maestri claimed that he and Austrian Toni Egger reached the summit in 1959 (Egger died in an avalanche, taking the camera with him), Italian Casimiro Ferrari made the first undisputed ascent in 1974.

From the Madsen pack station, the more demanding **Sendero Río Blanco** trail rises steeply at the outset before leveling out through boggy beech forest and continuing to the Fitz Roy base camp, climbing 350 vertical meters in 10 kilometers. About midway to Río Blanco, a signed lateral trail leads south to **Laguna Capri,** which has backcountry campsites.

From Río Blanco, a vertiginous zigzag trail ascends 400 meters in just 2.5 kilometers to **Laguna de los Tres,** a glacial tarn whose name commemorates three members of the French expedition—René Ferlet, Lionel Terray, and Guido Magnone—who summited Fitz Roy in 1952. Truly a top-of-the-world experience, Laguna de los Tres offers some of Patagonia's finest Andean panoramas.

From the Río Blanco campground (reserved for climbers), a northbound trail follows the river's west bank north to **Laguna Piedras Blancas,** whose namesake glacier continually calves small icebergs. The trail continues north to the Río Eléctrico, beyond the park boundaries, where a westbound trail climbs the river to Piedra del Fraile and a possible circuit of the Campo de Hielo Sur. This is only for experienced snow-and-ice trekkers. At the Río Eléctrico, it's also possible to rejoin the road from El Chaltén to Lago del Desierto.

From the park visitors center, a short ascent (about 45 minutes) leads to the **Mirador de los Cóndores,** for good views of El Chaltén and the confluence of the Río de las Vueltas and the Río Fitz Roy.

From the same trailhead, the hike to **Loma del Pliegue Tumbado** is a 500-meter elevation gain that yields some of the area's best views. Weather permitting, the panorama takes in Fitz Roy, Cerro Torre, Cerro Solo, Glaciar Torre, and Lago Torre, but the wind at the overlook can be overpowering. Four hours is about right for an average hiker, but the truly fit can do it in three. The descent takes about 2.5 hours.

GLACIAR VIEDMA

From Lago Viedma's north shore, south of El Chaltén, the park's best lake excursion is the *Viedma Discovery*'s full-day catamaran to **Viedma Glacier,** which can include an ice-climbing component. The less ambitious can settle for just a boat trip.

Sailing from Bahía Túnel, the vessel rounds the ironically named **Cabo de Hornos** (Cape Horn) to enter an iceberg-cluttered area before anchoring in a rocky cove. After disembarking, visitors hike to an overlook (the glacier is Argentina's largest, though its lakeside face is small) with additional views of 2,677-meter Cerro Huemul. Those who want to can strap on crampons and continue onto the glacier for about 2.5 hours (even some sedentary city dwellers do so).

The bilingual guides know glaciology. While prices here do not include lunch, they do provide an aperitif on the glacial rocks.

Departure time from El Chaltén is 8:30am, while the boat sails from Bahía Túnel at 8:15am; the cost is US$160 pp, including transportation from El Chaltén. The more demanding "Viedma Pro" version, which involves ice climbing, costs US$200 pp. The twice-daily "Viedma Light" boat trip alone is US$55 pp. For details, contact **Patagonia Aventura** (Av. San Martín 56-B, tel. 02962/49-3110, El Chaltén, www.patagonia-aventura.com).

EL CHALTÉN

Billing itself as Argentina's national trekking capital, **El Chaltén** has become popular for easy access to Fitz Roy range trailheads. Many trails are suitable for overnight backpacking, but access is so easy that day hikers can cover nearly as much ground.

the Fitz Roy range

El Chaltén

To Laguna Capri,
Laguna de Los Tres,
and Cerro Fitz Roy

To Lago del
Desierto

AV. SAN MARTIN

E. BRENNER

EL MURO

VIENTO OESTE

To Laguna Torre

ALBERGUE
RANCHO GRANDE

HOTEL POINCENOT

LOS CÓNDORES

LA
WAFLERÍA

CALLE 3

POSADA
ALTAS CUMBRES

EL RELINCHO

LA CASITA

HOSTEL PIONEROS DEL VALLE

KALENSHEN FITZ ROY INN

HOSTERÍA
KALENSHEN

CAL TUR

L. TERRAY

HOSTERÍA EL PUMA

TRAVELLERS' HOSTEL PATAGONIA

FONROUGE

FUEGIA

LA CERVECERÍA

LAGO SAN MARTÍN

Río de las Vueltas

CALLE 8

To Laguna
Torre

BOCATTO

DON LOS
CERROS
BOUTIQUE
HOTEL & SPA

RITUAL DEL FUEGO

SAINT EXUPERY

DOMO BLANCO

LA LUCINDA

AYLEN AIKE HOSTEL

SERAC

TREVISAN

CAMPING
CENTER

ANTONIO ROJO

ARBILLA

CERRO SOLO

PORTER

AV. SAN MARTIN

HOTEL LUNAJUIM

GARCIA

CHALTÉN SUITES
HOTEL

ESTEPA

CABO

FITZ ROY
EXPEDICIONES

HOTEL LAS PIEDRAS

HOTEL CUMBRES
NEVADAS

LA TOSTADORA
MODERNA

HOSTERÍA KAU SI AIKE

EL GRINGUITO

TAOSA/MARGA

IQUELME

PANGAEA

EL SUPER

LA VINERIA

LA TAPERA

LA
SENYERA

CHALTÉN
TRAVEL

POST
OFFICE

CALLE 10

TECHADO NEGRO

HIKE
PATAGONIA

AHONIKENK
CHALTÉN

CONDOR DE LOS ANDES

HOSTERÍA
INFINITO SUR

LAGO DEL DESIERTO

PIZZERÍA
PATAGONICUS

AV. M. DE GÜEMES

TRANSPORTE
LAS LENGAS

TELECABINAS JAVIER

NOTHOFAGUS
BED & BREAKFAST

HOTEL
LA ALDEA

MARCO
POLO

PERITO MORENO

HOSPEDAJE LA BASE

LA CHOCOLATERÍA
JOSH AIKE

HOSTERÍA
THIAMALU

RÍO DE LAS VUELTAS

TERMINAL DE ÓMNIBUS

0   200 yds

0   200 m

Río Fitz Roy

To Laguna Torre

To RN 40 and
El Calafate

© AVALON TRAVEL

To Loma del Pliegue
Tumbado

ADMINISTRACIÓN DE
PARQUES NACIONALES

Exposed to fierce westerlies and to potential floods from the Río de las Vueltas, El Chaltén has somehow managed to achieve a sense of permanence in what, just a few years back, seemed a bleak outpost of government offices aimed to uphold Argentina's presence in a disputed border zone (the last of many Chilean-Argentine territorial quarrels, over Lago del Desierto to the north, was finalized several years ago). With the highway from the RN 40 junction now paved, it's growing so rapidly that some fear it will become the next El Calafate, where real estate development and speculation are rampant.

With the highway completely paved, travel time from El Calafate has fallen to about three hours. Meanwhile, the town is enjoying improvements as the streets are paved to keep down the dust, and a new bus terminal is one of many new and improved services.

El Chaltén (permanent pop. about 1,100) is 220 kilometers northwest of El Calafate via eastbound RP 11 to the Río Bote junction, northbound RN 40, and westbound RP 23 along Lago Viedma's north shore. It's worth mentioning that, while street addresses are increasingly common, locals pay little attention to them.

Entertainment and Events

El Chaltén celebrates several events, including **Aniversario de El Chaltén** (Oct. 12), marking its formal founding in 1985; **Día de la Tradición** (Nov. 10), celebrating the gaucho heritage; and the weeklong **Fiesta Nacional del Trekking** in late February or early March.

Shopping

Marco Polo (Av. Güemes 120, Local 5, tel. 02962/49-3122) sells books, maps, and CDs, with English-language titles that include guidebooks and novels.

Recreation

In addition to the usual hiking and climbing opportunities in nearby Parque Nacional Los Glaciares, it's possible to arrange lengthier nine-day guided hikes on the Campo de Hielo Sur, the Southern Continental Ice Field, with **Fitz Roy Expediciones** (Av. San Martín 56, tel. 02962/49-3178, www.fitzroyexpediciones.com.ar). **Serac** (Av. San Martín 175, tel. 02962/49-3371, www.serac.com.ar) has similar offerings. **Lago San Martín** (Av. San Martín 275, tel. 02962/49-3045, www.lagosanmartin.com) arranges excursions to and from Lago del Desierto.

looking down on El Chaltén

At the north end of town, **Viento Oeste** (San Martín 898, tel. 02962/49-3200, vientooeste1993@gmail.com) rents and sells climbing, camping, and wet-weather gear, as do the **Camping Center** (Av. San Martín 70, tel. 02962/49-3264) and **Hike Patagonia** (Lago del Desierto 250, tel. 02962/49-3359, www.patagoniahikes.com).

Food

Hikers and climbers stock up on supplies at **El Super** (Lago del Desierto 248, tel. 02962/49-3039), **El Gringuito** (Cerro Solo 108), or **La Tostadora Moderna** (Av. San Martín 36). For its size, El Chaltén offers a fine and improving restaurant selection.

La Chocolatería Josh Aike (Lago del Desierto 105, tel. 02962/49-3008, roughly 10am-7pm daily) is more than it sounds—the desserts are good enough, but the breakfasts and pizzas are also excellent, and the Bailey's-spiked hot chocolate is comforting on a cold night. **La Senyera del Torre** (Lago del Desierto 240, tel. 02962/49-3063, breakfast, lunch, and dinner daily) prepares Argentine comfort food such as *locro* (a hearty stew) and excellent desserts.

In bright new quarters, **Domo Blanco** (San Martín 164, tel. 02962/49-3368, 1pm-midnight daily) serves exceptional ice cream, with local ingredients such as raspberries and strawberries. It also serves coffee drinks and pastries.

Porter (San Martín 84, tel. 02962/49-3167, lunch and dinner daily) has pub grub and draft beer. **La Cervecería** (San Martín 320, tel. 02962/49-3109, lunch and dinner daily, US$8) is a pizza pub with its own microbrew beer. It also prepares an outstanding *locro,* a meal-in-itself northwestern Argentine stew that is ideal for a cool Chaltén evening.

Chaltén's first wine bar, **La Vinería** (Lago del Desierto 265, tel. 02962/49-3301, 4pm-2am daily) also serves empanadas, sandwiches, and platters of cheeses, cold cuts, and smoked Patagonian meats—not to mention great cycling advice in English, from a couple who cycled from Ushuaia to Alaska and lived several years in Anchorage. **La Lucinda** (San Martín 175, tel. 02962/49-3202, 7am-1am daily) is an art-themed café that displays photographs and works by local talent.

★ **La Tapera** (Antonio Rojo 76, tel. 02962/49-3138, lunch and dinner daily, US$15) is an exceptionally friendly restaurant-tapas bar with a small but excellent menu of fixed-price dinners that include soup and a choice of four entrées. This is one of the best values in town.

Informal but pleasant and subdued, with only a few small tables and one long one flanked by equally long benches, **La Waflería** (San Martín 640, tel. 02962/49-3093, lunch and dinner daily, US$12) prepares savory waffles such as roast lamb, but most of the rest are suitable for desserts.

Lamb is the specialty at **La Casita** (San Martín 430, tel. 02962/49-3042, lunch and dinner daily), which otherwise serves a standard Argentine menu of beef, pizza, pasta, and the like, but it's a bit cramped. In midsummer it can be hard to get a table at popular **Pizzería Patagonicus** (Güemes 57, tel. 02962/49-3025, www.patagonicusbyb.com.ar, lunch and dinner daily), one of few Argentine eateries to have lamb on the pizza menu. The decor, with natural wood and mountaineering photos, embodies Chaltén's evolving style. **Pangea** (Lago del Desierto 330, tel. 02962/49-3084, lunch and dinner daily) has decent pizza and a really excellent wine list.

Reservations are advised for ★ **Fuegia** (San Martín 342, tel. 02962/49-3019, from 7pm daily, US$15), the Patagonia Hostel's bistro-style restaurant, for dishes like rack of lamb and Patagonian trout. Likewise, plan ahead for the unpretentious and recently expanded ★ **Estepa** (Cerro Solo 86, tel. 02962/49-3069, noon-midnight daily, US$10-16), still a small eatery that offers home-style cooking at a high level. Its signature dish is the *cordero estepa* (US$22), lamb with *calafate* sauce, but there are also pizzas and empanadas. In daytime hours, it has an adjacent sandwich shop.

The best new choice in town, **Techado Negro** (Av. Antonio Rojo and Riquelme, tel.

02962/49-3268, noon-midnight daily, US$10) prepares a diversity of dishes, including outstanding lamb ravioli with a mushroom sauce and a vegetarian risotto. The decor is informal, with colorful paintings on the walls. The service is exemplary.

At the north end of town, the tiny but luminous **El Muro** (San Martín 948, tel. 02962/49-3248, lunch and dinner daily, US$14) is a bistro-style restaurant that gets crowded. The service can be distracted when it gets busy—especially with only two waitresses—but dishes such as grilled lamb or lamb and mushroom lasagna are well worth minor inconveniences. Special mention goes to the light-crusted empanadas, including lamb and beef.

Ritual del Fuego (San Martín 219, tel. 02962/49-3173, lunch and dinner daily, US$13) is a small if noisy bistro with a diverse menu of well-presented and flavorful dishes such as lamb curry and sirloin in a rhubarb sauce with scalloped sweet potatoes. Other choices include arugula gnocchi in a sauce of tomato, eggplant, basil, and mozzarella, and the standard *bife de chorizo*. The service is attentive.

Accommodations

El Chaltén has a reasonable selection of accommodations, some of them very good. High summer demand makes reservations advisable. Most places close in winter, but there's usually something available. Wi-Fi is almost universal but often slow because of heavy demand on limited bandwidth.

UNDER US$25

Camping El Relincho (San Martín 505, tel. 02962/49-3007, www.elrelinchopatagonia.com.ar, US$6.50 pp adults, US$5 children, plus US$3 per vehicle) offers shelters for cooking and 24-hour hot showers. There are other campgrounds along the road to Lago del Desierto.

At the south end of town, **Ahonikenk Chaltén** (Güemes 23, tel. 02962/49-3070, US$10 pp dorm, US$32 d) is the cheapest of hostel accommodations.

US$25-50

Several of El Chaltén's dozen or so hostels also offer private rooms that are excellent values for around the same price or a little more.

The Hostelling International affiliate ★ **Travellers' Hostel Patagonia** (San Martín 376, tel. 02962/49-3019, www.patagoniahostel.com.ar, Oct.-mid-May, US$25 pp dorm, US$60-95 s, US$88-100 d) provides utilitarian dorms with four beds per room. It also has shared-bath doubles and a separate wing of more spacious and comfortable doubles and twins with private baths; the latter include continental breakfast. On the hostel side, it also provides cooking facilities, laundry service, a small book exchange, and bike rentals, and organizes excursions. Its main drawback is that the hostel restroom and shower facilities, while good enough, are arguably too few. English and Dutch are spoken.

Having more than doubled its capacity by adding a second floor, the HI affiliate **Albergue Rancho Grande** (San Martín 724, tel./fax 02962/49-3005, www.ranchograndehostel.com, US$25 pp dorm, US$105 s or d) has drawn some flak for failing to insulate the between-floors gap for sound. It does offer B&B packages with transportation from El Calafate; for reservations, contact Chaltén Travel (Av. Libertador 1174, El Calafate, tel. 02902/49-2212, www.chaltentravel.com).

Owned and operated by Cal Tur, **Hostel Pioneros del Valle** (San Martín 451, tel. 02962/49-3079, US$16 pp dorm, US$60 d, with breakfast) now has a limited number of private rooms to compensate for otherwise cramped sleeping quarters. Its spacious common areas are notable. **Aylen Aike Hostel** (Trevisán 125, tel. 02962/49-3317, aylen-aike@hotmail.com, US$23 pp) is a dorms-only hostel with attractive common areas.

Cóndor de los Andes (Av. Río de las Vueltas and Halvorsen, tel. 02962/49-3101, www.condordelosandes.com, US$23 pp dorm, US$90 d) has four- and six-bed dorms, each with its own bath, kitchen facilities, and spacious common areas with exceptional views. It has also added private rooms.

US$50-100

Expanded **Posada Altas Cumbres** (Lionel Terray 227, tel. 02962/49-3060, www.altascumbreschalten.com, US$73 s, US$86 d) has a dozen spacious rooms and friendly management. Several rooms are underfurnished, and those closest to the reception area have thin walls (though it doesn't draw a noisy crowd).

Cozy, friendly ★ **Nothofagus Bed & Breakfast** (Calle 10 No. 40, tel. 02962/49-3087, www.nothofagusbb.com.ar, US$60-73 s, US$70-93 d, with breakfast) has seven rooms in a handsome house with convivial common areas. Rates depend on whether the room has a shared or private bath.

Hostería Kalenshen (Lionel Terray 30, tel. 02962/49-3108, www.kalenshen.com, US$60 s, US$100 d, with breakfast) has 17 rooms with handmade furniture and another six *cabañas* (US$145 for up to 4 people). Uncommon for this town, it has a heated swimming pool.

Other accommodations have surpassed the venerable (by Chaltén standards) **Kalenshen Fitz Roy Inn** (San Martín 545, tel. 02966/15-52-5743, www.kalenshen.com, US$80 s, US$100 d). It also has multiple-day packages with two or all meals included, but those options would preclude eating at other good places.

Friendly **Hostería Thiamalu** (Lago del Desierto 99, tel. 02962/49-3136, www.thiamalu.com.ar, US$100 d, with breakfast) isn't up to the level of the Nothofagus, though all its rooms do have private baths. Prices may be negotiable.

US$100-150

Combining a traditional Patagonian style with contemporary comforts in its standard rooms, **Hostería Kau Si Aike** (Lago del Desierto 365, tel. 02962/49-3279, www.hosteriakausiaike.com.ar, US$109 s or d) also has split-level apartments suitable for four or five guests at rates that are only slightly higher.

Now operated by Travellers' Hostel Patagonia, **Hotel Cumbres Nevadas** (Av. Antonio Rojo 131, tel. 02962/49-3210, www.elchalten.com/cumbresnevadas, US$105 s, US$110 d) offers private rooms comparable to those at the other location. For better or worse, Hotel Cumbres Nevadas lacks Patagonia's informal atmosphere.

Rates have risen at expanded, upgraded **Hotel Las Piedras** (Lago del Desierto 423, tel./fax 02962/49-3015, www.laspiedraspatagonia.com.ar, US$112-290 s, US$120-330 d),

Travellers' Hostel Patagonia

which provides large and comfy but tackily decorated rooms with private baths. It has well-tended grounds and is quiet, since the nearby power plant has a noise-reducing structure.

★ **Hostería Infinito Sur** (Riquelme 208, tel. 02962/49-3325, www.infinitosurelchalten. com, US$140 s or d) is a boutique-style hotel with just nine rooms in a building of quarried stone and rough-hewn wood. Only the bar-breakfast room enjoys views of Fitz Roy. Rates fall by about 20-25 percent outside January-February.

US$150-200

In a new building with clean modern lines, **Hotel Poincenot** (San Martín 688, tel. 02962/49-3252, www.hotelpoincenot.com, US$175-200 s or d) has cozy midsize rooms, some with wheelchair access. Its bar has a sandwich menu and a good wine selection, but no elaborate meals.

The 12-room ★ **Hostería El Puma** (Lionel Terray 212, tel. 02962/49-3095, www. hosteriaelpuma.com.ar, US$160 s, US$180 d) is one of the better options, though its Terray restaurant is now open only occasionally.

North of town, in an out-of-the-way location bordering the Lago del Desierto road, ★ **Hostería El Pilar** (RP 23 s/n, tel./fax 02962/49-3002, Buenos Aires tel. 011/5031-0755, www.hosteriaelpilar.com.ar, Oct.-Apr., US$160 s, US$180 d, with breakfast) has the classic style of a Patagonian big house, but it's a recent construction, dating to 1996. Reservations are essential for this cozy and increasingly popular place. It's possible to dine in the restaurant without being a guest, although reservations are advised. Shuttle transportation from El Chaltén is free for guests.

With improved landscaping and several new rooms, **Hotel Lunajuim** (Trevisán 45, tel. 02962/49-3047, www.lunajuim.com, US$135 s, US$165 d) continues to make a good impression with appealing common areas (including a bar-restaurant), central heating, and breakfast.

OVER US$200

Atop a hillock with panoramic views of the Río de la Vueltas, the **Don Los Cerros Boutique Hotel & Spa** (San Martín 260, tel. 02962/49-3182, Buenos Aires tel. 011/5236-9092, www.loscerrosdelchalten.com, US$205-252 s or d) works mainly with multiple-day packages and tour groups, but takes other guests on a space-available basis. Spacious and luminous, with baths all featuring whirlpool tubs, the rooms have massive picture windows. The common areas, many of them decorated with historic maps, have soaring cathedral ceilings that flood them with natural light.

The 14-room **Chaltén Suites Hotel** (Av. San Martín 27, tel. 02962/49-3213, www. chaltensuiteshotel.com, US$278-290 s or d) is a rustically handsome building whose four superior suites all have whirlpool tubs. The standard upper floor rooms all have balconies with views of Cerro Fitz Roy or the Río de las Vueltas valley.

Information and Services

At the bus terminal, El Chaltén's **Dirección de Turismo, Medio Ambiente y Pesca** (Perito Moreno 28, tel. 02962/49-3370, www. elchalten.com, 8am-11pm daily summer, 9am-5pm Mon.-Fri. fall-spring) has maps and other information, and will help phone for accommodations.

Correo Argentino (Andreas Madsen 22) is the post office. **Telecabinas Javier** (Antonio de Viedma 52) is the main long-distance phone option (although Movistar and Personal cell phones finally work here). Wi-Fi is now routine in many accommodations and restaurants; bandwidth is improving, but high demand can still slow connections.

There are no formal exchange houses, but **Banco de Santa Cruz** operates an ATM in the bus terminal; still, as it often runs out of bills, it's better to bring as much cash as is feasible. Some businesses will accept U.S. dollars, euros, Brazilian *reais*, and Chilean pesos in exchange for services, and Albergue Rancho

Grande changes money informally, but few places handle credit cards.

Transportation

All buses now leave from the **Terminal de Ómnibus** (Perito Moreno 28, tel. 02962/49-3370), at the southern edge of town. Several companies connect El Chaltén with El Calafate (3.5 hours, US$40), including **Cal Tur** (tel. 02962/49-3150), **Chaltén Travel** (tel. 02962/49-3392), and **Taqsa/Marga** (Antonio Rojo 88, tel. 02962/49-3294). There are several buses daily in summer, but this can fall to about one daily in winter.

With Chaltén Travel and Cal Tur, it's possible to travel north on RN 40 (La Cuarenta) to the towns of Perito Moreno and Los Antiguos in Chubut province (12 hours, US$70); on uneven dates, the former continues to Esquel (19 hours, US$112), El Bolsón (22 hours, US$120), and Bariloche (24 hours, US$130). Chaltén Travel leaves Chaltén daily at 8pm in summer; passengers from El Calafate can board the bus at the RN 40 junction, but continuing beyond Perito Moreno requires an overnight at Perito's Hotel Belgrano. Fall to spring, there may be only one bus weekly. Taqsa now does the same route.

Transporte Las Lengas (Viedma 95, tel. 02962/49-3023, laslengaselchalten@yahoo.com.ar) provides direct service to El Calafate and to Aeropuerto Internacional El Calafate (every 2 hours 5:30am and 7:30pm daily, 3 hours, US$31).

When the national park shuttles don't meet your needs, consider a meterless taxi service, such as **Remises Aires del Fitz** (tel. 02962/49-3356), an economical option if shared by several riders.

LAGO DEL DESIERTO AND VICINITY

Beyond the park borders, 37 kilometers north of El Chaltén, **Lago del Desierto** is a scenic end-of-the-road destination with hiking trails, boat excursions, and even a challenging border crossing to the Chilean hamlet of Villa O'Higgins. **Travellers' Hostel Patagonia**

(San Martín 392, tel. 02962/49-3019) offers a morning rental bicycle shuttle to the lake so that riders can return to town with the wind at their backs.

Hiking

From the lake's south end, a short trail winds west through dense southern beech forest to a vista point and the hanging glacier at **Laguna Huemul** (US$7, admission collected at the Estancia Lago del Desierto campground). A longer route follows the eastern shore to the border, a 20-kilometer trek over gentle terrain. Every year several hundred cyclists and hikers cross the Argentine-Chilean border in a zone that was once so contentious that a Chilean Carabinero even lost his life in a firefight with Argentine Gendarmes (border guards) in 1965. Despite objections by a handful of Chilean nationalists, the matter is resolved, the border is peaceable, and determined hikers or even mountain bikers can readily reach Villa O'Higgins (though most do the trip north to south).

About midway to Lago del Desierto, **Estancia Los Huemules** (RP 23, Km 17, Buenos Aires tel. 011/4765-8085, www.loshuemules.com, trail use US$12.50 pp per day) is a hybrid real estate development and nature reserve. More than 95 percent of its 5,786 hectares is devoted to forest and high country preservation. Four of five planned trails, up to four or five hours one-way, are open to the public, and one new rustic shelter is available for overnighters. There is a professionally arranged **visitors center** (9am-6pm daily, free).

Camping

At the south end of the lake, **Camping Estancia Lago del Desierto** (tel. 02962/49-3245, US$13 pp) offers wooded sites with fire pits and toilets with hot showers.

Transportation

From El Chaltén, **Zona Austral** (Av. Güemes 173, tel. 02962/49-3155, www.zonaaustral-turismo.com.ar) minibuses go to Lago del

Crossing into Chile

Several years ago, Argentina's previous government pledged to pave the entirety of RN 40 in Patagonia. When it found the promise easier to make than to honor, it fudged the issue by re-numbering the already paved RP 5 and RP 7 as RN 40—renumbering the far shorter gravel RN 40 as RP 7. Most southbound transportation to Chile, Puerto Natales, and Torres del Paine still uses the old route to Tapi Aike, a wide spot in the paved road where there's another gas station and a convenience store.

From Tapi Aike, the road continues southwest toward the border crossing at **Cancha Carrera,** the easiest access to Torres del Paine, with occasional direct summer buses. Most travelers, however, enter Chile from **Río Turbio,** an otherwise bleak coal town with a mining museum, a historical narrow-gauge railroad, and a small but modern ski resort.

Río Turbio (pop. 9,000) is 242 kilometers south of El Calafate via RN 40 and RP 7, and 30 kilo-meters north of Puerto Natales. Chile-bound buses from El Calafate almost all cross the border here, where motorists should fill the tank (gasoline is notably more expensive in Chile). There are frequent local buses to Natales.

For those who speak Spanish, miners conduct 45-minute tours of the **Museo Minero Anatol Kowaljow** (Mina 3, 8am-5pm Mon.-Fri., donation), on RN 40 about three kilometers east of town. Part of the school used to train miners, the museum gives a good introduction to underground mining, its evolving technologies, and its dangers.

Desierto (US$27 one-way or round-trip) at 8:30am and 3pm daily, returning at 2:30pm and 8:30pm. Hitching is feasible, but ve-hicles are few and often full. At the lake it-self, **Exploradores Lago del Desierto** (tel. 02966/15-46-7103, www.exploradoresla-godeldesierto.com) operates the 40-passen-ger *Huemul,* which carries passengers to the north end and back (US$32 pp).

Northwestern Santa Cruz Province

About 30 kilometers east of El Calafate, northbound RN 40 covers some 600-plus kilometers of once rugged gravel road in the Andes's arid eastern foothills before arriving at the cow town of Perito Moreno near Lago Buenos Aires, the oasis of Los Antiguos, and the Chilean border town of Chile Chico. Now more than half paved, this desolate highway is seeing more and more overland travelers, but it's not for ev-eryone. The unrelenting westerlies bowl over bicyclists and motorcyclists alike, sharp rocks still blow tires and shatter windshields, and vehicles can break down in the middle of nowhere.

Running from Río Gallegos almost to the Bolivian border, RN 40 is Argentina's longest interior highway. This segment of La Cuarenta (RN 40) has a mystique all its own. Some love it, some loathe it, and others are ambivalent, but no one forgets it.

LA LEONA AND VICINITY

Since 1916, the landmark **Hotel de Campo La Leona** (junction of RN 40 and west-bound RP 21, Buenos Aires tel. 011/5032-3415, www.hoteldecampolaleona.com.ar, US$75 s, US$110 d, with breakfast) has been a rural roadhouse where today's travelers brake for chocolate and lemon pie, banana bread, and tea and coffee. Though the ex-terior looks much as it did a century ago, a Buenos Aires investor totally transformed the interior, with a small souvenir shop in addition to a more spacious and cheerful dining room (with equally cheerful personnel). The four remodeled rooms have private baths. Camping (US$20 pp, breakfast not included) is also an option here. Little more than a wide turnout alongside the road, Hotel de Campo La Leona is a useful stop for cyclists, either northbound or southbound, who don't care to set up the tent and want amenities like Wi-Fi.

Under the same ownership, west of the highway, the more luxurious **Estancia La Estela** (tel. 011/5032-3415 in Buenos Aires, www.estancialaestela.com.ar, US$135 s, US$230 d) offers custom-built accommodations with views of Lago Viedma and the Fitz Roy range, plus activities that include rafting, riding, and even archery.

Nearby, the **Bosque Petrificado La Leona** is a badlands reserve of petrified forests and dinosaur fossils on nearby Estancia Santa Teresita, visited by guided tour only. For details on this full-day excursion (US$110, including transportation and lunch), contact El Calafate's **Morresi Viajes** (Av. del Libertador 932, tel. 02902/49-2276, www.morresiviajes.com.ar).

TRES LAGOS AND VICINITY

Beyond La Margarita, northbound RN 40 climbs over the volcanic Meseta Escorial before dropping into the enigmatically named hamlet of **Tres Lagos** ("Three Lakes," though the only nearby water is the humble Río Shehuen). Northbound motorists *must* fill up at the service station, which has the only gasoline until Gobernador Gregores, about 210 kilometers northeast, and Bajo Caracoles, 338 kilometers north.

Tres Lagos has few other services, though its municipal **Camping Don Jorge Cepernic** (US$10 per tent) has seen a major upgrade, with new baths and a café. Sandwiches, empanadas, and lesser snacks are available at the service station.

LAGO CARDIEL AND VICINITY

North of Tres Lagos, RN 40 winds north over the Meseta Cascajosa before coming within sight of **Lago Cardiel,** a deep interior drainage lake that's a bellwether for ongoing climate-change studies. It also enjoys a certain popularity for fishing, and it's so remote that there's little competition.

Hotel de Campo La Leona

The Changing Cuarenta

From the Bolivian border near La Quiaca to its terminus near Río Gallegos, RN 40 has been Argentina's great unfinished interior highway: "La Cuarenta." In the central Cuyo provinces, segments have long been smoothly paved, while others in the Andean northwest remain rough and rugged. None of those, though, has enjoyed the notoriety of the segment between the El Calafate junction and the town of Perito Moreno, on the cusp between the Patagonian steppe and the icy southern Andes.

It's no longer Argentina's loneliest road—some of the cul-de-sac tracks that spin off it seem simply abandoned—but for Argentines and foreigners alike it's been the standard for adventurous driving and cycling thanks to its secluded Andean lakes, isolated *estancias,* plentiful wildlife, and sights like the pre-Columbian rock art of Cueva de las Manos. Even the advent of ever more frequent public transportation has not diminished its mystique.

The summer season sees a growing procession of motorists, motorcyclists, and bicyclists (though most cyclists prefer the Chilean side). Some, at least, appreciate Charles Darwin's insight that the appeal of the bleak Patagonian plains was "the free scope given to the imagination."

A trip on La Cuarenta still requires preparation. With accommodations and supplies few and far between, bicyclists and motorcyclists *must* carry tents and cold-weather gear, even in midsummer, and plenty of food. A GPS receiver and maps, like ACA's newest regional sheets, are essential. Motorists might feel more comfortable with two spare tires. Also carry extra fuel—between El Calafate and Perito Moreno, the only reliable supplies are at El Chaltén (a 90-kilometer detour),

On the west side of the highway, 22 kilometers south of the RP 29 junction to Gobernador Gregores, **Estancia La Siberia** (Estrada 368, Río Gallegos tel. 02966/15-35-2521, tel. 02966/15-55-5308, jfquinteros1@yahoo.com) has long been the casual version of the stereotypical tourist *estancia.* With little livestock, set among an aging orchard of apricot, cherry, pear, and plum trees, it's now only open erratically, but may have moderately priced accommodations, camping, and meals.

ESTANCIA LA ANGOSTURA AND VICINITY

About 60 kilometers northwest of La Siberia on RN 29, which used to be RN 40 and is still a more direct route north than the paved route via Gobernador Gregores, an eastbound dirt road drops into the Río Chico marshlands. The marshlands are dotted with birds that include upland geese, coots, and lapwings. Sheltered by densely planted trees, **Estancia La Angostura** (RP 29, Km 91.5, tel. 02902/49-1501, www.estancialaangostura.com.ar,

mid-Oct.-Mar., US$90 s or d, with breakfast, camping US$10 pp) has six comfortable guest rooms and also a decent campground on a farm that leans toward the rustic end of the *estancia* continuum. The food is heavy on Argentine standards like *milanesa* (breaded cutlet). With RN 40 rerouted to Gobernador Gregores, this will be an off-the-paved-track shortcut to experience the old highway.

North of La Angostura, the 200-or-so-kilometer stretch of northbound RN 40 to Bajo Caracoles has few services. The landmark **Hotel Las Horquetas** (US$25 pp), a picturesque roadhouse near the junction with westbound RP 37, has reopened; meals are also available. Some campers like the free sites beneath the bridge over the Río Chico near the junction of RN 40 and RP 29, but best spots go early.

GOBERNADOR GREGORES

Though it's 60 or 70 kilometers east of the former RN 40 shortcut, **Gobernador Gregores** (pop. 4,900) can be an essential detour for bikers or motorists running short of gasoline.

Tres Lagos, Gobernador Gregores (which sometimes runs out), and Bajo Caracoles (which also sometimes runs out). Some tourist *estancias* will sell gasoline to their clients in an emergency, but don't count on it.

Hazards remain. Powerful winds can knock over cyclists in an instant. Deep gravel adds to the danger in some spots. Even high-clearance vehicles are vulnerable to flipping on loose gravel, especially when braking suddenly. Although a 4WD vehicle is not essential, some drivers prefer it to avoid fishtailing on gravel.

Chipped, cracked, and even shattered windshields are par for the course. Normally, rental-car insurance policies do not cover such damage, and replacements are expensive in Argentina (though reasonable in Punta Arenas, Chile). Approaching vehicles usually brake to minimize the possibility of damage, but some drivers find they need to play chicken to slow down an onrushing pickup truck or SUV.

About half of this segment of RN 40 is paved and the rest of it seems likely to be completed within a few years. Because of rerouting, it now passes through Gobernador Gregores (anyone nostalgic for the old route can still take on the graveled shortcut of RP 29).

If driving or cycling doesn't appeal to you, but you still want to see the "loneliest highway," summer bus and minivan services now connect El Calafate and El Chaltén, at the south end, with Perito Moreno and Los Antiguos, at the north end of Santa Cruz province, and with Bariloche.

It's also the easiest place to obtain other supplies and to hire a car and driver to Parque Nacional Perito Moreno, some 200-plus kilometers northwest. RN 40's paving and rerouting via Gregores figures to reinvigorate the town as a service center, especially as a base for improved park access.

The **Camping Municipal Nuestra Señora del Valle** (Roca and Chile, tel. 02962/49-1228, free) has hot showers. The best accommodations are at **Hotel Cañadón León** (Roca 397, tel. 02962/49-1082, US$28 s, US$41 d), which also has the best restaurant. The next best dining is at **Pizzería Chicho** (Belgrano 319, tel. 02962/49-1391).

The **Dirección Municipal de Turismo** (tel. 02962/49-1259) keeps a kiosk at the western approach to town. In new quarters, the **APN** (Paseo 9 de Julio 610, tel. 02962/49-1477, peritomoreno@apn.gov.ar) deals with Parque Nacional Perito Moreno.

Cerro San Lorenzo (San Martín and Alberdi) has buses to San Julián (6pm Mon.-Sat., US$30). **Taqsa** (Alberdi 678, tel. 02962/49-1102) goes to Río Gallegos (1:40am Sun.-Fri., 5.5 hours, US$38).

★ PARQUE NACIONAL PERITO MORENO

The Sierra Colorada's intensely colored sedimentary summits are the backdrop for the lake-laden, wind-whipped, and wildlife-rich high country of **Parque Nacional Perito Francisco P. Moreno,** named for the founder of Argentina's park system. Possibly Patagonia's wildest park, where Paleo-Indians covered cave walls with images of guanacos and human hands, it's a major reason travelers have braved the past rigors of La Cuarenta.

Comprising 115,000 hectares of Patagonian steppe, sub-Antarctic forest, glacial lakes and fjords, and high Andean pastures, the park is 220 kilometers northwest of Gobernador Gregores via RN 40 and RP 37. It's 310 kilometers southwest of the town of Perito Moreno via RN 40 and RP 37.

At 900 meters, its base elevation is higher than Los Glaciares, and its climate is colder, wetter, and more unpredictable. Its highest summit is 2,254-meter Cerro Mié. Snowcapped 3,700-meter Cerro San Lorenzo, north of the park boundary, is even higher.

In the drier eastern steppes, the dominant

vegetation consists of bunch grasses known collectively as *coirón*. To the west there's a transitional wind-flagged forest of *lenga* and *ñire*, the ubiquitous southern beeches. In more sheltered areas, there are dense and nearly pure *lenga* stands along the shores of Lago Azara and Lago Nansen.

Troops of guanacos patrol the steppes and even some of the high country where there is summer pasture; the *huemul* (Andean deer) grazes the uplands in summer but winters at lower elevations. The puma is the top predator, but there are lesser killers in red and gray foxes. The *pilquín* or *chinchillón anaranjado* is a species of viscacha unique to Santa Cruz province and southernmost Chile.

The largest birds are the Andean condor and the flightless rhea. Other impressive species include the *águila mora* (black-chested buzzard eagle), the large *ñacurutú* owl, Patagonian woodpeckers, and the *carancho* (crested caracara). The many lakes and streams support abundant wildfowl, including flamingos, black-necked swans, grebes, wild geese, and steamer ducks. Unlike other Patagonian lakes, those within the park have remained free of introduced fish species.

Sights and Recreation

While **Lago Burmeister** is worth a visit, the cave paintings are closed to public access. There are large troops of guanacos on **Península Belgrano,** reached by an isthmus immediately west of Estancia Belgrano (which is no longer a tourist ranch).

One of the best day hikes is 1,434-meter **Cerro León,** a 2.5-hour climb immediately north of Estancia La Oriental, which offers the area's best, easily accessible panoramas (be prepared for changeable weather). The volcanic overhang known as the **Cerro de los Cóndores** is the flight school for condor chicks.

Food and Accommodations

There are free but barren campsites with pit toilets at the APN's Centro de Informes, at the park entrance. The more appealing

Lago Burmeister campground consists of Tehuelche-style lean-tos in dense *lenga* forest. The water is potable, but no supplies are available—campers must bring everything.

On Lago Belgrano's north shore, **Estancia La Oriental** (Rivadavia 936, San Julián, Buenos Aires tel./fax 011/4152-6901, www. laorientalpatagonia.com.ar, Nov.-Apr., US$150 d, US$70 dorm for up to 4 people, camping US$30 per tent for up to 3 people, with hot showers) has both conventional accommodations (seven rooms sleeping up to 22 guests) and protected campsites near the lodge. The breakfasts (US$10) of homemade scones, bread, jam, ham, and cheese deserve a detour, but the dinners (US$35) are nothing special.

Transportation and Services

Rangers at the Centro de Informes, at the park entrance, provide maps and brochures and offer guided hikes and visits; they can also be reached through the **APN** (Paseo 9 de Julio 610, tel./fax 02962/49-1477, peritomoreno@ apn.gov.ar) in Gobernador Gregores. There is no admission charge, but the park closes to the public from May to October.

Rental cars offer the greatest flexibility, though it's possible to hire a car and driver in Gobernador Gregores or the town of Perito Moreno. Hitching from the highway junction is feasible but uncertain.

BAJO CARACOLES

Midway between Las Horquetas and the town of Perito Moreno, barren **Bajo Caracoles** is an oasis for automobiles and motorcycles, with the only gas station in nearly 500 kilometers (though the newly designated RN 40 via Gobernador Gregores offers an alternative). Southbound travelers should fill the tank here; others should buy enough to reach Perito Moreno, 128 kilometers north.

Bajo Caracoles is also the southern gateway to the rock-art site of Cueva de las Manos, 41 kilometers northeast via RP 97, but there are alternative access points farther north. RP 39 leads east to the hamlet of Hipólito Yrigoyen and **Lago Posadas,** near the Chilean border. RP 41, a short distance north of Bajo Caracoles, goes directly to the border crossing at **Paso Roballos.**

Better than expected in this remote outpost, the classic roadhouse **Hotel Bajo Caracoles** (tel. 02963/49-0100, US$40 s, US$55 d) fills up early. It has surprisingly good meals, groceries, and modernized baths. There is also cheap camping nearby.

★ CUEVA DE LAS MANOS AND VICINITY

Beyond Baja Caracoles, RN 40 traverses the northern steppe until the point where, over millions of years, the Río Pinturas has cut a deep, scenic canyon. In the process, erosion has left countless *aleros,* rocky overhangs often mistakenly called *cuevas* (caves). One of these is the **Cueva de las Manos,** a UNESCO World Heritage Site where stencils of hundreds of human hands, guanacos, and abstract forms cover the walls in orange, red, and yellow hues.

Dating from around 7370 BC, the oldest paintings represent hunter-gatherers from immediate postglacial times. The more abstract designs, which are fewer, are more recent.

Oddly enough, nearly all the hands from which the site takes its name are left hands.

Along with Parque Nacional Perito Moreno, this is one of La Cuarenta's finest detours, with three main access points. From Bajo Caracoles in the south, gravel RP 41 goes directly to the **visitors center** (www.cuevadelasmanos.org, 9am-7pm daily, foreigners US$10, Argentines US$5), where the province collects an admission fee for an obligatory guided tour. The center itself contains informational panels in imperfect but passable English. Metal screens now block close access to the paintings, to discourage vandalism and prevent repeated touching that could damage the paintings, but they do not obstruct the view.

Another access point is Estancia Cueva de las Manos, another 23 kilometers north and 4 kilometers east in the Pinturas drainage. From there, another 18-kilometer access road leads to a parking area and a trailhead, where it's a 2-kilometer hike that includes a sandy, slippery descent, with many loose rocks. By this route, mountain bikers can avoid backtracking to RN 40 by walking their bikes down the slope and then over the river (there's a suspension footbridge, but the stream is usually shallow) and out the other direction. There

The pre-Columbian paintings at Cueva de las Manos have made it a UNESCO World Heritage Site.

is a new and shorter access road midway between the Bajo Caracoles and Estancia Cueva de las Manos.

Estancia Cueva de las Manos (Buenos Aires tel. 011/5237-4043, www.cuevadelasmanos.net, Nov.-Mar., US$80 s, US$100 d, with breakfast) has nine attractive, modern rooms with private baths, as well as hostel accommodations (US$25 pp, with breakfast) in two vast dorms, each with 18 beds, three toilets, and three showers. Its restaurant (US$30) serves lunch and dinner, including dishes such as pumpkin-stuffed pasta and excellent desserts. The wine list has some good but moderately priced vintages.

Estancia Cueva de las Manos is open November-March and sometimes for Semana Santa (the week before Easter). It also offers additional excursions besides Cueva de las Manos. It has no phone or Internet access, but they have a Perito Moreno contact in **Zoyen Turismo** (Av. Juan Perón 1008, tel. 02963/43-2207, zoyenperitomoreno@hotmail.com).

LAGO POSADAS

Bajo Caracoles is not known for its beauty, but it's hard to improve on aquamarine **Lago Posadas,** 90 kilometers west, and nearby Lago Pueyrredón, nudging the Chilean border. While the main route from Bajo Caracoles to the border passes Lago Ghío, along RP 41 to the north, southerly RP 39 via Lago Posadas is a more scenic alternative. The westbound road continues to Paso Roballos, a spectacular border area with access to Valle Chacabuco, the audacious new conservation project poised to become Chile's Parque Nacional Patagonia.

PERITO MORENO

Where RN 40 meets the smoothly paved international highway from Comodoro Rivadavia to Chile Chico, nondescript **Perito Moreno** marks the return to civilization for northbound travelers and the start of the adventure for the Calafate-bound. Often confused with its namesake national park, as well as the eponymous glacier in Parque Nacional Los Glaciares, it has decent services, but many visitors prefer the lakeside town of Los Antiguos to the west.

Perito Moreno (pop. 4,617) is 398 kilometers southwest of Comodoro Rivadavia via Caleta Olivia, and 58 kilometers east of Los Antiguos via paved RP 43. It is 124 kilometers south of Río Mayo, Chubut province, where RN 40 continues toward Esquel and the Andean Lake District. There is only infrequent public transportation between Perito Moreno and Río Mayo.

Early February's **Festival Folklórico Cueva de las Manos** is a musical event that capitalizes on the proximity of the world heritage site. A new **Museo Regional de la Cueva de las Manos** remains under construction; part of it already occupies the **Salón Iturrioz** (San Martín and Rivadavia, tel. 0297/624-0603), a café in a handsome brick structure.

Food and Accommodations

The **Salón Iturrioz** (San Martín and Rivadavia) has snacks, sandwiches, drinks, and Wi-Fi in a museum atmosphere. **Urbano** (San Martín and Juan D. Perón, lunch and dinner daily) has the most diverse menu in agreeable surroundings (except when they pump up the volume). The pizzas will feed two hungry diners.

Opposite Laguna de los Cisnes, the city park at Perito's south end, the sheltered **Camping Municipal** (Roca and Moreno, tel. 02963/43-2130, US$2 pp plus US$3 per tent, plus US$10 per vehicle) is small but has flawless baths with hot showers for a small extra charge.

Otherwise, the pickings are slim. **Hotel y Restaurante El Viejo Bar** (Av. San Martín 990, tel. 02963/43-2538, US$32 s, US$45 d) has leapt ahead of most local competitors in its accommodations and bar-restaurant facilities. Used by Chaltén Travel buses for the overnight break between El Calafate and Bariloche, **Hotel Belgrano** (Av. San Martín 1001, tel. 02963/43-2019, hotelbelgrano@hotmail.com, US$16 dorm, US$38 s, US$57 d) also has a restaurant. The best option is the charming ★ **Kaiken Lodge** (Hipólito Yrigoyen 2012, tel. 02963/43-2079, www.chakrakaiken.com.ar, US$97 s, US$107 d), operated by the semiretired former owners of Estancia Telken.

Information and Services

In new quarters, the **Dirección de Turismo** (Av. San Martín 2005, tel. 02963/43-2732, turismoperitomoreno@yahoo.com.ar, 7am-midnight Mon.-Fri., 9am-9pm Sat.-Sun. summer, 7am-midnight Mon.-Fri., 10am-7pm Sat.-Sun. fall-spring) keeps long hours.

Banco Santa Cruz (Av. San Martín 1385) has an ATM. The postal code for **Correo Argentino** (Av. Juan D. Perón 1331) is 9040. **Cyber Ruta 40** (Av. San Martín 1401) has telephone and Internet access.

Zoyen Turismo (Av. Perón 1008, tel. 02963/43-2207, cell tel. 0297/15-623-8811, www.zoyenturismo.com.ar) offers local excursions including Cueva de las Manos (US$56 pp plus the admission fee) via Estancia Cueva de las Manos and a short end-of-the-road hike. Bilingual **Harry Nauta** (Perito Moreno 1087, tel. 02963/43-2303, cell tel. 0297/15-429-0950, jarinauta@yahoo.com.ar) freelances on excursions that include Cueva de las Manos and Cañadón del Arroyo Feo.

For medical services, try the **Hospital Distrital** (Colón 1237, tel. 02963/43-2045).

Transportation

LADE (Av. San Martín 1065, tel. 02963/43-2055) has occasional flights into and out of Perito Moreno but is hard to rely on.

The sharp new **Terminal de Ómnibus** is at the north end of town, where RN 40 (Av. San Martín) meets RP 43. **CMC** (tel. 02963/43-2638) and **Sportman** (tel. 02963/43-2177) have westbound service to Los Antiguos (1 hour, US$7) and eastbound service to Comodoro Rivadavia (5 hours, US$31). Sportman and **Taqsa** (tel. 02963/43-2675) both have daily service to Río Gallegos (14 hours, US$72). Taqsa goes to El Chaltén (US$70) and El Calafate (US$70) at midnight on even-numbered days.

Chaltén Travel (El Calafate tel. 02902/49-2480) buses from Los Antiguos to El Calafate will pick up passengers at the terminal here; the service runs on alternate days December-April or so. Passengers from El Chaltén can board the northbound bus from El Calafate at the junction of RN 40 and RP 23 without having to return to El Calafate. Buses depart Calafate on odd-numbered days and return from Los Antiguos on even-numbered days. For southbound travel to El Chaltén, Chaltén Travel links up with its own buses between El Calafate and El Chaltén. It now takes passengers onward to Bariloche, but they have to spend the night at Hotel Belgrano here. **Cal Tur** now has similar services to and from El Calafate, and onward to Los Antiguos, but does not go to Bariloche.

LOS ANTIGUOS

Rows of upright poplars announce the approach to **Los Antiguos,** a garden spot where vivid flowerbeds fill the median strip of Avenida 11 de Julio; flats of soft fruits like raspberries, cherries, and strawberries go for a song; and baskets of apples, apricots, peaches, pears, plums, and prunes adorn the storefronts. Its microclimate has made it a getaway since Tehuelche times.

On Lago Buenos Aires's south shore, Los Antiguos (pop. about 7,000) is 58 kilometers west of Perito Moreno via RP 43. Entering town, the highway becomes Avenida 11 de Julio, which continues to the Chilean border. The Argentine border post is at the western end, while Chilean immigration and customs are across the Río Jeinimeni, about five kilometers farther.

Early January's three-day **Fiesta de la Cereza** (Cherry Festival) can put a strain on accommodations. **Día de los Antiguos** (Feb. 5) marks the town's anniversary, while **Día del Lago Buenos Aires** takes place on October 29.

For fresh fruit as well as preserves, try any of several farms, such as **Chacra El Porvenir** (walking distance from Av. 11 de Julio).

Food and Accommodations

Dutch-run **Viva El Viento** (Av. 11 de Julio 477, tel. 02963/49-1109, www.vivaelviento. com, US$20) is a new restaurant and wine bar, with live music and Wi-Fi. It does a superb leg of lamb with rosemary and garlic potatoes. The service can be distracted, though it does offer live music (including traveling invitees) on Tuesday nights.

A short walk to the west, **Taura** (Av. 11 de Julio 571, tel. 0297/15-625-0912) adds a touch more sophistication with its slow-cooked deboned Patagonian lamb (US$18) and fish and shellfish stew (US$16).

Protected by poplars and cypresses, the lakeshore **Camping Municipal** (Av. 11 de Julio s/n, tel. 02963/49-1265, US$2 pp, plus US$7 per tent, plus US$3.50 per vehicle) provides picnic tables and fire pits at every site. Midway between town and the border post, **Hostel Sol de Mayo** (Av. 11 de Julio 1300, tel. 02963/49-1232, chacrasoldemayo@hotmail. com, US$12 pp dorms, US$48 d) has dorms and some private rooms.

Hotel Antiguos Cerezos (Av. 11 de Julio 850, tel. 02963/49-1132, hotel_losantiguoscerezos@hotmail.com, US$48 s, US$71 d) is a utilitarian hotel with a decent restaurant. On the eastern outskirts of town, **Hostería Antigua Patagonia** (RP 43 s/n, tel. 02963/49-1038, www.antiguapatagonia. com.ar, US$92 s, US$110 d) is a three-story lakeshore hotel with a restaurant. **Chacra Refugio de Rocas** (Chacra 127, Parcela 10, tel. 0297/15-401-0787, www.refugioderocas. com.ar, US$65 s, US$115 d) is a spa hotel on a traditional berry farm parcel.

Information and Services

The **Secretaría de Turismo** (Lago Buenos Aires 59, tel. 02963/49-1261, turismolosantiguos@gmail.com, 8am-midnight daily Dec.-Apr., 8am-8pm daily May-Nov.) occupies spacious new quarters. Perito Moreno's **Zoyen Turismo** (Av. 11 de Julio 427, Local 8, tel. 02963/43-2207, www.zoyenturismo. com.ar) has established an office here to offer tours to Cueva de las Manos and other regional attractions.

Banco de Santa Cruz (Av. 11 de Julio 531) has an ATM here, but note that it does not read chip-enabled cards and that some businesses change informally at better rates. The postal code for **Correo Argentino** (Gobernador Gregores 19) is 9041. **Locutorio Los Antiguos** (Alameda 436) has long-distance telephone services. Wi-Fi is abundant but still slow and balky.

Transportation

At present, because of a tax issue with Santa Cruz province, minibuses from Chile Chico no longer shuttle back and forth across the border here, so it's a six-kilometer hike from the Argentine border post to Chilean customs and immigration. From there, it may be possible to phone a cab to downtown Chile Chico.

From the **Terminal de Buses** (Av. Tehuelches 157), on the other hand, an increasing number of bus companies offer services throughout the province and even a bit beyond. **CMC** (tel. 0297/15-416-4001) shuttles four times daily between Los Antiguos and Perito Moreno (1 hour, US$7). **Sportman** (tel. 02963/49-1175) also provides service to Perito Moreno and to Caleta Olivia (5 hours, US$23) and Comodoro Rivadavia (6 hours, US$30). Sportman also has daily service to Río Gallegos (14-15 hours, US$70).

In season, **Chaltén Travel** (tel. 0297/15-623-4882, analiakruk@gmail.com) goes daily to El Chaltén (13 hours, US$85) and El Calafate (14 hours, US$85) via southbound RN 40, and to northbound destinations as far as Bariloche. At the terminal, **Cal Tur** (tel. 0297/15-623-4882) has similar services to Calafate Tuesday, Thursday, and Saturday, while **Taqsa** (tel. 02966/15-41-9615) goes on odd-numbered days, and also daily to Río Gallegos from Perito Moreno.

El Pingüino/Andesmar/Tramat (tel. 0297/15-492-9590) goes to Perito Moreno and Caleta Olivia (12:15pm Mon.-Fri.).

Magallanes

Look for ★ to find recommended
sights, activities, dining, and lodging.

Highlights

★ **Casa Braun-Menéndez:** Magallanes's regional museum occupies what was once the mansion of Patagonia's wool aristocracy (page 397).

★ **Monumento Natural Los Pingüinos:** In the summer season, penguins occupy every square centimeter of Isla Magdalena, also home to a historic lighthouse (page 406).

★ **Parque Nacional Pali Aike:** Hugging the Argentine border, the volcanic caves of northern Magallanes's steppe feature some of the continent's prime early human sites (page 410).

★ **The Fjords of Fuegia:** Cruise the ice-clogged inlets of the Tierra del Fuego archipelago, from Punta Arenas to Ushuaia, Cape Horn, and back. Even backpackers sometimes splurge for a leg of this unforgettable itinerary (page 412).

★ **Torres del Paine:** These granite needles rising above the Patagonian steppe are a beacon drawing travelers from around the world to Chile's premier national park (page 432).

★ **Cuernos del Paine:** This jagged interface between igneous and metamorphic rock is some of the world's most breathtaking alpine scenery (page 432).

★ **Parque Pingüino Rey:** This colony of majestic king penguins has established itself at Estancia San Clemente, on Bahía Inútil (page 440).

★ **Puerto Williams:** Across the Beagle Channel from Ushuaia, tiny Williams provides access to the rugged hiking trails of the Dientes de Navarino, a series of summits that rise like inverted vampire's fangs (page 441).

T hanks to the Torres del Paine, the magnificent granite needles that rise above the Patagonian plains, Chile's most southerly region has acquired international fame. Pacific storms drench the nearly uninhabited western cordillera,

feeding glaciers and rushing rivers, but relentless winds buffet the rolling eastern grasslands of the Andean rain shadow.

Along the Strait of Magellan, the city of Punta Arenas is the center for excursions to various attractions, including easily accessible penguin colonies and Tierra del Fuego's remote fjords. The region has no direct land connections to the rest of Chile. Travelers arrive by air, sea, and through Argentine Patagonia.

Administratively, Region XII (Magallanes) includes all Chilean territory beyond 49 degrees south latitude—technically to the South Pole, as Chile claims a slice of Antarctica between 53 and 90 degrees west longitude. It also takes in the Chilean sector of the Tierra del Fuego archipelago.

Improved communications have meant that many visitors to southern Argentina also visit Chile to see Puerto Natales, Torres del Paine, and other attractions. January and

February are the peak months, but the season is broadening. Prices drop in winter, though many places also close.

PLANNING YOUR TIME

Punta Arenas can be a sightseeing base, but usually for a day or two. For those who haven't seen Magellanic penguins elsewhere, it's worth scheduling or waiting for the boat to Isla Magdalena, or taking a day trip to see king penguins on Tierra del Fuego. It's also the home port for the spectacular cruise to Tierra del Fuego's remotest fjords and Cape Horn via Ushuaia (Argentina), a three- or four-day excursion in either direction. Based on an island in the western Strait of Magellan, summer whale-watching is drawing a small but growing crowd on three-day excursions.

Exploring the thinly populated Chilean sector of Tierra del Fuego requires a vehicle or an airplane. Connections to Puerto Williams,

Previous: Estancia Puerto Consuelo; fisherman at ruins of Puerto Natales's pier. **Above:** Estancia Yendegaia in the Cordillera Darwin.

Magallanes

PACIFIC OCEAN

ATLANTIC OCEAN

CHILE

ARGENTINA

Ferry to
Caleta Tortel &
Puerto Yungay

Isla Hanover

Isla Jorge
Montt

Isla Diego de
Almagro

Reserva
Nacional
Alacalufes

Isla
Desolación

Isla
Santa Inés

Parque
Nacional
Torres del
Paine

Glaciar
Torres del Moreno
Paine

El Calafate

TORRES DEL PAINE
CUERNOS DEL PAINE

Glaciar
Balmaceda

MONUMENTO NATURAL
CUEVA DEL MILODÓN

Península
Muñoz
Gamero

Lago
del Toro

Cerro Paine Grande

Puerto Natales

Villa Cerro
Castillo

Río Turbio

To Puerto San Julián and
Comodoro Rivadavia

Puerto
Santa Cruz

CASA BRAUN-
MENÉNDEZ

RN Magallanes

Isla
Riesco

Villa
Tehuelches

RN Laguna
Parrillar

Pingüinera

PUNTA
ARENAS

Seno Skyring

Seno Otway

Río Verde

Laguna
Blanca

PARQUE NACIONAL
PANAIKE

Estrecho de Magallanes

FUERTE
BULNES

MONUMENTO NATURAL
LOS PINGÜINOS

Isla
Dawson

Porvenir

Cerro
Sombrero

ESTANCIA
SAN GREGORIO

Punta
Delgada

RÍO GALLEGOS

Canal Cockburn

Parque Nacional
Alberto de
Agostini

THE FJORDS
OF FUEGIA

Cordillera
Darwin

Parque
Nacional
Yendegaia

Camerón

Lago
Blanco

Onaisín

PARQUE
PINGÜINO REY

Cabo
Vírgenes

PN Tierra
del Fuego

Bahía Inútil

Bahía San Sebastián

Isla Hoste

Puerto
Navarino

USHUAIA

Paso
Radman

MUSEO
SALESIANO

Río Grande

Bahía

Grande

PUERTO WILLIAMS

Canal Beagle

Lago
Fagnano
(Kami)

Tolhuin

ESTANCIA
HARBERTON

Isla Navarino

ESTANCIA
VIAMONTE

Isla
Grande de
Tierra del Fuego

Isla Nueva

Parque Nacional
Cabo de Hornos

Cabo de Hornos

Península Mitre

ESTANCIA
POLICARPO

Estrecho de Le Maire

Isla de los
Estados

Estrecho de Magallanes

RP 9

RP 7

RN 40

RP 2

RP 5

RN 40

RN 3

255

RN 3

0   60 km

0   60 mi

although it's not far from Ushuaia as the crow flies, are haphazard except by air from Punta Arenas. Once you're there, hiking the Dientes de Navarino circuit takes at least a week.

Puerto Natales, the urban gateway to Torres del Paine, is mainly a place to prepare for trekking. Its seaside setting, youthful exuberance, and nearby hiking excursions tempt visitors to extend their stay. The park deserves no less than a week, for day-hikers and overnight trekkers alike, but even an abbreviated day trip—some people do it, despite the time and difficulty of getting here—is worth the trouble.

Another attraction is the *Skorpios III* cruise through the fjords on the west side of the Campo de Hielo Sur, across the ice from Torres del Paine. In summer, this five-day, four-night excursion visits many otherwise inaccessible areas.

HISTORY

Some of the continent's oldest archaeological evidence for human habitation comes from volcanic rock shelters in and near Parque Nacional Pali Aike, along the Argentine border. Pleistocene hunter-gatherers once stalked now-extinct species such as giant ground sloths and native American horses, but they later switched to a broader subsistence that included marine and coastal resources. These peoples were the predecessors of the few surviving Tehuelche and Kawéskar (Alacaluf) peoples and the nearly extinct Selk'nam (Ona) and Yámana (Yahgan), who gathered shellfish and hunted guanaco and rhea with bows and arrows and *boleadoras* (rounded stones tied together with leather thongs).

The European presence dates from 1520, when Portuguese navigator Fernando Magalhaes, under the Spanish flag, sailed through the strait that bears his name (Magallanes in Spanish, Magellan in English). Ranging 3 to 25 kilometers in width, the strait became a major maritime thoroughfare to the Pacific.

Spain's colonization attempts failed, as did early Chilean and Argentine efforts. The city of Punta Arenas took hold after 1848, thanks partly to the fortuitous discovery of gold in California just a year later. Gold fever quickly subsided, but the introduction of sheep brought a wool and mutton boom that benefited from the 1870s Franco-Prussian War and helped create sprawling *estancias* (ranches) that dominated the region for nearly a century.

While the livestock industry hangs on, commercial fisheries, the state-run oil industry, and the tourist trade have superseded it in the economy. Even these industries have proved vulnerable to fluctuations, declining reserves, and international developments beyond their control. Chile's energy shortages have spurred new exploration and investment. The Zona Franca free-trade zone, which once drew immigrants from central Chile, is not what it once was, but Magallanes still has one of Chile's lowest unemployment rates at about 3.6 percent.

Punta Arenas

Patagonia's largest city, Punta Arenas is also the regional capital and the traditional port of entry, whether by air, land, or sea. Stretching north-south along the Strait of Magellan, the city boasts an architectural heritage that ranges from the Magellanic vernacular of corrugated metal-clad houses with steeply pitched roofs to Francophile mansions commissioned by 19th-century wool barons. Home to several museums, it's a base for excursions to historical sites, nearby penguin colonies, and whale-watching areas.

The diverse economy depends on fishing, shipping, petroleum, duty-free retail, and tourism. Historically, it's one of the gateways to Antarctica for both research and tourism,

Punta Arenas

ENRIQUE WEGMANN HANSEN

ZENTENO

To Ferries, Airport,
Pingüinera Otway, Puerto
Natales, and Río Gallegos
(Argentina)

To Cementerio Municipal, Museo del Recuerdo,
Zona Franca, Ferries, Airport, Pingüinera Otway,
Puerto Natales, and Río Gallegos (Argentina)

AV. BULNES

MUSEO REGIONAL
SALESIANO MAYORINO
BORGATELLO ★

LAVASECO
VICARS

SARMIENTO   DE   GAMBOA

ARMANDO

SANHUEZA

CHILOE

CARLOS
BORIES

DON BOSCO

IGNACIO

JOSÉ

PASAJE EMILIO TURINA

ARAUCO

MANUEL SEÑORET

AVENIDA

AVENIDA

REPUBLICA

CISCUTTI

ESPAÑA

SALA
ESTRELLA

CROACIA

PATAGONIA

TURISMO OTWAY ■

AVENIDA

REPUBLICA

MEJICANA

CROACIA

Río de las Minas

VALESSE

LATAM
AIRLINES ■

LOMIT'S ▼

JOSÉ

CIBER CLUB ■

MENÉNDEZ

TURISMO LAGUNA AZUL ■

CARLOS BORIES

POST
OFFICE ■

HOSTAL
CALAFATE ■

HOTEL JOSÉ
NOGUEIRA ■

★ CASA BRAUN-
MENÉNDEZ

HERNANDO DE

LUBAG ■

CASA JOSÉ
MENÉNDEZ ★

EX-SOCIEDAD
MENÉNDEZ BEHETY ★

SARA BRAUN
MANSION ■

PEDRO

MONTT

MAGALLANES

BANCO
SANTANDER ■

GOBERNACIÓN ★

Plaza
Muñoz
Gamero

BUSES FERNÁNDEZ,
BUSES EL PINGÜINO
& TURIBÚS ■

HOTEL
CÓNDOR DE
PLATA ●

HOTEL
TIERRA DEL
FUEGO ●

HOTEL
FINIS
TERRAE ■

HOTEL
MONTECARLO ●

SANTINO ▼

CHOCOLATTA ■

LA CARIOCA ▼

SEE DETAIL

HOTEL CHALET
CHAPITAL ■

PJE DUBLE ALMEYDA

CASTILLO MILWARD ★

HOTEL REY
DON FELIPE ●

WALDO SEGUEL

INTERNATIONAL
RENT A CAR ■

HOTEL
LA YEGUA
LOCA ★

FAGNANO

MIRADOR
LA CRUZ ★

HOTEL
TURISMO ORO
FUEGUINO ●

RESIDENCIA DEL ★
GOBERNADOR

IGLESIA MATRIZ ★

Plaza
Muñoz
Gamero

PALACIO
MONTES ★

HOTEL
PLAZA ●

PJE J
PEDRALS

PATAGONIA

ARAUCO

MANUEL SEÑORET

AVENIDA

ARMANDO

SANHUEZA

ERRÁZURIZ

ERRÁZURIZ

SOLO EXPEDICIONES ■

CHILOE

NOGUEIRA

BALMACEDA

To Reserva Nacional
← Magallanes

AVENIDA   INDEPENDENCIA

ESPAÑA

AVENIDA   INDEPENDENCIA

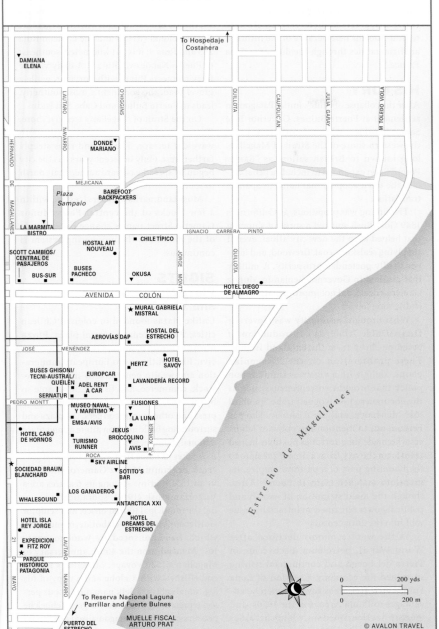

To Hospedaje
Costanera

DAMIANA
ELENA

LAUTARO

O'HIGGINS

QUILLOTA

CAUPOLICÁN

JULIA GARAY

M TOLEDO VIOLA

NAVARRO

DONDE
MARIANO

HERNANDO

MEJICANA

Plaza
Sampaio

BAREFOOT
BACKPACKERS

DE

MAGALLANES

LA MARMITA
BISTRO

IGNACIO CARRERA PINTO

SCOTT CAMBIOS/
CENTRAL DE
PASAJEROS

HOSTAL ART
NOUVEAU

CHILE TÍPICO

JORGE MONTT

QUILLOTA

BUSES
PACHECO

BUS-SUR

OKUSA

HOTEL DIEGO
DE ALMAGRO

AVENIDA

COLÓN

MURAL GABRIELA
MISTRAL

HOSTAL DEL
ESTRECHO

AEROVÍAS DAP

JOSÉ

MENÉNDEZ

BUSES GHISONI/
TECNI-AUSTRAL/
QUEILÉN

EUROPCAR

HERTZ

HOTEL
SAVOY

ADEL RENT
A CAR

LAVANDERÍA RECORD

SERNATUR

PEDRO MONTT

MUSEO NAVAL
Y MARÍTIMO

FUSIONES

EMSA/AVIS

LA LUNA

HOTEL CABO
DE HORNOS

TURISMO
RUNNER

JEKUS
BROCCOLINO

PJE KÖRNER

AVIS

ROCA

SOCIEDAD BRAUN
BLANCHARD

SKY AIRLINE

SOTITO'S
BAR

WHALESOUND

LOS GANADEROS

ANTARCTICA XXI

HOTEL ISLA
REY JORGE

HOTEL
DREAMS DEL
ESTRECHO

21

EXPEDICION
FITZ ROY

LAUTARO

DE

PARQUE
HISTÓRICO
PATAGONIA

NAVARRO

MAYO

Estrecho de Magallanes

To Reserva Nacional Laguna
Parrillar and Fuerte Bulnes

MUELLE FISCAL
ARTURO PRAT

0   200 yds

0   200 m

PUERTO DEL
ESTRECHO

© AVALON TRAVEL

but the Argentine port of Ushuaia has absorbed much of that traffic. Ironically, in a region that grazes millions of sheep, it's hard to find woolens here because of the influx of artificial fabrics through the duty-free Zona Franca.

HISTORY

After the collapse of Chile's initial Patagonian settlement at Fuerte Bulnes, Governor José Santos Mardones relocated north to a site on the western shore of the Strait of Magellan, long known to British sailors as "Sandy Point." Soon expanded to include a penal colony, the town adopted that name in Spanish translation.

The timing was propitious, as California's 1849 Gold Rush spurred a surge of shipping that helped keep the new city afloat, even if supplying sealskins, coal, firewood, and lumber hardly portended prosperity. A mutiny that resulted in Governor Benjamín Muñoz Gamero's death did not improve matters, and traffic soon fell off.

What brought prosperity was Governor Diego Dublé Almeyda's introduction of breeding sheep from the Falkland Islands. Their proliferation on the Patagonian plains, along with a vigorous immigration policy that brought entrepreneurs such as the Portuguese José Nogueira, the Spaniard José Menéndez, and the Irishman Thomas Fenton, not to mention the polyglot laborers who made their fortunes possible, helped transform the city from a dreary presidio to the booming port of a pastoral empire. Its mansions matched many in Buenos Aires, though the maldistribution of wealth and political power remained an intractable issue well into the 20th century.

As the wool economy declined after World War II, petroleum discoveries on Tierra del Fuego and commercial fishing sustained the economy. Creation of Zona Franca duty-free areas gave commercial advantages to Punta Arenas in the 1970s, and tourism has flourished since Pinochet's dictatorship ended in 1989.

ORIENTATION

Punta Arenas (pop. 130,704) is 210 kilometers southwest of Río Gallegos via the Argentine Ruta Nacional (RN) 3 and the Chilean Ruta 255 and Ruta 9; it is 241 kilometers southeast of Puerto Natales via Ruta 9. A daily vehicle ferry connects Punta with Porvenir, while a gravel road, the continent's most southerly, leads to Fuerte Bulnes and Cabo San Isidro.

On the Strait of Magellan's western shore, Punta Arenas occupies a narrow north-south wave-cut terrace. The ground rises steeply farther west. Only in recent years has the city begun to spread eastward rather than north to south.

Most landmarks and services are within a few blocks of the central Plaza Muñoz Gamero. Street names change on each side of the plaza, but the numbering system is continuous.

SIGHTS
Plaza Muñoz Gamero and Vicinity

Unlike plazas founded in colonial Chilean cities, Punta Arenas's central plaza, **Plaza Muñoz Gamero,** was not the initial focus of civic life, but thanks to European immigration and wealth generated by mining, livestock, commerce, and fishing, it became so by the 1880s. Landscaped with Monterey cypress and other exotic conifers, the plaza and surrounding buildings constitute a *zona típica* national monument.

It takes its name from early provincial governor Benjamín Muñoz Gamero, who died in an 1851 mutiny. Among its features are a Victorian kiosk (1910), sporadically housing the municipal tourist office, and sculptor Guillermo Córdova's elaborate monument, which was sponsored by wool magnate José Menéndez on the 400th anniversary of Magellan's 1520 voyage. Magellan's figure, embellished with a globe and a copy of his log, stands above a Selk'nam indigenous person representing Tierra del Fuego, a Tehuelche person symbolizing Patagonia, and a mermaid with Chilean and regional coats-of-arms.

According to local legend, anyone touching the Tehuelche's toe—enough have done so to alter its color—will return to Punta Arenas.

After about 1880, the city's burgeoning elite began to build monuments to their own good fortune, such as the ornate **Palacio Sara Braun** (1895) at the plaza's northwest corner. Only six years after marrying José Nogueira, Punta's most prominent businessman, the newly widowed Sara contracted French architect Numa Mayer, who applied contemporary Parisian style to create a two-story mansard that helped upgrade the city's earlier utilitarian architecture. Now home to the Club de la Unión and Hotel José Nogueira, the building retains most original features, including the west-facing winter garden that now serves as the hotel's bar-restaurant.

Mid-block, immediately east, the **Casa José Menéndez** belonged to another of Punta's wool barons. At the plaza's northeast corner stands the former headquarters of the influential **Sociedad Menéndez Behety** (Magallanes 990). Half a block north, dating from 1904, the **Casa Braun-Menéndez** (Magallanes 949) houses the regional museum.

On the plaza's east side, immediately south of Hotel Cabo de Hornos, the **Instituto Antártico Chileno** is the site of Chile's Antarctic research entity. Several other buildings in surrounding streets bear plaques attesting to their role in exploration of the frozen continent. On the south side, directly opposite the Victorian tourist kiosk, the former **Palacio Montes** holds municipal government offices. At the southeast corner, the **Sociedad Braun Blanchard** belonged to another powerful commercial group (as the names suggest, Punta Arenas's first families were, commercially at least, an incestuous bunch).

At the southwest corner, the **Iglesia Matriz** (1901) now enjoys cathedral status. Immediately north, both the **Residencia del Gobernador** (Governor's Residence) and the **Gobernación** date from the same period, filling the rest of the block with offices of the Intendencia Regional, the regional government.

★ Casa Braun-Menéndez

Like European royalty, Punta's first families formed alliances sealed by matrimony, and the 1904 **Casa Braun-Menéndez** (Magallanes 949, tel. 061/224-2049, www.museodemagallanes.cl, 10:30am-5pm Wed.-Mon., free) is a classic example: the product

Casa Braun-Menéndez

I Heard It Through the Grapevine

When the Patagonian wool barons built their mansions and *cascos* (manor houses on ranch estates) in the 19th century, one amenity they all required was a glassed-in greenhouse or conservatory. In a region where high winds, hail, and snowstorms might happen in any season, they could enjoy balmy indoor sunshine on long summer days and grow vegetables like eggplants and tomatoes that could never survive outdoors.

Both Argentina and Chile are famous for grapes (thanks largely to their wine industries). The two countries can also boast the world's southernmost grape arbors. The most readily seen is the one at La Pérgola, the conservatory restaurant at Punta Arenas's **Hotel José Nogueira,** the former Sara Braun mansion, at 53 degrees 9 minutes south. So far, though, even visiting specialists have been unable to identify its origins.

According to Sara Braun's descendant, Julia Braun, vines at the *casco* of Estancia Sara, on the Argentine side of Tierra del Fuego, push the grape line to 53 degrees 25 minutes south. The original *casco* at Estancia María Behety (53 degrees 48 minutes south), west of the city of Río Grande, may have had vines, but the house burned to the ground several years back.

One of the most luxuriant austral grapevines flourishes in **Government House** in Stanley, in the Falkland Islands. Introduced by Governor Cosmo Haskard in the 1960s, at 51 degrees 45 minutes south, it's not so far south as Punta Arenas or Estancia Sara, but its Black Hamburg table grapes may provide the most abundant harvest of any of them. In the Islands, grapes have been such a luxury that Government House dinner guests eat them dipped in chocolate during the March-April harvest.

of a marriage between Mauricio Braun (Sara's brother) and Josefina Menéndez Behety (daughter of José Menéndez and María Behety, a major wool-growing family in Argentina, though international borders meant little to the wool barons).

Still furnished with the family's belongings, preserving Mauricio Braun's office and other rooms virtually intact, the house boasts marble fireplaces and other elaborate architectural features. The basement servants' quarters expose the early-20th-century's upstairs-downstairs divisions. Part of it now serves as a gallery for special exhibits.

Today, the Casa Braun-Menéndez serves as the regional museum, replete with panels on pre-Columbian peoples, pioneer settlers' artifacts, and historical photographs. There are imperfect but readable English descriptions of the exhibits. On some days, a pianist plays beneath the atrium's stained-glass skylight.

Museo Regional Salesiano

From the 19th century, the Salesian order played a key role in evangelizing southern Patagonia and Tierra del Fuego, on both sides of the border. Punta Arenas was their base. While their rosy view of Christianity's impact on the region's indigenous people may be debatable, figures such as the Italian mountaineer priest Alberto de Agostini (1883-1960) made key contributions to both physical geography and ethnographic research.

Today, a sizable collection of Agostini's photographs can be found in the **Museo Regional Salesiano Mayorino Borgatello** (Av. Bulnes 336, tel. 061/222-1001, musborga@123mail.cl, 10am-12:30pm and 3pm-6pm Tues.-Sun., free), which also has a library and a regionally oriented art gallery. Permanent exhibits deal with regional flora and fauna (including the whaling industry), a handful of early colonial artifacts, regional ethnography with dioramas, the missionization of Isla Dawson and other nearby areas, cartography, and the petroleum industry. For Darwinians, there's a scale model of the *Beagle* and, for Chilean patriots, one of the *Ancud*, which sailed from Chiloé to claim the region in 1843.

Museo Naval y Marítimo

Pleasantly surprising, the **Museo Naval y Marítimo** (Pedro Montt 981, tel. 061/220-5479, www.museonaval.cl, 10am-5:30pm Tues.-Sun., US$1.50 adults, US$0.50 children) provides perspectives on topics like ethnography in the context of the Strait of Magellan's seagoing peoples, even while stressing its military mission. It features interactive exhibits, such as a credible warship's bridge, a selection of model ships, and information on the naval history of the southern oceans.

Museo del Recuerdo

Run by the Instituto de la Patagonia, part of the Universidad de Magallanes, the **Museo del Recuerdo** (Av. Bulnes 01890, tel. 061/220-7056, www.institutodelapatagonia.cl, 8:30am-11:30am and 2:30pm-6:30pm Mon.-Fri., 8:30am-12:30pm Sat., free) is a mostly open-air facility of pioneer agricultural implements and industrial machinery, reconstructions of a traditional house and shearing shed, and a restored shepherd's trailer house, hauled across the Patagonian plains on wooden wheels. In addition to a modest botanical garden, the institute has a library-bookshop with impressive cartographic exhibits.

The museum can be reached from downtown Punta Arenas by *taxis colectivos* to the duty-free Zona Franca, which stop directly opposite the entrance.

Other Sights

For a panoramic overview of the city's layout, the Strait of Magellan, and the island of Tierra del Fuego in the distance, climb to **Mirador La Cruz,** four blocks west of Plaza Muñoz Gamero via a staircase at the corner of the Fagnano and Señoret.

Four blocks south of Plaza Muñoz Gamero, naval vessels, freighters, cruise ships, Antarctic icebreakers, and yachts from many countries dock at the **Muelle Fiscal Arturo Prat** (at the foot of Av. Independencia), until recently the city's major port facility. It's still a departure point for cruises to the fjords of Tierra del Fuego and to Antarctica, but,

unfortunately, international security hysteria has closed it to spontaneous public access.

The late Bruce Chatwin found the inspiration for his legendary vignettes of *In Patagonia* through tales of his eccentric distant relative Charley Milward, who built and resided at the **Castillo Milward** (Milward's Castle, Av. España 959). Described by Chatwin as "a Victorian parsonage translated to the Strait of Magellan," with "high-pitched gables and gothic windows," the building features a square street-side tower and an octagonal one at the rear.

The seven-meter **Mural Gabriela Mistral** (corner of Av. Colón and O'Higgins) graces the walls of the former Liceo de Niñas Sara Braun (Sara Braun Girls' School) in honor of Chile's Nobel Prize-winning poet.

Ten blocks north of Plaza Muñoz Gamero, the **Cementerio Municipal Sara Braun** (Av. Bulnes 029) is home to the extravagant crypts of José Menéndez, José Nogueira, and Sara Braun. The multinational immigrants who worked for them—English, Scots, Welsh, Croat, German, and Scandinavian—repose in more modest circumstances. A separate monument honors the vanished Selk'nam (Ona) people who once flourished in the Strait, while another memorializes German fatalities of the Battle of the Falklands (1914).

ENTERTAINMENT

Except on Sunday, when the city feels deader than the cemetery, there's usually something to do. Punta Arenas has one surviving cinema, the **Sala Estrella** (Mejicana 777, tel. 061/222-5630).

Santino (Av. Colón 657, tel. 061/271-0882, www.santino.cl, 6pm-3am daily) is a spacious and informal pub where everyone feels welcome; there's also food, but it's not the main attraction. The Sara Braun mansion's basement **Taberna Club de la Unión** (Plaza Muñoz Gamero 716, tel. 061/261-7133) is popular on weekends.

The **Club Hípico** (Av. Bulnes 0601, tel. 061/221-2968, www.clubhipicopuntaarenas.cl), the sadly moribund municipal racetrack, is north of downtown. Professional soccer matches take place at the **Estadio Fiscal** (Enrique Abello 785, tel. 061/221-4900), a few blocks north on a perpendicular street off the avenue.

SHOPPING

Though it's faltered in recent years, Punta's major shopping destination is the duty-free **Zona Franca** (Av. Bulnes, Km 3.5, tel. 061/236-2000, www.zonaustral.cl), four kilometers north of downtown but easily reached by *taxi colectivo* from Calle Magallanes. Consumer electronics were once the big attraction—Santiaguinos even flew here for the bargains—but price differentials are smaller now.

For crafts such as metal (copper and bronze), semiprecious stones (lapis lazuli), and woolens, visit **Chile Típico** (Ignacio Carrera Pinto 1015, tel. 061/222-5827).

FOOD

Punta Arenas's fast-improving gastronomic scene ranges from fast food to haute cuisine. Lamb and seafood are becoming expensive.

The best fast-food is ★ **Lomito's** (José Menéndez 722, tel. 061/224-3399, US$6-10), a sandwich-and-beer joint that's almost always packed. **La Carioca** (José Menéndez 600, tel. 061/222-4809) is another sandwich outlet that also serves passable pizza, pasta, and draft beer.

Friendly **Chocolatta** (Bories 852, tel. 061/224-8150, www.chocolatta.cl) has the best coffee drinks and hot chocolate, along with desserts and muffins, and good Wi-Fi. It also has a branch in the Hotel Dreams alongside the casino.

Dónde Mariano (O'Higgins 504, tel. 061/224-5291, lunch and dinner daily, US$14) delivers on its modest pretensions, serving simply prepared fish entrées and a king crab casserole.

★ **La Luna** (O'Higgins 1017, tel. 061/222-8555, www.laluna.cl, noon-3:30pm and 7pm-11:30pm daily, US$22) buzzes with activity, good humor, and good food. Pins on wall maps indicate the origins of its clientele. The *chupe de centolla* (king crab casserole) remains the signature dish, but the slightly spicy *ostiones al pil pil* (a scallop appetizer) deserves special mention.

Alongside La Luna, the **Restaurant y Pub Jekus** (O'Higgins 1021, tel. 061/224-5851, www.restaurantypubjekus.cl, US$14) has a sunken bar and dining room of natural woods. The food is demonstrably Patagonian in dishes such as the king crab cannelloni and roast lamb.

In classic quarters, ★ **Okusa** (O'Higgins 787, tel. 061/222-1965, www.okusarestaurant. cl, noon-3pm and 7pm-midnight Mon.-Sat., noon-4pm Sun., US$15) is a hybrid restaurant and wine bar-shop that specializes in lamb and seafood, with nice complements such as a savory *pebre* spread. The pork loin with rhubarb chutney (US$10) is a pleasant surprise.

★ **La Marmita Bistro** (Plaza Sampaio 678, tel. 061/222-2056, www.marmitamaga. cl, 12:30pm-3pm and 7pm-11pm Mon.-Thurs., 12:30pm-3:30pm and 7pm-midnight Fri.-Sat., US$15) has risen to near the top of Punta's restaurant scene for creative seafood (no Italian would recognize the scallop appetizer as "lasagna," but it's outstanding), unusual vegetarian plates, a lamb casserole, and even game dishes such as guanaco. With a casual historical atmosphere, it also serves varied desserts.

Merged with the former Puerto Viejo (the two had the same owners), **Los Ganaderos** (O'Higgins 1166, tel. 061/222-5103, www.parrillalosganaderos.cl, lunch and dinner daily, from US$10) is a classy *parrilla* specializing in succulent Patagonian lamb grilled on a vertical spit. There is also a more diverse mixed grill for two, pasta dishes with simple sauces, and Puerto Viejo's specialties such as *centolla* (king crab) and *merluza* (hake). Try the regional Patagonian desserts, such as *mousse de calafate* and *mousse de ruibarbo* (rhubarb).

For beef and other meats, though, the current innovator is the inconspicuous ★ **El Fogón de Lalo** (21 de Mayo 1650, tel. 061/237-1149, www.elfogondelalo.cl, 8pm-11pm Tues.-Fri., 1pm-2:30pm and 8pm-11pm

Sat., 1pm-3pm Sun.)—there's no sign on this reddish metal-clad building with greenish window frames—just beyond the conspicuous Buddhist temple a few blocks south of the Muelle Prat. It excels in every aspect of its meat-oriented menu, and the service is attentive and good-natured but not overbearing. The *entraña* (skirt steak, US$15 and big enough for two) deserves special mention, but the *provoletta* makes a great appetizer, and the desserts are exquisite. Reservations advised, and essential on the weekend.

For a more diverse cuisine, there's the upstairs ★ **Fusiones Gastrobar** (O'Higgins 1011, tel. 061/237-1202, www.fusionesgastrobar.cl, US$20), where whimsical decor surrounds sturdy tables and chairs. Exceptional entrées includes *chupe de centolla* (crab casserole) and lamb ravioli, the drinks are outstanding (especially its spectacular Peruvian pisco sour). Except for ice cream, though, the desserts are forgettable.

Broccolino (O'Higgins 1049, tel. 061/222-4989, lunch and dinner daily, from US$15) serves a fine rack of lamb, plus fish dishes such as conger eel with crab and scallops in a white wine sauce. Traditionally, the expanded **Sotito's Bar** (O'Higgins 1138, tel. 061/224-5365, www.restaurantsotitos.cl, lunch and dinner daily, US$15) has set the seafood standard here, and it still deserves consideration for dishes such as king crab cannelloni.

In a magnificent period house whose several small dining rooms give it a real intimacy, ★ **Damiana Elena** (Magallanes 341, tel. 061/222-2818, from 8pm Mon.-Sat.) is the city's best restaurant. There is no longer a listed menu; rather there are half a dozen or so nightly specials that go beyond regional specialties. It also has gracious ownership. The wine list focuses on big producers such as Errázuriz and Concha y Toro; with a half-bottle of wine, dinner runs about US$30 pp.

ACCOMMODATIONS

Sernatur maintains a complete list of accommodations but no longer divulges prices to the public. What in many other parts of Chile would be called *residenciales* are called *hostales* (B&Bs) here. Some relatively expensive places have cheaper rooms with shared baths that can be excellent values.

Under US$25

Finding truly shoestring accommodations has become more difficult, but friendly **Barefoot Backpackers** (O'Higgins 646, tel. 09/6303-2147, US$15 pp) occupies an old but well-kept

Occupying a historic house, Damiana Elena offers some of the finest food in Punta Arenas.

house, with four to eight beds per room. It offers kitchen access, decent baths, Wi-Fi, and abundant computers, but can't seem to manage an online presence.

US$25-50

East of the racetrack at the foot of Quillota, the shoreline **Hospedaje Costanera** (Rómulo Correa 1221, tel. 061/224-0175, www.hospedaje-costanera.hostel.com, US$22 pp dorm, US$27-30 s, US$47-59 d) has drawn favorable commentary. The cheaper singles and doubles have shared baths.

Rehabbed **Hotel Montecarlo** (Av. Colón 605, tel. 061/222-2120, idamayorga@hotmail.com, US$26-41 s, US$44-59 d) is a plain but pleasant option that has maintained modest standards over the years. The more expensive rooms have private baths.

US$50-100

Six blocks south of the plaza, once a military brothel, **Hotel Hain** (Nogueira 1600, tel. 061/224-1357, www.hotelhain.cl, US$56 s, US$75 d) has become an indigenous-themed boutique B&B with views onto the elevated Plaza Lautaro, a former cemetery now studded with topiary cypresses. Its restaurant, though, is now only open for catered group meals.

Less pretentious than it sounds, **Hostal Art Nouveau** (Lautaro Navarro 762, tel. 061/222-8112, www.hostalartnouveau.cl, US$57 s or d, with breakfast) is a restored period house with appealing common spaces. Some rooms lack exterior windows, and others are on the small side, but there is a sheltered garden.

The art deco-style **Hotel Cóndor de Plata** (Av. Colón 556, tel. 061/224-7987, www.condordeplata.cl, US$70 s, US$80 d) has long been a good choice at a modest price.

US$100-150

Half a block south of Plaza Muñoz Gamero, **Hotel Plaza** (Nogueira 1116, tel. 061/224-1300, www.hotelplaza.cl, US$85 s, US$110 d) is a classic of its era, but it would benefit from a restoration.

Overlooking the rejuvenated waterfront, the modern **Hotel Diego de Almagro** (Av. Colón 1290, tel. 061/220-8800, www.dahoteles.com, US$100 s, US$110 d) is a welcome addition to Punta's accommodations roster. The spacious corner rooms have especially panoramic views, and the service is exemplary.

The 11-room ★ **Hotel Chalet Chapital** (Sanhueza 974, tel. 061/273-0100, www.hotelchaletchapital.cl, US$110 s, US$120 d) occupies a handsomely restored historic building, with contemporary furnishings, Wi-Fi, and whirlpool tubs in every room.

Long a favorite with foreign tour groups, **Hotel Isla Rey Jorge** (21 de Mayo 1243, tel. 061/224-8220, www.islareyjorge.com, US$119 s, US$143 d) appears to be recovering from years of relative neglect.

US$150-200

Hotel Finis Terrae (Av. Colón 766, tel. 061/222-8200, www.hotelfinisterrae.com, US$137-202 s or d) is another fine newer hotel. One the same block, the contemporary **Hotel Tierra del Fuego** (Av. Colón 716, tel./fax 061/222-6200, www.puntaarenas.com, US$165 s, US$200 d) is a business-oriented facility that is spacious, comfortable, and well-managed.

Punta's best view accommodations may be the **Hotel La Yegua Loca** (Fagnano 310, tel. 061/237-1734, www.yegualocal.com, US$160 s or d), a boutique option on the hillside overlooking downtown. Each of its eight rooms takes a theme from the region's ranching tradition, as does the restaurant (though it also serves seafood, including ceviche).

Hotel Dreams del Estrecho (O'Higgins 1235, tel. 061/220-4500, www.mundodreams.com, US$175-240 s or d) is a glass palace casino hotel with 88 rooms, including 16 suites. From the outside, it contrasts shockingly with the old waterfront, but it's agreeable within, except for the adjoining casino, a kitschy remodel of an historic gymnasium's neoclassical skeleton. In addition to the slots and tables, it has a restaurant, a convention center, a rooftop bar, and a heated pool, plus subterranean parking.

Built by the Sociedad Ganadera Tierra del Fuego, the 1960s high-rise ★ **Hotel Cabo de Hornos** (Plaza Muñoz Gamero 1025, tel. 061/271-5000, www.hoteles-australis.com, US$176 s, US$196 d) has undergone not just a facelift but a full-scale makeover under current ownership (the same owners as the Cruceros Australis cruise line). The public spaces are spectacular and the rooms attractive, and they now include improved Wi-Fi connections.

Over US$200

The most historic accommodation is the ★ **Hotel José Nogueira** (Bories 959, tel. 061/271-1000, www.hotelnogueira.com, US$180 s, US$200 d), which occupies part of the Sara Braun mansion. Its conservatory bar-restaurant, with its serpentine grape arbor, merits a visit even if you don't book a room (some of which are small).

Directly across from the Hotel Chalet Chapital, **Hotel Rey Don Felipe** (Armando Sanhueza 965, tel. 061/229-5000, www.hotelreydonfelipe.com, US$225 s, US$250-320 d) is a fine contemporary hotel, but not notably superior to some cheaper alternatives.

INFORMATION

One block east of the plaza, **Sernatur** (Lautaro Navarro 999, tel. 061/222-5385, info-magallanes@sernatur.cl, 8:30am-8pm Mon.-Fri., 9am-1pm and 2pm-6pm Sat.-Sun. high season, 8:30am-6pm Mon.-Fri. off-season) is one of Chile's better regional offices, with English-speaking personnel and up-to-date accommodations and transport information. **Conaf** (Av. Bulnes 0309, 4th Fl., tel. 061/223-8554) provides national parks info.

SERVICES

Punta Arenas is one of the easier Chilean cities in which to change both cash and traveler's checks, especially at travel agencies along Lautaro Navarro. Most close by midday Saturday, but **Scott Cambios** (Av. Colón

and Magallanes, tel. 061/224-5811) will cash traveler's checks then. Several banks around Plaza Muñoz Gamero have ATMs, such as **BancoEstado** (Plaza Muñoz Gamero 799).

Just north of Plaza Muñoz Gamero, **Correos de Chile** (Bories 911) is the post office. The **Ciber Club** (José Menéndez 882) provides Internet access. The **Argentine consulate** (21 de Mayo 1878, tel. 061/226-1912, 9am-6pm Mon.-Fri.) is in town.

For clean clothes, try **Lavandería Record** (O'Higgins 969, tel. 061/224-3607) or **Lavaseco Vicars** (Sarmiento de Gamboa 726, tel. 061/224-1516).

The **Hospital Clínico Magallanes Dr. Lautaro Navarro Avaria** (Av. Los Flamencos 01364, tel. 061/229-3000, www. hospitalclinicomagallanes.cl) occupies new quarters north of downtown.

TRANSPORTATION

Punta Arenas has good air links with mainland Chile, frequent flights to Chilean Tierra del Fuego, infrequent flights to Argentine Tierra del Fuego, and regular weekly service to the Falkland Islands. There are roundabout overland routes to mainland Chile via Argentina, regular bus service to Argentine Tierra del Fuego via a ferry link, direct ferry service to Chilean Tierra del Fuego, and expensive (but exceptionally scenic) cruise-ship service to Ushuaia, in Argentine Tierra del Fuego.

Air

Aeropuerto Presidente Carlos Ibáñez del Campo (PUQ) is 20 kilometers north of town on Ruta 9, the Puerto Natales highway. **Transfer Austral** (Av. Independencia 595, tel. 061/272-3358, transfer@transferaustral. com) arranges door-to-door transfers (US$7 pp in a shared van). Taxis (US$15) may also be shared. Buses returning from Puerto Natales will normally drop passengers at the airport to meet outgoing flights on request, but make arrangements before boarding. Natales-bound buses will also pick up arriving passengers, but again, make advance arrangements.

Air Antarctica

For many visitors, one of the great disincentives to Antarctic travel is the fact that, even though southern South America offers the closest approach to the frozen continent, it usually involves two days of a stomach-churning crossing of the stormy Drake Passage—in each direction. Chilean entrepreneurs, though, now offer well-heeled travelers a chance to skip the seasickness.

In the summer of 2004, Punta Arenas-based Antarctica XXI organized the first commercial air-sea excursion to the South Shetland Islands, eliminating the Drake Passage segment. Arriving at the Base Aérea Presidente Eduardo Frei Montalva, the Chilean air force's main Antarctic base on Isla Rey Jorge, passengers almost immediately board the Danish-built, 62-passenger *Ocean Nova* for a five-day cruise in the relatively sheltered waters between the South Shetlands and the Antarctic Peninsula.

The convenience comes at a price. Rates for the all-inclusive tour start at US$10,995 pp, triple occupancy. For more details, contact **Antarctica XXI** (O'Higgins 1170, Punta Arenas, tel. 061/261-4100, U.S./Canada tel. 877/994-2994, www.antarcticaxxi.com).

LATAM (Bories 884, tel. 061/224-1232) flies several times daily to Santiago, normally via Puerto Montt. Some flights stop at Balmaceda, near Coyhaique. It also flies Saturday to the Falkland Islands. In each direction, one Falklands flight per month stops in the Argentine city of Río Gallegos. **Sky Airline** (Roca 935, tel. 061/271-0645) flies north to Balmaceda-Coyhaique, Puerto Montt, and Santiago, with connections to northern Chilean cities.

Aerovías DAP (O'Higgins 891, tel. 061/261-6100, www.aeroviasdap.cl) flies seven-seat Cessnas to and from Porvenir (Mon.-Sat., US$39), in Chilean Tierra del Fuego, at least daily except Sunday, and more often in summer. It flies 20-seat Twin Otters to and from Puerto Williams on Isla Navarino (Mon.-Sat., US$99). In high season, in addition, it now flies twice weekly to Balmaceda-Coyhaique (US$71-143) and to Ushuaia (US$199). It also operates extensive charter services and occasionally goes to Antarctica.

Bus

Punta Arenas has no central terminal, though some companies share facilities and the **Central de Pasajeros** (Av. Colón 806, tel. 061/224-5811) sells tickets for all of them. Most terminals are within a few blocks of each other, north of Plaza Muñoz Gamero. Services vary seasonally but are most numerous in January and February.

Carriers serving Puerto Natales (3 hours, US$9) include **Bus Sur** (Avenida Colón 842, tel. 061/261-4224, www.bus-sur.cl), with 8 to 10 buses daily; **Buses Fernández** (Armando Sanhueza 745, tel. 061/224-2313, www.busesfernandez.com), up to 14 buses daily; and **Buses Pacheco** (Av. Colón 900, tel. 061/222-5527, www.busespacheco.com), 2 buses daily.

Queilen Bus (Lautaro Navarro 975, tel. 061/222-2714, www queilenbus.cl) travels to the Chilean cities of Osorno (9am Fri., 27 hours, US$56), Puerto Montt, and Castro, via Argentina. **Turibús** (Armando Sanhueza 745, tel. 061/222-7970) goes to Osorno (9:30am Tues., Thurs., and Sat., US$45) and beyond.

Several carriers go to Río Gallegos (US$22, four hours): Bus Sur, **Buses El Pingüino** (Armando Sanhueza 745, tel. 061/222-3898), **Buses Ghisoni** (Lautaro Navarro 975, tel. 061/261-3420, www.turismoghisoni.com), and Buses Pacheco.

Tecni-Austral (Lautaro Navarro 975, tel. 061/222-2078) goes to Río Grande (9am Tues., Thurs., and Sat., 8 hours, US$30) and Ushuaia (11 hours, US$60), in Argentine Tierra del Fuego. **Buses Pacheco** goes to Río Grande (9am Mon.-Sat.), with connections to Ushuaia. It also has direct services (9am Tues.,

Thurs., and Sat.). Bus Sur has also added services to Ushuaia.

Sea

Transbordadora Austral Broom (Av. Bulnes 05075, tel. 061/221-8100, www.tabsa. cl) sails from Punta Arenas to Porvenir (9am Mon.-Sat., 9:30am Sun., 2.5 hours, US$9 adults, US$5 children, US$60 vehicles, US$17 motorcycles, bicycles free). The driver's fare is included in the vehicle fare. Vehicle reservations are advised for *Crux Australis* ferry, which leaves from Terminal Tres Puentes, easily reached by *taxi colectivo* No. 15 from the Casa Braun-Menéndez, on Magallanes half a block north of Plaza Muñoz Gamero.

Broom also operates the ferry *Bahía Azul* to Puerto Williams (6pm Thurs., 32 hours, sofabed seat US$220 adults, US$110 under age 11, reclining Pullman seat US$160 adults, US$80 under age 11), returning at 4pm Saturday.

It's neither a cheap nor conventional way of getting to Argentina, but the luxury cruisers *Ventus Australis* and *Stella Australis* spend the summer shuttling to Ushuaia as part of a weeklong circuit through the fjords of Chilean Tierra del Fuego, and passengers can disembark in Ushuaia (or board there, for that matter). Normally both vessels require reservations well in advance: contact **Cruceros Australis** (www.australis.com).

Car Rentals

Punta Arenas has numerous car-rental options, including **Adel Rent a Car** (Pedro Montt 962, tel. 061/222-4819, www.adelrentacar.cl), **Europcar** (O'Higgins 964, tel. 061/220-2720, www.europcar.cl), **Avis** (Pedro Montt 969, tel. 061/261-4381, www.avis.cl), and **Hertz** (O'Higgins 931, tel. 061/261-3087, www.hertz.cl).

Vicinity of Punta Arenas

Punta Arenas's myriad travel agencies operate excursions to nearby destinations such as Reserva Nacional Magallanes, Fuerte Bulnes, the Seno Otway penguin colony, Río Verde, Estancia San Gregorio, and even Parque Nacional Torres del Paine. The most popular half-day excursions, such as Fuerte Bulnes and Otway, cost around US$25 pp, while full-day trips such as Pali Aike cost around US$100 pp, with a three-person minimum. The latest sensation, though, is the full-day excursion to Tierra del Fuego to view the king penguin colony at Bahía Inútil (US$70 pp).

Among Punta's established operators, some are now accessible only by phone or online. Among the choices are **Turismo Laguna Azul** (Plaza Muñoz Gamero 1011, tel. 061/222-5200, www.turismolagunaazul. cl), **Turismo Runner** (Lautaro Navarro 1077, tel. 061/271-2102, www.turismolagogrey.cl), and **Turismo Yámana** (www.yamana.cl).

RESERVA NACIONAL MAGALLANES

Eight kilometers west of downtown, 13,500-hectare **Reserva Nacional Magallanes** (tel. 061/223-8875, US$6 adults, US$2 children) is a combination of Patagonian steppe and southern beech forest that, in good winters, amasses enough snow for skiing. Despite its proximity to Punta Arenas, it gets barely 10,600 visitors per year. Only about 1,700 of them are foreigners.

Westbound Avenida Independencia, a good gravel road that may require chains in winter, climbs gradually to a fork whose southern branch leads to the local Club Andino's **Centro de Esquí Cerro Mirador** (tel. 061/224-1479, www.clubandino.cl), which includes a single chairlift, a ski school, and a *refugio* (shelter) that serves meals. In summer, try the **Sendero Mirador,** a two-hour loop hike that winds through the forest and crosses the ski area, offering panoramas east toward the city, the strait, and Tierra del Fuego, and west toward Seno Otway. The northwesterly **Sector Las Minas** includes a gated picnic area. A longer footpath links up with the El Mirador summit trail. The area is also suitable for mountain biking.

PINGÜINERA SENO OTWAY

Barely an hour from Punta Arenas, the closest penguin-breeding site to any of the continent's major cities contains roughly 5,000 burrowing Magellanic penguins. Numbers have declined slightly in recent years due to feral dog attacks and, perhaps, overfishing. From mid-October, when the first arrive, to April, when the last stragglers head to sea, **Pingüinera Seno Otway** (8am-6:30pm daily) draws upward of 40,000 visitors. The peak season is December to February.

While the site is fenced to keep human visitors out of critical habitat, the birds are relatively tame and easy to photograph. During the season, Punta Arenas operators shuttle visitors to and from Otway (US$35 pp, including US$11 pp admission). Half-day tours take place either in morning (which photographers may prefer) or afternoon. For visitors with private vehicles, there's a small toll.

For more details, contact **Turis Otway** (Mejicana 122, tel. 061/261-4650, www.turisotway.cl) or another local travel agency. Otway is only about 65 kilometers northwest of Punta Arenas via Ruta 9 and a gravel road leading west from a signed junction at Parque Chabunco, about 19 kilometers north of the city. It was closed for the 2016-2017 season, however.

★ MONUMENTO NATURAL LOS PINGÜINOS

From early October, about 60,000 breeding pairs of Magellanic penguins paddle ashore and waddle to burrows that cover nearly all of 97-hectare **Isla Magdalena,** 37 kilometers northeast of Punta Arenas, before returning

Magellanic penguins at Isla Magdalena

to sea in April. Also the site of a landmark lighthouse, Isla Magdalena is the focal point of **Monumento Natural Los Pingüinos,** one of Conaf's smallest but most interesting reserves.

While the mainland Otway colony gets upward of 40,000 visitors per year, Isla Magdalena gets only about 30,000 because of its relative inaccessibility. Of the visitors, about 70 percent are foreigners. In summer, the ferry *Melinka* visits daily from Punta Arenas. Though more expensive than Otway tours, these excursions also offer the chance to see penguins and dolphins in the water, as well as black-browed albatrosses, cormorants, kelp gulls, skuas, South American terns, and other seabirds in the surrounding skies.

From a floating dock on the island's leeward side, a short trail leads along the beach and up the hill to Scottish engineer George Slight's **Faro Magdalena** (1901), a lighthouse whose iron tower rises 13.5 meters above the island's highest point. Still functioning, the light has a range of 10 nautical miles (19

Penguin Colonies

Chilean Patagonia's largest city, Punta Arenas, is close to two breeding colonies of the burrowing Magellanic penguin, *Spheniscus magellanicus*. The Otway Sound colony (Pingüinera Seno Otway) is about a 45-minute drive from the city, and is interesting enough. The larger colony on Isla Magdalena (Monumento Natural Los Pingüinos), an island in the Strait of Magellan, is two hours away by ferry or slightly less by bus and rigid inflatable.

Also known to English speakers as the jackass penguin because its call resembles that of a braying burro, the Magellanic is present from October to April. They are most numerous in January and February, when chicks hatch in the sandy burrows that parents dig beneath the coastal turf. After hatching, parents alternate fishing trips in search of food that they later regurgitate to their young (combined with the scent of bird droppings, this makes any visit an olfactory as well as a visual and auditory experience).

While the birds appear tame, they are wild animals and their sharp beaks can draw blood—maintain a respectful distance for photography. Though both colonies have fenced walking routes to restrain tourists, the birds themselves frequently cross these routes.

Besides the countless seabirds and dolphins en route, the Magdalena trip has the added bonus of a historical lighthouse that's now a visitors center on an island that is saturated with burrows. While neither trip is strenuous, any walk in Patagonia's roaring winds can be a workout.

kilometers). A narrow spiral staircase ascends the tower, now closed to the public.

In the building's first five decades, a resident caretaker maintained the acetylene light, but after its automation in 1955 the building was abandoned and vandalized. In 1981, the navy entrusted the building to Conaf. Declared a national monument, it has since become a visitors center that provides good accounts of the island's history, including discovery, early navigation, cartography, the lighthouse's construction, and natural history in both Spanish and decent English. U.S. archaeologist Junius Bird, best known for his 1930s work at the mainland site of Pali Aike, also undertook excavations here.

For ferry excursions to Isla Magdalena, contact **Turismo Comapa** (Magallanes 990, tel. 061/220-0215, www.islamagdalena. com). In December, January, and February, the ferry *Melinka* normally makes a 4pm daily passengers-only trip to Isla Magdalena (US$60 adults, US$30 children) from Terminal Tres Puentes. There are sometimes morning departures (bring food—the *Melinka*'s snack bar is pretty dire). Visitors spend about 1.5 hours on the island, returning to Punta Arenas before 9pm.

Passengers on Cruceros Australis voyages stop here on the return from Ushuaia, but there's also an intermediate alternative. **Solo Expediciones** (José Nogueira 1255, tel. 061/224-3354, www.soloexpediciones. com) offers half-day excursions (US$90 pp) that shuttle passengers from the mainland in covered Zodiacs and include an approach to nearby Isla Marta, where the overflow from penguin-saturated Magdalena has migrated; there are also southern sea lions.

FUERTE BULNES

In 1584, Spanish explorer Pedro Sarmiento de Gamboa organized an expedition of 15 ships and 4,000 men to control the Strait of Magellan. After a series of disasters, only three ships with 300 colonists arrived to found **Ciudad del Rey don Felipe** at Punta Santa Ana, south of present-day Punta Arenas. Even worse for the Spaniards, the inhospitable climate and unsuitable soils made agriculture impossible. When British privateer Thomas Cavendish landed three years later, in 1587, he found just a handful of survivors and gave it the name Port Famine, which has survived as the Spanish **Puerto de Hambre.**

For many years, the consensus was that

starvation alone determined Port Famine's fate, but regional historian Mateo Martinic has suggested that disease, mutual acts of violence, Tehuelche attacks, and a sense of anguish or abandonment contributed to its demise. The area then remained unsettled until 1843, when President Manuel Bulnes ordered the cutter *Ancud* south from Chiloé with tools, construction materials, food, and livestock to take possession for the expansionist Chilean state. The result was **Fuerte Bulnes,** a military outpost that survived only a little longer than the original Spanish settlement before relocation to Punta Arenas in 1848.

Archaeologists located nearby remnants of Ciudad del Rey don Felipe in 1955, and later excavations turned up human remains, bullets, tombs, and ruins of the church. A more recent plaque (1965) celebrates the 125th anniversary of the Pacific Steam Navigation Company's ships *Chile* and *Perú* and their routes around the Horn.

Today, Fuerte Bulnes is a national monument, with reconstructions of 19th-century buildings and the defensive walls—with sharpened stakes—that surrounded them. Among the structures were residences, stables, a blockhouse, a chapel, a jail, and a warehouse.

It has been resurrected as **Parque Histórico Patagonia** (21 de Mayo 1261, Punta Arenas, www.phipa.cl, 9:30am-6pm daily, US$21 pp), under a 25-year lease to develop it as an historical site for its role in settlement of the strait. A visitors center and café-souvenir shop are now open, there are several short footpaths, and archaeological excavations are proceeding at the cemetery.

Parque Histórico Patagonia is 58 kilometers south of Punta Arenas via Ruta 9, which is now fully paved. There is no regular public transportation, but Punta Arenas operators offer half-day excursions.

RESERVA NACIONAL LAGUNA PARRILLAR

About 45 kilometers southwest of Punta Arenas via paved Ruta 9 and a gravel westbound lateral road, **Laguna Parrillar** (tel. 061/223-8875, US$6 adults, US$2 children) attracts about 3,500 visitors per year to its 18,000 hectares of forest and wetland with its picnic areas, hiking trails, and campsites.

PARQUE MARINO FRANCISCO COLOANE

For decades, the great whales have drawn travelers to Mexico's Baja California lagoons,

Fuerte Bulnes

the shallows of Argentina's Península Valdés, and other breeding and feeding sites. From late December to April, Chile's Parque Marino Francisco Coloane, in the Strait of Magellan southwest of Punta Arenas, joins the whale-watching sweepstakes.

Established in July 2003 and named for a Chilean author who chronicled the southern seas, this 67,000-hectare maritime park, **Parque Marino Francisco Coloane,** is the result of five years' biological investigations that pinpointed the area around Isla Carlos III, in the southwestern Strait of Magellan, as summer feeding grounds for southern humpbacks. In addition to the humpbacks, which migrate south from Colombia, the park's seas and shores are home to breeding Magellanic penguins, cormorants, many other southern seabirds, fur seals, and sea lions. Orcas are also present.

Carlos III itself is a sheltered island of bonsai beeches that is also home to the world's southernmost conifer, the *ciprés de las Guaitecas* (Guaitecas cypress, *Pilgerodendron uviferum*). At low tide, a fur seal colony is only 20 minutes away on foot.

From mid-December to late April, **Whalesound** (Lautaro Navarro 1191, Punta Arenas, tel. 09/9887-9814, www.whalesound.com) offers overnight expeditions (US$1,500 pp, minimum 2 people) and some longer trips to the park, where guests sleep in geodesic dome tents, with comfortable Japanese beds and solar-powered electricity, on Isla Carlos III. Rates include daily excursions with specialized bilingual guides and gourmet meals. Sea kayaks are also available.

The 15-meter yacht *Tanu* sails from Punta Carrera, an hour south of Punta Arenas by road, near Fuerte Bulnes. The *Tanu* has a galley, four bunks, and an open-air observation deck (not always ideal on the stormy Strait of Magellan). If seas are too rough, they may go overland via Isla Riesco and then a shorter hop to Carlos III on rigid inflatables.

A rather different product, **Expedición Fitz Roy** (Roca 825, Oficina 3, tel. 061/261-3932, www.expedicionfitzroy.com, from US$650 pp for 1-day, 2-night packages) offers similar services. Passengers sleep aboard the reconditioned M/V *Forrest,* which once hauled wool around the Falkland Islands. **Solo Expediciones** (Jose Nogueira 1255, tel. 061/271-0219, www.soloexpediciones.com) has begun to offer very long full-day excursions (US$290 pp) in fast motor boats from Punta Arenas.

RÍO VERDE

Some 43 kilometers north of Punta Arenas on Ruta 9, a gravel road loops northwest along Seno Otway to Seno Skyring and **Estancia Río Verde,** which has seemingly made the transition from a shipshape sheep farm to a model municipality of exquisitely maintained public buildings in the Magellanic style. Note particularly the manicured gardens surrounding the **Escuela Básica,** the local boarding school.

In one wing of the boarding school, the **Museo Comunal Río Verde** (open erratically, nominal admission) has exhibits on local history, natural history (taxidermy), ethnology, and local and regional literature.

Across from the former *hostería* (small hotel), a small ferry (8am-noon and 1:30pm-8pm daily) shuttles vehicles and passengers to **Isla Riesco** (warning: it's free to the island but costs US$45 to get your vehicle back to the mainland). Nearby, Paola Vizzani González's **Escultura Monumental,** a beached whale built of concrete and driftwood, recalls the region's early colonists. Also nearby, the **Hito El Vapor** marks the final resting place of the steamer *Los Amigos,* which carried coal to outlying farms until it ran aground in a storm.

The loop road rejoins Ruta 9 at Villa Tehuelches, a wide spot in the road about 90 kilometers from Punta Arenas. This makes a good alternative route north or south for both motorists and fat-tire cyclists. The terrain is comparable, but the loop—about 13 kilometers longer—is more scenic.

Accommodations

The Chilean-Uruguayan ★ **Estancia Río Verde** (Km 98 Norte, tel. 061/231-1123 or 061/221-5671, www.estanciarioverde.cl, Nov.-Mar., US$130 s, US$160 d) offers stylish accommodations (one suite has a sunny tower with sea and Pampas views), day tours that can include horseback riding and fishing, lunches, and tea in its restaurant. A bargain by *estancia* standards, it also has gracious English-speaking ownership, but advance reservations are essential—no drop-ins, as it mainly hosts groups.

ESTANCIA SAN GREGORIO

From a highway junction about 45 kilometers north of Punta Arenas, paved Ruta 225 leads east-northeast to the Argentine border at Monte Aymond, passing the former **Estancia San Gregorio,** once one of Chilean Patagonia's largest landholdings. Part of the Menéndez wool empire, San Gregorio dates from the 1890s, reaching its peak between 1910 and 1930. Besides wool, it produced frozen mutton, hides, and tallow.

Now run as a cooperative, 120 kilometers from Punta Arenas, San Gregorio is a *zona típica* national historical monument. It exemplified the Anglo-Scottish Patagonian sheep ranch, in which each unit was a self-sufficient hierarchy with a nearly omnipotent administrator at the top. Geographically, it consisted of discrete residential and production sectors: The former included the administrator's house, employee residences, shearers' dormitories, chapel, and the like, while the latter comprised the shearing shed, warehouses, a smithy, a company store, and similarly functional buildings. It had its own pier and railroad to move the wool clip directly to freighters.

Most of San Gregorio's constructions date from the 1890s. A descendant of the Menéndez dynasty still occupies French architect Antoine Beaulier's **Casa Patronal** (1925). The farm featured an extensive system of windbreaks ranging upward of five meters in height, later planted with Monterey cypress for beautification.

While technically not open to the public, many of San Gregorio's buildings line both sides of the highway to Monte Aymond. Beached on shore are the corroded hulks of the British clipper *Ambassador* (a national monument) and the company steamer *Amadeo,* which gave up the ghost in the 1940s.

PUNTA DELGADA

About 30 kilometers east of San Gregorio, paved Ruta 257 leads southeast to **Punta Delgada,** the port for the ferry crossing to Tierra del Fuego via the Primera Angostura narrows. Depending sometimes on tidal conditions, the ferries *Patagonia, Fueguino,* and *Crux Australis* shuttle across the channel every 1.5 hours, 8:30am-1am daily (US$3 adults, US$22 cars, US$7 motorcycles or horses). Buses to Argentine Tierra del Fuego use this route because the Porvenir ferry goes just once daily and is subject to delay or cancellation for rough seas.

★ PARQUE NACIONAL PALI AIKE

Hugging the Argentine border north of Kimiri Aike and west of the Monte Aymond border crossing, little-visited **Pali Aike** (tel. 061/223-8875, parque.paliaike@gmail.com, US$4.50 pp) is an area of volcanic steppe and rugged lava beds that once supported megafauna such as the ground sloth *Mylodon* and the native American horse, both of which disappeared soon after humans first inhabited the area some 11,000 years ago.

While Paleo-Indian hunters probably contributed to their extinction, environmental changes after the last major glaciation may also have played a role. In the 1930s, Junius Bird, of New York's American Museum of Natural History, conducted the earliest systematic excavations of Paleo-Indian sites such as Cueva Pali Aike, within the park boundaries, and Cueva Fell, a short distance west. These archaeologically rich volcanic shelters (not caves in the strictest sense of the word) are the prime reason Chilean authorities have nominated the area as a UNESCO World Heritage Site.

Findings at Pali Aike include human remains that have yielded insights on Paleo-Indian funerary customs. Materials from Cueva Fell have helped reveal the transition from relatively simple hunting to more complex forms of subsistence. These include sophisticated hunting tools such as the bow and arrow and *boleadoras* (rounded stones tied together with leather thongs), and a greater reliance on coastal and marine resources. There are also indicators of ceremonial artifacts.

Part of arid eastern Magallanes, 5,030-hectare Pali Aike consists of rolling steppe grasslands whose porous volcanic soils and slag absorb water quickly. Almost constant high winds and cool temperatures make it a better summer or autumn excursion.

While the *Mylodon* and native horse may have disappeared, the park's grasslands swarm with wild guanacos and flocks of rheas, upland geese, ibis, and other birds. Pumas and foxes are the major predators.

Sights and Recreation

Accessible by road, **Cueva Pali Aike** is a volcanic tube seven meters wide and five meters high at its mouth. It is 17 meters deep but tapers as it advances. In the 1930s, Bird discovered both human and megafauna remains, at least 8,600 years old and probably much older, in the cave.

Tours from Punta Arenas visit Cueva Pali Aike and usually hike the 1.7-kilometer trail through the **Escorial del Diablo** (the appropriately named Devil's Slag Heap, which is hell on hiking boots). The trail ends at the volcanic **Crater Morada del Diablo.**

From Cueva Pali Aike, a nine-kilometer footpath leads to **Laguna Ana,** where waterfowl are abundant, and the main road, five kilometers from the park entrance. Mountain bikes should be ideal for this sort of rolling terrain, but it could be even tougher on tires than it is on boots.

Practicalities

A great destination for solitude seekers, Pali Aike officially gets only about 2,300 visitors per year, about 40 percent of them foreigners. At the main entrance, Conaf has a ranger station but often neglects to collect the admission

guanacos, Parque Nacional Pali Aike

fee. There are rudiments of a campground, but no tourist services as yet, so bring supplies (particularly water).

Parque Nacional Pali Aike is 196 kilometers northeast of Punta Arenas via Ruta 9, Ruta 255, and a graveled secondary road from the hamlet of Cooperativa Villa O'Higgins, 11 kilometers beyond Kimiri Aike. Just south of the Chilean border post at Monte Aymond, a hard-to-follow dirt road also leads to the park. There is no public transportation, but Punta Arenas travel agencies can arrange visits. Hiring a car, though, is probably the best option, especially if shared among several people.

★ THE FJORDS OF FUEGIA

Short of Antarctica itself, some of the southern hemisphere's most awesome scenery occurs in the Beagle Channel and southern Tierra del Fuego. And as usual, Charles Darwin left one of the most vivid descriptions of the channel named for the vessel on which he sailed:

> The lofty mountains on the north side compose the granitic axis, or backbone of the country, and boldly rise to a height of between three and four thousand feet, with one peak above six thousand feet. They are covered by a wide mantle of perpetual snow, and numerous cascades pour their waters, through the woods, into the narrow channel below. In many parts, magnificent glaciers extend from the mountain side to the water's edge. It is scarcely possible to imagine anything more beautiful than the beryl-like blue of these glaciers, and especially as contrasted with the dead white of the upper expanse of the snow. The fragments which had fallen from the glacier into the water, were floating away, and the channel with the icebergs presented, for the space of a mile, a miniature likeness of the Polar Sea.

Even today, few visitors see Tierra del Fuego's splendid fjords—little changed since Darwin described them in 1833, except for the receding glaciers. Many of those who do

see the fjords do so onboard weeklong excursions from Punta Arenas to the Argentine port of Ushuaia and back on the Chilean cruise ships *Ventus Australis* and *Stella Australis* (all cabins have picture windows, and there are additional lounges with audiovisual gear).

Unlike the Navimag ferry from Puerto Montt to Puerto Natales, these are cruises in the traditional sense. The passengers are waited on hand and foot, and they're not cheap. Yet for the foreseeable future, this remains the only way to see the area short of sailing your own yacht or chartering someone else's, and for that reason it's worth consideration even for those with limited finances.

One common alternative is to do either leg of the voyage separately—either five days and four nights from Punta Arenas to Ushuaia, or four days and three nights from Ushuaia to Punta Arenas. The boats sometimes undertake variants, and there's usually some duplication. Both legs, for instance, usually visit Cape Horn and the western Beagle Channel's **Glaciar Pía.** Routes can also vary depending on weather conditions in this notoriously capricious climate, and there are occasional routes exclusively within Chilean waters.

After an evening departure from Punta Arenas's Muelle Prat, the vessel usually crosses the Strait of Magellan to enter the **Seno del Almirantazgo** (Admiralty Sound), a westward maritime extension of the freshwater Lago Fagnano trough. Passengers usually go ashore at **Bahía Ainsworth,** near the **Glaciar Marinelli,** where there's a short hiking trail through what was once forest until feral beavers dammed the area into a series of ponds. For many visitors, the most interesting sight is a small elephant seal colony. Farther west, at **Isla Tucker,** there's a Magellanic penguin colony (observed from an inflatable Zodiac), and it's also possible to see the rare striated caracara, *Phalcoboenus australis.*

After a night's sailing that includes Canal Cockburn, where open ocean swells can rock the boat at least briefly, the vessel turns into the calmer **Canal Ocasión** and eventually enters the Beagle Channel's north arm, sailing past the so-called **Avenida de los Glaciares,** a series of glaciers named for various European countries. After entering **Fiordo Pía** (Pía Fjord), where dozens of waterfalls cascade down sheer metamorphic slopes, passengers normally disembark at **Glaciar Pía,** where a short hike leads to an overlook as angular seracs collapse off the glacier's face and into the sea.

Darwin, again, described the dangers of travel in a land that sea kayakers are just beginning to explore:

> The boats being hauled on shore at our dinner hour, we were admiring from the distance of half a mile a perpendicular cliff of ice, and were wishing that some more fragments would fall. At last, down came a mass with a roaring noise, and immediately we saw the smooth outline of a wave traveling toward us. The men ran down as quickly as they could to the boats; for the chance of their being dashed to pieces was evident.

After traveling through the night, the ship anchors at **Cabo de Hornos** (Cape Horn), and, wind permitting (less than 45 knots), passengers disembark in a rocky cove to hike to the stylized iron albatross silhouette that symbolizes sailors who lost their lives "rounding the Horn." At the lighthouse, tended by a Chilean naval officer with his family, there's now a small gift shop.

Again, weather permitting, the captain can choose to round the Horn before proceeding north to **Bahía Wulaia,** on Isla Navarino's western shore. Here passengers visit the site of an early mission where, in a notorious incident, the Yámana massacred all but one of the Anglicans and their crew. There is then the option of a short but steep hike with panoramic views of the bay, or an easier shoreline walk to see birdlife, including Magellanic oystercatchers.

Before continuing to Argentina, the vessel stops at **Puerto Navarino,** at the western end of **Isla Navarino,** for immigration formalities (the crew shuttles the documents ashore and back by Zodiac). Proceeding to **Ushuaia,** passengers spend the night aboard; those returning to Punta Arenas have the day free in Ushuaia before reboarding the ship, while new passengers check their bags downtown before boarding in late afternoon.

Stella Australis passengers view Glaciar Pía.

After reentering Chile at Puerto Navarino, the ship sails south to Cape Horn again for an early disembarkation and stops again at Wulaia as well. Returning to the Beagle Channel, it veers westward through the north arm, again passing the Avenida de los Glaciares. It reenters Canal Cockburn, rounding Península Brecknock to the **Fiordo Chico** (Little Fjord), where passengers board Zodiacs for an easy shoreline walk to the receding **Glaciar Águila**. On the final morning, the boat sails north to **Isla Magdalena** before returning to Punta Arenas.

Practicalities

Well-organized but not regimented, the cruise is informal in terms of dress and behavior. At the start, passengers sign up for meal tables; places are fixed for the duration, though some small groups join their tables. In general, passengers are grouped by language, though they often place together people who speak English as a second language. The staff themselves can handle Spanish, English, German, French, and some other languages.

After introduction of the captain and crew, and an obligatory safety drill, there's a welcome drink and a brief folklore show (in Punta Arenas) or tango demonstration (in Ushuaia). Smoking is prohibited everywhere except the exterior decks. The package includes bar consumption.

The cabins themselves are spacious, with either a double bed or twin beds, built-in reading lights, a closet with hangers and shelves (with a small lock box for valuables), and a private bath with an excellent hot shower. Some also have a fold-down bunk for children or a third person. The food is abundant and often

excellent, though breakfasts can be a little monotonous. The wine is superb, and the service exceptional. Vegetarian menus are available on request.

For those who tire of the landscape or when weather is bad, onboard activities include karaoke, slide lectures on history and flora and fauna, engine-room tours, knot-tying demonstrations, and documentary films on topics such British explorer Ernest Shackleton and local wildlife. The farewell dinner is a fairly gala affair, followed by champagne on the top deck.

Punta Arenas is the home port for fjord-bound cruises. Check-in takes place at **Turismo Comapa** (Magallanes 990, tel. 061/220-0200) 1pm-5pm, while boarding takes place 5pm-6pm at the entrance to **Muelle Prat.** Some passengers begin or end the trip in **Argentine Tierra del Fuego,** where check-in takes place at **Comapa's Ushuaia office** (San Martín 409, tel. 02901/43-0727, 9am-4pm); boarding takes place 5pm-6pm at the Muelle Comercial (at the foot of 25 de Mayo).

Often this popular cruise runs full September to April. In December and January, days are so long that it's possible to enjoy the landscape until after 11pm, and there's sufficient light to read by 4am.

Make reservations through **Cruceros Australis** (Av. Bosque Norte 0440, 11th Fl., Las Condes, Santiago, tel. 02/2442-3110, www. australis.com), which also has representatives in Buenos Aires (tel. 011/5128-4632) and in the United States (U.S. tel. 877/678-3772). Per-person rates for four days and three nights start at US$1,189 and reach US$4,054 in high season. For five days and four nights, rates start at US$1,800 and reach US$4,054.

Puerto Natales

Over recent decades, Puerto Natales has changed from a sleepy wool and fishing port on Seno Última Esperanza (Last Hope Sound) to a bustling tourist town whose season has lengthened well beyond the traditional summer months. Its proximity to Torres del Paine, coupled with its status as the southern terminus for the scenic ferry from Puerto Montt, has placed it on the international travel map, transforming the local economy.

Natales has no knockout attractions in its own right, but it enjoys a magnificent seaside setting, with the snowcapped Cordillera Sarmiento and Campo de Hielo Sur, the southern Patagonian ice cap, visible over the water to the west. The waterfront is increasingly presentable, and numerous nearby excursions make it more than just a stopover en route to Paine.

In addition, it's a more attractive town than it once was with its rejuvenated Plaza de Armas, including a sunken amphitheater, and the main commercial street, Eberhard, now features wider and handsomely tiled sidewalks. New park benches along Eberhard and other central streets increase its pedestrian appeal, along with new and upgraded hotels and an improving gastronomic scene.

For visitors to Paine and other regional sights, Natales has abundant services, including tour operators and rental equipment, plus convenient connections to Argentina's El Calafate and Parque Nacional Los Glaciares and Glaciar Perito Moreno. The new airport has improved connectivity with northern Chile, including the Aisén region.

HISTORY

Última Esperanza acquired its name because expeditions led by 16th-century explorers Juan Ladrilleros and Pedro Sarmiento de Gamboa failed to find a westbound route to the Pacific here. Puerto Natales proper dates from the early 20th century, a few years after German explorer Hermann Eberhard founded the area's first sheep *estancia* at Puerto Prat. Within a few years, the Sociedad Explotadora de Tierra del Fuego had built a slaughterhouse at nearby Bories to process mutton for export. While the livestock economy declined in the second half of the 20th century, the tourist boom has reactivated and diversified the economy.

ORIENTATION

On the eastern shores of Seno Última Esperanza, Puerto Natales (pop. 18,741) is 250 kilometers northwest of Punta Arenas via paved Ruta 9. It is 150 kilometers south of Parque Nacional Torres del Paine, also by Ruta 9, which is paved as far as the town of Cerro Castillo.

Entering town from the north, Ruta 9 becomes the north-south Costanera Pedro Montt. Most services and points of interest are within easy walking distance to the east. The principal commercial streets are east-west Manuel Bulnes and Eberhard, and north-south Avenida Baquedano. A new northwesterly route has cut the distance to the park border and made a loop through the park feasible.

SIGHTS

The Sociedad Explotadora de Tierra del Fuego, owner of large pasture tracts in both Chile and Argentina, financed construction of Natales's gingerbread-style municipality, dating to 1929. (Many might have said the powerful Sociedad Explotadora was the region's de facto government.) It's been rededicated as the **Espacio Cultural Natalis.** Immediately east, dating from the same era and undergoing restoration, the **Iglesia Parroquial María Auxiliadora** shares its Magellanic style.

In the same exterior fashion but with a roomier interior that displays its holdings to

Puerto Natales

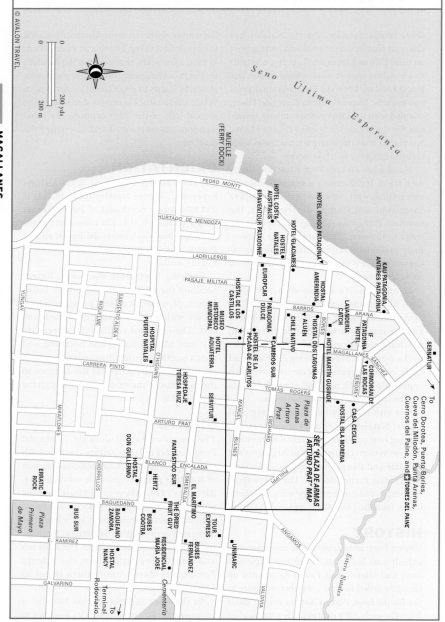

Seno Última Esperanza

MUELLE
(FERRY DOCK)

PEDRO MONTT

HURTADO DE MENDOZA

LADRILLEROS

PASAJE MILITAR

HOTEL COSTA
AUSTRALIS
KIPAVENTOUR PATAGONIE

HOTEL
NATALES

HOTEL GLACIARES

HOTEL INDIGO PATAGONIA

KAU PATAGONIA,
ANTARES PATAGONIA

EUROPCAR

HOSTAL DE LOS
CASTILLOS

MUSEO
HISTORICO
MUNICIPAL

PATAGONIA
DULCE

HOTEL
AGUATERRA

HOSTEL DE LA
PICADA DE CARLITOS

HOSPITAL
PUERTO NATALES

HOSTAL
AMERINDIA

CAMBIOS SUR

HOSPEDAJE
TERESA RUIZ

SERVITUR

BARROS

BORIES

CHILE NATIVO

ALUEN

HOSTAL DOS LAGUNAS

LAVANDERIA
CATCH

CORMORAN DE
LAS ROCAS

IF
PATAGONIA
HOTEL

HOTEL MARTIN GUSINDE

MAGALLANES

ARANA

SANCHEZ

SEÑORET

HOTEL ISLA MORENA

CASA CECILIA

HOSTAL ISLA MORENA

SERNATUR

To
Cerro Dorotea, Puerto Bories,
Cueva del Milodón, Punta Arenas,
Cuernos del Paine, and ✈ TORRES DEL PAINE

TOMAS ROGERS

Plaza de
Armas
Arturo
Prat

SEE "PLAZA DE ARMAS
ARTURO PRAT" MAP

CARRERA PINTO

ARTURO PRAT

HOSTAL
DON GUILLERMO

FANTASTICO SUR

BLANCO

ENCALADA

HERTZ

ERRATIC
ROCK

BAQUEDANO

Plaza
Primero
de Mayo

BUS SUR

BAQUEANO
ZAMORA

BUSES
COOTRA

EL MARITIMO

THE DRIED
FRUIT GUY

RESIDENCIAL
MARIA JOSE

E. RAMIREZ

HOSTAL
NANCY

GALVARINO

To
Terminal
Rodoviario

Cementerio

TOUR
EXPRESS

BUSES
FERNANDEZ

UNIMARC

YUNGAY

SARGENTO ALDEA

RIQUELME

O'HIGGINS

MIRAFLORES

CHORRILLOS

MANUEL

EBERHARD

BULNES

PHILLIPPI

ANGAMOS

VALDIVIA

Estero Natales

0   200 yds
0   200 m

Plaza de Armas Arturo Prat

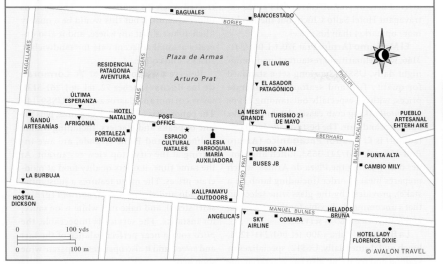

BAGUALES

BANCOESTADO

BORIES

Plaza de Armas

EL LIVING

RESIDENCIAL
PATAGONIA
AVENTURA

Arturo Prat

EL ASADOR
PATAGÓNICO

ÚLTIMA
ESPERANZA

HOTEL
NATALINO

LA MESITA
GRANDE

TURISMO 21
DE MAYO

PUEBLO
ARTESANAL
EHTERH AIKE

ÑANDÚ
ARTESANÍAS

AFRIGONIA

POST
OFFICE

FORTALEZA
PATAGONIA

ESPACIO
CULTURAL
NATALES

IGLESIA
PARROQUIAL
MARÍA
AUXILIADORA

TURISMO ZAAHJ

EBERHARD

PUNTA ALTA

CAMBIO MILY

BUSES JB

LA BURBUJA

HOSTAL
DICKSON

KALLPAMAYU
OUTDOORS

ANGÉLICA'S

MANUEL BULNES

SKY
AIRLINE

COMAPA

HELADOS
BRUNA

0   100 yds

0   100 m

HOTEL LADY
FLORENCE DIXIE

© AVALON TRAVEL

advantage, the **Museo Histórico Municipal** (Bulnes 285, tel. 061/220-5934, muninata@ct-cinternet.cl, 8am-7pm Mon.-Fri., 10am-1pm and 3pm-7pm Sat., US$1.50) offers displays on natural history, archaeology, the region's indigenous peoples, European settlement, the rural economy (including the Sociedad Explotadora), Natales' own urban evolution, and the Carabineros police, who played a role in the museum's creation. Noteworthy individual artifacts include a Yámana (Yahgan) dugout canoe and Aónikenk (Tehuelche) *boleadoras* (rounded stones tied together with a leather thong), plus historical photographs of Captain Eberhard and the town's development.

ENTERTAINMENT

Baguales (Bories 430, tel. 061/241-1920, www.cervezabaguales.cl, 6pm-3am daily Sept.-Mar.) is a stylishly casual brewpub, with its own light and dark draft made on the premises. It also offers a pub-grub menu of burgers, sandwiches, and salads, plus a handful of Mexican dishes such as *carnitas* tacos and quesadillas. The music's not normally so loud as to inhibit conversation, but the service can be inconsistent.

SHOPPING

Ñandú Artesanía (Eberhard 301, tel. 061/241-4382) sells maps and books in addition to a selection of quality crafts. It occupies larger quarters at the corner of Eberhard and Prat that also includes a bar-restaurant. The **Pueblo Artesanal Ehterh Aike** (Philippi 660) has a variety of crafts but is also the best place in town to buy fresh fruit and other produce.

FOOD

Known for seafood, Natales has several moderately priced eateries and improving mid-range to upscale choices.

To stock up on supplies for that Paine trek, visit **Unimarc** (Bulnes 742). More specialized, for trail mix, is **The Dried Fruit Guy** (Baquedano 443).

On the east side of the Plaza de Armas, the vegetarian option is ★ **El Living** (Arturo Prat 156, tel. 061/241-1140, www.el-living.com, 11am-11pm daily, mid-Oct.-Apr.,

US$7-8), which serves breakfast, economical sandwiches, and desserts. The British owner arrived here by way of Torres del Paine's extravagant Hotel Salto Chico, but the food is more upmarket than his prices.

El Marítimo (Arturo Prat 370, tel. 061/241-3166, www.elmaritimo.restaurant, noon-midnight daily, US$13) has long set a standard for quality fish and seafood at moderate prices, with an especially outstanding *chupe de centolla* (king crab casserole), but it lacks ambience and flair. The best *parrilla* (grill restaurant) is **El Asador Patagónico** (Arturo Prat 158, tel. 061/241-3553, lunch and dinner daily), facing the Plaza de Armas, which prepares meat to order (including lamb on a stake), provides a by-the-glass wine selection that's uncommonly flexible for the provinces, and features assiduous service.

La Burbuja (Bulnes 300, tel. 061/241-4204, lunch and dinner daily, US$12) specializes in seafood and meats but also has vegetarian offerings. For an appetizer, try the mildly spicy *ostiones al pil pil* (scallops). For an entrée, try the *paila marina* (seafood stew) or the grilled *congrio* (conger eel).

Rarely does Chilean pizza merit special mention, but the thin-crusted pies at ★ **Mesita Grande** (Arturo Prat 196, tel. 061/241-1571, www.mesitagrande.cl, lunch and dinner daily, US$7-13) do. Individual pizzas with four ample slices range from simple mozzarella to spinach and garlic to ground lamb and just about everything in between. Diners sit at either of two long but solid tables that encourage conversation with neighboring parties.

Underrated **Última Esperanza** (Eberhard 354, tel. 061/241-3626, noon-3:15pm and 6:30pm-11:30pm daily, US$14) deserves more credit for exceptional seafood at modest prices with outstanding service. Sample dishes include scallop and squid appetizers, conger eel, and grilled Patagonian lamb and potatoes.

★ **Angélica's** (Bulnes 501, tel. 061/241-0007, lunch and dinner daily, US$15) has comparably fine fish and seafood, such as king crab cannelloni. The service is an anomaly—often great when it's crowded, but distracted when it's nearly empty. The decor is underwhelming, but this would be a quality kitchen just about anywhere, and it also operates a small adjacent café for sandwiches, snacks, and coffee.

Reserve a window table at ★ **Cormorán de las Rocas** (Sánchez 72, tel. 061/261-5131, www.cormorandelasrocas.com, US$9-14). The panoramas of Última Esperanza, plus the line of peaks and glaciers, including Monte Balmaceda and Paine Grande, are awe-inspiring at the city's top view restaurant. At the same time, it offers quality food at moderate prices. The menu features a substantial avocado and shrimp salad, *entraña* (grilled skirt steak), and hake in a white wine sauce, for instance. The service is impeccable, the *pisco* sour a near perfect balance of the tart and sweet, and it also operates a separate wine shop here.

In expanded quarters, the surprising ★ **Afrigonia** (Eberhard 343, tel. 061/241-2232, noon-2:30pm and 7pm-11pm daily, from US$15) attempts to fuse Patagonian standards with East African touches in dishes such as shrimp and scallop curry, and grilled lamb rump with port and apricot sauce. It's certainly Natales's most sophisticated restaurant and, by consensus, probably its best. Some premium wines go for nearly US$200, but most are more affordable.

★ **Patagonia Dulce** (Barros Arana 233, tel. 061/241-5285, US$3-6) serves several variations on coffee, tea, and hot chocolate, plus exquisite pastries and desserts (mostly chocolate but also with fresh fruit), along with rich homemade chocolates by weight. Unfortunately, it doesn't open until 11am. For fine days, there are outdoor tables.

At **Helados Bruna** (Bulnes 585), *calafate* and rhubarb are the regional ice cream specialties, and **Aluén** (Barros Arana 160, www.aluenpatagonia.com, 2pm-7:30pm Tues.-Sun.) has made some inroads with artisanal ice cream. Patagonia Dulce also has ice cream.

ACCOMMODATIONS

Natales has developed one of Chile's densest accommodations offerings. This is especially true in the budget category, where competition keeps prices low, and in stylish new options. Off-season rates can drop dramatically at upscale places, but many close at least briefly. Nearly every place now offers Wi-Fi.

US$25-50

Residencial María José (Esmeralda 869, tel. 061/241-2218, patagoniamj@hotmail.com, US$12-15 pp) has simple doubles, triples, and quadruples, with either shared or private bath. **Hospedaje Teresa Ruiz** (Esmeralda 463, tel. 061/241-0472, freepatagonia@hotmail.com, US$15 pp with shared bath, US$18-22 pp with private bath) gets high marks for congeniality, cleanliness, and outstanding breakfasts with homemade rhubarb preserves.

Friendly **Residencial Patagonia Aventura** (Tomás Rogers 179, tel. 061/241-1028, www.apatagonia.com, US$19 pp, US$44 s or d) affords more privacy than others in its range, with knowledgeable operators who also rent equipment. Unlike many hostels, though, it provides no kitchen access.

The expat-operated hostel **Erratic Rock** (Baquedano 719, tel. 061/241-0355, www.erraticrock.com, US$24 pp, US$37 s, US$48 d) occupies a creaky house with character. It also serves a better-than-average breakfast, has a large book exchange, and rents quality gear for Paine-bound travelers. It also has a unique special: Anyone who can do 150 pushups nonstop gets one free night.

All rooms at popular **Hostal Nancy** (Ramírez 540, tel. 061/241-0022, hostalnancy@gmail.com, US$30 s, US$53 d, with breakfast) now have private baths.

At friendly **Hostal Dickson** (Bulnes 307, tel. 061/241-1871, www.hostaldickson.net, US$44 s, US$66 d), inspect the rooms first—some have windows so small that they evoke prison cells. On the other hand, there's central heating, the beds are good, all rooms now have private baths, and rates include breakfast in a nicely remodeled nook.

US$50-100

Despite the near elimination of its signature rose garden, **Hostal de los Castillos** (Bulnes 241, tel. 061/241-3641, www.hostaldeloscastillos.com, US$60 s, US$90 d, with breakfast) remains both friendly and immaculate. All rooms now have private baths, central heating, cable TV, and Wi-Fi.

Despite its hostel history, the 14-room **Hostal de la Picada de Carlitos** (Bulnes 280, tel. 061/241-4885, www.hostelpicadadecarlitos.cl, US$37 s, US$59 d) is more of a B&B. All the rooms have fine furniture, small flat-screen TVs, and private baths. There are three legitimate singles for solo travelers, but those go early.

Now a Natales institution, the Swiss-Chilean B&B ★ **Casa Cecilia** (Tomás Rogers 60, tel. 061/261-3560, www.casaceciliahostal.com, US$36-75 s, US$55-80 d) deserves credit for improving accommodations standards here. The rooms are simple, and some are small, but all enjoy central heating and most have private baths and cable TV with upgraded showers. The luminous atrium is a cheerful gathering place, and rates include a diverse breakfast with fresh homemade bread.

Open year-round, in an older house with substantial character and attentive ownership, ★ **Hostal Dos Lagunas** (Barros Arana 104, tel. 061/241-5733, hostaldoslagunas@gmail.com, US$19 pp dorm, US$37 s, US$47 d) is steadily upgrading. Rates include an ample and varied breakfast, which gets even better with longer stays. Owner Alejandro Cárdenas, who speaks English and German, helps book tours and conducts his own off-season trips to Paine.

Hotel Isla Morena (Tomás Rogers 68, tel. 061/241-4773, hotelislamorena@gmail.com, US$37 s, US$71 d) enjoys fine natural light in modern rooms with private baths. A couple of rooms lack exterior windows but have skylights. It also has a restaurant with a limited nightly menu.

Some years ago, **Hostel Natales** (Ladrilleros 209, tel. 061/241-0081, www.hostelnatales.cl, US$24 pp, US$59 s, or d) transformed the dreary Hotel Palace into warm, luminous accommodations with private baths. Some rooms have two or four bunk beds—expensive by hostel standards—while others have double beds for couples. The lobby and atrium are spacious and inviting, with comfortable chairs and sofas, but sounds carry from the lobby to the nearest of the sparsely furnished rooms.

Expanded **Hostal Amerindia** (Barros Arana 135, tel. 061/241-1945, www.hostelamerindia.com, US$40-47 s, US$55-70 d, 6 percent surcharge for credit cards) is an artfully decorated 13-room B&B in two buildings separated by a garden that may become an expanded reception area. It serves a diverse buffet breakfast. Seven rooms have private baths, but the other six share three baths. Free tea and cookies are available all day.

In a quiet location six blocks east of the plaza, the utilitarian rooms at **Hostal Álamo Patagónico** (Balmaceda 254, tel. 061/241-5069, www.hostalalamopatagonico, US$62 s, US$70 d) are good value, with secluded gardens and an outstanding breakfast.

In an off-the-beaten-sidewalk location, the immaculate ★ **Hostal Don Guillermo** (O'Higgins 657, tel./fax 061/241-4506, www.hostaldonguillermo.com, US$20 s, US$37 d with shared bath, US$56 s or d) is underpriced compared to nearby competitors. Though the singles are small, some rooms now have private baths, and the breakfast is excellent.

US$100-150

Some years ago, the purpose-built ★ **Hotel Aquaterra** (Bulnes 299, tel. 061/241-2239, www.aquaterrapatagonia.com, US$93 s, US$120 d), a 13-room hotel that combines style (native woods) and substance (comfortable furnishings), was almost unique. Though the competition has more than caught up, it's still worth consideration, though prices have risen recently.

Having rejuvenated the over-the-hill Hotel Ladrilleros, ★ **Kau Patagonia** (Pedro Montt 161, tel. 061/241-4611, www.kaulodge.com, US$100-115 s or d) is a cozy nine-room

B&B. Guests take breakfast at the on-the-premises café, The Coffee Maker, which is also open to nonguests for snacks, sandwiches, and espresso drinks.

Hotel Lady Florence Dixie (Manuel Bulnes 659, tel. 061/241-1158, www.hotelflorencedixie.cl, US$114-136 s, US$136-160 d) has expanded and upgraded what was already a good hotel. **Hotel Glaciares** (Eberhard 104, tel. 061/241-1452, www.hotelglaciares.com, US$128 s, US$141 d) is comparable.

US$150-200

Clearly drawing inspiration from nearby Hotel Indigo (despite assertions to the contrary), the luminous 15-room **IF Patagonia Hotel** (Magallanes 73, tel. 061/241-0312, www.hotelifpatagonia.com, US$140 s, US$150 d) includes two suites and seven rooms with panoramic sea views. The rest of the rooms face the city or Cerro Dorotea. The fourth-floor terrace offers both sorts of views. The standard rooms are on the small side.

Since being acquired by the neighboring casino, the expanded **Hotel Martín Gusinde** (Bories 278, tel. 061/271-2180, www.martingusinde.com, US$163 s, US$197 d) has lost some of the subdued character it once had. Arguably, the improvements have lagged behind hotel trends here.

On a deep, narrow lot, **Hotel Natalino** (Eberhard 371, tel. 061/241-4345, www.hotelnatalino.com, US$134 s, US$180 d) offers 23 mostly small but maximally efficient rooms, reached by a gently rising staircase (with its own gentle waterfall) along one side of the building. Behind the facade, where blue-lighted slabs of glass mimic a glacier's face, the third floor has a spa and small pool, and a deck for fine weather. One room is suitable for disabled access.

Over US$200

About two kilometers north of town, on the Paine highway, at the hillside **Hotel Altiplánico del Sur** (Ruta 9 Norte, Huerto 258, tel. 061/241-2525, www.altiplanico.cl, from US$170 s, US$220 d), only the windows

Hotel Costa Australis

and roof rise above ground level. Blocks of peat insulate the concrete structure and help camouflage it. The common areas, rooms, and furnishings all display an elegant simplicity.

★ **Hotel Indigo Patagonia** (Ladrilleros 105, tel. 061/241-3609, www.indigopatagonia. com, from US$206 s or d) is a minimalist-design hotel with 29 rooms, including half a dozen suites. Most rooms are surprisingly small but efficient and striking. The glassed-in showers, for instance, have huge copper showerheads, and the top-level spa offers great sea and sierra views.

On the waterfront, the best rooms at the Francophile classic **Hotel Costa Australis** (Costanera Pedro Montt 262, tel. 061/241-2000, www.hoteles-australis.com, from US$196 s, US$224 d) have sea views, and the highest rates correspond to suites. While comfortable and efficient, with an excellent buffet breakfast, it's hard-pressed to keep up with newer choices such as the Altiplánico and

Indigo. The rooms are arguably overheated, but on some days that's comforting here.

INFORMATION

The local delegation of **Sernatur** (Pedro Montt 19, tel. 061/241-2125, infonatales@sernatur.cl, 8:30am-6pm Mon.-Fri., 10am-4pm Sat.) has helpful personnel, including English speakers, and thorough information on accommodations, restaurants, transportation, and excursions.

SERVICES

Puerto Natales has several exchange houses, including **Cambio Mily** (Blanco Encalada 266) and **Cambios Sur** (Eberhard 285). On Plaza Arturo Prat, **BancoEstado** (Bories 492) has an ATM. **Correos de Chile** (Eberhard 429), at the southwest corner of Plaza Arturo Prat, is the post office. Internet connections are improving and costing less, and Wi-Fi is ubiquitous.

Lavandería Catch (Bories 218, tel. 061/241-1530) can do the washing. **Hospital Puerto Natales** (Ignacio Carrera Pinto 537, tel. 061/241-1582) handles medical emergencies, but new facilities, near the bus terminal, are due to open in 2017.

TRANSPORTATION
Air

Punta Arenas-bound buses will drop passengers at that city's Aeropuerto Presidente Carlos Ibáñez del Campo, but Natales now has its own Aeropuerto Teniente Julio Gallardo (PNT, tel. 061/241-1980), seven kilometers north of town. It has begun to receive commercial flights from Santiago with LATAM/LAN, which no longer keeps a separate office here, but **Turismo Comapa** (Bulnes 541, tel. 061/241-4300, www.comapa.com) handles reservations and tickets. Flights from Santiago continue to Punta Arenas before returning to the Chilean capital.

In summer, **Sky Airline** (Bulnes 531, tel. 061/241-0646, www.skyairline.cl) offers three flights weekly from Santiago, stopping in Punta Arenas before continuing to Puerto Natales and then back.

Bus

There's frequent service to and from Punta Arenas and Torres del Paine, and regular but less frequent service to the Argentine destinations of Río Turbio, Río Gallegos, and El Calafate. Buses leave from the new **Terminal Rodoviario** (Av. España 1455, tel. 061/241-2554), though some individual companies still have more central ticket offices.

Carriers serving Punta Arenas (3 hours, US$9) include **Bus Sur** (Baquedano 668, tel. 061/241-0784, www.bus-sur.cl), **Buses Fernández** (Ramírez 399, tel. 061/241-1111, www.busesfernandez.com), and **Buses Pacheco** (tel. 061/241-4800 at the terminal, www.busespacheco.com). Round-trip tickets offer small discounts but less flexibility. In summer, Pacheco goes directly to Ushuaia in Argentina (9am Tues., Thurs., and Sun., 12 hours, US$56); additional services require changing buses in Río Grande. Bus Sur offers similar services, but with them it's sometimes necessary to change buses in Punta Arenas.

Services to Torres del Paine (2.5 hours, US$22 round-trip) vary seasonally, and there is frequent turnover among agencies. Carriers include Bus Sur, **Buses J.B.** (Prat 258, tel. 061/241-2824), **Buses Gómez** (tel. 061/241-1971, www.busesgomez.com), and **Buses María José** (tel. 061/241-0951, www.busesmariajose.com).

For the Argentine border town of Río Turbio (1 hour, US$10), where there are connections to El Calafate and Río Gallegos, try **Buses Cootra** (Baquedano 454, tel. 061/241-2785), which has service at 8:30am daily.

To El Calafate (5 hours, US$25), the carriers are Buses Cootra, Buses Pacheco, and **Turismo Zaahj** (Prat 236, tel. 061/241-5443, www.turismozaahj.co.cl). Services are frequent in high season, but in winter they may be weekly only.

Ferry

In new offices at the bus terminal, **Navimag** (tel. 061/241-4300, www.navimag.cl) operates the weekly car-passenger MV *Evangelistas* to the mainland Chilean city of Puerto Montt (US$550-$2,100 pp with all meals, bicycles free, motorcycles US$122, passenger cars US$396, light trucks US$421). Fares vary by season and level of accommodations. Northbound departures are normally around 8am Tuesday, but check-in takes place the night before, and passengers spend the night

Terminal Rodoviario, Puerto Natales

on board. Those with vehicles must report earlier, to complete an internal customs check.

As of mid-2016, there is also weekly ferry service to Puerto Yungay with the ferry *Crux Australis* (US$180 adults, bicycles US$15, passenger vehicles US$36 per linear meter). Avoiding the rougher waters of the Golfo de Penas, through which northbound Navimag ferries must pass, the vessel leaves Natales at 5am Thursday, arriving at Yungay at 1am Saturday. For reservations, contact

Transbordadora Austral Broom (tel. 061/272-8100, www.tabsa.cl).

Car Rentals

The rental car fleet is growing, but reservations are essential. Agencies include **Europcar** (Bulnes 100, tel. 061/241-4475), **Hertz** (O'Higgins 632, tel. 061/241-4519) in the Hotel Alberto de Agostini, and **Punta Alta** (Blanco Encalada 244, tel. 061/241-0115, www.puntaalta.cl).

Vicinity of Puerto Natales

A growing number of operators arrange excursions to nearby sites of interest and, of course, to Torres del Paine and even Argentina's Parque Nacional Los Glaciares. Day tours of Paine, more feasible since completion of a new road permits loops rather than time-consuming backtracking to return to Natales, cost around US$45 pp plus the park entrance fee. The most reliable are **Tour Express** (Manuel Bulnes 769, tel. 061/241-0734, www.tourexpress.cl), **Turismo Comapa** (Bulnes 541, tel. 061/241-4300, www.comapa.com), and **Kipaventour Patagonie** (Bulnes 90-B, tel. 061/241-3615, www.kipaventourpatagonie.com).

Several operators supply services, including accommodations and meals at park *refugios* (shelters), and activities within the park. These include **Fantástico Sur** (Esmeralda 661, tel. 061/261-4184, www.fslodges.com), with its own accommodations; **Chile Nativo** (Eberhard 230, tel. 061/241-1385, www.chilenativo.travel) for riding, trekking, and birding; **Fortaleza Patagonia** (Tomás Rogers 235, tel. 061/241-3395, www.fortaleza-patagonia.cl); and **Servitur** (Prat 353, tel. 061/241-1858, www.servitur.cl). **Baqueano Zamora** (Baquedano 534, tel. 061/261-3530, www.baqueanozamora.cl) specializes in horseback trips in the park.

Two companies operate as the **Centro de Turismo Aventura de Patagonia** (Pedro

Montt 161, tel. 061/241-4611): **Antares Patagonia** (www.antarespatagonia.com) for trekking and ice hiking, and **Big Foot Patagonia** (www.bigfootpatagonia.com) for kayaking. **Kallpamayu Outdoors** (Arturo Prat 297, tel. 061/241-5891) has a large supply of rental gear.

FRIGORÍFICO BORIES

Between 1912 and 1914, the Sociedad Explotadora de Tierra del Fuego built this state-of-the-art (for its time) meat freezer to process livestock, primarily sheep, for shipment to Europe. Four kilometers north of Puerto Natales, the brick complex is the only plant of its kind in a reasonable state of preservation. After its 1971 expropriation by the Allende government, the plant was partially dismantled and finally shut down a few years back.

Among the remaining structures are the rendering plant, which converted animal fat into tallow; the tannery, which prepared hides for shipment; and the main offices, smithy, locomotive repair shop (Bories had its own short line), freight jetty, power plant, and boilers.

Today, the complex is part of a 57-room luxury hotel, ★ **The Singular Patagonia** (tel. 061/272-2030, www.thesingular.com, from US$365 s, US$445 d), seamlessly integrated into the context of **Museo y**

Colección Privada (10am-1pm and 3pm-6:30pm daily, US$7.50 pp), which is open to nonguests. A registered historical monument, the on-site facility includes a tour of the tannery, boiler room, and power plant, among other structures.

No Bories employee could ever have imagined napping in the spacious accommodations, with panoramic views of Última Esperanza, that guests at The Singular now enjoy. Overnight guests are welcome, but the hotel focuses on multiple-day packages and also offers a highly regarded restaurant-bar and a spa, both open to nonguests.

Meanwhile, the next best accommodations are at **Bories House** (tel. 061/241-2221, www.borieshouse.com, US$150-195 s or d), a stylish expansion of an existing Patagonian house that offers large, comfortable, well-furnished rooms and is only a short cab ride from Puerto Natales. It is due to add a restaurant and spa to its offerings. The Anglo-Chilean owners also offer horseback excursions from their ranch at Puerto Consuelo, about 15 minutes north.

PUERTO PRAT AND VICINITY

About 15 kilometers northwest of Puerto Natales via a gravel road, sheltered **Puerto Prat** is the nearest thing to a beach getaway here. On rare hot days, its shallow waters warm up enough to let the truly intrepid dip their toes into the sea. It's also the paddling point for half-day sea kayak trips to **Fiordo Eberhard** (about US$105 pp); for details, contact any of several kayaking companies in Puerto Natales.

A short distance north, settled by Captain Hermann Eberhard, **Estancia Puerto Consuelo** was the area's first sheep farm. It's open to the public for horseback excursions, including a beginner's two-hour ride through scenic rolling seaside terrain (US$33), a half-day excursion to the Cueva del Milodón and back (US$80, including lunch), and a full-day combination of kayaking and riding (US$100-125, including lunch). For details, contact **Estancia Travel** (tel. 061/241-2221, www.estanciatravel.com), which has native and Chilean English-speaking personnel, at Puerto Bories.

DIFUNTA CORREA SHRINE

About six kilometers east of Puerto Natales, on the south side of Ruta 9, the spreading mountain of water-filled plastic bottles at this spontaneous roadside shrine suggests one of

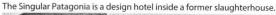

The Singular Patagonia is a design hotel inside a former slaughterhouse.

two things: Either many Argentines are traveling here, or Chileans are becoming devoted to Argentina's favorite folk saint, a woman who presumably died in the desert, with a live baby suckling at her breast, in the 19th century. Or it may be a changing combination of the two, ever since recurring Argentine economic crises have altered the traditional flow of neighboring tourists here.

CERRO DOROTEA

About seven kilometers east of town on Ruta 9, nudging the Argentine border, the hike to the Sierra Dorotea ridge makes an ideal half-day excursion, offering some of the area's finest panoramas. Well-marked with red blazes and signs, the route to **Cerro Dorotea**'s 549-meter summit is, after the initial approach, unrelentingly uphill but never exhaustingly steep. This is not pristine nature, though. Much of the lower slopes consists of cutover *lenga* forest, some of which has regenerated itself into an even-aged woodland. The ridge itself is barren, with a telephone relay antenna on the top.

Trailhead access is over private property, where farmer Juan de Dios Saavedra Ortiz collects US$18 pp. The fee includes a simple but welcome Chilean *onces* (afternoon tea with homemade bread, butter, ham, and cheese) on your return from the hike. **Baqueano Zamora** (Baquedano 534, tel. 061/261-3531, www.baqueanozamora.cl, US$45) offers the option of riding to the ridge.

MONUMENTO NATURAL CUEVA DEL MILODÓN

Northwest of present-day Puerto Natales, on the shores of a small inlet known as Fiordo Eberhard, the giant Pleistocene ground sloth known as the *Mylodon (Mylodon darwini)* took shelter in this wave-cut grotto some 30 meters high and 80 meters wide at its mouth, and 200 meters deep. This sight is now called **Monumento Natural Cueva del Milodón** (foreigners US$7.50 adults, Chileans US$4, nominal rates for

children). While the *Mylodon* has been extinct for nearly as long as humans have inhabited the area—some 11,000 years—the discovery of its remains caused a sensation, as their state of preservation induced some European scientists to speculate the animal might still be alive.

German pioneer Hermann Eberhard gets credit for discovering the cave in 1895, but Erland Nordenskjöld was the first scientist to study the *Mylodon*, taking sample bones and skin back to Sweden. Its manure has been carbon-dated at roughly 10,400 years BCE, meaning the large herbivore coexisted with humans, but it was most definitely not a domesticate. In all probability, hunting pressure contributed to its demise, and that of other Pleistocene megafauna. Oddly enough, no complete skeleton exists.

The *Mylodon* has gained a spot in the Western imagination, among both scientists and the general public. U.S. archaeologist Junius Bird described the beast in his journals, published as *Travel and Archaeology in South Chile* (University of Iowa Press, 1988), edited by John Hyslop. Family tales inspired Bruce Chatwin to write his masterpiece *In Patagonia*, which relates far-fetched legends that Paleo-Indians penned the *Mylodon* in the cave and that some specimens survived into the 19th century.

Conaf's **Museo de Sitio** (no phone, 8am-8pm daily, admission included with park entrance fee) has excellent information on the 192-hectare park, which attracted 110,833 visitors in 2013, about 30 percent of them foreigners. A kitschy life-size replica of the *Mylodon* stands in the cave itself.

Many Natales-based tours take in the sight, but there is no scheduled public transportation. Mountain-bike rental can be a good alternative.

GLACIAR BALMACEDA

Chile's largest national park, **Parque Nacional Bernardo O'Higgins,** covers 3.5 million hectares of islands and icecaps from Aisén to Magallanes but has only a few easy

The Channels of the Kawéskar

From the Golfo de Penas to Tierra del Fuego, southwestern Patagonia is one of the planet's most thinly peopled, least visited areas. Its pre-Columbian inhabitants were "Canoe Indians," a term applied to the Yámana and Kawéskar peoples, who used precarious vessels to hunt seals and gather shellfish. Never numerous, they prospered on local resources until catastrophic contact with Europeans—first violence and then disease—nearly obliterated them.

Today, ironically enough, it's possible to explore the dramatically scenic channels and icy fjords of the Kawéskar, also known as the Alacaluf, on a comfortable cruiser. Long known for its voyages from Puerto Montt to Laguna San Rafael, the Skorpios line has incorporated the glacial fjords between Puerto Natales and Puerto Edén into a **Ruta Kawéskar** itinerary that pays symbolic homage, at least, to the last sad survivors.

The *Skorpios III* normally sails late Saturday from the company jetty, four kilometers north of Puerto Natales. At the beginning, it follows Navimag's northbound ferry route as far as Isla Chatham, where it veers east to enter **Parque Nacional Bernardo O'Higgins** and anchor briefly at the fishing camp of **Caleta Villarrica.** It then enters **Fiordo Amalia,** where **Glaciar Amalia**'s floating tongue protrudes from the southern continental ice field, almost directly opposite Torres del Paine. Here passengers transfer onto double-hull, flat-bottomed vessels that are really mini-icebreakers, slicing through pack ice to approach the glacier's face (flat roofs keep off the rain and snow, except when wind makes the rain horizontal). Passengers can also catch a glimpse of South America's longest glacier, **Glaciar Pío XI,** a staggering 62 kilometers in length and 6 kilometers wide.

access points. The **Balmaceda Glacier** at the Río Serrano's outlet is one of them. From Puerto Natales, the closest approach is a four-hour sail northwest, past Puerto Bories, several wool ranches accessible only by sea, and nesting colonies of seabirds and breeding colonies of southern sea lions, while Andean condors glide above U-shaped valleys with glaciers and waterfalls. This route is where Juan Ladrilleros and Pedro de Sarmiento de Gamboa ended their futile quests for a sheltered entrance to the Pacific.

At the end, passengers disembark for an hour or so at **Puerto Toro,** where a half-hour walk through southern beech forest leads to the fast-receding Glaciar Balmaceda. Visitors remain for about an hour before returning to Natales, unless they take advantage of the option to travel upriver to Torres del Paine, weather permitting. Torres del Paine is visible in the distance.

Another option for visiting remote parts of the park, in comfort, is the five-day, four-night *Skorpios* cruise on the so-called Ruta Kawéskar.

Food and Accommodations

The park proper lacks formal accommodations. Across the sound from Puerto Toro, though, in virtually the most peaceful location imaginable—but for the wind—is **Hostería Monte Balmaceda** (c/o Turismo 21 de Mayo, Eberhard 560, Puerto Natales, tel. 061/241-1978, www.turismo-21demayo.com, US$180 s, US$210 d with breakfast, US$35 extra per meal for lunch and dinner).

As it's mostly accessible by sea, a stay here is usually part of a package that includes a visit to Balmaceda or Torres del Paine. There is, however, a footpath suitable for a two-day trek to or from Paine.

Transportation

Natales operators sail up the sound to the Balmaceda Glacier, usually daily in summer, less frequently the rest of the year. Bad weather and high winds may cause cancellations at any time of year.

The traditional operator is **Turismo 21**

From Amalia, the *Skorpios III* sails north to **Fiordo Calvo,** a site of magnificent hanging glaciers, a sea lion colony, and a rock cormorant colony. Unfortunately, when the icebreakers' noisy diesels approach too closely, the lions and their pups scramble over the rocks and into the sea.

Retracing its route and then sailing south, the ship eventually enters the **Fiordo de la Montaña,** a sheer-sided canyon between the Cordillera Sarmiento and Cordillera Riesco, just west of Puerto Natales. Also reachable by day trips from Natales, it includes the cruise's only other shore-based stop: a hike to the relatively small **Glaciar Bernal.** The last night, which includes a dinner-dance, is spent en route to and at anchor in Natales, where guests spend the night aboard ship.

Accommodating only 110 passengers in 48 cabins, *Skorpios III* is small for a cruise ship. Decorated with handsome wood veneer, with view windows rather than portholes, the cabins also have excellent baths and showers. The food and wine are excellent, and the service personalized.

The Kochifas family, Greek-Chilean shipbuilders based in Puerto Montt, have pioneered an appealing itinerary. What the Ruta Kawéskar trip lacks is information. The guides' main task seems to be pointing out photo opportunities. The *Skorpios III* would benefit from presentations on history, environment, and ecology. Instead, it's "eat well, sip your *pisco* sours, and snap your shutter."

The *Skorpios III* sails Tuesday and Friday early September to late April on four-day, three-night voyages. High-season is mid-December to late February. Fares range US$1,690-2,775 pp, depending on the season and level of accommodations. For more detail, contact **Cruceros Skorpios** (Augusto Leguía Norte 118, Las Condes, Santiago, tel. 02/2477-1900, www.skorpios.cl).

de Mayo (Eberhard 560, tel. 061/241-1978, www.turismo21demayo.com, US$125 pp), which sails its eponymous cutter or the yacht *Alberto de Agostini* from a new pier at Puerto Bories. On the return, the boat stops for lunch at Estancia Los Perales.

Agunsa Patagonia (Blanco Encalada 244, tel. 061/241-5940, www.agunsapatagonia.cl, US$90 pp without lunch, US$125 pp with lunch) provides competition with newer catamarans that cover the route faster, in greater comfort, with decent food on board, and a barbecue on the return.

PUERTO EDÉN AND VICINITY

Thanks to nearly incessant rains, **Puerto Edén** is as verdant as Adam and Eve's biblical garden, but red-tide conditions have placed the shellfish livelihood of the remaining handful of Kawéskar people at risk. Their only other income sources are government handouts and some crude crafts—tiny carved canoes and shells, for instance. Alcoholism is sadly common.

"Vicinity" is a relative term with respect to this last Kawéskar outpost (pop. 300), which is some 400 kilometers northwest of Puerto Natales. It is on the weekly Navimag ferry route to and from Puerto Montt and also private yachts, which can explore the ice fields of the Campo de Hielo Sur, in Parque Nacional Bernardo O'Higgins, from the west.

Along the shore, the subsidized Proyecto Yekchal built a now weathering boardwalk over soggy terrain to an overlook where, on clear days, the view is magnificent. There's also a replica of a traditional Kawéskar dwelling, but nobody lives in these anymore.

CERRO CASTILLO AND VICINITY

North of Natales, one of Chile's most thinly populated municipalities, the *comuna* (political subdivision) of Torres del Paine has only a few hundred inhabitants. More than half reside in the hamlet of **Cerro Castillo,** 60 kilometers north of Puerto Natales on Ruta

9, alongside the Río Don Guillermo border crossing. Called Cancha Carrera on the Argentine side, this is the most direct route from Parque Nacional Torres del Paine to El Calafate (Argentina) and Parque Nacional Los Glaciares. Previously seasonal, it's now open year-round, but it has no scheduled public transportation.

Formerly an *estancia* of the powerful Sociedad Explotadora de Tierra del Fuego, Cerro Castillo has an assortment of services, including decent cafés, a dismal museum at the municipal **Departamento de Turismo** (Av. Bernardo O'Higgins s/n, tel. 061/269-1932, oficinaturismo@torresdelpayne.cl), and the only gas station north of Puerto Natales (if continuing to Argentina, fill up there; gasoline is notably cheaper on the Argentine side, diesel less so).

En route to and at Cerro Castillo, **Hotel Tres Pasos** (Ruta 9, Km 283 Norte, tel. 09/9644-5862, www.hotel3pasos.cl, US$167 s or d) is a contemporary roadside inn that's above average for the area. It also has a restaurant (US$17) serving lunch and dinner.

On what is still a working sheep ranch on Estancia Cerro Guido, about midway between Cerro Castillo and Torres del Paine, **Estancia Cerro Guido** (tel. 09/6588-1314, www.cerroguido.cl, US$350-400 s or d) has rehabbed and modernized its historical *casco* and another structure into attractive guesthouses with 16 total rooms. About 12 kilometers north of the road that leads to the park's Laguna Amarga entrance, Cerro Guido gets less traffic than Paine's accommodations, but its facilities are equal or better than most of them. There's also a restaurant-bar whose wines come from the owners' own Matetic family vineyards near Valparaíso. Rates include breakfast, while lunch or dinner costs extra. Activities include horseback riding (multiple-day excursions are possible), hiking, and observing farm activities such as summer shearing.

Parque Nacional Torres del Paine

Some years ago, when a major Pacific Coast shipping company bought a two-page spread in Alaska Airlines' in-flight magazine, the landscape chosen to represent Alaska's grandeur was . . . Torres del Paine! A photo editor may have made the error as, fittingly enough for a southern hemisphere destination, the image was reversed. Nevertheless, the granite spires of Chile's premier national park have truly become an international emblem of alpine majesty.

But there's more. Unlike many South American parks, Torres del Paine has an integrated network of hiking trails suitable for day trips and backpacking treks, endangered species such as the wild guanaco in a UNESCO-recognized World Biosphere Reserve, and accommodations options from rustic campgrounds to cozy trail huts and five-star luxury hotels. It's so popular that some visitors prefer the shoulder seasons of spring (Nov.-Dec.) or fall (Mar.-Apr.). The park receives over 210,000 visitors annually, more than half of them foreigners. While Paine has become a major international destination, it's still wild country.

Almost everybody visits the park to behold extraordinary natural features such as the **Torres del Paine,** the sheer granite towers that defy erosion even as the weaker sedimentary strata around them have weathered, and the jagged **Cuernos del Paine,** with their striking interface between igneous and metamorphic rocks. Most hike its trails uneventfully, but for all its popularity, this can still be treacherous terrain. Hikers have disappeared, the rivers run fast and cold, the weather is unpredictable, and there is one documented case of a visitor killed by a puma.

Parque Nacional Torres del Paine

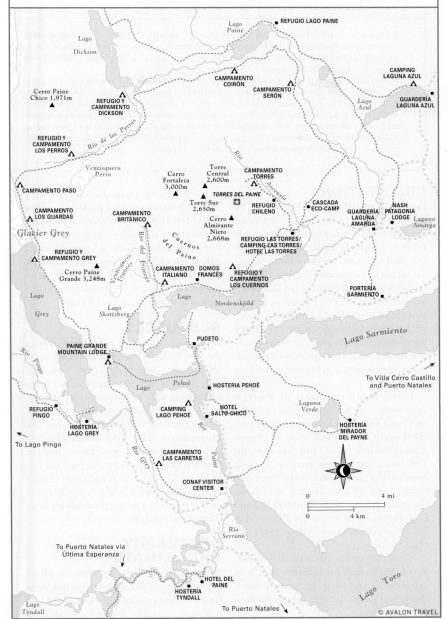

REFUGIO LAGO PAINE

Lago Paine

Lago Dickson

CAMPING LAGUNA AZUL

CAMPAMENTO COIRÓN

CAMPAMENTO SERÓN

Cerro Paine Chico 1,971m

REFUGIO Y CAMPAMENTO DICKSON

Lago Azul

GUARDERÍA LAGUNA AZUL

REFUGIO Y CAMPAMENTO LOS PERROS

Río de los Perros

Ventisquero Perro

Torre Central 2,600m

CAMPAMENTO TORRES

Río

Cerro Fortaleza 3,000m

CAMPAMENTO PASO

CAMPAMENTO LOS GUARDAS

CAMPAMENTO BRITÁNICO

TORRES DEL PAINE

Torre Sur 2,650m

REFUGIO CHILENO

Ascensio

CASCADA ECO-CAMP

NASH PATAGONIA LODGE

Laguna Amarga

GUARDERÍA LAGUNA AMARGA

Cerro Almirante Nieto 2,668m

REFUGIO LAS TORRES/ CAMPING LAS TORRES/ HOTEL LAS TORRES

Glacier Grey

Cuernos del Paine

REFUGIO Y CAMPAMENTO GREY

Cerro Paine Grande 3,248m

Río del Francés

CAMPAMENTO ITALIANO

DOMOS FRANCÉS

REFUGIO Y CAMPAMENTO LOS CUERNOS

PORTERÍA SARMIENTO

Ventisquero Francés

Lago Grey

Lago Skottsberg

Lago Nordenskjöld

Lago Sarmiento

PUDETO

PAINE GRANDE MOUNTAIN LODGE

Río Pingo

Lago Pehoé

To Villa Cerro Castillo and Puerto Natales

HOSTERÍA PEHOÉ

REFUGIO PINGO

CAMPING LAGO PEHOÉ

HOTEL SALTO CHICO

Laguna Verde

HOSTERÍA LAGO GREY

HOSTERÍA MIRADOR DEL PAYNE

To Lago Pingo

Río Grey

CAMPAMENTO LAS CARRETAS

Río Paine

CONAF VISITOR CENTER

0   4 mi

0   4 km

To Puerto Natales via Última Esperanza

Río Serrano

Lago Toro

HOTEL DEL PAINE

HOSTERÍA TYNDALL

Lago Tyndall

To Puerto Natales

© AVALON TRAVEL

The Torres del Fuego: Wildfires in the National Park

In 2005, in an incident that will have consequences for decades, a careless camper overturned his camp stove, starting a fire that burned for nearly a month in Parque Nacional Torres del Paine. The conflagration scorched 15,470 hectares of native vegetation, including forest, scrubland, and steppe, in the park's popular northeastern sector.

Most of the burned area consisted of steppe grasses and shrubs that are recovering nicely, but the 2,400 hectares of slow-growing southern beech forest are more problematic. West of the Río Paine and the Lago Paine road, Conaf is placing priority on restoring 800 hectares of *lenga* and *ñire*. In 2006, at a cost of about US$1,700 per hectare, the government forestry agency collected seeds and built several greenhouses to nurture seedlings for transplanting to the burned area; 100,000 seedlings remain fenced off to prevent humans trampling them and guanacos from eating them. Some parts of the park may still be off-limits to hikers.

ORIENTATION

Parque Nacional Torres del Paine is 112 kilometers northwest of Puerto Natales via Ruta 9 through Cerro Castillo. Thirty-eight kilometers beyond Castillo, a westbound lateral road traces the southern shore of Lago Sarmiento de Gamboa to the park's isolated **Laguna Verde sector.** Three kilometers beyond the Laguna Verde junction, another westbound lateral road leaves Ruta 9 to follow Lago Sarmiento's north shore to **Portería Sarmiento,** the main gate; it continues southwest for 37 kilometers to the Administración, the park headquarters at the west end of Lago del Toro.

Twelve kilometers east of Portería Sarmiento, another lateral road branches northwest and, three kilometers farther on, splits again. The former leads to Laguna Azul, in the little-visited **northern sector.** The latter enters the park at Laguna Amarga, the most common starting point for the popular **Paine Circuit,** and follows the south shore of Lago Nordenskjöld and Lago Pehoé on the way to the visitors center. Most public transportation takes this route.

A bridge over the Río Serrano now permits access to park headquarters via Cueva del Milodón and Lago del Toro's western shore, but this has not affected regular public transportation.

For foreigners, Torres del Paine is Chile's most expensive national park—the **entry fee** is US$31 per person October to April, US$16 May to September. Rangers at Portería Lago Sarmiento, Guardería Laguna Amarga (where most inbound buses stop), Guardería Lago Verde, or Guardería Laguna Azul collect the fee, issue receipts, and provide a 1:100,000 park map that is useful for trekking.

RESOURCES

In English, the best available trekking guide is Rudolf Abraham's *Torres del Paine* (Milnthrope, Cumbria, UK, 2010; www.cicerone.co.uk), which has fine full-color maps and photographs to accompany a thorough text. Climbers should look for Alan Kearney's *Mountaineering in Patagonia* (Seattle: The Mountaineers, 1998), which includes both historical and practical information on climbing here and in Argentina's Parque Nacional Los Glaciares. Gladys Garay N. and Oscar Guineo N. have collaborated in *The Fauna of Torres del Paine* (1993), a locally produced guide to the park's animal life.

GEOGRAPHY AND CLIMATE

Parque Nacional Torres del Paine comprises 181,414 hectares of Patagonian steppe, lowland and alpine glacial lakes, glacier-fed torrents and waterfalls, forested uplands, and nearly vertical granite needles. Elevations range from 50 meters above sea level along the lower Río Serrano to 3,050 meters atop Paine Grande, the central massif's tallest peak.

Paine has a cool temperate climate with frequent high winds, especially in spring and summer. The average summer temperature is about 11°C, with highs reaching around 23°C, while the average winter minimum is around freezing. Averages are misleading, though, as the weather is changeable. The park lies in the rain shadow of the Campo de Hielo Sur, where westerly storms drop most of their moisture as snow, so it receives only about 600 millimeters of rainfall per year. Still, snow and hail can fall even in midsummer. Spring is the windiest season; in autumn—March and April—winds tend to moderate, but days are shorter.

It should go without saying that at higher elevations temperatures are cooler and snow likelier to fall. In some areas it's possible to hut-hop between *refugios* (shelters), eliminating the need for a tent and sleeping bag but not for warm clothing and impermeable rain gear.

FLORA AND FAUNA

Less diverse than in areas farther north, Paine's vegetation still varies with elevation and distance from the Andes. Bunch grasses of the genera *Festuca* and *Stipa,* known collectively as *coirón,* cover the arid southeastern steppes, often interspersed with thorny shrubs such as *calafate (Berberis buxifolia),* which produces edible fruit, and *neneo.* There are also ground-hugging *Calceolaria* orchids, such as the *zapatito* and *capachito.*

Approaching the Andes, deciduous forests of southern beech *(Nothofagus)* species such as *lenga* blanket the hillsides, along with the related evergreen *coigüe de Magallanes* and the deciduous *ñire.* At the highest elevations, little vegetation of any kind grows among alpine fell fields.

Paine's most conspicuous mammal is the llama-relative guanaco, whose numbers—and tameness—have increased dramatically. Many of its young, known as *chulengos,* fall prey to the puma. A more common predator, or at least a more visible one, is the gray fox, which feeds on the introduced European hare and, beyond park boundaries, sheep. The endangered *huemul* (Andean deer) is a rare sight.

The monarch of South American birds, of course, is the Andean condor, not a rare sight here. Filtering the lake shallows for plankton, the Chilean flamingo summers here after breeding in the northern altiplano.

Torres del Paine

The *caiquén* (upland goose) grazes the moist grasslands around the lakes, while the black-necked swan paddles peacefully on the surface. The flightless *ñandú* (rhea) scampers over the steppes.

★ TORRES DEL PAINE

Some of the Andes's youngest peaks, the **Torres del Paine** are among the range's most emblematic sights. Some 10 million years ago, a magma intrusion failed to reach the earth's surface, cooling underground into resistant granite. In the interim, water, ice, and snow have eroded softer terrain to liberate the spires as one of the world's most dramatic landscapes.

So strong a draw are the Torres that some visitors pressed for time settle for day tours that allow only a few hours in the park. Others walk to their base from Hostería Las Torres, a relatively simple day hike where it's hard to avoid the crowds. A longer and more tiring alternative, up the steep Río Bader canyon, provides a different perspective and the Andean solitude that many hikers seek.

★ CUERNOS DEL PAINE

Many park visitors misidentify the **Cuernos del Paine** (Horns of Paine) as the Torres. Located almost immediately south of the

Torres proper, the saw-toothed Cuernos retain a cap of darker but softer metamorphic rock atop a broader granitic batholith that, like the Torres, never reached the surface before cooling. It's the contrast between the two that gives the Cuernos their striking aspect.

As with the Torres, day-trippers can admire the Cuernos from the park highway. The best views, though, come from the "W" trail along the north shore of Lago Nordenskjöld, between Hostería Las Torres and Lago Pehoé.

HIKING
Paine Circuit

Nearly three decades ago, under a military dictatorship, Chile attracted few foreign visitors, and hiking Torres del Paine was a solitary experience. On a 10-day trek over the now-famous **Paine Circuit,** this author met only three other hikers. Parts of the route were easy to follow, while others were barely boot-wide tracks on steep slopes, or involved scrambling over granite boulders and fording waist-deep glacial meltwater.

Today, much has changed. At peak season, hikers are so numerous that the route can approach gridlock (hyperbole intentional). Rudimentary and not-so-rudimentary

the Cuernos del Paine

bridges make water crossings easier. In addition to the lean-tos that once sheltered shepherds, there are enough comfortable *refugios* (shelters) and organized campgrounds that it's theoretically possible to complete most of the circuit without a tent or even a sleeping bag. Still, hikers must remember that this is rugged country with unpredictable weather and come well-prepared.

Most hikers tackle the circuit counterclockwise from Guardería Laguna Amarga, where buses from Puerto Natales stop for passengers to pay the park admission fee. An alternative is to continue to Pudeto and take a passenger launch to Refugio Pehoé, or else to the park's Administración (involving a longer and less interesting approach). Both of these mean doing the trek clockwise.

A trail along Lago Nordenskjöld's north shore provides access to the Torres's south side, offering easier access up the Río Ascencio and Valle del Francés on the shorter "W" route to Lago Pehoé. The circuit follows the river's west bank south to Laguna Amarga. (A Laguna Azul, exit or entrance is feasible as well by crossing the Río Paine by a cable raft at the river's Lago Dickson outlet, with help from the staff at Refugio Dickson.)

The full circuit takes at least a week to complete. Before beginning, hikers must register with park rangers. Camping is permitted only at designated sites, a few of which are free. Purchase supplies in Puerto Natales, as only limited goods are available within the park, at premium prices.

FOOD AND ACCOMMODATIONS

For counterclockwise hikers beginning at Laguna Amarga, there is no *refugio* (shelter) until Lago Dickson (roughly 11 hours), though there is a fee campground at **Campamento Serón** (4-5 hours, US$14 pp).

All the park's *refugios* are presently under concession to **Vértice Patagonia** (Ladrilleros 209, tel. 061/241-2742, Puerto Natales, www.verticepatagonia.cl), including **Refugio Lago Grey** and **Refugio Lago**

Dickson, where there are also campgrounds and backpackers still crash at the rustic *puesto,* plus the **Campamento Río de los Perros** (US$7.50 pp).

Both *refugios* (US$30 pp) resemble each other, with 32 bunks with kitchen privileges and hot showers, but without sheets or sleeping bags. Bedding is technically available for rental but is sometimes scarce. Meals (breakfast US$12, lunch US$15, dinner US$20) are available separately, or you can rent a bunk with meals included (US$70 pp). Campers pay US$7.50 each (*refugio* guests have shower priority). Rental tents, sleeping bags, mats, and camp stoves are also available.

Replacing the cramped and overcrowded Refugio Lago Pehoé, the **Paine Grande Mountain Lodge** (tel. 061/241-2742 in Natales, US$48-70 pp, without breakfast) is now open year-round. Meals (breakfast US$12, lunch US$15, dinner US$20) are available separately, but three-meal packages (US$40 pp) mean a small savings. Camping costs US$9 pp (US$42 more with three meals), with rental tents, pads, and sleeping bags available. There's also phone and even expensive Internet access.

The "W" Variant

From Guardería Laguna Amarga, a narrow undulating road crosses the Río Paine on a narrow suspension bridge to the grounds of **Estancia Cerro Paine**, at the foot of 2,640-meter Monte Almirante Nieto. The *estancia* operates a hotel, *refugios* (shelters), and campgrounds, and the staff also shuttles hikers back and forth from Laguna Amarga (US$5.50 pp).

From Estancia Cerro Paine, a northbound trail parallels the route from Guardería Laguna Amarga, eventually meeting it just south of Campamento Serón. The *estancia* is more notable, though, as the starting point for the **"W" route** to Lago Pehoé, a scenic and challenging option for hikers lacking time for the full circuit. On the western edge of the grounds, the footbridge crosses the Río Ascencio to a junction where a northbound lateral trail climbs the river canyon to Campamento Torres, where a short but steep trail ascends to a nameless glacial tarn at the foot of the Torres proper. Weather permitting, this is a recommended day hike from the *estancia,* though many people prefer to camp or spend the night at the *refugio.*

From the junction, the main trail follows Lago Nordenskjöld's north shore, past another *refugio* and campground, to the free Campamento Italiano at the base of the **Río del Francés** valley. While the main trail continues west toward Lago Pehoé, another northbound lateral trail climbs steeply up the valley, between the striking metamorphic Cuernos del Paine to the east and the 3,050-meter granite summit of Paine Grande to the west, to the free Campamento Británico.

Hikers in search of peace and quiet can make a strenuous detour up the **Valle Bader,** a steep rugged river valley that's home to a climber's camp at the Cuernos' base. The route is mostly unmarked, but experienced cross-country walkers can handle it.

FOOD AND ACCOMMODATIONS

Technically outside park boundaries, most of the "W" route belongs to **Fantástico Sur** (Esmeralda 661, Puerto Natales, tel. 061/261-4184, www.fslodges.com), which runs the 96-bunk **Refugio Las Torres Norte** and the new, nearby **Refugio Las Torres Central** on the *estancia*'s main grounds; the 36-bunk **Refugio Chileno** in the upper Río Ascencio Valley; the 24-bunk **Domos El Francés;** and the 28-bunk **Refugio Los Cuernos,** all of which also have campgrounds.

Bunks at Fantástico Sur *refugios* cost US$61-95 pp, US$103-119 pp with three meals. Camping costs US$7-11 pp with hot showers. Refugio Los Cuernos also has two-person cabañas (US$155 d with breakfast and hot tub; US$203 s, US$251 d, with 3 meals), and has added nearby domes (US$55 pp, US$103 pp with 3 meals).

Meals (breakfast US$15, lunch US$21, dinner US$28, full-meal package US$64) are available separately. Rental tents, sleeping bags, mats, and stoves are also available.

Other Trails

After heavy runoff destroyed the once-sturdy bridge at Lago Paine's outlet in the early 1980s, the Río Paine's north shore became isolated from the rest of the park. A good road, though, still leads from Guardería Laguna Amarga to Laguna Azul's east end, which has a campground and cabañas, as well as the **Sendero Lago Paine,** a four-hour walk to the lake and a simple *refugio* (shelter). A trekkers' alternative is the **Sendero Desembocadura,** which leads north from Guardería Laguna Amarga through open country to Laguna Azul's west end and continues to Lago Paine, but this takes about eight hours. From the north shore of Lago Paine, the **Sendero Lago Dickson** (5.5 hours) leads to the Dickson Glacier.

Several easy day hikes are possible near Guardería Lago Pehoé, directly on the road from Laguna Amarga to the visitors center. The short **Sendero Salto Grande** trail leads to the thunderous waterfall, at Lago Sarmiento's outlet, that was the circuit's starting point until unprecedented runoff swept away the iron bridge to Península Pehoé in 1986. From Salto Grande, the **Sendero Mirador Nordenskjöld** is a slightly longer but still easy walk to a lakeshore vista point, directly opposite the stunning Cuernos del Paine.

From Guardería Lago Grey, 18 kilometers northwest of the visitors center by road, a short footpath leads to a sandy beach on Lago Grey's south shore, where steady westerlies often beach icebergs from Glaciar Grey. The longer and less visited **Sendero Lago Pingo** ascends the Río Pingo Valley to its namesake lake (5.5-6 hours). A basic *refugio* and two free campgrounds are along the route.

CLIMBING

Though popular, hiking is not the only recreational option. Despite similar terrain, Paine attracts fewer climbers than Argentina's neighboring Parque Nacional Los Glaciares, perhaps because fees for climbing permits have been high here. At present, permits are free of charge; before being granted permission, climbers must present Conaf with climbing résumés, emergency contacts, and authorization from their consulate.

When climbing in sensitive border areas (meaning most of Andean Chile), climbers must also have permission from the Dirección de Fronteras y Límites (Difrol, www.difrol.cl) in Santiago. It's possible to do this through a Chilean consulate overseas or at Difrol's Santiago offices or, preferably, online. If you arrive in Puerto Natales without permission, it's possible to request it through the **Gobernación Provincial** (tel. 061/241-1423), the regional government offices on the south side of Plaza Arturo Prat. The turnaround time is 48 hours.

While climbing and mountaineering activities may be undertaken independently, local concessionaires can provide training and lead groups or individuals with less experience on snow and ice. **Big Foot Adventure Patagonia** (tel. 061/241-4611 in Natales, www.bigfootpatagonia.com) has a Refugio Grey base camp, where it leads half-day traverses of Glaciar Grey's west side (US$140) and 2.5-hour kayak excursions (US$90). It also operates guided three-day, two-night descents of the Río Serrano (US$795-1,090 pp, depending on group size). Except for weatherproof clothing, the company provides all equipment.

FOOD AND ACCOMMODATIONS

Park accommodations range from free trailside campgrounds to first-rate luxury hotels with just about everything in between. In summer, reservations are almost obligatory at hotels and advisable at campgrounds and *refugios* (shelters).

Camping

At Estancia Cerro Paine, **Camping Las Torres** (US$11 pp, US$59 pp with all meals) draws hikers heading up the Río Ascencio Valley to the Paine overlook or west on the "W" route to Lago Pehoé, or hikers finishing up the circuit here. Formerly insufficient shower and restroom facilities have improved.

On a bluff above Refugio Las Torres, the **Cascada EcoCamp** (www.ecocamp.travel) is a geodesic dome-tent facility designed for minimum-impact accommodations. It's generally available through package deals only but, occasionally, there's availability on a nightly basis. On raised platforms, each tent is five meters wide, with wooden floors and two single beds with towels and bedding, including down comforters. Two larger domes contain a common living area, dining rooms, and a kitchen. The separate baths have hot showers and composting toilets (from some domes, it's a long walk for middle-of-the-night toilet visits).

Electricity comes from solar collectors, windmills, and a small hydroelectric turbine. Cascada's organized tour clients have priority, but its half-dozen luxury "Dome Suites" (with woodstoves, king beds, private baths and showers, and exterior decks with views of the Torres) are available to private parties on a space-available basis. Contact them through the website or, alternatively, through their Puerto Natales office (Barros Arana 166, tel. 061/241-4442).

On the small peninsula on its namesake lake's eastern shore, just west of the road to the Administración, sites at concessionaire-run **Camping Lago Pehoé** (tel. 02/1962-0377, www.campingpehoe.com, US$15 pp) hold up to six people. Fees include firewood and hot showers. About six kilometers south of park headquarters, **Camping Río Serrano** (tel. 02/1962-0447, rio.serrano@cajalosandes.cl, US$12 pp) has undertaken considerable improvements, including cooking shelters at each site.

Hosterías, Hotels, and Lodges

At the Laguna Amarga entrance to the park, **Nash Patagonia Lodge** (tel. 061/241-4276 in Puerto Natales, www.nashpatagonia.com, US$120 pp with breakfast and dinner) is a frills-free seven-bedroom lodge with four bunks per room and shared baths; sleeping bags are the default choice here, and available for rent at US$7 each. Bring your own towel; shower times are 7am-9am and 7pm-9pm only.

Reachable by road along Lago Sarmiento's south shore or by foot or horseback from the Río Paine, well-regarded **Mirador del Payne Lodge** (tel. 09/9640-2490, www.miradordel-payne.cl, US$200 s, US$245 d) lies in the isolated southeastern Laguna Verde sector.

Where Lago Grey becomes the Río Grey, the 60-room **Hotel Lago Grey** (US$290-358 s, US$344-399 d, with breakfast) hosts visitors to the park's lesser-visited western sector; its restaurant is open to nonguests. The higher prices correspond to more contemporary lake-view rooms. For reservations, contact **Turismo Lago Grey** (tel. 061/271-2100, www.lagogrey.cl).

The park's oldest hotel, on a five-hectare island linked to the mainland by a footbridge, the 40-room **Hostería Pehoé** (US$165-195 s, US$185-240 d) has improved since the operator began to reinvest in what had been a run-down facility with substandard service in an undeniably spectacular setting. For reservations, contact **Turismo Pehoé** (José Menéndez 647-A, Punta Arenas, tel. 061/272-2853, www.hosteriapehoe.cl).

At Estancia Cerro Paine, seven kilometers west of Guardería Laguna Amarga, the sprawling but well-run ★ **Hotel Las Torres** (Sarmiento 846, Punta Arenas, tel. 061/236-0360, www.lastorres.com, US$357-422 s or d) is a gem for its setting beneath Monte Almirante Nieto, its professionalism, a spa offering saunas and massages, and even Wi-Fi access (expensive because of a costly satellite link). While it's an elite option that's leaning toward all-inclusive packages, it's conscientiously eco-friendly in terms of waste disposal, and management is constantly seeking feedback. Off-season hotel rates fall by about half. Open to both guests and nonguests, the restaurant prepares quality food in cruise-ship quantities.

Open for packages only, ★ **Hotel Salto Chico** (from US$7,984 s or d for 4 nights in the least expensive room; US$13,440 s or d for

Hotel Las Torres is the starting point for hikes into the backcountry.

8 nights in the costliest suite) is a mega-luxury resort that somehow manages to blend inconspicuously into the landscape while providing some of the globe's grandest views. Rates include transfer to and from Punta Arenas and unlimited excursions. Low-season rates are about 20 percent cheaper. For details and reservations, contact **Explora Hotels** (Américo Vespucio Sur 80, 5th Fl., Las Condes, Santiago, tel. 02/2395-2800, www.explora.com).

At the east end of Lago Sarmiento, with panoramic views of the towers near the park's Laguna Amarga entrance, **Tierra Patagonia Hotel & Spa** (tel. 02/2207-8861 in Santiago, U.S. tel. 800/829-3325, www.tierrahotels.com, from US$2,540 s, US$3,465 d for 3 nights) is an all-inclusive spa resort with extensive excursions, including hiking and horseback riding, with transfers.

Just beyond the park's eastern boundary, **Awasi Patagonia** (Tercera Barranca, Torres del Paine, tel. 02/2233-9641 in Santiago, U.S. tel. 800/880-3219, www.awasipatagonia.com, from US$5,055 s, US$6,740 d for 3 nights) is an all-inclusive resort modeled on the company's predecessor in San Pedro de Atacama (though its architecture differs dramatically). Packages include all meals and all excursions with individualized guide service for three nights in its hillside lodge and villas, all of which have views of the Torres and Lago Sarmiento. Programs up to six nights are possible.

Just beyond park boundaries, reached by launch over the Río Serrano, the stylish **Hotel Lago Tyndall** (tel. 061/261-4682, www.hotel-tyndall.cl, US$160-180 s, US$230 s or d) enjoys peace, quiet, and magnificent views. Nearby is the rather less stylish **Hotel del Paine** (tel. 061/272-3303, www.hoteldelpaine.com, US$200-250 s or d).

INFORMATION

Conaf's principal facility is its **Centro de Informaciones Ecológicas** (tel. 061/269-1931, www.parquetorresdelpaine.cl, 8am-8pm or later daily summer, 8am-6pm daily fall-spring), at the Administración building on the shores of Lago del Toro near the Río Paine outlet, with good natural-history exhibits. The private Hostería Las Torres (Estancia Cerro Paine) has an excellent audiovisual salon with sophisticated environmental exhibits.

Ranger stations at Guardería Laguna Amarga, Portería Lago Sarmiento, Guardería Laguna Azul, Guardería Lago Verde, and Guardería Lago Grey can also provide information.

TRANSPORTATION

Most people find the bus the cheapest and quickest way to and from the park. The route up Seno Última Esperanza and the Río Serrano by cutter and Zodiac is a viable, more interesting alternative. Tour companies from Puerto Natales usually enter the park at Laguna Amarga and loop back on the new road. Regular bus services continue to use the old highway.

Bus

Natales bus companies enter the park at Guardería Laguna Amarga, where many hikers begin the Paine Circuit, before continuing to the Administración at Río Serrano and then returning by the same route. Round-trips are slightly cheaper, but companies do not accept each other's tickets.

Buses to and from Puerto Natales will also carry passengers along the main park road, but as their schedules are similar, there are extended daily periods with no public transportation. Hitching is common, but competition is heavy and most vehicles are full with families. There is a regular shuttle between Guardería Laguna Amarga and Estancia Cerro Paine (Hostería Las Torres, US$5.50 pp) that meets arriving and departing buses.

River

Transportation up and down the Río Serrano by a combination of catamaran and Zodiac, between the park and Puerto Natales, has become an interesting if more expensive alternative to the bus. Visitors who only want to see this sector of the river, without continuing to Puerto Natales, can do so as a Zodiac trip to Puerto Toro and back.

The traditional operator is **Turismo 21 de Mayo** (Eberhard 560, Puerto Natales, tel. 061/241-1978, www.turismo21demayo.com, US$160 pp), which sails its eponymous cutter or one of the motor yachts *Alberto de Agostini* or *Joaquín Álvarez* from a new pier at Puerto Bories to Puerto Toro and the Balmaceda Glacier, and then continues upstream by Zodiac.

October to April, reliable transportation is available from Pudeto to Refugio Pehoé (30 minutes, US$27 one-way, US$41 round-trip) with the catamaran *Hielos Patagónicos* (Avenida España 1455, 2nd Fl., Puerto Natales, tel. 061/241-1133, www.hielospatagonicos.com). In October and in April, there is one departure at noon daily from Pudeto, returning at 12:30pm. The first two weeks of November and the last two weeks of March, there's an additional service at 6pm daily, returning at 6:30pm. From mid-November to mid-March, there are departures at 9:30am, noon, and

6pm daily, returning at 10am, 12:30pm, and 6:30pm. Schedules may be postponed or canceled due to bad weather, and there are no services on Christmas Day and New Year's Day. Also mid-November to mid-March, the catamaran *Grey II* goes daily from Hotel Lago Grey to Glaciar Grey (one-way US$90 adults, US$45 ages 5-12, round-trip US$105, US$53 ages 5-12) at 8am, noon, 3pm, and 6:15pm daily.

Chilean Tierra del Fuego

Across the Strait from Punta Arenas, thinly populated Chilean Tierra del Fuego has only one major settlement, the town of Porvenir, on its northerly steppes. To the south, its rugged alpine terrain is a westward extension of the Argentine cordillera, with scenic fjords that few other landscapes can equal. Across the Beagle Channel, Isla Navarino's Puerto Williams, the world's southernmost permanent settlement, is part of an archipelagic maze that stretches south to the celebrated Cape Horn.

PORVENIR

Chilean Tierra del Fuego's main town, Porvenir, sits on a sheltered harbor on the Strait of Magellan's eastern shore. It dates from the 1880s, when the area experienced a brief gold rush, but stabilized with the establishment of wool *estancias* around the turn of the 20th century. After the wool boom fizzled in the 1920s, it settled into an economic torpor that left it a collection of corroding metal-clad Magellanic buildings. Construction of a salmon-processing plant has jump-started the local economy, and it's more presentable now.

Porvenir's inner harbor is ideal for spotting kelp geese, gulls, cormorants, steamer ducks, and other seabirds, but the lack of public transportation to the Argentine border has marginalized the tourist sector. All buses from the mainland to Argentine Tierra del Fuego take the longer Primera Angostura route, which offers a shorter and more frequent ferry crossing.

Only 30 nautical miles (56 kilometers) east of Punta Arenas, Porvenir (pop. 5,907) occupies a protected site at the east end of Bahía Porvenir, an inlet of the Strait of Magellan. Its port at Bahía Chilota is five kilometers west of the town site. Because the Sunday ferry to Punta Arenas sails late (at 5pm), it allows curious visitors to spend the day here rather than return immediately.

From Porvenir, Ruta 215 (a smooth gravel road) leads south and then east along the Bahía Inútil shoreline to the Argentine border at San Sebastián, 150 kilometers away. An alternative route leads directly east through the Cordón Baquedano before rejoining Ruta 215 about 55 kilometers to the east. If it's too late to catch the ferry back to Punta Arenas, another gravel road follows the coast to Puerto Espora, 141 kilometers northeast.

Sights

Directly on the water, **Parque Yugoslavo** memorializes the earliest gold-seeking immigrants, mostly Croatians. It's also one of Porvenir's best birding spots. The tourist office provides a small map-brochure, in English, of the city's architectural heritage; many of its houses and other buildings were also built by Croatians.

Most public buildings surround the neatly landscaped **Plaza de Armas,** two blocks north of Parque Yugoslavo. Nearby, the luminous **Museo de Tierra del Fuego Fernando Rusque Cordero** (Jorge Schythe 79, tel. 061/258-1800, 8am-5:30pm Mon.-Thurs., 9am-4pm Fri., 10:30am-1pm and 3pm-5pm Sat.-Sun. and holidays, US$1) deals with the island's natural history, indigenous heritage, the early gold rush, the later but longer-lasting wool rush, and even cinematography. German-born filmmaker José

Bohr went to Hollywood in 1929 and enjoyed a long if inconsistent career. It also features a skillfully produced replica of an early rural store and a good photographic display on local architecture.

Food and Accommodations

Other than hotel restaurants, the main dining options include the basic **Puerto Montt** (Croacia 1169, tel. 061/258-0207, lunch daily, dinner Mon.-Sat.) and the **Club Social Catef** (Zavattaro 94, tel. 061/258-1399, lunch daily, dinner Mon.-Sat.). On the waterfront, the slightly more formal **Club Social Croata** (Señoret 542, tel. 061/258-0053, lunch daily, dinner Mon.-Sat., US$14) serves good fish in ample portions. Try the conger eel in a king crab and scallop sauce.

There's no sign outside expanding **Hospedaje Shinká** (Santos Mardones 333, tel. 061/258-0491, US$22 s, US$41 d), but this still homey place offers better facilities and amenities for less money than any other place in town. Immaculate midsize rooms come with comfortable beds, private baths, and cable TV. The breakfast is forgettable, but that's a minor fault for a place this good.

All rooms have private baths at expanded **Hotel España** (Croacia 698, tel. 061/258-0160, www.hotelespana.cl, US$30 s, US$45 d), whose utilitarian addition masks large new rooms. In the older sector, some slightly smaller rooms are still adequate. It also has a restaurant.

In a restored Magellanic house with greater character than any other local lodging, **Yendegaia House** (Croacia 702, tel. 061/258-1919, www.yendegaiahouse.com, US$51 s, US$81 d) has spacious rooms in their original configuration, with high ceilings and contemporary comforts, including flat-screen TVs. It also displays an impressive local crafts selection, for sale, and a selection of books on the area.

At the north edge of town, Porvenir's newest option is the purpose-built **Hotel Barlovento** (John Williams 2, tel. 061/258-1000, www.hotelbarlovento.cl,

US$87 s, US$105 d), which has 16 rooms with all contemporary conveniences, plus an Italian restaurant with a diversity of pastas, and a bar.

Information and Services

In the same offices as the museum, Porvenir's attentive **Oficina Municipal de Turismo** (Padre Mario Zavattaro 434, tel. 061/258-1800, www.muniporvenir.cl, 10:30am-5pm Mon.-Thurs., 10:30am-4pm Fri., 10:30am-1pm and 3pm-5pm Sat.-Sun. and holidays) keeps the same hours as the museum.

BancoEstado (Philippi 263) has an ATM. **Correos de Chile** (Philippi 176) is at the southwest corner of the Plaza de Armas. There is free but erratic municipal Wi-Fi on and around the plaza. For medical services, try the **Hospital Dr. Marco Antonio Chamorro** (Carlos Wood 480, tel. 061/258-0034).

Transportation

Porvenir has regular but infrequent connections to the mainland but none to the San Sebastián border crossing into Argentina. Visitors with their own vehicles (including cyclists) will still find this a shorter route from Punta Arenas to Ushuaia.

Aerovías DAP (Manuel Señoret s/n and Muñoz Gamero, tel. 061/258-0089) operates air taxi service to Punta Arenas (15 minutes, US$38) at least daily, often more frequently.

There's a municipal bus from the DAP offices on Señoret to Camerón and Timaukel (6am and 4pm Tues., 6am and 4pm Fri., 3pm Sun., 2 hours, US$3) in the southwestern corner of the island. Another goes to **Cerro Sombrero** (5pm Mon., Wed., and Fri., 1.5 hours, US$4) from Zavattaro 432.

In the same building as DAP, **Transbordadora Broom** (Manuel Señoret s/n, tel. 061/258-0089) sails the comfortable car-passenger ferry *Pathagon* to Punta Arenas (2.5 hours, Tues.-Sun. US$10 adults, US$5.50 children, US$60 vehicle and driver, US$17 motorcycles), seas permitting. The ferry leaves from Bahía Chilota, about five kilometers west of town.

From Bahía Chilota, there are shared taxis or minivans to town (US$2 pp). A local bus (4pm Sun.) connects to the port from the Plaza de Armas.

VICINITY OF PORVENIR

"Vicinity" is a relative term on Tierra del Fuego, as some fascinating locales are difficult or expensive—or both—to reach. To reach the remote south-side fjords, the main option is the luxury cruises on the Cruceros Australis line.

Monumento Natural Laguna de los Cisnes

International birding groups often detour to this 25-hectare saline lake reserve, which sometimes dries out, just north of Porvenir. While **Monumento Natural Laguna de los Cisnes** takes its name from the elegant black-necked swan, it's home to many other species.

Cordón Baquedano

In 1879, after Chilean naval officer Ramón Serrano Montaner found gold in the rolling hills east of Porvenir, panners from Chile and Croatia flocked to the Río del Oro valley, between the **Cordón Baquedano** and the Sierra Boquerón. Living in sod huts that shielded them from the wind and cold, hoping to eke out a kilogram per year, more than 200 worked the placers until they gave out. By the turn of the century, California miners introduced dredges and steam shovels, but decreasing yields ended the rush by 1908-1909. A century later, though, a few hardy panners hang on.

From Porvenir, the eastbound road through the Cordón Baquedano passes several gold-rush sites, some marked with interpretive panels. The literal high point is the **Mirador de la Isla,** an overlook at 500 meters elevation. In many places, gua-nacos, which seem to outnumber sheep, gracefully vault meter-high fences that stop the sheep cold.

Onaisín

About 100 kilometers east of Porvenir, a major north-south road crosses Ruta 215 at Onaisín, a former Sociedad Explotadora *estancia* whose **Cementerio Inglés** is a national historical monument. It contains the graves of several 19th-century British colonists (despite the name, some of them were probably Scots). Northbound, the road goes to the petroleum company town of Cerro Sombrero, while southbound it goes to Camerón and Lago Blanco.

★ Parque Pingüino Rey

About 10 kilometers south of Onaisín, Estancia San Clemente is home to the **Parque Pingüino Rey** (www.pinguino-rey.cl), home to an accessible colony of the rare king penguin on Bahía Inútil. Visits are most easily arranged through Punta Arenas's **Turismo Ghisoni** (Lautaro Navarro 975, tel. 061/261-3420). Returning at 10pm, they have a full-day trip (US$71 pp), which also stops at Porvenir for lunch (not included) and returns via Cerro Sombrero and Primera Angostura.

Lago Blanco

Some 50 kilometers southwest of Onaisín, the road passes through **Camerón,** an erst-while picture-postcard *estancia* that is now a municipality. The road then angles south-east to **Lago Blanco,** an area known for its fishing, and continues toward Yendegaia, though it'll be a while before it's finished. In summer, there's a bumpy border crossing to Río Grande, Argentina, via a dirt road with many livestock gates and a ford of the Río Rasmussen. The Argentine border post is called Radman.

Estancia Yendegaia

Visited primarily by Chilean cruise ships and private yachts, **Yendegaia** conserves 44,000 hectares of Fuegian forest in the Cordillera Darwin between the Argentine border and Parque Nacional Alberto de Agostini. While the owners hope to establish a private national park and create an unbroken preservation corridor along the Beagle Channel (Yendegaia borders Argentina's Parque Nacional Tierra

I f Patagonia is exciting, the archipelago of Tierra del Fuego (Land of Fire) is electrifying. In days of sail, the reputation of its sub-Antarctic weather and ferocious westerlies obsessed sailors whether or not they had ever experienced the

thrill—or terror—of "rounding the Horn." After surviving the southern seas en route to California in November 1834, Richard Henry Dana vividly recounted conditions that could change from calm to chaos in an instant:

> "Here comes Cape Horn!" said the chief mate; and we had hardly time to haul down and clew up, before it was upon us. In a few moments, a heavier sea was raised than I had ever seen before, and . . . the little brig . . . plunged into it, and all the forward part of her was under water; the sea pouring in through the bow ports and hawse-hole, and over the knight-heads, threatening to wash everything overboard. . . . At the same time sleet and hail were driving with all fury against us.

In Dana's time, that was the price of admission to one of the planet's greatest groupings of sea, sky, land, and ice. In a landscape whose granite pinnacles jut nearly 2,000 meters out of the ocean, only a handful of hunter-gatherers foraging in the fjords and forests could know the area with any intimacy. Today, fortunately, there are ways to reach Tierra del Fuego that involve less hardship—not to mention motion sickness—than Dana and his shipmates suffered.

In his memoirs, pioneer settler Lucas Bridges labeled Tierra del Fuego the "uttermost part of the earth" for its splendid isolation at the continent's southern tip. It's still a place where fur seals, sea lions, and penguins cavort in the choppy seas of the strait named for global navigator Ferdinand Magellan, where Darwin sailed on the *Beagle*, and the first 49ers found their route to California. From the seashore, behind its capital of Ushuaia, glacial horns rise like sacred steeples. The beaches and southern beech woodlands of Parque Nacional Tierra del Fuego, west of the city, are the terminus of the world's southernmost highway.

Previous: rock cormorants in the Beagle Channel; the harbor at Ushuaia. **Above:** southern sea lions on the islands of Tierra del Fuego.

Argentine Tierra del Fuego

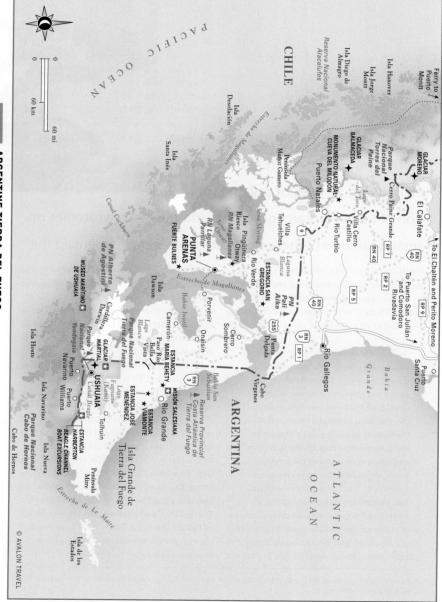

PACIFIC OCEAN

CHILE

Ferry to Puerto Montt

Isla Diego de Almagro
Reserva Nacional Alacalufes

Isla Hanover

Isla Jorge Montt

Isla Desolación

Isla Santa Inés

Estrecho de Magallanes

Península Muñoz Gamero

MONUMENTO NATURAL CUEVA DEL MILODÓN

Parque Nacional Torres del Paine

GLACIAR BALMACEDA

Puerto Natales

Cerro Paine Grande

GLACIAR MORENO

El Calafate

Lago del Toro

Villa Cerro Castillo

Río Turbio

To El Chaltén and Perito Moreno

To Puerto San Julián and Comodoro Rivadavia

Villa Tehuelches

Isla Pingüinera

RN Laguna Parrillar

RN Riesco

RN Magallanes

PUNTA ARENAS

FUERTE BULNES

PN Alberto de Agostini

MUSEO MARITIMO DE USHUAIA

Canal Cockburn

Cordillera Darwin

Isla Dawson

Seno Otway

Seno Skyring

Río Verde

ESTANCIA SAN GREGORIO

Laguna Blanca

PN Pali Aike

Punta Delgada

Cabo Vírgenes

RN 40

RP 7

RP 2

RP 5

RN 40

RN 3

RP 1

Río Gallegos

Puerto Santa Cruz

Grande

Bahia

Camerón

Porvenir

Onaisín

Cerro Sombrero

Bahía Inútil

Paso Río Bella Vista

Lago Blanco

Parque Nacional Tierra del Fuego

ESTANCIA MARÍA BEHETY

Río Grande

MISIÓN SALESIANA

ESTANCIA JOSÉ MENÉNDEZ

ESTANCIA VIAMONTE

Lago Fagnano (Kami)

Bahía San Sebastián

Reserva Provincial Costa Atlántica de Tierra del Fuego

ARGENTINA

GLACIAR MARTIAL

USHUAIA

Yendegaia

Parque Nacional Tierra del Fuego

Puerto Navarino

Puerto Williams

Isla Navarino

Isla Hoste

Parque Nacional Cabo de Hornos

Cabo de Hornos

Canal Beagle

Tolhuin

ESTANCIA HARBERTON

BEAGLE CHANNEL BOAT EXCURSIONS

Península Mitre

Isla Grande de Tierra del Fuego

ATLANTIC OCEAN

Estrecho de Le Maire

Isla Nueva

Isla de los Estados

© AVALON TRAVEL

0 60 km

0 60 mi

Tierra del Fuego is not just one island, but an archipelago, though the Isla Grande de Tierra del Fuego is South America's largest island. Chile shares the territory with Argentina. While parts of the Argentine side are urbanized, the Chilean side has just a few small towns and isolated ranches. Roads are few but improving, and some are now paved, especially on the Argentine side. The unpaved roads can be hell on windshields, which are most cheaply replaced in the Chilean mainland city of Punta Arenas.

Two ferry routes connect the Chilean mainland to Tierra del Fuego: a shuttle from Punta Delgada, only 45 kilometers south of Argentina's Santa Cruz province, across the Primera Angostura narrows to Puerto Espora, and a daily service from Punta Arenas to Porvenir, over one of the widest parts of the strait.

PLANNING YOUR TIME

Like the rest of southern South America, Tierra del Fuego deserves all possible time, but most visitors have to make choices. Ushuaia is the best base for sightseeing in Tierra del Fuego proper, given its access for excursions to the nearby national park, the Beagle Channel,

and Estancia Harberton, with a minimum of three days. Hikers may wish to spend several days more and fly-fishing aficionados, who may prefer the vicinity of Río Grande, often stay a week or two.

HISTORY

European familiarity with southernmost South America dates from 1520, when Portuguese navigator Fernando Magalhaes, under the Spanish flag, sailed through the strait that now bears his name (Magallanes in Spanish, Magellan in English). Ranging 3-25 kilometers in width, the strait became a maritime thoroughfare to the Pacific.

Prior to Magellan's "discovery," southern South America's insular extremes were inhabited by hunter-gatherer bands of Selk'nam (Ona), Kawéskar (Alacaluf), and Yámana (Yahgan) peoples. They lived off maritime and terrestrial resources that they considered abundant—only European eyes saw a land of deprivation. The archipelago acquired its name from the fires set by the region's so-called "Canoe Indians," the Kawéskar and Yámana peoples, for heating and cooking. In this soggy region, though, Tierra del Humo (Land of Smoke) might have been more accurate.

king cormorant colony on an Island in the Beagle Channel

Early navigators dreaded Cape Horn's wild seas, and their reports gave their countrymen little reason to settle in or even explore the area. In the early 1830s, on the *Beagle's* first voyage, Captain Robert FitzRoy abducted several Yámana people, including the famous Jemmy Button, to England. He subjected them to missionary indoctrination before returning them to their home two years later. On that later voyage, a perplexed Charles Darwin commented on the simplicity of their society: "The perfect equality among the individuals composing the Fuegian tribes, must for a long time retard their civilization."

The first to try to bring European civilization to the Yámana people, rather than the opposite, were Anglican missionaries from the Falkland Islands, some of whose descendants still live here. After abortive attempts that included both Fuegian assaults and the starvation of evangelist Allen Gardiner, the Anglican Thomas Bridges settled at present-day Ushuaia, on the Argentine side of the Isla Grande, where he compiled an English-Yámana dictionary. His son Lucas, who grew up with Yámana playmates, wrote the extraordinary memoir *The Uttermost Part of the Earth,* published shortly before his death in 1950.

In the meantime, both the Chilean and Argentine governments established their presence, and enormous sheep *estancias* (ranches) occupied the sprawling grasslands where indigenous people once hunted guanaco and other game. As the guanaco declined and the desperate Fuegians began to hunt domestic sheep, they often found themselves facing the wrong end of a rifle. Introduced European diseases such as typhoid and measles killed more indigenous people than did bullets.

In 1979, the two countries nearly went to war over three small Beagle Channel islands in an archipelago whose borders were never clearly defined. Positions were uncompromising—one adamant Argentine poster proclaimed "We will never surrender what is ours!"—but papal mediation brought a peaceable settlement within a few years. Since then, travel to the uttermost part of the earth has boomed, especially on the Argentine side in the summer. Other important economic sectors on both sides are sheep farming and petroleum.

Ushuaia

Beneath the Martial range's serrated spires, on the Beagle Channel's north shore, the city of Ushuaia is both an end (the virtual terminus of the world's southernmost highway) and a beginning (the gateway to Antarctica). The surrounding countryside attracts activities-oriented visitors for hiking, mountain biking, fishing, and skiing. In the summer season, the city gets hundreds of thousands of visitors, many of them merely day-trippers from the hundreds of cruise ships that anchor here.

After more than two decades of economic growth and physical sprawl, the provincial capital is both declining and improving. On the one hand, the duty-free manufacturing, fishing, and tourist boom that transformed a onetime penal colony and naval base into a bustling city has weakened. On the other, it has spruced up the waterfront and restored historic buildings, some of them becoming hotels or B&Bs. The streets are cleaner (though Avenida San Martín is tourist-trap ugly) and there are more parks, plazas, and green spaces. Still, Ushuaia has particulate pollution problems because high winds kick up dust in its newer unpaved neighborhoods.

HISTORY

Ushuaia dates from 1870, when the South American Missionary Society decided to place the archipelago's first permanent European settlement here. Anglican pioneer

Ushuaia

To GLACIAR MARTIAL

LUIS VERNET

Avenida Leandro N. Alem

O V ANDRADE

PAZ

FLORENCIA

SANCHEZ DE CABALLERO

LUGONES DE

ONACHAGA

JAINEN

DARWIN

HOSTERÍA
AMERICA

J. GOMEZ

CHILEAN
CONSULATE

AUTOMOVIL CLUB
ARGENTINO

HOSPITAL
REGIONAL

To Airport, and Parque
Nacional Tierra del Fuego

25 DE AGOSTO

AVENIDA SAN MARTIN

Plaza
Piedra
Buena

CASA BEBAN

Paseo de
las Rosas

Parque
Centenario

Paseo del

CEMENTERIO
MUNICIPAL

Plaza
General
San
Martín

Plaza
Gendarmería
Nacional

Perito Moreno

EL TURCO

Plazoleta

ONAS

GOBERNADOR

GOBERNADOR

SARMIENTO

MAGALLANES

Bahía Encerrada

Plaza Islas
Malvinas

ADMINISTRACION
DE PARQUES
NACIONALES

PATAGONIA

LA
CASA

PAZ

BELGRANO

PIEDRABUENA

CAMPOS

DON BOSCO

FAGNANO

MONSEÑOR

SOLIS

Parque
Aborigen

TOLKEYEN
BUSES
PACHECO

HELADOS
GADGET

MARIA
LOLA

BOUTIQUE
DEL LIBRO

LIDER

DE LAS
ARTES

SEE "USHUAIA WATERFRONT" MAP

JM DE ROSAS

9 DE JULIO

JUANA FADUL

25 DE MAYO

GOBERNADOR DELOQUI

AVENIDA SAN MARTIN

GOBERNADOR

LASSERRE

MAGALLANES

HOTEL
POSADA
FUEGUINA

KAUPÉ

RIVADAVIA

KALMA

To RN 3, Ski Areas, Lago Kami/
Fagnano, Río Grande, and
ESTANCIA HARBERTON

USHUAIA
BOATING

MUSEO MARÍTIMO
DE USHUAIA

YAGANES

AVENIDA PREFECTURA NAVAL ARGENTINA

ROCA

GODOY

TANTE SARA
RESTO BAR

137 PIZZA
& PASTA

ANTARTIDA

ARGENTINA

MUSEO DEL FIN
DEL MUNDO

Bahía Ushuaia

To Aeroclub
Ushuaia

MUELLE
DEPROTIVO/
CLUB NÁUTICO

MUELLE
COMERCIAL

OFICINA
ANTARCTICA,
INFUETUR

MUELLE
TURÍSTICO

0   200 yds

0   200 m

© AVALON TRAVEL

Ushuaia Waterfront

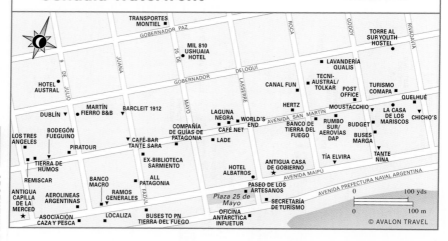

TRANSPORTES MONTIEL ■
GOBERNADOR PAZ
ROCA
GODOY
RIVADAVIA
TORRE AL SUR YOUTH HOSTEL ●
MIL 810 ● USHUAIA HOTEL
25 DE MAYO
JUANA
9 DE JULIO
LAVANDERÍA QUALIS ■
DELOQUI
HOTEL AUSTRAL ●
GOBERNADOR
LASSERRE
CANAL FUN ■
TECNI-AUSTRAL/TOLKAR ■
POST OFFICE ■
TURISMO COMAPA ■
QUELHUÉ ■
DUBLÍN ▼
MARTÍN FIERRO B&B ●
BARCLEIT 1912 ▼
MAYO
HERTZ ■
MOUSTACCHIO ▼
LA CASA DE LOS MARISCOS ▼
CHICHO'S ▼
LOS TRES ANGELES ■
BODEGÓN FUEGUINO ■
COMPAÑIA DE GUÍAS DE PATAGONIA ■
LAGUNA NEGRA ■
WORLD'S END ■
AVENIDA SAN MARTÍN
BANCO DE TIERRA DEL FUEGO ■
RUMBO SUR/ AEROVÍAS DAP ■
BUDGET ■
BUSES MARGA ■
PIRATOUR ■
CAFÉ-BAR TANTE SARA ▼
CAFÉ NET ■
LADE ■
TIERRA DE HUMOS ■
EX-BIBLIOTECA SARMIENTO ■
ANTIGUA CASA DE GOBIERNO ■
TÍA ELVIRA ▼
TANTE NINA ▼
REMISCAR ■
BANCO MACRO ■
ALL PATAGONIA ■
HOTEL ALBATROS ■
AVENIDA MAIPÚ
ANTIGUA CAPILLA DE LA MERCED ★
AEROLINEAS ARGENTINAS ▼
RAMOS GENERALES ▼
FADUL
PASEO DE LOS ARTESANOS ■
AVENIDA PREFECTURA NAVAL ARGENTINA
Plaza 25 de Mayo
SECRETARÍA DE TURISMO ■
ASOCIACIÓN CAZA Y PESCA ■
LOCALIZA ■
BUSES TO PN TIERRA DEL FUEGO ■
OFICINA ANTÁRCTICA INFUETUR ■
0   100 yds
0   100 m
© AVALON TRAVEL

Thomas Bridges and his descendants have left an enduring legacy in Bridges's Yámana (Yahgan) dictionary, his son Lucas's memoir, and the family *estancia* at nearby Harberton (the Yámana people whom Thomas Bridges hoped to save, though, succumbed to introduced diseases and conflict with other settlers).

Not long after Ushuaia's settlement, Argentina, alarmed by the British presence, moved to establish its own authority at Ushuaia with a penal colony for its most infamous criminals and political undesirables. It remained so until almost 1950, when Juan Domingo Perón's government created a naval base to support Argentina's Antarctic claims. Since the 1976-1983 dictatorship ended it has become a tourist destination, visited by cruise ships as well as overland travelers and air passengers who come to see the world's southernmost city.

ORIENTATION

Stretching east-west along the Beagle Channel's north shore, Ushuaia (pop. 56,500) is 3,220 kilometers south of Buenos Aires and 212 kilometers southwest of Río Grande, the island's only other city.

Bedecked with flowerbeds, the main thoroughfare is westbound Avenida Maipú, part of Ruta Nacional (RN) 3, expanded into a divided boulevard whose southerly side is eastbound Avenida Prefectura Naval Argentina. It continues west to Bahía Lapataia in Parque Nacional Tierra del Fuego. The parallel San Martín, one block north, is the main commercial street. It's also the focus of Ushuaia's nightlife, and gets gridlocked on summer nights as surely as any avenue in Buenos Aires. From the shoreline, the perpendicular northbound streets rise steeply—some so steeply that they become staircases.

SIGHTS

Even if it has leveled off, Ushuaia's economic boom provided the wherewithal to preserve and even restore some of the city's historic buildings. Two are now museums: Dating from 1912, the waterfront former branch of the **Banco de la Nación** (Av. Maipú 173) houses the historical Museo del Fin del Mundo, while the former **Presidio de Ushuaia** (Yaganes and Gobernador Paz), dating also from the early 20th century, is now the misleadingly named Museo Marítimo (while not insignificant, its maritime exhibits are less interesting than those on the city's penal genesis).

Three blocks west of the Museo del Fin del Mundo, dating from 1893, the classically Magellanic **Antigua Casa de Gobierno** (Av. Maipú 465) once housed the provincial government and is now part of the museum. Five blocks farther west, the **Antigua Capilla de la Merced** (Av. Maipú and Rosas) is a chapel originally dating from 1898, restored in 1999. Municipal offices now occupy the 1926 **Biblioteca Sarmiento** (San Martín 674), the city's first public library (built by prisoners). At the west end of downtown, the waterfront **Casa Beban** (Av. Maipú y Plüschow) is a reassembled pioneer residence dating from 1913; it now houses an exhibition center.

Museo del Fin del Mundo

Its block exterior handsomely restored, the evolving **Museo del Fin del Mundo** (Av. Maipú 173, tel. 02901/42-1863, www.tierradelfuego.org.ar/museo, 10am-7pm Mon.-Fri., 1pm-7pm Sat.-Sun. and holidays Oct.-Apr., noon-7pm Mon.-Sat. May-Sept., US$8) features exhibits on the Yámana, Selk'nam, and other Fuegian indigenous people and on early European voyages. There remain permanent exhibits on the presidio, an early general store, Banco de la Nación's original branch (which occupied the building for more than 60 years), and natural history, including run-of-the-mill taxidermy. Its star artifact is a copy of Thomas Bridges's Yámana-English dictionary.

An open-air sector recreates a Yámana encampment and dwellings alongside machinery used in early agriculture and forestry projects. There are also a bookstore/souvenir shop and a specialized library focused on southernmost Argentina, the surrounding oceans, and Antarctica.

Guided tours (11am and 2pm daily Oct.-Apr.) are available. Admission includes access to the former **Casa de Gobierno** (Government House, Av. Maipú 465), also with guided tours (noon and 3:30pm daily).

★ Museo Marítimo de Ushuaia

Somewhat misleadingly named, the **Museo Marítimo y del Presidio de Ushuaia** (Yaganes and Gobernador Paz, tel. 02901/43-7481, www.museomaritimo.com, 9am-8pm daily Jan.-Mar., 10am-8pm daily Apr.-Dec., US$22 pp, US$16 students, US$48 family) most effectively tells the story of Ushuaia's inauspicious origins as a settlement for prisoners. Alarmed over the South American Missionary Society's incursions among the Beagle Channel's indigenous peoples, Argentina reinforced its territorial claims in 1884 by building a military prison on Isla de los Estados (States Island), across the Strait of Lemaire at the southeastern tip of the Isla Grande.

Barely a decade later, in 1896, it established Ushuaia's civilian Cárcel de Reincidentes for repeat offenders. After finally deciding that Isla de los Estados was a hardship post even for prisoners, the military moved its own facility to Ushuaia in 1902. Then, in 1911, the two institutions fused in this building, which held some of the country's most famous political prisoners, celebrated rogues, and notorious psychopaths of the early 20th century, until closing in 1947.

Divided into five two-story pavilions, with 380 cells intended to house one prisoner each, it held up to 600 prisoners at a time. Its most famous inmates were political detainees, such as Russian anarchist bomber Simón Radowitzsky, who killed Buenos Aires police chief Ramón Falcón in 1909; Radical politicians Ricardo Rojas, Honorio Pueyrredón, and Mario Guido (the deceptively named Radicals are an ineffectual middle-class party); and Peronist politician Héctor Cámpora, who was briefly president in the 1970s.

Many, if not most, prisoners were long-termers or lifers, such as the diminutive strangler Cayetano Santos Godino, a serial killer dubbed "El Petiso Orejudo" for his shortness and oversize ears (the nickname also describes a large-eared bat native to the archipelago).

Life-size figures of the most infamous inmates, department-store mannequins clad in prison stripes, occupy many cells. One intriguing exhibit is a wide-ranging comparison with other prisons that have become museums, such as San Francisco's Alcatraz and South Africa's Robben Island.

The museum does justify its name with a collection of scale models of ships that have played a role in local history, such as Magellan's galleon *Trinidad,* the legendary *Beagle,* the South American Missionary Society's three successive sailboats, each known as the *Allen Gardiner,* and Antarctic explorer and conqueror Roald Amundsen's *Fram.* In addition, there are materials on Argentina's Antarctic presence since the early 20th century, when the corvette *Uruguay* rescued Otto Nordenskjöld's Norwegian expedition, whose crew included the Argentine José María Sobral. On the grounds stands a full-size replica of the Faro San Juan de Salvamento, the Isla de los Estados lighthouse that figures in Jules Verne's story "The Lighthouse at the End of the World."

In addition, the museum contains a philatelic room, natural history and marine art exhibits, and admirable accounts of indigenous peoples. It has two drawbacks: There's too much to see in a single day, and the English translations could use some polishing to say the least.

Tickets are valid for two days and, since there's so much here, splitting up sightseeing sessions makes sense. The museum has an excellent book and souvenir shop, and a café for snacks and coffee.

ENTERTAINMENT AND EVENTS

Ushuaia has sprouted a plethora of pubs, some but not all with Irish aspirations or pretensions, such as **Dublin** (9 de Julio 168, tel. 02901/43-0744), with a standard menu of *minutas* (short orders).

The **Festival Internacional de Ushuaia**

Boutique del Libro, Ushuaia

(www.festivaldeushuaia.com) is a varied program of classic music concerts by Argentine and international artists, held at Las Hayas Resort Hotel in April for two weeks. It always includes a free concert at a local stadium.

SHOPPING

In spacious quarters, the **Boutique del Libro** (San Martín 1120, tel. 02901/42-4750) offers a wide choice of literature in Spanish, plus Argentine and imported books in Spanish, English, and other languages on the "uttermost part of the earth" and its surroundings (including Moon Handbooks at moderate markups). There are also novels for that long voyage across the Drake Passage to Antarctica.

One of several similar venues along the main shopping street, **World's End** (San Martín 505, tel. 02901/42-2971, www.worldendshop.com.ar, with a branch at the Museo Marítimo) sells kitschy souvenirs but also maps and books. Nearby **Laguna Negra** (San

Martín 513, tel. 02901/43-1144) specializes in locally produced chocolates.

Tierra de Humos (San Martín 861, tel. 02901/43-3050, www.tierradehumos.com) stocks locally produced leather, fleeces, handicrafts, and silverwork. For purchases directly from the artisans, there's the **Paseo de los Artesanos** (Av. Maipú and Lasserre), at the entrance to the Muelle Comercial port.

Quelhué (San Martín 214, tel. 02901/43-5882, www.quelhue.com.ar) carries a fine selection of Argentine wines and imported duty-free liquors.

FOOD

Dining here can be expensive. The financially challenged should look for *tenedor libre* (all-you-can-eat) specials or be cautious with extras like dessert and coffee.

Hotel Cap Polonio's **Marcopolo** (San Martín 746, tel. 02901/43-6612) is a café-restaurant that serves excellent coffee, chocolate, and croissants for breakfast. Try the *submarino* (a bar of chocolate dissolved in steamed milk) for a cold morning's pickup.

El Turco (San Martín 1440, tel. 02901/42-4711, lunch and dinner Mon.-Sat., entrées US$7-12, pizzas from US$10), though lacking variety, is a good shoestring choice. Well-established **Barcleit 1912** (Juana Fadul 148, tel. 02901/43-3015, lunch and dinner daily, from US$10) has fallen a step behind some of the other pizzerias, but also offers moderately priced short orders and a convenient fixed-price menu.

In luminous quarters, **Tante Sara Resto Bar** (San Martín 175, tel. 02901/43-3710, www. tantesara.com, lunch and dinner daily, US$11-18) made its name in sweets and snacks, which are still abundant. It also produces a limited menu of well-crafted lunch and dinner dishes, such as a rib-eye with a Malbec sauce. For breakfast, coffee, sandwiches, and desserts, try its **Café-Bar Tante Sara** (San Martín 701, tel. 02901/42-3912).

★ **137 Pizza & Pasta** (San Martín 137, tel. 02901/43-5005, lunch and dinner daily, US$9-15) still sets the pace in diverse pastas

with a broad selection of imaginative sauces (US$5-10 extra), as well as pizza. Entrées include ravioli with king crab.

Facing the waterfront, ★ **Ramos Generales** (Av. Maipú 749, tel. 02901/42-4317, www.ramosgeneralesushuaia.com, 9am-midnight daily, US$12-20) is a bar and restaurant that recreates a pioneer general store with humor and museum-quality artifacts. It may romanticize the era, but its snacks (including sandwiches) and sweets reinforce the style to make it a must for any Ushuaia visitor. The menu is not elaborate, but the quality is outstanding.

In an artfully restored historical house, **Bodegón Fueguino** (San Martín 859, tel. 02901/43-1972, lunch and dinner daily, US$20) specializes in Fuegian lamb prepared in a variety of styles, but it also has pasta, pizza, tangy beef empanadas, and good desserts.

La Rueda (San Martín 193, tel. 02901/43-6540, lunch and dinner daily, US$22 pp buffet) features a buffet *parrilla* (grill) and cold dishes. Drinks are not included in the buffet price. The well-established **Moustacchio** (San Martín 298, tel. 02901/42-3308, lunch and dinner daily, US$19-25) stresses seafood, such as king crab, but also serves beef and other meats, including lamb.

Ushuaia has a wider choice of seafood restaurants than almost any other Argentine provincial city. **La Casa de los Mariscos** (San Martín 232, tel. 02901/42-1928, lunch and dinner daily, US$13-23) specializes in *centolla* (king crab) but has many other fish and shellfish options.

With a 30-year history and portside views, **Tante Nina** (Gobernador Godoy 15, tel. 02901/43-2444, www.tanteninarestaurant. com.ar, lunch and dinner daily, from US$23) focuses on Fuegian fish and seafood, including 10 preparations of king crab. The food is fine and the service is efficient, but the ambience feels institutional. **Chicho's** (Rivadavia 72, tel. 02901/42-3469, lunch and dinner daily, US$20) also handles large crowds efficiently, serving dishes such as king crab, hake, and

Fuegian trout stuffed with crab, prawns, and mushrooms.

Other possibilities include **Tía Elvira** (Av. Maipú 349, tel. 02901/42-4725, www.tiaelvira. com, king crab US$25) and ★ **Kaupé** (Roca 470, tel. 02901/42-2704, www.kaupe.com.ar, lunch and dinner daily, US$20-25), which serves an exclusively (and exclusive) à la carte menu. Kaupé has specialties such as king crab crêpes in saffron sauce, exquisite lemon ice cream, and wine by the glass.

Equally top-of-the-line, both literally and geographically, is the dining room with a panoramic view at ★ **Chez Manu** (Luis Martial 2135, tel. 02901/43-2253, www.chezmanu.com, lunch and dinner daily, from US$15), on the road to the glacier. Using local ingredients such as king crab and lamb, the French-run restaurant is *the* place for a truly elaborate meal. This is one Ushuaia restaurant with food to match its views, although portions are on the small side.

On a promontory, in a recycled building that once transmitted Argentina's first-ever color TV program—the 1978 World Cup—★ **María Lola** (Deloqui 1048, tel. 02901/42-1185, www.marialolaresto.com.ar, lunch and dinner Mon.-Sat., US$15-20) may be Ushuaia's best restaurant. Period. Items range from relatively simple but delicate pastas to more elaborate dishes, such as stir-fried Patagonian lamb with vegetables. The bar serves a diversity of mixed drinks at moderate prices.

In rustically fashionable surroundings on the semi-industrial eastern waterfront, **Küar** (Perito Moreno 2232, tel. 02901/43-7396, www.kuaronline.com, US$25) has an elaborate menu of fish and seafood specialties, including items such as king crab soup (US$9) and hake ravioli (US$8), plus an extensive wine selection.

Reservations are essential at the tiny **Kalma** (Gobernador Valdez 293, tel. 02901/42-5786, 7pm-11pm Mon.-Sat., www. kalmaresto.com.ar, US$30), where the young chef Jorge Monopoli creates a diversity of sophisticated dishes, such as black hake in rich

sauces, but also unconventional appetizers such as beaver (introduced from Canada for pelts, they have become a pest). Works by local artists cover the walls.

In bright new quarters, **Helados Gadget** (San Martín 1256, tel. 02901/43-4864) has all the conventional Argentine ice cream flavors—good enough in their own right—but also incorporates regional specialties such as *calafate*.

ACCOMMODATIONS

Ushuaia has abundant accommodations, but it has long been one of the country's most expensive destinations. Demand is also high, especially in January and February, when reservations are advisable. One heartening development is the proliferation of good but moderately priced backpacker hostels and the arrival of several bed-and-breakfasts, known by the semi-English acronym ByB. Wi-Fi services are widely available.

US$10-25

In new and more central quarters, **Torre al Sur Youth Hostel** (Gobernador Paz 855, tel. 02901/43-0745, www.torrealsur.com.ar, from US$23 pp dorm, US$79 d) deserves another look. Rooms have two to six beds as well as lockers; there's free luggage storage.

US$25-50

The Hostelling International affiliate ★ **Albergue Los Cormoranes** (Kamshen 788, tel. 02902/42-3459, www.loscormoranes. com, US$25-30 pp dorm, US$85 d with private bath) has attractive common areas, including a wind-sheltered garden, and some of the dorms have private baths. Most easily reached by climbing Don Bosco to its end and then taking a left, it's about eight steep blocks north of the waterfront (arrival transfers are free).

US$50-100

Only a short walk from downtown, in an oasis neighborhood of sheltered gardens, ★ **Galeazzi-Basily B&B** (Gobernador Valdez 323, tel. 02901/42-3213, www.

avesdelsur.com.ar, US$46 s, US$68 d) is a comfortable family house where its few private rooms share baths. It also has exterior *cabañas*, which are excellent value (from US$95 for 2 people in low season). The hosts speak fluent English and are a great source of information on the entire island, especially Estancia Harberton.

Owner, designer, and host Silvia Casalaga has created the homey **La Casa** (Gobernador Paz 1380, tel. 02901/42-3202, www.lacasaenushuaia.com, US$65 s, US$80 d), which is far enough from noisy San Martín, but still central. All six rooms share a bath.

US$100-150

On the hillside, the contemporary ★ **Martín Fierro B&B** (9 de Julio 175, tel. 02901/43-0525, www.martinfierrobyb.com.ar, US$63 s, US$101 d) offers downstairs "apart-hotel" rooms with separate kitchens, sleeping up to three people each. In the upstairs, where additional rooms with shared bath may be available, a diverse breakfast takes place in tasteful common areas that are simultaneously spacious and cozy.

Hotel Austral (9 de Julio 250, tel. 02901/42-2223, www.hotel-austral.com.ar, US$135 s or d) is a 10-room hotel with soaring, light-filled common areas that offer panoramic views of the Beagle Channel (at least until new constructions block them in the future). Painted in pastels, the rooms themselves are spacious and comfortable.

US$150-200

Though other buildings block its views, the 30-room **Mil 810 Ushuaia Hotel** (25 de Mayo 245, tel. 02901/43-7710, www.hotel1810. com, US$150 s or d) is a central design hotel on a prominent hillside site just a couple of blocks from the waterfront. Just beyond the congested downtown, it's close enough to walk everywhere.

Hillside **Hotel Ushuaia** (Lasserre 933, tel. 02901/43-0671, www.ushuaiahotel.com. ar, US$170 s or d) offers good value in its price range and has a restaurant. Responsive

Hostería América (Gobernador Paz 1665, tel. 02901/42-3358, www.hosteriaamerica. com.ar, US$120-185 s or d) is a decent choice in a fine location above the Parque Paseo del Centenario. The highest rates correspond to suite with channel views.

The spacious, rejuvenated **Hotel Albatros** (Av. Maipú 505, tel. 02901/43-7300, www.albatroshotel.com.ar, US$198 s or d) is the pick of downtown's waterfront options, with a spa and a restaurant.

Over US$200

On the Martial Glacier road, the **Las Hayas Resort Hotel** (Luis Martial 1650, tel. 02901/43-0710, www.lashayashotel.com, from US$206 s or d) enjoys nearly all conceivable amenities, including an elaborate buffet breakfast, a gym, a sauna, a hot tub, and a heated indoor pool. It picks up guests at the airport and offers a regular shuttle to and from downtown. Behind its surprisingly utilitarian exterior, some of its 93 rooms and suites suffer from hideous decor (the wallpaper is to cringe at), but all are comfortable. The hotel's staff is highly professional.

From its cul-de-sac perch, **Hotel Posada Fueguina** (Lasserre 438, tel. 02901/42-3467, www.posadafueguina.com.ar, US$135-180 s, US$225-280 d) offers awesome views, especially from its deluxe rooms, which also have jetted tubs. It has *cabañas* as well to handle any overflow, but it falls short of others in its price range.

About four kilometers west of downtown, in a mostly residential neighborhood, family-run ★ **Hotel Tierra de Leyendas** (Tierra de Vientos 2448, tel. 02901/44-6565, www. tierradeleyendas.com.ar, US$198-258 s or d) is a seven-room boutique hotel with expansive views of the Beagle Channel. Owner Sebastián García Cosoleto, who cooked for eight years at the Buenos Aires Marriott Plaza Hotel, is also chef of its Francophile restaurant (for guests only). There are significant discounts for stays of three days or more.

In a densely wooded residential area about 1.5 kilometers northeast of downtown,

Bound for the Ice

Ushuaia has become the main jumping-off point for Antarctic excursions, using ships such as Russian icebreakers. (Despite being chartered under U.S. officers, the Russian vessels sometimes still show the Soviet Union's hammer and sickle on their bows.) For travelers with flexible schedules, it has been possible to make last-minute arrangements at huge discounts. No ship wants to sail with empty berths. Heavy demand has made it difficult to pay anything less than about US$5,000 for 10 days, including several days' transit across the stormy Drake Passage (seasickness medication advised).

On the waterfront Muelle Comercial, Ushuaia's **Oficina Antártica Infuetur** (tel. 02901/43-0015, antartida@tierradelfuego.org.ar) has the latest information on Antarctic cruises. At present, even last-minute arrangements go through Ushuaia travel agencies for the October-March season.

★ **Patagonia Villa Lodge** (Bahía Buen Suceso 563, tel. 02901/43-5937, www.patagoniavilla.com, US$220-300 s or d, with breakfast) has just four rooms in luminous semidetached cabins and a new lodge with magnificently rustic architecture and comforts that include whirlpool tubs in two of its suites. There is one double (US$110 s, US$180 d) with limited natural light that suffers only by comparison with the others; elsewhere, it would count among the best in town. Owner Luciana Lupotti, a former Florida exchange student, speaks fluent English.

INFORMATION

Ushuaia's well-organized municipal **Secretaría de Turismo** (Av. Prefectura Naval Argentina 470, tel. 02901/43-7666, www.turismoushuaia.com, 8am-9pm daily) occupies spacious quarters opposite the tourist pier. English-speaking staff are normally present. An airport office (tel. 02901/42-3970) is open for arriving flights only.

The **Administración de Parques Nacionales** (APN, San Martín 1395, tel. 02901/42-1315, tierradelfuego@apn.gov.ar, 9am-4pm Mon.-Fri.) is in town. At the waterfront Muelle Comercial, the **Oficina Antártica Infuetur** (tel. 02901/43-0015, antartida@tierradelfuego.org.ar, 9am-6pm Mon.-Fri.) provides the latest information on Antarctic sailings and tours.

Motorists can consult the **Automóvil**

Club Argentino (ACA, Malvinas Argentinas and Onachaga, tel. 02901/42-1121, 24 hours).

SERVICES

Several banks have ATMs, including **Banco Macro** (Av. Maipú 761) and **Banco de Tierra del Fuego** (San Martín 396); the latter accepts traveler's checks at a 2 percent commission. **Correo Argentino** (San Martín 309) is the post office. **Café Net** (San Martín 565, tel. 02901/43-0037) provides telephone, fax, and Internet access, including Wi-Fi.

The **Dirección Nacional de Migraciones** (Fuegia Basket 187, tel. 02901/42-2334, 9am-5pm Mon.-Fri.) and the **Chilean consulate** (Jainén 50, tel. 02901/43-0909, 9am-1pm Mon.-Fri.) are open weekdays only.

Los Tres Ángeles (Juan Manuel de Rosas 139, tel. 02901/43-5262) offers quick and reliable laundry service but can be overwhelmed in high season; if so, try **Lavanderías Qualis** (Deloqui 368, tel. 02901/42-1996).

The **Hospital Regional** (12 de Octubre and Fitz Roy, tel. 02901/44-1000, tel. 0107 for emergencies) handles medical issues.

TRANSPORTATION

Ushuaia has air links to Buenos Aires and intermediate points, and improving overland transportation from mainland Argentina and from Chile. Maritime transportation is either tenuous or expensive.

rumbosur.com.ar), **Tolkar** (Roca 157, Local 1, tel. 02901/43-1408, www.tolkarturismo.com.ar), and **Tolkeyén** (San Martín 1267, tel. 02901/43-7073, www.tolkeyenpatagonia.com).

Aerovías DAP (San Martín 350, tel. 02901/42-1139, ventas.ush@dap.cl) now connects with Punta Arenas Wednesday and Saturday. **LADE** (San Martín 542, Local 5, tel. 02901/42-1123) flies irregularly to Río Gallegos, El Calafate, Comodoro Rivadavia, Bariloche, and Buenos Aires.

For Puerto Williams, across the Beagle Channel in Chile, it may be possible to arrange a private charter through the **Aeroclub Ushuaia** (tel. 02901/42-1717 or 02901/42-1892, www.aeroclubushuaia.org.ar).

Bus

At the foot of Juana Fadul, a parking area now serves as a bus station, even though companies have their offices elsewhere. **Líder** (Gobernador Paz 921, tel. 02901/43-6421, www.lidertdf.com.ar) and **Montiel** (Gobernador Paz 605, tel. 02901/42-1366) have several daily services to Tolhuin (1.5 hours, US$15) and Río Grande (3.5 hours, US$23).

Represented by Tolkar (Roca 157, tel. 02901/43-1408), **Tecni-Austral** goes at 5am daily to Río Grande (US$22) and Río Gallegos (12 hours, US$50). **Marga** (Gobernador Godoy 41, tel. 02901/43-5453) also goes at 5am daily in high season (with a few weekly services off-season) to Tolhuin (US$16), Río Grande (US$22), and Río Gallegos (US$44), continuing to El Calafate (US$73).

Several carriers go to Punta Arenas early in the morning (12 hours, US$57), including Tecni-Austral, Pacheco, Bus Sur, and Barría, whose tickets can be purchased at travel agencies **Tolkar** (Roca 157, tel. 02901/43-1408), **Tolkeyén** (San Martín 1267, tel. 02901/43-7073), **Comapa** (San Martín 245, tel. 02901/43-0727), and at Marga's office (Gobernador Godoy 41, tel. 02901/43-5453). Some services may require changing buses at Río Grande. Some companies offer connections to Puerto Natales (changing buses in Punta Arenas, US$75).

ship serving the Antarctic tourist trade

Air

A causeway links the city with **Aeropuerto Internacional Malvinas Argentinas** (USH). Taxis and *remises* (meterless taxis) cost about US$7 with **Remiscar** (San Martín 895, tel. 02901/42-2222, www.remiscar.com.ar).

Aerolíneas Argentinas (Av. Maipú 823, tel. 02901/42-1218) normally flies two or three times daily to Buenos Aires's Aeroparque Jorge Newbery, adding more services in high season, sometimes via Trelew or El Calafate and Bariloche; it also flies twice weekly to Río Gallegos. Occasional Buenos Aires-bound flights land at the Ezeiza international airport instead of Aeroparque.

LATAM Argentina flies daily to Buenos Aires's Aeroparque, and in high season it flies to El Calafate. LATAM tickets can be purchased online or at any local travel agency, including **All Patagonia** (Juana Fadul 60, tel. 02901/43-3622, www.allpatagonia.com), **Canal Fun** (Roca 136, tel. 02901/43-7395, www.canalfun.com), **Rumbo Sur** (San Martín 350, tel. 02901/42-1139, www.

From the staging point at Avenida Maipú and Juana Fadul, **Transporte Lautaro** (tel. 02901/44-4293) and **Transporte Ushuaia** (tel. 02901/15-60-8600) alternatively run hourly services (9am-4pm or later daily summer) to Parque Nacional Tierra del Fuego (US$22-25 pp round-trip); it's normally possible to camp in the park and return the following day.

Sea

The Chilean cruisers **MV *Stella Australis*** and **MV *Ventus Australis*** offer luxury sightseeing cruises to Puerto Williams, Cape Horn, and through the fjords of Chilean Tierra del Fuego to Punta Arenas. While not intended as simple transportation, they can serve that purpose for those who can afford them. It's possible to either disembark in Punta Arenas (four days) or return to Ushuaia (in a week). These cruises are sometimes booked far in advance, but on occasion—normally just before Christmas—it may be possible to make on-the-spot arrangements. If business is slow, there may be last-minute bargains.

For Puerto Williams, across the Beagle Channel, **Ushuaia Boating** (Gobernador Paz 233, tel. 02901/43-6193 or 02901/15-60-9030, www.ushuaiaboating.com) shuttles passengers across the channel to Puerto Navarino and then overland to Puerto Williams (9am Mon.-Sat. summer, 2 hours, US$125 pp one-way plus US$6 boarding tax).

Car Rental

Car rentals start around US$50 per day and range up to US$210 per day for 4WD vehicles. Agencies generally limit mileage to 200 kilometers per day, so read carefully before signing any contract.

Rental agencies include **Budget** (Gobernador Godoy 49, tel. 02901/43-7373, ushuaia@budget.com.ar), **Hertz** (San Martín 409, tel. 02901/43-7529, hertzushaia@infovia. com.ar), and **Localiza** (Av. Maipú 768, tel. 02901/43-7780, localizaush@speedy.com.ar).

Vicinity of Ushuaia

Ushuaia has more than a dozen travel agencies offering excursions in and around Ushuaia, ranging from double-decker-bus city tours (1 hour, US$10) to Parque Nacional Tierra del Fuego (4 hours, US$38) and historic Estancia Harberton (8 hours, US$125). They also organize activities such as hiking, climbing, horseback riding, fishing, and mountain biking.

Local operators include **All Patagonia** (Juana Fadul 60, tel. 02901/43-3622, www. allpatagonia.com); **Canal Fun** (Roca 136, tel. 02901/43-7395, www.canalfun.com); **Rumbo Sur** (San Martín 350, tel. 02901/42-1139, www.rumbosur.com.ar); **Tolkar** (Roca 157, tel. 02901/43-1408, www.tolkarturismo. com.ar); and **Tolkeyén** (San Martín 1267, tel. 02901/43-7073, www.tolkeyenpatagonia.com).

The **Compañía de Guías de Patagonia** (San Martín 628, tel. 02901/43-7753, www. companiadeguias.com.ar) specializes in trekking.

★ BEAGLE CHANNEL BOAT EXCURSIONS

From the Muelle Turístico, at the foot of Lasserre, there are boat trips to Beagle Channel wildlife sites such as **Isla de los Lobos,** home to the southern sea lion (*Otaria flavescens*) and the rarer South American fur seal (*Arctocephalus australis),* and **Isla de los Pájaros,** a cormorant nesting site. These excursions cost around US$70-115 pp for a 2.5-hour trip on oversize catamarans such as the *Ushuaia Explorer, Mariana I,* and *Ana B.* With summer extensions to the penguin colony at Estancia Harberton and a visit to the *estancia* itself, returning overland, the cost is about US$125 plus Harberton's admission fee (US$15).

Rumbo Sur, Catamaranes Canoero, and Tolkeyén sell tickets for these excursions from offices at the foot of the Muelle Turístico, where Héctor Monsalve's **Tres Marías** (tel. 02901/43-6416, www.tresmariasweb.com) operates four-hour trips (US$75 pp) on smaller vessels (4-passenger minimum, 10-12 maximum) that can approach Isla de los Lobos more closely than the large catamarans. They also land on Isla H, a small island with a diverse birdlife. A short walk on Islas Bridges is part of the conventional itinerary in a few excursions operated by Rumbo Sur, as well as on **Catamaranes Canoero** (tel. 02901/43-3893, www.catamaranescanoero.com.ar) and **Patagonia Adventure Explorer** (tel. 02901/15-46-5842, www.yatespatagonia.com.ar) on their four-hour excursions (US$57 pp) on boats with up to 26 passengers.

A US$1.50 boarding tax is added to all excursion fees; ask whether Harberton or national park admission charges are included.

TREN DEL FIN DEL MUNDO

During Ushuaia's early days, prison labor built a narrow-gauge steam-driven railroad, Ferrocarril Austral Fueguino, west into what is now Parque Nacional Tierra del Fuego, to haul the timber that built the city. Only a few years ago, commercial interests rehabilitated part of the rail bed to create an anodyne tourist version of the earlier line that pretty much ignores its unsavory history to focus on the Cañadón del Toro's admittedly appealing forest scenery.

What's today known as the **Tren del Fin del Mundo** (US$45 pp tourist class, free under age 5, US$77 pp 1st class, US$100 pp with food service) leaves from the **Estación del Fin del Mundo** (tel. 02901/43-1600, www.trendelfindelmundo.com.ar), eight kilometers west of Ushuaia. From September to April there are two or three departures daily; May to August there's only one, or perhaps two if demand is sufficient. The ride takes over two hours. Fares do not include the US$14 park entry fee, payable in Argentine cash only.

SKI AREAS

Most visitors see Ushuaia in summer, given its proximity to the mountains, but it's also becoming a winter sports center. Downhill skiing, snowboarding, cross-country skiing, and even dogsledding are possibilities.

The major ski event is mid-August's **Marcha Blanca.** Luring upward of 400 skiers, it's a 21-kilometer cross-country race along the Valle de Tierra Mayor.

There are two downhill ski areas. The aging **Centro de Montaña Glaciar Martial** (Luis Martial 3995, tel. 02901/15-50-3767, www.escuelaushuaia.com), seven kilometers northwest of town at the end of the road, has a single 1,130-meter run on a 23-degree slope, but the double-seat chairlift hasn't operated in nearly three years—it's a hike-up, ski-down proposition.

East of town, **Cerro Castor** (RN 3, Km 26, tel. 02901/49-9301, www.cerrocastor.com, lift ticket US$50 high season) has more modern facilities, including four lifts and 25 different runs. In high season (July), look for discounts for multiple-day packages. In low and shoulder seasons, there are additional discounts.

Other areas east of town, along RN 3, are for cross-country skiers. These include **Tierra Mayor** (RN 3, Km 21, tel. 02901/43-7454, www.tierramayor.com), **Villa Las Cotorras** (Km 25, tel. 02901/49-9300), **Haruwen** (RN 3, Km 36, tel. 02901/42-1306, www.haruwen.com.ar), and several other options. All of them rent equipment and offer transfers from Ushuaia. Access is free.

★ ESTANCIA HARBERTON

Harberton (no phone, www.estanciaharberton.com, tours 10am-7pm daily mid-Oct.-mid-Apr. except Christmas Day, New Year's Day, and Easter, US$16) dates from 1886, when missionary Thomas Bridges resigned from Ushuaia's Anglican mission to settle at his new *estancia* at Downeast, later renamed for the Devonshire hometown of his wife, Mary Ann Varder. Thomas Bridges, of course, was the author of the famous English-Yámana dictionary, and their son Lucas continued their literary tradition with *The Uttermost Part of the Earth,* a memoir of his boyhood and life among the indigenous Yámana and Ona (Selk'nam) peoples.

Harberton continues to be a family enterprise. Its present manager and part-owner, Abby Goodall, is Thomas Bridges's great-great-granddaughter. While the wool industry has declined, the *estancia,* which still has about 1,000 cattle, has opened its doors to organized English- and Spanish-language tours of its grounds and outbuildings; these include the family cemetery, flower gardens, woolshed, woodshop, boathouse, and a native botanical garden whose Yámana-style lean-tos are more realistic than their Disneyfied counterparts along the Ferrocarril Austral Fueguino. Photographs in the woolshed illustrate the process of cutting firewood with axes and transporting it by raft and oxcart, and the tasks of gathering and shearing sheep.

In addition, the late U.S. biologist Rae Natalie Prosser, Tommy Goodall's wife, created the **Museo Acatushún de Aves y Mamíferos Marinos Australes** (www. acatushun.com, 10am-7pm daily mid-Oct.-mid-Apr.), a bone museum stressing marine mammals but also seabirds and a few shore-birds. It's also possible to visit Magellanic and Gentoo penguin rookeries at **Isla Martillo** (Yécapasela) with Ushuaia's Piratour (US$55 pp).

Estancia Harberton, 85 kilometers east of Ushuaia via paved RN 3 and gravel RC-j (now Ruta Provincial 33), is open for guided tours, included in the admission fee. Because of its isolation, there is no telephone, but it has added Internet service at the farm.

With written permission, free **camping** is permitted at unimproved sites; the *estancia* also offers accommodations at the **Shepherd's House** (two triple rooms with private baths, US$325 s, US$580 d with all meals and tours; US$220 s, US$400 d with two meals; US$150 s, US$240 d with breakfast). There are also B&B accommodations at **Uribe's House** (US$80 s, US$120 d), whose three double bedrooms share a bath and a small kitchen.

Harberton's restaurant, **Acawaia,** serves a three-course lunch (US$30 without drinks) and the farm's separate teahouse is open until 7pm daily. Not far from the farm, the **La Mesita de Almanza** (Ruta K, Km 5, tel.

Estancia Harberton is one of Patagonia's most historic ranches.

02901/15-41-0659) offers surprisingly so-phisticated food near the hamlet of Puerto Almanza—the *volcán de centolla* is a tasty king crab casserole.

In summer, several companies provide round-trip transportation from Ushuaia, but renting a car is more convenient. From Ushuaia's Muelle Turístico, **Piratour** (San Martín 847, tel. 02901/43-5557 or 02901/15-60-4646, www.piratour.com.ar) offers a US$160 package with overland trans-portation and a visit to the penguin colony, returning by sea, but without time for the one-hour farm tour.

Catamaran tours from Ushuaia include the farm-tour fee. The amount of time spent on land can vary depending on the operator.

Parque Nacional Tierra del Fuego

For pilgrims to the uttermost part of the earth, mecca is Parque Nacional Tierra del Fuego's **Bahía Lapataia,** where RN 3 ends on the Beagle Channel's north shore. It's a worthy goal, but most visitors see only the area on and around the highway because most of the park's mountainous interior, with its alpine lakes, limpid rivers, blue-tinged glaciers, and jagged summits, is closed to public access.

GEOGRAPHY AND CLIMATE

About 12 kilometers west of Ushuaia, Parque Nacional Tierra del Fuego hugs the Chilean border as its 63,000 hectares stretch from the Beagle Channel north across Lago Fagnano (Kami). Elevations range from sea level to 1,450 meters on the summit of Monte Vinciguerra.

The park has a maritime climate, with fre-quent high winds. Rainfall is moderate, about 750 millimeters per year, but humidity is high, as cool temperatures inhibit evapotranspira-tion. The summer average is only about 10°C. The record maximum temperature is 31°C, while the minimum is a fairly mild -12°C. At sea level, snow rarely sticks, but higher eleva-tions have permanent snowfields and glaciers.

FLORA AND FAUNA

As on the Chilean side, dense southern beech forests cover the Argentine sector of Tierra del Fuego. Along the coast, the deciduous *lenga (Nothofagus pumilio)* and the Magellanic evergreen *coigüe* or *guindo (Nothofagus betu-loides)* are the main species. At higher eleva-tions, the stunted, deciduous *ñire (Nothofagus antarctica)* forms nearly pure stands. In some low-lying areas, where cool annual tempera-tures inhibit complete decomposition, dead plant material compresses into sphagnum peat bogs with a cover of ferns and other moisture-loving plants. The insectivorous *Drosera uni-flora* swallows unsuspecting bugs.

In Argentina's first coastal national park, thick kelp beds help incubate fish fry. Especially around Bahía Ensenada and Bahía Lapataia, the shoreline and inshore waters swarm with cormorants, grebes, gulls, kelp geese, oystercatchers, flightless and flying steamer ducks, snowy sheathbills, and terns. The black-browed albatross skims the Beagle's waters, while the Andean condor sometimes glides overhead. Marine mammals, mostly sea lions but also fur seals and elephant seals, cavort in the ocean. The rare southern river otter *(Lontra provocax)* exists here.

Inland areas are fauna-poor, though foxes and guanacos are present in small numbers. The most conspicuous mammals are the European rabbit and the Canadian beaver, present-day pests that were introduced for their pelts.

★ GLACIAR MARTIAL

Technically within park boundaries but also within walking distance of Ushuaia, the **Glaciar Martial** is the area's best single hike, offering expansive views of the Beagle Channel and even the jagged peaks of Chile's Isla Navarino. Reached by the zigzag Camino al Glaciar (also known as Luis Martial), which climbs northwest out of town, the trailhead begins at the Aerosilla del Glaciar, the ski area's chairlift, which is now closed. Although the trail is easy to follow, it is steep—especially the middle segment—and the descent requires caution because of loose rocks and soil. There is no park admission charge here, and taxis will drop off passengers at the chairlift.

OTHER SIGHTS AND ACTIVITIES

Where freshwater Lago Roca drains into the sea at Bahía Lapataia, the park's main sector has several short nature trails and a few longer ones. Most of the backcountry is off-limits to casual hikers. Slightly less than one kilometer long, the **Senda Laguna Negra** uses a boardwalk to negotiate boggy terrain studded with ferns, wildflowers, and other water-tolerant species. The 400-meter **Senda de los Castores** (Beaver Trail) winds among southern beeches gnawed to death to form dams and ponds where the beavers themselves occasionally peek out of their lodges.

The five-kilometer **Senda Hito XXIV** follows Lago Roca's northeastern shore to a small obelisk that marks the Chilean border. If authorities can someday get it together, this would make an ideal entry point to Chile's new Parque Nacional Yendegaia, but at present it's illegal to continue beyond the marker. From a junction about one kilometer up the Hito XXIV trail, **Senda Cerro Guanaco** climbs four kilometers northeast up the Arroyo Guanaco to its namesake peak's 970-meter summit.

From Bahía Ensenada, near the park's southeastern edge, there are boat shuttles with **Isla Redonda Navegaciones** (tel. 02901/42-2932, tel. 02901/25-56-1455, correodeaventuras@yahoo.com.ar, 10am-5pm daily summer, US$44 pp) for a hike on its namesake island, with the option of disembarking at Bahía Lapataia.

hikers at Glaciar Martial

FOOD AND ACCOMMODATIONS

Camping is the only option in the park itself, where there are free sites with little or no infrastructure at **Camping Bahía Ensenada, Camping Río Pipo, Camping Las Bandurrias,** and **Camping Laguna Verde.** Unfortunately, the organized campground at Lago Roca is presently closed.

INFORMATION

At the park entrance on RN 3, the APN collects a US$14 pp entry fee; Argentine residents get a 75 percent discount. Farther west, 700 meters from the shores of Lago Roca, the **Centro de Visitantes Alakush** (RN 3, Km 3057, tel. 02901/15-51-9727, www.centroalakush.com.ar) contains exhibits on the park's natural history and ethnography. It also has a restaurant, a bookstore, and a gift shop.

Several books have information on the park, including William Leitch's out-of-print *South America's National Parks* (Seattle: The Mountaineers, 1990). Two useful hiking guides are the 5th edition of Tim Burford's *Chile & Argentina: The Bradt Trekking Guide* (Chalfont St. Peter, UK: Bradt Travel Guides, 2001) and the 4th edition of *Trekking in the Patagonian Andes* (Melbourne: Lonely Planet, 2009). Both could use updates, however.

Birders may want to acquire Claudio Venegas Canelo's *Aves de Patagonia y Tierra del Fuego Chileno-Argentina* (Punta Arenas: Ediciones de la Universidad de Magallanes, 1986), Ricardo Clark's *Aves de Tierra del Fuego y Cabo de Hornos* (Buenos Aires: Literature of Latin America, 1986), or Enrique Couve and Claudio Vidal Ojeda's bilingual *Birds of the Beagle Channel and Cape Horn* (Punta Arenas: Fantástico Sur Birding & Nature, 2000).

TRANSPORTATION

From their Ushuaia staging point at Avenida Maipú and Juana Fadul, **Transporte Lautaro**

(tel. 02901/44-4293) and **Transporte Ushuaia** (tel. 02901/15-60-8600) alternate hourly buses (9am-4pm or later daily summer) to Parque Nacional Tierra del Fuego, (US$22-25 pp round-trip). It's normally possible to camp in the park and return on another day.

Car rental agencies in Ushuaia include **Budget** (Gobernador Godoy 49, tel. 02901/43-7373, ushuaia@budgetargentina.com.ar), **Hertz** (San Martín 409, tel. 02901/43-7529, hertzushcentro@speedy.com.ar), and **Localiza** (Sarmiento 81, tel. 02901/43-7780, localizaush@speedy.com.ar). Some agencies offer unlimited mileage within Tierra del Fuego province, but others limit mileage to as few as 100 kilometers per day. Verify mileage limits before signing any contract.

Río Grande and Vicinity

Most visitors who stay in and around Río Grande, on the Isla Grande's blustery Atlantic shoreline, do so for the fishing. For the rest, this once-desolate city is more a place to change buses. Thanks to smoothly paved streets, the huge dust clouds that once blew through this wool and oil burg have subsided. There are limits to beautification, though, and all the trees in Plaza Almirante Brown are stiffly wind-flagged.

Bus schedules used to dictate that travelers spend the night here, but recent improvements mean quicker overland connections to Ushuaia. Still, services have improved, and there's enough to do that an afternoon spent here need not be a wasted one.

On the north bank of its namesake river, Río Grande (pop. 67,000) is 89 kilometers southeast of the Chilean border post at San Sebastián via paved RN 3 and gravel RC-i, and 212 kilometers northeast of Ushuaia via RN 3, which is now completely paved.

SIGHTS AND ENTERTAINMENT

Occupying the former storehouses of the Asociación Rural de Tierra del Fuego, the **Museo Municipal Virginia Choquintel** (Alberdi 555, tel. 02964/43-0647, 9am-5pm Mon.-Fri., free) does a lot with a little, with good natural history materials, sophisticated exhibits on ethnology and indigenous subsistence, and historic displays on maps and mapmaking, island communications, and astronomy.

Río Grande has few architectural landmarks, or few buildings of any antiquity, for that matter. Dating from the Juan Perón era (circa 1954), at Plaza Almirante Brown's northeast corner, the **Obras Sanitarias** waterworks tower (Lasserre 386) now holds the local tourist information office.

El Cine 1 & 2 (Av. Perito Moreno and 9 de Julio, tel. 02962/43-3260) shows current films. It sometimes cranks up the volume to excruciating levels; bring or improvise ear plugs, just in case.

FOOD

Mamá Flora (Av. Belgrano 1101, tel. 02964/42-4087, breakfast and lunch daily) is a good breakfast choice that also has coffee and exquisite chocolates. Also good is **Bonafide Café** (Piedra Buena 520, tel. 02964/42-5910, 9am-9pm Mon.-Sat.).

Tante Sara (Av. Belgrano 402, tel. 02964/42-4366, 8am-midnight daily, US$10-15), like its homonymous counterpart in Ushuaia, is a fine café-restaurant with a varied menu. **La Nueva Colonial** (Av. Belgrano 489, tel. 02964/42-5353, lunch and dinner daily, from US$10) serves abundant pastas, such as lasagna, plus sauces.

Leymi (25 de Mayo 1335, tel. 02964/42-1683, lunch and dinner Mon.-Sat., US$18) serves fixed-price lunches (US$10, drinks not included) and has a broad *parrilla* (grill) and pasta menu, plus good homemade desserts.

Several hotels have their own restaurants, most notably ★ **Posada de los Sauces** (Elcano 839, tel. 02964/43-2895, lunch daily, dinner Mon.-Sat., US$17), which deserves special mention for superb service and the cooked-to-order *lomo a la pimienta* (pepper steak). There's also a 10 percent cash discount.

Canela (Moyano and Libertad, tel. 02964/42-5570) is a fine ice creamery.

ACCOMMODATIONS

Accommodations options are few. Nearly every mid-range-to-upscale place offers discounts for cash payment.

The family-run **Hospedaje Noal** (Obligado 557, tel. 02964/42-7516, US$28-32 d, no breakfast) has simple but spotless and spacious rooms with plenty of closet space and good beds. Rooms with private baths are only slightly costlier than those with shared bath.

Perhaps the best value for money, re-habbed **Hotel Villa** (Av. San Martín 281, tel. 02964/42-4998, hotelvilla@live.com, US$61 s or d) has cheerful contemporary rooms and

assiduous service. There are discounts for cash payment.

Río Grande's most professional operation, **Posada de los Sauces** (Elcano 839, tel. 02964/43-2895, www.posadadelossauces. com, US$82-101 s, US$101-140 d) is easily top of the line. One of the suite baths could hold a hot-tub party, and the restaurant is the city's most elegant.

Despite the garish exterior, suites at the **Status Hotel Casino** (Av. San Martín 268, tel. 02964/43-5700, www.statushotelcasino. com, from US$105 s or d) are comfortable, plainly decorated, and have all the amenities of a hotel of its range, with attractive promotional rates.

On the airport road, the top-end **Grande Hotel** (Echelaine 251, tel. 02964/43-6500, www.grandehotel.com.ar, from US$118 s or d) has 64 contemporary rooms and suites, all with whirlpool tubs, a restaurant, and an indoor pool.

INFORMATION

On Plaza Almirante Brown, Río Grande's helpful **Dirección de Turismo** (Lasserre 386, tel. 02964/42-9528, www.riogrande.gob. ar, 9am-8pm Mon.-Fri.) has moved to the historic water tower opposite the plaza.

SERVICES

Banks with ATMs include **Banco de Tierra del Fuego** (Av. San Martín 193) and **HSBC** (Av. San Martín 194). **Correo Argentino** (Rivadavia 968) is two blocks west of San Martín; the postal code is 9420. The **Centro Integral de Comunicaciones** (Av. Belgrano 556, tel. 02964/42-0357) has long-distance telephone and Internet services.

Welcome (Moyano 343, tel. 02964/43-2936) handles the washing. For medical services, contact the **Hospital Regional** (Ameghino 755, tel. 02964/42-2086).

TRANSPORTATION

Aeropuerto Internacional Río Grande (RGA, tel. 02964/42-0699) is a short distance west of downtown. City bus Línea A (US$1)

The historic Misión Salesiana, north of Rio Grande , has an outstanding museum

(8:30am Mon., Wed., and Fri., US$41), to Río Gallegos (8:30am daily, 9 hours, US$38), and to Ushuaia (4pm daily, 3 hours, US$20). **Buses Marga** (tel. 02964/43-4316) goes to Río Gallegos (daily, US$40) and to Ushuaia (daily, 3 hours, US$20).

Hertz (Av. San Martín 236, tel. 02964/42-6754) provides rental cars.

VICINITY OF RÍO GRANDE

As the surrounding area lacks well-developed transport infrastructure, consider renting a vehicle.

Reserva Provincial Costa Atlántica de Tierra del Fuego

From Cabo Nombre, at Bahía San Sebastián's north end, to the mouth of the Río Ewan, southeast of Río Grande, the Isla Grande's entire shoreline is a bird sanctuary, the **Reserva Provincial Costa Atlántica de Tierra del Fuego,** because of the abundant plovers and sandpipers in summer. Birds include the two-banded plover (*Charadrius falklandicus*), whimbrel (*Numenius phaeopus*), Hudsonian godwit (*Limosa haemastica*), redknot (*Calidris canutus*), and white-rumped sandpiper (*Calidris fuscicollis*), some of which cover one of the world's longest migration routes yearly between the Arctic and South America.

★ Misión Salesiana

One exception to Río Grande's lack of historic sites is the **Misión Salesiana** (RN 3, Km 2800, tel. 02964/42-1642, www.misionrg. com.ar), founded to evangelize the Selk'nam people. After the indigenous people died out from unintentionally introduced diseases and intentional slaughter, the priests turned their attention to educating rural youth in their boarding school. The well-preserved **Capilla** (chapel), a national historic monument, and similar Magellanic buildings form part of the mission's **Museo Monseñor Fagnano** (11am-4:30pm Tues.-Fri., 1:30pm-5:30pm Sat., foreigners US$6, under age 13 free), which presents its natural history, ethnography, and

goes directly there. A cab charges around US$5.

Aerolíneas Argentinas (Av. San Martín 607, tel. 0810/2228-6527) flies nonstop to Buenos Aires several days a week. Puddle-jumping **LADE** (Lasserre 447, tel. 02964/42-2968) flies to Ushuaia, Río Gallegos, and El Calafate, and to other northbound destinations, including Buenos Aires.

The **Terminal Fueguina** (Obligado and Finocchio) is Río Grande's bus terminal, but companies also keep some more central offices. **Líder** (Av. Perito Moreno 635, tel. 02964/42-0003, www.lidertdf.com.ar) and **Transportes Montiel** (25 de Mayo 712, tel. 02964/42-0997) have multiple departures to Tolhuin (1.5 hours, US$8) and Ushuaia (3.5 hours, US$22). At the terminal, **Buses Pacheco** (tel. 02964/42-5611, www.busespacheco.com) goes to Punta Arenas, Chile (10am Tues., Thurs., and Sat., 9 hours, US$44-50), and has connections to Puerto Natales, Chile.

Tecni-Austral (Moyano 516, tel. 02964/43-0610) goes to Punta Arenas

history collections far better than in the not-too-distant past.

From Río Grande, the Línea D bus goes hourly (7:30am-8:30pm daily) to the Misión Salesiana, about 11 kilometers north of Río Grande.

Historic *Estancias*

Several of the region's largest and most important *estancias* are in the vicinity of Río Grande. Founded by the Menéndez dynasty's Sociedad Explotadora de Tierra del Fuego, **Estancia María Behety** (tel. 02964/42-4215, www.maribety.com.ar), 17 kilometers west via gravel RC-c (now RP 5), is home to the world's largest shearing shed. Though it no longer offers guided tours itself, it's possible to arrange one through the Río Grande office of **Infuetur** (Av. Belgrano 319, tel. 02964/42-2887). The *estancia* also welcomes drop-ins interested in taking a look around.

Also Sociedad Explotadora property, **Estancia José Menéndez,** 16 kilometers southwest of town via RN 3 and RC-b (now RP 8), is one of the island's most historic ranches with its exclusive **Villa María** fishing lodge (Buenos Aires tel. 011/4801-1008, U.S. tel. 877/637-8420, www.vmarialodge.com) on the shores of the Río Grande. RP 8 continues west to an obscure border post (open Nov.-Apr. only) at **Radman,** known also as **Río Bella Vista,** where few visitors of any kind cross the line, best done in a 4WD vehicle, to Lago Blanco on the Chilean side.

Lago Fagnano (Kami)

Named for the priest who spearheaded Salesian evangelism among the Selk'nam people, the elongated **Lago Fagnano** fills a structural depression that stretches across the Chilean border to the west. Also known by its Selk'nam name, Kami, its shoreline is nearly 200 kilometers long, and its surface covers nearly 600 square kilometers.

The lake's most westerly part, along the Chilean border, lies within Parque Nacional Tierra del Fuego but is virtually inaccessible

---

Fishing in Fuegia

Fishing for Atlantic salmon, brown trout, and rainbow trout is a popular pastime throughout Argentine Tierra del Fuego. Fees differ according to the period of time, the lake or river in question, and residence status.

The season runs November-April. Daily rates are US$30 for nonresidents; there's a weekly license for US$91, and seasonal rates are US$121. Residents of neighboring countries and Argentina pay a fraction of these rates.

In Ushuaia, licenses are available at the **Asociación Caza y Pesca** (Av. Maipú 822, tel. 02901/42-3168, cazpescush@infovia.com.ar). In Río Grande, contact the **Asociación Riograndense de Pesca con Mosca** (Montilla 1040, tel. 02964/42-1268, arpmosca@ciudad.com.ar).

---

except by boat. As might be expected, the lake is popular with fishing enthusiasts.

At the east end, about midway between Río Grande and Ushuaia, pilgrims pause at the town of **Tolhuin** to sample the goods at ★ **Panadería La Unión** (Jeujepén 40, tel. 02901/49-2202, www.panaderialaunion. com), a legendary bakery that has the usual fine bread but also loads of *facturas* (pastries), *alfajores* (cookies sandwiched around sweet fillings like *dulce de leche*), and sandwiches; what it lacks, astonishingly for Argentina, is any coffee other than machine-dispensed instant. Photos on the walls attest to the constant arrival of Argentine show-biz celebrities.

For accommodations and a full meal, five kilometers west of Tolhuin on the shores of Lago Fagnano, try rehabbed **Hostería Kaikén** (RN 3, Km 2958, tel. 02964/15-61-5102, www.hosteriakaiken.com, US$75-141 s or d), which has comfortable doubles with lake views, of which the most expensive ones have whirlpool tubs. Its restaurant (US$15-20) serves regional specialties such as lamb and trout.

The Falkland Islands

Look for ★ to find recommended sights, activities, dining, and lodging.

Highlights

★ **Historic Dockyard Museum:** In just an hour or so, visitors can get a grasp of the islands' history, with a touch of Antarctica to boot (page 478).

★ **Johnson's Harbour and Volunteer Point:** Johnson's Harbour's large and growing king penguin colony spends the entire year at the scenic Volunteer Point lagoon (page 485).

★ **Bleaker Island:** For visitors on a budget, Bleaker has excellent accommodations and much of the same wildlife as Sea Lion Island, but its penguins, cormorants, and petrels are more dispersed (page 488).

★ **Sea Lion Island:** Sea Lion may be one of the most expensive options, but there's more wildlife in a smaller area than any other easily accessible part of the islands (page 488).

★ **Port Howard:** Enjoy the comforts of Port Howard Lodge, the former manager's house in the last of the large sheep farms that once monopolized the islands' wool industry (page 489).

★ **Pebble Island:** The island's endless crescent beaches and lagoons are full of wildfowl, including penguins and petrels, all within easy reach of one of the islands' best lodges (page 491).

★ **Saunders Island:** Both the hiking and the wildlife—especially the black-browed albatrosses—are extraordinary on mountainous Saunders, whose historic resources include ruins of Britain's original 18th-century outpost (page 492).

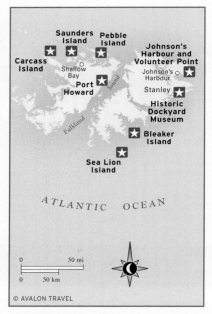

© AVALON TRAVEL

★ **Carcass Island:** This family ranch on wildlife-rich West Falkland feels like a throwback to the days when no Islander would have even considered charging for bed and breakfast (page 494).

I n 1982, the isolated Falkland Islands made world headlines when Britain and Argentina fought a 10-week South Atlantic war that ended in a decisive British victory and, serendipitously, ended a brutal military dictatorship. The territorial dispute over the islands, which Argentina claims as the Malvinas, has not gone away, but the islands' tourism profile has risen as a destination for cruise ships and a select group of independent travelers interested primarily in sub-Antarctic wildlife.

As a Patagonian outlier 500 kilometers east of the South American continent, the Falklands offer enormous colonies of seabirds (five penguin species, including easy access to the uncommon king and gentoo, black-browed albatrosses, and several species of cormorants in particular) and marine mammals (including elephant seals, sea lions, and fur seals). Most of these are rarely seen on the continent, and seeing many of them would require a trip to either remote South Georgia or Antarctica.

Despite their small permanent population, only about 3,400, the islands have good visitor infrastructure in the capital city of Stanley and in main island and offshore lodges, close to wildlife sites, that are the local counterpart to Argentine and Chilean *estancias* (ranches). The big drawback is that most, though not all, of these sites are only accessible by relatively expensive air taxis that require good timing.

PLANNING YOUR TIME

Because of infrequent international commercial flights, weekly at best, organizing your itinerary before arrival is essential, unless your time is almost unlimited. Without your own plane or yacht, visits shorter than a week are nearly impossible, and two weeks would be desirable. Charter flight passengers from the United Kingdom can take Ministry of Defence (MOD) charters that arrive every five or six days.

Most visitors enjoy the islands between October and March, when migratory seabirds and marine mammals return to the shoreline to breed. The concentrations of penguins, cormorants, albatrosses, elephant seals, and other

---

Previous: view from Kidney Cove; king penguins at Volunteer Point. **Above:** Cape Pembroke Lighthouse.

The Falkland Islands

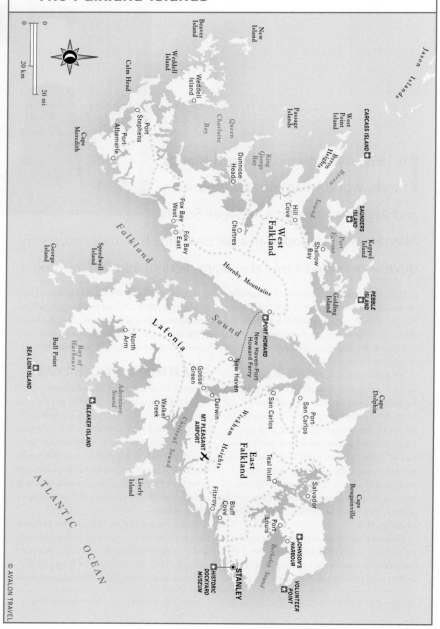

0
0

20 km
20 mi

Jason Islands

New Island
Beaver Island
Weddell Island
Calm Head
Weddell Island
Port Stephens
Port Albemarle
Cape Meredith

West Point Island
Passage Islands
CARCASS ISLAND

Queen Charlotte Bay
King George Bay
Dunnose Head
Byron Heights
Byron Sound

Fox Bay West
Fox Bay East
Chartres
Hill Cove

West Falkland

Keppel Island
SAUNDERS ISLAND
PEBBLE ISLAND

Port Egmont
Shallow Bay
Golding Island

Hornby Mountains

Falkland

George Island
Speedwell Island

Lafonia

North Arm

Bull Point

SEA LION ISLAND

Bay of Harbours

Sound

PORT HOWARD
New Haven-Port Howard Ferry

Goose Green
New Haven

Walker Creek

Adventure Sound

BLEAKER ISLAND

Choiseul Sound

Darwin

MT PLEASANT AIRPORT

Port San Carlos
San Carlos

Wickham Heights

East Falkland

Teal Inlet

Salvador

Cape Dolphin

Cape Bougainville

Cape Berkeley Sound

Lively Island

Fitzroy
Bluff Cove

Port Louis

JOHNSON'S HARBOUR
VOLUNTEER POINT

HISTORIC DOCKYARD MUSEUM
STANLEY

ATLANTIC OCEAN

© AVALON TRAVEL

species are greatest in December and January, when chicks and pups are present; these are also the longest days of summer, with more flexibility for wildlife-watching. That said, signature bird species such as the king penguin are present year-round.

Given the fickle climate, warm and waterproof clothing, such as woolen sweaters and windbreakers, is essential. Rubber boots ("wellies") are useful for slogging over peaty ground. It's sometimes possible to borrow them.

GEOGRAPHY AND CLIMATE

Consisting of two main islands (East Falkland and West Falkland) and some 700 smaller ones, the total land area is about 4,700 square miles (12,173 square kilometers). Roughly the size of Connecticut, they measure about 155 miles (250 kilometers) east to west. The Falkland Sound separates the two main islands.

Except for East Falkland's softly undulating southern peninsula of Lafonia, the topography ranges from hilly to mountainous, though the highest point, East Falkland's Mount Usborne, reaches only 2,312 feet (705 meters). The most striking landforms are the

periglacial "stone runs," quartzite boulder fields that descend like rivers from the ridges and summits of the two main islands. The heavily indented coastline, with its sandy and gravelly beaches, bays, estuaries, inlets, and scenic headlands, provides abundant wildlife habitat.

Over the past decade, the road network on both main islands has improved dramatically, making some destinations more accessible. Air taxis still link the relatively populous East with the West and smaller offshore islands, only a handful of which are inhabited. A regular ferry from East to West Falkland now connects the two.

While it might be fair to describe the climate as "sub-Antarctic" because low annual average temperatures, around 6°C (around 43°F), inhibit both plant growth and decomposition, the latitude is comparable to that of London, and the surrounding South Atlantic mitigates the winter chill. Summer temperatures average around 15°C (59°F), while winter temperatures rarely remain below freezing for days on end. Humidity is high but rainfall is moderate, reaching about 24 inches (600 millimeters) per year at Stanley. West Falkland is drier. The climate's most trying feature is the almost incessant

a nesting colony of gentoo penguins at Cape Dolphin

Eight Days in the Falklands

For visitors to southernmost Patagonia, the Falklands make an intriguing detour, but an inflexible one. There is only one weekly flight, on Saturday, from the Chilean city of Punta Arenas to the Mount Pleasant International Airport (MPN). Likewise, travel within the islands requires, for the most part, using air taxis whose itineraries depend on demand rather than fixed schedules. For a visit this short, and with limited accommodations, advance arrangements are nearly essential. Depending on availability, other sites could be substituted for those mentioned.

Day 1

Arrive at Mount Pleasant and make an immediate FIGAS flight connection to Pebble Island, West Falkland. Overnight at Pebble Island Lodge, with a visit to 1982 combat sites and nearby seabird and marine mammal colonies. Alternatively, fly to Saunders Island, with self-catering accommodations; visit 18th-century ruins of the earliest British settlement and the bird-rich shoreline.

Day 2

Enjoy a full-day exploration of Pebble Island wildlife sites, with gentoo and rockhopper penguins, the occasional king penguin, and sea lions. Alternatively, on Saunders, take a long but rewarding hike to diverse penguin and black-browed albatross colonies at "The Neck" or to similar wildlife at "The Rookery."

Days 3-4

Catch a FIGAS flight to Carcass Island, West Falkland, with elephant seal colonies and many birds,

---

westerlies—the average annual wind speed is nearly 14 knots (26 km/h).

FLORA AND FAUNA

The islands' relatively simple flora comprises mostly extensive grasslands and prostrate shrubs; there are no native trees. Fringing parts of the coastline is the high, dense tussac grass *(Parodiochloa flabellata)*, a prime wildlife habitat so dense and verdant that passing European mariners mistook it for forest. Given it vulnerability to fire and overgrazing, its range has diminished and its abundance has declined. Most native pasture is "white grass" *(Cortaderia pilosa)*, which covers much of the interior but is less nutritious for livestock.

It's the fauna, though, that draws visitors. Five penguin species breed here, of which only the Magellanic is readily sighted on the South American continent. The gentoo, the majestic king, and the crested rockhopper are easily found, while the occasional macaroni nests among rockhoppers, which it resembles. Other species, such as the chinstrap, make the odd appearance but do not breed here.

Large numbers of king cormorants nest among the rockhoppers, while predatory skuas raid the colonies to steal eggs. The most interesting bird of prey, though, is the striated caracara or Johnny rook, so fearless that it will approach humans on foot and steal small, shiny objects. The most striking of breeding birds is the black-browed albatross, so flawlessly beautiful that photographs can make living individuals look like perfectly preserved museum specimens.

Other common shoreline birds include rock cormorants, giant petrels, various gulls, black and Magellanic oystercatchers, snowy sheathbills, kelp geese, and flightless steamer ducks. The grasslands and wetlands are home to crested caracaras, red-backed hawks, black-necked swans, peregrine falcons, and several species of sheldgeese. Nearly all the birds are surprisingly tame and easily photographed.

In addition, marine mammals include breeding populations of elephant seals, southern sea lions, and southern fur seals (whose inaccessible colonies are more difficult to visit), six species of dolphins, and orcas. The large South Atlantic whales are uncommon, however.

including an abundance of the striated caracara, a rare but remarkably tame raptor. Stay at Carcass Island ranch.

Day 5
Take FIGAS to Sea Lion Island, East Falkland, home to three penguin species, large elephant seal and sea lion colonies, giant petrels, uncommon small birds, and large stands of native tussac grass, more than two meters high. Stay at Sea Lion Lodge.

Alternatively, visit Bleaker Island, which has most of the same wildlife as Sea Lion, with less expensive but still comfortable accommodations.

Day 6
Do morning sightseeing on Sea Lion or Bleaker, with an afternoon FIGAS flight to Stanley. Find hotel or B&B accommodations in town.

Day 7
Take a full-day overland excursion to Volunteer Point to visit the king penguin colony, also with gentoos and Magellanics, returning to Stanley in the afternoon. Do a Friday-night pub crawl, if desired.

Day 8
Morning is free for sightseeing in Stanley, with an early-afternoon departure for Punta Arenas.

HISTORY

The Falklands' early history is murky. Pre-Columbian Fuegian people conceivably reached them in bark canoes, but there is no evidence of permanent occupation. An unidentified ship from Magellan's 1520 expedition may have wintered here after being blown off course. Various Spanish, Dutch, British, and French navigators frequented the area over the next two centuries.

Nobody established a settlement until Frenchman Louis de Bougainville brought colonists to Port Louis, East Falkland, in 1764 (the islands' Spanish name, Malvinas, is an adaptation of St. Malo, a key French port).

In 1766, unaware of the French presence, Britain built its own garrison at Port Egmont on Saunders Island, West Falkland. In 1767, meanwhile, Spain replaced France at Port Louis after invoking the Treaty of Tordesillas (1494), under which the pope had divided the New World between Spain and Portugal. In 1770, after happening upon the Port Egmont settlement, the Spaniards ejected the British but, under threat of war, permitted them to return.

In 1774, the British left Port Egmont without relinquishing their claims. A desolate penal settlement for nearly four decades, the islands became a haven for whalers and sealers after Spain's departure in 1811. A decade later, the newly independent United Provinces of the River Plate sent a governor whose tenure was short, while Buenos Aires businessman Louis Vernet asserted rights to the seal fishery and the feral livestock, cattle, and horses that the Spaniards had abandoned. When Vernet attempted to enforce those rights against American sealers, a U.S. naval officer wrecked the Port Louis settlement and forced Vernet's return to Buenos Aires.

In early 1833, a British naval vessel evicted the United Provinces' remaining forces, but its Argentine successor state has maintained its claim to the islands, usually diplomatically. It never became an overt issue until Juan Perón took power in the 1940s and, more aggressively, when a military dictatorship launched a surprise invasion in 1982. Without renouncing its claims, Argentina's current government has been more conciliatory.

After the British takeover, Montevideo-based Englishman Samuel Lafone created the Falkland Islands Company (FIC) to commercialize the cattle herds and then transformed the economy by introducing wool-bearing sheep. For well over a century, the FIC owned nearly half the property and dominated shipping as well, though other immigrants created similar large sheep farms with a resident labor force.

About half the population, which grew slowly and has never exceeded about 3,400, lived on the farms. The other half resided in the port capital of Stanley, established in 1844. Starting in the 1970s, political uncertainty and the declining wool industry led farm owners to sell off their properties; most are now family farms, but the population has shifted toward the capital for reasons having only partly to do with the wool industry.

The South Atlantic Conflict

The Falklands' peculiar political status, as an isolated British possession in the decolonization era that followed World War II, led to negotiations that might have resulted in their absorption by Argentina despite Islanders' determination to remain British (perhaps a dozen Argentines, nearly all of them married to Islanders or other British subjects, resided on the Falklands). Granting Argentina's military airline, LADE, the first regular routes from the continent to the islands, a 1971 communications agreement also gave Buenos Aires a de facto say in immigration and other matters.

The 1976-1983 military dictatorship, which increased Islanders' misgivings about Argentine instability, was collapsing beneath the weight of its own brutality, corruption, and ineptitude when it made a last-gasp grab for domestic popularity by invading on April 2, 1982. The generals and admirals, though, underestimated British prime minister Margaret Thatcher's resolve. Even worse, they misjudged her military's ability to organize the task force that retook the islands within 10 weeks (Argentine forces, for their part, had not fought a real shooting war since 19th-century conflicts with Paraguay and the Mapuche people).

The Postwar Period

In the conflict's aftermath, Britain's new fisheries protection zone and licensing regime made the islands in general, and Stanley in particular, one of the world's most prosperous places on a per-capita basis. While Islanders themselves did not crew the ships that came from Europe and Asia, the revenue from squid licenses and joint ventures enabled local government to invest in schools, medical care, and roads, and individuals to improve their living standards. Tourism revenues also rose rapidly, as round-the-Horn and Antarctica-bound cruise ships anchored at the islands' capital and enjoyed the spectacular coastal wildlife.

Meanwhile, relations with the continent improved in the 1990s as Argentine president Carlos Menem's administration attempted to persuade skeptical Islanders of its goodwill. The biggest step forward was a communications agreement allowing Chile's LAN Airlines to fly weekly from Santiago and Punta Arenas to the islands' Mount Pleasant International Airport. That remains the only commercial international air link, and subsequent Argentine governments took a harder line. In 2010, president Cristina Fernández even ordered that ships en route to the Falklands could not pass through Argentina's 200-mile (320-kilometer) maritime economic zone without permission. Since Mauricio Macri replaced the term-limited Fernández in late 2015, there's speculation of additional flights.

Stanley benefited most from the newfound prosperity and the population shift, as family-owned farms did not need—and could not afford—the large labor force employed by traditional sheep ranches. More recently, there has been offshore oil exploration, probably the main reason for Argentina's maritime embargo, and commercial extraction appears increasingly likely.

RECREATION

For most visitors, **wildlife-watching** is the main activity. Because of the islands' isolation and small human population, many species show little fear of humans. The Falkland Islands Countryside Code, adapted from rules for comparable sites in Antarctica, recommends that visitors get no closer than six meters to birds and marine mammals. Be especially cautious with southern sea lions, which can be aggressive and surprisingly quick on land.

Hiking opportunities are almost limitless, but government and some landowners discourage camping because of fire danger and livestock disturbances. Since nearly all land is privately held, hikers must seek permission from the landowner; the Tourist Board (tel. 22215, info@falklandislands.com) in Stanley can provide a list of contacts. **Fishing** for sea trout no longer requires a license, but there are daily limits. For more information, also contact individual landowners, who control access.

Golfers seeking a real challenge can take on the 12-green, 18-tee course at Stanley, as the islands' nearly constant winds complicate play even more. Greens fees are modest; for further information, contact the **Stanley Golf Club** through Roy Smith (tel. 51136, construction@fic.co.fk).

HEALTH AND SAFETY

Probably one of the world's safest destinations, the Falklands pose no major health problems and have good medical infrastructure in case of illness or injury. Serious crime is virtually nonexistent. It is worth mentioning, though, the unfortunate legacy of **landmines** laid by the Argentine military. Though dangerous, minefields are fenced and clearly marked, and no civilian has been injured since hostilities ceased in 1982.

Recently, a team of Zimbabwean specialists have cleared many of the remaining minefields. Entering remaining minefields or tampering with signs, though, can still expose you to fines of £1,500 and a year in jail. To report landmines or other questionable objects, contact Joint Service Explosive Ordinance Disposal (tel. 53940).

While the weather can be changeable, intense sunshine and brisk winds make visitors vulnerable to sunburn even with very brief exposure. A good sunscreen is imperative.

TRANSPORTATION

Chile's **LATAM Airlines** (www.latam.com) offers the only regular commercial flight to the Falklands' **Mount Pleasant International Airport** (MPN), 35 miles (60 kilometers) southwest of Stanley, every Saturday from Santiago and Punta Arenas; it turns around on arrival. One Saturday per month in each direction, it picks up passengers in Río Gallegos, Argentina; the following Saturday, it drops them off.

LATAM fares from Santiago start around US$1,200 round-trip; from Punta Arenas, it's US$800 round-trip. Through fares from Europe or North America can work out cheaper for those already planning to visit South America. From the United Kingdom, the economy fare is £1,092 round-trip, with one stopover permitted. From Río Gallegos, though, the fare is only US$240.

LATAM also has good connections from North America, Mexico, Australia, and New Zealand. LAN's U.S. gateways are Miami (US$1,299 to Mount Pleasant), New York (US$1,675-2,749, depending on routing), and Los Angeles (US$2,570-3,225). From Toronto, the fare starts at US$2,339; from Sydney, it's US$4,450; and from Auckland, US$5,190.

Britain's **Ministry of Defence** (MOD) charters six or seven flights per month from RAF Brize Norton, near Burford, Oxfordshire, via the tiny South Atlantic island of Ascension. The flight takes 18 hours, including a two-hour stopover for refueling on Ascension. Non-resident fares start around £2,244 round-trip, considerably more expensive than the Santiago-Punta Arenas route, but Chile-bound travelers can purchase one-way tickets. The MOD baggage limit is normally 60 pounds (27 kilograms). Enforcement is sporadic, but overweight charges run £20 per kilogram.

For reservations on MOD flights, contact the Travel Coordinator at **Falkland House** (14 Broadway, Westminster, London SW1H 0BH, UK tel. 020/7222-2542, UK fax 020/7222-2375, travel@falklands.gov.fk); in the islands, contact the **Falkland Islands Company West Store** (Ross Rd., tel. 27633, flightbookings@fic.co.fk). In the Falklands, for both LAN and MOD flights, contact **International Tours and Travel Ltd** (1 Dean St., tel. 22041, fax 22042, www.falklandislands.travel.com).

Passengers flying from Mount Pleasant pay an international **departure tax** of £22 or its equivalent in U.S. dollars or euros. Credit card payments are not accepted. This tax can also be prepaid at Customs & Immigration in Stanley.

Except between Stanley and Mount Pleasant International Airport, there is no regular public transportation on roads, though **taxis** and **rental cars** (with or without guides) are available on both East and West Falkland. Rental cars are not allowed off-road. In any event, driving is not advisable for drivers without local experience, who frequently get "bogged" in the soggy terrain and have to call or trek for help. Visitors may use their own state or national driver's licenses in the Falklands for up to 12 months.

To West Falkland and offshore islands, the only regular public transportation is the **Falkland Islands Government Air Service** (FIGAS, tel. 27219, operations@figas.gov.fk), an air-taxi service that flies 10-seater Norman-Britten Islander aircraft to grass airstrips throughout the islands. At the approximate rate of £1.80 per minute, the fare from Stanley to Saunders Island, north of West Falkland, is about £230 round-trip. For safety reasons, pilots enforce the baggage limitation of 30 pounds (14 kilograms) per passenger.

The freight-and-passenger ferry **MV Concordia Bay** (Globe Offices, Philomel St., Stanley, tel. 22300, www.workboat.co.fk) operates between the East Falkland port of New Haven and the West Falkland settlement of Port Howard (round-trip £20 adults, £10 under age 16, £5 under age 5) up to four or five times weekly. The vehicle rate (£50 round-trip) includes the driver's fare; motorbikes cost £10 round-trip.

Stanley and Vicinity

Its setting often compared with the moorlands of Scotland's outer isles, thriving Stanley claims to be the "world's smallest capital." It's modernizing rapidly as commercial fishing, tourism, and (perhaps) oil supplant wool in the islands' economy. The sweet scent of smoldering peat no longer permeates the evening atmosphere, as kerosene now warms the houses and fuels the cookstoves of most aging stone cottages and newer kit houses alike, and streets once lined with utilitarian Land Rovers now sport shiny new SUVs.

While few Islanders work directly in the fishery, their joint ventures with overseas fishing companies and local government's infrastructural investments have, since the 1982 South Atlantic conflict, transformed a forlorn-looking village into a much more presentable place. Many local residents have remodeled and repainted their houses or built new ones. Many continue their tradition of self-sufficiency by tending tidy kitchen gardens even though more commercial produce is now available. Pending oil development may bring even greater changes.

HISTORY

In 1844, after the Colonial Office shifted the islands' capital from Port Louis to sheltered Port Jackson (soon renamed Stanley Harbour), Stanley became the new seat of government. Its permanent population was a

Stanley

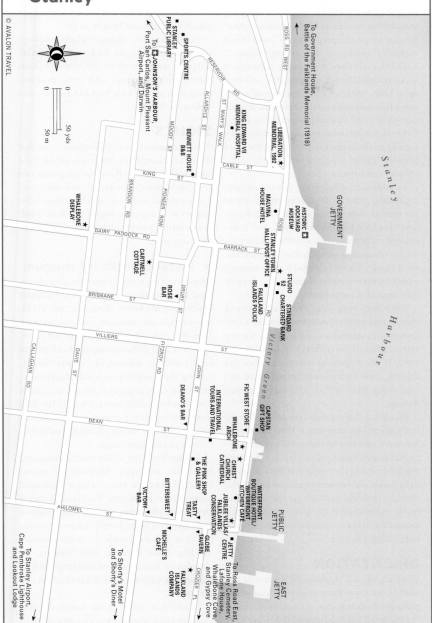

© AVALON TRAVEL

0   50 yds
0   50 m

To STANLEY
PUBLIC LIBRARY

To JOHNSON'S HARBOUR,
Port San Carlos, Mount Pleasant
Airport, and Darwin

SPORTS CENTRE

To Government House,
Battle of the Falklands Memorial (1918)

ROSS RD WEST

RESERVOIR RD

ALLARDYCE ST

ST MARY'S WALK

MOODY ST

KING ST

BRANDON RD

PIONEER ROW

DRURY ST

FITZROY RD

JOHN ST

DAVIS ST

CALLAGHAN RD

KING EDWARD VII
MEMORIAL HOSPITAL

BENNETT HOUSE
B&B

WHALEBONE
DISPLAY

DAIRY PADDOCK RD

CARTMELL
COTTAGE

ROSE
BAR

BRISBANE ST

VILLIERS ST

DEAN ST

PHILOMEL ST

DEANO'S BAR

INTERNATIONAL
TOURS AND TRAVEL

FIC WEST STORE

WHALEBONE
ARCH

CHRIST
CHURCH
CATHEDRAL

THE PINK SHOP
& GALLERY

BITTERSWEET
BAR

VICTORY
BAR

MICHELLE'S
CAFE

LIBERATION
MEMORIAL, 1982

CABLE ST

MALVINA
HOUSE HOTEL

STANLEY TOWN
HALL/POST OFFICE

HISTORIC
DOCKYARD
MUSEUM

ROSS RD

BARRACK ST

STUDIO
52

FALKLAND
ISLANDS POLICE

STANDARD
CHARTERED BANK

CAPSTAN
GIFT SHOP

Victory Green

JUBILEE VILLAS/
FALKLANDS
CONSERVATION

TASTY
TREAT

FALKLAND
ISLANDS
COMPANY

GLOBE
TAVERN

CROZIER PL

WATERFRONT
BOUTIQUE HOTEL/
WATERFRONT
KITCHEN CAFE

JETTY
CENTRE

PUBLIC
JETTY

EAST
JETTY

GOVERNMENT
JETTY

Stanley

Harbour

To Shorty's Motel
and Shorty's Diner

To Stanley Airport,
Cape Pembroke Lighthouse
and Lookout Lodge

To Ross Road East,
Stanley Cemetery,
Lafone House,
Whalebone Cove,
and Gypsy Cove

ragtag assortment of roving mariners, hold-over gauchos, and military pensioners. Except in emergencies, round-the-Horn shipping avoided the islands as they gained a reputation for cargo-shipping losses—"condemned at Stanley" became a cliché among insurers.

In the early days, feral cattle rather than sheep roamed the islands' pastures, and low-value hides attracted little commercial interest. After midcentury, the Falkland Islands Company (FIC) shifted from cattle to sheep. Other farms followed suit, and Stanley grew rapidly as the transshipment point for wool between "camp" (the local term for the countryside) and Britain.

In addition to being the islands' largest landholder, the FIC dominated commerce as the islands' only significant merchant house and Stanley's biggest employer, and it remained so for more than a century. Its impact on the townscape was palpable. Many if not most Stanley houses belonged to the company, whose workers lived in them only so long as they remained employees.

With declining wool prices after World War II, and political uncertainties due to relations with Argentina in the 1970s, Stanley stagnated until the outbreak of hostilities in 1982. While Argentine troops occupied the capital, their last-minute surrender to approaching British forces avoided serious damage.

Stanley still transships the islands' wool, but fisheries income since 1986 has transformed it into one of the world's most prosperous communities of its size. It's far from pretentious, and the boom-and-bust of squidding makes the economy vulnerable, but the changes since the conflict are the most dramatic in the capital's history. Only oil, still unconfirmed in commercial quantities, could have a bigger impact.

ORIENTATION

Stanley (pop. 2,634, about 80 percent of the islands' total permanent population) occupies a north-facing slope on Stanley Harbour, the sheltered inner harbor of the larger Port William. Most points of interest and businesses are on Ross Road, which stretches east-west along the waterfront, and the parallel John Street and Fitzroy Road.

From Stanley Common's windy ridgetop, south of town, roads lead east to Stanley Airport and west to Mount Pleasant International Airport and camp destinations such as Darwin, Port San Carlos, and Volunteer Point.

SIGHTS

Stanley is pedestrian-friendly in the sense that it's small, though it's more spread out than some expect, and walking the steep hills can be tiring (especially for aging cruise-shippers). The perpetual wind can also be trying. Most visitors start along the waterfront Ross Road, at the Jetty Centre tourist office, and work their way west.

★ Historic Dockyard Museum

Now occupying recycled quarters, directly behind the Penguin News office, the **Historic Dockyard Museum** (Ross Rd., tel. 27428, www.falklands-museum.com, 10am-4pm Tues.-Fri., 9am-11am and 2pm-5pm Sat., 2pm-5pm Sun., £5) dedicates separate exhibits to local, maritime, military, and natural history. Among the standouts are a well-stocked replica of an early general store, an admirably even-handed audiovisual account of the 1982 war from the local perspective, and exhibits on camp life, including changing communications and transportation.

Dating from the 1950s on the Antarctic Peninsula, one prize exhibit is the reconstructed **Reclus Hut,** which sheltered researchers from the Falkland Islands Dependencies Survey (FIDS), later renamed and still active as the British Antarctic Survey (BAS). It now sits inside the main museum building. Apart from the main building, the complex includes restored buildings such as the radio-telephone office, the print shop, and the smithy.

In addition to its regular hours, the museum is open whenever cruise ships are in port. It occasionally has special exhibits, such as 2016's centennial of Antarctic explorer Ernest Shackleton's epic escape from Antarctic shipwreck on a lifeboat to South Georgia, and the subsequent rescue of his crew.

Ross Road and Ross Road West

Dating from 1887, built to celebrate Queen Victoria's 50th year on the throne, the **Jubilee Villas** (Ross Rd. and Philomel St.) were private homes that, with their British brick, bay-window, terraced-row style, seem to have been plucked out of working-class London boroughs. The easternmost of them is now home to Falklands Conservation.

One block west, dating from 1892, the capital's most imposing building is the Anglican **Christ Church Cathedral** (Ross Rd. and Dean St.), local seat of the Church of England. Built of brick and stone, with a soaring steeple and stained-glass windows, its interior also memorializes local men who died in the two world wars. The cathedral overlooks an open green graced by **Whalebone Arch,** a sculpture joining the jawbones of two blue whales, erected for the colony's 1933 centennial.

Stretching west along the waterfront from Dean Street, **Victory Green** commemorates the Allied triumph in World War I. Several cannons from the Port Louis settlement, functional 19th-century Hotchkiss guns (fired on ceremonial occasions), and the mizzenmast of HMS *Great Britain* punctuate the neatly trimmed lawns.

One block west, the rehabbed **Stanley Town Hall** is home to the post office, public meetings, and events such as May dances; behind it stands the **Historic Dockyard Museum.** A block farther, the **Liberation Memorial** (1982) reveres the British soldiers and sailors who died in the 1982 conflict with Argentina. Every June 14, Stanley residents gather for a memorial service here.

Appointed by London, the territory's highest officials have resided in **Government House** (Ross Rd. W.) since the mid-19th century. Bright yellow in summer, spiny gorse hedges and broad lawns separate the house from the street. Not long ago it was customary for all island visitors to sign the guest register. With all the economic activity and personnel movement since the 1982 war, the governor has more to do than just socialize, and it's now open by invitation only.

Stanley's Jubilee Villas date from Victorian times.

On the shoreline side of Government House, the **Monument to the Battle of the Falklands** (1918) is an obelisk commemorating the 1914 confrontation in which British naval forces surprised and sank several German vessels. Farther west, one of few still-identifiable Stanley Harbour shipwrecks, the deteriorating Liverpool-built bark *Jhelum* was scuttled here in 1870. On the green itself, a **Solar System Sculpture** walk begins with a replica of the sun, made of recycled materials.

Central Stanley

Many of Stanley's surviving stone houses from the 19th century line John Street, one block south of Ross Road. Erected for the Chelsea pensioners, mid-19th century kit houses line **Pioneer Row,** directly uphill from Stanley Town Hall. One of these, **Cartmell Cottage** (7 Pioneer Row, by appointment only, £1 or included in Historic Dockyard Museum £5 admission), is part of the Historic Dockyard Museum.

Two blocks farther uphill, local conservationist Mike Butcher displays part of his salvaged **whalebone collection,** including the skull, jaws, and teeth of a gigantic sperm whale, in his yard at Dairy Paddock Road and Davis Street. The exhibit also includes a harpoon gun that, according to Butcher, killed 20,000 whales between 1936 and 1965.

Ross Road East and Vicinity

East of Philomel Street, the **Falkland Islands Company** headquarters occupies most of block-long Crozier Place, beyond which Ross Road resumes as Ross Road East and passes **Stanley Cemetery,** whose weathering tombstones tell a great deal about the origins of the islands' immigrant population. Immediately behind the cemetery, the **Memorial Wood** honors the British military who died in the 1982 war.

At the east end of Stanley Harbour, **Whalebone Cove** is the final resting place for several rusting hulks, most notably the handsome three-masted freighter *Lady Elizabeth,* left here after striking a reef in 1913. To the north, still a feasible walk from town, **Gypsy Cove** is home to hundreds of breeding pairs of Magellanic penguins, as well as cormorants, night herons, oystercatchers, and small birds. Stick to the signed nature trail, as landmines left by the Argentines in 1982 are still a potential hazard on the beach and in some other areas.

Farther east, about seven miles (11 kilometers) from town, **Cape Pembroke Lighthouse** (1854) is a bit distant for most hikers, but it's a common destination for tours out of Stanley. During the 1982 conflict, its keeper, Reginald Silvey, used a hidden radio to keep British forces informed of Argentine movements. Visitors can enter the lighthouse with the loan of a key (£5, nonrefundable) from the museum.

ENTERTAINMENT

There's always a pub crawl starting at the relatively low-key **Victory Bar** (1-A Philomel St., tel. 21199, www.victorybar.com), commonly known as "the Vic." One block north, the **Globe Tavern** (Crozier Place and Philomel St., tel. 22703) is the capital's traditional and, in some ways, most colorful watering hole. To the west, **Deano's Bar** (40 John St., tel. 21296) and the **Rose Bar** (1 Brisbane Rd., tel. 21067) are additional options. Live music with local bands, and occasional visitors, takes place in the pubs and on occasion in Stanley Town Hall.

EVENTS

New Year's Day is an occasion for the annual **Sea Cadets Raft Race,** for which competitors build their own vessels. Under the sponsorship of the Falkland Islands Horticultural Society, March's **Horticultural Show** is a competitive event, which, at the end of the day, finishes with an auction of produce and baked goods from Stanley and the countryside outside Stanley.

August's Town Hall **Crafts Fair** showcases the efforts of leatherworkers (whose bridles, stirrups, and other gear resemble

Falklands Philately

Until the 1982 South Atlantic conflict, the Falklands had a low international profile except among one near-obsessive constituency—they made their mark with stamp collectors. Since the islands' first postage stamps appeared in 1878, collectors have treasured Falklands issues, and for more than a century, they were one of the colony's main revenue earners. Economically, they're no longer so important, but neither are they insignificant.

Unlike many newly independent countries in postcolonial Africa and Asia, the Falklands never flooded the market, and thus they've kept their credibility among collectors. Falklands stamps are also works of art, thanks to local talents like illustrators Ian Strange and Tony Chater.

In Stanley Town Hall, adjacent to the post office, the **Philatelic Bureau** (Ross Rd., tel. 27159, www.falklandstamps.com, 9am-noon and 1:15pm-4pm Mon.-Fri.) sells Falklands stamps and first-day covers for up to a year after their initial appearance. It keeps longer hours when cruise ships are in port.

those of early gauchos), weavers, artists, and photographers.

On Boxing Day, the day after Christmas, **Stanley Sports** features horse racing (betting is legal), footraces, and gymkhana competitions. **Camp Sports** takes place in late February or early March, after the end of shearing, at venues such as Goose Green (East Falkland) and Port Howard, Hill Cove, or Fox Bay (West Falkland).

SHOPPING

Locally produced items include knitted woolens and leatherwork, and children's toys with penguin motifs. Many souvenirs are imported from the United Kingdom.

Stanley has a growing number of outlets, starting with books and maps at the **Jetty Centre** (Ross Rd. and Philomel St.). Across Philomel Street, next to the Waterfront Boutique Hotel, **The Harbour View Gift Shop** (Ross Rd., tel. 22217) carries local souvenirs and photographic equipment, as does the FIC's **Capstan Gift Shop** (Ross Rd. and Dean St., tel. 27654), on Victory Green opposite The West Store.

Studio 52 (Ross Rd., tel. 51552, www. studio52.co.fk), on Victory Green alongside Town Hall, is a photo print gallery and souvenir shop. **The Pink Shop & Gallery** (John St., tel. 21399) has prints and crafts by local artists, as well as books and maps.

SPORTS AND RECREATION

Immediately south of Government House, Stanley's **Sports Centre** (Reservoir Rd., tel. 27291, hours vary) includes a public swimming pool. Phone ahead or ask the tourist office regarding hours.

For **fishing,** the nearest site is the Murrell River at the west end of Ross Road. The improved road network has made other East Falkland sites almost equally accessible.

FOOD AND ACCOMMODATIONS

Reservations are almost essential, since accommodations are limited even though quality is good to excellent. For emergencies, the tourist board keeps a list of local people who will take in roomless visitors. Many accommodations also offer food and even full-scale restaurants. It's worth mentioning that, while the food has improved dramatically over the last decade-plus, the restaurants can have their ups and downs.

Bittersweet (3 Philomel St., tel. 21888) is a hybrid tapas bar-wine bar-pizzeria that also serves Sunday brunch and British fast food (such as Cornish pasties) in pleasant surroundings. Though not at the level of the Waterfront or Malvina, it's decent enough. Down the block, **Tasty Treat** (Waverley House, Philomel St., tel. 22500, 11am-2pm and 6pm-8:30pm Mon.-Thurs., 11am-2pm and 6pm-9pm Fri.-Sat.) is a bakery, pizzeria, and sandwich shop with some offbeat items such as plo (£7.50), a curried Saint Helenan version of pilaf.

There are several fast food and takeaway choices, starting with **Michelle's Café** (2 Philomel St., tel. 21123), which also serves breakfast and lunch. **Deano's Bar** (40 John St., tel. 53296, 10am-11pm Mon.-Thurs., 10am-11:30pm Fri.-Sat., noon-10:30pm Sun.) serves pub grub including fish-and-chips, burgers, and curries and fishcakes.

For the largest selection of groceries, there's the FIC's **West Store** (Ross Rd. and Dean St., tel. 27660), which also has a café and a delicatessen.

Where Davis Street East intersects the Airport Road, the converted Portakabin (military container-style housing) rooms at **Lookout Lodge** (VPC Rd., tel. 22834, £50 pp with breakfast, £80 pp with all meals) cater primarily to groups of visiting contractors, but will accommodate tourists if space is available.

Bennett House B&B (14 Allardyce St., tel. 21191, celiastewart@horizon.co.fk, £60-70 pp) is a comfortable house whose charming hostess, Celia Stewart, has one spacious quadruple room with an external private bath, plus two slightly smaller doubles with private baths in the room. Camping (£25 pp) is also possible here, with full house access throughout the day. All guests enjoy a filling English breakfast.

At the east end of town, **Shorty's Motel** (West Hillside, tel. 22861, £65 s, £70 d, with breakfast) is an immaculate prefab often used by visiting military from Mount Pleasant. Its adjacent **Shorty's Diner** (Snake Rd., tel. 22855, www.shortys-diner. com, 8:30am-8:30pm Mon.-Fri., 8am-8pm Sat.-Sun. and holidays, short orders £7.50) has panini and other sandwiches, a diversity of short orders such as sweet-and-sour pork and squid rings with chili sauce, and desserts. It's licensed to serve alcohol with meals only.

The Falklands Beerworks supplies brews to local pubs.

In a quiet location beyond the cemetery, ★ **Lafone House** (Ross Rd. E., tel. 22891, arlette@horizon.co.fk, £79 s, £106 d with shared bath, £95 s, £120 d with private bath, both with breakfast) is an immaculate and spacious five-room B&B with coffee, tea, and cookies available all day. Proprietor Arlette Betts may be Stanley's most hospitable innkeeper.

The upgraded, centrally located **Waterfront Boutique Hotel** (36 Ross Rd., tel. 22331, www.waterfronthotel.co.fk, £175-199 s, £225-250 d, with private bath) offers upgraded accommodations in a rambling house with harbor views. The modernized rooms are attractive but have design limitations. In its ★ **Waterfront Kitchen Café**, also open to nonguests, Chilean owner-chef Alex Olmedo provides an increasingly sophisticated menu; reservations are advised for dinner.

Widely considered Stanley's best, now undergoing a major expansion, the 35-room ★ **Malvina House Hotel** (3 Ross Rd., tel. 21355, www.malvinahousehotel.com, £157.50-203 s, £198-256 d, with breakfast, suite £230 s or d) is a contemporary lodging on attractive grounds, with a cozy bar and Wi-Fi throughout. Its ★ **Sunroom Restaurant** (lunch £8-12, dinner £20) vies with the Waterfront for the top spot among Stanley eateries, with full meals as well as excellent lunch specials. Appetizers include reindeer-upland goose pâté and pineapple shrimp. Entrées start with succulent roast lamb in a country where the default option used to be aging mutton, but roast reindeer is also a possibility. It's popular enough that reservations are advised for both lunch and dinner.

INFORMATION

At the foot of Philomel Street, the **Jetty Visitors Centre** (Ross Rd., tel. 22281, www.visitorfalklands.com, 10am-12pm and 1pm-4pm Mon.-Fri., 9am-5pm Sat., 10am-4pm Sun.) keeps longer hours when cruise ships are in port. The annual *Visitor Guide,* a glossy full-color booklet with brief descriptions of sights and services both in Stanley and throughout the islands, is free of charge here.

Falklands Conservation (41 Ross Rd., tel. 22247, www.falklandsconservation.com) is the leading conservation organization, offering advice and information on visiting wildlife sites throughout the islands; it also has a small shop in its Jubilee Villas headquarters.

In the Falkland Islands Community School, the **Stanley Public Library** (Reservoir Rd., tel. 27290, 9am-noon and 1:30pm-5:45pm Mon.-Tues. and Thurs., 9am-noon and 2:30pm-5:30pm Wed., 9am-noon and 3pm-6pm Fri., 1:45pm-5pm Sat.) holds a large collection of books and papers relating to the Falklands (including this author's 781-page doctoral dissertation!) and Antarctica.

SERVICES

Standard Chartered Bank (Ross Rd. between Barrack St. and Villiers St., 8:30am-3pm Mon.-Fri.) changes U.S. dollars and euros to pounds sterling and local pounds (local banknotes, though at par with pounds sterling, are not valid in the UK). There's no ATM, but they'll issue cash advances against MasterCard and Visa. The Falkland Islands Company's **West Store** (Ross Rd. and Dean St.) will also change money with purchases, but adds a £3 surcharge for cash-back transactions.

The **post office** (Ross Rd. at Barrack St., tel. 27180, 8am-noon and 1:15pm-4:30pm Mon.-Fri.) occupies part of Town Hall. It keeps longer hours, and weekend hours, when cruise ships are in port.

Public phones, in the FIC West Store (Ross Rd. and Dean St.) and some other locations, require prepaid Sure phone cards. Internet access is only available through prepaid phone cards (£10 per hour) on your own computer, tablet, or smartphone. It's possible to buy a local SIM card for £30, which includes an initial £10 pay-as-you-go credit toward phone calls and data usage.

For efficiently arranging a visit to the islands, especially for short-term guests, try **International Tours and Travel** (1 Dean St., tel. 22041, www.falklandislands.travel), which is also the LATAM Airlines rep here. **Falkland Islands Holidays** (Airport Rd., tel. 22622, www.falklandislandsholidays.com) is also reliable.

East of Philomel Hill, the **Customs & Immigration Department** (3 H Jones Rd., tel. 27340) sells nautical charts of the islands. For emergencies, contact the **Falkland Islands Police** (Ross Rd. between Barrack St. and Villiers St., tel. 28100).

King Edward VII Memorial Hospital (St. Mary's Walk, tel. 28000) has 90 staff members and 28 beds. In true emergencies, British military specialists are also available. Care is on a fee-for-service basis. Visitors must have insurance, including medical evacuation coverage, to enter the islands.

The hospital **pharmacy** (tel. 28011) can fill prescriptions, also on a fee-for-service basis.

TRANSPORTATION

For several years after the 1982 war, the only way to reach the islands was an expensive Royal Air Force flight from England via Ascension Island. That route still exists, with

Making the Continental Connection

Because Buenos Aires has prohibited Chilean charters from using Argentine airspace en route to the Falklands, LATAM's scheduled Saturday flights to and from Punta Arenas are increasingly full of cruise-ship passengers. This means that independent travelers need to make travel plans carefully or they might have to remain longer than expected in the Falklands.

If disembarking in Río Gallegos, Argentina, insist that immigration officials stamp your passport; some travelers exiting Argentina at more northerly border posts have had problems with immigration officials who have accused them of entering the country illegally or overstaying their visas. Some, on the other hand, have backdated entry stamps to the date the individual arrived in the Falklands—which Argentina considers its territory.

There is one advantage in flying from Río Gallegos to the Falklands: Since Argentina considers this a "domestic" route, the fare is about one-third the cost of that from Punta Arenas.

an irregular schedule, but for the last several years **LATAM/LAN** (www.latam.com) has offered Saturday flights to and from Punta Arenas (US$800 round-trip); one flight per month picks up and drops off passengers in the Argentine city of Río Gallegos (less than US$300 round-trip).

FIGAS (tel. 27219, tel. 27303 at check-in desk) flies 10-seat Norman-Britten Islanders to grass airstrips around the islands on demand. With an excellent safety record, the government airline covers every remote settlement, though weight restrictions limit access to some airstrips, particularly on small islands like West Point and New Island. These flights are a treat. There's no better overview of the islands. Because flight schedules are demand-driven, passengers need to ber flexible, but may enjoy a lengthy aerial tour before reaching their final destination.

Stanley Airport is about four kilometers east of town. Typical FIGAS destinations and one-way fares from Stanley include Bleaker Island (£75), Port Howard (£91.50), Sea Lion Island (£92.60), Pebble Island (£100.30), Saunders Island (£116.80), and Carcass Island (£138.80). Tourists are allowed 20 kilograms (44 pounds) baggage pp, but overweight charges are £1.40 per kilogram per flight segment.

For international flights, **Falkland Islands Tours & Travel** (tel. 21775, fitt@ horizon.co.fk) and **Penguin Travel** (tel. 27630) offer door-to-door bus service (£17 pp) to Mount Pleasant International Airport. **Stanley Cabs** (tel. 51001) provides service around town; the average fare is about £3, but Stanley airport transfers cost £6.

For rental cars, try the FIC's **Falklands 4X4** (Crozier Place and Hebe St., tel. 27663), **Stanley Services** (tel. 22622, www.stanley-services.co.fk), or **Raymond Poole** (tel. 51037). Rates start around £40 per day.

East Falkland

East Falkland still has the islands' best road network, though little beyond town is paved. The best is the Stanley-Mount Pleasant Highway, which links the capital with the airport, continuing to Darwin and Goose Green, but even this is mostly gravel and requires caution. From Pony's Pass, about eight miles (13 kilometers) west of town on this route, the North Camp Road leads to Estancia, where it forks north to Port Louis and Johnson's Harbour, and west to Teal Inlet, Douglas Station, and Port San Carlos. Rental cars may not be taken off-road.

Several Stanley-based operators offer tours in and around Stanley, and overland on East Falkland by road and off-road. In alphabetical order, they include Patrick Watts's **Adventure Falklands** (P.O. Box 223, Stanley, tel. 21383, pwatts@horizon.co.fk), which covers Stanley, wildlife sites at Volunteer Point and Cape Bougainville, and 1982 battlefields (Patrick manned the local radio coverage during the 1982 Argentine invasion); Tony Smith's **Discovery Falklands** (33-A Davis St., tel. 21027, www.discovery-falklands.com), which does natural history, historical, and battlefield excursions throughout East Falkland; and **Harbour Excursions** (57 Fitzroy Rd., tel. 55380, cheryl@beauchenefishing.co.fk) for boat trips around Stanley Harbour, Port William, and Berkeley Sound.

KIDNEY COVE

For visitors stuck in Stanley, whether by weather, unavailability of flights, or camp accommodations shortages, nearby **Kidney Cove** is more than just a consolation prize. Bird-watchers can count on seeing gentoo, Magellanic, and rockhopper penguins here. On a good day, they can also bag kings and macaronis for their life lists, although there's no guarantee given the relatively small numbers of those species here.

Murrell Farm owners Adrian and Lisa Lowe live close enough to Stanley that they can pick up passengers in town and Rover them to a large gentoo colony with the occasional king that also has plenty of Magellanics nearby. Alternatively, they can head overland to Berkeley Sound's scenic southern shore, where rockhoppers scale the steep headlands to an exposed site where, in the spring hatching season, skuas swoop down to steal newborn chicks. Either trip costs £50 pp. For £70 pp, the Lowes will combine the two for an excursion that can be done comfortably in about five hours. That said, they place no time limit at any site. The visitors themselves determine when to move on; for more than four people, there are discounts.

The Lowes have also added the king penguin rookery at Volunteer Point (full-day, £115 pp) to their programs. In addition, there are fishing trips on the Murrell (£90 pp, gear included), battlefield tours (£60 pp), and shorter excursions to Gypsy Cove and the Cape Pembroke lighthouse (£40). There are also full-day minibus tours to Goose Green, San Carlos, and back via Teal Inlet (£70 pp, minimum 3 people). For more information, contact Adrian or Lisa Lowe at **Kidney Cove Safari Tours** (Murrell Farm, tel./fax 31001, www.kidneycove.com). When cruise ships are in port, individual tours are on hold.

★ JOHNSON'S HARBOUR AND VOLUNTEER POINT

Northeast of Port Louis settlement by a good road, **Johnson's Harbour** (£15 pp per day access fee) is a 36,000-acre (14,570-hectare) sheep farm that's more notable as an essential stop on the islands' tourism circuit for its thousands-strong colony of king penguins. The kings are present year-round at its easterly **Volunteer Point** sector. In addition,

The Camp

Traditionally, in the Falklands, everything outside Stanley is "camp," and *camp* has been a synonym for hospitality. The term itself derives from the Spanish *campo* (countryside), and it's a common usage among Anglo-Argentines and Anglo-Chileans as well.

In the heyday of sheep farming, Falklands settlements were small company towns on or near sheltered harbors. Since the land reform and subdivision of the 1980s, though, this pattern has changed; many campers have moved to Stanley, the settlements have fewer residents, and many farmers now live in isolated homesteads, once "outside houses." Still, on East and West Falkland, an improved road network has partly compensated for the decline of traditional settlements and their social amenities.

While many camp residents are still involved in sheep farming, an increasing number work wholly or partially in tourism and cottage industries. Some of the best wildlife sites—Sea Lion, Bleaker, Pebble, Saunders, and Carcass Islands, for instance—now boast comfortable lodges or self-catering accommodations.

Not so long ago, the idea of charging someone who came to spend a weekend in camp was almost unthinkable, although it was customary to present the host with rum or another small gift. Now, for better or worse, the custom of a free bed has nearly disappeared. Pebble Island Hotel's former manager Allan White once told me that "I preferred the old way," but the pressure for economic diversification has nearly, though not entirely, eliminated that option. Even so, the hospitality remains.

there are gentoos, Magellanics, cormorants, and many other birds.

The colorful king, the islands' largest penguin, has an unusual breeding cycle that can range from 10 months (in the Falklands, at the northern limit of its range) to 14 months (at sub-Antarctic South Georgia). Moreover, that cycle is much less season-specific than that of its migratory counterparts or even the gentoo, which is also present throughout the year. At the site itself, do not enter the stone circle intended to mark an undisturbed king penguin area.

The tour season runs November to March; from the settlement, the soggy 4WD track is open for tour operators only and can be difficult even for locally experienced drivers. Accommodations with food are available at Lee and Martha Moldenbuhr's **Johnson's Harbour Cottage** (tel. 31398, mjf_farming@hotmail.com, £35-40 pp, with higher rates corresponding to weekends) and more rustically at Derek Petterson's **Volunteer Point** (tel. 32000, drp@horizon.co.fk, £70 pp with all meals, £10 pp one-time charge for camping).

SALVADOR AND CAPE BOUGAINVILLE

Northwest of Stanley via Estancia, Teal Inlet, and Douglas Station, **Salvador** is the gateway to **Cape Bougainville,** home to large rockhopper colonies and the occasional macaroni, plus other seabirds and a plethora of sea lions. In the hands of the same family since its Gibraltarian founder, Andrés Pitaluga, arrived from South America in the 1830s, it also has elephant seal and sea lion colonies on Centre Island in the estuary of Port Salvador (Salvador Water), near the settlement.

From Stanley, Cape Bougainville is a full-day excursion. There are no accommodations, but it has a Portakabin shelter, with sofas and chairs, in case of rough weather.

PORT SAN CARLOS AND CAPE DOLPHIN

At the end of the North Camp Road, the settlement of **Port San Carlos** is the gateway to **Cape Dolphin,** a wildlife-rich area that's a long day's excursion from Stanley. Its long white-sand beach and headlands are home to gentoo penguins, king and rock cormorants, and sea lions, while black-necked swans, grebes, and teal paddle its ponds.

A protected wildlife reserve, Cape Dolphin is irregularly open to the public, so it's best to go with a tour from town or at one of the farms. At **Race Point Farm** (tel. 41012, jh-jones@horizon.co.fk, £35 pp, discounts for 2 nights or more), John and Michelle Jones offer self-catering accommodations, plus coastal tours for up to three people (£125), farm work permitting.

Ben Berntsen also provides self-catering at Elephant Beach Farm's nearby **James Cabin** (tel. 41020, benebf@horizon.co.fk, £25 pp adults, £10 ages 5-15, camping £10 pp). Dinner (£15), usually a roast with vegetables, breakfast (£10) and boxed lunches (£10) are also available. Coastal tours (£120 per vehicle for up to 4 people) with a guide are available. Landing fees (£10 pp adults, £5 ages 10-15) are charged for visitors with their own vehicles. Stanley pickups and drop-offs cost £70 for a single passenger, £60 pp for two, £50 pp for three, and £40 pp for four.

From Stanley, Port San Carlos (commonly known as "KC" for the initials of founder Keith Cameron) is about two hours by road, but the overland track to the cape is slower.

DARWIN AND GOOSE GREEN

Where a slender isthmus links East Falkland's mountainous north with its undulating southern peninsula of Lafonia, about 60 miles (100 kilometers) west of Stanley, **Darwin** once had a population of nearly 200 that has fallen to just a few, as most of the farm buildings and houses shifted to nearby **Goose Green** in the 1920s. The peninsula, whose highest point is only 90 meters above sea level, takes its name from Montevideo merchant Samuel Fisher Lafone, founder of what became the Falklands Islands Company (FIC). Lafone's gauchos hunted feral cattle to be slaughtered and their hides processed at his *saladero* (meat-salting plant).

Darwin is a historic site, starting with the circular **corral** that dates from *saladero* days before sheep replaced cattle, and it became the center of the FIC's camp operations for more than a century; weathering headstones at **Darwin Cemetery** tell part of the story. In 1982, the South Atlantic war's deadliest combat took place at Goose Green. Military landmarks include a **monument** to British Colonel H Jones, who died leading an assault on Argentine positions, and the **Argentine military cemetery.**

Cape Dolphin

At Goose Green itself, at the end of the FIC jetty, the last visible remains of the bark *Vicar of Bray* (1841) belong to the only surviving ship to have served San Francisco during the California Gold Rush. After spending several decades coasting the islands, it was blown ashore here in 1912 and incorporated into the jetty.

South of Goose Green, dating from 1927, the **Bodie Creek Bridge** is the world's southernmost suspension span. In the middle of the FIC camp, it simplified communications with the outlying Walker Creek and North Arm settlements, but it's now a precarious monument.

All six rooms in tastefully-modernized ★ **Darwin Lodge** (tel. 31313, www.darwin-house.com, £48 pp B&B, £85 pp with two meals; £105 pp with all meals; £20 solo occupancy supplementary charge) now have private baths. Common areas include a sunny north-facing conservatory, large sitting and dining rooms, a substantial library, and a small bar. Managers Al and Lorraine Campbell also offer tours of nearby battlefield sites, wildlife-rich lagoons, and Mount Usborne, the islands' highest summit.

★ BLEAKER ISLAND

For wildlife-oriented visitors on a budget, **Bleaker** is an exceptional alternative to more distant and costly destinations like Sea Lion and Carcass Islands, which require longer flights and have more expensive accommodations and food. Bleaker can't quite match the diversity of those islands, but it has a scenic rocky shoreline with Magellanic, rockhopper, and gentoo penguins, as well as the occasional king and macaroni, plus king cormorants and night herons, and a breeding colony of giant petrels. Black-necked swans have recently made an appearance.

Because Bleaker has no cats, it also has thriving populations of small birds. Owners Mike and Phyl Rendell have removed rats from offshore islands to further encourage the diminutive species like tussock birds, and rat

eradication is underway on the main island. While there are no breeding sea lions or elephant seals, Bleaker gets occasional visitors.

At its closest, Bleaker is barely half a mile (800 meters) from East Falkland. FIC managers used to ride 20 miles (32 kilometers) southeast from North Arm and row across to Bleaker, but today's visitors prefer FIGAS air taxis. Most wildlife is within easy walking distance of the settlement, but there's a Land Rover available for rent (on Bleaker's "hard camp," unlike much of East Falkland, getting stuck is not a serious issue). Orientation tours (£30 pp) are available.

Bleaker's ★ **Cobb's Cottage** (tel. 32491 or 21084, www.bleakerisland.com, £57.75 pp self-catering, £99.75 pp with all meals) is a comfortable and attractive kit house with two twin bedrooms. A newer and more spacious alternative, the nearby four-room **Cassard House** takes its name from a French ship that was wrecked at the south end of the island in 1906. Amenities include radiant floor heating, an ample sitting room, a sunny conservatory (which can get overheated), and an honesty bar.

From October to the end of February, the all-meal package is the only option; there's a small store for supplementary needs.

★ SEA LION ISLAND

For wildlife-lovers who can afford it, **Sea Lion** offers more in a smaller area than any other destination in the islands. Five miles (8 kilometers) long and barely a mile (1.6 kilometers) wide, with landscapes ranging from broad sandy beaches to rocky tussac-topped cliffs, it can boast 47 breeding bird species (including three penguins and five predators), plus large breeding colonies of elephant seals and sea lions.

Sea Lion's single most impressive feature may be the sprawling mixed colonies of rockhopper penguins and king cormorants—for both their visual impact and their odor. But the most exciting feature may be the plantations of native tussac grass that sometimes conceal the bull sea lions that gave the island its name. An unexpected encounter with these large, fierce beasts can be disconcerting.

In the summer breeding season, some 2,000 elephant seals nearly blanket the sandy beaches within a few minutes' walk of the island's comfortable lodge. Frequenting the nearby tussock, the striated caracara or Johnny rook *(Phalcoboenus australis)* is one of the world's rarest predatory birds. It's remarkably tolerant of the human presence.

After purchasing Sea Lion from Terry and Doreen Clifton, who had restored the native tussock for both wildlife habitat and controlled grazing (there are no longer any sheep), the Falkland Islands Development Corporation (FIDC) chose it for the islands' first dedicated wildlife lodge. Those who are staying only a day can see a bit of everything, while those spending several days can orient themselves and then choose where they wish to concentrate their explorations.

Under a 150-year lease, a British company now operates ★ **Sea Lion Lodge** (tel. 32004, www.sealionisland.com, £100-170 pp with all meals). Purpose-built from a kit, with mostly Chilean staff, the 10-room lodge is probably the most economically successful of the islands' wildlife destinations. Rates vary seasonally, with the highest in November through February.

West Falkland

Beyond the Falkland Sound, which runs northeast-southwest, the west was the site of Britain's first settlement, at Port Egmont on Saunders Island. Nobody settled West Falkland proper, though, until J. L. Waldron founded the Port Howard sheep station in the late 1860s, and settlements like Fox Bay, Hill Cove, and Port Stephens followed in short order. Some of these farms remained in the same hands for over a century, while others became FIC property. Several offshore islands, some of them exceptional wildlife destinations, were home to small independent farmers. One of them, Keppel Island, witnessed a curious experiment in missionizing indigenous people from Tierra del Fuego.

While the population of West Falkland has been declining since the agrarian reform of the 1980s, there's hope that the improved road network and the establishment of Fox Bay Village, on the south coast, as a wool transshipment point will revitalize the island. The only other surviving large settlement, still run as a traditional sheep station, Port Howard has fewer than 20 permanent residents. One local humorist has suggested that it would be easy to repopulate the west by enforcing prohibition in Stanley and declaring open licensing hours here.

★ PORT HOWARD

Every house has a view at **Port Howard,** West Falkland's only surviving large farm and the starting point for an improving road system. Most wildlife sites are a bit distant, but a visit here offers insights into how the large sheep stations worked. Since its sale to former employees in 1987, hard times in the wool industry have caused unemployment, population has fallen from 40 into the 20s, and the school closed because there was only a single school-age child (served by a traveling teacher and radio instruction).

One of Howard's outstanding features is the former **manager's house,** now a visitors' lodge. In its present state, this is a gem, but in the past it could also be a burden. According to one experienced observer, a large house was not necessarily a luxury, especially as labor became more scarce and expensive:

Managers' houses have tended to be large not for the convenience of the managers—rather the opposite. They

The Falklands Bookshelf

For a good general account of history and natural history, look for Ian J. Strange's *The Falkland Islands* (London: David & Charles, 1983); however, it barely anticipates the dramatic economic and political changes since the 1982 South Atlantic war. Robert Fox's *Antarctica and the South Atlantic: Discovery, Development and Dispute* (London: BBC Books, 1985) places the territorial controversy in historical context. For military and political details on the war, try Max Hastings's and Simon Jenkins's *Battle for the Falklands* (London: Pan, 1983). Graham Bound's *Fortress Falklands* (Barnsley, South Yorkshire: Pen & Sword, 2012) brings the controversy up to date.

For detail on natural history, try Strange's *Field Guide to the Wildlife of the Falkland Islands and South Georgia* (London: Harper Collins, 1992), illustrated with the author's exceptional color and black-and-white illustrations and black-and-white photographs. Also well illustrated, Robin Woods's *Guide to Birds of the Falkland Islands* (Oswestry, Shropshire, United Kingdom: Anthony Nelson, 1988) focuses exclusively on birds, while Strange covers marine mammals, introduced land mammals, and flora as well.

For a Darwinian perspective, based on archival research at Cambridge, there's Patrick Armstrong's *Darwin's Desolate Islands: A Naturalist in the Falklands, 1833 and 1834* (Chippenham, United Kingdom: Picton, 1992). Based on private papers, Michael Mainwaring's *From the Falklands to Pata-*

have been used as free hotels by official visitors—OK when servants were obtainable but a burden on wives in particular since in general they were not.

Still, as it grazes 42,000 sheep on about 200,000 acres (81,000 hectares), Port Howard offers possibilities for hiking near **Mount Maria,** fishing in the **Warrah River,** and highway and off-road tours. Occupied by 1,000 Argentines in 1982, it saw no serious combat, but there's a small **war museum** here, and the British military's occasional live-fire exercises are a reminder of the continuing territorial dispute.

Port Howard Lodge (tel./fax 42187, porthowardlodge@horizon.co.fk, £125 pp with all meals, discounts for children depending on age) provides a glimpse into the apparent comforts that came with privilege: spacious, well-furnished bedrooms with private baths, a large sitting room that now serves as a bar, a dining room that's now the restaurant, and a sunny conservatory that yields luscious grapes in summer. The operators have preserved historic features like the antique crank telephone exchange (since replaced by a digital network). A handsome assortment of gaucho-style horse gear adorns the walls.

In addition, Port Howard Lodge offers **farm tours** (£10 pp) and eight-hour **4WD and wildlife tours** (£90 pp, 2-person minimum). Other farms have better access to wildlife, however.

Another option is the self-catering **Head Shepherd's House** (tel. 42181, phfarm@horizon.co.fk, £50 for up to 4 people).

HILL COVE

Almost directly west of Port Howard, now reached by a good road, **Hill Cove** acquired a certain fame for being the only place in the islands where a forest plantation, primarily conifers such as pines and Sitka spruce, has been successful. Some specimens reach 50 feet (15 meters) in a land where most ornamentals are stunted and wind-flagged, but recently they've suffered parasitic attacks that have killed many of them.

Since its subdivision and sale, the settlement is a lesser focus than the outside houses, some of which offer accommodations. On the site of the initial settlement, northeast of Hill Cove proper, Paul and Davina Peck's **Shallow Bay Guest House** (tel. 41007, psb@horizon.co.fk, £25 pp self-catering, children free) occupies one of the islands' oldest stone houses.

gonia (London: Allison & Busby, 1983) chronicles one 19th-century shepherd's family's departure from the islands to pioneer an *estancia* on "The Coast" of Argentine Patagonia.

In cooperation with the Falkland Islands Trust, the small British publisher Bluntisham Books (www.bluntishambooks.co.uk) has a series of well-illustrated booklets that include T. H. Davies's and J. H. McAdam's *Wild Flowers of the Falkland Islands* (1989), John Smith's historical *Those Were the Days* (1989) on Stanley's past, and Julian Fisher's *Walks and Climbs in the Falkland Islands* (1992).

The annual *Falklands Islands Journal* covers a variety of historical and natural-history topics, including local memoirs. It's available in Stanley or in the United Kingdom from Jim McAdam (Department of Applied Plant Science, Queens University, Newforge Lane, Belfast BT9 5PX, Northern Ireland, jim.mcadam@afbini.gov.uk).

Beautifully illustrated with color photographs, and with contributions from local writers, Debbie Summers's excellent *Visitor's Guide to the Falkland islands* (2nd ed., London: Falklands Conservation, 2005) makes an ideal souvenir; it's available in the islands for £12. There's a growing number of expensive coffee table books such as French photographer Stanley Leroux's *Furious Fifties* (Stellar Editions, 2016).

PORT STEPHENS

Now accessible by road, from Port Howard via Fox Bay Village, the far western settlement of **Port Stephens** lies on the edge of one of the islands' most scenic and wildlife-rich areas. Unfortunately, it lacks formal tourist facilities, but for visitors with time and flexibility, it's worth exploring the options. One option is to rent a vehicle at Port Howard, about three hours away.

Just southwest of the settlement, the wildlife sites include **Wood Cove** and **Stephens Peak,** home to enormous mixed colonies of cormorants and rockhopper penguins, Magellanic and gentoo penguins, and even a small contingent of kings. **Calm Head,** about two hours from the settlement, provides some of the islands' most spectacular coastal panoramas. Peter and Anne Robertson, who own this area, do not permit vehicles to enter it: Visitors must hike from the settlement.

Formerly part of Port Stephens, **Port Albemarle** was the site of an industrial sealing station, a Colonial Development Corporation fiasco that, fortunately, failed to commercialize sea lion oil after World War II. Most of its ruins have been dismantled, but

the factory was a suitable metaphor for the misjudgments and neglect that so long characterized London's attitude toward the Islands.

Beyond the former sealing station, a large gentoo colony faces the stunning **Arch Islands,** where the South Atlantic seas have eroded a passageway in the largest of the group.

Prospective visitors need permission from landowners **Peter and Anne Robertson** (tel. 42307, par@horizon.co.fk) at the settlement, and **Shaun May and Tanya Ford** (tel. 42012) at Albemarle Station. When it's not needed for shearers, the Robertsons rent the **Cadet's Quarters** (£25 pp, £13 under age 16) on a self-catering basis.

★ PEBBLE ISLAND

Just off West Falkland's north coast, **Pebble Island** takes its name from the colorful agates, sometimes polished and turned into jewelry, that litter its westernmost beaches. Visitors come to the 24-mile-long (39-kilometer) offshore island for its diverse wildlife and landscape: East of the settlement isthmus, a pond-filled plain teems with wildfowl while sea lions breed along the shore; to the west, several penguin species have colonized the coastal greens and headlands, along with giant petrels. There are more than 40 resident bird species.

Immediately north of the settlement, horseshoe-shaped **Elephant Bay** has no elephant seals, but its white crescent beach is the starting point for a two-hour walk to **Little Wreck Point.** At the end, there's a shoreline graveyard of beaked whale skulls, ribs, and vertebrae. Magellanic penguins breed here and swim in the large pond.

On the night of May 14-15, 1982, Pebble was the site of a British commando raid that destroyed 11 Argentine spotter planes, an action that made their naval counter-invasion of East Falkland feasible. On the slope of **First Mount,** just west of the settlement, there's a monument to HMS *Coventry,* which sank with at least 10 British helicopters onboard after being hit by a missile, about 10 miles (16 kilometers) to the north. A nearby gravesite marks the resting place of two Argentine pilots whose Learjet came down a short distance from here, but the remains went undetected until 1992.

Some distance west, on a coastal green, there's a substantial gentoo colony with the occasional king, and a midsize rockhopper colony with the odd macaroni. Giant petrels also nest on a nearby slope, but

visitors should not approach too closely as these easily disturbed birds may abandon their nests.

The former manager's house, ★ **Pebble Island Lodge** (tel./fax 41093, www.pebblelodge.com, £144 pp adults, £72 ages 5-15, with all meals) has six spacious doubles and one odd compact single entered through its own bath. All baths are private but have showers rather than tubs. The enormous sitting room, with excellent natural light, has a self-service bar on the honor system. There is 24-hour electricity from a wind turbine and storage batteries, and 24-hour hot water.

For hikers, the lodge has Land Rover drop-off service; the cost depends on the distance from the settlement.

★ SAUNDERS ISLAND

Better than any other island in the archipelago, **Saunders** blends the attractions of natural history and history. Its wildlife is abundant and accessible, but it's also a case study in the Falklands-Malvinas controversy.

The Falklands' second-largest offshore island, at 31,000 acres (12,500 hectares), Saunders is a roughly U-shaped landmass nearly cut into unequal segments by the east-west Brett Harbour. The settlement occupies

rockhopper penguin colony on Pebble Island

A rockhopper penguin showers with a friend on Saunders Island.

a site near Port Egmont, on the relatively sheltered east coast, almost facing Keppel.

History

British marines first established themselves here in 1765. After France withdrew from Port Louis, Spain discovered and expelled the Port Egmont settlement two years later—nearly sparking a shooting war in Europe. Under pressure, the Spaniards restored the Saunders settlement, but, in 1774, Britain suspended its presence for, it said, budgetary reasons. After the British departure, Spanish forces leveled the settlement.

Just north of the current settlement, Port Egmont's surviving ruins include extensive foundations and even some walls, jetties, and garden terraces that, by one account, yielded plentiful produce. The produce was mostly root crops such as potatoes and carrots, but also green vegetables such as broccoli, celery, lettuce, and spinach.

Ironically enough, long after Britain regained the islands from Buenos Aires,

Saunders became Argentine property. Scottish sheep farmer John Hamilton, who came to the islands as an FIC shepherd in the late 19th century, reemigrated to Santa Cruz territory, where he became a major *estanciero* (ranch owner); never losing interest in the Falklands, he purchased several island properties, including Saunders. When Hamilton died, his Argentine children inherited the property, and until its sale to resident employees in 1987, its ownership was a sore point among Islanders.

Sights

For wildlife-oriented visitors, one big attraction is **The Neck,** a sandy isthmus about four hours' walk from the settlement on the north side of Brett Harbour. Facing the open ocean to the north, a large gentoo colony and a smaller contingent of 30 or so kings breed. For some years, a solitary chinstrap penguin made its home among the gentoos, but it has apparently headed back to the Antarctic.

The Neck's real highlight is the enormous breeding colonies of rockhopper penguins, cormorants, and especially black-browed albatrosses, who need the steep cliffs and stiff northwesterlies beneath **Mount Richards** to launch themselves into flight. On land, these stunningly beautiful birds are ungainly but, nearly fearless of humans, they will reward photographers by waddling into close-up range.

For tireless hikers, this scenic northeastern coastline is an ideal way to return to the settlement, but its steepness, slipperiness, and high winds make it potentially hazardous. Beneath **Rookery Mountain,** more albatrosses, rockhoppers, and king cormorants breed near a new house and an old Portakabin (military container-style housing) that both offer accommodations; it is more easily accessible from the settlement.

Immediately west of The Neck, Magellanic penguins burrow in the coastal greens en route to **Elephant Point** (another four hours on foot), which has a substantial elephant-seal colony, as well as kelp gulls, skuas, and other birds.

From February to May, there are whales offshore.

Food and Accommodations

In the settlement, farm owners and managers David and Suzan Pole-Evans (tel. 41298, www.saundersfalklands.com, £30 pp) rent the self-catering 6-bed **Stone Cottage,** dating from 1875 but with a modernized interior, and **The Settlement,** a 10-bed unit sometimes used by military guests from Mount Pleasant.

Wildlife-lovers usually prefer ★ **The Neck** (£70 pp), whose converted Portakabin that has electricity and hot water and can sleep up to eight. It also has a gas cook-stove and a full bath with a shower and a flush toilet. Tent camping (£20 pp) is also possible nearby.

Beneath Rookery Mountain, about 50 minutes' ride north from the settlement near rockhopper and albatross colonies, the **Rookery Inn** (£70 pp) is a comfortable modern house with two ample bedrooms, plus a combination living-dining room and kitchen.

The Pole-Evanses also permit **camping** (£20 pp) anywhere except near the accommodations at The Neck proper (though it's possible not too far away, where there's piped spring water and a latrine). The farm has a small store and may sell fresh milk and eggs, but visitors should bring most supplies from Stanley. Payment is possible in local currency, UK pounds sterling, or U.S. dollars. Children under age 10 pay half price for accommodations, with children under 5 free.

For those staying in the settlement, an all-meal package is available (£70 pp, minimum 6 people). Individual precooked meals are also available on request.

Transportation

Farm schedules permitting, the Pole-Evanses can provide Land Rover transfers to The Neck (£70 pp round-trip) or to The Rookery for visitors who stay at the settlement (£30 pp). Children under age 16 go free of charge.

★ CARCASS ISLAND

Remote and tiny **Carcass** is the favorite island of many Islanders and visitors alike. At the archipelago's northwestern edge, it's full of wildlife, but at the same time, it's equally notable for a home-style hospitality that belies its dependence on the tourist trade.

On the island's south shore, Carcass settlement is a sheltered beauty spot whose

elephant seal pups, Northwest Point, Carcass Island

honeysuckle aroma and 10-foot dracaenas lend it a semitropical aura. Curious caracaras perch in the Monterey cypress windbreaks outside the lodge's dining-room windows, the younger ones playing like kittens with string that droops from the limbs.

Unlike the larger islands, Carcass has always been a family farm, though it's changed hands several times in nearly a century and a half. The present owners, Rob and Lorraine McGill, run relatively small numbers of sheep and make much of their living from brief cruise-ship visits and overnight guests. On meeting FIGAS flights, Rob McGill even offers chocolates and juice on the Rover ride into the settlement.

On the settlement shoreline, the birdlife is abundant and diverse, with kelp geese, steamer ducks, Magellanic oystercatchers, Patagonian crested ducks, Cobb's wren, and tussock birds (small birds flourish in the absence of cats, rats, and mice). South of the settlement, there's a large tussock grass plantation with gentoo and Magellanic penguins.

At **Northwest Point,** several miles from the settlement but not far from the airstrip, there's a colony of perhaps 200 elephant seals. The highest point, 723-foot **Mount Bing,** yields views of the uninhabited Jason Islands to the northwest.

Carcass, which takes its name from the 18th-century naval vessel HMS *Carcass,* has half a dozen rooms with private baths—two doubles, three twins, and a triple—in the **main house** (£115 pp Oct. and Mar., £125 pp Nov.-Feb., with all meals). Rates include all transportation on the island, but not wine or other drinks from the honesty bar. Thanks to a wind turbine and backup generator, it now enjoys 24-hour electricity. For reservations and information, contact **Rob or Lorraine McGill** (tel. 41106, lorraine@horizon.co.fk).

WEST POINT ISLAND

Southwest of Carcass, separated from West Falkland by a narrow strait called The Woolly Gut, **West Point Island** has been in the same family since 1879. Like Carcass, it gets plenty

of cruise-ship visitors to see its black-browed albatrosses, Johnny rooks, Magellanic penguins, and rockhoppers. Owner Roddy Napier replanted native tussock grass on much of the shoreline. Unfortunately, because of its short and thrilling airstrip—probably too thrilling for timid fliers—FIGAS cannot land more than two passengers on it, but Carcass-based **Michael Clarke** (jeannetteclarke@horizon. co.fk) will shuttle passengers here by sea (£250 pp for 2 passengers, £100 pp for larger groups); he also runs more expensive excursions to remote Steeple Jason Island.

WEDDELL ISLAND

On the southwestern edge of the archipelago, sprawling **Weddell** is the Falklands' third-largest island, with a representative sample of wildlife and an intriguing history. Like Saunders Island, Weddell belonged to Argentina-based Scotsman John Hamilton, and he and his managers undertook audacious agricultural experiments here.

Some of these projects, such as replanting native tussock grass, cultivating experimental forests, and diversifying the livestock with dozens of Highland cattle and more than a hundred Shetland ponies, were well-meaning even if they achieved limited success. Others, such as introducing Patagonian foxes, were foolish; expected to provide pelts, the proliferating foxes not only caused high lamb mortality but also preyed on bird eggs.

Like Saunders, Weddell became Argentine property, but after the war it was sold to its resident managers. It has since changed hands again to a British resident and then to a local owner. Visitors can go to Loop Head, the best wildlife site, for its gentoo and Magellanic penguins, giant petrels, great skuas, night herons, and striated caracaras. Open to visitors once again, **Weddell Island** (tel. 42398, www.weddellisland.com) offers self-catering accommodations at **Sea View Cottage** (£170, sleeping up to 4 people) and **Mountain View Cottage** (£200, sleeping up to 8).

The Staats Island Guanacos

West of Weddell, uninhabited Staats Island is notable for supporting a population of roughly 300 guanacos, first introduced by John Hamilton in the 1930s. In such a restricted habitat, as its 1,200 acres (500 hectares) of natural vegetation declined under grazing pressure, biologists would expect large die-offs to keep the population in equilibrium. Into the 1950s, though, hunting kept the population in check—on sporadic visits, Islanders culled upward of a hundred in a week.

The culling records are, in fact, scratched into the walls of **Waldron's Shanty,** where the hunters sought shelter from wind and rain. The remarkably stable numbers since then have piqued biologists' interest in the species' population dynamics in what is, for all practical purposes, an ideal natural laboratory. The current owners have still been culling occasionally to maintain the numbers, and plan to fence off the island's north end for tussock restoration. There has been talk, though, of eliminating the guanacos entirely.

NEW ISLAND

In more than one sense, **New Island** has always been the Falklands' "Wild West." Its rugged, precipitous headlands burst with wildlife, including rockhopper penguins, black-browed albatrosses, and southern fur seals. It was also a lawless refuge for British and North American sealers and whalers in the late 18th and early 19th centuries. In one celebrated case, during the War of 1812, New England whaler Charles Barnard spent 18 months marooned here after being abandoned by British marines he had rescued from a shipwreck.

Remains of **Barnard's House** (now a visitors center) still stand here, as do rusting ruins of an early-20th-century **Norwegian Whaling Factory** that folded for lack of whales. In all, New Island has 41 breeding bird species, including crested and striated caracaras, and the rare thin-billed prion.

Most New Island visitors come from cruise ships, though the improved airstrip now permits FIGAS to land here, but with no more than two passengers. The owners manage the property as nature reserves, and there are no remaining sheep. No smoking is permitted anywhere on the island.

Ian J. Strange established the **New Island South Conservation Trust** (www.newislandtrust.co.uk) to protect wildlife colonies and historical constructions on the island. Visitor housing is under construction; for latest details, contact John and Charlene Rowland (tel. 42317, rowland@horizon.co.fk).

For an account of Barnard's New Island stranding, look for his memoir *Marooned* (Middletown, CT: Wesleyan University Press, 1979), edited and with an illuminating introduction by Bertha S. Dodge.

Background

The Landscape

Patagonia's diverse geography rises from sea level through desert steppe to Andean forests and fell-fields to continental glaciers. On the Chilean side, west of the Andes, it's a well-watered and often lushly forested region, while the sparsely vegetated eastern Argentine side lies mostly in the rain shadow of the cordillera.

GEOGRAPHY

Because there's no agreement as to Patagonia's boundaries, it's hard to calculate its size, but it's larger than most of the world's countries. From its northernmost point at the source of Argentina's Río Colorado, around 36 degrees south latitude, it's about 2,200 kilometers as the crow flies to Cape Horn, at nearly 56 degrees south. At the widest point, roughly 40 degrees south, it measures nearly 1,000 kilometers from the Atlantic to the Pacific, but it narrows to barely 400 kilometers toward the tip of the continent.

Argentine Patagonia, traditionally comprising the provinces of Neuquén, Río Negro, Chubut, Santa Cruz, and Tierra del Fuego, has an area of 786,983 square kilometers, larger than Texas and about the same size as Turkey. This calculation excludes similar areas of Buenos Aires province north of the Río Negro and south of the Río Colorado, Argentine Patagonia's traditional boundary. Some contemporary sources include La Pampa province and even parts of Mendoza.

Chilean Patagonia's limits are even more imprecise. South of the traditional Mapuche frontier on the Río Biobío, La Araucanía, Los Lagos, and the new Los Ríos region, plus the more southerly regions of Aisén and Magallanes, add up to 339,914 square kilometers, a little smaller than present-day Germany. Counting only the "truly" Patagonian regions of Aisén and Magallanes, though, it would be just 241,058 square kilometers—still as large as the United Kingdom.

Together, the Argentine and Chilean sectors would total 1,126,897 square kilometers, about the size of France, Germany, and the United Kingdom combined, or of California and Texas combined.

Mountains

Patagonia's most imposing feature is the longitudinal Andean range that extends the length of the continent, and gradually disappears beneath the Pacific Ocean. The southern Patagonian Andes are lower than the uplands of Peru, Bolivia, and northernmost Chile and Argentina, but still have many glaciated peaks because of their higher latitude.

One of the world's most seismically active countries, Chile lies at the juncture of the Nazca and South American tectonic plates. Positioned along the so-called Pacific "ring of fire," it also has many active volcanoes—some very active—and many active earthquake faults. The 1960 earthquake centered near the southern city of Valdivia brought a tsunami that devastated coastal areas from Concepción to Chiloé and left many thousands homeless. The more northerly 2010 quake had similar consequences. Seismic safety has improved, but earthquakes are not going to disappear.

Steppes

In Patagonia's high latitudes, in the Andean rain shadow, bunch grasses and shrubs punctuate the arid, mostly level *meseta* (Patagonia steppe) tablelands that stretch to the Atlantic.

In a few areas, eastward-flowing rivers have cut deep, scenic canyons through the bedrock.

Rivers

On both sides of the Andes, rushing transverse rivers create recreational rafting runs and water to irrigate the vineyards of Neuquén. Some Argentine rivers reverse direction to flow through gaps into the Pacific on the Chilean side, while others, like the Río Negro and the Río Santa Cruz, traverse the Patagonian steppe to reach the Atlantic.

Chile's largest and most important rivers are the Futaleufú, still providing recreational thrills, and the remote Baker, which carries the largest flow of any Chilean river. Both, as well as other rivers, face the threat of major hydroelectric projects.

Lakes

Both Argentina and Chile are famous for their Andean lakes districts, where the melting ice of Pleistocene glaciers has left a legacy of indigo-filled troughs. Chile's remote Aisén region and Argentina's Chubut and Santa Cruz provinces have countless large lakes barely touched by anglers. There are also large interior drainage lakes such as Chubut's Lago

Musters and Lago Colhué Huapi, and Santa Cruz's Lago Cardiel.

CLIMATE

In Patagonia, the northern hemisphere seasons are reversed: The summer solstice falls on December 21, the autumn equinox on March 21, the winter solstice on June 21, and the spring equinox on September 21. For most Argentines and Chileans, the summer months are January and February, when schools are out of session and families take their holidays.

In far southern latitudes, blustery maritime conditions are the rule and seasonal variations can be dramatic, but it's difficult to generalize about climate. Moreover, elevation plays a major role in all areas.

Because its receding glaciers are sensitive to warming, Patagonia is a living laboratory for climate-change studies. While it's the coolest part of both countries, its inclemency is often overstated. Despite a geographical position at the southern tip of the continent, it is not Antarctica. Eastern portions of Argentina's Patagonian provinces are even arid steppe, with little rainfall but frequent high winds, especially in summer. Climatically, Tierra del Fuego is an extension of mainland Patagonia.

Flora and Fauna

Much of Patagonia's flora and fauna will be novel to foreign visitors, especially those from the northern hemisphere.

CONSERVATION ORGANIZATIONS

Argentina, Chile, and the Falkland Islands all have their own conservation-oriented entities, both governmental and nongovernmental.

Argentina

For information on protected areas and national parks, contact the **Administración de Parques Nacionales** (Av. Santa Fe 690,

Retiro, Buenos Aires, tel. 011/4314-0303, www.parquesnacionales.gov.ar).

Argentina's main wildlife advocacy organization is the **Fundación Vida Silvestre Argentina** (Defensa 251, 6°-K, Monserrat, Buenos Aires, tel. 011/4331-3631, www.vidasilvestre.org.ar, membership from US$10 per month). It publishes the quarterly magazine *Revista Vida Silvestre*, which is excellent reading for those proficient in Spanish.

For birders, there is the **Asociación Ornitológica del Plata** (Matheu 1246/1248, Buenos Aires, tel. 011/4943-7216, www.avesargentinas.org.ar, 10:30am-1:30pm and 2:30pm-8:30pm Mon.-Fri.).

The international conservation organization **Greenpeace** (Zabala 3873, Chacarita, tel. 011/4551-8811, www.greenpeace.org.ar, 10am-6pm Mon.-Fri.) also has a Buenos Aires branch.

For general information on mountaineering, contact the **Centro Andino Buenos Aires** (Rivadavia 1255, Oficina 2, tel. 011/4381-1566, www.caba.org.ar, 6pm-10pm Tues.-Thurs.). There are also local and provincial mountaineering clubs.

Chile

Chile's primary government environmental organization, in charge of national parks and other protected areas, is the **Corporación Nacional Forestal** (Conaf, Av. Bulnes 291, Santiago, tel. 02/2390-0282 or 02/2390-0125, www.conaf.cl), which provides information and also sells maps, books, and pamphlets at its Santiago offices. It also has offices in every regional capital and some other cities, and visitors centers or ranger stations at nearly all its units.

Chile's oldest nongovernmental environmental organization is the **Comité de la Defensa de Flora y Fauna** (Committee for the Defense of Flora and Fauna, or Codeff, Ernesto Reyes 035, Providencia, Santiago, tel. 02/2777-2534, www.codeff.cl). Since 1968, it has focused on practical projects to preserve and restore native plants and animals, often in cooperation with government agencies such as Conaf.

The highly professional **Fundación Terram** (General Bustamante 24, 5-I, Providencia, Santiago, tel. 02/2269-4499, www.terram.cl) emphasizes sustainable development.

Falkland Islands

Falklands Conservation (Jubilee Villas, 41 Ross Rd., P.O. Box 26, Stanley FIQQ 1ZZ, tel. 22247, www.falklandsconservation.com) is the main conservation organization. It also has a UK office (1 Waterloo Close, Abbotsley, Cambridgeshire PE19 6UX, tel. 01767/679-039).

VEGETATION ZONES

Floral associations are strongly, but not perfectly, correlated with latitude and elevation.

Broadleaf and Coniferous Forest

In the Patagonian lakes region, various species of broadleaf southern beech *(Nothofagus),* both evergreen and deciduous, are the most abundant trees. Conifers include the araucaria *(Araucaria araucana),* called *paraguas* (umbrella) or monkey-puzzle tree because its crown resembles an umbrella and its limbs the form of a monkey's curled tail. The long-lived *alerce* or *lawen (Fitzroya cupressoides)* is an endangered species because of its high timber value, though most stands are now protected. It is more common on the well-watered Chilean side.

Except for specialists, Argentines and Chileans refer indiscriminately to conifers as *pinos* (pines), even though the southern hemisphere's only true pines (of the genus *Pinus)* occur as garden ornamentals or plantation timber.

Temperate Rainforest

In southwestern Chilean Patagonia, heavy rainfall supports dense and verdant coastal and upland *Nothofagus* forests, though there are other broadleaf trees and even the occasional conifer, such as the *ciprés del los Guaitecas* (Guaytecas cypress). In some areas, this forest has suffered severe depredations at the hands of corporations and colonists.

Patagonian Steppe

In the Andean rain shadow, on the eastern Patagonia plains, Chilean Magallanes, and parts of Tierra del Fuego, decreased rainfall supports extensive grasslands where the wind blows almost ceaselessly. In some areas, thorn scrub such as the fruit-bearing barberry *calafate (Berberis buxifolia)* is abundant. From the late 19th century, sheep grazing for wool degraded these natural pastures, but some are recovering as some *estancias* (ranches) have folded.

Magellanic Forest

From southern Patagonia to the tip of Tierra del Fuego, Argentine and Chilean woodlands consist primarily of dense *Nothofagus* forests that, because of winds and climatic extremes, are nearly prostrate except where high mountains shelter groves of them.

FAUNA

As with the flora, Patagonian wildlife is largely correlated with latitude and elevation.

Marine, Coastal, and Aquatic Fauna

The temperate to sub-Antarctic southern Atlantic and Pacific, with their lengthy coastlines and many estuaries, are a storehouse of biological wealth. That wealth is more abundant in sheer numbers than in species diversity.

Upwelling nutrients and the north-flowing Peru (Humboldt) Current make Chile's coastline one of the world's richest fishing grounds (giving Chile's cuisine its character). In the far south, indigenous peoples such as the Yámana and Kawéskar lived largely on maritime resources.

The main pelagic **fish** in the southern oceans include *congrio* (conger eel), *cojinova*, *corvina*, and the overexploited *merluza* (hake) and *merluza negra* (Chilean sea bass or Patagonian toothfish). Shellfish and crustaceans, all of them edible, include the commonplace mussel, *centolla* (king crab), the *ostión* (scallop), and *calamares* (squid, both *Loligo gahi* and *Ilex argentinus*), target of a burgeoning fishery between the Argentine mainland and the Falklands. Particularly notable in Chile are the *loco* (false abalone), *erizo* (sea urchin), and *picoroco* (giant barnacle). On occasion, red tide conditions limit or reduce shellfish harvests and consumption.

Marine mammals include the *lobo marino* (southern sea lion), which inhabits the coastline from the Río de la Plata all the way south to Tierra del Fuego and well north into the Pacific. From Argentina's Chubut province south, the southern elephant seal and southern fur seal both appear on Appendix II of the Endangered Species List (CITES), classified as threatened or regionally endangered.

The most notable cetacean is the southern right whale, which breeds in growing numbers in the waters around Argentina's Península Valdés. Others found in southern waters include the blue whale, humpback whale, fin whale, sei whale, minke whale, pygmy right whale, and beaked whale. The orca or killer

elephant seal at Northwest Point, Carcass Island

whale is also present, along with smaller marine mammals such as Commerson's dolphin.

Terrestrial Fauna

Patagonia's land animals, especially large mammals, are often nocturnal or otherwise inconspicuous, but they are a diverse lot.

The largest, most widely distributed carnivore is the secretive puma or mountain lion. The smaller Andean cat *(Felis jacobita)* is an endangered species.

The southern river otter is an endangered species, while the Argentine gray fox qualifies as threatened.

Wild grazing mammals include the widely distributed guanaco *(Lama guanicoe),* related to the domestic llama and alpaca, which is most abundant on the Patagonian steppe but also inhabits parts of the high Andes. Domestic livestock like cattle, horses, burros, and goats are, of course, common.

The South Andean *huemul,* a member of the deer family that appears on Chile's coat-of-arms, is the subject of a joint conservation effort between the two countries. In the mid-19th century, there were some 22,000 in both countries, but at present only about 2,500 survive because of habitat destruction,

contagious livestock diseases, and unregulated hunting.

The *pudú* is a miniature deer found in densely wooded areas on both sides of the Patagonian Andes. Like the *huemul,* it's difficult to spot.

Chile lacks poisonous snakes, but some species of the venomous, aggressive pit vipers known collectively as *yarará* range into the northernmost parts of Argentine Patagonia, even south of Península Valdés. They are less common in their southernmost range than in the subtropical north, however.

Freshwater Fish

In the Andean lakes district and Tierra del Fuego, introduced species include brook trout, European brown trout, rainbow trout, and landlocked Atlantic salmon. Native species (catch-and-release only) include *perca bocona* (big-mouthed perch), *perca boca chica* (small-mouthed perch), *puyén,* Patagonian *pejerrey,* and *peladilla.*

Birds

Southern Patagonia's steppes, seacoasts, oceans, and forests can be a wonderland for birders. For dedicated birders from the

gentoo penguins at Wood Cove, Port Stephens, in the Falkland Islands

northern hemisphere, the great majority are new additions to their life lists.

The Argentine Pampas' signature species may be the southern lapwing or *tero,* whose local name derives from its call, but it and other similar species have a wide distribution. With its curved beak, the buff-necked ibis or *bandurria* is a striking presence.

The Andean condor soars along the length of the cordillera, while migratory birds like flamingos, along with coots, ducks, and geese, frequent shallow steppe lakes like Lago Musters and even much smaller bodies of water.

In northern Patagonia's dense forests, some birds are heard as often as seen, especially the reticent songbird *chucao.* Others, like the flocks of squawking Patagonian parakeets that flit through the woods, are more conspicuous.

Some 240 bird species inhabit the south Atlantic coastline and Tierra del Fuego, including the wandering albatross, with its four-meter wingspan; the black-necked swan; Coscoroba swan; flightless steamer duck; kelp gull; and several penguin species, most commonly the Magellanic or jackass penguin. Its close relative, the Humboldt penguin, is an endangered species that ranges far north on the Chilean side. Several other penguin species breed in the Falklands.

The ostrich-like *choike* or *ñandú* (greater rhea) strides across some less densely settled parts of Argentine and Chilean Patagonia. Its numbers were reduced on the Pampas, where it roamed before cattle, horses, and humans turned native grasslands into ranches and granaries. The smaller *ñandú petiso* (lesser rhea) is fairly common in Neuquén, Río Negro, Chubut, and Santa Cruz provinces.

Invertebrates

For purely practical purposes, visitors should pay attention to pests and dangers like mosquitoes, flies, and ticks, which can be disease vectors, even though maladies like malaria and dengue are almost unheard of (the mosquito vector for dengue has been spreading southward from the tropics, but the disease itself has not yet been detected). In well-watered rural areas, mosquitoes can be a plague, so a good repellent is imperative.

The reduviid, or assassin bug, which bears trypanosomiasis (Chagas' disease), is present in Argentina, though it is hardly cause for hysteria. In the lakes districts, in early summer, the aggressive *tábano* is an annoying biting fly.

The Cultural Landscape

While Patagonia's natural landscapes, flora, and fauna are fascinating and enchanting, the region also has a cultural landscape, one transformed by human agency over the millennia. Few areas are truly pristine, but their landscapes are no less interesting for all that.

Most of pre-Columbian Patagonia was a thinly populated place of hunter-gatherers who left few conspicuous landmarks, notwithstanding globally significant aboriginal rock-art sites such as Santa Cruz province's Cueva de las Manos. Some of the continent's most important early archaeological sites are just over the border from Santa Cruz, in Chile's Magallanes region, and at Monte Verde near Puerto Montt.

In immediate pre-Columbian times, nomadic hunter-gatherers peopled much of Patagonia. Living in smallish bands, they relied on wild game like the guanaco and the flightless *ñandú* (rhea), as well as fish, for subsistence. What remains of their material culture is primarily lithic (arrowheads, spear points, and the rounded stone balls known as *boleadoras*).

AGRICULTURE AND THE LANDSCAPE

From the Pampas south, the European invasion transformed Argentina's landscape first into an open range cattle zone, then into fenced sheep and cattle ranches known as *estancias* that dominated the rural economy for over a century. In Patagonia, this took the form of the sheep *estancia,* which produced wool for export to Europe and North America.

Beyond the Biobío, in the Andean lakes district, southern Chile's pre-Columbian peoples were shifting cultivators whose impact on the landscape was not always obvious. Because they cut the forest and used fire to clear the fields before planting, their impact was significant, but long fallow periods allowed the woodlands to recover. Much of what seems virgin forest today may in fact be secondary growth.

Because Mapuche people on both sides of the Andes resisted the advance of the Spaniards and then the Argentines and Chileans, agricultural colonization was spotty until the late 19th century (this did not prevent the Mapuche from adopting European livestock and planting orchards of European fruits such as apples). By the early

1880s, however, Argentine general Julio Roca's ruthless military campaign against them and Chile's advance south of the Biobío ended the autonomy of indigenous peoples.

On the Chilean side, European settlers transformed the landscape by deforesting large areas for dairy farms and croplands. In the Aisén region, government incentives encouraged settlers to slash and burn the forest even when they lacked the labor resources to produce crops that, in any event, had no market.

On the drier Argentine side, irrigation was necessary to develop the Patagonian fruit basket in localities such as the Río Negro and Río Chubut valleys. A few remote localities achieved a certain success, such as Argentina's Los Antiguos and, just across the border, Chile Chico, but their remoteness made it difficult to get produce to market.

The greatest factors in transforming the natural landscape of the Falklands have been the introduction of domestic animals, first cattle and then sheep, and the impact of fire. Both have nearly eliminated the lush and nutritious native tussock grass, which fringed virtually the entire coastline before the islands were settled. Other plant species, better adapted to grazing and trampling, have flourished over the landscape.

sorting sheep at Estancia Monte Dinero, Argentina

SETTLEMENT LANDSCAPES

When the Spaniards took control of present-day Argentina and Chile, they tried to institute a policy of *congregación* or *reducción*. This meant concentrating indigenous populations in villages or towns to achieve political control, impose tribute or taxes, and stimulate religious evangelization. This model had limited success in Chile's northernmost lakes district, and small dispersed populations made it utterly impractical elsewhere in Patagonia.

Cities, of course, differ from the countryside. By royal decree, Spanish-American cities were organized according to a rectangular grid surrounding a central plaza where all the major public institutions—cabildo (town council), cathedral, and market—were located. The logical outgrowth of *reducción* policies, Buenos Aires, Santiago, and other cities were no exception to the rule. The transformation from colonial city to modern metropolis obliterated some landmarks, but the grid pattern became an almost universal model for the former Spanish empire.

In the Mapuche countryside beyond the Biobío, traditional *rucas* (plank houses with thatched roofs erected with community labor rather than by individual families) have nearly disappeared; they are more common on the Chilean side, where the indigenous population is larger and more cohesive. On the Chiloé archipelago, some neighborhoods of precarious *palafitos* (fishers' houses on stilts or pilings) have withstood earthquakes and tsunamis.

In colonial cities and towns, houses fronted directly on the street or sidewalk, with an interior patio or garden for family use; any setback from the street was rare. This general pattern has persisted, though building materials have mostly changed from adobe to concrete, and high-rise apartment blocks have replaced single-family houses in many urban neighborhoods. Covered by metal cladding and topped by corrugated zinc roofs, southernmost Patagonia's wood-framed, 19th-century Magellanic houses affect a Victorian style.

In recent decades, wealthier Argentines and Chileans have built houses with large gardens, on the North American suburban model, in a frenzy of conspicuous consumption. These houses are surrounded by high fences and state-of-the-art security. Some lie within so-called "gated communities," known in Argentina as *"countries,"* but these are uncommon in Patagonia.

On the Falkland Islands, in the "camp" (anything outside the capital of Stanley is the camp), settlement landscapes resemble those of Patagonia's sprawling *estancias*. In fact, these were the prototype for the mainland as landless shepherds emigrated to take up farming in Chile and Argentina. In the Falklands' case, they sat close to the shore, to simplify the transfer of wool to Stanley.

Stanley, the islands' only real "urban" settlement, reminds some visitors of towns and villages in Scotland or Ireland, because of its older stone houses. But the Magellanic style of brightly painted, metal-clad houses is as common here as it is on the Patagonia mainland.

Environmental Issues

Like other countries, Argentina and Chile suffer from environmental degradation, though not all indicators are negative.

AIR, WATER, AND NOISE POLLUTION

Aging diesel buses may be the primary culprit in deteriorating urban air quality, but private vehicles and taxis contribute more than their share (many taxis and private vehicles, though, run on natural gas). Superannuated factories, with subsidized smokestacks, are another source but, especially in Chile, the widespread use of firewood for cooking and heating is a public health issue.

In Patagonia, a different sort of atmospheric problem is critical. Deterioration of the Antarctic ozone layer has exposed both humans and livestock to dangerous UV radiation in summer. Though ozone depletion from aerosols is a global problem over which Argentines and Chileans have relatively little control, they suffer the consequences of the growing ozone hole.

Just as motor vehicles cause urban air pollution, so do they produce most of its noise pollution, due partly to inadequate mufflers. Buses and motorcycles are the worst offenders, but Jet Skis and other personal watercraft on otherwise limpid, placid lakes are a source of growing concern.

Drinking water is normally potable, but a historical legacy of polluted waterways derives from, first, the proliferation of European livestock, followed by the processing of hides and livestock, and then by industry. Mining is also a factor. Near the city of Esquel, Chubut, there was vociferous opposition to a Canadian project that would have used cyanide, which might find its way into streams and aquifers, to extract gold from local ores.

Salmon farming, a booming and increasingly concentrated industry, causes problems with runoff, from Chile's Andean lakes region south into Aisén. Moreover, salmon often escape to colonize streams and seas at the expense of native fish, and some farmers have been accused of killing sea lions that prey on the caged fish.

SOLID WASTE

Like other urban and rural areas, Patagonian cities can produce prodigious amounts of garbage. Though the landfills are isolated, gusting winds can carry their contents for dozens of kilometers or more.

Despite the disposal problems, city streets are relatively clean even if, in the rush toward "development," there's an unfortunate reliance on disposable beverage containers and other undesirable packaging. The Patagonian towns of El Calafate (Argentina) and Pucón (Chile) have banned plastic bags.

ENERGY

Argentina has been nearly self-sufficient in fossil fuels and has substantial hydroelectric resources in the subtropical north and along the Andean foothills, but recently it's had to import petroleum from Venezuela because low prices have discouraged local producers from exploration and extraction. Now it's encouraging fracking (hydraulic fracturing) in Neuquén's Vaca Muerta shales, north of the town of Zapala.

Argentine governments have promoted nuclear power since the 1950s. Not known for its transparency, the **Comisión Nacional de Energía Atómica** (CNEA, National Atomic Energy Commission) is located in San Carlos de Bariloche.

Even hydroelectricity is no panacea, as it threatens key natural sites in both Argentina and Chile. The most threatened areas are the basins of Chile's Río Futaleufú, one of the world's top white-water rivers, and the isolated Río Baker, but Argentina's Río Santa

Cruz is due to become the site of a major Chinese-built dam.

DEFORESTATION AND SOIL CONSERVATION

Native forest conservation is a hot-button issue for many Chilean activists, who have led determined and successful opposition to schemes like the Cascada Chile wood chip project in Region X (Los Lagos), which was canceled in early 2001. Clandestine logging of protected *alerce* trees in the Andean lakes district has caused occasional scandals.

According to the industry-oriented Corporación de Madera (Corma), 90 percent of the timber that arrives in Chilean factories comes from forest plantations and only 10 percent from native forests. This figure is misleading in that plantations of eucalyptus and Monterey pine have replaced heavily logged native woodlands. Moreover, of the 10 million cubic meters of wood used annually for heating and cooking in Chilean households, 70 percent comes from native forests. Hydroelectric projects proposed for Aisén, near the town of Cochrane, would require a 2,300-kilometer power line that would deforest a lengthy strip along the Carretera Austral.

Centuries of livestock activities, both grazing and trampling, have already caused serious erosion even in areas where there were never native forests, such as the Pampas and the Patagonian steppes. Even today, some forested national parks, most notably Argentina's Lanín and Los Glaciares, have failed to eliminate grazing. There has been pressure to create presumably sustainable forest-exploitation projects in Tierra del Fuego's Magellanic woodlands, and road-building in these areas has caused substantial damage.

FISHING

What happens beneath the seas may be less observable than deforestation or air pollution, but there is serious concern that both small and large fisheries are overfished on both sides of the Andes. Pelagic species such as the Patagonian toothfish (often known as Chilean sea bass) are vulnerable to industrial overfishing, and inshore shellfish such as *locos* (false abalone) are traditionally at risk of exploitation.

This has repercussions in the region's natural assets. Overfishing for squid, for instance, may have contributed to Magellanic penguin deaths in the Falklands, but this controversial issue is a reasonable hypothesis rather than proven fact. Such issues, unfortunately, often get tied up in political disputes, such as Argentina's territorial claims to the Falklands or Chilean fishers' assertions that predation by sea lions is reducing their catches.

For most of the Falklands' history, the big environmental issue had been the deterioration of overgrazed pastures, due to high stocking rates and insufficient fencing. In the 1980s, though, the "Squid Rush" of Asian and European fishing fleets forced the British government to declare a conservation zone and licensing regime in offshore waters that had previously been a free-for-all. Commercial fishing has revolutionized the economy and given the islands some of the world's highest per-capita income and living standards. At the same time, some have worried that the fishery could collapse if, under pressure to maintain those standards, authorities grant too many licenses.

Meanwhile, petroleum exploration in the Falkland Islands' turbulent offshore waters could also put fish and other wildlife at risk.

History

Patagonia has an epic and complex multinational history that started long before it lodged in the European imagination.

PREHISTORY

Human occupation of the Americas is relatively recent. The earliest immigrants reached North America from East Asia more than 12,500 years ago, when sea levels fell during the last major continental glaciation and united the two continents via a land bridge across the Bering Strait. Some researchers believe this migration, interrupted by various interglacials during which rising sea levels submerged the crossing, began tens of thousands of years earlier. Still, by the time the bridge last closed about 10,000 years ago, the entire western hemisphere was populated, at least thinly, with hunter-gatherer bands occupying environments ranging from torrid deserts to sopping rainforests to frigid uplands and everything in between.

One of the continent's oldest confirmed archaeological sites is at Monte Verde, Chile, near present-day Puerto Montt. Radiocarbon dating here has given a figure of 14,000 years at a site that, according to archaeologist Tom Dillehay, has some of the continent's earliest evidence of architecture, as well as use of wild potatoes and other native tubers. The most geographically proximate early human sites—later than Monte Verde—are 900 kilometers or more to the north.

At least 11,000 years ago, and probably several thousand years earlier, the first inhabitants arrived as aboriginal hunter-gatherers who subsisted on guanaco, rhea, and other wild game and may even have contributed to extinction of megafauna like the ground sloth (*Mylodon*) and the native American horse (*Onohippidium saldiasi*).

In cave sites ranging from present-day Neuquén to Tierra del Fuego, they left clues as to the peopling of Patagonia. Their successors left vivid visual evidence of their way of life in rocky overhangs like Cueva de las Manos, in Santa Cruz province. These were essentially self-sufficient bands; only much later, around AD 1000, does ceramic evidence suggest contact between northernmost Patagonia and the central Andean civilizations.

As important as hunting was to the earliest inhabitants, gathering wild foods probably contributed more to the diet. As the population gradually reached saturation point under hunter-gatherer technology, they began to rely on incipient agriculture, one of whose hearths was the Peruvian highlands. Sedentary farming arrived much later in what is now Patagonia.

In any event, from around 6000 BC, beans, squash, and potatoes became the staples of an agricultural complex that, as the population grew, supported a settled village life and, eventually, great Andean civilizations. Maize was a later addition, acquired from Mexico.

When the Spaniards finally arrived, according to one scholar, they found "the richest assemblage of food plants in the western hemisphere." Domestic animals were few, with only the dog (sometimes raised for food), the guinea pig (definitely raised for food), and the llama and alpaca (both raised for food and fiber, with the llama also serving as a pack animal).

Slower to develop than the Andean region, at least partly due to late demographic saturation, most Patagonian peoples remained nomadic or semisedentary until shortly before the Spanish invasion. Some sustained a hunter-gatherer way of life into the 20th century.

PRE-COLUMBIAN CULTURES

In Pre-Columbian times, present-day Chile and Argentina comprised a diversity of native peoples who ranged from isolated bands of hunter-gatherers to semi-urbanized outliers of Inca Cuzco (in present-day Peru). The Incas' southernmost penetration took them beyond present-day Santiago, but they never managed to conquer the semisedentary Mapuche and the closely related Pehuenche and Puelche peoples, who withstood both the Inca expansion and, for more than three centuries, the invading Spaniards and their successors. More numerous on the Chilean side of the Andes, they survived because of the distance from Cuzco, their mobility as shifting cultivators, and their decentralized political structure, not easily conquered or co-opted by the bureaucratic Inca.

In Patagonia, groups like the Chonos, Tehuelche (Aónikenk), Kawéskar (Alacaluf), Yámana (Yahgan), and Selk'nam (Ona) peoples subsisted by hunting, fishing, and gathering. Introduced European diseases and outright extermination devastated their already small numbers, while sheep displaced the guanaco and rhea on which their livelihood depended.

Toward the end of the 15th century, just prior to the Spanish invasion of the New World, southernmost South America was a mosaic of remote peoples who either resisted domination from "civilized" outsiders or had little or no contact with them.

EARLY HISTORY

Multiple currents of European exploration and settlement made early Patagonian history complex. Ferdinand Magellan's legendary expedition spent the winter of 1520 in San Julián, Santa Cruz province, before rounding the Horn. Magellan died before returning to Spain on the first circumnavigation of the globe, but his Italian chronicler, Antonio Pigafetta, aroused European imaginations with exaggerated tales of Patagonian "giants." This first meeting between Europeans and Patagonians was cordial, but many succeeding encounters were not.

Pigafetta's fanciful description of the Tehuelche was not the only one of its kind, and it took more than two and a half centuries for

this sort of exaggeration to fade away. As late as the 1770s, John Byron, grandfather of the celebrated poet Lord Byron, fabricated tales of Patagonians whose "middle stature seemed to be about eight feet; their extreme nine feet and upwards."

The word *Patagonia* itself is a matter of confusion. One explanation is that it derived from the Tehuelches' supposedly oversize feet, but the Spanish word *pata* more correctly means "paw." More probably, it came from the Spanish romance *Primaleón,* in which a giant named Patagón inhabits an island of fur-wearing hunter-gatherers.

Though little explored, the Patagonian interior was also a source of tall tales, like the kingdom of Trapalanda or Trapananda, a southern El Dorado. Ironically, no European saw real geographical marvels such as the Glaciar Perito Moreno until the 19th century. If Patagonia was a source of tall tales, though, it also saw scientifically serious expeditions like those of the Englishman John Narborough, the Frenchman Louis de Bougainville, the Spaniard Alejandro Malaspina, and, of course, Charles Darwin on the *Beagle*. It was Darwin who credibly debunked the lingering legends of Patagonian giants:

> We had an interview at Cape Gregory with the famous so-called gigantic Patagonians, who gave us cordial reception. Their height appears greater than it really is, from their large guanaco mantles, their long flowing hair, and general figure; on an average their height is about six feet, with some men taller and only a few shorter; and the women are also tall; altogether they are certainly the tallest race which we anywhere saw.

From the North
Christopher Columbus's so-called "discovery" of the New World was, of course, one of the signal events of human history. While he may have bungled his way into fame—according to geographer Carl Sauer, "The geography in the mind of Columbus was a mixture of

fact, fancy, and credulity"—the incompetently audacious Genoese sailor excited the imagination of Spaniards and others who, within barely half a century, brought virtually all of present-day Latin America under at least nominal control.

Europeans had roamed the Caribbean for more than three decades after Columbus's initial voyage, but the impulse to conquer South America came from Mexico and especially Panama, which Francisco Pizarro and his brothers used as a base to take Peru. From Peru, in 1535, Pizarro's partner and rival Diego de Almagro made the first attempt to take Chile by traveling south through what is now northwestern Argentina. Crossing the 4,748-meter Paso de San Francisco from the east, Almagro's expedition ended in grisly failure. Most of his personnel, retainers, and even livestock perished, but this marked the start of the Spanish presence in Argentina and Chile.

Four years later, after defeating an uprising by Almagro, Pizarro designated Pedro de Valdivia to undertake Chile's conquest, and by 1541 Valdivia had founded Santiago. In short order, he founded several other cities on or south of the Biobío, including Concepción, Villarrica, and his namesake city, Valdivia.

Valdivia met his match, his own former Mapuche slave Lautaro, at the Battle of Tucapel. According to some accounts, Valdivia pleaded for his life by offering his captors unimaginable wealth before suffering a fatal blow to the head. Before his death, though, he had laid the groundwork for the country that was to become Chile.

Spanish institutions were most easily imposed in areas that had been under Inca influence, as a long history of hierarchical government made it possible for the Spaniards to place themselves atop the pyramid. In much of Spanish America, peoples accustomed to paying tribute to the Inca's delegate now paid it to the *encomendero*, the Spanish crown's representative, but Patagonia developed differently.

COLONIAL PATAGONIA

Not permanently settled until 1580, Buenos Aires was not Patagonia, but what happened there affected Patagonia. On the surrounding Pampas, the Querandí people and other indigenous groups had subsisted on guanacos, rheas, and other game, in addition to edible fruits and plants they gathered, but these resources were inadequate for the Spaniards, and culturally alien to them.

In 1535, the failed Pedro de Mendoza expedition left behind horses that proliferated on the lush but thinly populated Pampas pastures, and the multiplication of escaped cattle from Juan de Garay's 1580 expedition transformed the Buenos Aires backcountry and northernmost Patagonia into a fenceless feral cattle ranch. Nearly free for the taking, the abundant horses and cattle fostered Argentina's famous gaucho culture.

After 1776, when Buenos Aires became capital of the newly created Virreinato del Río de la Plata (Viceroyalty of the River Plate), the Spaniards began to establish a presence in Atlantic Patagonia, founding the cities of Carmen de Patagones and Viedma.

South of the Chilean heartland, the Mapuche people soon adopted the Spanish-introduced horse, bringing mounts across the Andes from Argentina, and staving off the Spaniards and then the Chileans for more than three centuries. In fact, the territory south of the Biobío was widely known as a separate country called "Arauco." In distant Patagonia and Tierra del Fuego, tentative Spanish colonization efforts failed because of poor planning and unfamiliar environmental conditions.

The Demise of Colonial Spain

When Napoleon invaded Spain in the early 19th century, the glue that held its colonial possessions together began to dissolve, leading to independence in stages. Patagonia was marginal to this struggle, in which an evolving sense of metropolitan identity contributed to political change.

In the early generations, people identified themselves as Spaniards, but over time criollos (American-born Spaniards) began to differentiate themselves from *peninsulares* (European-born colonists). It bears mention that while the mestizos and even the remaining indigenous population may have identified more closely with Argentina or Chile than Spain, independence appealed most to the criollo intelligentsia.

The South American independence movements commenced on the periphery, led by figures such as Argentina's José de San Martín, Venezuela's Simón Bolívar, and Chile's Bernardo O'Higgins, but their heroism rested on widespread support. In Buenos Aires, the base developed as opportunistic and unauthorized British forces, taking advantage of Spain's perceived weakness, occupied the city in 1806 and 1807. A grassroots uprising ejected the invaders and gave the Porteños confidence.

Returning from Spain, San Martín led criollo forces against royalist armies deployed from Peru, in what is now northwestern Argentina and over the Andes into Chile. As both countries soon declared independence, the polities that would rule Patagonia began to take shape. San Martín honorably declined to head the new Chilean government, leaving it to his colleague O'Higgins.

THE SETTLEMENT OF PATAGONIA

Political independence meant less in Patagonia than in the rest of Argentina and Chile, though the isolationist dictator Juan Manuel de Rosas of Buenos Aires dominated a loose confederation of provinces from 1829 until his overthrow in 1852. In the 1830s, he drove the Mapuche people westward out of Buenos Aires province toward the Andean lakes district, but the real challenge was the Patagonian frontier to the south and west.

In immediate pre-Columbian times, the semisedentary Mapuche and their allies crossed the northern Patagonian Andes freely, occupying Tehuelche territory and mixing with them, and they continued to do so after the Spanish invasion. Their mastery of the Old World horse allowed them to keep their autonomy even as the Spaniards and then the Argentines advanced southward. Still, after Darwin met Rosas, he sorrowfully foretold the aborigines' demise:

> Every one here is fully convinced that this is the justest war, because it is against barbarians. Who would believe that in this age in a Christian civilised country that such atrocities were committed? ... Great as it is, in another half century I think there will not be a wild Indian in the Pampas north of Río Negro.

The Argentines and their European immigrant allies advanced on several fronts, by differing means. In the 1860s foreign minister Guillermo Rawson struck a deal granting Welsh dissidents farms in coastal Chubut, from where they moved westward, upriver, toward the Andes. General Julio Argentino Roca wanted to complete the job begun by Rosas, while the Mapuche, for their part, continued to raid the frontier for cattle and horses.

In 1879, the ambitious Roca initiated his euphemistically titled Conquista del Desierto (Conquest of the Desert), a merciless military campaign that displaced the Mapuche and other indigenous people in favor of settlers' cattle and sheep. This was also a preemptive strike against Chilean territorial ambitions. On the strength of his success, Roca became president in 1880. The subsequent arrival of the railroad from the coast accelerated the process and opened the fertile Río Negro valley to agricultural development.

Around the same time, the government began to encourage Scottish settlers, many from the Falkland Islands, into the southern territories of Chubut, Santa Cruz, and Tierra del Fuego, to conquer Patagonia with sheep. With the settlement of southern Patagonia, Argentina reached its maximum territorial expansion, though precise boundaries with Chile remained to be settled.

Meanwhile, at the same time Chile warred with Bolivia and Peru for control of nitrate-rich northern deserts, it also turned attention to the troublesome Mapuche frontier and, soon thereafter, consolidated its position in Patagonia. In 1881, treaties with the Mapuche people paved the way for European, largely German, immigration beyond the Biobío. The war with Bolivia and Peru probably cost Chile much of what is now far southern Argentina, but the growth of Punta Arenas, thanks to the California Gold Rush and the subsequent wool boom, contributed to a new-found prosperity.

Argentine Patagonia remained peripheral to, though hardly exempt from, the turmoil of 20th-century Argentine phenomena like Peronism and the countless coups that eventually culminated in the 1976-1983 "Dirty War," in which a bloodthirsty military dictatorship tortured and killed thousands of mostly leftist opponents and presumed opponents. It also led the country into a foolish war with Great Britain over the Falklands (known to Argentines as the Malvinas).

Only a few years earlier, in 1978, the Argentine and Chilean dictatorships had nearly gone to war over three small Beagle Channel islands, south of Ushuaia. Papal mediation resolved that conflict without bloodshed, but General Augusto Pinochet's regime looked the other way when British forces used Chilean territory to conduct mainland commando operations against Argentina in 1982.

Southernmost Patagonia also played a role in the campaign against "subversives" that followed Pinochet's 1973 coup against constitutional president Salvador Allende. Once a Salesian missionary outpost, remote Isla Dawson, southwest of Punta Arenas, served the regime as an inescapable prison camp.

PATAGONIA TODAY

Today, thanks to fishing, industrial preferences, and tourism, Argentine Patagonia, including Tierra del Fuego, is the country's fastest-growing region, with the most positive demographic indicators. Between 1980 and 2010, Tierra del Fuego's population more than quadrupled, while Neuquén's and Santa Cruz's more than doubled. Chubut grew by 79 percent.

Patagonia now has some of Argentina's highest employment rates outside of Buenos Aires, and some of the highest mean monthly incomes, lowest poverty rates, and lowest mortality rates. It has the highest percentage rate of potable water and sewer service, and the highest literacy rates, though many observers consider that Argentine education is declining.

Ironically, the Argentine economic implosion of 2001-2002 revived the wool industry, as the new exchange rate made the Argentine clip more competitive internationally. At the former one-to-one rate with the U.S. dollar, production costs were impossibly high. At the same time, Australia's drought-depleted flocks and wool stocks raised demand elsewhere, and oil price increases made wool more competitive with petroleum-based fibers: Prices that were US$3 per kilogram rose to US$9 per kilogram and, in peso terms, earnings quadrupled. This stagnated under the government of Cristina Fernández Kirchner, who suppressed the exchange the rate, but its recent liberation under her successor Mauricio Macri could favor sheep farmers again.

Before World War II, Santa Cruz province had 1,500 *estancias* (ranches) with 7.5 million sheep, a figure that fell in the 1990s from 4 million sheep on 1,200 *estancias* to 2 million on 600. After a series of bad winters and a natural disaster in the ash-laden 1992 eruption of Chile's Volcán Hudson, some farms were abandoned. Some economically desperate *estancieros* (ranch owners) may have even set fires to collect on insurance, and perhaps set outbuildings afire to avoid their designation as historic structures that they would have been obliged to maintain with no economic assistance.

More recently, however, a promotional sheep law and low-interest loans with easy terms have helped repopulate Patagonian pastures, which now graze roughly six million sheep, half of them in Chubut province. Some beneficiaries of the boom have been foreign companies that bought the best properties at bargain prices. In Santa Cruz, sheep still outnumber humans by 10 to 1, and Patagonia's largest wool producer, the Italian conglomerate Benetton, owns flagship ranches like Estancia El Cóndor near Río Gallegos. Now running more than 200,000 sheep on about 900,000 hectares, Benetton has introduced sustainable production techniques on its pastures, planted windbreaks against erosion, and purchased a 30 percent interest in an Italian-owned wool-processing plant in Trelew so that it can export its produce with at least primary processing (combed as wool tops). They are also partners with a Río Gallegos exporting abattoir, and all their lamb and mutton production (in addition to wool) is organically certified.

Devaluation also made tourism competitive. For much of the 1990s, Argentines took their vacations in Chile or other "inexpensive" countries like the United States. The exchange rate trend has since reversed, so that Chileans and other foreigners are flocking to Argentine Patagonia. Summers since 2003 have been a bonanza for Patagonian tourism; increased demand has brought steadily rising prices, but they're still reasonable by international standards. The previous government's exchange rate manipulation threatened the sector, but recent devaluations in both Argentine and Chile, and the elimination of exchange controls in Argentina, have made the region more appealing to visitors. Inflation remains a serious issue in Argentina, however.

Chilean Patagonia's population has also grown, but less dramatically than Argentina's. Since the 1982 census, thinly settled Aisén's population has grown by 50 percent, but Magallanes by only 22 percent. Closer and more accessible to Santiago than comparable Argentine provinces, the regions of La Araucanía and Los Lagos grew by 31 and 47 percent, respectively.

Government and Politics

In both Chile and Argentina, Patagonian politics differ from those of the rest of the country. Argentine federalism has encouraged a certain provincial autonomy, while Chilean unitarianism has engendered skepticism and even resentment in both Aisén and Magallanes. In the latter case, it's not unusual to see unofficial flags and bumper stickers of the "República Independiente de Magallanes" (Independent Republic of Magallanes).

These are not just theoretical issues. During Argentina's 2001-2002 financial collapse, for instance, Santa Cruz's then-governor (later president), Néstor Kirchner, managed to shift US$660 million in provincial oil revenues to overseas banks, thus avoiding the devaluation of the province's financial assets (it's worth adding that Santa Cruz residents objected to President Kirchner's meddling in provincial issues). Chilean citizens of Magallanes, meanwhile, argue that decisions affecting their daily lives take place in Santiago, not Punta Arenas.

Traditionally, one of Patagonia's hot-button issues has been "territorial integrity," as the two countries squabbled over borders for nearly a century. In the 20th century, border guards even died in shootouts, and full-scale war nearly erupted over three small Beagle Channel islands in 1978. All these disagreements have been settled, but a handful of extreme nationalists on both sides still grit their teeth and grimace. Some Chileans fret and the more extreme seethe over the late U.S. environmental philanthropist Douglas Tompkins's initiatives to create private nature reserves and national parks in continental Chiloé (Los Lagos region) and Aisén, worried that these compromise Chile's territorial integrity.

The highest-profile territorial issues, though, are Argentina's claims to the Islas del Atlántico Sur (including the British-ruled Falkland or Malvinas Islands and South Georgia) and Antártida Argentina (an Antarctic wedge below 60 degrees south latitude between 25 and 74 degrees west longitude). Many Argentine politicians and citizens of the southern Patagonian provinces, especially Santa Cruz and Tierra del Fuego, are vociferous on the Malvinas controversy—especially since petroleum exploration has begun there.

While Argentina is persistent and vocal on Falklands and South Georgia, it acknowledges that Antarctic claims are on hold by international treaty. Chile reserves an Antarctic wedge between 53 and 90 degrees west longitude, but the oldest Antarctic claim belongs to Great Britain: British Antarctic Territory lies between 20 and 80 degrees west latitude. Fortunately, these overlapping claims have not precluded international cooperation on the frozen continent.

ORGANIZATION
Argentina

Argentina's federal system superficially resembles that of the United States, with executive, legislative, and judicial branches at the national level and parallel institutions for each of the 23 provinces and the Ciudad Autónoma de Buenos Aires (Autonomous City of Buenos Aires).

At the national level, the Congreso Nacional (legislative branch) consists of a 257-member Cámara de Diputados (Chamber of Deputies) and a 72-member Senado (Senate, with three members for each province and the city of Buenos Aires). As head of the executive branch, the president wields great discretionary powers, often governs by decree, and frequently intervenes in provincial affairs.

Provincial governments establish their own budgets, but the federal government funds them through revenue-sharing, a formula that has led to irresponsibly large deficits in some provinces that the feds are obliged to cover. This varies according to province. Oil-rich Santa Cruz, for instance, is solvent, but Neuquén's social services have put a strain on local revenues.

Chile

Chile's national government consists of separate and legally independent executive, legislative, and judicial branches, but its 14 regions, plus the Metropolitan Region of Santiago, lack the autonomy of Argentina's provinces. The president's Santiago office appoints their governors, for instance. At the same time, municipalities do have autonomy in local matters.

At the national level, the bicameral Congreso Nacional (National Congress) consists of a 38-member Senado (Senate) and a 120-member Cámara de Diputados (Chamber of Deputies), both based in Valparaíso. Based in Santiago, the 21-member Corte Suprema is the highest judicial authority.

Falkland Islands

As a British Overseas Territory, the Falkland Islands are a political anomaly. The governor is an appointee of the Foreign and Commonwealth Office (FCO) in London. The United Kingdom controls foreign and civil service affairs, but the local Legislative Council (Legco) is an elected eight-member body with substantial autonomy. Legco members serve four-year terms, and selected members advise the governor as part of his Executive Council (Exco), along with the chief executive (usually an expatriate Briton recruited and appointed by local government) and financial secretary.

Local political issues are mostly practical matters, including education and public works. On an international level the biggest concern is Argentina, distrusted by most Islanders even before the 1982 invasion. Related practical issues include air links with Chile, on which Islanders rely for both their own convenience and for the tourism and fisheries industries. Connections with

Punta Arenas, their preferred airport, must have permission to overfly Argentine territory. The South Atlantic fishery, which is the Falklands' main revenue source, relies on migratory stocks that move from Argentine offshore waters into local seas, and vice versa.

In a 2013 referendum, Islanders voted overwhelmingly to remain British, but some are disposed toward friendlier commercial and political relations than others. Those opposed argue that there needs to be greater reciprocity on the Argentine side; the new Argentine administration of President Mauricio Macri has been less overtly hostile toward the Islanders, but has made no substantive changes.

BUREAUCRACY

The government institutions most travelers are likely to come into contact with are immigration, customs, and police. Most visitors have little contact with the Argentine or Chilean military, who were notorious for political repression in the 1970s and 1980s but now keep a low profile.

Argentina

Argentine immigration and customs generally treat foreigners fairly, but the police are notoriously corrupt. The Policía Federal are generally superior to provincial forces, some of whom are infamous for shaking down motorists for bribes for minor equipment violations, but this is less common in the Patagonian provinces.

Chile

Unlike most other Latin American countries, Chile has a reputation for honesty in public administration. The country regularly receives the region's highest rating from the anticorruption organization Transparency International.

Chile's immigration, customs, and police are trustworthy as institutions; the Carabineros (national police) might be best categorized as "firm but fair." There have been instances, though, of renegade cops who rob, steal, and intimidate, especially in lower-class neighborhoods.

Falkland Islands

The Falklands bureaucracy is exemplary in terms of honesty, but unyielding in enforcing rules "by the book." Immigration officials, for instance, invariably question arriving visitors as to their local accommodations, admit them for exactly the time their resources permit, and make it clear that nonresidents may not work. Like the Chilean Carabineros, local police are firm but fair (and do not carry firearms).

Economy

ARGENTINA

To most observers, Argentina's economy is an enigma. Rich in natural resources, with a well-educated populace and modern infrastructure, it has lurched from crisis to crisis for over seven decades, with the notable exception of the stable, prosperous 1990s. In late 2001, it stunned the world and even many Argentines by defaulting on part of its US$141 billion foreign debt, triggering a political and economic meltdown comparable to the Great Depression of the 1930s.

Much of the problem was attributable to high-level corruption and a rigid exchange policy that was particularly tough on Patagonia, where production costs for wool soared in international terms. The subsequent devaluation, though, made Patagonian wool an attractive international commodity, and competitive prices spurred a tourism boom throughout the country, but especially in Patagonia. Under the government of former President Cristina Fernández de Kirchner, though, arbitrary currency exchange rates and regulations complicated travel on the Argentine side.

International tourism, which accounts for about 6.1 percent of Argentine exports, and domestic travel are significant economic factors. As Argentina's main gateway, the city of Buenos Aires benefits more than any other locality from the tourist trade, but Patagonia is the ultimate destination for many of the more than 2.3 million who pass through the capital each year.

CHILE

While not Latin America's largest economy, Chile is one of the region's most stable and dynamic. For more than two decades, its economic performance has been one of almost uninterrupted growth. However, the dramatic 7.6 percent average for the decade that ended in 1998 has slipped into the 2.3 percent range. With a fishing and retail boom, augmented by coal mining, Region XII (Magallanes) has recently experienced double-digit economic growth and an unemployment rate of barely 4.1 percent in late 2016.

Perhaps the economy's most obvious weakness is its continuing dependence on mining in general and copper in particular. It's also vulnerable to energy shortages, which have fostered pressure to develop Aisén's remote rivers for hydroelectricity, with high transmission costs and even greater environmental risk. Despite recent setbacks, though, the threat never goes away entirely.

After mining, the single most important export contributor is forestry. It's a controversial sector for environmental reasons, as overharvesting of native forests and their subsequent replacement by plantations of exotics like Monterey pine and eucalyptus have created biological deserts. It's also controversial for social and political reasons, as forestry companies have occupied ancestral lands of the Mapuche people, who are increasingly vocal in seeking their return.

One interesting agricultural development is a plan to establish organic agricultural standards for all of Region XI (Aisén), which would ease the export of products like beef to the European community. This could also apply to fruit growing in the small but productive "banana belt" around Lago General Carrera, and even to fish farming.

Thanks to the productive north-flowing Humboldt or Peru Current, which parallels the coast, Chile has become one of the world's leading fisheries, though there's been criticism of management of resources such as "Chilean sea bass" (Patagonian toothfish). A more recent development is salmon farming in the cool ocean inlets and glacial lakes from the Andean Lakes district south through Aisén and into Magallanes, but this flourishing industry has had high environmental costs.

Tourism is a key economic sector from the lakes district to the tip of Cape Horn. Once nearly limited to January and February, the season is lengthening, and adventurous overseas visitors, in particular, have flocked to Aisén and Magallanes. Chile's lakes district lost much of its traditional market, at least temporarily, with the Argentine economic collapse of 2001-2002, and Argentine foreign exchange controls in recent years. With the unification of exchange rates, though, Argentine visitors are rapidly returning.

According to most surveys, poverty is declining throughout Chile, but there are regional variations. In 2013, Aisén and Magallanes (Region XI) had relatively low rates of 6.2 and 4.3 percent compared with the region of La Araucanía (Region IX), where the rate was 25.1 percent. The level in La Araucanía, the country's highest, correlates with the impoverished Mapuche population.

FALKLAND ISLANDS

For more than a century, wool dominated the Falklands' economic life through sprawling sheep farms that closely resembled or were even the forerunners of the Patagonian sheep *estancia*. Since 1986, wool is a distant second or even third to fishing and tourism. There are almost 500,000 sheep on 84 farms, with an average of around 6,400 sheep on about 25,000 acres (10,000 hectares). Most of the population lives in Stanley, however, where the main employers are government, the Falkland Islands Company (FIC), and small businesses.

In 1986, establishment of an exclusive fishing zone around the islands led to a licensing regime whose revenues transformed the economy into one that, given the small population, now enjoys one of the world's highest per-capita GDPs (around US$34,500 pp) and standards of living.

In 2012, fisheries revenue amounted to £20.5 million (about US$32.8 million). Although it's the economy's most vigorous sector, it's also vulnerable to boom and bust as squid, the most valuable species, has a short life cycle. Some observers worry that a collapse in squid and other fish stocks could cause revenue shortfalls that would make it impossible to support the infrastructure of ports, roads, schools, and a new hospital, not to mention the 600 or so civil servants who administer and maintain them. Offshore petroleum has promise, but also brings environmental and perhaps political complications (especially from Argentina). In addition, the global decline in oil prices could make the Falklands fields economically marginal for exploitation.

For an isolated archipelago, the tourism sector is well developed. In the 2014-2015 season, 43,437 cruise-ship passengers disembarked in the wildlife-rich islands at £21 per head in landing fees. The total revenue of some £912,177 (about US$1,428,469) made this the local government's second-largest revenue earner after fishing, and total leisure travel expenditure was approximately £4.7 million in 2014. Private-sector farmers with wildlife sites also earn landing fees (around £10-15 per head), a valuable supplement to wool and mutton income. Service providers such as wildlife lodges, bus and taxi services, a market garden, and a butcher have also benefited.

People

ARGENTINA

According to the October 2010 census, Argentina has 40,091,539 inhabitants. The Patagonian provinces are thinly populated—among them, Neuquén, Río Negro, Chubut, Santa Cruz, and Tierra del Fuego total slightly more than 5 percent of the country's population in nearly 30 percent of its territory.

Argentina is a country of immigrants, both recent and not-so-recent, and Patagonia's population reflects that history. Spaniards first colonized what is now Argentina, but a 19th-century tsunami of Italians, Basques, English, Irish, Welsh, and other nationalities have spread throughout the country. In Patagonia, Anglo-Argentines and Yugoslavs have a high profile, along with working-class Chilotes from the Chilean archipelago of Chiloé.

Argentina has the smallest indigenous population of any South American country except Uruguay, though certain provinces and regions have significant concentrations. There are no definitive statistics, but perhaps 40,000 to 90,000 Mapuche people reside in La Pampa, Neuquén, and Río Negro provinces, with far smaller numbers of Tehuelche people and others in the southern provinces of Chubut, Santa Cruz, and Tierra del Fuego.

CHILE

Chile's 2012 census has drawn severe criticism but, according to preliminary figures, the population is 16,572,475. As in Argentina, the distribution is skewed. More than 40 percent of Chileans live in the Santiago Metropolitan Region, and about a third in the capital city itself. Only 2.3 million, about 14 percent, live in the regions of La Araucanía, Los Ríos, and Los Lagos, and the Patagonian regions of Aisén and Magallanes, which together compose about 45 percent of Chilean territory.

In the prime Patagonian jurisdictions of

Aisén and Magallanes, the statistics are even more extreme; only about 260,000 people, barely 1.5 percent of the population, live on nearly one-third of the country's surface. In Aisén alone, some 98,000 residents, barely half a percent of all Chileans, inhabit about 15 percent of the country's territory.

Chile's population is largely mestizo, of mixed Spanish and indigenous heritage, but roughly one million Mapuche people inhabit the area south of the Biobío, not to mention Santiago boroughs such as Cerro Navia, La Pintana, El Bosque, Pudahuel, and Peñalolén (80 percent of Chile's indigenous population lives in urban areas, only 20 percent in the countryside).

The Mapuche people, whose language, Mapudungun, is vigorously used, constitute about 90 percent of Chile's total indigenous population. There are small surviving communities of the Kawéskar (Alacaluf) and Yámana (Yahgan) peoples in the southern fjords and rainforests of Aisén and Magallanes.

The surnames of Chile's nonindigenous populations suggest a potpourri of nationalities, from Spanish to Basque, Italian, German, Anglo, and many others, but they do not form such obvious ethnic communities as, say, Italian-Americans in New York or Irish-Americans in Boston. Chilean Patagonia's population resembles that of Argentine Patagonia, with a particularly strong representation of Croatians.

FALKLAND ISLANDS

On a much smaller scale, the Falklands' population distribution is even more extreme than that of either Argentine or Chilean Patagonia. According to the 2016 census, the resident population is 3,032 (not including workers at the Mount Pleasant military base). Mount Pleasant is home mostly to British troops, both officers and "squaddies" on short tours of duty.

Of the Falklands' permanent residents, 2,634 (about 80 percent) live in the capital of Stanley. The rest are dispersed among the 12,173 square kilometers of the two main islands, East Falkland and West Falkland, and smaller offshore islands. About 53 percent were Falklands-born, some with upward of seven generations of history in the islands. Most of the rest came from the United Kingdom, but there is a Chilean contingent of 150, as well as nearly 60 other nationalities. Many Mount Pleasant support workers came from the South Atlantic island of St. Helena. Slightly more than 1 percent identify as Argentine.

Most of the original 19th-century immigrants were English and Scottish laborers and shepherds, some of whom migrated to "The Coast" of Patagonia, as they referred to it. At the same time, Britain has long remained "home," and prosperous landowners traditionally sailed there to escape the austral winter and even sent their children there for secondary and university education.

Today, Falklands schools are on a United Kingdom schedule, so that students who finish their A levels here may now continue their university education in the United Kingdom without a break. Thanks to fishing revenues, local government funds university education—"even their beer money," according to one local commentator—even for indifferent students. This, ironically, is the other extreme from the time when university education was the privilege of landowners' children.

LANGUAGE

Spanish is Argentina's official language, but English is widely spoken in the tourism and business sectors. Foreign language use is also vigorous among ethnic communities such as Italian-Argentines, Anglo-Argentines, and German-Argentines. The Anglo-Argentine and business communities even support a weekly tabloid, *The Buenos Aires Herald,* while the German-Argentine community has the weekly *Argentinisches Tageblatt.* Welsh is making a comeback in Chubut province.

Spanish, likewise, is Chile's dominant language, but perhaps 400,000 speak the Mapuche vernacular of Mapudungun, with

El Voseo

Along with Uruguayans, Paraguayans, and some Central Americans, Argentines commonly use the distinctive second-person familiar form of address known as *el voseo* (use of the pronoun *vos*). Spaniards and most other Latin Americans, by contrast, employ the *tuteo* (use of the pronoun *tú*) in most circumstances.

Use of the *voseo*, a mostly archaic form dating from the 16th and 17th centuries, involves different verb endings for all regular and most irregular verbs. This means adding a final-syllable accent for stress—instead of *tú hablas*, for instance, Argentines will say *vos hablás*. Likewise, with an irregular verb such as *decir* (to say), Argentines will also say *vos decís* rather than *tú dices*.

In the imperative form, there are also differences—instead of *ven* (come), Argentines say *vení*. Negative imperatives, though, are the same in both *tuteo* and *voseo*, e.g., *no vengas* (don't come). Some common verbs, such as *ir* (to go) and *estar* (to be) are similarly irregular in both *voseo* and *tuteo*, but others are not. In the *voseo*, for instance, *tu eres*… becomes *vos sos*….

Despite differing verb forms, Argentines still use the possessive article *tu* and the reflexive or conjunctive object pronoun *te* (¿*te vas?*). Alert travelers will recognize the differences but should hesitate before using the form, considered substandard in some contexts. Visitors may wish to refrain from using *voseo* unless absolutely certain it's appropriate. The *tuteo* is never incorrect, though it may sound quaint in some contexts.

half of those active users. English is a fairly common second language in tourism and business, and government policy is to broaden use of the language.

In the Falklands, English is the official language and the language of preference. Many locals handle basic Spanish or better, but some are reluctant to speak it because of antipathy toward Argentina. Others, though are taking Spanish lessons to improve business communications with the South American continent, particularly with Chile.

Arts and Culture

Both Argentina and Chile have made contributions to the arts and literature well beyond the size of their relatively small populations (there are about 17 million Chileans and 40 million Argentines). Patagonia, though, is still a frontier in Southern Cone arts and entertainment.

LITERATURE

Much Argentine literature is urban and urbane, but not all of it. In the 19th century, even as the free-roaming gaucho was becoming a wage laborer on the *estancias,* José Hernández enshrined his most positive qualities in the epic poem *Martín Fierro* (1872 and 1879), available in many editions and in English translation. This so-called *gauchesco*

(gauchesque) tradition has never completely disappeared.

Born of U.S. immigrant parents in Buenos Aires province, William Henry Hudson (1841-1922) left Argentina for London at the age of 33, but his memoir *Long Ago and Far Away* (1922) is a staple of Argentine public education. An accomplished amateur naturalist, he also wrote *Idle Days in Patagonia* (1893), about his birding explorations. Argentines know him as Guillermo Enrique Hudson.

Chile is famous for its poets. Their progenitor was the conquistador Alonso de Ercilla (1533-1594), who paid his indigenous adversaries tribute in the 16th-century epic *La Araucana*, about the southern frontier that is now the lakes district. The first Chilean-born poet of note was Pedro de Oña (1570-1643), whose *Arauco Domado* (Arauco Tamed) extols the Spaniards' martial achievements, particularly those of García Hurtado de Mendoza (disparaged by Ercilla).

VISUAL ARTS

Buenos Aires is a city of monuments. Unfortunately, many if not most are pretentious busts of ostensible statesmen and colossal equestrian statues of military men like Patagonian invader Julio Argentino Roca, who also makes a horseback appearance in Bariloche's landmark Centro Cívico.

Chilean public art can be comparably pompous, but there are agreeable surprises like Castro's Museo de Arte Moderno (Modern Art Museum), on the Isla Grande de Chiloé.

ARCHITECTURE

Argentine architect Alejandro Bustillo, who designed many luxurious Buenos Aires buildings, also created a magnificent northern Patagonian style with Bariloche's landmark Centro Cívico. His many imitators have failed to achieve the same harmony of nature and culture, and many Euro-Andean structures are derivative.

Indigenous architecture survives in thatched Mapuche *rucas,* plank houses that are more common on the Chilean side of the Andean lakes district. In Chilean towns like Puerto Varas, 19th-century German immigration has left a legacy of shingled houses that seem straight out of Bavaria. The archipelago of Chiloé has become a UNESCO World Heritage Site for its churches and chapels. The diversity of shingle designs is truly extraordinary, but Chiloé's remaining *palafitos* (houses on stilts or pilings) are a treasure of vernacular architecture.

Southernmost Patagonia, especially the Chilean city of Punta Arenas, is notable for the mansions erected during the late 19th and early 20th century wool boom, but also for more modest wooden-framed, metal-clad Magellanic houses. Some of the best are in the town of Porvenir, on the Chilean side of the Isla Grande de Tierra del Fuego, but many remain along Argentine Patagonia's Atlantic coastline and on its side of Tierra del Fuego.

MUSIC

It's hard to identify a distinctive Patagonian music, but even high culture has reached the provinces. Punta Arenas tenor Tito Beltrán (born 1965), a resident of Sweden for a decade

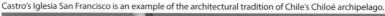

Castro's Iglesia San Francisco is an example of the architectural tradition of Chile's Chiloé archipelago.

and a half, is widely considered one of the world's best opera singers in his range and has sung alongside Luciano Pavarotti.

CINEMA

Like the American West, thinly populated Patagonia has a hold on the imagination, but that hasn't quite translated into a comparable cinematic notoriety. Nevertheless, cinephiles can explore the region on video and occasionally the big screen.

Chileans have played a greater role in global cinema than most people realize, though it's best not to exaggerate. It has its origins in the tiny Tierra del Fuego town of Porvenir, where German-born José Bohr made an early movie before eventually finding an erratic career in Hollywood.

With state support in the late 1960s and early 1970s, talented but noncommercial Chilean filmmakers, such as Miguel Littín (born 1942), did some truly audacious work. Littín is best known for *Alsino and the Condor* (1983), filmed in exile in Nicaragua, which earned an Academy Award nomination for Best Foreign Film. He has characterized *Tierra del Fuego* (2000) as an "existentialist western." Filmed on both sides of the Argentine-Chilean border, Chilean director Alex Bowen's *Mi Mejor Amigo* (My Best Enemy, 2005) is a tragicomedy about the 1978 near-war between the two countries.

The classic Patagonian film, though, is Argentine director Héctor Olivera's *La Patagonia Rebelde* (1974), based on Osvaldo Bayer's fictional treatment of an early 1900s anarchist uprising in Santa Cruz province. Tristan Bauer's *Iluminados por el Fuego* (Blessed by Fire, 2005) recounts the 1982 Falklands war between Argentina and Britain from the viewpoint of Argentina's maltreated conscripts; the closing scenes were actually shot in the islands.

Fans of the offbeat can look for director Emilio Vieyra's *Sangre de Virgenes* (Blood of the Virgins, 1967), presumably the finest vampire flick ever filmed in Bariloche, available on DVD through British distributor MondoMacabro (www.mondomacabrodvd.com). In Brazilian director Walter Salles's *The Motorcycle Diaries* (2004), a young Ernesto "Che" Guevara tours the region. Starting with a bungled Buenos Aires bank robbery, Marcelo Piñeyro's *Wild Horses* (1995) becomes a road romance that ends with a chase in the Patagonian province of Chubut.

Elaborately carved stirrups are standard equipment for Chilean *huasos*.

CRAFTS

The artisanal heritage of Argentina and Chile, especially in Patagonia, is less evident than, say, the indigenous textile traditions of the Peruvian or Guatemalan highlands. Still, both the city and the countryside have characteristic crafts.

Indigenous weaving traditions are apparent in Mapuche blankets, ponchos, sweaters, and similar garments on both sides of the Andean lakes district. Mapuche silversmiths are heir to an equally impressive tradition.

Befitting their origins on the Río de la Plata (literally, River of Silver), Argentine silversmiths create intricate jewelry, as well as adornments such as the large-bladed *facón* (knife) and *espuelas* (spurs) that accompany traditional gaucho clothing.

Expert leatherworkers, in turn, produce gaucho-style clothing and horse gear such as *rastras* (belts), reins, and saddles. Both these traditions come together in the production of paraphernalia for *mate,* the herbal "Paraguayan tea," whose consumption is a cultural bellwether. Traditionally, *mate* (the herb) is sipped with a silver *bombilla* (straw) from a *mate* (gourd, the same word in a different context), which may be mounted in a leather holder.

Throughout the Chilean heartland and well into the south, *huaso* horse gear has its own unique features; look for the elaborately carved wooden stirrups in particular. Carvers in the Chiloé archipelago produce model *dalcas* (dugouts), *palafitos* (houses on pilings), and dolls.

ENTERTAINMENT

Even in the Patagonian provinces, Argentines are night people. Discos and dance clubs, for instance, may not even open until 1am or so and stay open until dawn. Chileans are less so, but by North American or Northern European standards, they keep remarkably late hours.

Bars, Clubs, and Discos

Patagonian cities like Bariloche have the largest numbers of places to dance and drink. Rock, techno, and sometimes Latin styles like salsa are the music of choice. Cavernous dance clubs *(boliches)* can have state-of-the-art sound systems and recorded techno. Some smaller, more interesting venues have live folk, rock, and even jazz.

In Argentina, the distinction between cafés and bars is not always obvious. In fact, it's often more a continuum than a dichotomy. Some of the more stylish (or pretentious) bars go by the English "pub" but call themselves Irish.

Cinemas

In some provincial cities, the central cinemas have closed but multiplexes have also opened in suburban areas. Cultural centers and universities in regional capitals often reprise classics or show less commercial movies.

Most imported films appear in the original language, with Spanish subtitles. The exceptions are animated and children's films, which are invariably dubbed into Spanish.

HOLIDAYS, FESTIVALS, AND EVENTS

Government offices and most businesses close on national holidays, most of which are religious observations. The summer months of January and February, when most leave on vacation, are a quiet time; things pick up after school starts in early March.

Traditionally, many Chileans take "sandwich holidays" between official holidays and the weekend, but the government is attempting to eliminate the practice by moving some holidays to the nearest Monday.

January 1 is **Año Nuevo** (New Year's Day), an official holiday in both countries and the Falkland Islands. **Semana Santa** (Holy Week, the week before Easter) is widely observed in both Argentina and Chile, though only the days from **Viernes Santo** (Good Friday) through **Pascua** (Easter) are official holidays. Many use the long weekend for a mini vacation. May 1 is **Día del Trabajador** (International Labor Day), an official holiday in both countries. October 12 is **Día de la Raza** (equivalent to Columbus Day), an official holiday in both countries. November 2's

Día de los Muertos (All Saints' Day or Day of the Dead) is the occasion for Argentines and Chileans to visit the graves of their loved ones. It's not the colorful event it is in, for example, Mexico or Guatemala. December 25 is **Navidad** (Christmas Day), an official holiday in both countries and the Falklands.

Argentina

On May 25, Argentines observe the **Revolución de Mayo** (May Revolution of 1810), when the Porteños of Buenos Aires made their first move toward independence by declaring the viceroy illegitimate. This is not, however, the major independence celebration, which takes place July 9. June 10 is **Día de las Malvinas** (Malvinas Day), an official holiday commemorating Argentina's claim to the British-governed Falklands. June 20, also an official holiday, is **Día de la Bandera** (Flag Day). July 9, **Día de la Independencia,** celebrates Argentina's formal declaration of independence at the northwestern city of Tucumán, in 1816. Later in the month, when school lets out, many Argentines take *vacaciones de invierno* (winter holidays), when flights and even buses out of the capital fill up fast. August 17 is **Día de San Martín,** observing the death (not the birth) of Argentina's independence hero.

Chile

On May 21, **Glorias Navales** commemorates the Battle of Iquique, a naval skirmish in the War of the Pacific with Peru. **Corpus Christi** (May 30) is a religious holiday, as are the **Día de San Pedro y San Pablo** (Saint Peter and Saint Paul's Day) on June 29 and **Asunción de la Virgen** (Assumption) on August 15. September 18's **Día de la Independencia Nacional** (Independence Day) is immediately followed by September 19's **Día del Ejército** (Armed Forces Day); together, they constitute the **Fiestas Patrias.** December 8 marks **Inmaculada Concepción** (Immaculate Conception), a religious holiday.

Falkland Islands

The Falklands celebrate many of the same holidays as Argentina and Chile, but several others are either derived from the British tradition or unique to the islands. January 10, for instance, is **Margaret Thatcher Day,** as Islanders acknowledge the birthday of the British prime minister who ordered the 1982 counter-invasion that dislodged Argentina from their home.

June 14 is **Liberation Day,** commemorating the date on which Britain forced the Argentine surrender. The first Monday of October is the **Spring Holiday.** December 8 acknowledges the **Battle of the Falklands,** a World War I confrontation with Germany that took place within sight of Stanley. The day after Christmas is **Boxing Day,** a movable holiday that can change if Christmas falls on a Saturday or Sunday.

Essentials

Getting There

Most overseas visitors arrive by air, via Buenos Aires or Santiago, but some will arrive overland and others by ship.

AIR

Buenos Aires and Santiago have regular air links with North America, Europe, Australia, and New Zealand, plus less-frequent routes from southern Africa across the Atlantic (some via Brazil). Both, though, are relatively expensive destinations during peak periods such as the Christmas-New Year's and Holy Week holidays. An Advance Purchase Excursion (Apex) fare can reduce the bite but may have minimum- and maximum-stay requirements, allow no stopovers, and impose financial penalties for changes. Economy-class (Y) tickets, valid for 12 months, are more expensive but allow maximum flexibility. Travelers staying longer than a year have to cough up the difference for any interim price increases.

Discount ticket agents ("consolidators" in North America and "bucket shops" in Britain) may offer the best deals through "bulk fares," but often have other drawbacks; they may not, for instance, allow mileage credit for frequent-flyer programs. Courier flights, on which passengers surrender some or all of their baggage allowance to a company sending equipment or documents to overseas affiliates or customers, may be even cheaper. Courier flights are available for short periods only; they often leave on short notice and are less common to South America than to other parts of the world.

Other options include Round the World (RTW) and Circle Pacific routes that permit numerous stopovers on longer multi-continental trips, but assembling an itinerary requires effort and patience. The 5th edition of Edward Hasbrouck's *The Practical Nomad* (Berkeley, CA: Avalon Travel, 2011) is a key resource for researching airfares and other aspects of international travel.

Many airlines reduced services to Argentina after the economic collapse of 2001-2002, as debt default and a steep devaluation meant fewer Argentines could splurge on overseas travel. Despite some recent setbacks, services have rebounded and even increased.

Popularly known as "Ezeiza" for its suburban location, Buenos Aires's international airport is **Aeropuerto Internacional Ministro Pistarini** (BUE), operated by the concessionaire Aeropuertos Argentinos 2000 (tel. 011/5480-6111, www.aa2000.com.ar). It is 35 kilometers southwest of downtown Buenos Aires.

In the western suburb of Pudahuel, Santiago's state-of-the-art **Aeropuerto Internacional Arturo Merino Benítez** (SCL, tel. 02/2690-1753, www.aeropuerto-santiago.cl) is 26 kilometers from downtown.

From North America

The main gateways to Buenos Aires are Miami, Atlanta, Washington DC (Dulles), New York (JFK), Dallas, Houston, and Los Angeles. Canadian passengers may also use Toronto.

Aerolíneas Argentinas is the traditional carrier, but other options include American Airlines, Avianca, Copa, Delta, Gol, LATAM, and United. Aerolíneas Argentinas, American, Delta, LATAM, and United have the only non-stop services; others require changing planes elsewhere in Central or South America.

Air Canada flies from Toronto to Buenos Aires via Santiago three or four times per week. By taking this route, non-Canadians

ESSENTIALS
GETTING THERE

Previous: Cerro Torre and Cerro Fitz Roy in Parque Nacional Los Glaciares; Narrow-gauge train La Trochita leaves the station at Esquel.

International Airlines in Buenos Aires

Unless otherwise indicated, the addresses below are in the Microcentro and vicinity.

- **Aerolíneas Argentinas:** Perú 2, Monserrat, tel. 011/4320-2000, www.aerolineas.com.ar
- **Aeroméxico:** Carlos Pellegrini 1259, tel. 011/5648-2205, www.aeromexico.com
- **Air Canada:** Av. Córdoba 656, tel. 011/4393-9090, www.aircanada.com
- **Air Europa:** Av. Santa Fe 850, tel. 011/5219-4545, www.aireuropa.com
- **Air France:** San Martín 344, 23rd Fl., Microcentro, tel. 011/4317-4711, www.airfrance.com
- **Alitalia:** San Martín 344, 23rd Fl., Microcentro, tel. 011/4310-9910, www.alitalia.com
- **American Airlines:** Av. Santa Fe 881, Retiro, tel. 011/4318-1111, www.aa.com
- **Avianca:** Carlos Pellegrini 1075, 4th Fl., Retiro, tel. 011/4360-8200, www.avianca.com
- **British Airways:** Av. del Libertador 498, 13th Fl., tel. 0800/222-0075, www.britishairways.com
- **Copa:** Emma de la Barra 353, 7th Fl., Puerto Madero, tel. 011/4132-3535, www.copaair.com
- **Cubana de Aviación:** Sarmiento 552, 11th Fl., tel. 011/4326-5291, www.cubana.cu
- **Delta:** Av. Santa Fe 899, Retiro, tel. 011/4898-8170, www.delta.com
- **Gol:** Cerrito 1134, Retiro, tel. 011/4815-4035, www.voegol.com
- **Iberia:** Carlos Pellegrini 1163, 1st Fl., Retiro, tel. 011/5984-0122, www.iberia.com
- **KLM:** San Martín 344, 23rd Fl., Microcentro, tel. 011/4317-4700, www.klm.com
- **LAN:** Paraguay 1102, Retiro, tel. 0800/999-9526, www.lan.com
- **Lufthansa:** Marcelo T. de Alvear 590, 6th Fl., Retiro, tel. 011/4319-0600, www.lufthansa.com
- **Qantas:** Av. Madero 900, 27th Fl., Puerto Madero, tel. 011/4114-5800, www.qantas.com.au
- **Swiss International:** Av. Santa Fe 846, Retiro, tel. 011/5354-2311, www.swiss.com
- **Transportes Aéreos de Mercosur (TAM):** Cerrito 1026, Retiro, tel. 011/4819-4800, www.tam.com.br
- **United Airlines:** Carlos Pellegrini 527, tel. 011/4316-0777, www.united.com

can avoid the nuisance of getting a U.S. visa just for transit purposes.

From Mexico, Central America, and the Caribbean

Services from Mexico to either Santiago or Buenos Aires almost always require changing planes in Central America or elsewhere in South America. The exception is LATAM, which flies nonstop from Mexico City to Santiago, with connections to Buenos Aires.

Other carriers from Mexico City include Aeroméxico; Copa (changing planes in Panama); and TACA, via Lima, Peru. Cubana has two or three flights weekly from Havana, while Avianca has connections to the Caribbean, Central America, and Mexico via Bogotá.

From Europe

From Europe, there are direct services with Aerolíneas Argentinas (from Rome and

Madrid); Air France (from Paris); Alitalia (from Milan and Rome); British Airways (from London); Iberia (from Barcelona and Madrid); KLM (from Amsterdam); Lufthansa (from Frankfurt via São Paulo); and Swiss International (from Geneva and Zurich). TAM has connections from Paris via São Paulo.

Many Buenos Aires services continue to Santiago, but there are also direct services to the Chilean capital with LATAM and Iberia. There are also connections via Brazil with Gol.

From Asia, Africa, and the Pacific

Aerolíneas Argentinas no longer flies from Sydney via Auckland, but LATAM now has direct flights from Australia and New Zealand. From Australia, Qantas links up with LATAM flights via Tahiti, Easter Island, and Santiago, or with LATAM via Los Angeles. Air New Zealand also links up with LATAM, and may soon be flying to Buenos Aires directly. From Japan, it's easiest to make connections via Los Angeles.

From Johannesburg, South African Airways flies five times or so weekly to São Paulo, where LATAM and Gol offer connections to Buenos Aires.

Within South America

Buenos Aires and Santiago have connections to neighboring republics of Uruguay, Brazil, Paraguay, Peru, and Bolivia, and elsewhere on the continent as well. There are no flights to the Guyanas, however.

For passengers on a Patagonian trip, the most important connections are between Buenos Aires and Santiago, which are frequent on many South American and trans-Atlantic carriers.

LAN has the only flights to the Falkland Islands, every Saturday from Santiago and Punta Arenas; they return the same day. Once a month, these flights also stop in Río Gallegos, Argentina.

OVERLAND

Overland travel from the north can be challenging, but once you reach Argentina or Chile, it's easy enough.

From North America, Mexico, and Central America

Overland travel from North America is problematic because Panama's Darien Gap to Colombia is time-consuming, impassable for motor vehicles, and difficult and potentially dangerous even for those on foot. Although Colombian security has improved, this route still passes through areas inhabited by drug smugglers, holdout guerrillas, and paramilitaries.

Those visiting Patagonia and other parts of the continent for an extended period should consider shipping a vehicle. To locate a shipper, check the Internet or the phone directory under Automobile Transporters, who are normally freight consolidators rather than the company that owns the ship, which will charge higher container rates. Since many more people ship vehicles to Europe than to South America, finding the right shipper may take patience; one reliable U.S. consolidator is **McClary, Swift & Co.** (360 Swift Ave., South San Francisco, CA 94080, U.S. tel. 650/872-2121, www.mcclaryswift.com), which has affiliates at many U.S. ports.

Argentine bureaucracy has improved in recent years, and clearing customs is simpler than it used to be. Vehicles arrive at the Puerto Nuevo's **Estación Marítima Buenos Aires** (Av. Quartino s/n, Retiro, tel. 011/4310-1428 or 011/4310-1431). Here it is necessary to present your passport, vehicle title, and the original *conocimiento de embarque* (bill of lading), and to fill out a customs application. You will then obtain an appointment with a customs inspector to retrieve the vehicle, which will cost about US$450 for port charges and another US$400 for the shipper. If the vehicle has been in port longer than five days, there will be additional charges. The vehicle can remain in Argentina legally for eight months, with an eight-month extension possible; any visit to

International Airlines in Santiago

This list includes airlines that fly to and from Santiago, though several other foreign airlines also have local representatives. Unless otherwise noted, the offices are in Santiago Centro.

- **Aerolíneas Argentinas:** Roger de Flor 2921, Las Condes, tel. 02/2210-9300, www.aerolineas.com.ar
- **Aeroméxico:** Av. Vitacura 2909, Oficina 305, Las Condes, tel. 02/2390-1000, www.aeromexico.com
- **Air Canada:** Andrés Bello 2687, 16th Fl., Las Condes, tel. 02/2690-1108, www.aircanada.com
- **Air France/KLM:** Joaquín Montero 3000, Vitacura, tel. 02/2580-9696, www.airfrance.com
- **Alitalia:** Av. Providencia 1998, Oficina 208, Providencia, tel. 02/2335-1010, www.alitalia.com
- **American Airlines:** Huérfanos 1199-B, tel. 02/2679-0000, www.aa.com
- **Avianca/TACA:** Isidora Goyenechea 3365, Oficina 1201, Las Condes, tel. 02/2270-6612, www.avianca.com
- **British Airways:** Don Carlos 2929, Oficina 1105, Las Condes, tel. 0800/83-2598, www.britishairways.com
- **Copa:** Av. El Golf 99, Oficina 101, Las Condes, tel. 02/2200-2100, www.copaair.com
- **Delta:** Joaquín Montero 300, 2nd Fl., Vitacura, tel. 02/2200-2700, www.delta.com
- **Gol:** Américo Vespucio 900, 9th Fl., tel. 02/2248-1800, www.voegol.com.br
- **Iberia:** Bandera 206, 8th Fl., tel. 02/2870-1000, www.iberia.com
- **LATAM:** Huérfanos 926, tel. 02/2526-3000, www.latam.com
- **Lufthansa:** Av. El Bosque Norte 500, 16th Fl., Las Condes, tel. 02/2630-1655, www.lufthansa.com
- **Qantas:** Cerro El Plomo 5420, Oficina 608, Las Condes, tel. 02/2817-9500, www.qantas.com.au
- **Sky Airline:** Av. El Bosque 0117, Las Condes, tel. 02/2352-5600, www.skyairline.cl
- **Swiss International:** Barros Errázuriz 1954, Oficina 810, Providencia, tel. 02/2940-2907, www.swiss.com
- **Transportes Aéreos Mercosur (TAM):** Isidora Goyenechea 2880, Las Condes, tel. 02/2676-7900, www.tam.com.br
- **United Airlines:** El Bosque Norte 0177, 19th Fl., Las Condes, tel. 02/2337-0000, www.united.com

a neighboring country restarts the clock. In event of any difficulty, consult a private *despachante de aduana* (customs broker), such as **José Angel Vidal Labra** (tel. 011/4345-7887, vidla@sinectis.com.ar).

Chile's ports are less bureaucratic and safer for the vehicle than those of Argentina. The likely ports of entry are San Antonio, southwest of Santiago, and Valparaíso, northwest of the capital. It pays to be there within a couple of days of the vehicle's arrival, or storage charges can mount. Leave the gas tank as empty as possible (for safety's sake) and leave no valuables, including tools, in the vehicle.

To arrange a shipment from San Antonio or Valparaíso, contact the Santiago consolidator **Ultramar** (Av. Bosque Norte 500, 18th Fl., Vitacura, tel. 02/2630-1000, www.ultramar.cl). For a trustworthy customs broker to handle the paperwork, contact **Juan Alarcón Rojas** (Fidel Oteíza 1921, 12th Fl., Providencia, Santiago, tel. 02/2328-5100, www.alarcon.cl).

Bicycles, of course, can be partially dismantled, packaged, and easily shipped aboard airplanes, usually for a small additional charge.

Getting Around

AIR

Argentina

In addition to international air service, Argentina has a large network of domestic airports and a handful of airlines centered on Buenos Aires; indeed, to fly between provincial cities, backtracking to Buenos Aires is often unavoidable. Most domestic flights use Aeroparque Jorge Newbery, the city airport, but a few use the international airport at Ezeiza. Foreigners are once again eligible for discounted fares that were only available to Argentine citizens and residents under the previous government.

The erratic Aerolíneas Argentinas has domestic as well as international flights, while its affiliate Austral (the two are almost indistinguishable) serves many Patagonian destinations from Buenos Aires south to Ushuaia, Tierra del Fuego. Both lose large amounts of money.

Other domestic airlines come and go, with the exception of Líneas Aéreas del Estado (LADE, www.lade.com.ar), the air force's heavily subsidized commercial branch. Miraculously surviving budget crises and privatizations, it flies to southern Buenos Aires province and out-of-the-way Patagonian destinations on a wing and an overdrawn bank account.

Other private airlines have consistently failed, but expanding LATAM Argentina, an affiliate of Chile's LATAM, seems likelier to survive. Colombia's Avianca is also looking to enter the Argentine market.

Available only in conjunction with international travel to Buenos Aires, Aerolíneas Argentinas' "Visit Argentina" pass offers a series of discount fares to foreigners and nonresident Argentines, which requires some planning to gain maximum advantage from them. Fares are notably lower if the international travel takes place on Aerolíneas Argentinas.

Chile

In addition to Santiago's international airport, there are domestic airports at Temuco, Osorno, Puerto Montt, Chaitén, Balmaceda (Coyhaique), Puerto Natales, and Punta Arenas; some of these have short international hops to Argentina. Coyhaique has a separate airfield for flights to Laguna San Rafael.

LATAM dominates the domestic market in a country whose longest domestic flight is only about three hours. There are discounts at inconvenient hours, such as the middle-of-the-night flight from Punta Arenas to Santiago.

No competitor has had sustained success challenging LATAM's supremacy, but budget-oriented Sky Airline now holds about 20 percent of the domestic market and serves Temuco, Puerto Montt, Balmaceda, and Punta Arenas.

Domestic airfares are generally reasonable, but purchasing tickets a few days ahead of time can mean substantial discounts. For overseas visitors, LATAM also has a "Visit Chile" pass that can mean substantial savings, but it's not promoting this as much as it has in the past.

BUS

In both Argentina and Chile, buses along the principal highways, and those connecting other main cities and resorts, are frequent and almost invariably spacious and comfortable, sometimes even luxurious. A handful on backroad routes may be infrequent but are still better than Central American "chicken buses," and distances are relatively short.

So-called Pullman buses have reclining seats, and for short to medium runs, up to six or seven hours, they're more than adequate. Seats are guaranteed. For the longest distances, many travelers prefer the more spacious *servicio diferencial* or the *coche cama* service, which provide greater legroom in seats that recline almost horizontally. Fares are reasonable by international standards.

Most cities have a central *terminal de buses* (bus terminal), but a few have multiple terminals for long-distance, regional, and rural services, or for individual companies. Some companies have separate ticket offices in more central locations than the terminals themselves.

Services are so frequent that reservations are rarely necessary except for some infrequently traveled routes and some international services, or during holiday periods like Semana Santa (Holy Week), September's Chilean patriotic holidays, Christmas-New Year's, and occasionally during the January-February summer and July-August winter vacation seasons. Fares can rise and fall with demand, depending on the season.

RAIL

Once the primary mode of interurban transportation, Argentine domestic rail service is now limited to a handful of long-distance domestic services. In Argentine Patagonia, the only long-distance service connects the Río Negro provincial capital of Viedma with the resort city of Bariloche.

In addition to regular passenger trains, there are also tourist excursions, including the narrow-gauge La Trochita (immortalized in Paul Theroux's *The Old Patagonian Express*), in Río Negro and Chubut provinces. Chile no longer offers rail service from Santiago to Temuco and Puerto Montt, but,

for possible changes, check the government's Empresa de Ferrocarriles del Estado's website (www.efe.cl).

CAR AND MOTORCYCLE

Driving conditions in Argentina and Chile have similarities, but there are also dramatic differences. In the Falkland Islands, where roads are few and many interesting destinations are inaccessible except by air or bad tracks best left to locals, driving is inadvisable for short-term visitors.

Note that members of the American Automobile Association (AAA), Britain's Automobile Association (AA), and other foreign automobile clubs are often eligible for limited roadside assistance through the **Automóvil Club Argentino** (ACA, Av. del Libertador 1850, Buenos Aires, tel. 011/4808-4000, www.aca.org.ar) and through the **Automóvil Club Chileno** (Acchi, Av. Andrés Bello Norte 1863, Providencia, Santiago, tel. 02/2431-1000, www.automovilclub.cl). Both have representatives in larger cities and many smaller towns, throughout each country.

Argentina

Driving in Argentina, especially Buenos Aires, is not for the timid. In the words of *Buenos Aires Herald* columnist Martín Gambarotta, this is a country "where pedestrians and not cars have to stop at a zebra crossing." According to the NGO Luchemos for la Vida (www.luchemos.org.ar), the traffic death rate of 1,066 per million vehicles is South America's highest, seven times greater than that of the United States.

Argentine highways are divided into *rutas nacionales* (abbreviated here as RN), maintained by the federal government, and *rutas provinciales* (RP), maintained by individual provinces. Generally, but not necessarily, federal highways are better maintained; one exception is in oil-rich Santa Cruz province.

Highway speed limits are generally around 100 kilometers per hour, but they are 120 kilometers per hour on four-lane divided roads (rare in Patagonia). Officially, helmets are obligatory for motorcyclists, but enforcement is lax.

Chile

The longitudinal Panamericana or Ruta 5, stretching from the Peruvian border to Puerto Montt and the Isla Grande de Chiloé, is Chile's main transport artery. On the mainland south of Santiago, it's a smoothly paved, four-lane divided highway. Even so, and despite the presence of call boxes, rest areas, and *peajes* (toll booths), there are occasionally loose animals, pedestrians crossing at unsuitable places, and even vendors hawking items ranging from sweets and ice cream to fresh produce and cheese to dressed kid goat, ready for barbecue.

Many more roads are paved or smoothly graded. Ruta 7, the Carretera Austral (Southern Highway), is often narrow, mostly gravel, and occasionally precarious (this author has wrecked two 4WD vehicles on it, with extenuating circumstances). Heavy truck traffic can make all these routes dangerous, but most Chileans are courteous and cautious drivers despite occasional road-rage incidents in Santiago. Watch for Argentine license plates, as many trans-Andean visitors drive more aggressively.

Speed limits on most highways are generally around 100 kilometers per hour, but they are 120 kilometers per hour on most segments of the Panamericana that are four-lane divided roads. Carabineros (national police) with radar guns are commonly seen along all highways.

Vehicle Documents, Driver's Licenses, and Equipment

Most South American countries, including Argentina and Chile, have dispensed with the cumbersome *Carnet de Passage en Douanes,* which required depositing a large bond in order to import a motor vehicle. Officials at the port of arrival or border post usually issue a 90-day permit on presentation of the vehicle title, registration, bill of lading (if the vehicle is being shipped), and your passport. For shipped vehicles, port charges can rise rapidly if the vehicle has been stored more than a few days.

Before traveling, many visitors obtain an International or Interamerican Driving Permit, available through the American Automobile Association (AAA) or your home country's counterpart and normally valid for one calendar year from the date of issue. Police in both countries, though, now acknowledge state and national driver's licenses.

The police pay close attention to vehicle documents: *tarjeta verde* (green card) registration for Argentine vehicles, customs permission for foreign ones, and liability insurance (though many Argentines drive without it). Vehicles without registration may be impounded on the spot. Argentine vehicles should have proof of a *verificación técnica* (safety inspection); Chile's equivalent is the *revisión técnica.*

At roadside checkpoints, Argentine police are rigid about obligatory equipment such as headrests for the driver and each passenger, *valizas* (triangular emergency reflectors), and *matafuegos* (1-kilogram fire extinguishers). In any instance of document irregularity or minor equipment violation, provincial police may threaten fines while really soliciting *coimas* (bribes). This is less common in Patagonian provinces. A firm but calm suggestion that you intend to call your consulate may help overcome any difficulty.

Chilean checkpoints are less common, but always stop when the Carabineros (national police) signal you to do so; this is usually a routine document check. Unlike many Argentine police, nearly all Carabineros will refuse bribes; offering one can get you in serious trouble. If you've committed an *infracción* (traffic violation), the best thing to do is reason with the officer, and you may get off unless your offense is truly flagrant or particularly dangerous. Note that the slang term *paco* for a police officer is widely considered an insult—never use it to a cop's face.

Be sure to obtain Chilean liability insurance, which is available in major cities. *Seguro mínimo,* a cheap, no-fault policy with limited personal injury coverage, is obligatory but inadequate for any serious accident.

Road Hazards

Argentine traffic can be fast and ruthless. Many roads are narrow with little or no shoulder, and others are poorly surfaced or potholed. Heavy truck traffic can make all routes dangerous, and not just because of excess speed. Impatient Argentine drivers often try to pass in dangerous situations, and head-on crashes are disturbingly common, even between passenger buses.

Porteño drivers in the city and stray cattle in the provinces might seem to be enough to deal with, but political protests often mean *piquetes* (roadblocks) of demonstrators protesting unemployment and other issues. *Piqueteros* (picketers), while they tend to focus on stopping commercial traffic, manage to slow everything else down as well. Never try to run a roadblock, which can raise their wrath. Rather, try to show solidarity and, in all likelihood, you'll pass without incident. Patagonia's main focus of picketing activity has been the western Neuquén oil town of Plaza Huincul.

Unleaded fuel is available everywhere. In remote areas where gas stations are few, carry additional fuel. In both the city and the countryside, watch for *lomas de burro* (speed bumps), also colloquially known as *pacos acostados* (sleeping policemen) in Chile. Night driving is inadvisable in some rural areas, as domestic livestock and inebriated campesinos may roam freely.

Expenses

In recent years, global fuel prices have stabilized or even fallen in dollar terms, but they're on the rise again in Argentina. Still, a tax break makes "Patagonian prices" for gasoline in the provinces of La Pampa, Neuquén, Río Negro, Chubut, Santa Cruz, and Tierra del Fuego provinces lower than in the rest of the country; there is no price differential for diesel.

Typical Patagonian prices per liter are about US$0.98 (US$3.71 per gallon) for super and US$1.11 (US$4.23 per gallon) for premium. At about US$1.06 per liter (US$4.04 per gallon), *gasoil* (diesel) is typically cheaper than most gasolines throughout Argentina, but that differential disappears in Patagonia, where it is not subsidized. Because gasoline prices are unregulated, they may rise quickly.

Partly because Chile imports over 90 percent of its oil, operating a gasoline-powered vehicle is more expensive than in the United States (though still cheaper than in Europe). Depressed oil prices in recent years, though, have meant that the cost of 93-octane *bencina* (gasoline) has fallen to about US$1.10 per liter (roughly US$4.15 per U.S. gallon) in Santiago. Prices generally increase with distance from the capital, reaching upward of US$1.25 per liter (US$4.85 per U.S. gallon) in remote Aisén. These prices are subject to exchange rate fluctuations and international crude oil prices.

Unleaded 93-octane fuel is available everywhere; higher octane versions are only slightly more expensive. Diesel fuel is about 20 to 30 percent cheaper than gasoline.

In both countries, repairs are cheap in terms of labor, but parts can be expensive, as many must be imported. Generally, parts are cheaper in Chile. Fortunately, Argentine and Chilean mechanics can rehabilitate virtually any salvageable part.

Car Rental

Both Buenos Aires and Santiago have such good public transportation that it's hardly worth risking aggressive drivers (especially in the Argentine capital), traffic congestion, and limited parking. In Patagonia's wide-open spaces, though, a car makes it easier to explore otherwise inaccessible areas with limited time. To rent a car, you must present a valid driver's license, a valid credit card, and be at least 25 years old.

Rental prices are generally lower and terms better in Chile, where unlimited mileage deals are more common. The most expensive options are 4WD vehicles, commonly referred to as *doble tracción* or *cuatro por cuatro* (the latter usually written "4X4"). On the other hand, if shared among a group, they can be fairly reasonable. International agencies such as Avis and Hertz have larger vehicle fleets and can usually guarantee a rental for overseas clients.

Local agencies may have somewhat lower rates, but insurance is normally additional and may not completely cover you against losses. There is almost always a deductible of several hundred dollars or more in case of serious damage, total destruction, or vehicle theft.

In Chile, camping vehicles ranging from pickup trucks with shells to fully equipped RVs are available through Santiago's **Holiday Rent** (tel. 02/2745-1988, www.holidayrent.cl) or **Wicked Campers South America** (Franklin 300, Santiago, tel. 09/4207-3790, www.wickedsouthamerica.com), which also has locations in Puerto Varas and Punta Arenas. Motorcycles are available through **Moto Aventura** (Argomedo 739, Osorno, tel. 064/224-9123, www.motoaventura.cl).

Note that taking a Chilean vehicle into Argentina, or vice versa, involves additional paperwork and a surcharge, as well as supplementary insurance. Returning a vehicle to an office other than the one you rented from, which is impossible with the cheapest local companies, usually means a hefty drop-off charge.

Buying a Vehicle

If you're visiting Chile or Argentina for several months, buying a vehicle might be worth consideration. Unfortunately, both Argentine and Chilean regulations now prohibit non-residents from taking vehicles out of the country—even if they have been legally purchased there—without notarial permission. Prices for used vehicles are much higher in Argentina than in Chile, and the selection is smaller.

Santiago has the largest selection. Be circumspect about purchasing a vehicle in Region XII (Magallanes), where *zona franca*

(duty-free) regulations may limit purchases to permanent residents. Only a vehicle that is legally *liberado* may be sold in and taken outside the region.

To purchase a Chilean car, you need a RUT (Rol Único Tributario) tax ID number, which takes only a few minutes at any Servicio de Impuestos Internos (SII, Internal Revenue Service) office; you need not be a Chilean resident. The SII issues a provisional RUT, valid for any purpose, and sends the permanent card to a Chilean address that you designate.

Before purchasing the vehicle, request a *Certificado de Inscripción y Anotaciones Vigentes* from any office of the Registro Civil (Civil Registry). This inexpensive document will alert you to title problems if any, as well as pending legal issues (such as accident settlements). To be licensed, the vehicle also needs an up-to-date *revisión técnica* (safety and emissions test).

Registering the sale, at any Registro Civil office, involves a *compraventa* (bill of sale, about US$10) and an official *Transferencia de Dominio de Vehículos Motorizados* (title transfer, about US$42), plus a transfer tax set at 1.5 percent of the sale price. The Registro then issues a provisional title and mails the permanent title, usually within a month, to the address on your RUT.

Unfortunately, the *compraventa* and other documents no longer entitle you to take the vehicle out of the country. Because purchase of a Chilean vehicle by foreigners is still uncommon, it may be worth making a special request to accelerate the issuance of the permanent title, which requires a brief letter to the head of the Registro. Personnel at the office can help with this.

BICYCLE

For the physically fit, or those intending to become physically fit, with enough time, cycling can be an ideal way to see Patagonia. Because so many roads are unpaved, a *todo terreno* (mountain bike) beats a touring bike. Cyclists should know basic mechanics, though the increasing availability of mountain bikes means that parts and mechanics are easier to find than they once were. In an emergency, it's easy to put a bicycle on board a bus.

Some cyclists dislike the main Argentine highways because their narrowness, coupled with fast drivers and the lack of shoulders, can make them unsafe. There are many alternative routes with less traffic. High winds can make cycling difficult on Argentine Patagonian roads, such as coastal RN 3 and the interior RN 40.

Likewise, some cyclists dislike Chile's busy Panamericana, much of which is relatively uninteresting. Its completion as a four-lane divided highway with broad paved shoulders has made it safer, at least. There are interesting alternatives: the scenic Carretera Austral, especially, is a mountain biker's delight, and the improving Ruta Interlagos connects lakes district destinations.

FERRY AND CATAMARAN

From Puerto Montt south through the Aisén and Magallanes regions, lacustrine and maritime transportation fills the gaps in Chile's highway network. This is true even in parts of the Andean lakes district, where passenger ferries on finger lakes like Todos los Santos form part of trans-Andean routes to Argentina. In addition to ferries, high-speed catamarans cover some routes and also serve some isolated tourist destinations.

From Puerto Montt, there are ferries to Chaitén and Puerto Chacabuco, where there are services to the ice fields of Parque Nacional Laguna San Rafael on the cruise ship *Skorpios* and the luxury passenger catamaran *Chaitén*.

Depending on the season, Navimag's *Evangelistas* and *Edén* connect Puerto Montt with Puerto Natales, a three-day journey through the scenic fjords of Aisén and northern Magallanes.

Transmarchilay runs a shuttle ferry across the mouth of the Reloncaví estuary, from La Arena to Puelche, about 45 kilometers southeast of Puerto Montt. The village of

Hornopirén, 60 kilometers farther southeast, is the port for Transmarchilay's summer-only ferry to Caleta Gonzalo, the gateway to Parque Pumalín, Chaitén, and the Carretera Austral. On this stretch, the Ruta Bimodal (www.taustral.cl) involves two ferry shuttles between Hornopirén linked by a road between Leptepú and Fiordo Largo.

Ferries also connect the mainland port of Pargua, southwest of Puerto Montt, with Chacao, on the Isla Grande de Chiloé. There are also ferries from Quellón, at the south end of the Isla Grande, to Chaitén and occasionally to Puerto Chacabuco.

From the Aisén village of Puerto Ingeniero Ibáñez, on Lago General Carrera's north shore, the car ferry *Pilchero* sails to the south shore border town of Chile Chico. While Chile Chico is also accessible by a road around the lake, the ferry is faster and cheaper.

In Magallanes, there's a daily ferry from Punta Arenas across the Strait of Magellan to Porvenir, on the Chilean side of the Isla Grande de Tierra del Fuego. A more frequent shuttle ferry crosses the strait from Primera Angostura, northwest of Punta Arenas.

LOCAL TRANSPORTATION

Though cars clog the streets of Buenos Aires and Santiago, many Argentines and Chileans still rely on public transportation to get around, even in small towns.

Underground

Buenos Aires and Santiago both have subway systems. Buenos Aires's **Subte** (www.metrovias.com.ar) dates from 1913, but carries city residents efficiently and is slowly expanding to underserved neighborhoods. Expanding even faster, Santiago's exemplary **Metro** (www.metrosantiago.cl) looks as good as the day it opened in 1975.

Colectivos and *Micros* (Buses)

Even small cities and towns are well served by local buses, which often run 24-7. Fares are inexpensive but vary according to distance.

Argentines use the term *colectivo,* while Chileans normally say *micro* or, for smaller buses, *liebres* (literally, hares). Santiago's integrated bus system, **Transantiago** (www. transantiagoinforma.cl), got off to a rocky start in 2007 but has since stabilized.

One of the great conveniences in Chilean public transport is the *taxi colectivo,* which operates like a city bus on a fixed route. Only slightly more expensive than a city bus, it's usually faster and often more comfortable. *Taxis colectivos* are identifiable by the illuminated plastic signs on top of their roofs, which show major destinations along the route.

In Buenos Aires and some other localities, rechargeable SUBE cards have replaced coin boxes. In other localities they may require *fichas* (tokens) or cards; on a few buses, drivers still handle the task.

Taxis and *Remises*

Buenos Aires, Santiago, and other cities have abundant taxis, mostly painted black with yellow roofs. Since a spate of robberies that began some years ago, nearly all Buenos Aires cabs are now *radio taxis*—some people prefer the security of phoning for a cab—but many Argentines still flag them down in the street. If in doubt, lock the back doors so that no one can enter by surprise.

All regular cabs have digital meters. In Buenos Aires, it costs about US$1.50 to *bajar la bandera* ("drop the flag"; i.e., switch on the meter) and another US$0.15 per 200 meters; provincial cities tend to be a little cheaper. Verify that the meter is set at zero.

Drivers do not expect tips. Sometimes, to avoid making change, they will even round the fare down. Carry small bills rather than rely on the driver to make change, especially if he has just come on shift. To deter a potentially dishonest driver when paying with a large note, ask whether he has the proper change for that amount.

Remises are Argentine radio taxis that charge an agreed-upon rate based on distance. The dispatcher will let you know the fare when you call, based on the pickup and drop-off points. Hotels, restaurants, and other businesses will gladly ring radio taxis and *remises* for customers and clients, especially when the hour is late.

On-demand services, most notably Uber, do exist in Buenos Aires, but they are often the target of protest and even aggression by taxi drivers.

Bicycle

Cycling may not be the safest way of navigating chaotic city traffic, but the number of cyclists is growing rapidly. If riding around Buenos Aires, Santiago, or other cities, side streets may be safer than fast-moving avenues, but they are also narrower, with less room for maneuvering. Weekend traffic is not so wild as on weekdays, and downtown areas may be virtually deserted on Sunday. There are increasing numbers of dedicated bike paths, but Buenos Aires drivers do not always respect them.

There are public bicycle-share programs in both Buenos Aires and Santiago, but they're oriented toward permanent residents. Both cities do have bicycle tour companies.

Walking

Most Argentine cities are compact enough that walking suffices for sightseeing and other activities. The first rule of pedestrian safety is that that you are invisible—for many Argentine drivers, crosswalks appear to be merely decorative. While making turns, they weave among pedestrians rather than slowing or stopping to let them pass. Jaywalking is endemic, perhaps because it's not much more hazardous than crossing at the corner with the light.

Compared with most Argentines, Chilean motorists respect crosswalks and are courteous to pedestrians. A substantial minority, though, seem to drive distractedly at times, so it pays to be attentive. Despite the hazards, pedestrians can often move faster than automobiles in congested areas.

Crossing Patagonian Borders

Argentina and Chile have numerous border crossings, in Patagonia and elsewhere. In both countries' lakes districts, trans-Andean bus service is fairly common, but many southerly crossings lack public transportation.

Crossing the border is normally routine and, given the similarities between the two countries' visa regimes, poses few unexpected obstacles for any nationality. It can take anywhere from five minutes to an hour or more, depending on how busy the given border post is. That said, Chilean customs and immigration posts tend to be quicker and more efficient than their Argentine counterparts, whose personnel are often poorly trained, with outdated technology (and technological skills). Argentina's customs regulations can also be more arbitrary than Chile's. While this mostly affects Argentine citizens, it slows everyone down. At some remote crossings, Chilean Carabineros (national police) and the Argentine Gendarmería (Border Patrol) handle all formalities.

In many border areas, especially where the towns are close together (as in Chile Chico and Los Antiguos, and Puerto Natales and Río Turbio), Chilean and Argentine currencies are accepted on both sides of the line. However, they are usually not accepted for official transactions, such as postal services.

OVERLAND CROSSINGS

In northern Patagonia, Argentina-bound buses cross from Temuco to Neuquén over the 1,884-meter-elevation Paso de Pino Hachado via Curacautín and Lonquimay; the alternative 1,298-meter Paso de Icalma is slightly to the south. Other options include a regular bus service from Temuco to San Martín de los Andes via the Paso de Mamuil Malal (Paso Tromen to Argentines); a bus-boat

combination from Panguipulli to San Martín de los Andes via the 659-meter Paso Huahum and Lago Pirehueico; a paved highway from Osorno to Bariloche via the Paso de Cardenal Samoré that's the second-busiest crossing between the two countries; and the classic bus-boat shuttle from Puerto Montt and Puerto Varas to Bariloche.

There are many southern Patagonian crossings, but roads are often bad and only a few have public transportation. Those with scheduled services include the mostly gravel road from Futaleufú, Chile, to Esquel (local buses only); Coyhaique to Comodoro Rivadavia on a mostly paved road via Río Mayo on long-distance coaches; Chile Chico to Los Antiguos; Puerto Natales to El Calafate via Río Turbio on a steadily improving route, much of it now paved; Punta Arenas to Río Gallegos via an entirely paved highway; and Punta Arenas to Río Grande and Ushuaia, a route that includes a ferry crossing on the Chilean side.

Many other crossings are suitable for private motor vehicles and mountain bikes, and a few by foot.

WATER

The main international crossings are the popular and scenic but increasingly expensive bus-boat-bus route between the Argentine resort town of San Carlos de Bariloche and the Chilean city of Puerto Montt, and the relatively short cruise (three-plus days) that carries passengers between Punta Arenas (Chile) and Ushuaia (Argentine Tierra del Fuego). There is also a rugged boat-bus route between Villa O'Higgins (Chile) and El Chaltén (Argentina) that also requires travelers to cover part of the route on foot, bicycle, or horseback.

Visas and Officialdom

ARGENTINA

Citizens of neighboring countries—Bolivians, Brazilians, Uruguayans, and Paraguayans—need only national ID cards, but most other nationalities need passports. U.S. and Canadian citizens, along with those of the European Union and Scandinavian countries, Switzerland, Israel, Australia, and New Zealand, and other Latin American countries need passports but not advance visas. Citizens of nearly every African and Asian country, except for South Africa and Japan, need advance visas.

Regulations change, however, and it may be helpful to check the visa page of Argentina's **Ministerio de Relaciones Exteriores** (Foreign Relations Ministry, www.mrecic. gov.ar), which also includes contacts of the most important Argentine embassies and consulates overseas. The most recent change is the application of a "reciprocity fee" for citizens of countries that collect visa fees from Argentine applicants: in this case, those of Australia (US$100, multiple entry for 1 year), and Canada (CDN$100, valid for 10 years or until expiration of the passport). It is now obligatory at all border crossings, and must be arranged online through the Dirección Nacional de Migraciones (www.migraciones. gov.ar/accesible).

Argentina routinely grants foreign visitors 90-day entry permits in the form of a tourist card. Theoretically, this card must be surrendered on departure; in practice, it's the passport stamp that counts. For 900 pesos, about US$60, entry is renewable for another 90 days at the **Dirección Nacional de Migraciones** (Av. Argentina 1355, Retiro, Buenos Aires, tel. 011/4317-0237, 8am-2pm Mon.-Fri.).

In the provinces, renewal can be done at any office of the Policía Federal (Federal Police), but in smaller towns the police may not be accustomed to doing so.

Formally, arriving visitors must have a return or onward ticket, but enforcement is inconsistent. If you have a Latin American, North American, or Western European passport, for instance, it's unlikely you will be asked to show the return ticket (in the western hemisphere, only Cubans need advance visas to enter Argentina). This author has entered Argentina dozens of times over decades, at Buenos Aires and some of the most remote border posts, without ever having been asked for a return or onward ticket.

Foreign airlines, though, may not permit a passenger without a round-trip ticket to board an Argentina-bound flight. Likewise, if the arriving passenger presents an Eastern European, Asian, or African passport, he or she may well be asked for proof of return transportation. Immigration officials have a great deal of discretion in these matters.

Always carry identification, since either the federal or provincial police can request it at any moment, though they rarely do so without reason. Passports are also necessary for routine transactions like checking into hotels, cashing traveler's checks, or even credit card transactions.

Dependent children under age 14 traveling without both parents presumably need notarized parental consent, but this author's minor daughter visited Argentina many times with only one parent and was never asked for such a document.

Argentine-born individuals, even if their parents were not Argentines or if they have been naturalized elsewhere, sometimes attract unwanted attention. Generally, they may enter the country for no more than 60 days on a non-Argentine document. Argentine passports renewed outside the country expire on reentry, often requiring a time-consuming renewal at the Policía Federal.

Lost or Stolen Passports

Visitors who suffer a lost or stolen passport must obtain a replacement at their own embassy or consulate. After obtaining a replacement passport, visit the Dirección Nacional de Migraciones to replace the tourist card.

Customs

Traditionally notorious for flagrant corruption, Argentina's improved customs system normally presents no obstacle to tourists. Short-term visitors may import personal effects, including clothing, jewelry, medicine, sporting gear, camping gear and accessories, photographic and video equipment, personal computers and the like, as well as 400 cigarettes, two liters of wine or alcoholic beverages (over age 18 only), and up to US$300 in new merchandise.

Customs inspections are usually routine, but at Buenos Aires's international airports, river ports, and at some land borders, incoming checked baggage may pass through X-rays. Fresh food will be confiscated at any port of entry.

At some remote border posts, the Gendarmería Nacional (Border Patrol) handles all formalities, from immigration to customs to agricultural inspections. Visitors arriving from drug-producing countries such as Colombia, Peru, and Bolivia may get special attention, as may those from Paraguay, with its thriving contraband economy.

Argentine Consulates in Other Countries

Embassies and consulates are often, though not always, at the same address. Consulates, rather than embassies, are primarily responsible for dealing with individuals traveling for either business or pleasure, however. Intending visitors should visit consulates for visas or other inquiries. This list includes overseas consulates and others in countries that border Argentina and Chile.

Australia

• 7 National Circuit, 2nd Fl., Barton, ACT, tel. 02/6273-9111, www.eaust.mrecic.gov.ar

• 44 Market St., Level 20, Sydney NSW, tel. 02/9262-2933

Bolivia

• Aspiazu 497, La Paz, tel. 02/241-7737, www.ebolv.mrecic.gov.ar

Brazil

• Praia de Botafogo 228, Sobreloja 201, Rio de Janeiro, tel. 021/3850-8150, http://crioj.cancilleria.gov.ar

• Av. Paulista 1106, Entrepiso, São Paulo, tel. 011/3897-9522, www.sanpablo.argentinaconsul.ar

Canada

• 81 Metcalfe St., 7th Fl., Ottawa, ON K1P 6K7, tel. 613/236-2351, www.ecana.mrecic.gob.ar

• 5001 Yonge St., Suite 201, Toronto, ON M2N 6P6, tel. 416/955-9075, www.consargtoro.ca

• 2000 Peel St., Suite 600, Montréal, QC H3A 2W5, tel. 514/842-6582, www.cmrea.mrecic.gov.ar

Chile

• Vicuña Mackenna 41, Santiago, tel. 02/2582-2606, www.csigo.mrecic.gov.ar

• Pedro Montt 160, 6th Fl., Puerto Montt, tel. 065/228-2878, www.cpmon.cancilleria.gov.ar

• 21 de Mayo 1878, Punta Arenas, tel. 061/226-1912

New Zealand

• 142 Lambton Quay, Level 14, Wellington, tel. 04/472-8330, www.enzel.mrecic.gob.ar

Paraguay

• Av. España and Perú, Asunción, tel. 021/21-2320, www.embajada-argentina.org.py

United Kingdom

• 27 Three Kings Yard, London W1K 4DF, tel. 020/7318-1340, www.clond.mrecic.gov.ar

United States

- 1811 Q St. NW, Washington, DC 20009, tel. 202/238-6460, www.embassyofargentina.us

- 5550 Wilshire Blvd., Suite 210, Los Angeles, CA 90036, tel. 323/954-9155, www.clang.cancilleria.gov.ar

- 1101 Brickell Ave., Suite 900, North Tower, Miami, FL 33131, tel. 305/373-1889, www.miam.cancillera.gov.ar

- 245 Peachtree Center Ave., Suite 2101, Atlanta, GA 30303, tel. 404/880-0805, http://catla.cancilleria.gov.ar

- 205 N. Michigan Ave., Suite 4208/09, Chicago, IL 60601, tel. 312/819-2610, www.cchic.mrecic.gov.ar

- 12 W. 56th St., New York, NY 10019, tel. 212/603-0400, http://cnyor.mrecic.gov.ar

- 2200 West Loop S., Suite 1025, Houston TX 77027, tel. 713/871-8935, http://chous.cancilleria.gov.ar

Uruguay

- Wilson Ferreira Aldunate 1281, Montevideo, tel. 02902-8623, http://cmdeo.cancilleria.gov.ar

- Av. General Flores 209, Colonia, tel. 04522-2093, http://ccolo.cancilleria.gov.ar

Foreign Consulates in Buenos Aires

As a major capital, Buenos Aires has a full complement of embassies and consulates providing services to foreign visitors. A country's embassy and consulate often shares an address. When the addresses are separate, this list provides the address of the consulate, as they are primarily responsible for dealing with individuals traveling for either business or pleasure. It includes major overseas consulates as well as those from countries that border Argentina.

Australia

- Villanueva 1400, Palermo, tel. 011/4779-3500, www.argentina.embassy.gov.au

Bolivia

- Bartolomé Mitre 2815, 1st Fl., Balvanera, tel. 011/5263-3790, www.consuladoboliviano.com.ar

Brazil

- Carlos Pellegrini 1363, 5th Fl., Retiro, tel. 011/4515-6500, www.conbrasil.org.ar

Canada

- Tagle 2828, Palermo, tel. 011/4808-1086, www.buenosaires.gc.ca

Chile

- Roque Sáenz Peña 547, 2nd Fl., tel. 011/4331-6228, http://chileabroad.gov.cl/buenos-aires

New Zealand

- Carlos Pellegrini 1427, 5th Fl., Retiro, tel. 011/5070-0700, www.nzembassy.com/argentina

Paraguay

- Viamonte 1851, Balvanera, tel. 011/4814-4803, www.mre.gov.py

Peru

- San Martín 128-136, Microcentro, tel. 011/4341-0020, www.consuladoperubaires.org

United Kingdom

- Dr. Luis Agote 2412, Recoleta, tel. 011/4808-2200, www.ukinargentina.fco.gov.uk

United States

- Colombia 4300, Palermo, tel. 011/5777-4533, http://ar.usembassy.gov

Uruguay

- Paraguay 1571, Microcentro, tel. 011/6009-5040, www.embajadadeluruguay.com.ar

Police and Military

Argentina is so notorious for police corruption that Argentines scornfully call both federal and provincial police *la cana*, an insult that should never be used to their face.

The Policía Federal (Federal Police) are marginally more professional than provincial forces, which are often despised for harassing motorists for minor equipment violations and, even worse, for their *gatillo fácil* (hair-trigger) response to minor criminal offenses. Cops often solicit *coimas* (bribes) at routine traffic stops. To avoid paying a bribe, either state your intention to contact your consulate, or else use broken Spanish even if you understand the language well. Either one may frustrate a corrupt official sufficiently to give up the effort.

Since the 1976-1983 dictatorship ended, the Argentine military has lost prestige and appears to have acknowledged its inability to run the country, despite occasional coup clamor by fringe figures. Still, security is heavy around military bases and photography is taboo—though the "Sentry Will Shoot" signs have mostly disappeared.

CHILE

Argentines, Brazilians, Uruguayans, and Paraguayans need only national identity cards, but every other nationality needs a passport. U.S. and Canadian citizens, along with those of the European Union, Switzerland, Norway, Israel, Mexico, Australia, and New Zealand, need passports but not advance visas.

Nationalities that must obtain advance visas include Indians, Jamaicans, Koreans, Poles, Russians, and Thais. For contacts of overseas Chilean embassies and consulates, see the website of the **Ministerio de Relaciones Exteriores** (Foreign Ministry, www.minrel.gov.cl).

Chile routinely grants 90-day entry permits to foreign visitors, in the form of a tourist card that must be surrendered on departure from the country. Formally, visitors must have a return or onward ticket, but this author has entered Chile dozens of times over many years, at many border posts, without ever having been asked for a return or onward ticket.

An unpleasant surprise, though, is the hefty *arrival* tax that the Foreign Ministry has imposed on certain nationalities: US$23 for Mexicans; US$95 for Australians; US$132 for Canadians. These are one-time fees, valid for the life of the user's passport and collected only at airports. Chile's acceptance into the Visa Waiver Program has reduced the fee to US$14 for U.S. citizens.

The rationale behind these fees, officially described as a *gasto administrativo de reciprocidad* (administrative reciprocity charge), is that the governments of those countries require Chilean citizens to pay the same amounts simply to apply for a visa (with no guarantee of being issued one). That's a reasonable argument, but the misunderstandings provoked when unsuspecting arrivals are diverted to a special line to pay additional fees often generate ill will.

Ninety-day extensions can take several days and cost roughly US$100, plus two color photos, at the **Departamento de Extranjería** (Moneda 1342, Santiago Centro, tel. 02/2672-5320) or in regional capitals. Visitors close to the Argentine, Peruvian, or Bolivian border may find it quicker and cheaper to dash across the line and return. For lost tourist cards, request a replacement from the **Policía Internacional** (General Borgoño 1052, Independencia, Santiago, tel. 02/2737-1292), or from offices in regional capitals.

Always carry identification, since the Carabineros (national police) can request it at any moment, though they rarely do so without a reason. Passports are also necessary for routine transactions like checking into hotels and cashing traveler's checks.

Lost or Stolen Passports

Visitors who suffer a lost or stolen passport must obtain a replacement at their own embassy or consulate. After obtaining a replacement, it's necessary to visit the Policía Internacional to replace the tourist card.

Customs

Visitors may import personal effects including clothing, jewelry, medicine, sporting gear, camping equipment and accessories, photographic and video equipment, personal computers and the like, and wheelchairs for individuals with disabilities, as well as 500 grams of tobacco, three liters of wine or alcoholic beverages (over age 18 only), and small quantities of perfume.

Customs inspections are usually routine, but at Santiago's international airport and some land borders, incoming checked baggage passes through X-rays; do not put photographic film in your checked baggage overland from Mendoza, Argentina, to Santiago, for instance. At the international airport, there are drug-sniffing beagles.

Travelers bound from Region XII (Magallanes) will undergo internal customs checks because the region has *zona franca* (duty-free) status. At many borders, the Servicio Agrícola Ganadero (SAG, Agriculture and Livestock Service) conducts agricultural inspections and sometimes levies a small charge for doing so. It confiscates fresh food.

At some remote border posts, Carabineros (national police) handle all formalities, from immigration to customs to agricultural inspections.

Chilean Embassies and Consulates Abroad

Chile has embassies and consulates throughout much of the world. Those listed here should be most useful to potential visitors. For a complete list, check the website of the foreign-relations ministry (Ministerio de Relaciones Exteriores, www.minrel.cl).

Argentina

• Roque Sáenz Peña 547, 2nd Fl., tel. 011/4331-6228, http://chileabroad.gov.cl/buenos-aires

Australia

• 10 Culgoa Circuit, O'Malley, ACT 2606, tel. 02/6286-4027, http://chileabroad.gov.cl/australia/en

• 80 Collins St., Level 43, Melbourne, Victoria 3000, tel. 03/9654-4982, www.chile.com.au

• 44 Market St., Level 18, Sydney, NSW 2000, tel. 02/9299-2533, http://chileabroad.gov.cl/sydney

Bolivia

• Calle 14 No. 8024, Calacoto, La Paz, tel. 02/279-7331, http://chileabroad.gov.cl/la-paz

Brazil

• Praia do Flamengo 344, 7th Fl., Flamengo, Rio de Janeiro, tel. 021/3579-9658, http://chileabroad.gov.cl/rio-de-janeiro

• Av. Paulista 1009, 10th Fl., São Paulo, tel. 011/3284-2148, http://chileabroad.gov.cl/sao-paulo

Canada

• 50 O'Connor St., Suite 1413, Ottawa, ON K1P 6L2, tel. 613/235-4402, http://chileabroad.gov.cl/ottawa

• 2 Bloor St. W., Suite 1801, Toronto, ON M4W 3E2, tel. 416/924-0106, www.congechiletoronto.com

• 1010 Sherbrooke St. W., Suite 710, Montréal, QC H3A 2R7, tel. 514/499-0405, http://chileabroad.gov.cl/montreal

• 1185 W. Georgia St., Suite 610, Vancouver, BC V6E 4E6, tel. 604/681-9162, http://chileabroad.gov.cl/vancouver

New Zealand

• 7th Fl., The Pencarrow House, 1-3 Willeston St., Wellington 6011, tel. 04/471-6270, http://chileabroad.gov.cl/wellington/en

Paraguay

- Capitán Emilio Neudelmann 351, Villa Mora, Asunción, tel. 021/60-0671, http://chileabroad.gov.cl/asuncion

United Kingdom

- 37-41 Old Queen St., London SW1H 9JA, tel. 020/7222-2361, http://chileabroad.gov.cl/londres/en

United States

- 1736 Massachusetts Ave. NW, Washington, DC 20036, tel. 202/530-4104, www.chile.glb.cl/washington

- 6100 Wilshire Blvd., Suite 1240, Los Angeles, CA 90048, tel. 323/933-3697, www.chile.gob.cl/los-angeles

- 870 Market St., Suite 1058, San Francisco, CA 94105, tel. 415/982-7662, http://chileabroad.gov.cl/san-francisco

- 800 Brickell Ave., Suite 1230, Miami, FL 33131, tel. 305/373-8623, http://chileabroad.gov.cl/miami

- 1415 N. Dayton St., 2nd Fl., Chicago, IL 60642, tel. 312/654-8780, www.chile.gob.cl/chicago

- 866 United Nations Plaza, Suite 601, New York, NY 10017, tel. 212/980-3366, http://chileabroad.gov.cl/nueva-york

- 1300 Post Oak Blvd., Suite 2330, Houston, TX 77056, tel. 713/621-5853, http://chileabroad.gov.cl/houston

Uruguay

- 25 de Mayo 575, Montevideo, tel. 02916-2346, http://chileabroad.gov.cl/montevideo

Foreign Embassies and Consulates in Santiago

All major European and South American states, plus many others, have diplomatic representation in Santiago. The bordering countries of Argentina, Bolivia, and Peru have consulates in several other cities.

Argentina

- Vicuña Mackenna 41, tel. 02/2582-2606, www.csigo.cancilleria.gov.ar

Australia

- Isidora Goyenechea 3621, Torre B, Las Condes, tel. 02/2550-3500, www.chile.embassy.gov.au

Bolivia

- Av. Santa María 2796, Providencia, tel. 02/2232-4997, www.consuladodebolivia.cl

Brazil

- Los Militares 6191, 1st Fl., Las Condes, tel. 02/2820-5800, http://santiago.itamaraty.gov.br

Canada

- Nueva Tajamar 481, 12th Fl., Las Condes, tel. 02/2652-3800, www.canadainternational.gc.ca/chile-chili

New Zealand

- Isidora Goyenechea 3000, 12th Fl., Las Condes, tel. 02/2616-3000, www.nzembassy.cl

Paraguay

- Carmen Silva 2437, Providencia, tel. 02/2963-6380

Peru

- Antonio Bellet 444, Oficina 104, Providencia, tel. 02/2940-2900, www.conpersantiago.cl

United Kingdom

- Av. El Bosque Norte 0125, 3rd Fl., Las Condes, tel. 02/2370-4100, www.ukinchile.fco.gov.uk

United States

- Av. Costanera Andrés Bello 2800, Las Condes, tel. 02/2330-3000, http://chile.usembassy.gov

Uruguay

• Pedro de Valdivia 711, Providencia, tel. 02/2223-8398, www.uruguay.cl

Police and Military

Chile's Carabineros (national police) are probably the continent's most professional police, with a reputation for integrity and a low tolerance for bribery and similar corruption (Argentine motorists, accustomed to bribing police following traffic violations in their own country, have had vehicles confiscated for trying to do so in Chile). Known popularly but scornfully as *pacos* by some Chileans (do not use this form of address to a Carabinero!), the Carabineros are normally polite and helpful in public, but can be stern with lawbreakers or individuals they suspect of being lawbreakers.

During the Pinochet dictatorship, the military were feared, but since the return to constitutional government and, especially, since Pinochet's detention and arrest in London, they keep a low public profile.

FALKLAND ISLANDS

All visitors, including Britons, must have passports to visit the Falklands. Visitors from the United States, Canada, Australia, New Zealand, Britain, the European Union, Chile, and the Mercosur countries do not need visas, but others should contact a British consulate. Tourists must have return tickets and sufficient funds to cover their stay, and may need to arrange accommodations in advance. Visa or MasterCard is proof of sufficient funds.

Visitors must have adequate medical coverage, including emergency evacuation insurance.

Lost or Stolen Passports

Visitors who suffer a lost passport here (theft is unlikely) may have problems, as there are no foreign consulates. United Kingdom and European Union citizens should be able to arrange a temporary passport through Customs and Immigration, but other nationalities could need to obtain a formal Declaration of Identity through their nearest embassy and obtain permission from any other country through which they might pass, with consular assistance required at the transit airport. Consequently, there could be delays in departing the islands.

Customs

Local customs regulations permit the importation of almost anything except illegal drugs. There are taxes on alcoholic beverages (which are readily available locally). For details, contact Customs and Immigration (3 H Jones Rd., Stanley, tel. 27340, admin@customs.gov.fk).

Police and Military

Police resemble their British counterparts; they do not carry firearms and rarely deal with anything more serious than a traffic violation or a bar brawl.

The British military presence is substantial at Mount Pleasant Airport, but visitors rarely come in contact with them elsewhere. Some soldiers do take advantage of R&R to visit wildlife sites, where they may meet tourists.

Recreation

Patagonia provides exciting options for hiking, climbing, and mountain biking in the Andes; bird-watching on its Atlantic and Pacific shorelines, the interior drainage lakes, the southern steppes, and southern rainforest fjords; and viewing marine mammals ranging from seals, sea lions, and dolphins to orcas and the great right and blue whales.

On both sides of the Andes, the runoff permits white-water rafting and kayaking from the Andean lakes district in the north to Chubut province and Aisén in the south, and there's sea kayaking in the southern fjords and glacier-fed lakes.

NATIONAL PARKS AND OTHER PROTECTED AREAS

Both Argentina and Chile have impressive rosters of national parks, reserves, and monuments, and some significant provincial reserves as well. In fact, Argentina and Chile were pioneers in setting aside land for conservation purposes, even if they haven't always provided sufficient funding and have sometimes surrendered to commercial pressures.

Given a land tenure situation in which nearly all its territory is privately owned, the Falkland Islands have no formal national parks, but the northwesterly Jason Islands and some other areas are Crown Reserves. Many farms protect their wildlife zealously, and some have designated parts of their properties, particularly offshore islands, as nature reserves.

Argentina

Argentina's main conservation agency is the **Administración de Parques Nacionales** (APN, Av. Santa Fe 690, Retiro, Buenos Aires, tel. 011/4311-0303, www.parquesnacionales. gov.ar, 10am-5pm Mon.-Fri.). While its selection of brochures on national parks and other protected areas continues to improve, the staff members are best informed on the highest-profile destinations, such as Parque Nacional Los Glaciares. The APN also maintains branches in cities such as San Martín de los Andes, San Carlos de Bariloche, El Calafate, and Ushuaia, while rangers staff information offices at many parks and reserves.

Argentina has three categories of protected areas: *parques nacionales* (national parks), *reservas nacionales* (national reserves), and *monumentos naturales* (natural monuments), though distinctions are not always clear. According to law, national parks are "areas to be preserved in their natural state, which are representative of biogeographical region and have natural beauty or scientific interest."

Often contiguous with national parks, national reserves may be buffers that permit "conservation of ecological systems . . . or the creation of independent conservation zones." Natural monuments are "places, things, and live animal or plant species, of aesthetic, historic, or scientific interest, to which is granted absolute protection." They usually have one outstanding feature, such as the petrified forest of Santa Cruz province, but may also be a rare or endangered species such as the southern right whale or the *huemul* (Andean deer).

Chile

Chile's main conservation agency is the **Corporación Nacional Forestal** (Conaf, National Forestry Corporation), which manages the Sistema Nacional de Áreas Silvestres Protegidas (Snaspe, National Protected Areas System). Within Snaspe, Chile has three categories of protected areas: *parques nacionales* (national parks), *reservas nacionales* (national reserves), and *monumentos naturales* (natural monuments). In addition, Chilean law allows for *reservas naturales privadas* or *santuarios de la naturaleza,* private nature reserves, which are growing in number.

Conaf defines each of its *parques nacionales* as "a generally extensive area where there exist either unique or biologically representative environments, not significantly affected by human intervention and capable of self-sustainability, whose flora and fauna or geological formations are of special educational, scientific, or recreational interest." Management objectives are to preserve samples of these environments, their cultural and scenic characteristics, the continuity of natural processes, and to promote activities associated with education, research, and recreation.

Monumentos naturales are generally smaller areas "characterized by the presence of native flora and fauna, or the existence of geologically relevant sites of scenic, cultural, or scientific interest." Management objectives resemble those of national parks.

Reservas nacionales are areas "whose

natural resources require special attention because of their susceptibility to degradation or importance to the welfare of nearby communities." The primary management objectives are soil and watershed conservation, preservation of endangered flora and fauna, and the application of appropriate technologies to those ends.

Falkland Islands

The Falklands have no national parks per se, but there are 27 "national nature reserves" totaling about 400 square kilometers. Several farms are de facto wildlife reserves, and a handful have formal designations, most notably the **New Island Wildlife Reserve.** The remote 790-hectare **Steeple Jason Island** belongs to the Wildlife Conservation Society of New York, while neighboring **Grand Jason Island** is government property, a Crown Reserve.

HIKING

Both Argentina and Chile have abundant hiking terrain, and the number of parks and reserves with integrated and well-maintained trail systems is increasing, but there are still shortcomings. Each country has an Instituto Geográfico Militar whose topographic maps,

at a scale of 1:50,000, are available for parts of the country, but there's been an upsurge in quality private mapping. Many trails lack clearly signposted junctions—multiple tracks are the rule. If necessary, try to contract a local guide.

Prime hiking and backpacking areas include the lakes districts on both sides of the Andes, where the season tends to be longer than in the far south; the Argentine side is generally drier than the Chilean side, which receives the brunt of Pacific storms. Of the northerly parks, the best for hikers are Nahuel Huapi and Lanín on the Argentine side, and Huerquehue, Villarrica, and Puyehue on the Chilean side.

South of the temperate lakes districts, Patagonia can be inclement at any time of year. In Argentina, the northern El Chaltén sector of Parque Nacional Los Glaciares has the best trail network. Matters are improving at hard-to-reach Parque Nacional Perito Moreno, which is much less crowded.

Farther south on the Chilean side, the best hiking destinations are Parque Pumalín, whose unique trails include ladders through vertiginously steep forest terrain; Reserva Nacional Cerro Castillo, the Aisén region's multiple-day hiking choice; and of course

Trailheads this way. . . .

Parque Nacional Torres del Paine, whose season is consistently lengthening. Popular Paine is Patagonia's most crowded hikers' destination, but motivated walkers can still find solitude on its lesser-known trails—or in winter.

In the Falklands, where wildlife-watching is the main tourist activity, the coastal sites are distant from each other. Most people travel by air taxi and 4WD vehicle. That said, there's plenty of open country and hiking opportunities for those willing to confront the incessant westerlies.

CLIMBING

In both Argentine and Chilean Patagonia, the Andean cordillera offers a climber's buffet, or for truly committed pilgrims it can be a mecca. For serious technical climbers, the biggest draws are the Fitz Roy range in Parque Nacional Los Glaciares's El Chaltén sector, or even Parque Nacional Nahuel Huapi's ice-covered 3,478-meter Monte Tronador. Other options include the rest of Parque Nacional Nahuel Huapi near Bariloche and 3,776-meter Volcán Lanín near Junín de los Andes. A warning: Even experienced mountaineers in prime condition have died on these peaks.

Across the Andes, Chile's volcanoes are a particular attraction: From the northernmost lakes district to remotest southern Aisén, Chile is part of the Pacific "ring of fire." But there is snow, ice, and rock climbing on all kinds of surfaces. Summer is the season for most climbers.

The most frequently climbed Chilean volcano, near the resort town of Pucón, is 2,847-meter Volcán Villarrica, which is also one of the most active. It's a day excursion that's sometimes canceled when Conaf decides the crater is a little too lively. A local guide is obligatory. The more technical Volcán Osorno, near the town of Puerto Varas, is also commercially climbed.

For general information on Argentine mountaineering, contact the **Centro Andino Buenos Aires** (Av. Rivadavia 1255, Oficinas 2/3, tel. 011/4381-1566, www.caba.org.ar).

There are also local and provincial mountaineering clubs.

Capable independent climbers can tackle many Chilean summits on their own, but peaks near international borders require clearance from the Foreign Ministry's **Dirección de Fronteras y Límites** (Difrol, Teatinos 180, 7th Fl., Santiago, tel. 02/2827-5900, www.difrol.cl). For permission, which may be done prior to arrival, each participant must present complete name, passport number, nationality, birth date, residence address, profession, arrival and departure dates in Chile, and a detailed itinerary. Issuing permission usually takes two to three days; climbers must present this permission to the nearest Carabineros police station before actually undertaking the climb.

For general information on climbing in Chile, including suggestions on dealing with the bureaucracy, contact the **Federación de Andinismo** (Almirante Simpson 77, tel. 02/2222-0888, www.feach.cl). See also the bilingual online **Chile Climbing Page** (www.chilemountains.info).

While the Falklands are not a climber's destination per se, the rocky summits of both main islands, though they barely reach 700 meters elevation, can provide rewarding recreation.

CYCLING AND MOUNTAIN BIKING

Both long-distance riders and recreational mountain bikers will find Patagonia's spectacular landscapes appealing and rugged terrain challenging. Because many roads have dirt or gravel surfaces, and because paved roads are often so narrow that riding on the shoulder is imperative, a mountain bike is the best option. Riders without their own bikes will find readily available rentals in towns like Bariloche and Pucón, but their condition varies widely. Check the brakes, tires, and everything else before renting.

If touring, carry rain gear, a tent, and supplementary camping gear, and acquire a knowledge of bicycle repairs—some of the finest riding areas have almost no services. Possible routes are countless, but the most popular area is the scenic lakes district on both sides of the Andes.

Increasing numbers of cyclists, some of them through riders from Alaska to Tierra del Fuego, are braving the changeable weather on Chile's Carretera Austral, a discontinuous 1,100-kilometer road from Puerto Montt that's now complete to the southern outpost of Villa O'Higgins, and even continuing to El Chaltén, on the Argentine side. North of the regional capital of Coyhaique, it's mostly paved, but it still requires several ferry crossings as it passes through some of the continent's most spectacular terrain. East of the Andes, between Esquel and El Calafate, Argentina's dusty but charismatic RN 40 parallels the Carretera Austral, but riders need stamina and sense of balance, as the powerful winds can either slow progress to a crawl or knock a rider over. Paving is proceeding rapidly here.

Feasible as early as October, the southernmost Patagonian routes are best December to April. As work progresses on the Sendero de Chile, intended to link the Andean uplands for pedestrians, bicycles, and horseback riders only, this will become an even more adventurous alternative.

HORSEBACK RIDING

Gaucho Argentina was born on horseback, and recreational riding is common even in and around Buenos Aires. It's most interesting in the provinces, though, especially in the rugged terrain of the Andean lakes around Junín de los Andes and Bariloche. Trips range from morning or afternoon trail rides to hard-riding excursions of several days, and nearly all *estancias* (ranches) offer riding as an optional activity.

Likewise, Chile's *huaso* tradition makes riding a popular pastime in many lakes district and southern Patagonian destinations. The most challenging options are around Pucón and the Cochamó area near Puerto Varas, and in Parque Nacional Torres del Paine.

SKIING

Since the seasons are reversed in southern South America, Patagonia's Andean slopes reach their peak in August. While Argentina's resorts may not have the reputation of Chile's best, the mountains near Bariloche have long drawn skiers from around the continent and the world. There are also options at San Martín de los Andes, Villa La Angostura, Esquel, and even Ushuaia.

Chile's top international ski resorts are close to the capital city of Santiago, but Parque Nacional Villarrica (near the town of Pucón), Corralco (east of Temuco), and Parque Nacional Puyehue's Antillanca (near the city of Osorno) are respectable choices.

BIRDING

Patagonia's diverse natural environments, ranging from Atlantic and Pacific shorelines to boundless steppes with surprising wetlands and from Andean woodlands to the sub-Antarctic, mean an opportunity to add lots of new species to your life list. The finest birding areas are the Atlantic and Pacific coasts, the arid eastern steppes, and both sides of the temperate Andean woodlands in the lakes district.

For birding suggestions in Argentina, contact the **Asociación Ornitológica del Plata** (Matheu 1246, Buenos Aires, tel. 011/4943-7216, www.avesargentinas.org.ar). **Hostería Las Torres,** in Chile's Parque Nacional Torres del Paine, is also a birding specialist with English-speaking personnel. Many tour operators offer birding excursions.

RAFTING AND KAYAKING

Descending steeply from the Andes, Chile's transverse Patagonian rivers are world-class. More than a few rafters and kayakers consider the powerful Futaleufú, in a remote area near the southern Argentine border, the world's best **white water.** The Trancura near

Pucón, the Fuy near Panguipulli, the Petrohué near Puerto Varas, and the Baker south of Coyhaique all blend wild water with exquisite scenery, but none of them quite matches the Futaleufú's adrenaline level.

On the rain-shadow side of the Andes, Argentine rivers lack the tremendous spring snowmelt that turns Chilean rivers into raging white water. But there are commercially viable rivers from the Aluminé in northern Neuquén to Esquel in northern Chubut, and the number is growing. The country's top river is the Class IV Río Manso, south of Bariloche.

Nearly all Patagonian rivers may be run from the first October runoff to the early days of April.

The Chilean village of Dalcahue, on the Isla Grande de Chiloé, is a center for commercial **sea kayaking,** though there are many other suitable locations, among them Puerto Natales and Tierra del Fuego's spectacular Cordillera Darwin. Pacific Chile offers exceptional opportunities, such as the river to ocean route from the Río Futaleufú's mouth to Chaitén via Lago Yelcho and the Río Yelcho.

While Argentine Patagonia's exposed coastline lacks the sheltered channels and inlets of Pacific Chile, Nahuel Huapi and other large glacial lakes make a more-than-adequate substitute for sea kayakers.

DIVING

Diving may not be an obvious activity in Patagonia, as much of the waters are cold and lack reefs, but in summer the Argentine city of Puerto Madryn, in Chubut province, has a cluster of diving outfitters and operators for the warm and shallow waters of the Golfo Nuevo.

SURFING

The good news is that, with a long coastline and small surfer population, Patagonia means little competition for waves; the bad news is that Argentina's Atlantic surf is generally tamer than Chile's Pacific, which is wilder but colder (wet suits are essential here).

Shallow waters and wide tidal ranges may be further deterrents in Argentine Patagonia. But places like desolate Cabo Raso (where competition is zero) are suitable. The waters of the Golfo Nuevo, at Puerto Madryn, are too sheltered for big waves, but the blustery Patagonian winds make it a windsurfer's dream.

Most Chilean surfers frequent areas well north of the Andean lakes district, but there are possibilities near the coastal city of Valdivia. Windsurfing is best on some of the lakes, rather than on the ocean.

FISHING

Both Argentine and Chilean Patagonia draw fly-fishing enthusiasts eager to test their skills on lakes, rivers, and fjords from both sides of the Andean lakes district to Tierra del Fuego's southernmost tip.

Along the eastern Andean slopes, the rivers of Neuquén and Río Negro provinces have Argentina's greatest concentration of fly-fishing choices. Along Chile's Carretera Austral, in the Aisén region, there are specialized fishing lodges and other resorts that include fly-fishing among their offerings.

Organized Tours

Because of Patagonia's complex logistics, organized tours can be a useful option for visitors with limited time, and many reputable U.S., Argentine, and Chilean operators offer and even coordinate tours on both sides of the border. Within each category, the companies appear in alphabetical order.

NORTH AMERICA

Primarily but not exclusively for cyclists, **Backroads** (801 Cedar St., Berkeley, CA

94710, tel. 510/527-1555 or 800/462-2848, www.backroads.com) offers a five-day Argentina's Lake District Biking tour that takes in Bariloche, Villa La Angostura, and the Siete Lagos area, and an eight-day Patagonia Walking trip, which stays at luxury lodgings in and around Argentina's Parque Nacional Los Glaciares.

Bio Bio Expeditions (P.O. Box 2028, Truckee, CA 96160, tel. 530/582-6865 or 800/246-7238, www.bbxrafting.com) offers weeklong kayaking and multi-sport programs at its cozy base camp on Chile's Río Futaleufú.

From its own deluxe camp on the Futaleufú, **Earth River Expeditions** (180 Towpath Rd., Accord, NY 12404, tel. 845/626-2665 or 800/643-2784, www.earthriver.com) offers 10-day rafting and multi-sport trips on and around the river.

Based commercially in Southern California and operationally in Bariloche, **Eureka Travel** (P.O. Box 7384, Burbank, CA 91510, tel. 818/841-8624 or 855/938-7352 toll-free, www.eurekatravel.net) is a family-run enterprise that shows patience in arranging flights and constructing itineraries.

A pioneer on the Río Futaleufú, former Olympian Chris Spelius's **Expediciones Chile** (P.O. Box 752, Sun Valley, ID 83353, tel. 208/629-5032, www.exchile.com) has its own sprawling and secluded but cozy Campo Tres Monjas on the river's south bank. While the company specializes in kayaking the Futaleufú, it also offers rafting and multi-sport holidays that include birding, hiking, and horseback riding. Weeklong stays at Tres Monjas include plenty of time and instruction on the river, and transportation from Esquel, Argentina, or from Puerto Montt, Chile. There are also shorter options, but a week is ideal here.

Mountain Travel Sobek (1266 66th St., Emeryville, CA 94608, tel. 888/831-7526, www.mtsobek.com) does a variety of Patagonian trips, including an 11-day Trekking the Paine Circuit Tour, a 14-day Hiker's Patagonia, and a 12-day Patagonia Explorer Tour that includes four nights

cruising through the Fuegian fjords of Tierra del Fuego on the *Terra Australis* and a variety of day hikes in southernmost Argentina and Chile.

Nature Expeditions International (7860 Peters Rd., Suite F-103, Plantation, FL 33324, tel. 954/693-8852 or 800/869-0639, www.naturexp.com) operates upscale "soft adventure" and culture-oriented tours to Argentina and Chile, among other destinations. Its 14-day Patagonia Wilderness Adventure visits Santiago, Torres del Paine, El Calafate, El Chaltén, and Buenos Aires.

Orvis (1711 Blue Hills Dr., Roanoke, VA 24012-8613, tel. 800/547-4322, www.orvis.com) arranges fishing holidays in the vicinity of the Argentine lakes district destinations of Junín de los Andes and Bariloche, as well as Chubut province, and along the Carretera Austral in Chile.

Owned by native Patagonians (from Neuquén and Río Gallegos), California-based **Patagonia Travel Adventures** (P.O. Box 22, Ben Lomond, CA 95005, tel. 831/726-8059, www.patagoniaadventures.com) focuses on small group tours to Península Valdés and Punta Tombo, Parque Nacional Los Glaciares, the little-visited Patagonian steppe along RN 40, and even Chile's Parque Nacional Torres del Paine.

Powderquest Tours (7108 Pinetree Rd., Richmond, VA 23229, tel. 888/565-7158, www.powderquest.com) runs five or six 9- to 13-day Southern Cone ski tours annually. Argentine Patagonia resorts include Chapelco, Cerro Bayo, Catedral Alta Patagonia, and Ushuaia, while Chilean Patagonia sites include Corralco (east of Temuco), and Pucón.

REI Adventures (P.O. Box 1938, Sumner, WA 98390, tel. 800/622-2236, www.rei.com/adventures) offers a diversity of Patagonian trips, including 11- to 13-day Fitz Roy and Paine Hiking tours, focusing on Argentina's El Chaltén area and Chile's Torres del Paine.

For travelers at least 55 years of age, **Road Scholar** (formerly Elderhostel, 11 Ave. de Lafayette, Boston, MA 02111, tel. 800/454-5768, www.roadscholar.org) offers a variety of southern South America trips, including a 13-day Hiking at the End of Earth trip that visits southern Argentine Patagonia and Tierra del Fuego, and a 24-day Falklands, South Georgia, and Antarctica expedition cruise.

Affiliated with the Smithsonian Institution, **Smithsonian Journeys** (P.O. Box 23182, Washington, DC 20077-0843, tel. 202/357-4700 or 877/338-8687, www.smithsonianjourneys.org) offers an 18-day land-and-sea Patagonia Explorer trip that visits Puerto Varas, Punta Arenas, Puerto Natales, Torres del Paine, El Calafate and the Glaciar Perito Moreno, and Ushuaia.

Wilderness Travel (1102 Ninth St., Berkeley, CA 94710, tel. 510/558-2488 or 800/368-2794, www.wildernesstravel.com) offers a diversity of options including a 16-day, hiking-oriented In Patagonia itinerary that focuses mostly on Argentina but also visits Torres del Paine.

Wildland Adventures (3516 NE 155th St., Seattle, WA 98155, tel. 800/345-4453, www.wildland.com) operates small group tours (2-8 people) through locally based guides. In Argentina, the 10-day Best of Patagonia tour takes in the Perito Moreno Glacier and other sights via Buenos Aires. The 13-day In the Wake of Magellan trip includes both Torres del Paine and a segment of the scenic luxury cruise between Punta Arenas and Ushuaia, as well as Argentina's Perito Moreno Glacier.

UNITED KINGDOM

Explore Worldwide (39 Steeple View, Swindon, Wiltshire SN1 3FH, tel. 07846/970-561, www.exploreworld.co.uk) organizes 13- to 18-day tours primarily to the northern Andean lakes district and the more southerly Torres del Paine and Argentina's El Calafate area.

Journey Latin America (401 King St., London W6 9NJ, tel. 020/3553-1554, www.journeylatinamerica.co.uk) specializes in small group tours throughout Latin America, including Argentina, Chile, and the Falkland Islands.

AUSTRALIA

Peregrine Adventures (7/567 Collins St., Melbourne, Victoria 3000, tel. 03/8601-4444, www.peregrineadventures.com) organizes tours to southernmost Patagonia, covering both sides of the border.

One of Australia's biggest operators, **World Expeditions** (71 York St., Level 5, Sydney, NSW 2000, tel. 02/8270-8400, www.worldexpeditions.com.au) has a variety of Patagonian tours. It also has branches in Melbourne (393 Little Bourke St., Melbourne, Victoria 3000, tel. 03/8631-3300, travel@worldexpeditions.com.au) and several other Australian cities, as well as Auckland, New Zealand (59-67 High St., Level 1, Auckland CBD, tel. 09/368-4161, enquiries@worldexpeditions.co.nz).

ARGENTINA

The operators listed here invariably have English-speaking personnel and services in many parts of the country. Many locally focused operators, though, have very good services as well. Argentina's country code is 54.

The Buenos Aires-based **Al Mundo** (Florida 825, Oficina 320, tel. 011/5199-7758, www.almundo.com) is Argentina's youth- and budget-oriented operator. Also in the capital, **Sayhueque** (Thames 2062, Palermo, tel. 011/5258-8740, U.S. tel. 718/395-5504, www.sayhueque.com) is a full-service agency that covers the whole country but is particularly strong on Patagonia.

Bariloche-based **Magellanica** (Calle 4, Meli 12040, San Carlos de Bariloche, tel. 0294/452-0669, www.magellanicatrips.com) is an adventure travel company whose custom-made journeys for solo travelers, small groups, or families make the most of the best hiking, sea kayaking, backcountry skiing, and mountaineering sites and itineraries in Patagonia and the lakes district of Chile and Argentina. Trained at Wyoming's National Outdoor Leadership School (NOLS), founder Diego Allolio and his staff adhere to "Leave No Trace" principles.

Based in El Chaltén, activity-oriented **FitzRoy Expediciones** (San Martín 56, tel.

02962/49-3178, www.fitzroyexpediciones.com.ar) focuses on that geographical area, organizing expeditions onto the southern Patagonian ice sheets and other less-demanding day trips.

CHILE

Several Chile-based operators focus on Chilean Patagonia and Tierra del Fuego, and some also work the Argentine side of the border. Chile's country code is 56.

AlSur Expediciones (Aconcagua and Imperial, Puerto Varas, tel./fax 065/223-2300, www.alsurexpeditions.com) operates tours and activities in the lakes district and specializes in Parque Pumalín and Parque Patagonia, the private nature reserves founded by Doug Tompkins and Kris McDivitt Tompkins.

Based in summer only at the town of Dalcahue on the Isla Grande de Chiloé, **Altué Sea Kayaking** (tel. 09/9419-6809, www.seakayakchile.com) has extensive itineraries around the archipelago's eastern shore and Parque Pumalín. For reservations, its Santiago contact is Altué Active Travel (Coyancura 2270, Oficina 801, Providencia, Santiago, tel. 02/2333-1390, www.altue.com).

Antares Patagonia Adventure (Pedro Montt 161, Puerto Natales, tel. 061/241-4611, www.antarespatagonia.com) operates activities-oriented trips to Patagonia, mostly but not exclusively in Torres del Paine, where it has concessions for activities like ice hiking, kayaking, and mountaineering. It also has a U.S. office (2726 Shelter Island Dr., San Diego, CA 92106, tel. 415/251-6198). Kayaking programs last 1-3 days.

French-owned **Azimut 360** (Eliodoro Yáñez 1437, Providencia, Santiago, tel. 02/2235-1519, www.azimut360.com) offers Patagonian excursions ranging from traditional lakes district trips to northern Patagonian ice fields and technical climbs of summits such as Aisén's 4,058-meter Monte San Valentín.

Campo Aventura (tel. 09/9289-4314, www.campoaventura.cl) offers four-day, three-night horseback explorations of the spectacularly scenic Cochamó backcountry southeast of Puerto Varas. Shorter and longer options are possible as well, and hiking trips are more common than they once were.

Santiago-based **Cascada Expediciones** (Don Carlos 3327-C, Las Condes, tel. 02/2923-5950, U.S./Canada tel. 888/232-3813, UK tel. 0800/051-7095, www.cascada.travel) offers activity-oriented excursions to destinations such as Pucón, Futaleufú, and Torres del Paine (where its domed Eco-camp is a distinctive accommodations option).

Aisén-based **Catamaranes del Sur** (Pedro de Valdivia Norte 0210, Providencia, Santiago, tel. 02/2231-1902, www.loberiasdelsur.cl) goes to Laguna San Rafael from its hotel at Puerto Chacabuco, and has longer programs with additional activities in the region.

October to April, **Cruceros Australis** (Av. Bosque Norte 0440, 11th Fl., Las Condes, Santiago, tel. 02/2442-3115, www.australis.com) offers three-, four-, and seven-day cruises from Punta Arenas through southern Tierra del Fuego's fjords to Ushuaia and Cape Horn on the luxury vessels *Ventus Australis* and *Stella Australis*. Rates change from low-season (Oct. and Apr.) to mid-season (Nov.-mid-Dec. and all of Mar.) and high-season (mid-Dec.-Feb.). Cruceros also has representatives in the United States (tel. 877/678-3772) and Europe (Spain, tel. 034-93/497-0484).

September to May, **Cruceros Marítimos Skorpios** (Augusto Leguía 118, Las Condes, Santiago, tel. 02/2477-1900, www.skorpios.cl) operates a fleet of small cruise ships (around 100 passengers) from Puerto Montt and Puerto Chacabuco to Laguna San Rafael, and from Puerto Natales to the fjords of Campo de Hielo Sur, the southern continental ice field west of Torres del Paine.

Explora Hotels (Américo Vespucio Sur 80, 5th Fl., Las Condes, Santiago, tel. 02/2395-2800, U.S. tel. 866/750-6699, UK tel. 0800/086-9053, www.explora.com) offers expensive, all-inclusive packages, ranging from three days to a week, at its magnificently sited hotel in Parque Nacional Torres del Paine, with overland extensions to El Chaltén on the Argentine side.

Navimag Ferries (Av. El Bosque Norte 0440, Las Condes, 11th Fl., tel. 02/2869-9900, www.navimag.com) sails between the Patagonian town of Puerto Natales and the mainland city of Puerto Montt. While these are not cruises in the traditional sense, they are more than just transportation as they pass through Pacific Chile's spectacular fjord lands.

U.S.-run, Puerto Bertrand-based **Patagonia Adventure Expeditions** (Casilla 8, Cochrane, tel. 09/8182-0608, www. adventurepatagonia.com) is a trekking, fishing, and white-water rafting operator. Its signature trip is the Aisén Glacier Trail, an exclusive 10-day hiking trip through the wild backcountry of Parque Nacional Laguna San Rafael and adjacent private lands.

Patagonia Connection (Fidel Oteíza 1951, Oficina 1006, Providencia, Santiago, tel. 02/2225-6489, www.patagonia-connection. com) offers four-day, three-night to six-day, five-night packages based at its Puyuhuapi Lodge & Spa hot-springs resort in Aisén. Prices are lower in the fall and spring shoulder seasons than in the January-February summer peak.

Puerto Williams-based, German-run **Sea & Ice & Mountains Adventures Unlimited** (tel./fax 061/262-1150 or 061/262-1227, www.simexpeditions.com) operates summer yacht tours through Tierra del Fuego and Cape Horn.

Accommodations

Argentine and Chilean Patagonia both have accommodations in categories ranging from campgrounds to youth-hostel dormitories to extravagant luxury suites and everything in between. Peak summer season demand can stress some localities. National and municipal tourist officials offer accommodations lists and brochures, but these often exclude budget options and may even omit some mid-range and high-end places.

Argentine prices may be negotiable; do not assume the *tarifa mostrador* (rack rate) is etched in stone. Visitors should not take hotel ratings too literally as they often represent an ideal rather than a reality, and some one- or two-star places are significantly better than others that formally rank higher.

Prices in Buenos Aires and Santiago often fall during the summer months of January and February, as business travel slows to a crawl. For Patagonian destinations, though, prices usually rise. Other peak seasons, when prices may rise, are Semana Santa (Holy Week), July's winter school vacations, which coincide with Argentine patriotic holidays, and mid-September's Chilean patriotic holidays.

In late 2016, Argentina decided to eliminate the *impuesto al valor agregado* or IVA (value-added tax) on accommodations by foreign visitors. This require payment in foreign currency or by credit or debit card (it's worth noting that, even before this measure took effect, many Argentine hotels gave de facto discounts to guests who paid in foreign cash).

Mid-range to upscale Chilean hotels levy 19 percent IVA but some can legally discount that to tourists with the appropriate documentation (passport and tourist card) who pay in dollars or by international credit card, and have been in the country for 60 days or less. Foreign residents of Chile are not eligible for this discount. At the same time, the discount can be smaller than expected if the hotel's exchange rate is unfavorable.

CAMPING

Organized camping is common throughout Patagonia. Campgrounds are generally spacious affairs, with shade, clean restrooms, baths with hot showers, and even groceries and restaurants. They can be surprisingly central and usually cheap, rarely more than a few dollars per person. Some Chilean campgrounds charge for a minimum of four or five people, however.

In the peak summer season and on weekends, the best sites can be crowded and noisy, as families on a budget take advantage of bargain prices. It's usually possible to find a quieter but less desirable site on the periphery. Remember that Argentines stay up late—very late—for their barbecues.

In the wilder, more remote areas like Santa Cruz and Aisén, it's possible to camp just about anywhere for free, although there are restrictions in popular destinations like Parque Nacional Los Glaciares and Parque Nacional Torres del Paine.

HOSTELS

For youth and budget travel, Argentina and Chile have growing hostel networks, plus there are many independent hostels, where bunks start around US$10-15 pp. In addition to the customary dorm accommodations, most hostels offer more expensive private rooms for individuals and couples.

Argentine hostels usually avoid the term *albergue;* in Argentine Spanish, an *albergue transitorio* means a by-the-hour hotel. Many have adapted the English word hostel, or Hispanicized it into *hostal,* a term more common in Chile, where it's a step above an *hospedaje* (family-run lodging).

For up-to-the-minute information on official Argentine hostels, contact **Hostelling International Argentina** (Florida 835, Oficina 107, tel. 011/4511-8723, www.hostels. org.ar). For their Chilean counterparts, contact **Hostelling International Santiago** (Cienfuegos 151, Santiago Centro, tel. 02/2671-8532, www.hostelling.cl).

Numerous independent hostels have opened in both countries, sometimes in loosely affiliated groups such as **Backpackers Chile** (www.backpackerschile.com). These

often have private rooms in addition to dorm-style accommodations.

BUDGET

Budget accommodations in Argentina and Chile can cost as little as US$10-15 pp. They go by a variety of names that may camouflage their quality, ranging from dingy fleabags with mattresses that sag like hammocks to simple but cheerful and tidy places with firm new beds.

An *hospedaje* is generally a family-run lodging with a few spare rooms; *pensiones* and *casas de huéspedes* (guesthouses) are comparable, nearly interchangeable terms. All may have long-term residents as well as overnight guests. *Residenciales* (singular *residencial*) are generally buildings constructed with short-stay accommodations in mind, but they may also have semipermanent inhabitants. All such places may even go by the term *hotel,* though that term usually means a more formal category.

All these categories have some exceptionally good values. Most will have shared bath and toilet *(baño general* or *baño compartido),* but some offer a choice between shared and private bath *(baño privado).* Bathtubs are unusual at these venues. In some cases, they will have ceiling fans and even cable TV, but there is often an extra charge for cable and almost always a surcharge for air-conditioning.

Travelers intending to stay at budget accommodations should bring their own towels, though some provide towels. Many but by no means all include breakfast in their rates; ask to be certain.

Showers

Many Argentine and Chilean showers use natural gas in an on-demand *calefón.* Opening the tap normally triggers the *calefón,* presuming the *piloto* (pilot) is lit. Some budget-conscious accommodations light the pilot only when someone wants to take a shower. Before getting in and turning on the tap, be sure the pilot is lit.

A Day (or More) in the Country

Over the past decade-plus, facing economic reality, many of Argentina's rural estates have opened themselves to the tourist trade. From the subtropical north to the sub-Antarctic south, diversification has become the word for *estancia* owners, some of which earn more income from hosting visitors than growing grain or raising livestock. For many visitors, staying at an *estancia* is their entire vacation.

According to the Buenos Aires-based Red Argentina de Turismo Rural (Ratur), more than 1,000 *estancias* are open to the public, and hundreds of thousands of people spend some time in the countryside every month. For nearly all of these farms, tourism makes up a significant portion of their income, and for some of them, most notably in Patagonia, it exceeds 90 percent.

Throughout the country, some *estancias* are reasonably priced places with limited services, but others are magnificent properties with castle-like *cascos* (manor houses), elaborate service that includes gourmet meals, and recreational activities such as horseback riding, tennis, and swimming. Some *estancias* aim at day-trippers—weekending in the countryside of Buenos Aires province has become an increasingly popular option for escaping the capital—but most prefer overnight guests.

Several *estancias* get detailed individual coverage in this book, but various others are open to the public. Several groups of them have formed networks to promote themselves as tourist destinations.

Affiliated with the Sociedad Rural Argentina, the traditionally powerful landowners' organization, the **Red Argentina de Turismo Rural** (Ratur, Florida 460, 4th Fl., Buenos Aires, tel. 011/4328-0499, www.raturestancias.com.ar) represents a number of *estancias* in Patagonia and elsewhere.

Estancias Argentinas (Diagonal Roque Sáenz Peña 616, Oficina 910, Buenos Aires, tel. 011/4343-2366, www.estanciasargentinas.com) has expanded in recent years, with a broader geographical representation than it once had, but not all of its members are *estancias*; some are even urban hotels.

The best-organized provincial group is **Estancias de Santa Cruz** (Reconquista 642, Oficina 417, Buenos Aires, tel./fax 011/5237-4043, www.estanciasdesantacruz.com). Most of its affiliates are in the southwestern corner of its home province, plus a few members on the Argentine side of Tierra del Fuego.

MID-RANGE

Mid-range hotels generally offer larger, more comfortable, and better-furnished rooms than even the best budget places. This category almost always includes a private bath. Ceiling fans, cable TV, and even air-conditioning are common, but there may not be on-site parking. Some mid-range lodgings have restaurants. Rates can range anywhere from US$50 up to US$100 for a double; some are better values than their high-end counterparts.

HIGH-END

Luxury hotels with top-flight service are most common in the capital cities of Buenos Aires and Santiago and major resort areas, but they are increasingly abundant throughout Patagonia. In capital cities, these will usually offer amenities like restaurants, swimming pools, gym facilities, business centers, Wi-Fi, and conference rooms. Outside capital cities, these are mostly resort hotels and may lack the business facilities. Invariably they will offer secure parking.

Some of the best options are hot-springs hotels and country-inn resorts on ranches, which offer traditional hospitality and ambience with style unmatchable at other high-end places. Prices range from US$100, often substantially higher.

Food and Drink

Stereotypically, the Argentine diet consists of beef and more beef. This common perception isn't entirely mistaken, but the diet has always had a Spanish touch and, for more than a century, a marked Italian influence with pizza and pasta. Over the past decade, the restaurant scene has become more cosmopolitan, adventurous, and nuanced, with Brazilian, Japanese, Thai, Vietnamese, and many other once-exotic cuisines, not to mention high-quality variations on regional dishes.

Chile's long, rich coastline and productive farmland provide seafood, meat, fresh fruit, and vegetables in abundance. While the everyday diet may have some shortcomings, in most areas visitors will have no difficulty finding appealing food and drink.

On both sides of the border, it's becoming more common to find "Patagonian" cuisine that stresses fresh regional products, including wild game, lamb, seafood, greens, and soft fruits like raspberries.

WHERE TO EAT

In Argentina, places to eat range from hole-in-the-wall *comedores* (eateries) or fast-food *bares* (unavoidably but misleadingly translated as "bars") with no formal menu, in bus and train stations, to *cafés, confiterías* (teahouses), and elegant *restaurantes* in Buenos Aires and other major tourist centers.

Likewise, in Chile, *restaurante* can cover a seemingly infinite range of possibilities. About the only hard and fast rule is to avoid places in which single men or groups of men sit and drink beer.

Restaurant terminology—the words used to describe various eateries—overlaps in Argentina and Chile, but there are some differences.

Argentina

Restaurante (occasionally *restorán* or, more fashionably, *restó*) usually means a place with sit-down service. Within this definition there can be great differences. Most often, the term refers to a locale with a printed menu and table service, but even this can range from any place with a basic beef and pasta menu to truly elegant settings with celebrity chefs, complex cuisine, elaborate wine lists, and professional service.

The usual international fast-food villains have franchises in Buenos Aires, but the best cheap food normally comes from *rotiserías* (delicatessens), which serve excellent takeaway fare and may have basic seating. Likewise, supermarkets such as Coto and Disco have *cafeterías* that are excellent budget options.

Bares and *comedores* are no-frills eateries, with indifferent service, offering *minutas* (short orders). The term *comedor* can also mean a hotel breakfast nook or dining room. A *café,* by contrast, is a place whose patrons may dawdle over coffee and croissants, but its real purpose is to promote social interaction in personal affairs, business deals, and other transactions, even though it also serves snacks, *minutas,* and alcoholic beverages.

Confiterías, by contrast, serve breakfast, light meals like sandwiches, snacks like cakes and other desserts, and coffee-based drinks. Generally more formal than *cafés*—some of them prestigious—they are suitable for afternoon tea; some have full-scale restaurant menus, often in a separate section.

Chile

Cocinería can be a synonym for *comedor,* but there are several other terms not used in Argentina. *Fuente de soda* (literally, "soda fountain") signifies a place with a modest menu that lacks a liquor license. *Cafeterías* provide plain meals, usually without table service, but the misleadingly named *salón de té* (literally, "teahouse") can be more like a European-style café, sometimes with sidewalk seating. *Hosterías* are generally country-style

Dining Vocabulary and Etiquette

In both Argentina and Chile, dining vocabulary is mostly straightforward. The usual term for menu is *la carta; el menú* is almost equally common but can also mean a fixed-price lunch or dinner. The bill is *la cuenta. Cubiertos* are silverware, while a *plato* is a plate and *vaso* a glass. A *plato principal* is a main dish or entrée.

Note that one might ask for a *vaso de agua* (glass of water), but never for a *vaso de vino* (literally but incorrectly, a glass of wine); rather, ask for a *copa de vino*. When speaking English, native Spanish speakers often make a comparable error in requesting "a cup of wine."

Many but not all Argentine restaurants assess a small *cubierto* (cover charge) for dishes, silverware, and bread. This is not a *propina* (tip). Generally, a 10 percent tip is the norm, but Argentines themselves often ignore this norm, especially in times of economic crisis. Women in a group will often tip little or nothing, but a good rule of thumb is that anyone able to afford a restaurant meal can afford a tip. In Chile, now, it's possible to add the tip to a credit card purchase, but in Argentina cash is the rule.

It's worth emphasizing that the occupation of waiter is traditionally male and professional, rather than a short-term expedient for university students or aspiring actors. This is changing in the new, stylish restaurants, where servers are just as likely to be young and female. Note, though, that *mozo*, a common and innocuous term for an Argentine waiter, implies an insulting servility in Chile. When in doubt, use *mesero* or *jóven*, even if the individual in question is not particularly young; for a female, use *señorita* unless the individual is at least of late middle age.

restaurants serving large numbers of customers on weekend or holiday outings. *Hostería* can also mean a type of lodging; such places often have restaurants as well.

One distinctively Chilean term is the *picada*, a small family-run eatery that begins informally, often with just a couple tables in a spare room facing the street, but can develop into something more elaborate. (In both Chile and Argentina, by the way, *picada* can mean a snack, and in Argentina, it can also refer to a trail or footpath.)

Marisquerías are simple but often very good fish and seafood eateries in locations where they can buy the morning's catch straight off the boat.

WHAT TO EAT

According to historian John C. Super, whatever the Spanish invasion's negative consequences, it actually improved a late pre-Columbian diet that was, by some accounts, nutritionally deficient (often protein-poor). In Super's opinion,

> The combination of European and American foods created diversified, nutritionally rich diets. Crop yields were higher than those in Europe, and longer or staggered growing seasons made fresh food available during much of the year. The potential for one of the best diets in the history of the world was evident soon after discovery of the New World. For Europeans, the introduction of livestock and wheat was an essential step in creating that diet.

When Europeans first landed in South America, in the densely populated Andean region, the staples were beans, squash, and a variety of potatoes and other tubers. The diet was low in animal protein—only the llama, alpaca, guinea pig, and wild game were readily available, and not in all areas. Spanish introductions such as wheat and barley, which yielded only a four-to-one harvest ratio in Europe, were usually double or triple that in the Americas.

The Spanish introductions blended with the indigenous base to create many edibles found on Argentine and Chilean tables today. Abundant seafood, combined with European animal protein and high-productivity European fruits like apples, apricots, grapes, pears, and many others, resulted in a diverse food production and consumption system, which, however, is changing today.

Cereals

Trigo (wheat), a Spanish introduction, is most common in *pan* (bread) but also appears in the form of pasta. *Arroz* (rice) is a common *agregado* or *guarnición* (side dish).

Maíz (maize or corn) is a main ingredient in many dishes, including the Italian-derived polenta. Maize leaves often serve as a wrapping for traditional dishes like *humitas,* equivalent to Mexican tamales in northwestern Argentina and throughout Chile.

Legumes, Vegetables, and Tubers

Salads are almost always safe, and all but the most sensitive stomachs probably need not be concerned with bugs from greens washed in tap water. In Argentine restaurants, green salads are usually large enough for two diners.

Porotos (beans of all sorts except green beans) are traditional in families of Spanish descent. Other common legumes include *chauchas* (green beans), *arvejas* (peas), *lentejas* (lentils), and *habas* (fava beans).

In many varieties, *zapallo* (squash) is part of the traditional diet, as is the *tomate* (tomato). Old World vegetables include *acelga* (chard), *berenjena* (eggplant), *coliflor* (cauliflower), *lechuga* (lettuce), and *repollo* (cabbage). *Chiles* (peppers) are relatively uncommon; neither Argentine nor Chilean cuisine is *picante* (spicy), except for dishes from Argentina's Andean northwest and those with the Mapuche spice *merkén,* and those rarely challenge palates accustomed to Mexican or Thai cuisine.

Native to the central Andes, *papas* (potatoes) grow in well-drained soils at higher elevations in northwestern Argentina and as far south as the Chilean archipelago of Chiloé; *papas fritas* (french fries) are almost universal, but spuds also appear as *purée* (mashed potatoes) and in Italian-derived dishes such as Argentine *ñoquis* (gnocchi). Other common

tubers include *zanahorias* (carrots) and *rábanos* (radishes).

Vegetarianism

Vegetarian restaurants are few outside of Buenos Aires and Santiago, but ingredients for vegetarian meals are easy to obtain, and many dishes such as pasta and salads are easily adapted to vegetarian preferences. Before ordering any pasta dish, verify whether it comes with a meat sauce; *carne* means "beef" in the Southern Cone. Waiters or waitresses may consider chicken, pork, and similar items another category, sometimes called *carne blanca* (literally, "white meat"). Faced with an unwilling kitchen, you can always plead *alergia* (allergy).

Fruits

As its seasons are reversed from the northern hemisphere, the temperate Southern Cone produces many of the same fruits, often available as fresh juices. Items like *manzana* (apple), *pera* (pear), *naranja* (orange), *ciruela* (plum), *sandía* (watermelon), *membrillo* (quince), *durazno* (peach), *frambuesa* (raspberry), and *frutilla* (strawberry) will be familiar to almost everyone. When requesting *jugo de naranja* (orange juice) in Argentina, be sure it comes *exprimido* (fresh-squeezed) rather than out of a can or box. In Chile, fresh-squeezed juice is a *vitamina.*

Also widely available, mostly through import, are tropical and subtropical fruits like banana and *ananá* (pineapple). Mango, *maracuyá* (passion fruit), cherimoya, and similar tropical fruits are less common but not unknown.

The *palta* (avocado), a Central American domesticate known as *aguacate* in its area of origin, often appears in Argentine and Chilean salads.

Meats and Poultry

Prior to the Spaniards, South America's only domesticated animals were the *cuy* (guinea pig, rare in contemporary Argentina and Chile), the llama and alpaca, and the dog,

Cattle Culture

From his hotel room on the Avenida de Mayo, U.S. poet Robert Lowell once wrote, he could hear "the bulky, beefy breathing of the herds." Ever since feral livestock changed the Pampas in the 16th century, displacing the native guanaco and rhea, cattle have been a symbol of wealth and the foundation of the Argentine diet. Riding across the Pampas, Charles Darwin found the reliance on beef remarkable:

> I had now been several days without tasting any thing besides meat: I did not at all dislike this new regimen; but I felt as if it would only have agreed with me with hard exercise. I have heard that patients in England, when desired to confine themselves exclusively to an animal diet, even with the hope of life before their eyes, have scarce been able to endure it. Yet the Gaucho in the Pampas, for months together, touches nothing but beef ? ... It is, perhaps, from their meat regimen that the Gauchos, like other carnivorous animals, can abstain long from food. I was told that at Tandeel, some troops voluntarily pursued a party of Indians for three days, without eating or drinking.

> Research has suggested that this diet has not been quite so universal as once imagined. Urban archaeologist Daniel Schávelzon has unearthed evidence that, for instance, fish consumption was much greater in colonial Buenos Aires than once thought. But there is no doubt that the *parrilla* (grill restaurant) is a culinary institution. Beef may not be healthy in the quantities that some Argentines enjoy—and many of them will even admit it—but few can bypass traditional restaurants, where flamboyantly clad urban gauchos stir the glowing coals beneath grilled meat on a vertical spit, without craving that savory beef.

> For most Argentines, *bien cocido* (well done) is the standard for steak, but *jugoso* (rare) and *a punto* (medium) are not uncommon. In Patagonia, though, the standard is just as often well-grilled lamb. Note that in Chile, however, *a punto* means rare.

sometimes used for food. The Spaniards enriched the American diet with their domestic animals, including cattle, sheep, pigs, and poultry (chickens and ducks).

Red meat consumption, the hallmark of the Argentine diet, may be decreasing among the more affluent but it remains the entrée of choice among lower classes. Thanks to the Italian immigrant influence, pasta is available almost everywhere. Traditionally, Chileans consume less red meat than Argentines, but it remains the entrée of choice for many.

Carne, often modified as *carne de vacuno,* or *bife* (beef), is the most common menu item in both countries. Specifically Argentine terms include *bife de chorizo* (sirloin or rump steak), *bife de lomo* (tenderloin), *asado de tira* (rib roast), and *matambre* (rolled flank steak). *Milanesa* is a breaded cutlet or chicken-fried steak that, at cheaper eateries, can be greasy.

The widest selection is usually available in the *parrillada* or *asado,* a mixed grill that includes prime cuts but also *achuras,* a broad term that encompasses offal such as *chinchulines* (small intestines, *chunchules* in Chile), *mollejas* (sweetbreads), *criadillas* (testicles), *morcilla* (blood sausage), and *riñones* (kidneys). *Asado* can also mean a simple roast. *Chimichurri* is a garlic-based marinade that often accompanies the Argentine *parrillada.*

Sausages such as the lightly spiced Argentine *chorizo* may also form part of the *asado;* in a hot-dog bun, it becomes *choripán.* *Panchos* are basic hot dogs, while *fiambres* are processed meats.

Cordero (lamb), often roasted on a spit over an open fire, is common in Patagonia. *Cerdo* (pork) appears in many forms, ranging from simple *jamón* (ham) to *chuletas* (chops) to *lomito* (loin) and *matambre de cerdo* (pork flank steak). *Chivo* (goat) or *chivito* (the diminutive) is a western Argentine specialty that sometimes appears on menus in the capital and occasionally in Patagonia. Note that the

Uruguayan *chivito* means something else: a steak sandwich or plate slathered with eggs, fries, and other high-calorie extras.

Argentine stews and casseroles include *carbonada* (beef, rice, potatoes, sweet potatoes, corn, squash, and fruit like apples and peaches) and *puchero* (beef, chicken, bacon, sausage, *morcilla,* cabbage, corn, garbanzos, peppers, tomatoes, onions, squash, and sweet potatoes). Broth-cooked rice serves as a garnish.

Ave (poultry) most often means *pollo* (chicken), which sometimes appears on menus as *gallina* (literally, hen) in a casserole or stew. Eggs are *huevos. Pavo* (turkey) is becoming more common.

In Chile, the most common poultry dish is *cazuela de ave,* a stewed piece of chicken in a thin broth with potato, corn on the cob, and other vegetables.

Fish and Seafood

Argentine fish and seafood may not have the international reputation of its beef, but the long coastline, territorial seas, and freshwater rivers and lakes provide abundant options. Buenos Aires and other coastal cities have fine seafood restaurants, but these are less common in the interior. Chilean cuisine makes better use of its abundant ocean resources.

Seafood, among the most abundant animal-protein sources in pre-Columbian times, includes both *pescado* (fish) and *mariscos* (shellfish and crustaceans). The most common fish are *congrio* (conger eel), sometimes called *abadejo; lenguado* (sole or flounder), *merluza* (hake), and freshwater *trucha* (trout); and *salmón* (salmon), which often comes from Patagonian fish farms.

The cheapest restaurants often ruin perfectly good fish by preparing it *frito* (deep fried), but on request almost all will prepare it *a la plancha* (grilled, usually with a dab of butter) or *al vapor* (steamed). Higher-priced restaurants will add simple or sometimes elaborate sauces, often including shellfish.

Among the shellfish, visitors will recognize the relatively commonplace *almejas* (clams), *calamares* (squid), *camarones* (shrimp), *cangrejo* or *jaiva* (crab), *centolla* (king crab), *mejillones* (mussels), *ostiones* or *callos* (scallops, but beware—*callos* can also mean tripe), *ostras* (oysters), and *pulpo* (octopus). Spanish restaurants normally serve the greatest variety of fish and shellfish.

Chile's *chupes* are seafood casseroles.

Chilean cuisine also makes use of *cholgas* and *choritos* (different varieties of mussels) and *machas* (razor clams), as well as more unusual items like the *choro zapato* ("shoe mussel," so called because of its enormous size); *erizos* (sea urchins, definitely an acquired taste, frequently exported to Japan); the oddly named *locos* (false abalone, literally "crazies"); *picoroco* (giant barnacle); and *piure* (resembling a dirty sponge, according to food writer Robb Walsh). Many shellfish have closed seasons.

Seafood often appears in the form of ceviche, raw fish or shellfish marinated in lime juice and spiced with cilantro. Other seafood specialties worth looking for are *chupes* (casseroles) of *congrio, jaiva,* and *locos,* and *curanto,* a kitchen-sink stew that can include fish, shellfish, beef, chicken, lamb, pork, potato, and vegetables.

"Fast Food" Snacks

Despite the invasion of international franchises, Argentina retains some of the continent's best snack food. Best of the best is the empanada, a flaky turnover most often filled with chopped or ground beef, hard-boiled egg, and olive, but it may also come with ham and cheese, chicken, onion, and (rarely) with tuna or fish. The spicier ground beef *salteña* comes from northwestern Argentina but may be available elsewhere; the tangy *empanada árabe* (lamb with a touch of lemon juice) is more difficult to find. Empanadas *al horno* (oven-baked) are lighter than *fritas* (fried, sometimes in heavy oil).

Argentine pizza can be crust-heavy, and is less diverse in toppings than in North America. For slices, try the cheeseless *fugazza* with Vidalia-sweet onions or its cousin *fugazzeta,* enhanced with ham and mozzarella. Argentines embellish their slices with *fainá,* a baked chickpea dough that fits neatly atop.

Chileans also eat pizza, but it generally lacks zest. Chilean empanadas are larger, with a heavier crust. The standard is the *empanada de pino* of ground beef, hard-boiled egg,

and olive, but ham and cheese is an option. Seafood usually appears only at Easter.

Desserts

At home, the standard Argentine *postre* (dessert) is fresh fruit, ranging from grapes (many single-family homes have their own arbors) to apples, pears, and oranges. In restaurants, this becomes *ensalada de frutas* (fruit salad) or, more elaborately, *macedonia. Postre vigilante,* consisting of cheese and *membrillo* (quince) or *batata* (sweet potato) preserves, is another fruit-based dessert; it also goes by the name *queso y dulce.*

Often topped with whipped cream, *arroz con leche* (rice pudding) and flan (egg custard) are also good choices, as is the Spanish custard *natillas.* An acquired taste is *dulce de leche,* which one international travel magazine referred to as "its own major food group." Argentines spread prodigious quantities of this sickly sweet caramelized milk, which Chileans call *manjar,* onto just about anything and even eat it directly out of the jar.

Though it stems from the Italian tradition, Argentine ice cream lacks the high international profile of gelato. When a pair of Porteños opened an ice creamery in this author's hometown of Oakland, California, they chose the compromise name of Tango Gelato, stressing its Italian roots without ignoring its Buenos Aires stopover. Argentina has countless ice creameries, and a diversity of flavors, ranging from the standard vanilla and chocolate (with multiple variations on those, including white chocolate and bittersweet chocolate) to lemon mousse, *sambayón* (resembling eggnog), *dulce de leche,* and countless others.

Chilean ice cream is also popular, but the quality is usually only so-so except in the capital, where *elaboración artesanal* (small-scale production) is more common, and in Patagonia, where regional flavors like *ruibarbo* (rhubarb) appear on the menu. Chile's German immigrants have left a legacy of kuchen (pastries such as apple strudel and raspberry tarts) in the south.

International and Ethnic Food

Buenos Aires and Santiago (an underappreciated gastronomic center) have the greatest variety of international food, though some tourist-oriented areas also have good selections. Italian and Spanish are the most common foreign cuisines, but French and Chinese venues are also numerous. Peruvian food—perhaps the continent's best—has become popular in Santiago and Buenos Aires, but it's rarer elsewhere.

Brazilian, Mexican, and Middle Eastern restaurants are less common. Some popular world-food cuisines, such as Japanese, Thai, and Vietnamese, have made inroads. Given the raw material that Chile's oceans offer, sushi can be a real treat here.

MEALS AND MEALTIMES

Despite some regional differences, Argentine food is relatively uniform throughout the country, except in Buenos Aires, where diverse ethnic and international cuisine is abundant. In Patagonia, game dishes are not unusual (most of this, such as venison, is either farmed or culled on ranches where populations have risen too high).

By North American and European standards, both Argentines and Chileans are late eaters except for *desayuno* (breakfast); Chileans, though, are notorious late risers. *Almuerzo* (lunch, sometimes called *colación* in Chile) usually starts around 1pm, and *cena* (dinner) around 9pm or later—sometimes much later in Argentina. Argentines bide their time between lunch and dinner with a late-afternoon *té* (tea) that consists of a sandwich or some sort of pastry or dessert. The Chilean counterpart is *onces*.

Since Argentines often eat *after* the theater or a movie, around 11pm or even later on weekends, anyone entering a restaurant before 9pm may well dine alone.

Breakfast and Brunch

Most Argentines eat a light breakfast of coffee or tea and *pan tostado* (toast, occasionally with ham or cheese) or *medialunas* (croissants) or *facturas* (pastries, also eaten for afternoon tea); *medialunas* may be either *de manteca* (buttery and sweet) or *salada* (saltier, baked with oil). *Mermelada* (jam) usually accompanies plain *tostados.*

As a side dish, eggs may be either *fritos* (fried) or *revueltos* (scrambled), or sometimes *duros* (hard-boiled). In some fashionable areas, a more elaborate Sunday brunch has become an option.

Chilean breakfasts are similar, but usually without the croissants or pastries; North American breakfast foods like corn flakes have also made inroads. *Avena* (oatmeal) is common in wintertime.

Lunch

Lunch is often the day's main meal, usually including an *entrada* (appetizer), followed by a *plato principal* (entrée, often *plato de fondo* in Chile), accompanied by a *guarnición* (side dish, *agregado* in Chile) and a *bebida* (soft drink) or *agua mineral* (mineral water) and followed by *postre* (dessert).

Upscale restaurants often offer fixed-priced lunches that make it possible to eat stylishly without busting the budget. It's also possible to find local fast-food items like *hamburguesas* (hamburgers), sandwiches, pizza, and pasta, without resorting to international franchises.

Té and Onces

Filling the time between lunch and the dinner, the Argentine *té* and the Chilean *onces* can range from a late-afternoon sandwich to a full afternoon tea, with cakes and cookies, and is often a social occasion. Presumably intended to tide people over until a relatively late dinnertime, it often becomes larger and more elaborate than the name would imply.

Dinner

Dinner resembles lunch, but in formal restaurants it may be substantially more elaborate (and more expensive), and it can be a major social occasion. Argentines and Chileans dine late—9pm is early, and anything before that may bring incredulous "What planet are you

ESSENTIALS
FOOD AND DRINK

from?" stares from waiters. One major exception is tourist-oriented areas like Buenos Aires's Puerto Madero complex, where restaurateurs have become accustomed to North Americans and Europeans who, lodged at nearby luxury hotels, can't wait any later than 7pm.

BUYING GROCERIES

In Argentina, supermarkets carry a wide selection of processed foods but often a lesser variety (and quality) of fresh greens than is available in produce markets. Many have cheap cafeterias with surprisingly good food.

In areas where supermarkets are fewer, almost all neighborhoods have corner shops with basic groceries and fresh produce, usually within just a few minutes' walk. Butchers are numerous; fishmongers, less so.

Virtually every Chilean city, town, village, and hamlet has a central market where it's possible to buy fresh produce. Even in locales without central markets, small shops almost always carry groceries.

BEVERAGES
Coffee, Tea, and Chocolate

Caffeine junkies feel comfortable in Argentina, where espresso is the norm even in small provincial towns. *Café chico* is a dark viscous brew in a miniature cup, supplemented with enough sugar packets to make it overflow onto the saucer. A *cortado* comes diluted with milk and follows lunch or dinner; for a larger portion, request a *cortado doble*. *Café con leche,* equivalent to a latte, is a breakfast drink; ordering it after lunch or dinner is a serious faux pas.

Most Chilean coffee, by contrast, has long been a disappointment, but that's changing—powdered Nescafé was long the norm, but espresso drinks are becoming more common. *Café negro* is Nescafé mixed with hot water; *café con leche* (coffee with milk) is usually Nescafé dissolved in warm milk.

Té negro (black tea) usually comes in bags and is insipid by most standards. Visitors wanting British-style tea with milk should ask for tea first and milk later; otherwise, risk getting a tea bag immersed in lukewarm milk. Herbal teas range from the nearly universal *manzanilla* (chamomile) and *rosa mosqueta* (rose hips) to *mate de coca* (coca leaf). *Yerba mate* (Paraguayan tea) is one of Argentina's most deeply embedded customs.

In addition to the usual, Chilean herbal teas also include specialties such as *llantén* (plantain), *cedrón* (lemon verbena), *paico* (saltwort), *boldo,* and many others. In Patagonia, some Chileans follow the Argentine custom of *mate.*

Chocolate lovers will enjoy the Argentine *submarino,* a bar of semisweet chocolate that dissolves in steamed milk from the espresso machine. Less flavorful powdered chocolate is also available.

It's possible to get a good cup of *chocolate* (hot chocolate) in Santiago and much of Chile's lakes district, where Swiss-German influence is most significant. Elsewhere, it will be powdered chocolate mixed with hot water.

Water, Juices, and Soft Drinks

Tap water is potable nearly everywhere. Ask for *agua de la canilla* in Argentina or *agua de la llave* in Chile. For ice, request it *con hielo.*

Visitors with truly sensitive stomachs might consider bottled water, which is widely available. Ask for *agua pura* or *agua mineral;* some brands are spring water, while others are purified. For carbonated water, add *con gas* or, in Argentina, the even cheaper *soda,* which comes in large siphon bottles.

Gaseosas (plural) are sweetened bottled soft drinks (including most major transnational brands but also local versions such as the Argentine tonic water Paso de los Toros).

Fresh-squeezed *jugos* (fruit juices) are good though limited in their diversity. *Naranja* (orange) is the standard; to ensure freshness, ask for *jugo exprimido* or, in Chile, a *vitamina.*

Chilean *licuados* are fruit-based drinks mixed with water or blended with *leche* (milk). Unless your sweet tooth is insatiable, ask to have them prepared without sugar *(sin azúcar, por favor);* this can be a problem even with fresh-squeezed juices other than orange.

Alcoholic Beverages

Argentina may be less famous for its wines than Chile, perhaps because domestic consumption traditionally overshadows exports. But it is the world's fifth-largest wine producer and its international profile is rising fast due to the red malbec. Most production takes place in the western and northwestern provinces of Mendoza, San Juan, and Salta, but the northern Patagonian provinces of Neuquén and Río Negro have earned a niche market.

Chile, of course, is one of the world's major wine producers, and exports have boomed since worldwide boycotts ended along with the Pinochet dictatorship. Its signature varietal is carménère, destroyed by phylloxera in France but rediscovered here in the 1990s (it had been misidentified as merlot).

Tinto is red wine, while *blanco* is white. The best restaurants have a wide selection, usually in full bottles, though sometimes it's possible to get a *media botella* (half bottle) or, increasingly, wine by the glass. Argentines often mix their table wines, even reds, with soda water or ice.

Christopher Fielden's *The Wines of Argentina, Chile, and Latin America* (New York: Faber and Faber, 2001) is a capable overview, though it doesn't account for recent developments. Laura Catena's English-language *Vino Argentino* (San Francisco: Chronicle Books, 2010) comes from the accomplished daughter of a wine-growing family in Mendoza, while Ian Mount's *The Vineyard at the End of the World* (Norton, 2012) tells the story of malbec through the experience of Laura Catena's father, Nicolás.

While the wines are more than worthwhile, both Argentines and Chileans are leaning more toward beer, which tastes best as *chopp*, direct from the tap, rather than from bottles or cans. Craft beers are becoming more common, especially in Patagonia.

Hard liquor is less popular in Argentina, but whiskey, gin, and the like are readily available. *Ginebra bols* (differing from gin) and *caña* (cane alcohol) are local specialties.

Chile is, along with Peru, a major producer of the potent grape brandy known as *pisco,* the base of the legendary *pisco* sour. Another popular aperitif is the *vaina,* a concoction of port, cognac, cocoa, and egg white that some Chileans consider a "woman's drink."

In both Argentina and Chile, as well as the Falklands, the legal drinking age is 18. The islands now have their own brewery.

Travel Tips

CONDUCT AND CUSTOMS

Argentines and Chileans have many things in common, but some traits differ dramatically. In both countries, politeness goes a long way with officials, shopkeepers, and others. It's always good form to offer the appropriate polite salutation: *buenos días* (good morning), *buenas tardes* (good afternoon), or *buenas noches* (good evening or good night), depending on time of day.

Both women and men should dress conservatively and inconspicuously when visiting churches, chapels, and sacred sites. This, again, is an issue of respect for local customs, even if locals themselves don't always observe it.

Argentines and especially Porteños (like New Yorkers) are notorious extroverts, with a stereotyped reputation for brusqueness; some even gripe about their compatriots that "nobody respects anybody here anymore." Chileans, by contrast, have a reputation as the "Victorians of South America" for their reluctance to display their emotions publicly. This is a stereotype as well—many Chileans are gregarious—but on balance Argentines are probably more outgoing.

Photographic Etiquette

Argentines are not exactly camera-shy, so, if a person's presence is incidental, as in a townscape, it's unnecessary to ask permission. However, if a person is the photograph's primary subject, try to establish a rapport before asking permission to photograph, if you can manage Spanish or have another language in common. If in doubt, ask; if rejected, don't insist. Photographers should be particularly respectful of Patagonia's indigenous peoples.

Likewise, Chileans in general are accustomed to cameras, but photographing the Mapuche people of the Andean lakes district or other indigenous people without first establishing a rapport would be a serious error of judgment.

If you're purchasing something from a market vendor, he or she will almost certainly agree to be photographed. Be cautious about photographing political protests, though. The police are notorious for cataloguing dissidents, so protestors may be suspicious of unknowns with cameras. Likewise, avoid photography near military installations, although "Sentry Will Shoot" signs are a thing of the past.

There is one absolute no-no: Without explicit permission, do not even think about photographing Israeli or Jewish community sites in Argentina. Since car-bomb attacks on Retiro's Israeli Embassy in 1992 and Once's Jewish cultural center in 1994, federal police are stationed outside all these sites. They vigorously discourage would-be clickers.

EMPLOYMENT OPPORTUNITIES

The unemployment situation may be better in Patagonia than elsewhere in Argentina or Chile, but well-paid work can be hard to come by even for legal residents, let alone visitors on tourist or student visas. Nevertheless, foreigners have found work in the tourist industry, or casual labor in bars or restaurants. Such jobs, though, may be seasonal (in the case of tourism) or poorly paid (in the case of restaurants, except in a handful of places where tips are high).

Ideally, obtaining a work permit from an Argentine consulate is better than attempting to obtain one in country, as employment may not begin until the permit is actually granted. Nevertheless, it still requires submitting documents and takes time.

Legal residence in Chile, which permits eligibility for a greater number of better-paying jobs, usually requires local or foreign sponsorship, a substantial investment, marriage to a Chilean spouse or other permanent resident, or a reliable retirement income. In theory, temporary working visas can lead to residency, but some workers have continued on them for several years, as the Interior Ministry bureaucracy turns slowly.

BUSINESS TRAVEL

Though distorted exchange rates are a thing of the past, Argentina's economy continues to suffer from high inflation and other structural issues. Chile's economy has remained the continent's most stable and one of the most productive.

There are few legal restrictions on foreign businesses operating in Argentina. Under the new government of President Mauricio Macri, the business climate has improved, but institutional weakness has discouraged investment by those unaccustomed to dealing with high risk. Political corruption continues to be a disincentive.

The best investment bets include travel and tourism services, a key Patagonian sector. Devaluation had made residential real estate a bargain but, in recent years, prices have rebounded. In any event, before signing any business deal, consult a local lawyer recommended by your embassy, consulate, or a truly trusted friend.

Chile's institutional stability and low corruption levels have made it an investor's favorite. That, however, does not eliminate the need to understand the cultural and legal context of investing in the country.

TRAVELERS WITH DISABILITIES

For people with disabilities, Patagonia can be problematic, as the infrastructure is mostly unsuitable in a region whose main attractions are outdoors. Even in cities, narrow and uneven sidewalks, not to mention fast-moving traffic, are unkind to people with disabilities, especially those who need wheelchairs. Public transportation rarely accommodates passengers with disabilities, though Avis Argentina offers rental vehicles with hand controls.

Few older buildings are specifically equipped for accessibility, but many of these are single-story and can often accommodate people with disabilities. In newer high-rise hotels, accessibility is obligatory.

TRAVELING WITH CHILDREN

Argentina and Chile are child-friendly countries. In fact, since many Argentines and Chileans enjoy large extended families, they may feel little in common with people in their late 20s and older who don't have children, and traveling with kids can open doors.

Many parks and plazas have playground equipment, and it's easy to mix with families there. What foreign parents may find unusual is that even toddlers may be out on the swings and slides with their families at 11pm or later, even in small isolated communities. Likewise, kids are off across the street, around the neighborhood, and even on the buses at ages when U.S. helicopter parents are driving their kids three blocks to school and waiting anxiously until the doors close safely behind them.

On public transportation, strangers may spontaneously but gently touch small children and even set them on their laps. While foreigners may find this disconcerting, it's not necessarily inappropriate in this cultural context.

WOMEN TRAVELERS

Like other Latin American societies, Argentina and Chile have strong *machista* (chauvinist) elements. Argentine and Chilean women are traditionally mothers, homemakers, and children's caregivers, while men are providers and decision-makers, but there are increasing numbers of professional and working women.

Many Argentine and Chilean men view foreign women as sexually available, but this is not necessarily discriminatory; they view women of their own nationality the same way. In Argentina, harassment often takes the form of *piropos*, sexist comments that may be innocuous and can even be poetic, but are just as likely to be vulgar. It's best to ignore verbal comments, which are obvious by tone of voice even if you don't understand them. If they're persistent, seek refuge in a café or *confitería*.

Despite problems, Argentine and Chilean women have acquired political prominence. The most prominent and notorious, of course, was Eva Perón, but her rise to the top was an unconventional one. The highest-profile women in current politics are Argentina's ex-President Cristina Kirchner, wife of the late president Néstor Kirchner and a formidable politician in her own right, and Chilean president Michelle Bachelet.

GAY AND LESBIAN TRAVELERS

Despite its conspicuous Roman Catholicism, Argentina is a fairly tolerant country for both gay men and lesbians, and public displays of affection—men kissing on the cheek, women holding hands—are common even among heterosexuals. In 2003, in fact, the city of Buenos Aires passed an ordinance permitting same-sex civil unions, and in 2010 the country enacted same-sex marriage equality.

This does not mean that gay people can always behave as they wish in public. The police have beaten and jailed individuals who have offended their sense of propriety. If in doubt, be circumspect.

Certain Buenos Aires districts, most notably Recoleta, Barrio Norte, and Palermo, have a number of openly gay entertainment venues and even accommodations, but these are less conspicuous in provincial cities. Conservative Chile may be less publicly tolerant, but Santiago has a lively (though not exclusively) gay scene in Barrio Bellavista.

Health and Safety

Mid-latitude Buenos Aires and Santiago offer no major health risks beyond those associated with any large city. Public health standards are good, and tap water is potable almost everywhere.

A good general source on foreign health matters is Dr. Richard Dawood's *Travelers' Health* (New York: Random House, 1994), a small encyclopedia on the topic. The 13th edition of Stuart R. Rose's and Jay Keystone's *International Travel Health Guide* (Northampton, MA: Travel Medicine, 2006) is regionally focused. Try also the 5th edition of Dirk G. Schroeder's *Staying Healthy in Asia, Africa, and Latin America* (Berkeley, CA: Avalon Travel, 2000).

For information on health issues throughout the Southern Cone, one source is the U.S. Centers for Disease Control (CDC, www.cdc. gov), though some of its Patagonian suggestions sound alarmist, with inappropriate boilerplate text (to cite two examples: there are no monkeys in Chile except in zoos, and nobody is likely to swim outdoors in the Falklands).

BEFORE YOU GO

Theoretically, Argentina and Chile demand no proof of vaccinations, but if you are coming from a tropical country where yellow fever is endemic, authorities could ask for a vaccination certificate.

Overseas travel without adequate medical insurance is risky. Before leaving your home country, purchase a policy that includes evacuation in case of serious emergency. Foreign health insurance may not be accepted in either country, so you may be required to pay out of pocket for later reimbursement. Usually, though, private medical providers accept international credit cards in return for services.

For an extensive list of carriers providing medical and evacuation coverage, see the U.S. State Department's website (www. travel.state.gov).

HEALTH MAINTENANCE

Common sense precautions can reduce the possibility of illness. Washing hands frequently with soap and water, and drinking only bottled, boiled, or carbonated water, reduces the risk of contagion, although Argentine and Chilean tap water are potable almost everywhere.

Where purified water is impossible to obtain, such as backcountry streams where there may be livestock or human waste problems, pass drinking water through a one-micron filter and further purify it with iodine drops or tablets (but avoid prolonged consumption of iodine-purified water).

FOOD-AND WATERBORNE DISEASES

Few visitors run into problems of this sort, but contaminated food and drink are not unheard of. In many cases, it's exposure to different sorts of bugs to which the body becomes accustomed, but if symptoms persist, the problem may be more serious.

Traveler's Diarrhea

Colloquially known as *turista,* the classic traveler's diarrhea usually lasts just a few days and almost always less than a week. Besides "the runs," symptoms include nausea, vomiting, bloating, and general weakness. The usual cause is the *Escherichia coli* bacterium from contaminated food or water. In rare cases *E. coli* infections can be fatal.

Fluids, including fruit juices, and small amounts of bland foods such as freshly cooked rice or soda crackers, may relieve symptoms and help regain strength. Dehydration can be serious, especially for children, who may need an oral rehydration solution of carbohydrates and salt.

Over-the-counter remedies like Pepto-Bismol, Lomotil, and Immodium (loperamide) may relieve symptoms but can also cause problems. Prescription drugs such as doxycyline and trimethoprim-sulfamethoxazole can also shorten the cycle. These may not, however, be suitable for children, and everyone should avoid them if at all possible.

Dysentery

Bacterial dysentery, resembling a more intense form of traveler's diarrhea, responds well to antibiotics. The more serious amoebic dysentery can lead to intestinal perforation, peritonitis, and liver abscesses. Like diarrhea, its symptoms include soft and even bloody stools, but some people may be asymptomatic even as they pass on *Entamoeba hystolica* through unsanitary toilet and food-preparation practices. Metronidazole, known by the brand names Flagyl or Protostat, is an effective treatment, but a physician's diagnosis is advisable.

Cholera

Resulting from poor hygiene, inadequate sewage disposal, and contaminated food, modern cholera is less devastating than its historical antecedents, which produced rapid dehydration, watery diarrhea, and imminent death without almost equally rapid rehydration. While today's strains are highly infectious, most carriers do not even suffer symptoms. Existing vaccinations are ineffective, so health authorities now recommend against them.

Treatment can only relieve symptoms. On average, about 5 percent of victims die, but those who recover are immune. It is not a common problem in either Argentina or Chile, and it's rare in Patagonia.

Hepatitis A

Usually passed by fecal-oral contact under conditions of poor hygiene and overcrowding, hepatitis A is a virus. Traditional gamma globulin prophylaxis wears off in just a few months, but newer vaccines are more effective and last longer.

Typhoid

Typhoid is a serious disease common under unsanitary conditions, but the recommended vaccination is an effective prophylaxis.

INSECT-BORNE DISEASES

Patagonia is malaria-free, but the disease may exist in northernmost Argentina. A few other insect-borne diseases may be present if not exactly prevalent.

Dengue Fever

Like malaria, dengue is a mosquito-borne disease of the lowland tropics, but it's less common than malaria and rarely fatal. Eradicated in Argentina in 1963, the mosquito vector *Aedes aegypti* is once again present as far south as Buenos Aires. The best prophylaxis is to avoid mosquito bites by covering exposed parts of the body with insect repellent or appropriate clothing.

Chagas' Disease

Also known as South American trypanosomiasis, Chagas' disease is most common in Brazil but affects about 18 million people between Mexico and Argentina; 50,000 victims die every year. It has a discontinuous distribution. Panama and Costa Rica, for instance, are Chagas-free.

Since Chagas spreads by the bite of the night-feeding conenose or assassin bug, which lives in adobe structures, avoid such structures (which still exist in the countryside); if it's impossible to do so, sleep away from the walls. DEET-based insect repellents offer some protection. Chickens, dogs, and opossums may carry the disease.

The disease's initial form is a swollen bite

often accompanied by fever, which soon subsides. In the long run, though, it may cause heart damage leading to intestinal constipation, difficulty in swallowing, and sudden death; there is no cure.

Zika Virus

In 2016, the U.S. State Department issued an Argentina travel advisory for elevations below 1,980 meters for mosquito-borne Zika, which can cause microcephaly and other problems. This would include Buenos Aires and most of the rest of the country. It specifically recommended that pregnant women avoid Argentina, and that others refrain from sexual activity if intending to become pregnant. The mosquito vector *Aedes aegypti* is present in Chile, but there have no cases of insect-borne Zika, though it's endemic on remote Rapa Nui (Easter Island).

HANTAVIRUS

Hantavirus is an uncommon but deadly disease contracted by breathing, touching, or ingesting feces or urine of the long-tailed rat. Primarily a rural phenomenon and most prevalent in Patagonia, the virus thrives in enclosed areas; when exposed to sunlight or fresh air, it quickly loses potency. Avoid places frequented by rodents, particularly abandoned buildings. There have been cases in which hikers and farm workers have apparently contracted the disease in open spaces.

RABIES

Rabies, a virus transmitted through bites or scratches by domestic animals (like dogs and cats) and wild mammals (like bats), is a concern; many domestic animals go unvaccinated in rural Patagonia. Human prophylactic vaccination is possible.

Untreated rabies can cause an agonizingly painful death. In case of an animal bite or scratch, clean the affected area immediately with soap and running water, and then with antiseptic substances like iodine or 40 percent-plus alcohol. If possible, try to capture the animal for diagnosis, but not at the risk of further bites. Where rabies is endemic, painful post-exposure vaccination may be unavoidable.

SNAKEBITE

Poisonous snakes are rare in Patagonia (Chile has none), but Argentina's aggressive pit viper *yarará* ranges into northern Chubut province. The venom paralyzes the nervous system, but strikes are uncommon. Death is not instantaneous and antivenins are available, but it's best to be alert and avoid confrontation. If bitten, get to medical facilities as quickly as possible, but avoid excessive movement that helps the venom circulate.

ALTITUDE SICKNESS

At the highest elevations, above about 3,000 meters, *apunamiento* or *soroche* can be an annoyance and even a danger, particularly for older people with respiratory problems. Most of the Patagonian uplands are lower than the central and northern Andes, but even among young, robust individuals, a quick rise from sea level to the sierra can cause intense headaches, vertigo, drowsiness or insomnia, shortness of breath, and other symptoms. Combined with hypothermia, it can be life-threatening.

For most people, rest and relaxation help relieve symptoms as the body adapts to reduced oxygen; aspirin or a similar painkiller will combat headache. Should symptoms persist or worsen, moving to a lower elevation usually has the desired effect. Do not overeat, avoid alcohol consumption, and drink extra fluids.

The 2nd edition of Stephen Bezruchka's *Altitude Illness, Prevention & Treatment* (Seattle: The Mountaineers, 2005) addresses the topic in detail; the 6th edition of James A. Wilkerson's edited collection *Medicine for Mountaineering & Other Wilderness Activities* (Seattle: The Mountaineers, 2010) discusses other potential problems as well.

HYPOTHERMIA

Hypothermia is a dangerously quick loss of body heat, most common in cold and damp weather at high elevations or high latitudes, with large day-to-night temperature variations. Symptoms include shivering, disorientation, loss of motor functions, skin numbness, and physical exhaustion. The best remedy is warmth, shelter, and food. Unlike cottons, woolen clothing retains warmth even when wet. Avoid falling asleep; in hazardous conditions, you may not regain consciousness. Carry high-energy snacks and drinking water.

SUNBURN

In southernmost Patagonia and Tierra del Fuego, ozone-destroying aerosols have increased the entry of ultraviolet radiation, contributing to skin problems (including melanomas) for people and even for livestock like cattle and sheep. For outdoor activities, use an SPF 30 sunblock with zinc. On city streets, walk in the shade whenever possible.

SEXUALLY TRANSMITTED DISEASES

While life-threatening HIV/AIDS is the most hazardous of the sexually transmitted diseases (STDs) and gets the most press, other STDs are more prevalent and serious if left untreated. All are spread by unprotected sexual conduct; the use of latex condoms by males reduces the possibility of contracting STDs but does not necessarily eliminate it.

Most STDs, including gonorrhea, chlamydia, and syphilis, are treatable with antibiotics, but some strains have developed immunity. If taking antibiotics, complete the prescribed course, since an interrupted or incomplete treatment may not kill the infection and could even help it develop immunity.

The most common STD is **gonorrhea,** characterized by a burning sensation during urination and penile or vaginal discharge; it may cause infertility. **Chlamydia** has milder symptoms but similar complications. **Syphilis,** the only major disease that spread from the Americas to Europe after the Spanish invasion, begins with ulcer and rash symptoms that soon disappear; long-term complications, though, can include cardiovascular problems and even derangement.

Herpes, a virus that causes small but irritating genital ulcers, has no effective treatment. It's likely to recur, easily spread when active, and can contribute to cervical cancer. **Hepatitis B,** though not exclusively an STD, can spread through the mixing of bodily fluids such as saliva, semen, and menstrual and vaginal secretions. It can also spread through unsanitary medical procedures, inadequately sterilized or shared syringes, during body piercing and tattooing, and similar circumstances. Like hepatitis A, it can lead to liver damage but is more serious. Vaccination is advisable for high-risk individuals but is expensive.

As in most countries, **HIV/AIDS** is an issue of increasing concern. It is not exclusively an STD (IV drug users can get it by sharing needles), but unprotected sexual activity is a common means of transmission. The use of latex condoms reduces the possibility of infection.

SMOKING

Slightly less than a third of Argentines smoke, with a marginally higher incidence among males. Tobacco directly causes 40,000 deaths per annum. According to a survey several years back, 3 of every 10 Argentine *cardiologists* smoke, and few of those make any recommendation to their own patients on the subject. Future fatalities start early—3 of 10 students between the ages of 13 and 15 are smokers.

Still, there is widespread recognition that the habit is unhealthy, and effective smoking restrictions are making rapid progress. In Buenos Aires, for instance, all restaurants and bars are, in principle, tobacco-free, though they may allow smoking in patio or sidewalk seating.

Enforcement hasn't been perfect, but it's been surprisingly good. Beyond the capital, provincial laws are a hodgepodge, though the trend is to restrict smoking. If faced with inappropriate secondhand smoke, it's best to appeal to courtesy with a white lie such as *"soy asmático"* ("I'm asthmatic").

Smoking is more widespread in Chile than in the United States, but less so than in Europe. A new law has significantly reduced tobacco consumption in public areas, including restaurants and bars. Chilean smokers generally respect limitations on their habit.

LOCAL DOCTORS

Top-quality medical services, with the latest technology, are readily available in Buenos Aires and Santiago, and even in provincial cities. Foreign embassies sometimes maintain lists of English-speaking doctors, who often have overseas training and are numerous in the capitals and other large cities.

PHARMACIES

Pharmacies serve an important public health role, but they also carry certain risks. Pharmacists may provide drugs on the basis of symptoms that they may not completely comprehend, especially if there's a language barrier. While the societal impact may be positive, individual recommendations may be erroneous.

Many medications available by prescription only in North America or Europe may be sold over the counter in Argentine or Chilean pharmacies. Travelers should be circumspect about self-medication even when such drugs are available; check expiration dates, as out-of-date drugs sometimes remain on the shelf.

In large cities and even some smaller towns, pharmacies remain open all night for emergency prescription service on a rotating basis. The *farmacia de turno* and its address will usually be posted in the window of other pharmacies or advertised in the newspaper.

CRIME

Many Argentines and Chileans believe homicides, assaults, rapes, and property crimes are increasing, but both countries are considered safe by international standards, and Patagonia particularly so. Because citizens keep late hours, there are plenty of people on the street at most times. Rarely will you find yourself walking alone down a dark alleyway.

Still, certain precautions almost go without saying. Most crimes are crimes of opportunity. Never leave luggage unattended, store valuables in the hotel safe, watch your belongings closely at sidewalk cafés, and carry a photocopy of your passport with the date of entry into the country. Avoid carrying large amounts of cash (money belts or leg pouches are good alternatives for hiding currency), leave valuable jewelry at home, and keep conspicuous items such as photo and video cameras out of sight. Do not presume that any area is totally secure.

If accosted by anyone with a firearm or other potentially lethal weapon, do not resist. While guns are uncommon—knives are the weapon of choice—and violent crime against tourists is unusual (almost unheard of in Patagonia), a misjudgment can have lethal consequences.

One phenomenon that has disturbed Argentines is the so-called *secuestro exprés* (express kidnapping), in which criminals hold an individual for a small ransom or, alternatively, force someone to withdraw money from an ATM. Far more common in Buenos Aires province than in the capital or elsewhere in the country, these crimes have not targeted tourists—rather, they appear to concentrate on individuals whose movements are familiar to the lawbreaker.

More common is the crime of distraction, in which an individual bumps into the victim and spills a substance like ice cream or mustard; while the perpetrator apologizes profusely, an accomplice surreptitiously lifts items of value. Pickpocketing is also common on public transportation. Carry wallets and other items of value in a front trouser pocket or, even better, an interior jacket pocket.

Information and Services

MONEY

While traveling in Patagonia, consider a variety of money alternatives. International credit cards are widely accepted, and foreign ATM cards work almost everywhere. Because ATMs are open 24 hours, many visitors prefer this alternative, but in remotest Patagonia there are sometimes no banks. It makes sense to have a cash reserve in U.S. dollars (rather than euros; although the European currency is gaining credibility, it's not an everyday item, especially outside Buenos Aires and Santiago). Traveler's checks may be the safest way to carry money, since they're usually refundable in case of loss or theft, but changing them outside Buenos Aires or Santiago can be a nuisance, especially in Argentina.

If carrying an emergency cash reserve, use an inconspicuous leg pouch or money belt—not the bulky sort that fits around the waist, which thieves or robbers easily recognize, but a zippered leather belt that looks like any other.

Currency

Argentina's unit of currency is the peso (Ar$). Banknotes exist in denominations of Ar$2, Ar$5, Ar$10, Ar$20, Ar$50, and Ar$100, Ar$500 and Ar$1,000. Coins exist in denominations of 1, 5, 10, 25, and 50 centavos, but 1-centavo coins have nearly disappeared and businesses generally round off prices to the nearest 5 or 10 centavos. There are also Ar$1 and Ar$2 coins.

Counterfeiting of both U.S. and local currency appears to be increasing in Argentina. Merchants will often refuse a U.S. banknote with the smallest tear or writing on it; ironically, they will accept any peso note that is not flagrantly *trucho* (bogus). On Argentine banknotes, look for the conspicuous watermark with the initials of the historical figure depicted—JSM for José de San Martín on the 5-peso note, for instance.

Chile's unit of currency is also the peso (Ch$), with coins in denominations of Ch$5, Ch$10, Ch$50, Ch$100, and Ch$500. Banknotes come in values of Ch$1,000, Ch$2,000, Ch$5,000, Ch$10,000, and Ch$20,000.

Pegged at par to the British pound sterling, the Falkland Islands pound (£) is the official currency, but U.S. dollars and euros are widely accepted, as are traveler's checks. MasterCard and Visa are also widely accepted, at least in Stanley, but other credit cards are not. Stanley's Standard Chartered Bank has no ATM, but British visitors with a guarantee card can cash personal checks up to £50.

ATMs

Foreign ATM cards work almost everywhere, but Argentina's economic instability and occasional regulations that limit cash withdrawals for Argentines have made Argentine ATMs iffy at times; carry a cash reserve in U.S. dollars. Argentine ATMs impose fees (up to US$8) on each withdrawal, so it pays to make fewer withdrawals of larger amounts. The maximum is Ar$1,000, but sometimes the ATM charge means you must withdraw a slightly smaller amount.

Conditions are similar in Chile, but some small villages do not even have banks, let alone ATMs, so be sure to change enough money to get you to the next major town. Likewise, in the countryside, carry smaller bills. For a small shopkeeper, changing a Ch$5,000 note may be impossible. All ATMs charge a fee here too, but Banco del Estado's is the lowest.

In the Falkland Islands, U.S. dollars, euros, and pounds are widely accepted, and Stanley's Standard Chartered Bank will change traveler's checks and give advances on Visa. There are no ATMs, however.

Exchange Rates

Patagonia covers three countries, each with its own currency. The **Argentine exchange rate** is the most challenging to predict because of its volatile politics and economy. Argentina made front-page news in 2014 after failing to persuade the US Supreme Court that its plans to pay debt from its 2001 default and 2005 restructuring conformed to the New York State laws under which much of that debt was contracted. In 2014, the Argentine peso fell from six to eight per US dollar, but that's not the whole story. At one point, it was still unclear whether the country would face a default that might result in another peso collapse.

Given Argentina's foreign debt problems, President Cristina Fernández de Kirchner's government instituted a series of patchwork measures to stem the flow of dollars, widely used in real estate transactions, and to preserve Argentines' savings in the face of inflation and a depreciating peso. One of these measures was the *cepo cambiario* ("currency clamp"), which made it difficult or impossible to purchase foreign currency—even for overseas travel, where Argentines had to use credit cards with purchases subject to a punitive tax.

This led to an active **black market** for the so-called **"blue dollar,"** which traded for 15 pesos or more. In late 2015, however, the incoming government of President Mauricio Macri unified the exchange rates, and changing at so-called *cuevas* ("caves") nearly disappeared. Do note that some businesses will only accept 50- and 100-dollar bills at the blue rate. For current rates, check an online currency converter such as www.oanda.com.

During 2016, the **Chilean exchange rate** versus the dollar strengthened from roughly 710 pesos per dollar to the 670 range. There is no black market. Barring unforeseen circumstances, both exchange rates and prices in Chile should remain relatively stable. The **Falkland Islands pound,** at par with the British pound sterling, is likely to remain the most stable of the currencies used in Patagonia, although Great Britain's planned exit from the European Union may change that.

Traveler's Checks and Refunds

Despite their safeguards, traveler's checks have drawbacks in Patagonia, particularly in the Argentine side. In addition to the time-consuming bureaucracy of changing them at banks and exchange houses, they may carry a substantial commission penalty, up to 3 percent or even more in some cases. Businesses other than exchange houses may not accept them, and in really out-of-the-way places, almost nobody will. Traveler's checks, unfortunately, should be a last-resort means of carrying and changing money here; cash (despite the risks) and ATM cards are better options.

Bank Transfers

Many Argentine exchange houses, post offices, and other businesses are affiliated with **Western Union** (www.westernunion.com), making it relatively straightforward to send money from overseas. For a list of Western Union affiliates in Argentina and Chile, see its website. The **American Express Money Gram** is another alternative; American Express has headquarters in Buenos Aires and Santiago, and affiliates throughout both countries. For visitors with U.S. bank accounts, **Xoom** (www.xoom.com) simplifies online transfers, but its payout points are few in Patagonia.

In an emergency, it's possible to forward money to U.S. citizens via the U.S. Embassy in Buenos Aires or Santiago by establishing a Department of State trust account through its **Overseas Citizens Services** (Washington, DC 20520, tel. 202/647-5225); there is a US$30 service charge for setting up the account. It's possible to arrange this as a wire or overnight-mail transfer through Western Union (U.S. tel. 800/325-6000). For details, see the State Department's website (www.travel.state.gov).

Credit and Debit Cards

Credit cards have been common currency for many years in both Argentina and Chile. During the 2002 peso crisis, when Argentines could not withdraw their savings from frozen bank accounts, their use became even more widespread. Under the foreign currency restrictions of the Kirchner de Fernández government, it was almost the only option for Argentines traveling abroad.

Visa and MasterCard are most widely accepted, but there are inconsistencies. Some businesses prefer American Express, sometimes to the exclusion of others, or even Diner's Club. Debit cards with Visa or MasterCard affiliation are also widely accepted.

There can be drawbacks to credit cards, though. During the 1990s boom, Argentine merchants generally refrained from the *recargo,* a surcharge on credit-card purchases because of slow bank payments; many have reinstituted the *recargo,* up to 10 percent, to cut potential losses due to slow bank reimbursement. Note that hotels may offer equivalent cash discounts.

Fluctuating exchange rates may also affect the charge that eventually appears on your overseas account. If the rate has changed in the interim between your payment in Patagonia and its posting to the home account, it may be either greater or smaller in terms of dollars (or other foreign currency), depending on the peso's performance.

In general, *propinas* (gratuities) cannot be added to charged Argentine restaurant meals, but Chile is more flexible. Still, keep some cash, preferably pesos, for tips.

Costs

For most of the 1990s, **Argentina** was South America's most expensive country, so much so that even North Americans and Europeans cringed at the cost. Wealthy Argentines, meanwhile, partied in Miami, Madrid, Rome, and other "inexpensive" destinations.

This anomaly was a function of then economy minister Domingo Cavallo's "convertibility" exchange-rate policy, which reduced previous hyperinflation to near zero. It also froze prices at a relatively high but unsustainable level, however, that eventually made Argentine exports noncompetitive and contributed to the late-2001 default.

After the 2002 peso float, Argentina became a bargain for visitors from hard currency countries. Though the peso solidified, travel remained relatively inexpensive by global standards until recently, when a dollar-starved government began arbitrary exchange control measures that caused some Argentines to seek refuge in the dollar again. As of late 2016, the official rate was roughly 16 pesos to the dollar.

Much depends on the traveler's expectations; there are suitable services for everyone from bare-bones budget backpackers to pampered international business travelers. Budget travelers will still find hostel beds for US$15 pp or so, and some excellent values for only a little more money. Prices have rebounded at hotels and resorts of international stature, such as the Hyatt and Sheraton chains and their local equivalents.

Likewise, meals range from a few dollars or less at the simplest eateries, but restaurants with sophisticated international cuisine can charge a lot more. Even the latter, though, often serve moderately priced lunchtime specials.

As of press time, true shoestringers could still get along on US$30 per day or conceivably less for accommodations and food. For US$50 or so per day, it's possible to live comfortably and eat a bit better, but a budget of over US$100 per day is far from extravagant. It's worth adding that economic volatility—hyperinflation was a recurrent phenomenon in the late 20th century and independent statistics show that it now exceeds 30 percent—makes it impossible to guarantee that prices will not rise.

By global standards, travel in **Chile** is moderately priced, but much depends on the traveler's expectations and where in the country he or she goes. Truly disciplined travelers in rural areas might get away with as little as US$25 or less per day by staying in the cheapest accommodations, buying groceries, and cooking for themselves, or eating market food. Public transportation is moderately priced, especially given the long distances on some routes, but the fact that Chile imports nearly all its oil makes the sector vulnerable to fluctuations.

The **Falkland Islands,** by contrast, are substantially more expensive than either Argentine or Chilean Patagonia, because accommodations are few, wages are high, and local transportation relies on costly air-taxis. For most visitors, US$100 per day for meals and accommodations alone will be a modest budget, though the pound's post-Brexit slump has made thing slightly cheaper.

Prices are comparable to those in the United Kingdom for hotels and wildlife lodges (the latter, with full board, cost upward of £100 pp per day). On the other hand, self-catering cottages in camp go for as little as £20-30 pp, and B&B accommodations in Stanley for only a little more. Camping is an option in a few areas, but nearly all land is private, and many farmers worry about fire.

Food costs, except for fresh meat (mainly mutton) are also high, as many items must be imported by air or sea, and Stanley's market garden is a capital-intensive hydroponic facility. Stanley's best restaurants would be good anywhere and have prices to prove it, but there are also moderately priced snacks like burgers and pub grub like fish-and-chips.

Internal transportation is expensive because of high capital investments for a relatively small market. Government air-taxi service links the two main islands and many smaller ones, but visitors pay higher rates than residents.

Taxes

Argentina imposes a 21 percent *impuesto al valor agregado* (IVA, value-added tax) on goods and services, though this is normally included in the advertised price. If in doubt, ask *"¿Incluye los impuestos?"* ("Does this include taxes?"). Tax evasion is a national sport, though, and hotel owners often ignore the tax for cash payments.

Tourists may request IVA refunds for purchases of Argentine products valued more than about US$25 from shops that display a "Global Refund" decal on their windows. Verify that the decal is not out of date.

When making any such purchase, request an invoice and other appropriate forms. Then, on leaving the country, present these forms to Argentine customs; customs will then authorize payment to be cashed at Banco de la Nación branches at the international airport.

At smaller border crossings, do not expect officials to be prepared to deal with tax refunds. Some crossings do not even have separate customs officials but rather are staffed by the Gendarmería (Border Patrol), a branch of the armed forces.

Chile levies a 19 percent IVA on goods and services. Most mid-range to upscale hotels, however, legally discount IVA for foreign visitors, who receive a *factura de exportación* (export receipt) with their hotel bill.

Tipping

In formal restaurants with table service, a 10 percent gratuity is customary, but in family-run eateries the practice is rare. Taxi drivers are customarily not tipped, but rounding off the fare to the next highest convenient number is appropriate. Where there is no meter, this is not an issue.

Bargaining

Bargaining is less common in Argentina and Chile than it is in some other Latin American countries, but in flea or crafts markets the vendor may start at a higher price than he or she expects to receive. Avoid insultingly low offers, or such a high offer that the vendor will think you a fool. Depending on your language and bargaining skills, you should reach a compromise that satisfies everybody.

Student and Senior Discounts

Student discounts are relatively few, and prices are so low for most services that it's rarely worth arguing the point. Students, though, may be eligible for discount international airfares. Visit a student-oriented travel agency to see if such a deal is available.

Travelers over age 62 may be eligible for *tercera edad* discounts for museums, transportation, and some other services. In some cases, though, you must be an Argentine or Chilean citizen or resident.

MAPS AND VISITOR INFORMATION

Argentina, Chile, and the Falkland Islands all have good sources for maps and tourist information, but others are available overseas.

Maps

International Travel Maps and Books (ITMB, 12300 Bridgeport Rd., Richmond, BC V6V 1J5, tel. 604/273-1400, www.itmb.com) publishes a series of maps that cover all or parts of Patagonia at a variety of scales, including Argentina (1:2,200,000), Chile (1:1,130,000), Patagonia (1:2,000,000) and Tierra del Fuego (1:750,000), and the Falkland Islands (1:300,000).

For **Argentina**, the **Automóvil Club Argentino** (ACA, Argentine Automobile Club, Av. del Libertador 1850, Palermo, Buenos Aires, tel. 011/4808-4000, www.aca.org.ar) publishes the most comprehensive series of highway maps, covering every province and including major city plans. Members of overseas affiliate automobile clubs, like the AAA in the United States, can buy these at discount prices. For official topographic maps, the source is the government's **Instituto Geográfico Nacional** (Av. Cabildo 381, Palermo, Buenos Aires, tel. 011/4576-5576, www.ign.gob.ar). Recent creations by Bariloche-based **Pixmap** (tel. 02944/15-64-2152, www.pixmap.com) are pretty much the best available recreational maps now, and also cover parts of Chile.

In **Chile**, the oil retailer Copec has recently taken over the annually updated three-volume *Turistel* guidebook series (Spanish only), which contains the most current road maps at the back of its *Norte* (North), *Centro* (Center), and *Sur* (South) volumes, along with numerous useful city maps, which, unfortunately, lack scales.

Chile's own **Instituto Geográfico Militar** (IGM, Dieciocho 369, Santiago Centro, tel. 02/2241-0963, www.igm.cl) publishes detailed topographic maps covering the entire country at a scale of 1:50,000; some of these, however, are "proprietary" as they adjoin what the military consider to be sensitive border areas. They are also expensive at about US$15 and up. The Instituto also sells a variety of city maps, road atlases, and books useful to the everyday visitor, and the staff members are professional and efficient.

Unofficially, Talca-based **Trekking Chile** (www.trekkingchile.com) publishes a very useful assortment of road and trekking maps for both sides of the border.

For the **Falkland Islands**, the locally available *Falkland Islands Explorer*, published in the United Kingdom, depicts the islands' roads and topography at a scale of 1:365,000, plus a basic city map of Stanley and text on history and natural history.

In Stanley, the **Secretariat** (Ross Rd., tel. 27242) offers Directorate of Overseas Surveys (DOS) topographic maps of the entire Falkland Islands at a scale of 1:50,000, but there's also a two-sheet (1:250,000) series that's adequate for most purposes. **Customs & Immigration** (3 H Jones Rd., tel. 27340) has maritime charts.

Tourist Offices

Argentina's **Ministerio de Turismo** (www.turismo.gov.ar), which was recently promoted to ministry status, has its main office in Buenos Aires. Every province also maintains a tourist-information representative in the capital:

- **Chubut:** Sarmiento 1172, San Nicolás, tel. 011/4383-7458, www.chubutpatagonia.gob.ar
- **Neuquén:** Maipú 48, Microcentro, tel. 011/4343-2324, www.neuquentur.gov.ar
- **Río Negro:** Tucumán 1916, Balvanera, tel. 011/4371-7078, www.rionegrotur.gob.ar
- **Santa Cruz:** 25 de Mayo 279, Microcentro, tel. 011/4343-8478, www.santacruz.tur.ar
- **Tierra del Fuego (Instituto Fueguino de Turismo):** Av. Córdoba 679, 2nd Fl., Depto. B, Retiro, tel. 011/4312-0631, www.tierradelfuego.org.ar

Each Argentine province also operates an information office in its own capital, and often in specific destinations as well. Even the smallest towns may have their own tourist office; these normally keep long summer hours but may be limited the rest of the year.

Sernatur (www.sernatur.cl), Chile's national tourism service, maintains public information offices in Santiago and all regional capitals, and in Puerto Natales. Most are normally open Monday to Friday only, but in summer and in some localities they are open weekends.

Many municipalities have their own tourist offices, especially in Andean lakes district resorts like Villarrica, Pucón, and Puerto Varas, which keep long summer hours but are limited the rest of the year. Smaller towns may have summer-only (Jan.-Feb.) offices.

The **Falkland Islands Tourist Board** (www.visitorfalklands.com) is a public-private partnership with offices in Stanley and representatives in the United Kingdom. For details on and suggestions for travel to, from, and in the islands, consult their thorough, well-organized website.

In the United Kingdom, **Falkland House** (14 Broadway, Westminster, London SW1H 0BH, tel. 020/7222-2542, reception@falklands.gov.fk) is the islands' official representative and de facto tourist office.

COMMUNICATIONS AND MEDIA
Telephone and Fax
Argentina's country code is 54; the *característica* (area code) for the Capital Federal and Gran Buenos Aires is 11, but there are a bewildering number of area codes for individual cities, smaller cities and towns, and rural areas. All telephone numbers in the Capital Federal and Gran Buenos Aires have eight digits, while those in other provincial cities and rural areas vary. When calling out of the area code, it's necessary to dial zero first.

Cellular phone numbers in Buenos Aires all have eight digits, prefixed by 15. In addition, certain toll-free and other specialty numbers have six or seven digits with a three-digit prefix. In the provinces, the cell phone prefix follows the area code.

Public telephones are rapidly disappearing; some operate with coins only, but most also accept rechargeable account cards. The basic local phone rate is Ar$0.25 (about US$0.07) for five minutes or so. Domestic long distance is more expensive. Phone cards are convenient for in-country calls but less useful for more expensive overseas calls.

For long-distance and overseas calls, and faxes, it's simplest to use *locutorios* (call centers), which are still abundant in both Buenos Aires and the provinces. Prices now tend to be much cheaper than placing *cobro revertido* (collect) or *tarjeta de crédito* (credit card) calls to the United States or any other country. Calls are more expensive during peak hours (8am-8pm Mon.-Fri., 8am-1pm Sat.).

Opening a cell-phone account without a permanent Argentine address is something of a nuisance, but "caller pays" card phones are a good alternative if you're going to be in-country for a while. Rental phones are available from Nolitel (tel. 011/4311-3500, www.nolitelgroup.com) in Buenos Aires.

Chile's country code is 56, but cell and landline phones now have nine-digit numbers beginning with 9 (cell) or 2 (landline). In addition, certain toll-free and other specialty numbers have six digits with a three-digit prefix.

Public telephones are also declining here; some operate with coins, but most also accept rechargeable account cards. The basic local phone rate is Ch$100 (about US$0.20) for five minutes or so; domestic long distance is inexpensive. For long-distance and overseas calls and faxes, it's simplest to use *centros de llamados* (call centers), which are also fewer than in the past.

The **Falkland Islands** country code is 500, valid for numbers in Stanley and in camp (the area outside Stanley). Sure operates both local and long-distance telephone services; all local numbers have five digits. Telecommunications are fairly expensive, though local technology is state-of-the-art; calls may be made from private phones or Stanley's Sure offices (Ross Rd. West, tel. 20800, www.sure.co.fk).

Local calls cost £0.06 per minute, £0.09 to mobile phones; calls to the United Kingdom are £0.90 per minute during business hours and £0.60 per minute weekends, holidays, and evenings. Calls to other countries are £1 per minute during business hours and £0.80 per minute weekends, holidays, and evenings. Operator-assisted calls are more expensive and have a three-minute minimum, so it's best to buy a phone card. There's also a surcharge for collect calls (local only).

Mobile phone packages are also available for visitors. For details, contact **Sure** (Ross Rd. West, tel. 20800, www.sure.co.fk).

Internet Access

In the last few years, public Internet access has become abundant and so cheap that, if price trends continue, providers will soon be paying customers to use their services. Rarely does access cost more than US$1 per hour, and it's often even cheaper. Many Argentine *locutorios* (call centers) offer access, and there are many Internet cafés in both Argentina and Chile. High-speed and Wi-Fi coverage are increasing rapidly in both countries.

In the Falklands, broadband Internet service remains relatively expensive. Some Stanley hotels have Wi-Fi hot spots, but it's necessary to purchase a card to use them.

Media

Buenos Aires newspapers are also—some to a greater degree than others—national papers sold throughout **Argentina.** The middle-of-the-road tabloid *Clarín* is the Spanish-speaking world's largest-circulation daily, while the *Buenos Aires Herald* is an English-language weekly, published on Friday, whose niche market correlates highly with hotel occupancy. It stresses commerce and finance but also produces intelligent analyses of political and economic developments.

What was once a state broadcast monopoly is now far more diverse, thanks to privatization and the advent of cable, but conglomerates like the Clarín and El Cronista groups control much of the content. The recent government of Cristina Fernández de Kirchner imposed a "media law" to give it greater control over both print and electronic media, but the advent of conservative President Mauricio Macri may refrain from rigid enforcement.

Chile may have emerged from dictatorship, but the press remains in the hands of large consortia like the pro-Pinochet El Mercurio group, which publishes its namesake daily and many other papers. Pinochet's arrest and subsequent legal troubles, however, opened up a whole new space for irreverently satirical papers such as *The Clinic,* whose widespread circulation is a remarkable success story (the paper named itself for the London clinic at which the late dictator was detained).

In contrast with the print media, radio and TV journalism are more pluralistic, at least in terms of ownership, as private media with foreign capital have competed with local sources since the early 1990s. That said, the state-run Television Nacional (TVN) and the Universidad Católica's Canal 13 (Channel 13) are still the most important broadcast outlets.

The only print medium in the **Falkland Islands** is the weekly *Penguin News,* which often raises the hackles of local politicians. The Falkland Islands Radio Service (96.5 FM or AM 550) provides local radio programming, but Islanders also get radio and TV from the BBC and the British Forces Broadcasting System (BFBS). The nightly radio announcements, at 6:30pm, include the following day's Falkland Islands Government Air Service flight schedules.

Postal Services

Though it's been renationalized, Correo Argentino is still more reliable than in the past. Domestic services remain generally cheap, international services more expensive. International couriers provide reliable services at premium prices.

General delivery at Argentine and Chilean post offices is *lista de correos,* literally a list arranged in alphabetical order. There is a small charge for each item addressed to you.

Note that, in Spanish-language street addresses, the number follows rather than precedes the name; instead of "1343 Washington Avenue," for example, a comparable Spanish-language address would read "Avenida Providencia 2134." Spanish speakers normally omit the word *calle* (street) from addresses; where an English speaker might write "499 Jones Street," for instance, a Spanish speaker would simply use "Tucumán 272." It's not unusual for street addresses to lack a number, as indicated by *s/n (sin número,* without a number), especially in provincial towns.

Falklands postal services are dependable but infrequent, as they rely on weekly flights from Chile and RAF charters from the United Kingdom. Large parcels go by sea four or five times per year. Air taxis deliver mail to outer settlements and islands, sometimes without landing.

WEIGHTS AND MEASURES

Time

The time in Argentina is three hours earlier than GMT year-round; daylight saving time is not observed. When the U.S. eastern time zone is on daylight saving time, during the northern hemisphere summer, Buenos Aires is one hour later than New York; the rest of the year, Buenos Aires is two hours later.

Across the Andes, Chile is four hours earlier than GMT and one hour earlier than Argentina, except in summer (Aug.-May), when Chile goes on daylight saving time and it's the same time as in Argentina. The Magallanes region now remains on daylight saving time all year.

The Falkland Islands are four hours earlier than GMT year-round.

Electricity

All outlets are 220 volts, 50 hertz. Converters are necessary for some North American appliances that do not have dual-voltage power supplies. Traditional plugs have two rounded prongs, but more recent Argentine plugs have three flat blades that form, roughly, an isosceles triangle; cheap adapters are widely available.

Falkland Islands outlets also run on 220 volts, 50 hertz, but the plugs are identical to those in the United Kingdom.

Measurements

The metric system is official, but this doesn't eliminate vernacular measures that Argentines and Chileans use in everyday life. Rural folk often use the *legua* (league), about five kilometers, as a measure of distance, and the *quintal,* 46 kilos, is also widely used, especially in wholesale markets and agricultural statistics.

Likewise, the metric system is now official in the Falklands, but locals still use vernacular English measures such as miles (but not Fahrenheit degrees).

Resources

Glossary

aduana: customs

aduana paralela: "parallel customs," corrupt Argentine customs officials

agregado: side dish

agua de la canilla: in Argentina, tap water; in Chile, this is *agua de la llave*

albergue juvenil: youth hostel; the word *hostel*, however, is now widely used in both Argentina and Chile.

albergue transitorio: a by-the-hour hotel, frequently used by couples in search of privacy

andén: platform at a train station or bus terminal

anexo: telephone extension

argentinidad: nebulous notion of Argentine nationalism, often associated with the gaucho

asado: generally, a barbecue; in context, can also mean short ribs or roast prime rib

autopista: freeway

avenida: avenue

balneario: bathing or beach resort

baño compartido: shared bath (in a hotel or other accommodations)

baño general: shared or general bath (in a hotel or other accommodations)

baño privado: private bath

barrio: borough or neighborhood

bodega: winery or storage cellar, depending on context

boleadoras: rounded stones, tied together with leather thong, used for hunting by Pampas and Patagonian peoples; also known as bolas

bronca: a singularly Porteño combination of aggravation and frustration; there is no precise English equivalent, the closest being "wrath" or, in Britain, "aggro"

cabildo: colonial governing council

cabotaje: full-fare domestic airline ticket

cacique: indigenous chief or headman

cajero automático: automatic teller machine (ATM)

calle: street

camarote: sleeper berth on a train

camioneta: pickup truck

campo: countryside

característica: in Argentina, telephone area code

carbonada: stewed beef

carne: in Argentina, beef; other kinds of meat are *carne blanca* (literally, "white meat")

carretera: highway

cartelera: in Argentina, discount ticket agency

casa chorizo: house on a deep, narrow lot in Buenos Aires

casa de cambio: official money-exchange facility, often just *cambio*

casco: manor house of an *estancia* (ranch)

casilla: post office box

caudillo: in early independence times, a provincial Argentine warlord, though the term is often used for any populist leader, such as Juan Domingo Perón

cazuela: traditional stew, such as *cazuela de ave*, with chicken, or *cazuela de vacuno*, with beef

cerro: hill

Chilote: inhabitant or native of the Chiloé archipelago

chivito: roast kid goat; alternatively, in Uruguay, a steak sandwich

chopp: draft beer

cobro revertido: collect or reverse-charge telephone call

coche cama: spacious, fully reclining long-distance bus seat

cocinería: small restaurant, often in a market complex

coima: bribe

colectivo: in Argentina, a city bus

comedor: simple eatery or dining room

comuna: political subdivision in Chile, ranging in size from the borough of a city to sprawling rural areas

confitería: in Argentina, a restaurant/café with a menu of *minutas* (short orders)

corralito: unpopular banking restrictions imposed by Argentine government during the debt default and devaluation of 2001-2002

costanera: any road along a seashore, lakeshore, or riverside

criollo: in colonial times, an American-born Spaniard; in the present, normally a descriptive term meaning "traditionally" Argentine or Chilean

cueca: traditional Chilean folk dance

curanto: meat and/or shellfish stew, cooked in the earth or a large pot

desaparecido: "disappeared one," victim of the military dictatorships of the 1970s and 1980s

día de campo: "day in the countryside" on a tourist *estancia* (ranch)

dique: deep-water basin dredged in the harbor of Buenos Aires

doble tracción: four-wheel drive, also known as *cuatro por cuatro* (the latter written as "4X4")

edificio: building

encomienda: in colonial times, a grant of indigenous labor within a given geographical area; the *encomendero* (holder of the *encomienda*) incurred the reciprocal obligation to provide instruction in the Spanish language and Catholic religion, though such obligations were rarely honored

estancia: cattle or sheep ranch controlling large extents of land, often with an absentee owner, dominant manager, and resident employees

estanciero: owner of an *estancia*

estero: estuary

facón: gaucho knife

farmacia de turno: pharmacy remaining open all night for emergencies, on a rotating basis

feria: artisans market, outdoor crafts or antiques fair; alternatively, an outdoor bookstall

filete: traditional colored sign painting of Buenos Aires

gasoil: in Argentina, diesel fuel

gauchesco: adjective describing romantic art or literature about, as opposed to by, gauchos

golfo: gulf

golpe de estado: coup d'état

Gran Aldea: Great Village; Buenos Aires prior to the influx of 20th-century immigrants

guarnición: side dish

heladería: ice creamery

hipódromo: horserace track

hospedaje: family-run lodging

hostería: B&B or a small hotel; can also mean a rural restaurant

huaso: Chilean counterpart to the Argentine gaucho or the American cowboy

humita: corn dish resembling Mexican tamale

indígena: indigenous person

indigenista: adjective describing romantically pro-indigenous literature, music, and art

infracción: traffic violation

isla: island

islote: islet

istmo: isthmus

lago: lake

laguna: lagoon

latifundio: large landholding, usually an *estancia* (ranch)

local: numbered office or locale, at a given street address

locutorio: in Argentina, a telephone call center

lunfardo: Porteño street slang that developed in working-class immigrant barrios but is now more widely used in Argentine Spanish, though not in formal situations

machista: male chauvinist

Magellanic architecture: traditional architecture of southernmost Patagonia, wooden houses with metal cladding

marisquería: a simple seafood restaurant

matambre de cerdo: pork flank steak

mate: the dried leaf of *Ilex paraguayensis,* a holly relative prepared in a gourd and sipped through a straw by Argentines, Uruguayans, and others in the Southern Cone countries

mate de coca: tea made from the coca leaf

media pensión: two-meal package or half board, at a hotel or guesthouse

menú: menu; also, a fixed-price meal

meseta: Patagonian steppe

mestizo: individual of mixed indigenous and Spanish ancestry

milonga: informal neighborhood dance club, which often includes tango as a participant rather than spectator activity

minuta: in Argentina, a short-order meal like pasta

mirador: overlook or viewpoint

mozo: in Argentina, a term of address for a restaurant waiter; in Chile, though, this would be extremely rude

museo: museum

oligarquía terrateniente: traditional landowning "aristocracy" of the Pampas

onces: Chilean afternoon tea

palacete: mansion

palafito: house on stilts or pilings, found in the Chiloé archipelago

Pampa: broad, flat expanse in and around Buenos Aires province

pampero: southwesterly cold front on the Argentine Pampas

parada: bus stop

parque nacional: national park

parrilla: grill restaurant

parrillada: mixed grill

pasarela: catwalk in wet or marshy area

paseaperros: professional dog walker in Buenos Aires

pastel de choclo: Chilean corn casserole with beef, chicken, onions, and/or hard-boiled egg slices

payador: spontaneous gaucho singer

peaje: tollbooth

peatonal: pedestrian mall

peña: a community meeting place, with cheap food and drink

pensión: family-run lodging

pensión completa: all-meal package or full board, at a hotel or guesthouse

picada: in Chile, a simple restaurant, usually in a private home; in both Chile and Argentina, a snack; alternative meaning in Argentina, a footpath

picante: spicy hot; the Argentine and Chilean tolerance for spicy food is low, however, and most visitors may find foods labeled as spicy relatively bland

pingüinera: penguin colony

piquete: protestors' roadblock

piropo: sexist remark, ranging from humorous and innocuous to truly vulgar; also, on *filete,* an aphorism

playa: beach

Portakabin: military container-style housing, brought to the Falklands after the 1982 war; now mostly used for storage

Porteño: native or resident of Buenos Aires

propina: tip, as at a restaurant

puchero: stewed meat and vegetables

puente: bridge

puerto: port

puesto: "outside house" on a sheep or cattle ranch, a rustic construction where shepherds slept; also, a market food stall

Pullman: first-class bus, with reclining seats and luggage storage underneath

pulpería: general store, often the only retail outlet in a rural area

quincho: an outdoor shelter, often featuring a fire pit for cooking

rastra: studded gaucho belt

recargo: surcharge on credit-card purchases, common in Argentina

reducción: colonial settlement where missionaries concentrated the indigenous population to be evangelized

remise: meterless radio taxi charging a fixed rate within a given zone

reserva nacional: in Chile, a national reserve, a category of Conaf-protected land

residencial: permanent budget accommodations, often also called "hotel"

restó: fashionable, even pretentious, term for a restaurant, especially in Buenos Aires

río: river

rotisería: delicatessen

ruca: Mapuche plank house with thatched roof

ruta: route or highway

ruta nacional: federal highway

ruta provincial: provincial highway

saladero: meat-salting plant of late-colonial and early republican times

sendero: footpath or trail

sorrentino: stuffed pasta resembling ravioli, but larger and round instead of square

tango canción: "tango song," with music and lyrics expressing nostalgia

tanguero: tango dancer

tarifa mostrador: hotel "rack rate," from which there are often discounts

tenedor libre: literally "free fork"; an all-you-can-eat restaurant

termas: hot springs

toldo: tent of animal skins, inhabited by mobile Pampas natives in pre-Columbian times

trucho: bogus, in Argentine slang

turco: Argentine of Middle Eastern descent

ventanilla: ticket window at bus terminal or train station

viveza criolla: in Argentina, "artful deception," ranging from small-scale cheating to audacious chutzpah

voseo: use of the second person singular pronoun *vos* and its distinct verb forms in Argentina, Uruguay, Paraguay, and some other countries; most others, though, use the *tuteo* (the pronoun *tú* and its forms)

ABBREVIATIONS AND ACRONYMS

ACA: Automóvil Club Argentino

APN: Administración de Parques Nacionales (National Parks Administration, Argentina)

Av.: *avenida,* or avenue

Codeff: Consejo de Defensa de la Flora y Fauna (Council for the Defense of Flora and Fauna, Chile)

Conaf: Corporación Nacional Forestal (National Forestry Corporation, Chile)

Conama: Comisión Nacional del Medio Ambiente (National Environmental Commission, Chile)

IVA: *impuesto al valor agregado* (value-added tax)

RN: Ruta Nacional (National Highway, Argentina)

RP: Ruta Provincial (Provincial Highway, Argentina)

s/n: *sin número,* a street address without a number

Spanish Phrasebook

Spanish is the official language of both Argentina and Chile.

Argentine Spanish is distinctive, often Italian-inflected, most notable for pronouncing both the "ll" diphthong and "y" as "zh." "Llegar" (to arrive), for example, is pronounced "zhe-gar," while "yo" (I) sounds like "zho." Another distinguishing feature is the familiar pronoun "vos" instead of "tú." Verb forms of the *voseo* differ from those of the *tuteo,* although Argentines will always understand speakers who use "tú." The stereotypical Porteño intonation, equivalent to a Bronx accent in New York, is unique, for better or worse.

In Chile, the local variant of Spanish often drops terminal consonants and glides over some internal ones. This may confuse those who learned Spanish elsewhere. At tourist offices, airlines, travel agencies, and upscale hotels in both countries, English is often spoken. In the provinces and regions, it's less common, though its use is spreading, especially in the travel-and-tourism sector.

PRONUNCIATION GUIDE

Spanish pronunciation is much more regular than that of English, but there are still occasional variations in pronunciation.

Consonants

c as c in "cat," before a, o, or u; like s before e or i

d as d in "dog," except between vowels, then like th in "that"

g before e or i, like the ch in Scottish "loch"; elsewhere like g in "get"

h always silent

j like the English h in "hotel," but stronger

ll like the y in "yellow"

ñ like the ni in "onion"

r always pronounced as strong r

rr trilled r

z like s in "same"

b, f, k, l, m, n, p, q, s, t, w, x   as in English

Vowels

a as in "father," but shorter

e as in "hen"

i as in "machine"

o as in "phone"

u usually as in "rule"; when it follows a q the u is silent; when it follows an h or g, it's pronounced like w, except when it comes between g and e or i, when it's also silent (unless it has an umlaut, ü, when it again is pronounced as English w)

Stress

Native English speakers frequently make errors of pronunciation by ignoring stress. Any Spanish vowel—a, e, i, o, and u—may carry an accent that determines which syllable gets emphasis. Often, stress seems unnatural to nonnative speakers. The surname Chávez, for instance, is stressed on the first syllable. Failure to observe this rule may make it difficult for native speakers to understand you.

NUMBERS

zero *cero*
one *uno*
two *dos*
three *tres*
four *cuatro*
five *cinco*
six *seis*
seven *siete*
eight *ocho*
nine *nueve*
10 *diez*
11 *once*
12 *doce*
13 *trece*
14 *catorce*
15 *quince*
16 *dieciseis*
17 *diecisiete*
18 *dieciocho*
19 *diecinueve*
20 *veinte*
21 *veinte y uno* or *veintiuno*
30 *treinta*
40 *cuarenta*
50 *cincuenta*
60 *sesenta*
70 *setenta*
80 *ochenta*
90 *noventa*
100 *ciento*
101 *ciento y uno* or *cientiuno*
200 *doscientos*
500 *quinientos*
1,000 *mil*
10,000 *diez mil*
100,000 *cien mil*
1,000,000 *millón*
one-half *medio*
one-third *un tercio*
one-fourth *un cuarto*

DAYS OF THE WEEK

Monday *lunes*
Tuesday *martes*
Wednesday *miércoles*
Thursday *jueves*
Friday *viernes*
Saturday *sábado*
Sunday *domingo*

MONTHS

January *enero*
February *febrero*
March *marzo*
April *abril*
May *mayo*
June *junio*
July *julio*
August *agosto*
September *septiembre*
October *octubre*
November *noviembre*
December *diciembre*

TIME

Chileans mostly use the 12-hour clock, but in some instances, usually associated with plane or bus schedules, they may use the 24-hour military clock. Under the latter, for example, *las nueve de la noche* (**9pm**) would be *las 21 horas* (**2100 hours**).

What time is it? *¿Qué hora es?*
It's one o'clock. *Es la una.*
It's two o'clock. *Son las dos.*
It's ten to three. *Son tres menos diez.*
It's ten past three. *Son tres y diez.*
It's three fifteen. *Son las tres y cuarto.*
It's two forty-five. *Son tres menos cuarto.*
It's two-thirty. *Son las dos y media.*
It's six am. *Son las seis de la mañana.*
It's six pm. *Son las seis de la tarde.*
It's ten pm. *Son las diez de la noche.*
today *hoy*
tomorrow *mañana*
morning *la mañana*
yesterday *ayer*
week *la semana*
month *mes*
last night *anoche*
the next day *el día siguiente*
after *después*
before *antes*

USEFUL WORDS AND PHRASES

Spanish speakers consider formalities important. When approaching anyone for information or some other reason, do not forget the appropriate salutation: good morning, good evening, etc. Standing alone, the greeting *hola* (hello) can sound brusque.

Most of the words listed below are fairly standard, common to all Spanish-speaking countries. Many, however, have more idiomatic Chilean equivalents.

Hello. *Hola.*
Good morning. *Buenos días.*
Good afternoon. *Buenas tardes.*
Good evening. *Buenas noches.*
How are you? *¿Cómo está?*
Very well, thank you. *Muy bien, gracias.*
Good. *Bien.*
So-so. *Más o menos.*
And you? *¿Y usted?*
Thank you. *Gracias.*
Thank you very much. *Muchas gracias.*
You're very kind. *Muy amable.*
You're welcome. *De nada.*
Good-bye. *Adios.*
See you later. *Hasta luego.*
please *por favor*
yes *sí*
no *no*
I don't know. *No sé*
It's fine; okay. *Está bien.*
more *más*
less *menos*
much, a lot *mucho*
large *grande*
small *pequeño, chico*
quick, fast *rápido*
slowly *despacio*
bad *malo*
difficult *difícil*
easy *fácil*
Just a moment, please. *Momentito, por favor.*
I'm sorry. *Lo siento.*
Pleased to meet you. *Mucho gusto.*
How do you say . . . in Spanish? *¿Cómo se dice . . . en español?*
What is your name? *¿Cómo se llama usted?*
Do you speak English? *¿Habla usted inglés?*
Is English spoken here? (Does anyone here speak English?) *¿Se habla inglés?*

I don't speak Spanish well. *No hablo bien el español.*
I don't understand. *No entiendo.*
How do you say . . . in Spanish? *¿Cómo se dice . . . en español?*

straight ahead *al derecho; adelante*
to the right *a la derecha*
to the left *a la izquierda*
Where (Which) is the way to . . . ? *¿Dónde está el camino a . . . ?*

TERMS OF ADDRESS

When in doubt, use the formal *usted* (you) as a form of address. If you wish to dispense with formality and feel that the desire is mutual, you can say *Me puedes tutear* (you can call me "tú").
I *yo*
you (formal) *usted*
you (familiar) *vos* (Argentina)
you (familiar) *tu* (Chile)
he/him *él*
she/her *ella*
we/us *nosotros*
you (plural) *ustedes*
they/them *ellos* (all males or mixed gender); *ellas* (all females)
Mr., sir *señor*
Mrs., ma'am *señora*
miss, young woman *señorita*
wife *esposa*
husband *esposo*
friend *amigo* (male); *amiga* (female)
sweetheart *novio* (male); *novia* (female)
son; daughter *hijo; hija*
brother; sister *hermano; hermana*
father; mother *padre; madre*
grandfather; grandmother *abuelo; abuela*

GETTING AROUND

Where is . . . ? *¿Dónde está . . . ?*
How far is it to . . . ? *¿A cuánto está . . . ?*
from . . . to . . . *de . . . a . . .*
How many blocks? *¿Cuántas cuadras?*
highway *la carretera*
road *el camino*
street *la calle*
block *la cuadra*
kilometer *kilómetro*
north *norte*
south *sur*
west *oeste; poniente*
east *este; oriente*

PUBLIC TRANSPORTATION

bus station *terminal de buses*
bus stop *la parada*
boat *el barco*
launch *lancha*
dock *muelle*
airport *el aeropuerto*
entrance *la entrada*
exit *la salida*
ticket office *la oficina de boletos*
I want a ticket to . . . *Quiero un pasaje a . . .*
I want to get off at . . . *Quiero bajar en . . .*
Where is this bus going? *¿Adónde va este autobús?*
round-trip *ida y vuelta*
What do I owe? *¿Cuánto le debo?*

ACCOMMODATIONS

hotel *hotel*
Is there a room? *¿Hay cuarto?*
May I (may we) see it? *¿Puedo (podemos) verlo?*
What is the rate? *¿Cuál es el precio?*
Is that your best rate? *¿Es su mejor precio?*
Is there something cheaper? *¿Hay algo más económico?*
single room *un cuarto sencillo*
double room *un cuarto doble*
room for a couple *matrimonial*
key *llave*
with private bath *con baño*
with shared bath *con baño general; con baño compartido*
hot water *agua caliente*
cold water *agua fría*
shower *ducha*
towel *toalla*
soap *jabón*
toilet paper *papel higiénico*
air-conditioning *aire acondicionado*
fan *ventilador*

blanket *frazada; manta*
sheets *sábanas*

FOOD

menu *la carta; el menú*
glass *taza*
fork *tenedor*
knife *cuchillo*
spoon *cuchara*
napkin *servilleta*
soft drink *agua fresca*
coffee *café*
tea *té*
sugar *azúcar*
drinking water *agua pura; agua potable*
bottled carbonated water *agua minera con gas*
bottled noncarbonated water *agua sin gas*
beer *cerveza*
wine *vino*
milk *leche*
juice *jugo*
eggs *huevos*
bread *pan*
cheese *queso*
salad *ensalada*
fruit *fruta*
mango *mango*
watermelon *sandía*
banana *banano*
plantain *plátano*
apple *manzana*
orange *naranja*
meat (without) *(sin) carne*
beef *carne de res*
chicken *pollo; gallina*
fish *pescado*
shellfish *mariscos*
shrimp *camarones*
fried *frito*
roasted *asado*
barbecued *a la parrilla*
breakfast *desayuno*
lunch *almuerzo*
dinner (or a late-night snack) *cena*
the check or the bill *la cuenta*

MAKING A PURCHASE

I need... *Necesito...*
I want... *Deseo...; Quiero...*
I would like... (more polite) *Quisiera...*
How much does it cost? *¿Cuánto cuesta?*
What is the exchange rate? *¿Cuál es el tipo de cambio?*
How much does it cost? *¿Cuánto cuesta?*
May I see...? *¿Puedo ver...?*
This one *ésta/ésto*
expensive *caro*
cheap *barato*
more *más*
less *menos*
a little *un poco*
too much *demasiado*
money *dinero*
money-exchange bureau *casa de cambio*
Do you accept credit cards? *¿Aceptan tarjetas de crédito?*

HEALTH

Help me please. *Ayúdeme por favor.*
I am ill. *Estoy enfermo.*
It hurts. *Me duele.*
Call a doctor. *Llame un doctor.*
hospital *hospital*
drugstore *farmacia*
pain *dolor*
fever *fiebre*
headache *dolor de cabeza*
stomach ache *dolor de estómago*
diarrhea *diarrea*
vomiting *vomitar*
medicine *medicina*
pill; tablet *pastilla*

VERBS

Verbs are the key to getting along in Spanish. They employ mostly predictable forms and come in three classes, which end in *ar, er,* and *ir,* respectively:

to buy *comprar*
I buy, you (he, she, it) buys *compro, compra*
we buy, you (they) buy *compramos, compran*

to eat *comer*
I eat, you (he, she, it) eats *como, come*
we eat, you (they) eat *comemos, comen*

to climb *subir*
I climb, you (he, she, it) climbs *subo, sube*
we climb, you (they) climb *subimos, suben*

Here are more (with irregularities indicated):

to do or make *hacer* (regular except for *hago,* I do or make)
to go *ir* (very irregular: *voy, va, vamos, van*)
to go (walk) *andar*
to love *amar*
to work *trabajar*
to want *desear, querer*
to need *necesitar*
to read *leer*
to write *escribir*
to repair *reparar*
to stop *parar*
to get off (the bus) *bajar*

to arrive *llegar*
to stay (remain) *quedar*
to stay (lodge) *hospedar*
to leave *salir* (regular except for *salgo,* I leave)
to look at *mirar*
to look for *buscar*
to give *dar* (regular except for *doy,* I give)
to carry *llevar*
to have *tener* (irregular but important: *tengo, tiene, tenemos, tienen*)
to come *venir* (similarly irregular: *vengo, viene, venimos, vienen*)

Spanish has two forms of "to be":

to be *estar* (regular except for *estoy,* I am)
to be *ser* (very irregular: *soy, es, somos, son*)

Use *estar* when speaking of location or a temporary state of being: "I am at home." *"Estoy en casa."* "I'm sick." *"Estoy enfermo."* Use *ser* for a permanent state of being: "I am a doctor." *"Soy doctora."*

Suggested Reading

ARCHAEOLOGY, ETHNOGRAPHY, AND ETHNOHISTORY

McEwan, Colin, Luis A. Borrero, and Alfredo Prieto, eds. *Patagonia: Natural History, Prehistory and Ethnography at the Uttermost End of the Earth.* Princeton, NJ: Princeton University Press, 1997. First published under the auspices of the British Museum, this collection of academic but accessible essays ranges from Patagonia's natural environment to early human occupation, the first encounters between Europeans and indigenous people, the origins of the Patagonian "giants," and even travel literature.

GUIDEBOOKS AND TRAVELOGUES

Burford, Tim. *Chile & Argentina: The Bradt Trekking Guide.* Chalfont St Peter, UK: Bradt Publications, 2001. Needs an update, but still a useful source for planning many hiking trips in the two countries.

Chatwin, Bruce. *In Patagonia.* New York: Summit Books, 1977. One of the continent's classic travelogues, even if, or perhaps because, Chatwin blurs the line between experience and fiction.

Crouch, Gregory. *Enduring Patagonia.* New York: Random House, 2001. Details one mountaineer's experiences on Cerro Fitz Roy and Cerro Torre in Parque Nacional Los Glaciares.

Darwin, Charles. *Voyage of the Beagle* (many editions). Perhaps the greatest travel book ever written, Darwin's narrative of his 19th-century journey bursts with insights on the people, places, and even politics he saw while collecting the plants and animals that led to his revolutionary theories.

Foster, Dereck, and Richard Tripp. *Food and Drink in Argentina*. El Paso, TX: Aromas y Sabores, 2006. A fine short introduction to Argentine food, with an extensive Spanish-English glossary, by the late restaurant critic of the *Buenos Aires Herald* and a U.S. collaborator.

Green, Toby. *Saddled with Darwin*. London: Phoenix, 1999. Audacious if uneven account by a young, talented writer of his attempt to retrace the hoofprints—not the footsteps—of Darwin's travels through Uruguay, Argentina, and Chile. Self-effacing but still serious, the author manages to compare Darwin's experience with his own, reflect on contemporary distortions of the great scientist's theories, and stay almost completely off the gringo trail.

Guevara, Ernesto. *The Motorcycle Diaries: A Journey around South America*. New York and London: Verso, 1995. Translated by Ann Wright, this is an account of an Argentine drifter's progress from Buenos Aires across the Patagonian Andes and up the Chilean coast by motorcycle and, when the bike broke down, by any means necessary. The author is better known by his nickname, "Che," a common Argentine interjection.

Keenan, Brian, and John McCarty. *Between Extremes*. London: Black Swan, 2000. During four years as hostages in Lebanon, Keenan and McCarty fantasized about riding through Patagonia on horseback. Years after their release, they did it.

Leitch, William. *South America's National Parks*. Seattle: The Mountaineers, 1990. Dated in detail, but still a good summary of several national parks in Chile and Argentina.

Lista, Ramón. *A Journey to the Southern Andes*. Olivos, Argentina: El Calafate Editores, 2000. Originally published in 1892, this journal by the governor of Santa Cruz territory recounts an arduous steamer navigation up the Río Santa Cruz, duplicating the route of FitzRoy, to Lago Argentino and Lago Viedma. Some of the naval officer's natural-history observations are badly mistaken.

McCarthy, Carolyn. *Trekking in the Patagonian Andes*. Melbourne: Lonely Planet, 2009. Another update would be desirable, but the maps are useful.

Meadows, Anne. *Digging Up Butch and Sundance*. 3rd ed. Lincoln, NE: University of Nebraska Press, 2003. The classic biography of the world's most famous outlaws since Robin Hood.

Moreno, Francisco Pascasio. *Perito Moreno's Travel Journal: A Personal Reminiscence*. Buenos Aires: Elefante Blanco, 2002. Absorbing translation of the great Patagonian explorer's northern Patagonian letters and journals, including his thrilling escape down the Río Limay from his indigenous captors.

Muir, John. *John Muir's Last Journey*. Washington DC: Island Press, 2001. Edited by Michael P. Branch, this annotated collection of Muir's correspondence and notes on his eight-month odyssey through South America and Africa includes his search for native araucaria forests in Chile's northern Andean lakes district.

Murphy, Dallas. *Rounding the Horn*. New York: Basic Books, 2004. A hybrid of historical and contemporary navigation in the world's wildest waters, Murphy's travelogue conveys the travails of advancing against the winds of the "Furious Fifties." But it also communicates the mystique of South America's southernmost tip.

Reding, Nick. *The Last Cowboys at the End of the World*. New York: Crown, 2001. Anthropological in its approach, this account of isolated gauchos in Chilean Patagonia's upper Río Cisnes rings true for the author's refusal to romanticize people with whom he clearly sympathizes and empathizes.

Roosevelt, Theodore. *A Book Lover's Holiday in the Open*. New York: Scribner's, 1916. After retiring from politics, the still vigorous U.S. president undertook numerous overseas adventures; among other stories, this collection retells his crossing of the Andes from Chile into the lake district of northern Argentine Patagonia, and his meeting with legends like Perito Moreno.

Symmes, Patrick. *Chasing Che: A Motorcycle Journey in Search of the Guevara Legend*. New York: Vintage, 2000. Symmes follows the tread marks of Che's legendary early 1950s trip from Buenos Aires through Argentina and Chile.

Wangford, Hank. *Lost Cowboys*. London: Victor Gollencz, 1995. A British country musician and experienced travel writer, whose band's name and book title are identical, follows the gauchos and other Latin American horsemen.

Willis, Bailey. *A Yanqui in Patagonia*. Palo Alto, CA: Stanford University Press, 1947. Out of print but well worth seeking, this U.S. geologist's memoir is a vivid account of the early 20th century's northern Patagonian frontier. It's also fascinating for his assessment of the region's potential, and for his account of intrigues within the Argentine governments of the day.

Crow, John A. *The Epic of Latin America*, 3rd ed. Berkeley, CA: University of California Press, 1980. A comprehensive history of the region, told more through narrative than analysis, in an immensely readable manner. Several chapters deal with Argentina.

Nouzeilles, Gabriela, and Gabriela Montaldo, eds. *The Argentina Reader: History, Culture, Politics*. Durham, NC: Duke University Press, 2002. It's too big and heavy to carry along on the road, but this diverse collection of essays and extracts is an excellent introduction to the country through the eyes of Argentines, and visitors to Argentina, since colonial times.

Parry, J. H. *The Discovery of South America*. London: Paul Elek, 1979. Well-illustrated account of early voyages and overland explorations on the continent.

Rock, David. *Argentina 1516-1987: From Spanish Colonization to the Falklands War and Alfonsín*. London: I. B. Taurus, 1987. Comprehensive narrative and analysis of Argentine history prior to Carlos Menem's presidency.

Slatta, Richard. *Cowboys of the Americas*. New Haven and London: Yale University Press, 1990. Spectacularly illustrated comparative analysis of New World horsemen, including both Argentine gauchos and Chilean *huasos*.

GOVERNMENT AND POLITICS

Caviedes, César. *The Southern Cone: Realities of the Authoritarian State*. Totowa, NJ: Rowman & Allanheld, 1984. Comparative study of the military dictatorships of Chile, Argentina, Uruguay, and Brazil of the 1970s and 1980s.

LITERATURE AND LITERARY CRITICISM

Aira, César. *The Hare*. London and New York: Serpent's Tail, 1998. Touching the dangerous territory of magical realism, Aira's novel of a wandering English naturalist on the Pampas is a complex tale that ties up neatly at the end.

Hudson, William Henry. *Far Away and Long Ago*. London: Eland, 1982. Originally published in 1922, this is Hudson's memoir of his childhood in Argentina, including trips to the edge of Patagonia.

Hudson, William Henry. *Idle Days in Patagonia*. Berkeley, CA: Creative Arts Book Company, 1979. Originally published in 1893, this title covers Hudson's travels and natural history observations in northern Argentine Patagonia.

Martínez, Tomás Eloy. *The Perón Novel*. New York: Pantheon, 1988. Based on the author's own lengthy interviews with the exiled caudillo, for which fiction seemed the appropriate outlet. According to Jorge Castañeda, "Whether Perón ever actually uttered these words is in the last analysis irrelevant: He could have, he would have, and he probably did."

Wilson, Jason. *Traveler's Literary Companion: South & Central America, Including Mexico*. Lincolnwood, IL: Passport, 1995. An edited collection of excerpts from literature, including fiction, poetry, and essays, that illuminates aspects of the countries from the Río Grande to the tip of Tierra del Fuego, including Argentina, Buenos Aires, and Chile.

ENVIRONMENT AND NATURAL HISTORY

Clark, Ricardo. *Aves de Tierra del Fuego y Cabo de Hornos*. Buenos Aires: Literature of Latin America, 1986. Spanish-language field guide to birds in "the uttermost part of the earth."

Couve, Enrique, and Claudio Vidal Ojeda. *Birds of the Beagle Channel and Cape Horn*. Punta Arenas: Fantástico Sur Birding & Nature, 2000. Bilingual field guide to coastal Tierra del Fuego.

Hudson, William Henry. *The Bird Biographies of W. H. Hudson*. Santa Barbara, CA: Capra Press, 1988. A partial reprint of the romantic naturalist's detailed description of the birds he knew growing up in Buenos Aires province, with illustrations.

Jaramillo, Álvaro. *Birds of Chile*. Princeton, NJ: Princeton University Press, 2003. The California-based Chilean author's outstanding field guide to Chilean bird life is also useful in Argentine Patagonia and the Falkland Islands.

Venegas Canelo, Claudio. *Aves de Patagonia y Tierra del Fuego Chileno-Argentina*. Punta Arenas: Ediciones de la Universidad de Magallanes, 1986. Well-illustrated field guide to the region's birds.

Internet Resources

ARGENTINE WEBSITES

Administración de Parques Nacionales (APN)
www.parquesnacionales.gob.ar
Primary government agency in charge of national parks and other conservation areas.

Aerolíneas Argentinas
www.aerolineas.com.ar
Home page for Argentina's flagship airline.

Aeropuertos Argentinos 2000
www.aa2000.com.ar
Private concessionaire operating most of Argentina's international and domestic airports, including Buenos Aires's Ezeiza and Aeroparque. In English and Spanish.

Argentina Travel Net
www.argentinatravelnet.com
Portal for Argentine travel sites, though not all of the links are closely related to travel. In Spanish and English.

Asociación Argentina de Albergues de la Juventud (AAAJ)
www.aaaj.org.ar
Argentine hosteling organization, with limited facilities throughout the country.

Asociación Ornitológica del Plata
www.avesargentinas.org.ar
Buenos Aires-based birding and conservation organization.

Automóvil Club Argentino (ACA)
www.aca.org.ar
Argentine automobile association, useful for both information and up-to-date road maps. Offers discounts for members of affiliated clubs, such as AAA in the United States and the AA in Britain.

Buenos Aires Herald
www.buenosairesherald.com
Abbreviated online version of the capital's venerable English-language paper, but it's now only a weekly.

Clarín
www.clarin.com
Outstanding online version of the capital's tabloid daily, the Spanish-speaking world's largest-circulation newspaper.

Festival de Tango
www.festivaldetango.com.ar
The capital's increasingly popular series of autumn (Mar.-Apr.) tango events, following Brazilian Carnaval.

Fundación Vida Silvestre Argentina
www.vidasilvestre.org.ar
Nongovernmental wildlife and habitat advocates.

Greenpeace
www.greenpeace.org.ar
Argentine affiliate of the international conservation organization.

Hostelling International Argentina
www.hostels.org.ar
Argentine Hostelling International affiliate, with information on travel and activities throughout the country.

Instituto Geográfico Militar
www.igm.gob.ar
Military Geographical Institute, preparing and selling maps of Argentina.

Instituto Nacional de Estadísticas y Censos
www.indec.mecon.ar
Website for the federal government's statistical agency.

Interpatagonia
www.interpatagonia.com
Probably the most complete site for content and services on both the Argentine and Chilean sides of the Southern Cone's southernmost region.

Líneas Aéreas del Estado (LADE)
www.lade.com.ar
Commercial passenger arm of the Argentine air force, which serves primarily Patagonian destinations.

Metrovías
www.metrovias.com.ar
Details on Buenos Aires's subway system.

Ministerio de Relaciones Exteriores
www.mrecic.gov.ar/consulares/pagcon.html
Argentine foreign ministry, with information on visas and consulates, in English and Spanish.

Páginas Amarillas
www.paginasamarillas.com.ar
Yellow pages for the entire country.

Ministerio de Turismo
www.turismo.gob.ar
National tourism authority, with information in Spanish and English.

CHILEAN WEBSITES

Automóvil Club Chileno
www.acchi.cl
Motorist organization that also provides services to members of overseas affiliates.

Comité de la Defensa de Flora y Fauna
www.codeff.cl
Well-established group oriented toward wildlife and habitat conservation.

Corporación de Promoción Turística
www.visitchile.org
Public-private Chilean site in English and Spanish.

Corporación Nacional de Desarrollo Indígena
www.conadi.cl
Official government page for indigenous affairs, in Spanish only.

Corporación Nacional Forestal
www.conaf.cl
Official page of quasi-governmental agency in charge of Chile's national parks and other protected areas; in Spanish only.

El Mercurio
www.emol.com
Santiago's traditional daily newspaper, with conservative editorial line; in Spanish.

Federación de Andinismo
www.feach.cl
Site devoted to climbing, including explanation of bureaucratic obstacles in sensitive border areas.

Fundación Terram
www.terram.cl
Nonprofit promoting sustainable development in Chile.

FutaFriends
www.futafriends.org
Nonprofit organization dedicated to preserving the Río Futaleufú.

Hostelling International Santiago
www.hostelling.cl
Chilean affiliate of Hostelling International, with information on hostels and activities throughout the country.

Instituto Geográfico Militar
www.igm.cl
Chilean government agency in charge of mapping, map sales, and general geographic information.

La Tercera
www.latercera.cl
Best of the Chilean tabloid dailies, serious but with a rigidly conservative editorial policy.

Parque Natural Pumalín
www.parquepumalin.cl
Exceptional site, in Spanish and English, for what may be the most audacious (and controversial) private conservation effort in the world.

Publiguías
www.amarillas.cl
Chilean yellow pages.

Renace
www.renace.cl
Alliance of Chilean environmental organizations.

Sernatur
www.sernatur.cl
Chilean government tourism bureau; in Spanish and English.

Viña Cousiño Macul
www.cousinomacul.cl
Classic winery within Santiago's city limits, open for tours and tastings.

FOREIGN AND GENERAL INTEREST WEBSITES

Centers for Disease Control
www.cdc.gov
U.S. government page with travel health advisories.

CIA Factbook
www.odci.gov/cia/publications/factbook
The world's most notorious spooks perform at least one admirable public service in their annual encyclopedia of the world's countries, which appears complete online.

Currency Converter
www.oanda.com
Present and historic exchange-rate information.

Department of Health
www.doh.gov.uk
British government agency with country-by-country health advice.

Department of State
www.travel.state.gov
Travel information and advisories from the U.S. government; while it has a great deal of useful material, its warnings are often exaggerated.

Latin American Network Information Center (LANIC)
http://lanic.utexas.edu
Organized by the University of Texas, this site has a huge collection of quality links to Argentina, Chile, and other Latin American countries.

Mercopress News Agency
www.falkland-malvinas.com
Montevideo-based Internet news agency covering politics and business in the Mercosur common-market countries of Argentina, Brazil, Uruguay, and Paraguay, as well as Chile and the Falkland/Malvinas Islands. In English and Spanish.

Index

N

QR

List of Maps

Photo Credits

Acknowledgments

Like my previous efforts on Argentina, Chile, and Buenos Aires, this guide owes its existence in its present form to numerous individuals in North America, Argentina, Chile, and elsewhere. I'll start with Bill Newlin, whose prerogative helped make this title a priority, and his Berkeley staff at Avalon Travel.

In the course of nearly 40 years' experience in South America, most of that as a guidebook writer, I owe enormous debts to friends, acquaintances, and officials throughout the region. My apologies to anyone I may have overlooked or perhaps omitted through an errant keystroke. Their names appear by region in no particular order, though some are grouped by workplace.

In Buenos Aires and vicinity, thanks to the late Joaquín Allolio and Eduardo Birabén; Dan Perlman; and my nephews José, Juan, and Manuel Massolo. A special mention to Nicolás Kugler, who contributed much of the coverage of Argentine Patagonia in the previous edition.

In Santiago, acknowledgments to Marcelo Puga of Cruceros Australis and Pilar Ojeda of Navimag; Yerko Ivelic and Javier López of Cascada Expediciones; Eduardo Núñez of Conaf; Pablo Negri Edwards for various suggestions; and my longtime friend Marializ Maldonado. Franz Schubert of Talca also provided help on several fronts.

In northern Argentine Patagonia, special mention to Diego Allolio of Bariloche and Sergio Rodríguez of Viñas Nant y Fall, Chubut. In southern Argentine Patagonia, I would add Matías Soriano of Bahía Bustamante; Juan Kuriger and the late Silvia Braun of Hostería Monte León; Ricardo Pérez of Puerto Deseado; María Elisa Rodríguez, Sebastián Bruna, and Dany Feldman of El Calafate; and Ricardo Brondo and Rubén Vasquez of El Chaltén. In Argentine Tierra del Fuego, regards to Alejandro Galeazzi, Javier Jury, Luciana Lupotti, to Débora Hirsch of the Secretaría de Turismo of Ushuaia, and to Abby Goodall of Estancia Harberton.

In the Chilean lakes district, special mention to Gina Rubio of Sernatur, Temuco; Hans Schoendorfer of the Andenrose, Curacautín; Sergio Pérez Menares of Malalcahuello; Hernán Verscheure of ¡École!, Pucón; Hans Liechti and Verónica Araneda of Travel Aid Pucón; Armin and Nadia Dübendorfer of Puerto Octay; Franz Schirmer of Petrohué; Andreas La Rosé and Carolina Morgado of Puerto Varas; Steve Anderson of Panitao; Britt Lewis of Ancud; and administrator Alan Bannister of Parque Tantauco.

In Chilean Patagonia, including Aisén and vicinity, thanks to Nicholas La Penna of Chaitén; Chris and Rosi Spelius of Futaleufú; Gabriela Neira Morales of Sernatur, Coyhaique; Jonathan Leidich of Puerto Bertrand; Alfredo Runín of Villa O'Higgins; Alejandro Cárdenas Lobos of Puerto Natales; Werner Ruf and Cecilia Chaura of Casa Cecilia, Puerto Natales; and Hernán Jofré of Antares Patagonia, Puerto Natales; and Lilian Riquelme of Punta Arenas.

In Stanley, Falkland Islands, thanks to tourism CEO Steph Middleton, Sally Ellis and Jennie Forrest of International Tours & Travel, María Strange, Richard McKee, Tony Smith, Ian Bury, and Ray and Nancy Poole. Peter and Annie Young deserve special mention for putting me up—and putting up with me—as their house guest. In camp, where I couldn't spend as much time as I might have liked, thanks to Mike and Phyll Rendell of Bleaker Island; and to Micky Reeves of Sea Lion Island.

And finally, thanks to my wife, María Laura Massolo for her patience, and to our aging Alaskan malamute Malbec, who still reminds me when I need to get out of my office for a walk.

Also Available

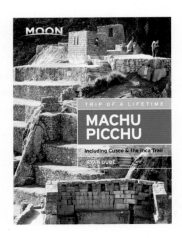

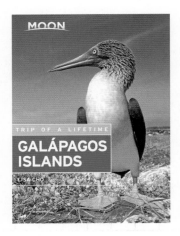

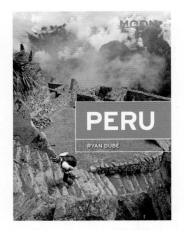

MAP SYMBOLS

═══ Expressway	○ City/Town	✈ Airport	⚓ Golf Course		
═══ Primary Road	◉ State Capital	✈ Airfield	🅿 Parking Area		
── Secondary Road	⊛ National Capital	▲ Mountain	⬜ Archaeological Site		
----- Unpaved Road	★ Point of Interest	✦ Unique Natural Feature	♟ Church		
── Feature Trail	• Accommodation		⛽ Gas Station		
------ Other Trail	▼ Restaurant/Bar	⬲ Waterfall	⬭ Glacier		
·········· Ferry		▲ Park	Mangrove		
═══ Pedestrian Walkway	■ Other Location	⬛ Trailhead	Reef		
▥▥▥ Stairs	▲ Campground	⛷ Skiing Area	Swamp		

CONVERSION TABLES

°C = (°F - 32) / 1.8
°F = (°C x 1.8) + 32
1 inch = 2.54 centimeters (cm)
1 foot = 0.304 meters (m)
1 yard = 0.914 meters
1 mile = 1.6093 kilometers (km)
1 km = 0.6214 miles
1 fathom = 1.8288 m
1 chain = 20.1168 m
1 furlong = 201.168 m
1 acre = 0.4047 hectares
1 sq km = 100 hectares
1 sq mile = 2.59 square km
1 ounce = 28.35 grams
1 pound = 0.4536 kilograms
1 short ton = 0.90718 metric ton
1 short ton = 2,000 pounds
1 long ton = 1.016 metric tons
1 long ton = 2,240 pounds
1 metric ton = 1,000 kilograms
1 quart = 0.94635 liters
1 US gallon = 3.7854 liters
1 Imperial gallon = 4.5459 liters
1 nautical mile = 1.852 km

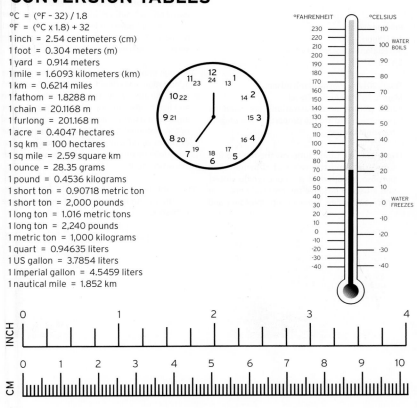

MOON PATAGONIA

Avalon Travel
Hachette Book Group
1700 Fourth Street
Berkeley, CA 94710, USA
www.moon.com

Editor: Kevin McLain
Series Manager: Kathryn Ettinger
Copy Editor: Christopher Church
Production Designer: Sarah Wildfang
Cover Design: Faceout Studios, Charles Brock
Interior Design: Domini Dragoone
Moon Logo: Tim McGrath
Map Editor: Mike Morgenfeld
Cartographers: Brian Shotwell, Austin Ehrhardt
Indexer: Greg Jewett

ISBN-13: 978-1-63121-631-2

Printing History
1st Edition — 2005
5th Edition — November 2017
5 4 3 2

Front cover photo: Zoonar GmbH / Alamy Stock Photo
Back cover photo: © Wayne Bernhardson
Printed in China by RR Donnelley